The Collected Works
of Ḥakham Dr. José Faur

The Horizontal Society and Political Thought

LJP

# The Library of the Jewish People

The Library of the Jewish People *presents primary, original voices of significant writers and thinkers in the fields of Rabbinics, the Arts, and Politics. These foundational Jewish writers will engage, inspire, and teach present and future generations.*

THE LIBRARY OF THE JEWISH PEOPLE

# JOSÉ FAUR

## THE GRAZI FAMILY EDITION

## THE HORIZONTAL SOCIETY AND POLITICAL THOUGHT

EDITORS, JOSEPH FAUR & ELI SHAUBI

*The Collected Works of of Ḥakham Dr. José Faur*
*The Horizontal Society and Political Thought*

First Edition, 2024

*The Library of the Jewish People*



POB 8531, New Milford, CT 06776-8531, USA
& POB 4044, Jerusalem 9104001, Israel
www.ljp.pub



ISBN 978-1-61329-227-3, *hardcover*

Printed and bound in Turkey

*In honor of*

*Leslie and Dr. Richard Grazi* הי"ו

*In joyous celebration of your 45th wedding anniversary,*
*and in recognition of your daily*
*devotion and exemplary living.*

*Mom and Dad,*
*Your love and respect for each other has been a source of*
*strength and inspiration throughout our entire lives.*

יְבָרֶכְךָ ה׳ מִצִּיּוֹן וּרְאֵה בְּטוּב יְרוּשָׁלָםִ כֹּל יְמֵי חַיֶּיךָ.
*May the Lord bless you from Sion;*
*and may you share the prosperity of*
*Jerusalem all the days of your life.*

וּרְאֵה־בָנִים לְבָנֶיךָ שָׁלוֹם עַל־יִשְׂרָאֵל.
*And may you see your children's children;*
*and peace be upon Israel.*

(Psalms 128)

*With endless love and gratitude,*
*Your children*

*In honor of*

# *Leslie and Dr. Richard Greer נ״י*

*In joyous celebration of your 45th wedding anniversary,*
*and in recognition of your daily*
*devotion and exemplary living*

Mom and Dad,

Your love and respect for each other has been a source of strength and inspiration throughout our entire lives.

יברכך ה׳ מציון וראה בטוב ירושלים כל ימי חייך

*May the Lord bless you from Zion,*
*and may you share the prosperity of*
*Jerusalem all the days of your life.*

וראה בנים לבניך שלום על ישראל

*And may you see your children's children;*
*and peace be upon Israel.*

(Psalms 128)

With endless love and gratitude,

Your children

# Contents

# Publisher's Preface

Always steadfast in his beliefs, deeply passionate, Ḥakham José Faur was a Sephardic Ḥakham (rabbi), a teacher and a scholar. He was born and raised in Buenos Aires, Argentina, as part of the Damascus community there, and taught Torah in the Syrian-Jewish community in Brooklyn for many years. Faur was educated at Syrian Yeshivot in Buenos Aires, he studied under Rav Aharon Kotler in Lakewood, and furthered his education at the University of Barcelona in Spain – one of the first Jews to be accepted since the expulsion of 1492.

Faur wrote over ten books and more than 100 essays and articles on a wide variety of subjects, ranging from linguistics to historiography to rabbinic law. His niece, Mijal Bitton, summarized some of his world views thus:

> "There were many aspects to Ḥakham Faur's rabbinic intellectual tradition. One of the important aspects central to his thinking was a focus on methodology. For Ḥakham Faur, it was not enough to have information: one needed to acquire wisdom in a systematic way and follow consistent and coherent rules for the application of knowledge. This is critical to

> Ḥakham Faur's philosophy and means two things: (1) memorizing data, or citing statements said by others, are not the most advanced approaches in rabbinic discourse, and (2) it is not enough to be smart: the caliber of a Jewish sage is built first and foremost upon allegiance to an intellectual tradition and command of its methodology. This approach was different from many of the non-Maimonidean streams in the Jewish tradition, according to which one can demonstrate that something is forbidden or permitted by citing some prominent names whose statements have been memorized, without explaining the statements themselves. So, for instance, for Ḥakham Faur, Maimonides was a giant of the rabbinic world not because of his IQ, but because he was methodical in his approach and an effective proponent of rabbinic tradition. So, too, students of Hakham Faur would not believe it is enough to quote Maimonides and cite his authority. Rather, they are tasked with following Maimonides' carefully laid out journey through the sources and understanding his conclusions."

It is fitting that this, the first of a five-volume *Collected Works*, is among the first in *The Library of the Jewish People*. I'm especially pleased to thank the sponsors of this volume, the Grazi Family of New York and Jerusalem. Dr. Richard Grazi has been one of the world's leading infertility specialists for a generation, and it is with pride that his children honor both Richard and his wife, Leslie Grazi, for enabling them to have made so great a contribution to the larger Jewish community. They are truly exemplars of what is a full Jewish life.

We thank the editors of this volume, Eli Shaubi and Joseph Faur, for their exhaustive and exhausting work in bringing this together. We also thank Ḥakham Abe Halevy Faur for his encouragement and editorial support regarding textual nuances.

We also thank Uri Bollag, our Managing Editor; Tani Bayer for designing the covers; Tomi Mager for creating the typography; and Rachel Miskin and Adina Karpuj for editing the works.

We hope that this volume will awaken new interest and appreciation of this remarkable, overlooked, and fearless Sephardi writer.

Matthew Miller, Publisher
Library of the Jewish People
2024

# Timeline

| | José Faur | Jewish Context | Global Context |
|---|---|---|---|
| 1910s | 1914: Faur's grandparents leave their ancestral home in Damascus and move to Argentina. A primary factor in their decision to emigrate was the prospect of being drafted into the Turkish army. | 1914: Yeshiva College (later: University) and the Rabbi Isaac Elchanan Rabbinical Seminary are established in New York City. | 1912: Carl Gustav Jung publishes *Psychology of the Unconscious*, outlining his theory of the unconscious mind.<br><br>1914: Archduke Franz Ferdinand is assassinated, instigating the start of World War I.<br><br>1916: Ferdinand Saussure's *Course on General Linguistics*, regarded as the starting point of structural linguistics, is published posthumously. |
| 1920s | 1921: R. Maṭloub 'Abadi, student of R. Yiṣḥaq Dayyan and future teacher of Faur, moves to Brooklyn, New York, to join its newly flourishing Syrian community.<br><br>1927: Faur's maternal grandfather, Jacob Joli, passes away in Argentina. Joli was the descendant of R. Jacob Joli (1689–1732), who composed the Tora anthology, *Me'am Lo'ez*. | 1921: R. David de Sola Pool becomes Senior Rabbi of Congregation Shearith Israel, the Spanish and Portuguese synagogue in New York City.<br><br>1925: R. 'Ezra 'Aṭṭieh is appointed head of the prominent Sephardic institution, *Yeshibat Porat Yosef*. Faur later recounts that R. Maṭloub 'Abadi was offered this position, but declined and recommended R. 'Aṭṭieh in his stead. | 1921: Ludwig Wittgenstein publishes his seminal treatise, which is published a year later in English, with the Latin title *Tractatus Logico-Philosophicus*.<br><br>1922: Following the death of Vladimir Lenin, Joseph Stalin assumes power over the Soviet Union.<br><br>1929: The Great Depression shakes the world economy, as US stock prices crash. |
| 1934 | September 19: José Faur is born on Yom Kippur, at the time of *ne'ila*. | Abraham Shalom Yahuda publishes *The Accuracy of the Bible*. | November 9–10: Kristallnacht, or the Night of Broken Glass, symbolizes for many the beginning of the Holocaust in Nazi Germany. |

| | José Faur | Jewish Context | Global Context |
|---|---|---|---|
| 1947 | Faur's paternal grandfather, Joseph Faur, arranges for his grandson to begin studying with the most prominent Syrian Rabbis of Argentina. His teachers include R. Eliyahu Freue, the spiritual head of the Community of Damascus in Argentina (1880–1957), R. Eliyahu Suli (d. 1966), R. Jamil Harari, and R. Aharon Ha-Kohen 'Ajami (d. 1978). | November 29: The UN General Assembly adopts Resolution 181, the UN Partition Plan for Palestine. The Jewish Agency for Palestine accepts the plan. The State of Israel is established in May 1948. | March 12: In a speech delivered before the US Congress, President Harry Truman announces "The Truman Doctrine," a policy with the primary goal of containing Soviet geopolitical expansion. For some, this marks the beginning of the Cold War, which would last over four decades. |
| 1950 | Joseph Faur, Faur's paternal grandfather and mentor in Tora, passes away. | | June 25: North Korea, supported by China and the Soviet Union, invades South Korea, supported by the US. The Korean War is one of the first major conflicts during the Cold War era. |
| 1951 | Following the passing of his grandfather, Faur leaves Argentina at the young age of 17 for Mexico City, where he is appointed principal of Talmud Tora Aram Ṣoba. | Through Operation Ezra and Nehemiah, around 125,000 Iraqi Jews immigrate to the State of Israel. | |
| 1952–1953 | Faur moves to the United States and begins studying at the Beth Medrash Govoha in Lakewood NJ, headed by the prominent Lithuanian Rabbi, R. Aharon Kotler. During this time, Faur was the *habruta* of R. Shlomo Carlebach. | 1953: R. David Chelouche, who would later become a close friend of Faur, is appointed Chief Rabbi of Netanya, a position he would hold until his death on June 8, 2016. | March 5, 1953: Joseph Stalin, the second leader of the Soviet Union, dies. |
| 1956 | Faur is hired to teach at Aḥi Ezer synagogue in the Syrian community of Brooklyn, NY. | Louis Finkelstein publishes his edition of the *Sifra*, the *midrash halakha* on the book of Leviticus. | The Suez Crisis: Egypt nationalizes the Suez Canal, leading to a tripartite attack by Israel, the United Kingdom, and France, in an effort to re-open the blocked Straits of Tiran and regain control of the Suez Canal for Western powers. |
| 1957 | Faur and some of his students attempt to establish a Sephardic Seminary. After fundraising for over a year, the project does not succeed, and Faur begins to pursue his academic studies. | | |

| | José Faur | Jewish Context | Global Context |
|---|---|---|---|
| 1958–1959 | Sometime in the late 1950s, Faur spends six months at Harvard University, where he meets Prof. Harry Wolfson. Wolfson, who was no longer taking students in his last years of teaching, recommends Faur pursue his academic studies at the University of Barcelona because of their strong Semitic Philology department.<br><br>Following suit, Faur begins his studies in Semitic Philology at the University of Barcelona. | 1958: The Aleppo Codex, one of the most accurate biblical manuscripts in existence, is secretly smuggled out of Syria to Jerusalem, Israel. Referred to as "The Crown of Aleppo," the manuscript was written in the 900s and was used by Maimonides in his laws for writing a Tora scroll. It was housed in Aleppo for about 600 years. | 1959: The overthrow of Cuban President Fulgencio Batisto by Fidel Castro and Che Guevara results in the creation of the first communist government in the Western hemisphere. |
| 1961 | Faur completes his M.A. in Semitic Philology. His master's thesis is titled: "La Espiritualidad Judia." He subsequently begins his Ph.D. studies. | | |
| 1963 | February 25: Faur marries Esther Cohen.<br><br>Faur receives *semikha* of *Yore Yore* from R. Suleiman Ḥuggi 'Abudi, head of the Bet Din of Jerusalem. The ordination letter is also signed by R. 'Ezra 'Aṭṭieh, R. Ya'aqob 'Ades, and R. 'Obadya Hidaya.<br><br>December 14: Faur's first daughter, Aura Faur Varon, is born. | | November 23: US President John F. Kennedy is assassinated.<br><br>Mircea Eliade, historian of religion, writes his *Myth and Reality*. |
| 1964 | August 8: Faur receives his doctoral degree in Semitic Philology from the University of Barcelona. His doctoral dissertation is titled: *The Masorah to the Targum Onqelos*.<br><br>Fall: Faur begins a three-year Post-Doctoral Fellowship at the Jewish Theological Seminary (JTS) under Saul Lieberman.<br><br>Faur is hired to teach classes at Congregation Shaare Zion, at the time the largest Syrian synagogue in Brooklyn, New York. | R. Yosef Messas migrates from Morocco to Haifa, where he and Faur later become friends. | Marshall Mcluhan publishes *Understanding Media*, his seminal work in media theory, proposing that media themselves, and not the content they carry, should be the focus of study: "The medium is the message." |
| 1965 | July 7: Faur's only son, Abe, is born. | Eli Cohen, an Egyptian-born Israeli spy in Syria, is uncovered by Syrian security forces and ultimately hanged. | Israel and West Germany establish diplomatic relations. |

| | José Faur | Jewish Context | Global Context |
|---|---|---|---|
| 1966 | Faur is ordained as *dayyan* in Family Law (*Eben Ha-'Ezer*) by R. Maṭloub 'Abadi. | R. Ḥayyim David Ha-Levi, Chief Rabbi of Tel Aviv, publishes the first volume of his five-volume series on Jewish Law, *Meqor Ḥayyim.* | Claude Lévi-Strauss publishes *The Savage Mind*, in which he lays out his theories of culture and mind, of history and social change, as well as of the nature of human freedom. |
| 1967 | On the advice of R. David de Sola Pool and R. Maṭloub 'Abadi, Faur accepts a faculty position at the Jewish Theological Seminary. Faur is the first Sephardic faculty member since the Seminary's founding in the days of R. Sabato Morais and R. Henry Pereira Méndes.<br><br>In response to Faur's inquiry, R. Maṭloub 'Abadi writes a responsum (*teshuba*) declaring it permissible to teach at a Conservative institution. | During the Six Day War, Israel captures the West Bank, the Golan Heights, the Gaza Strip, and the Sinai Peninsula. It annexes East Jerusalem, reuniting Jerusalem under Jewish control for the first time since the Second Temple period. | Jacques Derrida publishes three of his most important works, *Speech and Phenomena, Writing and Difference,* and *Of Grammatology.* |
| 1968 | Faur publishes his first English article, "Understanding the Covenant."<br><br>Faur receives rabbinic ordination (*semikha*) from R. Aharon Ha-Kohen 'Ajami. | | Roland Barthes writes his seminal essay "The Death of the Author."<br><br>Following the Second Vatican Council, Spain formally and symbolically revokes the 1492 Edict of Expulsion. |
| 1969 | Faur is ordained as *dayyan* in Civil Law (*Ḥoshen Mishpaṭ*) by R. Suleiman Ḥuggi 'Abudi.<br><br>In response to a question posed by R. Abraham Hecht, Rabbi of Shaare Zion, R. Moshe Feinstein issues a responsum (*teshuba*) declaring that someone teaching at a Conservative institution should not be allowed to teach Tora classes at an Orthodox institution. | | Émile Benveniste, a French structural linguist and semiotician, publishes *Indo-European Language and Society.*<br><br>The US becomes the first country to put a man on the moon, as part of the Apollo 11 mission. |
| 1970 | Shortly after R. Maṭloub 'Abadi's death, Faur stops teaching at Shaare Zion. | January 1: R. Maṭloub 'Abadi, one of Faur's primary teachers, passes away. | |
| 1973 | February: Faur establishes the World Institute for Sephardic Studies (WISS), an organization dedicated to disseminating Sephardic Tora throughout the Jewish world.<br><br>Fall: Faur begins a sabbatical year in Haifa, where he would teach Tora in various institutions and become close with R. Yosef Messas and R. Yosef Dana. | R. 'Obadya Yosef becomes Sephardic Chief Rabbi of Israel.<br><br>The Conservative Movement's Rabbinical Assembly (RA) allows women to be counted for a *minyan*, contrary to JTS policy at the time. | October 6: Egypt launches a surprise offensive against Israel, starting the Yom Kippur War. |

| | José Faur | Jewish Context | Global Context |
|---|---|---|---|
| 1974 | Fall: Faur moves from Israel to Manhattan and, at this time, does not yet return to the Syrian community. | | May 31: Israel and Syria sign the Agreement on Disengagement, officially ending the Yom Kippur War and the attrition period on the Syrian front. |
| 1975 | At the request of his students from the Syrian community, including Dennis Dweck, Faur moves back to Brooklyn, New York, and resumes teaching Tora classes in private venues within the Syrian community. | | Jorge Luis Borges publishes *The Book of Sand*.<br>The Lebanese Civil War begins.<br>April 30: The Vietnam War ends with the fall of Saigon. |
| 1977 | Faur publishes his first book, *R. Yisrael Moshe Ḥazzan: The Man and His Works* (Heb). | Pressured by the Conservative Movement's Rabbinical Assembly, JTS Chancellor Gerson Cohen establishes the Commission for the Study of the Ordination of Women as Rabbis, to examine the issue of women's ordination. | Menachem Begin is elected Prime Minister of Israel.<br>November 19–21: Egyptian President Anwar Sadat addresses the Israeli Knesset, becoming the first Arab leader to visit Israel. |
| 1978 | Faur publishes *Studies in the Mishne Tora* (Heb) on Maimonides' *Sefer ha-Madda'* (Book of Knowledge). | | At Camp David, near Washington D.C., Israel and Egypt sign a comprehensive peace treaty, The Camp David Accords, which includes the withdrawal of Israel from the Sinai. |
| 1982 | October 10: The Foundation for Sephardic Studies, of which Faur is nominated President, is established, with the purpose of providing daily Tora classes to the public, as well as training Rabbis and *ḥazzanim*. | | June 6: IDF forces invade southern Lebanon, beginning the First Lebanon War. |
| 1983 | Faur's father, Abraham Faur, passes away in Argentina. | R. Mordechai Eliyahu becomes Sephardic Chief Rabbi of Israel.<br>March: Prof. Saul Lieberman, mentor and close friend of Faur, passes away.<br>October 24: The JTS faculty votes to begin admitting women to their program for rabbinic ordination. | |
| 1984 | Following the JTS decision to begin ordaining women as Rabbis, Faur takes a leave of absence. | R. Ezra Baṣri, *Ab Bet Din* of Jerusalem, establishes *Mekhon Ha-Ketab*, a publishing house dedicated to printing works of Sephardic Rabbis. | January 24: The first Macintosh home computer is introduced. |

| | José Faur | Jewish Context | Global Context |
|---|---|---|---|
| 1985 | Faur formally resigns from his faculty position at JTS, and sues the institution for breach of contract.<br><br>In an effort to prevent Faur from teaching at Congregation Shaare Zion, a question is sent to R. 'Obadya Yosef about whether it is permitted for someone who has taught at a Conservative institution to be appointed to teach classes within an observant community.<br><br>February 18: R. 'Obadya responds that such a person should not be appointed, and if he was already appointed, he should be removed from his post. | Amy Eilberg is ordained by JTS, becoming the first female Rabbi ordained through the Conservative Movement. | |
| 1986 | Faur publishes his first English book, *Golden Doves with Silver Dots: Semiotics and Textuality in Rabbinic Tradition.* | | April 26: The Chernobyl nuclear disaster occurs in the Soviet Union. |
| 1987 | Faur takes a position as Visiting Professor at the Spertus Institute for Jewish Learning and Leadership in Chicago, to which he commutes from New York on a regular basis. He maintains this position until 1993.<br><br>September 7: At Faur's request, R. Shalom Messas, Chief Rabbi of Jerusalem, convenes the Rabbinical Court of Jerusalem to examine allegations brought against Faur. The Court concludes that "Rabbi Faur is innocent from all the accusations against him."<br><br>One day later, R. Mordechai Eliyahu, then Chief Rabbi of Israel, approves of the Jerusalem Court's decision and issues his own letter of support for Faur.<br><br>After mounting pressure, two of the court's signatories later retract their support for Faur. | A Palestinian uprising, known as the First Intifada, begins in the territories of the Gaza Strip and the West Bank. The Intifada lasts until 1993. | |

| | José Faur | Jewish Context | Global Context |
|---|---|---|---|
| 1988 | January: After much political strife, Faur is hired a second time to teach Tora at Congregation Shaare Zion.<br><br>February 12: *Yated Ne'eman*, an Israeli ultra-Orthodox newspaper, publishes a letter signed by seventeen rabbis, in which they condemn Shaare Zion for allowing Faur, "a Conservative Rabbi," to teach Tora at its premises, and assert that Faur's "books emit an odor of heresy."<br><br>March: Faur is removed from his rabbinic position teaching Tora at Shaare Zion.<br><br>Faur's close students, through the Foundation for Sephardic Studies, decide to begin fundraising to establish a new beit midrash in which Faur would be the primary teacher. In the meantime, Faur continues teaching Tora in homes, synagogues, and other private venues. | | |
| 1990 | The decision is made that the beit midrash would also incorporate a synagogue. In 1995, the synagogue was ultimately named Bnei Yitzhak. | | The Gulf War begins as Iraq invades Kuwait, leading to a military response by a coalition of countries, including the United States and Israel. The Gulf War continues until 1991. |
| 1992 | Faur publishes *In the Shadow of History*.<br><br>September: The synagogue has its grand opening before Rosh HaShana.<br><br>Faur teaches at the synagogue for one year, and some controversies ensue. | Syrian President Hafez al-Assad allows the remaining Jews of Syria to leave unrestricted. Over the following year, the Syrian Jewish community's institutions are closed and the final 4,000 Jews immigrate to the United States and Israel. | |
| 1993 | October 21: As a result of the controversies, Faur is removed from the synagogue, after which he decides to move to Israel. | | Israel and the PLO sign the first Oslo Accords.<br><br>November 1: The Maastricht Treaty comes into effect, formally establishing the European Union. |
| 1994 | Faur begins teaching Talmud part-time at Bar-Ilan University, until 2003. | | |

| | José Faur | Jewish Context | Global Context |
|---|---|---|---|
| 1995 | After having lived in Israel for one year, Faur formally makes *'aliyya*. | November 4: Israeli Prime Minister Yitzhak Rabin is assassinated. | |
| 1996 | Faur begins teaching Jewish Law (*mishpaṭ 'ibri*) in the Department of Law at the Netanya Academic College. He maintains his teaching position until 2007, when he becomes Professor Emeritus. | | |
| 1997 | Faur's mother, Sofia Aurora, passes away in Argentina. | | |
| 1998 | Faur publishes *Homo Mysticus: A Guide to Maimonides' Guide for the Perplexed*. | | |
| 2003 | Faur publishes the article "Anti-Maimonidean Demons." | | The US invasion of Iraq marks the first stage of the Iraq War. |
| 2005 | R. Adin Steinsaltz invites Faur to become a member of the Nascent Sanhedrin, which was established in 2004. After attending one meeting, Faur declines the invitation. | August 15: The forcible evacuation of the Gush Katif settlements begins, continuing until August 22, when the last residents are evicted from the settlement of Netzarim. | |
| 2006 | Faur publishes the article "On Martyrdom in Jewish Law: Maimonides and Nahmanides." (Heb.) | Marc Shapiro publishes *Saul Lieberman and the Orthodox*, a segment of which discusses the Faur controversy. | |
| 2008 | Faur publishes *The Horizontal Society: Understanding the Covenant and Alphabetic Judaism*. | December: The State of Israel initiates Operation Cast Lead, also known as the Gaza War, a three-week IDF military operation in the Gaza Strip, with the stated purpose of stopping Palestinian rocket fire into Israel. | The economic recession of 2008, also known as the Global Financial Crisis, affects markets around the world. |
| 2009 | Faur publishes *The Naked Crowd: The Jewish Alternative to Cunning Humanity*.<br>Faur finishes writing his previously unpublished work, *Forbidden Meditations: Popular Essays on Unpopular Subjects*. | | |
| 2012 | Faur publishes *The Gospel According to the Jews*. | | |

| | José Faur | Jewish Context | Global Context |
|---|---|---|---|
| 2016 | Faur finishes writing his as-of-yet unpublished work on Maimonides' Introduction to the *Mishne Tora, Va-Ya'an Yosef.* | | |
| 2018 | Faur finishes writing his as-of-yet unpublished work *Oedipal Paul.* | | |
| 2020 | June 9: Ḥakham José Faur passes away at the age of 85, leaving behind 3 children, 13 grandchildren, and 3 great-grandchildren.<br>July 6: Less than one month later, Faur's eldest sister, Angelica, passes away in Argentina. | Numerous important figures pass away: R. Jonathan Sacks, R. Adin Steinsaltz, R. Nachum Rabinowitz, and Prof. Yaacov Choueka.<br>September 15: Joint normalization agreements, known as The Abraham Accords, are signed between Israel and the United Arab Emirates, as well as Israel and Bahrain.<br>In December, Morocco joins the accords and normalizes relations with Egypt. Sudan follows suit in January 2021. | March 11: The World Health Organization declares the Covid-19 outbreak a pandemic. |
| 2021 | May 2: *Yafe Be'iṭo: Ḥakham Dr. José Faur Studies Foundation* was established by Faur's family and close students, with the purpose of preserving and disseminating the Tora of Ḥakham Faur. | | |

# General Introduction

*Ḥakham Abe Halevy Faur*

In describing the different levels of prophecy, Maimonides writes that there were prophets upon whom the flashing light of prophecy appeared once in a lifetime, or in the words of Maimonides, "one time in the entire night: They prophesied [once] but then no more' (Num. 11:25)." Even a once in a lifetime prophecy is a rare experience. Rarer still, there were those illuminated by the prophetic lightning flashes continuously throughout their lives, with the intervals between flashes varying from prophet to prophet. Indeed, a prophet's prominence may be described as a function of the duration of time between the lighting flashes.

Significantly, no prophet (other than Moses, who was of a unique class) had control over the number of lightning flashes that he/she would experience. Rather, the prophet would prepare himself/herself for the prophetic experience, and pray for God's grace to descend upon him/her. Whether or not God's grace would then descend upon the prophet(ess) was a matter of God's wholly autonomous decision. God's internal decision-making process, whether or not to bestow His grace upon a worthy individual, as well as the "logic" (if any) for such a decision, was never revealed to man. Moses himself did not receive an explanation for how God decides whether or not to bestow His grace upon a worthy individual, other than God's cryptic comment, "I shall bestow grace upon whom I bestow grace" (Ex. 33:19). To be sure, we do know what kind of individual is *worthy* of prophecy, since Maimonides describes this in a fairly detailed manner at the beginning of the *Mishne Tora*. What we don't know is why some worthy people receive God's prophetic grace and others don't; and, in the case of those who do receive such prophetic grace, we cannot predict what the frequency of such prophetic experiences will be.

As in the case of prophecy, the Tora attributes *ḥokhma*, i.e., original insights and conceptions, as coming from God: "He grants intelligence (*ḥokhmeta*) to the insightful and understanding to those who possess discernment." At first blush, the verse seems to be tautological: intelligence is granted to the insightful, and understanding is granted to those who possess discernment. However, in view of the above quoted cryptic comment by God to Moses, "I shall bestow grace upon whom I bestow grace," we can gain a clearer understanding of the verse in Daniel. Specifically, Daniel is teaching us two things. First, insightful people do not have an internal mechanism which they volitionally activate to generate new ideas and concepts, but rather, intelligent ideas and concepts are given from the outside by God, as an act of grace and kindness to the insightful person. Hence, new ideas and concepts do not spring wholly formed out of an individual's mind, even if he or she tries really hard, but are inspired in the person's mind by God. Hard work and concerted effort may be preconditions for insightfulness and original conceptions, but efforts are not enough. Rather, as Daniel teaches, intelligence and understanding are gifts from God that are bestowed upon whomever He chooses to bestow such gifts.

The second lesson is that beyond our knowing that God bestows original insights upon those whom He chooses, we know little of *why* God chooses to bestow *ḥokhma* upon one person and not upon another. In fact, God did not reveal, even to Daniel himself, the reason or the "logic" for why specific people are chosen for *ḥokhma* and others are not. Therefore, we cannot detect any logical pattern in either who is graced with *ḥokhma* or the number of brilliant insights that a *ḥakham* may be graced with. As God told Moses, "I shall bestow grace upon whom I bestow grace."

Interestingly, unlike prophecy, even non-God-fearing individuals (Jews and gentiles alike) may receive the gift of *ḥokhma*: an agnostic musician may compose a sublime and never before thought of musical composition; a painter who thinks little of God may paint water lilies (the ones first painted by God) as no one has before him; a theoretical physicist who sees design in the universe and (oddly) expressly denies the existence of an intelligent designer, may think of the space-time boundaries of the universe in a new and original way. At the same time, a pious man who cares deeply about the Creator of the universe and its secrets may discover nothing new about the universe, its design, its direction … and might not even have the intellectual skills to apprehend, let alone appreciate, discoveries made by the aforementioned theoretical physicist.

It is said that subsequent to Albert Einstein's discoveries of the special and general theories of relativity (and a few other related items), the last 30 years of his life were spent in the futile search for a unified theory that would reconcile his theories with those of quantum mechanics. Famously, Einstein could not reconcile himself to the new concepts of quantum mechanics, decrying that "God does not play dice with the universe." Regretfully, nothing came of Einstein's efforts during these last decades. The same genius brain that revolutionized and forever transformed our understanding of the space-time matrix of the universe could not generate a significant, original insight for decades. Why, one may ask? If these original thoughts spring through effort (and nothing else) from the inside, from the very depths of Einstein's brain, why would this brain-machine stop generating new ideas? Similarly, we may ask, why do writers experience extended periods of "writer's block," during which the mind feels like it is shut off, with no interesting words flowing from pen to paper? The answer offered by Daniel is that such insights come from the outside. Hence, God graced Einstein's brain with brilliant insights during a certain period of his life, but (for whatever reason) chose to no longer grace him with new insights during later periods of his life. Similarly, a writer is graced from the outside with a message, an idea, a string of words, which impel him or her to write, but when these stop, the pen goes dead.

Nikola Tesla, probably one of the greatest inventors of the last several centuries, famously said: "My brain is only a receiver. In the Universe there is a core from which we obtain knowledge, strength and inspiration. I have not penetrated into the secrets of this core, but I know that it exists." The Tora would say that there is a God who communicates with people, gracing them with original ideas and beautiful insights.

In a class on the Jewish idea of *ḥokhma*, my father, Rabbi Dr. José Faur, contrasted Einstein's relatively short-lived period of intellectual creativity with Isaac Newton's far greater span of creativity: the latter not only discovered the laws of motion (which established the foundation for modern classical mechanics) but also discovered and quantified gravity, validated Kepler's laws and the heliocentric Copernican model of the solar system, discovered (or co-discovered) calculus, and moreover authored various treatises on subjects as diverse as optics, the temple of King Solomon, the validation of historical predictions contained in the book of Daniel, and others. As it turned out, Newton's mind was prodigiously creative for an extended period of time. And again, we may ask: why did God choose to grace Newton with intelligent creativity for an extended period of time, while Einstein's creativity ended abruptly? But, as we know from Daniel, that question is pointless, for God did not reveal to us how or why He exercises His own free will.

***

Rabbi Dr. José Faur, or as he was known by his students, "the Ḥakham," was intellectually creative for around seven decades. To be sure, this does not include any original thoughts that he may have had before his *bar miṣva,* and having spoken to him about his childhood, I believe that his creativity may have commenced before he turned 13 years of age.

We do know that for the 70 years after, until the very end of his life, the Ḥakham was illuminated with God's grace and, in turn, illuminated those around him with his grace, in the form of daily *ḥiddushim* (original insights on the Tora). These *ḥiddushim* were recognized by those who received them as beautiful jewels to be cherished and enjoyed. They were cherished because they could not be found anywhere else: they were original thoughts and insights! His words, spoken even in a fleeting moment, had the power to change the life trajectory of many, penetrating hearts and souls, instilling within his students a new reverence for Tora and a deeper consciousness of the presence of the Creator.

The Ḥakham's creativity as an author was founded on two axes, which at first appear contradictory. One axis, "Axis Y," affirms a fierce fealty to the traditions of the Jewish Judiciary, including:

a. The Tora received by Moses from Sinai and then transmitted to the High Court of Israel;
b. The Oral Law formulations of the *Tanna'im,* which, after the dissolution of the Supreme Court in Jerusalem and under the leadership of R. Judah the Prince, reformulated the *Tora Shebe'al Pe,* the Oral Law, into the Mishna;
c. Talmudic Judaism, which deliberated and expounded upon the Mishna, as well as related aspects of Jewish traditions and beliefs;
d. the Babylonian *Geonim,* who, while located in the same cities and communities where the Talmud was formulated, faithfully and accurately explained the Talmud;
e. the Andalusian *ḥakhamim,* who brought talmudic Judaism into the Iberian Peninsula, North Africa and to other parts of the Mediterranean Basin.

My father was particularly attentive to, and held a special (but by no means exclusive) deference for, the teachings of the Andalusian *ḥakhamim*. The greatest of these, for whom my father devoted much of his life's works, was Maimonides, who left behind the monumental, complete (indeed the only complete) restatement of Jewish law in his *magnum opus* the *Mishne Tora*.

In considering the above stages, the following pattern emerges: each stage faithfully received, studied and transmitted the teachings of the previous stage, but each subsequent stage also built upon and further developed the teachings of the previous stage. Thus, the Tora was always relevant and compelling not only to past generations, but also to each new generation. We will elaborate on this last point in our discussion of the other axis ("Axis X") below.

* * *

Let us first consider what allowed for the historical transmission, progression and development of the Oral Law. To begin with, the Oral Law does not exist in a vacuum; it is not some transcendent platonic idea (or ideal) existing out there in some realm beyond our own. Therefore, no great philosopher, no pious rabbi (imbued though he may be with holiness) and not even a true prophet of God, has the authority, by virtue of such greatness, piety or prophetic insight, to transmit the Oral Law to the Jewish people.

How then is the Oral Law transmitted? Scriptures emphasize that the law is "not in the heavens!" Hence, the Oral Law, including the proper performance of the *miṣvot,* is not determined by individuals having spiritual insights or by ancient private family traditions.

Correspondingly, the Oral Law is not determined through "cultural transmission," as it is not a cultural feature of the Jewish people. Cultural values and features, such as the type of fish one eats on Shabbat, or which melodies to sing before the Shabbat *Birkat HaMazon,* are of little interest to one seriously considering the transmission of the Oral Law. This is not to minimize the importance of cultural values and features, which are, to be clear, important. Rather, this observation is meant to place these cultural values and features in their proper place, which is not in the Oral Law system.

What, then, is the authorized body through which the Oral Law is to be transmitted? In fact, there is a precise answer to that question: the authoritative medium through which the Oral Law is formally transmitted is the Jewish judiciary, and more specifically, the Supreme Court of Israel. To be precise, the Supreme Court serves as the recipient, repository, trustee, and transmitter of the Oral Law. Hence, each Supreme Court of Israel receives the Oral Law from the previous Supreme Court and transmits it to the subsequent Supreme Court. As the repository of the Oral Law, declarative statements by the Supreme Court in conformance with the Oral Law are legally binding. Moreover, as the trustee of the Oral Law, the Supreme Court has the sole prerogative to promulgate new rules, decrees and regulations related to the Oral Law and to Scripture, perhaps to protect the Oral Law itself, or perhaps to address specific contemporary challenges. These new rules, decrees and regulations are, in turn, incorporated into and become part of the Oral Law, transmitted forward to the subsequent Supreme Court. Hence, the Oral Law received by a given Supreme Court in one generation will not be identical to the Oral Law transmitted to a Supreme Court of a future generation.

***

To understand this matter more deeply, it should be noted that Moses was not only the first head of the Jewish Supreme Court of Israel, but was also the founder of the Jewish judiciary, as well as the Jewish constitutional law system.

In order to understand the Jewish constitutional law system and how this is related to the Jewish judiciary, it is important to start with the Theophany at Sinai. At the beginning of the Theophany, Moses acted as a duly authorized agent appointed by the Jewish people to represent them before God, and as a duly authorized agent appointed by God to represent Him before the Jewish people. The purpose of this dual-agency was to negotiate a covenant between God and Israel, under which Israel would accept the Tora, particularly, the *miṣvot*/instructions contained in the Tora, and God would award Israel with the role of "a nation of priests and a holy people," with all that that entails.

In his capacity as the agent of both God and Israel, Moses was the sole and exclusive (i) recipient of the Tora from the Almighty and (ii) transmitter of the Tora to the Jewish people.

The receipt of the Tora by Moses commenced at Sinai in the year 2449. It is important to note that during this initial stage, the Tora took the form of an oral law, i.e., the "Oral Law," and it was not yet set forth in a written medium. In addition to Moses' role in receiving the Tora from the Almighty, Moses was invested with the sole and exclusive authority to transmit the Tora that he received from the Almighty to the Jewish people. The transmission of the Tora by Moses to the Jewish people took place in the *Ohel Moed* (the Tabernacle built by Moses and the Jewish people in the desert). To elaborate, the *Ohel Moed* was not only the place where Moses transmitted the Tora to the Jewish people, but also the place where God transmitted additional laws to Moses post-Mt. Sinai. For example, the laws of the second Paschal sacrifice were not received by Moses at Mt. Sinai, but rather were transmitted to Moses in the *Ohel Moed* almost a year after the Theophany.

The Oral Law received by Moses from God (also known as the *de-'oraita* laws) established the Jewish Constitutional Law system, which in turn established the monarchy, the priesthood and the judiciary. The Oral Law not only established the various branches of Jewish government, but clearly and carefully separated the powers of these branches from one another and placed limitations on their respective roles and authority. Hence, unlike say, European monarchies from the Middle Ages, where authority was predicated upon power, might and violence, the Jewish government in general, together with its various branches, were predicated upon a pre-existing law, the Tora, which itself gives authority and legitimacy to the various branches of government. Hence, the Tora received by Moses serves as a Jewish constitution, alternatively establishing and delineating the various branches of government and the different centers of, and limits on, authority.

Since the judiciary's authority is predicated upon and constituted by the Tora, it may only function in a role that is subservient to, and within the specific limitations and confines outlined by the Tora. Accordingly, if the Supreme Court of Israel was to try to abrogate a law from the Tora (i.e., a *de-'oraita* law) received by Moses from God, this attempt would be of no effect, and the *de-'oraita* law that was the object of the Supreme Court's illegal effort would remain in full force and effect. If this was to happen, as a matter of Jewish constitutional law, citizens of the Jewish state who were aware of this illegal effort would be under an obligation to continue following the *de-'oraita* law and to ignore the Supreme Court's attempted abrogation of that same law.

* * *

Having considered the authority of the Supreme Court, let us now consider the location of the Supreme Court. In the book of Numbers we learn that Moses established the first Jewish Supreme Court of Israel, which sat in the *Ohel Moed.* Subsequently, after the completion of the Temple in Jerusalem, the address of the Supreme Court (the Sanhedrin) was moved to the Temple.

This last point is important. With the conquest of the land of Israel and the establishment of the Jewish monarchy, the *Ohel Moed* was replaced with the Jewish Temple in Jerusalem, and the Ark of the Tabernacle, together with the holy utensils, were moved from the *Ohel Moed* to the Temple. Placing the Sanhedrin first in the *Ohel Moed,* which is where Moses himself transmitted the Oral Law to Israel, and later in the Temple in Jerusalem, which was the functional equivalent of the *Ohel Moed,* meant that the Sanhedrin sitting in the Temple was a continuation of the transmission and development of the Oral Law taught my Moses to Israel. Placing the Sanhedrin in the

Temple confirmed the supreme and exclusive authority of every Sanhedrin to receive, transmit and develop the Oral Law to the nation of Israel just as Moses received, transmitted and developed the Oral Law from the *Ohel Moed.*

Moreover, functionally there is no legal distinction between the authority of the Sanhedrin established by Moses and the authority of the later iterations of the Sanhedrin in each subsequent generation. The Sanhedrin, the Supreme Court of Israel, is authorized as an *institution* to receive and interpret the laws of Israel. It is not the individual members of the Sanhedrin that are authorized (either because of their superior knowledge or their charisma) to transmit or interpret the laws but the institution of the Sanhedrin. It is for this reason that the Talmud states, "Yiftah in his generation is like Samuel in his generation." While each may have been the head of the Supreme Court of his respective generation, it is clear that Samuel was far greater than Yiftah. Nevertheless, the authority of the Supreme Court as an institution does not depend on the stature of its individual members but on the authority vested in it by the Tora received by Moses from the Almighty. It is specifically the institution that has the authority with respect to transmission of the Oral Law, and not the individual justices in their individual capacity. Yiftah, serving as the head of the Supreme Court of his generation, was vested with the same authority as Samuel, who also served as the head of the Supreme Court of his generation. Hence, although on an individual level Samuel was far greater than Yiftah, the institution that they both led, the Sanhedrin, was the same institution vested with the same authority, irrespective of whether the individual members of this institution were average or great.

* * *

We discussed earlier that the Sanhedrin derives its authority from the Tora, and more precisely from the *de-'oraita* laws received by Moses. Thus, the Sanhedrin's authority is predicated upon the *de-'oraita* laws received from Moses. It is worth re-emphasizing that because of the

Sanhedrin's subservient position in relation to the Tora received by Moses, the Sanhedrin does not have the authority to revise, add to, or subtract from the *de-'oraita* laws received from Moses.

However, the authority of the Sanhedrin, includes the following primary functions:

a. Maintaining the integrity of the *de-'oraita* laws by receiving them from the previous generation and transmitting them to future generations;
b. Interpreting (or re-interpreting) scriptural verses for legislative purposes;
c. Implementing regulations with respect to details of the *de-'oraita* laws not explained by Moses; and,
d. Legislating new *derabbanan* laws.

The Sanhedrin could legislate *derabbanan* laws for various reasons, including in order to augment and fortify the *de-'oraita laws,* as well as to address contemporary societal needs and issues. While such *derabbanan* laws were legislated by the Sanhedrin and were not part of the traditions received from Moses, the authority to legislate such *derabbanan* laws is itself *de-'oraita.* In the view of Maimonides and the Andalusian *ḥakhamim,* there is a *de-'oraita* obligation to accept and observe the instructions and decrees (i.e., the *derabbanan* laws) legislated by the Sanhedrin. Hence, every *derabbanan* law is in effect *de-'oraita,* insomuch as it is the word of God, spoken to Moses that obligates every Jew to accept and comply with such Supreme Court dictates.

* * *

As seen above, the Tora is constituted as a two-tiered system of laws. It may be useful to compare the Tora's two-tier system of laws to the two tiers that cause the variety of weather on Earth: (i) the sun; and (ii) the hydrosphere (which includes the atmosphere and the oceans). One tier, the *de-'oraita* laws, is as immutable and eternal as the sun rising and setting. The second tier, the interpretations of the Sanhedrin, together with their various promulgations, revocations and decrees, is dynamically changing like the Earth's weather. Together, these two systems create the weather we observe here on Earth, from the changing shapes of white cumulus clouds traveling against a blue springtime sky, to darker storm clouds that bring forth torrential rains.

The sun, as noted, is stable and eternal, but its specific effect on the Earth's atmosphere depends on many variables, including cloud cover, water vapor content, ocean temperatures (which in turn can be related to underwater volcanic activity, such as in the areas of the pacific ocean known as the "ring of fire"), atmospheric dew points, jet stream configurations, various atmospheric cyclical oscillations, blocking systems, etc. So, while the sun exerts a definite and profound effect on Earth's weather, this effect is conditioned and subject to the variables noted above. Still, while the sun is relatively stable, its influence on the Earth's meteorological systems is also dependent on various solar-related variables, including the position of the Earth in its orbit around the sun, sunspot frequency, the strength and angle of the sun's rays, solar flares, Milankovitch cycles, etc. The two systems, which interact dynamically and often unpredictably, are inseparable from each other, and are together responsible for the incredible variety of the weather conditions on Earth.

Like the sun, the *de-'oraita* laws given by Moses are eternal, stable and hierarchically superior to the *derabbanan* laws to the judiciary. Within the Tora system itself there are cycles and fluctuations, such as the 7 year Sabbatical cycle, the 50 year Jubilee cycle, laws that apply only in Israel, laws that change for areas outside of Israel, laws that apply when all the Jews are in Israel, etc. Like the changing atmospheric configurations and systems, the judiciary develops new laws, decrees, and practices, offers new interpretations of scriptures and abrogates old ones. The variety of *derabbanan* laws, with their fluctuations, permutations, shifts and alterations are too numerous to even begin to categorize. There is a dynamic interaction between the eternal *de-'oraita* laws and the activities of the judiciary, resulting in a panoply of laws, regulations, decrees and practices, some immutable and some changing and developing and some previously revoked. Like the great variety of weather on Earth caused by the sun and the hydrosphere, the two tiers of *de-'oraita* and judiciary affect each other dynamically, and form the incredible system of laws that govern the Jewish nation.

* * *

With the destruction of the Jewish government in Judea at the end of the Second Commonwealth came the waning of the Sanhedrin. To be sure, to be functional and effective, the Jewish judiciary does not require Jewish sovereignty in Jerusalem or Judea – indeed, the Jewish judiciary was fully functional in the desert before the Israelites reached the land of Israel. Hence, even after the destruction of the Second Commonwealth, together with the loss of Jewish autonomy in Israel, the Sanhedrin continued to function in various cities outside of Judea, such as the cities of Yabne and Usha.

However, with the increasing difficulty of life in Israel, and the exile of the majority of Jews to outside of Israel, the Sanhedrin was discontinued. Nevertheless, the Jewish judiciary continued through the Babylonian academies, or *yeshibot*. Although the *yeshibot* were located outside of Israel, they acted as the high court of Israel, authoritatively receiving and transmitting the laws of Israel, and convening to discuss the Mishna, as well as to settle matters of Jewish law. It should be noted that the authority of the Babylonian academies was based upon the fact that the vast majority of the Jewish people, together with a majority of the *ḥakhamim,* were physically located in Babylonia. Through the *yeshibot,* the *ḥakhamim,* acting as faculty members of these academies, convened to constitute the last High Court of Israel, which had legal jurisdiction over the Jewish people by virtue of their physical presence in Babylonia.

The *yeshibot* not only settled matters of Jewish law and interpreted the Mishna, but they formally recorded their rulings and interpretations, together with the Oral Law traditions of Israel, into an edited textual format known as the Babylonian Talmud. Thus, the Babylonian Talmud represents the final authoritative recording of the Oral Law of Israel. A similar, parallel project took place in Israel in the form of the Jerusalem Talmud, but due to adverse historical circumstances this project was never completed.

In conclusion, the authority of the Babylonian Talmud does not lie in the fact that the protagonists of the Talmud were pious, insightful, or brilliant – even though they were all of these things, that's not where Jewish legal authority lies. Rather, the authority of the Babylonian Talmud lies in the fact that it collected, organized and authoritatively recorded the rulings of this last High Court of the Jewish people.

It follows that material external to the Talmud, whether spoken or written, even if logical, convincing, holy, and inspiring all at once, is not legally binding, at least as a matter of Jewish law. Absent the reconstitution of the Sanhedrin, the legal authority of the Talmudic rulings continue until today. To be sure, a new Sanhedrin, once established, would have the authority to review some of the Talmudic rulings, and if it so chooses, to update them and issue new rulings to deal with contemporary issues and developments that the Talmud did not deal with.

* * *

Upon the completion of the Babylonian Talmud, the further dispersion of the Jewish people to places outside of Babylonia lead to the concomitant dissolution of the Jewish judiciary. Hence, with the completion of the Talmud there was no further authorized transmission of the Oral Law. The reason for this is that there was no legally authorized body that could either receive, transmit or to further develop the Oral Law. Hence, with the final editing of the Babylonian Talmud, so ended the period of the transmission of the Oral Law started by Moses. Correspondingly, the authority of the High Court was, in a sense, deposited into the Babylonian Talmud, since the Talmud now became the final authority in matters related to the Oral Law and to Jewish law.

The *Geonim* that came after the editing of the Talmud contributed to the Oral Law by providing precise explanations of the talmudic text and descriptions of how Jewish law was practiced in their communities, which substantially mirrored the talmudic rulings.

Later, from Andalusia, Spain, and following on the teachings of R. Yosef ibn Megas, Maimonides embarked upon the formulation of the greatest, and perhaps the most impactful, rabbinic work ever written (certainly after the Talmud): the *Mishne Tora*. In it, he restated the entirety of Jewish law and practice as set forth in the Talmud, lucidly, completely, fully, and faithfully. The impact of the *Mishne Tora* on the preservation of talmudic Judaism cannot be overstated.

Prior to the *Mishne Tora*, laymen, not sufficiently adept in the study of Talmud to understand its rulings, were forced to rely on a professional clergy who would inform them of the law in any given situation. Because the laymen asking the questions did not have the expertise to question such rulings, the clergy exerted strong influence over many Jewish communities. Of concern to the Andalusian *ḥakhamim* was that certain elements within this clergy did not view the Talmud as the ultimate or the sole source of authority. Hence, the legal rulings of this clergy were sometimes based on extra-talmudic sources, such as the personal ideas and notions of charismatic or pious leaders. The result was that there was a divergence between the requirements of talmudic law and some practices that were developing in various Jewish communities.

By setting forth talmudic law in simple, clear language, Maimonides at once freed Jewish communities from the halakhic rulings of the clergy, and at the same time removed the clergy from the powerful perch of being the sole arbiters of Jewish law. It is not particularly difficult to understand why some members of this clergy were critical of Maimonides, as he broke their monopolistic powers and influence over many Jewish communities.

In conclusion, Maimonides ensured the continuation of talmudic

Judaism by establishing talmudic law as the sole basis for rulings related to Jewish law. Significantly, because of Maimonides, scholars and non-scholars alike could now open the *Mishne Tora* and determine what the talmudic law was in any given situation. Because of its prominence and growing popularity, the *Mishne Tora* established talmudic law as the basis for normative practices in certain Jewish communities, such as the Yemenite Jewish community, who chose to follow the *Mishne Tora* in all matters of Jewish law. However, even for communities that did not strictly adhere to the *Mishne Tora* in all matters, the *Mishne Tora* became the gold standard for anyone interested in finding out what the pure unadulterated talmudic position was in any given situation. Divergent legal rulings that were based on extra-talmudic material were now easy to identify and scrutinize critically, simply by shining the light of the *Mishne Tora* upon such rulings. This meant that there was now a limit to how far Jewish practice could stray from talmudic law without raising some eyebrows. Specifically, because the *Mishne Tora* expressed talmudic law clearly and precisely, opinions and practices that diverged from the *Mishne Tora* would now need to be defended.

I will illustrate the above with a simple example. There is a widespread practice among some Jewish communities to slaughter a white chicken on the eve of Yom Kippur. Putting aside the non-trivial similarity of this practice to certain pagan practices, it is not recorded in the *Mishne Tora*. It is not recorded in the *Mishne Tora* because it is not recorded in the Talmud. It is not recorded in the Talmud because this practice was never part of the valid traditions transmitted by the Jewish judiciary. A simple Jew living in a Jewish community where this practice is widespread, not being well versed in the study of Talmud, would believe, incorrectly that this practice is required under Jewish law. With the publication and availability of the *Mishne Tora*, this same simple Jew could now easily determine that this practice is not recorded in the *Mishne Tora*, and, given its absence from the *Mishne Tora*, would conclude that it is not required under Talmudic law. He or she may then, perhaps, choose to eschew this practice as not part of the formal legal traditions of Israel but as a later addition.

* * *

Let us summarize some of the above. The *Mishnayot,* edited by R. Judah the Prince, allowed for the continuity of the Oral Law traditions during (and after) the Roman destruction of Jewish national life in Israel by transferring it from the Sanhedrin to a precise fixed text. Since this text was accessible to all of Israel, the Oral Law traditions became accessible to the public at large and no longer depended on the Sanhedrin for its existence. Somewhat analogously, the preparation and presentation of the *Mishne Tora* by Maimonides transferred the talmudic interpretations and legal rulings from the academies of Babylonia to the pages of the *Mishne Tora.* Hence, the *Mishne Tora* transformed the complex talmudic text into precise and clear legal instructions. This amounted to a transference of authority from the Talmud to the *Mishne Tora,* which, as noted, freed people from clergy leaders.

* * *

Let us now return to our earlier discussion. In contradistinction to Axis Y, that describes the development of the Oral Law traditions (through the judiciary) over the course of time, Axis X looks at the Tora as a synchronic system of knowledge that organically combines axiomatic/intellectual principles with *miṣvot*/rules of behavior.

This organic synchronic system of knowledge is often referred to as an "*eṣ ḥayyim,*" a "tree of life." This metaphor affirms that a successful system of knowledge and understanding should be like a flourishing tree. A flourishing tree dynamically extracts the right nutrients from the surrounding soil, from a spring of freshwater, from the falling rain, benefiting as well from the warmth of the sun or an ever gentle breeze, growing in strength while extending its branches into a growing canopy of green. This green canopy in turns provides shade and oxygen for the surrounding environment, shelter for birds and small animals, while the roots beneficially transform the soil so as to promote the growth of other plants, generating new life in the surrounding area. Hence, King Solomon compares the Tora to a tree of life: "It is a tree of life for those who uphold it."

Significantly, the Tora does not run away from new ideas and intellectual trends, but instead engages with them. It does so by dynamically deducing such ideas and trends from the contemporary landscape while critically analyzing and evaluating the intellectual and spiritual dimensions of such ideas and trends. Rather than avoid, it evaluates; if found lacking, it debates and pushes back or rejects; but, at times it adopts and adapts new intellectual trends and currents into the Tora system; or, alternatively, it may reveal that they were already part of the Tora system.

By way of illustration, today, based on cosmological observations and theories, we know that the Universe is incredibly vast in size, beyond comprehension. This view of the Universe augments our understanding of the Tora's description of creation and is fully compatible with the Tora system of thought. Therefore, the study of modern cosmology can be used for purposes of understanding the descriptions of creation contained at the beginning of Genesis. On the other hand, the hypothesis proposed by evolutionary biologists that incredibly complex information systems (also known as prokaryotic and eukaryotic cells) somehow just appeared through random processes, is incompatible with God being the supreme Creator. Therefore, the Tora would reject this hypothesis, much as the roots of a tree would not absorb harmful substances into the tree.

This rejection, however, is expressed in terms of intelligent discourse and not dogmatic bickering. In this way, the Tora, through the *ḥakhamim* who are its spokespersons, contributes to the contemporary landscape and discussions, and raises questions and considerations that any intelligent person (Jewish or gentile) would want to confront and consider. Hence, by engaging rather than ignoring, the Tora acts eternally to guide man and mankind towards a higher understanding of the created world and a consciousness of the Creator.

* * *

Although Axis Y expresses fidelity to the past while Axis X focuses on the contemporary landscape, the two axes are not contradictory. Let us return to the metaphor of the tree. Its branches grow larger, spreading in new and often unexpected directions, but they always remain attached to the trunk. Similarly, the Tora dynamically incorporates new concepts and ideas from the surrounding landscape, growing new branches, generating new ideas, and attaining knowledge that previous generations could not fathom. However, these new branches and directions always remain attached to the original trunk. The original trunk is always present, permanently serving as the foundation for everything that comes afterwards. Thus, there is no contradiction between Axis Y, which affirms the traditions of the past, and Axis X, which extends these traditions from the present into the future.

* * *

My father's perennial calling to me was and until today is: "There is no [such thing as a] *midrash* (a study session) with no new insights". Hence, on a daily basis, he would ask me: "Tell me a *ḥiddush* (an original and creative Tora insight)!" He would not take no for an answer. He prodded me and urged me to be fruitful with *ḥiddushim,* and to grow new branches on the "tree of life," insisting that I should not just read the texts of the Tora (be it the weekly *parasha,* a talmudic *sugya,* or even one of his own writings) but that I think about what I read, form new connections, generate insights, and compellingly articulate them. Thus, for the Ḥakham, allegiance to the past was not an obstacle to but rather a springboard for new knowledge and ideas.

In explaining this, my father taught me the verse in Ecclesiastes: "The words of *ḥakhamim* (the wise teachers of Israel) are like prods, and planted nails, masters of the assembled are they, all coming from one shepherd." Their words are like prods, which guide the sheep away from the dangers of the desolate and deadly desert, towards restful waters and lush fields. So, too, the words of the *ḥakhamim* guide the Jewish people away from harmful ideas and destructive notions offered by unintelligent leaders (cf., politicians) and towards the life-giving springs of the Tora. Still, while a prod moves the flock towards lush grass and promised water, the sensation caused by the prod is painful but fleeting; when the prod is gone, it leaves nothing behind. In contrast to the fleeting sensation of the prod, the words of the *ḥakhamim* are like "nails," as they serve to imbed the Tora system powerfully and permanently into the national psyche of Israel and into the mental constructs of those individuals that receive them, structuring their internal intellectual apparatus, linguistic faculties, as well as epistemological outlooks and concepts.

However, nails are but dead metallic items; they do not grow, they are static and offer no future promise. Tellingly, King Solomon added a single word to describe these nails: "planted." The words of the *ḥakhamim* are like "*planted* nails." Rather than being inanimate and static, they are alive and growing. How can this be? The words of the *ḥakhamim* are an extension of the Tora system of knowledge, which itself is a "tree of life." Therefore, these words are themselves alive, growing and part of a living organic system.

Like a majestic tree that draws different animals and birds to its shade, the words of the *ḥakhamim* draw those who seek knowledge of God's Tora to the Tree of Life! Hence, the words of the *ḥakhamim* are "masters of the assembled." To be precise, these words gather the people and orient them towards the center of the garden, when they can partake of the Tree of Life, and enjoy the presence of their Creator.

***

There is another aspect to the "masters of the assembled." Consider that in hierarchical societies, which includes almost every Western political system, masters of men are other men who are above them, and who therefore have a right (by virtue of the monopoly of violence that they yield) to tell those below them what to do, what to think, how to behave.

Gentile societies and nations are organized vertically, with an elite class that abuses and uses those beneath them: from Pharaoh's ministers in Egypt to the Roman Emperor's financial patrons, to the members of the World Economic Forum, the elites are usually above and operate outside the law, standing in a hierarchically superior position over others. Men lording over other men, acting like their "masters," is a ubiquitous dimension of Western civilization, where words such as "democracy" and "equity" are bandied around so as to create the illusion of freedom and caring.

In contrast, King Solomon envisions a world, a horizontal society, where intelligent words pronounced by intelligent people call upon other intelligent people to hear, to listen, to think and to respond – nay, to join the conversation and meaningfully contribute their own intelligent words! For Western politicians, it is essential that the masses be composed of unlearned people – otherwise, how can they be fooled by words such as "democracy!"

Consider King Solomon's vision of a nation that is animated by intelligent words spoken by the King himself, words that illuminate the nation of Israel. Contrast that vision with the contemporary political landscape in the United States (circa 2022) and other Western "democracies," where insipid speeches of petty buffoons and senile politicians, and the narratives offered by other intellectually and spiritually bankrupt "woke" overlords, seek to keep their constituents away from even the possibility of intelligence, by shutting down (or shall we say, by "canceling") free thought and dialogue. Compellingly, they tell us that "you are a racist!" if you think otherwise.

The reason for promoting low intellect and dull critical judgment is obvious: intelligence on the part of the populace would expose the leaders as evil and incompetent. "Eat the fruit! It's good for you!" screams the snake. "You'll become like one of us!" I, for one, choose to walk back towards the Tree of Life.

The Ḥakham, my father, envisioned a civilization, a Jewish civilization. This civilization would not be composed of analphabetic people who subserviently bow before the dictates of tyrants, petty politicians and unlearned spiritual leaders of whatever religious denomination. Rather, it would be composed of an alphabetic people who are interested in the knowledge expressed by the words, and even letters, of the Tora, by the words of the *ḥakhamim*, people who are looking not for abstract philosophical concepts but for the wisdom expressed in concrete words and in allegorical sign posts.

Note that the "masters" in the aforementioned verse, "Masters of the assembled," are not the wise men but the *words* of the wise men! Hence, a free man does not accept a human master or overlord. A free individual accepts wise words as his or her master. Words are intelligent, not because of who said them, but because our minds recognize these words as containing wisdom. "Receive the truth from whomsoever spoke it," says Maimonides.

We present before you in these volumes the wise words written by Ḥakham Dr. Rabbi José Faur. These words are meant to free you, the reader, from the manipulation of unlearned (but very shrewd) individuals seeking that you blindly and uncritically accept whatever is told to you by *that* person, because he is above you, because he knows better than you.

The Ḥakham's words seek an intelligent individual: they seek an individual who wishes to be free from the shackles of ignorance imposed by those who know better than we do because they are in positions of political power, standing hierarchically above us. Submitting to these shackles is a *sine qua non* to be a member in good standing of modern Western polities and cultural systems. Through these volumes, you are hereby invited to free yourself from these shackles, to join the linguistically intelligent members of the Jewish people, and to begin to listen closely to the masters of the assembled.

Manhattan Beach, NY
Tebet 26, 5783
January 18, 2023

# The Horizontal Society

## Understanding the Covenant and Alphabetic Judaism

### Volume I

# Contents

SECTION V: THE FOLLY OF ISRAEL

# Introduction
# Recovering the Straight and the Good

*Alan J. Yuter*

This two-volume work is in reality many books in one, encompassing many methods and modes of discourse as it addresses and explicates radically different constructions of social and religious reality. José Faur writes formally as a secular, critical scholar, decoding the past, arguing his theses, and presenting an anthropology of the Judaism that he contends is encoded in Israel's sacred library. However, Faur personally, normatively, and passionately identifies with that canonical library's encoded culture, which serves as the benchmark by which other Judaisms are measured, decoded, and evaluated.

This formally modern, scholarly work is also a *derasha*, an exercise in the rhetoric of rabbinic argument, analysis, and non-authoritarian persuasion. Faur's magisterial *derasha* both explicates and exemplifies

Judaism's canonical version,[1] which is conceived as a horizontal society of covenanted Israelites who are citizens but not subjects, all of whom are invested with the image of God and subject to God's law over and above the human tyrant's self-interested caprice. Using historiography, literary criticism, philosophy, philology, and anthropology, Faur first decodes the normative culture prescribed by this Judaism's sacred canon and then contrasts the horizontal, egalitarian society that this canon commends, with special, explicit attention to the politics of pagan structures, to Christianity as a theological political construction of reality, to Orthodox Judaism as it presents itself in Jewish non-rabbinic mysticism, the anti-Maimonidean movement,[2] and, as I argue in the footnotes, to the contemporary religion of Orthodox Judaism's street culture. In other words, Faur's description of events past is an implicit polemic opposing what is [mis]taken to be Orthodox Dual Torah Judaism.

The narrative's secular academic format deals with descriptive explication; the *derasha* presents the argument, based on explication, and an *apologia,* defending the canonical Covenant that constitutes

1. This Judaism is identical to what Neusner calls the "Judaism of the Dual Torah," defined in his *Judaism: The Evidence of the Mishnah* (Chicago and London: University of Chicago Press, 1981); see pp. 14–24. Neusner defines the social and theological construction of Jewish reality envisioned by the Mishnah, based on a New Criticism reading, i.e., based upon internal evidence that the Mishnah actually provides. Faur argues that this Judaism is preserved in old Sepharad and has its source in the Written Torah, the Aramaic Targum Onqelos, and was made explicit by Maimonides. Just as Neusner addresses the dead end paths of G.F. Moore and E.E. Urbach, who used categories borrowed from Christian theology that are not intrinsic to the Mishnah's encoded world construction, Faur contrasts the phenomenology of this Judaism to its competitors, those Judaic systems that sought to suppress and supersede the Judaism of the Dual Torah. For a statement of this terminology, see Neusner, *Economics of the Mishnah* (Chicago: University of Chicago Press, 1990), p. 12. See also *Judaism: The Evidence of the Mishnah*, p. 14, for a gracious appreciation of Moore's seminal efforts, which also exposes Moore's inappropriate conceptual paradigm.
2. See Faur, "Anti-Maimonidean Demons," in *Review of Rabbinic Judaism* 6 (2003), pp. 3–52.

the polity called "Israel." Faur applies academic methodology when addressing Rabbinic literature and appears as a precise, astute, and accomplished philologist. However, as a matter of nationalist Jewish pride, Faur refuses to submit Biblical Hebrew writing to secular, critical analysis. Avoiding even the lower criticism of R. Abraham ibn Ezra, Faur even treats Isaiah as a singular, unified document.[3] However, Faur cites higher critics approvingly on occasion,[4] indicating to the astute reader that the author is keenly aware of the critical school as well as its nonacademic and occasionally anti-Jewish culture biases.[5] By affirming that the Hebrew Bible is best read with the tools applied to fiction, and by astutely noting that as long as the Jew observes the *mitsvot,* which are presented not as commandments but as teachings/precepts of covenantal Judaism, Faur the narrator emerges as an "Orthodox" post-modern thinker who is not a fundamentalist. Indeed, for Faur, fundamentalism is the rhetoric of tyrannical leaders to create compliant, controllable crowds.

This review essay surveys and explicates the five sections of Faur's

3. While many critical scholars regard Ephesians, Timothy I, II, and Titus to be post-Pauline, many fundamentalist Christians regard the ascriptions to be divinely inspired and therefore inerrant. Faur, on ideological grounds, refuses to treat his canon, or "Book," as a pedestrian document. Indeed, he treats all New Testament books ascribed to Paul as Pauline, because, even as an adversary, he is meticulous regarding protocol.
4. On p. 150, n. 31, Faur uses *Diqduqei Soferim,* the variant readings from the Munich MS. Faur does not flinch from academically defensible and responsible lower text criticism.
5. See, e.g., p. 156, n. 57, where he castigates Rimon Kasher, Bar Ilan University, who argued that to be considered sacred, books of Scripture were said to have been composed with the Holy Spirit. But see T. Sot. 13:3. For Faur, academic critics often internalize a Christian hermeneutic that is alien to the ethos of Israel's canonical library, a criticism that Neusner has astutely identified in the writings of Moore and Urbach (see n. 1, above). For Faur, " 'Jewish history' needs to have been first regurgitated by non-Jews" regarding the issue of canonization, which, for Faur, is a term not found in Israel's Dual Torah canon. Critics whom Faur treats with respect are William F. Albright, Elias Bickerman, Robert Gordis, E. Speiser, and Mayer Gruber.

work: The God of Israel, the Books of Israel, the governance of Israel, the memory of Israel, and the folly of Israel.

## 1. The God of Israel

Faur portrays the God of Israel as a writer who appears to Israel in a book, i.e., the Torah. Opening with a discussion of the Book of Creation [*Sefer Yesira*], which Faur understands to be an epistemological hermeneutic regarding creation and not a work of theosophic mysticism, because *Sefer Yesira* views creation as an act of writing. Tellingly, Faur argues that fiction is the closest form of writing to Torah, the building of worlds with words. In his introduction, Faur introduces the core theme that pervades his work, that unalphabetic societies "produce fanatics, not sages" (p. 67). The Greeks are unalphabetic, their gods do not read. This astute observation is corroborated by Antigone, who pleads before the gods of the unwritten law and for the Greeks; memorization is more valuable than written texts. The Torah is for Faur a legal document that embodies the bilateral contract/covenant between God and Israel. Those who do not understand the "Book" reflect "godless and soulless ideologies" of "German historiography and the Documentary Hypothesis." It must be stressed that Faur's opposition to the Documentary Hypothesis is epistemological and political but not theological. This point is made by Faur's identifying Jacob Neusner (p. 66) as the author of the insight that there are descriptively various and often competing Judaisms. When a Bible critic would not subject the American Constitution to critical analysis "because we live under it," Faur retorted that there are Jews who choose to live under Torah. Furthermore, Neusner also endorses the Documentary Hypothesis and astutely distinguishes between Judaisms that are in fact conflicting and competing systems. Faur affirms that his own Judaism is that of Old Sepharad, Maimonidean, and is for Faur alphabetic, a term to be unpackaged, explicated, and applied to decode the religion that in post-Rabbinic times is the most direct successor to what Neusner calls "the Judaism of the Dual Torah."[6]

In M. Ab. 5:6, at that liminal moment between the Creation week and the first Sabbath, God endowed humanity with "two separate faculties," *Ketab*, script, and *mikhtab*, writing (p. 73). By reading the text that binds both God and Israel, the reader him or /herself becomes a writer by generating meaning through reading. Because Judaism has a published, linguistically fixed, and uniformly accepted "Book,"[7] it develops through conversation and persuasion regarding the Book's meaning; the Book's norms are precepts that are observed as acts of human willful compliance and not as commandments of compulsion. The individual human is endowed with the image of God, which is the capacity to be a reader, a copartner with God the Author in the ongoing generation of meaning.

No other god in antiquity was a writer. God wrote the covenant Book with the Divine finger (Exod. 31:19, 34:1, Deut. 9:10) and also writes on the wall (Dan. 5:5–6). Thus Faur ends his prologue with the core idea that animates the Judaism he presents in both academic discourse and with didactic diction, that God does not communicate with an analphabetic audience (p. 77), because God communicates through and by means of His Book (p. 80). Meaning is what emerges from the reading/engagement with the Book on the part of the reader. God wrote the Book of Life, which for R. Levi b. Gershon is "everything that exists" (p. 80). Faur argues that Isaac Newton[8] and Francis Bacon subscribed to this same system, that the world is a

6. Neusner, *supra.*
7. See Moshe Halbertal, *People of the Book: Canon, Meaning and Authority* (Boston: Harvard University Press, 1997), where the distinction between an open as opposed to closed canon is developed.
8. Faur develops this thesis in "Esoteric Knowledge and the Vulgar: Parallels between Newton and Maimonides," in *Trumah* 12 (2002), pp. 183–191; "Newton, Maimonidean," in *Review of Rabbinic Judaism* 6 (2003), pp. 215–249; "Sir Isaac Newton–'A Judaic Monotheist of the School of Maimonides,' " in Gorge K. Hasselhoff and Otfied Fraisse, eds., *Moses Maimonides (1138–1204)* (Germany: Ergon Verlag, 2004), pp. 289–309.

Book written by God (p. 83) through "decoding (*ketab*) and reading (*mikhtab*)."

Analphabetic speech maintains that the word is a "thing;" that the signified and signifier are identical (p. 88). The copula "be" expresses this identity, which makes mythic thinking possible, as in the origin, the metaphysic *arche*.[9] Writing and reading are not only alien to the Greek mind and ethos (p. 89) but also to Western culture in general and what is taken to be religious Orthodoxy,[10] both Christian and Jewish, in particular. Faur correctly calls attention to Plato's preference for memory over the written word in antiquity (p. 92) and the intellectual successor of Platonic analphabetic Edmund Husserl, the father of phenomenology, according to which "becoming" is a mystical idea (p. 93).

Faur rejects the discipline called "Theology" because it is, to apply G.E. Moore's term, a category error. The alphabetic God who is a writer cannot be addressed analphabetically, with an epistemology modeled on and molded by Greek language and conceptual structures. Hence, Scripture is a book, "not a totem" (p. 98), and Scripture is to be read as a novel, with Adam the [initial] hero (p. 99). In classical Maimonidean tradition, Faur here reveals to the attentive reader that he is hardly a fundamentalist, that he not only does not believe that the written biblical word is an exact, exhaustive, documentable historical record; he would argue that such a mimetic inclination is itself a symptom of the analphabetic thinking that fuses and confuses the signified with the signifier. By viewing the doctrine that humankind is created in God's image, after the Akkadian *ṣalmu* ,[11] Faur insightfully turns the idiom on its head, having God in His Book proclaiming an anti-pagan polemic. For the pagan, the idol is the totem for

9. John 1:1 is an exquisite example of this phenomenon.
10. As will be suggested below, Faur *never* directly addresses Jewish Orthodoxy, but when addressing other subjects, he *always* addresses the dissonance between Judaism's canonical religion and its popular reconstruction in everyday life.
11. Faur's doctorate is from University of Barcelona in Semitic Philology. Unlike

the god; in God's Book given to Israel, the human is a visible totem of the divine, with this quality not to be monopolized by a hierarchical elite, but shared by every single human being. It is Adam and not God who gives name to God's creations. It is by reading that God and humankind engage in conversation. In the books written by God, the Torah and the cosmos, God has dominion because God made the world. Therefore, the divine politics–not theology!–declare that no human has a right of dominion over others. But God is ultimately unknowable even though God, like the novel's author, is always and everywhere present.

For the Greek mind, memory recovers speech, which in the mind of the muse and the mouth of the poet is the truth revealed in the enthrallment of the audience. In this world construction no critical analysis may be tolerated; the mind of the masses is worthless (p. 113). For Faur, this scheme requires a leisure class that is free to be political because all others are slaves (p. 114).

In contrast, Hebrew speech is neither theatrical nor dramatic; after all, Moses was rhetorically challenged [Exod. 4:10]. According to Faur, "the shield against the call to barbarism is alphabetic discourse" (p. 128). With this seemingly innocent idiom, the overture to the argument ends, introducing the line of argument that will unfold. God dominates by dint of creation; by being Book based, humanity has a shared benchmark for truth as well as a grammatical grid for communication. Power is expressed in the persuasive word and not the brutal fist. Having introduced the two competing anthropologies, the culture of the Divine Book and brutal, human force, Faur then turns to the Books of Israel.

---

most Orthodox readers, who impose *a priori* beliefs *on* the textual canon, Faur uses philology to formulate as innocent a reading of the canon as possible in order to understand its normative claims.

## 2. The Books of Israel

Faur opens the second section of his work by describing Adam's choice to live in a world of rules promulgated by God or to inhabit a world in which a human master/*Adon* speaks in a divine voice in order to subjugate other humans. While both cultures have divinities and rules, the former system is hierarchical, and rules are enforced with the threat of violence. In the latter system, the Book provides the values and premises whereby the reader, the Ruler meets the ruled in dialogue (p. 129).

There are three principles that are central to the Jewish theory of the Book:

1. The book is a national publication, published by the nation and validated by the people,
2. The *ketab* or writing is public, accessible, and is the source of religious, political, and legal authority, and
3. The right to apply, through *meliṣa,* the rhetoric of persuasion, the reading of the *mikhtab,* the writing is given to the Jewish people and not to a hierarchical elite.

This reading is necessarily *synchronic,* localized at a moment *in* time.[12] Commands, or what Faur calls precepts, occur in the present. Note that the imperative, grounded upon the imperfect tense (popularly but incorrectly understood as future tense) is itself out of time and therefore without tense. By historicizing and attempting to describe an essentially unrecoverable past as a thing-in-itself, "historians" who study the Jewish Torah not as Book but as an artifact are for

12. This sensibility underlies Faur's rejection of *"Historical"* Jewish scholarship, which imposes, like Urbach on the Oral Torah, unwarranted conjectures while missing the fact that the object of study is a real Judaism, a Judaic system that makes normative claims.

Faur engaging in an ideological polemic but not in an academic pursuit of truth discovery. Therefore, challenging the authority of the Book would be akin to arguing for the de-authorization of the Bill of Rights, because they were forged at their historical origins out of earlier versions. Alternatively, other religions presume and indeed validate hierarchy, while Torah, the Jewish national Book, is given to all Israel and may be accessed to hold leaders to account. After all, the *ketab,* referring to the Written law, is static; the *michtab,* the vowel-less writing that requires reading–not recitation[13]–is the domain of the oral law, whereby the reader participates in the assignation of meaning–to the Book.

Since "religion" carries with it a semantic field that originates with Christianity,[14] applying Christian categories to Judaism is, for Faur, singularly inappropriate. Whatever the intellectual constructs regard-

---

13. In Judaism, the Scriptural text is preserved without vowels. If the vowels would be inscribed in the Torah text and subsequently erased, the scroll would remain invalid. Readers are required to supply the vowels in reading and, through reading, interpreting. In contrast, the Quran contains the vowel marks and one recites what one sees, and the *Koine* Greek of the Gospels is a vocalized documentary trove.
14. According to Max Weber, religions begin with charisma and are established with institution building. This "theory" is a reification of the Christian experience, where the shamed, crucified Messiah, thought by Jews to be a political redeemer, is repacked, re-presented, and marketed to non-Jews by the salesmanship of Paul. As seen above, Israel's leadership is anti-charismatic; Moses is not a good speaker until his concluding soliloquy in Deuteronomy, where he does not appear as speaker/prophet but as a teacher, anticipating the role the Rabbis will assign him. So too Islam; Muhammad is both charismatic *and* an institution builder. Faur's point is that academics compose academic rhetoric while engaging in ideological polemics; however, making the reader aware that he is engaging in *meliṣa,* Faur alerts the attentive reader to his actual agenda, to write an *apologia/derasha* exposing the official world construction of Judaism in starkly contemporary terms. However, this position is also polemical.

ing the ancient religion of Israel might be,[15] Faur finds that the content of the Book is a contract/ *berit* covenant, consisting of (p. 135):

1. A proposal that Israel would follow God's precepts, and Israel would be preserved as a holy people, a kingdom of priests. Clergy do not have monopoly access to the sacred.[16] Israel freely accepts the terms,[17] so Moses transmitted the decision to God. By needing to be "informed" of Israel's decision to accept the covenant, God appears not as not all knowing but as not coercing, intimidating or imposing the Torah upon Israel.
2. The theophany at Sinai is to be seen as instruction, as precepts, and not as coerced commands, which are proposed to Israel for acceptance.
3. Israel accepts the bargain, agreeing to live in accordance with those precepts. Moses then records the covenant content, and a ratification ceremony took place,
4. and the covenant is then ratified, without the divine fireworks of fire and thunder, which could be taken to be coercive. Moses ordered the erection of twelve pillars, representing the tribes, and one altar, representing God. This covenant is seen as a binding

15. See Faur, "Idolatry," in *Encyclopaedia Judaica* (1973), vol. 8, cols. 1227–1232, and "Thie Biblical Idea of Idolatry," in *Jewish Quarterly Review* 69 (1978), pp. 1–26.
16. Before forcing Aaron to build a golden calf, the *'am*, the non-covenented *ethnoi'* rise up on or over him (Exod. 32:1). Moses restores order by reconvening Israel as *et adat kol benei Yisrael* (Exod. 35:1). In addition to the hierarchical *'al*, meaning "on," Moses restores order and meaning with *et*, the Hebrew direct object marker, cognate to the Akkadian *itti*, meaning "with," indicating horizontality. According to Num. 16:3, Qorah and his cohorts congregated over/ on Moses and Aaron. In this narrative, Qorah reads hierarchy into Moses' intent, revealing to the attentive reader his own power hungry intention. In Faur's *Horizontal Society* II, the excurses both define and corroborate the first volume's thesis. The test of a theory's validity is its ability to explain as yet unexamined phenomena, and it appears that Faur's theory explains Hebrew Scripture's narration rather well.
17. See B. Shab. 88a and Rashi to Exod. 19:17. Rashi's reading of the B. Shab. passage reflects a penchant for coercion over persuasion.

> preliminary compact, as later stipulations, including penalties for covenantal breach (Lev. 26:3–46).

For Faur, the rest of the precepts were given over the next forty years[18] and are subject neither to addition nor to subtraction.[19] In recompense for following God's rules, Israel merits God's special attentive care (p. 138).

Ever the attentive lawyer, Faur's *meliṣa*/legal brief offers a supremely crafted argument, suggesting that in paganism, commandments are enforced with violence; the pagan gods perform miracles to demonstrate power.[20] There is no word in Hebrew for "obedience." It is the fulfillment of the precept, or instructional norm, that is called *qiyyum*, a fulfillment of the norm. Since God is eternal, so is the Covenant. Israel may be punished for not obeying the Covenant, but God will not abrogate the Covenant.[21] Thus the King of the universe does not claim sovereign immunity; therefore no human sovereign may ever claim to be beyond or above the law.[22] Gods who change their

18. Faur seems to be endorsing the view that the Torah was given scroll by scroll over the forty year desert sojourn. See B. Git. 60a. It is however possible that for Faur the written Torah was given as occasional oral oracles during the wilderness sojourn with the Torah document being given whole at the end of Deuteronomy, which is apparently Maimonides' view (Introduction to MT). See also Deut. 31:24, where it is reported that the Torah was then completed.
19. Deut. 13:1, according to which Moses takes Pharaoh's words ironically and out of context. See Exod. 5:7–8. Pharaoh adds to the Israelite work load without diminishing quota requirements, changing a human law in order to assert human authority. In God's law, one who changes the rules is a rebel against God.
20. In Mark and Matthew, Jesus performs miracles to impress the *Greek* reader; Jews would not be so impressed. In John, Jesus is talking over Jews to Greeks, and miracles demonstrate his agency and divinity.
21. The Christian claim that the Covenant has been modified is for Faur impossible. He addresses this below.
22. Consider Richard M. Nixon's angry retort in the screenplay *Frost/Nixon*, "If I [the president, taken or mistaken to possess sovereign immunity] do this, it is not illegal." Faur notes that this doctrine is explicit in Y. R.H. 2:5, 57b..

mind willy-nilly are no more than self-absorbed tyrants,[23] and the king, or ultimate sovereign of Israel, is not really the current human representative of the Davidic line, but the law itself (p. 139). In pagan thought,[24] there is a cosmic power that when mastered and manipulated by men "compels the deity" (p. 139). Faur's diction is critical; a humanly defined "deity" is for Israel no God at all, and that it is for the Hebrew mind "profoundly irreverent" to suggest that humans are able to read God's mind (p. 139).

The ideal of "the Book" is manifest in Hebrew Scriptures. The Torah is the Law or Constitution of Israel, which governs the political, judicial, and ecclesiastical aristocracies of Israel, the Prophets record the political history or memory of ancient Israel, and humans address God and Israel in the Wisdom or "sacred" Writings. The speaker in the first two sections is God, in the third section, humans. These national books of Israel are preserved and protected by special notes, with fixed official texts, and are given to *derasha*, or publically accessed and persuasive argumentation. The oral law, the system whereby the written law is parsed[25] and protected, is expressed primarily in the Mishnah and Talmud. The Judaism of the sages, of the "Dual Torah," regards the written text and the mental/oral law as a signified/signifier system, to be [1] the Judaism of the Book, [2] that is a published, accessible national text, that is [3] read in and

23. Hesiod concedes as much in Theogeny, in which the gods are interested in station, sex, power and control. See also Enoch 7.

24. At this stage of his narrative, Faur artfully contrasts *avoda zara*, the opiate of the masses that justifies human authority by authorizing humans to speak [falsely] in God's voice. Furthermore, when Faur refers to covenant with Israel as a people, it is the people and no self appointed elite. Consider the dictum of Num. 16:1, where Qorah appoints himself to be Moses's challenger and, without believing in God, speaks in God's voice. It is a narrative irony that, on the one hand, Faur, like Maimonides, eschews artful and crafty narrations, but at his argument's beginnings one finds the groundwork of his well-developed conclusions.

25. This observation corresponds to Neusner's descriptive idiom, "the Judaism of the Dual Torah."

by a people, that [4] is alphabetic, i.e., is endowed with both the right and ability to read. Faur advances this definition clearly and without ambiguity: "God's words ... are conditioned to the linguistic apparatus of *the people* " [my emphasis; p. 148]. A reading of the "Book" is that sense in which the people, i.e., all Israel, apply the *mikhtab*/meaning generating system to the *ketab,* or fixed, textually protected sacred covenant that provides the benchmark/meaning grid for interpretive reading exposition, or *derasha,* covenantally authorized and dynamic inquiry into God's word.[26] What Scripture means as a "thing-in-itself" is, for Faur, unknowable and inconsequential; what is ultimately normative is how the text is surrendered to [*mesura*] and processed by a people (p. 148). The process of *perush,* or unfolding of meaning, makes the reader and Writer copartners in the generation of meaning. Analphabetic minds operate under the ideological and metaphysical allusion and delusion that the mind of the writer (human) or Writer (God) can be objectively read and understood. Meaning is not determined or coerced by the first person, but for Israel's freedom giving God is processed and negotiated through the reading generated by the Writer/reader engagement.

Obliquely alluding to the contemporary doctrine of *Daas Torah,* Faur's core argument is here articulated in précis form. Greek, and its spiritual and political successors, Imperial Rome, Pauline Christianity, the secular "Enlightenment," which revivifies Greek culture and epistemology, kabbalistic Judaism, and implied throughout the line of argument, contemporary popular religion Orthodox Judaism, all claim that the betters, i.e. the aristocrats, have the right of rule because [1] they have the power, kingdom, and glory at their disposal, [2] they are rightly "ordained" and read the mind of God "correctly," as

26. Although not noted by Faur, the analphabetic Greeks, who do not have a canon of sacred books and for whom the memorized rather than written word carries great valence, produced a Herodotus, for whom inquiry is "history." He is known as "the father of history" and "the father of lies." His retelling of the Persian war is his opinion, based on an *a priori* world view; it is not a national book with normative valence.

*orthodox*, and [3] they exercise their right of rule with the threat of the exercise of coercive violence. For Israel the oral and written law are "equally divine," God having committed God's self not "to neither invade the *mind* of the reader nor to *dictate the meaning* of the covenant" (p. 148). The Jewish interpretive system excludes divine intervention in determining what the covenant means, because the "exposition" of the Book is given to the people (p. 149). The Book does not lay at rest in a guarded archive; it is the public property of Israel, it was formally presented by God and accepted by Israel. Israel studies and interprets[27] the text of the Book and does not meekly and obsequiously obey coerced commandments but willingly fulfills God's mediated precepts (p. 150).[28] Thus, God agrees not to dictate the covenant's meaning (p. 151).

To ensure textual stability, the Torah's official template version was placed in the holy place, the *Qodesh*, hence Scripture refers not to the holy books but the books safeguarded and preserved at the holy place. Torah scrolls that are copied from authorized copies carry the same legal valence as the originals.[29] And since Samuel, the

27. Faur cites B. B.M. 59b, where R. Eliezer the Great is put under the ban for invoking God's will. Even though God, in an oracle, confirmed R. Eliezer's opinion, the expressed will of God outside the covenant carries no force. In Hartian terms, divine intervention as a source of law is not a "rule of recognition" in the Judaism of the Dual Torah. See H.L.A. Hart, *The Concept of Law* (Oxford: Clarendon, 1979), pp. 97–106. For Hans Kelsen, R. Eliezer's claim would be an "ideology," a disfiguring of the legal order. See Hans Kelsen, *Pure Theory of Law*, trans. Max Knight (Berkeley: University of California Press, 1967), pp. 208–10. In the legal order of Torah, lower-grade norms may not violate higher norms. In the Maimonidean version of halakhic jurisprudence, judicial discretion does apply to the gaps in the law, i.e., where there is no statutory rule. The local judge/*dayyan* carries the valence of a *bet din shel yahid*, whose rulings are valid as long as the canonical statute remains inviolate. See Maimonides, *Yad, Introduction.*
28. Following B. Meg. 7a.
29. Although not noted by Faur, the touching/kissing of the waters of one *miqveh* with another filled with drawn water bestows the fit pool's ritual status on the second pool. See M. Miq. 6:1–3 and Maimonides, Miqvaot 8:7.

sage of Nehardea, opined that while the Scroll of Esther is divinely inspired, it is not a Book, or given to *derasha* or exposition. For a tradition to be "canonical" or official, it must be published, or recited and accepted in the plenum session of the Court. By making this point at this juncture of his argument, Faur brilliantly foreshadows his discussion at Section V, the Folly of Israel, where the speculative gnostic intuitions of mystics are presented to the Jewish people as *Kabbalah,* or [false] "Tradition," lacking reference to the Book or vetting by the norm creating Court, which determines whether or not this or that rule, idea, or doctrine is in fact "Tradition."[30] Although written down, memoranda[31] are not given to interpretive exposition; for Faur, "only a duly published text, [approved by the court and] available to the general public, may be included in the Scripture and used for *derasha* (p. 164)."

After probing what the Scriptural text means to the linguistic community, Faur discusses *peshat,* commonly taken to be the "plain" or philological meaning of the text. For Faur, *peshat* actually refers to the "manifest tenor" or "commonly accepted" sense of Scripture, which the sages distinguished from *derasha.* Note well that just as one can read God's Book but not God's mind, *peshat* of Scripture is not an "objective" thing-in-itself, meaning that is discovered, uncovered, or recovered from the text; it is the sense of Scripture to which the Sadducees, i.e., those "unorthodox" Jews who rejected the Judaism of the

30. Regarding Faur's view, which is based upon Maimonides, of those who claim to possess "Tradition" by dint of individual charisma and intuition, even though said Tradition was not given to the collective of Israel the people, see Maimonides, Repentance 3:7. The claim that individuals are capable of reading God's mind outside of referencing a persuasive reading of the Book is, as Faur argues, theological fraud.

31. This seemingly innocent remark also anticipates the critique of kabbalistic Judaism that will be the subject of this work's Section V. Take for example the current idiom used by many orthodox rabbis, "the holy Zohar," "the holy Baal Shem Tob," "the holy Or ha-Hayyim." No one speaks of the holy tractates of *Kereitot, Mei'la,* or *Baba Batra.* Faur argues that Jewish mystics make claims that conflict with the religion of the Dual Torah.

Dual Torah in late antiquity, concur (p. 165).[32] Since *peshat* reflects the popular sense of Scripture and not the discovery of the thing-in-itself, the *derasha* may actually generate subsequent, evolving *peshat* understandings, which themselves unfold with the evolution of the linguistic community. In perhaps the most profound observation in the monograph, Faur states that other literature changes flow from the community to the text, while, in Israel, when Hebrew was displaced by Aramaic and was preserved in the *Qodesh,* or sacred precinct, the flow of ideas went from the text to the community. In other words, *derasha* generates *peshat* by over time becoming the manifest tenor of the text (p. 173).[33]

The written law as a static text cannot be taken as an unmediated direct command but must be addressed with the *derasha,* in this case, *Midrash Halakhah.* The *mitzvah* is the judicial application of the written law (p. 174).[34] Anticipating his subsequent critique of pagan political law, Faur here argues that the *Kabbalah,* the authentic Oral Law Tradition, is active and not, as required by pagan coercive authority, passive.[35] And because the Torah was given to the people, the Court is held to account and must offer a sin-offering after breaking the law. Indeed, a scholar who defers to the Court when he knows the court to be in error is a deliberate sinner (p. 175).[36] Only with regard to the gaps in the law, where there is no

32. B. San. 33b and B. Hor. 4a-b. Faur astutely calls attention to Maimonides, Sanhedrin 10:9, where he notes that the Pharisees and Sadducees' agreement was based upon persuasion and not "the actual literal sense of the Scripture."
33. Long ago, Professor Daniel Boyarin graciously explained to me in a private communication that *peshat* is not really objective but conditioned by the subjectivity of the reader.
34. Faur cites Mishneh Torah, Introduction, as the source of this insight (p. 174).
35. Although unaddressed by Faur, because the discussion does not follow his line of argument, the Scroll of Esther corroborates his theory. The pagan king in Esther is active, while his subjects are almost uniformly described in passive voice.
36. B. Hor. 2b. The Israelite hero obeys the law thoughtfully and actively, not passively or obsequiously. There is not one Hebrew Scriptural hero who was weak or passive. See Lev. 4:13 and Rashi, *ad. loc.*

objective right or wrong, does the Court have ultimate and final jurisdiction. In other areas, the Court has limited jurisdiction. The Law, not the Court, clergy, or monarchy, in Israel is sovereign. Since Scripture never may be shorn of its *peshat*/manifest tenor [see B. Shab. 11b, B. Yeb. 11b and 24a], the judiciary assigns but does not reveal meaning to the Written Law text.

While Maimonides believes that there are real Jewish articles of faith,[37] he does not regard deniers of doctrine to be ineligible to testify,[38] but only disqualifies those who violate behavioral norms.[39] Matters of doctrine are given to persuasion but not coercion; the court deals with deeds, not doctrine or dogma. Here Faur, the anti-Bible critic, astutely signals that his own intellectual and theological commitments notwithstanding, Judaism stresses deed, not doctrine, and these matters are subject to conscience.[40] Consequently, Faur

---

37. Laws of Torah Foundations, Introduction to Heleq.
38. See Choshen Mishpat Bet Yosef and Shulhan 'Aruch 34 for the codified values regarding who is a "good" Jew.
39. Laws of Testimony 10:1–4. Faur astutely references at p. 181, n. 123, Repentance 3:7, which is a verbatim application of M. San. 10:1, where the articulated denials of Jewish legal dogmas is forbidden but not the denial of dogma itself.
40. Although following the Maimonidean disposition against literary creativity and poetry in particular, Faur lays the groundwork here in his frontal criticism of the Pauline doctrine that maintains that salvation derives from faith and not action. And Faur is also signaling to the academic community of which he is a part, that he is [1] not a fundamentalist and [2] open to a persuasive conversation. Stressing this intellectual affirmation, Faur references R. Joseph Albo, Iqqarim, 1,2, who maintains that people who are obedient to Jewish law are not disqualified because of heretical views. For the contrasting view reflecting conventional Orthodox Judaism, see J. David Bleich, *With Perfect Faith: The Foundations of Jewish Belief* (New York: KTAV, 1983), who cites R. Bahya regarding "correct belief" [*ortho + doxa*] as duties of the intellect. Citing (the mystic (!)) Nahmanides and R. Elchonon Wasserman, 1–11, Bleich believes that heresy is a real category in Jewish *law*. Note that Bleich cites post-Talmudic opinion with which he agrees and avoids, unlike Faur, a philological reading and application of the canon. Following this "tradition" of heresy assignation, R. Bleich concedes that Rabbi Hillel denies the doctrine regarding the coming of the Messiah, with the messianic chit having been cashed in during Hezekiah's

cites approvingly the Bible critic Robert Gordis (p. 225)[41] and the Talmudic scholar Jacob Neusner (p. 442),[42] who accept higher biblical criticism.[43] Faur does accept lower criticism of rabbinic texts.[44]

## 3. The Governance of Israel

The God of Israel is the Writer of the Torah, which defines the governance of Israel. This Book serves as Israel's constitution, which is premised on the principle that Law rather than violence is to be applied in order to resolve conflict. According to Faur, the "nations" hate Israel because of its governance, its unwillingness to "surrender… [its] *ketab* system," its national values, and its intuitive recognition that in Egypt it is in bondage, an unnatural and therefore intolerable political state of affairs (p. 192). In Faur's scheme, paganism sees humanity as the creation and possession of the State, while for Israel humanity begins with *one* individual, who joins in family creation and which congeal into a nation and, in the case of Israel, decided by non-violent means to be bound by the humanizing law that God

reign [B. San. 99a]. Bleich argues [p. 4] that the Halakhah was decided that this lack of belief is heretical. I am unable to find a definitive ruling in Pereq Heleq that reflects Bleich's position.

41. "Democratic Origins in Ancient Israel–The Biblical *Edah*," in *Alexander Marx Jubilee Volume* (New York: Jewish Theological Seminary of America, 1950), pp. 369–388.
42. See *The Horizontal Society*, vol. 2, p. 994, where Faur lists seven entries of Professor Neusner, who is one of the more regularly cited scholars in this volume.
43. See Jacob Neusner, *Introduction to Rabbinic Literature* (New York, London, Toronto, Sydney, and Auckland, 1994), who argues, "the Pentateuchal system addressed one reading of the events of the sixth century" (p. 111), and who refers to the "writers of… Genesis, Exodus and Deuteronomy" (p. 112), and "the power of the biblical myth" (p. 114). See also p. 99, where Neusner associates the Mishnah's concern with things cultic in Rabbinic culture with the "Priestly document" that academic Biblicists find in Leviticus.
44. Faur cites *Diqduqe Soferim*, p. 150, and see his comment at p. 183, n. 129.

had presented. Faur reports that Tacitus was outraged[45] that the Jews did not recognize the Roman "right of Conquest."[46]

Faur argues that unlike pagan political structures, in which power is monopolized by a monarch and elite who rule hierarchically over the monarch's population, Israel's Torah constitution creates a horizontal society of equals under the Law; hence the title and mission of this monograph. The holiday of freedom, Passover, focuses on the *seder*, order, which is the antithesis of the chaos that is inherently violent. The symbols of slavery become symbols of freedom, because the symbols are celebrated with freedom-like gestures and words (p. 202). True political freedom requires political sovereignty in the land of Israel; lacking that freedom, the Jew recites a benediction praising God "who has not made me a slave." This formula reminds the Jew that political bondage is unnatural and requires correction (p. 202).

Whereas pagan societies are organized hierarchically, the horizontal society of Israel is ruled by rules and not a ruler. For the pagan, rule is enforced with the sword; for Israel rule is accepted by covenant and national acclaim. And for the pagan, specifically Hobbes (p. 212), the Deity rules by dint of coercive power, not because the deity is the beneficent Creator. The God of Israel is Himself bound by Law and is not above the law,[47] while for human hierarchies, the

45. *The Complete Works of Tacitus* (New York: Modern Library, 1942), V, 5, cited in Faur, p. 195.
46. Tacitus, V, 10. Consider the argument of Thucydides in his discussion of the Athenian conquest of Meilos, where like the Persians who tried to conquer Athens, Athens claimed the right to conquer Meilos, because they possessed the requisite might to do so.
47. Faur astutely alludes to Gen. 18:25, but does not develop the theme, which depicts Abraham audaciously challenging God, the judge of the earth, to act in a way that is just. Thus Abraham assumes that God does not and indeed cannot maintain sovereign immunity. Note well that according to the Scriptural narrative, there indeed were not even a quorum of ten decent men in Sodom, Gen. 19:5. Although not addressed by Faur, Num. 16:22 eloquently proves his thesis, as Moses, even more audaciously than Abraham, challenges God by calling attention to what he takes to be inequity, that one man act wrongly and God's anger be unleashed, unfairly, upon the Israelite collective.

king is above the law which binds all but him (p. 218).[48] For this reason, Israelite society is founded upon the individual, who creates a family that emerges into a nation (pp. 221–34).

In the Torah, personal property belongs to the Creator sovereign and not to the human sovereign (p. 235). Alms are given to God, through the priests, and not to the monarchy. God, not the king, apportions the land, having commanded Israel to possess the land before establishing a monarchy. The king thus remains a limited, not absolute, enslaving monarch. The Israelite monarchy must not be linked "with might and violence" (p. 238). Thus Israel ensures the freedom and autonomy of every Israelite (p. 239), who is the "master of the good name" (M. Ab. 4:12), the benchmark whereby the crowns of priesthood, judiciary, and monarchy are held to account. Moses divested himself of the monarchical and priestly crowns, and the monarchy and priesthood could not, according to Dual Torah Judaism, coalesce in any one individual. The northern Kingdom in Samaria espoused the doctrine of unlimited, i.e., pagan monarchical sovereignty, with the priesthood serving as an instrument of the state.[49] In Judah, where there is no doctrine of sovereign immunity for God, the human establishment institutions have limited powers and are ruled by the Torah.

Faur explains how the Torah covenant, "Horizontal Society,"

48. See Faur's comparison of the "fear of God," or moral boundaries, with Pharaoh, who portrays himself as a divine right monarch (p. 218). In contrast to the all powerful Pharaoh, the midwives "feared God," Exod. 1:17.

49. Faur, a Rabbinics scholar who emphasizes the legal aspects of Jewish law, has devoted a great deal of energy to mastering the method and mind of the English legal system, which in both religious and secular versions reflects the hierarchical, and therefore violent, qualities of ancient Roman and Church law. In these systems, the ruler and pontiff stand outside of the law. In Hans Kelsen's pure theory of law, the basic norm is outside the law. Fiefs are owned by the king and what the human king gives, he can by whim take away. At the dawn of modernity, England tried to weaken the nobility in order to centralize power in the absolute monarch, who used religion as a tool but, like Machiavelli's ideal, rules in order to rule, without restraints, and not to be a good shepherd if the situation does not so permit.

actually functions. Israel's governance is defused, anticipating Federalism, in three branches, called "crowns" (M. Ab. 4:12). These parallel executive branches, the monarchy, the priesthood, and the judiciary, are to work together. When Moses, representing the Law, raised his hands when praying for God's help against Amaleq,[50] he was supported by Aaron, the priest, and Hur, of the monarchical Judean tribe (p. 242). While in pagan antiquity, church and state were fused,[51] Moses divested himself of both priestly and monarchical roles.[52] Often taken with the brute power in their possession, Israelite and Judean kings are frequently reminded by prophets that their powers are limited by legal statute (pp. 244–5).[53] The crown of the good name, which stands above the three executive branches, is the "public opinion" that holds the executives accountable with the right and obligation to offer criticism (p. 259).

Here we find the point of Faur's polemic, the target never mentioned but always in the crosshairs of his many faceted argument. Faur is offering an **academic alternative to what passes for Orthodox Judaism in contemporary Jewish culture.** For popular Orthodoxy, authority resides in the rabbinic *person*, whereas for Faur and the canonical *evidence*[54] he musters, authority resides in the documented rabbinic *principle.* For the pagan monarch, loyalty is directed to the royal *person;* in Israel, the king must submit to his people. Theocracy

50. M. R.H. 3:8. Thus, the Israelite king may not break the law by subjugating Israel, because the king, like Israel, is subject to the law. See Sifra, *be-Har* VI, 106b.
51. The medieval theory of the "Great Chain of Being" corroborates Faur's contention. Ideally, religion legitimates the state and, in turn, the state supports religion, because it relegates its laity to docility and hierarchical exploitation.
52. The only pagan model for principled divestiture of power was the lawgiver of Athens, Solon.
53. Faur astutely corroborates his distinction between pagan/hierarchical and Israelite/hori- zontal political structures by referencing Henry Frankfort, *Kingship of the Gods* (Chicago: University of Chicago Press, 1978), pp. 338–339.
54. Recall that Neusner, an often cited voice in this monograph, speaks about defining Judaism based on *evidence* rather than ideology. See *Judaism: The Evidence of the Mishnah* (Chicago: University of Chicago Press, 1981).

is the rule of God by means of the Law as opposed to the absolute power claimed by the pagan king. Now, pagan hierarchies, absolute monarchies, and that "Orthodox" Judaism that is the target of Faur's polemic, regard evaluative criticism as "bashing."[55] Faur contrasts the pagan claim that the king is *above* the law to the legal statutes that are applied when the King, Priest, or Court actually make an error (p. 262). Faur suggests, usually implicitly and occasionally explicitly, that no stream in modern Jewish life follows the canonical model but elements of that model remain, making the growth of Israel possible, "*in spite* of a thoroughly inept leadership" (p. 692). Most academic scholars of Judaism would nevertheless regard Faur's system as "Orthodox," because of his unflinching commitment to, reverence for, and philological study of Jewish law. Orthodox rabbis who oppose philological study appeal to their charismatic[56] or intuitional authority,[57] which transcends covenantal textual evidence.

55. It is slander to articulate negative thoughts regarding those who are hierarchically superior on the rabbinic "chain of being." Only the elite can call others heretics. See the corroborating passage in Mayer Israel Kagan, *Shemirat ha-Lashon 8:7*.
56. See, e.g., Rabbi Herschel Schachter of Yeshiva University, who makes the astounding claim that great rabbis may "rule from the gut," using intuition, while lesser rabbis do not have a right to an opinion or reasoned argument." See his postings at www.torahweb.org.
57. *In the Shadow of History: Jews and Conversos at the Dawn of Modernity* (Albany: SUNY Press, 1992), p. 13. Faur here assigns this type of truth divined by intuition to Nahmanides. For all of his protest against critical study, Faur associates with that world where conversations take place with regard to evidence. Menachem D. Genack, ed., *Rabbi Joseph B. Soloveitchik, Man of Halakha, Man of Faith* (Hoboken: KTAV, 1998), p. 104. Mayer Twersky, a grandson of R. Soloveitchik, argues that tradition continues after the close of the canon in the intuition of sacred sages, and Genack, p. 208, affirms that the Raabad and Nahmanides are the source of the Soloveitchik "Tradition." Ahron Soloveitchik, *Logic of the Heart, Logic of the Mind* (Chicago: Genesis, 1991), p. 46, argues that the critics "deny the sanctity of the Torah." In point of fact, a religion based on evidence rather than privileged intuition denies the charismatic his power. For R. Soloveitchik, Maimonides was a "religious" but not a Halakhic man. See Joseph B. Soloveitchik, *Halakhic Man*, trans. Lawrence Kaplan (Philadelphia: JPS, 1983),

Faur's most seminal insight is his understanding of Judaism *not as theology* but as *politics*.[58] By living according to its own law, without political power or the threat of violence, Israel survived exile (p. 265). Law was accepted and valued but "not imposed" (p. 268). The Jewish people retained their ethno/religious identity over the ages precisely because they were governed by the same Toraitic and Rabbinic laws, with local enactments, or customs reflecting particular local needs and expressing individuating local autonomy. The theology underlying this political structure "posits that the God of the Jewish nation, whose capital is Jerusalem, is the God of the whole world" (p. 269). Therefore, for Israel, God is sovereign and rules by means of Law (p. 271). [59]

For Faur, "pagan political sovereignty is unlimited" (p. 276) In this

---

p. 11. At p. 23, he claims that Halakhic concepts are *a priori* and not legislation and that his version of Halakhic Man did not accept Maimonides's objection to *piyyutim*, the Gnostic liturgical poetry that has infiltrated the popular liturgy. In this way, Torah is not determined by evidence but by *a prioiri* principles. Thus, God's will is divined by Masoretic sages, not demonstration or evidence. Faur's monograph must be read and understood as a polemic against the Judaic system that affirms that the Judaism of the Book, the canonical library, is superseded by a Judaism of culture. In the remarks that follow, the qualities exhibited by the popular version of Orthodox Judaism is challenged by Faur on the basis of evidence that this Judaism is neither canonical nor covenantal.

58. The understanding of Hebrew Scripture and the Rabbinic canon as politics rather than theology conforms to and confirms the understanding of Neusner that the Mishnah is best understood as a work of philosophy; see Neusner, *Rabbinic Literature*, pp. 97–99. See his *Judaism: The Evidence of the Mishnah*, where the theological approaches of G.F. Moore and E.E. Urbach are shown to be inappropriate projections of authorial bias onto the text under examination. Ironically, Faur, who on nationalist and political grounds avoids criticism of the Torah, shares Neusner's consistent proclivity for evidence when making synthetic interpretations. See Faur's *Studies in the Mishneh Torah: Book of Knowledge* (Hebrew) (Jerusalem: Mossad Harav Kook, 1978), pp. 194–210, where the ideological biases of Yehezkel Kaufmann's view of idolatry is examined. For an English version, see his "The Biblical Idea of Idolatry," in *The Jewish Quarterly Review* 69 (1978). For a discussion in medieval terms of the political dimension of idolatry, see Maimonides, *Aboda Zara* 1:1–2.

59. Since the land of Israel belongs to God, it cannot be transferred to another

scheme, "the king is a god, having powers not shared by any other human being" (p. 278). Clearly implicit is the unmentioned reference to the Jesus of the historical Church. In hierarchical societies, where the king is a god, "there are no individuals" (p. 281). This sovereign "has absolute power" (p. 282). In Israelite thought, "Adam and his descendants are self-sufficient creatures endowed with God's image (Gen. 1:26) (p. 327–8).

Hierarchical societies, Jewish or gentile, are antithetical to Torah, which views every person as God's image. For Faur, all hierarchical societies, regardless of origins, are "hated worship," *Aboda Zara*.[60] In these societies, the human king reigns as if above the law (p. 301). Faur finds this structure in Paul (pp. 323–4), associating all hierarchical systems to human invention.[61]

Faur then explains why Europe rejected religion. "In the West 'faith' was identified with Christianity," and "it did not take long for 'religion' to be associated with cruelty and intolerance" (p. 331). The sword of state defended the Church, which validated the status quo and privileged hierarchy. Faur's extensive excurses on Paul, who invented a religion with power but without law (pp. 314–44), is central to his critique. Antisemitism is *not* theological, but political (p. 345). The religious phony, the *min* (p. 299), speaks in the name of a god he or she denies.[62]

---

sovereignty (p. 273). Here Faur makes two points, one explicit, that Israel "did not (and indeed could not) forfeit" its homeland rights, and "Scripture [= God] explicitly prohibits the transfer of (Israel's) real estate in perpetuity" (p. 273).

60. Faur's insight is corroborated by philology. The root *nkr* means both "stranger" and "hated" in Akkadia. See Ps. 137:4.

61. See MT 'Aboda Zara 1:1–2. Note well that Faur does cite 1:3 (p. 294), following Maimonides' encoded narrative calling attention to passages that are strategically deleted or uncited. By citing this passage regarding *minnut*, the heresy of religious fraud, the astute reader will realize that Faur's paradigm is a contemporary restatement of false, invented religion.

62. Although not cited or addressed by Faur, Faur's reading is corroborated by Scripture. At the beginning of the Golden Calf episode, the idolatrous quest finds the people "gathering themselves *on/over*" Aaron, expressing a demand to return to the vertical society of tyrannical Egypt, in the *nif 'al*, or passive

Freedom without law necessitates that law serves as an instrument of power rather than a condition of power. Therefore, Faur claims that under the Torah law, where the Creator is both law giving and law-abiding, no human may claim a sovereign immunity because the ultimate sovereign, God, rejects such immunity. According to Faur's reading of Paul, there is an "essential inequality" of humankind (p. 323), which is assumed and adopted by pagan political systems. All Christian systems "posit the *essential inequality* of men" (p. 325). Obedience requires that the inferior submit to the superior; faith is expressed socially as well as doctrinally – faith in God requires deference to God's self-proclaimed vicar, surrendering both individuality and dignity before the superior ranking person.[63]

Faur "credits" Paul with the doctrine that Jesus the king is also god (p. 325).[64] The pagan Rex stands above the law and is not bound by the law.[65] On the contrary, the God of the Hebrew Scripture rejects sovereign immunity for God's self in order to deny the hierarchical thinking so typical of paganism.[66] Indeed, Paul nowhere protests

---

conjugation (Exod. 32:1). Moses's response was to restore order, to render the *am*/"people" again into a sacred, horizontal community; Exod. 35:1. Also note that this verse's second phrase, "these are the matters that the Lord commanded to do them," carries very specific qualities. Like Deut. 1:1, the "matters" are defined by a demonstrative pronoun, so that the Lord's commands, and in Faur's system, precepts, are too obvious and public to be subject to manipulation for an alphabetic public. Qorah, in Num. 16:3 gathers his cohorts with the identical verb, *on* Moses and Aaron, speaking in the voice of the very God whose being they deny. Not the last part of the verse, "why do you raise yourselves over the Lord's community," where Moses and Aaron, appointees of the Lord, are accused of the very usurpation that Qorah intends to accomplish.

63. See the discussion in *In the Shadow of History*, pp. 32–37.
64. Matthew, Mark, and Q, and, for that matter, the Coptic Nag Hammadi "Gospel," know nothing of Jesus' divinity; Luke portrays a Jesus who is godly, i.e., walking with equanimity to his demise, while the last canonical Gospel, John, indeed portrays Jesus as a god (so John 1:1, where Jesus is *logos*). Peter regards Jesus as an object of worship. Acts 2:38 describes Jesus as a god.
65. Matt. 5:17. Here Jesus "knows" what the *telos* of the law happens to be.
66. Gen. 18:25, Num. 16:22, Ps. 22:1, Job 3, and Lam. 5:20.

pagan law (p. 327), only Jewish law. After all, one must "render unto Caesar"[67] that which belongs to the secular authorities, and, unlike Torah, according to which the sovereign God does *not* demand immunity, every human – and not just every Israelite – is endowed with God's image (Gen. 1:26). For Paul, without the Rex/Christ, the human being is utterly worthless (p. 327).[68] Being a Christian requires belonging to a Roman corporation; since Israel is also a corporation, Israel is eternally guilty and worthy of condemnation for the killing of Jesus/god. To de-authorize the Law and the Book of Israel, the ability to read must be undermined; the sword of the Rex and not the Book of the Covenant reigns supreme. In Israel, the intellectual atheist is preferred to the false religionist.[69] The former, the king/god, speaks in God's name; the latter neither knows nor claims to know God.[70] Paul taught that the letter of the Law kills (2 Cor. 3:6), he cannot control what he does or does not do (Rom. 7:15, 23), and he condemned circumcision (Gal. 5:1–3) in order to de-authorize the original apostles, who, as Jews, were themselves in all likelihood circumcised. For Faur, "Paul [and all Western civilization, including

67. Matt. 22:21 and Luke 20:25. This aphorism shared by Matthew and Luke is a doctrine first found in Mark 12:17. As Acts is a continuation of Luke, the scribe of Paul, we note Acts 17:7, where the kingship of Jesus is correctly perceived to be a political threat to Rome.
68. This notion is advocated by the alienated, rejected, and not ordained sage, Aqabia b. Mehallalel, M. Ab. 3:1. The eastern European Morality movement's school of Novgorod, or Navorodok, also internalized this perspective. But, as noted above, Faur's present scientific monograph is a normative polemic against Jews who speak and preach like Paul.
69. See p. 331, n. 271, where Faur cites Bertrand Russell, *Why I Am Not a Christian* (New York: Simon and Schuster, 1957), p. 20. Faur credits Russell and Haim H. Cohn, "Religious Human Rights," in *Dine Israel* 19 (1997–98), p. 107, for noting that the great religions caused suffering in world history but chides the latter thinker for imputing the sins of the persecuting Church upon historical Israel, the victim.
70. See Kallah Rabbati 5:1, according to which God prefers correct deeds to correct doctrine, and we recall that Moses did not believe in God until he met God at the burning bush. God chose Moses for his character, not his creed.

the Jews who have internalized the Pauline mindset!] succeeded in creating something more powerful and enduring than religion: a crowd ready to gain grace by faulting the hierarchically 'inferior,' preferably Jews. If not, other despicable minorities would do" (p. 338).[71] Antisemitism is *political* and not *theological* because the Jew cannot regard what is human as god (p. 346). Because America did not enforce religion, American Christendom is significantly less anti-Jewish than its European counterparts (p. 348).

By juxtaposing the Western and Jewish theory of rights with the contrasting Pax Romana and Pax Hebraica, Faur contrasts two conflicting normative orders, a hierarchical society enforced with coercive threat and the *horizontal* society with its stress on persuasion. For the pagan, the state is the giver of rights, and what the state gives it can take away (p. 352). The biblical person has both duties and rights and is a carrier of human dignity (p. 353). Faur insightfully cites the case of Constantine, arguing that Christianity was advanced by the sword and not persuasion.[72] What is demanded is compulsory submission

71. The discerning reader will recall that at p. 99, the God that Faur finds in the Torah affirms the personhood of the "other," the singular individual. Faur then finds this same non-rabbinic ideology in Nahmanides (p. 623), who argues that sin pollutes and immersion in water absolves one of guilt, a doctrine unattested in rabbinic thought (see Num. Rabbah 19:8) but reflected in Mark 1:4. Thus Faur deftly makes his point without appearing to be radical, a literary/political technique perfected by Maimonides in the Introduction to the *Guide*. Most Orthodox Jews identify with Nahmanides, who subordinates the public, exoteric covenantal *law* to the intuitively private, esoteric theosophic mysticism, which reflects Pauline rather than Hebrew Scriptural doctrine. For the Biblical predilection for an exoteric covenant, see Deut. 30:12.
72. Faur references Walter Nigg, *The Heretics: Heresy through the Ages* (New York: Dorset Press, 162), p. 354. Thus doctrine is a tool to manipulate and pacify the people; good order is useful to the political order. Implied is that dogma is an instrument of mental control. For example, note the translation of "*Moshe qibbel Torah mi-Sinai*" as "Moses received *the* Torah" [with the definite article, thus: the Pentateuch], adopted by the ArtScroll prayerbook. The Mishnah's meaning is that "Moses received Torah [without the definite article] at Sinai,"

(p. 356) not principled autonomy.[73] After all, pagan gods, like pagan rulers, rule by imperial might, while Israelite sovereignty is based on the right of the Creator to dispense kindness and maintain the covenant.

Ever the very close reader of *every* Scripture, Faur understands Paul's second coming of Jesus as military victory (1 Cor. 15:57). Because Israel's Pax Hebraica exposes the facts that pagan religion invents gods as state propaganda, "which is grounded on might and the subjugation of the weak" (p. 361),[74] its "Messiah is no Cosmocrator fuming fire and brimstone fire," which is the post-Jesus Revelations depiction of Jesus who violently breaks the seven seals (Rev. 6:1–8:5). Faur here describes the ways of Rome with the metaphor of Revelations, seeing both cultures as affirming the same construction of reality, where real rule is enforced by violence. The Israelite alternative that empowers individuality is both seditious and subversive, because it exposes the politics of tyranny for what it is (Rev. 19:11–21, 20:10). Consequently, Christian liberty "lies in the realm of the intangible" (p. 365) or the unreal. Israel's God's Sabbath is a matter of Law, which cannot be abolished because God has eminent domain over Creation.

---

presumably a reference to the Oral Law. Exod. 46:10, Lev. 1:1, and Deut. 1:3 suggest that the Orthodox reading is itself unorthodox: the claim that the Torah was *written* at Sinai is contradicted by the Torah itself.

73. Faur's contention is corroborated by a close reading of Exodus 1–2, which depict Pharaoh as a murderous tyrant who would kill his human property, his Israelite slaves. His three decrees are to break the Hebrews with hard work, to have the Hebrew midwives kill the male children, and to drown the Israelite male babies. Thus, Pharaoh exemplifies the *hierarchical* model. In contrast, Moses in Exodus 2 kills an Egyptian to save an Israelite; he then threatens an Israelite who, mimicking the oppressor, oppresses a fellow Israelite; and he rescues Midianite women from the bullying of Midianite men. Thus, Moses exemplifies what Faur calls the *horizontal* model. No orthodox ideology will tolerate Moses's types, who privilege good behavior over high station. Note that the Judaism of the *Dual Torah* accesses both biblical and rabbinic writings to proclaim its world view.

74. See Maimonides, *Avoda Zarah* 1:1–2 and *Teshuva* 3:7 for Maimonides' – and Faur's – view of coercive, invented religion in all of its varieties and manifestation.

The violation of Shabbat or forcing the poor and meek to work for a superior shows contempt for the Lawgiver/Creator (p. 366).[75] Alternatively, when the state defends the Catholic/universal faith, the leader of the state determines the faith of his subjects (p. 369). The king rules by divine right but not human consent. Israelite monarchy requires the king to represent the people and is "king in name only" (p. 372).[76] This idiom is shorthand for a rule of law that allows for freedom of religious conscience.

## 4. The Memory of Israel

For Faur, the Memory of Israel does not refer to an accurate recollection of past chronology; it is how the past is recalled in order to generate meaning.

Thus, creation creates the idea of the Sabbath (p. 384).[77] This means that the work of many academics is to undermine Israel's Book as a means of eradicating Israel's generative memory (p. 386).

Israelite memory is recorded in a public text; Greek memory is oral (p. 390). The former memory is collective and horizontal; the latter is hierarchical, imperial, universal and, for Faur, "obnoxious." Here Faur advances his polemic. "Universal" alludes to the Roman church, and "obnoxious" refers to the propensity for arrogance and the threat of violence. The converts Shemaya and Abtalion are part

---

75. In his incisive n. 325, Faur notes that B. Hul. 5a and Maimonides, Shabbat 30:15, make this connection. Note that the death penalty is incurred for murder, sexual crimes, and idolatry, each which deny the image of God, and Sabbath violation, which denies the sovereignty of God.
76. R. Solomon ibn Verga, *Shevet Yehuda*, Azreil Schochet and Y. Baer, eds. (Jerusalem: Mosad Bialik, 1847), VII, 71, and Faur's "*El pensamiento Sefardi frente a la ilustracion Europea*," in Judit Targarona Borras, et al., eds., *Pensamiento y Mistica Hispanojudia y Sefardi* (Cuenca: Ediciones de la Universidad de Castilla-La Mancha), pp. 323–327.
77. See Yosef Hayim Yerushalmi, *Zakhor: Jewish History and Jewish Memory* (Seattle: University of Washington Press, 1982).

of Israel, while the ethnically related Esau and Ishmael are not (p. 394). In order to attack the governance of Israel, antisemites combat the memory of Israel. Faur finds that Israel was first presented as a nation of philosophers but, once the Septuagint was published, the horizontal ideals of Israel were manifest and Israel became demonized because its political theology is subversive (p. 392).[78] Thus Antiochus IV Epiphanes established a religion for the Jews that required the violation of Torah (p. 398).[79]

Faur then reports that gentiles were adopting Jewish practices like the Sabbath,[80] scandalizing elites who realized that that the Torah and its egalitarian ideology is "not only under state control" but is available to a larger public. Faur cites Tacitus who has disparaging things to say about Jewish practice.[81] By offering individuals dignity, Israel threatens all hierarchical regnant elites.[82]

Israel's founding event was the memory of Sinai, which is to be transmitted to future generations.[83] For Israel, education is presented to the public in the format of national values; for the Greek, the narratives are stories for elites.[84] And for Israel, faith is a matter of free choice, not submission to another human being. Ever the encoding

78. Philo, *Contra Apion* II 282.
79. Faur cites Elias Bickerman, *The God of the Maccabees* (Leiden: E.J. Brill, 1979), pp. 12, 78, 81, and 83–88: "The Hebrew memory recorded in the Jewish Hanukkah prayer reports that the Greek monarch tried *le-hashkicham toratecha*, to coercively bring Israel to forget its Torah, its Book, and its memory."
80. Philo, *supra.*, II 282–284.
81. Tacitus, *History* V 659–660.
82. A comparison of Plato's *Symposium* and the Passover seder validates Faur's assertion. For Plato, Socrates speaks about love philosophically, holds his alcohol, rejects homosexual advances, and speaks at a drinking party where only Greek male aristocrats are welcome, At the seder, poor men and women are welcome, they are given provisions, and the horizontal Hebrew Book, the Torah, is recalled, reviewed, and its narrative remembered.
83. Deut. 29:13–14 and Josh. 8:35. Faur understands *morasha* to be the national duty to transmit its values to subsequent generations, a project which the United States also succeeded but Europe did not.
84. Philo, *supra*, I 181.

literary virtuoso, Faur is not only describing Christianity but every hierarchical society.[85] Recognizing Israel's subversive disposition, i.e., its stubborn inability to submit to imperial power because of its Book, memory, and horizontal construction of social reality, the Roman state assaulted the Jewish body and the Church attacked that uniquely Jewish memory, which recalled and revered its autonomous past.[86]

---

85. See R. Herschel Schachter, "Preserving the Mesorah," in *Jewish Action* 71:2 (Winter, 2010), pp. 38–40. He argues that one must submit to one's teacher and to the great sage of the generation because the Shulhan Aruch YD 242:4 said so. Actually Tosafot to B. Ber. 31b affirms, without Oral Torah warrant, that the great sage of the generation is everyone's teacher. Alternatively, in Maimonides, "great sage" is an honorific term [Introduction to the Code]. Given that Tannaitic rabbis were deposed for bad behavior (B. B.M. 59b), the Maimonidean view reflects the position of the Dual Torah. Alternatively, Schachter views the persons of Torah to have virtual canonicity and requires submission to their legal and theological views. He adds to the medieval innovation that requires respect for the great sage to require submission to his views. For Schachter, changes that violate "tradition" as defined by the great sages are reforms, and those that do not are called *hiddushim*, innovations. Schachter offers no verifying hermeneutic whereby the great sage may be evaluated. Thus, for instance, mixed seating in synagogues copies Christian practice and, in Schachter's reading of his mentor, R. Joseph Soloveitchik, is forbidden by biblical law. This law, like the Dead Sea Pesher readings, gives the charismatic the authority and power to update God's otherwise unchanging law. Faur's presentation must therefore be understood not only as a critique of the Church, which demands submission of mind and deed to charismatic, hierarchical human authority, but also of Jews who have internalized hierarchical thinking. Calling upon the name of the Lord means calling the Lord of Israel by name (Pss. 116:12–13, 17; Joel 2:12). Acts 2:21–22 seems to refer to calling on the name of Jesus who is taken to be Lord. The plain sense of the Psalms and Joel passages can hardly refer to Jesus. In Hab. 2:4, "the righteous shall live by faith" in God; in Rom. 3:24–26, this refers to faith in Jesus. Anticipating Christian exegesis, CD I-VIII/XIX-XX and 1Q Pesher Habakkuk (1QpHab) understand this idiom to refer to the Qumranic Teacher of Righteousness, a flesh and blood charismatic.
86. Faur explains that Jewish education inculcates critical thinking and, with it, intellectual responses to the Book through *knowing* the text of the canon that rules the rulers (Ruth Rabbah 1:1). In contrast, Schachter, in his tape, "The P' sak Process," argues that only great rabbis have a right to have an opinion justified by intuition. Laity and rabbis who are not great do not have a right to such an

By placing the locus of Jewish sovereignty in the Book, Israel holds potential tyrants to the equalizing benchmark of the Jewish book. After the abortive anti-Roman rebellion of 135–137,[87] R. Aqiba asked those who can learn to come forth to learn and those who could to come forward to teach.[88] The published text of the Mishnah rendered the document "legal tender," with universal acceptance.[89]

Faur then offers an anthropology of text to explain the macro structure of the Mishnah: The Division of seeds, refers to space; Holy Days, to time; Women, to family law, the first and immediate relationship of the child; Damages, to interactions with the the totality of humankind, viewed as a family; Holy things, to sacred space; and Purities, to the human's approach toward God in sacred space. By affording all Israel an ethos encoded in its national memory, Jewry is

opinion. This view is echoed by Rabbi J. David Bleich, *Contemporary Halakhic Problems* (New York: KTAV and Yeshiva, 1977), p. xvii. See Hart, *The Concept of Law*, p. 9, for a discussion of the "rule of recognition" or how one knows what a norm actually is in the legal order, designated by Hart as a rule of obligation, a *mitzvah*, a command, or a precept. Faur's system is based upon the Horizontal society ruled by the Book; in contrast, Schachter's system reconstructs Torah by investing the ruler with the sole right to read and apply the Book, as there is no room for conversation or persuasion in Schachter's system, only dutiful submission to the man who speaks with and in God's voice.

87. In n. 116 Faur properly credits Professor Neusner's seminal anthropology of Rabbinic literature: *The Philosophical Mishnah* (Atlanta: Scholars Press, 1988–89), vol. 1, p. 223. In these three volumes, Neusner examines the basic philosophical frame of the Mishnah. For a substantive discussion of the economic, political, theological, and philosophical outlook of the Mishnah, see idem, *The Social Study of Judaism* (Atlanta: Scholars Press, 1988), vol. 2, pp. 3–125. On the Judaism of the Mishnah in general, see there, vol. 1, pp. 29–55.
88. Canticles Rabbah 2:3, 15b–c.
89. This understanding contrasts with Schachter's alternative system, which shields the Book from mass review, because the Book means that the great sages, who themselves are not subject to review, displace the actual content of the Book and the legal order recorded therein. See Faur, "Reading Jewish Texts with Greek Eyes," in *Sh'ma* 18/342 (November 27, 1987), pp. 10–12, and "De-Authorization of the Law: Paul and the Oedipal Model," in *Journal of Psychiatry and the Humanities* 11 (1989), pp. 22–243.

immunized from paganism's subordinating mindset.[90] "Fear of God" means recognizing God's sovereignty. Such recognition is implied in Sabbath observance and taking the words of the Covenant seriously.[91] Faur then contrasts pagan societies, where laws are the possession and instrument of elites, with Jewish law, which Moses made the accessible possession of the people.[92] The Mishnah was recited in public making it the property of *the* public.[93]

The authenticity of tradition for Faur is verifiable and testable: It is minted by the legislature as legal tender; traditions had to be certified;[94]

---

90. Consider Schachter's alternative view in "Preserving the Mesorah," *supra*, "Changes in practice require delicate evaluations that *only a master Torah scholar, a gadol baTorah, can properly conduct.* Only someone with a broad knowledge and a *deep* [a code word for esoteric] understanding of the corpus of halakhah, with an intimate familiarity with *both the letter and the spirit of the law*, with a mastery of both the *rules and the attitudes of the mesorah*, can determine when a change is acceptable or even required. The more wide-reaching the proposed change, the greater the expertise required to approve it. The evaluator must not only be a master of the *mesorah*, but he must also be able to consider new practices based *solely on values internal to the mesorah*, removing external influences from the deliberation" (p. 39; my emphasis). Schachter invokes no rule of recognition other than to claim that there are traditional attitudes, a spirit of the law, and a hierarchy of personal authority whereby it is the intuition of the sage and not the cogency of the claim that is ultimately normative.
91. See the Maimonides, Repentance 3:11.
92. In nn. 124 and 125, Faur cites his canonical proof texts for his assertion. See Deut. 31:12; T. Sot. 7: 9; B. Hag. b3a; and *AdRNA*, XVIII, 67–68. Cf. Deut. 29:10. B. Erub. 54b. Cf. Exod. 24:1; Midrash Tanhuma, *Va-Yaqhel*, 8, vol. 2, 124; and *Saadya's Commentary on Genesis*, 186.
93. See Faur's documentation, B. San. 5a and B. Hor. 11b; IShG, 76–77, and *Genizah Studies*, vol. 1, p. 22. The parallel in Gen. Rabbah XCVII, 10, vol. 3, 1219, is a later interpolation, not found in Gen. Rabbah Vat. Ebr. 30 (Jerusalem: Makor, 1971), pp. 187–188. *Targum Neophyti* 1 on Gen. 49:10, vol. 1, 331, renders "scribes who teach the Law" in general, without any allusion to Hillel's dynasty. The discerning reader will compare and contrast the competing systems of Faur and Schachter.
94. Faur references B. San. 68a and M. Naz. 7:4. Alternatively, in a web posting (www. torahweb.org), Schachter affirms that God fearing rabbis are assisted by God "to see to it that they don't err… we assume that God is there behind the scenes guiding the rabbis in each generation in the development of the

it required acceptance by the people; the metal of the coin supports the inscription on the coin, so that tradition must be seen as honest and authentic; the content of the metal – the meaning of the canon's words – is the measure of meaning; "special measures must be taken against forgery";[95] one must formulate words densely, so that a minimum of words maximizes information; the text of tradition must be stable.[96] Just as the Written Torah is inscribed on a ritually kosher hide, the Oral Torah is inscribed in the memory of Israel. The first level of learning is *girsa,* getting the text right, the second is mastering textual intent, and the third identifies the the texts' inhering principles.

*halachah.*" He cites in his post, "Masorah and Change," Rabbi Soloveitchik, who said there are *hiddushim* [innovations that are legitimate] and changes [which are not], and a great sage alone knows the difference. Note well that the structure of Schachter's theory and attitudes regarding changes in Jewish law is actually similar to Conservative Judaism's position. He differs with that community in his social non-egalitarian agenda. According to the Judaism of the Dual Torah, B. Meg. 2a, and codified by Maimonides, *Mamrim* 2:2, laws are changed *only* by a court greater in number and wisdom than the court of original jurisdiction, but not the unvetted intuition of the great sage. 1QpHab 2:1–2 finds the Qumranide Teacher/Oracle of Righteousness receiving updated revelations from "the mouth of God." Hab. 2:4 reads "the righteous shall live by faith," presumably in God. But 1QpHab 8:1–2 assigns the locus of this faith in the Teacher/Oracle and Paul, in the "Tradition" of Qumran, (Rom. 1:17 and Gal. 3:11) assign the locus of this faith to Jesus. The shared feature of these interpretations is that the locus of authority shifts from the canonical *Book* that is sealed, certified, inscribed, the measure by which the Oral Torah reads the Written Torah, and, perhaps alluding to Christian Scripture and the Qumranide *Pesher* writings, forgery. B. Yeb. 23b maintains that the plain sense of Scripture does not lapse, as it does in the *Pesher* and Christian writings. Perhaps the sages' *doresh be-haggadot shel dofi,* B. San. 99b, is directed to this form of "interpretation" in which the charismatic speaks in God's voice and centralizes power and authority in his person which is not subject to review.

95. This seemingly innocent statement underlies Faur's global argument; the mission of this monograph is to identify forgeries of Torah.

96. For the Church and Qumran, the canon is open and therefore unstable; for Schachter, the rabbinic hermeneutic must be *unstable*/given to change in order that the Orthodox social culture remain stable.

In order to safeguard a free conscience, Dual Torah law dealt with actions, while dogma is not legally enforced.[97]

The institutionalization of Israelite horizontality is the Law, the mandated behavioral gesture that expresses value. For example, teachers and students all sit on chairs or on the ground, choreographing the common equality under the Law.[98] For the Church, there is neither Jew nor gentile in the person of Jesus.[99] But once salvation is found in Jesus, in the ideology of hierarchy, and in the Jewish version of this ideology, theosophic Kabbalah, Israel abandons its classical model and succumbs to folly. Faur distinguishes between the tradition called Kabbalah, which corresponds to what Neusner terms the "Judaism of the Dual Torah," and Kabbalah, the alternative Judaism that, like Qumran and early Christianity, replaced sacred text with the saintly canonical person.[100] Faur begins his account of Israel's anti-Rabbinic folly by exposing what he regards as a Jewish assault on Judaism by rabbis who ruled on the basis of unauthorized texts, who underwent

97. At n. 176, Faur documents his claim: *MT* "Introduction," ll. 2–4; cf. ll. 95–97, 156–157. Similarly in *Mamrim* 1:1: "the *actions* of the Law," and in 1:2: "*to act* in accordance…" see quotation from *Guide* 1:71. R. Se'adya Gaon Exod. 18:20 used Ar. *'anuil* to translate Heb. *Ma asseh.*

98. B. Meg. 21a and codified by Maimonides, Torah Study, 4:2.

99. Gal. 3:28. See also Rom. 10:12. For Schachter, "Preserving the Mesorah," p. 38, one must submit to the authority of one's teacher and not search texts or the internet for views that are more appealing. Unaddressed by Schachter and maintained by Faur, is that the student may respectfully disagree. R. Berlin in Ruah Hayyim 1:3 maintains that the student may disagree with the teacher because sometimes the student is correct.

100. Faur finds that these Jews believe that God has a body. See his documentation at n. 6. See Bernhard Blumenkranz, *Les auteurs chretiens latins du moyen age sur les juifs et le Judaism* (Paris: Mouton, 1963), p. 165, n. 63, and R. Hayye Gaon, in *Teshubot ha-Ge onim ha-Hadashot,* #155, 67, pp. 219–220, regarded people holding this type of belief as *minim*. For Maimonides' view on God's having a body, see Repentance 3:7. Independent of Faur, Nathan Slifkin has convincingly argued that Rashi believed God has a body. See his, "Was Rashi a Corporealist?" in *Hakirah, The Flatbush Journal of Jewish Law and Thought* 7, 2009, pp. 81–105. See my comments at http://viewpoints.utj.org/?p=597.

bad training, exhibited poor manners, and challenged the authority of the Babylonian Yeshivot.[101]

Citing the root *bida* as theological distortion as well as Maimonides,[102] Faur views these pretenders to be bereft of authentic tradition.[103] Furthermore, these pretenders, for Faur the anti-Maimonideans, are described by R. Samuel ha-Nagid[104] as people who wear ritual fringes, rabbinical garb, a beard and hat, yet who mispronounce Hebrew and are arrogant and gullible.[105] These people are bellicose and poorly mannered and teach Torah without the discipline of grammar, using verbal violence rather than reasoned persuasion.[106] After presenting his own criticism, Faur goes on to cite the confirming view of R. Yonah b. Janah, which presents the same image.[107]

---

101. It is the "Tradition" of the Gaonim that is reliable. This contrasts with Schachter's tradition, "Preserving the Mesorah," p. 36, where tradition is passed down from teacher, and the *godol ha-dor* is everyone's teacher and therefore must be as if he were a pope. The fact that Ben Sira and the Damascus Document were both found at Qumran and in the Cairo Geniza indicates that we may have two very old contending Judaisms at continuous war with one another.
102. Laws of Kings 11:3. In Arabic, the root means "heresy." See Job 11:3.
103. See R. Joseph B. Soloveitchik, *Shenei Sugei Masoret,* in Joseph B. Soloveitchik, *Shiurim le-Zecher Abba Mori, z"l* ( Jerusalem, 5743), where the author, Schachter's teacher, first defines Tradition in Maimonidean terms, and then in terms of culture Traditions that are not subject to review.
104. Diwan R. Shemu'el ha-Nagid, Ben-Tehillim, #83, 228–229.
105. This thick description of a medieval phenomenon plainly describes the Orthodox Jewish present, which is, as I argue, Faur's subliminal polemic.
106. In his tape, "The P'sak Process," Schachter eloquently confirms Faur's contention, couched in his commentary on a poem. For Schachter, the great rabbi may rule on the basis of intuition, i.e., "from the gut," while other rabbis who are not "great" do not have the right to an opinion. In Schachter's system, there does not seem to be a place for open conversation or persuasion. The narrative of Lev. 10:17–20 would seem to indicate that at least for the Written Torah, conversation and persuasion carry greater valence than charisma or office. See also Jeffrey Rubenstein, *The Culture of The Babylonian Talmud* (Baltimore: Johns Hopkins University Press, 2003), for the precedent for rhetorical bellicosity as evidenced by the Stammaim of the Bavli.
107. Translation of R. Yonah's *Kitab al-Luma,* p. 3, with Faur's consultation with the Hebrew translation by R. Judah ibn Tibbon, *Sefer ha-Riqma,* vol. 1, pp. 11–12.

Like the Church, the anti-Maimonideans valorized martyrs, or holy men.[108] In these systems, the devotee is required to surrender critical thinking and act the way the authority commands. Saints are venerated, their words displacing the Dual Torah canon, which, when read charismatically rather than grammatically, only means what the religious hero says it means.

After describing "heroic" Judaism,[109] Faur boldly asserts that "Judaism does not recognize 'heroes' or 'heroism.'" In Rabbinic Judaism, an ignorant person cannot be pious (M. Ab. 2:5). However, the medieval piyyut seems to "celebrate salvation through penitence and martyrdom."[110] This suggests that the celebrants of this literature are using Christian rather than Jewish categories. This heroic disposition changed the "concept and function" of the rabbi from the master of the law to the carrier of mystic knowledge and "supernatural power."[111]

---

Faur here recalls "several occasions when Professor Lieberman would mention with great admiration some of the sharp notes on rabbinic lexicography made by this outstanding linguist." I suspect that Faur is here arguing that Lieberman's preference for lexical correctness also indicates a shared antipathy for the anti-Maimonideans.

108. Corroborating Faur's claim is the citation from Theodore Gaster, *The Holy and the Profane* (New York: William Morrow, 1980), pp. 185–188. For an overview of this literary *genre*, see *European Literature and the Middle Ages*, pp. 425–428.
109. Which is the Judaism of Schachter's great sage, described above.
110. See Salo W. Baron, *A Social and Religious History of the Jews* (Philadelphia: Jewish Publication Society, 1957), vol. 4, p. 95. In vol. 2, pp. 145–150, Faur notes with more than a little irony that it is claimed that Targum is not recited because it is not understood but *piyyutim* are recited even though they are understood perhaps only by those who have taken seminars in the literature. In point of fact, the *piyyut* literature reflects that gnosticism of popular religion rejected by Targum Onqolos. For a discussion of Rabbi Joseph B. Soloveitchik's endorsement of this writing, without justification, see my "The Nuanced Ambiguities of R. Joseph B. Soloveitvchik's Thought, A Review Essay of Dov Schwartz, *Religion or Halakha: The Philosophy of Rabbi Joseph B. Soloveitchik*," in Review of Rabbinic Judaism 12.2 (2009), p. 231.
111. Recall that Schachter reads between the lines of the canon and rules "from the gut," and his teacher, R. Soloveitchik, issues an apodictic ruling regarding *piyyut*.

This esoteric knowledge is not subject to review. But the canon could be changed because (like the Church's and Qumranide treatment of revealed Scripture) it is the canonical person who defines the canonical Book.[112] The "decline of the generations" doctrine denies access to the rights afforded by the canon and its law.[113] For the Judaism of the Dual Torah, generations may but do not necessarily decline[114] and will not and cannot decline in a fashion that alters Israel's legal system because Samuel, who ruled after Jepthath, was both subsequent and superior to Jepthath.[115] The Hebrew sage can make an error; but the mystical hero cannot.[116] These rabbinic heroes are the anti-Maimonidean rabbis whose Kabbalah/Tradition is esoteric, elitist, inaccessible and therefore not given to review.[117]

Rather than state his own view explicitly, Faur approvingly cites

112. Faur references Israel Ta-Shma, " *Qelitatam shel sifre ha-Rif, ha-Rah, ve-Hilkhot Gedolot be-Sarfat wub-Ashkenaz bemeot ha-Yod-Alef-Yod-Bet,*" in *Qiryat Sefer* 55 (1980), pp. 191–201; and idem, "*Sifriyyatam shelhakhme Ashkenaz bene ha-Me a ha-Yod Alef-Yod Bet,*" in *Qiryat Sefer* 60 (1985), pp. 298–309.

113. See Faur's n. 92: "This doctrine had been anticipated by Horace, *Odes and Epodes*, tr. and ed. Niall Rudd (Loeb Classical Library), III, 6,105, who wrote: 'Our fathers' age, worse than our grandfathers', gave birth to us, inferior breed, who will in due course produce still more degenerate offspring.' Maimonides had nothing to do with this doctrine. For a coherent discussion of the subject, see Menachem Kellner, *Maimonides on the Decline of the Generations and the Nature of Rabbinic Authority* (Albany: SUNY Press, 1996); for a shorter version, see idem, "Maimonides on the Decline of the Generations," in *Hazon Nahum* (New York: Yeshiva University, 1998), pp. 163–185.

114. As evidenced by R. Pinehas b. Yair's observation, which *does not* carry the valence of rabbinic dogma, B. Shab. 112b.

115. B. R.H. 25b.

116. The Tosafist and Schachter version of *gadol ha-dor*, who, being everyone's magisterial teacher, must be honored *and* obeyed.

117. See R. Joseph B. Soloveitchik, "*Shenei Sugei Masoret*" ("Two Types of Tradition"), in *Shiurim le-Zecher Abba Mori* (Jerusalem: Akiva Yosef, 1993), and his son, Prof. Haym Soloveitchik, "Rupture and Reconstruction: The Transformation of Contemporary Orthodoxy," in *Tradition* 28:4 (Summer, 1994). For Faur, *only* the canonical Tradition is absolutely normative; for Schachter and the Soloveitchiks, both canon and culture are normative.

R. Samuel ha-Nagid, who held that these rabbis suffered from aspects of heresy.[118] The most eminent French rabbi was R. Moses b. Nahman, or Nahmanides, who speaks dogmatically and tolerates no dissent;[119] these rabbis are infallible.[120] By affirming Kabbalah as esoteric dogma, these rabbis' political power derives from their esoteric knowledge,[121]

---

118. Faur cites *Sefer ha-Ittim 267* and explains the significance of the Targum at appendix 61, vol. 2, pp. 933–40.

119. See Faur's references, "*Milhemet ha-Dat*," in J.I. Kobakak, ed., *Jeshurun* VIII (Bamberg, 1875), p. 29; and the second from ibid., p. 40. See appendix 67, vol. 2, pp. 953–61. A close reading of Nahmanides indicates a belief in a "law beyond the law." Nahmanides' view is not uncontested and it lacks convincing precedent in the Oral Torah canon. For Nahmanides, being holy requires fulfilling the commandments, and more; commentary to Lev. 19:2. The law for the intuitionist school is *private*, esoteric, and ultimately not subject to review. For the view of biblical Israel, see Deut. 33:4, where all Israel is given the Torah as a collective. It is one matter to entertain this claim and quite another to demonstrate that it is creedal, covenantal, or even true. Maimonides argued that sanctity is attained by observing the commandments. See *Guide* 3:7. While Nahmanides offers no citation in support for his view, Maimonides cites his source in the rabbinic canon, *Sifra Qedoshim* 10:9, the case of Nadab and Abihu, who tragically applied their religious intuition by performing a ritual act that was "not commanded to them.

    Lev. 10:1 seems to support Maimonides' thesis. Similarly, the formulae of the sacred Jewish library also anticipate the Maimonidean view: *asher qeddishenu be-mitsvotav, qaddeshenu be- mitsvotecha* and the wearing of the liturgical tassels remind Israel to observe the commandments and *thereby* "become holy," Num. 15:39. See the important work of Menachem Kellner, *Maimonides' Confrontation with Mysticism* (Oxford: Litman Library of Jewish Civilization, 2006), the thrust of which is that there are two competing religions of Israel in Medieval Judaism.

120. Faur's description of the French rabbi's ideology is corroborated by our reading of Schachter. In his post "Mesorah and Change," Schachter concedes that Jewish law changes when the change represents continuity. The great sage alone may make this determination. In the post, "Can Women Be Rabbis" we are told that rabbis derived laws by "reading between the lines of the text of the Torah," In the post, "Did the Rabbis Distort the Psak," Schachter maintains that it is the moral equivalent of showing disrespect to sages by attributing motives or subjecting them to review because, like the French rabbis described by Faur, Schachter's rabbis are guided by God and are therefore not to be evaluated by lesser rabbis.

121. In a private communication, R. Stuart Grant, a former student and one time aid to R. Joseph B. Soloveitchik, Schachter's mentor, reported that R. Soloveitchik

reflecting Christian patterns of thought and intellectual independence with doctrinal heresy. In order to suppress Maimonides' viewpoint, R. Jonah Gerondi sought the aid of the Church to suppress this heresy.[122] R. Abraham Maimonides is cited as criticizing esotericist abandonment of Jewish law, falsehoods, ignorance, polluted faith, and asking Christians to burn Jewish books.[123] According to Nahmanides's protege, R. Solomon Adret, "the true Tradition is received our hands"[124] and not the other, i.e., Maimonidean rabbis, and thereby undermined all rabbinic authority. After all, Maimonides maintained that the earth would not be destroyed because the laws of nature are stable,[125] and R. Ardeti regards the view and its holder to be heretical.[126] R. Ardeti's position is echoed by R. Asher of Toledo, who maintained that rabbis

---

saw himself as a follower of Nahmanides and not Maimonides.

122. When listing the sinners who have no part in the eternal life [Repentance 3:6], Maimonides first lists ideological heretics and then enumerates anti-social types who cause the public to sin, who separate themselves from the community, who sin openly, brazenly and defiantly, *those who inform against Jews to non-Jewish authorities*, who intimidate the public for personal rather than pious reasons, shedders of blood, malicious gossip, and hiding one's membership in the Jewish people. The core value this list shares is that damage to the Jewish collective is a denial of the communal Covenant. For a latter day example of Orthodoxy's ignoring Jewish law when it conflicts with social policy, see B. Sot. 44b, which requires female conscription and which is codified by Maimonides, Kings 7:4, and R. Abraham Karelitz, *Igrot he-Hazon Ish*, 3:96–99. From this narrative we see how Faur may disagree with critical biblical scholarship while maintaining a cordial and collegial dialogue with this school.

123. Responsum R. Abraham b. ha-Rambam, n. 75. When citing this responsum at n. 141, Faur cites Professor Mayer Gruber, who claimed that Ashkenazi rabbis "make things up as one goes along." Gruber lumps all modern streams, Orthodox, Conservative, and Reform, in this anecdotal observation.

124. *Teshuvot ha-Rishba* 1:9, 94, 423.

125. *Guide* 2:7–289.

126. *Supra*, 1:9 3b-4a. In the "Tradition" of R. Ardeti, Schachter associates those who deny the divinity of the Torah with those who contradict its teachers. See Maimonides, Repentance 3:8, where Maimonides views those who contradict the Dual Torah sages to be heretics. In the name of his mentor, R. Joseph B. Soloveitchik, Schachter argues, as per Faur's view of kabbalistic rabbis, that lesser lights may neither contradict nor assign motives to great rabbis like R.

who were infected with worldly wisdom were corrupt and will deny "law of Moses."[127] After documenting in detail Judaism's rejection of the occult, Faur notes the kabbalistic rabbis' belief in the occult, particularly Nahmanides,[128] who believes in "spiritism." Faur astutely notes that while Nahmanides' mental intent cannot be reconstructed, the Nahmanidean claim that the Torah's subtext consists of magical names of God[129] is suggestive of the Pauline distinction between the letter and spirit of the law (2 Cor. 3:6), whereby the charismatic person replaces Torah by intuiting divine intent. Faur then reports that for R. Samuel ibn Tibbon, this disposition is pagan.[130] After all, the Nahmanidean claim that one might be a "depraved within the confines of the law"[131] implies that there is a law beyond the law known to the mystic but not to the less spiritually endowed.

For Faur, this alternative "mystical" Judaism rests upon five pillars, a faith the goal of an idiom suggestive of the Five Pillars of Islam أركان الإسلام, which is to demand total submission to God:[132] Kabbalah is the supreme theology of Israel; Law is subordinated to this theology; hermeneutics displaces the text of Torah; dismantling and reconstructing the words of the Torah. This Judaism demands submission to kabbalistic rabbis. The norm created by the mystical "method" associates the ten spheres of God's body with the Christian Trinity by dismantling and reconstructing words. Failure to accept this esoteric

Ardeti, who, because he has correct Tradition, may dismiss Maimonides as a heretic. Schachter would have his readers believe that God assists pious rabbis to rule correctly; see "Did the Rabbi Distort the Psak."

127. *Teshuvot ha-Rosh* 55:9.

128. Commentary to Lev. 16:8. For Nahmanides on the "science of necromancy," see his commentary to Exod. 20:3. And Faur reminds the reader that for R. Nissim Gerondi, magic is a science; *Derashot ha-Ran* 3:105.

129. *Kitve ha-Ramban* 1:168.

130. Faur cites the appendix to his Hebrew translation of the *Guide*, s.v. רוחניות. For further background, see *Kuzari*, I, 79, pp. 23–24; I, 97, p. 34; IV, 23, p. 178.

131. Commentary to Lev. 19:2.

132. Recall that for Maimonides, Idolatry 1:1–2, the sin of hated/strange worship is *political*, and *theology* is merely state propaganda. In official religion Islam, submission is before God; in folk religion Islam, one submits to God's spokesmen.

reading is seen as insubordination. In contrast, Dual Torah Judaism accepts truth based upon on the merits of the claim, not the charisma of the claimant. To document this observation, Faur cites the view of R. Asher,[133] who rejects Maimonides' system, philosophy, and the plain semantic sense of words, because, for Faur, R. Asher knew that he "was Torah incarnate with supreme mastery of the Law." Faur's use of the "incarnate" idiom[134] in the context of infallible rabbis whom he finds offering faulty readings of the canon now becomes clear. The very act of holding the great rabbi to account is a mental act of heresy.[135] By associating R. Asher's views to *Church v. Galileo* and by referring to R. Asher as "saintly", Faur identifies science, philosophy, and critical thinking with the horizontal Rabbinic tradition, while

133. *Teshuvot ha-Rosh* 55:9. Faur's incisive comment, pp. 640–1, n. 271, illustrates R. Asher's method and mindset: "The view of R. de Toledo appears in *Teshubot ha-Rosh*, 55:9. The underlying thesis is that the *text* of a *private agreement between two parties* ought not to be interpreted according to Talmudic hermeneutics and rabbinic linguistic connotations, but according to the semantic field of the particular *language*, as well as the *place* and *time*, in which the document was written. The requirements for the proper interpretation of such a document are two: "common sense" (סברא), which is familiarity with the syntactical and semantic apparatus of the speakingcommunity; and proficiency in classical Arabic, the language in which the pre-nuptial agreement was written. To substantiate his argument, R. de Toledo pointed out that the basic terms of the pre-nuptial agreement in question, such as "marriage," "wife," "inheritance," have a semantic field of their own (within the speaking-community), *independent* of the peculiar legal lexicon (of both the Jewish and non-Jewish communities), which is more restrictive and specialized. Forgetting with whom he was dealing, the poor rabbi made the fatal mistake of employing the term "reason" (שכל) to indicate the syntactical relations determined by the linguistic apparatus. Cleverly, R. Asher grabbed this term and associated it with infamous "philosophy"–something akin to "communist," "capitalist" in some political quarters–and used it to launch a devastating attack on the poor translator.

134. I suspect that Faur's idiom implies a Christian influence similar to his claim that [esoteric] Kabbalah is not part of the authentic Kabbalah, or rabbinic Tradition.

135. Schachter, "Did the Rabbis Distort the Psak?" Faur argues that indeed they did, that anyone and everyone is subject to truth and Torah, including charismatic rabbis, and that rational discourse may be employed to explicate rabbinic opinion.

associating the authoritarian R. Asher with the hierarchical Church culture.[136] Viewing himself as the defender of the Geonic tradition, which he believes has been subverted, Faur is not shy when subjecting R. Asher to criticism:

> As the presiding judge, R. Asher had the authority to overrule the [document's] translators' testimony.... He preferred to muzzle the translator by crying "Philosophy"! and imputing [sic][137] the integrity of Old Sefard! The fact that neither the saintly rabbi nor our learned historians had the foggiest ideas about the halakhic issues speaks for itself.

Because R. Asher is learned and carries the rabbinic office, Faur accords him the respect required by halakhic protocol.[138] Nevertheless, since Israel is ruled by the Book and not the charismatic person who intuits the mind God, R. Asher, who subjected others, including Maimonides, to review, is now subject to review. The "saintly" adverbial epithet also becomes contextually clear: By citing *Church v. Galileo*, by defining R. Asher's self-understanding as Torah "incarnate," and his character as "saintly," a leitmotif term in Faur's writing, Faur affirms his conviction that elements of what is taken to be rabbinic "Orthodoxy" reflects a Christian construction of religious reality. Since this conflict is a matter of political/theological principle, even R. Asher cannot claim privilege.[139] Faur does *not* regard this conflict to be an ethnic dispute between Sepharadim and Ashkenazim; there

---

136. In support of this daring thesis, in n. 272 Faur cites Israel Ta-Shma, "*Shiqulim Pilosofim be-Hakhra'at ha-Halakha bi-Sfarad*," *Sefunot* 18 (1985), pp. 99–109.
137. Faur probably intended to write "impugning."
138. See B. San. 99b, where the classical definition of the heretic/*apiqoros* is one who exhibits disdain for the rabbinic scholar. Note the *pi'el*/ intensive participle form.
139. Prov. 23:30 as understood by B. Ber. 19b, that even the honor due the rabbi pales before and is of no account when the human rabbinic honor conflicts with the honor due the Deity. Therefore, Faur is subject to censure if and only if his reading of the documentary evidence is shown to be faulty.

are Sephardic rabbis who were anti-Maimonideans and the Ashkenazi decisor, R Moses Isserles, actually endorsed the study of philosophy. According to the Dual Torah as cited by R. Isserles, the wise of the nations are called "wise,"[140] and he praises Maimonides in spite of those who wrongly burn his writing.[141] Thus, if studying philosophy and engaging in critical thinking is sinful, then if Maimonides is wrong, then R. Isserles is of necessity also wrong.[142]

Faur maintains that the anti-Maimonideans called the Maimonideans heretics, implying that the real deviants were the former rabbis who demanded obedience and who outlaw critical thinking and personal accountability. For the Andalusian/Sephardic school, for Faur the heir to the Geonic Tradition–and for every pre-Christian cult–religion is Orthoprax and not Orthodox.[143] On the one hand, Faur argues that the heresy of which Maimonides was guilty

140. B. Meg. 16a. See also B. Ber. 58a, which requires a benediction upon seeing a wise sage from among the nations of the world.

141. *She'elot wu-Tshubot R Moshe Iserlich* (Amsterdam, 5471/1711), #7, 4c.

142. See Faur's nn. 285, 400, "Maran Joseph Caro, *Bet Yosef, Yore Dea* CLXXXI s.v. *haqafat,* rejected a disparaging remark against Maimonides made by R. Jacob, in the *Tur* (for dealing with the reason for one of the Scriptural Precepts, in the *Guide*). It is pertinent to our discussion that Maran began his reply by rejecting the view that R. Jacob *imputes* to Maimonides–a classical anti-Maimonidean tactic: "It is unworthy [to suggest] that Maimonides held this!" Then Maran proceeded to challenge him with this fundamental question: "Who had actually cared for the honor of the Torah and precepts, more than him?" Finally, it is important to recall the scientific activities of R. David Gans (1541–1613)–a worthy disciple of Rama! By the way, if we are to judge the Rama's approach to the study of Talmud by the commentary on Tractate *Holin* by his disciple, R. Eliezer Ashkenazi, *Dammeseq Eliezer* (Lublin, 1607), which I had the privilege to study–one would have to admit that his methodology is very close to that of R. Menahem Meiri, having nothing to do with the pilpulistic hodgepodge of bogus-Talmudists. Here Faur describes the anti-Maimonidean tactic of claiming that the opposition maintains a position that it does not and then attacking that wrongly imputed position.

143. Since for Christianity, Jesus the person replaces Torah (Ac. 2 and John 14:6), knowing who Jesus is becomes essential and this orientation explains why for the Church, doctrine is more critical than deed.

is not cited by his detractors. By informing the reader that the anti-Maimonideans doctored texts to suit their ends, *after* making faith in the saintly great rabbi who is Torah incarnate a dogma, the discerning reader realizes that Maimonides' "heresy," which empowered critical thinking, creates individuals and communities who will hold their leaders to account and not tolerate charlatans. His sharpest criticisms are found in the notes. In n. 299 Faur observes that "Violence and zeal, both intellectual and emotional, are supreme testimony of religiosity according to the Islamic-Christian concept of *jihad,* but it was flatly rejected by the Maimonideans and the Andalusian school."[144] Faur opens his comments[145] on the Maimonidean Mishneh Torah with a

---

144. Faur's statement recorded above is a précis of his, "Law and Hermeneutics in Rabbinic Tradition," in *Cardozo Law Review* 14 (1993), pp. 1662–1666. In his post, "Ego and Humility in Torah Study," Schachter notes with approval that in dialectic study yeshiva students are "extremely belligerent toward each other, seemingly angry and even abusive." When the study is over, the students appear as friends. When studying, one does not discover truth; one wins a battle. Real Torah is for Schachter not found in sacred texts but in atextual/analphabetic Masorah and the great sages. Only those vetted to be great sages by the great sages have the right to even express an opinion. Posting at www.torahweb.org, "Masorah and Change." Schachter believes that when the right rabbis enact change, the word *hiddush* [innovation] applies and when the wrong rabbis enact change the word *shinnui* [change] applies. We find in Schachter's postings regarding Orthodox in modernity the incarnation of Torah, culture bellicosity, and suppression of critical thinking. In this posting, the good Jew emulates the past practice of sacred people. This Judaic system is not the Judaism of the Dual Torah. Lam. 5:7 reminds the reader that the "ancestors sinned and are no more" and B. Pes. 116a reports the words of Rav, who reminds the Seder celebrants to expound "our ancestors were originally idolaters."

145. " Earlier studies of Faur on this topic are "Understanding the Covenant," in *Tradition* 9 (1968), pp. 33–55, *"De-Oraita, de-Rabbanan ve-Dinim Muflaim be-Mishnato shelha-Rambam,"* in *Sinai* 67 (1972), pp. 20–35, *Iyyunim be-Mishneh Torah le-ha- Rambam* [*Studies in the Mishne Tora*] ( Jerusalem: Mossad Harav Kook, 1978), *"Iyyunim be-Hilkhot Teshuba le-Harambam," Sinai* 61 (1969), pp. 259–266, "The Fundamental Principles of Jewish Jurisprudence," in *The Journal of International Law and Politics,* New York University, 12 (1979), *"De-Oraita, de-Rabbanan ve-Dinim Muflaim be-Mishnato shel ha-Rambam,"* in *Sinai* 67 (1972),

critique of the anti-Maimonidean school, which in passing outlines his own academic method:

- Studying the anti-Maimonidean readings of the Mishneh Torah–a work based on a meticulous examination of the Talmud and juridical traditions of the Geonim
- One cannot help but wonder whether they had any idea of what halakhah is or if they actually cared about it.
- They were unfamiliar with the rudiments of Semitic grammar and philology, knew no rabbinic rhetoric and jurisprudence, and they were not conversant with the major halakhic and hermeneutic principles developed in the academies of the Geonim and Old Sepharad.
- If one were to judge their level of comprehension by the grammar of their writings, one would have to admit that textual analysis and cohesiveness were not part of their mental apparatus.
- In addition, the texts they studied, including Scripture and the Talmud, had been subjected to whimsical doctoring by careless and semi-lettered scribes.
- Generally, their objections rest on faulty texts, analphabetic readings, and unfamiliarity with Geonic scholarship.

For Faur – as opposed to conventional Orthodoxy, Maimonides's compendium, the Mishneh Torah, encapsulates the authentic Jewish Dual Torah Tradition with meticulous care; academic seriousness is essential because words do have actual meaning. By boldly declaring that the anti-Maimonideans did not know or care about Halakhah, Faur rejects their *bona fides* and existential position. It is the Mishneh Torah that represents the "Horizontal Society," because it is an "alphabetic" book-based culture statement, whose very horizontality

pp. 20–35, "Maimonides on Freedom and Language," in *Helios* 9 (1982), pp. 73–94, "Law and Hermeneutics in Rabbinic Jurisprudence: A Maimonidean Perspective," in *Cardozo Law Review* 14 (1993), pp. 1657–1679.

threatens all vertical/hierarchical analphabetic alternatives. With the lapse of political sovereignty, the Talmud became the corpus that was promulgated by rabbis who represented the last national authority of the Jews. The law in real life and the law on the books, Faur concedes, do not always cohere;[146] thus Maimonides' Mishneh Torah is less a code and more a guide to normative practice. Legal decisions are justified by reason and not by "*ex Cathedra*" decrees. While real life realities account for the discrepancies between the law in the schools and legal application,[147] judicial discretion is part of the legal order. The Mishneh Torah was written *for* the public as a compendium to be followed by reasoned conversation and persuasion. The anti-Maimonideans did not want the public to have access to the law, because no one may have access to God's mind but them. In classical Maimonidean fashion, Faur first exposes the error of the anti-Maimonideans, i.e., their enshrining of "hierarchic truth." The discerning reader will also note that this "hierarchic truth" is the political doctrine shared both by the Church and contemporary anti-Maimonidean "Orthodox" rabbis. Noting Rabad's aggressive and rude remark,[148] Faur observes with seething sarcasm, "for an impassioned panegyric of this towering figure, by a most worthy representative, see I. Twersky, *Rabad of Posquieres*."[149] By referring to Twersky as "worthy" and Rabad as

146. Faur notes that Rabban Gamliel taught the law differently in school than he applied the law in everyday life, as in M. Ber. 2:5–7.

147. Faur cites the case of Maimonides' allowing a twice widowed woman to remarry. See 411 and n. 315, and Alan J. Yuter, "*Horaat Sha'ah*: The Emergency Principle in Jewish Law and a Contemporary Application," in *Jewish Political Studies Review* 13:3–4 (Fall 2001), internet edition. See also Maimonides, *Responsa*, n. 181, Blau, pp. 329–330.

148. See Raabad's attack of *Maimonides* at Teshuva 3:7, "greater and better fellows than he [= Maimonides] actually believed that God has a body." On the one hand, calling Raabad "rude" is for this school considered to be rude; on the other hand, Raabad's comment would be considered to be rude if it were made by a hierarchically inferior person. Faur's "horizontal society" radically rejects "hierarchical truth," and therefore subjects Raabad to the treatment that Raabad accorded Maimonides.

149. Cambridge: Harvard University Press, 1962.

"towering," Faur alludes with the "towers" idiom to Rabad's confident and hierarchical sense of self; Twersky is a "worthy" or fitting acolyte, because he regards Rabad's tradition to be authentic.

Recall that while, for the Maimonideans, scholarly argument is collegial and respectful, medieval [and contemporary!] anti-Maimonideans are not, and for good reason:

> Anti-Maimonidean truth is hierarchic… anti-Maimonideans possess a higher truth – nobler,[150] and more archaic than that of the vulgar. It must be acknowledged by those standing below, not because it is true–those of lesser rank are too stupid to understand–but because a superior man had told them so. Truth is a matter of personal status: who says it is of the essence.[151]

Consequently, the rabbi may not defer to authority, but, if capable of making an autonomous reading, must give in to the most reasonable reading of the Dual Torah canon.

---

150. Faur is cleverly, in the allusive rhetoric of Maimonides, reminding the discerning that medieval and modern "nobles" were members of a warrior class.
151. Consider the corroborating view of Schachter, "Preserving the Mesorah [Tradition]," in *Jewish Action*, 21:2 (Winter 2010), p. 39: "Changes in practice require delicate evaluations that only a master Torah scholar, a *gadol baTorah*, can properly conduct. Only someone with a broad knowledge and a deep understanding of the corpus of halachah, with an intimate familiarity with both the letter and the spirit of the law, with a mastery of both the rules and the attitudes of the *mesorah*, can determine when a change is acceptable or even required. The more wide- reaching the proposed change, the greater the expertise required to approve it. The evaluator must not only be a master of the *mesorah*, but he must also be able to consider new practices based solely on values internal to the *mesorah*, removing external influences from the deliberation." According to Maimonides, a new rule may be issued by a local rabbi [*bet din shel yahid*] as long as the canonical limits remain in force [Introduction to the Code]; according to M. Ed. 2:2 codified in Bet Yosef Yoreh Deah 1:1, an act must be explicitly forbidden in order to be forbidden. Schachter's theory of Tradition, like Raabad's, invests the authoritative *person* with the right to innovate. He, no less than the anti-Maimonideans described by Faur, requires submission to the person but offers no hermeneutic whereby judgment of the judge, i.e., himself, may be judged.

At stake in this pointed conversation is the very nature of Jewish theological discourse. Is Jewish knowledge based on "submission to authority" or "rational understanding"? Now, Raabad argues that Maimonides erred by failing to cite the name of the authority on whom Maimonides' view is based. Not only does Rabad reconstruct Judaism from a system of legal norms to an oligarchy of charismatic rabbis, he rejects the Dual Torah norm that requires the judge not to defer to the authority of others but to rule as "his eyes see."[152] Rabad and those who adhere to his Judaism believe that others should defer to him because of his age and superior wisdom.[153] The ideological/ theo- logical hero for anti-Maimonidean Judaism is the "inerrant saint."[154] While in the Judaism of the Dual Torah, no human is infallible and no being, not even God, is endowed with sovereign immunity, these new rabbis, being saintly, are self-defined to be virtually

152. B. B.B. 131a.

153. Raabad, *Strictures to Maimonides, Code, Introduction.*

154. Raabad, *Teshuvot u-Pesaqim* (Jerusalem: Rav Kook, 1964), p. 65, n. 20. Faur now directs his reader to 2:155–162, appendix 67, where Nahmanides rejected the rabbinic right to legislate but regarded rabbinic commentary of Torah to Torah, a view consistent with Raabad's view and for that matter, Schachter as well. Faur then cites the unpublished paper of R. Josh Yuter, who argued that Nahmanides' view is sourced in Tertullian's *De Padicta*, 21, tr. Henry Bettenson, *The Later Christian Fathers: A Selection from the Writings of the Fathers from St. Cyril of Jerusalem to St. Leo the Great* (Oxford: Oxford University Press, 1977), p. 113. Faur locates this doctrine that the post-Talmudic sages speak in God's voice to *Sefer ha-Hinnuch*, 492, and law derives from the superior [as if measurable] knowledge of the rabbi and not the judicial, i.e., legal right to legislate office that is the norm creating body. Faur then turns to Rashi's view [B. R.S. 25b] that the latter sages must be obeyed as if they are members of the Sanhedrin. Ever the neo-Maimonidean advocate, Faur will show that Raabad contracted the Oral Torah by requiring deference to charisma over reason, and Rashi, whose present claim contradicts both I Chronicles 9:20, and Gen. Rabbah 60:13, where it is the judiciary, the norm creating body, and not the sages who, following Raabad, Nahmanides, and today, Schachter, who is able to intuit God's law by reading between the lines of Scripture. These rabbis cannot "not know" or make an error [2:160.]

immune from error.[155] By referring to R. Asher[156] as "saintly," Faur accomplishes two ends: he identifies rabbis who use saintliness as a cloak for their authority and he explains why the Judaism of Law, with a public set of rules, is so threatening to the charismatic. Disagreeing with R. Asher, the Torah incarnate is an act of apostasy, even if one affirms the letter of the law.[157]

R. Asher, like Rabad and Nahmanides, is also able to read the mind of God; consequently, disagreeing with the great rabbi is the theological equivalent of defying God. According to old Jewish law, host country Gentiles are not to be lent money with interest. R. Nisim Gerondi could not find a rational for money lending for profit that was accepted in his community.[158] Faur refers to R. Asher's "altruistic" and "principled" ' justification for lending money to Gentiles for profit, that if he did not lend money to Gentiles for profit, other Jews would do so.[159] Faur's diction is syntactically proper while his polemic is seethingly sarcastic.

---

155. It has become fashionable in contemporary Orthodox conversation to speak of "holy rabbis," like the "holy Rabbi Baal Shem Tov," the holy "Or ha-Hayyim," or the "holy Zohar." Since these rabbis are holy and presumably others are not, their authority resides in their personal charisma and not in their power to persuade. I have not heard people speak of "the holy Maimonides," "the holy Bible," or "holy Mishnah." It seems that the "holy" epithet is only applied to mystical rabbis.
156. *Teshuvot ha-Rosh* 55:9.
157. *Supra*, 21:8. Note the case of the rabbi who ruled correctly that a public thoroughfare requires a door, *tsurat ha-petah*, to permit carrying on Shabbat. Note well that Faur is deftly implying that the Orthodox, saintly, and inerrant R. Asher is, when measured against the Dual Torah benchmarks, a Reformer and not Orthodox at all. In his "The Psak Process," Schachter argues that even if it appears that a great rabbi distorts the ruling, since the rabbi issuing the ruling is inerrant, finding error is both error and shows the shower of the error to be in error. This doctrine of virtual inerrancy is found in R. Mayer Yisroel Kagan, *Chofetz Chaim* 8:7, where no one can criticize another except the great rabbi, who, in the "tradition" of R. Asher, is authorized to identify the heresy of the others who are dissenters.
158. *Teshuvot ha-Ran*, 56, 47b.
159. *Hilkhot ha-Rosh, Moed Qatan* 1:24.

By presenting R. Asher's actual words after his discussion regarding Nahmanides, Faur implies that this alternative Judaic system is neither altruistic nor principled but is "saintly" in the Christian sense of the term. The inability to tolerate dissent, coupled with the readiness to override settled, Dual Torah law, indicates that, for Faur, this Judaic system is hierarchical and not consistent with Torah. In his Epilogue, Faur addresses his reader not as a scholar but as a guide, asking which Judaism, the Maimonidean or the anti-Maimonidean, advocates the horizontal society. Canon, *shari'a,*, and anti-Maimonidean laws are instruments of power that serve elites; in Torah, the Law is the religion. And in the Torah religion of the horizontal society, elites are themselves judged by the Law because they stand under the law; Faur judges R. Asher, Rabad, and Nahmanides by the benchmarks of the law. By requiring the Jew to confirm that the soul of humans is pure in the morning liturgy, the rabbinic sages offered a religion very different from R. Asher, who declared that people are wretched.[160] Like the Christian who needs Jesus to be saved, Jewry then and now is told to submit not to the religion of the sacred canon, but to the human canons who claim to control that library. Faur concludes that America was founded in the principles of the horizontal society, challenging his readers to read, challenge political elites, and to think for themselves.

Following Maimonides' *Guide,*[161] where different ideas must be connected from disparate passages, Faur's appendices "*Minim and Minut* ("About 'Strict Talmudists' ") [2:23–127] and the juxtaposed "Semantic Assimilation" [2:127–132] provide the category definition that fits the description of the anti-Maimonidean rabbis provides the essence of his critique:

Maimonides [*Teshubot ha-Rambam,* #263, vol. 2:499], defined *min* "as someone who rejects one of the principles of the Torah; one of

160. Besamim Rosh n. 192, 65b-c. The actual authorship of this source has been debated. See http://seforim.blogspot.com/2006/11/bizzare-case-of-censoring-besamim-rosh.html

161. Introduction.

whom is someone postulating that the Torah is not from Heaven"... In the rabbinic mind, a *min* is the most shameful type of "heretic"– more wretched and evil than even the infamous epicurean (the *apiqoros* of rabbinic literature). What makes the *minim* particularly odious is their method of cunning; luring the prey, as in hunting and fishing. They are perfidious: they use Scripture not to teach, but as a lure to beguile the gullible; exposing a single aspect of their beliefs to block the prey's judgment, driving him/her to do things that he/she will lament for the rest of his/her life. They are the supreme masters of the art of cunning. Their manifest reliance on the Hebrew Scripture and use of Jewish terms are baits designed to entrap the dull-witted. In spite of their pretentious religiosity, they are cynics who believe in no religion. In brief, for them the end justifies the means [2:119–120].

Faur's monograph is a *derasha/* legal brief that aims to defend the honor of the Maimonidean Judaism that be believes is the descendant of the Judaism of the Dual Torah, and to persuade the reader with facts, analysis, documentation, and reasoned argument. The test of a thesis is its ability to predict. The reader will not only learn a great deal from this monograph; the reader will learn how to read medieval and contemporary Jewish arguments critically.

# Preface

This work endeavors to show that whereas all social and political organizations are structured on the basis of hierarchic considerations, the Jewish people alone were organized along horizontal lines. This was possible because of two overwhelming principles. First, the Hebrew Scripture alone proposes that every human being is created in the image of God. Jewish belief in a single Creator necessitates the absolute equality of every human being. Second, the covenant at Sinai establishes the Law as the supreme authority of Israel. Accordingly, whereas in other societies, might is the source of authority, in Judaism all forms of authority, whether social or political, are limited by the Law. Both these principles were summarized by the last Prophet of Israel: "Have we not all one father? Has not one God created us? Why do we deal treacherously every man against his brother, profaning the covenant of our fathers?" (Mal 2:10).

José Faur
Nisan 14, 5767
April 2, 2007
Netanya, Israel

# Hebrew Transliteration Table

| א | ’ |
|---|---|
| ב | b |
| ג | g |
| ד | d |
| ה | h |
| ו | v, w |
| ז | z |
| ח | ḥ |
| ט | ṭ |
| י | y |
| כ, ך | k, kh |

| ל | l |
|---|---|
| מ, ם | m |
| נ, ן | n |
| ס | s |
| ע | ‘ |
| פ, ף | f, p, ph |
| צ, ץ | ṣ |
| ק | q |
| ר | r |
| ש | sh, s |
| ת | t |

# Abbreviations

| | |
|---|---|
| *Ac.* | *Acts* |
| *AdRN* | *Abot de-Ribbi Natan* |
| *Am.* | *Amos* |
| Ar. | Arabic |
| *Chr.* | *Chronicles* |
| *Col.* | *Colossians* |
| *Cor.* | *Corinthians* |
| *Dan.* | *Daniel* |
| *Deut.* | *Deuteronomy* |
| *Eccl.* | *Ecclesiastes* |
| *Eph.* | *Ephesians* |
| *Est.* | *Esther* |

| | |
|---|---|
| *Lev.* | *Leviticus* |
| *Lk.* | *Luke* |
| *Mac.* | *Maccabees* |
| *Mal.* | *Malachi* |
| *Matt.* | *Matthew* |
| *Mic.* | *Micah* |
| *MT* | *Mishne Tora* |
| *Mk.* | *Mark* |
| n.d. | no date |
| n.p. | no place |
| | no pagination |
| *Neh.* | *Nehemiah* |

| *Ex.* | *Exodus* |
|---|---|
| *Ezek.* | *Ezekiel* |
| *Gal.* | *Galatians* |
| *Gen.* | *Genesis* |
| *Hab.* | *Habakkuk* |
| Heb. | Hebrew |
| *Hos.* | *Hosea* |
| *Is.* | *Isaiah* |
| *IShG* | *Iggeret Sherira Gaon* |
| *Jer.* | *Jeremiah* |
| *Jn.* | *John* |
| *Josh.* | *Joshua* |

| *Num.* | *Numbers* |
|---|---|
| *Pet.* | *Peter* |
| *Ps.* | *Psalms* |
| *Prov.* | *Proverbs* |
| *Sam.* | *Samuel* |
| *Song.* | *Song of Songs* |
| *Thess.* | *Thessalonians* |
| *Tim.* | *Timothy* |
| *Tit.* | *Titus* |
| *Zech.* | *Zechariah* |
| *Zeph.* | *Zephaniah* |
| | |

# Prologue

"If a man could pass through Paradise in a dream," wrote Samuel Taylor Coleridge (1772–1834), "and have a flower presented to him as a pledge that his soul had really been there, and if he found that flower in his hand when he awoke Ay! – and what then?" [1] The first man to have dreamt, so the Hebrew Scripture tells us, was Adam. Some time after discovering that he was unlike any other animal, God put him "in a deep sleep" (תרדמה) and Adam dreamt that Eve was made "bone of his bones and flesh of his flesh." He also dreamt that he had welcomed her and loved her and God blessed them both, and they were "one flesh," and for her sake he sinned and lost Paradise. Later, when he awoke, he opened his hand and – lo and behold! – there it was: the flower that God presented to him in Paradise! And Adam "knew" (וידע) – in the sense of 'recognizing' – "his wife, Eve" for what she really was: the pledge of having been in the presence of God and visited Paradise! (See Gen. 2:19–4:1). To commemorate this primordial dream the rabbis instituted seven blessings at the wedding ceremony, evoking the joy shared by the first parents of humanity, and praying that God should "bring forth happiness to this loving pair,

1. Cited by Jorge Luis Borges, "The Flower of Coleridge," in his *Other Inquisitions*, trans. Ruth L. C. Simms (Austin: University of Texas Press, 1964), pp. 10–11.

as Thou have brought happiness formerly to Thy creatures in Paradise." That primordial joy is in fact the matrix, not only of human faith in "God, Ruler of the Universe and Creator of humans in His image," but also of "bliss and happiness, bridegroom and bride, love, brotherhood, elation and jubilation, peace and fellowship." In a word, of all those basic feelings that make an individual a part of humanity.

Patriarch Abraham, too, was put into "a deep sleep" (תרדמה). Then, God came and told him that his children would be enslaved and oppressed, and in the end "they would come out with a great wealth." This time God required a pledge from Abraham, to confirm that *He* had actually been present at *his* dream. The circumcision is Abraham's pledge that God had been in *his* presence. God, in turn, reciprocated and gave Abraham the most wonderful pledge: Sarah would bear him a son, Isaac (see Gen. 15:12–17:19). In Hebrew, reciprocal acknowledgement and commitment is designated 'covenant' (ברית). Thus, at the circumcision ceremony, the father of the new-born child gives thanks to God, "for having enjoined us to have him [the child] to partake in the covenant of Abraham our father." Eventually, as it was announced in the "deep sleep" (תרדמה), Abraham's children were enslaved and oppressed. Later, when they heard God's voice and contracted a 'covenant' (ברית) with Him at Sinai, they discovered the meaning of "great wealth." It is the way out from the realm of the bestial freedom of pagan humanity, and towards life as a free people under "one Law for you and the alien residing in your midst." Next, when Moses and the Tabernacle and the Pillar of Fire and the Cloud guiding them through the Desert vanished from their sight, the children of Israel opened their hands. And – lo and behold! – there it was: the Law that God presented to them at Sinai! "Ay! – and what then?"

Dummies cannot dream. They resent the fact that others can and rail with malice against those who dare. Desperately, they spend their lives trying to convince Adam that Eve is nothing more than a chimpanzee in fancy lingerie; to convince Eve that her beloved is a gorilla unworthy of any of the rabbis' blessings; to convince Israel that they are not really Israel, or that they have forged the Law, or that it is nothing more than an assortment of gibberish; to convince the nations that bestial freedom, anarchy, and might are better than God, Paradise, and Sinai; and to convince anyone who would lend them an ear that the rabbis' seven blessings are a chimera. Thus, countless people – from godless pagans to heartless divines – are obsessed with a single goal: denying Israel the right to dream. The freedom preached by dummies is bestial and illusory. Can you imagine a more tyrannical purpose than denying a people the right to dream? Without this basic right, 'freedom' of speech and of conscience is nothing more than empty words.

Giambattista Vico (1688–1744), the father of modern humanism, called attention to the "conceit of nations" and the conceit "of scholars, who will have it that what they know is as old as the world."[2] Vico endeavored to show that the basic sentiments of humanity "were later perverted by the conceit of scholars and the conceits of nations – conceits we have sought throughout this work to discredit."[3] The realm of the dreamless is ruled by the proverbial "little foxes" (acting under the vigilant eye of the Big-Fox). These are the "learned fools," who, unable to do anything meaningful with their lives, devote their energies to destroying the "vineyards" planted by Israel.

They approach the Hebrew Scripture and Jewish tradition with the supreme arrogance of barbarous times: like warriors, in search of weak points to attack. Bereft of legal training and philology, and armed with scores of ideas gained from outmoded notions of historiography and literary criticism, they focus on a single aim: discrediting Jewish texts and institutions. In this vein, ideas are wrongly framed; words are pried from their semantic context, and books torn into infinitesimal fragments. On behalf of their 'objectivity' they offer their abject contempt for all that is sacred to Jews and Judaism. The purpose of "little foxes" is to tear down, not to build up (see Song. 2:15). Professor

---

2. *The New Science of Giambattista Vico,* trans. by Thomas Goddard Bergin and Max Harold Fisch (Ithaca, N. Y.: Cornell University, 1968), ##126–127, p. 61.
3. *New Science* #1111, p. 426.

Abraham Joshua Heschel (1907–1972) called attention to the devastating effect of the negative approach to Jewish studies.

> Judaism today is the least known religion. Its rare splendor has been so frequently adjusted to the trivialities of changing opinions that what is left is commonplace. There are only a few who still perceive the vanishing *niggun* of its perennial yearning.[4]

Alarmingly, the reduction of Judaism to trivialities has affected some of our most distinguished Rabbinic Colleges. The upshot is what Professor Neusner described as "Rabbis, but no Tora." He began this essay with this eye-opening paragraph:

> The failure of the Rabbinical schools, Reform, Conservative, Reconstructionist, and integrationist-Orthodox, over the past generation to set forth a coherent intellectual structure and system resting on Tora-learning has produced a generation of rabbis with little or no Tora to teach. By "Tora" I refer not to some knowledge of the Hebrew Scriptures, which the liturgy requires rabbis to gain. I speak of a basic philosophy – a core-theology – of conviction that coheres and that guides the everyday encounter with the crises of life, both public and private.[5]

The Hebrew Scripture, the Law, Tora, Judaism – or whatever which way you wish to call the values, texts, and traditions of Israel – is *not* for dummies. In the First Section of this work, we focus on a simple idea, unnoticed in contemporary thought: "The God of Israel" can read and write! This means that His speech is alphabetic, that Creation itself ought to be conceived in terms of a text in which the reader is the writer. Conversely, the analphabetic mind cannot grasp the God

4. Abraham Joshua Heschel, *The Earth is the Lord's* (New York: Henry Schuman, 1950), p. 107.
5. Published in *National Jewish Post and Opinion*, 2004.

of Israel; and of necessity, the posture of an unlettered public towards a 'sacred' text, be it the Scripture or a Constitution, borders on myth and the fabulous. Analphabetic 'faith' in an unread text produces fanatics, not sages. The Hebrew Scripture urges Israel to be "a wise and understanding people." To remind us of this purpose, the first blessing of the daily prayer asks God, "to graciously award us wisdom, understanding and comprehension." By way of contrast, Greek rational-ideality excludes 'reading.' Therefore, it can grasp neither the God nor the Scripture of Israel. Or what amounts to the same, analphabetic crowds will invariably choose the magic of heroes and poets over the wisdom of scribes and sages.

The Second Section invites the reader to consider a key dimension of "The Books of Israel," barely grasped by modern scholarship. They are *national* texts: published by the governing institutions of and for the people of Israel. The Tora is 'sacred' not simply because it comes *from* God, but because it was confirmed in a solemn covenant *with* God, in *the presence of the entire population and governing bodies of Israel.* In this specific sense, there is an abysmal difference between the Hebrew Scripture and a 'book' in western tradition, just like there is a difference between a 'book' and a *national* document, be it the Constitution or the Magna Carta. The *political* dimension of "The Books of Israel" renders 'Israel/Tora' a single entity, so that text and people interlace and further expand – semantically and historically – one another. It would follow, therefore, that purloining the Scripture from the people of Israel is no less an offense than purloining the US Constitution or Magna Carta from their respective people would be.

The Third Section, "The Governance of Israel" is a follow up. For Israel, the source of all forms of authority is the Law contracted at Sinai. This means, above all, that all forms of sovereignty are limited, and that political authority is not the fact of might *but of the consent of the governed.* Accordingly, Judaism refused to extend a helping hand to despotic regimes or to muzzle political criticism. Although commonly seen as a 'religious' phenomenon, hatred against Israel is political in its motivation. (How can a Rex or Pontifical ruler be expected to exercise absolute sovereignty over his subjects, when a high-profile radical minority refuses to subject itself to the absolute sovereignty of anyone?) In due course, we shall draw attention to the fact that antisemitism is the preferred strategy of political and religious systems claiming unlimited sovereignty.

The Fourth Section focuses on the political and judicial crises facing Israel, after suffering a most devastating defeat at the hands of the Romans. Specifically: how a people divested of earthly power and living under ruthless tyrants were able to maintain a modicum of judicial and political autonomy. "The Memory of Israel" traces the strategy of survival mapped out by the rabbis, and seeks to show the triumph of wisdom over might and cunning. An important factor in the development and preservation of Israel's Memory was the official publication of the Mishna: establishing, thus, a formal distinction between national and vernacular memory. The medium of Israel's National Memory is rabbinic discourse (מליצה). Rather than to 'demonstrate,' as in Greek rational-ideality, the point of rabbinic discourse is to state a view or tradition – calmly, clearly, and without theatrics. The purpose is to initiate a dialogue, which will result in a flow of ideas leading to consensus. In the course of rabbinic discourse, the principles and values that sustain the biblical text and tradition were identified, and the National Memory of Israel was kept alive and further expanded. Thanks to the system of governance developed by the rabbis, Jews in captivity enjoyed more freedom and higher standards of material and social living than the general population under the Rex. Given that the most representative depositary of the rabbinic system is the Talmud, there arose the need to malign the 'Talmud,' 'rabbis,' and 'Jews' in general.

The last Section examines some of the events and ideas leading to the collapse of Iberian Jewry. They illustrate what may happen to a well-organized society when, out of complacency and gullibility, it surrenders its leadership to "little foxes" – both 'religious' and 'secular.' The underlying thesis is that "little foxes" are to a democratic political and legal system the equivalent to entropy in the second law of thermodynamics. Hence, the urgency for education and critical thinking in Judaism and in all systems based on freedom, equality, and the rule of law. "The Folly of Israel" examines the seduction of unreason, the might of analphabetic crowds, the foolishness of inerrant teachers, and the turpitude of heroic leadership. (In the end, Jewish leadership proved so oppressive and inept that many chose to abdicate self-autonomy under the Law on behalf of the unlimited sovereignty of the State. Or what amounted to the same, to rely on the proverbial 'Kindness of Strangers' and the wisdom of the fabulous *europaischen Menschentums*[6] rather than on their own institutions. Thus, giving rise to a chain of blunders, ending with the Holocaust.)

In this work we treat the Tora as a legal document, setting forth the fundamental laws and institutions governing the public and private life of the Jewish people; in short, as the Constitution of the children of Israel. Its literary and semantic integrity is a given. I find it personally demeaning to accept a doctrine, popular in some 'scholarly' circles, that to be 'scientific,' an idea needs first to be regurgitated by godless and soulless ideologues. 'German historiography' and the 'Documentary Hypothesis' are the children of Greek rational-ideality: anti-book and anti-humanism. They are the product of dismal spirits, preferring the rule of tyrants and demagogues to the seven blessings of the rabbis. The purpose is to discredit Jewish history and Jewish texts on behalf of the legendary *europaischen Menschentums* – the glorious 'European man' who brought about the First and Second World Wars and through turpitude and insatiable greed may bring about the Third. I once pointed out to a celebrated biblical scholar that if we were to apply German historiography to the history of the

6. The term comes from Edmund Husserl, "Philosophy and the Crisis of European Man," printed in his *Phenomenology and the Crisis of Philosophy* (New York: Harper & Row, 1965); see José Faur, *Golden Doves with Silver Dots: Semiotics and Textuality in Rabbinic Tradition* (Bloomington: Indiana University Press, 1986), p. 155 n. 45. In this work it stands for the European sense of superiority, both cultural and political. See below, Section I n. 55.

'Philadelphia Convention,' it no longer would be possible to believe that it had ever taken place! Similarly, if we were to apply the 'Documentary Hypothesis' to the text of the *Federalist Papers* or the US Constitution, these documents would have zero standing. In fact, if this type of textual analysis would be accepted in a court of law, it would render most legal contracts null and void! "Our Constitution is different," the biblical scholar responded, "because we live under it." To which I retorted: "The same applies to Jews for whom the Tora is their Constitution, and who strive with all their soul to live under it."

I fully concur with Professor Neusner that "we cannot hope to define a single Judaism that sets the standard for all competing versions," for the simple reason that Judaism requires communities. Since there are "many communities of Judaism, and they differ from one another," we must speak of 'Judaisms' – in the plural. With one *caveat*, "there is no such thing as 'mine alone.'"[7] The same principle applies at the purely intellectual level. My own Judaism has its roots in 'Old Sepharad,' generally described as 'Maimonidean.' I prefer to call it 'Alphabetic Judaism,' because it *generates* 'Jewish knowledge and values' from a scrupulous and delicate study of the *texts* of Israel: alphabetically, where every letter and linguistic nuance counts. Therefore, as will be obvious through the course of this work, my understanding of Jewish texts, including the Scripture and Talmud, is not always congruent with current interpretations – both traditional and scholarly. Let me begin by stating that I don't regard Judaism as a 'religion' in the standard, Christian sense of the term. For better or for worse, the primary structure of Judaism is *not* theological. The term does not exist and it cannot even be coined in classical Hebrew. This is not to say that the Hebrew Scripture and rabbinic texts are not bursting with concepts that one can treat theologically and philosophically. However, as with the 'philosophy' of science or law, the subject itself – *science* or *law* – is *not* philosophy. In this regard it is instructive to notice that Maimonides (1134/5–1204) classified 'belief in God' as one of

7. Published in *National Jewish Post and Opinion*, 2004.

the 613 'precepts' (מצוות) of the Tora, which presupposes a primary political and judicial context, having nothing to do with theology. To render the 'God' of the Hebrew Scripture asunder from its original context, would be no less misleading than doing the same with "In God we trust" on our dollar bills, "So help me God" in our courts of justice, "under God" and "all men are created equal" in the Declaration of Independence – and then proceeding to develop an 'American Theology,' and refusing to acknowledge the context of these terms.

The purpose of law, whether Jewish or non-Jewish, is to build bridges. "Disciples of sages," taught the rabbis, "increase peace in the world." The purpose of theology is to point at 'differences' between various creeds, and explain why one system is superior or inferior to another. There is another reason for not focusing on 'theology.' The subject interests only theologians who teach other theologians, who would want to teach other theologians... *ad infinitum*. Today, people are more interested to know what the Tora and rabbis have to teach about limited sovereignty, division of power, distribution of wealth, pseudo-democracies, dictatorship, the right of privacy, equality before the Law, constitutional interpretation, consensus understanding, world peace, etc., rather than theological niceties. If, for the sake of reference and illustration, parallel works are needed, it would be more helpful to consult modern constitutions, legislation, and judicial decisions, than works on theology and religious hermeneutics.

This book is written for a public sharing the primordial dream of humanity. The style is of rabbinic discourse (מליצה). The objective is not to demonstrate – for every argument there will be a counter-argument – but to open a dialogue, which, hopefully, will result in a new flow of ideas.

To facilitate a better grasp of the subject at hand, every section is accompanied by Introductory Remarks and Concluding Reflections. The Appendices at the end of the book intend to further document and analyze rabbinic concepts and terms, which are treated differently than standard scholarly and rabbinic interpretation. The Epilogue seeks to relate some of the ideas and values discussed in this work to contemporary issues. I cherish the standard translations of "The Hebrew Scripture." However on many occasions I rendered my own translation to underline some semantic or grammatical nuances essential to the point at hand. Unless specified, translations of all other texts are mine.

I wish to conclude this Prologue with a story, told to me by my friend Dr. Philip Miller. It illustrates the peculiar burden facing Jewish scholars today.

> Once there was a Master who would give classes on high philosophy and love of God. During these classes, the temple cat would crawl affectionately into the laps of the students, distracting them. So to help their concentration, the Master would tie the cat to a tree outside the temple and then release it after the class.
>
> Master passed away, but his successor continued to tie the cat to the tree out of devotion to the memory of his Master. Some time later, the cat also died and another cat was procured and tied to the tree during class.
>
> The next generation of the lineage began to debate the spiritual powers achieved by tying a cat to a tree outside of philosophy classes, and the next Master in the line wrote a thick book of theological speculations on the essential esoteric practice of cat-tree-tying. The following generation, of course, changed the lineage's seal to an emblem of a cat tied to a tree.

Much of contemporary Jewish learning concerns the holy cat. The following chapters aim at the arduous task of trying to liberate Judaism from the cat's claws.

# Section I

# The God of Israel

## Introductory Remarks

The first Sabbath signaled the end of Creation and the beginning of *historical* time, when God "rested *away* from all His works" (Gen. 2:2).[1] Among the ten things "created at twilight" – the instant marking the end of Creation preceding the beginning of the Sabbath – the rabbis counted "*ketab* and *mikhtab*," two separate faculties that God endowed on humanity (Abot 5:6; see Pesaḥim 54a).

1. See José Faur, *Homo Mysticus* (Syracuse: Syracuse University Press, 1999), pp. 144–145.

Usually, these terms are taken as synonymous; *ketab* standing for 'script' and *mikhtab* for 'writing,' resulting in a tautology. The correct interpretation was given by R. Ḥanan'el (d. ca. 1055/6), quoted by R. Judah al-Bargeloni (or al-*Barṣeloni,* 11th-12th centuries). The first term, *ketab,* refers to the alphabet, "the [particular] letters that you write; for example, *'Alef, Resh, Ṣadi.*" The second term, *mikhtab* stands for 'reading,' and is the faculty that enables "you to read [the above mentioned letters] as: *'EReṢ* (= ארץ 'earth')." Thus, 'writing' and 'reading' are two extraordinary faculties bestowed on humankind at "the twilight" of Creation. These faculties border on the miraculous. The first is the faculty to devise a *visual* system (the alphabet) in which each sign (= the letter) stands for a phonetic *sound.* To gain a better insight of the 'miraculous' aspect of the *ketab* and *mikhtab* we must remember that the Hebrew alphabet consists only of *consonants*: vowels are excluded (see appendix 1). Thus, the *ketab* consists of symbols, each standing for a consonant – an *unpronounceable phonetic* sound. The *mikhtab* system is the faculty of synthesizing the *ketab* into something transcending the symbols themselves and *reading* them as a *word.* To accomplish this, the reader must mentally provide the *vowels* to an unpronounceable set of consonants. After citing R. Ḥanan'el, R. Judah al-Bargeloni expounded these points further. The *ketab* system stands for the faculty of devising,

> The shape of each letter, as with [our] alphabet, [in which] each [individual] letter [stands] for and by itself; given that speech is composed of phonetic sounds emitted from different places, all the way from the internal larynx to the external lips. At 'twilight' God bestowed on Adam and his posterity the faculty to devise different symbols (the alphabet) in which each (symbol) stands for one of these phonetic sounds. [In Hebrew] this [system] is designated *ketab*. The word that is [phonetically] synthesized out of these symbols (the alphabet) is designated *mikhtab* ('reading'), which is the [phonetic]

> fusion of the letters [= consonants], [thus] reading a [written] term as a word.[2]

The Hebrew alphabet breaks the grid 'signifier/signified.' An important feature of the Hebrew alphabet is that it excludes vowels. A scroll of the Tora containing vowels is ritually void (see appendix 1). This bears directly on the Hebrew concept of 'reading' (*qeri'a*). It involves interaction between the *mikhtab* system, whereby the reader mentally supplies the vowels, and the *ketab* or 'unreadable' consonantal system. The 'word,' therefore, is the creation of the reader.

Paraphrasing Roland Barthes (1915–1980), we may say that in Hebrew the reader is the writer.[3] In a vocalized text, such as that of the Christian and Moslem Scriptures, where the consonants have been

---

2. Edited by R. Israel Moses Ḥazzan, *Iyye ha-Yam* (Leghorn, 5629/1869), 113a from a Geonic manuscript, Part I, #14; see *Perush R. Ḥanan'el, Pesaḥim* (Jerusalem: Makhon Leb Sameaḥ 5751/1991), p. 124 n. 186. This *responsum* is found also in *Teshubot ha-Ge'onim*, ed. R. Musafia (Lyck, 5624/1864), #119, 36a; cf. R. Jonathan b. Yeḥiel, *'Arukh*, s.v. *ketab*; and R. Judah al-Bargeloni, *Perush Sefer Yeṣira* (Berlin: Mekize Nirdamim, 1885), p. 215. The authority for this tradition is R. Sherira Gaon; see *Teshubot ha-Ge'onim*, ed. Abraham E. Harkavi (Berlin, 1887), #29, p. 11. Cf. *Golden Doves*, p. 171 n. 29. See also *Oṣar ha-Ge'onim, Pesaḥim*, p. 153. For Maimonides' view, see Maimonides, *Dalalat al-Ḥa'irin*, ed. Issachar Joel and Solomon Munk (Jerusalem, 1931; henceforth cited as *Guide*) I, 66. Generally, the term *mikhtab* stands for 'writing.' Our case is different because here *mikhtab* appears together with *ketab*. Were we to interpret *mikhtab* in its usual sense, it would be redundant. According to R. Ḥanan'el's interpretation, the *mem* in *mikhtab* is a performative of *ketab*. On these noun formations, see R. David Kimḥi (Qimḥi), *Hebrew Grammar* (*Mikhlol*), trans. and annotated by William Chomsky (New York: Bloch Publishing, 1952–5713), p. 277. This type of noun is composed of [i] a performative *mem* + [ii] a verbal-root in the function of the infinitive. In my view, the performative *mem* renders the noun a *performative* of the *verbal-root*; as with *mishpat* which is the performative of *shafat*; *mishna* which is the performative of *shana*; *miqra* which is the performative of *qara*, standing for 'recitation' of the *Shema'*, see Mishna Berakhot 2:1, Mishna Sota 7:2; cf. below n. 62. Thus, the expression *em la-miqra* for the 'vocal *reading*' of Scripture, in contradistinction to *em la-masoret*, which stands for the consonantal text; see Sukka 6b, etc.; and appendix 2.
3. See *Golden Doves*, pp. 2, 10–12, 121.

provided with vowels, the reader is passive. His role is marginal and submissive. He just 'lifts up' the sound from the script and 'recites' it.[4]

In Judaism, writing is not an instrument for memorization.* The rabbis distinguished between 'writing' (*koteb*) and a mnemonic 'marking' (*roshem*).[5] Writing is structurally connected to a 'word' – not a 'thing.' A 'word' in Hebrew comprises two or more consonants. Therefore, writing must comprise at least two consonants. A single letter abbreviating a word or representing a number is *not* 'writing.'[6] 'Writing' is independent of the intention of the writer. Someone intending to write *GaDdi'EL* [consisting in Hebrew of four consonants: ג/ד/א/ל], for example, had effected 'writing' upon completing *GaD*, since it is a meaningful term[7] (see appendix 2).

The preceding considerations permit a clearer understanding of writing and reading in Hebrew intellectual tradition. Reading' is the result of the interaction of the *ketab* and *mikhtab* systems. By mentally uniting two signs (in themselves unpronounceable and void of connotation), the reader *generates* meaning (see appendix 2). This leads to what Paul Ricoeur (1913–2005) designates as the "semantic autonomy of the text";[8] and consequently, the "disconnection of the mental intention of the author from the verbal meaning of the text, of what the author meant and what the text means."[9] Thus, Hebrew 'meaning' is contained in, but not determined by, the written text. As

4. This fundamental aspect of vocalized reading has been overlooked by Ivan Illich and Barry Sanders, *ABC: The Alphabetization of the Popular Mind* (San Francisco: North Point Press, 1988), pp. 12–13. Cf. *Golden Doves*, pp. 6–7.

* Thus at the "beginning," God writes the Tora!

5. See Mishna Shabbat 12:3; Maimonides, *Perush ha-Mishnayot*, ed. and trans. R. Joseph Qafiḥ, 7 vols. (Jerusalem: Mossad Harav Kook, 1967), vol. 2, p. 62; *MT Shabbat* 11:17. This means that 'writing' stands above 'marking' in the hierarchic system of ideas. It also means that people employing marking systems will not necessarily evolve into alphabetic societies.

6. See *MT Shabbat* 11:13

7. Mishna Shabbat 12:3; *Perush ha-Mishnayot*, vol. 2, p. 62.

8. Paul Ricoeur, *Interpretation Theory* (Fort Worth, Texas: The Texas Christian University Press, 1976), p. 75.

9. *Interpretation Theory*, pp. 29–30.

we shall see, this rule applies even to texts authored by God: meaning is a function of reading.*

The God of Israel is the only God who can write and read. When King Belshazzar saw "the handwriting on the wall" he knew that it was a message coming from the God of Israel and not from a pagan deity. Therefore he panicked (see Dan. 5:5–6). The Tablets of the Covenant were "written with the finger of God" (Ex. 31:18; 34:1; Deut. 9:10). The rest of the Tora, although copied by Moses, was actually written by God: Moses was merely acting as God's amanuensis.[10] God's memory, too, is recorded in an alphabetic system. God does not 'remember' in abstract. Whatever transpires in the world is written in "a Book of Memories," which is "read before Him" (Mal. 3:16; cf. Dan. 7:10; 12:1). Once a year, God assesses humankind (Mishna Rosh HaShana 1:2). Thereupon, the righteous are inscribed in the "Book of Life," the wicked in the "Book of Death," and those in the middle in a third "Book," whose final verdict God pronounces on Yom Kippur.[11] Every individual action and behavior, too, undergoes a similar process. A heavenly "eye sees, an ear listens, and all your actions are written in a Book" (Abot 2:1).

The God of Scripture does not communicate to an analphabetic void. The audience must not only *hear* the sound of His words but actually *read* them. More precisely: it is only by *reading* His words that one can actually *hear* His voice. Thus, when God spoke at Sinai, Israel simultaneously *heard* His voice and *read* them, "written in black letters, against the white parchment of the sky."[12] During the Theophany at

* By means of the Oral Law, "reading" consists of the application of vowels (*qore*) to *mute* consonants by the *outside* reader.

10. See Sifre Debarim, ed. Louis Finkelstein (New York: The Jewish Theological Seminary, 5717–1956), #357, p. 427; Baba Batra 15a, and cf. Jer. 36:4. Thus Moses is referred to as "the Great Scribe of Israel;" see *Targum* to Deut. 33:21, Sota 13b, and *Targum* to Song. 1:2. As it were, Moses was the 'pen' moved by God. In such a case, the 'writer' is not the person holding the pen, but the person moving the hand holding the pen; see *MT Shabbat* 11:14.

11. Rosh HaShana 16b; *MT Teshuba* 3:3.

12. See José Faur, "Maimonides' Starting Precept," in Shamir Yona, ed., *Or le-Mayer:*

Sinai, the people simultaneously read/heard His words. Commenting on the verse, "And all the people saw the voices" (Ex. 20:14), R. 'Aqiba (50–135) explained: "They saw, and they heard what they saw. They saw the word of fire coming out from the mouth of the Almighty being inscribed on the tablets."[13] Later, rabbinic tradition explained this to mean that the people actually *read* the voices as they were enunciating the Decalogue.[14] At Sinai, not everybody could alphabetize God's speech. When God first proposed the Covenant to the people, they responded: "we shall do," (Ex. 19:8; cf. 24:3) – but they did not say 'we shall hear!' The people had to ask Moses to articulate God's speech, so that they "could hear" (Ex. 20:15), i.e., alphabetize, His words. It was later, when Moses read "the Book of the Covenant" "into the ear of the people" that they responded: "everything that God spoke we shall do and we shall *hear*" (Ex. 24:7).

Before having been endowed with the *ketab* and *mikhtab* faculties, mankind lacked the linguistic instruments to analyze speech. Given that the alphabet consists of consonants alone, diction, sound and all those elements that are not comprehended within the *ketab* and *mikhtab* systems are linguistically irrelevant. This implies that staging, voice manipulation, and non-linguistic elements associated with oratory, are not germane to alphabetic meaning. An important consequence of this view is that within an alphabetic system, speech and writing are fundamentally one and the same.[15] Accordingly, a public unable to generate meaning from the written word of God will find

---

*Studies In Bible, Semitic Languages, Rabbinic Literature, and Ancient Civilizations* (Beer Sheva: Ben-Gurion University, 2010), (Heb.) p. 286, n. 11.

13. *Mekhilta de-R. Yishma'el*, eds. H. S. Horovitz and I. A. Rabin (Jerusalem: Wahrmann Books, 1970), *Yitro*, IX, p. 235. Cf. R. Se'adya Gaon's translation to Deut. 4:12.

14. Accordingly, R. Se'adya Gaon translated Deut. 4:9 "not to forget 'the things' (הדברים) that your eyes saw" at Sinai, as: "not to forget *the words* (הדברים) that your eyes saw," i.e. "read." See "Maimonides' Starting Precept," p. 286, n. 11; and cf. *Homo Mysticus*, pp. 148–150.

15. That is why in rabbinic literature alphabetized speech is referred to indiscriminately either as "it was written" or "it was said." For instance, referring to King

it impossible to make head or tail out of His speech, either at Sinai or in the rest of Scripture.

The purpose of this Section is to explore the *ketab* and *mikhtab* systems in the intellectual tradition of Israel. A fundamental premise of this investigation is the principle that signification is conditioned by the mode in which the events making up God's speech are processed and subsequently stored in the Collective Memory of Israel. This would afford a better understanding of the role of the scribes, in contradistinction to that of poets in analphabetic societies.

---

Solomon's writings, Shir ha-Shirim Rabba, I, 7, 2a affirms: "King Solomon *said* three books, Song of Songs, Proverbs, and Ecclesiastes." Cf. *Golden Doves*, p. 171 n. 29.

# Chapter 1
# The Book of Creation

The Tora is not the only Book written by God. To the Hebrews the whole of creation is a semiological system: it signifies. Meaning, however, is not a given: it is the effect of reading and interpretation.[16] The world in which we live appeared to Moses as a 'Book' written by God. When pleading with God to forgive Israel for having worshipped the golden calf, he said: "and if not, erase me (מחני) please, from the Book which you [God] have written" (Ex. 32:32). Commenting on this verse, R. Levi ben Gereshom (1288–1344) remarked: "Behold the 'Book' that God wrote is everything that exists."[17] The Tora given to Israel represents God's primeval wisdom, as it was alphabetically expressed and organized before Creation.[18] God created the world by glancing at it. R. Hosha'ya (2nd century) explained:

> When a king wishes to build a palace, he will not build it in an unplanned fashion, but would consult with an artisan. [In turn,] the artisan would not build it in an unplanned fashion, but from plans and notes at his disposal... In the same fashion, God glanced at the Tora, creating the world.[19]

---

16. See *Golden Doves*, pp. 23–26.
17. In his *Perush 'al ha-Tora* (Venice, 5307/1547), 113b.
18. See Pesaḥim 54a. Obviously, this is related to 'deconstruction' as exposed by Jacques Derrida, in *Writing and Difference* (Chicago: Chicago University Press, 1978).
19. Bereshit Rabba I, 1, vol. 1, p. 2. Cf. Abot 3:14.

According to the psalmist, the human embryo, too, is a book that God shapes by glancing at it – simultaneously 'reading/writing' – the different organs and limbs that will make up the newborn. "At my shapeless embryo you have set your eyes, and on your book (i.e., the embryo) all (the organs and limbs) proceeded to be written." The divine glancing, as yet imperceptible to the human eye, will emerge as the shape of the embryo unfolds: "they [the organs] will be formed in the coming days"; although at the moment of inception "– not even one of them was there!" (Ps. 139:16). The rabbis, too, compared the human embryo to "a notebook, folded and (appropriately) placed."[20]

Given that life equals 'writing,' it stands to reason that the supreme penalty is to be 'deleted' from God's Book. Thus, when Moses requested to be 'erased' from God's Book, He replied: "He who had sinned against me I shall delete him from my Book" (Ex. 32:33). This doctrine is central to the Hebrew Scripture. The wicked, the psalmist tells us, will be "deleted from the book of life" (Ps. 69:29, cf. Ex. 17:14, Deut. 9:14, 25:19; II Kings 21:13). To 'erase' is the act of blotting out something written (cf. Num. 5:23). As during the Flood, when God "erased" life from earth (Gen. 6:7; 7:4, 23), commencing thereafter with a new beginning, or *palingenesis*. Concerning the desecration of the Sabbath, the rabbis define 'erasing' (מוחק) as deleting writing, a scribble, or a spot from a parchment for the purpose of writing in its place.[21] Since sins are inscribed in the celestial registrar, to 'forgive' is to 'erase' (see Is. 43:25; 44:22; Ps. 51:3, 4; 109:14; Neh. 3:37).

Speech and writing are not marginal to creation. God's creations *are* His speech/writing. Commenting on the verse, "And all the people saw the voices" (Ex. 20:15), Philo explained:

> ... for in the case of men is [only] audible, but the voice of God is truly visible. Why so? Because whatever God says are not

20. Nidda 30b.
21. See *MT Shabbat* 11:9.

> words but deeds, which are judged by the eyes rather than the ears.[22]

In the same vein R. Eleazar (d. 279) asked: "How do we know that the word [of God] is actions? – because it is written: 'By the word of God heavens were made'" (Ps. 33:6).[23] Thus, the rabbis referred to "the letters with which the heavens and the earth were created."[24] God's alphabet, as well as His 'speech/writing,' constitutes a kind of meta-language comprising the alphabet and the numeral system. In *Sefer Yeṣira* (a book containing material from the end of the 2nd century, but whose present form is from ca. 8th century), the divine alphabet consists of "thirty-two paths of wisdom," i.e., the twenty-two letters of the Hebrew alphabet and the ten basic ciphers of the decimal system.[25] Referring to the central doctrine of *Sefer Yeṣira*, R. Judah ha-Levi (ca. 1075–1141) explained that God's writings are in fact His creations. Similarly, given the identity speech/writing, God's words are one and the same with His writings. To illustrate:

> At the instant that God said, "Let it be light" (Gen. 1:3), or "Let it be space" (Gen. 1:6) the speech became actuality. This actuality is designated 'Book' – a term involving 'writing.' Thus God's writings are His creations, and God's speech His writing, and His words are the mathematical value.[26]

---

22. *The Decalogue*, 47, *Philo*, vol. 7, pp. 29–31. The same is with its equivalent, the Aramaic *memra* of the rabbis.
23. Shabbat 119b; cf. A. E. Harkavi, *Ḥadashim gam Yeshanim* (Jerusalem: Karmiel, 5730/1970), (II, p. 157), p. 418; *Golden Doves*, pp. xxi-xxii; 25–26; 167.
24. Berakhot 55a.
25. See *Golden Doves*, p. 59. Cf. *The Mishna of Rabbi Eliezer* (Heb.), ed. H. G. Enelow (New York: Bloch Publishing, 1933), XIV, p. 268, and ibid., "Introduction," p. 53.
26. *Kuzari*, ed. and trans. Yehuda Even Shmuel (Tel-Aviv: Dvir Publishing, 1994), IV, 25, p. 180. For the rabbinic sources, see *Golden Doves*, p. 167 n. 1. Simply put, this means that humans can grasp God's works through a system comprehending speech and mathematics. On the simultaneity of God's words/actions, see *Golden Doves*, pp. 23–24.

The idea that the world is a Book written by God was subsequently introduced to Western thought by Francis Bacon (1561–1626) in his *Proficiency and Advancement of Learning* (1605). This should be of particular interest to modern secularists who correctly see Bacon as the founder of empiricism, but often forget that he was a man of God, of the Judaic monotheistic persuasion, like Isaac Newton (1642–1727).[27]

Philo's *logos* is dynamic: it does not *reveal* but creates – not as an absolute, but as ciphers and consonants from which the reader must spawn meaning. This is why the Universe is not a *given*, but, as the Scripture states: "that God Created, to be made (לעשות)" (Gen. 2:3).[28] Since the God of Scripture does not address an analphabetic vacuum, 'knowledge,' 'truth,' etc., even when proceeding from the mouth of the Almighty, must undergo a process of decoding (*ketab*) and reading (*mikhtab*), whereby the reader assumes the function of writer. When this process fits the divine plan, as when a judge renders a just verdict, man becomes "a partner with the Holy One in the acts of Creation."[29] A consequence of this doctrine is that 'artificiality' – "the doings of man" in the language of the rabbis – is "superior to the doings of God."[30]

The Tora that Moses brought down to Israel, too, is the effect of a special *ketab-mikhtab* reading. R. Joshua b. Levi (3rd century) taught

27. The secularist notion, positing that 'science' and 'religion' are mutually exclusive is flawed, historically and conceptually. The reason for this misconception is that the secular concept of 'religion' is Christian – through and through; see our quotation from Wittgenstein, Section III at n. 270. On Newton's religious views and his close affinity to Judaism, I dealt extensively in the following three articles: "Esoteric Knowledge and the Vulgar: Parallels between Newton and Maimonides," *Trumah* 12 (2002), pp. 183–191; "Newton, Maimonidean," *Review of Rabbinic Judaism* 6 (2003), pp. 215–249; "Sir Isaac Newton – 'a Judaic Monotheist of the School of Maimonides,'" in Gorge K. Hasselhoff and Otfried Fraisse eds., *Moses Maimonides (1138–1204)* (Germany: Ergon Verlag, 2004), pp. 289–309.

28. See *Golden Doves*, pp. 22, 138. Concerning Philo's *logos* and the Aramaic *memra* of the rabbis; see *Golden Doves*, pp. 24–25, and p. 163 n. 1.

29. *Mekhilta de-R. Yishma'el, Yitro*, p. 196; *Mekhilta de-R. Shim'on b. Yoḥai*, eds. J. N. Epstein and E. Z. Melamed (Jerusalem: Mekize Nirdamim, 1955), on 18:13, p. 132.

30. See Baba Batra 10a, and *Golden Doves*, pp. xxii–xxiii.

that when Moses went up to heaven to receive the Tora, the angels objected that a mere human could merit such privilege. God told Moses to respond. Addressing God, Moses asked:

> – Master of the Universe! The Tora that Thou gavest me, what is written in it, "I am the Lord your God who took you out of the land of Egypt, from a household of slaves" (Ex. 20:2).
> Turning to the Angels he then asked them:
> – Have you ever come down to Egypt? Have you ever been a slave to Pharaoh? Why should the Tora be yours?!
> He then proceeded to repeat the same with the rest of the Decalogue.
> – "Thou shalt have no other deities before Me!" (Ex. 20:3). 'Do you dwell among pagans?'
> – "Remember the Sabbath and declare it holy!" (Ex. 20:8). 'Do you do any kind of work requiring you to rest?' And so on.[31]

At first glance the position of the angels makes little sense. Weren't they aware that the Decalogue could not possibly apply to heavenly beings? The key to this riddle lies in the fact that the *ketab* making up the alphabet of the Cosmic Tora requires *reading*. Moses' reading of the Cosmic Tora was unlike the angels' precisely because he read it from the unique perspective of an earthly being – something that no celestial creature could equal. What was unique about Moses and the Jewish people was that they used their *own historical experience* as the vowels to synthesize the Cosmic Consonants. Generating, thereby, a specific *meaning*, according to their own *mikhtab*. This peculiarly human reading was approved by God. Thus, the Tora states that the Tablets containing the Decalogue, "are the doing of God, and the *mikhtab* " – the linguistic apparatus permitting the processing of the writing on the Tablets, too – "is God's *mikhtab*" (Ex. 32:16) – that is,

31. Shabbat 88b–89a.

it corresponded to the system that He had endowed on humanity at the twilight of Creation.

The Cosmic Tora that God wrote before Creation "was written with black fire on white fire."[32] Moses "kindled" our Tora from the Cosmic Tora. This could be best understood in light of Julia Kristeva's definition of text in terms of 'phenotext/genotext.' As with biology, the written text is a 'phenotext' projecting the original 'genotext.' In her words:

> Let us designate as a text any linguistic *practice* in which the operations of the genotext appear in laminar form in the phenotext, so that the phenotext serves as a projection of a genotext and invites the reader to reconstruct from it the entire signifying process.[33]

Similarly, "The Tora that God gave to Moses," taught a Talmudic sage, "was white fire inscribed with black fire: it was of fire enveloped in fire."[34]

A fundamental characteristic of consonantal writing is that meaning is not immanent in the text. Consequently, a term may be correctly interpreted in various ways (see below, chapter 9). When pertaining to the Cosmic Book, consonantal density is utmost: the grouping and possible arrangement of the letters, countless. Citing Ps. 62:12: "God uttered a single word, which I heard as two, since might is God's," Abayye (278–338) proposed the principle that "a single scriptural term (*miqra*) may give expression to various meanings." In support, the Talmud quotes a source from the school of R. Ishmael. Referring to

---

32. *Midrash Tehillim*, ed. Salomon Buber (New York: Om Publishing, 1947), XC, 12, p. 391.
33. In ed. A. J. Greimas, *Essais de semiotique poetique* (Paris: Larousse, 1972), p. 216, quoted in David Michael Levin, "The Living Body of Tradition," *Religious Tradition* (University of Sydney), 5 (1983), p. 46.
34. Yerushalmi Sheqalim VI, 1, 49d. For some interesting variants, see Yerushalmi Sota VIII, 3, 22d; Debarim Rabba, ed. Saul Lieberman (Jerusalem: Wahrman Books, 1974), p. 89, etc.

the verse, "Isn't My word akin to fire, said the Lord, and to a hammer smashing a rock?" (Jer. 23:29), the rabbis explained: "Just like a hammer that produces numerous sparks, so a single scriptural word (*miqra*) may give expression to numerous meanings."[35]

A corollary of the preceding is that the minimum requirement for apprehending God's *speech/writing* is the faculty to discern two distinct consonants and generate meaning thereof. Israel ascertained that the Tora is a true reflection of the Cosmic Tora *because the people read it* with the *ketab* and *mikhtab* faculties endowed by God at the twilight of Creation. This proposes that meaning is not evident, that the *ketab* requires continuous processing, and that the Book is always 'in the making.' What is unique about the people of Israel is the fact that throughout their history they continuously generated meaning and stored it in their Collective Memory, at all periods and under all circumstances: from glorious Exodus to Inferno Auschwitz.

35. Sanhedrin 34a.

# Chapter 2
# Monolingualism and the Analphabetic Mind

Alphabet is to language what numbers are to quantity. Analphabetic man can apprehend the auditory contour of words, as if they were phonetic slabs, but cannot analyze them linguistically. In analphabetic speech, the grid signifier/signified is inviolable. The word, more accurately, the phonetic contour of a word *is* the thing it signifies. For that reason, analphabetic man dwells in the realm of myth and metaphysics. This is how Ernst Cassirer (1874–1945) described the mental process underlying mythmaking:

> The notion that name and essence bear a necessary and internal relation to each other, that the name does not merely denote but actually *is* the essence of its object, that the potency of the real thing is contained in the name – that is one of the fundamental assumptions of mythmaking consciousness itself. Philosophical and scientific *mythology*, too, seemed to accept this assumption[36] (Italics in original).

36. Ernst Cassirer, *Language and Myth* (New York: Dover Publications, n.d.), p. 3; cf. ibid., pp. 51–57.

The grid signifier/signified reigns supreme even in the realm of numbers. "Things were not only related to or expressible by numbers," observed Cassirer, "they *were* numbers"[37] (Italics in original).

Myth and metaphysics are not peripheral to analphabetic speech. They are the source and justification for a whole plethora of theories and models spanned around the verb 'to be' in the function of copula.[38] This is why, as noted by Ludwig Wittgenstein (1889–1951), the 'philosophical problems' raised around this verb are perennially the same, with the same inconclusive solutions.

> People say again and again that philosophy doesn't really progress, that we are still occupied with the same philosophical problems as were the Greeks. It is because our language has remained the same and keeps seducing us into asking the same questions. As long as there continues be a verb 'to be'

37. Ernst Cassirer, *An Essay on Man* (Garden City, N.Y.: Doubleday, n.d.), p. 266. That is why mathematical thinking cannot be apprehended by the analphabetic mind.
38. See Émile Benveniste, *Problems in General Linguistics* (Coral Gables, Florida: University of Miami, 1971), pp. 61–63. Benveniste's position irritated philosophers all over; see Jacques Derrida, "The Supplement of the Copula: Philosophy *before* Linguistics," *The Georgia Review* 30 (1976), pp. 527–564. [Reprinted in ed. Josué V. Harari, *Textual Strategies* (Ithaca, New York: Cornell University Press, 1979), pp. 82–120]. The source of the conflict 'language/ thought' pertains to what I call the 'splitting of the *logos*' inaugurating western philosophical thought; see my "The Splitting of the *Logos*: Some Remarks on Vico and Rabbinic Tradition," *New Vico Studies* 3 (1985), pp. 85–103. In my view, after the inaugural split of the *logos*, the function of the verb 'to be' is to 'reunite' – *re-ligare* in theological parlance – the two realms of the 'split' *logos*. Derrida's arguments are unpersuasive, because through and through he expresses a 'truth' assuming that 'to be' is fundamentally not different than the verb 'to eat' and 'to drink'; see the quotation from Wittgenstein in the following note. That is why Derrida's verb 'to be' involves the proto-logical and essentially analphabetic universe central to Husserl's "*europaischen Menschentums*" that we described in this chapter. Philip Slater, *The Pursuit of Loneliness* (Boston: Beacon Press, 1976), p. xii, called attention to patterns of thought and feelings "that enslave the mind and sap the will" – they apply to philosophers in particular.

> that looks as if it functions in the same way as 'to eat' and 'to drink,' people will keep stumbling over the same difficulties and find themselves starting at something which no explanation seems capable of clearing up.[39]

In fact, the 'demythitization' of the pagan mind is itself a myth created by the pagan mind. The "'demythitization' of Greek religion and the triumph, with Socrates and Plato, of strict and systematic philosophy," noted Eliade, "did not finally do away with mythical thought." Adding:

> In all probability, the Greek genius left to itself and its own devices could not have exorcised mythical thought, even if the last God had been dethroned and his myths brought down to the level of children's tales. For, on the one hand, the Greek philosophical genius accepted the essence of mythical thought, the eternal return of things, the cyclic vision of cosmic and human life, and, on the other hand, the Greek mind did not consider that History could become the object of knowledge. Greek physics and metaphysics developed some basic themes of mythical thought: the importance of the origin, the *arche*; the essential that precedes human existence; the determinative role of memory, and so on. This of course, does not mean that there is no solution of continuity between Greek myth and philosophy. But we can easily understand that philosophical thought could employ and continue the mythical vision of cosmic reality and human existence.[40]

Thus, the 'myth' of Greek rationality. Within the grid signifier/signified, speech and thought are one and the same. It has been shown that the celebrated Aristotelian 'canons of logic' are nothing more than

39. Ludwig Wittgenstein, *Culture and Value* (Chicago: Chicago University Press, 1984), p. 15e.
40. Mircea Eliade, *Myth and Reality* (New York: Harper Torchbooks, 1975), pp. 112–113.

the "fundamental categories of the language in which he thought."[41] Because the analphabetic mind perceives speech in terms of sound alone, 'meaning' is determined by the non-linguistic aspects of speech: voice, diction, staging and all the paraphernalia connected to oratory (see below). This gives rise to what may be properly described as monolingualism, that is, the notion of a superior language, which alone could express the truth, the whole truth, and nothing but the truth. It is "the living heroic language" spoken by the Greeks, Romans, Arabs, and Germans. Given that speech is nothing more than a conglomerate of certain phonetic patterns, our 'truth' cannot possibly be expressed in a different language. By implication, those speaking a different language are inferior, exhibiting lesser standards of thought and humanity.[42]

Writing and reading are alien to Greek ethos and civilization. To the Greek mind, writing is some sort of counterfeit, at best to be tolerated as an aid for memorization, but always falsifying and distorting. The written word, Socrates tells Phaedrus, is "a reminiscence of what we know" and of what had been previously "taught and communicated orally." Oral communication alone is genuine, since it is "written in the soul, which is the true way of writing" and has "clearness and perfection and seriousness."[43] To the Egyptian god purported to have invented writing, it was told: "this invention of yours will create forgetfulness in the learner's souls, because they will not use their memories; they will trust to the external written characters and not remember of themselves."[44] On behalf of the analphabetic memory it was argued:

41. *Problems in General Linguistics*, p. 57. For further analysis and references, see *Golden Doves*, pp. 7–8.

42. See *New Science* #445, pp. 148–149; *Golden Doves*, pp. 7–8, 23–37; and *In the Shadow of History*, pp. 4–7.

43. *Phaedrus*, in *Collected Works of Plato*, trans. by B. Jowett (New York: Greystone Press, n.d.), vol. 3, p. 447.

44. *Phaedrus*, in *Collected Works of Plato*, vol. 3, p. 442. The Greeks preferred not to use writing even as an aid to memory. The art of memory founded by Simonides of Ceos (ca. 556–468 B.C.E.), and subsequently adopted by all rhetorical

> The memory and knowledge acquired through writing are hollow: You have found a specific, not for memory but for reminiscence, and you give your disciples only the pretense of wisdom; they will be hearers of many things and will have learned nothing; they will appear to be omniscient and will generally know nothing; they will be tiresome, having the reputation of knowledge without the reality.[45]

The alphabet and the written word are pernicious (see appendix 21). As with the Platonic ideals, the Greek *logos* as well as the 'truth' (or *aletheia* which 'unveils') are absolute and static.[46] In reading, the Greek merely "picks the sound from the page"; passively 'gathering' the sense standing motionless 'out there.'[47] 'Knowledge' is reducible to the tautology 'A = A.' The Socratic theory of knowledge as 'recollection' expresses this fundamental proposition: what is known was already known.[48] In the physical-metaphysical system of the Greeks, things *are,* and don't signify. Meaning is both superfluous and intrusive to beingness. "Reading the Socratic dialogues," remarked Wittgenstein, "one has the feeling: what a frightful waste of time! What's

---

schools, consisted of imprinting a building and all its images in the memory of the student, and then proceeding to associate the words of the composition at hand with the already-memorized building and images; see *Golden Doves,* p. 32.

45. *Phaedrus,* in *Collected Works of Plato,* vol. 3, pp. 442–443. Concerning the various interpretations of Socrates' idea of recollection, see the valuable analysis of Kenneth Seeskin, *Dialogue and Discovery: A Study in Socratic Method* (Albany, N.Y.: SUNY, 1987), particularly, pp. 103–110.
46. That is the underlying thesis for the scholastic view of a 'universal' and 'natural' law valid for all men, at all times and places. The same basic idea is present in 'secular' thinkers such as Descartes, Spinoza, Hobbes, and others.
47. *The Alphabetization of the Popular Mind,* p. 13. See M. Heidegger, lively essay in *Early Greek Thought* (San Francisco: Harper & Row, 1975), pp. 59–78.
48. Particularly as developed in the *Symposium* and the subsequent theory of *cognoscere* leading to the mythical notion of 're-integration' and magic, developed by the celebrated Pico della Mirandolla in his *Apologia*; cf. Isaiah Berlin, *Vico & Herder* (New York: The Viking Press. 1976), pp. 14–15. Art, too, is mimesis or 'replication' of nature.

the point of these arguments that prove nothing and clarify nothing."[49] The same, to my mind, applies to mimetic art.

Reading exercises a negative influence, interfering with memory and true knowledge. In support of Plato's outcry at the danger of reading, two modern scholars offered this eloquent defense:

> Plato was not Greece's first author. But he was the first uneasy man of letters. He was the first to write with the conviction of the superiority of thought unrelated to writing. He was anguished by the effect the alphabet was exerting on his pupils. Their reliance on silent, passive texts could not but narrow the stream of their remembrance, making it shallow and dull. Earlier, this mistrust of the alphabet had been reflected in Aeschylus' *Prometheus Bound*: Zeus punished Prometheus for bringing the alphabet – "the combining of letters, creative mother of the Muses' art, wherewith to hold all things in memory" – to mankind. Zeus had engendered his daughters in the pond of Mnemosyne so that they might bubble and flow, not to be blocked up in script.[50]

Since analphabetic language apprehends only the auditory contour of words, Greek 'truth' is *a-letheia* 'discovery' of a metaphysical reality lying 'out there.' The function of the Greek *logos* is *apophansis* "pointing out," "showing," and "letting things be seen from themselves," passively 'gathering' the manifest sense 'out there.'[51] The 'truth' of the philosopher, we are told, is "alone apprehended in the pure concept,"[52] i.e., analphabetically. Greek deities, too, were analphabetic: essentially

49. *Culture and Value*, p. 14e.
50. *The Alphabetization of the Popular Mind*, p. 24.
51. Joseph J. Kockelmans, "Language, Meaning, and Ek-sistence," in Joseph J. Kockelmans, *On Heidegger and Language* (Evanston: Northwestern University Press, 1972), p. 27; see *Golden Doves*, pp. 18, 24 and p. 160 n. 5.
52. Ernst Cassirer, *The Philosophy of Symbolic Forms*, (New Haven: Yale University Press, 1957), vol. 3, p. 16, cf. ibid., p. 36.

and fundamentally. They possessed knowledge and cunning intelligence, but none of them could either write or read. Speech, too, could not, should not, be alphabetized. The alphabet dismembers the word. It decapitates it and wrenches the life away from it. In defense of analphabetic speech, Miguel de Unamuno (1864–1936) repeated Paul's claim, "For the spirit, which is the oral tradition, breathes life; but the letter, which is the book, kills."[53] We should not be surprised to find, therefore, that Greeks treated scribes as outcasts.[54]

Monolingualism is the matrix of the "*europaischen Menschentums*," a discovery that is to be credited to Edmund Husserl (1859–1938), the father of phenomenology. According to this celebrated philosopher, their superiority springs from their "sense of infinity" – the gift that Greek philosophy had endowed on them.[55] (Let us remark, in passing, that to the analphabetic mind, 'infinity' is more or less analogous to the connotation of this term in linguistic communities not yet familiar with numbers.) This quality, like all that is precious in humanity, is connected to the verb 'to be.' It is the finality "toward which in secret the collective spiritual becoming, so to speak, strive."[56] The 'becoming' is a purely 'mystical' phenomenon, somehow connected to the 'cosmic sacrality' of pagan religiosity lingering among South European peasantry.[57] For that reason, it is universal, embracing "not only men and animals and other infra-human and infra-animal beings (*Wesen*) but also the supra-human." This results in a hierarchic structure, on top of which stands *europaischen Menschentums* – a being analogous to, but not as brazen as, Nietzsche's superman. "The spiritual *telos* of European Men (*europaischen Menschentums*), lies in infinity; it is an

53. "The Word and the Letter," skillfully translated into English by Anthony Kerrigan, *The Agony of Christianity* (Princeton: Princeton University Press, 1974), p. 23. Cf. the citation from Rousseau, below, n. 113.
54. See David Nunes Carvalho, *Forty Centuries of Ink* (New York: Banks Law Publishing, 1904), p. 19, and *Golden Doves*, p. 8.
55. Edmund Husserl, "The Crisis of European Man," p. 163. See appendix 58.
56. "The Crisis of European Man," p. 158.
57. See *Homo Mysticus*, p. 3. That is somehow similar to "the great sea" mentioned in Dan. 7:2.

infinite idea." Because of their hierarchic supremacy, *europaischen Menschentums* actually *know* that other 'philosophies,' although apparently similar to that of the Greeks, are worthless. Obviously, those standing below in the human ladder could not possibly understand this. Hence, Husserl issued a stern warning:

> ... it is a mistake for someone brought up in the scientific modes of thought initiated in Greece and progressively developed in modern times [i.e., *europaischen Menschentums*] to speak of Indian and Chinese philosophy (astronomy, mathematics) and thus to interpret India, Babylonia, and China in a European way.[58]

We can thus arrive at a more colorful definition of monolingualism. It is the faculty endowing *europaischen Menschentums* with the undisputed right to ascertain the insignificance of Indian, Chinese, etc., cultures and civilizations without having read an iota of these languages.

In Hebrew tradition, the consonantal-*ketab* can only *indicate* a sense which needs to be processed by the *mikhtab*-reader acting as a writer. God, too, is not manifest in His creations: they only point towards Him. This fundamental doctrine was taught by King Solomon. In his address celebrating the inauguration of the Temple, he proclaimed: "Behold the heavens and the heavens of heavens cannot contain You – and surely not this house which I have built" (I Kings 8:27). Neither the Temple in Jerusalem nor the Universe nor the Tora that He created can manifest God. In a vocalized word,

58. "The Crisis of European Man," p. 171. I don't share the view that Husserl's conversion to Christianity was a matter of expediency. The ideology of a super-*Menschentums*, etc., is structurally the same as those professed by some Christians. A most tragic epilogue of this ideology was the fact that he met his end in a concentration camp – a direct result of the culture of monolingualism and intellectual intolerance that he defended so vigorously. It is not accidental that Martin Heidegger, his most famous disciple, as well as Paul de Man and other luminaries of the time were full-fledged members of the Nazi Party.

meaning is manifest. To the Hebrew mind, a Name manifesting God would be indistinguishable from an icon or an idol. We can now better appreciate the wisdom behind the 'ineffability' of God's Name (the Tetragrammaton) in Jewish tradition.[59] It has nothing to do with "the anonymous deities" of pagan antiquity (cf. Acts 17:23). In a pagan environment a new deity remained 'anonymous' until it had been identified with one of the local deities. Within the context of an alphabetic society, 'ineffability' means something radically different.[60] It is the rule disallowing "voicing (להגות) the Tetragrammaton *alphabetically*[61] (באותיותיו)"; that is, enunciating the consonants with the corresponding vowels.[62] This ruling expresses the belief that granting the reader the right to process the consonants of the Tetragrammaton and supply them with vowels, as with other consonantal terms, borders on blasphemy.[63] The rule can be best understood in the light

59. Samaritans pronounced the Tetragrammaton; see Y. Sanhedrin X, 1, 28b and R. Judah al-Barṣeloni, *Perush Sefer Yeṣira*, p. 115.

60. See Elias Bickerman, "Anonymous Gods," in his *Studies in Jewish and Christian History*, 3 vols. (Leiden: E. J. Brill, 1986), vol. 3, pp. 270–281, especially pp. 279–281.

61. See Mishna Sanhedrin 10:1, Sanhedrin 101b, 'Aboda Zara 18a, and Pesaḥim 50a. For some additional insights, see *Oṣar ha-Ge'onim*, *Sanhedrin*, ed. R. Ch. Z. Tobias (Jerusalem: Mossad Harav Kook, 1966), pp. 525–526; and my "Maimonides' Starting Precept," p. 312, n. 128.

62. See *Perush ha-Mishnayot*, *Soṭa* 7:4, vol. 3, p. 267; *MT Tefilla* 14:10. The term *qore* in Hebrew stands for both 'reading' and 'calling forth' for signification of the consonantal text. As it were, the reader 'calls forth the signification' encoded in the *ketab* system, transforming it thereby into *mikhtab*; cf. *Golden Doves*, pp. 11, 119–123. The rabbis distinguished between consonantal reading in general, which includes the enunciation of vowels, and consonantal reading excluding vowels, which they designated, "קורא להגיה"; see above n. 2. In the latter, only when the reader 'focused his heart' (כיוון לבו) on the text, had he discharged the duty of reciting the *Shema'*; see Berakhot 13a; Rosh HaShana 28b.

63. The High Priest pronounced the Tetragrammaton at the Yom Kippur services; see Mishna Yoma 6:2. Since to the analphabetic mind the 'Name of God' is nothing more than abracadabra, the High Priest took special care to "muffle it in the chants of the other priests"; see Y. Yoma III, 7, 40d. It was pronounced also in the priestly blessing at the Temple, but not outside the Holy Precinct;

of Wittgenstein's seminal distinction between what can be said and what can only be indicated. "What expresses *itself* in language," he wrote, "we cannot express by means of language." And vice versa: "what can be indicated by words cannot be manifest in words."[64] The Tetragrammaton (as well as the Cosmic Book) can only point towards Him, but cannot *manifest* Him.*

Greeks and Hebrews each propose a different approach for the understanding of reality and of ourselves: one is metaphysical, the other semiological. The difference is huge. In the realm of metaphysics things *are*, but don't signify. Only questions pertaining to the verb 'to be' are relevant. 'Truth' is a function of 'necessary' and vice versa, as with a geometrical theorem. 'Choice,' as well as the 'possible' and the 'probable' and issues pertaining to 'meaning' and 'purpose' are irrelevant. Reality is imposed on us *necessarily*, by mechanics that we cannot change and must learn to accept, as with a Greek drama. Within the context of a Book, every item in Creation is *significant*. Life is *purposeful*: meaning is a function of *choice*. The real is a series of letters challenging the reader. It would be up to her/him to connect them and generate meaning.

To sum up our discussion thus far. At the pre-twilight stage of humanity, man had the faculty of speech and understanding. Those on top could dictate 'the truth' to those below, and the way for 'spiritual becoming.' Communication, however, was not possible. Discourse of any kind, warranted a Cosmic Book, permitting a common situ-

---

see Mishna Soṭa 7:6, Tamid 7:2, and Soṭa 38a. That is why Josephus, when referring to the Name that God revealed to Moses, added: "and of which I am forbidden to speak"; see *Jewish Antiquities,* II, 276, *Josephus* (Loeb Classical Library), vol. 4, p. 285. In rabbinic mysticism, the 'synthesis' giving meaning to the consonants of the Tetragrammaton is intellectual, not vocal. The rabbis would transmit the key to this process to especially qualified students; see Qiddushin 71a. For some insights, see *Guide* I, 61.

64. Ludwig Wittgenstein, *Tractatus Logico-Philosophicus,* trans. D. F. Pears and B. F. McGuinness (London: Routledge and Kegan Paul, 1961), 4.121; cf. 6.522. See *Homo Mysticus*, p. 6.

* This relates to the distinction between *peshaṭ* and *derash.*

ational reference, as well as a *ketab* system by which to apprehend the code, together with a *mikhtab* system of interpretation. The Tora that Moses brought down to earth addresses post-twilight humanity. It not only presupposes the Cosmic Book, but also the *ketab* and the *mikhtab* systems, accessible to all; in the absence of which neither communication nor meaning is possible.

# Chapter 3
# God as a Writer

To an alphabetic public, 'writing' and 'book' are instruments of communication and self-expression. For the analphabetic mind they are magical devices pertaining to the paranormal and mysterious. Classical theology ignores the *ketab* and *mikhtab* systems and the meaning of literature. Its task is an oxymoron: to 'validate' the Book according to the canons peculiar to analphabetic thinking. The issues it raises pertain to a world inhabited by analphabetic deities and men who haven't got the foggiest notion about reading/writing (see below chapter 4). How relevant are questions about causality, determinism, and all the array of ontological and epistemological notions, for the understanding of Blake's *Songs of Innocence* or Kafka's *Metamorphosis*? In what way could it be helpful to know the chemical composition of the paper and ink of Shakespeare's first edition, for the understanding of *Hamlet* or *Julius Caesar*?

As per its Hebrew designation, *Sefer* (Book), the Scripture is a *literary* work – not a totem.[65] The God of Scripture is the Writer. In which case, the insights of modern authors could be more helpful for the understanding of Scripture than that of theologians. Speaking about the novel – to my mind the closest literary *genre* to the Hebrew

65. Bearing this in mind we can understand Maimonides' opposition to using verses and the script of the Hebrew Scripture for 'ornamentation' and 'magical' purposes; see *Teshubot ha-Rambam*, ed. and trans. J. Blau, 4 vols. (Jerusalem: Mekize Nirdamim, 1975–1986), #268, vol. 2, pp. 510–515. Cf. below, n. 121, and appendix 2. Concerning the expression *Kitbe ha-Qodesh*; see below, chapter 7.

Scripture – Unamuno asked: "Why write a novel?" His answer sheds light on the principal objective of God, the Cosmic Writer.

> To become a novelist! And why does one become a novelist? To create the reader, to become one with the reader! And only by becoming one can the novelist and the reader of the novel be saved from the radical solitude.[66]

A book worth reading should be – following King Solomon's counsel – like "Golden apples enclosed in a silver net" (Prov. 25:11), concealing under the surface a sketchy autobiography of the author. In the words of Unamuno:

> Yes, every novel, every work of fiction, every poem, when alive is autobiographical. Every fictional character, every poetic personage that an author creates becomes a part of the author himself. And if he happens to bring into the poem a man of flesh and blood that he knew, this is so after he had made him his own, a part of himself. The great historians are also autobiographical. The tyrants that Tacitus described are himself... The supposed impersonality or objectivity of Flaubert is a lie. All the poetic personages of Flaubert are Flaubert and Emma Bovary more than anyone else.[67]

The main character of God's 'novel' is Adam, father of humankind. The Scripture stipulates that unlike other creatures, he was made "in the image (*ṣelem*) of God" (Gen. 1:27). This term is related to the Akkadian *ṣalmu* (pl. *ṣalme*), standing for an image consecrated to a deity.[68] Through a special ritual of consecration, the *ṣalmu* becomes

66. Miguel de Unamuno, "Cómo se hace una novela?" in *Obras Completas,* ed. M. Garcia Blanco, vol. 10 (Madrid: Afrodisio Aguado, 1958), p. 922.
67. "Cómo se hace una novela?" pp. 861–862.
68. See José Faur, "God as a Writer: Omnipresence and the Art of Dissimulation," *Religion & Intellectual Life* 6 (1989), p. 39, where I called attention to the impor-

the abode of the spirit of the deity to which it was consecrated.[69] The *ṣalme* could be statues or figurines, or inscribed *stelai* without any figurative representation.[70] A human being, too, could be consecrated as the *ṣalmu* of a god. We know of an Assyrian king who was addressed as "the very image (*ṣalmu*) of the god Shamash."[71] The fact that we find personal names with the component *ṣalmu*, suggests that common people, too, could become the *ṣalme* of gods.[72] The *ṣalmu* needed not be a pictorial representation.[73] Following a ceremony known as "the opening of the mouth," the god infused its spirit onto the *ṣalmu*; at precisely the moment in which the spirit touches the inert *ṣalmu*, the *ṣalmu* is 'born,' acquiring the attributes of the god.[74]

The preceding could help us understand the sense of "image (צלם, *ṣelem*) of God" (Gen. 1:27). As with the *ṣalmu*, God infuses His own spirit into the inert body of Adam: "and He blew into his (Adam's) nostrils a breath of life" (Gen. 2:7). It is precisely at that moment that Adam became "a living soul" (Gen. 2:7). How? The *Targum* or Aramaic version of the Tora rendered "a living soul" as "speaking spirit"

---

tance of Douglas Van Buren, "The *Ṣalme* in Mesopotamia in Art and Religion," *Orientalia*, n.s., 10 (1941), pp. 65–92, for the proper understanding of the Hebrew *ṣelem*. Cf. Professor Mayer Gruber, "God, Image of," in *Encyclopaedia of Judaism*, Supplement #1.

69. See "The *Ṣalme* in Mesopotamia in Art and Religion," pp. 75–79. See ibid., pp. 80–91 about *ṣalme* of deified kings, and of important people, animals, and constellations.
70. See "The *Ṣalme* in Mesopotamia in Art and Religion," pp. 65–66.
71. See "The *Ṣalme* in Mesopotamia in Art and Religion," p. 70.
72. See "The *Ṣalme* in Mesopotamia in Art and Religion," pp. 75–76.
73. There were ṣalme of objects which could not be pictorial representations of the original, such as light; see "The *Ṣalme* in Mesopotamia in Art and Religion," p. 70; of natural and architectural features, ibid., pp. 81–90; and even of moral qualities, ibid., pp. 90–91. This confirms Maimonides' view that ṣelem in the Scripture is not a pictorial representation of the original; see Guide I, 2.
74. See "The Ṣalme in Mesopotamia in Art and Religion," pp. 81, 91. On the ceremony of 'the opening of the mouth'; see José Faur, "Idolatry," Encyclopedia Judaica, vol. 8 (1973), 1227–1232, reprinted in Jewish Values (Israel Pocket Library, 1974), pp. 52–60. Idem, "The Biblical Idea of Idolatry," Jewish Quarterly Review, 69 (1978), pp. 1–26.

(רוח מללא) – the faculty of speech that God awarded to Adam and his posterity.[75] This is not mere communication. What rendered Adam and his posterity unique is the faculty of *linguistic subjectivity*, allowing for self-consciousness and introspection. Specifically, this faculty permits the speaker to pose himself as a *subject* and say '*I*' in syntagmatic opposition to a '*you*.' Thus, both 'speaker' and 'addressee' constitute a 'person.' Addressing this fundamental concept, Émile Benveniste (1902–1976) wrote:

> Consciousness of self is only possible if it is experienced by contrast. I use *I* only when I am speaking to someone who will be a *you* in my address. It is this condition of dialogue that is constitutive of *person*, for it implies that reciprocally *I* becomes *you* in the address of the one who in his turn designates himself as *I* (italics in original).

Linguistic subjectivity involves reciprocity between the persons: there cannot be *I* without a corresponding *you* and vice versa.

> Language is possible only because each speaker sets himself up as a *subject* by referring to himself as *I* in his discourse. Because of this, *I* posits another person, the one who, being, as he is, completely exterior to 'me,' becomes my echo to whom I say *you* and who says *you* to me[76] (italics in original).

Adam's self-awareness came in stages. At first, he realized his own differentiation within the animal kingdom. A sense of differentiation, however, is not equivalent to self-consciousness and subjectivity. This leads to an overwhelming question. Since linguistic subjectivity and the faculty of self-reflection are grounded on the syntagmatic opposition '*I*/*you*,' whom did Adam address as '*you*?' Put another way: who

---

75. See our discussion in *Golden Doves*, p. 171 n. 29.
76. Problems in General Linguistics, pp. 224–225. See *Golden Doves*, pp. 41–49, 80.

first addressed Adam as '*you*!' warranting him to reply '*I*!?' Within the context of Scripture, it was the syntagmatic opposition '*I*/*you*' to God, that permitted Adam to realize his own subjectivity and become a "living" *I* (= רוח מללא). According to the rabbis, Adam's subjectivity came in two stages. At first, he only realized his own differentiation within the animal kingdom, but was not yet conscious of his subjective '*I*.' The rabbis, in their own way, recount how this unique phenomenon came about. Before creating Adam, God consulted with the Angels.

> He (God) asked them: 'Shall we make Adam?'
> They replied to Him: 'This Adam, what type [of creature] is he?'
> God told them: 'His wisdom is greater than yours.'

To demonstrate to them the merits of the new creature, God initiated a dialogue involving the Angels and Adam.

He then proceeded to parade before them beasts, wild animals, and birds.

> He asked them: 'This! What is it called?' And they did not know! 'This! What is it called?' And they did not know! He then paraded them before Adam.
> He asked him: 'This! What is it called?'
> 'This is an ox!'
> 'This, what is it called?'
> 'This is a camel!'
> 'This, what is it called?'
> 'This is a donkey!'
> 'This, what is it called?'
> 'This is a horse!'...

In this fashion it was shown that Adam had the linguistic faculty to structurally connect the signifier (sound-image) or 'name' with signified (linguistic concept) and create thus a linguistic sign.[77]

77. See *Golden Doves*, pp. xix, 71.

Interaction of these signs permitted humankind to communicate and develop linguistic knowledge *without* comprehension. Man's 'superiority' to angels rests in the faculty to converse about matters which he does not comprehend (generating, thereby, the possibility of progress and human development). At this stage, Adam did not demonstrate self-consciousness. His own subjectivity he apprehended later, when he posited himself as 'Adam' in syntagmatic opposition to God, in quality of *Adon* ('Lord, Master'). Addressing Adam, God asked:

> 'And you, what is your name?'
> He answered Him: 'To me it would be fit to call Adam, since I was created from *Adama* (dust).'
> 'And what is my name'? – asked God.
> 'To you it would be fit to call *Adon* (Master), since You are the Master over all your creations.'[78]

In Hebrew intellectual tradition, recognition of God's Dominion is a fundamental human condition. Failing to realize the syntagmatic opposition Adam/*Adon,* man will fall short from forging his own '*I*' and the "image of God (*Elohim*)" within: people failing to recognize God's Dominion will fall prey to human dominion[79] (see Concluding Reflections below).

The God of Scripture, as with Unamuno's writer, is replicated by endowing Adam – the first character of His 'novel' – with the faculty to communicate and establish a syntagmatic relation ' *I/you.* ' The election of Israel, too, can be best understood within the perimeter of creative writing. God, the Supreme Author, identifies (cf. Is. 4:1) with Israel, the principal protagonist of *His* book. The biblical expres-

78. Bereshit Rabba XVII, 4, vol. 1, pp. 155–156. See José Faur, "Newton, Maimonidean," pp. 246–247. Celebrating this primordial dialogue, in the prayer *Elohai Neshama* said every morning, the faithful confesses that God is "... *Adon* of every soul."
79. Cf. *Homo Mysticus*, pp. 4–5, 8, 15–16, 127–128, 138–142.

sion, "the name of the Lord was called upon" Israel (Deut. 28:10; cf. Jer. 7:10 ff; Am. 9:12; Dan. 9:19; II Chr. 7:14), means that the people of Israel are the protagonist with whom God empathizes. The history of Israel is the unfolding dialogue between God and the people who first *chose* to call up to Him and to whom He *chose* to reply. The imperfections in the world are not the effect of a subaltern god, as per Gnostic theology, but the consequence of human failure to realize the "image of God" within. So, as pointed out by R. Ḥayyim ben 'Aṭṭar (1696–1743), God's manifestation is conditioned by the quality and disposition of the people.[80] R. Ḥayyim Palaggi (1788–1869) developed this doctrine further. Moses could not perceive God as Merciful and Compassionate and Forgiving until he himself became merciful and compassionate and forgiving.[81] Thus, the rabbis taught: "Just as God is Compassionate, you, too, must become compassionate."[82] This doctrine also involves the reverse proposition: "Just as you are compassionate, God, too, is (i.e., will reveal Himself to you as) Compassionate." In classical theology one can only 'follow the gods' in a series of pathological projections, as in political and religious mass-hysteria.[83] In Scripture, 'God' is existentially always 'in the making,' in terms of the syntagmatic relation 'Adam/*Adon*.'

The preceding leads to a second concern peculiar to writing. A consummate writer who has mastered the skills of his trade is faced with the problem of his own omnipresence and omniscience. An author not only has the power to replicate himself in the reader, but also to affect the events and final outcome of the story. Thus, replication warrants dissimulation. To be readable, the writer must appear as a

80. See his commentary to the Tora, *Or ha-Ḥayyim* (Warsaw, 5671/1911), on Ex. 33:11.
81. See his *Re'e Ḥayyim*, vol. 2 (Izmir, 5624/1864), 121b, and Tosefta Baba Qamma 9:30, p. 49.
82. Shabbat 133b. For a comprehensive analysis of this doctrine, see George F. Moore, *Judaism*, 3 vols. (Cambridge: Harvard University Press, 1966), vol. 2, pp. 109–111; and Harry A. Wolfson, *Philo*, 2 vols. (Cambridge: Harvard University Press, 1948), vol. 1, pp. 194–196.
83. See *Homo Mysticus*, pp. 10–13, 121; cf. ibid., p. 60.

disinterested party, indifferent to the plot. "The artist," wrote James Joyce (1882–1941), "like the God of creation remains within, behind, or beyond or above his handiwork, invisible, refined out of existence, indifferent, paring his fingernails."[84] A similar concern was expressed by T. S. Eliot (1888–1965). A writer should simultaneously be thoroughly omnipresent and thoroughly hidden: "The world of a great poetic dramatist is a world in which the creator is everywhere present and everywhere hidden."[85] Dissimulation is the art by which the author hides his presence. "The poet is each one of the people of his fictitious world," wrote Borges (1900–1986). "He is every breath and every detail. One of the tasks, certainly not the easiest, is to hide or dissimulate that omnipresence."[86] At the cosmological level, too, the God of the Hebrews is "everywhere present and everywhere hidden." "God, where shall I find Thee, and Thine place is lofty and hidden?" asked R. Judah ha-Levi. "And where I shall not find Thee, and Thine Glory fills the World!"[87] Regarding God and dissimulation, Derrida (1930–2004) noted: "Whether He is Being or the master of beings, God himself is, and appears as what He is, within difference, that is to say, as difference and within dissimulation.[88] Francisco Sánchez (1550/51–1623), the son of *conversos* and the father of modern skepticism, pointed at the perennial game of dissimulation played by nature:

> The variety is so great that nature seems to be playing with it, and delighting in our bewilderment; as we search for it here and there, it stands before our eyes, laughing and teasing us.[89]

84. In his *A Portrait of the Artist as a Young Man* (New York: Modern Library, 1928), p. 252.
85. "The Three Voices of Poetry," in his *On Poetry and Poets* (New York: Farrar, Strauss and Cudahy, 1957), p. 112.
86. Jorge Luis Borges, *Nueve Ensayos Dantescos* (Madrid: Espasa-Calpe, 1982), pp. 93–94.
87. In *The Liturgical Poetry of R. Yehuda ha-Levi,* (Heb.), ed. Dov Jarden, vol. 1 (Jerusalem, 1978), #97, p. 215.
88. Jacques Derrida, *Writing and Difference*, p. 74.
89. *Quod nihil scitur,* in his *Opera Omnia,* ed. Joaquim de Carvalho (Coimbra:

The Supreme Writer is also the Supreme Master of Dissimulation: even in the midst of the most portentous 'revelation.' The rabbis taught that after splitting the sea at the Exodus, the waters returned to their original condition, thus concealing the miracle. The miracle of concealing a miracle was sung about by the psalmist. Referring to the splitting of the sea, he sang: "Thy pathway was in the sea, and thy trails in many waters. And yet, Thy footsteps were unknown!" (Ps. 77:20). There is a rational explanation for this marvel. R. Joseph ibn Sanṭas ibn Abitur (10th century), the first Jewish biblical commentator to emerge from Europe, explained that a phenomenon in nature leaves a 'trace' because there is resistance to it. Thus,

> A human being when walking upon a substance will inevitably leave footprints. This, however, is not the case with the God of the Universe. As it is written: "Thy pathway was in the sea... And yet, Thy footsteps were unknown" (see Ps. 77:20).[90]

The Tora teaches that the Cosmos hangs "from the arms" of the Creator (Deut. 33:27). The rabbis explained that "God is the place of the world, and" – in the Hebrew sense of 'consequently' – "the world is not the place of God." The same principle was reiterated by Isaac Newton. "Bodies," he explained, "find no resistance from the omnipresence of God."[91] Only pagan deities leave footprints.

One of the ways that Scripture accomplishes dissimulation is by the use of the third person. As mentioned earlier, 'person' is the effect of the syntagmatic opposition *I/you*. In Hebrew, the third person is

Universidade de Coimbra, 1955), p. 44. For some notes on this very important thinker, see José Faur, "Francisco Sánchez's Theory of Cognition and Vico's *verum/factum*," *New Vico Studies* 5 (1987), pp. 131–146; idem, "The Jewish Mentality of Francisco Sánchez," *Mentalities* 7 (1992), pp. 26–38; and *In the Shadow of History*, pp. 91–106.

90. See *Homo Mysticus*, pp. 13–14.
91. Isaac Newton, *Principia* (Berkeley and Los Angeles: University of California Press, 1962), vol. 2, p. 545. See "Sir Isaac Newton," pp. 296–297, and *Homo Mysticus*, pp. 13–14.

designated 'absent' (נסתר), given that he is excluded from the act of speech. Therefore, it stands for the grammatical 'non-person.' Since one cannot enter into a dialogue with a non-person, the Hebrew 'absent' (נסתר) expresses impersonal language, which one can either accept or reject, but cannot negotiate or enter into a dialogue with.[92] Bearing this in mind, let us consider the opening passage of Scripture: "In the beginning God created the heavens and the earth" (Gen. 1:1). Here God, Creator of the Universe, uses the third person narrative to record the moments of Genesis which only He could know. The use of the non-person 'absent' (נסתר) rendered the Creator "invisible, refined out of existence" – as with Joyce's writer. The rabbis, too, taught that when God passed in front of Moses and revealed to him His practice of Mercy, God spoke of Himself in the third person. It was God who proclaimed to Moses: "The Lord, the Lord is Merciful and Compassionate... " (Ex. 34:6).[93] Within the context of absolute monotheism of the Scripture, even such terms as 'Satan' and 'evil' must be interpreted as devices designed to hide divine omnipresence.[94]

God's unknowability pertains to literature. The answer that God gave Moses: "You cannot see My face and live" (Ex. 33:20), expresses the absolute distance that must separate a literary character from the author: neither Hamlet nor Othello could see the face of Shakespeare and live. A case in point is Borges' *Inferno*, I, 32. Both the leopard that inspired Dante to write 'leopard' and Dante could grasp their respective roles in dreams, which they had to forget upon awakening: it was

92. See José Faur, "The Third Person in Semitic Grammatical Theory and General Linguistics," *Linguistica Biblica Bohn* 46 (1979), pp. 106–113. That is why someone who had made a vow not to 'speak' (ידבר) with a friend may speak to another person in the presence of said friend, even with the expressed intention that his friend should hear. Nevertheless, he would not be breaking his vow. Since the friend is not the second person, they are not 'speaking' to each other; see *MT Nedarim* 6:18.

93. See Rosh HaShana 17a.

94. See *Golden Doves*, p. xxi.

as difficult for Dante to understand his inclusion in Creation, as for the leopard to understand its inclusion in Dante's *Inferno*.[95]

In sum, for the Hebrews the universe is a semiological system, where things *signify*.[96] Central to the system is the "image of God" (*Elohim*), rendering man a "speaking spirit" (רוח מללא). This involves not only speech and communication but linguistic subjectivity, i.e., the faculty of a speaking subject to pose himself as '*I*' to a '*you*.' A fundamental principle of linguistic subjectivity is the principle of reciprocity. The faculty permitting the speaking subject to posit himself as *I* to a *you*, awards the addressee the right to say *I* to the speaker and render him *you*. In this sense "the image of God" implies absolute *equality* between the persons – not in metaphysical or ontological terms as per pagan theology – but *linguistic* equality, based on the *difference* and *individuation*, postulated by the personal pronouns 'I/you.'[97] It also implies *freedom*: "speaking spirit" is operative only when both parties *choose* to posit themselves in syntagmatic opposition to each other.[98] We will see in the course of this work that freedom and equality are the axis around which the Tora and Tradition of Israel orbit.

95. In *Obras Completas*, p. 807. Cf. the incisive note in his *Nueve Ensayos Dantescos*, p. 120 n. 1.
96. See *Golden Doves*, chapter II.
97. For a detailed analysis, see José Faur, "The Hebrew Personal Pronoun," in *Perspectives on Jews and Judaism* (New York: Rabbinical Assembly, 1979), pp. 45–59; see also *Golden Doves*, pp. 41–47; idem, "Person and Subjectivity: A Linguistic Category," *Mentalities* 6 (1990), 15–18.
98. See the sources cited in the preceding note and *Homo Mysticus*, pp. 3–5. The fact that the linguistic apparatus is not given *in* nature, rendered Adam free *from* nature; see Sandra Rudnick Luft, *Vico's Uncanny Humanism* (Ithaca, N.Y.: Cornell University Press, 2003), p. 146 n. 80.

# Chapter 4
# Of Scribes and Analphabetic Poets

Hebrew intelligence is alphabetic. The early sages, we are apprised, "were called *soferim* (scribes) because they counted every single letter of the Tora."[99] A special concern of the scribes was to promote accurate reading of Scripture. Reflecting on that early period, R. Hayye Gaon (939–1038) explained: "In that generation," when Jews returned from the Babylonian Exile to the Land of Israel, "most [of the people] were ignorant and read the Scripture incorrectly, except for the scribes (*soferim*), who were in the minority. Accordingly, the accurate reading of Scripture was referred to as the 'reading of scribes'

99. Qiddushin 30a; cf. Ḥagiga 15b, Sanhedrin 106b. They further expounded the alphabetic character of the word; see *Midrash Tanḥuma, Beshallaḥ,* XVI, vol. 1, p. 146; *Golden Doves,* pp. 84–85. Hence the relevance of the children's playful songs on the alphabet, in Shabbat 104a. An illuminating example of an alphabetic approach to the text of the Scripture is provided by R. Jonah ibn Jannaḥ's works and methodology. See, for instance, his *Kitab al-Luma'*, ed. Joseph Derenbourg (Paris: F. Vieweg, 1886), Heb. translation, R. Judah ibn Tibbon, *Sefer ha-Riqma,* ed. M. Wilensky (Berlin: Akademie-Verlag, 1930, facsimile edition, 2 vols. Jerusalem: Academy for the Hebrew Language, 5724/1964). A good beginning would be studying his chapter 32 (31), in conjunction with Ma'arabi Pereṣ, "*Ledarko ha-Parshanit shel R. Yona ibn Jannaḥ,*" *Sinai* (Jubilee Volume) 100 (5748/1988), pp. 661–681.

(*soferim*)."[100] Hence the position of prominence that scribes occupy in Jewish tradition.[101]

Among Greeks, the idea of an 'oral law' emerges as a result of their dissatisfaction with writing in general, and the belief that a written law would be necessarily imperfect. While there is no consensus as to when alphabetic writing first appeared in ancient Greece, one thing is for sure: Greek poets, as well as the Muses inspiring them, were analphabetic. 'Memory' was the exclusive patrimony of the poet not because he 'remembered,' but because the Muse who once inspired him to sing his song will help him recall it, again and again. When Homer asked the Muses to help him remember things past (see *Iliad* II, ll. 484–492, 760–762; XI, ll. 218–220; XVI, ll. 112–113), he was not referring to historic times but to the songs he had sung. Since there was no written text, to recall his songs the poet needed the assistance of the Muses.[102] Given that analphabetic language only apprehends the auditory contour of words, as if they were phonetic slabs (see above chapter 2), nuance and multiple understandings are not

---

100. Cited in *Sefer ha-'Ittim*, p. 257. It would appear that Maimonides, in his *Sefer ha-Miṣvot*, ed. R. Joseph Qafiḥ (Jerusalem: Mossad Harav Kook, 1971), II, p. 15, gives a different interpretation of *soferim*. Upon consideration, I am inclined to believe that the legal niceties discussed by Maimonides were in fact encoded in the meticulous 'reading of the scribes.'

101. The first sages of Israel, beginning with Ezra, are called 'scribes'; see Sanhedrin 106b. Cf. *Forty Centuries of Ink*, p. 19.

102. See Marcel Detienne, *The Masters of Truth in Archaic Greece* (New York: Zone Books, 1996), pp. 39–52. According to Vico, *The New Science*, V, #410, pp. 131–132, 'poetic' discourse reflects the "inability to abstract forms or properties from subjects." cf. ibid. #209, pp. 74–75, and #816, p. 312. At this early period, 'memory' pertained to the realm of the sacred and was related to religion and rituals; see ibid., pp. 44–50. It was only after Simonides developed a technique for remembering, that memory became independent from religion. For some background, see ibid., pp. 107–134, and *Golden Doves*, pp. 32–33. The poetic tradition continued in various forms throughout European society until relatively recent times; e.g., the epic songs and bards in Welsh tradition; see Prys Morgan, "From a Death to a View: The Hunt for the Welsh Past in the Romantic Period," in eds. Eric Hobsbawm and Terence Ranger, *The Invention of Tradition* (Cambridge: Cambridge University Press, 1992), pp. 43–100.

tolerated. At that level of linguistic development, the grid signifier/signified is inviolable. "In the poem," wrote a distinguished thinker of our times, "it is impossible to dissociate meaning from sound."[103] Analphabetic poetry functions like a slogan or graffiti. That is why it is essentially untranslatable. "I emphasize," he added, "that it is not only untranslatable into other languages but also into the language in which it is written." In fact, "The translation of a poem is always the creation of another poem; it is not a reproduction of, but a metaphor equivalent to, the original."[104]

An important factor in analphabetic speech is the range of emotions that the speaker can elicit: fear, pity, anger, etc. These emotions do not belong to language proper, but to the irrational aspect of speech: rhythm, voice, imagery, etc. As with sorcery and the occult, a skilled orator can suspend rationality and *charm* the audience. This explains the close, intimate relation between rhetoric and magic, leadership and charisma, politics and the divine, truth and the supernatural: belief is a consequence of *seduction*. Philo observed that poetry and art are forms of idolatry designed to charm and seduce the foolish.

> But not only are wealth and glory and the like idols and unsubstantial shadows, but also all the personages, wherewith mythmakers have invented and spread delusion, building up their false imagination into a stronghold to menace the truth, and staging as by machinery new gods, in order that the eternal and really existing God might be consigned to oblivion. And to promote the seductiveness, they have fitted the falsehood into melody, meter and rhythm, thinking thereby to cajole their audience. Furthermore, they have brought in sculpture and painting to co-operate in their deception, in order that with colors and shapes and artistic qualities wrought by their fine workmanship they may enthrall the spectators and

103. Octavio Paz, *Claude Lévi-Strauss: An Introduction* (New York: Dell Publishing, 1978), p. 59.

104. *Claude Lévi-Strauss: An Introduction*, pp. 59–60. See *Golden Doves*, pp. 1–3.

> so beguile the two leading senses, sight and hearing – sight through lifeless shapes of beauty, hearing through the charm of poetry and music – and thus make the soul unsteady and unsettled and seize it for their prey.[105]

Poetic consciousness unfolds in the realm of myth and magic. "Nothing is dearer to poets," noted Vico, "than singing the marvels wrought by sorceresses by means of incantations."[106] The ground of analphabetic speech is metaphysics/myth. At this level of human development, the word *is* the thing it signifies. The poet's speech creates; 'poets,' noted Vico, is Greek for 'creators.'[107] Poetic speech "is the essence of language where language is, where man is bespoken, in the antique, strong sense of the word."[108] Myth and metaphysics are two methods by which to 'explain' the copula *is*, and thus the cohesiveness thing/name (see above chapter 2). Poets have been described as "interpreters of the gods."[109] Upon some thought, they

105. *Philo*, "The Special Laws," I, 28–29, vol. 7, p. 115. On the specific association of oratory to magic, see "The Worse Attacks the Better," 35–40, *Philo*, vol. 2, pp. 227–233. Cf. Jacqueline de Romilly, *Magic and Rhetoric in Ancient Greece* (Cambridge, Mass.: Harvard University Press, 1975). On Bruno's views on magic and memory, see Ignacio Gómez de Lino, ed. *Mundo, Magia, Memoria* (N.p.: Taurus, 1981). There is an essay by Jorge Luis Borges on the novel and magic, "El arte narrativo y la magia," in his collection, *Discusión* (Buenos Aires: Emecé, 1964), pp. 81–91. On the 'charismatic leader,' see the seminal article by George Devereux, "Charismatic Leadership and Crisis," *Psychoanalysis and the Social Sciences*, 4 (1955), pp. 145–157. That is why, popular opinion notwithstanding, Judaism does not recognize the legitimacy of charismatic leadership.
106. *The New Science*, #383, p. 120. On the relation between magic and poetry in Vico, see Gustavo Costa, "Fantasía y Magia Diabólica en Vico," *Cuadernos sobre Vico*, 15–16 (2003), pp. 15–30.
107. *The New Science* #376, p. 117; cf. Giambattista Vico, *On the Study Methods of Our Time* (Ithaca, New York: Cornell University Press, 1990), IX, p. 45. See Martin Heidegger, "... Poetically Man Dwells..." in *Poetry, Language, Thought* (New York: Harper & Row, 1975), p. 214.
108. George Steiner, *Martin Heidegger* (New York: Viking Press, 1978), p. 146. Steiner, however, was not aware that Heidegger's 'poetry' is fundamentally anti-writing.
109. See *The New Science*, #381, p. 120.

are more than 'interpreters': they *create* the gods. After examining a problematic term (*kraíno*) in the "Homeric Hymn to Hermes," Émile Benveniste concluded:

> The god is singing of the origin of things and by his songs the gods 'are brought into existence.' A bold metaphor, but one which is consistent with the role of a poet who is himself a god. A poet causes to exist; things come to birth in his song.[110]

In fact, the poet creates something more durable and transcendent and potent, without which no god could come to be: the analphabetic crowd. Beguiled by the 'spell' of the contour of words – absolute, dense, and iridescent – the crowd will adore any god sung by the poet. Poets do not merely articulate the mind and experiences of society: they forge one by creating the other – simultaneously.

To the analphabetic mind, writing and reading are passive instruments tolerated in order to record and retrieve *speech*. Since writing cannot possibly evoke the charm created by the speaker, reading is but a pale and unreal shadow of the original. Staging and theatrics, so essential to poetic discourse, are designed to halt rationality and make the 'impossible' possible. To retrieve the past, the poet 'enthralls,' evoking a series of dramatic images designed to thwart critical analysis. The memory of ordinary men is worthless. The public can gain access to the past only through the office of the poet. The 'past' that the poet retrieves precludes intelligent consideration and interpretation. The poet can reclaim the past, but he can neither confront it nor explain it. The public, as with a Passion play, can relive the poet's past and repossess it again and again, but can never access it. Not only the 'facts' of history, but also those affecting the economic and political conditions of a people, are justified by poetic logic, rather than reason. To be 'enthralled,' the public must be sequestered inside myth. Therefore it is incumbent upon the ruling authorities to prevent the

110. *Indo-European Language and Society*, p. 331.

masses from gaining access to alphabetic discourse – at all costs and by all means.

There are political consequences to analphabetic discourse. Given that agreement is attained by manipulating the dramatic features of speech, political decisions could only be reached after a long, intense debate. By excluding the dramatic aspects of speech, writing dissipates the voice of the people. Consequently, pagan political tradition associates writing with tyranny.[111] Rousseau (1712–1778) refers to the ideal (and essentially analphabetic) law inscribed "in the heart of the citizens; a law which creates the real constitution of the State."[112] To the pagan mind, the ultimate tyrant is someone attempting to translate analphabetic discourse into writing. Thus wrote Rousseau "to replace these 'internal inscriptions' with an outside text, to silence the inner voice with a visible written sign, [is] to kill the spirit with the letter."[113]

The same is the case with political representation. As with writing, it cannot possibly convey the full voice of the people in all its dramatic features. "Sovereignty," Rousseau explained, "consists essentially in the general will, and the will cannot be represented."[114] To help carry on a proper political discourse, the ideal society must provide its citizens with unrestricted leisure to assemble, debate, and direct their civic affairs.[115] A vital requisite for achieving this ideal is slave labor. "There are circumstances so unfortunate," Rousseau explained, "that people can preserve their freedom only at the expense of that of others, and the citizen cannot be completely free except when the slave is enslaved to the utmost."[116] This ideology underlies the dichotomy *civita dei*/*regnum* of Augustine; superman/masses, as proposed by

111. See Deborah Tarn Steiner, *The Tyrant's Writ* (Princeton: Princeton University Press, 1994), chapter 4.
112. Rousseau, *Social Contract*, II, 12, in ed. Charles M. Andrews, *Famous Utopias* (New York: Tudor Publishing, n. d.), p. 48.
113. Rousseau, *Social Contract*, II, 12, in *Famous Utopias*, p. 48; see *The Tyrant's Writ*, p. 250, and above n. 53.
114. *Social Contract*, III, 15, in *Famous Utopias*, p. 84.
115. See *The Tyrant's Writ*, chapter 5.
116. *Social Contract*, III, 15, in *Famous Utopias*, p. 86.

Nietzsche in his groundbreaking *Genealogy of Morals*; and countless variations of superior/inferior, present in all hierarchic societies.[117]

We mentioned earlier that the Hebrew alphabet excludes vowels (see appendix 1). Reading involves choice and semantic analysis. The text of Scripture is structured into semantic units or sentences known as 'verses' (פסוקים). Unlike analphabetic terms which are immediately 'recognized' by all, the semantic value of Scripture is *processed* on the basis of cogent linguistic data in the 'verse' (פסוק), requiring linguistic analysis and *interpretation*. Given the plurality of meaning and multiple understandings inherent in semantic analysis, consensus is a function of *persuasion*. Marginal factors, such as emotion, theatrics, and anything that could cloud rational analysis are formally excluded from alphabetic discourse. This is true even when coming from God. For that reason, the pact at Sinai was not ratified in the Presence of God, but on the following morning, when God was conspicuously absent, and no phenomena, natural or divine, could affect the will of the people (see chapter 5).

The linguistic apparatus of Israel is a highly alphabetized system (see appendix 3). Words are processed and broken down into their ultimate component: consonant-letters; vowels are to be supplied mentally by the reader. (This is consistent with the transitive sense of the Hebrew verb 'to read,' see appendix 2.) In this fashion, grammatical classification, differentiation, nuance, and a whole range of linguistic analyses are possible, elevating the semantic sense of the 'verse' (פסוק), thereby, to an order exceeding and excelling the sum total of each term in isolation.[118] Semantic reading warrants continuous interpretation on the basis of cognitive data. For that reason, the 'meaning' of a 'verse' (פסוק) cannot be retrieved by active rehearsal and mere repetition, as with the epic recollections of analphabetic poets, but by extending its semantic context and information units to the ideas, cultural conceptions, and challenges of the day. The pur-

117. See Richard Wolin, *The Seduction of Unreason* (Princeton, N. J.: Princeton University Press, 2004).

118. See *Golden Doves*, pp. 1–2.

pose is not to retrieve the past, but to structure the present: "Every generation, and its own commentators, every generation and its own sages, every generation and its own leaders."[119] To make sense, interpretation must stimulate rationality and point to hitherto unnoticed nuances in the 'verse' (פסוק). Therefore, far from restricting the individual, the Scripture bestows *eloquence* (see below Section IV). Commenting on the verse, "The Tree of Life is medicine to the tongue" (Prov. 15:4), the rabbis taught:

> *Tree of Life* stands for 'Tora,' as it is written: "It (the Tora) is (the) Tree of Life, for those who uphold it" (Prov. 3:18). The tongue of the Tora sets free the tongue (of men). Let it be known that in the future God will grow fine trees from the Garden of Eden, and all those who are mute will chew them. Immediately, they would excel in the words of the Tora. As it is written: "[And on the banks of the river (passing through the Garden of Eden) will grow], on either side [every edible tree, whose leaves will not wither and whose fruits will never end]" (Ezek. 47:12). *On either side* – refers to the Tora. As it says [about the tablets containing the Decalogue] "on either side" [they were written] (Ex. 32:15).[120]

Given that the Hebrew alphabet rules out vowels, *speech* is outside script representation. Slogans are excluded, once and for all, and with them the whole gamut of theatrics, intrinsic to speechmaking: Moses stuttered, for he was "heavy of mouth and heavy of speech"

119. Sanhedrin 38b, 'Aboda Zara 5a. Cf. Berakhot 63b; *Pesiqta de-Rab Kahana* XII, 5, ed. Bernard Mandelbaum, 2 vols. (New York: The Jewish Theological Seminary, 1962), vol. 1, pp. 206–207.
120. My translation comes from the text quoted by R. Moses Almosnino, in his *Tefilla le-Moshe* (Israel: Hamakhon le-Ḥeqer Yahdut Saloniki, 5748/1988), p. 147; which is different than the versions in Debarim Rabba (Vilna) I, 1, vol. 2, p. 193; and Debarim Rabba (Lieberman) I, 7, p. 5. Cf. *Tana de-Be Eliyahu* (Lublin, 5657/1897), XVIII, pp. 339, 347.

(Ex. 4:10).[121] The Hebrew alphabet excludes monolingualism. We had the opportunity to examine the centrality of monolingualism among the Greeks (see above chapter 2). It was shared by other people, such as Arabs and more recently Germans. 'Monolingualism' is central to the language of the analphabetic crowd, 'enthralled' by the 'charm' of the myth-making poet. At that level of consciousness, the 'truth' is 'obvious' – as with slogans and graffiti – and will not tolerate analysis. Among the most successful monolinguistic movements are those of the Greeks, Arabs and Germans. Noticeably, they each had a long tradition of analphabetic poetry *before* writing. It is not haphazard that they, too, share the ideal of imperial domination and coercive ideologies. In such civilizations, later alphabetization is marginal to their national ethos. At the poet's song, cultivated intelligence and scientific thought vanish, as if by magic. Once possessed by the poetic truth, the analphabetic crowd will march to the beat of the poet's drum, silently, obediently (see appendix 21).

In the Book of Ecclesiastes (9:13–18), King Solomon presented a radical thesis, designed to challenge popular wisdom. "The following thesis I also wish to propose – a subject that one may wish to ponder, under the sun: quite amazing in my view" (v. 13). Let us imagine, "a small town scarcely populated," that suddenly had to face "a mighty king," who "besieged it and built great bulwarks against it" (v. 14).

---

121. That is why the rabbis censured those "singing" a verse of the Song of Songs, or "reciting" a verse from the Tora in a drinking bout; see Sanhedrin 101a. Cf. Bereshit Rabba LXXXV, 2, vol. 2, p. 1033, where concern is expressed that people should not believe that the book of Daniel is like a "work of poetry" (דברי פיוטין). In my view, this is the reason why R. Jacob Zahalon, *A Guide for Preachers*, ed. and trans. R. Henry Adler Sosland (New York: The Jewish Theological Seminary of America, 1987), p. 138, advised that a sermon should be delivered "without any chant or melody." Noting: "Chanting is appropriate with prayers, not in a sermon." see editor's note ad loc. Finally, it is important to call attention to the rabbinic doctrine stipulating that "the principal" (עיקר) dimension of the Temple songs are the psalmist's words, not the music. To emphasize this point, no musical instruments were played at the time that the Levites sang; see 'Arakhin 11a; and *MT Kele ha-Miqdash* 3:2–3. Cf. above n. 65.

King Solomon submits that it could be saved, provided that "it were found in it a man who is poor-wise (מסכן-חכם)," that is, someone *with no* might *and* at the same time wise. These two qualities are essential to "save the town by his wisdom." It means that to render an intelligent and unbiased judgment of the situation, and devise a plan of action, the sage must be "poor"; i.e., he should have no share in the power-structure and management of the city. Hence the paradox: 'poverty' – the very condition enabling the sage to offer intelligent advice – will render him unfit to give advice. Simply put, even in a small town, the governing leadership would prefer to capitulate to the "mighty king," rather than acknowledge the assistance of a "*poor* man." To succeed, the poor-wise man would have to accept anonymity: "and nobody would remember that poor man" (v. 15). King Solomon explained: Although we all agree that "wisdom is better than might," nonetheless, the fact remains that "the wisdom of a poor man," that is, someone without power, "is despised and his words are not heard" (v. 16). If so, how could the town be saved? King Solomon offered a solution, formulated as a "riddle" (חידה, cf. Prov. 1:6 and appendix 31), which the keen reader will be able to unravel. "The words of wise men softly (בנחת) spoken are more persuasive than the scream (מזעקת) of a ruler (addressing) fools" (v. 17). Both, the wise men and the ruler, address a public made up of fools. The difference is in the *way* the message is conveyed. Wise men convey their words "softly" (בנחת), that is, calmly and clearly, without anger and antagonism. Having this type of leadership in mind, R. Eleazar (Sanhedrin 92a) taught:

> Every leader who leads the public softly (בנחת) will have the merits to lead them in the World to Come. As it is written: "For he who loves them shall lead them, and by a spring of water he shall guide them" (Is. 49:10; cf. Ps. 23:2).

The public, even when made up of fools, would eventually absorb his message. This, however, would take place a long time after he is gone. When he is forgotten and forsaken, and dwelling in the divine abode, his ideas would be guiding the people. According to this interpretation, "softly" (בנחת) pertains not only to the manner in which the sage delivered the message, but also to the manner in which the public is persuaded to admit the message: 'softly,' at their own pace, without force and anxiety. (For this sense of the term 'בנחת,' see Berakhot 56b and Yoma 86a.)

Unlike the sage, the ruler does not 'speak,' but screams (מזעקת). His purpose is not to enlighten the folks but to beguile and manipulate them. A close reading of the text will reveal that the ruler in question is no other than the king "besieging" the little town. Invariably, this type of political leadership builds "great bulwarks" to 'protect the people' from some imminent danger, created by him, and thus justifies his dysfunctional and corrupt leadership. Put another way, without staging a 'mortal enemy,' analphabetic leadership has no chance of success, even with fools! In this context, it would be important to take note that Esau, the paradigm of pagan leadership, was a master of staging and theatrics. To gain sympathy from his father: "he cried with an exceeding great and bitter cry" (ויצעק צעקה גדולה ומרה, Gen. 27:34; cf Gen. 33:1–16).

By way of conclusion, King Solomon ascertained: "Wisdom is better than weaponry." With one caveat: "A single wicked man (חוטא) could destroy much good" (v. 18). (This last point is further developed in the following chapter, Eccl. 10. See also Introductory Remarks, Section V.)

The sages of Israel, from the early *soferim* (scribes) to the latest congregational rabbi – regardless of denomination – are the anonymous sages offering the public the choice of alphabetic wisdom, rather than pageantry, theatrics, and preachy sermons. (see Section V, n. 543).

# Concluding Reflections

'Creation' is an expression of freedom. Not only is there no compulsion on the part of God to create, but neither is there any ontological or metaphysical link between Him and what He created.[122] R. Abraham ibn 'Ezra (1089–1164) observed that the Hebrew verb 'created' (ברא), designating God's primeval act of creation, actually means 'to cut, to sever.'[123] The function of this verb is to negate any sort of link, metaphysical or physical, relating God to His creatures: causality is the effect, not the ground, of Creation.[124] Creation belongs to the realm of the semiological. The Universe, as well as the things and events crisscrossing history, *signify*. Signification, however, is not a given. It requires discerning a *ketab* system that excludes vowels, and challenges the *reader* to interpret it by means of a *mikhtab* system, becoming thereby the writer. The purpose of Creation, as far as the Hebrew Scripture is concerned, is for men and God to transcend their "radical solitude." To accomplish this, Adam and his posterity were endowed with the "image of God" and the faculties to enter into a syntagmatic dialogue '*I/you*.' There are two basic conditions to this dialogue. It involves choice, whether the parties wish (or don't wish) to establish a syntagmatic relation. It also involves *concealment*

122. See *Homo Mysticus*, pp. 89–93.
123. In his *Commentary* on Gen. 1:1.
124. See *Homo Mysticus*, pp. 111–115.

between person '*I*' and person '*you*.'[125] Moses understood this well. Therefore, he "concealed his face from looking at Him, because he feared to look at God" (Ex. 3:6).[126] (In psychoanalysis, too, patient and doctor are *not* to see each other's faces.) Moses was told that he could only see God's "back" as He was "passing by" (Ex. 33:22–23; cf. 34:6). Within a dialectical context, not only is man precluded from 'seeing' the face of His Maker, but God, too, exercises a *willful disconnection from omniscience, refraining from 'seeing' the face of the interlocutor*. Without God's *willful disconnection from omniscience,* no dialogue between Him and man could take place.

The best metaphor that I know to illustrate God's relation to humankind is *The Orchestral Conductor,* by Canetti.[127] During the entire performance the conductor stands with his back to the public. Only the orchestra, seated in front of him, has access to his presence and can interpret his directions, sometimes given by both hands, sometime by a single hand and the baton. In this fashion, the conductor *conducts* the audience and *leads* it to the realm of music.

> During a concert, and for the people gathered together in the hall, the conductor is a leader. He stands at their head with his back to them. It is him they follow, for it is he who goes first. But, instead of his feet, it is his hands which lead them. The movement of the music, which his hands bring about, represents the path his feet would be first to tread. The crowd in the hall is carried forward by him.

The audience cannot know what the members of the orchestra see, or how they actually interpret the various movements.

---

125. Rather than 'opacity,' which is a condition of ontology; see *Golden Doves,* p. 28.
126. To dispel any notion that he was some sort of a deity, Moses would uncover his face when speaking to the public; see Ex. 34:33.
127. In Elias Canetti, *Crowds and Power* (Middlesex, England: Penguin Books, 1973), pp. 458–460, from where the following quotations proceed.

> During the whole performance of a work they never see his face. He is merciless: there are no intervals for rest. They see his back always in front of them, as though it were their goal.

One thing is evident. The conductor is the supreme master of the orchestra and the audience. The musical score – like the Cosmic Book of Creation – lies before his eyes alone. He alone has the power to interpret the score and transmit it to the members of the orchestra in a series of *directions*, which in turn they must *interpret* and convey to the audience in the form of music. The conductor is absolutely omniscient and absolutely omnipotent.

> He has the power of life and death over the voices of the instruments; one long silent will speaks again at his command. Their diversity stands for the diversity of mankind; an orchestra is like an assemblage of different types of men. The willingness of its members to obey him makes it possible for the conductor to transform them into a unit, which he then embodies.

Only at the end of the concert, the conductor shows his face and the public responds in ovation. Similarly, God told Moses that he could perceive His face only *after* "He passed over His face" (Ex. 34:6) – never before.

Having a dialogue with God postulates that God *ad intra*, as He is to Himself, is outside the realm of dialogue and above and beyond comprehension. Paraphrasing Maimonides, Borges said:

> I felt that the First Being, the *En-Sof*, cannot be defined. It cannot even be said that He exists. Even that is too concrete. Then you cannot say that He is wise or that He knows. Because if He knows, then there are two things – the known and the One who knows.[128]

128. Amelia Barili, in an interview with Borges, "Borges on Life and Death," *New*

Before eating the forbidden fruit, Adam inhabited a theocentric world. Unlike man in the 'state of nature,' Adam knew the canons of human conduct – "good and evil" in the language of Scripture – by virtue of the "image of God" within. The snake proposed another method. Adam could know the basic norms of conduct simply by "becoming as God (*Elohim*), knowing good and evil" (Gen. 3:5). Adam-*Elohim* is a formal repudiation of Adam/*Adon*.[129] It is also a forfeiture of the "image of God" (*Elohim*) within. The difference between the two classes of "good and evil" is huge. Previously, "good and evil" was a function of Adam/*Adon*. Within this context, the Scripture teaches that "the beginning of wisdom is fear – in the Hebrew sense of 'reverence and deference' – of God" (Ps. 111:10; Prov. 1:7; 9:10; cf 14:27; 15:33; Job 28:28). The purpose of "Fear of God," as the psalmist teaches, is to assist "a man who craves life; [and] loves days to see goodness." This 'fear' is translated into the basic norms of human life and fellowship: "Keep your tongue from [speaking] evil, and your lips from uttering deceit. Keep away from wickedness and do good, seek peace and pursue it" (Ps. 34:12–15). By contrast, a heartless man – *nabal* in the language of the psalmist – is one who "had said in his heart: there is no *Elohim*" (Ps. 14:1; cf. 53:2): 'heartless/godless' are two sides of the same coin.

*Elohim* stands for 'authority' in general (cf. Ps. 82:6).[130] The key for deciphering this term in conjunction with Adam is provided by the *Targum*. Usually, *Elohim* refers to 'God' or a 'deity.' Occasionally, it refers to a 'political' or a 'judicial' authority. It is also used in the sense of 'angel, messenger,' given that an agent, human or celestial, stands for the authority which it *represents*, civil or divine. The *Targum*

*York Times Review*, July 13, 1986, p. 28. Cf. *MT Yesode ha-Tora* 2:10, and *Teshuba* 5:5. On the niceties of this doctrine, see *Guide* I, 57–60.

129. Cf. *Saadya's Commentary on Genesis*, (Heb.), ed. Moshe Zucker (New York: Jewish Theological Seminary, 1984), pp. 288–292.

130. That is why in rabbinic tradition *Elohim* is associated with 'stern justice' (מידת הדין).

(Gen. 3:5) rendered the above *Elohim*, neither 'god' nor 'angel,' but 'princes, political leaders'[131] (רברבין).

The message is clear: repudiation of "the image of God" (*Elohim*) within renders man an *Elohim* – the hero of pagan humanity, or a "*europaischen Menschentums*" – in poetic discourse. By expelling "the image of God" (*Elohim*) from within, Adam expelled himself from Eden.

The object of Scripture is the dialogue *I/you* within the context Adam/*Adon*, in its fullness. Given that the God of Israel does not communicate to an analphabetic vacuum, Hebrew reading, in the sense of mentally joining two consonants and generating meaning thereof, is the minimum intellectual requirement for apprehending God's word. Within the *ketab/mikhtab* system, meaning is a *performative* category. Applying Vico's principle of *verum/factum*, stipulating that 'knowledge' is a function of 'making,' we may say that in Hebrew, the reader believes because she/he *created* meaning.[132] The inalienable right to 'join two consonants,' authorizes even the "simple believer" to voice the words of God. The rabbis taught:

> ... If one has heard a word (דבר) from the mouth of the meekest Israelite (= "simple believer"), he must regard it as if he had actually heard it from a great sage.... He should not regard it

131. The hero is Adam-*Elohim*, who, as per the Aramaic rendition רברבין, indicates hierarchic 'superiority.' In Dan. 7:8, 11, 20 it is associated with 'pompous,' and 'pretentious' speech. Therefore, it is also used in the sense of a 'high rank dignitary,' and 'prince'; see ibid. 4:33; 5:1, 2, 3, 9, 10, 23, etc. The *Targum*, too, uses it to translate 'prince'; see Gen. 17:20; 25:16; and 'officers'; see Num. 7:2, 3; 22:15; *Pseudo-Jonathan* on Num. 22:15; and *Targum Jonathan ben 'Uzziel* on II Sam. 8:18, cf. Radaq ad loc.; *Guide* I, 3; and *Homo Mysticus*, pp. 65, 108. In Yerushalmi Berakhot VII, 2, 11b, it is found in the sense of dignitaries, officers.'

132. See *Homo Mysticus*, pp. 92–92. On the performative utterances in general, see *Problems in General Linguistics*, pp. 231–238. On the legal status of such utterances, see José Faur, "Performative and Descriptive Utterances in Jewish Law" (Heb.), in ed. Arye Edrei, *Studies in Jewish Law in Honor of Professor Aaron Kirschenbaum* (*Dine Israel* 20–21, 5760–5761), pp. 101–121.

> only as if had actually heard it from a single sage, but as if he had actually heard it from all the sages ... and not only as if he had actually heard it from all the sages, but as if he had actually heard it from the *Sanhedrin* [Supreme Court] ... and not only as if he had actually heard it from the *Sanhedrin,* but as if he had actually heard it from Moses the Shepherd ... and not only as if he had heard it from Moses the Shepherd, but as if he had actually heard it from the mouth of God, blessed be He![133]

By contrast, the world of Adam-*Elohim* is hierarchic, through and through. Within such an organization,

> the word of the simple believer has no sanctity. Everything he expects, everything which is to free him from the manifold burdens weighing on him, comes to him from a higher authority. He only understands what is explained to him.[134]

'Understanding,' 'knowledge,' 'faith,' is a function of obedience – as per scholasticism, where the 'truth' is demonstrated by quoting an 'authority.' By denying the individual the basic right to see the reality with her/his own eyes, the 'truth' of Adam-*Elohim* enslaves rather than liberates, rendering its possessor more obnoxious, rather than more humane.

People inhabiting an anthropocentric world can see their gods but cannot establish a dialogue with them. Their gods are as silent as their idols and the worshippers as blind and deaf as their idols (see Ps. 115; cf. 135).[135] Given that these gods cannot utter an intelligible word – let alone write or read – to know 'good and evil,' etc., man

133. *Sifre* #41, p. 86; see *Golden Doves,* p. 56.

134. *Crowds and Power,* p. 182.

135. See the lively discussion between a Jew and a pagan in *Genizah Studies,* ed. Louis Ginzberg, 2 vols. (New York: Jewish Theological Seminary, 1928–1929), vol. 1, pp. 222–223. The same basic story is transmitted in Sephardic folklore, as taking place between a *converso* and an 'old' Christian. When the latter asked

needs the assistance of what Vico calls "theological poets." The task of these poets is to "enter" the mind of the gods – as with Balaam the sorcerer (see Num. 24:16) – and transmit to the sovereign the "divine mysteries."[136] The apex of such a labor is a mystical vision (i.e., outside alphabetic analysis), that enthralls and captivates the audience.

> The first [jurisprudence] was a divine wisdom called mystic theology, which means the science of divine speech or the understanding of the divine mysteries of divination. This science of auspicial divinity was the vulgar wisdom whose sages were the theological poets, who were the first sages of the gentile world. From this mystic theology they [the poets] were called *mystai*, or mystics, which the well-informed Horace translates as interpreters of gods. To this first jurisprudence belonged the first and proper interpreting, called *interpretari* for *interpatari*; that is, "to enter into the fathers," as the gods were at first called. Dante would call it *indiarsi*, to enter into the mind of God (*Paradise* 4.28).[137]

Paul Tillich (1886–1965), one of the great religious thinkers of modern times, distinguished between 'transitory groups,' bound together either by common interest or family ties, and 'a community of faith.' The former will disappear as soon as the conditions that give rise to their existence vanish. By contrast, 'a community of faith' will continue on the strength of its own faith, regardless of circumstances (cf. Abot 5:16).

> In a community of faith these conditions are not decisive; the only condition of its continuation is the vitality of its faith.

---

the neophyte how he felt as a Christian, pointing at the crucifix he answered: 'Now I can see god, but he cannot see me. Before I could not see God, but he surely saw me.'

136. See *Homo Mysticus*, p. 5. In Jewish tradition Balaam represents the religious prophet that works hand in hand with the political sovereign.

137. *The New Science*, #938, p. 343.

> That which is based on an ultimate concern is not exposed to destruction by preliminary concerns and the lack of their fulfillment. The most astonishing proof of this assertion is the history of the Jews. They are, in the history of mankind, the ultimate and unconditional character of faith.[138]

The same distinction applies to the realm of the spirit. Analphabetic crowds are 'transitory.' Although bound by common symbols, rituals, and spiritual values, since the people are precluded from examining them alphabetically, they will fall back into barbarism as soon as they are summoned by the call of the poet or politician. Witness the wholesale conversion to Islam by the Christian intelligentsia in the Ancient Near East, in the Mediterranean Basin, and in North Africa;[139] the effervescence of morality and ideals, characterizing European history; and the mass desertion from religion and ethics in favor of materialistic secularism in modern times. The return to barbarism, warned Tillich, "can happen at any moment even in the highest culture."[140] The reason is that whatever the character of one's faith may be, unless it is grasped alphabetically, it would not stand up to the call of barbarism.

Underneath the culture of barbarism lurks a pathological obsession with death, threatening human continuity. At the end of a panegyric on Wisdom, King Solomon called attention to this overwhelming principle. "He who shall find me [wisdom], shall find life, and will extort good-will from the Lord. But he that blunders against me has wronged his soul: All those who hate me [wisdom] do love death" (Prov. 8:35–36).* The following story illustrates the intelligence of these words. It took place at the University of Salamanca,

138. Paul Tillich, *Dynamics of Faith* (New York: Harper & Row, 1958), p. 119.
139. See Patricia Crone and Michael Cook, *Hagarism* (Cambridge: Cambridge University Press, 1977), chapter 9.
140. Paul Tillich, "The Decline and the Validity of the Idea of Progress," in ed. Jerald C. Brauer, *The Future of Religions* (New York: Harper & Row, 1966), p. 69.

* Cf. The "Palestinians" in modern times.Cf. The "Palestinians" in modern times.

Spain, in 1936. A prominent fascist general who was crippled during the Spanish Civil war had a favorite motto: *Viva la muerte!* ('Long live death!'). As he began to deliver a speech, one of his followers shouted the motto in token of support. After the general concluded, Miguel de Unamuno, Rector of the University, replied:

> ... Unfortunately there are too many [war] cripples in Spain just now. And soon there will be even more of them if God does not come to our aid.... A [war] cripple who lacks the spiritual greatness of a Cervantes [who had lost an arm in battle] is wont to seek ominous relief in causing mutilation around him.

As if to confirm King Solomon's principle, the general retorted: "*Abajo la inteligencia!*" ('Down with intelligence!'), to which Unamuno responded:

> This is the temple of the intellect.... It is you who profane its sacred precincts. You will win, because you have more than enough brute force. But you will not convince. For to convince you need to persuade. And in order to persuade you will need what you lack: Reason and Right in the struggle. I consider it futile to exhort you to think of Spain.[141]

The shield against the call to barbarism is alphabetic discourse, *meliṣa* in the language of the Hebrews, Vichian eloquence in humanistic discourse (see Section IV). The vitality of the Jewish faith, applauded by Tillich, rests on a simple fact: the alphabetic mind is immune to analphabetic blabber and poetic logic. It would be futile to try to engage in a dialogue with someone marching to the beat of *Viva la muerte!* And *Abajo la inteligencia!* – being immune to alphabetic reason and all that jazz.

141. The citations proceed from Eric Fromm, *The Anatomy of Human Destructiveness* (New York: Holt, Rinehart, and Winston: 1973), pp. 331–332. Cf. idem, *The Heart of Man* (New York: Harper & Row, 1964), pp. 35–38.

# Section II

# The Books of Israel

## Introductory Remarks

The crisis created by Adam presented humankind with two mutually exclusive options. Humankind can either inhabit a world governed by a set of rules – the 'good and evil' of Scripture – resulting from the dialogue Adam/*Adon*, or a world governed by rules hierarchically imposed by a super-Adam. The first is a theocentric universe, where every human being is conceived to be 'in the image of God.' Given that there is One God, this proposes the absolute equality of all of humankind. The second is an anthropocentric universe, rigidly controlled by a hierarchic system on top of which reigns Adam-*Elohim* (or "*europaischen Menschentums*"). Both universes recognize a divinity and the need for a set of regulations. The difference is in the method.

A hierarchic system is grounded on violence and the threat of violence. The linguistic apparatus of Adam-*Elohim* is geared for the processing of orders issued from a first to a third person or 'absentee,' excluding the possibility of dialogue. The realm of Adam/*Adon* is a universe grounded on a dialogue '*I/you*.' The 'Book' is to serve as a contextual point* of reference allowing for the dialogue Adam/*Adon*. As such, the Book is a Jewish invention: the only alternative to hierarchic violence. It both precedes and transcends a text or a given document. At the linguistic and intellectual levels it contains the constitutive values and primary premises without which the *ketab* and *mikhtab* of a linguistic community are non-operative. Using a rabbinic metaphor, we may say that the Book stands for the "Golden Doves," permitting articulation in the form of linguistic subjectivity as '*I/you*' or "silver dots." Outside such a contextual apparatus, man can communicate *hierarchically*, as master to slaves and subalterns: either issuing or accepting orders. Within such a system the function of first → third person communication is to block linguistic subjectivity: 'good and evil' are the sole prerogative of Adam-*Elohim*. Similarly, within this context, the function of religion is to block the Adam/*Adon* dialogue.[1]

There are three fundamental principles pertaining to the theory of Book. First, to serve as the contextual point of reference of a people, the Book must be a *national publication*. The Tora is the National Book of Israel because it was *published* by the Nation of Israel and fully validated by the *people* in a *national* covenant. To question its authority on the basis of some literary hypotheses would be as valid as questioning the authority of the Magna Carta, the American Constitution, or the *Code Napoleon* on similar grounds (cf. *Introductory Remarks*, Section IV). Second, in an alphabetic society, authority – whether political, ecclesiastical, or judicial – is a function of the Book. Therefore, a fundamental principle of Book is *accessibility* and

* Hence, Tora comprises [1] *min ha-shamayim* and [2] Mental Law.

1. See above Section I n. 92. Thus the relation of religion to political power, cf. *Homo Mysticus*, pp. 96–98. This, rather than ingesting a peculiar fruit, was Adam's sin; see ibid., pp. 58–65, and below chapter 30.

*distribution* of the text, or *ketab* system, to the general public. Third, the right to apply *derasha,* 'exposition' or the *mikhtab* system, to the text or *ketab* of the Book. We will see in the course of this Section that the *mikhtab* system corresponds to the synchronic axis of the linguistic community, and the *ketab* to its diachronic axis. Thus, to serve as the point of reference for private as well as national dialogue, the Book has to be intellectually accessible to the people. Hence, the right of the people to interpret the Book and to expound it. A corollary to this principle is the paramount importance of education; public and private (see Appendices 37–39, 50).

Bearing these principles in mind we can understand why Eupolemus (2nd century B.C.E.), the earliest known Jewish historian, believed that the Law written by Moses was the first book ever.[2] Obviously, he did not mean that it was the first written text, but that it was the first *Book,* i.e., a *nationally published text,* intended for general distribution and 'exposition,' that is *derasha* (pl. *derashot*) or 'the right to ascribe meaning to the text.' Western tradition confirms this view. The Hebrew Scripture is known as the 'book' (*biblos*), from which 'Bible' is derived. In Section III we will show that, in fact, the Tora was the first book available, textually and linguistically, to both the Jewish public and pagan humanity.

"Religion," a distinguished scholar taught, "is generally accepted as a system of rank, implying dependence, subordination and submission to unseen powers."[3] Given that the purpose of Scripture is the dialogue *I/you* within the context Adam/*Adon* in all its fullness, the Book serves to establish horizontality, both in relation to God and in relation to man. At the center of the Book stands the *berit* ('covenant') – a horizontal alliance between God and Israel. Just as the Ark was designed as an instrument to hold and enclose the "two

2. See *Golden Doves*, pp. 10, 120. Similarly, Josephus, *Against Apion*, II, 154, *Josephus,* vol. 1 (Loeb Classical Library), p. 353 maintained that Moses, "our legislator is the most ancient of all legislators in the records of the whole world."
3. Walter Burkert, *Creation of the Sacred* (Cambridge, Mass.: Harvard University Press, 1996), p. 81.

tablets of the covenant" (Ex. 25:16), and in turn the Tabernacle and later the Temple in Jerusalem were made to hold and enclose the Ark containing the tablets, the Tora, too, was designed to hold and enclose the covenant between God and Israel, thereby establishing a complementary relationship with the people: the Tora was given to Israel and Israel was given to the Tora. They perpetuate one another by means of transmission: the people perpetuate the Tora by passing it from one generation to the next, and the Tora perpetuates the people by producing a generation capable of carrying on the process of transmission, in the face of new circumstances and historical situations. 'Tora/people' are unique concepts. The interaction results in a special, non-hierarchic realm: the Book establishes a horizontal relationship between God and Israel and between the individual and the nation. The uniqueness of the Sinaitic covenant rests on the fact that it alone is a *bilateral* alliance between God and *an entire nation*. Previously, God made a unilateral covenant with Noah not to upset the forces of nature (Gen. 9:8–17). He had also contracted a covenant with the Patriarchs to bestow on their children the Land of Israel and make them "His" people, i.e., to contract a bilateral *berit* with the entire nation. When the children of Israel cried to the Lord because of their enslavement, the first act of God was to "remember," i.e., to acknowledge, the covenant that He had contracted with the Patriarchs (Ex. 2:24). Never, before or after, has God established a *bilateral* covenant with *an entire nation*. The Tora is the Book documenting the *berit* ('covenant') God/Israel. The *berit* constitutes a formal expansion and indenture of the Adam/*Adon* dialogue.

Usually, Scripture is regarded as a 'religious' work – with all the semantic accessories that this term had acquired via Christianity. It is taken as a given, therefore, that it is proper to freely apply to the Hebrew Scripture ideas and insights gained from the teachings and disciplines associated with 'religion.' The method is flawed. This will be obvious upon considering that the plethora of concepts applied to Scripture, including those of 'religion,' 'spirituality,' and the like, originate in an analphabetic environment, fundamentally inimical to the culture of writing and Book. Thus, in the attempt to 'interpret' the content of Scripture, critics and theologians often overlook the fact that the Scripture is first and foremost a *national* Book published *by* the *national institution* of Israel, *for* the people of Israel. The purpose of this Section is to examine the principles underlying the idea of 'publication,' 'distribution,' and other substantial principles connected with the concept of Book. We hope to show that whereas the 'Written Law' functions as the *ketab* system, governing the text of the Book, the 'Oral Law' is the *mikhtab* apparatus by which the Book is interpreted and ascribed with legal meaning.

# Chapter 5
# The *Berit* ('Covenant') Sinai-Moab

Israel was constituted by a duly drawn document or bilateral *berit* ('covenant'), formally contracted by the people and God. Let us note, at the outset, that in accordance with Jewish and standard legal procedure, the covenant registered the *date* and *locale* where it was negotiated – the first document in history duly listing [i] the chronological time, *and* [ii] the geographical locale in which the transaction took place: [i] "On the first day of the third month of the Exodus of Egypt, on that very day, [ii] they arrived at the Sinai Desert" (Ex. 19:1).[4] As in contract law, the *berit* was grounded on the principle of 'offer and acceptance.' It was executed in four steps.

Proposal. At God's request, Moses offered Israel to establish a bilateral covenant. The terms of the covenant were as follows. Israel, on her part, would accept God's Law as binding; God, on His part, would recognize Israel as a kingdom of priests and a holy nation. The proposal was accepted. Thereupon, Moses transmitted their decision to God (Ex. 19:3–6).

The Theophany at Sinai. Three days after accepting the proposal, God revealed Himself amidst thunders, lightning, and turmoil "before the eyes of all Israel," and verbally uttered the Decalogue to them

4. On the significance of the space-time continuum for the unfolding of historical time, see *Homo Mysticus*, pp. 142–147.

(Ex. 19:16–25, 25:1–13), "face to face" (Deut. 5:4). The consequence of this revelation was *instruction* – rather than demands imposed by virtue of might. This is the central theme of the liturgy (*musaf*) of Rosh HaShana:

> You have revealed Yourself to Your holy people with the cloud of Your Glory, to speak with them. From the heavens You permitted them to hear Your voice, and revealed Yourself to them in an iridescent cloud (ערפלי טוהר). The whole world, too, trembled before You. And the creatures of Genesis stood in awe before You, when You, O our King, revealed Yourself at Mt Sinai to teach your people the Law and the precepts (תורה ומצות).

Acceptance of God's precepts. After God's Theophany, Moses ascended to the "thick darkness" (ערפל) to receive representative precepts of the Law – a series of rituals, as well as moral and judicial legislation. Upon descending from the "thick darkness" (ערפל), Moses transmitted these precepts to the people. The people accepted, replying: "All the words which God had spoken we shall do" (Ex. 20:17–24:3). During the night, Moses put the articles of the covenant into writing. The document read by Moses is known as "the book of the *berit*" (Ex. 24:4, 7).

Ratification of the Pact. The following morning the pact was ratified. Moses ordered the erection of twelve pillars, representing the tribes of Israel, and an altar, representing God. Then, Moses sent young men to offer sacrifices. Half of the blood of the sacrifices was poured into basins and the rest was sprinkled onto the altar. Thereupon, Moses proceeded to read to the people "the book of the *berit*." At this ceremony, God was conspicuously absent. The morning was quiet, there was no thunder, lightning, or anything that could coerce, frighten, or intimidate the people. Freely and in unison the people broke the stillness of the morning with these words: "Everything that God will tell us we shall execute and we shall hear" (נעשה ונשמע).

Moses took the rest of the blood and sprinkled it on the people, saying: "Behold, the blood of the *berit* that God made with you, on all these words" (Ex. 24:4–8).

Thus took place an event with no parallel in history: a bilateral covenant between God and an entire people. The Scripture has recorded revelations and covenants between God and individuals, but only at Sinai did God speak to an entire people and establish a covenant with them. To understand the nature of the covenant we must focus on the last word spoken by Israel: ונשמע – "and we shall hear." It meant, as properly understood by the rabbis, that the contract at Sinai was a 'binding preliminary commitment' sanctioning, thereby, the introduction of new terms, conditions, and provisions to be negotiated afterward.[5] In effect, later, before leaving the Sinai Desert, the considerations and penalties contained in the covenant were stipulated (Lev. 26:3–46). The rest of the precepts were delivered during the following forty years. These precepts were duly exposed and promulgated by Moses and the elders at the *Ohel Mo'ed* (Tent of Assembly; see Section IV, n. 78) to the entire Community of Israel. At the end of forty years, in the fields of Moab, before crossing the Jordan into the Promised Land, Moses and the people sealed with another *berit* the precepts that were received during these forty years (Deut. 28:69). It, too, contains a series of blessings and sanctions reiterating the considerations and penalties of the covenant (Deut. 27:11–28:68). The Scroll of the Law, which Moses presented to the Priests and which was deposited next to the Ark of the Covenant (Deut. 31:25–26, see below chapter 7), is designated "written to its

5. In my "Maimonides' Starting Precept," p. 296–297 n. 60, I offered a detailed examination of Shabbat 88a-b, as read by R. Simon b. Ṣemaḥ Duran, *Tashbeṣ* (Amsterdam, 5498/1738), III, #310, 63a and the Geonim. A preliminary agreement is much more than a 'letter of intent' or an 'agreement to agree.' It is a binding and enforceable contract that contemplates being superseded by a subsequent agreement of broader scope and more detailed provisions. On preliminary agreements in American law, see Alan Schwartz and Robert E. Scott, "The Law and Economics of Preliminary Agreements," *Harvard Law Review*. Forthcoming. Available at SSNR: http: //ssrn.com/abstract= 921620.

conclusion" (עד תמם; Deut. 31:24); i.e., a technical term standing 'for a fully redacted agreement, with all the remedies upon breach, and the institutions in place, charged with performance.' Thus the Tora constitutes a sealed *berit* or entire agreement, which cannot be amended or altered in any respect by any of the parties, and no one can either add to or subtract from it (see below).[6]

The *berit* at Sinai was contracted by God and "the household of Jacob," i.e., "the children of Israel" (Ex. 19:3), directly linking every Israelite to God. At Moab, before crossing the Jordan into the Holy Land, the *berit* was contracted by God and the *nation* of Israel. This is the first case in recorded history in which the term 'nation' includes men and women, children and alien residents, as well as the political, judicial, and ecclesiastical authorities. Accordingly, as in all *national* covenants, this *berit* is binding upon *all* members of the *nation* or corporation of Israel, present as well as future (Deut. 29:9–14; cf. Josh. 8:35). In similar fashion to the covenant contracted at Sinai, it, too, was contracted in the "presence of God" (Deut. 29:9), with a significant

---

6. An "Entire Agreement Clause" is regularly appended in modern contracts stipulating that this Agreement constitutes the "entire, complete, and exclusive agreement of the parties and supersedes all prior communications, understandings and agreements relating to the subject matter hereof, whether oral or written." This is the precise sense of 'עד תמם.' A similar point was made in *Ezra* 7:12, where Ezra is described as "the Scribe that concluded (גמיר) the Law of the God of Heavens." R. Samuel Masnut, *Midrash Daniel wu-Midrash 'Ezra*, eds. I. S. Lange and S. Schwartz (Jerusalem: Mekize Nirdamim, 1968), p. 128, observed that the verb "גמיר" refers to "the Law" and it is an exact parallel of 'עד תמם' in Deut. 31:24: "גמיר" [in *Ezra*] has the same sense of the *Targum* that rendered "completely blue" (Ex. 28:31) as 'גמיר-blue.' It means that (Ezra) wrote all the Tora of God and its laws completely (עד תמם). A similar interpretation was given independently by R. Samuel Isaac Reggio, *Be'ur Yashar* (*Debarim*), vol. 5 (Vienna, 5581/1821), on Deut. 31:24, 153a. In the same vein, the Aramaic Version, *Ms. Neophyti* 1, vol. 5. Ed. Alejandro Díez-Macho (Madrid: Consejo Superior de Investigaciones Científicas, 1978), on Deut. 31:24, p. 263, renders: "והוה כד אשלם משה למכתב ית [כל] מילי אורייתה הדה בגו ספר עד זמן די אשלם יתהון". Cf. variants ad loc. The term "גמיר" stands at the basis of גמר/גמרא; see appendix 48.

difference. Ever since God handed Moses the tablets containing the Decalogue, the Law became the hyperspace where God's revelation unfolds. God communicates with Moses from *within* the "Ark of the Testimony" (see Ex. 25:22; Num. 7:89; cf. Ex. 31:18). Therefore, at Moab, God does not reveal His presence amidst thunder, lightning and turmoil as at Sinai, but from within the hyperspace of the Ark of the Covenant. As noted by R. Abraham ibn 'Ezra, in the "presence of God" (Deut. 29:9) actually means "around the Ark containing the tablets of the Law" (see his *Commentary* on Deut. 29:9). The *berit* at Moab, too, was formally accepted by the people. However, instead of manifesting their approval with the words "we shall do and we shall hear" (נעשה ונשמע), as at Sinai (Ex. 24:7), this time they replied: "The hidden," that is, transgressions committed in secret, are "for God our Lord," i.e., they are not our responsibility. "But what is evident," that is, public offenses, are "upon us and our children forever" (Deut. 29:28).[7] If there ever were a people that contracted a judicial and political system freely and without coercion, it was Israel at Sinai-Moab. The Tora is the fundamental Law of Israel, containing the 'precepts' (*miṣvot,* sing. *miṣva*) defining the rules of action and the institutions which have been sanctioned by the entire people in a solemn covenant before God.

The *berit* involves mutuality and consideration. At Sinai and Moab the people agreed, on their part, to follow a set of rules and regulations. God, on His part, will extend upon them His special care. Transgression of the terms of the national *berit* at Moab, as in all contracts, involves *sanctions* (Deut. 29:11) and *penalties* (Deut. 29:15–28), but not the *dissolution* of the covenant. In fact, God assured Israel that no matter what, He would redeem them and restore them to their land. To confirm this promise, God confirmed that He had "Promised in a solemn oath, to your fathers, to Abraham, to Isaac and to Jacob, to give to them the Holy Land" (Deut. 30:15–20; cf. Jer. 46:16). In the

7. See *Mekhilta de-R. Yishma'el, Ba-Ḥodesh,* V, p. 219. This is the basis for the doctrine establishing that matters of faith are not justiciable by the Jewish Court; see below chapter 11.

blessing pronounced by Moses before his death, he reminded the people of the Sinai-Moab covenant. First, he reminded them that God gave them the Tora at Sinai (Deut. 33:1–4). Then, he reminded them of the covenant contracted at Moab in the presence of the entire nation. At that supreme instant, a "king" was installed in Israel (Deut. 33:5). We have mentioned earlier that at Moab, God made His presence manifest from within the Ark of the Law. Therefore, as noted by R. Judah ha-Levi, the "king" installed by the people was none other than the Tora itself.[8] In this connection it is particularly illuminating to note that the place where the Tora is deposited at the Synagogue is called *Hekhal*, 'palace of residence of the sovereign.'[9] This term signals not only God's heavenly abode (see Hab. 2:20, Ps. 11:4, etc.) and His Temple in Jerusalem (see II Kings 24:13, Zech. 6:14, 15, etc; Mishna Pesaḥim 4:9, Yoma 3:10; etc.), but also the official residence of pagan monarchs (see II Kings 20:18; Dan. 4:26; 5:5; Ezra 5:14). By designating the place of the Tora *Hekhal*, every single Synagogue is in fact proclaiming that the Law *is* Israel's Supreme authority.

The Tora also defines Hebrew worship and devotion. Simply put, the God of Israel can be worshipped only as stipulated in the *berit*: Hebrew monotheism warrants *monolatry*. This means that devotion is to be expressed through the fulfillment of the *miṣvot* established at Sinai-Moab. In religion, the cult derives its power from some sort of a 'cosmic sacrality' that, as in magic, can manipulate and compel the deity. To the Hebrews, there is something profoundly irreverent in the notion that men can 'penetrate' the mind of God and determine the manner in which *it* ought to be worshipped.[10] Rather, the God of Israel is worshipped by following the precepts concluded at

---

8. Cited by R. Abraham ibn 'Ezra on Deut. 33:5. Cf. Quotation at Section III, n. 123.
9. See *MT Tefilla* 11:2; *Shulḥan 'Arukh, Oraḥ Ḥayyim*, CLIII, 2. Tyrants, old and new, too, believe this to be true. Hence, the effort to 'kill' the Tora, either by the sword (see the Talmudic story at Section III, n. 12,) or through theological blabber (see below chapter 29).
10. See *Homo Mysticus*, pp. 10–11.

Sinai-Moab. Hence, the close, intimate relationship between Hebrew monotheism and monolatry: the *one* God must be worshipped *only as it was established* in the covenant, i.e., through the fulfillment of the *miṣvot* (see appendix 4). Accordingly, the difference between pagan and Jewish devotion is huge. It was plainly explained by the Prophet Samuel. Defending himself for having disobeyed God's order to destroy the sheep and cattle of 'Amaleq, Saul argued that some of the beasts had been used for sacramental offerings (I Sam. 15:21). To which Samuel replied:

> Is it that God wishes burnt-offerings and sacrifices, or to comply with the voice of God? Behold, to comply is better than a sacrificial offering; to hearken [better than offering] the fat of a sheep. Because the sin of magic is defiance, and the evil of idolatry is compulsion (I Sam. 15:22–23; cf. Hos. 6:6).

Given that the purpose of ritual is compliance (rather than theological and or cultic compelling), details are of the essence. The purpose of halakha, or legal definition of a *miṣva,* is to spell out these details – otherwise it would be 'alien worship' – another human effort to manipulate the deity by doing what man deems 'good' (see appendix 11). To stress this fundamental doctrine, a blessing is pronounced before the performance of a ritual, ascertaining that God "has sanctified us with His *miṣvot* and prescribed us" to perform that particular ceremony. With Wittgenstein, this proposes that "Good is what God orders" – not the other way around.[11] Hence, the rabbinic norms invalidating a ritual performed by committing a sin (מצוה הבאה בעברה; see appendix 4).

In conclusion, the Tora is the final and complete written agreement of the Sinai-Moab covenant contracted by God and Israel. Once sealed, neither God nor the people may add, subtract, or introduce

11. Ludwig Wittgenstein, "Lecture on Ethics," *Philosophical Review* 74 (1965), p. 15.

modifications (Deut. 13:1).[12] It is *sui generis*: the first and last Constitution of its class (see appendix 10).

Outside the *berit*, the link with the divine is predicated on the logic of hierarchy: the inferior *must* submit to the will of the superior by the fiat that *ipso facto* an inferior *must* submit to the will of the superior. Pagan devotion sanctions not only hierarchic *violence* but also redemption through violence (see below Section III). In Israel, God is not obeyed by virtue of a prophetic oracle or a miracle (= proof of might), but because of a freely negotiated covenant. The Hebrew lexicon does not have a term for 'obedience.' Rather than 'obedience,' Judaism proposes' fulfillment' (קיום) – implying contractual responsibility (see appendix 4). According to this view, compliance to God's Law is the effect, not the cause, of the *berit*. Thus, pre-Sinaitic rituals, although coming from God, are not binding since they were not grounded on a national *berit*.[13] The miracles performed by Moses, too, are recognized because they were performed "before the eyes of *all* Israel" (Deut. 34:12), i.e., they were authenticated *by the people* – not *imposed* by some hierarchic authority. An accord or set of rules issued by a Rex, binding *his* subjects, but granting *de jure* or *de facto* immunity to some, is *not* a *berit*. Thus, the Law rejects the notion of 'Sovereign Immunity.' Rather, God Himself is bound to the *berit* that He contracted with Israel. Quoting a Greek proverb, "That the law is not written for the king," i.e., it is not binding, the rabbis taught:

> Ordinarily, when a human king issues a decree, if he chooses, he observes it, otherwise [only] others observe it; but when the Holy One, blessed be He, issues a decree, He is the first to observe it.[14]

---

12. See Megilla 2b; *MT Yesode ha-Tora* 8:2–3; 9:1–2.
13. Y. Mo'ed Qaṭan III, 8, 82c. See *Studies in the Mishne Tora*, p. 14 n. 5, and pp. 148-151. Cf *MT Ebel* 1:1.
14. Y. Rosh HaShana I, 3, 57b. The correct version is found in Louis Ginzberg ed., *The Talmud Yerushalmi Fragments of the Genizah* (New York: The Jewish Theo-

Since God Himself is bound to the *berit,* the *berit* is eternal. Neither God nor the people can abrogate it or introduce any additions to it. A deity that can dissolve a covenant, reinterpret it, or change one contracting party for another, is one more tyrant in the long history of tyranny – not the God who contracted the *berit* with Israel at Sinai-Moab. Members of other monotheistic religions *have* to believe. Jews *choose* (בחר) to be Jews. More precisely, they and God *choose* (בחר) to believe in each other. The Tora is the document attesting to the *berit,* or choosing, of God-Israel.

logical Seminary, 1909), p. 145. The correct interpretation of this passage was given by Saul Lieberman, "How Much Greek in Jewish Palestine?" in *Biblical and Other Studies* (Cambridge, Mass.: Harvard University Press, 1963), p. 128.

# Chapter 6
# Scripture and the Mental Law of Israel

The Jewish people possess a corpus of written literature, the Hebrew Scripture, known as 'Written Law' (תורה שבכתב). It comprises three different classes. The first and most authoritative is the Tora or Five Books of Moses. It is the 'Law,' more precisely, the 'Constitution' of Israel, and the source of all political, judiciary and ecclesiastic authority.[15] Next, we have the *Nebi'im* ('Prophets'), containing the books relating to the *political* history of Israel – from the conquest of Canaan until the fall (597 B.C.E.) and destruction (586 B.C.E.) of Jerusalem. This collection also contains the literature of the major prophets of Israel. In these writings God addresses the people; hence their 'prophetic' character. In the third class, known as *Ketubim* ('Hagiography'), man addresses God and his fellow men. Therefore, it represents the 'wisdom literature' of Israel. It also contains the chronology of the Jewish people, from their very beginning until their return to Israel after the first Exile (538 B.C.E.). The threefold division of Scripture is ancient. It was mentioned as early

15. For Philo's views on this matter, see Wolfson, *Philo*, vol. 2, pp. 374–395. For a modern perspective on this issue, see Jacob Neusner, "The Constitutions of Judaism in Ancient Times: The Pentateuch and the Mishna," *Journal of Reform Judaism* 36 (1989), pp. 55–63; and idem, *Understanding seeking Faith*, vol. 3 (Atlanta, Georgia: Scholars Press, 1988), pp. 145–162.

as the year 130 B.C.E. The Hebrew canon closed about the year 100.[16] Thereafter, no other writings would be admitted into this collection. The reason is *political.* The texts included in Scripture are *national* books. Publication of a Scriptural text requires *national* approval by a properly constituted political body (see below chapter 9). This is why, after the destruction of the Second Temple (68 C.E.) and subsequent loss of political power, the rabbis at Yabne 'closed' the Scripture. To ensure textual authenticity and forestall forgery, subsequent generations would append the *Masora* system to the published text of the Scripture (see appendix 3). Future works would be regarded as a surrogate for the spoken word, and be classified as 'expositions' (פירוש) of the Scripture, lacking textuological dimensions.[17]

The works included in the Scripture have a special status. By rabbinic decree, books contained in the Scripture defile the hands (see appendix 5). Therefore, they must be handled with care. Externally, these texts are to be wrapped within a special cover or case, designed to prevent defilement of the hands. In addition, they are to be read according to the rules of biblical prosody (טעמים). This type of reading was reserved for the works of the Scripture. In this regard, we should note the prohibition to read Christian and heretical texts in the mode of biblical prosody (טעמים), since this may be taken as evidence that they are part of Scripture.[18] Externally, the different status was signaled by the prohibition to place a copy of *Nebi'im* or *Ketubim* on top of the *Tora,* or a copy of *Ketubim* on top of *Nebi'im* (see appendix 6). In addition, it is required to stand up before the Scroll of the Tora and treat it with reverence.[19] Internally, they were distinguished by the fact that the Tora is to be read in public every Sabbath

16. See Roger T. Beckwith, "Formation of the Hebrew Bible," in ed. Martin Jan Mulder, *Mikra* (Philadelphia: Fortress Press, 1988), pp. 51–61. Cf. below, appendix 58.
17. See *Golden Doves,* pp. 132–133.
18. See José Faur, "Concerning the Term *Qore be-Iggeret*" (Heb.), *Alei Sefer* 15 (1988–89), pp. 21–30, and *Golden Doves,* p. 10.
19. See *MT Sefer Tora* 10:2–10.

morning by at least seven readers in a forum of no less than ten men, and three times a week (including Sabbath afternoon) by three readers. The *Nebi'im* are to be read publicly only on Sabbath morning, after the reading of the Tora has been completed. Although portions of the Psalms were incorporated in the liturgy, there is no obligation to publicly 'read' *Ketubim*, i.e., from a properly written scroll. In fact, a rabbinic legislation prohibited private readings of *Ketubim* on Sabbath afternoon at the time of the public homily.[20]

The most authoritative texts of the Oral Law are the Mishna and the Talmud. Principally, these works deal with matters pertaining to public and private law, known by the generic term of *halakha*, 'law'; they are authoritative and may be enforced by the judiciary (see below Section IV). The bulk of rabbinic exegeses of the Scripture were brought together in special collections known as *Midrashim* (singular *Midrash*). They are generally divided into *Midrash Halakha* or 'Legal Hermeneutics,' and *Midrash Aggada* 'Exegetical Hermeneutics.' The former contains exegeses that explicate the legal elements of Scripture. The *Mekhilta* (on Exodus), *Sifra* or *Torat Kohanim* (on Leviticus), and *Sifre* (on Numbers and Deuteronomy), are the most important collections of this type of Midrashim. There are numerous collections of *Midrash Aggada*. The best known are *Midrash Rabba* on the Pentateuch and "Five Scrolls" (Song of Songs, Ruth, Ecclesiastes, Lamentations, and Esther), and *Midrash Tanḥuma*.

These works were not officially published, and the materials they contain fall outside the perimeter of public right and the jurisdiction of the court (see below chapter 45).

The structure 'Written/Oral' Law, or *ketab/mikhtab*, concerns a principle of general linguistics. The processing of a written text or *ketab*-system is based on an *unwritten* frame of reference or *mikhtab*-system giving the written text meaning and textuological dimension. It follows a principle whereby writing – any kind of writing – involves

20. See Shabbat 116b; *MT Shabbat* 23:19. See Charles Perrot, "The Reading of the Bible in the Ancient Synagogue," in *Mikra*, pp. 127–159.

a mental, unwritten context. "My work consists of two parts," wrote Wittgenstein, "the one present here plus all that I have not written. And it is precisely this second part that is the important one."[21] Spanish-speaking Sepharadim designate the Oral Law, serving as the unwritten context of the Scripture, *Ley Mental*, or 'Mental Law.' The Mental Law is grounded on the linguistic apparatus giving psychological and epistemological cohesion to a speaking community, permitting certain syntactic connections and rejecting others. It is akin to Vico's *sensus communis*. Both, *sensus communis* and *Ley Mental* originate in a pre-linguistic (and therefore a pre-voluntary) state. Its judgments are primary. In the words of Vico, they form "judgment without reflection, shared by an entire class, an entire people, an entire nation, or the entire human race."[22] As with Vico's *sensus communis*, the Mental Law was not communicated verbally, but "taught to the nations by divine providence."[23] It is by virtue of its linguistic apparatus that a community processes speech and effects meaning, establishing certain syntactic connections and rejecting others. A free people – even when in abject condition – are the ultimate source of meaning, since they provide sense and connotation to the laws of the sovereign. In the words of Vico:

> In virtue of this [the people's] sovereignty over languages and letters, the free people must also be masters of their laws, for they impose on the laws the senses in which they constrain the powerful to observe them, even against their will.... It is naturally not in the power of monarchs to deprive the people of this sovereignty, but, in virtue of this very inalienable nature

21. Ludwig Wittgenstein, *Worterbuch fur Volkess Schulen* (Vienna: Holder-Picher-Tempsky, 1977), p. xvii.
22. *The New Science*, # 142, p. 63.
23. *The New Science*, #145, p. 63. For a lively, insightful discussion of this topic, see *Vico's Uncanny Humanism*, pp. 53–55. For our discussion, it is important to bear in mind that, as with the rabbinic *peshat*, Vico's *sensus communis* serves as the basis of order and authority; see ibid., pp. 138–140.

> of human civil affairs, such sovereignty, inseparable from the people, contributes largely to the power of the monarchs, for they may issue their royal laws, which the nobles must accept, according to the senses that their peoples give to them. This sovereignty over vulgar letters and languages implies that, in the order of civil nature, the free popular commonwealths preceded the monarchs (see appendix 7). [24]

Functioning as *mikhtab*, the Mental Law renders not only the interpretation of the Written Law, but also the canons by which the Israelites processed God's consonantal speech at Mount Sinai and ascribed meaning to it (see Section I). Without a prior Mental Law (= *mikhtab*), providing the textuological dimensions of writing, there is no text (= *ketab*).

The Mental Law cannot become a 'written text.' Otherwise it could no longer function as *mikhtab*/interpreter and it will become the object of 'exposition.' In simpler terms, a semiotic relationship prevails between the Mental Law/*mikhtab* as interpreter and the Written/*ketab* or interpreted system. The relationship cannot be reversed: the interpreter system cannot be interpreted in terms of the interpreted system. For example, the Morse and Braille systems are interpreted in terms of the alphabet, but the alphabet cannot be interpreted in terms of the Morse or Braille systems. Similarly, in modern science, we interpret physical and chemical phenomena in mathematical terms, but we cannot interpret mathematics in terms of physical and chemical phenomena.[25] The Mental Law, too, is a primary system, and cannot be understood in terms of the Written Law or any other system.[26]

It is this initial comprehension, and not the bare text barren from

24. *The New Science*, #936, p. 342.
25. See *Golden Doves*, pp. 111–112.
26. Accordingly, the Mental Law cannot be the object of hermeneutics; see *Golden Doves*, p. 88. Furthermore, as a primary system reflecting the intellectual apparatus of a people, it cannot be 'deduced' from a text. It must be known

sense, which is the constitutive of the Sinai-Moab *berit*. R. Johanan (ca. 180–ca. 279), one of the great sages of Israel, formulated this doctrine: "God did not contract a covenant with Israel, but an account of the oral words," that is, the Mental or Oral Law.[27] God's words, too, are conditioned to the linguistic apparatus of the people. Thus, the actual covenant is not the barren written text, pried from the linguistic apparatus of Israel, but as processed by, and recorded in, Israel's Mental Law. From this point of view, the question 'what does the text mean?' is inconsequential. What matters is 'how was the text processed' in the mind of Israel? This is the place to point out that popular wisdom notwithstanding, the purpose of interpretation in Judaism is not to 'discover' the mind of the author, as per analphabetic hermeneutics, but, as indicated by the Hebrew term *perush*, 'to unfold' and *generate* meaning in a forward direction (see below chapter 41). Underlying this theory is the principle that meaning is not determined by the first person. The speaker puts forward only the *ketab* of the utterance. Although its semantic perimeters are established by language and culture, its specific meaning is conditioned by the *mikhtab* process generated by the second person. Thus, the act of speech cannot take place unless the first person accepts the decoding system of the second person, and thereby the reciprocity principle (see above Section I). Hence, the rabbinic doctrine: "God had revealed two Toras to Israel, a written and an oral one."[28] The 'written,' expresses the mind of the first person, God, whereas the 'oral' expresses the mind of the second person: the people of the covenant. By positing that both the Written and the Oral Laws are equally divine, the rabbis upheld the horizontality of the covenant. This ascertains that God, the first party of the covenant, shall neither invade the *mind* of the second

through a special form of instruction, designated by Arabic speaking Jews as *talqin*. Without this special type of instruction, every reading is a misreading – a deviation from the Mental Law; see below chapter 43.

27. Giṭṭin 60b.
28. *Sifre* #351, p. 408. Cf. *Sifra*, ed. Isaac Hirsch Weiss (Vienna, 5622/1862), *Be-Ḥuqqotai* 2 (Lev. 26:46), 112c; Shabbat 31a; Berakhot 5a.

party, Israel, nor *dictate the meaning* of the covenant. It also upheld the principle that Israel shall provide the mental apparatus by which the terms of the covenant are processed and acquire meaning – exactly as with every linguistic communication.

The preceding leads to what may be properly described as breaking of the grid 'author/text.' It was enunciated by R. Joshua (1st and 2nd centuries), who declared that the "Tora is not within the realm of Heaven!" i.e., God cannot determine the interpretation of the Tora. A fundamental condition for rabbinic discourse, or *meliṣa,* is the exclusion of divine intervention (in the form of either supernatural oracles or miracles). To establish 'meaning,' authorial perspective must be excluded.[29] The same principle underlies every aesthetic experience. Only upon the dissolution of the grid 'author/text,' the conjunction 'reader/text' takes place and the "aesthetic fact" is realized. It is at this very moment, and not before, that the book is born (see above chapter 3).[30]

One of the objectives of publication is the dissolution of the grid 'text/author.' Another objective is the formal introduction of the text into the *ketab* system of Israel, thus rendering it qualified for 'exposition' by the *mikhtab* system of the people.

---

29. Baba Meṣi'a 59b; cf. *Golden Doves,* pp. 13–14, 119. Cf. above, Section I, n. 8. A similar argument was proposed by Hobbes to justify why it would be improper to acknowledge any prophecy that would contradict Christian Scripture and tradition, see *Leviathan* XXXII, p. 414 [198].
30. See *Borges, Oral* (Buenos Aires: Emecé Editores, 1979), p. 66.

# Chapter 7
# The Publication of Scripture

A book is much more than a document deposited in a royal archive. The rabbis relate that the story of Purim was "written (כתובה) and deposited (ומנחה, root NWḤ) in the Chronicles of the Kings of Mede and Persia." And yet, Queen Esther requested from the Jewish authorities that it be "written in a book"[31] (כתבוני על ספר). Why? A document deposited in a royal archive is unavailable to the public. In Hebrew, 'depositing' is connected to the root NWḤ (see appendix 6), 'placing an object ceremoniously' in a sacred precinct, *away* from the general public; precisely as with the document containing the laws regulating the monarchy written by Samuel, and subsequently "deposited" (וינח, root NWḤ) in a holy precinct, "before the Lord" (I Sam. 10:25). Since it was not intended for circulation, it was eventually lost, like similar writings deposited in the royal archives of Israel. By contrast, a 'book' (ספר) is designed for circulation. That is why, although Queen Esther's story had been already "written and deposited" (כתובה ומנחה, root NWḤ) in the royal "archives," she requested that it "be written in a book" (ספר), i.e. "to be recorded for future generations."[32]

The terms used for the publication of a written document are

---

31. Megilla 7a, this is the correct version; see *Diqduqe Soferim,* ad loc., the printed text is faulty. On the archival system of the ancient Near East, see N. Schneider, "Die Unkundenbehalter von Ur III und die archivalische Systematik," *Orientalia* N.S. 9 (1940), pp. 1–28.
32. Megilla 7a, see *Diqduqe Soferim,* ad loc., the printed text is faulty; cf. below nn. 60, 86.

connected to the root NTN (for the publication of oral texts see below chapter 43). Primarily, this root conveys 'giving,' 'presenting,' and 'bestowing.'[33] In Scripture and rabbinic literature, terms stemming from this root are used for the 'promulgation' of either a civil law,[34] or divine precepts.[35] In the function of 'publication,' to 'present' (נתן) involves a *dynamic* process of 'presenting/accepting'[36] (נתן/ קיבל). Within this context, 'acceptance' is not to passively acknowledge certain duties, but to *study* the text in question. (To an analphabetic public, 'acceptance' of a text is meaningless – the equivalent of a blind man 'looking' at a painting.) This is why the presentation of the proposal of the Covenant, as well as acceptance of the Tora at the Theophany in Sinai, included the resolution "we shall do and we shall hear (ונשמע)" (Ex. 19:8, 24:7), which in Hebrew means also 'understanding' and 'compliance.'[37] Addressing himself to the blessing declaring "that God presented (נתן) the Tora to us," Maimonides explained: "the implicit meaning [of נתן] is our duty to study it [the Tora]; this is what was intended by declaring that [God] had presented [נתן, the Tora] to us."[38] A similar term, ניתנה (root NTN) is used in reference to the 'publication' of the Tora.[39] When elucidating R. Joshua's doctrine that the Tora is no longer in Heaven, R. Jeremiah (4th century) explained that since the Tora had "already been presented (נתנה) at Mount Sinai," God could no longer dictate its mean-

---

33. In rabbinic literature it is used also for 'defining' or establishing a 'measurement,' see Shabbat 35b and parallels; 'Erubin 23b; Baba Batra 75b etc.; or to establish a 'standard,' see, for instance Yoma 35b; Sukka 5a; Mo'ed Qaṭan 3b; Sanhedrin 76b; Keritot 27a, Ḥolin 32a, etc.
34. See Est. 3:14; 8:13; cf. 9:14.
35. See Eccl. 12:11 and Ḥagiga 3b; Shabbat 154a and parallels; Yebamot 71b; Makkot 13b, etc.
36. Cf. Ta'aniyot 25a; Giṭṭin 14b; and therefore 'consent,' see Qiddushin 12b–13a.
37. See Shabbat 88a-b; *Golden Doves*, p. 12.
38. Maimonides, *Teshubot ha-Rambam*, #182, vol. 2, p. 333. Cf. Baba Batra 11b.
39. As with the tablets of the Law given by God to Moses (Ex. 31:18; Deut. 9:11; 10:4); cf. Berakhot 62a; Shabbat 87a; Yoma 4a, etc.

ing.[40] This doctrine establishes the separation of powers between the primary legislator, God, and the judiciary in charge of interpreting and adjudicating the terms of the *berit* (see below chapter 18).

The publication of a Book is executed in three steps. First, is the presentation of the text (נתן) by the author to the authorities. The purpose is to formally break the grid 'author/text.' This is germane to rabbinic hermeneutics according to which the purpose of interpretation is not to discover 'authorial intention' but *to generate* meaning from the published text (see below chapter 8). Applying this principle to the Scripture, this means that since the Tora has been 'published,'[41] it no longer remains within the domain of Heaven. Consequently, it shall be interpreted according to the mental apparatus of the second person, Israel. The next two steps are linked to the Hebrew sense of 'to present' (נתן). Essential to it is the object of the verb denoting 'frontal acceptance' (קבלה, see appendix 32). In the context of a national publication, it implies the responsibility of both guarding and conveying (מסירה) the text of the Tora and its interpretations to future generations, in perpetuity (see appendix 12). Moses, taught the rabbis, "accepted (קיבל) the Tora" from God "at Sinai" and then conveyed it (ומסרה) to subsequent authorities (Abot 1:1, see chapter 8).[42]

The rabbis designate the Theophany at Sinai as 'the presentation' (מתן, root NTN, in the infinitive) of the Tora, which comprises both God's 'bestowing' (מתן), and Israel's 'accepting' the Tora (קבלת התורה).[43] The latter involves two distinct responsibilities: guarding the text, and transmitting its meaning and accumulated interpretations

40. Baba Meṣi'a 59b.
41. See Berakhot 63b; Shabbat 86b; Beṣa 25b; Baba Batra 110b; Sanhedrin 21b, 22a; Menaḥot 99b; Zebaḥim 116a, etc.
42. On the semantic proximity of נתן to מסר, see Shabbat 89a.
43. Berakhot 58a; Pesaḥim 118a; Sukka 13a; 'Aboda Zara 19a, 24a; Zebaḥim 116a; etc. This is a nuanced term, with highly technical connotations. It can refer to the 'ritual placing' of the sacramental blood on the altar; see 'Erubin 100a; Makkot 19a; Zebaḥim 6b, 11a, 37a, etc. It can also refer to the money that the groom presents as part of the wedding agreement, requiring formal 'acceptance' and 'consent' on the part of the bride; see Qiddushin 12b-13a. It is also used

to the next generation. The publication of the text of the Tora was made by Moses shortly before his death. It consisted of [i] presenting the Scroll of the Tora (ויתנה, root NTN), [ii] to the priests, [iii] in the presence of the elders (Deut. 31:9). Subsequently, the Scroll was placed next to the Ark (Deut. 31:26).[44]

The responsibilities of the priests and the elders differed. The priests were charged with the supervision of the *ketab* or text of the Tora, while the elders were charged with the supervision of the *mikhtab*, or *interpretations*. Among the responsibilities of the priests was to oversee the text of the Scroll of the Tora,[45] to be carried out by the Jewish monarch (Deut. 17:19) as "an ensign of sovereignty."[46] On their part, the elders – not the priests – had the responsibility of having the king read the Tora and impart its meaning to the entire nation. This ceremony was a national event performed in the Temple at the end of the Sabbatical year. Immediately after delivering the Tora to the priests, Moses charged "all the elders of Israel" with the task of having the king read "this Tora." In addition to its proper reading, the king had to convey its meaning "into their ears of all Israel" – including women, children, and proselytes. In this fashion, the Theophany at Sinai was renewed in perpetuity (Deut. 31:10–13; cf. II Chr. 34:30–33 and *MT Ḥagiga* 3:6). Similarly, after publishing the Tora, God told Moses "to write down this song," which the rabbis interpret as an allusion to the Tora, and to "put it in their mouths"

---

for money 'given' as part of a contractual obligation; see Baba Meṣi'a 66a; Baba Batra 176b, etc. Finally, it can stand for 'reward' for the fulfillment of the precepts; see Shabbat 87a, 'Erubin 21a, Beṣa 16a, etc. Cf. appendix 4.

44. See *Hellenism in Jewish Palestine*, p. 86.

45. This is what Josephus, *Against Apion*, I, 29, vol. 1, p. 175, had in mind when he wrote that the priests and prophets are the custodians in charge of keeping the records of Israel, which "were preserved with scrupulous accuracy."

46. Philo, *The Special Laws*, IV, 164, p. 111. See ibid., 160, p. 109 where Philo correctly explained that this involves writing a "summary" of the Law. The standard interpretation 'the *Book of Deuteronomy*' is incorrect; see *Golden Doves*, pp. 52–54; cf. however Wolfson, *Philo*, vol. 2, p. 384.

(Deut. 31:19, cf. 22).[47] The interpretation of the Tora, Moses conveyed (מסירה) to Joshua, the political head of Israel, who in turn conveyed it to the elders, etc. (see chapter 41).

Authorized copies of the Tora were made and kept at the Temple's library.[48] As a legal instrument, the publication of the Tora involves the responsibility of safeguarding it from blunders, forgeries, and interpolations. A primary responsibility of the authorities was the establishment of national libraries where official copies of the text were kept and made available for authorized reproductions. Upon returning to the Holy Land from Exile, Nehemiah (5th century B.C.E.) founded a national library to house the texts of Israel and make them available for authorized reproductions. Judas the Maccabee followed his example.

> [Nehemiah] founded a library and collected the books about the kings and the prophets, and the books of David, and letters of the kings about sacred gifts. Even so did Judas collect for us all the writings which had been scattered owing to the outbreak of war. They are with us. So, if you need them, send some messengers to fetch them for you. (II Maccabees 2:13–15)

With this purpose in mind, the text of the Tora was safeguarded in a sacred place, first at the Temple (cf. II Chr. 34:14–33) and national libraries, and later on in the Synagogue.[49] Every Jewish community kept authorized copies to serve as the authorized text of Scripture. Throughout the ages, Oriental and Old Sephardic communities kept in the Synagogue's archive (standing in place of the Temple) certified copies of the Scripture, known by the Arabic term *taj* ('crown'), from

47. See *Golden Doves,* p. xxvi.
48. See "Formation of the Hebrew Bible," pp. 40–45.
49. See *Hellenism in Jewish Palestine,* pp. 85–86, 200. On the scroll at the Temple, see *Midrash ha-Gadol, Deuteronomy,* ed. S. Fisch (Jerusalem: Mossad Harav Kook, 1972), p. 5. The purpose was to guard against tampering and falsification; see R. David Pardo, *Sifre Debe Rab* (Salonika, 5559/1799), 234a.

which authorized reproductions of the text were made, and Scrolls were checked for possible blunders.[50] Special attention should be drawn to two regulations concerning authorized copies. First, "it is prohibited to write even a single letter not from a written copy,"[51] i.e., from an *authorized* copy. Second, and as a consequence of the first, a properly executed copy of the Tora has the same status as the original text published by Moses. Thus, a Scroll of the Tora must be treated with special deference, since "the very words that are in the Tablets of the Covenant, are in every Scroll [of the Tora]."[52]

In its own way each generation of Jews accepts the accumulated learning that the elders and sages conveyed to them so that in turn they will convey it to the next, in perpetuity.[53] This is the place to note that the duty to "study" and "teach" Tora to one's children includes two distinct obligations: to have the child know how to *read* proficiently the *text* of "the entire Written Law," and know its "interpretation."[54] By accepting the responsibility of safekeeping the text of the Tora and its meaning, Israel not only became 'the people

---

50. See *MT Sefer Tora* 8:4; and *Perush ha-Mishnayot*, vol. 1, pp. 3–4, where it is said that Moses gave a copy of the Scroll of the Tora to each tribe ליקתצ'י בהא "to be regulated by it"; that is, to control future copies of the Tora.
51. *MT Sefer Tora* 1:12. For the source of this law, see Megilla 18b, particularly Yerushalmi Megilla IV, 1, 74d. The correct text is found in *Midrash Daniel wu-Midrash 'Ezra*, p. 150.
52. *MT Sefer Tora* 10:9; cf. ibid. 10:11. According to tradition, the Scroll found at the Temple in the time of King Josiah (II Kings 22:8) was the Tora written by Moses; see R. Joshua ibn Shu'eb, *Derashot 'al ha-Tora* (Constantinople, 5283/1523), *Ḥayye Sara*, at the beginning.
53. See *Golden Doves*, pp. xxv-xxvi, 13–14.
54. *MT Talmud Tora* 1:7, 12. The curriculum includes proper reading of *all* the Scripture, including the *qabbala*, see ibid. 1:12; which includes the Prophets, see Mishna Ta'aniyot 2:1; and Hagiography, see Tosefta Kippurim 2:4, p. 231; 2:15, p. 238; and Nidda 25a. In Rabbinic Hebrew, 'reading' includes proper Hebrew diction and prosody; see "Concerning the Term *Qore be-Iggeret*," pp. 21–30. This is not an easy task, cf. R. Abraham ibn 'Ezra, *Yesod Mora ve-Sod Tora*, eds. Joseph Cohen and Uriel Simon (Ramat-Gan: Bar-Ilan University Press, 2002), pp. 74–75, and editor's note on l. 72. Cf. appendix 58.

of the Book,' i.e., the people guarding the Book, but also the people guarded by the Book. Hence the unique reverence professed by the Jews for both the text and the teachings of the Tora. As attested by Josephus:

> We have given practical proof of our reverence for our own Scriptures. For, although such long ages have now passed, no one has ventured either to add, or to remove, or to alter a syllable; and it is an instinct with every Jew, from the day of his birth, to regard them as the decrees of God, to abide by them, and, if need be, cheerfully to die for them. Time and again ere now the sight has been witnessed of [Jewish] prisoners enduring tortures and death in every form in the [Roman] theaters, rather than utter a single word against the laws and the allied documents.[55]

Historians neglect to assess the function of publication in Jewish tradition. According to the doctrine that to be legitimate, 'Jewish history' needs to have been first regurgitated by non-Jews, attention was focused on the 'canonization' of the Hebrew Scripture – a non-operational idea for which Hebrew has neither a term, nor a definition, nor a tradition, nor a ceremony.[56] Consequently, it is generally assumed that 'sacred writings' are texts believed to have been "written by prophets, that is, by men who had the Holy Spirit."[57] The assumption is incorrect. Although Jews believed that their books were inspired by the Holy Spirit, not all texts inspired by the Holy Spirit

55. *Against Apion*, I, 42, vol. 1, pp. 179–181.
56. See Sid Z. Leiman, *The Canonization of Hebrew Scripture* (New Haven: The Connecticut Academy of Art and Sciences, 1991).
57. *Judaism*, vol. 1, p. 238. Bereft of Jewish learning and lacking a genuine understanding of Western culture and tradition, pseudo-Jewish intellectuals meekly mimic Christian tradition; see for example, Rimon Kasher, "The Interpretation of Scripture in Rabbinic Literature," *Mikra*, pp. 548–549.

form part of Scripture.[58] Let us note, at the outset, that the 'holiness' of a text is the result, not the cause, of its publication. Concerning the Book of Esther, R. Joshua ben Levi taught: "The earthly Court effected it and the Heavenly Court approved their decision." Put in different words, "They certified above [in Heaven] what they [the authorities] have concluded below"[59] – not the other way around![60]

To be inducted into the National Library of Israel, a text must be published by *the national authorities of Israel,* like the Scroll of the Tora which Moses "presented to the priests the sons of Levi, and to all the elders of Israel" (Deut. 31:9). The national authorities have a three-fold responsibility. First, they must determine that the proposed work was divinely inspired. Second, they must investigate whether the alleged author could have written such a work (and did not plagiarize it). Finally, there is a need for a *national* commitment to preserve the text and convey it together with the accumulated interpretations developed around it, like the priests and elders of Israel. This is how R. Se'adya Gaon (882–942) described the publication of the Sacred Books of Israel:

> There are three basic fundamentals to [the publication of] Prophetic Writings. One of them is allusion to prophecy, e.g., "And God said..." or the teaching of some [previously] unknown matter [thereby indicating divine inspiration], as with Proverbs, Ecclesiastes, and Esther.[61] The second is proof that the [alleged] author of the book is in fact a prophet [and

58. See Tosefta Yadayim 2:14, p. 683; Megilla 7a; Y. Megilla I, 1, 70a and the explanation in *Golden Doves,* pp. 105–106. The expression 'Holy Spirit' is a mistranslation of 'Spirit from the Holy,' i.e., from the 'Holy Precinct' or Temple in Jerusalem; see below n. 70.
59. Makkot 23b.
60. See *Golden Doves,* pp. 108–110. We have seen that a text although 'placed' (מנחא) in the royal archives is not yet a book; see Megilla 7a and above n. 32. There is a misprint in Y. Megilla I, 7, 70d; 'בארכיים' should read: בארכיונים, "written in the archives... of the kings of Persia and Mede."
61. Cf. Megilla 7a: "*Tanya* R. Eli'ezer says..." and the subsequent discussion.

> has not plagiarized someone else's work] .... The third is that the Nation admits that book [as part of] the Sacred Books, and conveys it authoritatively. If [all] these three [conditions] are not met, but one was omitted,[62] that book is not a prophetic book.[63]

The Hebrew idea of publication reflects the special relationship 'people/Book.' As indicated earlier, implicit in the verb 'to present' (נתן) is the idea of 'conveying' (מסירה) – a technical term indicating the delivery of a bill or document to the Court, empowering the Court to interpret it and execute it.[64] "The Tora that Moses conveyed" was given with the title of "legacy" (מורשה, see appendix 12) to "the community of Jacob" (Deut. 33:4); meaning – as accurately rendered in the *Targum* – that Moses "conveyed it in perpetuity" to the community of Israel.[65] Israel's right to apply *derasha* to the Tora is a consequence of having been the duly appointed recipient of such conveyance (מסירה). Only texts "published to be written" (ניתנו [root NTN] להיכתב),[66] that is, duly published with certified copies accessible to the public, may be the subject of 'interpretation' (ניתן [root

62. In the original Arabic there was a *shadda*. The editor (ibid. n. 3) detected a stroke on top of the word, which he interpreted as a mark to indicate that the word should be deleted. Consequently, he skipped it. His translation: "If these three are not met but only one," does not cohere. Rather, the stroke stands for a *shadda* on top of the last consonant as per our translation.
63. *Sefer ha-Galui*, in *Zikhron la-Rishonim*, vol. 5, ed. Abraham E. Harkavi (St. Petersburg, 1892), p. 163.
64. See *Golden Doves*, p. 88. This term stands also for an 'oral deposition' given before an officer of the court.
65. This term is conceptually akin to 'fee tail estate' in English law, see appendix 13. The Aramaic translation of 'מורשה' as 'מסרה ירותא' is conceptual rather than lexical. (Obviously, one cannot receive in 'inheritance' a constitution or a set of values!) The rabbinic doctrine that "Moses received (קיבל) the Tora at Sinai, and then מסרה to Joshua" (Abot 1:1), is lexically and thematically linked to this *Targum*. The other times in Scripture in which this term appears (Ex. 6:8 and Ezek. 36:3; cf. Mic. 1:14) is rendered by the *Targum* as plain 'inheritance.'
66. About these types of documents, see *Golden Doves*, pp. 103, 107, 133, 189.

NTN] להידרש). Other writings, although containing valuable data, e.g., the Book of Ecclesiasticus, may not be the object of *derasha* since they were not formally published.[67] In a similar vein, to become an instrument of the court, a deed (or deposition) must be duly "conveyed" (מסירה) to the judicial authorities. It is through the act of conveyance that it acquires the status of a "published text, and may be subsequently expounded" (ניתן [root NTN] להידרש), i.e., it can be duly interpreted and executed by the judiciary.[68] In this respect, 'exposition' of Scripture parallels that of a court's interpretation of legal documentation submitted to it. Since the Scripture was 'conveyed in perpetual deposition' to Israel alone, Israel alone has the authority to expound and execute it.[69]

Finally, the expression *Kitbe ha-Qodesh* used in rabbinic literature to designate 'Scripture,' does not mean 'Sacred Writings,' but 'Writings at the *Qodesh*' or 'Sacred Precinct,' i.e., the Temple. *Qodesh* is a noun, not to be confused with the adjective *qadosh*.[70] Similarly, *Kitbe ha-Qodesh* stands for the "Books at or from the *Qodesh*," i.e., properly published books that were originally deposited at the Temple's library, and their authorized copies.

In short, these and only these books, form part of the *ketab*-system of Israel. As we will see in the following chapter, not all Jewish texts form part of this system and can be the object of *derasha*.

---

67. See *Golden Doves*, pp. 100–110; "Concerning the Term *Qore be-Iggeret*," pp. 21–30.
68. See *Golden Doves*, pp. xxv, 109, 123–124.
69. See *Golden Doves*, pp. 2, 13, 119–120.
70. Similarly, לשון הקודש does not mean 'sacred' language but, as per its Aramaic translation, לישנא דבי קודשא, 'the language spoken at the Temple'; see below n. 96. The same is the case with רוח הקודש. It does not mean 'Holy Spirit' but a 'Spirit [coming from] the *Qodesh*,' i.e., the Temple.' see *Homo Mysticus*, p. 201, and appendix 58.

# Chapter 8
# Epistles and Memoranda

Not all nationally published texts have the status of 'Book' (ספר). To gain an adequate grasp of the subtleties of publication it would be necessary to consider some of the issues surrounding the publication of Esther. Its status was debated in Talmudic times and later on throughout the Middle Ages.[71] A close reading of the rabbinic sources shows that the basis for including Esther in the Scriptures was a verse stating that it had been "certified" (קימו) and then "accepted" (וקבל[ו] Est. 9:27). The two great Talmudic masters of Babylonia, Rab and Samuel (2nd and 3rd centuries), disputed whether it had been "certified" by the official authorities or only by Heaven. 'Certification' is a technical term referring to a judicial process whereby recognition is extended to a document submitted to the court[72] (קיום שטרות). Samuel maintained that "certification" of Esther was made in Heaven, but not by the official authorities. In his view, the people had only "accepted" the text, but it had not been certified as a 'book' (ספר). In Samuel's words: "They certified above [in Heaven] what was [only] accepted below" by the people. Rab disagreed. Following the sequence of the words "certified" (קימו) and then "accepted" (וקבל[ו]), he maintained that it was *first* "certified" by the people (hence the plural), and *then* it was "approved" (הסכים) in Heaven.[73] Pointing out the defective spelling of וקבל[ו] in the singular, Rab

71. See "Concerning the Term *Qore be-Iggeret*," pp. 24–26.
72. See *Golden Doves*, pp. 107, 143.
73. Megilla 7a.

remarked: "it is spelled וקבל [in the singular]: it was the Lord of the Jews (i.e. God) who approved it!" – i.e. after it had been certified by the earthly authorities (hence: *qiyyemu*, in the plural).[74] Rab reflected the view that the Book of Esther "was from Sinai,"[75] i.e., that it had been officially published and given the status of a 'book' (ספר). Therefore, he maintained that Esther ניתנה [root NTN] להידרש ('it may be the object of *derasha*').[76] Both arguments are circular. As we shall see shortly, Rab assumed that Esther had been published with all the textuological dimensions of a 'Book' (ספר). Therefore, he proposed a *derasha* on the basis of the defective and full spelling of the written text. On the other hand, Samuel believed that Esther was published only as an 'epistle' (אגרת), not a book, and therefore one cannot build an argument on the basis of the written text.

Before embarking on an analysis of Samuel's thesis, we must dispose of some preliminary considerations. Samuel, too, recognized the obligation to read Esther on the feast of Purim, and that it had been divinely inspired.[77] Nonetheless, he maintained that since it had been published as an 'epistle' and not as a 'book,' it could not be the object of *derasha*. In the course of discussing Samuel's view, the Talmud examined the following argument:

> Said R. Judah, said Samuel: – [The scroll of] Esther does not defile the hands [i.e., it is not part of Scripture, see appendix 5].
> – Shall we then assume that Samuel maintains that [the scroll of] Esther was not pronounced by the Holy Spirit? But Samuel had said: "[the scroll of] Esther was pronounced by the Holy Spirit!
> – It was pronounced for reading, but it was not pronounced for writing (נאמרה לקרות ולא נאמרה להיכתב).[78]

74. Ruth Rabba IV, 5 (33d).
75. Y. Megilla I, 7, 70d. See appendix 33.
76. Y. Megilla I, 1, 70a; cf. *Golden Doves*, pp. 103–108.
77. See *Golden Doves*, p. 104.
78. Megilla 7a.

Within this context, נאמרה 'to pronounce,' means 'to publish' – a reference to the practice whereby the author publishes the text by *reciting* it to a scribe (see Jer. 36:4 and appendix 8). Therefore, although divinely inspired, since the text of Esther "was pronounced" for reading purposes and not for writing (נאמרה לקרות ולא נאמרה להיכתב), it lacks the textuological dimension of a book. This was the position of the Academy of Nehar De'a where Samuel presided: Esther is not a "book" (ספר) but an "epistle"[79] (אגרת). One of the implications of this thesis is that Esther cannot be the object of *derasha.* The legal model for Samuel's thesis is to be found in the chancelleries of Ancient Persia.

The writing of memoranda (Hebrew זכרון, Aramaic ,דוכרן ,דוכרניא זכרן, etc.) was common in antiquity. A number of business memoranda from the fifth century B.C.E. from Persia were found and published.[80] When Prophet Malachi wanted to teach that even casual conversations of the righteous are precious in the eyes of God, he said that "God takes note and listens, and it is written before Him [in] a memorandum-book (ספר זכרון, *Targum*: דוכרניא)" – a royal record containing the memoranda of outstanding events (Mal. 3:16). Similarly, when Mordechai alerted King Ahasuerus of a plot against his life, the deed was recorded "in the book of times-past, which is before the king" (Est. 2:23, 6:1; *Targum,* ad loc., and *Targum Sheni,* 22b, 25a: דוכרניא). Memoranda were written in a concise style, and the details and eventual outcome were left to the memory of the archivists (see Est. 6:1–3).[81] In Persian chancelleries, official memoranda were recorded and filed under their own particular headings, and then arranged either chronologically or according to subject matter. They were designated by the Aramaic term *dikhrona,* 'memorandum,' paralleling the Greek *hypomnematismos,* and recorded in scrolls (see

---

79. See "Concerning the Term *Qore be-Iggeret,*" pp. 25–26.
80. See, for instance, A. Cowley, *Aramaic Papyri of the Fifth Century B.C.* (Oxford: Clarendon Press, 1932), pp. 123 (ll. 1, 2), 164 (l. 1), 165 (l. 10), 166 (l. 4), 167 (1l. lo, 12, 14), 176 (no. 11). The rabbis refer to this type of memoranda as דוכרן פיתגמי; see Baba Batra 136a and Sanhedrin 29b.
81. As a kind of *perush* or 'oral tradition.'

Ezra 6:2).[82] Official memoranda were not available to the general public. To ensure confidentiality they were sent in epistles (*iggera, iggerta,* see Ezra 4:8, 11; 5:6; 6:2; Neh. 2:7–9; 6:5,19) rolled as scrolls (Ezra 6:2).[83] Government decisions that had to be made known to the public were delivered *orally* by heralds reciting from written "epistles" (*iggeret,* see II Chr. 30:6).[84] Copies of the epistles were not available to the public. This meant, in rabbinic terminology, that the text "was pronounced for reading purposes but it was not pronounced for writing" (נאמרה לקרות ולא נאמרה להיכתב). Samuel and the members of his Academy maintained that Esther was published as an *iggeret* (see Est. 9:29), not a book. Following the model of Persian chancelleries, Samuel proposed that Esther was published as an *iggeret*: not "for writing" – as a text which could be reproduced from authorized copies – but only for "reading" purposes, as the official epistles read by heralds. To highlight the fact that Esther is an epistle rather than a book, the communities that followed Samuel's view recited Esther in the style of heralds: [i] *without* the traditional cantillation used for reading a *sefer*; [ii] and by *unfolding* the scroll *before* it was read, as it was habitually done by heralds.[85]

Samuel's view is connected to R. Joshua who maintained that Esther has the status of a 'memorandum' (זכרון, cf. Mal. 3:16) – the

82. On this type of documentation, see the illuminating discussion of Elias Bickerman, "The Edict of Cyrus in Ezra 1," in *Studies in Jewish and Christian History,* vol. 1 (Leiden: E. J. Brill, 1976), pp. 72–76.

83. Although occasionally it was sent as "an opened epistle" for propaganda purposes, see Neh. 6:5. In Aramaic, *iggeret* may indicate the material containing the text, or just the text, or both; cf. *Midrash Daniel wu-Midrash 'Ezra,* p. 118.

84. On the oral proclamations by heralds, see "The Edict of Cyrus in Ezra 1," *Studies in Jewish and Christian History,* vol. 1, pp. 74–76.

85. The present status of the Scroll of Esther is a compromise between *iggeret* and *sefer*; see *Halakhot Gedolot,* ed. Ezriel Hildesheimer, vol. 1 (Jerusalem: Mekize Nirdamim, 1971), Megilla, p. 406–407; and "Concerning the Term *Qore be-Iggeret,*" p. 26. For example, according to Maimonides, the *text* of Esther has the status of a 'book' (ספר), see *MT Megilla* 2:9, 11. However, the *reading* is to be conducted as that of an *iggeret*; cf. *MT Megilla* 2:7, 12.

Hebrew equivalent of the Aramaic *dikhrona* – not of a 'book!'[86] R. Joshua arrived at this view by associating the Hebrew term *zikkaron* (*Targum*: *dukhrana*) that Moses requested to be placed "in the *ears* of Joshua," (Ex. 17:14) with Esther. Moses did not request that the entire text of the order should be conveyed to Joshua, but, only a *zikkaron* of it (ושים, not ושימו! cf. Deut. 31:19) should be transmitted to him *orally*.[87] The *Targum* clarified this point by rendering *zikkaron* as *dukhrana* – a dialectical variation of *dikhrona*. Literally understood, it meant that Moses had ordered that the memorandum should be filed as a diplomatic document, and only the gist should be conveyed *orally*; hence: "in the *ears* of Joshua."[88] Accordingly, Samuel proposed that the Book of Esther, too, was a kind of memorandum following the model prescribed by Moses.

The rabbinic disagreement about Esther concerned historical facts: was it certified by the proper authorities? If so: was it certified as a written document or as a memorandum, for reading purposes only? Consequently: could it serve as the basis of *derasha*? There was no disagreement, however, on the principle itself: only a duly published text, available to the general public, may be included in the Scripture and used for *derasha*. For the purpose of the present discussion it is important to take note that according to the rabbis, the book of Chronicles was published for *derasha* purposes alone.[89]

86. See Megilla 7a. The printed text is corrupt, see *Diqduqe Soferim* ad loc., and *Golden Doves*, pp. 108–109.
87. This *zikkaron* is recorded in the second half of the verse, "that God will blot out the memory of 'Amaleq."
88. Pointedly, R. Se'adya Gaon translates ושים as "ואתלה," that is "to recite it"; cf. his translation of Ex. 19:7, 21:1 and Deut. 31:19.
89. Vayyiqra Rabba I, 3, ed. Mordecai Margulies (Jerusalem: American Academy for Jewish Research, 1960), 5 vols., vol. 1, pp. 7–8; see editor's note, and the discussion in *Iyye ha-Yam*, 99b-100a.

# Chapter 9
# Interpreting the Books of Israel

Conceptually, *derasha* is the application of the *mikhtab,* or synchronic axis of the linguistic community, to its *ketab,* or diachronic axis. We have seen in the preceding chapter that not all published texts have the status of 'Book' (ספר), and could be the object of *derasha.* Rabbinic tradition recognizes two modes of textual interpretation: *derasha,* 'exposition,' and *peshaṭ* or 'manifest tenor,' i.e., the 'commonly accepted' sense of Scripture (see appendix 28). The oldest expression for 'a commonly agreed interpretation' is "something which the Sadducees concur" [with the Pharisees], that is, a consensus understanding of Scripture.[90] *Peshaṭ* is a universal concept. It corresponds to the *sensus communis,* shaping the logical and psychological factors binding the collective mind of a linguistic community. Thus, whereas *peshaṭ* conveys the consensus understanding of the text, *derasha* proposes an interpretation transcending the conventional meaning. The semantic boundaries of *peshaṭ* and *derasha* are determined by the linguistic community – some interpretations represent 'general consensus,' whereas others are idiosyncratic. Structurally, *derasha* and *peshaṭ* define themselves in terms of paradigmatic

90. Sanhedrin 33b; Horayot 4a, 4b. According to Maimonides, the legislation agreed upon by the Sadducees and Pharisees was not grounded on the actual literal sense of the Scripture, but on a *derasha;* see *MT Sanhedrin* 10:9 and cf. pseudo-R. Ḥanan'el on Horayot 5b.

opposition to each other: without *derasha* there is no *peshaṭ,* and vice versa. In fact, the very idea of 'exegesis' implies a '*peshaṭ*-sense' accepted by the linguistic community.[91]

*Derasha* and *peshaṭ* correspond to two types of perceptual processes. At one level of consciousness, the processing of data is conditioned by the cultural, psychological, and linguistic factors determining the sense of 'reality' of the linguistic community. The result is the kind of 'absolute experience' transcending analysis and interpretation.[92] From this perspective, 'perception' is a (special) type of 'reading' of a (special) 'text' by a process shared by the entire community.[93] At both the literary and perceptual levels, the process unfolds without a deliberate methodology. By contrast, there are creative and critical methods of interpretation, usually acquired through instruction, whereby a set of data is processed differently, involving a subcode accessible only to a segment of the linguistic community. The tension *derasha/peshaṭ* is somehow analogous to the tension marking individual and collective views. A similar phenomenon takes place in the fields of art, science, etc. The tension subsides when the community assimilates that idiosyncratic view into its linguistic apparatus. Accordingly, *peshaṭ* evolves from *derasha*. This is evident from the

91. See "Basic Concepts in Rabbinic Hermeneutics," *Shofar* 16, (1997), pp. 1–12; and *Golden Doves*, pp. xviii, xxv, 2, 122–124. This runs contrary to Professor David Weiss Halivni's thesis that these two forms of exegesis represent different "Interpretative States of Mind"; see his *Peshaṭ and Derash* (New York: Oxford University Press, 1991), pp. 7–9.
92. These two levels of perception were discussed by R. Moses Albelda, *Darash Moshe* (Venice, 5363/1603), 35a-b. For a more contemporary treatment of the subject, see Patrick A. Heelan, "Perception as a Hermeneutical Act," in eds. Hugh J. Silverman and Don Ihde, *Hermeneutics and Deconstruction*, (Albany: State University of New York Press, 1985), pp. 43–54. Nietzsche, too, rejected the distinction 'literal/figurative,' and concluded that all words are metaphors. On this point, see the valuable study of Ranjit Chattarjee, "Before and Beyond Linguistics: The Case of Professor Nietzsche, Philologist," in eds. Colin E. Nicholson and Ranjit Chattarjee, *Tropic Crucible: Self and Theory*, (Singapore: University of Singapore, 1984), pp. 25–35.
93. See "Perception as a Hermeneutical Act," p. 52.

*Targum* version of the Scripture, representing the conventional sense of the text, which has absorbed many *derashot*.[94] The same linguistic phenomena took place in the Middle Ages when the *peshaṭ* of the Tora was identified, among Arabic speaking Jews with R. Se'adya Gaon's translation, and in European communities, with Rashi's commentary.

The semantic evolution *derasha* → *peshaṭ* of a text is not exclusive to Scripture. It pertains to all texts read throughout the ages. In a lecture on "The Book," Borges noted the semantic fluidity of literary texts:

> Heraclites said (I had mentioned this several times) that since the waters change, no one goes down to the same river twice. Much more terrible is [the fact] that we are no less fluid than the river. Each time that we read a book, the connotations of the words have changed.... *Hamlet* is not exactly the *Hamlet* that Shakespeare had conceived at the beginning of the XVII century, *Hamlet* is the *Hamlet* of Coleridge, of Goethe and Bradley. *Hamlet* had been reborn. The same is the case with *Don Quixote*.... The readers had enriched the book.[95]

There is a radical difference, however, between the unfolding of *derasha*→*peshaṭ* in general literature and in rabbinic literature. In general literature, the original language of the text continues to be spoken. The semantic changes are first assimilated linguistically and then projected semantically onto the text. Therefore, the reading community is unaware that its own *peshaṭ* is in effect a *derasha*. Since semantic changes go undetected, *derasha* appears disguised as *peshaṭ* – as a collective reality imposing itself on the text. A movement in the opposite direction took place with the rabbis. According to tradition, Hillel (died ca. 20 B.C.E.) was the first sage to have applied *derasha*

94. E.g. "don't cook a kid in its mother's milk" (Ex. 23:19) is rendered by the *Targum* "don't eat meat cooked in milk." Likewise, the verse "an eye for an eye" (Ex. 21:24), was rendered by the *Targum*: the "monetary value of the eye." These phenomena are more common in the *Targumim* used in the Holy Land.

95. *Borges, Oral*, p. 24.

to Scripture. This took place at the time when Hebrew began to be displaced as the spoken language of the Jews, and the language of the Scripture was confined to *leshon ha-qodesh,* or more precisely, *lishana de-be qudsha* 'the language [spoken at] the Temple.[96] Since there no longer was a linguistic community where the language of Scripture could record the semantic changes, the new linguistic connotations were first made in the text of Scripture and later on projected via *derasha* onto the public. Thus, whereas in general literature, semantic changes are projected from the linguistic community onto the text, in rabbinic tradition they pass from the text-*derasha* onto the general public. In this fashion, new interpretations continue to broaden the *mikhtab* or synchronic axis of the community. If and when the community incorporates the *derasha* elements into its *mikhtab* they, in turn, would become *peshaṭ*. These changes would further affect the understanding of the text, raising fresh tensions which would result in new *derashot*.

In short, a linguistic community is unaware of its own hermeneutical idiosyncrasies, and the circumstances underlying the process *derasha* → *peshaṭ*. As an effect of historical circumstances, when Hebrew ceased to be spoken, the flow of ideas and semantic fluctuations could no longer be registered in the language of the Scripture and be projected onto the *text*. The process had to be reversed: first the *derasha* was applied onto the text and then the new semantic fluctuations were projected onto the mental apparatus of the public. One of the effects of this process was a greater awareness on the part of the educated public of the *derasha* origin of the *peshaṭ*.

---

96. Later on it was further reduced to לשון חכמים 'the language of sages'; see *Golden Doves*, p. xx, and above n. 70.

# Chapter 10
# Law and the Judiciary

The Tora is the first Constitution establishing an independent judiciary system with full judicial authority (Deut. 16:18–20). The Supreme Court is the last word in the *interpretation* and *application* of the Law. It is also the highest court of appeal in the settling of legal controversies (Deut. 17:8–10). The judiciary, however, does not approach the text of the Law from an intellectual vacuum, but according to well established legal doctrines and principles. Given that a law – any law – warrants interpretation, the *written* text in and of itself cannot be an imperative. Hence, the distinction between the *written* aspect of the Law, and a *miṣva* ('precept') conveying its *judicial* application. The *miṣva*-aspect of the Tora is synonymous with what eventually will be known as 'the Oral Law' (see appendix 44). In the words of Maimonides:

Every precept that was presented (שניתנו, root NTN) to Moses at Sinai, was given (ניתנו) with its explanation. As it is written: "And I presented (ואתנה) you (Moses) the stone-tablets, and the Tora, and the precept (מצוה)" (Ex. 24:12): *and the Tora* – refers to the Written Law; *and the miṣva* [refers to] its explanation. [God] prescribed us to implement the *Tora* in accordance with *the miṣva*. The *miṣva* is [commonly] designated 'Oral Law.'[97]

Essential to the judicial process is the Mental Law forming the nucleus of the covenant (= *de-'Oraita*). It conditions all subsequent

97. *MT*, Introduction, ll. 2–4. Cf. R. Abraham Maimonides, *Perush*, pp. 382–384.

understanding of the Law. As mentioned earlier (chapter 7), *qabbala* of the Tora is not a passive 'acceptance.' It includes the responsibility to pass it on to the next generation, who in turn will pass it on to the next, in perpetuity. Therefore, departure from the Mental Law constitutes a breach of the covenant. These primary 'explanations' are grounded on the *sensus communis* or 'Mental Law' – forged by the collective mind of Israel at Sinai. In this precise sense, the Oral Law instructed by the Supreme Court is the actual *perush* of the Written Law – not a 'commentary' in its conventional meaning, but in its original connotation of 'unfolding' and 'promulgating.' Again, quoting Maimonides:

> The Supreme Court in Jerusalem is the foundation (עיקר) of the Oral Law. It is the pillar of judicial decision and from it comes forth the legislation and judgments [binding] on all Israel.[98]

The authority of the judiciary presupposes constancy with the doctrines defined by the Sinaitic nucleus (= *de-'Oraita*). Were the court to violate this trust, its pronouncements would be null and void. Addressing this fundamental aspect of the Law, the rabbis taught:

> Could it be that if they [the Supreme Court] will tell you that the right is left, or that the left is right, that you should comply with them? That is why the Scripture stated: "do not sway off from the pronouncement that they [the Supreme Court] tell you, either to the right or to the left" (Deut. 17:11). Only when they ascertain that the right is right and the left is left, you must comply with them![99]

98. *MT Mamrim* 1:1.

99. Y. Horayot I, 1, 45d. See *Studies in the Mishne Tora*, pp. 21–24. This doctrine has been upheld by the Geonim, see appendix 10. In this sense, the Mental Law is absolute. Accordingly, a Talmudic dispute constitutes evidence that the issue in question was not part of the original Mental Law; see *MT Mamrim* 1:3; *Studies in the Mishne Tora*, p. 38 n. 35.

The fact that the Tora stipulates that if the Supreme Court issued a 'declaratory judgment' (הוראה) contrary to the Law, that they must bring an expiatory atonement acknowledging their error is clear evidence that there is an objective Law transcending their own say.[100] A consequence of this doctrine is the rule stipulating that if a legal scholar were to follow a faulty judgment, under the presumption that it is necessary to comply with a view of the Supreme Court even in error, he is a 'deliberate transgressor'[101] (פושע). Second, the Tora charged the Supreme Court with the right to interpret the ambiguous elements of the Law, requiring further definition and clarification (Deut. 17:11). Maimonides called the penumbra elements of the Law, 'ambiguous regulations' (*dinim mufla'im*). Through judicial exegesis (*derasha*) the ambiguous terms of the Law acquire concrete meaning and the force of law. For the purpose of the present discussion it is important to note that unlike the Zadokites, the rabbis recognized the right to apply exegesis to Scripture. It is a judicial right. "The Tora itself," noted the rabbis, "granted the sages the right to interpret" the Law.[102] A distinctive mark of judicial exegesis are the 'thirteen rules' (שלוש עשרה מדות) used in developing the justification for these definitions (see appendix 52). Given that the Tora is a polysemic text (see the following chapter), hermeneutical issues cannot be conclusive

100. *Hora'a* is a declaratory judgment about an existing law, issued in response to a formal query submitted to the court. Unlike a *din* 'judgment' seeking execution and performance, *hora'a* seeks to resolve doubts and to instruct about the meaning of a law or legal text.
101. Horayot 2b; Y. Horayot I, 1, 45d; cf. *MT Shegagot* 13:1. For a further discussion, see José Faur, "Law and Hermeneutics in Rabbinic Tradition," *Cardozo Law Review* 14 (1993), pp. 1670–1674; "One-Dimensional Jew," pp. 32–37.
102. Sifre Bemidbar, ed. H. Horovitz (Jerusalem: Wahrman Books, 1966), #134, p. 179 and variants. See Sifre Zuṭa, ed. Menaḥem Kahana (Jerusalem: Magnes Press, 2002), pp. 234, 254–255; and *Studies in the Mishne Tora*, pp. 21–24. On the authority of the Supreme Court to interpret and execute the Tora, see appendix 10. It parallels the right of the court to interpret and execute *all* documents under its jurisdiction; see *Golden Doves*, pp. 123–124. By way of contrast we should note that the authority of the U.S. Supreme Court to interpret the Constitution is not grounded on the Constitution, see appendix 10.

in and of themselves. Therefore, conflicting judicial interpretations are to be resolved by a majority vote (עומדים למניין). The principal constituents of this doctrine are contained in a homily delivered by R. Yannai (ca. 200), a member of the same Supreme Court that published the Mishna.

> R. Yannai said: If the Tora would have been delivered (by God to Israel) categorically [חתומה, that is, without any ambiguity] not a single leg could stand [i.e., its continuity would be impossible]. What is the source for this? "And God spoke to Moses *to say*!(לאמור)[103]
> – He (Moses) said to Him:
> – "Lord of the Universe, teach me what the halakha is!"
> – He (God) replied: "(You) must follow the majority (opinion)! If the majority (issues a verdict of) innocence, they have absolved [the accused]! If the majority (issues a verdict of) guilt, [the accused] is guilty! In this fashion the Tora may be expounded in forty-nine modes (concluding that the matter is) impure, and in forty-nine modes (concluding that the matter is) pure.[104]

---

103. That is, to *say,* i.e., to further develop and *communicate* to others; see R. Samuel Yafe Ashkenazi, *Yefe Mar'e* (Berlin, 5485/1725), 186c.

104. Y. Sanhedrin IV, 2, 22a. See *Massekhet Soferim* XVI, 5; pp. 287–289; and cf. Rosh HaShana 21a; Sanhedrin 36a; and the bibliographic note in *Ekha Rabbati,* p. 20, n. 28. Cf. below Section IV, n. 194 and appendix 52. The reason why forty-nine faces are revealed is because rabbinic tradition reckons fifty grades of intelligence. Grade number fifty represents absolute wisdom which excludes both interpretation and variation. Cf. the text published by Moses Zucker, "*Iyyunim,*" *Proceedings of the American Academy for Jewish Research* 49 (1982), pp. 101–102. This doctrine may be related to the thesis that the Tora was first published as *megillot* and only later acquired the status of "Tora חתומה"; see Giṭṭin 60a. For further analyses, see R. Ḥanan'el on Sanhedrin 36a; R. Nissim Gaon, *Sefer ha-Mafteaḥ* on 'Erubin 13b s.v. *ve-diglo,* 56b. On the position of the Geonim on this matter, see *Rav Saadya Ga'on's Translation of the Tora,* p. 109 n. 461; cf. Maimonides, *Perush ha-Mishnayot, Terumot* 6:3, vol. 1, pp. 294–295.

Two principles follow. First, there are elements in the Tora that were not defined by Sinaitic tradition (= *dinim mufla'im*). Second, conflicting judicial exegeses of the Law and judicial uncertainties are to be resolved by the majority opinion. Since these elements were never defined by the judicial tradition, the decisions of the court are binding "even when the right appears to you to be the left and the left to be the right, you must comply with them."[105]

Judicial exegesis cannot displace the *sensus communis* of the text, nor displace semantic ambiguities, nor acquire the status of Scripture, even when proceeding from the highest court of the nation.[106] "A verse cannot be unbound from its manifest tenor (פשוטו),"[107] i.e., exegesis does not displace the *sensus communis* of the text.[108] This is why, although conditioning the *law* of Scripture, exegesis cannot eliminate the fundamental ambiguity of a text. *Derasha* belongs to the realm of rhetoric, not metaphysics: it seeks to persuade, rather than *demonstrate* (see below chapter 44). The primary task of *derasha* is not to resolve the ambiguities (*dinim mufla'im*) but to *generate* meaning by pointing out fresh semantic possibilities suggested by new circumstances. R. Joseph ibn Megas (1077–1141) – one of the foremost rabbinic authorities from the Iberian Peninsula – established the principle that the Oral Law (including the exegeses it transmits) "does not equal the true [i.e., the actual text of the] Tora."[109] The interpretative

105. *Sifre* #154, p. 27. See *Studies in the Mishne Tora*, pp. 21–25.
106. See *Studies in the Mishne Tora*, pp. 183–186.
107. Shabbat 63a; Yebamot 11b, 24a. See R. Joseph ben Judah ibn 'Aqnin, ed. and trans. A. S. Halkin, *Hitgallut ha-Sodot ve-Hofa'at ha-Me'orot* (Jerusalem: Mekize Nirdamim, 1964), p. 143.
108. This point is germane to the issue raised by R. Se'adya Gaon (and others) concerning precepts whose *peshaṭ* differs from the definition established by the judiciary – are they also binding according to their *peshaṭ*? For example, the rabbis explained that the prohibition "to put a stumbling block before a blind person" (Lev. 19:14) is an injunction against aiding someone to transgress the law, see 'Aboda Zara 6a-b. What about someone actually obstructing the path of a blind person, could he be charged for having violated the above injunction?
109. *She'elot wu-Tshubot R. Yosef ibn Megas* (Salonika, 5546/1786), #92, 13a.

mission of the judiciary is to *institute* the legal meaning of the text. Its function is to implement the law, not to resolve textual ambiguities, past or future, or impose interpretations on the *meaning* of the text. Therefore, as long as the law is implemented in accordance with the norms ascribed to it by the judiciary, the text may be interpreted differently. Hence the doctrine stipulating that the judicial exegeses of Scripture (*dinim mufla'im*) are never Scriptural (*de-'Oraita*). The purpose of hermeneutics is to serve as a tool by which the judiciary can ascribe meaning to the legal text – not to 'reveal' it![110]

Third, the Law grants the judiciary authority to legislate new rules and develop legal doctrines (דרבנן). The Geonim and Maimonides maintained that this authority was granted to the judiciary by the Tora (Deut. 17:11).[111] The purpose of this type of legislation is to meet new political, economic, and social circumstances facing Israel, particularly after the Exile and the Destruction of the Temple.

Laws and rules promulgated on the basis of judicial exegesis (*dinim mufla'im*), differ from regulations enacted by legislation (דרבנן) in a major point. According to standard judicial practice, the rules, etc., enacted on the basis of legislation could only be abrogated by a more senior court. This restriction does not apply to 'ambiguous regulations' (*dinim mufla'im*) promulgated on the basis of judicial exegesis. Legislation promulgated on the basis of judicial exegesis may in fact be abrogated by a less senior court. Addressing the question as to how a lesser court was authorized to abrogate an earlier statute (about Sabbatical law), the rabbis explained: "(Since) they (the more senior court) based it [the law] on the authority of Scripture... (the lesser court, too) may base the abrogation [of the statute] on the authority

110. See *MT* Introduction, ll. 102–104; cf. *Studies in the Mishne Tora*, pp. 25–32, 47, 132. Let us notice, in passing, that occasionally Maimonides justifies a law by citing a different verse than the rabbis. See, for example, *Kesef Mishne* on *MT Ma'ase ha-Qorbanot* 5:3; *Leḥem Mishne* on *MT Melakhim* 1:1; see R. Jacob Mal'akhi, *Yad Mal'akhi* (New York: Keter, 5706/1946), *Kelale ha-Rambam* #iv.

111. See *MT Mamrim* 1:2; *Studies in the Mishne Tora*, pp. 19–25.

of Scripture."[112] Underlying this principle is the doctrine stipulating that the function of judicial exegesis is not to capture 'authorial intention,' but to *generate* meaning. Otherwise, judicial exegesis would be rewriting the Tora. More grievously, the 'elimination' of legal ambiguities by judiciary fiat would impair the further unfolding of the Law and the resolutions of new situations. As per R. Yannai, without the possibility to look at legal ambiguities each time anew, legal development is impossible and "not a single leg could stand."[113]

The laws *de-'Oraita*, as defined by judicial tradition and the Mental Law, from Sinai onwards, narrow judiciary power and the potential for judicial abuse. The doctrine establishing that their authority is only valid when declaring "that the right is right and the left is left," establishes that the ultimate depository of the Law and tradition – the *ketab* and *mikhtab* of Israel – are the people (see Deut. 33:4), not the institutions *representing* the people! Accordingly, a verdict by the Supreme Court that is palpably wrong is worthless. To wit, if they would declare that the Sabbath has ended,

> On the basis that the sun was clouded, and they presumed that the sun had [actually] set, and then the sun shone – this is not a judgment (הוראה) but an error.... Likewise, if they permitted a woman to remarry on the basis of the testimony of witnesses who testified before them that her husband had died, and later on the husband appeared – this is not a judgment (הוראה) but an error.... The same is the case with other such cases.[114]

---

112. Y. Shebi'it I, 1, 33a. Cf. Y. Megilla I, 1, 70b. See below, Section IV, n. 177. For further analyses and sources, see *Studies in the Mishne Tora*, pp. 25–32; *Golden Doves*, pp. 15–16.
113. See the very wise comments of David Werner Amram, *The Jewish Law of Divorce* (London: David Nutt, 1897), pp. 19–20. On the status of these laws, see *Studies of the Mishne Tora*, pp. 25–32.
114. *MT Shegagot* 14:3. Accordingly, an instruction about something patently clear in the Law, is not to be regarded as הוראה; see *Keritot* 13b and *MT Bi'at ha-Miqdash* 1:3. Some of the great rabbinic jurists upheld this principle; see for example

This type of mistake renders the pronouncement of the court not merely erroneous, but void, requiring no reversal or judicial review. Otherwise, the people of Israel would be slaves under men, rather than a free people under the Law!

Laws *de-'Oraita* offer stability and protection against judicial abuse. The elucidation and development of 'ambiguous regulations' (*dinim mufla'im*), permit the promotion of new standards. These two groups of laws constitute the two pillars of modern jurisprudence. "If a body of law were in existence, adequate for the civilization of today," proposed Justice Cardozo, "it could not meet the demands of the civilization of tomorrow." He explained further:

> Society is inconstant. So long as it is inconstant, and to the extent of such inconstancy, there can be no constancy in law. The kinetic forces are too strong for us. We may think the law is the same if we refuse to change the formulas. The identity is verbal only. The formula has no longer the same correspondence with reality. Translated into conduct, it means something other than it did. Law defines a relation not always between fixed points, but often, indeed oftenest, between points of varying position. The acts and situations to be regulated have a motion of their own. There is a change whether we will it or not.[115]

To meet the challenge of social inconstancy and ensure that the kinetic forces moving society will not reduce the law to the dictates

---

the note by R. Moses Isserles on *Shulḥan 'Arukh, Eben ha-'Ezer* CLVI, 4; and the note of R. Samuel Isaac Reggio, *Thora et Philosophia* (Heb.) (Vienna, 1827), p. 62. For a similar argument, see the citation in *Kesef Mishne, MT Ma'akhalot Asurot* 1:20. In general, the rabbis avoided issuing legal opinions on matters that could be determined empirically; see Y. Terumot III, 1, 42a and cf. Ḥalla I, 1, 57a.

115. Benjamin Cardozo, *The Paradoxes of Legal Science* (New York: Columbia University, 1928), pp. 10–11.

of men, the rabbis kept on expanding the 'ambiguous regulations' (*dinim mufla'im*) to new standards. Quoting Judge Cardozo again:

> The pressure of society invests new forms of conduct in the mind of the multitude with the sanction of moral obligation, and the same pressure working upon the mind of the judge, invest them finally through his action with the sanction of the law.[116]

The rabbis accomplished this not from the bench, by fiat and authority, but through a special form of discourse: *derasha*. In this manner, the social and political pressures bearing on Israel kept on strengthening, rather than weakening, the pristine covenant forged by the collective mind of the people. That is why the definitions of 'ambiguous regulations' (*dinim mufla'im*) are invariably accompanied by *derashot*, encoding the linguistic and intellectual rationale for the new unfolding of the Law (see Concluding Reflections).

116. *The Paradoxes of Legal Science*, p. 18.

# Chapter 11

# The Boundaries of *Derasha*

The right to *derasha* is derived from the conveyance (מסירה) whereby one generation *submits* to the following generation the Tora (= *ketab*) it had received, and with it the right to interpret it (= *mikhtab*). Fundamental to the concept of conveyance (מסירה) are the cumulative teachings and traditions of Israel. Therefore, a condition *sine qua non* to propose a *derasha* is to be a 'sage' (חכם) who has mastered the Mental Law and cumulative wisdom of Israel.[117] Without this knowledge, every reading of Scripture is a misreading. *Derasha* is subjective. It belongs to the realm of the *possible*, not the necessary. This is why the rabbis taught, "One cannot raise an objection against a homily."[118] *Derasha* is a semantic composition, bordering on the aesthetic, which may be accepted or rejected, but it can be neither imposed nor demonstrated. As in music and painting, the terms incorporated into the *derasha* acquire a new level of meaning transcending the original sense of each term in isolation: the whole is larger than the parts.[119] In this fundamental respect, *derasha* differs from Western 'exegesis.' In Greek literary theory, the purpose of interpretation is to 'uncover' the 'original' mind of the author and to remove the ambiguities intrinsic to written texts. 'Interpretation' simultaneously explains the text and displaces it: as with a code that

117. See *Golden Doves*, p. xviii; cf. *Homo Mysticus*, p. 26.
118. Cited in *Oṣar ha-Ge'onim*, Pesaḥim, p. 71 and n. 3.
119. See José Faur, "The Limits of Readerly Collusion in Rabbinic Tradition," *Soundings* 76 (1993), pp. 156–157. Cf. *Golden Doves*, pp. 118–123.

once cracked becomes superfluous. This view postulates that the text is unisemic: once 'deciphered,' alternative interpretations are spurious.

Fundamental to rabbinic tradition is the belief that the Tora is polysemic. There are "seventy faces to the Tora," that is, seventy modes of interpretation, corresponding to the seventy nations making up humankind. Moreover, within each mode there are as many variations as individuals.[120] Concerning the parity of conflicting interpretations, the rabbis taught:

> A single verse could unfold into many senses.... [Someone] from the school of R. Ishmael transmitted: "[Is not my word like fire, said the Lord] and like a hammer that shatters the rock? (Jer. 23:29). – Just as each blow of a hammer strikes forth many sparks, likewise a single verse, too, unfolds into many senses.[121]

Notably, when the court forewarns a prospective witness of the moral gravity of giving false testimony, particularly in capital cases, it not only delivers to him the *derasha* supporting the view of the court, but also the alternative *derasha* of the text (Mishna Sanhedrin 4:5).

These considerations lead to one of the most remarkable aspects of judicial authority. In Israel, the judiciary does not embody the spirit of some sort of *europaischen Menschentums* in charge of administering the 'truth.' Their authority to adjudicate and promulgate new rules on the basis of exegesis is limited to areas that fall within the jurisdiction of the court, what is commonly known as public law, not to matters of faith and dogma. This fundamental doctrine was formulated by R. Baḥye ibn Faquda (11th century), one of the great rabbinic figures flourishing in the Iberian Peninsula. He pointed out that when defining the authority of the Supreme Court, the Scripture (Deut. 17:8–11) limited its jurisdiction to legal matters, what he designated 'duties of

120. See *Golden Doves*, p. 120.

121. Sanhedrin 34a; cf. 'Erubin 13b and *Golden Doves*, pp. xiii-xiv.

the limbs,' i.e., external obligations – not to matters of personal faith or 'duties of the heart.' After analyzing the text awarding authority to the highest court, seated at the Temple of Jerusalem, he concluded:

> Upon examining the types of laws included in the first verse (Deut. 17:8) you will notice that these pertain to matters requiring (the type of judicial) analysis and definition, entailing legal tradition, not inductive reason. Haven't you noticed that it (the Tora) does not mention [in this context] matters that could be resolved through reason (alone)? It does not say, 'When you have doubts about the unity of God,' or about [the meaning] of 'the Creator's names and His attributes,' or about one of 'the doctrines of faith' (Ar. *uṣul al-din*)... – matters that one can resolve through analysis and reason – that you have to accept the authority of the sages who transmit the laws [i.e., the judiciary], and that you must rely only on what it [the judiciary] had transmitted about them.[122]

This position was upheld by Maimonides. The Supreme Court of Israel has jurisdiction over matters pertaining to "the implementation of the law (*dat*)," that is, judicial matters (= Ar. *uṣul al-fiqh*) in contradistinction to "the doctrines of faith" (= Ar. *uṣul al-din*):

> The Supreme Court (sitting at the Temple) in Jerusalem is the foundation of Oral Law. They [the judges seated at the Supreme Court] are the pillars of judicial instruction, and from them come forth law and jurisprudence to all Israel. About them the Tora gave assurance, as it is written: "In accordance to the Law that they instruct you..." (Deut. 17:10). Whoever believes in Moses our Teacher and in his Law is bound to

122. Our translation comes from *Kitab al-Hadaya ila Fara'id al-Qulub*, ed. A. S. Yahuda (Leyden, 1912), p. 16. Cf. R. Joseph Qafiḥ, ed. and trans. *Torat Ḥobot ha-Lebabot* (Jerusalem, 5733/1973), pp. 26–27.

> entrust (them) [with the matters concerning] the implementation (*ma'ase* = Ar. *a'mal*) of the *dat* [= law] and to rely on them.[123]

Consequently, when defining the precept instructing compliance with the Supreme Court, Maimonides was careful to set down that its authority is valid in areas concerning the "prohibited and permitted" – something analogous to 'duties of the limbs.'[124] Similarly, when defining the injunction against someone refusing to comply with the Supreme Court (see Deut. 17:11), Maimonides made it clear that the authority of the judiciary is confined "to the implementation (Ar. *a'mal*) of the Law"; i.e., of external actions, not of beliefs.[125] In the *Guide*, too, when delineating the authority of the Supreme Court, Maimonides pointed out that its authority is in the area of *fiqh* – an Arabic term mistranslated as either 'Talmud' or 'Oral Law,' but actually meaning 'jurisprudence' – in contradistinction to *uṣul al-din* or doctrines of faith.[126] The Tora awards authority to "the Supreme Court" in the area of *fiqh*, i.e., "in all these matters" where there could rise "uncertainty as to *its implementation* " (= *al-'amal*).[127] Thus, matters of faith are not justiciable. Obviously, people can be 'wrong' and hold 'heretical' views contrary to commonly held doctrines. But this

123. *MT Mamrim* 1:1. Maimonides stipulated this principle in the 'Introduction,' *MT* ll. 3–4, 8–9. The Mishna Sanhedrin 10:1 censures someone "...who *says*" (האומר), i.e. professes – not "who believes..." The same formula was adopted by Maimonides *MT Teshuba* 3:7, 8 when cataloging the various types of heresies. Accordingly, the doctrines and articles of faith are a matter of education and persuasion. The notion that they are to be enforced by the judiciary is the result of anti-Maimonidean reading and analphabetic theology, old and new. Concerning Heb. *ma'ase* = Ar. *a'mal*, see below n. 127 and Section V, n. 317.

124. See *Sefer ha-Miṣvot*, positive precept #174, p. 147.

125. *Sefer ha-Miṣvot* negative precept #312, p. 325.

126. *Guide*, III, 51, p. 455 (l. 24); see *Studies in the Mishne Tora*, p. 147. Wittgenstein, too, was emphatic about not 'mixing faith and reason'; see Ranjit Chatterjee, *Wittgenstein and Judaism* (New York: Peter Lang, 2005), p. 106.

127. *Guide*, I, 71, p. 121 (ll. 9–19). See ibid., III, 49, p. 409 (ll. 3–16); José Faur, "Monolingualism and Judaism," *Cardozo Law Review* 14 (1993), pp. 1736–1737. Cf. above n. 123.

would be the responsibility of the school and teachers to explain and advise – not of the judiciary. R. Joseph Albo (14th century), one of the most illustrious philosophers to emerge from Christian Spain, addressed this fundamental issue. Upon analysis it will be discovered that some of the most prominent sages held opinions which, according to standard beliefs, are to be regarded as 'heretical.' Nonetheless, these men, concluded Albo, were not 'heretics' since they arrived at those beliefs in good faith. Here is what he wrote on this matter:

> But a person who upholds the law of Moses and believes in its principles, that when he undertakes to investigate these matters with his reason and scrutinizes the texts, is misled by his speculation and interprets a given principle otherwise than it is taken to be meant at first sight; or denies the principle because he thinks that it does not represent a sound theory which the Tora obliges us to believe; or erroneously denies that a given belief is a fundamental principle, which however he believes as he believes the other dogma of the Tora which are not fundamental principles; or entertains a certain notion in relation to one of the miracles of the Tora because he thinks that he is not thereby denying any doctrines which is obligatory upon us to believe by the authority of the Tora, – a person of this sort is not an unbeliever (כופר 'heretic'). He is classed with the sages and pious men of Israel, though he holds erroneous theories. His sin is due to error and requires atonement.[128]

128. R. Joseph Albo, *Sefer ha-'Iqqarim*, ed. and trans. Isaac Husik (Philadelphia: The Jewish Publication Society, 1946), I, 2, vol. 1, pp. 48–50. This is why Maimonides and his son treated with deference and appropriate respect, Jewish sages who held, from the point of view of Maimonidean tradition, 'heretical beliefs'; see Section V, n. 308. I found the same attitude among some outstanding sages of our time, representing both the Ashkenazic and the Sephardic traditions.

There is an exception to this rule. A *derasha* must unfold within the perimeters of the *mikhtab* and the *ketab* systems. Therefore, a *derasha* intending to impugn either of these systems is unlawful and criminal. Among the people who have forfeited the World-to-Come and fellowship with Israel, the rabbis included those engaging in "faltering expositions" (דרשות של דופי). It includes Gnostic, as well as Christological and Antinomian exegeses, intended to delegitimize Israel and the Tora of Israel.[129]

This point merits explanation. The right to apply *derasha* is a condition of the principle establishing that a people have the right to interpret its *ketab* system according to its *mikhtab*. Both 'strict' and 'liberal' methods of interpretations would agree that the Supreme Court could not render an opinion according to which the Constitution is no longer legitimate and the Commonwealth of the United States of America is hitherto dead and illegitimate. The case in Israel is a bit more complex. The legitimacy of *derasha* parallels the principle awarding the Court of Justice the authority to determine the sense of contracts, statutes, and other documents under its jurisdiction. Since the Tora was given to the Jewish people, it follows that they, too, have the right to interpret it and determine its meaning, judicially by the courts, and morally and doctrinally through their schools and sages. By rendering the Jewish Constitution void and the Jewish nation dead, those proposing "faltering expositions" (דרשות של דופי) have denied themselves all legal standing. In a similar fashion, if

129. See Sanhedrin 99b, and *Golden Doves*, p. xxi. There are two different versions of מגלה פנים. In Abot 3:14 Maimonides had "מגלה פנים בתורה"; see *Perush ha-Mishnayot*, vol. 4, p. 433. Accordingly, he explained it to mean "one who transgresses the Law in open defiance," in the same sense that 'open defiance,' "מגלה פנים," is used in 'Erubin 69a. Maimonides incorporated this version in *MT Teshuba* 3:11. It is probable that that was the version he had in Sanhedrin 99b. The more popular version, in both Abot and Sanhedrin, is: "מגלה פנים בתורה שלא כהלכה," "unveiling in the Tora directions contrary to the law," i.e., subversive homilies designed to void a particular law. See *Golden Doves*, pp. 123–124; and "The Limits of Readerly Collusion in Rabbinic Tradition," pp. 153–161.

one were to recognize Gnostic, Christological, and Antinomian exegeses, then the *ketab* of Israel would be illegitimate and the *mikhtab* system null and void. A consequence of these *derashot* is that the Jewish Commonwealth would be *ipso facto* dissolved and the nation of Israel dead and deadly.

# Concluding Reflections

Fundamental to rabbinic discourse is compatibility with other modes of human knowledge and intelligence. "If they tell you there is wisdom among the nations, believe it," taught the rabbis. The distinctiveness of Israel lies in its legal and political systems. Thus, continued the rabbis, "But if they tell you there is Law (Tora) among the nations, do not believe it."[130] Why? The question is particularly poignant in light of the fact that the Jewish legal system coincides in many significant points with other legal systems, past and present. In an alphabetic society, the governing institutions of the nation, including the judiciary and the political, have only limited sovereignty. Their authority is grounded on, and therefore conditioned by, the Law. A *sine qua non* for the proper functioning of the Law is a society with full access to its own *ketab* and *mikhtab* systems, both linguistically and intellectually. Alluding to the fact that the (Eastern) Roman Empire was composed of numerous ethnic groups speaking a multitude of languages, the rabbis classified it "an unfair empire" (מלכות שאינה הוגנת; Mishna Giṭṭin 8:5) because the people "have neither [their own] writing (*ketab*) nor [their own] language."[131] In such a vacuum, the administration of justice is more a matter of manipulation than fairness and judicial integrity.[132] Within such a system, violence and

130. *Midrash Ekha Rabbati*, ed. S. Buber (Vilna, 1899), II, [9], p. 114.
131. Giṭṭin 80a. See appendix 7.
132. See the humorous and highly illustrative story, Shabbat 116a-b.

military might are not only the ultimate basis of the judiciary, but, in a perverse way, 'law and justice' become a pretext for military conquest and the extermination of other people and civilizations. As noted by René Cassin (1887–1976), in spite of its "exalted principles" and elaborated code of law,

> The Roman Empire, nevertheless, carried on its expansion by fierce conquests – even to the point of total destruction of any adversary who resisted and of its civilization as well. Gaul is one illustration. At the eastern end of the Mediterranean, the destruction of the State (Kingdom) of Israel and the dispersion of its population constitute an even more perfect example.[133]

For the Jews, the Law contracted at Sinai-Moab is the great equalizer system because it stands above all governing institutions: political, ecclesiastical and judicial. The ultimate depository of the Law is the people (Deut. 33:4), not the governing authorities. The fact that the Tora stipulates that even when the supreme political chief or the High Priest errs, or if the Supreme Court would issue a 'declaratory judgment' (הוראה) contrary to the Law, they must bring an expiatory atonement acknowledging their error, clearly shows that there is an objective Law transcending national institutions.[134] We have noticed earlier (chapter 10) the principle that if the judiciary would declare that "the right is left" the people have the *duty* to disobey. Were the authorities to persist in their error, it would then result in a national crisis – as was demonstrated during the Maccabean uprising (annually celebrated on the holiday of Ḥanukka). By way of contrast, in

---

133. René Cassin, "From the Ten Commandments to the Rights of Man," in ed. Shlomo Shoham, *Of Law and Man* (Sabra Books: Tel Aviv and New York, 1971), p. 17.

134. *Hora'a* is a declaratory judgment about an existing law, issued in response to a formal query submitted to the court. Unlike a *din*, 'judgment,' seeking execution and performance, *hora'a* seeks to resolve doubts and to instruct as to the actual law.

pagan political thought, sovereignty is a function of might and the threat of violence. Briefly, the Law of Israel is not merely what the authorities dictate (see appendix 10). In Psalms 82 sung by the Levites on Tuesdays at the Temple, God looks over every trial, as well as over the judges sitting in judgment. The Hebrew Scripture designates the seat of justice *Elohim*, 'God,' not because *the judges* are God, but because God Himself looks over the trial: while they are judging, the judges are judged by the Supreme Judge. This fundamental doctrine was formulated by R. Simon ben Shaṭṭaḥ (1st century B.C.E.), Chief Justice of Israel's Supreme Court. Confronting the King of Israel in Court, he addressed him with this admonition:

> You should know that not before us (the Supreme Court of Israel) you stand, but before the One who spoke and the Universe was! Because it is written, "*Elohim* stands over the Congregation of God. Inside the guts of the Justices (*Elohim*), He is judging" (Ps. 82:1).[135]

If the people of Israel had acquiesced to the absolute supremacy of the judiciary, then, borrowing from Thomas Jefferson (1743–1826), "the people will have ceased to be their own rulers, having to that extent practically resigned their government in the hands of that eminent tribunal."[136] Psalm 94 sung by the Levites at the Temple on Wednesdays underscores this fundamental doctrine: the Law is not simply what the political and legal bureaucracies declare. The first part of the opening title, "The Lord is a God of Vengeance" (v. 1), introduces the theme. In Hebrew, 'vengeance' (נקמה) is not synonymous with 'revenge' and settling scores. It means extrajudicial retribution, principally, against the 'haughty,' believing they are hierarchically superior and above the law. The second half of the title, "the God of Vengeance has appeared!" expresses the psalmist's hope that those flaunting the

135. Sanhedrin 19b a-b; see Josephus, *Antiquities* XIV, 168, vol. 7, pp. 537–539; and cf. *Em la- Miqra*, vol. 5, 15b-16a.

136. Letter Sep 28, 1820 to William C. Jarvis.

Law would be judged by the Supreme Judge. Thematically, the psalm is divided into three parts. In the first part (vv. 2–7), the psalmist invokes God "Judge of the earth," and prays for the punishment of the haughty who abuse their power. These are the 'enlightened' elite, who regard themselves hierarchically superior (יתאמרו) to others, and use the bench to crush and suppress the meek: the widow, the alien, the orphan. Projecting their own psyche onto God, they foolishly assume that since He is hierarchically superior to men, He would not care about what they in turn do to those 'below.' In the second part (vv. 8–11), the psalmist addresses the corrupt magistrates. Pointing to God's exquisite providence, he asks them: "He, who has planted the ear, wouldn't He listen? He, who has crafted the eye, wouldn't He observe?" Concluding, "The Lord knows the doings of men, although they may be trivial." In the third part (vv. 12–23), the psalmist proceeds to describe the misery brought on the people by justices, rich in foibles and follies, incapable of nuance and critical judgment (see appendix 69). He goes on to depict their office as "the chair of violence (כסא הוות)." In Hebrew, as well as in Aramaic and Arabic, "chair" (כסא) stands for the 'seat of justice.' Instead of administering justice, the 'enlightened elite' pervert the law. In the words of the psalmist, they "craft inequity by means of law" (יצר עמל עלי-חק); i.e., they use their office to bestow on injustice the cloak of 'legitimacy.' According to the Hebrew Scripture, a court of justice supposes to 'bond' with God insofar as it brings justice on earth. This is not the case with a judiciary system that perverts justice by rationalizing violence against the weak. Turning to God, the psalmist asks (vv. 20–23):

> Would a chair of violence (כסא הוות) bond with You? – [those who] craft inequity by the means of law (יצר עמל עלי-חק)? They pass verdicts against the life of the righteous, and declare the blood of the innocent 'guilty!' The Lord has become my shelter, my God is the rock of my fortress! He will punish them for their inequities, and with their own evil He shall obliterate them. Our Lord God shall destroy them!

There is another aspect of Tora that renders it a unique system of government. It has to do with *derasha* and the hermeneutics of 'ambiguous regulations' (*dinim mufla'im*). If, as Philo tells us, "…violence is the enemy of law,"[137] then *intellectual* violence, or *belehrt* ('instruction of truth') imparted by *europaischen Menschentums* in black robes, cannot be used to teach and promote justice. This would help us understand the rabbinic strategy of *derasha*. Sovereignty, in pagan political thought, is a function of might. By virtue of his hierarchic superiority, the sovereign issues orders which his subjects must obey. Or he founds a State, and then proceeds to frame a series of laws and legal principles whose objectives would be to further strengthen the political institutions of the State. Concerning both methods, Philo noted:

> Now, other legislators are divided into those who set out by ordering what should or should not be done, and laying down penalties for disobedience, and those who, thinking themselves superior, did not begin with this, but first founded and established their state as they conceived it, and then, by framing laws, attached to it the constitution which they thought most agreeable and suitable to the form in which they had founded it.

These methods invoke the fiat of hierarchic power, and were therefore unacceptable to the Hebrews, who were the first to discover the meaning of bondage. Accordingly, the Law of Moses followed neither of the above courses.

> But Moses, thinking that the former course, namely issuing orders without words of exhortation, as though to slaves instead of free men, savored of tyranny and despotism, as indeed it did, and that the second, though aptly conceived, was evidently not entirely satisfactory in the judgment of all, took a

137. *Moses* II, 13, *Philo*, vol. 6, p. 457.

> different line in both departments. In his commands and prohibitions he suggests and admonishes rather than commands, and the very numerous and necessary instructions which he essays to give are accompanied by forewords and afterwords, in order to exhort rather than to enforce.

Moses sought to persuade, rather than impose. Philo continued:

> Again, he considered that to begin his writings with the foundation of a man-made city was below the dignity of the laws, and, surveying the greatness and beauty of the whole code with the accurate discernment of his mind's eye, and thinking it too good and godlike to be confined within any earthly walls, he inserted the story of the genesis of the 'Great City,' holding that the laws were the most faithful picture of the world-polity.[138]

The rabbinic system is a follow up of the above. Although Moses was shown "even what a skilled student would expose before his teacher,"[139] many Mosaic laws and regulations were only encoded as a 'clue' (רמז) in the *ketab* system of the Tora (see appendix 31), to be decoded by the *mikhtab* system of Israel, at a later time, when acceptance of these laws would be a matter of conviction rather than imposition. We can thus understand the exquisite care that Jews took of their *ketab* system (through the *Masora*), given that even minute orthographic irregularities may supply the proper 'clue' (רמז), via *derasha,* in the promotion of a higher standard of behavior. This tradition has been continued in modern times. In their Sabbath sermons, congregational rabbis of all denominations find and develop 'clues' in the weekly *Parasha* (to the chagrin of historians and philologists) destined to upgrade the standards of the people – not by the fiat of authority, but through the persuasion of *derasha.*

138. *Moses* II, 49–51, *Philo*, vol. 6, pp. 473–475.

139. Y. Pe'a II, 4, 17a. See *Studies in the Mishne Tora*, p. 21 n. 11.

# Section III

# The Governance of Israel

## Introductory Remarks

The three greatest miracles in Israel were comprised of an initial discovery, which led to a strategic decision, which then culminated in personal and national commitment. Respectively, these miracles involved the *ketab* and *mikhtab* systems and recognition of a national Book. The first miracle was Israel's discovery that they were slaves in Egypt. Thanks to their *ketab,* Jews alone were able to 'read' their situation: they were slaves, plain and simple. The second miracle has to do with the *mikhtab*. It was so wondrous that even today it is difficult to apprehend, let alone comprehend. It took place in the Desert before the Theophany at Sinai. Scripture relates that the morning after Jethro came to meet Moses, he saw him sitting as judge to the people, "and the people stood before Moses, from morning to evening" (Ex. 18:13). For reasons that are difficult to explain by standard logic, the people made the most significant decision any society – past and present – could make. Somehow, the people had come to perceive their wondrous redemption from Egypt as "judgments" (שפטים) brought about by God on their behalf (see Ex. 6:6; 7:4, 12:12). In response, Israel resolved to settle their differences through the process of law – the only alternative to bondage/violence (cf. Gen. 18:17–19). The resolution carried everlasting consequences for Israel and the rest of humanity. Jewish history is nothing but a record of the subsequent unfolding of this resolution (cf. Am. 3:2). The third miracle pertains to the genesis of the Book. It involved a commitment, *berit,* 'covenant,' between the people and God: out of this commitment emerged the Tora. This commitment rests on the premise that Law, the alternative to bondage/violence, will be for naught unless the people are willing to undertake a solemn commitment – in the presence of God, freely and unrestrained – to accept, for all time to come, a set of rules by which to govern and moderate their lives. In Hebrew, the set of rules negotiated by God and the people at Sinai is designated 'Tora'; usually translated 'Law,' but more accurately, 'the Constitution' of the Nation of Israel. The Jews were *chosen* by God because they alone *chose* to discover that they were slaves, and then they *chose* to resolve their conflicts through law, and finally they *chose* to contract a *berit* with God (see above chapter 5). To celebrate this *choice* every Jewish man and woman includes in the morning prayers a blessing thanking God for "*choosing* us from among all the peoples and giving us His Tora." People *choosing* to remain in a state of bondage, needing somebody above to tell them what they are seeing, hearing, and feeling, would invariably be *choosing* to resolve their differences through violence and the threat of violence, and would end up not *choosing* to accept the responsibility and accountability central to Tora and Sinai.

Jews discovered their own bondage because they refused to surrender their own *ketab* system. Consequently, they saw with their own eyes and not through their masters' eyes, and concluded that Pharaoh abused his authority,

> … making serfs of men who were not only free but guests, suppliants and settlers, he showed no shame or fear of the God of liberty and hospitality and of justice to guests and suppliants, Who watches over such as these.[1]

The second miracle involved the recognition of a shared *mikhtab*, permitting the resolution of conflicts through a legal system. The third miracle has to do with the idea of Book. Namely, that no legal or political system can function without a Book serving as the ultimate context, sanctioned by God and freely accepted by the people. The threefold process: discovery of enslavement → *ketab*, settling differences through a legal process → *mikhtab*, and a firm commitment to a set of governing values → Tora, is the reason why the gentile nations hate Jews. The rabbis taught that when the Tora was given at Sinai, the "kings of the nations trembled in fear in their palaces." Their fear was politically motivated: a Law whose ultimate principles lie beyond the Rex and the State. In a Machiavellian maneuver, tyrants hid their fear and "sang a song."[2] "What is the meaning of 'Sinai'?" asked the rabbis. They replied: "that hatred [against Israel] overtook the nations of the world."[3] The term "nations" is to the point. We are dealing with systems regarding humans as a creation of the state and nothing more (see below chapter 33).

There is no record of a people, other than the Jews, who have been the continuous object of persecution and vilification from antiquity to the present. In this Section we propose that the reason for discrediting Judaism and applauding violence against them is not inspired by religion (see below chapter 25) but by Israel's system of law and governance. Judaism is tolerant of other religions. "For it is

1. *Moses* I, 36, *Philo*, vol. 6, p. 295.
2. Zebaḥim 116a.
3. Shabbat 89a.

our traditional custom," writes Josephus, "to observe our own laws and to refrain from criticism of those of aliens."[4] Other forms of worship are designated 'עבודה זרה.' Under Christian influence, this term has been mistranslated as 'idolatry.' The interpretation is erroneous and misleading. It actually means 'alien cult' (see appendix 11). It would be well to remember that at the Temple there were images of Cherubim. Furthermore, as a result of the Hebrew idea of monolatry, the Tora prohibited not only the worship of images or of another deity, but also the worship of the true God with an 'alien cult,' that is, with a ritual that was not prescribed by the covenant (see above chapter 5). From the perspective of Scripture, it makes no difference whether Israel worships God with images, or with an unprescribed cult, or through an angel, intercessor, etc. These acts are an 'alien cult' (עבודה זרה) to *Jews*, simply, because these cults were not prescribed in the covenant (see appendix 11). The Tora is not an imperial religion. Therefore, although open to all, it is not binding on all. Unlike Christianity that is universally binding, but excludes people of other faiths from Salvation, the Tora, although binding only on Jews, is first (and last?) to proclaim that "the pious among the nations of the world have a portion in the World to Come."[5] Rather than having contempt for idolatrous men and women, Judaism expresses hope that they would come to recognize God and worship Him. The rabbis taught that,

> Upon seeing a place… from where an idol has been removed, one should say: 'Blessed is He who had removed idols from *our land* (the Land of Israel). May Your Will be, O God our Lord,

4 *Against Apion*, II, 237, *Josephus*, vol. 1, p. 389. Explicitly, the Tora confines the precept of 'censuring' the faults of "*your own people*" (עמיתך; root 'AM, 'nation,' Lev. 19:17) – not of 'others'; while you, by default, remain immaculately pure.

5. Tosefta Sanhedrin 13:2, ed. M. S. Zuckermandel (Jerusalem: Wahrman Books, 5035/1975), p. 434. See Sanhedrin 105a; *MT Teshuba* 3:5. Our position here is contrary to the view proposed by R. Abraham b. ha-Rambam, *Perush*, p. 302; cf. editor's note 14.

> that idols should be removed from all the places of Israel, and that You should turn the hearts of your servants to serve You.[6]

Therefore, unless Jews argue *ad hominem,* they are at a disadvantage. Whereas gentiles speak about their religion and institutions in absolute terms, Jews are circumspect and prone to admit their own subjectivity. And yet, as over two millennia of unparalleled persecution have demonstrated, Jews are not easily swayed by other religions. Why?

The sin of the Jews is political. The principles upon which the Governance of Israel rest are anathema to pagan political ideology. Tacitus (ca. 55–ca. 117), hailed as "the greatest Roman historian," described the Jews as "The most degraded of the other races."[7] What infuriated Tacitus was the fact that the Jews refused to recognize Rome's "right of conquest."[8] Cicero, too, was baffled by that. "Even when Jerusalem was still standing and the Jews at peace with us, the demands of their religion were incompatible with the majesty of our Empire, the dignity of our name and the institutions of our ancestors."[9] Tacitus confessed, "Our indignation was heightened by the circumstance that the Jews alone had not submitted." What made the Jews and their faith unbearably hideous was the fact that they paid respect to God over kings, and "do not allow any images to stand in their cities, much less in their temples." Adding in ire, "This flattery is not paid to their kings, nor this honor to our Emperors."[10] In this respect, the celebrated historian was

6. Tosefta Berakhot 6:2, p. 33; see Mishna Berakhot 9:1; Berakhot 57b; and *MT Berakhot* 10:9. Cf. *MT Melakhim* 11:4 quoted in full below, chapter 36, p. 211 . See *Homo Mysticus*, p. 151.
7. Tacitus, *History,* V, 5, p. 659. All our references and quotations proceed from ed. Moses Hadas, *The Complete Works of Tacitus* (New York: Modern Library, 1942). For a critical appraisal of Tacitus' views, see Hans Levy, "Tacitus on the Origin and Manners of the Jews," (Heb.) *Zion* 8 (1943), pp. 1–34, 61–80.
8. Cf. Tacitus, *History,* V, 9, p. 662.
9. Cicero, *Pro Flacco,* 69, in *Cicero* (Loeb Classical Library), vol. 10, pp. 517–519. For a detailed analysis of Cicero's argument, see Hans Levy, "Cicero on the Jews in his Speech for the Defense of Flaccus," (Heb.) *Zion* 7 (1942), pp. 109–134.
10. Tacitus, *History,* V, 10, p. 663; and 5, p. 660; cf. 9, p. 663.

following standard antisemitic propaganda. "Apion has consequently attempted to denounce us on the ground that we do not erect statues of the emperors," wrote Josephus, further explaining:

> He (God) did not, however, forbid the payment of homage of another sort, secondary to that paid of God, to worthy men; such honors we do confer upon the emperors and the people of Rome. For them we offer perpetual sacrifices; and not only do we perform these ceremonies daily, at the expense of the whole Jewish community, but, while we offer no other victims in our corporate capacity, even for [imperial] family, we jointly accord to the emperors alone this signal of honor which we pay to no other individual.[11]

The Jewish form of governance enrages tyrants and their worshippers. Hatred of the Tora goes beyond madness and the purely pathological. To the high and mighty, to obliterate Jews and what they stand for in every which way is a solemn duty bordering on the spiritual and the sublime. Jewish tradition relates that upon entering the Holy of Holies at the Temple in Jerusalem,

> Titus seized (תפס) a whore in hand and entered the Holy of Holies. Then he proceeded to spread out a Scroll of the Tora on the ground and performed a sin on top of her. Thereafter, he grabbed a sword and slashed the Curtain (of the Sanctuary). A miracle happened and blood gushed forth. He thought: he killed himself (a circumlocution for God).[12]

There is some irony in this story. The mighty general could not impose his will even on that unfortunate Jewish woman. The term "seized"

11. *Against Apion*, II, 73, 76–78, vol. 1, pp. 321–325.
12. Giṭṭin 56b. In token of admiration, Constantine the Great, who made Christianity the religion of the State, placed his triumphal arch next to his; see Section IV n. 93.

(תפס) indicates 'overpowering someone, and dragging him against his will' (cf. Deut. 21:19).

Dreading the impact of Jewish legal and political institutions on their own people, pagan writers refused to recognize the merits of men such as Moses. Referring to this fact, Philo noted:

> Greek men of letters have refused to treat him (Moses) as worthy of memory, possibly through envy, and also because in many cases the ordinances of the legislators of the different states are opposed to his.

These men, explained Philo, "have abused the powers which education gave them ... to widespread disgrace." There is "malice" in their writing about Moses.[13]

The political dimension of Roman persecution was already noted by the father of modern political thought, Thomas Hobbes (1588–1679):

> And therefore the Romans, who had conquered the greatest part of the then known World, made no scruple of tolerating any Religion whatsoever in the City of *Rome* it selfe; unlesse it had something in it, that could not consist with their Civil Government; nor do we read that any Religion was there forbidden, but that of the Jewes; who (being the particular Kingdome of God) thought it unlawful to acknowledge subjection to any mortal King or State whatsoever. And thus you see how the Religion of the Gentiles was a part of their Policy.[14]

The underlying thesis of this Section is that antisemitism is not a clash between spiritual systems, but of certain political views intrinsic to European ethos and society (or *europaischen Menschentums*).

---

13. *Moses* I, 2, *Philo,* vol. 6, p. 277; see ibid., I, 3–4, *Philo,* vol. 6, p. 277–279. Cf. appendix 20.
14. Hobbes's *Leviathan,* XII, p. 90.

Specifically, that the idea of Law and liberty put forward by the Tora and embraced by the Jews constituted a challenge to hierarchic government and administration. This rendered Israel a unique nation *because* of its legal and political apparatus. The Scripture, as it was understood in the Synagogue, said so. It recounts that when Balak, the *political* leader of Moab, asked Balaam to curse Israel, Balaam received an oracle, part of which said: "Lo, it is a people that shall dwell (ישכן) alone (לבדד), *and* shall not be reckoned among the nations" (Num. 23:9). Given that by definition every nation dwells separately, what is the point that Israel "shall dwell alone?" And what does it mean that Israel shall not "be reckoned among the nations?" The Aramaic versions of the Tora, which were officially recited in the Synagogue, shed light on the matter. We have three such versions. Let us begin with Ms. *Neophyti* 1, which was recited in the ancient Holy Land. It reads: "...Behold this people shall dwell by themselves and" – in the sense of 'since' – "with the system of governance of the nations (ובנימוסי) are not engaged." Patently, Jews believed that their uniqueness was the result of their exceptional political-legal system. A similar interpretation was given by the *Targum* used in the Diaspora. Taking "to dwell alone" (ישכן) in the future tense, it paraphrases: "this nation alone *shall* inherit the world." To appreciate this version, it would be important to recall that a similar term "בדד" appears in Deut. 32:12: "The Lord alone (בדד) shall lead them (ינחנו)" – the people of Israel. Properly, the *Targum* interpreted "ינחנו" as a future verb, and "בדד" as a reference to God. Accordingly, the verse is foretelling the future palingenesis of the world: "Them alone" – that is, the people of Israel – "God will preserve in the world which He will renew in the future." The key term connecting Num. 23:9 with Deut. 32:12 is לבדד/בדד. By linking these two verses we can discover the nature of this brave new world, and the reason that Israel shall inherit it. It is a *politically* new world that Israel shall inherit by virtue of being guided by God, i.e., of having a political system unlike that of the nations. In sum, these verses are saying that God "alone" (בדד) leads Israel towards a "renewed world" which they alone "shall inherit" because they alone (לבדד) *don't* partake in the political system of the nations. The *Targum* Pseudo-Jonathan, which was composed some time later, synthesized the preceding, and rendered Num. 23:9: "...this people alone shall inherit the [renewed] world *because* they are not governed (מדברין) in accordance with the system of governance (דבנימוסי) of the nations"[15] (see appendix 57).

In the following chapters we will be examining the principal differences between the political and legal institutions of Israel and those of pagan humanity. It is because of this unique system of governance that the Jews were and continue to be targeted by the nations. And yet, as noted by René Cassin:

> Centuries have passed. Judaism has, throughout unparalleled trials, preserved its passion for justice and its desire to contribute to the defense of the rights of men of all races and origins, along the lines of the very principle with which it was entrusted two thousand years ago. The Ten Commandments, the first Code of the essential duties of man, have suffered many an outrage in history and continue to suffer. Their moral authority remains intact.[16]

This may well be Israel's fourth miracle. (see Section V, Concluding Reflections.)

---

15. The first quotation is from ed. Alejandro Díez Macho *Neophyti 1*, vol. 4 (Madrid: Consejo Superior de Investigaciones Cientfficas, 1974), p. 221. The second quotation is from ed. M. Ginsburger, *Pseudo-Jonathan* (Berlin: S. Calvary, 1903), p. 273. The term 'נימוס' which I translated as 'governance,' is usually rendered a 'law,' 'legal practice,' 'norm,' etc.; see Daniel Sperber, *A Dictionary of Greek & Latin Legal Terms* (Ramat Gan: Bar-Ilan University, 1984), s.v. *nomos*, pp. 113–117. However, in conjunction with 'מדברין,' from 'דבר' 'political leader,' it would be more accurate to translate it as 'governance.'
16. René Cassin, "From the Ten Commandments to the Rights of Man," p. 25.

# Chapter 12

# Of *Ḥerut*

From the beginning of time, the relationship between the various elements of society was determined by a vertical system of superior/inferior. *Authority* and *obedience* are functions of hierarchic systems: those occupying a higher echelon have *authority* over those below by the fiat of rank. At the top of the scale stands the Rex (absolute sovereign) exercising total dominion. At the bottom stand the lower strata. They are the marginal folks peculiar to vertical systems. Hierarchy may be based on race or blood (aristocracy); on ecclesiastical or military structures; on political bureaucracies (communism, socialism); on economics (capitalism); or on cultural enlightenment and spiritual superiority (oligarchy). The result is a pyramidal organization on top of which stands an absolute Rex. Hierarchic systems depend on violence and the threat of violence – which include cultural and religious intimidation.[17] At the political level, 'legitimacy' is established by an initial act of violence, simultaneously determining the rules of normalcy and excluding others from the use of violence. 'Obedience' is secured through violence for non-compliance. A government which ceases to control violence lacks legitimacy: might *is* right. At the theological level, too, polytheistic systems postulate a perennial conflict between independent cosmic forces. Order is the result of one or more forces *overpowering* other forces. 'Cosmogony'

17. See José Faur, "Of Cultural Intimidation and Other Miscellanea: Bar-Sheshakh v. Raba," *Review of Rabbinic Judaism* 5 (2002), pp. 34–50.

celebrates the birth and battles waged by forces dominating the world. 'Victory' announces the formal installation of the triumphant party and its subsequent monopoly of violence. Without monopoly of violence all hierarchic structures collapse.

Israel does not recognize the legitimacy of a law standing upon violence. "Violence," noted Philo "is the enemy of law"; namely: *Jewish* Law.[18] The Hebrew people were the first [a] to realize their own bondage and [b] seek freedom *under* the Law. People too dense to acknowledge their bondage will eschew the *responsibility* implied in this type of freedom. "A slave favors lawlessness," said a minority opinion in the Talmud. Since in a state of bondage man has no *responsibilities*, he would rather enjoy libertine relations with another slave than assume the *responsibilities* of wedding a free woman. A rabbi explained: "She [the female-slave] is of little value to him [the male slave], she is readily available to him, and she is promiscuous with him."[19] Addressing himself to those seeking freedom without first realizing their current enslavement, David Nassy (1747–1806) noted:

> Liberty is the most favorite word of our generation, used at every instance, but without knowing what it means. Some think that by virtue of this term they could do whatever they wish. Others imagine that they have [already] shaken off the yoke of slavery, but which, I believe, they never had felt its weight.[20]

18. *Moses* II, 2, 14, *Philo*, vol. 6, p. 457. Cf. R. Saul Levi Mortera, *Providencia de Dios con Yisrael*, Ms. Etz Hayyim 48C 20 (Hebrew University Library), chapters 65–66; Josephus, *Against Apion*, II, 168–174, pp. 359–363; and Herbert Marcuse, "Repressive Tolerance," in ed. R. P Wolff et al, A *Critique of Pure Tolerance* (Boston: Beacon Press, 1969), pp. 115–117.
19. Giṭṭin 13a.
20. David Nassy, *Lettre politico-theologico-morale sur les Juifs* (Paramaribo, ca. 1789), pp. XVIIIXX. For a full treatment of his views, see José Faur, "David Nassy: On Prejudice and Related Matters," in *Neveh Ya'akov: Jubilee Volume Presented to Dr. Jaap Meijer*, eds. Lea Dasberg and Jonathan N. Cohen (Assen, The Netherlands: Van Gorcum, 1982), pp. 87–116.

The rabbis designate the freedom proposed by the Tora and pursued by the Jewish people *ḥerut* (חרות). It is not wanton freedom, but liberty *under* the Law (see Abot 6:2). The Passover holiday comes to commemorate "the time of our *ḥerut*." The Seder (סדר) celebrated on the night of Passover includes a formal dinner, conducted according to strict Jewish etiquette. It centers on the Haggada – a kind of symposium where the participants exchange ideas about bondage and the Exodus from Egypt. It would be appropriate to take note that Seder (סדר) means 'order'– the antithesis of anarchy![21] Whereas in Egypt Israelites were subject to slavery (violence), Seder serves to underline that *order* is essential for freedom. During Passover the unleavened bread – symbol of slavery – is transformed into a symbol of liberty, not by changing its substance, but by eating it "in the way of *ḥerut*." The four cups of wine, too, are to be drunk not in dissipation and debauchery, but "in the way of *ḥerut*." The message is clear: the difference between bondage and freedom is not in *what* you eat and drink, but in *how* you eat and drink. The Seder concludes with a blessing thanking God for "taking us from slavery to *ḥerut*." Similarly, in the blessing pronounced every evening after the recitation of the *Shema'*, thanks are offered for "having taken His people out from slavery to everlasting *ḥerut*."

*Ḥerut* requires political sophistication. The Haggada opens with a phrase encoding the two fundamental dimensions of *ḥerut*: "This year, here, slaves. Next year free, in the Land of Israel." The first segment expresses awareness of one's personal bondage. The second conveys the belief that without a political and territorial sovereignty, freedom is impossible. In this fashion, hope is expressed that *ḥerut* will soon

---

21. The rabbis applied this term to mathematical order and probabilities, as in Mishna Qinnim 1:1. See the illuminating Introduction of Professor Moshe Koppel, *Seder Kinnim* (Israel: Aluma Publishing, 1998). It is also used in the sense of a 'properly executed ceremony,' as in that of the Passover meal. It may be of some interest to note that in Judeo-Arabic, the bridal bath ceremony is designated *sidr al-ḥammam*, that is, 'the *seder* of the [bridal] bathing.' see appendix 36.

be realized in the Land of Israel. To celebrate the *ḥerut* that the Law bestows, Jewish men and women thank the Lord every morning not only for *not* being a 'gentile,' i.e., a member of a hierarchic system,[22] but also for *not* having been made a 'slave.' The latter, as with the opening paragraph of the Haggada, suggests that we may be slaves even when people around us are too dense to sense their own bondage. In a state of bondage, the worst slave is someone unwilling to acknowledge his condition, supposing it to be the 'natural' result of a fate beyond control. By blessing God for *not* having made us a slave, the individual ascertains that human bondage is *not* the work of Heaven.

Without the context and content of law, 'liberty,' 'equality,' etc., are empty slogans, leading to mayhem and wantonness. Because at the heart of the Enlightenment there were men such as Voltaire (1694–1778) and Rousseau, for whom anything remotely 'Jewish' was anathema, they failed to point out that without *a* Law the ideology they were preaching would unleash some of the darkest aspects of man. Their desire to discredit Jewish tradition was so fanatical that they went out of their way to savagely attack the very ethos and integrity of Israel. No lesser a figure than Sir Henry Maine (1822–1888) took notice of their shameful behavior:

> There was but one body of primitive records which was worth studying – the early history of the Jews. But resort to this was prevented by the prejudice of the time. One of the few characteristics which the school of Rousseau had in common with the school of Voltaire was utter disdain of all religious antiquities; and, more than all, of those of the Hebrew race. It is well known that it was a point of honour with the reasoners of that day to assume not merely that the institutions called after Moses were not divinely dictated, nor even that they

22. In Hebrew, 'gentile' (*goy*) refers to a *political,* not an ethnic group, see E. A. Speiser "'People' and 'Nation' of Israel," *Journal of Biblical Literature* 79 (1960), pp. 157–163. The other appellative, 'nations of the world,' too, refers to the political system peculiar to pagan humanity; see below chapter 16.

> were codified at a later date than that attributed to them, but that they and the entire Pentateuch were a gratuitous forgery,* executed after the return from the Captivity. Debarred, therefore, from one chief security against speculative delusion, the philosophers of France, in their eagerness to escape from what they deemed the superstition of the priests, flung themselves headlong into the superstition of the lawyers.[23]

This explains the rationale for excluding Jewish and rabbinic law from the study of ancient law. In addition to the mutual influences pointed out by scholars of the rank of Professor Boaz Cohen (1899–1968) *et al*, there are significant analogies between the Tora and other legal and political systems worthy of study. Few would dispute, for instance, that the idea that national and legal documents require publication by a national institution, and that they must be made accessible to the general public, is best exemplified by the Hebrew Scripture and Jewish tradition. Israel is the earliest model for placing its national texts, first in the Temple and national libraries, and then in the *Hekhal* at the Synagogues (see above chapter 7). This is somehow analogous to the British Magna Carta, the American Declaration of Independence, the Constitution and laws promulgated by the Congress, etc. And yet, although Scripture is the most read book in history, law schools and legal scholars rarely care to consider the Jewish dimension of modern legal and political thought.[24]

Joseph Salvador (1796–1873) envisioned a showdown between Moses (the Law) and Voltaire (the *philosophe*). In this vision, Voltaire suddenly finds himself in a desert covered with piles of bones and corpses. In between, there are rows of green trees. As Voltaire glances carefully, he notices that at the end of each row is standing a

---

* Cf. Biblical criticism.

23. Henry Maine, *Ancient Law* (New York: Dutton, 1965), pp. 52–53.
24. On the anti-Jewish ideologies and feelings among the *philosophers*, see William Nicholls, *Christian Antisemitism* (Northvale, N. J.: Jason Aronson, 1993), pp. 296–299.

Patriarch, crying. When Voltaire asks what they are doing, he is told to wait. Moses then appears:

> 'Is it over?' – cried Moses, in a louder tone than before; without waiting for an answer he took the arm of the philosopher and told him: 'You have asked what these great, venerable Patriarchs with tearful eyes are doing at the end of the rows of green trees? Come and see!' On one of them there was an enormous stone with an engraved inscription: 'Carnage of the French Revolution.'[25]

With this background in mind, David Nassy questioned the 'liberty' espoused by the *philosophes*. To be meaningful, freedom must operate within the context of law. There is malice in an ideology designed to inflame the masses without teaching that freedom needs to unfold within the boundaries of law and reason.

> Finally, the majority think that this pretended liberty shall award them free rein of their savage passions. And in their blind madness they don't consider the obstacles standing in the way of their senseless desires, or the consequences of such a liberty; exposing themselves to the suspicion of advocating the criminal and illegitimate desire of freedom from virtue as well as from mores. But liberty, what is it? Is it license? Is it the dissolution of mores? Undoubtedly not! It is the faculty of having the right to follow reason and the law without incurring the risk of being tyrannized by the stronger.[26]

When God spoke at Sinai, He specified that He was addressing those individuals whom He "had taken out from the land of Egypt, from the house of slaves" (Ex. 20:2) – people too dull to recognize their

---

25. Joseph Salvador, *Paris, Rome et Jerusalem*, vol. 1 (Paris: Michel Levy Freres, 1860), pp. 253–254.
26. *Lettre politico-theologico-morale sur les Juifs*, pp. xviii-xx.

personal bondage cannot possibly 'hear' the voice of God, let alone be free.[27] The freedom awarded by European revolutions (from first to last) and celebrated by the masses is symptomatic of a people too obtuse to sense their perennial unfreedom: before and after. The net result was replacing one set of masters for another. Quoting Nassy again:

> All the people of France and Holland before and after the Revolution were, are, and shall eternally be subordinated to their magistrates. They will be forced to pay taxes, to defend their homes, and to make the sacrifices demanded by their legislators. They are and shall be slaves of the views of those to whom they have entrusted the government, and perhaps more so [after the Revolution] than they were in former times.[28]

27. See R. Se'adya Gaon, *Commentary on Exodus* (Heb.), ed. Y. Ratzaby (Jerusalem: Mossad Harav Kook, 1998), p. 87; Cf. Herbert Marcuse, *One-Dimensional Man* (Boston: Beacon Press, 1964), pp. 7, 32–33.
28. *Lettre politico-theologico-morale sur les Juifs*, p. xx. In their own way the *philosophes* were actually promoting the Christian ideology of freedom *without* law; see appendix 22.

# Chapter 13
# Hierarchic Humanity

There are three major issues dividing Jewish from pagan thought. These are: sovereignty, law, and the status of the individual. Pagan society is organized hierarchically; at the top stands a Rex, or absolute sovereign, from whom the law and rights derive. The Rex antecedes law, society, and the individual. Without a Rex, human society and civilization are impossible.

Man's survival depends on a sovereign and the institutions that he establishes. The basis of hierarchic organization is the right of might. I think that it was Callicles (4th B.C.E.), quoting Pindar, who first defended this principle.

> ... right consists in the superior ruling over the inferior and having the upper hand. By what right, for example, did Xerxes invade Greece and his father Scythia, to take two of the countless instances that present themselves? My conviction is that these actions are in accordance with nature; indeed, I would go so far as to say that they are in accordance with natural law, though not perhaps with the conventional law enacted by us. Pindar seems to me to express the same thought as mine in the poem in which he speaks of 'Law, the king of all, men and gods alike,' and goes on to say that this law 'carries things off with a high hand, making might to be right.'[29]

29. In *Gorgias* 484, (Penguin Classics), p. 79. See below n. 32.

To be meaningful, sovereignty must be grounded on might. As it was argued so forcefully by Hobbes:

> For the Lawes of Nature (as *Justice, Equity, Modesty, Mercy,* and (in summe) *doing to others, as we would be done to,*) of themselves, without the terrour of some Power, to cause them to be observed, are contrary to our naturall Passions, that carry us to Partiality, Pride, Revenge, and the like. And Covenants, without the Sword, are but Words, and of no strength to secure a man at all.[30]

Bereft of the sword embodied in the sovereign, accords are meaningless.

> Covenants being but words, and breath, have no force to oblige, contain, constrain, or protect any man, but what it has from the publique Sword; that is, from the untied hands of that Man, or Assembly of men that hath the Sovereignty, and whose actions are avouched by them all, and performed by the strength of them, in him united.[31]

30. *Leviathan*, XVII [85], p. 223.
31. *Leviathan*, XVIII [89–90], p. 231. Similarly, concerning the heroic idea of 'law,' writes Vico, *The New Science*, #923, p. 338: "This law of force is the law of Achilles, who referred every right to the tip of his spear." The preceding will permit a better understanding of Patriarch Jacob's condemnation of Simeon and Levi (Gen. 49:5). They first deceived the children of Shechem, and then resorted to war (Gen. 34). The correct interpretation of this verse was given by R. Jacob b. El'azar (ca. 1160–ca. 1240) of Toledo, one of the most celebrated grammarians of the period. It was cited from the Arabic by R. Abraham b. ha-Rambam, *Perush*, pp. 197–199. According to his interpretation, Jacob said: "Weapons of violence are their pledges (*muba'i'hom*)" (Gen. 49:5). That is, the pledge that Simeon and Levi made to Shechem was a ruse to excuse violence. The focus of his interpretation is the Hebrew מכרותיהם (root מכר) which he rendered by the Arabic *muba'i'hom* 'contracts, pledges,' root *ba'a* 'pledge, agreement' – a term which in the form *ba'i'a* stands for 'assurance, promise,' and 'transaction.' This term comes from the Aramaic, בעא 'to request, to question' (see Is. 21:12).

"Sovereignty is a matter of fact," noted an eminent legal scholar, that is, the violence that the Rex controls.[32] His legitimacy does not derive from an institution. On the contrary, all political and legal institutions gain legitimacy from the Rex. Thus, sovereignty is absolute and indivisible. This becomes evident upon considering that he has the inherent right to choose all "Counsellours, Ministers, Magistrates, and Officers. Both in Peace, and War."[33]

Second, and as a consequence of the preceding, law expresses the Rex's free and unrestricted will. In the words of medieval teachers: "the king is the law" (*Rex est lex*).[34] Not only does the sovereign not depend on the law, but, actually, the law depends on the sovereign. There cannot be a law or legal system without a Rex who commands it.

---

It also denotes 'to reveal one's inner thoughts and expose them to the outside'; see Baba Qamma 3b. Hebrew מכר 'transacted, sold,' stands also for 'source, quarry,' and 'family,' 'countryman'; see Ezek. 16:3; 21:35; 29:14 and *Targum* ad loc.; cf. Deut. 18:8; II Kings 12:6; Rashi on Ezek. 16:3; *Guide* I, 17, and R. Abraham b. ha-Rambam, *Perush*, pp. 197–199. (The same Hebrew root MKR appears in Arabic with the meaning, 'cunning'; see Se'adya Gaon's translation to Gen. 27:35.) Hence, both the Arabic *ba'i'a* and the Hebrew מכר are semantically parallel, having both the sense of a 'pledge, promise' and 'transaction,' as well as 'bringing something concealed and out of sight, into the open.' The following is a translation of R. Jacob b. El'azar's words: "Weapons of violence are their pledges (*muba'i'hom*)" (Gen. 49:5). He (Patriarch Jacob) meant to say that their (Simeon and Levi) personal 'pledge' (*ba'i'a*) [was predicated] on violence. Indicating, thus, that their course of action, their exploits, and their schemes, stemmed from their (Simon and Levi) reliance on war and their preference for it. I.e., the very pledge that they made to the children of Shechem was in fact a tool of violence. Concerning making a pledge with no intention of keeping it, but to use it as a pretext to war, see Vico's quotation from Plautus [*Pot of Gold* 260], and *The New Science*, #966, p. 357, when "An agreement is not an agreement, and no agreement is an agreement."

32. H. F. Jolowicz, *Lectures on Jurisprudence* (London: University of London, 1963), p. 26.
33. *Leviathan*, XVIII [92], p. 235; cf. ibid. XX [104–105], pp. 256–257.
34. See Ernst H. Kantrowicz, *The King's Two Bodies* (Princeton: Princeton University Press, 1957), chapter 4.

> The theory does not merely state that there are *some* societies where a sovereign subject to no legal limits is to be found, but that everywhere the existence of law implies the existence of such a sovereign.[35]

The purpose of legal systems and institutions is to execute the will of the sovereign.

> The judges therefore act only by the sufferance of the sovereign, and what the sovereign permits he commands; so that indirectly, the rules they lay down are the commands of the sovereign.[36]

The judiciary is not an autonomous institution, independent of the sovereign. The last word in legal matters belongs to the sovereign who alone has,

> The Right of Judicature; that is to say, of hearing and deciding all Controversies, which may arise concerning Law, either Civill, or Naturall, or concerning Fact.[37]

Similarly, his alone is the right to remunerate and punish anyone at his discretion. Whether deservedly or not, the Rex may reward anyone

> … with riches, or honour; and of Punishing with corporall, or pecuniary punishment, or with ignominy every Subject according to the Law he hath formerly made; or if there be no Law made, according as he shall judge most to conduce to the encouraging of men to serve the Commonwealth, or deterring of them from doing disservice to the same.[38]

---

35. H. L. Hart, *The Concept of Law* (Oxford: Clarendon Press, 1994), p. 66.
36. *Lectures on Jurisprudence*, p. 23.
37. *Leviathan*, XVIII [91], p. 234.
38. *Leviathan*, XVIII [92], p. 235. This theory is akin to the doctrine of grace es-

Third, as a consequence of the preceding, humans in a 'state of nature'; i.e., *outside* the realm of the political and legal apparatus established by the Rex, have no rights and must be regarded as in a perennial state of war[39] (cf. below chapter 33).

> [T]hat during the time men live without a common Power to keep them all in awe, they are in that condition which is called Warre; and such a warre, as is of every man against every man. For Warre, consisteth not in Battell onely, or the act of fighting; but in a tract of time, wherein the Will to contend by Battell is sufficiently known: and therefore the notion of *Time*, is to be considered in the nature of Warre; as it is in the nature of Weather.[40]

It is freely assumed that in such a state, man's life and possessions are in peril of utter destruction, and could not possibly survive without the protection of the Rex. Therefore, men stand in respect to the sovereign as slaves in reference to their master.

> The Master of the Servant, is Master also of all he hath; and may exact the use thereof; that is to say, of his goods, of his labour, of his servants, and of his children, as often as he shall think fit. For he holdeth his life of his Master, by the covenant of obedience; that is, of owning, and authorizing whatsoever the Master shall do. And in case the Master, if he refuse, kill him, or cast him into bonds, or otherwise punish him for his disobedience, he is himselfe the author of the same; and cannot accuse him of injury.[41]

---

poused by the Church, whereby salvation may be imputed regardless of merits. Similarly, guilt and eternal perdition may be imputed freely by the right of might; cf. the quote below at n. 48 and "Concluding Reflections."

39. See Walter Ullmann, *The Individual and Society in the Middle Ages* (Baltimore: John Hopkins Press, 1966), pp. 3–50; and *In the Shadow of History*, pp. 32–34.
40. *Leviathan*, XIII [62], pp. 185–186.
41. *Leviathan* XX [104], p. 256.

The point has been eloquently argued by Socrates, in *Crito* (Jowett, *The Works of Plato,* vol. 3, p. 152):

> Can you deny … that you are our [the State's] child and slave, as your fathers were before you? And if this is true you are not on equal terms with us; nor can you think that you have the right to do to us what we are doing to you. (see below chapters 16, 33).

Sovereignty is absolute and indivisible. As per the judicial doctrine of sovereign immunity, the laws that a Rex commands are binding on others, but not on him. Not only that the "king is the law" (*Rex est lex*), but he is "above the law" (*supra legem*).[42] The logic is quite simple. Sovereignty "is a matter of fact," i.e., might; therefore "it cannot be limited by law."[43] This point had been argued by Hobbes. "It is true, that they that have Soveraigne power, may commit Iniquite, but," he adds, "not Injustice, or Injury in the proper signification."[44] In plain words, the Rex is "legally unlimited and illimitable."[45] If there would be any legal limitations on the Rex, then he would cease to be a sovereign. Here is what a renowned legal scholar wrote on this fundamental concept:

> There are, and can be, no legal limits on his law-creating power. It is important to understand that the legally unlimited power of the sovereign is his by definition: the theory simply asserts that there could only be legal limits on legislative power if the legislator were under the orders of another legislator whom he habitually obeyed; and in that case he would no longer

42. For the sources of this basic concept, see *The King's Two Bodies*, p. 163 n. 223; and ibid., pp. 494–495.
43. *Lectures on Jurisprudence*, p. 26.
44. *Leviathan*, XVIII [90], p. 232.
45. *The Concept of Law*, p. 51. Cf. *Lectures on Jurisprudence*, pp. 26–27.

> be sovereign. If he is sovereign he does not obey any other legislator and hence there can be no legal limits on his legislative powers.

Whatever limitations there are on the sovereign, fear of revolt, morality, etc., have no basis in law and cannot be enforced in a Court of Justice.

> He is under no legal duty to abstain from such legislation, and law courts, in considering whether they have before them a law of the sovereign, would not listen to the argument that its divergence from the requirements of popular opinion or morality prevented it from ranking as law.[46]

The Rex cannot injure any of his subjects because the injuries befalling a victim, although executed by the sovereign or one of his agents, *ought* to be imputed on the victim. There is a perfectly logical explanation to this:

> But by this Institution of a Common-wealth, every particular man is Author of all the Soveraigne doth; and consequently he that complaineth of injury from his Soveraigne, complaineth of that wherof he himself is Author; and therefore ought not to accuse any man but himselfe; no nor himselfe of injury; because to do injury to one selfe, is impossible.

Consequently, the Rex cannot be prosecuted in a Court of Justice, or punished for alleged crimes against his subjects.

> ... no man that hath Soveraigne power can justly be put to death, or otherwise in any manner by his Subjects punished. For

46. *The Concept of Law*, p. 67.

> seeing every Subject is Author of the actions of his Soveraigne; he punisheth another, for the actions committed by himselfe.[47]

There is a major theological implication to Hobbes' thesis. Contrary to the Hebrew Scripture, Hobbes maintained that "God reigneth over men … not from his Creating them … but from his *Irresistible Power.*" Therefore, he concluded, God is to be obeyed "… not as a Creator, and Gracious; but as Omnipotent." There is a political agenda to this theology: the authority of the Rex, too, is a function of might. Fundamental to Hobbes' theology is that God punishes not always because of sin, but also because He has the power to do so. In Hobbes' words: "Right of Afflicting, is not always derived from *mens Sinne*, but from God's Power."[48] Obliquely, we learn not to be critical of earthly sovereigns failing to adhere to common standards of justice. Thus, 'might' is 'right' in a double sense: it bestows absolute authority on the Rex and releases him from accepted standards of justice. (Hence the modern doctrine of 'Sovereign Immunity.')

Let us review some of the ideas discussed thus far. The Rex has absolute sovereignty due to the fact that he has absolute might and the power to exclude others from sharing his might. Other areas of power within the state occupy a subordinate position, operating based on the sufferance of the sovereign. Given that sovereignty is unlimited and indivisible, the diverse areas of authority within the state are structured as a pyramid, converging onto a single focal point under the absolute control of the sovereign. Fundamental to pyramidal organization is the division 'superior/inferior,' and 'obedience' owed by a 'subordinate' to his 'superior' by the fiat of rank (as per *fidelis christianus*, see below chapter 28). That is why, in pagan legal theory, law and the power to legislate are inextricably connected to a sovereign standing *above* the law. 'Sovereign' is a man or group of men with the authority to impose laws on others while remaining

47. *Leviathan*, XVIII [90], p. 232. Cf. above the quotation in n. 41.
48. *Leviathan* XXXI [187–188], pp. 397–398. Cf. above the quotation in n. 31.

legally immune, unlimited and illimitable. Accordingly, a situation of 'political unfreedom' (whether resulting from a democratic or non-democratic process) is essential for the proper functioning of hierarchic systems. Since everyone, regardless of rank, is in a position of 'submission,' the people are in a state of political unfreedom.[49] This is why Scripture (Ex. 20:2) characterizes Egypt not as 'a house of bondage' (עבדות) in the abstract, but as "a house of slaves" (עבדים)': a system binding the different elements of society in a vertical structure of 'superior/ inferior.'

49. See F. A. Hayek, *The Road to Serfdom* (London: Routledge & Kegan Paul, 1962), chapter 6.

# Chapter 14
# Horizontal Man

The Tora rejects all of the foregoing. Sovereignty is not the effect of might. The Hebrew Scripture puts forward the principle that God's sovereignty is grounded on the fact that He is the *Creator* of everything (see quotation below in n. 204). His Dominion is positively different from that of the Rex. The latter's claim for dominion is based on might. "The nations," noted the rabbis, "their lives [depend] on their swords."[50] Moreover, the Law was not imposed but was freely negotiated (see above chapter 1). Thus the overwhelming principle: Law is not a consequence of dominion, but of an agreement contracted between two consenting parties. This is manifest in the fact that although God has dominion over the whole universe by virtue of Creation, His Law is not binding on the rest of humanity since they were not a party to the *berit* (see *MT Melakhim* 8:10). This leads to another principle: God does not govern according to whim and want but exclusively according to the Law. Indeed, the whole dialogue between God and man in the Tora presupposes that He is not *above* the Law or the accepted standards of justice (e.g., Gen. 18:25; Ex. 32:12; Deut. 32:4, etc.). Fundamental to Judaism is the belief that God Himself observes the Tora (see above chapter 5).[51] Neither God nor any other member

50. Bemidbar Rabba (Vilna: Jerusalem, 5735/1975), XX, 13, 85b, s.v. *vayyiḥar. Cf. On the Special Laws,* IV, 213, *Philo*, vol. 8, p. 141.
51. This is the legal basis for Maimonides and the sages that the laws given in the Tora are not an expression of divine whim (as proposed by the anti-Maimoni-

of the Covenant can either subtract or add to it. Consequently, if one would express a legal opinion *in the name of God,* he could be charged as a false prophet.[52] Finally, the individual does not depend on the sovereign. In the Hebrew economy of ideas the *individual* creates the *family* that eventually would create the *state.* Prior to the foundation of state, man was not a forsaken creature left alone in a hostile environment, as per pagan wisdom. Rather, he was placed in an environment that "was very good" (Gen. 1:31), and was endowed with the faculty to "rule" over other animals (Gen. 1:28–30; 9:1–7). Before there was a national government in Israel, a young shepherd who would become king proclaimed that God had put all of His creations "under his [man's] feet" (Ps. 8:7). As can be gathered from Genesis and Exodus, basic human rights, such as property, life, freedom from bondage, as well as the institution of marriage, were a given, anteceding the state (see the following chapter). In actuality, properly read, the first two books of the Tora constitute the Hebrew 'bill of rights' *establishing the rights and institutions fundamental to humankind, prior to government, and therefore immune from government.*[53] Thus, according to the rabbis, every human (and not only a Jew) is a "complete and total universe" (Mishna Sanhedrin 4:5).[54]

---

deans). Given that, the Law prohibits ordering a slave to do something for no reason other than for the sake of exercising dominion over him; see *Sifra* VI, 2, 106b-107a; *MT 'Abadim* 1:6; cf. 9:8. Consequently, if God were to issue *miṣvot* for no reason other than whim, He would be abusing His authority. See below, vol. 2, appendix 59, p. 915.

52. See *MT Yesode ha-Tora* 9:1. The same principle applies to someone wishing to substantiate a legal view on the basis of 'divine inspiration,' see ibid. 9:4.

53. Cf. Alan M. Dershowitz, *The Genesis of Justice* (New York: Warner Books, 2000), especially chapter 12.

54. This is the correct text; see *Perush ha-Mishnayot,* vol. 4, pp. 166–167; and *MT Sanhedrin* 12:3; cf. Mishna Abot 3:17, where God's image is associated with 'humankind' and not exclusively with 'Israel.' On the authenticity of this text, see Menachem Kellner, "A New and Unexpected Textual Witness," (Heb.) *Tarbiz* 75 (2006), pp. 565–566. Fundamental to this conception is 'individuation,' i.e., the uniqueness of each individual, see Tosefta Berakhot 6:2, p. 33 (ll. 13–14) and *Tosefta Ki-Fshuṭah, Berakhot,* p. 104. To indicate the exceptionality of every

The supremacy of certain fundamental rights served to establish the sacredness of the individual and the boundaries of authority. A consequence of belief in God's sovereignty is the recognition of certain norms standing above rank (Gen. 42:18) and power (cf. Deut. 25:18 and above n. 1). The expression "fear of God" serves to indicate the basic norms standing above human authority. When Sarah was taken forcefully by a king, Abraham apologized for having misled him because he had thought that "there was no fear of God in this place" (Gen. 20:11) and he would have been murdered. This was not a mere excuse but a fundamental principle: sovereignty disintegrates when "fear of God" is not operative. Let us recall that *Elohim* is the appellation given to God who "created the heavens and the earth" (Gen. 1:1), and therefore Supreme Sovereign over all creation. Remarkably, in a similar incident that had taken place previously in Egypt, when Pharaoh asked Abram why he misinformed him and said that Sarah was his sister, he kept silent and did not reply that he had thought that "there was no fear of God in this place" (Gen. 12:19). Why? In fact, there was plenty of fear of *Elohim* in Egypt – not of God the Creator of the heaven and the earth, but of Cosmocrator-Pharaoh. Hence the function of atheism (see Ps. 14:1; 53:2; and below chapter 33): negation of God will invariably lead to belief in an Adam-*Elohim* (see below chapter 25).

Early in Jewish history, during the bondage in Egypt, a clash took place between the mightiest of the mighty and the lowest of the low. On one side of the arena stood Pharaoh, King of Egypt. To appreciate the magnitude of this encounter, it should be remembered that Pharaoh was not a mere human, but as Ezekiel would later teach, a Cosmocrator with dominion over the whole universe (see below chapter 28). Referring to the Nile, Egypt's god and source of sustenance, Pharaoh declared: "Mine is the Nile." Unlike other humans, a Cosmocrator is not engendered by a biological father (see the

---

single individual, the psalmist referred to the soul as יחידתי ("my uniqueness") (Ps. 22:21; 35:17); see Radaq ad loc. The source of this idea is Patriarch Jacob, see Gen. 49:6. Cf. *Golden Doves*, pp. 140–142; and *Homo Mysticus*, pp. 2–3.

quotation below at n. 170). He owes nothing to anyone and has the inherent right to rule over everything and everyone with unlimited power (see below chapters 31, 33). Thus, Pharaoh boasted: "and I had begotten myself" (Ezek. 29:3).[55] On the other side of the arena stood what in the hierarchic mind represents the lowest echelon of existence: two *Hebrew women*, each challenging "Pharaoh, King of Egypt." Pharaoh issued a direct order to those lowly beings: kill every male infant during delivery! For the first time in history a Rex was disobeyed. It was a matter of fear of God: "and the midwives feared God" and therefore they refused to comply with Pharaoh's command (Ex. 1:15–17). Other cases of non-violent refusals to obey pagan as well as Jewish authorities crisscross throughout the Hebrew Scripture. According to Jewish law there is a duty – not simply the right – to disobey such an order.[56]

In light of the preceding, the rabbinic statement, "On account of righteous women our ancestors were redeemed from Egypt," gains depth and precision.[57] In the footsteps of the two Hebrew midwives,

---

55. See Gen. 40:20: 'הלדת' and the note by A. S. Yahuda, *The Language of the Pentateuch* (Oxford: Oxford University Press, 1933), p. 111. Concerning the ritual by which Pharaoh engendered himself, see R. G. Bauval, "The seeding of the Star Gods: A Fertility Ritual inside the Cheops's Pyramid?" in *Discussions in Egyptology* 16 (1990), pp. 9–21. On the idea of a king-god-Cosmocrator of the world, see below nn. 95, 320.
56. See Milton R. Krovitz, "Conscience, Natural Law and Civil Disobedience in the Jewish Tradition," in *Of Law and Man*, ed. Shlomo Shoham, (New York and Tel Aviv: Sabra Books, 1971), pp. 159–175; particularly pp. 168–172. The first case of military men refusing to obey a king's order as a matter of conscience is registered in I Sam. 22:17. In Dan. 6 Daniel not only refused to obey the king, but he actually went ahead and prayed in violation of his order. The book of Maccabees registered many dramatic cases of civil disobedience. What is significant about this type of civil disobedience is the readiness to submit to legal punishment. To break the law and then refuse to submit to the proper authorities is not civil disobedience but rebellion. For a detailed analysis of the halakha on this matter, see José Faur, "On Martyrdom in Jewish Law: Maimonides and Nahmanides," (Heb.) *Annual of Bar-Ilan University*: In Memory of Prof. Meyer Simcha Feldblum, 30–31 (2006), pp. 373–407.
57. See Soṭa 11b. Cf. the reading in *Yalquṭ Shim'oni*, 2 vols. (Jerusalem: Ch. Vegshel,

Jews throughout the centuries kept on saying 'No!' to the Pharaohs of their time.

n.d), on Ezek. #354, vol. 2, 419c; Ps. #795, vol. 2, 464b. See "On Martyrdom in Jewish Law," n. 25.

# Chapter 15
# The Household of Israel

Genesis, the first book of the Hebrew Scripture, begins with a single individual, Adam, and concludes with the establishment of the first family, the household of Jacob, progenitor of the *children* of Israel. God *creates* the individual, who in turn *creates* the family, which eventually *creates* the State. The man of Genesis is not a helpless creature. He was endowed with "the image of God" (Gen. 1:26–27; 9:6), bestowing on him self-reliance and the faculty to "rule" over the animal world (Gen. 1:28–30; 9:2–5). The environment he inhabited was "very good" (Gen. 1:31). Above all, Adam was endowed with an extraordinary faculty permitting him to establish an institution that would upgrade the quality of human life and make this world a friendlier environment. To fully appreciate this faculty it should be noted that "all" that God made was "very good" (Gen. 1:31). And yet, about Adam it was written "that it is not good for man to be alone, I will make for him a parallel-complementary (כנגדו) mate" (Gen. 2:18).[58] The purpose of having this class of mate was not biological reproduction. Other members of the animal kingdom reproduce without a "parallel-complementary mate." The "not good" of Adam

58. As with a pair of organs and limbs 'complementary' to one another, thus enabling each other to function properly; e.g., right and left hands or feet, that are not *identical*, but *complementary* to each other. In this connection, the expression "and Adam knew his wife Eve" (Gen. 4:1) is not merely a euphemism for marital relations, but serves to indicate that Adam had the psychological and intellectual capacity to actually *know* his mate.

pertains to his mental and psychological development. As if without this special class of mate he would remain unfulfilled and incapable of reaching individuation. With this purpose in mind, man was endowed with the mental and psychological apparatus that would enable him to establish an organic, psychosomatic relationship. "Thus a man will leave his father and mother and cleave (ודבק) unto his wife; and they shall become a single flesh" (Gen. 2:24). The operative term 'to cleave,' 'to bond' (ודבק) refers to a unique human faculty whereby one "an-other" may be horizontally linked (כנגדו) to a second "an-other" and form a psychosomatic entity (see appendix 13).

'Family' is the first human institution. Its purpose is to upgrade human life and permit Adam's children to attain individuation. In this fundamental aspect, the 'family' of Scripture is not a 'privilege' awarded by a political, social, or religious organization, without whose recognition the offspring is to be regarded as 'illegitimate' – the *bestioni* or 'monstrous' and 'bastard' children of pagan humanity; but an institution intrinsic to the very 'image of God' innate in all humans. The stories about the Patriarchs in Genesis attest to this primary institution: the family is independent of a political and social establishment. The Hebrew term for 'household' (בית, rather than משפחה standing for the extended family, cf. Gen. 12:3; Am. 3:2; etc.) means not only 'house' but 'inside' (in opposition to 'outside'). It also stands for 'corporation,' as in the 'fellowship' of individuals sharing a common bond; particularly, that of 'immediate family' and 'household.' Exodus opens with a statement, on the surface of little significance, stating that together with Patriarch Jacob, his children came down to Egypt, "a man and his household" (Ex. 1:1). It encodes a key concept, essential for the understanding of the book: prior to their arrival, each of Jacob's sons succeeded in organizing his own 'house.'[59] The syntax is revealing. The Hebrew suffix *-o-* 'his' (in the construct בית/ו) refers to both subjects of the sentence: Patriarch Jacob and the sons. In plain words, the Hebrew household had been patterned according

59. See the *midrash* published in *Geonica*, vol. 2, p. 326.

to the archetype of Jacob, *and* individually shaped by each son. This archetype must be conceived of, more or less, in terms of the 'genotype/phenotype' model of biology, admitting a level of morphological diversity and individuation, while retaining at the same time the characteristic of the biotype. The future families constituting the Household of Jacob, too, are conceived of in terms of בית/ו. Jews do not reproduce clones, but in terms of 'genotype/phenotype,' admit variation and differentiation within the original archetype.[60] The fact that prior to their arrival to Egypt the Hebrews were organized as a 'household' (בית) will explain the first recorded miracle – a miracle without which no other miracle could have taken place: Israel's discovery that they were slaves! Jews were not the only slaves in Egypt. To pagan humanity slavery is a 'natural' condition. All Egypt was a big "household (בית) of slaves" – from the lowliest servant to the highest officer.[61] In Plato's cave, the truth was discovered by an individual who broke loose from his shackles and discerned light shining above the cave. In Egypt, Israel discovered the light while *deep inside* the cave

60. On this fundamental concept, see José Faur, "The Hebrew Species Concept and the Origin of Evolution: R. Benamozegh's Response to Darwin," *Rassegna Mensile di Israel* 63 (1997), pp. 43–66. The same characteristics are found in "God's seal," see Mishna Sanhedrin 4:5 cited above in n. 54 and *Golden Doves*, pp. 140–142.

61. On the Greek attitude toward slavery, see M. I. Finley, "Was Greek Civilization Based on Slave Labour?" in *Slavery in Classical Antiquity: Views and Controversies* (Cambridge: Cambridge University Press, 1960); Victoria Cuffel, "The Classical Greek Concept of Slavery," *Journal of the History of Ideas* 27 (1966), pp. 323–342. Eccl. 10:17 alludes to the fact that within a tyrannical system the king himself is a slave. Therefore, Pharaoh was not free to choose; see Ex. 7:3, 13, 14, 22, etc. and *MT Teshuba* 6:2. The same idea was echoed by Elias Canetti, *Crowds and Power*, p. 358. Concerning the anxiety peculiar to despots he wrote:

> It is the strongest in the mightiest. The concentration of anxiety is greatest in one who is a source of commands, who creates *orders* and receives them from no one above him. A ruler can keep it hidden, or under control, for a long time, but, in the course of a life, it can increase until, as with certain Roman emperors, it suddenly manifests itself as madness.

(cf. Deut. 4:20, 35; I Kings 8:51; Jer. 11:4). Since everyone was a slave, how did *they* discover that *they* were in bondage?

In utopian societies, old and new, crying for the wrongs of the system equals insubordination. Expressions of grief are controlled by the state. Unexpectedly, an opportunity arose. "And it came to pass in the course of many days that the king of Egypt died." People were expected to lament Pharaoh's death. Israel seized the moment and gathered to grieve. But instead of lamenting the king's death, "the children of Israel came to weep over their bondage, and they cried; and their supplication ascended to God from their enslavement."[62] Only upon acknowledging their bondage, "God remembered His covenant with Abraham, and with Isaac, and with Jacob," and sent Moses to save them (Ex. 2:23–25; cf. I Sam. 12:6, and *Kuzari* II, 56). Moses was the *outcome* – not the *cause* – of Israel's momentous discovery! Again: what brought about this discovery?

The Hebrews recognized Egyptian society for what it was, because *prior* to their arrival they had been organized as the "household (בית) of Jacob." The realization that they were in a "household (בית) of slaves" came through opposition to the "household (בית) of Jacob." It will be clear now why, before leaving Egypt, God ordered the Hebrews to bring in celebration a Passover lamb (Ex. 12:1–14) and eat it "in a single house" (בית, Ex. 12:46). Right to the point, the Aramaic version rendered it 'a corporation' (חבורה), that is, an 'association of individuals engaged in common pursuit and responsibilities.' (In Jewish law the family is conceived of as a corporation). It is by virtue of being incorporated as a 'household' (בית) that the Hebrews merited freedom from Egypt. Accordingly, the Passover lamb is incumbent upon "the household" (בית; see Ex. 12:3–4, 7). During the Passover night, God protected not individual Israelites but the "houses" (בית; Ex. 12:13). Similarly, when God sought to establish a covenant with the Jews, He charged Moses to first bring the proposal "to the household (בית) of Jacob" (Ex. 19:3).

62. This point was brought up to me in a conversation with my friend Benny Dweck over half a century ago.

During the Egyptian bondage the Hebrew 'household' (בית) was further organized into a 'consortium of households' (בית אבות). At the head of each consortium stood an 'elder' (זקן, pl. זקנים), representing their respective consortium. God acknowledged their authority. When God announced to Moses the Salvation of Israel, He ordered him to report to the "elders of Israel" and include them in his mission to Pharaoh (Ex. 3:16–18; cf. 4:29–30; 12:21; 17:6; 18:12; 24:14). More significantly, God's proposal to make an alliance with Israel was first brought "to the elders of the people" (זקני העם) for approval (Ex. 19:7; cf. ibid. 24:1, 9, 14). Later, God ordered Moses to establish an assembly of "seventy elders" (Num. 11:24–25) to govern jointly with him (Num. 11:16–17, 24; cf. Ex. 24:14).[63] Collectively, these elders are designated the 'Congregation' (עדה) of Israel (Lev. 4:13), and constituted the highest judicial and political authority of Israel.[64] Alluding to the organic connection between the elders and the people, the Scripture referred to them as "the eyes of the congregation" (Num. 15:24, cf. Lev. 4:13).[65] Through the elders, the people expressed their supreme judicial and political will. Concerning the authority of the 'Congregation' a Biblical scholar commented:

---

63. The 'Congregation' or Senate of Israel consisted of six representatives per tribe. The excess two were eliminated as follows. Each elected officer picked a scroll from a box containing seventy scrolls with the word 'elder' and two with the word 'blank' (חלק). The two elders picking up these two scrolls were rejected; see Sanhedrin 17a. On the office of the 'elders,' see Hanoch Reviv, *The Elders in Ancient Israel* (Heb.) (Jerusalem: The Magnes Press, 1983).
64. See Robert Gordis, "Democratic Origins in Ancient Israel – the Biblical *'Edah,"* in *Alexander Marx Jubilee Volume*, English Section (New York: The Jewish Theological Seminary of America, 1950), pp. 369–388. On the difference between *'eda* and *qahal*, see ibid., pp. 376–380; and *Em la-Miqra*, vol. 4, 34a; vol. 5, 50b-51a.
65. See *Sifre* #41, pp. 86–87; #306 and *Em la-Miqra*, vol. 3, 8b-9b; vol. 4, 38a-b. This term implies also 'fountain,' because from the elders *flow* not only political and judicial guidance, but also knowledge and wisdom. In this context it would be instructive to note that *Targum*, Rashi, and Maimonides, *Guide* I, 30, p. 43 (ll. 16–22), interpreted "מעיני" in Is. 12:3 in accordance with "מעיני" in Num. 15:24, above. On the rationale for this interpretation, see Maimonides ibid.

> The Sabbath violator is brought before Moses, Aaron and the *'eda* (Num. 15:33 ff.) and it is they who execute the blasphemer (Lev. 24:14 ff.). That the *'eda* is judicial rather than ecclesiastical in character is clear from the fact that the daughters of Zelophehad appear before Moses, Eleazar, the princes and all the *'eda* to demand the rights of inheritance (Num. 27:2 ff.), as do the Transjordan tribes bringing their plea for pasture land (Num. 32:2 ff.).[66]

Through the Congregation, the elders conferred legitimacy on the decisions taken by the national leaders, including Moses (Num. 32:2 ff.) and Joshua (Josh. 15:1, 16:1, 17:1, 18:1, 22:12 ff.). They also confirmed the appointments of kings (see I Kings 12:20; I Chr. 11:3), and expressed formal approval by participating in the coronation ceremony.[67]

Alone in the ancient world, Israel was not organized into 'social classes.' A renowned Biblical scholar points out the uniqueness of Israel's society:

> But it would be a mistake to see in ancient Israelite society the contrasts found in other societies, past or present, between 'nobles' and 'plebeians,' 'capitalists' and 'proletariat.' In Israel, there never really existed social classes in the modern sense of groups conscious of their particular interests and opposed to one another.[68]

A decisive factor in the internal cohesiveness of Israel was the belief in their common ancestry. All members of the original twelve tribes were regarded as 'children' of Patriarchs Abraham, Isaac and Jacob. This, however, was an *inclusive* element, transcending ethnicity.

66. "Democratic Origins in Ancient Israel – the Biblical *'Edah,*" p. 381. See Chief Rabbi J. H. Hertz, *The Pentateuch and HafToras* (London: Soncino Press, 5758–1997), pp. 929–930.
67. See "Democratic Origins in Ancient Israel – the Biblical *'Edah,*" pp. 384–387.
68. Roland de Vaux, *Ancient Israel*, vol. 1 (New York: McGraw-Hill, 1965), p. 68.

People from diverse backgrounds were assimilated into the original tribes. Let us recall that among those coming out with the Israelites from Egypt were the "mixed multitude" consisting principally of intermarried couples (see Ex. 12:38; and cf. Neh. 13:3). Proselytes were fully-fledged members of the nation, sharing also the history of Israel. Each proselyte, too, had to offer the Paschal sacrifice and celebrate the miracles that God wrought for 'his' ancestors (see Ex. 12:48–49; Num. 9:14).[69] Consistent with this doctrine, Maimonides issued a legal decision to a proselyte ascertaining that he may lead in the prayers and say: "Our God and the God of our Fathers, since the Patriarch Abraham is *your* father – and of all those who join Israel."[70] Given that ethnicity was not exclusive, later, under the monarchy, the 'tribe' became 'clan,' in the wide, non-ethnic sense of this term.

> This territorial disposition of the tribes was itself modified by the administrative organization under the monarchy. Sure, everyone remembered to which tribe he belonged, but the unit of society which survived, and which to some extent retained the ancient customs, was the clan. In practice, after the settlement, the village stood for the clan, and in many genealogies of Chronicles, names of villages replace names of ancestors.[71]

By the end of the monarchy, Israel society was close to that of a modern state, rather than to European monarchies. Here is what Professor Morton Smith wrote:

> Accordingly, 'Israel,' before the Assyrian and Babylonian conquests, seems to have been about as distinct an entity as 'Austria' is today. That is to say, there was a nucleus of persons

69. See Samuel David Luzzato, *Commentary to the Pentateuch* (Heb.) (Tel-Aviv: Dvir, 1965), p. 453.
70. *Letters and Essays of Maimonides* (Heb.), vol. 1, p. 234; cf. *Homo Mysticus*, pp. 127–131. Cf. *Perush ha-Mishnayot*, on Bikkurim 1:4, vol. 1, p. 417; *MT Bikkurim* 4:3; *Homo Mysticus*, pp. 127–131.
71. *Ancient Israel*, vol. 1, p. 13.

> united by common interest, common language, common tradition, common religious feeling (loyalty to local shrines and to the national god), and such ethnic uniformity as can be produced by the amalgamation of many elements, but on every side this nucleus blended into the surrounding population.[72]

Let us review some of the ideas discussed above. Humanity began with Adam, an individual created with the 'image of God' within. Given that for the Hebrews there is only One God, and given that Adam is the progenitor of *all* humanity, it follows that every human is created in God's image (cf. Gen. 9:6). A consequence of this view is belief in the dignity of the common man and woman, and rejection of all forms of racial and ethnic discrimination (see appendix 18). This gave rise to the principle of *justice* and *equality*. Hence the fundamental juridical principle – the first in legal history – declaring that "a single Law and a single judicial procedure must apply to you and the alien sojourning among you" (Num. 15:16, cf. ibid. v. 29). Josephus has an important passage about this principle:

> The considerations given by our legislator to the equitable treatment of aliens also merits attention. It will be seen that he took the best of all possible measures at once to secure our own customs from corruption, and to throw them open and ungrudgingly to any who elect to share them. To all who desire to come and live under the same laws with us, he gives a gracious welcome, holding that it is not family ties alone which constitute relationship, but agreement in the principles of conduct.[73]

By way of illustration, let us point out the remarkable fact that the rabbis included two proselytes, Shema'ya (1st century B.C.E.) and

72. Morton Smith, *Palestinian Parties and Politics That Shaped the Old Testament* (New York: Columbia University Press, 1971), p. 18.
73. *Against Apion* II, 209–210, vol. 1, pp. 377–379; cf. ibid. 261, p. 397.

Abṭalion (1st century B.C.E.), in the chain of tradition stemming from Moses (Mishna Abot 1:10). Moreover, the rabbis declared that every single human being – not only Jews – "constitutes a complete world" (Mishna Sanhedrin 4:5; Jew or gentile as in the original text, see above n. 54). 'Slaves' too are included. It is worthy of note that the Hebrew *'ebed* is the equivalent of a 'domestic' in Western society, rather than 'slave' in its common semantic connotation:

> To us it means hideous cruelty, the selling of a human being into the absolute possession of another person who could do with him exactly as he pleased. We think of the terrible slave-trade which existed a century ago, and we shudder. We, who love the Bible, may perhaps feel some regret that it tolerates slavery; and when noble-hearted men tried to abolish it, even leaders of religion opposed them with the argument that it had the sanction of God's Revelation. They who dared to argue in this manner either spoke in shameful ignorance or told consciously a conscious lie. In fact the Hebrew term *'ebed* does not correspond to the modern term 'slave.'[74]

The Hebrew *'ebed* was not plain 'property' to be disposed of by the owner as he pleased. It would suffice to point out that if in the course of chastising a 'slave' he died under the master's whip, the master was subject to capital punishment (see Ex. 21:20).

74. R. Abraham Cohen, *Sabbath Sermons* (London: Soncino Press, 1960), p. 240, see ibid., pp. 239–243. Cf. *The Special Laws*, 34, *Philo*, vol. 7, p. 327, and the note of Chief Rabbi J. H. Hertz, *The Pentateuch and HafToras*, pp. 404–405.

# Chapter 16
# Humanity *before* Statehood

Jewish institutions emerged from the sacredness of the individual, expressed in the doctrine that every human is created in "the image of God" (see Gen. 9:6). The individual, in turn, established the household and family, which in turn contracted the 'Law' or Constitution of Israel, which is both 'divine' and 'everlasting' – two legal doctrines having nothing to do with theology. In reference to the quality of 'divine,' the Tora requires no promulgation by a *political* authority, and therefore is immune from *government* intervention. Consequently, it is 'everlasting' in the sense that it cannot be abrogated by any authority, civil or divine. Later, the people, through their respective elders, representing the households of Israel, constituted themselves as a nation; and thereafter, with David, into a monarchy. The evolution individual → household → law → state → citizen is exceptional. It means, above all, that human rights are a given, inherent in the image of God within. It proposes that the individual does not depend on the state. But, rather, that he *creates* the household which will then *create* the state. A corollary of this principle is the belief that the ruling authorities are not hierarchically superior to anyone: they, too, are equally bound to the same Law (see below chapter 33).

The first book of Scripture begins with the story of a single individual, Adam, ending with the establishment of the first family, Patriarch Jacob's *household* (בית), progenitor of the *children* (בני) of Israel. The second book documents the genesis of the *nation* of Israel. How Patriarch Jacob's *household* created a nation in two strategic movements:

freedom from bondage and the establishment of a primeval covenant. The Exodus involved two distinct elements, "journeying three days into the desert" and "serving" God (Ex. 5:3). Moses did not ask Pharaoh to free the people, but to let them "serve" God in the "desert" (Ex. 5:3). Moses rejected Pharaoh's offer to "serve" God in Egypt (Ex. 8:21), insisting that they must "serve" God in the desert (Ex. 8:23). Why? The primary sense of 'desert' in Hebrew is not 'an arid track of land,' but 'a territory not under the rule of a political entity.' In pagan thought there is an uninfringeable relationship between 'sovereign' and 'territory': the ruler of the land *owns* the people inhabiting *his* domain. It was clear to both Moses and Pharaoh that once outside Egypt's boundaries there could no longer be any claim over the people. To ensure that no claim would be lingering, Israel would journey a distance of "three days into the desert" (Ex. 5:3, 8:23), proclaiming, thus, the forfeiture of any Egyptian claim over them. The second element, "serving God," meant that the Jewish people would formally accept God as their supreme sovereign. In the Hebrew mind, God's sovereignty concerns the realms of the legal and political, and not merely the 'spiritual' as in Christianity. (It also suggests the impossibility of worshipping God under Pharaoh or any absolute monarch, see below chapter 26.)

Acceptance of God's sovereignty took place in Sinai's *desert* where Israel was in a state of political freedom. Regarding this fundamental doctrine, the rabbis taught:

> The Tora was given in a state of liberty, [in a state of] autonomy, in a site under no government. If it had been given in the Land of Israel, the nations of the world would have said: 'They [the people of Israel] do not [yet] possess it!' That is why it was given in the desert: [in] a state of liberty, [in a state of] independence, in a site under no government. Whoever wishes to accept [the Tora] let him step forward and accept [it].[75]

---

75. *Mekhilta de-R. Yishma'el*, p. 205; cf. *Mekhilta de-R. Shim'on b. Yoḥai*, p. 137.

The Jewish political system rests on this pivotal point. Allegiance to the Law renders the Jew free from man. The rabbis taught, "No one can enjoy liberty (בן חורין) unless he is engaged (עוסק) in the Tora" (Abot 6:2). The rights and freedom awarded by pagan states are predicated on personal unfreedom: subjection to the sovereign (see below chapter 33). On this fundamental principle the rabbis taught:

> Whoever accepts upon himself the authority of Heaven (i.e., the Law), political and mundane authority would be lifted up from him. Whoever removes from upon himself the authority of Heaven (i.e., the Law), political and mundane authority would be imposed on him.[76]

In pagan political thought the individual is a creation of the State: freedom is awarded by the State to its subjects. Without statehood the individual, the family, and society have no standing. Social and individual rights are established by the Rex and predicated upon the recognition of his absolute authority. 'Freedom,' 'rights' – whatever their actual content may be – is a condition of unfreedom. Socrates, as portrayed in *Crito*, is first and foremost an *Athenian citizen*. Everything, including his father and mother, as well as his personal status as a human being, and his education, etc., he owes the state. By contrast, a biblical person (regardless of religion) is first and foremost an individual. "It is not merely that man *has* a soul. It is that man *is* a soul – a divinely-created being, invested with rights and dignities at

76. Abot 3:5. There is no ground in between. For some significant insights on this subject, see Israel Abrahams, *Studies in Pharisaism and the Gospels, Second Series* (Ktav: New York, 1967), pp. 4–14. *Shema'* – the most solemn Jewish prayer – begins with a paragraph proclaiming full acceptance of "the authority of Heaven," followed by another paragraph proclaiming full acceptance of God's precepts (see Mishna Berakhot 2:2). For further references and sources, see José Faur, "The Status of Jewish Real Estate outside Israel's Territory" (Heb.), *In Honor of Prof. Avner H. Shaki*, ed. Chief Justice Aharon Barak, *Law Review Netanya Academic College*, vol. 4 (2005), pp. 767–769.

birth, subject to God-made laws and ordinances, and responsible to his Maker" (italics in original), wrote Professor Konvitz. He added:

> The time may come to him to become a citizen of Athens or Rome or Jerusalem, but his citizenship will not be all-absorbing. He will always retain for himself certain liberties, certain powers and dignities – prerogatives which he enjoys as gifts from the giver of gifts, and which he can never lose.[77]

Mindful of the encroachment of gentiles under their political systems, the rabbis refer to gentile humanity as 'the nations of the world' (אומות העולם). As with Socrates, nationality takes precedence over everything else, including their professed ideals and religion.

To an Athenian, a member of a different state is an alien. To a Jew, a member of a different state is another individual in the image of God, Creator of Heaven and Earth. When he meets people from different cultural environments exhibiting different ethnic characteristics, as with Native Americans, the Jew regards them as brothers, "members of the ten lost tribes."[78] In Indo-European societies, *alien*, *enemy*, and *guest* are linguistically and legally interrelated.[79] The idea of 'humanity' – let alone radical concepts such as "families of the world" (in contradistinction to the politicized 'families of *nations*' at the U.N.; cf. below chapter 33) branching from a single human (see Gen. 10:32; 12:3; 28:14; Ezra 20:32; Am. 3:2; Ps. 22:28; 96:7; I Chr. 16:28) – is alien to pagan thought. For millennia, the bond uniting Indo-European societies was blood. Henry Maine called attention to this fact:

---

77. Milton R. Konvitz, "A Philosophy of Human Rights," in eds. Abraham I. Katsh and Leon Nemoy, *Essays on the Occasion of the Seventieth Anniversary of the Dropsie University* (Philadelphia: Dropsie University, 1979), pp. 297–299. This is a most important essay on the subject.
78. Not like the Spaniards, who regarded Native Americans with as much rights as hogs or a dog-litter; see José Faur, "Jews, *Conversos*, and Native Americans: The Iberian Experience," *Annual of Rabbinic Judaism* 3 (2000), pp. 95–121.
79. Émile Benveniste, *Indo-European Language and Society* (Coral Gables, Florida: University of Miami Press, 1973), p. 294.

> If a man was not of kin to another there was nothing between them. He was an enemy to be slain, or spoiled or hated, as much as the wild beasts upon which the tribe made war, as belonging indeed to the craftiest and cruelest order of wild animals. It would scarcely be too strong an assertion that the dogs which followed the camp had more in common with it than the tribesmen of an alien and unrelated tribe.[80]

Israel became the target of persecution because of its political dimension. Throughout the Diaspora, Jews were regarded as a radical minority – not because of their religious peculiarities – but because they alone refused to bow down to the tyranny of the majority. Concerning this type of minority, Herbert Marcuse (1894–1979) observed:

> The tolerance which is the life element, the token of a free society, will never be the gift of the powers that be; it can, under the prevailing conditions of tyranny by the majority, only be won in the sustained effort of radical minorities, willing to break this tyranny and to work for the emergence of a free and sovereign majority – minorities intolerant, militantly intolerant and disobedient to the rules of behavior which tolerate destruction and suppression.[81]

Camouflaged under theo-political noise by the enemies of Israel lies a simple fact: Jews lived under the Law, whereas pagan humanity lived under a man or a group of men. For almost two millennia Jews lived without a government. How long do you suppose other nations could survive without a police force patrolling their streets?

80. Henry Maine, *Lectures on the Early History of Institutions* (Port Washington, N.Y.: Kennikat Press, 1966), p. 65.
81. "Repressive Tolerance," p. 123.

# Chapter 17
# God's Territory

Professor Levine showed that the special laws attached to the territory of Israel must be understood in light of the feudal system common in the region. In the Ancient Middle East, the territory was the *personal* property of the sovereign. From Hammurabi and Hittite law, as well as from commercial documentation from Nuzi and Ugarit, we learn that the sovereign would parcel fiefs to his lieutenants in return for personal servitude and dues from the land and products. The sovereign, however, retained absolute ownership of the fief, and it never became the personal property of the user. This is essential to understanding the status of the territory of Israel. God is the proprietor of the Promised Land: "The Land is mine," said God (Lev. 25:23). A constituting factor in the intellectual and juridical apparatus of Israel is the *exclusionary* principle – a fundamental semantic connotation, overlooked in modern scholarship. In the case of property, this means that the owner has the absolute right to *exclude* others from his property.[82] In the same vein, God stipulated "that the land should not be sold in perpetuity, because the land is mine" (Lev. 25:23; cf. I Chr. 25:8). The people of Israel received the land in title of *Morasha* – something akin, but not identical to fee-tail

82. Best defined in modern jurisprudence by Sir William Blackstone, *Commentaries on the Laws of England* (Facsimile 1765 edition, Chicago University Press, 1972), II p. 2: ... the right of property ... comprised that sole or despotic dominion which one man claims and exercises over the external things of the world, in total exclusion of the right of any other individual in the universe.

inheritance in English Medieval law – in fulfillment of the promise that God made to the Patriarchs (see appendix 13). The people are not absolute proprietors. In God's terms: "that you are like aliens or tenants in respect to Me" (Lev. 25:23). The Sabbatical laws, as well as the dues and agricultural tithes to be paid to the priests and the poor, serve to establish that the fiefs' tenants acknowledge God as the legal proprietor of the estate and pay the tithes and tariffs due to Him.[83]

There are legal and political consequences to this principle. God promised the Land to the Patriarchs. As their legal heirs, the Jewish people took possession of the land by right of succession (see Ex. 3:6–8, 14–17). The Promised Land is the "hereditary succession" (נחלה) of the Jewish people (see Num. 18:24; Deut. 4:21, 38; 15:4; 20:16; 26:1; etc.). The Executor of the inheritance (מנחיל) is God Himself (see Deut. 12:10; Jer. 3:18; 12:14; Zech. 8:12; Ps. 78:54; 135:12, etc.). Upon crossing the Jordan, the Jewish people took possession of what was strictly theirs (see Josh. 1:11). The Tora excludes the king from either the acquisition or the parceling of the territory of Israel. The land was parceled among the tribes of Israel by "lot" (Num. 26:55, 56; 33:54; 34:13; 36:2; Josh. 17:17, 18; 18:8, 11, etc. etc.). In Scripture, the lot has an exclusionary function.[84] In our case, it excludes the king. Since among the neighboring nations, the king would parcel the land among his lieutenants by lot,[85] the Tora stipulates that the lot was to be cast out "before God" (see Josh. 18:10; cf. Ps. 16:5). To stress that the lot represented God's will, rather than the earthly sovereign's, the lot was cast in the presence of the High Priest, implying divine approval. Joshua, the military leader, stood *next* to him (Num. 34:17). It was a widespread belief even among common people that this procedure was established by God, not by the king (Num. 34:13). When

83. Etan Levine, *Heaven and Earth, Law and Love: Studies in Biblical Thought* (Berlin: Walter de Gruyter, 2000), pp. 60–63.

84. E.g., the lot for resolving which goat would be offered to God and which one would be sent to the desert; see Mishna Yoma 4:1; cf. 6:1. On the principle of indeterminacy in Judaism, see *Homo Mysticus*, pp. 111–115.

85. See *Heaven and Earth, Law and Love*, p. 61.

the daughters of Zelophehad approached Moses requesting their father's inheritance, they said: "God had ordered my lord [Moses] to parcel the land in hereditary succession to the children of Israel by lot" (Num. 36:2).

After entering the Promised Land, the children of Israel had to "take possession" (לרשת) of the land; this term (root YRSh) has various connotations. In Rabbinic Literature, it means 'to inherit' by means of succession. In the Tora, particularly in connection to the Land of Israel, it means 'to take possession of one's inheritance, and dislodge squatters and illegal residents, if necessary by force of arms.'[86] This operation was to be carried out by the people under God's direction (see Deut. 8:7–18; 9:1–3). In accordance with the exclusionary principle, this meant that God – *not the military leader* – defeats the enemy (see Ex. 34:10–16) in fulfillment of the promise He made to the Patriarchs (Deut. 1:21; 4:37–38).[87] Obliquely, it serves as a disclaimer for authority on the basis of military victory. When Gideon was offered the monarchy in recognition of his military victory, he responded: "I shall not rule over you, nor shall my son rule over you. The Lord shall rule over you" (Judges 8:23). Gideon's logic was premised on the belief that the Conquest of Israel's territory is the result of God's promise to the Patriarchs, which He executed through His might (see Deut. 8:7–18; 9:1–3). God – not the military leader – defeats Israel's enemy (see Ex. 34:10–16, and appendix 14).

The preceding permits resolution of what seems to be a contradiction between Deut. 17:14–20, prescribing the appointment of a monarch, and I Sam. 8:1–22, where the prophet censures the people for requesting such an appointment. To avert any linkage between the political sovereign and military victory, Scripture requires setting up the monarchy *after* the territory of Israel was secured and

---

86. See Num. 14:22; 21:32. For further sources, see W. Gesenius, *Hebrew and English Lexicon* (Oxford: Clarendon Press, 1907), s.v. '*yarash*,' pp. 439–440.

87. Therefore, the inheritors are not the Israelites taking possession of the land at the time of Joshua, but their parents who originally left Egypt; see Baba Batra 117b.

tenure established – not before. Addressing this point, R. Judah (d. 299) pointed out that although this is "a precept" (מצוה), the Israelites at the time of Samuel were punished "because they (requested) beforehand" (הקדימו על ידם); i.e., *before* they had conquered the land.[88] A close reading of the passage in Deuteronomy substantiates this view. "When you come to the land that the Lord your God gives you, and you have taken possession of it and established tenure on it; and you would (then) say: I shall appoint for me a monarch, as all the nations around me" (Deut. 17:14). Establishing the monarchy before securing tenure of the land would link sovereignty with military might and violence. At the time of Samuel, Israel's territory was not fully secured. The request to appoint a monarch was motivated by military considerations. The intent of the people was to have a king "to rule over us as [it is done] among all other nations" (I Sam. 8:5). In this case, the principal task of the king would be military, as with pagan nations. The point was explicitly made: "And we also shall be like all other nations. And our king shall rule over us, *and he shall go forth before us, and he shall fight our battles*" (I Sam. 8:20). This constituted a vote of no-confidence in God's ability to fulfill His promise, and a formal dismissal of God as Commander in Chief of Israel. "They have not rejected thee," replied God to Samuel, "but they have rejected Me, that I should not be king over them" (I Sam. 8:7). Sovereignty would have been then linked to military power – intrinsically and perennially. It is noteworthy that Saul, the monarch whom they appointed, fell in battle and his reign was dissolved. Pagan sovereigns claim absolute *dominium* over the land and thereby absolute *imperium* over the people of the land.[89]

---

88. *Sifre* #156, p. 208. The alternative explanation of R. Nehora'e, ibid. that "They requested a king to have them serve Alien Worship," reflects the fact that conquest of the land by a king would set him as an absolute monarch, and thus a *de facto* deity, displacing the God of Israel; see appendix 11.
89. In Roman law, *dominium* is an aspect of *potestas* ('power'); see *Digest* 50. 16. 215. On the relation of *dominium* to *imperium*, see *Digest* 2.1.3. For further reference, cf. A. Borkowski, *Textbook on Roman Law* (Oxford: Blackstone, 1997), pp.

Unlike the nations, the people of Israel do not own their territory by the grace of kings. The doctrine establishing that God is the sole sovereign of the Land of Israel is a repudiation of pagan sovereignty. The land is the 'inheritance' of the people and was secured by them through God's intervention, not by the king! Given that the king is *not* the proprietor of the land, as the case of Ahab and Nabot amply demonstrates (I Kings 21:1–24), he could not claim *imperium* over the people.[90] Following the covenant contracted at Sinai, God declared that the people of Israel are *His* slaves (Lev. 25:42, 55). Assuming the exclusionary principle, the rabbis explained this to mean that Jews *would not be* "slaves to slaves" – including the monarch and the state![91]

There are economic consequences to this doctrine. Since the territory does not belong to the king and cannot be transferred in perpetuity to anyone (Lev. 25:23), the possibility of an oligarchy based on the accumulation of wealth is excluded (see below chapter 25). The Sabbatical and Jubilee laws give further emphasis to this doctrine (Lev. 25:1–55). Since without economic autonomy freedom is not factual, the Tora called attention to the fact that these laws were issued "at Mount Sinai" (Lev. 25:1): together with the Decalogue they serve to ensure the personal autonomy of every Jew. Oscar Solomon Straus (1850–1926), the first Jew to be appointed a member of the US cabinet, explained the significance of the Sabbatical and Jubilee laws. His words carry special weight in light of the fact that he had also served as Secretary of Commerce of the US.

---

160–161. On the idea of *dominium* in feudal law, see Walter Ullmann, *Law and Politics in the Middle Ages* (Ithaca, N. Y.: Cornell University Press, 1975), pp. 216–218.

90. For an incisive analysis of this episode, see Chief Rabbi J. H. Hertz, *The Pentateuch and HafToras*, pp. 926–928.

91. Baba Meṣi'a 10a. This doctrine is the source of R. Judah ha-Levi's famous poem, "Slaves of time." There is a beautiful English rendition of this poem by Nina Salaman, *Selected Poems of Jehudah Halevi* (Philadelphia: Jewish Publication Society, 1928), #66, p. 121. Cf. *Kuzari* V, 25.

> In that year, likewise, all agricultural property and all realty other than real estate located in walled cities was to revert to the original owner or to his heirs at law, discharged from all liens, debts, and encumbrances. In this wise the permanent accumulation of large tracts of lands in single hands or families was rendered impossible, and thereby would have been prevented the species of slavery known as the feudal system.

He added: "No better law than that of Moses could have been devised to maintain political equality."[92]

Without the economic basis guaranteed by the Sabbatical and Jubilee laws, the Jewish people would fall prey to what Marcuse referred to as "the realities of the prevailing societies":

> The only authentic alternative and negation of dictatorship (with respect to this question) would be a society in which the 'people' have become autonomous individuals, freed from the repressive requirements of a struggle for existence in the interest of domination, and as such human beings choosing their government and determining their life. Such a society does not yet exist anywhere. In the meantime, the question must be treated *in abstracto* – abstraction, not from the historical possibilities, but from the realities of the prevailing societies.[93]

Alone among the nations, Israel rejected the notion of absolute sovereignty, either over persons (*imperium*) or over properties (*dominium*). All forms of sovereignty are necessarily limited. It is a matter of law: "My jurisdiction (שיטרי) over them (the people of Israel)," declared God, "takes precedence over" (any other jurisdiction).[94] The people

92. Oscar Straus, *The Origin of the Republican Form of Government in the United States* (New York: G. P Putnam's Sons, 1885), p. 115. See below, chapter 25.
93. "Repressive Tolerance," p. 105.
94. *Sifra, Behar*, VI, 106b. Accordingly, if the king would issue an order to do

of Israel never became the *subjects* of political and ecclesiastical rulers. Political subjection of the nation of Israel or judicial subjection of Jews constitutes a challenge to the exclusionary principle implicit in God's sovereignty.

something contrary to the law, such order is illegal; see *MT Melakhim* 3:9. This principle has been the topic of numerous dissertations. Those that I have read exhibit lack of familiarity with legal and political ideas, Jewish and otherwise..

# Chapter 18
# The Three Crowns of Israel

In Israel all forms of authority derive from, and therefore are limited by, the Law. The rabbis described the three executive bodies governing Israel as "three crowns" (שלושה כתרים) representing the monarchy, the priesthood, and the judiciary. None of these bodies have unlimited power.[95] The idea of 'three crowns' was first suggested in an event taking place after crossing the Red Sea, when Israel was attacked by 'Amaleq. To encourage the people in their first battle, Moses ascended a hill and raised his hands in prayer (see Mishna Rosh HaShana 3:8). When Moses tired, Aaron and Hur helped him keep his arms up (Ex. 17:17). The setting became the model for the governing structure of Israel. To function properly, Moses, representing the Law, would require the active support of the other executive

95. See *Sefer ha-Qabbala*, (Heb.) p. 16. The first two crowns are hereditary, unlike the crown of the Tora, which "anyone who wishes to take may come and do so" (*AdRN* A, XLI, p. 130). A similar idea was proposed by R. El'azar ha-Moda'i, Ḥolin 92a. Since the Law is the source of all authority, it follows that "the crown of the Tora" is above the other two, see Yoma 72b; *MT Talmud Tora* 3:1. This fundamental idea was first developed by R. Israel Moses Ḥazzan; see José Faur, *Israel Moses Ḥazzan: The Man and his Works* (Heb.) (Haifa: Academic Publishers, 1978), pp. 64–65. On the separation of power in ancient Israel, see R. Lelio della Torre, "Quelques mots sur la peine de mort et la séparation de pouvoirs chez les anciens Juifs," in *Scritti Sparsi*, 2 vols. (Padova: P. Prosperini, 1908), vol. 2, pp. 292–300. The Christian model of the absolute autocracy, expressed in a "God-Messiah-King" reflect pagan ethos and ideology – not the Scripture of Israel!

branches: Aaron representing the priesthood, and Hur (of the tribe of Judah) representing the political arm of Israel. Later, before ascending Mt. Sinai to receive the Tablets of the Law, Moses charged Aaron and Hur with the administration of the people in his absence (Ex. 24:14; cf. Lev. 4:3, 13, 22).

At the beginning of his ministry, Moses was the "King of Israel," invested with these three crowns: he stood at the head of the Jewish Court, the Sanctuary, and the Nation. Shortly after the Theophany at Sinai, Moses complained that the burden of governing Israel was too heavy to carry alone (Num. 11:10–15). Subsequently, he was charged to appoint seventy elders known to be representative of the people – more or less like the early electoral college in the US – to carry on with him in the government of Israel (Num. 11:16, 24; cf. Ex. 17:5–6). Together with Moses, the elders partook in "the spirit" coming down from God to the Tabernacle. In this fashion, Moses enabled them to share the responsibilities of government (Num. 11:25). At the end of his ministry, Moses appointed Joshua as the next leader of Israel in the "presence" of the congregation of Israel (Num. 27:16–23; Deut. 31:7), implying, thereby, their consent and approval.[96]

In antiquity, the sovereign was also the Supreme Pontiff. Early in the journey towards the Promised Land, Moses divested himself from the priesthood. In a ceremony lasting eight days, he invested Aaron and his children with pontifical authority; divesting himself, at the same time, from the priesthood (see Ex. 28–29). The ceremony consisted of two rituals. First, Moses had to bathe, anoint and clothe the new priests (Ex. 29:4–9). Then, he offered an elaborate sacramental sacrifice where he sprinkled Aaron and his children with the blood of the sacrifice. The ceremony concluded with a ritual meal where the consecrated priests consumed the sacrifice (Ex. 29:32–34). The ceremony was executed by Moses *personally*, for the following two reasons. First, the consecration of the priesthood was a national issue. Therefore, it had to be executed by the head of the

96. See Berakhot 55a; *MT Melakhim* 1:3.

nation together with the Supreme Court.[97] Second, by executing all facets of the rituals, including the bathing and anointing, Moses was solemnly declaring his divestiture from the priesthood.[98] Following their consecration, God charged Aaron and his sons with the government and management of the Sanctuary (Num. 18:1–7). Later, when a dispute arose between Moses and Aaron concerning the propriety of a sacramental meal, Moses conceded and the matter was settled in Aaron's favor (see Lev. 10:12–20). In this manner, the autonomy of the priesthood from the realm of the political was established. Referring to this momentous step in political history, Straus commented:

> Having crossed the Red Sea, the first significant step taken by Moses is the separation of Church and State, by causing the priestly duties to devolve upon Aaron, and the military command upon Joshua, while Moses retains the entire charge of the civil administration, until about the third month of wanderings, when they arrived at the foot of Mount Sinai.[99]

The three crowns are formally and irrevocably autonomous from one another; they may not infringe on each other's authority or usurp it. This leads to one of the most important developments in political history: the separation of kingship from divinity (much more significant than our modern separation of Church and State).

97. See Tosefta Sanhedrin 3:4, p. 418; *MT Kele ha-Miqdash* 4:23; cf. Rashi on Yebamot 61a s.v. *minnahu*; Tosafot on Yoma 12b s.v. *kohen,* and Megilla 9b s.v. *ve-lo*.
98. See Vayyiqra Rabba XI, 6, vol. 1, pp. 226–228. Cf. Zebaḥim 120a; Ta'aniyot 11b; and the sources discussed by R. Ḥayyim Palaggi, *Re'e Ḥayyim*, vol. 2, 13c-14b. Although the laws of purity were legislated by Moses, they were issued and executed by the priesthood; see Num. 31:21; cf. 19:1–2.
99. *The Origin of the Republican Form of Government in the United States*, p. 104. In this regard we should note that the tribe of Levites and priests was not included with the rest of the tribes; see Num. 1:49.

> In the light of the Egyptian, and even Mesopotamian, kingship, that of the Hebrews lacks sanctity. The relation of the Hebrew monarch and his people was as nearly secular as is possible in a society wherein religion is a living force.[100]

The Hebrew king was not the head of the sanctuary, and was not involved in the rituals. King Saul was severely censured by Samuel for participating in the sacrament of a sacrifice (see I Sam. 13:8–14). Although non-priests were permitted to officiate before the building of the Temple in Jerusalem, Samuel forbade Saul to officiate, lest the people assume that the Jewish king could head the sanctuary, like pagan monarchs. When King Uzziah tried to burn incense at the Temple, the High Priest with a group of eighty priests rebuffed him: "it is not for you, Uzziah, to burn incense to the Lord, but for the priests, the sons of Aaron" (II Chr. 26:16–21).[101] Similarly, the rabbis rebuffed a Maccabean king: "It should be enough for you the crown of kingdom. Let the crown of priesthood stay with the children of Aaron!"[102] Conversely, the rabbis declared: "Priests may not be anointed as monarchs!"[103]

Pagan sanctuaries were under the official tutelage of the monarch. "When the Egyptians ruled over Palestine," wrote Professor Bickerman, "the Pharaohs likewise cared for the local gods, and built them

100. Henry Frankfort, *Kingship and the Gods* (Chicago: Chicago University Press, 1948), p. 341.
101. Cf. Shabbat 31a, Hillel's explanation to the proselyte, why he could not become a High Priest. For an incisive analysis of this doctrine, see R. Ḥayyim Alfandari, *Esh Dat* (Constantinople, 5478/1718), 51b-52a.
102. Qiddushin 66a. The standard explanation, that the rabbis objected because of rumors that his mother had been defiled, makes little sense. Jewish law does not invalidate the status of a priest on rumors; see the discussion ibid., a-b. There were other grounds for opposing Maccabean priesthood; see Yoma 72b, and *In the Shadow of History*, p. 201.
103. Yerushalmi Sheqalim VI, 1, 49d. See *Yefe Mar'e*, 93b; *Esh Dat*, 51b; and Harry Wolfson, *Philo*, vol. 2, pp. 338–339.

temples, for instance to 'Mekal, the great god, the lord of Betshan.'"[104] The close relationship between the realms of the political and the religious may be seen in the fact that, "For the ancients a city was the dominion of its tutelary gods."[105] By contrast, the administration and running of the Jewish Temple was not financed by the political ruler. To ascertain the independence of the Temple from the monarch, the Law authorized the Temple to institute a half-shekel annual tax upon every Israelite to finance the public sacrifices (see Ex. 30:11–16; 38:25–26; cf. Neh. 10:33). This tax was levied by the Temple, not the king. The tithes and other contributions levied from the people for the administration and maintenance of the priests and Levites served to ensure their independence from the monarch and the mighty. These taxes, too, were not given to a government agency under the control of the political ruler, but were paid directly by the Israelites to the priests and Levites. In this manner, the separation of the priesthood from the political was further enhanced. Christian criticism of these taxes (see Matt. 17:24–27) fails to consider that the alternative is surrendering the clergy and religious institutions to the control of the mighty.[106] In the mind of the Hebrews, the maintenance of the poor and needy is not the responsibility of the state, but a personal responsibility from one human being to another. Accordingly, the different tithes and alms for the poor are to be given directly to them, not to a government agency. In this fashion, the power of the state was further restrained.

---

104. Elias Bickerman, "The Edict of Cyrus in Ezra," in *Studies in Jewish and Christian History*, vol. 1, p. 93.
105. "The Edict of Cyrus in Ezra," in *Studies in Jewish and Christian History*, vol. 1, p. 92.
106. Jesus' thesis that since the Jews are God's children they should not have to pay tax to the Temple is oblivious of the fact that this would have reduced the Temple and the priesthood to the mercy of the monarch and the rich and powerful, and consequently it would have to suffer the same vicissitudes as the Church and Christian clergy. See, however, Richard Bauckham, *The Bible in Politics* (Louisville, Kentucky: John Knox Press, 1989), pp. 73–79. Cf. below Section IV n. 145.

In ancient Israel, the monarch, as with King Jehoshaphat, was responsible for the organization and supervision of the judiciary.[107] However, unlike the pagan monarch, the Jewish king was not above the Law, and when manipulating the law he was severely rebuked.

> From the beginning of the monarchy, the king was at any moment in peril of rebuke, even of rejection, by the prophets, who reminded him that the king's sovereignty was not unlimited, that over the king's *mishpaṭ* (law) stood the *mishpaṭ* of the Lord – an idea that frequently clashed with the exigencies of government.[108]

Limited sovereignty was the point of contention between the kingdom of Judah and Northern Israel. Unlike Judea, where the Temple was under the control and administration of the priesthood, in the North the sanctuaries and priests were under the control of the monarch. On this basis, Amaziah, the high priest of the local sanctuary in northern Bet El, sought to muzzle Amos since (unlike the Temple at Jerusalem) it was "the king's sanctuary and a royal abode." Absolute sovereigns can thrive only in hierarchic societies. The Scripture portrays northern Bet El under the rule of idolatrous Jeroboam, as a city surrounded by "a vertical (אנך) wall." In Hebrew, this term means also 'plumb line.' In retribution, God would take a 'plumb line' and measure the inequities performed by hierarchic oppression against "*my* people Israel." The latter is an exclusionary expression. According to pagan ideology the sovereign has *imperium* – 'rule and power' – over *his* subjects. By designating Israel as "*my* people," Amos was rejecting the pagan idea of sovereignty. Belief in the God of Israel constitutes a repudiation of the notion of *imperium* whereby the people 'belong' to

107. See II Chr. 19:4–11. Cf. W. F. Albright, "The Reform of Jehoshaphat," in *Alexander Marx's Jubilee Volume* (New York: The Jewish Theological Seminary, 1950), pp. 61–82.

108. *The Prophets*, p. 478. See, for example, Jer. 22:13–19 and Radaq ad loc. See above, Section II, *Concluding Reflections*.

the sovereign. Israel is "*my*" – not the ruler's – "people," declared God! (see Ex. 5:1; cf. 3:10 etc. and above n. 89). Since hierarchic societies are in fact grounded on the oppression of the weak, they are doomed to collapse.[109] In vertical organizations and pseudo-democracies, 'conspiracy' is a code-term designed to muzzle dissenting opinions: invariably, criticism is construed as incitement. Symptomatically, the high priest Amaziah asked the king to intervene, charging: "Amos has conspired against you" (Am. 7:7–13).

By way of conclusion, we may notice that Moses, the first sovereign of Israel, was also the first sovereign in history to divest authority from himself out of his own volition, without violence or the threat of violence. Hence, he is described as "the most humble person on the face of earth" (Num. 12:3). The rabbis, too, were not interested in the accumulation of power. R. David Nieto (1654–1728) showed that instead of seeking to extend their own authority, the rabbis, of their own volition, sought to further limit their own authority and jurisdiction, time and again.[110]

109. See Vayyiqra Rabba XXXIII, 2, vol. 4, pp. 758–760.
110. See *Maṭṭe Dan* II, #150–157, 45a-48a.

# Chapter 19
# Hebrew Theocracy: Sovereignty *under* the Law

Monarchy was not essential to Hebrew culture and civilization. The 'golden period of Israel' came before the monarchy. Historically, it was the people who demanded the establishment of the monarchy to deal with a military crisis (see I Sam. 8:10, 19, 22; 10:17–27; 11:14–12:25). For other nations, monarchy, standing for absolute power, is essential for their notion of civilization and culture. Without a king, nationhood, order and progress are inconceivable. Invariably, the birth of a country is connected with kingship, one way or another. In this fundamental aspect, the Hebrew people and civilization differed. Before having a king, the Hebrews had been a duly constituted nation, with well-established political and juridical institutions. According to Jewish historiography, the eventual destruction of Israel was the result of wicked monarchs.[111] For that reason alone, despite the obvious similarities between Israel and neighboring countries, the political organization and national ethos of the Hebrews were exceptional.

> [F]or the Hebrews, though in the Near East, were only partly of it. Much is made nowadays of Canaanite and other Near Eastern elements in Hebrew culture, and a phenomenon like

111. Cf. Debarim Rabba (Lieberman), pp. 98–99.

> Solomon's kingship conforms indeed to the type of glorified native chieftainship which we have characterized in the preceding paragraph. But it should be plain that the borrowed features in Hebrew culture, and those which have foreign analogies, are least significant. In the case of kingship they are externalities, the less important since they did not affect the basic oddness of the Hebrew institution.[112]

The monarchy was not imposed. David was crowned King of Israel and his dynasty was instituted by virtue of a "covenant," negotiated by him with the elders representing *all* the tribes of Israel (see II Sam. 5:1–3). Later, kings were installed in a threefold public ceremony. First, there was the coronation and anointment ceremony performed at the Sanctuary (see I Kings 1:32–48 and II Kings 11:12–20). It was followed by an official acclamation from the people. In celebration, they sounded the horn and trumpet, clapping hands and shouting: 'Long live the king!' (I Kings 1:34, 39; II Kings 11:12, 14; cf. 9:13). Finally, the king left the Sanctuary and sat on the throne, assuming power.[113] Since the people of Israel had been constituted as a nation independent of the monarchy, they never felt subservient to it.

> If kingship counted in Egypt as a function of the gods, and in Mesopotamia as a divinely ordained political order, the Hebrews knew that they had introduced it on their own initiative, in imitation of others and under the strain of emergency.[114]

The king was expected to act according to previously agreed norms. With this purpose in mind, after appointing Saul, Samuel wrote a document, "the king's rule," instituting the norms of conduct of the monarch and the people, which he deposited "before the Lord" (I Sam. 10:25). These norms were not permanent and were negotiated

112. *Kingship and the Gods*, pp. 338–339.
113. See *Ancient Israel*, vol. 1, pp. 102–107.
114. *Kingship and the Gods*, p. 339.

by the king and the elders. David negotiated the terms of the monarchy with the elders of Israel (see II Sam. 5:1–3). Similarly, Jehoiada "negotiated a covenant between God, the king and the people" (see II Kings 11:17). Rehabam's refusal to comply with the advice of the elders and with the request of the people led to the secession of ten of the tribes of Israel (see I Kings 12). When Rehabam sent his personal representative to collect taxes from the people, they stoned him to death and the king had to run for his life (I Kings 12:18). Ideally, the monarch, as the elders advised Rehabam, ought to be the "slave" (עבד) to the people: their loyalty to him was conditioned on *his* submission to *them* (see I Kings 12:7; II Chr. 10:7). The same is true with other government officers. In this spirit, Rabban Gamliel II (1st and 2nd centuries), when appointing two rabbis to a communal position, told them: "Do you imagine that I am investing you with a mandate? I am investing you with enslavement! (עבדות)"[115]

We have previously seen that the Hebrew monarch was not an absolute sovereign. Early in their political history, the people exercised political and judicial power through the institution of the elders. For that reason alone, the government of Israel may be properly described as a *democracy* – at least on a par with any other government in antiquity, including Greece and Rome. This is how a leading biblical scholar described the government of Israel:

> The Biblical concept of the state can be described as 'democratic' with at least as much justice as the Mesopotamian form of government. It is the people (i.e. *demos*) of Israel who have a decisive say as to how and by whom they are to be ruled; it is they who set up their kings time and again.[116]

Above all, the government of Israel was *representative*. The elders were in fact the spokespersons and delegates of the people. Explicitly, God

115. *Sifre Debarim* #17, p. 26; Horayot 10a-b. Cf. *Sifre Zuṭa*, p. 146. Cf. Mk. 10:43.
116. E. A. Speiser, "The Biblical Idea of History in Its Common Near Eastern Setting," in Judah Goldin ed., *The Jewish Expression* (New Haven: Yale University Press, 1976), p. 9.

charged Moses to appoint elders whom "you know that they are the elders of the people and their officials" (Num. 11:16). Likewise, the rabbis established: "No public officer may be appointed unless the public is consulted."[117] The term "הבו" used by Moses when instructing the people to appoint their officers (Deut. 1:13), was properly explained by Oscar Straus. It means:

> ... take for you or select for you, not that I (Moses) will make rulers over you of my own selection... and such as you select I will make them rulers.[118]

One may argue that the elders and public officers were not formally elected, but only appointed. In this connection it would be well to remember that the members of the Electoral College, beginning with the election of George Washington in 1789, were also appointed and not elected.

Those inimical to political Israel dismiss with lofty contempt the Jewish form of government with the alleged reason that it was a 'theocracy.' Addressing these writers, Oscar Straus noted:

> Many writers fall into the error of defining this theocratic government by priests, or a purely religious commonwealth. The very fact that the Levites, the tribe of priests, were separated from other tribes, and that, with the single exception of Eli, no priest was ever elected to the chief magistracy during the entire period of the Commonwealth, decidedly negates any such interpretation.[119]

117. Berakhot 55a. Cf. *Rav Saadya's Commentary on Exodus*, p. 246.
118. *The Origin of the Republican Form of Government in the United States*, p. 105.
119. *The Origin of the Republican Form of Government in the United States*, pp. 108–109; see quotation below in n. 346. The worst book that I have read on the subject is by Gershon Weiler, *Jewish Theocracy* (Leiden: E. J. Brill, 1988). On contemporary Jewish bigotry against Israel and Zionism, see Edward Alexander, *The Jewish Wars: Reflections by One of the Belligerents* (Carbondale: Southern Illinois University Press, 1996).

Since the principal leader organizing the return of the Jewish people to their ancestral home was Ezra (flourished 5th century B.C.E.), a scholar-priest (see below chapter 21), some argue that the Second Commonwealth was nothing more than an ecclesiastical state. To this allegation, Professor Bickerman responded:

> Nevertheless, it would be erroneous to regard the district of *Yehud* in the fourth century as an ecclesiastical state. While in Egypt, at the same date, a very large part of the soil belonged to the temples, and even a tithe of custom duties was assigned to them, the sanctuary of Jerusalem does not appear to have possessed any real estate outside its own site, and the emoluments of the priests were offerings of the believers.[120]

There is malice in divines and historians who, by virtue of imperial might, appropriate Jewish terms as their own, and then charge them with obscurantist connotations derived from pagan and Church ideology (see below chapter 29). Thus, luminaries of all persuasions effect a quantum jump backwards in time, and freely apply all the negative nuances accrued by Christian governance to *Jewish* theocracy. The method is essentially flawed. 'Theocracy' was never a part of the Greek political lexicon. It was first coined by Josephus, precisely, because Greek political lexicon lacked adequate terminology to describe the political system of Israel. This term, as pointed out by Professor Wolfson (1887–1974), was most probably suggested by a passage in Philo. Referring to the people at the time of the 'Tower of Babel,' Philo wrote that they were under "the government of God" (*Theou kratos*) – an expression almost identical to 'theocracy.' Vico, too – probably with the same passage in mind – wrote that these people were "under the government of God, which Philo has elegantly named *Theokratia*."[121] At any rate, other than anti-Jewish bias, there

120. Elias Bickerman, *From Ezra to the Last of the Maccabees* (New York: Schocken Books, 1962), p. 14; see ibid., p. 9.
121. *The First New Science*, in *Vico Selected Writings*, ed. and trans. by Leon Pompa

are no bases for assuming that Christian (or Greek) political theory could elucidate the sense of 'theocracy' in Josephus. To ascertain its meaning, it seems, it would be best to *read* the paragraph in question. Here is what Josephus wrote:

> There is endless variety in the details of the customs and laws which prevail in the world at large. To give but a summary enumeration: some peoples have entrusted the supreme political power to monarchies, others to oligarchies, yet others to the masses. Our lawgiver, however, was attracted by none of these forms of polity, but gave to his constitution the form of what – if a forced expression be permitted – may be termed a 'theocracy,' placing all sovereignty and authority in the hands of God.[122]

The sense is clear. Since the Law was given by God, and since said Law represents His will, God is in fact governing Israel. Bearing the same idea in mind, Philo wrote:

> It is a king's duty to command what is right and to forbid what is wrong. But to command what should be done and to forbid what should not be done is the peculiar function of law; so that it follows at once that the king is a living law, and the law a just king.[123]

This is a corollary of the belief "that the Father and Maker of the world was in the truest sense also its Lawgiver."[124] The Scroll of the Law

(Cambridge: Cambridge University Press, 1982), p. 91. See Wolfson, *Philo*, vol. 2, p. 382; and the incisive comments of Samuel Belkin, *In His Image* (New York: Abelard-Schuman, n.d.), pp. 15–19.

122. *Against Apion*, II, 165–166, *Josephus*, vol. 1, p. 359.
123. *Moses* II, 4–5, *Philo*, vol. 6, p. 453. Cf. *Em la-Miqra*, vol. 5, 15b-16a; and above Section II, n. 8.
124. *Moses* II, 48, *Philo*, vol. 6, p. 473. See below n. 204.

that the Jewish monarch must carry at all times is the "ensign of sovereignty which none can impeach, formed in the image of its archetype the kingship of God."[125] The same belief was voiced by Josephus:

> For us, with our conviction that the original institution of the Law was in accordance with the will of God, it would be rank impiety not to observe it. What could one alter in it? What more beautiful one could be discovered? What improvement imported from elsewhere? Would you change the entire character of the constitution? Could there be a finer or more equitable polity than one which sets God at the head of the universe, which assigns the administration of its highest affairs to the whole body of priests, and entrusts to the supreme high-priest the direction of the other priests?... But this charge further embraced a strict superintendence of the Law and of the pursuits of everyday life; for the appointed duties of the priests included general supervision, the trial of litigation, and punishment of condemned persons.[126]

Since in this passage Josephus identifies 'God' with 'Law'– a monstrous impiety in analphabetic theology – it has been described as a "long and rather rambling discussion of the topic [theocracy]."[127] Wolfson, however, has shown that Philo held the same belief: "On the basis of scriptural terminology, then, the constitution of the [Jewish] state as outlined by Moses should be called a government by God." This does not mean that the people are directly governed by God, as those seeking to deprecate Hebrew political thought claim: in Israel, God's *will* – not His person – is embodied in the *Law,* not in *people* representing the Law (see above, Section II, Introductory Remarks). As was shown by Wolfson, Philo was saying that since the Jewish State is "ruled by a law revealed by God," which has "its source of authority

125. *The Special Laws,* IV, 164, *Philo,* vol. 8, p. 111.
126. *Against Apion.,* II, 184–186, *Josephus,* vol. 1, p. 367.
127. James F. Driscoll, "Theocracy," *The Catholic Encyclopedia,* vol. 14, p. 568.

in God," it should "be described as a state ruled by God."[128] In this connection it is important to consider that in Hebrew semantics you have received the letter from the sender, not from the postman who hands it to you. Likewise, the ticket for a traffic violation is in fact given to you by the Traffic Authority, not by the police officer.[129] People living in hierarchic systems regard the final effect as the product of its immediate cause. Some of the Hebrews coming out from Egypt, (who had not yet shed the slave mentality), blamed Moses and Aaron for some of the vicissitudes encountered on the way. To which Moses responded: "And what are we? Your complaints should not be (addressed) against us, but against the Lord" (Ex. 15:8). Eventually, Israel overcame pagan semantics. A case in point is the blessing that the faithful offers in thanks to God for "having taken the bread out of the earth." Obviously, the intention is not that the actual loaf of bread was not made by the baker but directly by God, but that He, the Creator of everything had initiated a chain of causes and events leading to this loaf of bread.[130]

*Hebrew* theocracy is in reference to God who, as author of the Law, initiated a course of events leading to the system governing Israel. This is standard Jewish belief. Expressions such as 'Kingdom

128. Wolfson, *Philo*, vol. 2, pp. 381–382. It could be argued that a more appropriate term would be 'nomocracy,' or 'government by the Law.' However, since 'nomocracy' meant a manmade law (bearing all the legal and political implications of pagan legal and political ideals), Josephus coined a new term to convey the belief in a Law coming from God and not from the political sovereign. It is on this basis that the Jewish government is designated 'theocracy,' i.e., a Nation governed by (a Law given by) God. This is the place to point out that according to Philo and the rabbis, the authority of the priests to interpret and apply the Law rests on their knowledge and expertise; see Wolfson, *Philo*, vol. 2, pp. 341–342; and "Performative and Descriptive Utterances in Jewish Law" (Heb.), p. 105 n. 25.
129. Therefore, "to write" the Book of Law (Deut. 17:18), could be implemented by appointing someone else to write it. The same is the case with a bill of divorce; see M. A. Friedman, "*Ve-Khatab lo...*" *Sinai* 84 (5739/1979), pp. 175–179.
130. See *Golden Doves*, pp. 18–21, and Section IV, n. 190. Cf. Tosefta, Berakhot 6:2, p. 33.

of the Almighty' (מלכות שדי) and 'Kingdom of Heaven' (מלכות שמים) in the liturgy and rabbinic literature, mean that God's *Law* – not a man or group of men incarnating a deity – is the supreme rule of Israel! This is precisely what Jesus had in mind by the "Kingdom of Heaven" (*basileia ton ouranon*; see Matt. 4:17; cf. 6:10; Mk. 9:1; Lk. 11:2) and "Kingdom of God" (*basileia tou theou*, see Mk. 1:15; Lk. 9:27; 21:31) – not the hallucinatory mystical visions of divines! With Oscar S. Straus, we can summarize the preceding as follows:

> The government under the Judges [= זקנים] was very much like our own Federal Government: each tribe had its own tribal or state government, which had jurisdiction over local affairs, and it sent its duly elected representatives to the national congress. This government, from the fact that God, the source of all power, the embodiment of the law, and not a king, was ruler of the nation, is termed by various writers a Theocracy, or Nomocracy (from *nomos* law), or a Commonwealth.[131]

Hence, "the spirit of equality" permeating the Hebrew Scripture. "Equality," reasoned the Jewish monarch, "will earn its just rewards." Conversely, "inequality will create the gravest perils and pitfalls." It is incumbent upon Jewish monarchs not merely to eschew, but actually "to hate inequality, the bestower of darkness and wars." It is on this ground that Philo maintained that democracy is "the most law-abiding and best of constitutions.... For inequality on the other hand is the cause of sickness and vices."[132] Whereas in pagan political thought everyone is subject to a man or group of men, Moses "made the Law the standard and rule that we might live under it as under a father

131. *The Origin of the Republican Form of Government in the United States*, p. 108.
132. *The Special Laws*, IV, 165–166, *Philo*, vol. 8, p. 111; and ibid., 237, p. 155. See also ibid., 168, pp. 113–115; and 231, p. 151; and *The Unchangeableness of God*, 176, *Philo*, vol. 3, p. 97. Philo's idea of 'democracy' does not derive from Greek sources, cf. translator's appendix, ibid., p. 489, but from Jewish political tradition.

and a master."[133] In conclusion, granting that the Jewish rituals and religious concepts are idiosyncratic,

> On the other hand, their form of government was constructed upon laws of universal humanity, upon the broad principles that all men are equal, that God alone is King; which were as true when the Declaration of Independence was adopted as in the times of Moses and Joshua, and as true in New England as they were in Canaan.[134]

An important corollary to the preceding is that all forms of sovereignty, including that of the Jewish monarch, are *under* the Law. Accordingly, in all and every Synagogue, the Tora or Law of Israel is seated on the *Hekhal* – a term standing for the official seat of residence of the sovereign (see above chapter 5).

133. *Against Apion* II, 174, *Josephus,* vol. 1, p. 363.
134. *The Origin of the Republican Form of Government in the United States,* p. 74.

# Chapter 20
# The Crown of a Good Name

We had occasion to see that each of Israel's "crowns" had limited authority. Playing on the term *zer* ('crown,' 'boundary')/*zar* ('alien') connected with these three crowns, R. Johanan expounded: "if (the bearer of the crown) has merit, it would be a crown (for him), but if not it (the crown) would alienate itself from him."[135] At its most fundamental level, this means that officials trespassing the 'boundary' of their authority and jurisdiction (= *zer*), have forfeited their authority and become 'alien' (*zar*) – that is, usurpers. Alluding to the inner dynamics of the "three crowns," the rabbis taught that "the crown (כתר) of a good name (שם טוב) stands above them" (על גביהם) (Abot 4:13), i.e., the crown of a good name should preside over the three crowns.[136] The latter is not a fourth 'crown' – an office with a designated chief executor and a staff empowered to carry out his decisions.[137] 'Good name' is the semantic equivalent of our 'public opinion.' What the rabbis were teaching is that to be functional, limited sovereignty requires a vigilant public, free to raise questions and express criticism. This goes to the heart of the Hebrew sense of government

135. Yoma 72b; see Shemot Rabba (Vilna: Jerusalem, 5735/1975) XXXIV, 2, vol. 1, 62c.
136. A similar expression was used to teach that Moses "stood over" (על גבם) the Jewish Court, in the sense that he presided over them; see Mishna Sanhedrin 1:6; cf. Mishna Horayot 3:3 and Horayot 12a at the end.
137. Cf. R. Isaac Abarbanel, *Naḥalat Abot* (New York, 5713–1953), on Abot 4:14, p. 252.

and good management. Opposing views should not be quashed, and those raising critical questions should not be muzzled. National officers and policy makers need to engage in dialogue and respond to criticism, rather than rule by the fiat of authority. The context of the fourth 'crown' is a culture of Law serving as the ground of discourse, criticism, and above all, recognition of the right for disagreement and diverse opinions. The best model for this type of discourse is the Talmud and classic rabbinic literature, where different opinions are given due consideration (see below Section IV).

In Biblical times it was the task of the Hebrew prophet, a private individual without an office, to express the voice of public opinion. To understand the role of the prophet with some degree of precision, we must distinguish between two aspects of the 'Law'– of *any* law. One is the norms and principles upon which government agencies and officials *should* act. Another is the norms and principles regularly *practiced* by the authorities in charge. Only this second aspect is 'law' in the strict legal sense. The first aspect corresponds, more or less, to a kind of positive morality upon which the governing authorities should act, but is not enforceable in a court of justice. The tension between the Law as *ought* and the Law as *is*, stands at the center of Jewish political history. When the Hebrew prophet challenged the king, the priest, and the judiciary in the name of the Law, he was in fact postulating the principle that the Law is not reducible to the whims and wants of the governing bureaucracies. It was the specific task of the prophet to serve as the spokesman for the ideal Law, and to remind the rulers that they were not immune from censure, that there is a Law above the law. Addressing himself to this fundamental point, Heschel explained:

> Of paramount importance in the history of Israel was the freedom and independence enjoyed by the prophets, their ability to upbraid the kings and princes for their sins. From the beginning of the monarchy, the king was at any moment in peril of rebuke, even of rejection, by the prophets, who

> reminded him that the king's sovereignty was not unlimited, that over the king's *mishpaṭ* ['law, justice'] stood the *mishpaṭ* ['law, justice'] of the Lord – an idea that frequently clashed with the exigencies of government.[138]

The denunciation of corrupt kings, unworthy priests, and dishonest judges by the prophets of Israel has no parallel in history. This was possible because of the freedom with which the prophets functioned, even when addressing the most powerful rulers of their time (see I Kings 22:3–29; Am. 7:7–17; Is. 1:10–31) – a level of freedom that would not be tolerated by any other society, past or present. Pagan prophets were soothsayers at the service of the monarch, tools to expand and justify government's policy (much like the media in pseudo-democracies). Since in the pagan world the temples were under the tutelage of the monarch, priests and prophets, too, were instruments at the service of the Rex.

> The prophets in Greece, the diviners in Babylonia, the Canaanite *nebiim* ['prophets'] stood in close association with the cult, and belonged in a sense to the staff of the sanctuary. Since the cult and the sanctuaries were subordinate to the kings, all three powers were united in the person of the king.[139]

Given that Jewish society is fundamentally horizontal, the prophet did not approach the mighty as a subordinate to his master but as an equal; nay, even as a superior, given that he was speaking in the name of a higher standard.

> What is more, the prophet was not a *primus inter pares,* first among his peers. By his very claim, his was the voice of supreme authority. He not only rivaled the decisions of the

138. *The Prophets,* p. 478.
139. *The Prophets,* pp. 480–481.

> king and the counsel of the priest, he defied and even condemned their words and deeds.[140]

One of the most significant principles introduced by the Hebrew prophets to the landscape of political ideas is that national officials and government agencies, including the ecclesiastical and the judicial authorities, should be held to a higher standard. Over and over, rulers were reminded that they would have to render account for their reckless leadership.

> Mercilessly Jeremiah condemned the kings, the princes, the priests, and the *nebiim*. Of the *nebiim* of Samaria he maintained that "they prophesied by Baal and led My people astray" (Jer. 2:8). Of the prophets in Jerusalem he said: "Both prophet and priest have become polluted, even in My house I have found their wickedness, says the Lord" (Jer. 23:11). And according to the author of the Book of Lamentations, the great calamity came over Jerusalem, "because of the sins of her *nebiim* and the iniquities of her priests" (Lam. 4:13).[141]

Because the culture of Law is paramount in Israel's intellectual tradition, it was clearly understood that 'Law' is not simply what the executive branches declare. That is why the High Priest, the King, and the Supreme Court of Israel are subject to *judicial* error (see above chapter 10). An entire Talmudic Tractate, *Horayot*, examines the niceties of this principle. In this defining principle the Law differs from all other legal systems. The Tora is "the inheritance (*morasha*) of the commonwealth of Jacob" (Deut. 33:4). It means that the Tora, a written document *encoded in the collective mind of the people*, is the ultimate regulatory source of Israel (see appendix 10). That is why the judiciary should consult with, and take account of, the legal

---

140. *The Prophets*, p. 480.
141. *The Prophets*, p. 482. Cf. Dan. 9:6–10.

views of the scholarly community.[142] This doctrine is consistent with the republican principle that the people – not the government – are the ultimate depository of the Law. Confrontation with established authority in the name of the Law continued in post-biblical times. Jews alone summoned the king to court and established norms and procedures designed to punish kings guilty of breaking the Law (see above Section II, *Concluding Reflections*). The clash with Alexander Jannaeus, one of the most powerful Maccabean Kings, acting also as High Priest, shows that Jews were not coy when confronting someone breaking the Law, even if the culprit in question happened to be invested with the mantles of monarchy *and* priesthood (see appendix 10).

In sum, the authority of Israel's crowns rests on a culture of Law and public reason developed around the Sinai-Moab covenant. Hence the radical principle: the Law is not binding because an executive branch of government, secular or ecclesiastical, says so, but because it was proposed by God and accepted by the people in a sacred covenant. Thus, all forms of authority depend on the Law – not the other way around.[143] A major consideration within the context of limited sovereignty is that public officers and administrators should be sensitive to the 'Crown of a Good Name.' This is contingent on a vigilant public willing to exercise its civic duty and enter into a dialogue with the authorities. In this manner, dialogue would replace strife, and discourse around the Law would replace the sword. To be effective, the dialogue must be allowed to unfold through time and place. A view proposed by a prophet or a sage, although ignored in certain periods of history, may be given due consideration at a future time and

142. See *MT Mamrim* 2:2 and cf. *MT Sanhedrin* 20:8. This is somehow analogous to our present "public reason," in the sense that the decision of the court is expected to be based on, and reflect canons of thoughts and doctrines understandable to, the legal community.

143. See above, chapter 16 and below, chapter 33. On this fundamental principle, see the remarkable essay by Chief Rabbi J. H. Hertz, "Monarchy and Freedom in Israel," in his *The Pentateuch and HafToras*, pp. 926–930.

under new circumstances. That is why rabbinic tradition considers relevant the transmission, not only of the accepted view, but also of the minority opinion (see Mishna ʿEduyot 1:5).

# Chapter 21

# *Galut*: Right *without* Might

Ever since the fall of Judea (587 B.C.E.), Israel confronted military defeat with the establishment of new and highly advanced legal and political institutions. Jews were the first (and only) people going into *Galut* ('Exile'); thus, introducing a new doctrine in international law and diplomacy: a nation is not extinguished by the fiat of sword and banishment. A vanquished nation, ejected from its territory, could preserve its political identity as long as it administers its internal affairs according to its *own legal and political institutions.* On the basis that might is right in pagan political thought, national integrity is linked to territorial and military control (see the following chapter). Therefore, military defeat and loss of territory equal forfeiture of self-government and nationality. Israel challenged this: although vanquished, the Jewish nation was not extinguished. Neither the destruction of Jerusalem, nor loss of territory, nor mass deportation dissolved the nation of Israel. To counter all these, a new type of political entity emerged – a nation in *Galut* – ready to face the challenges posed by nations claiming that nationhood is a function of the sword. Firm in their conviction, the Jewish people remained a 'radical minority' refusing to bow down to pagan might. Two thousand years of ignominy and persecution lay bare the fortitude of this belief.

The doctrine of *Galut* springs from the belief that the Law contracted at Sinai-Moab is Israel's sole Constitution. *Galut* is the manifesto that although defeated in battle and forcefully uprooted from their territory, Jews will go on and live as full members of political

Israel. At the existential level, this means that Israel would rather subsist as an entity bereft of power, than succumb to a system whose ultimate authority is the point of a sword. It also serves to ascertain that Jewish nationhood is predicated on the ability of the people to rule themselves according to their Law *without* an army or police force patrolling their streets. Two major developments contributed to the rise and development of this doctrine: one intellectual, pertaining to the autonomy of the Law, another historical, structuring a unique type of polity that could meet the new and unprecedented set of circumstances.

A series of national catastrophes, beginning with the collapse of the monarchy, mass deportation to Babylonia (between the years 601 and 584 B.C.E.), and banishment from their own homeland, brought about the realization that the Law is the sole dimension of Jewish political and personal authority. It was not by chance that Ezekiel – a priest who as a young child was deported to Babylonia – became the prophet who inculcated the momentous relevance of the Law *after* exile (see appendix 15). It was observed that Ezekiel was not only "the father of Jewish legalism," but also the prophet who implanted in the Jews the faith that, "They were some day to return to their own land." Both these items are interrelated. We shall now quote the pertinent passage at length:

> The law and its rigorous observance have in some quarters been felt to be a declension from the high spiritual levels of the Prophets, and so, in a sense, they may have been. Yet Israel had to pass through terrible experiences before the consummation of her faith was come, and it may be doubted if she could have withstood the flood of heathen persecution which threatened her in the second century B. C. [E.] unless she had some external standard to which to cling. The seed of truth was there, and the function of the Law was to provide a rigid shell which should protect the kernel till the time of its sprouting.[144]

144. Theodore H. Robinson, *Prophecy and the Prophets in Ancient Israel* (London:

*Galut* involves *political* strategy. The political genius who reorganized Israel and set up a unique model of government was the priest-scribe Ezra. His strategy was grounded on three facts. First, Babylonia had been conquered by Cyrus I (539 B.C.E.), and the land as well as the people were under Persian domination. Shortly after his victory, Cyrus issued an edict (538 B.C.E.) urging Jews to return to their ancestral home and rebuild the Temple.[145] Second, Jews had been scattered all over the empire, among diverse lands and peoples. How can one bring *national* cohesiveness to people strewn all over the empire, among diverse ethnic and religious populations? Third, some Jews had responded to Cyrus' call and returned to Jerusalem. Since they were geographically disconnected from the majority of Jews, this could turn out to be a major liability: the detachment of the Jewish capital from the rest of the people. Ezra exploited these facts, establishing a Diaspora with a plurality of centers, united by a *single national capital*, under the rule of a *single Law*. He arrived in Jerusalem in August 458, with a royal letter

---

Duckworth, 1923), p. 157; cf. ibid., p. 195. For Robinson, ibid., p. 156, this meant, "the supreme manifestation of God in Jesus," etc. Because some Biblical historians operate within strict theological coordinates, and are neither philologians nor jurists, they fail to realize the mindboggling disparities of some of their remarks.

145. There were two versions of this proclamation. One was a public proclamation issued throughout the empire in the year 540 B.C.E. (Ezra 1:2–4). A second version was an internal memorandum addressed to the royal treasury, concerning the expenses for rebuilding the Temple (Ezra 6:2–5). Since it was an internal memorandum, this version was not made public. Elias Bickerman, "The Edict of Cyrus in Ezra," *Studies in Jewish and Christian History*, vol. 1, p. 76, wrote:

Thus there were (at least) two orders of Cyrus relevant to the Return from Captivity: a royal proclamation addressed to the Jews and published by the heralds everywhere and in many languages, including Hebrew (Ezra 1); and on the other hand a *memorandum* to the royal treasurer, in Aramaic, which was *not* made public at the time."

After a close examination of the documentation in question, Bickerman, ibid., p. 98, concluded: "This detailed examination of Cyrus' proclamation has shown that all the arguments advanced against its authenticity are faulty and fallacious."

permitting the establishment of a Jewish commonwealth in Judah *and* the right of Jews throughout the entire Empire to be governed according to the Law. Henceforth, the Law, rather than territory, would be the basis of Jewish cohesiveness.

> The spiritual unity of the Jews could hardly be established around Jerusalem if the whole Orient, from the Indus to Ethiopia, had not been one world obeying the orders issued by the Persian king. By its influence at the royal court, the Diaspora in Babylonia and Persia could act on behalf of Jewry everywhere and impose a uniform standard of faith and behavior.[146]

The Law was not imposed. Rather, it was proposed by Nehemiah (governed between ca. 445–430 B.C.E.) in a general assembly. True to the principle of democratic government by the people (see above chapter 19), Nehemiah convoked a general assembly that included: "our officers, our Levites, and our Priests" (Neh. 10:1), together with "the heads of the people" (Neh. 10:15), and "the rest of the people" (Neh. 10:29). The proposal was adopted. As one, the assembly proclaimed the Tora as the *only* source of authority (Neh. 10:1–37, especially verses 1, 29–30; cf. ibid., chapter 13:1–3). The proclamation was formalized in an אמנה or "National Accord" (Neh. 10:15).[147] Eighty-four signatories, headed by Nehemiah himself, confirmed the covenant (Neh. 10:2–28). (By contrast, there were about 30 signatories to the US Constitution.) In this fashion, the Tora was formally recognized as the Constitution of the Jewish people.[148] Jerusalem became the capital of the Jewish Diaspora: "dispersed and divided" among dif-

146. *From Ezra to the Last of the Maccabees*, pp. 8–9.
147. For the root 'AMN in the sense of 'binding' and 'joining permanently, separate items face to face,' see José Faur, "Maimonides' Starting Precept," pp. 308–309 n. 109.
148. See Elias Bickerman, *The Jews in the Greek Age* (Cambridge, Mass.: Harvard University Press, 1988), chapter 6.

ferent nations (see Est. 3:8), yet *united* under a single Law. What initially constituted an obstacle, impossible to resolve in terms of pagan political ideology, was transformed into a singular advantage. *Galut* gave the Jew exceptional mobility. Henceforth, a Jew could opt to reside at any place within the vast Persian Empire, yet remain under the jurisdiction of the same Law. Bickerman referred to this anomaly as a "rewarding polarity":

> That period is marked by a unique and rewarding polarity: on the one hand, the Jerusalem center and, on the other, the plurality of centers in the Diaspora. The Diaspora saved Judaism from physical extirpation and spiritual inbreeding. Palestine united the dispersed members of the nation and gave them a sense of oneness. This counterpoise of historical forces is without analogy in history.[149]

The unique polarity of the Diaspora stemmed from the prophetic tradition ascertaining that the God of the Jewish nation, whose capital is Jerusalem, is God of the whole world, and vice versa. Addressing the exceptionality of the Jewish Diaspora, Bickerman explained: "The Diaspora clung to its unique God and to Jerusalem, the unique center of lawful worship." At the same time, every Jew maintained that the God of Zion was not only God of the Jews but of all humanity.

> He was the sole God in heaven and earth, the so-called deities of the pagans were nothing but vain idols. Hence, the polarity of Jerusalem and the Dispersion had its ideological counterpart in the paradoxical combination of universal theism and particularism, in the conception that the sole Lord of the Universe dwells on the hillock of Zion. This theological paradox held the Jews in the Dispersion together, and from

149. *From Ezra to the Last of the Maccabees*, p. 3.

> all points of the compass they directed their eyes to the Lord's Temple in Jerusalem.[150]

Hence the exceptionality of a nation without territorial boundaries; united in the recognition of Jerusalem as its national capital, and the Tora as its supreme Law. This explains the extraordinary fact that other foreign colonies and peoples in the empire soon assimilated and lost all traces of their former nationality. Among all the people deported to Assyria and Babylonia, the Jews alone preserved their own national unity and integrity. Ezra was the brain who, in a quantum intellectual jump, transformed an insurmountable political problem – dispersion and lack of geographical contiguity – into a finer, highly organized national entity. The result was a nation that although "scattered and dispersed" countered with a *fixed geographical capital*, Jerusalem. By the end of the Second Temple, Jerusalem is described as

> the mother city not of one country Judaea but of most of the others in virtue of the colonies sent out at diverse times to the neighboring lands Egypt, Phoenicia, the part of Syria called the Hollow and the rest as well and the lands lying far apart, Pamphylla, Cillicia, most of Asia up to Bithynia and the corners of Pontus, similarly also into Europe, Thessaly, Boeotia, Macedonia, Aetolia, Attica, Argos, Corinth and most of the part of Peloponnese. And not only are the mainlands full of Jewish colonies but also the most esteemed of the islands of Euboea, Cyprus, Crete. I say nothing of the countries beyond the Euphrates, for except for a small part they all, Babylon and of the other satrapies those where the

150. *From Ezra to the Last of the Maccabees*, p. 8. For a comprehensive treatment of this subject, see Bickerman, "The Edict of Cyrus in Ezra," *Studies in Jewish and Christian History*, vol. 1, pp. 72–108; *From Ezra to the Last of the Maccabees*, pp. 3–40; idem, "Nebuchadnezzar and Jerusalem," *Studies in Jewish and Christian History*, vol. 2, pp. 282–298; idem, "The Generation of Ezra and Nehemiah," ibid., pp. 299–326.

> land within their confines is highly fertile, have Jewish inhabitants. So that if my own home-city [Jerusalem] is granted a share of your goodwill, the benefits extend, not to one city but to myriads of the others situated in every region of the inhabited world whether in Europe or in Asia or in Libya, whether in the main lands or on the islands, whether it be seaboard or inland.[151]

Given that the element bestowing national structure and cohesiveness was the Law, not geography, a Jew could be a full member of the Jewish nation regardless of provenance and place of residence.[152] In this fashion, geographical dispersion and instability were transformed into social and economic mobility, both upwards and downwards. The result was a type of kinetic economy by which a small enterprising group could accomplish much more than large static groups. With Haman, antisemites perceived Jewish economic kinetic mobility as unfair. Typical of the static mind, instead of emulating their more successful neighbors and upgrading their own affairs, antisemites, past and present, propose to massacre those who excel (see Est. 3:8). Max Weber (1864–1920), the darling of modern sociology, kindly classified Jewish economics as 'pariah-capitalism' – a decisive thesis in the formulation of antisemitic policies by Nazi Europe. Contrasting Jewish capitalism (which is evil) with Puritan capitalism (which is good), he wrote:

> In fact the difference may, in general, with necessary qualifications, be formulated: that Jewish capitalism was speculative pariah-capitalism, while the Puritan was bourgeois organization of labor.[153]

---

151. *The Embassy to Gaius*, 281–283, *Philo*, vol. 10, p. 143.
152. See *From Ezra to the Last of the Maccabees*, p. 13. The rabbinic doctrine: "Every single (member of) Israel is a guarantor to all the others," Shebu'ot 39a, should be taken in its strict connotation of the term, since default or miscarriage of debt, etc., by one Jew was imputed *de facto* on all Israel. See appendix 13.
153. Max Weber, *The Protestant Ethic and the Spirit of Capitalism* (New York: Charles

# Chapter 22
# Jewish Dominion over the Land of Israel

"From the beginning," noted a modern rabbinic thinker, "Judaism included both the possibility of exile as well as the certainty of redemption."[154] It is a uniquely Jewish concept. No other nation entertained the view that it *may* be vanquished, and that its people *may* be taken into exile and scattered throughout the four corners of the globe. Certainly, no other people made a *national* commitment that in such an eventuality they will *surely* return to their ancestral territory and reestablish their kingdom.[155] This concept rests on two concerns. First, the awareness that in a world ruled by Pharaohs and Caesars, a nation based on Law, espousing the ideals of limited sovereignty and individual freedom, is vulnerable to both psychological and military warfare. Second, confidence that the Jewish people will not acquiesce to be ruled by absolute sovereigns and that they will return home to reestablish their own government. Since a state such as the Jewish nation will never find acceptance in a world of Pharaohs

Scribner's Sons, 1958), p. 271. Jewish capitalism is also classified as "irrational and speculative," etc.; see ibid., pp. 20–22. On Weber's classification of Jews as 'pariah,' see below 'Introductory Remarks,' Section IV.

154. Eliezer Berkovitz, *Essential Essays on Judaism* (Jerusalem: Shalem Press, 2002), p. 184.

155. Some of the Biblical sources were cited in Yehudah Elitzur, *Israel and the Bible* (Heb.) (Ramat-Gan: Bar-Ilan University Press, 1999), pp. 280–293.

and Caesars, it stands to reason that it would not find permanent security until the Messianic Age (or *Pax Hebraica,* in contradistinction to *Pax Romana,* see below chapter 34).

God is the Supreme Sovereign of Israel's territory (see above chapter 17). In agreement with the exclusionary principle, it postulates that the land cannot pass to another sovereign, no matter what. Hence the fundamental principle establishing that military conquest, banishment of the people, etc. does not *extinguish* Jewish rights over the Land of Israel. A fundamental aspect of *Galut* is that the Jewish people did not forfeit their rights over their homeland, and that they intend to return and establish there their government, again and again. This doctrine rests on six principles.

First, real estate forcibly seized belongs to the original owners and legal heirs, never to those who robbed the land, nor squatters and the like. This principle is applicable to the Land of Israel as well as to real estate owned by gentiles outside the Land of Israel.[156]

Second, the people of Israel alone are the legitimate proprietors of the Land of Israel.

Third, the families of nations gave international recognition to Israel's right over its territory by the fact that they continuously designated their territory "the Land of Israel," even after banishment of the people from the land. This is particularly true after the spread of Christianity and the Hebrew Scripture.[157]

Fourth, Scripture explicitly prohibits the transfer of real estate in

---

156. See Sukka 30a-b and *Tosafot* on Sukka 30b s.v. *ve-qarqa'.*

157. 'Palestine' is an antisemitic designation designed to "extinguish" Jewish title from their homeland. It was introduced by Imperial Rome in late antiquity to extinguish Jewish rights. Concerning this fact, Yehoshafat Harkabi, *The Bar Kokhba Syndrome* (Chappaqua, N.Y.: Russel Books, 1983), p. 48 writes:

> The suppression of the rebellion was even given verbal symbolism: the name of the country was changed from 'Judea' to 'The Syrian province of Palestine' (derived from the earlier inhabitation of it by the Philistines), a move intended to obliterate the last traces of the Jewish settlement from memory.

With the same purpose in mind, it was reintroduced by Imperial England in the 19th century. The parroting of this name by illustrious Jewish leaders is another

perpetuity. Accordingly, the Land of Israel could not be transferred to non-Jewish ownership even with the explicit consent of the people.

Fifth, the Biblical principle, "the earth is the Lord's" (Ps. 24:1) rejects the pagan ideology, whereby territorial ownership is established by military conquest (see above Introductory Remarks and n. 8).

Sixth, the Jewish people never relinquished their claim to their land, and they intend to return and take possession of it.

These principles were brought together in a *responsum* issued by R. Naḥshon Gaon (who served as head of the Academy at Sura, 871–879). It was issued in connection with a special kind of transaction known as 'conjointly' (אגב). According to Jewish law, one may transfer movables and other valuables 'conjointly' with real estate property. It would appear that such a transaction should be restricted to a seller owning land. However, the practice of the Court had been to avail this form of transaction to all Jews, regardless of whether they were landowners or not. The legal basis for such a transaction is the principle that every Jew owns "four cubits of real estate in the Land of Israel." Here is the *responsum* issued by the Gaon:

> Rabbinic authorities maintain that there is no Jew who does not own four cubits [of land] in Israel's territory. Were you to object: [but] the Gentiles have taken possession of it and we are in Exile! [1] It is a well-established Rabbinic doctrine that real estate property cannot be tortuously possessed, [2] and therefore it [the Land of Israel] remains under Israel's tenure. [3] Moreover, the Land of Israel is called by the name of [the people of] Israel. [4] Furthermore, even at the time when [the people of] Israel possessed their land, they had no authority to sell their fields in perpetuity, as it is written: "And the land shall not be sold in perpetuity [because mine is the land]" (Lev. 25:23). [5] In addition, it is written, "To God belongs the earth

---

example of the mental alertness and political sophistication of the 'enlightened Jewry.' For an informative overview of the history and connotations of this designation, see *Israel and the Bible*, pp. 415–417.

> and what is contained therein" (Ps. 24:1). [6] And lastly, we intend to return to it and take possession of it.[158]

The doctrine of *Galut* determined the standing of Jews in the Diaspora. Central to *Galut* is the principle that a nation is constituted by the *people,* not by its territory. Hence the supreme *political* authority of the Jews needs not necessarily reside in the Land of Israel. After the destruction of the Second Temple, and following Roman genocide of the Jewish people and subsequent Christian hounding intended to extinguish Jewish rights to their homeland, the majority of Jews took up residence in Babylonia. In accordance with the principle that authority is of the people, the supreme political authority of the Jews was the Exilarch in Babylonia, where the majority of Jews resided, *not* the Patriarch in the Land of Israel.[159] Since a people in exile cannot establish permanent residence in the host country, the status of the Jewish nation outside Israel was that of a 'tribe' (שבט) – a nation *without* territorial claims over its place of residence.[160] A further consideration concerning the status of real estate owned by Jews outside Israel will clarify this point. Jews recognized only limited sovereignty. However, outside Israel, land acquisition implied the recognition of a hierarchic system at the top of which stands an absolute sovereign (see below). To avert this problem, a Talmudic decision issued between

158. In ed. B. M. Lewin, *Oṣar ha-Ge'onim,* vol. 9, Qiddushin (Jerusalem, 1939), #146, pp. 59–60. See *Teshubot ha-Ge'onim* (Harkavi), #199, p. 90; R. Judah al-Barṣeloni, *Sefer ha-Sheṭarot,* ed. S. J. Halberstam (Berlin: Mekize Nirdamim, 1898), p. 43. For an analysis of the dissenting opinion, see "The Legal Status of Jewish Real Estate outside Israel's Territory," p. 779 n. 150.
159. A judge appointed by the Exilarch in Babylonia had judicial authority in the Land of Israel, but not the other way around; see Sanhedrin 5a-b and *MT Sanhedrin* 4:14. Cf. *MT Melakhim* 5:12.
160. This explains why, although Jews were well established in many areas throughout Europe, Asia, and the Middle East, they never laid territorial claim over the territory in which they lived. Hence, Jewish real estate outside territorial Israel has the status of movable property. See following note.

the years 259 and 279 declared that Jewish landed property outside Israel's territory has the status of chattel – not real estate.[161]

A major problem regarding *Galut* was the fact that Judaism recognizes only limited sovereignty (see above chapter 18). Pagan rulers, however, claim unlimited sovereignty (see below chapter 23). Jews in the Diaspora insisted that the ruler of the host country could exercise only limited sovereignty over them. The issue is clearly exposed in the book of Daniel, chapter 3. There are matters, especially those regarding cult and worship, which lay beyond the authority of a monarch. Jews fully recognized limited sovereignty in the realm of taxation and the like, but did not concede subjection to a Rex. Therefore, they refused to obey a direct order of Nebuchadnezzar to bow down to an idol. According to the rabbis, they explained their position as follows: "Whichever taxation you may want to impose on us, we shall obey. But what you are demanding of us, to insubordinate against God's [sovereignty] – we shall not obey!"[162] Another source offers a slightly different version: "You are our sovereign (in matters of taxation), but to us, in the matter that you are ordering us to do (to worship the idol), you and a dog are one and the same!"[163]

161. See 'Arakhin 29a; *MT 'Arakhin* 8:11. For a comprehensive treatment of the subject, see "The Status of Jewish Real Estate Property outside Israel's Territory," pp. 743–791.
162. *Midrash Tanḥuma*, ed. S. Buber, 2 vols. (Vilna, 5645/1885), *Noaḥ* XV, p. 20.
163. Vayyiqra Rabba, XXXIII, 6, vol. 4, pp. 769–770. See Salomon Schechter, *Aspects of Jewish Theology* (New York: Schocken, 1961), p. 106; Israel Abrahams, *Studies in Pharisaism and the Gospels*, p. 62; *In the Shadow of History*, p. 185. Popular wisdom notwithstanding, the principle, "a law of the civil government is binding," applies only outside Israel's territory, and it is restricted to taxation and nothing else; see *MT Gezela* 5:8–18. It is interesting to note that a Christian Greek martyr addressed his judge as 'dog'; see Ernst Robert Curtius, *European Literature and the Middle Ages* (Princeton: Princeton University Press, 1973), p. 427.

# Chapter 23
# Pagan Political Thought

In pagan political thought, sovereignty is unlimited. Quoting Pindar, Callicles tells Socrates: "Law, the king of all, men and gods alike… carries things with a high hand, making might to be right."[164] On behalf of Caligula it was said that "Sovereignty cannot be shared, that it is an immutable law of nature." This principle stems from the notion that might is the ultimate source of authority. "He [Caligula] being the stronger," it was explained, "promptly did to the weaker what the weaker would have done to him." It follows that the assassination of those who were supposed to share power with Caligula was an act of "self-defense, not murder." People who might moralize to the contrary should consider that the elimination of potential rivals is designed to avoid "disturbances and wars both civil and foreign. And what is better than peace?"[165]

The Rex's authority is absolute. Apotheosis of kings and the worship of rulers in pagan humanity indicate the close, intimate relation between the realm of the political and the divine. Addressing this aspect of pagan sovereignty, Heschel noted:

> God and king are two conceptions so nearly coupled in the oriental mind that the distinction is constantly blurred. The God Re, according to mythology, was the first king in Egypt,

164. *Plato's Gorgias* (Penguin Classics), p. 79.
165. *The Embassy to Gaius,* 68, *Philo,* vol. 10, p. 35.

> and gods were among the rulers in Sumeria after the Flood. Thus, in historic times the king's majesty was equaled to that of a god. The king was held to be a god, begotten by his heavenly father, the sun god Re, who assumed the form of the living king for the purpose of procreation of an heir to the throne.[166]

At that level of political organization there is no actual 'state' or properly structured government. The king *is* god and in all circumstances *his* will is supreme. The norms and administrative rules of government do not have the force of law in regard to the sovereign. As with Pharaoh:

> He as a god *was* the state. To be sure, it was necessary for a new state to have rules and regulations for administrative procedures and precedents, but our negative evidence suggests that there was no codification of law, impersonally conceived and referable by magistrates without consideration of the crown. Rather, the customary law of the land was conceived to be the word of the pharaoh…. The authority of codified law would have competed with the personal authority of the pharaoh.[167]

The Rex is a supernatural being, the possessor of magical powers, not shared by any other human being.

> The kings were regarded as gods, sacrifices were offered to them, and their worship was celebrated in special temples by special priests. Indeed the worship of the kings sometimes cast worship of the gods into the shade…. The king was also the high priest of each god, who for practical purposes delegated his functions to the professional priesthood.[168]

166. *The Prophets*, p. 474.
167. Wilson, as quoted by E. A. Speiser, "The Biblical Idea of History in Its Common Near Eastern Setting," p. 5.
168. *The Prophets*, p. 474. See *Kingship and the Gods*, pp. 33–34. The same was the

In states organized on the basis of hierarchically structured power, the sovereign is god. This principle rests on impeccable logic. As argued by Caligula:

> Those who have charge of the herds of other animals, ox herds, goat herds, shepherds, are not themselves oxen, nor goats nor lambs, but men to whom is given a higher destiny and constitution, and in the same way I who am in charge of the best of herds, mankind, must be considered to be different from them and not of human nature but to have a greater and diviner destiny.[169]

Men destined to rule are hierarchically superior and above fault and criticism. Bearing this principle in mind, we can understand Caligula's indignation at those who dare offer him counsel.

> And then does anyone dare to teach me, who even while in the womb, that workshop of nature, was modeled as an emperor, ignorance dare to instruct knowledge? How can they who were but now common citizens have a right to peer into the counsels of an imperial soul? Yet in their shameless effrontery they who would hardly be admitted to rank as learners dare to act as masters who initiate others into the mysteries of government.[170]

Pagan sovereignty is a function of a monopoly of violence *within* the territorial boundaries of the state, and it is limited to the territory in which it can effectively exercise this monopoly. By virtue of this power, the entire territory of the state is the personal property of the sovereign. This is the source of feudalism: the land belongs to the Conqueror who, by virtue of his sword, becomes the proprietor and

---

case with Jesus, see below chapter 34.

169. *The Embassy to Gaius*, 76, *Philo*, vol. 10, p. 39.

170. *The Embassy to Gaius*, 56, *Philo*, vol. 10, p. 29.

sole ruler of the territory. Let us consider, for the sake of illustration, the case of William of Normandy.

> In 1066, William of Normandy crossed the English Channel, defeated King Harold at the battle of Hastings, and claimed England as his own. William – called the Conqueror by history – imposed on England a feudal system that was more strictly organized than the previous system, and it is from this system that the law of real property developed.[171]

Thereafter, the king parceled his territory to his lieutenants in return for their services and loyalties. In turn, they parceled their lands to others, creating a pyramid on top of which stood the Conqueror.

> William, claiming all England as his, parceled out great tracts of land to his chief supporters who became William's *tenants-in-chief.* In exchange for land each tenant-in-chief agreed to render the king specified *services,* such as providing forty knights each year to fight for the king, or sounding a horn when the king's enemies approached from Scotland, or furnishing the king with ten fat geese or other foodstuffs for his household. The services provided the king with military and economic support to govern England. Each tenant-in-chief, holding an immense acreage, parceled out portions of the land to subtenants, extracting from each *subtenant* a promise to render services. These services might support the tenant-in-chief in running his household or they might provide the tenant-in-chief with knights to fight for the king, thus meeting the tenant-in-chief's obligation to the king. The subtenant in turn might *subinfeduate* to another tenant, extracting services from him. In this way, a feudal ladder was built up, with the

171. Jesse Dukeminier, *Property* (Gilbert Law Summaries), p. 57.

> possessor of the land at the bottom and the lords above him entitled to various services.[172]

Within a hierarchic society there are no individuals. The people ought "to reduce all their Wills, by plurality of voices, into one Will... and therein submit their Wills, everyone to his Will, and their Judgments to his Judgment."[173] Rather than individuals, society is formed by various groups, strata, or castes. A tenant can sue neither his lord nor have direct access to the king save through his immediate superior.[174] To secure personal allegiance, the lord granted his tenants access to himself on condition that they swore direct allegiance to him.

> Each military tenant did homage to his lord in a solemn ceremony. He knelt, put his hands between the lord's hands, swore a binding oath of loyalty, and thereby became the lord's man. William and his successors shrewdly required a separate oath of loyalty to the crown. Therefore the tenant might say: 'I become your man from this day forward for the tenement which I hold of you, and I will bear you faith in life and limb and earthly worship against all men, saving only the faith I owe to our sovereign lord the king.' Since a man gave his allegiance to the king, he deserves the king's protection in a dispute with his lord.[175]

Consequently, William imposed a feudal system from which the law of English real estate developed, parceling the land to his lieutenants and in turn they parceled it to others. The sovereign stood on top of the

172. *Property* (Gilbert Law Summaries), p. 57. According to Vico, *The New Science*, IV, 489, p. 164, "the first fiefs were introduced by the ecclesiastics."

173. *Leviathan* XVII [87], p. 227. See below n. 267.

174. As per Christian theology, where the faithful can reach the Father only through Jesus; see Matt. 11:27.

175. Jesse Dukeminier and James E. Krier, *Property* (Boston: Little, Brown, and Company, 1988), p. 150.

system wielding absolute power. The system of land tenure and allocation of real estate property served to structure society hierarchically.

> A central feature of the system was land tenure; each person's position was defined in terms of relationship to land. Each person, save the king, was deliberately made subservient to another, his landlord. And all were subservient to the crown, from whom all land titles derived.[176]

This system, particularly in land based economies, awarded the upper echelons enormous financial power and influence.

> In the Middle Ages land law is the basis of all public law. You will have already observed how the system of tenure provides the king with an army and with a reverence – men owe military service by reason of tenure, they pay aids reliefs, scutages by reason of tenure, by reason of tenure the king sets profitable wardships, and marriages, and escheats – he is the supreme and ultimate landlord.[177]

In this manner the entire legal apparatus, both at the legislative and judiciary levels, were in fact tools designed to protect and enhance these interests.

> But the influence of tenure does not stop here; the judicial system is influenced by tenure. Every lord claims a right to hold

176. Dukeminier and Krier, *Property*, p. 146. There is a fine summary of English real estate theory in Jesse Dukeminier, *Property* (Gilbert Law Summaries), pp. 57–65. The connection between 'rex' and 'territory' is implicit in the fact that in Indo-European, "the *rex*" was "more of a priest than a king in the modern sense"; principally, he "was the man who had authority to trace out the sites of towns and to determine the rules of law," *Indo-European Language and Society*, p. 307. See appendix 17.
177. F. W. Maitland, *The Constitutional History of England* (Cambridge: Cambridge University Press, 1950), p. 38.

> a court of and for his tenants. This is an important principle, but we can hardly speak of its working until we have spoken of the courts older than feudalism – the courts of the shire and the hundred which continue to exist during the feudal period.[178]

The situation had direct bearing on the development of law and the judiciary. Due to this fact, English constitutional law was developed around the real estate system, rather than the other way around. This is how one of the foremost authorities on the English Constitution saw it:

> If we are to learn anything about the constitution it is necessary first and foremost that we should learn a good deal about the land law. We can make no progress whatever in the history of parliament without speaking of tenure, indeed our whole constitutional law seems at times to be an appendix to the law of real property.[179]

The doctrine stipulating that the territory of a country belongs to the sovereign by virtue of the sword excludes private ownership of real estate, and stands at the basis of English real estate law. As it was taught by one of its most eminent teachers:

> The first thing then the student has to do is to get rid of the idea of absolute ownership. Such an idea is quite unknown to the English law. No man is in law the absolute owner of lands. He can only hold an estate in them.[180]

The right of conquest and the subsequent principle that no man is absolute owner of his land is accepted by all modern states, including

178. *The Constitutional History of England*, p. 38.
179. *The Constitutional History of England*, p. 538.
180. Joshua Williams, *Principles of the Law of Real Property* (London: Hodges, Smith and Co., 1865), p. 17.

the USA (see appendix 16). The doctrines of Eminent Domain and Sovereign Immunity remind us that ultimately our property belongs to the Sovereign and that the Sovereign is above the Law. Private ownership, as an institution immune from government intervention, is a Jewish invention, guaranteed by the Decalogue at Sinai. The same is true of the doctrine that no one, Rex included, can claim immunity from the Law (see appendix 17).

# Chapter 24
# A Perfect Tora

The Tora, sang the psalmist, "is perfect" (Ps. 19:8), in the sense of being a 'meticulous' and 'all-encompassing' system. The Tora is not only perfect in and of itself, but it also *bestows* perfection on those who follow it. That is why, continued the psalmist, "it will enable me to accomplish *my* individual perfectibility (איתם)" (Ps. 19:14).[181] Concerning this ideal, Philo wrote:

> That Moses himself was the best of all law-givers in all countries, better in fact than any that have arisen among either the Greeks or the barbarians, and that his laws are most excellent and truly come from God, since they omit nothing that is needful.

The eternity of the Law – a pillar of Judaism – is a corollary of its perfectibility. Philo continued:

> But Moses is alone in this, that his laws, firm, unshaken, immovable, stamped, as it were, with the seal of nature herself, remain secure from the day when they were first enacted to now, and we may hope that they will remain for all future

181. See R. Joseph Albo, *Sefer ha-'Iqqarim,* I, 8; and *Shemona Peraqim* IV, *Perush ha-Mishnayot,* vol. 4, p. 383. For a further development of this theme, see R. Manasseh ben Israel, *The Conciliator* (London: 5602–1842), Part I, pp. 235–243. Hebrew איתם is similar to the Arabic *atamm* 'to be more complete, more perfect.' see *Homo Mysticus*, pp. 2–3.

> ages as though immortal, so long as the sun and moon and the whole heaven and universe exist.[182]

Hebrew 'perfection' involves 'autonomy.' Prior to Philo, the Jewish historian Eupolemus ascertained that the Law of Moses was the *first* 'Book' or literary composition designed for transmission and *open* circulation (in opposition to inscriptions on the walls of sanctuaries or documents in private archives). Eupolemus, too, believed that the Hebrew script used by Moses was the first alphabet system (see above Section II Introductory Remarks). To function as *ketab,* an alphabet must be something more than a group of symbols available to a selected few: it must be *of* the people. Therefore, both 'writing' and 'book' involve 'publication' (see above chapters 4, 6, 7). A *sine qua non* for 'book' is a 'published' alphabet, and vice versa: there cannot be an 'alphabet' unless published in a 'book.' As the *first* Book, the Tora is predicated neither on *another* book nor on *another* alphabet outside the reach of the general public.[183] There are overreaching implications to this view. Drawing on the fact that the Scripture designates God as *Shadday* ('Autonomous,' 'Omnipotent'), R. Saul Levi Mortera (ca. 1596–1660) pointed out that the Tora, too, is autonomous, in the sense of being a total and self-contained system (see appendix 10).

> The Law of Moses (is autonomous in respect to others). In this aspect it bears a resemblance to God, blessed be He. This is not the case with other religions claiming to be divine, because only the Law of Moses declares itself to have been made by God [but not the Christian and Moslem Scriptures]. This can be demonstrated by the fact that the Law of Moses is autonomous in respect to others, given that it does not appropriate either the spirit or the principles of any of the earlier religions

182. *Moses* II, 2, *Philo,* vol. 6, p. 457. According to the rabbis it even antecedes Creation, see Pesaḥim 54b. Cf. R. Saul Levi Mortera, *Providencia de Dios con Yisrael,* Ms. Etz Hayyim 48C 20 (Hebrew University Library), pp. 120, 138–139.

183. See *Golden Doves,* pp. 10, 120.

> or scriptures, but only from God Himself, the cause of all beings. Unlike other religions that appropriate their principles and fundamentals from the Law of Moses, so much so, that if one were to imagine the Law of Moses to be spurious, then all of these religions would have to be regarded as spurious. On the other hand, if one were to imagine that these religions are spurious, it [the Law of Moses] would not be affected. The same correspondence [prevails] between the Omnipotent and Autonomous [God], and all other [divine] entities, because in the same manner that God, blessed be He, had been from never-ending eternity, independent from anything that came to be, the Law of Moses, too, was from the start what it is now – before any of the religions claiming today to be divine were established.[184]

A similar point was made by Josephus. When discussing the difference between the Jewish system and that of pagan legislators, he noted:

> Religion governs all our actions and occupations and speech; none of these things did our lawgiver leave unexamined or indeterminate.[185]

"The words of the Tora are life for this world and for the next," taught the rabbis.[186] From the perspective of the *ketab* and *mikhtab*, 'perfection' means also that the Tora is a holistic, two-dimensional system. One, which for lack of a better term we may call 'spiritual,' embracing the institutions, doctrines and precepts intended to develop the mind and spirit of the individual. And a second dimension, 'political,' consisting of the institutions, doctrines, and rules needed for

---

184. *Providencia de Dios con Yisrael,* chap. 2, fol. 3a. Cf. R. Judah ha-Levi, *Kuzari,* I, ##4–10.
185. *Against Apion,* II, 171, *Josephus,* vol. 1, p. 361; cf. ibid., 172–175, pp. 361–363.
186. Midrash Shir ha-Shirim Rabba (Vilna) I, 3, 7a.

the administration of national and social life.[187] Both dimensions are indispensable. Access to only one of these systems would hinder personal autonomy. Quoting R. Mortera:

> ... the Law that He gave them provided them with everything they needed concerning the government of their soul, their body, their domicile, police, morality, and all that which is required and indispensable for the education of the human mind. Not requiring in any matter [pertaining to the affairs] of their republic to consult with anyone else, except the divine Law. There is no situation in which they may be required to depend on other sciences, or on other philosophies, or on other documents in the world [to achieve this], save the Law which God, blessed be He, is author of [and which] provided everything required to achieve human happiness.[188]

In this respect the Tora finds no parallels in either the ancient codifications or modern legal codes.

The preceding considerations can help us gain a better grasp of the doctrines, prescriptions and prohibitions of the Tora, known by the general term *miṣva*. Let us begin by pointing out that a *miṣva* is *not* the semantic equivalent of 'command.' Rather, it stands for *compliance*, resulting from a pledge. It involves personal *responsibility* – moral and legal – and *accountability* before God and men (see appendix 4). It presupposes 'freedom,' i.e., the faculty to choose without internal or external compulsion.[189] In Hebrew thought, freedom of choice entails *teshuba* 'repentance,' a central doctrine in Judaism.[190] In a kernel, it teaches that the Tora grants the offender the possibility of redressing

187. See Maimonides' *Guide* II, 40 and III, 27.

188. *Providencia de Dios con Yisrael*, chapter 63, fol. 159b.

189. Freedom of choice is a dimension of the divine image within, which God had endowed every human being; see *Golden Doves*, pp. 66–69.

190. See *MT Teshuba* 5:1–4; 7:1–6.

a breach.[191] Specifically, that if the transgressor would render himself *accountable* and acknowledge his *responsibility,* although "he had sinned all his life, and repented at the end of his life, he will not be reproached for any of the evil he did."[192] Even at his deathbed, the penitent's contrition is accepted and "all his sins will be forgiven."[193] Actually, *teshuba* effects a kind of palingenesis, by which the penitent is regenerated and newly born.[194] Thus, the penitent is "loved and prized by his Maker as if he had never sinned." What is more, "his reward is high since he had savored sin and brought his evil habits under control."[195] *Teshuba* pertains to freedom. Within the realm of a 'command,' freedom of choice and *teshuba* are non-operative. *Obedience* and *submission* excuse a subaltern from personal *responsibility* and *accountability*. By the same token, obedience and submission exclude discernment and the appeal to reason. Within the realm of a 'command,' the "image of God" is inconsequential: even beasts and brutes (as well as machines) can be made to obey and submit to a commanding force.[196] Failure to execute a command cannot be redressed. Disobedience renders the subject guilty, regardless of intention. The only recourse to guilt is escape from the wrath of the commanding force by taking refuge elsewhere.[197]

Summing up some of the points discussed above: for the Hebrews, the beginning of humanity is the individual – not the State and the

191. See Qiddushin 30b.

192. *MT Teshuba* 1:3. See *Homo Mysticus,* p. 80 and the citation from R. Emanuel Aboab, in *Golden Doves,* p. 68; cf. *MT Teshuba* 2:4; 5:1–2.

193. *MT Teshuba* 2:1; this is so even when repenting secretly; see ibid. 3:14.

194. See Yerushalmi, Rosh HaShana IV, 8, 59c; Vayyiqra Rabba XXX, 3, vol. 4, p. 698; *MT Teshuba* 2:4. On the Hebrew idea of palingenesis, see *Homo Mysticus,* pp. 137–142.

195. *MT Teshuba* 5:4; see ibid. 7:1–7.

196. Thus, rabbinic law distinguishes between 'speech,' which is exclusively human, and a 'command,' which can be given even to a beast, and does not have the legal status of 'speech.' see "Performative and Descriptive Utterances in Jewish Law," pp. 112–114.

197. See *Crowds and Power,* pp. 351–357. On 'escapism,' see Erich Fromm, *Escape from Freedom* (Avon Books, 1965), chapter 5 and *Homo Mysticus,* pp. 4–5.

Rex. Accordingly, the principal objective of the Tora is to award autonomy to the *individual* at all levels: personally, in his relationship to others, as well as socially and politically. Essential to personal autonomy is freedom of choice and its concomitant, *teshuba*; i.e., the possibilities of redressing breaches and attaining spiritual palingenesis. The perfectibility sung by the psalmist is a dynamic and never-ending process.

# Chapter 25
# The Five Doctrines Taught by Patriarch Abraham

In the Hebrew balance of ideas, acceptance of a Rex with absolute sovereignty is one and the same with apostasy and idol worship. In the course of this chapter we will see that the opposite of Hebrew monotheism is not merely polytheism, but belief in a monarch with unlimited sovereignty.

Israel did not come into conflict with pagan priests, but with pagan monarchs. In the books of Daniel and Maccabees, the Babylonian Talmud, and the Yerushalmi and Midrashim, antisemitic measures are ascribed to pagan *monarchs* – not to priests! When the prophets and later the sages challenged the earthly and ecclesiastical powers in the name of the Tora, they were rejecting the notion that one can claim immunity under the cover of 'sovereignty.' The rabbinic principle, "The Tora is not in the Heavens" ascertains that the judicial authorities may not be uncritically accepted even when invoking the name of God (see above chapter 6 and below Section IV, Concluding Reflections). Absolute sovereigns, not men of faith, would be prone to find themselves threatened by such a doctrine! In accordance with the principle that there is "wisdom among the nations," the rabbis treated "the sages from the nations" with deference. In token of respect, when meeting a pagan sage one should say: "Blessed art thou God, King of the Universe for having given of His Wisdom to a human being."[198] The rabbis did not refrain from consulting with "sages from among the nations" as expert witnesses in matters concerning Jewish law. On one such an occasion, when a dispute arose between "the sages of Israel and the sages from among the nations," the Jewish Court relied on the expert testimony of the sages among the nations against the Jewish sages.[199] The rabbis taught that when King Ahasuerus "consulted with the sages from among the nations" whether to proceed with Haman's plan to exterminate the Jews, they replied:

> Who has counseled you with the folly of destroying Israel? Were you to destroy them, the world will no longer subsist, since it subsists but for Israel and the Tora which was given to Israel.[200]

Pagans, too, are God's children, endowed with the same celestial image within. At his inaugural speech at the Temple in Jerusalem, King Solomon declared that it is also open to the prayers of "the alien, who is not of your people Israel" (I Kings 8:41). "My House," said Isaiah referring to the Temple, "will be called a 'House of Prayer' for all the people" (Is. 56:7). Whether conscious or not, they, too, direct their rituals to the Maker of everything (see Mal. 1:9; cf. Jer. 10:7–8, and Radaq's *Commentary*, ad loc.). Accordingly, a sacramental holocaust offered by a pagan was duly accepted at the Temple. "A pagan," explained the rabbis, has "his heart towards Heaven."[201]

Primarily, Hebrew monotheism pertains to the realm of the legal

198. Berakhot 58a; see *MT Berakhot* 10:11; *Shulḥan 'Arukh, Oraḥ Ḥayyim*, CCXXIV: 7.
199. Pesaḥim 94b. For an extensive treatment of this subject, see José Faur, "*Ve-Niṣḥu Ḥakhme Ummot ha-'Olam et Ḥakhme Yisrael*," eds. Chief Justice of Israel Aharon Barak and Professor Menashe Shawa, *Minḥa Le-Yiṣḥaq* (Jerusalem: Lishkat 'Orkhe-Din, 1999), pp. 113–133.
200. Midrash Rabba, Esther VII, 13, 12c; *Aggadat Ester* (S. Buber), 16b-17a.
201. Menaḥot 73b.

and political more than anything else. A basic premise of Hebrew monotheism is that Creation was inaugurated by an initial act of free volition – 'love' in the language of Scripture and the rabbis – by a supremely caring God. This idea leads to two irreconcilable concepts of divine sovereignty. In the pagan mind, "The Right of God's Sovereignty is derived from his Omnipotence."[202] According to Scripture, God's Sovereignty derives from the fact that He alone created and gives sustenance to everything – not because He is Almighty. The primary objective of the story of Creation is not metaphysical, but, as pointed out by Philo, to show "that the Father and Maker of the world was in the truest sense also its Lawgiver."[203] 'Might' does not bestow authority; only Creation, *ex nihilo*. This principle was formulated with precision and elegance by R. Isaac Abendana (ca. 1640–ca. 1710): "Whereas God Almighty is the Lord and Governor of the Universe, as having by Right of Creation the Supreme Dominion over all Creatures."[204] Given the exclusionary principle underlying Hebrew thought, this means that no one else may claim absolute sovereignty. Human sovereignty must be *consensual* and *limited*. The trend against anthropomorphism and positive attributes involving God and man serves to further disallow for a 'divine' aspect that could link a man – particularly monarchs – with God[205] (see below chapter 26). In this connection the exclusionary principle gives rise to two overwhelming doctrines. First, the only ground for absolute sovereignty is creation *ex nihilo*. Second, the Supreme Sovereign did not impose His Law by the fiat of His power, but through a covenant freely negotiated between Him and Israel, establishing thereby the principle that [1] consent and [2] clearly published laws are the only basis of legitimate government.

202. *Leviathan* XXXI, [187], p. 397.

203. *Moses* II, 48, *Philo*, vol. 6, pp. 471–473; *The Embassy to Gaius*, 115, *Philo*, vol. 10, p. 55; see ibid., 293, p. 147.

204. R. Isaac Abendana, *Discourses on the Ecclesiastical and Civil Polity of the Jews* (London, 1706), p. 126.

205. See *Homo Mysticus*, pp. 20–24, and below, chapter 26.

God, the rabbis taught, declared: "I am the Sovereign over all of humankind."[206] Only despots – not men of faith, whether monotheists or not – could feel threatened by this doctrine. Hebrew monotheism bears on the dialogue Adam/*Adon,* in contradistinction to Adam-*Elohim.* The rabbis taught that when Abraham realized that the celestial bodies were not deities, and there is "a Sovereign (*Adon*) and a God over them," he renounced idol worship and decided to take shelter "under the shade of his Maker." The one taking offense was the king – not the priests!

> He (the king) summoned our Patriarch Abraham, and asked him:
> – 'Are you Abraham, the son of Teraḥ?'
> – He answered: 'Yes'!
> – He asked him: 'Are you the one who opposes me, and destroyed my gods? Don't you know that I am the Sovereign (*Adon*) over everything? That on my say, the Sun comes out as well as the Moon, the Stars, and Constellations?'[207]

What worries despots is a dialogue Adam/*Adon* displacing the rule of Adam- *Elohim*. Before Abraham was graced with His presence he knew that the state sponsor-idols were not God. By the same token, although not all can tell *who God is,* everyone could tell *who God is not*!

Abraham was not the first man to discover that there is One God, but the first man, since Enoch, to have discovered that God is the Supreme Sovereign, and consequently that only He should be worshipped. Patriarch Abraham taught five basic doctrines, that Maimonides summarized as follows:

---

206. *Mekhilta de-R. Shim'on b. Yoḥai,* p. 146.

207. *Midrash ha-Gadol, Bereshit,* ed. Mordecai Margulies (Jerusalem: Mossad Harav Kook, 5727/1967), p. 205. Similarly, in *MT 'Aboda Zara* 1:3 (l. 46), the one seeking to kill Abraham was the "king." In the *Guide* III, 29, p. 375 (ll. 8–10), we learn that the king imprisoned Abraham and then expelled him because he was afraid that Abraham "would wreck his policies."

> [i] he discovered that there is a God and He is the Sovereign (of everything), [ii] that He created everything, [iii] that there is no God but Him, [iv] that everyone is wrong [for believing that God is corporeal and has a shape], [v] and the error [about corporality] came about because they worshipped the stars and [their] images [as intermediaries].[208]

Denial of any of these five doctrines constitutes *minut*, 'dissension, profanation,' something analogous with, but not identical to, 'heresy.' A *min* – someone professing *minut* – is 'a religious impostor.' Not because he lacks faith (like the epicurean in rabbinic literature), but because he is *deceitful*: overtly pretending to speak in the name of the Tora, while covertly denying one of these five doctrines.[209]

Given that in Judaism absolute sovereignty is a function of creation *ex nihilo*, conceptually there is no difference between someone [i] postulating that "there is no God or that there is no sovereign (of the universe)." It follows that an atheist and someone denying God's absolute Sovereignty is one and the same. Similarly, there is no difference between someone admitting that there is a God, but postulating that [ii] "there are two or more sovereigns"; e.g., an absolute sovereign for heavenly matters, and an absolute sovereign for the government of earthly things (= שתי רשויות). Or what amounts to the same, someone professing that the Sovereign of the Universe is [iii] "corporeal," [iv] or that He did not create everything *ex nihilo*;

208. *MT 'Aboda Zara* 1:3.

209. The rabbinic source is Shabbat 116a. For an analysis of this source, see José Faur, "Don Quixote: Talmudist and *mucho mas*," *The Review of Rabbinic Judaism* 4 (2001), pp. 141–145. That is why *minut* is associated with "toxic waters," Abot 1:11; i.e., they appear crystalline and pure whereas in fact they are fatal and venomous; see *Perush ha-Mishnayot*, ibid., vol. 4, p. 414; cf. ibid. Nedarim 10:8, vol. 3, p. 154. An essential element of *minut* psychology is that the end justifies the means; see *The Undiscovered Self*, p. 35; and pp. 33–34 cited below at n. 225. Accordingly, deception for a good purpose is justified. Thus, Paul could appear as a Jew to Jews, see I Cor. 9:20; and a Roman to Romans, see Acts 22:25–29; cf. ibid. 23:27; 16:37–38; and appendix 55.

[v] or that somehow, He shares or handed some of His sovereignty over to someone else, e.g., a star or a deity (and therefore it would be proper to worship God via that hierarchic superior object; see Is. 42:8). This is how Maimonides defined *min*.

> Five are classified *min*: [i] someone postulating (האומר) that there is no God or that the Universe has no Sovereign; [ii] someone postulating (האומר) that there is a Sovereign but that there are two or more (sovereigns); [iii] someone postulating (האומר) that there is a single Sovereign but it is corporeal and has a shape; [iv] someone postulating (האומר) that He alone is not the First and the Designer of all. [v] In addition, someone who worships a star or a constellation or something else besides Him, to serve as an intermediary between him (the worshipper) and the Sovereign of the Universe. Any of these five is a *min*.[210]

Those who oppose the rule of Law end up, vicariously or directly, as Adam-*Elohim*. Israel rejects the deification of kings (see Ezek. 28:1–2, 7–9; cf. Is. 14:13–14). Jews were expected to be aware of the abysmal difference between Jewish and pagan kings. To experience the difference, the rabbis permitted priests, even to

> Jump over coffins to go and glimpse Jewish kings. Not only were they permitted to go and glimpse Jewish kings but also to go and glimpse pagan kings. Possibly, if one would be privileged, he would then discern the difference between Jewish and pagan monarchs.[211]

---

210. *MT Teshuba* 3:7. For further sources and analysis, see "Maimonides' Starting Precept," pp. 299–306. For the term 'האומר' in the sense of 'postulating,' see *Perush ha-Mishnayot*, vol. 2, p. 108.

211. Berakhot 19b.

Concerning the conceit of pagan monarchs, Judge Mayer Sulzberger (1843–1923) remarked:

> Absolute autocracy, the lordly disregard of the humble, the exclusive concern of the individual for himself, these are all attributes which appear to us to be present in the great and powerful of Eastern lands, and they repel us.

Contrasting the attitude of these kings with the behavior of Jewish kings, Judge Sulzberger continued:

> In the Hebrew polity the ideals are the reverse. The King was to live for his people, was governed by a fixed law which he had not made and which he could not unmake, and was checked by a national council, representative of the people.[212]

In the words of Heschel: "If elsewhere the king was god, in Israel it was God [through the Law that He established] who was king."[213] This strategic point is the focus of every single Jewish blessing, proclaiming that God – and God alone – is the sole 'King of the Universe.'

212. Mayer Sulzberger, *The Polity of the Ancient Hebrews* (Philadelphia: Julius H. Greenstone, 1912), p. 2.

213. *The Prophets*, p. 476.

# Chapter 26

# The Two-Realm Governance

The rupture of Christianity with Judaism was not based on theological considerations, but on the fact that Christians opted to identify themselves with the Roman government, refused to assist Jews in tragic times, and gloated over the fall of Judea and the ensuing massacre of the Jewish population.[214] The Talmud classifies Christianity as *'aboda zara* – not because it worships images (at that time icons were not fully integrated in the Christian liturgy), but because it imposes a *hierarchic mediator* between man and His Maker. It is also identified with *minut*, which in turn is associated with a doctrine known as "two-realm governance"[215] (שתי רשויות). The term 'governance' (רשות) stands for 'political authority' (Abot 1:10; 2:3). It also stands for an area ruled by an autonomous set of regulations, as

214. See *In the Shadow of History*, p. 200.

215. For the Talmudic sources, see *Studies in the Mishne Tora*, pp. 230–237. There is important material on the subject in Anthony Byer and Judith Herein, eds., *Iconoclasm* (Birmingham: University of Birmingham, 1975). Postulating the "two-realm" doctrine is the same as rejecting Patriarch Abraham's doctrine [v] disallowing for the worship of an intermediary between the worshipper and God. On the association 'Christianity/*minut*', see *Mekhilta de-R. Yishma'el*, p. 220. For further sources and analysis, see R. Travers Hertford, *Christianity in Talmud and Midrash* (London: Williams & Norgate, 1903), especially pp. 376–381. Cf. *Perush ha-Mishnayot*, Ḥolin 1:2, vol. 5, p. 175; and appendix 55. On the association 'two realms/*minut*,' see Berakhot 33b; Megilla 25a; Bereshit Rabba VIII, 9, vol. 1, pp. 62–63; *Midrash Tanḥuma*, (Buber), Qedoshim IV, vol. 2, p. 75. Similarly, the "two-realm" doctrine is a repudiation of Patriarch Abraham's doctrine [ii]. See the following note.

a 'public' in opposition to a 'private' area in reference to torts, purity, and Sabbath's rules of carrying. At the theo-political level, the 'two-realm governance' proposes that there are self-governing areas, independent of each other; e.g., one for things material and another for things spiritual. Addressing members of the Christian communities, R. Nathan (2nd century) pointed out that the Theophany at Sinai "is a disclaimer against the *minim* who profess two governances [one for Heaven and one for earth]. When God [= Heaven] stood [at Mt. Sinai = earth] and said: 'I am God your Sovereign,' who stood up and contested Him?"[216] Accordingly, the doctrine "that the Son of man hath the power on earth to forgive sins" (Matt. 9:6) is an affront to God's Supreme Sovereignty. It also presupposes that 'the Son of man' is above the law and can therefore absolve transgressors at will (see appendix 22), publicans and tax-collectors in particular (see appendix 60). To contravene ideologies, as those proposed by Luther and Calvin, the Mishna (Sanhedrin 4:5) explains that one of the reasons that the Tora teaches that Adam is the single father of all humanity, created by a single God, is to counterview "the *minim* who ascertain that there are various authorities in heaven," e.g. one for those who 'merit' salvation and another for those who 'merit' damnation.

Because of its own theo-political agenda, post-Jesus Christianity chose to equate "Render unto Caesar the things which are Caesar's" (Matt. 22:21) with absolute sovereignty: no matter what.[217] In the

216. *Mekhilta de-R. Yishma'el, Ba-Ḥodesh* V, pp. 219–220. See Ḥagiga 15a; Sifre Debarim #329, p. 379 and variants. Particularly significant is the version that reads: "there is no kingdom of heaven" since the 'Son of man' can absolve sinners on his own. See also *Mekhilta de-R. Yishma'el, Shira* IV, pp. 129–130. The term 'אלוהיך,' commonly translated 'your God,' actually stands for 'your Sovereign'; see "Maimonides' Starting Precept," pp. 309–310.

217. Jesus meant only to acquiesce to the demands of tax-collectors; see appendix 60. I don't think for a minute that he meant absolute submission to Caesar. Compare Rom. 13:1–7 with Matt. 6:24: "No man can serve two masters: for either he will hate the one and love the other, or else he will hold to the one and despise the other. Ye cannot serve God and mammon." The idea is rabbinic. See Tosefta Baba Qamma 7:5, p. 30, stipulating that someone who has sold himself

Hebrew balance of ideas, absolute sovereignty is one and the same with idol worship: in either case God's image within rescinds in favor of someone in the function of Adam-*Elohim*. At the very moment that you have forfeited your own senses and gone on to acknowledge that a given object, be it natural, like a star or a mountain, or man-made, like an icon or a statue, is a god because someone told you so, you have surrendered the image of God within and the right to see and to hear and to sense on your own (see Ps. 115:1–8; 135:15–18; and cf. Deut. 4:28). Invariably, in such a system, there would be someone above telling you what *you* have seen and what *you* have heard and what *you* have felt. Within such a system, the faithful 'knows' and 'believes' because someone, in the function of Adam-*Elohim*, told him so! (Thus the significance of State-sponsored *'aboda zara*; see appendix 11.)

The doctrine of "two governance" (שתי רשויות) is the basis of the Christian dichotomy: Rex's 'governance' (רשות) or *regnum* (State) on the one hand, and God's 'governance' (רשות) or *civita Dei* (= Church) on the other (see appendix 24). A consequence of this dichotomy is 'The Divine Right of Kings,' awarding the Rex total immunity and unlimited sovereignty. By accepting Caesar's 'governance' (רשות) as ultimate in matters pertaining to the *regnum* (State), Christianity ended up making the king a *de facto* god. If in the Scripture "God is King," in Christendom "the King is God"; if in Scripture God is "Mighty" and "Great," etc., then the "Mighty" and the "Great," too, *is* God. The monarch is "represented as if it were the image of God upon earth," and "absolute princes, such as the sovereigns of England, were a species of divinity"; kings "represent unto us the person even

---

to an earthly master is as if "he had removed from over himself the authority of Heaven, and crowned over himself a king of flesh and blood." cf. James M. Robinson, ed. *The Nag Hammadi Library* (New York: Harper & Row, 1977), p. 123 (47). Jesus would have said the same about people acknowledging the absolute sovereignty of a Caesar or a Rex.

of God Himself."[218] Premised on this logic, King James I (1567–1625) of England concluded:

> It is atheism and blasphemy to dispute what God can do; ... so it is presumption and high contempt in a subject to dispute what a king can do, or say that a king cannot do this or that.[219]

In point of fact, the Rex *was* God (see above chapter 23 and below chapter 32). He could not even *think* something wrong. This doctrine was put forward by no lesser an eminence than William Blackstone (1723–1780), the father of modern English jurisprudence:

> The king is not only incapable of doing wrong, but even thinking wrong: he can never mean to do an improper thing: in him is no folly or weakness.[220]

There is one meaningless difference between the Rex and God: the earthly sovereign is a "Mortall God" whereas the other is an "Immortall God."[221]

The two-realm doctrine whereby the Rex's 'governance' is immune

---

218. Cited in, *The Prophets*, p. 475.

219. Quoted by E. R. Goodenough, *The Politics of Philo Judaeus* (New Haven: Yale University Press, 1935), p. 4. An old English law abolished in 1846, established certain fines called *deodans* ('giving to God') to be paid to the king; see "Of Cultural Intimidation," p. 42 n. 24. Significantly, the fine was not current in the American Colonies. Within this context, it should be noted that the Greek *krainein* meant both 'divine sanction' and 'royal authority'; see *Indo-European Languages*, pp. 327–333, and the following note.

220. Sir William Blackstone, *Commentaries on the Laws of England* (Facsimile 1765 edition, Chicago University Press, 1972), I, c. 7, p. 237.

221. *Leviathan* XVII [87], p. 227. It is important to bear in mind that the "Mortall God" had also absolute power over religion. Here is what Hobbes wrote in *Leviathan* XII, [57–58], p. 178:

> But where God himselfe, by supernaturall Revelation, planted Religion; there he also made to himselfe a peculiar Kingdome; and gave Lawes, not only of behaviour towards himselfe; but also towards one another; and thereby in

from criticism bears on the concept of law. Unlike the God of Israel who complies with the laws of the Covenant (see above, chapter 5), the Rex "creates laws for others and so imposes legal duties or 'limitations' upon them whereas he is said himself to be legally unlimited and illimitable."[222] (The doctrine of Sovereign Immunity bears this thesis.) Again, whereas the God of the Hebrews adheres to the Law (see above chapter 5), the Rex is *above* the law. Alluding to this legal theory, Heschel remarked:

> As a consequence of this conception it was assumed that the king stood above the law. According to the fourteenth-century Italian jurist, Baldus, the prince had *plenitude potestatis,* and he could therefore do anything *supra jus et contra jus, et extra jus*. From the time of the English Reformation we have Tyndale's statement that "the King is, in this world, without law; and may at his lust do right or wrong, and shall give account but to God only." James I (1567–1625) declared that "the King is above the Law." "That the king can do no wrong is," according to the famous jurist Sir William Blackstone "a necessary and fundamental principle of the English constitution." Some German scholars have held that the state is the creator of the law and thus superior to the law, and that acts of government officials are therefore not subject to the jurisdiction of the courts.[223]

---

the Kingdome of God, the Policy, and lawes Civill, are part of Religion; and therefore the distinction of Temporal, and Spirituall Domination, hath there no place.

On the association 'king/god,' see Mary Daly, *Beyond God the Father* (Boston: Beacon, 1973), p. 19. On the paleologic mode of thought permitting this type of association, see Sylvano Arieti, *Creativity* (New York: Basic Books, 1976); chapter 5, and *Homo Mysticus*, pp. 66–67, 79–82. Cf. *The Origin of the Republican Form of Government*, pp. 12–15.

222. *The Concept of Law*, p. 51.
223. *The Prophets*, p. 475.

The preceding, whereby the Rex is a *de facto* deity is the basis for the Judeo-Christian conflict. "With those who maintain that there are two gods in the world," counseled the rabbis, "don't get involved."[224]

Given that the Rex imposes the law by the fiat of his *dominion*, and given that no one can have dominion over him, the laws that he creates can have no legal limitations on him (see above chapter 13). There is an immediate consequence to this doctrine. In their long and enduring collaboration with the earthly governance, the ecclesiastical authorities not only learned from the Rex, but also taught him a lesson or two. An important lesson that the State learned from Christianity is that in accordance with *minut* ideology, the end justifies the means. The result, as noted by Jung (1875–1961), was that "Free opinion is stifled and moral decision ruthlessly suppressed, on the plea that the end justifies the means, even the vilest." When the Church was finally displaced by secularism, totalitarian states adopted many of the methods of their former spiritual mentors. Referring to the dictatorial forms of governments at his time, Jung wrote: "The State has taken the place of God; that is why, seen from this angle, the socialist dictatorships are religions and State slavery is a form of worship." Jung explained, "You can take away a man's gods, but only to give him others in return. The leaders of the mass State cannot avoid being deified."[225] In this fashion, the two-*rashut* doctrine helped pagan political ideology to flourish, in one form or another, until modern times.

> Through the apotheosis of the Roman emperor as *Dominus et Deus* and medieval traditions, down to modern times, one may trace the tendency to deify the king or to garb him with the trapping of divinity.[226]

224. Bemidbar Rabba, XV, 14, vol. 2, 66c.
225. *The Undiscovered Self*, p. 35; see ibid., pp. 33–34. On Loyola, see ibid., p. 49; the second quotation is from ibid. This was true even in societies professing to be secular and atheistic; see below n. 273.
226. *The Prophets*, p. 475.

Another consequence of the two-governance doctrine was blocking political discourse as trivial and unworthy. The Church Fathers did not contribute either to political or legal philosophy. Abrogation of the Law also meant the impossibility of questioning the legitimacy of a political system from within. The upshot was tolerance of pre-established inequalities and abandoning the faithful to the whims and cravings of dictators and megalomaniacs. Eventually, people realized that beside theo-political noise, those inhabiting *civitas Dei* had little to contribute to the conduct of civil society and government. This led to the separation of Church and State. Erwin R. Goodenough (1893–1965), one of the most perceptive writers on Jewish thought and history in late antiquity, wrote this curious passage:

> The modern world has increasingly tried to separate Church and State, the sacred and profane, by asserting that traditional revelation has no bearing upon or relation to the conduct of law and government. Those of you who know the history of this problem best will know how deeply the working out of a secular State has always been challenged by the Biblical tradition living on in the Churches and hearts of most men of the West. Marxists have tried to clear the air by discarding the Bible and all traditional forms of religious organization and cult. Whether they will eventually succeed, or will have to make concessions to the Bible, with its Christian and Jewish conception of divine rule, or have not really continued it under new terminology, I shall not say. All I am pointing out is that the Old Testament still keeps alive in modern society one of the most important aspects of antiquity, the conception that law and government never cease to be divine prerogatives, even when administered in executive mansions and human courts; that the distinction between the sacred and the profane, made by many scholars the very definition of religion, is an artificial distinction, a recent and modern one. As long as the Old Testament carries on its influence, both sides, the

> ancient and modern, have much compelling to say. As one who is by no means ecclesiastic I fear very deeply the power for evil of individuals or institutions which try to conduct the affairs of men in terms of a special knowledge that they have of divine will or cosmic right. Yet courts of law which support precedent *qua* precedent and ignore dreams of men for justice and mercy can be quite as destructive. If Old Testament law seems to us often antiquated and useless, it has recorded for us as no other document has the ancient dream of a society and a law which would not call ultimate the fallible judgments of human beings. We moderns who believe in human judgment must also believe in a better society than any we have ever seen and work for it, else our very institutions will shrivel of dry rot. For this we shall find inspiration in Aristotle, the Roman legists, the Greek democracies (at their best), but also in Sinai, and in the prophets' impassioned dreams of justice and mercy as recorded in the Old Testament.[227]

Professor Goodenough failed to notice, however, that the "artificial distinction" excluding the political and legal teachings of Israel from civil discourse was not the doing of "the modern world," or "Marxists," but of a long and intensive Christian denigration of the *Old* Testament and the *Law* – both political and civil – of the Tora; a denigration based on the naive presumption that it is possible to tear man into two, and "Render" one slice "unto Caesar" and the other "unto God" (see Matt. 22:21).

R. Elie Benamozegh (1823–1900) placed the failure of Christianity and Islam in their inability to grasp the two-dimensionality of the Tora and the close, intimate relation between the political and the spiritual. Instead, each proceeded to dismember Judaism, casting away this and cherry-picking that:

227. Erwin R. Goodenough, "The Bible as Product of the Ancient World," in *Five Essays on the Bible* (New York: American Council of Learned Societies, 1960), p. 7.

> If Jesus took from Judaism its moral, interior and spiritual side, and thereby showed himself the disciple of the Pharisees than of Moses, Mahomet, on the other hand, took from it its social and worldly side, and thereby attached himself to the Bible and to Moses rather than to tradition and the Pharisees.[228]

By focusing on the spiritual and discarding the political and legal aspects of the Tora, Christianity succeeded to present a

> Judaism, ever mutilated, ever deprived of that element connecting it with this life, namely, of the body, the family, society, country; of life, in short, in all its various aspects! Ever the exclusive culture of the spiritual side of Judaism, of faith proper, of the individual conscience, in which man, despising the forenamed relations of the present life, shuts himself up and intrenches himself!

Islam took the legal and political dimensions of Judaism, which had been abandoned by Jesus, and discarded the spiritual:

> A phenomenon, just the reverse of this, awaits us in Islamism. It is the other side of Judaism, the one abandoned by Jesus, that Mahomet selects for his chief principle, for the cornerstone of his system.

One-half of 'Judaism' is nothing more than a mutilated, dysfunctional scheme. In the beginning, this method will lead to either spiritual or political barbarism, and in the end to both. Again,

> Islamism, by excluding the spiritual side of Judaism, has barbarized its polity; Christianity, by soaring beyond the social

228. Elie Benamozegh, *Jewish and Christian Ethics* (San Francisco: Emanuel Blochman, 5633-1873), II, p. 4.

> life of Judaism, has transformed its religion into ascetism. In both cases is a Judaism mutilated – deprived of one of its essential members.[229]

There is cunning in presenting Judaism as a dysfunctional and spiritually wanting system. In the next chapter we will see that the focus of 'monotheistic religions' is silencing the Jewish Scripture – not teaching the word of God. Crushed under the military might of Rome, pillaged and plundered, banished from their homes, Israel's sole possession was the Book. 'Monotheistic religions' took advantage of the weak, and under the protection of the sword, proceeded to rob the Jews of their most valued possession: the Tora. Under the banner of 'monotheism' they took on the tone of a neutral and omniscient posture and proceeded to steal God's Word to Israel at Sinai. Chopping up this and distorting that would make the task easier, particularly when exposing these 'facts' to an analphabetic public, who were barred from reading the text itself! That is why, noted Nietzsche, the greatest crime ever perpetrated against the literary heritage of humankind was the Christian binding of the 'Old' with the 'New' Testament. In his own words:

> In the Jewish 'Old Testament,' the book of divine justice, there are human beings, things, and speeches in so grand a style that Greek and Indian literatures have nothing to compare with it. With terror and reverence one stands before these tremendous remnants of what man once was, and will have sad thoughts about ancient Asia and its protruding little peninsula Europe, which wants by all means to signify as against Asia the progress of man. To be sure, whoever is himself merely a meager, tame domestic animal and knows only the needs of domestic animals (like our educated people of today, including the Christians of 'educated' Christianity-) has no cause for amazement

229. *Jewish and Christian Ethics*, II, pp. 3, 4. See "One Dimensional Jew," pp. 47–50.

> or sorrow among these ruins – the taste for the Old Testament is a touchstone for 'great' and 'small'– perhaps he will find the New Testament, the book of grace, still rather more after his heart (it contains a lot of the real, tender, musty true-believer and small-soul smell). To have glued this New Testament, a kind of rococo of taste in every respect, to the Old Testament to make one book, as the 'Bible,' as 'the book as such' – that is perhaps the greatest audacity and 'sin against the spirit' that literary Europe has on its conscience.[230]

230. Friedrich Nietzsche, *Beyond Good and Evil* (New York: Carlton House, n.d.), 52, pp. 59–60. I believe that the whole idea of Nietzsche's antisemitism was a ruse to divert attention from his profound aversion for Christianity; see idem, *Why I am so Wise* (Penguin Books), pp. 51, 66–69. Much more hateful than an anti-Christ, is an anti-Christ who values Judaism.

# Chapter 27
# Silencing Scripture

To discredit the Law (mutilated and deformed), monotheistic religions chose to present their case to analphabetic crowds (see appendix 2). Islam was revealed to the *jahiliya* or analphabetic pagans populating the Arabian Peninsula before the advent of Muhammad (7th century). Insofar as Christianity is concerned, I would like to offer as evidence an incident casually mentioned in the Christian Scripture. One would presume that to a Christian, the most important word ever written would be a word written by Jesus himself. Jesus wrote such a word: with his own finger. Jn. 8:6 attests that when the scribes and Pharisees submitted a question to Jesus, he "stooped down, and with *his* finger wrote on the ground." To me, the fact that no one cared to register what Jesus wrote is clear evidence that we are dealing with an analphabetic crowd (see Appendices 20, 22). Indeed, the whole notion that God's "Word (*logos*) was with God" and it became "flesh" (Jn. 1:1, 14), makes as much sense as saying that *Paradise Lost* or the *Principia* became flesh. Consider the following corollary derived from the preceding, as worked out in Jn. 6:53–58:

> Verily, verily, I say unto you, Except ye eat the flesh of the Son of man, and drink his blood, ye have no life in you. Whoso eateth my flesh, and drinketh my blood, hath eternal life; and I will raise him up at the last day. For my flesh is meat indeed, and my blood, dwelleth in me, and I in him. As the living Father hath sent me, and I live by the Father: so he that

> eateth me, even he shall live by me. This is that bread which came down from heaven: not as your fathers did eat manna, and are dead: he that eateth of this bread shall live forever. (cf. 1 Cor. 11:24–34).

To a lettered public such a claim would be akin to someone proposing that the *Divine Comedy* and *Paradise Lost* have become flesh, and now they can be known by ingesting, respectively, Dante and Milton. One can only speculate about the sensitivities and visceral concerns of a crowd that finds spiritual edification in a metaphor of human blood and flesh to be consumed through the mystery of transubstantiation. By "Jewish standards," remarked a distinguished historian, it was "an atrocity that can have been conceived only by a circle bent on demonstrating its freedom from the Law."[231] The change in venue pushed Jesus' doctrines aside. Instead of the preacher of love, he became "the conqueror of demons, the exorcist, who at the end of time will render the Devil and his demons powerless." 'Salvation' became a code-term for the manipulation of demons. Baptism "had an exorcist function: it was meant to keep demons from the child being baptized" (see 1 Jn. 3:8; Col. 2:12–15).[232] To harvest the psychic potentiality from these masses, the psychic complexes swarming in the pagan mind were endowed with 'religious' significance.

We can now proceed to analyze a fundamental dilemma confronting monotheistic religions. On the one hand, these religions took as a point of departure the Tora and subsequent history of Israel. On the other hand, to substantiate their claim for 'improvement' and justify delegitimizing the Tora, a certain basic knowledge of Scripture would

231. *Jesus the Magician*, p. 123. See Morton Smith, *The Secret Gospel* (New York: Harper & Row, 1978), p. 95; and idem, *Studies in the Cult of Y...*, 2 vols. ed. Shaye J. D. Cohen (Leiden: E. J. Brill, 1996), vol. 2, pp. 101–102. Cf. appendix 22.

232. Alfred Ribi, *Demons of the Inner World* (Boston: Shambala, 1990), p. 25. Predictably, Gibbon, who followed Pagan and Christian anti-Jewish diatribe religiously, described Christian rite, in *The Decline and Fall of the Roman Empire*, vol. 1, p. 388 as "a pure and spiritual worship." see appendix 20.

be necessary. And yet, anti-Tora arguments are submitted, invariably, to analphabetic crowds. How difficult it would it be to shred into pieces a document – even as stirring and compelling as the Declaration of Independence or the Bill of Rights – to an illiterate public, crowded with demons and inspired by metaphors about eating human flesh and drinking human blood? The worst victim of these types of 'reasoning' was the faithful Christian. By addressing a public that was encouraged to demonize Jews but was forbidden to read the Tora, delegitimization of Judaism was effected via hatred. A principal difference between Judaism and other monotheistic religions is that one needs not to hate any religion or deprecate anyone to be a good Jew. On the contrary, "One who is in the habit of honoring himself by deprecating another," taught the rabbis, "has no portion in the world to come."[233] By contrast, hatred is an essential element of Christian salvation. "If a *man* come to me, and hate not his father, and mother, and wife, and children, and brethren, and sisters, yea, and his own life also," said Jesus, "he cannot be my disciple" (Lk. 14:26). In fact, regardless of variation in detail, *all* 'monotheistic' religions acquired their standing by attacking Jews. This may explain the telling fact that there was no antisemitism whatsoever in Asia before the arrival of Christian and Moslem missionaries. (Until the beginning of the 20th century, natives in some Spanish and Portuguese dominions in Latin America were taught to hate Jews and despise the *Old* Testament, but were forbidden from reading the Bible.) Considering these points, a critical question comes to mind. Why do monotheistic religions find it necessary to belittle the Tora and deride the Jewish people? At first glance it seems odd, given that the Tora does not claim to be binding on anyone except Jews. Not only is a gentile not bound to fulfill any of the precepts of the Tora, but, as noted earlier, a "pious from among the nations" can obtain salvation (see above Introductory Remarks).

---

233. Y. Ḥagiga II, 1, 77c; cf. *Guide* I, 59. Maimonides codified this doctrine in *MT De'ot* 6:3; *Teshuba* 3:7, 14; 4:4. On the policy of making the God of Israel the object of hatred and deprecation among the public, see *Sifre* #331, p. 381.

Why not, then, start afresh, and develop their spiritual systems without needing to attack the Jewish Law – like Buddhism and Taoism?

The reason moving these religions to claim to be 'monotheistic' has nothing to do with 'religion.' Rather, it is to silence the Jewish Scripture, particularly since it was used in the Synagogue to educate the masses.[234] By 'recognizing' the Tora – choosing this and thrusting aside that – monotheistic religions could tell their faithful, in quality of *minut*, that they were actually speaking in the voice of God. This, in turn, would permit them to claim possession of the Scripture, not to make the Good Book available to the masses, but the reverse: to prevent the educated public from reading the Scripture with their own eyes. "Winning the struggle meant co-opting the book from the Jews," observed Professor Nicholls, and "denying them the right to it." It could no longer be a book for either Jews or the faithful Christian. "It must become the book of the Church."[235] In this fashion, the Church abducted the Scripture and used it as a tool to attack undesirables and muzzle dissenting opinions. In the apostolic age, the faithful were organized in assemblies, like the Jewish Synagogue.[236] Since this gave too much power to the congregants, the Church organized itself as a Roman corporation, claiming the exclusive monopoly of interpreting the Scriptures. This claim is based neither on the Scripture nor on tradition, but on the imperial might awarded by the Rex's sword (see below chapter 31). Later, the Protestant Reformation challenged the Church's claim for exclusive right of interpretation. Professor Moore (1851–1931) explained:

---

234. On the propagation of Scripture and education of the masses through the Synagogue; see *Judaism*, vol. 1, pp. 281–283.

235. *Christian Antisemitism*, p. 119. Cleverly, the Church used the Hebrew Scripture to promote hatred against Jews among the unsuspecting masses. It is on account of the *minim* emphasis on hatred that the rabbis refer to them as 'hate-mongers' (משנאי); see Shabbat 116a and *Sifre* #331, p. 381.

236. See George F. Moore, *History of Religions*, vol. 2 (Edinburgh: T. &T. Clark, 1920), p. 149.

> The final authority of Scripture was, however, not the real issue, but the authority to interpret Scripture. The church claimed this as its exclusive right. The reformers asserted this right for themselves, and, in principle, for every Christian man – practically, they meant for those who interpreted as they did.[237]

This policy continued until relatively recent times.

> Historically, the Church has not placed primary emphasis on the Bible. The position of the church has been that the Church itself stands as the center of Christianity – the Church which, the Church says, was founded by Jesus, who named Peter the first Bishop of Rome, who, therefore, became the first Pope. According to Roman Catholic beliefs, it is tradition – as maintained and transmitted by the Church – that determines the character of Christianity. It is tradition, with the Church as its carrier and guardian that determines the place, role, and meaning of the Bible. The Church has never been Bible-centered; and in its reading of the Bible, it has never been fundamentalist. *The Bible must be interpreted by the priests (the Church); the Bible does not speak directly to every man; the Bible speaks through the Church, its priests and its tradition* (Italics added).

Thus, "...the Church continues to claim that it, and not the Bible, is the source of Christian teaching; that it alone has the authority to interpret and proclaim the teaching of the Bible."[238] In this fashion the ecclesiastic authorities built up a constituency which could digest Jesus' "flesh and blood" with their own bodies, but could not read the Scripture with their own eyes.

The effect that the Hebrew Scripture could have had on the gentile population, and which monotheistic religions tried so desperately to

237. *History of Religions,* vol. 2, pp. 312–313. See *Christian Antisemitism,* chapter 5.
238. Milton R. Konovits, *Religious Liberty and Conscience* (New York: Viking Press, 1968), pp. 8, 10.

prevent, can be estimated from the impact it had in Puritan England, when the faithful began reading the Bible on their own. It is then that "England became the people of a book, and that book was the Bible." It penetrated all levels of intellectual and public life. "What the revival of classical learning had done on the Continent," noted a distinguished scholar "was done in England in a far profounder fashion by the translations of the Scriptures."[239] This is why, unlike the rest of Europe, England did not need a revolution, *a la* French, to upgrade and reform its governing institutions. The most important result of the translation of Scripture was the American Revolution and the establishment of the USA. It is a historical fact that the ideals upon which the new country was founded came from reading the Jewish – not the Christian – Scripture (see below chapter 31 and Concluding Reflections). Let us hear what no lesser a historian than William Lecky (1838–1903) had to say on this matter:

> It is, at least, an historical fact, that in the great majority of instances the early Protestant defenders of civil liberty derived their political principles chiefly from the Old Testament, and the defenders of despotism from the New. The rebellions that were so frequent in Jewish history formed the favorite topic of the one – the unreserved submission inculcated by St. Paul, of the other. When, therefore, all the principles of right and wrong were derived from theology, and when by the rejection of traditions and ecclesiastical authority, Scripture became the sole arbiter of theological difficulties, it was a matter of manifest importance, in ascertaining the political tendencies

239. The first quotation comes from Green's *Short History of the English People*, cited in W. B. Selbie, "The Influence of the Old Testament on Puritanism," in eds. I. Abrahams et al, *The Legacy of Israel* (Oxford: Clarendon Press, 1928), p. 407; the second quotation is from Selbie himself, ibid. Cf. *Origin of the Republican Form of Government*, chapter 4.

> of any sect, to discover which Testament was most congenial to the tone and complexion of its theology.[240]

Were it not for the great efforts made by the monotheistic religions in silencing the Jewish Scripture, many of the ideals and institutions enjoyed in the free world today would have taken root earlier in history. Conversely, were it not for the Puritan reading of the Jewish Scripture, history in the Americas and the rest of the world would have followed a similar course and development as post-revolutionary France and Russia, where one set of rulers, enjoying unlimited sovereignty, are exchanged for another one under a different rubric.

Puritan theology was arrayed against the politico-theological tenets of the Established Church. The divine supremacy of the Law, as embodied in, and illustrated by, the Hebrew Commonwealth, was brought in conflict with the 'Divine Right' of kings, as exhibited in the absolutism of George III, and out of the struggle came to life American liberty.[241]

240. Quoted in the *Origin of the Republican Form of Government*, n. 2, pp. 19–20, from Lecky, *Rationalism in Europe*, vol. 2, p. 168. Cf. below n. 313.

241. *Origin of the Republican Form of Government*, pp. 99–100.

# Chapter 28

# The Road to Serfdom: Freedom *without* Law

Limited sovereignty, as with the three autonomous crowns of Israel, can function only within the perimeter of the Law and properly codified regulations. In turn, the Law entails a Book serving as the ultimate point of reference, where conflicts can be resolved without the resort to violence. To function thus, the Book must be grounded on a national covenant, like the *berit* of Israel, accessible to the *ketab* and *mikhtab* of the people. Otherwise, it would be under the aegis of the sword, rather than under the "crown of a good name." What makes documents such as the US Constitution and the Magna Carta efficient tools of government is not their content alone, but the relative autonomy of the national institutions, particularly the judiciary, to interpret and implement these documents; and above all, the commitment on the part of the *people* to safeguard their integrity. Without such a national commitment, a Constitution, regardless of the ideals it proclaims, cannot be an effective tool of government. Proclamations of human rights, etc. are worthless in governments where there is neither an independent judiciary system nor a solid constituency committed to safeguarding and implementing these ideals. This was the focus of David Nassy's criticism of the French Revolution. Its failure was due to the "... unbridled ambition, infamy and vanity of a great number of obscure Men," whom he described as a bunch of "ambitious Demagogues, Cannibals, Anthropophagites" (cannibals who devour each other).[242] The problem lies not in the ideals themselves but in the moral vacuum of the people – what Nassy refers to as lack of mores. This is why, he maintained, it was useless to discuss which form of government may be best in abstract without taking into consideration the fact that without an ethical constituency and leadership all forms of government are doomed to failure:

> Meanwhile I am far from wanting to decide which is the best [form] of Government; the greatest writers have failed in this matter, and my limited talents make me find this question very difficult; it only seems to me that they cannot be more than probably good or bad, because, I repeat, Men only determine everything; their ambition and their vices, or their *mores* and their virtues alone, will always decide this question.[243]

In abstract, the political principles of many nations as well as their religious systems may appear lofty and sublime. Their failure is due to the moral vacuum characterizing their leadership and general population:

> ...France, and perhaps even Holland itself, offer us striking examples of this unfortunate truth; their system of liberty and equality is undoubtedly beautiful and sublime; their principles, in my opinion, are comparable to those of our Religions, all are based on nature, and on the ethics which derive there from; but the vices of man have tainted them all, have turned them all upside down, they made us forget the basis of their principles, to remember nothing but their hideous result: The Religions, which through the fanaticism, ambition and the stinginess of most of its adherents, who know how to terrify the people with vain chimeras, and to plunge them into superstition, seem to

242. *Lettre*, pp. xxxii-xxxiv.

243. *Lettre*, pp. xxviii-xxx.

> have generated nothing but insolent priests, fanatics, scoundrels, and dangerous prejudices.[244]

David Nassy was one of those early political thinkers who recognized that the *American* Revolution had nothing to do with the *French* Revolution. In a letter of August 18, 1799, addressing the *American Philosophical Society* in Philadelphia, he lauded the "application of the grand principles of Liberty and Equality, of which the United States has given the first example to the whole world." In his view, the success of the United States lies not merely in the ideals themselves, but in the *mores* of the people. These *mores* came before the establishment of the US, paving the way to the formation of the state. Therefore, they could guarantee the integrity of its laws and institutions. In the same letter, Nassy declared: "Fortunate is the place where the good Laws are sanctioned by the *mores* of the People! Fortunate are the People, whose *mores* are guarantee of their Laws!" Alluding to the advocates of similar ideals in Europe, Nassy pointed out that they were proclaimed by "Philosophers and Politicians," implying opportunism and lack of popular support:

> It is then to the United States in general, and to the State of Pennsylvania in particular, to those States which had *mores*, before having had positive Laws, that the world owes the first and great result put in action, of that sweet Philanthropy, of that wise and enlightened Philosophy which makes no distinction among men, except that which is demanded by virtue, useful talents, and good *mores*.[245]

The foregoing is essential to understanding Paul's (d. 68) attitude towards the Law from a Jewish perspective. Early in their history, Jews understood what John Locke (1632–1704) would later teach, that

244. *Lettre*, p. xxxii.

245. In a letter of August 18, 1799, quoted in "David Nassy," p. 100.

there cannot be liberty without law: "For *Liberty* is to be free from restraint and violence from others; which cannot be, where there is no Law."[246] The freedom advocated by Israel lies in the realm of the political and it centers on an inviolable Law.[247] The point of the Tora and the rabbis is that without the benefit of Law, 'freedom' leads to the rule of the sword, persecution and corrupt leadership. Rather than a state of freedom, the people are reduced to a state of abject slavery, lacking any recourse except for escapism (= religion) and/or violence (= the Rex). Paul and his followers – not Jesus – rejected the Law. Although a Jew, Paul was a "citizen of no mean city" in Cilicia (Acts 21:39); and he identified himself as "a Roman" (Acts 22:25–29; cf. ibid. 23:27; 16:37–38). To ingratiate himself with the political authorities, he proposed that 'freedom' pertains to the realm of the intangible (= religion).[248] In a persuasive and systematic fashion, he laid out the theoretical basis for an ideology that would be the earmark of Christianity throughout the ages. Under the Law, one is in a state of "bondage" (Gal. 4:3, cf. ibid., vv. 9, 21), and no more than a "servant" (v. 7). Jews are the children "of the slave-woman… born after the flesh" (v. 23). Rather than the grounds for liberty, the covenant at Sinai is pure enslavement, symbolized by Sarah's maid Hagar. Displaying his uncanny wit, he declared: "Mount Sinai brings forth to slavery, which is Hagar" (v. 24). Adding: "For Hagar is Mount Sinai in Arabia, and corresponds to the present Jerusalem, and she

246. John Locke, *Two Treatises of Government* (Cambridge: Cambridge University Press, 1988), *Second Treatise*, 57, p. 306. See appendix 17.

247. See the valuable note of Israel Abrahams, *Studies in Pharisaism and the Gospels*, pp. 213–214.

248. See *Christian Antisemitism*, pp. 11–17. This explains why some of Jesus' early supporters were connected to Roman political circles; see Sanhedrin 43a (שאני ישו דקרוב למלכות הוה), and appendix 60. Later, after Jesus' death, these same circles must have been particularly interested in promoting Paul's policies (and delegitimizing Jesus' disciples). Ironically, Paul was executed by the Romans, the very people whom he wanted to serve and on whose behalf he blasphemed the God of Israel. On his trial, see Paul W. Walaskay, *'And so we came to Rome,'* (Cambridge: Cambridge University Press, 2005), chapter 4.

is in slavery with her children" (v. 25). Over and higher than earthly Jerusalem stands "the Jerusalem from above" which is "free" (v. 26). On the basis of this doctrine, the Church accorded Jews the status of 'slaves.' Although the Church does not dwell in hair-splitting legalities (as Pharisees do), it concluded that as 'slaves' the institution of ownership does not apply to Jews. It stands to reason, therefore, that there could not be a moral objection to plundering and despoiling Jewish property. This doctrine was enunciated with candor and precision by Thomas Aquinas (1225–1274), one of the most ethical minds to grace Christendom. Briefly and to the point, he wrote: "Since Jews are the slaves of the Church, the Church may take disposition of their property."[249] Paul's spirituality rests on a simple axiom: freedom and Law are mutually exclusive.

The faithful must choose one and eschew the other. In a passage echoing a spirit that would resonate throughout the ages, Paul addressed the faithful with this touching sentence: "Then stand firm in the freedom with which Christ made us free, and do not again be held with a yoke of slavery" (Gal. 5:1).[250] According to Paul – I don't think this idea has anything to do with the historical Jesus[251] – the freedom that Jesus proposed equals absolute submission to *earthly* masters. Thus, he summoned the faithful: "Servants! Obey in all things your Masters according to the flesh!" Reformulating a rabbinic aphorism not to serve God as slaves do with an eye on earthly reward (Abot 1:3), Paul urged the faithful to serve their *earthly* masters, "Not with eye-service, as men-pleasers; but in singleness of heart, as fearing the Lord" (Col. 3:22; cf. Rom. 13:1–7; 1 Cor. 9:27; 1 Pet. 2:13–21; Tit. 3:1, etc.). Later, Martin Luther (1483–1546) extended this doctrine to include Christian slaves owned by Muslims. Sternly, he warned them

249. *Summa Theologica* II, 2, 10, 10. Since the original could prove a bit unsettling, the English version, in ed. Timothy McDermott, *Summa Theologicae* (London: Eyre and Spottiswoode, 1989), p. 341, reads: "The church has the right to dispose of the Jew's property since he is the subject of the church."

250. See *Em la-Miqra*, vol. 2, 53a-b.

251. See *Christian Antisemitism*, pp. 11–17.

not to disobey their earthly masters since they were their *property*. Addressing Christian slaves, he said:

> You are robbing and stealing your body from your master who has bought it or acquired it in some other way so that it is no longer yours but his property, like cattle or other possession.[252]

In this fashion, Paul's words and ideas served as the basic defense in support of Christian slaveholders[253] (see appendix 22).

252. Quoted by Walter Kaufmann, *Religions in Four Dimensions* (New York: Reader's Digest Press, 1976), p. 157. This doctrine could not extend to Jewish owners since they themselves are to be regarded as *slaves* of the Church and thus without the right of property, see above n. 249.
253. See Forrest G. Wood, *The Arrogance of Faith* (New York: Alfred A. Knopf, 1990), pp. 67–83.

# Chapter 29
# Paul's Theo-Politics

Paul, as recorded by Luke, "offers the early church an *apologia pro imperio*: he opposed an anti-Roman attitude in order to help the church to survive in a given political order."[254] His agenda consisted of accommodating theology to the exigencies of the empire. It was fully developed by Augustine (354–430) into the dichotomy *regnum* (state)/*civita Dei* (city of God) (= two-realm governance), and served as the basis for the sustained continuation of political unfreedom. This dichotomy led to the separation of law from ethics and of positive law or *lex temporalis* from *lex aeterna*. Christian withdrawal into *civita Dei* permitted the Rex to have absolute control of the judicial and political institutions of the state. Since the affairs of the *regnum* were outside the scope of *civita Dei*, the sovereign was immune from criticism. Consequently, it was impossible to question the legitimacy of a political system from within. As argued by Marcuse in a different context:

> And indeed, there is no enforceable law that could deprive such a constitutional government of its legitimacy and legality. But this means that there is no (enforceable) law other than that

254. Klaus Wengst, *Pax Romana* (Philadelphia: Fortress Press, 1987), p. 105. On the association of various Churches with un-democratic ideologies in colonial America, see *The Origin of the Republican Form of Government in the United States*, pp. 54–69.

> which serves the *status quo,* and that those who refuse such service are *eo ipso* outside the realm of the law.[255]

Rather than battle political oppression and pre-established inequalities – rampant throughout the Roman Empire – Paul went on to develop a theology designed to support pagan political ideology against Israel and the Tora. In this fashion, Pauline theology became an indispensable tool for the Roman domination and future totalitarian governments. His efforts were fully appreciated, as exemplified by the continuous anti-Jewish measures sanctioned by Ecumenical Councils. Later, the symbiosis Rex/Church was formally consecrated into a theo-political entity known as the 'Holy Roman Empire.'[256]

Paul's theology rests on three pillars designed to uphold pagan political ideology *contra* the Law. These are: sovereignty, law, and the individual.

First, man's *essential inequality*. Christianity's most basic premise is the hierarchic principle positing that humanity is structured vertically in a chain of 'superior/inferior.' All forms of Christian organization, regardless of denomination, posit the *essential inequality* of men.[257] Upon this premise rests the doctrine of *obedience,* whereby the *inferior* must submit to the hierarchic *superior* by the fiat that the *inferior* must submit to the *superior*. It equals the whole of Christian faith: the faithful (*fidelis christianus*) expresses his faith (*fidelitas*) simply by submitting to the authority of the superior.[258] The principle of *obedience,* demanded by hierarchic logic meant, above all, that the *fidelis*

---

255. Herbert Marcuse, *An Essay on Liberation* (Pelican Books), p. 71.
256. See *In the Shadow of History*, p. 29.
257. See *The Individual and Society in the Middle Ages*, pp. 12–16. This doctrine served to justify the racist policies against Jews in Spain and Portugal, and the genocide of Native Americans; see "The Iberian Experience: Jews, *Conversos* and Native Americans," pp. 1–11. In more recent times this ideology was revived by the Nazis; see *Escape from Freedom*, p. 109.
258. See *In the Shadow of History*, pp. 32–34, 37.

*christianus* must surrender his individuality on behalf of authority. This is how a modern psychologist described Luther's idea of faith:

> Luther's relationship to God was one of complete submission. In psychological terms his concept of faith means: if you completely submit, if you accept your individual insignificance, then the all-powerful God may be willing to love you and save you. If you get rid of your individual self with all its shortcomings and doubts by utmost self-effacement, you free yourself from the feeling of your own nothingness and can participate in God's glory.[259]

'Submission' is nothing less than the "annihilation of the individual self as a condition for salvation." There are consequences to this theology. Implicit in this demand is training the faithful to do as he is told and to acquiesce to the 'superior': *obedience* is a matter of *faith*.[260] Against the teaching of the Tora that God had endowed every human with "the image of God," Luther's God was bent on depriving "man of self-confidence and the feeling of human dignity which is the premise for any firm stand against oppression of secular authorities."[261] A similar doctrine was developed by John Calvin (1509–1564). Preying on the feeling of insecurity inherent in vertical societies, he taught that the most pertinent message of Christianity is that "by complete submission and self-humiliation he [the individual] could hope to find new security."[262] All major denominations concur in this overwhelming principle, including the Catholic Church:

---

259. *Escape from Freedom*, p. 100. See idem, *Psychoanalysis and Religion* (New Haven: Yale University Press, 1950), p. 17 where Fromm defines Jung's concept of religion, as "the submission to powers higher than ourselves." cf. ibid., pp. 19, 34–37.
260. See *The Individual and Society in the Middle Ages*, pp. 10–15.
261. *Escape from Freedom*, pp. 100, 102.
262. *Escape from Freedom*, pp. 106–107.

> Like Protestantism and Calvinism, the Catholic Church had always denied that man, on the strength of his own virtues and merits alone, could find salvation that he could do without the grace of God as an indispensable means for salvation.[263]

The *human* aspect of Jesus reinforced the hierarchic principle. Christian doctrine assumes, as a *sine qua non,* man's essential inequality. Consider the following: Christian salvation is granted to some by virtue of grace, and eternal damnation to others by imputing sin on them; even more, the notion of a mystical body of Jesus ranking the faithful according to strict hierarchic order, in correlation to the body's limbs and organs, etc. Moreover, Jesus' demeanor, as portrayed in the Christian Scripture, is not of a common man but of a Rex. He is free to award riches and honors to some, and condemn others to eternal torment by his say: whether deservedly or not. Paul posited a human scale on the top of which stands Jesus. However, Jesus is not to be worshipped *qua* God but *qua Christ*. The distinction is crucial. 'Christ' is the Greek translation of the Hebrew *mashiaḥ* (משיח) 'anointed' – a term referring to the 'anointing ceremony' performed at the installation of the monarch and high priest. I would like to propose a question concerning the *semantic* content of *mashiaḥ/Christ*: is it that of a Hebrew king or of a pagan Rex? By postulating that Jesus *qua Christ* is god, and that Jesus *qua Christ* is to be worshipped as god, Paul was substantiating the pagan ideology Rex/god. At this point it would be relevant to raise a second question. Does Jesus' kingship, as depicted in Christian tradition, correspond to a *Jewish* monarch of the House of David, or to a pagan Rex? Jesus' miraculous birth and eventual apotheosis conform to that of a pagan Rex claiming bodily supremacy as a testimony to his hierarchic authority, as it was claimed by Caligula (see below chapter 32) and Pharaoh. This is contrary to

263. *Escape from Freedom*, p. 87. On the impact of this ideology in western thought, see Eric Fromm, *Man For Himself* (New York: Henry Holt and Company, 1947), chapter 4.

everything that the Tora and prophets taught, thus confirming pagan political theory *contra* the Law.

The second pillar erected by Paul concerns the indisputable right of the Rex to abrogate the Law, including the Jewish Law contracted at Sinai – not to speak of other Laws. We have seen that the whole idea of a Law based on consent (*berit*) and proposing limited sovereignty was offensive to pagan ideology, where the Rex *imposes* his will on his subjects by virtue of his might. What was particularly odious about the Tora is the principle that the Rex and his subjects are under the rule of Law. A particularly obnoxious aspect of the Law is the right (and responsibility) of the judiciary to summon the authorities, Rex included, to render account before the court of justice. More repellent was the fact that the Law recognized that certain basic rights are immune from the Rex's intervention.[264] Within this context, the first question that springs to mind is whether the abrogation of the Tora presupposes a Christ/Rex, yielding absolute and unlimited sovereignty, or a Christ/Jewish king with *limited* sovereignty *under* the Law? A follow-up question: was the basis for Jesus' authority a matter of *might* or *right*? Did it depend on *consent*, or on his alleged *power* to exorcise demons and perform all sort of magical acts, as attested by so many trustworthy witnesses (questioned only by feeble minded Jews and odious Pharisees)? A Christ based on might is a Rex – not a king of the House of David – regardless of alleged pedigree! We can now proceed to examine a matter of the highest importance. Paul snidely dismissed the Law *qua* Jewish, while honoring Roman law. Why? Not all historians are aware that Christianity is organized according to Roman corporate law. Regardless of whatever interpretation theologians wish to consider, it is an undisputable fact that the whole

264. Something more or less analogous to our 'Bill of Rights.' The denomination 'Law' to the Pentateuch has perplexed modern writers, since many passages in the Tora, particularly Genesis and the first part of Exodus, have nothing to do with 'law.' The purpose of these sections is to expose the human rights and social institutions anteceding legislation and political organization, and therefore immune from government intervention; cf. Radaq on Ps. 19:8.

idea of *corpus Christi* or 'Christ's mystical body'– the holy of holiest of Christianity – is nothing more than a Roman *commercial* corporation. The chief authority of said *corporation* has the same rights and duties as any other CEO in a Roman corporation. The faithful are stockholders, under the structure and regulations of stockholders in a Roman corporation. 'Salvation' is awarded to members of *corpus Christi,* exactly as 'dividends' in a *commercial* corporation. This is why although 'universal,' Christianity does not award salvation to non-members, as it would not be expected of any corporation to distribute its profit to outsiders. Simply put, 'baptism' is the formal induction into a corporation (Latin *corporatio*) known as 'the *corpus,* or body, of Christ.' Addressing this fundamental ideal, Augustine taught that salvation is achieved by *incorporating* into a corporation – the Christian Church – known as *corpus Christi.* The 'Holy Spirit' brings salvation and unity only to members of the *corpus*-corporation. By analogy, those who are not part of said corporation, or have been separated from said corporation, cannot be the recipients of salvation.[265] In short, Paul is not against pagan law but only against *Jewish* Law – a system that could hamper the policy of rendering "that which belongs" to the Rex, regardless of content and circumstances. Thus, confirming pagan political theory *contra* the Law.

The third pillar, human essential wretchedness. It derives from the belief that at the top of hierarchic-man stands perfect Jesus. This dogma confirms the thesis that the individual is doomed to failure without a Rex. No matter how one wishes to interpret Paul's doctrine of original sin (Rom. 5:14, 19; cf. 1 Cor. 15:21) it postulates the worthlessness of man and the impossibility of salvation without a Christ/Rex. Jesus functions in the realm of the spiritual as the Rex in the realm of the political. Without this doctrine, Paul's Christianity is pointless. To ascertain human worthlessness, Paul rejected the most fundamental doctrine of the Tora, i.e., that Adam and his

---

265. For sources, see *In the Shadow of History,* pp. 28–29, 32–34. Cf. *Christian Antisemitism,* pp. 34–36; and appendix 30.

descendants are self-sufficient creatures endowed with God's image. The theoretic basis of this doctrine is connected to the fact that Paul was not only a Roman citizen but thought and felt and sensed like a Roman. Therefore, he looked at people not as individuals but as members of a corporation, as seeds of wheat that have been ground and made into flour and kneaded into bread, and lost their individuality. "For we being many are one bread, and one body" (1 Cor. 10:27). A *corporatio* does not tolerate individuation. At the theological level, it means that Adam is not a single individual but the conglomerate of all human souls. Therefore, in impeccable Roman logic, his sin was committed by the corporation which he embodied. This doctrine affected how gentiles looked at people: they were not viewed as individuals but as members of a caste or corporation. Professor Ullman explained:

> The individual became absorbed in and by the corporation itself, by the Church, which itself, however, was governed on the monarchic principle, according to which original power was located in one supreme authority, from which all power in the public sphere was derived.[266]

This is why Jewish guilt for 'killing' Jesus applies to the entire membership of the corporation: past and present. Since there are no individuals, a 'sin' committed by a single Jew is to be imputed on the entire Jewish corporation. This point was elucidated by King Ferdinand. In the Edict of the Expulsion of Jews from Spain, 1492, he reasoned that although the "horrendous crime" of trying to instruct *conversos* in the ways of the Tora was

> committed by [only] a member of a college or university [= corporation], it is reasonable that the [said] college or university should be dissolved and annihilated, and that the

266. *The Individual and Society in the Middle Ages*, p. 9; cf. ibid., p. 12.

> young should be punished on account of the old, and some on account of others.[267]

A question springs to mind. What moved Paul to oppose Scriptural and rabbinic teaching establishing that every person is a distinct individual made in "the image of God?" Why did he postulate that without a Christ/Rex man is doomed to eternal damnation? It seems that by instilling the conviction of personal wickedness and inevitable failure, the faithful would incline to withhold personal judgment and submit to a hierarchic authority, thus confirming pagan political theory *contra* the Law.

Upon these three Pillars was fostered a policy tending to make the faithful more docile and the leadership more commanding. Jung's view on this matter is particularly illuminating.

> Anyone who has once learned to submit absolutely to a collective belief and to renounce his eternal right to freedom and the equally eternal duty of individual responsibility will persist in this attitude, and will be able to set out with the same credulity and the same lack of criticism in the reverse direction, if another and manifestly 'better' belief is foisted upon this alleged idealism.[268]

In fact, it is hardly possible to distinguish between the 'city of God' ruled by the Church, and the 'empire' ruled by the Rex. Quoting Jung, again:

267. Cited in *In the Shadow of History*, p. 39; see ibid., pp. 37–40. Hence the peculiar status of the *conversos* in Spain, although Christian, they 'belonged' to 'another caste'; see ibid., pp. 53–57. This bears on the question of 'honor' dividing 'new' from 'old' Christians. No matter what the particular accomplishment of an individual new Christian, he belonged to an inferior caste; see ibid., pp. 34–37, 66–70, 111–112. Cf above n. 173.

268. C. G. Jung, *The Undiscovered Self*, pp. 50–51.

> The absolutist claim of a *Civitas Dei* represented by man bears an unfortunate resemblance to the 'divinity' of the State, and the moral conclusion drawn by Ignatius Loyola from the authority of the Church ('the end justifies the means') anticipates the lie as a political instrument in an exceedingly dangerous way. Both demand unqualified submission to faith and thus curtail man's freedom, the one his freedom before God and the other his freedom before the State, thereby digging the grave of the individual.[269]

By bringing its theo-political message to a public bereft of a *ketab* and *mikhtab*, Hebrew or otherwise, Christianity gave religion a bad name. People in a state of bondage, unable to see and think on their own will necessarily render Scripture an incomprehensible blabber. The net result was the enslaving of faithful from without, by abandoning him to the earthly Caesar, and from within by imparting religion through the imperial might of dogma. Wittgenstein had something very important to say about it:

> The effect of making men think in accordance with dogmas, perhaps in the form of certain graphic propositions, will be very peculiar: I am not thinking of these dogmas as determining men's opinions but rather as completely controlling the *expression* of all opinions. People will live under an absolute, palpable tyranny, though without being able to say that they are not free. I think the Catholic Church does something rather like this. For dogma is expressed in the form of an assertion, and is unshakable, but at the same time any practical opinion *can* be made to harmonize with it; admittedly more easily in some cases than in others. It is not a *wall* setting limits to what can be believed, but more like a *brake* which, however, practically serves the same purpose; it's almost as though someone

269. *The Undiscovered Self*, pp. 49–50.

> were to attach a weight to your foot to restrict your freedom of movement. This is how dogma becomes irrefutable and beyond the reach of attack[270] [Italics in original].

Because in the West 'faith' was identified with Christianity, it did not take long for 'religion' to be associated with cruelty and intolerance. This is how Bertrand Russell (1872–1970) saw it:

> You find this curious fact that the more intense has been the religion of any period and the more profound has been the dogmatic belief, the greater has been the cruelty and the worse has been the state of affairs. In the so-called ages of faith, when men really did believe in the Christian religion in all its completeness, there was the Inquisition, with its tortures; there were millions of unfortunate women burned as witches; and there was every kind of cruelty practiced upon all sorts of people in the name of religion.[271]

There is an important consideration to all this. Just as Christianity could have hardly survived without the Rex's sword (see below chapter 31), the Rex, too, could have hardly survived without the

270. *Culture and Value*, p. 28e. On Wittgenstein's Judaism, see the masterful work of Ranjit Chatterjee, *Wittgenstein and Judaism: A Triumph of Concealment* (New York: Peter Lang Publishing, 2005).

271. Bertrand Russell, *Why I am not a Christian* (New York: Simon & Schuster, 1957), p. 20. A similar opinion was expressed by the late Supreme Court Justice of Israel, Haim H. Cohn, "Religious Human Rights," *Dine Israel* 19 (1997–98), p. 107: "The general consensus on the blessings and the eternity of religion is marred by the undisputed fact that the great religions brought much misery and suffering into the world." Russell and Cohn, however, gave no sense of the problem. Cruelty and persecution are not exclusive to religion: they are endemic to all systems, including those professing to be secular and rational, in which the authorities and magistrates operate with impunity as pagan gods. See *Introductory Remarks*, Section V. There is also something terribly unfair, particularly in the case of Justice Cohn, in imputing the sins of Christianity, in quality of persecutor, to Israel, the victim.

sustained efforts of the Church to quash Jewish ideas and rabbinic tradition. (This type of cooperation is best exemplified in the establishment of the Inquisition and decrees of *pureza de sangre* designed to exclude Christians of Jewish descent from the political, economical, and intellectual life of the country.) Christianity became an instrument for the advancement of political unfreedom. The overall effect was indulgence of tyrants acting as 'Defenders of the Faith.' It also provided the training of bullies and built a platform for dishonest politicians masquerading as defenders of the faith. In recent times it provided the model for what has been properly described as the "Psychology of Nazism."[272] In fact, "the father of Marxists philosophy," too, "makes use of exactly the same spiritual assumptions, and the same arguments and aims" as the Church.[273]

272. See *Escape from Freedom*, chapter 6.
273. *The Undiscovered Self*, p. 47.

# Chapter 30
# Escape from Guilt

"Christianity," writes Professor Nicholls, "does not rest on what Jesus taught himself, still less on what he taught about himself. It rests on what his followers began to teach about him after his death."[274] It was principally Paul and his followers who transformed the teaching of Jesus into the Christianity of history. The source of his theology was his tormented soul. It pertains to psychology, rather than Scripture.[275] He could not control his impulses. By his own admis-

---

274. *Christian Antisemitism*, p. 44.

275. On Paul's psychological background, see "De-authorization of the Law: Paul and the Oedipal Model," pp. 222–243. There is absolutely no evidence, except his say, that he had any rabbinic training, and least of all that he sat at the feet of R. Gamli'el the Elder. In fact, there is not a shred of evidence that he was familiar with the Scripture in the original or that he could read the Hebrew alphabet. Only someone with zero Tora education could have said that "the letter killeth" (II Cor. 3:6); see appendix 21. Most probably he was born to heathen parents barely converted to Judaism. I don't believe that he had been circumcised. Otherwise, how could he have pronounced the following tirade against circumcision, Gal. 5:1–3:

> Stand fast therefore in the liberty wherewith Christ hath made us free, and be not engaged again with the yoke of bondage. Behold, I Paul say unto you, that if ye be circumcised, Christ shall profit you nothing. For I testify again to every man that is circumcised, that he is a debtor to do the whole law.

This was said, so that he could pass himself as "a Roman" (Acts 22:25–29; cf. ibid. 23:27; 16:37–38). Incidentally, his attack against circumcision was intended to degrade Jesus' disciples, all of whom were circumcised. About Paul's flagrant ignorance of basic Tora, see *Judaism*, vol. 3, pp. 150–151, cited below at

sion, he was "captive by the law of sin" (Rom. 7:23) and not free to choose: "For what I do not will, this I do. But what I hate, this I do" (Rom. 7:15). To meet his situation, he developed a five-point theological apparatus that would be the guideline of much of Christianity throughout history.

a. "Christ is the end of law for righteousness to everyone who believes" (Rom. 10:4). I.e., personal behavior is inconsequential.
b. Therefore, 'faith' (which for Paul means 'submission,' see Rom. 10:3; 11:30–33, and appendix 22) suffices for salvation (see Rom. 1:17; 3:20–28; 4:15–16; 10:10, 13). In practical terms this means that whoever "believes with his heart" will be "justified" regardless of behavior (Rom. 10:9, cf. 1:16; 3:22–28; 5:1–2; Gal. 5:5; I Pet. 5:9–10; Jn. 6:27–29).
c. 'Sin' produces 'guilt' and 'guilt' can only be expiated by death (see Rom. 7:4–5).
d. Jesus "gave Himself on our behalf, that He might redeem us from all iniquity, and purify unto himself a peculiar people, zealous of good works" (Tit. 2:14, see Rom. 3:25; Gal. 1:4; Eph. 5:2).
e. Christians lose their personal individuality once incorporated into Jesus, gaining salvation through him (see Rom. 5:6–11; I Cor. 12:12; Eph. 5:14, 30; Col. 3:1–4; I Tim. 1:15).[276]

The notion that there could be salvation with faith alone, without actions is incompatible with Scripture and the rabbis. The rabbis made especial reference to people who don't live by the Tora, and misrepresent it (*minut*) to promote their own ideology. "Woe unto those who are hateful of rabbinic scholars, and engage in Tora-studies but have no fear of Heaven!" i.e., people who cite Scripture but don't

---

n. 288; and *Christian Antisemitism*, pp. 34, 129152. Let us point out, by way of contrast that one of Jesus' explanations satisfied R. Eli'ezer; see 'Aboda Zara 17a (uncensored editions). Cf. appendix 55.

276. See *The Individual and Society*, chapter 1.

live by it.[277] Having in mind men of the ilk of Paul, R. Yose (second half of 2nd century) taught that people entrenched in sin will invariably fall under the rule of their evil inclinations: "The righteous are ruled by their good inclination, while the wicked are ruled by their evil inclination."[278] Similarly, R. Banna'a (end 2nd century to mid-3rd century), who served as a judge in Galilee, taught that only "when someone is engaged in (the study) of Tora *and* acts of loving kindness" would he be able to overcome his evil impulses.[279] In simple terms: the Tora is not a magic potion that would heal regardless of personal behavior. Study of the Tora could be an elixir of life or the opposite, depending on whether it is accompanied by proper behavior and works. R. Joshua ben Levi (3rd century) who had close contacts with Christians and was familiar with Paul's ideology, explained: "If one merits (זכה) it, it [the Tora] would be for him an elixir of life. [But] if he does not merit (זכה) it, it would be a deadly poison for him."[280] A similar point was made by R. Banna'a: "Whoever is engaged in the (study of) Tora for its own sake," that is, with the intention to fulfill it, "his Tora would be for him an elixir of life." Conversely, "whoever engages in the Tora not for its own sake," that is, without any intention to fulfill it, "it would be for him a deadly poison."[281] Thinking of Paul and his followers, the rabbis censured gentiles for using the Tora to prop up their personal ideology, while promoting disrespect

277. Yoma 72b; cf. *Sifre* #306, p. 338. See *Bet Yosef* and *Shulḥan 'Arukh, Yore De'a* CCXLIII, 3.
278. Berakhot 61a.
279. 'Aboda Zara 5b.
280. *Sifre* #306, p. 338 and Yoma 72b; cf. Shabbat 31a and 'Erubin 54a. The term 'merit' (זכה) indicates merits gained through the fulfillment of *miṣvot*, i.e., 'works'; see *Targum* to Deut. 6:25.
281. Ta'aniyot 7a. A similar view is expressed in Y. Shabbat I, 2, 3b: "One who studies (*Tora*) to fulfill it – not who studies Tora not to fulfill it; because one who studies (Tora) not to fulfill it, it would be better for him had he not been born." cf. 'Aboda Zara 17b: "Whoever occupies himself only with Tora (without acts of love and kindness), is equal to someone having no God."

for the *miṣvot* (see 1 Cor. 9:19–23): "It [the Tora] is life for Israel but death to the nations."[282]

In the rabbinic economy of ideas, someone entrenched in evil and claiming impotence for self-control equals a corpse. "The wicked while alive is regarded as dead."[283] Echoing this doctrine, Paul cried in despair: "Who shall deliver me from the body of this death?" (Rom. 7:24). Rather than seeking to come to grips with his infirmities, he denied personal responsibility: "But if I do what I do not desire, it is no longer I working it out, but sin dwelling in me" (Rom. 7:21). Thus he began a process of guilt transference, designed to rationalize, rather than to redress, his faults. At this state of psychological turmoil the 'outside' is the effect of a series of psychological projections: inner self and outer world are interchangeable. Referring to Paul's state of mind, a distinguished psychiatrist explained:

> Because it often appears as something unconscious that is independent of, and often counter to, my conscious intentions, it is experienced as something happening outside of me. That is the demons. As Paul says, they cause me not to do the good that I would do and to carry out the evil that I would not (Rom. 7:19). Since they often thwart my will, I experience them as alien to my ego.[284]

A concomitant to the freedom awarded by the Law is accountability and personal responsibility. The Tora cannot help those who sequester themselves "inside" their own tree of knowledge, as Adam-*Elohim*, and proceed to wave an accusing finger at the 'outside.' One can only speculate about the character of Paul's transgressions. However, instead of following the psalmist's advice and facing his sins (see Ps. 51:5; cf. Prov. 28:13), he refused to accept responsibility. He could have followed the message of the Tora, repented, and asked

282. Debarim Rabba (Lieberman), p. 4.
283. Berakhot 18a. Cf. *MT Teshuba* 6:3 and *Homo Mysticus*, p. 127.
284. *Demons of the Inner World*, p. 192.

God for forgiveness. Instead, he chose to escape, taking refuge in Jesus (Rom. 7:25) under the presumption that there he would no longer be accountable. For there is "no condemnation to those" in Jesus (Rom. 8:1), since they are "free from the law of sin and of death" (Rom. 8:2). However, there is nothing in Jesus' words indicating that he would have consented to be used as 'refuge' for people refusing to be accountable and unwilling to take responsibility for their own behavior.

The Tora teaches that at the beginning, God made the "Tree of Life inside the garden [of Eden] grow." In the Hebrew original there is a semi-colon [*zaqef qaṭon*] separating these words from the end of the sentence: "and the Tree of Knowledge of Good and Evil" (Gen. 2:9) – implying, thereby, that the Tree of Knowledge of Good and Evil was *outside* the garden.[285] This will help us understand the plot of the story. Adam and Eve decided to forage *outside* the garden. Scripture hints at this by pointing out that the snake was the most "cunning animal from among all the animals of the meadow," (Gen. 3:1, 14). Here "meadow" stands in opposition to "garden." Later, when returning to the garden and hearing God's voice, Adam and Eve took refuge "inside a tree of the garden" (Gen. 3:8) – not *the* Tree of Life. One of the effects of eating from the Tree of Good and Evil was the faculty to hide "inside" a tree to avoid accountability and responsibility. By virtue of hiding "inside" the tree, Adam-*Elohim* believes himself to be above the Law and immune from prosecution, no matter what. When Adam-*Elohim* discovered that he could not escape trial, he resorted to excuses and finger pointing (Gen. 3:9–13): this, rather than ingesting a particular fruit, is Adam-*Elohim*'s sin (see above Introductory Remarks, Section II). Paul never understood the nature of the original sin. Rather, he became trapped within it: he could pin fault on others, but not look at himself, acknowledge responsibility and repent.

Because Paul and historic Christianity function as Adam-*Elohim*, they refuse accountability. Instead, they assume the indisputable right

285. Cf. *Guide* II, 30, p. 251 (ll. 8–17), and *Homo Mysticus*, pp. 9, 137–138.

to accuse everyone else. An indispensable dimension of this tactic is an analphabetic audience, eager to hear the poet's truth (cf. Jn. 8:32, and above chapter 4). The merit of this method is akin to someone criticizing Verdi's *La Traviata* to a public with no music education, or Goya's 'black paintings' to an audience ignorant of art. The allegation that the Law requires perfect conformity (see Gal. 3:10–12) is fraudulent. The same is true of the proposition that according to the Tora salvation is impossible without total fulfillment of all the *miṣvot* (see Rom. 3:19–20). The allegation that failure to comply with a single *miṣva* warrants death – as when disobeying a tyrant or a superior officer (cf. II Pet. 2:4, 11–12) – is malicious deception. Paul was not "a Biblical man of faith." "The Biblical man of faith," noted a legal scholar, "believed that God does not play moral tricks; that in the moral realm He is as subtle as in the physical realm, and that in neither realm is He malicious."[286] Paul depicts the God of Israel as a sado-masochistic deity, wickedly deceiving Israel by giving them an impossible system. Professor Moore – one of the great Christian Hebraists in modern times –explained:

> Paul's definition of righteousness as perfect conformity to the law of God would never have been conceded by a Jewish opponent, to whom it would have been equivalent to admitting that God had mocked man by offering a salvation on terms that they both knew to be impossible.[287]

His theology pertains to the pathological. The 'malicious god' that he portrayed was conceived and gestated deep inside his tormented mind. His argument rests on two premises, both of which are alien to the Law and Prophets. First, that under the Law righteousness stands for perfect conformity (see, for example, Gal. 3:10–12). Second,

286. Milton B. Konvitz, "A Philosophy of Human Rights," in eds. Abraham I. Katsh and Leon Nemoy, *Essays on the Occasion of the Seventieth Anniversary of the Dropsie University* (Philadelphia: Dropsie University, 1979), p. 301.

287. *Judaism*, vol. 1, p. 495.

that God in his righteousness cannot freely forgive the penitent. The second assumption is less explicit than the first. On it rests, however, the necessity of Jesus' expiatory death (see, for example, Rom. 3:25). The Christianity of history, too, rests on these two premises. More precisely, as pointed out by Professor Moore, on two "postulates which the predetermined conclusions demand." We can now appreciate why the Christian message could only be delivered to an analphabetic crowd: these postulates stand in flagrant contradiction to the most critical message of the Hebrew Scripture. Quoting Professor Moore again:

> How a Jew of Paul's antecedent could ignore, and by implication deny, the great prophetic doctrine of repentance, which, individualized and interiorized, was a cardinal doctrine of Judaism, namely, that God, out of love, freely forgives the sincerely penitent sinner and restores him to his favor – that seems from the Jewish point of view inexplicable.[288]

Thus, the inviolable link between Paul's vilification of the Tora, his message of 'salvation,' and a structurally analphabetic crowd: outside such a forum his words make little sense.

There is an eerie parallelism between Adam's and Eve's taking escape *into* the tree of the Eden, and Paul's escape *into* Jesus' mystical body. Adam and Eve *ingested* the Tree of Knowledge outside the garden. At that stage of mental stupor, *hubris*– the destructive haughtiness gripping the doomed hero of Greek tragedy – took over. In their frenzy, they believed that their Lilliputian knowledge of "good and evil" awarded them divine status and immunity from the Law. God revealed their inner thoughts: "Behold man regards himself as if he were (היה כ-) one of us, since he (now) knows good and evil" (Gen. 3:22).[289] Christianity, too, came to believe that one could escape guilt

288. *Judaism*, vol. 3, p. 151.

289. Here the Hebrew preposition ל- in ל-דעת stands for 'given that.' Accordingly, the sense of the verse is, "given that man now knows good and evil, he believes

gastronomically (albeit with faith and contrition), by ritually ingesting the Eucharist, first by incorporating the *Corpus Christi* into the eater, and then the eater becoming incorporated into the *Corpus Christi* or body of Jesus (see 1 Cor. 11:23–27; see appendix 23).

In systems governed by Adam-*Elohim*, people are in a state of unlimited submission, doubly: by the law of the earthly ruler, without, and by the world of myth created by the spiritual ruler, within. From that perspective, the idea of a Law resting on a negotiated *berit* is an oxymoron: there are only commands, *imposed* on the hierarchically inferior. In that realm, *guilt* substitutes for responsibility. Guilt, however, has nothing to do with the actual behavior of the accused: it is *imputed* by the hierarchically superior and cannot be appealed. The antidote to guilt is ritual *death*. In the realm of myth this can take place by ingesting certain magical victuals and *imputing* guilt on others, as Adam and Eve before they were expelled from Eden. Grace/guilt interlock: it is only by *imputing*, i.e., finger pointing at hierarchically inferior beings, that one gains 'salvation' from those standing hierarchically above. The logic of imputing guilt on the hierarchically inferior is protected by the principle of inequality before the law. "The inequality of the members of society showed itself most manifest in the unequal treatment before the law," wrote Professor Ullman, "for a superior was treated differently from an inferior"; given that "no inferior could legitimately bring any accusation against a superior."[290]

In the end, Paul succeeded in creating something more powerful and enduring than religion: a crowd ready to gain grace by faulting the hierarchically 'inferior,' preferably Jews. If not, other despicable minorities would do.

---

himself to be a godlike creature, like one of us," and therefore *above* the law. Here the Tora is identifying the knowledge gained in quality of Adam/*Elohim*, as the source of human *hubris* and self-destruction.

290. *The Individual and Society in the Middle Ages*, p. 15. See *In the Shadow of History*, pp. 4–8, 199–200.

# Chapter 31
# Imperial Religion

The primary perspective of Luke, wrote a well-known scholar, is that "church and empire are coeval and contemporary."

> According to this perspective, the Christian church and the Roman empire need not to fear or suspect each other, for God stands behind both institutions given to each the power and the authority to carry out His will. That the Christian church survived that first crucial century may be due in large measure to the cautious wisdom of Luke in this regard.[291]

The Christianity of History is an imperial religion, not merely because of its association with imperial power, but because of the rationale that imperial might awards spiritual supremacy, *ipso facto.* It was by imperial logic that Christianity assumed that it could 'abrogate' the Law *contracted* – not by them but by Jews at Sinai, and *impose* a "King of Kings and a Lord of Lords" on humanity (see below chapter 34). It was by imperial logic that it imagined that it could strip a people from its national constitution – the Tora – and arrogate to itself the title *Verus Israel* (see appendix 30, and below chapters 39, 40). Because Christian 'love' is fundamentally imperial (and psychologically narcissistic), it tolerates no rejection. "Once the apostle Paul

291. *'And so we came to Rome,'* pp. ix-x. The Roman Empire, however, did not fare that well; see appendix 20.

had laid down universal love between all men as the foundation of Christian community," noted Freud, "the inevitable consequence in Christianity was the utmost intolerance towards all who remained outside of it."[292] In virtue of imperial love, you either capitulate to it or else you will be the object of damnation and infamy and persecution and torment and slow and agonizing death. In law, such love is defined as rape. To merit love the faithful must degrade God's image within, abolish its own individuality, and confess to be sinful and evil and immoral and aberrant. Christianity would not have gained even a footnote in history, were it not for imperial *might*. The following passage by Bertrand Russell makes our point:

> In the Church as it existed at the time of the fall of the Western Empire (i.e. in the 5th Century) there were elements derived from three sources, Jewish, Greek and Roman. The Church took over from the Jews their sacred books and sacred history, their belief in a Messiah (whom the Christians, but not the Jews, believed to have already appeared), their somewhat fierce morality, and their intolerance of all religions but one. The Hellenic element appeared especially in the realm of dogma. St. John, St. Paul, and the Fathers gradually developed, by adaptations of Greek philosophy, an elaborate theology, wholly foreign to the Jewish spirit.... Without the strength derived from Roman governmental methods, it is doubtful whether the Church could have survived the shock of barbarian invasion.[293]

To secure imperial support, Christianity promoted the infamous doctrine proclaiming the Divine Right of Kings. In accordance with

---

292. Sigmund Freud, *Civilization and Its Discontents* (New York: Doubleday, 1958), p. 65. See *In the Shadow of History*, pp. 6–7.

293. Bertrand Russell, "How to Read and Understand History," in his *Understanding History* (New York: Philosophical Library, 1957), pp. 43–44. Scholars and intellectuals are not aware that the 'intolerance' of Judaism is a myth created by Christianity to justify its intolerance to Judaism and everybody else.

the two-realm governance (see above chapter 26), insubordination against the Rex equaled rebellion against God. The logic is obvious: might equals right. This will explain the fact that while Christian Scripture applauded disobedience of *Jewish* authorities (see Acts 4:19, cf. 5, 6; 5:21, 29, cf. 5, 6, 17), it urged the faithful unconditional submission to Roman authorities. "And he (Jesus) said to them, The kings of the Gentiles exercise lordship over them; and they that exercise authority upon them are called benefactors" (Lk. 22:25; cf. Mk. 10:43, and above chapter 27). Addressing the faithful, Paul said:

> Let every soul be subject unto the higher powers. For there is no power but of God: the powers that are ordained of God. Whosoever therefore resisteth the power, resisteth the ordinance of God: and they that resist shall receive to themselves damnation. For the rulers are not a terror to good works, but to evil. Wilt thou then not be afraid of the power? Do that which is good, and thou shalt have praise of the same: For he is the minister of God to thee for good. But if thou do that which is evil, be afraid; for he beareth not the sword in vain: for he is the minister of God, a revenger to execute wrath upon him that doeth evil. Wherefore ye must be subject, not only for wrath, but also for conscience sake (Rom. 13:1–5; cf. I Pet. 2:13–19).

This view is based on the theory that *might* confers *right*. Hence, the Divine Right of Kings.

Pagan rulers caught up with the advantages of Christian 'religious' teachings. A direct consequence of the axis cross-sword was the suppression of ideas, not only from Sinai, but also from pagan humanity. The result was the steady economic, political, and military decline of the Roman Empire. In less than one hundred and fifty years of Christianity, the West descended to a level of chaos and disintegration, euphemistically known as the Dark Ages. The glorious cities, the schools and libraries, as well as the celebrated political and judicial institutions of the Roman Empire were replaced by the dingy insight of cloisters. There were further consequences affecting the political and social life of the empire. We will mention two: in the realm of the political, the Divine Right of Kings, thriving in modern times in upgraded versions, such as Fascism, Marxism, or other less pompous nomenclatures. In the realm of the socio-economic, it would suffice to point out that already by the 10th century the accumulation of wealth and economic control of vast territories in Europe were consolidated in the hands of a few families.

# Chapter 32
# The Political Dimension of Antisemitism

A major point of this Section is the proposition that antisemitism, whether sponsored by the State or by a State-religion, is a political – not a spiritual – enterprise. Thanks to the two-realm governance, Christianity awarded the pagan Rex the status of a *de facto* god on earth. Concerning this pivotal point, Oscar S. Straus wrote:

> The might, the right, and the power, of the people having been wrested from them in the dawn of history and exalted so high over their heads by the art of designing princes, that they prostrated themselves before this trinity of their own creation and worshipped it under the form of 'Divine right of kings.' The usurper's title, through ages of wrongs and bloody oppressions, by the servility of cunning ecclesiastics, went through an evolution of fanatical consecration, and thereby transformed its bearer into a demi-god under the appellation of 'King by the Grace of God.'[294]

Imagine a Hitler or Mussolini addressing a mass rally. Is there any cogent difference between them and a deity? Theologians and philosophers may propose some elaborate nuances to 'show' the

294. *Origin of the Republican Form of Government*, pp. 12–13.

dissimilarity. But are these insights meaningful to a public shouting 'Hail to Caesar'? Picture a

> victorious Roman imperator rolled on the chariot by four white horses from Campus Martius to the Capitol – a living god clothed in the embroidered purple toga of Jupiter Capitolinus, in his hand the eagle scepter of the god, and his face painted red with cinnabar – the slave riding with him on the chariot and holding the golden wreath over his head, whispered to him: "Look behind thee. Remember thou art a man."[295]

Does anyone believe that the whisper of a slave would have an effect on Adam-*Elohim* riding the chariot? Theological and philosophical blabber aside: how is one to distinguish between a god and a Pharaoh? Within the boundaries of the *here-and-now*: is there any command that, if issued by a God, *here-and-now* would be obeyed, but if issued by a Caesar or Pharaoh would be rejected?

In antiquity and throughout the ages, Jews and Jews alone recognized absolute sovereigns for what they truly were. Jews alone refused to bow down to them. Surely, when Caligula proclaimed that he was a god and demanded to be worshipped, there were among the pagan intelligentsia those who recognized his folly. However, none, except Jews, refused to worship him. It is on this ground alone – and not because of their 'religion' – that Jews were targeted for persecutions. Philo, who was a witness to one of those not infrequent episodes in pagan political history, wrote:

> For he (Caligula) looked with disfavor on the Jews alone because they alone opposed him on principle, trained as they were we may say even from the cradle, by parents and tutors and instructors and by far higher authority of the sacred laws and also of the unwritten customs, to acknowledge one God

295. *The King's Two Bodies*, p. 496.

> who is Father and Maker of the world. For all others, men, women, cities, nations, countries, regions of the earth, I might almost say the whole inhabited world, groaning though they were at what was happening, flattered him all the same and magnified him out of all proportion and augmented his vanity. Some too even introduced into Italy the barbarian practice of prostrating themselves, a degradation of the high tradition of Roman freedom. One nation only standing apart, the nation of the Jews, was suspected of intending opposition, since it was accustomed to accept death as willingly as immortality, to save them from submitting to the destruction of any of their ancestral traditions, even the smallest, because as with buildings if a single piece is taken from the base, the parts that up to then seemed firm, are loosened and slip away and collapse into the void thus made.[296] *But that displacement was of nothing petty, but of the greatest of that exists, when the created and corruptible nature of man was made to appear uncreated and incorruptible by a deification which our nation judged to be the most grievous impiety, since sooner could God change into a man than man into God*[297] [italics added].

We can now understand the fury of Tacitus, the rage of Cicero, the indignation of the haughty at the Jews – the "vilest" and "most degraded" of all races – for refusing to give emperors the honor they give God.

The truism promoted by classical antisemites and pseudo-Jewish intellectuals, that Jewish hatred was motivated by some sort of

---

296. Tacitus, *History* V, 13, p. 665, noted perhaps with jealousy about the quality of the Jewish people: "All who were able bore arms, and a number, more than proportionate to the population, had the courage to do so. Men and women showed equal resolution, and life seemed more terrible than death, if they were forced to leave their country. Such was this city [Jerusalem] and nation [Judea]."

297. *The Embassy to Gaius, Philo*, vol. 10, XVI, 115–118, pp. 57–59.

'religious' problem, is untrue and fraudulent. 'Religion' as an antisemitic factor does not operate in a political vacuum. Catholics and Protestants in the United States are as devoted as their coreligionists in continental Europe, and yet they do not share their antisemitic ideologies. The difference is not in their religion but in the *political context* of their religion. It was in Colonial America, when Christians no longer felt the Rex's sword, that men of the ilk of Reverend Roger Williams (ca. 1603–1684) – founder of the State of Rhode Island and of the first Baptist Church in America – began to blossom. Banished and persecuted by militant ecclesiasts, he dedicated his life to promoting absolute freedom of religion, not as a *concession* on the part of the authorities, but as a *cardinal principle of faith*. In an address commemorating him (rightly described as "the pioneer of religious freedom"), Charles Evans Hughes (1862–1948), Chief Justice of the United States, said:

> The hardest lesson mankind has had to learn is that religious truth which is held to be most precious cannot prosper by attempts forcibly to impose it upon others. Strong convictions, especially religious convictions, are apt to develop tyrannical purpose, and no faith is so pure but that it is ever in danger of being made the instrument of the mistaken zeal of those who would deny to others the right to think as they choose.[298]

It was thanks to the spirit kindled by William Roger that a new type of spirituality blossomed. In a short time, fundamental ideas affecting our understanding of human rights and the human spirit set up in motion a series of events culminating in the greatest political success in modern history. A principal argument against those advocating submission to England was the Christian doctrine of "Divine Rights of Kings," etc. In the debate ensuing between those advocating

298. In Oscar S. Straus, *Roger Williams* (New York: D. Appleton-Century, 1936), p. xiii. There is an interesting note on him in Luigi Luzzatti, *God in Freedom* (New York: Mac Macmillan Company, 1930), pp. 126–128.

overthrowing the British government and those defending the Crown, a pattern began to emerge. Those advocating rebellion against George III supported their views from the Hebrew Scripture; whereas those advocating "Unlimited Submission," etc., cited the Christian Scripture. This is how Oscar Straus put it:

> George III, so far as his claims over the colonies were concerned, relied as much upon the kingly prerogatives, the doctrine of 'Divine Right,' as ever did James I. All of these pretensions, all of the questions of right and liberty, had to be argued. To refute this false theory of kingly power it was not only expedient but necessary to revert to the earliest times, to the most sacred records, the Old Testament, for illustrations and argument, chiefly because the doctrine of 'Divine Right,' 'King by the Grace of God,' and its corollaries, 'unlimited submission and non-resistance,' were deduced, or rather distorted from the *New Testament,* having been brought into the field of politics with the object of enslaving the masses through their religious creed.[299]

In a kernel, a perennial task facing Christians in modern societies is "to choose between Jesus and Paul."[300] At the core of this choice is the policy of two-governance (שתי רשויות) developed by Paul and his followers, whereby the tyrant is a *de facto* god. Reverend Jonathan Mayhew (1720–1766), one of the spiritual fathers of the American Revolution, gave expression to the feeling of revulsion of "such a monstrous, unaccountable doctrine." In a famous sermon that he

299. *Origin of the Republican Form of Government,* pp. 18–19.

300. *Christian Antisemitism,* p. xxvii. A close reading of Maimonides' *Epistle to Yemen,* ed. Abraham S. Halkin (New York: American Academy for Jewish Studies, 1952), p. 14 will reveal that he regarded Christian *theology* as proceeding from Paul and his followers, not from Jesus and his disciples; cf. ibid., n. 15 and below n. 308.

delivered on the 30th of January, 1750, he showed the absurdity of such a position. Let me quote one of the pertinent passages at some length:

> If we calmly consider the nature of the thing itself, nothing can well be imagined more directly contrary to common sense, than to suppose that *millions* of people should be subjected to the arbitrary, precarious pleasure of *one single man*; (who has *naturally* no superiority over them in point of authority) so that their estates, and everything that is valuable in life, and even their lives also, shall be absolutely at his disposal, if he happens to be wanton and capricious enough to demand them. What unprejudiced man can think, that God made ALL to be thus subservient to the lawless pleasure and frenzy of ONE, so that it shall always be a sin to resist him! Nothing but the most plain and express revelation from heaven could make a sober impartial man believe such a monstrous, unaccountable doctrine, and, indeed, the thing itself, appears so shocking – so out of all *proportion,* that it may be questioned, whether all the *miracles* that ever were wrought, could make it credible, that this doctrine *really* came from God. At present, there is not the least syllable in Scripture which gives any countenance to it.

It is highly suggestive that in rejecting the doctrine of the Divine Right of Kings, Reverend Mayhew associated it with the central pillar of Paul's theology: transubstantiation. I don't think that the connection was either casual or superficial.

> The hereditary, indefeasible, divine right of kings, and the doctrine of non-resistance which is built upon the supposition of such a right, are altogether as fabulous and chimerical as transubstantiation; or any of the most absurd reveries of ancient or modern visionaries. These notions are fetched neither from divine revelation, nor human reason; and if they are derived from neither of those sources, it is not much matter

> from *whence they come, or whither they go.* Only it is a pity that such doctrines should be propagated in society, to raise factions and rebellions, as we see they have, in fact, been both in the *last,* and in the *present,* REIGN.[301]

And now a defining question. Whom do you suppose a Rex would favor, members of the Hebrew nation, whose forbearers said 'No!' to Pharaoh and Caligula, or a religion proclaiming the principle, "Render unto Caesar the things which are Caesar's?" (Matt. 22:21).

301. Reverend Jonathan Mayhew, *Discourse, Concerning Unlimited Submission and Non-Resistance to the Higher Powers,* reprinted in *Religion in America* (New York: Arno Press, 1969), pp. 38–39.

# Chapter 33
# Two Concepts of Human Rights

In pagan political thought, rights evolve from the sovereign → state → law → family → citizen → individual. Without a state, the individual, family and society have no standing. Social and individual rights, etc., are predicated upon the recognition of the sovereign's absolute authority. 'Freedom,' 'rights' – whatever its actual content may be – is a condition of unfreedom. Socrates, as portrayed in *Crito* is first and foremost an Athenian citizen. Everything, including his father and mother, his status as a human being, as well as his personal education, etc., he owes the state. By contrast, a biblical person (regardless of religion) is firstly an individual. "It is not merely that man *has* a soul. It is that man *is* a soul – a divinely-created being, invested with rights and dignities at birth, subject to God-made laws and ordinances, and responsible to his Maker" [italics in original] – writes Konvitz, adding:

The time may come to him to become a citizen of Athens or Rome or Jerusalem, but his citizenship will not be all-absorbing. He will always retain for himself certain liberties, certain powers and dignities – prerogatives which he enjoys as gifts from the giver of gifts, and which he can never lose.[302]

'Human rights' proclaimed by governments and institutions rest

302. "A Philosophy of Human Rights," pp. 298–299. This is a highly cogent and most valuable essay.

on personal subjection to a man or a group of men representing the government and institutions awarding the alleged rights. The case of René Cassin illustrates our point. He was President of the European Court for Human Rights, winner of the Nobel Peace Prize, and a founding father of the United Nations. And yet, he was unable to persuade the United Nations to recognize the "Ten Commandments" as one of the sources for the Declaration of Human Rights adopted by the United Nations. "The spirit prevailing during the preparation of the Universal Declaration," wrote Cassin, "was completely at variance with any intention of drawing deliberate and direct inspiration from the Ten Commandments." In fact, "there was no mention of or reference to such monuments of the ancient religious history as the Ten Commandments. Only modern juridical instruments of a national character were alluded to." Why? As suggested by Cassin himself, the key lies in the abysmal difference between *duties* and *rights*. The Tora establishes duties, entailing responsibility and redress for failure. 'Duties' imply 'rights'– but not the other way around! "A man against whom the commission of murder or robbery is forbidden," noted Cassin, "has therefore implicitly the right to his life and his property!"[303] The 'universal human rights' proclaimed by the United Nations are platitudes, in essence not different than the protection offered by a Rex or a ruling lordship: the individual having no power to summon for default and breach of trust.[304] People demanding freedom are not aware that within the system, "the Lawes are of no power to protect them, without a Sword in the hands of a man, or men, to cause those laws to be put in execution." Freedom is not a

303. See "From the Ten Commandments to the Rights of Man," pp. 14, 13, 22.

304. For an eye-opener on the actual performance of the UN as a guardian of human rights, see William Korey, "Human Rights at the U.N.: Illusion and Reality," in ed. Sh. Shoham, *Of Law and Man: Essays in Honor of Haim H. Cohn* (New York: Sabra Books, 1971), pp. 27–45. Recent events show that performance has not yet improved, only the rhetoric. For some examples, see David P. Forsythe, "The Politics of Efficacy: The United Nations and Human Rights," in ed. Lawrence S. Finkelstein ed., *Politics in the United Nations System* (Durham and London: Duke University Press, 1988), pp. 246–273.

given, but lies "only in those things, which in regulating their actions, the Sovereign hath permitted."[305] Since individuals are powerless, we must conclude with Hobbes that the liberty discussed by classical authors "is not the Libertie of Particular men; but the Libertie of the Common-wealth."[306] In simpler words, individual freedom is a condition of unconditional submission to the Rex. It is clear now why the United Nations would not recognize the "Ten Commandments" (or any such document), since recognition of a non-political source for human rights would deprive the institutions that it represents of claiming absolute sovereignty over the subjects on whom they bestow 'universal human rights.' In this connection we should note that the Bill of Rights of the U.S. does not mention 'citizens' – a creature of the State – but *people* with certain rights and prerogatives enjoyed by all. Similarly, in the American Declaration of Independence, "all men" – not merely citizens – "are created equal." Their rights "are endowed by their Creator" – not by a political entity.[307] By contrast, in the Declaration of the Rights of Man made by the National Assembly of France, August 1791, protection of these rights is the "end of *political* society" [italics added].

Students of Christianity often overlook the fact that the spread of Christianity and the power it accrued is the result of the *might* conferred on it by the Rex. It was thanks to Constantine (and not some ecclesiastical figure) presiding over the first ecumenical council at Nicea in 325 who made Christianity the religion of the empire. It is bewildering that a

> … universal creed should be instituted solely on the authority of the emperor, who as a catechumen was not even admitted to the mystery of the Eucharist and was totally unempowered to rule on the highest mysteries of faith.[308]

---

305. *Leviathan* XXI, [109], p. 264.
306. *Leviathan* XXI, [110], p. 266.
307. See "A Philosophy of Human Rights," p. 299.
308. Walter Nigg, *The Heretics: Heresy Through the Ages* (New York: Dorset Press,

Let it be noted that Constantine's conversion to Christianity was not the result of spiritual illumination but of the emperor's *military* victory.

Under the government of a Rex all power is State power. Institutions may be tolerated on condition that they occupy a subordinate position, hierarchically inferior to the 'superior.' For this reason, it was imperative to control the flow of ideas and assure that new perspectives and values would not affect the running of the state. As was so persuasively argued by Hobbes:

> ... it is annexed to the Sovereignty, to be Judge of what Opinion and Doctrines are averse, and what conducting to Peace; and consequently, on what occasions, how farr, and what, men are to be trusted withal, in speaking to Multitudes of people; and who shall examine the Doctrines of all bookes before they are published. For the Actions of men proceed from their Opinions; and in the well governing of Opinions, consisteth the well governing of mens Actions, in order to their Peace, and Concord. And though in matter of Doctrine, nothing ought to be regarded but the Truth; yet this is not repugnant to regulating of the same by Peace. For Doctrine repugnant to Peace, can no more be True, than Peace and Control can be against the Law of Nature.[309]

The preceding applies all the more so to ideas and values emerging from religion. Therefore, all religious systems and institutions ought to be under the absolute control of the Rex.[310] In hierarchic systems the

1962), p. 127. Some educated Jews were aware that Christianity is *not* the product of Jesus and his disciples, but of Constantine's Council; see *Midrash Daniel*, p. 92. Cf. above n. 300.

309. *Leviathan* XVIII, [91], p. 233.

310. See *Leviathan* XXXIX. The idea originated in Plato's banishment of the poet, in *Republic* III. For a comprehensive and eminent discussion of the subject, see Kenji Yoshino, "The City and the Poet," *Yale Law Journal* 114 (2005), pp. 1835–1895.

status of an institution is a function of its ability to assist the Rex, either by consolidating or by acquiring and preserving power. Religion could be an effective tool in the hands of the Rex. The result of this unique association was desecration of religion and degradation of the government. A principal consequence of this partnership was the subjection of the faithful Christian to the ruling power under the doctrine of "unconditional submission." In this manner the two-realm governance was the source of violence, mayhem and carnage throughout the world.

By attempting to impose itself by the fiat of imperial power, the two-realm doctrine ended up empowering despots claiming the 'Divine Right of Kings.' In this fashion, Christianity succeeded in making religion something odious, something associated with hypocrisy and falsehood and cruelty. One need not be Jewish to share this view. Thoughtful people looking at Christian history from the perspective of freedom and equality may arrive at a similar conclusion. One of these men was Thomas Jefferson (1743–1826).

> Millions of innocent men, women, and children, since the introduction of Christianity, have been burnt, tortured, fined, imprisoned; yet we have not advanced one inch towards uniformity. What has been the effect of coercion? To make one half of the world fools, and the other half hypocrites. To support error and roguery all over the earth.[311]

There were lasting effects to the above, well after the nations decided to terminate the alliance cross/sword. Constantine's Christianity had succeeded in rendering the public numb to the rule of soulless men and women acting as raving gods. This is true even in societies professing to be secular and atheistic.

> The policy of the State is exalted to a creed, the leader or party boss becomes a demigod beyond good and evil, and his

311. Cited in Forrest G. Wood, *The Arrogance of Faith*, p. 27.

> votaries are honored as heroes, martyrs, apostles, missionaries. There is only *one* truth and besides it no other. It is sacrosanct and above criticism. Anyone who thinks differently is a heretic, who, as we know from history, is threatened with all manner of unpleasant things. Only the party boss, who holds the political power in his hands, can interpret the State doctrine authentically, and he does so just as it suits him.[312]

It seems, as far as planet Earth is concerned, that Paul's theo-political ideology served to justify oppression and the rule of the mighty more than anything else. "This unfortunate union of Church and State, of the crosier and the sword," noted Straus, "has been the prime source of more bloodshed in Europe than all other causes combined."[313]

312. *The Undiscovered Self*, p. 35.

313. *Origin of the Republican Form of Government*, p. 91.

# Chapter 34
# *Pax Romana* and *Pax Hebraica*

The difference between polytheism and Hebrew monotheism is not a matter of addition and subtraction.[314] Polytheism rests on the theo-political belief that the world is divided into two or more independent governances, positing an essential conflict between autonomous and self-regulating forces. Any form of order is the effect of one or more forces overpowering the rest; *order* is a function of *might*. In this spirit, *Pax Romana* is nothing more than the terms imposed on the vanquished by the right of the sword. A basic premise of Hebrew monotheism is that Creation was an act of free volition, executed by a supremely caring God. Sovereignty is not a function of might, but of creation (see above chapter 25). Order is the effect of a Law synonymous with *Shalom* – meaning not only 'Peace,' but 'Harmony,' 'Wholesomeness,' and 'Concordance.' Those who seek "the Law," taught the rabbis, "will be rewarded with *Shalom*." Conversely, those who seek the *Shalom* "will be rewarded with the Law." Because the Jew seeks peace based on Law rather than might, he is the focus of hatred. The nations "hate us because we love *Shalom*."[315] The alternative to Law is violence. At its barest, accepting the rule of Law is a most solemn pledge that conflicts will be resolved through *discourse* and *dialogue* around the Law. In this respect, Israel differs from the children of Esau, symbolizing pagan ethos and ideology.

314. See *Homo Mysticus*, pp. 140–142.

315. *The Mishna of Rabbi Eli'ezer*, IV, pp. 67, 77. Cf. Section IV, n. 121.

The rabbis taught that God offered the Tora to the children of Esau, but they refused. The dialogue went on as follows:

> God said to the children of Esau: 'Would you accept my Tora?'
> They replied: 'What is written in it?'
> He responded: "Do not murder" (Ex. 20:13).
> They replied to Him: 'On it [the sword] we trust!' It [the sword] we received from our Patriarch [Esau], as it is written: "and by your sword you shall live" (Gen. 26:40).[316]

Later, on their way to the Promised Land, the children of Israel asked the children of Esau to allow them to pass through their territory. They refused and challenged Israel to battle. Israel declined and went in a roundabout way to avoid conflict (Num. 20:14–21). The rabbis tell that the children of Esau argued that they were clinging to the culture of the sword just like the Hebrews were clinging to the culture of 'the voice' (i.e., dialogue and communication). Each side was pursuing its own ancestral tradition. This is how the children of Esau explained their position to Israel:

> You pride yourself on following the legacy of your father Isaac, as it is written "the voice is the voice of Jacob" (Gen. 26:22); and "God heard our voice" (Deut. 26:7). We, too, pride ourselves of the legacy of our father Isaac, as it is written: "the hands are the hands of Esau" (Gen. 27:22); "and by the sword you shall live" (Gen. 26:40). In this context it is written: "And Edom [Esau's children] said to him [the Israelites]: "Do not trespass into my [domain] lest I shall meet you, sword in hand" (Num. 20:18) – because they [Esau's children] trust only the sword. Also here [when Pharaoh's troops wanted to annihilate them], it was said: "And they were very much afraid, and the

316. Debarim Rabba (Lieberman), pp. 82–83.

> children of Israel cried to God" (Ex. 14:10) – they pursued their ancestors' vocation.[317]

To repudiate authority based on the sword, the Tora established the principle that triumphs in battle are God's – not the army's (see above chapter 14). The military victories of Israel, taught the rabbis, were not the result of superior weaponry: "they had neither a sword nor a spear, and all of their strength lay in their lips; and they overcame all other nations with nothing more than their lips."[318] Jewish leaders are not honored for their military victories but because of their wisdom, kindness, and humility. Israel did not celebrate the monarchy by parading its army and weaponry, but by having the monarch read the Tora to the general public. This was done at the end of the Sabbatical year, on the holiday of Sukkot, when the people left the luxury of their houses and dwelled in huts, in commemoration of their Wandering through the Desert (see Deut. 31:10–13; cf. II Chr. 34:30–33 and above chapter 8).

Israel's nemeses are not the "*families* of the earth" (Gen. 12:3; cf. Am. 3:2; Jer. 10:25; Ezek. 20:32) or "the *families* of the nations" (Ps. 96:7; I Chr. 16:28) – all of whom are Noah's children, the single father of *all* humanity (see Gen. 28:14). It is worthy to note that Israel was never defeated by a nation, but only by empires: Assyria, Babylonia, Greece, and Rome; each one claiming dominion over 'the nations of the world' (אומות העולם). Israel alone dared to confront these empires. The celebration of Israel's defeat by antisemitic ideologues is the celebration of the rights of empires to govern over weaker nations, not by consent, but by the right of the sword. The essence of this imperial ethos is best depicted in Nebuchadnezzar's dream: a colossal idol with a golden head, and a body made up of lower metals, ending in clay feet (Dan. 2). These empires, so teaches the book of Daniel, will be reduced to a puff of dust by a "stone" (אבן) striking at the colossus'

---

317. *Mekhilta de-R. Yishma'el, Beshallaḥ*, II, p. 93.

318. *Midrash Aggada*, ed. S. Buber, *Bemidbar* XXII, s.v. *va-yomer mo'ab*, p. 132. Cf. Ps. 44:3–4.

feet (Dan. 2:44). The there are two distinct features to this "stone" (אבן): it was [i] "cut from *the* mountain" (מטורא) – an obvious reference to Sinai; [ii] "*not* by hands" (Dan. 2:48, cf. 2:34). The latter is a reference to the "two tablets of the testimony, tablets of stone (אבן), written by the finger of God" (Ex. 31:18; cf. 32:16; Deut. 5:18; 10:4); i.e., "*not* by hands." This is the "stone" (אבן) that the "builders" of the nations "deride," but it actually "became the chief cornerstone" of the nation built by King David (see Ps. 118:22). Thus, *Pax Hebraica* is an offshoot of Israel's second miracle. We may recall that after crossing the Red Sea, the second most portentous miracle in history took place when the people decided, *on their own*, to resolve their differences through the process of Law (see Introductory Remarks). *Pax Hebraica* will be realized when the nations of the world, too, renounce violence and resolve to settle their conflicts through the process of Law. The first step in that direction consists in establishing the Law as "the chief cornerstone" (אבן) of the state, as did David of yore. Unlike *Pax Romana* this peace is not – it cannot be – grounded on might and the subjugation of the weak. Thus, the Hebrew Messiah is not a Cosmocrator fuming fire and brimstone fire, but a teacher who will impart to the nations of the world (אומות העולם) knowledge and intelligence and wisdom that would enable them to realize, *on their own*, the futility of war and violence.[319]

A corollary of the Christian abrogation of the Law was the displacement of *Pax Hebraica* on behalf of *Pax Romana*, and the substitution of the Jewish Messiah for a Cosmocrator revealed in supreme violence. According to Matt. 10:34–36, Jesus said:

> Think not that I am come to send peace on earth: I came not to send peace, but a sword. For I am come to set a man at variance against his father, and the daughter against her mother,

319. See Is. chapter 2, Mic. chapter 4; cf. Mishna Shabbat 6:4; and *MT Melakhim* 12:1–5; and the comments of R. Menaḥem 'Azarya di Fano, *Teshubot* (Venice, 5360/1600), #15.

> and the daughter-in-law against her mother-in-law. And a man's foe *shall be* they of his own household (cf. Mishna Soṭa 9:15).[320]

In short, rather than emulate King David and found the post-Messianic society on the basis of Law, the Christian Cosmocrator will impose his authority by might. In the *Book of Revelation* 19:11–21 we read:

> And I saw heaven opened, and behold a white horse; and he that sat upon him was called Faithful and True, and in righteousness he doth judge and make war. His eyes were as a flame of fire, and on his head were many crowns; and he had a name written, that no man knew, but he himself. And he was clothed with a vesture dipped in blood: and his name is called The Word of God. And the armies which were in heaven followed him upon white horses, clothed in fine linen, white and clean. And out of his mouth goeth a sharp sword, that with it he should smite the nations: and he shall rule them with a rod of iron: and he treadeth the winepress of the fierceness and wrath of Almighty God. And he hath on his vesture and on his thigh a name written, KING OF KINGS, AND LORD OF LORDS. And I saw an angel standing in the sun; and he cried with a loud voice, saying to all the fowls that fly in the midst of heaven, Come and gather yourselves together unto the supper of the great God; That ye may eat the flesh of kings, and the flesh of captains, and the flesh of horses, and the flesh of all men, both free and bond, both small and great. And I saw the beast, and the kings of the earth, and their armies, gathered

320. For a reinterpretation of this troubling passage, see Klaus Wengst, *Pax Romana and the Peace of Jesus Christ* (Philadelphia: Fortress Press, 1987), pp. 61–62. I personally don't believe that Jesus delivered such a horrendous message; cf. *Homo Mysticus*, pp. 125–126, and p. 230 n. 194. Anticipating the Christian Messiah, Sargon (ca. 2251–2196 B.C.E.), too, proclaimed himself King of the Universe; see *The Ancient Near East*, pp. 74–75, and above n. 168.

> together to make war against him that sat on the horse, and against his army. And the beast was taken, and with him the false prophet that wrought miracles before him, with which he deceived them that had received the mark of the beast, and them that worshipped his image. These both were cast alive into a lake of fire burning with brimstone. And the remnants were slain with the sword of him that sat upon the horse, which sword proceeded out of his mouth: and all the fowls were filled with their flesh.

This is why Jesus' Second Coming is viewed in terms of military victory; see I Cor. 15:57; cf. vv. 54, 55.

By associating itself with imperial power the Church forfeited its status of 'religion' and became *minut* (see above chapters 25–26). A rabbinic source, with the Church/Rex alliance in mind, taught: "This is the Empire of Evil (מלכות הרשעה), which recognizes neither the yoke of Heaven nor the yoke of the Law."[321] Thus, while overtly speaking in the name of 'God,' its primary task is to strengthen the earthly powers. Accordingly, the eleventh benediction of the Daily Prayer (*'Amida*) includes the *minim* – a usual reference to Christians in Rabbinic literature – together with "The Empire of Evil"[322] (מלכות הרשעה). Concerning this alliance, Oscar S. Straus noted:

> The public establishment of Christianity by Constantine in the beginning of the fourth century had the effect of placing the altar on the throne, and the ultimate result was the desecration of the one and the degradation of the other.

A principal consequence of this partnership was the subjection of the faithful Christian to the ruling power, under the doctrine of "unconditional submission." Quoting Straus, again:

---

321. *Midrash Mishle*, ed. Salomon Buber (Vilna: 5653/1893), 24a.
322. See Louis Ginzberg, *A Commentary to the Palestinian Talmud*, (Heb.), vol. 3 (New York: The Jewish Theological Seminary of America, 1941), p. 280.

> It carried with it as a state doctrine the unconditional submission on the part of the governed to the powers that be, as preached by the apostle in the reign of Nero. While the establishment in its inception may have had the effect of fostering and spreading the light of the new faith in the pagan world, it proved on the other hand a hindrance to the development of civil liberty for twelve centuries and more, distinct traces of which are yet to be found in the despotic governments of the Old World. Its immediate consequences were the augmentation of the power of the Pope and the subjection of every Christian country, in matters temporal as well as ecclesiastical, to the throne of Peter.[323]

323. *The Origin of the Republican Form of Government in the United States*, pp. 88–89.

# Chapter 35
# The Sabbath is the Lord's

Christian liberty lies in the realm of the intangible. One would need all the accumulated wisdom of Luther and Kant and Hegel and Heidegger – plus a host of less exotic thinkers – to make heads or tails of what liberty, in the "absolute inwardness of the person" is all about. At the end of journeying through mazes of words on words, the poor soul will be in such a state that he/she could hardly tell north from south. Because Christian liberty rejects the Law, it disenfranchises the meek and the poor on behalf of the mighty. A case in point is the abolition of the Hebrew Sabbath under the formula, "the Son of man is Lord even of the Sabbath day" (Matt. 12:8; cf. Mk. 2:24–28. This position may be linked to Jesus' strong association with tax-collectors who deeply resented the fact that the people were 'idle' on the Sabbath and Jewish holidays and that they could not collect enough revenue for the Roman masters; see Appendices 22 and 60). The story, as reported by Matthew and Mark, cannot withstand critical analysis. The disciples appear in a state of mental disarray, without the foggiest idea about what the Sabbath's rules are or what the Sabbath is all about. Referring to the impact that the Law had on the daily lives of the people, Josephus took note that it had also established "... what period should be devoted respectively to strenuous labor and to rest [the Sabbath]." Of particular importance was the fact that knowledge of the Law was well spread among the people. He added:

> For ignorance he left no pretext. He appointed the Law to be the most excellent and necessary form of instruction, ordaining that it should be heard once for all or twice or on several occasions, but that every week men should desert their own occupations and assemble to listen to the Law and to obtain a thorough and accurate knowledge of it.[324]

Jesus' disciples were clueless about all this. Clearly, their behavior shows that they were more interested in eating and frolicking than in instruction. They were unaware of even the most minimal knowledge of the Sabbath's regulation, as if aliens to the whole ambit of Jewish habits and beliefs.

Let us begin by pointing out that the God of Scripture is the Creator of everything, time included. Creation unfolds within the realm of time: One Day, Second Day… Sixth Day. Therefore, God exercises eminent domain *even* over time. From this perspective, time is public property awarded by the Creator for the use of people, over which He exercises supreme dominion. The Seventh Day, prohibiting all type of work, is inherent in God's Sovereignty and His eminent domain on *earth,* time included. As in all matters pertaining to eminent domain, the consent of the individual proprietor is irrelevant. Refusal to comply, resulting in the desecration of the Sabbath, equals contempt of God's eminent domain. Therefore it is one and the same with idolatry.[325] A major purpose of the Sabbath is to curb the greedy and opportunistic from robbing the poor and disenfranchising her/him of one day a week in which he/she could experience freedom and realize that she/he, too, is a full human in God's image.[326] Before the advent of

---

324. *Against Apion,* II, 174–175, *Josephus,* vol. 1, p. 363. See Y. Megilla I, 1, 70b; cf. Baba Qamma 82a, and *MT Tefilla* 12:1.

325. See Ḥolin 5a and *MT Shabbat* 30:15. Desecration of the Sabbath is the only crime in Scripture not connected with idolatry, sexual crimes, and bloodshed, in which the transgressor may be liable for capital punishment.

326. On its purpose, see Is. 58:13–14:

> If your foot would rest on the Sabbath, from doing your wants in My Holy

Christianity the Hebrew Sabbath spread among the gentile population, as reported by Philo:

> For, who has not shown his high respect for that sacred seventh day, by giving rest and relaxation from labor to himself and his neighbors, freemen and slaves alike, and beyond these to his beasts? For the holiday extends also to every herd, and to all creatures made to minister to men, who serve like slaves their natural master. It extends also to every kind of trees and plants; for it is not permitted to cut any shoot or branch, or even a leaf, or to pluck any fruit whatsoever. All such are set at liberty on that day, and live as it were in freedom, under the general edict that proclaims that none should touch them.[327]

None of the socialists' or Marxists' schemes purportedly designed to improve the proletariat could be remotely comparable to what the Jewish Sabbath accomplished.[328] Submitting the Sabbath to "the Son of man" robbed the poor and disenfranchised them from a day of rest. Also, it constituted an affront to God's eminent domain.[329] In the end, Christianity exchanged actual freedom for dissertations on topics such as 'transcendental liberty.' Who could benefit from such

---

Day. And you would call to the Sabbath: a delight, for the sanctification of the honorable God. And you would honor it by not doing your ways, (by abstaining) from carrying on your business or speaking about it. Then you shall delight yourself in God, and I will lift you up to the heights of the earth, and I shall nourish you the heritage of your father Jacob.

cf. Y. Shabbat XV, 3, 15a.

327. *Moses* II, 21–22, *Philo*, vol. 6, pp. 459–461; cf ibid. I, 206, p. 383.
328. Obviously, a second day of rest or an extra month vacation over Jewish holidays may be an improvement, but they do not equal the *first* day of rest or the *first* three annual holidays awarded by the Law! On the meaning of the Jewish Sabbath, see *Golden Doves*, pp. 51–52; *In the Shadow of History*, p. 188; and *Homo Mysticus*, p. 144.
329. See Sanhedrin 58b and *MT Melakhim* 10:9.

an exchange? – certainly not the faithful enslaved by the mighty and the wealthy!

God's image within is uninfringeable. Thus, the primary purpose of the Law is not to award 'inner freedom'– that is a given – but to shelter both the individual and society from Adam-*Elohim*. "Space is exposed to our will; we may shape and change the things in space as we please," observed Heschel. "Time, however, is beyond our reach, beyond our power. It is both near and far, intrinsic to all experience. It belongs exclusively to God." The Hebrew Sabbath serves to acknowledge all this. "Time is the presence of God in the world of space, and it is within time that we are able to sense the unity of all beings."[330] It is the time-space continuum permitting each and every human to experience *actual* freedom, as a full-fledged individual in the image of God. Imagine substituting that for hallucinatory dissertations on "transcendental liberty." What a joke!

330. Abraham Joshua Heschel, *The Sabbath* (New York: Harper & Row, 1952), pp. 99, 100.

# Chapter 36
# Separating *Church* from State

In societies where the Rex is *Fidii Defensor,* or "Defender of [the Catholic] Faith" – as with the Papal Bull of 1516 conferring this title on Henry VIII – matters pertaining to faith and personal consciousness are to be regulated by the State.[331]

A consequence of this principle is that the faith of the subjects of the state is to be determined by the political leader. It should not be surprising to discover, therefore, that 'religious wars' were fought not for the sake of faith, but to satisfy the conflicting claims of local princes and lords. In a lecture delivered in 1868, John Lothrop Motley (1814–1877), exposed the absurdity of this position:

> 'Whoever governs you his religion shall be yours!' *Cujus region, ejus religio*. Were ever more blasphemous and insulting words hurled in the face of mankind? Yet this was accepted as the net result of the Reformation, so far as priests and princes could settle the account. This was the ingenious compromise by which it was thought possible to remove the troublesome question of religion forever from the sphere of politics ... Not freedom of religion, but freedom of princes to prescribe religion to their slaves – for this so many tens of thousands had died on the battlefield, or been burned and buried alive.[332]

331. See the quotation from *Leviathan* XVIII [91], p. 233, above at n. 309.
332. In *Origin of the Republican Form of Government*, p. 89 n. 1. See *Leviathan* XXXIX.

Ideas develop and unfold in the course of history. The modern doctrine of separation of Church and State is no exception. It has its source in Judaism. It began firstly with the idea of limited sovereignty, stipulating that the king has no authority in matters pertaining to faith (see above chapter 22). In this connection it is well to remember that the Jewish Supreme Court has no jurisdiction in matters of conscience (see above chapter 11). Given that the monarch is not the source of law, he is not above the law (see above chapter 13). More particularly, as head of the state, he has a *fundamental responsibility* to uphold the law (see above chapter 19). In opposition to this, the doctrine of the "Divine Right of Kings" proposes that the monarch derives his authority neither from the people nor the law, but only from God, and therefore for all practical purposes he is *immune* from the law and from the people. (Hence the modern doctrine of Sovereign Immunity.)

We can now best appreciate the position of Jews and *conversos* in Spain and the reason for their banishment and eventual demise. They alone maintained that the monarch derived his authority from the law and the people; and therefore it is incumbent on him to protect *all* of his subjects, including Jews. R. Sanṭob de Carrión, known in Hebrew as R. Shem Ṭob ben Isaac Arduṭiel (ca. 1290–1369), first voiced this fundamental doctrine. He was an admirable Hebrew poet and liturgist – a long 'confession' (וידוי) of his forms part of the Yom Kippur service at the Sephardic Synagogue. He was the author of an outstanding book, *Proverbios morales,* known also as *Consejos y documentos al rey don Pedro,* "Advices and Documents to Don Pedro the King" (ca. 1355–1360). Because it was written in Spanish, in a sharp and witty style, these proverbs enjoyed wide circulation, and were often quoted by both Jews and Christians. To the end of his book, he appended an epilogue addressing the king:

> May God give life to the King, our sustainer, who upholds the law and is our defender.

> May he lead all the peoples of his land to his service and remove war and evil and unrest.[333]

As noted by the translator and editor of the *Proverbios*, the gist of 'upholding the law' is that the king is to be *under* the law. "Santob typically supports those in power, but he also insists that the King is not above the law."[334] This doctrine runs contrary to the Christian doctrine "that the king's power itself was derived not from the people or the kingdom or any individuals, but from divinity"[335] – rendering the king immune to the law and the people. There is another revolutionary idea proposed by R. Santob. The king is "our" defender, alluding to the monarch's responsibility to protect also Jews and not only Christians. The king is *of all* the people and not of a segment of the population. Given that sovereign authority is of the people, and not a 'divine privilege,' and given that the task of the sovereign is to serve the people, not the other way around (see above chapter 19), religious pluralism within the state is not a concession, but a fundamental condition of political authority. The theoretic roots of this doctrine are to be found in *Shebeṭ Yehuda*, a book written by R. Solomon ibn Verga (d. ca. 1520). (Latin translations circulated in manuscript during the

333. *The Moral Proverbs of Santob of Carrión*, ed. trans. and annotated by T. A. Perry (Princeton: Princeton University Press, 1987), l. 2761, p. 58. This is a very fine and cogent translation, accompanied by a detailed study and critical appraisal of the principal ideas of this work. For the original text, I consulted the critical edition with notes by Agustín García Calvo, *Don Sem Tob Glosas de Sabiduría* (Madrid: Alianza Editorial, 1974). I would like to point out that the rendition "who upholds the law" is not literal. The Spanish text, p. 146 reads: "guarda desta grey," that is: "protects this flock," i.e., the Jewish people. For the king as guardian of the law, see ibid., ll. 385, 2749; and Leopold Stein, *Untersuchungen uber die Proverbios Morales* (Berlin: Mayer & Muller, 1900), pp. 80, 108. García Calvo, the Spanish commentator, used to the authoritarian concept of monarchy, could make no head or tail of these ideas; see *Don Sem Tob*, p. 221. For a highly intelligent overview of the life and works of this rabbi, see Sanford Shepard, *Shem Tov: His World and His Words* (Miami: Ediciones Universal, 1978).
334. *The Moral Proverbs of Santob of Carrión*, p. 163.
335. *The Individual and Society in the Middle Ages*, pp. 18–19.

lifetime of the author; I know of two printed Latin editions.) The work was widely read by Christian scholars, among them probably Machiavelli.[336] R. Solomon ibn Verga proposed the radical thesis that "A monarch is anointed to give to his people and subjects grace and honor." He must rule in "name" only, the actual authority is of the people. "In reality," wrote ibn Verga, "the king is [the representative of the] people, and he is king in name only."[337] Inherent to political authority are certain responsibilities. Primary among them is to *defend* and *protect* the individual rights of the people, not to impose his religion on them. Therefore, he must distinguish between his personal convictions and his duties and responsibilities as a monarch. As a king, "I would risk my life to save them [the Jews from false accusations], because they are my subjects."[338] This should not be construed as if the king was wavering in his religion. He is a faithful Christian, fully committed to Christian doctrines.

> By it I live, and by it I shall die, and by it I shall be buried, and it will save me and award me a seat in Paradise with the kings before me. I am not saying this to intercede on their behalf [the Jews], but only to state that we have no power to make them transgress their religion.[339]

At the philosophical level, R. Solomon ibn Verga maintained that religion and cultural variability belong to the realm of 'imagination.'

336. See José Faur, "Imagination and Religious Pluralism: Maimonides, Ibn Verga, and Vico," *New Vico Studies* 10 (1992), pp. 36–51. On the Latin translations, see ibid., p. 44, and p. 50 n. 57. For an in-depth analysis, see *In the Shadow of History*, chapter 9.
337. R. Solomon ibn Verga, *Shebeṭ Yehuda*, eds. Azriel Shochet and Y. Baer (Jerusalem: Mossad Bialik, 5707/1947), VII, p. 41. See José Faur, "El pensamiento Sefardí frente a la iluminación Europea," in *Pensamiento y Mística Hispanojudía y Sefardí* (Cuenca: Ediciones de la Universidad de Castilla-La Mancha, 2001), pp. 324–327.
338. *Shebeṭ Yehuda*, VII, p. 26.
339. *Shebeṭ Yehuda*, VII, p. 38.

Therefore they cannot be disposed of, or proven by, 'logical' and 'rational' demonstrations. In an imaginary argument between a Jew and a Roman, the Jew conceded: "I cannot make you believe in monotheism, but neither can you make me believe in polytheism."[340] Similarly, in an imaginary argument between a Jew and the king, the king responded:

> I think that your words are excellent. Nonetheless they are not compelling. Therefore, we as Christians shall remain in [the religion] that we have received as genuine, and you shall remain in what you deem to be the genuine [religion], and you shall receive your [heavenly] reward since your hearts are directed towards Heaven. If you would have had a proof denying your creed you would have returned to us.[341]

The political situation in the West did not permit questioning the sovereign's authority on religious matters. Therefore, R. Solomon ibn Verga raised the issue in relation to an event taking place between Muhammad ibn Tumart (ca. 1080–1130), a Berber king, and the Jewish community. The king wanted to impose Islam on the Jews by the point of the sword. R. Solomon ibn Verga relates that the king issued

> ...a proclamation declaring that whoever would not accept Islam would be executed by the sword and his property would

---

340. *Shebeṭ Yehuda*, XII, p. 58.

341. *Shebeṭ Yehuda*, XXXII, p. 90. Similarly, Wittgenstein, *Culture and Value*, p. 29e wrote:

> Religion says: *Do this! – Think like that!* – But it cannot justify this and once it even tries to, it becomes repellent; because for every reason it offers there is a valid counterreason. It is more convincing to say: 'Think like this! However strangely it may strike you.' Or: 'Won't you do this? However repugnant you find it.'

On the idea that non-Jews, too, "direct their hearts towards Heaven," see above n. 201.

> be confiscated to the king's treasury. Then all Jews, together with their children and infants marched toward the king's gate. When they reached the king's gate, they cried: 'Save us, O king!'
> –The king responded: 'O stupid and ignorant people! Am I not summoning you to my religion, but to save you so that you shall not go down to hell?'
>
> –The Jews responded: 'Our salvation depends on our religion which we were commanded [to keep]! You, however, are our lord over our bodies [= *imperium*] and our properties [= *dominium*], but over our souls which [God] sent to us and which [He] will return back to Him, He [alone] is the sovereign who shall pass judgment over them. And you, our lord, seated in your throne [of government] are not accountable [for our souls]!'
>
> –The king responded: 'O stupid people! I don't wish to argue with you, because I know that you will put forward Jewish replies. My plain wish is that you should accept my religion. If not, the sword!'[342]

In the course of time, 'the Jewish reply' became the cornerstone of modern democracy. The first president of the first true democracy in modern times wrote:

> Every man, conducting himself as a good citizen, and being accountable to God alone for his religious opinions, ought to

342. *Shebeṭ Yehuda*, IV, pp. 21–22. See *In The Shadow of History*, pp. 184–185. This point is particularly significant in light of the fact that, as was observed by Américo Castro, the whole notion of a 'holy war' in Christendom comes from Islam; see *La Realidad Histórica de España* (Mexico City: Editorial Porrua, 1975), pp. 419–429. The episode in question concerned Muhammad ibn Tumart's efforts to force the Jews to embrace Islam; see R. Abraham ibn Daud, *Sefer ha-Qabbala*, ed. trans. and annotated by Gerson D. Cohen (Philadelphia: The Jewish Publication Society, 1967), VII, ll. 448–468, pp. 87–88.

> be protected in worshipping the Deity according to the dictates of his own conscience.
>
> President George Washington, 1789

Jews in America were particularly appreciative of the milestone in the field of civil and religious liberties inaugurated by the new republic. Let us read a paragraph of a letter by Moses Seixas, Warden of the Hebrew Congregation in Newport, Rhode Island, August 17th, 1790, addressed to George Washington:

> Deprived as we heretofore have been of the invaluable rights of free Citizens, we now with a deep sense of gratitude to the Almighty disposer of all events behold a Government, erected by the Majesty of the People – a Government, which to bigotry gives no sanction, to persecution no assistance – but generously affording to all Liberty of conscience, and immunities of Citizenship: deeming every one, of whatever Nation, tongue, or language equal parts of the great government Machine: This so ample and extensive Federal Union whose basis is Philanthropy, Mutual confidence and Public Virtue, we cannot but acknowledge to be the work of the Great God, who ruleth in the Armies of Heaven, and among the Inhabitants of the earth, doing whatever seemeth him good.

George Washington responded:

> The Citizens of the United States of America have a right to applaud themselves for having given to mankind examples of an enlarged and liberal policy: a policy worthy of imitation. All possess alike liberty of conscience and immunities of citizenship. It is now no more that toleration is spoken of, as if it was by indulgence of one class of people, that another enjoyed the exercise of their inherent natural rights. For happily the Government of the United States, which gives to

> bigotry no sanction, to persecution no assistance requires only that they who live under its protection should demean themselves as good citizens, in giving it on all occasions their effectual support.

A corollary of the above was formulated a few years later by the third president of the USA:

> I contemplate with sovereign reverence that act of the whole American people which declared that their legislature should 'make no law respecting an establishment of religion, or prohibiting the free exercise thereof,' thus building a wall of separation between Church and state.
>
> President Thomas Jefferson, 1802

Such policy benefits all, religion in particular. The fourth president of the same republic explained:

> Religion flourishes in greater purity without than with the aid of government.
>
> President James Madison, 1822

The logic of this principle was elucidated by one of the Founding Fathers. A religion in need of the Rex's sword to persuade the faithful is flawed, fundamentally and irreversibly.

> When a religion is good, I conceive it will support itself; and when it does not support itself, and God does not take care to support it so that its professors are obliged to call for help of the civil power, 'tis a sign, I apprehend, of its being a bad one.
>
> Benjamin Franklin

In the mind of the Founding Fathers, the ideals upon which the United States was founded, although 'religious,' were specifically and categorically *not* Christian. This fundamental point was made by George Washington. In the "Treaty of Peace and Friendship between the United States of America and the Bey and Subjects of Tripoli of Barbary", November 4, 1796–January 3, 1797, art. XI, 1796 U.S.T. LEXIS 4; 11 Bevans 1070, approved by the U.S. Senate in 1797, and ratified by President George Washington, we read: "The government of the United States is not, in any sense, founded on Christian religion."[343] Similarly, in a letter to Thomas Cooper (1804), Jefferson wrote: "We may safely affirm that Christianity neither is, nor ever was, a part of the common law."[344]

The term 'Church' in the famous clause establishing the separation of "Church and State" meant to exclude doctrines idiosyncratic to religious institutions, i.e., the *Church*, such as the divine right of kings – not *religion* as presently argued. Principally, it is a repudiation of the union cross/sword. It means not only freedom to worship or not to worship, but above all, rejection on the part of the civil authorities to use religion or religious institutions to either promote or attack matters of the state.[345] Unlike in Europe, the Church was not used as a tool for attacking Jews; rather, on many occasions it became a strong voice in the fight against antisemitism. This allowed for a less constricted relationship between Jews and Christians, and ended up promoting greater respect and cooperation between members of all faiths and persuasions, non-religious included. The upshot was the discovery of a common source bonding humanity – the "image of God" within. Reflecting this ideal, Maimonides, the most representative spokesman for rabbinic tradition, envisioned the Messianic Age

343. Source of Information: *Treaties and other International Acts of the United States of America, Volume 2, Documents 1–40; 1776–1818*, ed. Hunter Miller (United States Government Printing Office, Washington: 1931), pp. 364–366. On the specific non-Christian aspect of American religiosity, see *The Origin of the Republican Form of Government*, pp. 67–69.

344. Quoted in *The Origin of the Republican Form of Government*, pp. 67–68.

345. In this connection, it will be well to read Sam Harris, *Letter to a Christian Nation* (New York: Alfred A. Knopf, 2006).

as a time in which the three monotheistic religions will be working together "shoulder and shoulder" for the benefit of humankind. Here is what he wrote *MT Melakhim* 11:4:

> All these matters (of Jesus), [omitted from standard printed texts for fear of Christian censorship!], and of the Ishmaelite (i.e. Muhammad) coming after him (Jesus), came to straighten the path for the King Messiah; and prepare the whole world to worship God *jointly* [italics added]. As it is written, "Because then I shall bestow upon the nations a clear speech, summoning all in the name of God, to worship Him with one shoulder" (Zeph. 3:9).

In a letter by Jefferson to Mordecai Noah, May 28, 1818, we read:

> I thank you for the Discourse on the consecration of the Synagogue in your city, with which you have been pleased to favor me. I have read it with pleasure and instruction, having learnt from it some valuable facts in Jewish history which I did not know before. Your sect by its sufferings has furnished a remarkable proof of the universal spirit of religious intolerance inherent in every sect, disclaimed by all while feeble, and practiced by all when in power. Our laws have applied the only antidote to this vice, protecting our religious, as they do our civil rights, by putting all on an equal footing. But more remains to be done, for although we are free by the law, we are not so in practice. Public opinion erects itself into an inquisition, and exercises its office with as much fanaticism as fans the flames of an *Auto-da-fé*. The prejudice still scowling on your section of our religion altho' the elder one, cannot be unfelt by ourselves. It is to be hoped that individual dispositions will at length mould themselves to the model of the law, *and consider the moral basis, on which all our religions rest, as the rallying point which unites them in a common interest; while the peculiar dogmas branching*

> *from it are the exclusive concern of the respective sects embracing them, and no rightful subject of notice to any other.* Public opinion needs reformation on that point, which would have the further happy effect of doing away the hypocritical maxim of "*intus et lubet, foris ut moris*" ["within as pleases, without how maintained"]. Nothing, I think, would be so likely to effect this, as to your sect particularly, as the more careful attention to education, which you recommend, and which, placing its members on the equal and commanding benches of science, will exhibit them as equal objects of respect and favor. I should not do full justice to the merits of your Discourse, were I not, in addition to that of its matter, to express my consideration of it as a fine specimen of style and composition. I salute you with great respect and esteem [Italics added].

Freedom, including the freedom to worship, was the result of a *Law* not predicated on the right of might, but on certain inviolable principles common to all humankind.

# Concluding Reflections

The political and legal systems of Israel, discussed above, may be summarized in the following quotation from Oscar S. Straus:

> The children of Israel having arrived in sight of the Promised Land, their great lawgiver summons them all before him; he recounts to them their whole eventful history, their hardships, their toils, their sufferings and their triumphs; he recapitulates and codifies their laws and causes them to be written in one brief book, the book of Deuteronomy, which are thereupon adopted by the whole people under the most solemn and awe-inspiring circumstances. He admonishes them to keep these laws fresh in their memory, and directs that they shall be read before all Israel at the end of every seven years, in the solemnity of the year of release on the Feast of Tabernacles.
>
> [...]Moses then commits the book of the laws into the custody of the Levites, the tribe especially set apart for the service of religion and as instructors and teachers of the nation, who, as Moses expressly declares: "Shall teach Jacob thy judgments, and Israel thy law." Moses is succeeded by Joshua, who leads his conquering armies over Jordan. Before settling in the Promised Land the law is again promulgated, and Joshua is succeeded by the Shophetim, or Judges, of whom the Scriptures enumerate fourteen in all, from Othniel to Samuel.
>
> The Judges were elected by the people, and summoned to

> power as the necessities of the times demanded: they were statesmen-heroes, and after the occasion for which they were called to assume the head of the confederate nation had passed away, they usually retired to their humble occupation, as was notable with Gideon. The government under the judges was very much like our own Federal Government: each tribe had its own tribal or state government, which had jurisdiction over local affairs, and it sent its duly elected representatives to the national congress.
>
> This government, from the fact that God, the source of all power, the embodiment of the law, not a king, was ruler of the nation, is termed by various writers a Theocracy, or Nomocracy (from *nomos,* meaning law), or a Commonwealth.[346]

Jesus was crucified. The execution was carried out by Roman soldiers under Roman authority. Crucifixion was used by the Roman authorities as a brutal warning *to affront Jews*. In the case of Jesus, he was crucified as a '*Jewish* king' to humiliate and mock – not Jesus personally – but the Jews.[347] Under the presumption that an *imperial* religion has the might to impute grace 'freely,' the Church imputed guilt on the Jews: 'freely.' It then proceeded to advance a series of theo-political doctrines aimed at discrediting the Tora and the political system of Israel. And now a conclusive question. Who actually crucified Jesus: Jews, or those who rejected the Law and Israel's political system, declared the image of God within null and void, and upheld the 'Divine Right of Kings?'

---

346. *The Origin of the Republican Form of Government in the United States,* pp. 106–108. See the quotation above at n. 119.

347. See Vamberto Morais, *A Short History of Anti-Semitism* (New York: W.W. Norton: 1972), pp. 24–25. To have exonerated the Romans and then turn the killing of Jesus as a *Jewish* crime against humanity, undoubtedly ranks as the most perfidious act in the annals of ignominy.

# Section IV

# The Memory of Israel

## Introductory Remarks

The word for National Memory in Hebrew is *Morasha* (see appendix 12). The National Memory of a people has nothing to do with 'history.' 'History' is what professional historians say to other professional historians about what 'really' happened. National Memory is what a people wish to transmit to their posterity. Together with Borges, this explains the simple fact that "The historical truth... is not what actually happened; it is what we judged to have happened."[1] One has to do

1. Jorge Luis Borges, "Pierre Menard," in *Ficciones, Obras Completas,* p. 449, our translation.

with the past, the other with the future. Reportedly, John Steinbeck said, "Texas has its own private history based on, but not limited by, facts." This is true not only of Texans but of all people having something special to communicate to their children and children's children. For a non-professional, reading 'history' is for the sake of pleasure, akin to reading Shakespeare or a novel. National Memory involves commitment to an ideal envisioned by your ancestors that you accept and wish to pass on to your children. It has to do with your ethos and national culture and matters transcending 'factual truth' and 'cold facts.' In Hebrew, the word for 'remember' (זכור) comes from the root (זכר) 'male.' It has to do with 'fertilization' and 'generation,' rather than *retrieving* an experience. When Scripture urges us to "remember (זכור) the Sabbath," explaining: "*Because* God had created the heavens and the earth in six days," it is not instructing us to 'recollect,' but to *transform* belief in Creation into a day of rest (see Ex. 20:8–11). Thus, when the liturgy proclaims that the Sabbath is "a reminiscence (זכר) of the acts of Creation," it is referring to a *generative process*, the *outcome* of such a belief – not the 'remembrance of things past.'

'History,' as we learn it today in school, is a modern invention made famous by Sir Edward Gibbon (1737–1794), and later on by German professors who desperately wanted to prove that they, too, could be historians, if they only tried hard enough (see appendix 20). Before that, few cared to know or believed that it was possible to know, what 'really' happened in the past. Philology could shed some light on the attitude of the ancients in this matter. Currently, 'superstition' and 'superstitious' are terms associated with 'dread and belief in the irrational.' In the original Latin, however, *superstitio* and *superstitiosus* had a different meaning. 'Superstition' was knowledge of a past event, and 'superstitious' was that individual who had the peculiar ability to 'testify' about an event at which he was not present. Here is how Émile Benveniste defines these terms.

> [T]he seer who speaks of past events *as if he had actually been present*: the 'divination'... did not refer to the future but to the

> past (italics in original). *Superstitio* is the gift of second sight which enables a person to know the past as if he or she had been present, *superstes*. This is how *superstitiosus* denotes the gift of second sight, which is attributed to 'seers', that of being a 'witness' of events at which he has not been present.[2]

In the last few centuries, mankind has been graced with a plethora of historians having, as pagan *superstitiosus*, the unique gift of knowing what happened and what did not happen in biblical times: precisely, unerringly. Although they can hardly read a single word of Hebrew without making errors of biblical proportions, these scholars have had the peculiar gift of second sight, and they could tell you with uncanny precision where and when any given passage in Scripture was or was not written, and by whom. Not only Jewish history and religion have been blessed with this labor of love. Other religions, particularly those of the 'underdeveloped' and more 'primitive' kind, have benefited from this class of wisdom. There is, however, one significant exception, noted by Arnaldo Momigliano (1908–1987).

> [I]t is perhaps characteristic of our time that we have so many discussions of the religious ideas of underdeveloped countries, but so little analysis of our own religious beliefs with the simple purpose of ascertaining their credibility. During recent years in Italy more scholarly books have appeared on heretical sects than on modern Catholicism. The men who would be able to illuminate the contemporary scene by talking about truth in its historical context have not yet found their public. Therefore we are left with the English nanny and the cargo cult for the expression of our nostalgias and dissatisfactions.[3]

2. *Indo-European Language and Society*, p. 527.
3. Arnaldo Momigliano, *Essays in Ancient and Modern Historiography* (Middletown, Conn.: Wesleyan University Press, 1982), p. 7. Theodor H. Gaster, *Festivals of the Jewish Year* (New York: William Morrow and Company, 1952), p. 11 rightly pointed out:

(The exception includes the respective *national* histories and institutions of these bully-savants. One can only wonder why.)

There may be an agenda to the 'historical reconstruction' of Scripture. Their methods vary and conclusions differ. They share, however, a single purpose: to prove that the Book is a non-Book; or what amounts to the same, to deny the Jewish people the right to 'remember.' I don't think it is unreasonable to ask why the spirit of selflessness displayed by these brilliant minds focuses invariably on their thankless task of enlightening 'other' less gifted religions, Judaism in particular. What could motivate academicians and intellectuals unsympathetic to the Hebrew Scripture and tradition – and in many cases openly belligerent to Judaism – to devote their precious lives to 'demonstrating' the fallacies of something that they personally repudiate? Is it some sort of beatific urge moving these noble souls to forego riches and glory and fame (and successful family life) to enlighten the mentally disadvantaged? Could it be that this noble enterprise, particularly as manifested by anti-Judaism Jews, is motivated by psychological, rather than intellectual reasons?

At any rate, Hebrews had little time to indulge in Gibbon's notion of history. The sight of the prophets and sages was on the *future* and the unfolding of "the days to come." That is why only Jews have the "end of days," apocalypses when their *National Memory* is fulfilled. The past that the *superstitiosus* witness is a past without a future. (Christianity appropriated the Hebrew idea of 'apocalypses,' but what can the "end of days" mean without an initial *National Memory*, or *Morasha*, unfolding in "days to come?") The Hebrew Scriptures are the *National Books* of Israel (see above Introductory Remarks, Section II). Their authority rests on a single fact: they were published by the Jewish *Nation* and accepted as such by the *Jewish* People. Other than malice,

---

Indeed, the assumption that the only validation of festivals lies in the factuality of their attendant legends is a piece of 19th century rationalism which we ought to have outgrown.

On p. 12, he added: "After all, there is no historical proof that Jesus was born on Christmas Day."

there is no justification to treat the *National* publications of Israel differently than the publication of the currency or postal stamps issued by the national agencies of any state. People having no confidence in the legal tender and/or postal services of a country would be best advised to avoid using them, rather than spend their lives criticizing and defaming the money and postage of a people that they despise. Can you imagine a group of bully-savants dedicated to the suppression of US currency and Postal services on the claim to have discovered portraits of Washington, Franklin, and Jefferson different than those appearing on our dollars and postage stamps?

The focus of the Hebrew Scripture and tradition is the National Memory of Israel. National Memory is the subject of Psalm 44. The time is around the fall of Judea, about 604 B.C.E. The events are depressing: devastation, death, torture, martyrdom, opprobrium. It is precisely at that pivotal moment of a *national* crisis, that the psalmist had the courage and vision to raise the issue of National Memory. His voice is distinctive and evocative. The style is lyric, the texture dense and vivid. The text is too rich and nuanced to be coherently summarized here.[4] For our purpose we shall present a brief sketch of the main points it raises. The translation is from the English version of the "Jewish Publication Society," with minor variations. The psalm opens with a title giving some technical detail, as to those in charge of executing the psalm and the type of musical composition ("For the Head-Musician, the children of Koraḥ, *Maskil* [a type of musical composition]"). It may be divided into five parts.

First (2–4) is a validation of National Memory. It rests on two facts. The first, "our fathers have recounted to us." By inference, rejection of National Memory equals rejection of a family trust. Obviously, in an oedipal society the argument is without merits, but in the Hebrew mind parents' love is always chaste and pure and without reproach. Second, it pertains to the *National Foundation* of Israel, when the

4. For an illuminating exposition of this psalm, see R. Joel ibn Shu'eb, *Nora Tehillot* (Salonika, 5329/1569), 101b-104b. For some specific views on the subject, see *In the Shadow of History*, pp. 207–215.

people first settled the land, and it has been transmitted ever since through family tradition. A *National Memory* that does not begin at the incipient moment of the state will remain dysfunctional and clueless, wobbling back and forth.

1. For the leader; [a Psalm] of the sons of Koraḥ. *Maskil.*
2. O God, we have heard with our ears, our fathers have recounted to us. A feat you have wrought for them in their days, days of old.
3. Thou with Thy hand didst drive out the nations [from the Land of Israel], and didst implant them [the Jewish people];
4. For not by their own sword did they [our fathers] get the land in possession. Neither did their own arm save them; But Thy right hand, and Thine arm, and the light of Thy countenance. Because Thou wast favorable unto them.

The second part (5–9) affirms God's sovereignty and Israel's unconditional commitment to His governance. National Memory is not a collection of amusing stories recounted for the purpose of entertainment and ego aggrandizement. It must be, first and foremost, a source of *national* inspiration in times of *national* crisis.

1. Thou art my King, O God; Command the salvation of Jacob.
2. Through Thee do we push down our adversaries, through Thy name do we tread them under, those who rise against us.
3. For I trust not in my bow, neither can my sword save me.
4. But Thou hast saved us from our adversaries, and hast put them to shame, those who hate us.
5. In God have we gloried all the day, and we will give thanks unto Thy name forever. Selah.

The third part (10–17) describes the horrific situation facing the people, and God's failure to assist.

1. Yet Thou hast cast us off, and brought us to confusion; and go not forth with our army.

2. Thou make us to turn back from the adversary; and they that hate us spoil us at their will.
3. Thou has delivered us like sheep to be eaten; and scattered us among the nations.
4. Thou hast sold Thy people for small gain, and hast not set their price high.
5. Thou make us a taunt to our neighbors, a scorn and derision for those who are round us.
6. Thou make us a byword among nations, a shaking of the head among the peoples.
7. All the day is my confusion before me, and the shame of my face has covered me.
8. Because of the voice of him that taunted and blasphemed; for the reason of [the abuse perpetrated against me by] the enemy and the revengeful.

A condition of National Memory is the *fortitude to remember* in the face of defeat. The fourth part (18–21) describes Israel's loyalty while facing abandonment and spiritual dislocation.

1. All these have befallen us, yet we have not forgotten Thee; neither have we been false to Thy covenant.
2. Our heart has not coiled back, neither have our steps departed from Thy path.
3. Though Thou has crushed us in a place of jackals, and covered us with the shadow of death.
4. Have we forgotten the name of our God? Have we stretched our hands to an alien god?

The last part (22–27) addresses God, praying for deliverance. Without hope and trust, National Memory is short lived. Hebrew martyrdom is dedication and loyalty to Israel's National Memory.

1. O God! Would Thou not search this out? For He knows the secrets of the heart.

2. Nay, but for Thy sake we are killed all the day. We are considered as sheep for slaughter.
3. Awake, why do You sleep, O Lord? Arouse Thyself, cast [us] not off forever.
4. Why do you turn Thy face away, and forget our affliction and our oppression?
5. For our soul is bowed down to dust; our belly cleaves unto the earth.
6. Arise for our help, and redeem us for Thy mercy's sake.

Living in *Galut* demands validating Jewish memory (see appendix 15). Israel's right to remember was challenged by despots and religious demagogues (and today by 'historians' and 'divines'). Exile meant living under "the Shadow of Death." The Jewish mind is essentially alphabetic, non-Greek and non-poetic. Wittgenstein (and others) understood this well.

> What Renan calls the '*bon sens précoce*' of the Semitic races (an idea which had occurred to me too a long time ago) is the *unpoetic* mentality, which heads straight for what is concrete. This is characteristic of my philosophy[5] [italics in original].

There is a radical difference between alphabetic and analphabetic memory; it affects even such basic concepts as 'truth.' Jewish 'National Memory' originated in a *written* text (see Ex. 17:14; Deut. 24:17–19).[6] The poet's memory and Greek 'rational-ideality' exclude writing (see above chapter 4). One presupposes human horizontality, the other human hierarchy, where the enlightened man dictates to those below. Greek truth is absolute, categorical, and universal. Not only does it render the privileged 'free,' but also obnoxious, especially as the enlightened (or 'illuminated' if you prefer) feel compelled to

5. *Culture and Value*, p. 6.
6. Therefore, Hebrew thought is non-geometrical and non-spatial, and is organized in terms of successive synthesis; see *Golden Doves*, pp. 32–37.

impose it on everyone else. When psychological and cultural coercion under the guise of 'persuasion' fails to quench the voice of the 'unenlightened,' brutal force is justified. Hebrew 'truth' is communicated through *meliṣa,* horizontal dialectics. It is a humanistic form of eloquence, which springs from the Hebrew doctrine that every human is created in God's image. To the alphabetic mind this means, first and foremost, the recognition of others as free and equal. The essence of *meliṣa* is a dialectic in which neither side must necessarily be wrong; or conversely, that both sides may indeed be uttering "the words of the Living God." The objective is to persuade, not to demonstrate; to open, rather than close the subject. See below chapter 46.

Alphabetic memory is impervious to analphabetic demagoguery and theo-political noise. Hence, the imperative to delegitimize Jewish National Memory by de-alphabetizing the Book. The 'Jewish problem' is a problem of memory. Maimonides called attention to the two-pronged strategy of military and psychological warfare, whose ultimate goal is not merely the extermination of the people but eradication of their National Memory. So, in addition to brutal force, dictators require the assistance of men skilled in psychological and cultural coercion and the management of violence. Thus the vital role of poets and intellectuals specialized in the organization and promotion of mythologies.[7] An important argument used by members of the enlightened elite, old and new, is '*You're* different!' (For the analphabetic, it is difficult to apprehend that if *B* is different from A, then *A* is different from B.) All that was required of the Jew was national lobotomy and everything would be 'peachy keen!' Six

7. For a well-focused and critical analysis of the subject, see Daniel Lerner, "The Coercive Ideologists in Perspective," in *World Revolutionary Elites,* eds. Harold D. Lasswell and Daniel Lerner (Cambridge, Mass.: M.I.T. Press, 1966), pp. 456–468. On cultural 'remembering' and 'forgetting,' see Jan Assmann, *Moses the Egyptian* (Cambridge, Mass. Harvard University Press, 1997), pp. 215–218. Obviously, 'cultural forgetting' is radically different than cultural lobotomy practiced in pseudo-democracies, via intimidation and misinformation. See below n. 80.

million witnesses attest to the worth of that promise. Accordingly, it would not be difficult to understand why traditionally, Jews chose to pray to the God of Israel; and although He does not always answer in the expected way, they refused to "stretch our hands to an alien god."

Denigration of Judaism and pigeonholing are essential to anti-Judaic discourse. Max Weber, one of the fathers of modern sociology, branded Jews "a pariah nation." His logic is impeccable. It is as if someone, after butchering, vandalizing and raping a people, were to go on and denigrate the survivors for being destitute. "If the word 'pariah' indicates a people who accept their position as inferiors in an alien social system and work out their own salvation through this acceptance," responded Momigliano, "the Jews were not pariahs." He added:

> The Jews went on giving laws to themselves and treated their pact with God as their own legal title to the future recovery of their own land in the messianic age. Their morality encompassed rebellion against injustice and martyrdom – attitudes one does not normally associate with pariahs.[8]

We can illustrate this view simply by pointing to the laws and regulations promulgated throughout the Jewish Diaspora (the famous *teqanot ha-qahal)*. For example: those enacted by *La Nazione Ebrea a Livorno e a Pisa* [*The Hebrew Nation at Leghorn and Pisa*] (1591–1700), edited and annotated by Professor Renzo Toaff (Florence: Leo S. Olschki, 1990), 729 pages. A study of these laws will reveal that in fact they were not inferior, and it would not be unfair to say that in many respects were far superior, to those regulating any major city in Germany and Italy. An additional point: according to Weber, Paul freed the Christians from the pariah status.[9] This is, no doubt, the effect of Paul's doctrine concerning the Divine Right of Kings and unlimited submission – so elegantly argued in the *Epistle*

8. Arnaldo Momigliano, "Judaism as a Pariah Religion," in *Essays on Ancient and Modern Judaism* (Chicago: Chicago University Press, 1994), p. 176. We should add that Weber was not only fair-minded but also consistent. Therefore, he classified Jewish capitalism as pariah capitalism. See above Section III n. 153.
9. "Judaism as a Pariah Religion," p. 173.

*to the Romans* (13, see above chapter 26). Reverend Jonathan Mayhew, however, referred to this doctrine "as fabulous and chimerical, as transubstantiation; or any of the most absurd reveries of ancient or modern visionaries" (see above chapter 32). Reverend Mayhew's Sermon inspired the American Revolution and the creation of the first truly democratic republic. By way of contrast, Weber's concept of 'pariah' became an excuse for antisemitism and the persecution of unwanted minorities. A fresher and more intelligent definition of 'pariah society,' I propose, would be 'a society which gives rise to political rulers of the ilk of Hitler, Mussolini, et al.' It is no wonder, then, why many Jews would "rather be free citizens of the small Jewish republic of the Ghetto," than subjects of an empire famous for the bigots and demagogues it produces.

The focus of this Section is the National Memory or *Morasha* of Israel: how it was formed, the efforts made to eradicate it, and the strategies developed to preserve it and transmit it to future generations. We will see that through and through, Jewish strategy has been one: confronting the Sword with the Law.

# Chapter 37
# National Memory

In Judaism, memory and loyalty to tradition – not race and territory – are the constitutive elements of nationalism and nationality: Shema'ya and Abṭalion, the proselytes, are fully-fledged members of Israel, whereas Ishmael and Esau, the biological children of Abraham, are not (see above chapter 15 and appendix 18). Early in their history, Jews discovered that a people deprived of National Memory are not a nation. A modern rabbinic thinker made this important observation:

> Historians marvel at this unique phenomenon – a small minority defying every threat of extermination during century after century. They admit that with no other people could the same result have been achieved. Why the difference? How explain the unique endurance of the Jew? What is the secret of his indestructibility so far? The answer is plain and simple; there is no mystery about it. The Jew *remembered* – he remembered the advice of Moses and his ancestors… He recalled his national past with its long series of incidents which proved beyond all doubt that his people had an Ally whose aid assured final triumph.[10]

Israel's enemies, too, knew this. To succeed, they would have to gain supremacy not only on the battleground but also on the field of ideas.

10. R. Abraham Cohen, *Sabbath Sermons* (London: Soncino Press, 1960), p. 225.

This never happened. Although numerically overpowered on the battlefield, Israel remained invincible in the field of ideas.

Antisemitism and the demonization of Judaism are tools used by totalitarian regimes to carry out their psychological onslaught against Israel. The intended goal is the erasure of Israel's memory by maligning the Jew and discrediting Judaism: the former is a consequence of the latter. Totalitarian regimes persecute Jews not because of what they are but because of what they represent.[11] This can help us understand the role of antisemitism in the Hellenistic world. When Jews were first mentioned by Greek writers, after the destruction of the Persian Empire, they were depicted as a race of philosophers and priestly sages.[12] All this changed drastically with the publication of the Septuagint (the Greek translation of the Tora) made by Jews under the patronage of Ptolemy II Philadelphus (285–246 B.C.E.).[13] It made

11. The tactic of maligning the Jews as a pretext to justify inflicting physical injury on them is alluded to in Scripture. The correct translation of Deut. 26:6 is: "And the Egyptians claimed that we were evil, and [thus] they tortured us"; see *In the Shadow of History*, pp. 193–198. The rabbis were quite aware that hatred against Jews was the result of political antagonism against 'Sinai,' see above Section III n. 3. For some insights into Hellenistic antisemitism, see Victor Tcherikover, *Hellenistic Civilization and the Jews* (Philadelphia: Jewish Publication Society, 1961), pp. 365–370. The same occurred in Spain and other European societies.
12. In *Against Apion*, II, 281, *Josephus*, vol. 1, p. 405 we read: "Our earliest imitators were the Greek philosophers, who, though ostensibly observing the laws of their own countries, yet in their conduct and philosophy were Moses' disciples, holding similar views about God, and advocating the simple life and friendly communion between man and man." Concerning the dialogue of Aristotle with the Jew, cited by Clearchus, in *Against Apion*, I, 176, *Josephus*, vol. 1, p. 235; see Johanan Hans Levy, *Studies in Jewish Hellenism* (Heb.) (Jerusalem: Bialik Institute, 1969), pp. 15–43, where he showed that although it cannot be proven that the encounter had actually taken place, it could be shown that the meeting, as *it was depicted*, could have indeed taken place. For the literature on the subject, see Menahem Stern, *Greek and Latin Authors on Jews and Judaism*, 3 vols. (Jerusalem: The Israel Academy of Science and Humanities, 1974–1984). See also the collection of articles in Hebrew, in *Hellenistic Views on Jews and Judaism* (Jerusalem: Zalman Shazar Center, 1974)..
13. On the historical accuracy of this tradition, see Elias Bickerman, "The Septuagint

an enormous impact on all levels of society, particularly among the masses. It was precisely at that time that Hellenistic antisemitic propaganda emerged. Suddenly, the 'Jewish philosopher' was replaced by a demon of mythological proportions. Arnaldo Momigliano called attention to the fact that:

> About 300 B.C. Greek intellectuals presented the Jews to the Greek world as philosophers, legislators and wise men. A few decades later, the alleged philosophers and legislators made public in Greek their own philosophy and legislation. The Gentile world remained indifferent… The failure of the LXX [Septuagint] to arouse the interest of the pagan intelligentsia of the third century B.C. was the end of the myth of the *Jewish philosopher.*[14]

No sooner had the Septuagint reached the general public than any mention of Jews and the Law became slanderous. The objective was the delegitimization of the Jew: only what *others* said about them (Manetho, Apion, Apollonius, Molon, and so forth) mattered: what Jews said about themselves was to be discarded. Jewish memory was tainted, and their accounts about themselves were to be systematically ignored.[15]

Greek thinkers refused to come to grips with Scripture and Jewish ideas and institutions. The first citation of the Septuagint by a Greek

---

as a Translation," *Studies in Jewish and Christian History,* vol. 1, pp. 167–200.

14. Arnaldo Momigliano, *Alien Wisdom* (New York: Cambridge University Press, 1975), p. 92; see also ibid., pp. 74–78, 82–87.
15. Presently, even writers sympathetic to Judaism assume *a priori* that Jewish writers (unless anti-Judaism) must be suspected of being 'biased.' Accordingly, when quoting a Jewish source they apologize or try to qualify it. Significantly, they never would pause to consider that they themselves might be biased for assuming that a Jewish source is *ipso facto* tainted. The logic for this is that since Jews have rejected the idea of 'immaculate conception' they cannot possibly develop an 'immaculate perception.'

author is much later, after the destruction of Jerusalem. Momigliano noted that:

> No Hellenistic poet or philosopher quoted it, although modern scholars have sometimes deluded themselves on this subject. The first certain quotation of the Bible in a Greek philosopher is to be found in the treatise *On the Sublime* attributed to Longinus, which is usually dated in the first century A.D. (98).[16]

The Tora was not just ignored. The Seleucid king Antiochus IV Epiphanes aimed at the total eradication of the Tora. About December 167 B.C.E. he planned the systematic destruction of Jewish life in Judea, making the observance of the Tora a capital offense. The population of Judea was subjected to torture, martyrdom, and grisly massacre. There was no precedent for this type of religious warfare. Hellenization never involved the forcible abolition of an existing cult or the imposition of a new one. It also ran contrary to the king's personal ideology. As a follower of the Epicurean school, he should have condoned the observance of traditional rites.[17] He sought to abrogate the Law, not merely by forcing the Jews to *abstain* from practicing it, but by *imposing* on them a new cult. There was no precedent for this type of action.

---

16. *Alien Wisdom*, p. 91. See *Golden Doves*, pp. 7–8. Similarly, during the 16th century, Inquisition officials banned rabbinic texts. Eventually, even the Bible was included in this ban. In some Spanish and Portuguese dominions this measure lasted until the beginning of the 20th century. Reflecting pagan bias, Martin Hengel, *Jews, Greeks and Barbarians* (Philadelphia: Fortress Press, 1980), p. 110 writes: "The fact that either is not mentioned at all in the Greek sources ... only shows their [Jewish] political impotence." This claim had been put forward by known antisemites, beginning with Apion and Manetho. The opposite is in fact the truth: if the Jews had been impotent, then Greeks would not have failed to mention them!
17. See Elias Bickerman, "The Maccabean Uprising: An Interpretation," in ed. Judah Goldin, *The Jewish Expression* (New Haven: Yale University Press, 1976), p. 68.

> The persecution meant not only the suspension of the previous law, but also the introduction of a new one. This is the point at which any attempt fails to explain the measures of Epiphanes on the basis of his own ideology or on the conditions of the age.[18]

The 'cult' imposed on Jews did not consist of fresh rituals and ceremonies, or the adoption of another religious system. It consisted, principally, of *transgressing* the laws of the Tora.[19] It was a carefully thought-out plan aimed at abolishing Judaism simply by forbidding what it prescribes and commanding what it forbids. The scrolls of the Law were ordered destroyed and their possession punishable by death. The sanctity of the Temple and priesthood was abolished. The laws regulating the spiritual life of Jews were prohibited under penalty of death. Jews caught observing the Sabbath or circumcising their children were subjected to horrific torture. What the Law had forbidden was now imposed on Jews as a *religious* duty. These activities were not motivated by antipathy to Jewish laws. Samaritans were free to observe the Sabbath, circumcise their children, and observe the same laws which were forbidden to the Jews under the death penalty.[20]

---

18. Elias Bickerman, *The God of the Maccabees* (Leiden: E.J. Brill, 1979), p. 78. Similarly, Iberian *conversos* who retained some Jewish habits, i.e., changing linens on Friday night, were *ipso facto* charged with heresy and burned at the stake for having committed an 'offense' against Christendom. In view of this, it would not be too difficult to understand why educated *conversos* regarded 'The Feast of Maccabeus' celebrated in the Christian liturgy (August 1st) as diabolical. Worse was the Church's celebration of the Jewish Maccabees as a prototype of Christian martyrs, and then their establishment of the Inquisition, designed to inflict horrendous tortures on Jews – far worse than what the pagans inflicted on the Maccabean martyrs.
19. The same logic was applied to the *converso*: the most important aspect of the 'new' religion was *violation* of the 'old' Law. True to its vocation, the Church was not interested in earthly happiness. This would probably explain why the only moment of joy entering the lives of *cristianos viejos* was when forcing *Jews* (but not Muslims) to eat pork. The same occurred with antisemites in ancient times; see the quotation, below n. 22, and *A Short History of Anti-Semitism*, p. 26.
20. See Martin Hengel, *Judaism and Hellenism* (Philadelphia: Fortress Press, 1974),

Antisemitic writers, from Diodorus to Tacitus to modern apologists, defend Antiochus on the grounds that he was only attempting to bring 'civilization' and 'enlightenment' to Jews. Bickerman showed that contemporary documentation, both Jewish and Greek, fails to mention that Antiochus had such a mission in mind: "We do not find a single reference to the civilizing mission of Epiphanes or the barbarism of the Jews."[21] A few questions raised by Professor Bickerman may help us evaluate the merits of that defense:

> Why was the circumcision of a Hellenized Jew forbidden, but not that of a Hellenized Arab? Why did Epiphanes consider it a crime that an inhabitant of Jerusalem should serve Zeus and, at the same time, abstain from pork? After all, the pig was considered unclean by all Syrians, and they were allowed to continue holding this view.[22]

It has been proposed that 'enlightened' Jews persuaded the king to take draconian measures to save their brethren from 'Jewish particularism.'[23] There were Jews, indeed, who had "abandoned the holy covenant" (I Mac. 1:15) and collaborated with the Greeks. At the same time, it is hardly conceivable that Jews – whether 'enlightened' or not – would have urged the king to perpetrate such heinous crimes as slaughtering newborn infants because they had been circumcised, tying them around their mothers' necks and then smashing them down the wall of the city (I Mac. 1:60–61) – all for the sake of 'enlightenment!' We can now proceed to introduce the following question. Previously, Greek writers praised Judaism and hailed Jews as a "race

---

vol. 1, pp. 293–294. I disagree with Professor Hengel, who ascribes the "zeal against the law" to "Jewish reformers" and not to the Greeks themselves. Unknowingly, he is pursuing the old tradition of exonerating the enemies of Jews by blaming the Jews for everything, including antisemitism; see *In the Shadow of History*, p. 233 n. 41.

21. *The God of the Maccabees*, p. 81; see pp. 12–14.
22. *The God of the Maccabees*, p. 77.
23. See *The God of the Maccabees*, pp. 83–88; *Judaism and Hellenism*, vol. 1, pp. 292–303.

of philosophers." Suddenly, with the publication of the Greek version of the Tora, a radical change took place, signaling the emergence of the first systemic attack against Jews and Judaism. Why?

The Septuagint was the first book available to the general public. The large number of proselytes and semi-proselytes from Greek-speaking communities is clear evidence of the impact that Jewish life-style and Jewish values made on the general population. The catalyst for this social phenomenon was the publication of the Greek translation of the Tora. Mention should be made of a festival in which Jews and non-Jews together offered thanks to God for this precious gift. It was celebrated annually on the island of Pharos where, according to local tradition, Jewish sages translated the Tora into Greek. This is how Philo describes this exceptional celebration.

> Therefore, even to the present day, there is held every year a feast and great assembly on the island of Pharos, whither not only Jews but multitudes of others cross the water, both to do honour to the place in which the light of that version first shone out, and also to thank God for the good gift so old yet ever young. But, after the prayers and thanksgivings, some fixing tents on the seaside and others reclining on the sandy beach in the open air feast with their relations and friends, counting that shore for the time a more magnificent lodging than the fine mansions in the royal precincts. Thus the laws are shewn to be desirable and precious in the eyes of all, ordinary citizens and rulers alike, and that too though our nation has not prospered for many a year.[24]

Veneration for the Tora and appreciation of Jewish life-style spread throughout the Hellenistic world. Concerning this unique development, Josephus noted:

---

24. *Moses* II, 41–44, *Philo*, vol. 6, pp. 469–471. Cf. quotation from *Philo* in appendix 20.

> The masses have long since shown a keen desire to adopt our religious observances; and there is not one city, Greek or barbarian, nor a single nation, to which our custom of abstaining from work on the seventh day has not spread, and where the fasts and the lighting of lamps and many of our prohibitions in the matter of food are not observed. Moreover, they attempt to imitate our unanimity, our liberal charities, our devoted labour in the crafts, our endurance under persecution on behalf of our laws. The greatest miracle of all is that our Law holds out no seductive bait of sensual pleasure, but has exercised this influence through its own inherent merits; and, as God permeates the universe, so the Law has found its way among all mankind.[25]

Western thought is essentially elitist. In this respect the Septuagint was exceptional. Written in the colloquial language and in an uncomplicated, flowing style, it offered a comprehensive value-system relevant to *all* – elite and the masses. Explaining the wide success of the Tora, in contrast to the works of philosophers, Josephus observed:

> These, however, addressed their philosophy to the few, and did not venture to divulge their true beliefs to the masses who had their own preconceived opinions; whereas our lawgiver, by making practice square with precept, not only convinced his own contemporaries, but so firmly implanted this belief concerning God in their descendants* to all future generations that it cannot be moved.[26]

What made the situation intolerable was that the Tora was not under state control, which the ruling authorities could manipulate. Therefore,

25. *Against Apion* II, 282–284, *Josephus*, vol. 1, pp. 405–407.

* This relates to the concept of Israel's "intuitive knowledge" (*'ilm al-ḍaruri*) of God; see José Faur, "Intuitive Knowledge of God in Medieval Jewish Theology," Jewish Quarterly Review, vol. 67, no. 2 (October 1976 – January 1977), pp. 90–110.

26. *Against Apion* II, 169–170, *Josephus*, vol. 1, p. 361.

it became a political imperative to discredit Israel. Anyone assisting the state in this mission would be rewarded. The rabbis noted: "Whoever would persecute Israel will surely be (appointed) chief."[27] Thus, Tacitus inaugurated a path that would be frequently trodden by many other 'great spirits' at the service of totalitarian governments: enlisting their services on behalf of state-persecution. Even before the Romans conquered Israel, "While the East was under the sway of the Assyrians, the Medes, and the Persians, the Jews were the most contemptible of the subject tribes." First, Tacitus described Jewish rituals as "tasteless and mean."[28] In his considered opinion, "all their other customs, which are at once perverse and disgusting, owe their strength to their very badness."[29] Judaism is nothing but a "national superstition," in contradistinction to "Greek civilization." The atrocities performed by Antiochus IV Epiphanes are worthy of praise: they were intended to *civilize* the Jews and *save* them from their own superstition. King Antiochus endeavored to abolish Jewish superstition and introduce Greek civilization; the war with the Parthians, however, prevented his improving this "basest of all people."[30] What is particularly significant is that in the minds of these scholars, these oddities justify annihilating a people, conquering their land, and plundering their wealth.[31]

---

27. Giṭṭin 56b; Sanhedrin 104b. Probably, the original statement was made having in mind the decision of the senate to appoint Vespasian to conduct the war against Jews. However, as it is known from recent history, the same applies to academicians, poets, intellectuals and religious quacks and politicians..
28. Tacitus, *History,* V, 5, p. 660.
29. Tacitus, *History,* V, 5, p. 659.
30. Tacitus, *History,* V, 8, p. 662; cf. 13, p. 665. See *The God of the Maccabean*, p. 14.
31. See Tacitus, *History,* V, 1–5, p. 657–660. One can only wonder at the level of the humanity of historians admiring a civilization that justifies annihilating a people because they were deemed 'unfriendly.' For a critical analysis of Tacitus' view, see Johanan Hans Levy, in *Hellenistic Views on Jews and Judaism* (Heb.), pp. 109–162. On Cicero's antisemitic views, see idem, ibid., pp. 83–108. For a lively discussion of the subject, see *A Short History of Anti-Semitism,* pp. 35–46. A serious problem with these studies is the naïve attitude, stemming from a profound sense of self-deprecation, accepting as an absolute dogma the intellectual honesty of authors bent on maligning Jews and Judaism. I would like to

Invariably, the victim is always wrong: the raped is responsible for the crimes of the rapist. To ensure that history treats the mighty kindly, it must be written by the victor. A principal task of this type of civilization is to foster the sort of intellectual ambiance that would effectively muzzle the vanquished and discredit his memory.[32] Thus, the categorical imperative to dishonor Jewish memory. Only others may know the true beliefs of Jews and what had taken place in their history. In Tacitus' footsteps, Christianity deemed Jewish practices and rituals human aberrations. In the spirit of Antiochus Epiphanes, it, too, became committed to the proposition that the Jew must be 'saved' at all costs; if warranted, by the Crusader's sword, the fire of the Inquisition, or other such appropriate means. The memory of Israel, too, is unworthy: Jews are not to be permitted to remember, (thus the function of Shoa denial).

Tacitus, far more than Jesus and Scripture, is the guiding light of Christianity. Islam followed in the footsteps of Christianity, but with intellectual consistency. If Israel's memory is corrupt, then the whole Scripture must be regarded as a sham. Hence the most basic doctrine of Islam, having preeminence over all other doctrines, including monotheism and the apostleship of their prophet. It is called *taḥrif:* the text of the Scripture has been tampered with by the Jews. An obvious example is the Jewish forgery alleging that Abraham sacrificed Isaac, when everybody knows that it was Ishmael! Similarly, the Jews tampered with the original text of the Tora, knowing that the

---

point out that Vico, *The First New Science*, in *Vico: Selected Writings*, pp. 86–87 referred to Tacitus' view on the Jews. However, in no way or form did he share these prejudices. On the contrary, he had the highest regard for everything Jewish, including rabbinic tradition. We should add that he maintained good relations with Jews, among them Joseph Attias; see my "Vico, el Humanismo Religioso y la Tradición Sefardita," *Cuadernos sobre Vico* 7 (1997), pp. 255–263. For a more recent discussion, see the learned study of Leonardo Amoroso, "Vico e l'antichissima sapienza degli Ebrei," in ed. Giovanni Matteucci, *Studi sul "De antiquissima Italorum sapientia di Vico"* (Bologna: Quodlibet, 2002), pp. 101–113.

32. See "Repressive Tolerance," p. 113; and *In the Shadow of History*, pp. 189–190.

sacrifice had really taken place in Mecca, and instead they wrote Mt. Moriah! (see *Koran* 2:70; 3:64; 5:16, 45; 6:91, etc.).[33]

The foes of Israel are not a specific nation or people. What was particularly obnoxious about 'Amaleq, Israel's arch-nemesis, was "its memory" (זכר) – the notion of military nobility and martial supremacy underlying their political ideology (cf. Num. 24:20). Jews are to "remember" (Deut. 25:17) – that is, to archive in their National Memory – what 'Amaleq did (Ex. 17:14) and never "forget" (Deut. 25:19). Israel's objective is "to extinguish the memory" (זכר) of 'Amaleq (Deut. 25:19; cf. Ex. 17:14) – the militaristic ideology which they introduced, not their biological descent! Israel achieves this goal by "remembering" (Deut. 25:17) and passing this commitment on "from generation to generation" (Ex. 17:16; see appendix 25).

To succeed, Israel had to make a strategic decision: choosing the Book rather than the Sword. Were Jews to falter, not only would they cease to function as an autonomous political entity, but they would fall prey to the sword. Israel's enemies, past and present, knew this, too. The rabbis taught:

A Book and a Sword that were wrapped together descended from Heaven.

[God] told them [Israel]:

– 'If you were to fulfill what is written in this [the Book] you would be saved from this [the Sword]. If not, you will be chastised by this [the Sword].'[34]

---

33. The best work on this basic doctrine in Islam continues to be the study of Ignazio di Matteo, "'Il Tahrif' ad alterazione della Biblia secondo I musulmani," *Bessarione* 38 (1922), pp. 64–111.

34. *Sifre* #40, p. 84 cf. ibid., p. 83; see 'Aboda Zara 17b and *Sifre* #323, p. 372.

# Chapter 38
# The Matrix of Jewish Memory

The most important event in Jewish memory is the Exodus. Throughout the Scripture, liturgy and rabbinic literature, Jews are continuously exhorted to "remember the Exodus from Egypt." The matrix of Israel's memory, from within which all national experience developed, is the Theophany at Sinai. Borrowing from Song of Songs (8:2), the rabbis referred to Sinai as "my mother's house," because, they explained, "it was there where Israel was gestated, as a newborn baby."[35] Certain facts rendered the Sinai experience a unique phenomenon in the annals of man. Accounts of people speaking to, or having been spoken to, by supernatural beings, are fairly common. Sinai is the only case where God addressed an entire nation. The words that Israel heard at Sinai are not some disjointed, incoherent gibberish to be duly explicated post-mortem. The Decalogue is the basis of all civilized societies. Indeed, with all the development gained through the cumulative knowledge of past and modern civilizations, there is yet to be a set of norms promulgated which is superior to, let alone independent of, what Israel first heard at Sinai (see above chapter 33).

To compensate for their insecurity, crowds in a state of neurosis try frantically to enlarge the circle of believers by psychological coercion and brutal force. This was never Israel's manner. More significantly, myths unfold outside the realm of space-time. Mind-harboring mythological structures and ontologies cannot recognize a

35. Shir ha-Shirim Rabba VIII, 1 (2), 39b.

space-time frame of reference. In such a mental disposition, neither the precise date of the alleged event nor the locale is recorded – let alone the interjection of these two dimensions. Invariably, the units of information it provides lack a time-space context. The Theophany at Sinai is the first event in recorded history unfolding in a particular time-space context. As per record, it took place *at* Mount Sinai, situated in the Sinai Desert (see Ex. 19:1), *exactly fifty days after the Exodus* (see Ex. 19:16. The said date was computed according to the Calendar instituted by Moses and Aaron, two weeks *before* the Exodus (see Ex. 12:1–2).[36]

The Theophany at Sinai is the crucible forging the collective memory of Israel, the inner guts of the people, and their behavioral patterns and mental representations. No event could match an experience whereby every member of the group has apprehended God's voice speaking directly to her/him. In Jewish tradition, the Theophany at Sinai is variously portrayed in sublime terms,[37] as the symbolic wedding between God and Israel,[38] or death and resurrection of the

36. See *Homo Mysticus*, pp. 142–146. This concern explains why Prophet Ezekiel's vision in Ezek. chapter 1 – standing for the highest form of Hebrew mystical experience – carefully registered the date (vv. 1–2), and place (vv. 1, 3. Cf. ibid. 8:1; 20:1; 24:1; etc.). By way of contrast, Scriptures of other 'monotheistic religions' did not care to register the *date* and *place* of the events marking the foundations of their faith.

37. See Deut. 33:2–5; Judges 5:2–5; Ps. 68. Cf. *Sifre* #343, pp. 394–400, and editor's notes ad loc.

38. The prophets refer to Israel as the symbolic wife of God, and her unfaithfulness as adultery; see Hos. 1–4; Is. 50:1ff; 54:1ff; Jer. 2:2ff; Ezek. 16–17, etc., etc. The rabbis saw the Theophany at Sinai as the symbolic wedding between Israel and God; see Mishna Ta'aniyot 4:8; Y. Ta'aniyot IV, 9, 69c; cf. Debarim Rabba II, 25, 7d; XII, 8, 4 II, 25, 7d; XII, 8, 48d; Shir ha-Shirim Rabba III, 2, 22d; etc. It is also alluded to in a poem by Moshe b. Asher (9th century), cited by Paul Kahle, *The Cairo Geniza* (Oxford: Basil Blackwell, 1959), p. 84 l. 11. In the Sephardic Synagogue it is customary to recite on the holiday of *Shabu'ot* a poem by R. Israel Najara where the Tora is compared to a metaphoric *Ketuba* at the symbolic wedding of God and Israel. There is another poem by R. David Pardo, in Hebrew and Ladino, "La Ketuba de la Ley," developing the same theme. The central theme is the Theophany at Sinai, as the symbolic wedding between God

people,[39] conveying the idea of palingenesis, where every Israelite perishes and comes to life as a new creature.[40] Medieval authorities regarded Sinai as the matrix of Jewish collective consciousness, from which the intuitive principles of Israel and its religious ontology derive. The most fundamental principles of Israel, such as prophecy and the idea of God as encoded in the Tetragrammaton, are intuitively known because of the Sinai experience. Fundamentally, faith in Moses and the Tora derives from the experience shared at Sinai. In the words of Maimonides:

> Israel's faith in Moses is not predicated on the miracles that he made, since one who believes in miracles cannot be sure that the miracle was not the effect of deception and magic. The miracles which Moses made in the Desert, however, were made because there was a necessity [e.g. crossing the Red Sea, quenching thirst, hunger, etc.] – not to validate his prophecy… What was then the basis for believing in him? The Theophany at Sinai! Because our own eyes witnessed – and not a stranger; and our ears heard – and not someone else: the fire, the voices, the lightning! As he approached the dense fog and the voice spoke to him, and we heard: 'Moses! Moses! Go, and say to them this and that!'… How is it known that only the Theophany at Sinai constitutes evidence that his prophecy is true, without a shade of doubt? Because it is written: "Behold I will come unto you in the thickness of the cloud. In order that the people shall hear as I speak to you, and thereby they

---

and Israel. The Tora stands for the *Ketuba*, or 'marriage contract,' regulating the conduct between the 'groom' (God) and the 'bride' (Israel). On this theme, see Isaac Cardoso, *Las Excelencias de los Hebreos* (Amsterdam, 1679), p. 5.

39. Shabbat 88b, cf. Ḥagiga 12b; *Midrash Tehillim*, LXVIII, 5, p. 159. For the correct meaning of the often cited, but in no way understood, passage in Shabbat 89a, where God is said to have "lifted Sinai" over the Jewish people, see "Maimonides' Starting Precept," pp. 296–297 n. 60.

40. See *Homo Mysticus*, pp. 137–142; 147–155.

> will believe in you forever" (Ex. 19:9). It follows, that the faith which they previously had in him was not a faith that could stand forever, but rather a faith which allowed for reservation and afterthought.[41]

Perceiving God's voice and hearing His Law left an everlasting impression on the collective consciousness of Israel. It served as the ultimate context of Israel's National Memory. Prior to Sinai there was no National Memory. Knowledge of Israel's pre-Sinaitic past and its formulation, too, is *post*-Sinaitic.[42] Future historical events and cultural developments are to be duly evaluated and processed into the collective consciousness of the people in the light of Sinai. Forging a National Memory is of little value unless the people are made conscious of the menace of national amnesia. The Jewish people were first, not only in forging their National Memory, but also in realizing the perils menacing a society detaching its present from its past. A nation privy to the solemn voice of God is duty-bound to transmit it to future generations, not in a haphazard, sporadic manner, but as a national responsibility, that is, as a *Morasha*.[43]

Before crossing into the Promised Land, Moses repeated the Decalogue, adding: "Be vigilant! Guard carefully your soul all the days of your life, lest you forget the things that your eyes have seen, lest they be removed from your heart." Cognizant that without a proper recording system and transmission, the memory and mental representations accrued at Sinai would dissipate, he further added: "Teach them to your children and children's children" (Deut. 4:9; cf. 6:12). Shortly before his death, when concluding the national covenant at Moab (see above chapter 5), Moses included the following article:

41. *MT Yesode ha-Tora* 8:1. Cf. *Conciliator*, Part I, pp. 303–304.
42. See *Homo Mysticus*, pp. 146–147; cf. Ḥolin 101b.
43. This is one of the reasons why European revolutions failed miserably, despite their noble ideals, whereas the ideals of the American Revolution continue to flourish within and outside the USA. See above chapters 12 and 28.

> Not with you alone am I contracting this covenant and this oath. But with whomever is present today before God our Lord and with whomever is not present with us today (Deut. 29:13–14; cf. Josh. 8:35).

Inclusion of future generations into the covenant implies the sacred duty of conveying the specifics to the next generation.[44] It is a national responsibility to be implemented both individually and collectively by Israel (see Deut. 4:9; 6:7; 7:21). Failing to transmit the norms and intuitive principles derived from Sinai is one and the same as "forgetting" God (see Deut. 8:11). A crisis of memory will inevitably lead to apostasy and national perdition (see Deut. 8:19). Thus, the storage, development and transmission of Israel's *Morasha* is the most sacred duty of the people. Sometime before the destruction of the Second Temple a blessing was instituted containing something analogous to our pledge of allegiance. It is to be recited daily after the morning *Shema'* – the most solemn of Jewish prayers – ascertaining the unity of God, the authority of the Law, and the experience of the Exodus. The pledge begins as follows:

> It is true! And permanent, and precise, and valid, and rightful, and trustworthy, and beloved, and endearing, and delightful, and pleasing, and awesome, and correct, and acceptable, and good, and beautiful! It is binding upon us! Forever!
>
> True! O Eternal God, our King! The Rock of Jacob and Shield of our savior! From generation unto generation, He is trustworthy, His name is trustworthy, His throne is permanent, and His kingdom and faithfulness are upright forever! His words are alive and compelling and dependable and delightful, forever and ever! [It was] *upon our fathers,* [and it is] *upon us,* [and it shall be] *upon our children*: *upon our generation and*

44. In his translation of Deut. 29:14, Se'adya added: "If [duly] transmitted to him." cf. *Sifre* #335, p. 385.

> *upon all the generations of the seed of Israel your servant!* (cf. Deut. 29:28) The earliest [duties] and the latter [duties, we acknowledge]. It is good and compelling: in truth and in faith, O God, God of our fathers! Our King! King of our fathers! Our Savior, Savior of our fathers! Our Creator, Author of our salvation! Our Redeemer and our Rescuer – from everlasting that was Your Name! We have no other God besides you! Selah![45]

The words in italics above express the solemn responsibility of reception/transmission from the former (*upon our fathers*) to ourselves (*upon us*) and from us to the next generation in perpetuity (*upon our children, upon our generation and upon all the generations of the seed of Israel your servant!*). Without such a mechanism neither the conceptual structures of a National Memory, nor the cultural constraints it contains, can function adequately (see appendix 12).

The central role of education in Jewish tradition is now clear. Although witnessing God's voice and His Law left an indelible impression on the collective consciousness of Israel, it required, nonetheless, continuous nourishment and development. It is the commitment to transmit the Sinai experience, translated in both cultural and social learning, which will make it endure forever. Within this context, it would be well to remember that the first public education system was established in Israel by the High Priest Joshua ben Gamla (died ca. 67).[46] Concerning the place of education in Israel, one of his contemporaries wrote:

> Above all we pride ourselves on the education of our children, and regard as the most essential task in life the observance of

45. At Moroccan Synagogues, this blessing is sung with a special melody. "The earliest" duties allude to the duties instituted in the Tora, whereas "the later" ones refer to those duties established afterwards by the legislative and judicial authorities of Israel; see Shebu'ot 39a and Tosefta, Soṭa 7:6, p. 192.
46. See Baba Batra 21a.

> our laws and of the pious practices, based thereupon, which we have inherited.[47]

Dedication to the cultivation and transmission of socially inherited structures gave definition and psychic unity to the Jewish persona. The primary goal of instruction was legal fluency. In this aspect the average Jew differs from other citizens,

> ... should anyone of our nation be questioned about the laws, he would repeat them all more readily than his own name. The result, then, of our thorough grounding in the laws from the first dawn of intelligence is that we have them, as it were, graven on our souls. A transgressor is a rarity; evasion of punishment by excuses an impossibility.[48]

The end result was a law-abiding society, essentially and fundamentally:

> Nowadays, indeed, violation of the laws has with most nations become a fine art. Not so with us. Robbed though we be of wealth, of cities, of all good things, our Law at least remains immortal; and there is not a Jew so distant from his country, so much in awe of a cruel despot, but has more fear of the Law than him.[49]

Moses succeeded where philosophers failed because they "addressed their philosophy to the few," whereas Moses made "practice square with precept."[50] We must consider another difference. For a Greek, his nation's writings and past records "are mere stories improvised

---

47. *Against Apion*, I, 60, *Josephus*, vol. 1, p. 187; cf. 74, p. 193.
48. *Against Apion*, II, 178, *Josephus*, vol. 1, p. 365.
49. *Against Apion*, II, 276, *Josephus*, vol. 1, p. 403.
50. *Against Apion*, II, 169–170, *Josephus*, vol. 1, p. 361.

according to the fancy of their authors."[51] For the Hebrews the Law represents the cultural foundations of the mind and the values that categorize Jewish personhood. For that reason, faith in the Law cannot be grounded on miracles. The impact of a miracle is short-lived and not free from doubt and reservation.[52] It is on this fundamental issue that Judaism is at variance, totally and fundamentally, with other monotheistic religions. Only when in a state of mental freedom can someone truly believe (or not believe). A faith that demands you to place your trust in a person or a Church, is in fact a faith that demands the faithful to surrender his mind and heart, and to think and feel vicariously through someone else. In such a context, 'faith' is nothing more than acquiescence to some sort of imperial *might*. Theologians speaking on behalf of a 'monotheistic faith' fail to understand that unless the people actually believe in the 'One and Supreme God' on *their own*, the performance of an alleged 'miracle' could not help them determine whether that person was in fact speaking in the name of the 'One and Supreme God.'[53] This is why first Israel "believed in God *and*" – in the Hebrew sense of

51. *Against Apion*, I, 44, *Josephus*, vol. 1, p. 181.
52. See *The Conciliator*, Part I, pp. 303–304.
53. Moses' first task was to *instruct* the people as to the meaning of this 'One and Supreme God,' *independently* of his mission; see Ex. 3:13–18; 4:29–31, and *The Conciliator*, Part I, p. 104. Later, at the crossing of the Red Sea, the people attributed the splitting of the waters to the God that *they* had previously known in the bosom of their own homes. Singing in unison, *they* declared: "This is my God, and I shall exalt Him, the Lord of my father, and I shall glorify Him" (Ex. 15:2). Conversely, imagine an international corporation wishing to negotiate with people in a remote corner of the world, about securing the rights for some of their natural resources. Let us suppose that to obtain their consent the corporation's agent performed some 'miraculous' feat and thereupon the village's elders concluded a contract with said corporation. I propose that since they did not have the slightest clue as to what a 'corporation' is all about, that there was no 'meeting of the minds.' Consequently, that their 'assent' would be deemed worthless and said contract would be dismissed in a court of law. The same procedure would follow with pagans accepting the authority of the God of the Hebrew Scripture because of an alleged miracle. Since they are

'then'– "in his servant Moses" (Ex. 14:31), not the other way around! Faith in Moses is not the effect of 'trust' (which is another term for dogma).[54] Rather, it is grounded on the collective experience gained at Sinai. "As a consequence of the Theophany at Sinai, all of Israel witnessed him (speaking to God), therefore he (Moses) was not required to perform a miracle" to prove to them his credentials.[55] Epistemologically, the human mind does not recognize a higher form of certainty than that which it derives from a collective input in which every individual hears the voice of God, jointly with his brothers and sisters and sons and daughters and fathers and mothers and uncles and aunts and neighbors and friends.

> Accordingly, if there should arise a prophet who would make great miracles and wonders, and would wish to cancel out Moses' prophecy, he is not to be listened to! We should know with certainty that the alleged miracles were made with deception and magic. Because Moses' prophecy was not authenticated by miracles, so that we should be required to match up his miracles to that [alleged] miracle, but because of what we have witnessed (the Theophany) with our own eyes, and what we have heard (the Theophany) with our own ears, the same that he [Moses] heard. To what may this be compared? To witnesses coming up to a man and telling him that what he had observed with his own eyes is not as he had observed. He would not pay attention to them, and he would certainly know that they are false witnesses.[56]

---

clueless as to what this 'God' is, there is no meeting of the minds, and their 'assent' is meaningless. To have merits, they would have to be first instructed in the meaning of said 'God,' exactly as Moses did with the children of Israel.

54. *Credo qua absurdum est* is in itself an absurdity and nothing more than an oxymoron; cf. *Sefer ha-'Iqqarim* I, 18.

55. *MT Yesode ha-Tora* 8:2.

56. *MT Yesode ha-Tora* 8:3.

The overwhelming sense gained from the collective experience of having perceived and categorized God's words was engraved on the Jewish psyche. In this manner every Jew acquired a personal knowledge that Moses was indeed *God*'s faithful messenger. Maimonides explained:

> It is a matter made clear and explicit in the Tora, that it is a precept binding for all eternity. It admits neither change, nor abrogation, nor addition… Therefore, if someone, either from among the nations or from Israel, were to arise and make a miracle, and claim that God had sent him to either add or abrogate a precept, or that he would want to interpret a precept in a manner that we had not heard from Moses, or if he were to claim that the precepts that were ordered to Israel are not binding for all time, but said precepts are only temporary, he is a false prophet since he is invalidating Moses' prophecy.[57]

This may explain the failure of 'clever arguments and theology' with those who witnessed Sinai – even when buttressed by Christian love and the Inquisition's fire.

The memory of Sinai is the matrix of Jewish collective consciousness. Consequently, quoting Josephus, the words of the Law are indelibly "engraved on our souls."[58] Similarly, on the basis of rabbinic sources, medieval authorities regarded the Theophany at Sinai as a kind of ontogenetic intuition, continuously activated by Tora learning and practices. They concluded, therefore, that whoever lacks this faith could not possibly be a descendant of those who had stood at Sinai.[59]

> God had already guaranteed us – and a worthy guarantor He is! – and informed us, that everyone present during the Theophany at Sinai, they as well as their children until the

57. *MT Yesode ha-Tora* 9:1.
58. *Against Apion*, II, 178, *Josephus*, vol. 1, p. 365.
59. See "Maimonides' Starting Precept," pp. 291–296.

> end of time, shall have faith in Moses our teacher, and all that he said. As it is written, "Behold I will come unto you in the thickness of the cloud; that the people shall hear as I speak to you, and thereby they will have faith in you forever" (Ex. 19:9). Thus, let it be known, that whoever reneges on the Law given at that awesome Theophany is not a descendant of that people. As our rabbis taught concerning someone entertaining doubts about Moses: "his ancestors had never stood at Mount Sinai."[60]

Sinai is the spring from whence flow the traditions and intuitions that have been the earmark of Jewish society throughout the ages. It should not be surprising, therefore, to learn that in the last epistle written by Maimonides, he penned these lines:

> Remember the Theophany at Sinai, which God urged us to recall continuously, and warned us not to forget. He charged us to make it known to our children, so that they would be nurtured with this knowledge. God said: "Be vigilant! Guard carefully your soul all the days of your life, lest you forget the things that your eyes have seen, lest they would be removed from your heart. Teach them to your children and children's children" (Deut. 4:9; cf. 6:12). Brethren! It is worthy of you to nurture your children with reflection about this awesome vision. Recount its significance and glory in every gathering! Since in effect, it constitutes the axis of the Law and the argument leading to the truth.[61]

60. *Iggeret Teman*, p. 61.
61. *Iggeret Teman*, p. 29.

# Chapter 39
# Walking Under the Fox's Shadow

Jews kept national records since their early beginnings. Shortly after crossing the Red Sea, and before the Theophany at Sinai, Israel was instructed to keep in its national archives a memorandum of the war with 'Amaleq (Ex. 17:14, see appendix 25). We are apprised as to the national documentations in King Solomon's archives (I Kings 11:41), in those of the kings of Northern Israel (I Kings 14:19; 16:5, 14, 20, 27; 22:39; II Kings 1:18; 10:34; 13:8, 12; 14:15, 28; 15:11, 31; II Chr. 27:7; 36:8), and in those of the kings of Judea (I Kings 14:29; 15:7, 23; 22:46; II Kings 8:23; 15:36; 20:20; 21:17, 25; 24:5; II Kings 12:20; 14:18; 15:6; II Chr. 28:26). Also, there were records of documents deposited in the archives of both the kingdoms of Israel and Judea (I Chr. 9:1; II Chr. 25:26; 32:32; 35:27; 36:8). The Levites had their own private archive (Neh. 12:23; cf. 7:5).[62] *Targum* to Deut. 33:21 (and to Song. 1:2, as well as Soṭa 13b,) designates

62. See *Against Apion*, I, 35, *Josephus*, vol. I, p. 177. Concerning the term *midrash* in II Chr. 13:22, according to Radaq ad loc., it refers to a book; cf. idem on II Chr. 24:27; and R. Jonah ibn Jannaḥ, *Sefer ha-Shorashim*, p. 114. R. Solomon ben Melekh, *Mikhlal Yofi* (Amsterdam, 5445/1685), on II Chr. 24:27, 217b, gives a similar interpretation. However, on II Chr. 13:22, 215b, he explains the term to refer to the private 'study' where prophets deposited their records for public consultation. For a discussion of this term, see I. Heinman, *Encyclopaedia Biblica* (Heb.), vol. 4, cols. 695–696. In my opinion, *midrash* is a text that was not published, and was only available for private consultation, exactly as in later rabbinic tradition.

Moses "the great scribe (ספרא) of Israel" – a title implying not only the popular meaning of 'scribe,' but, as per Jewish tradition, that of 'archivist.' As can be learned from the Aramaic translation to the Scripture, at an earlier period of Jewish history the head archivist was also designated with the title *nabi*, 'prophet' (see appendix 26). In some instances, the Scripture preserved the name of the 'prophet' under whose charge these documents were redacted (see I Chr. 29:29; II Chr. 9:29; 12:15; 20:34; 26:22; 32:32; 33:19), a fact mentioned by Josephus. Hence the quality and reliability of Jewish records.

> But that our forefathers took no less, not to say even greater, care than the nations I have mentioned in the keeping of their records – a task which they assigned to their chief priests and prophets – and that down to our times these records have been, and I may venture to say so, will continue to be, preserved with scrupulous accuracy.[63]

Jewish authorities knew of documentation pertaining to Israel in foreign chancelleries (see Est. 6:1; 10:2).[64] Modern research has shown

---

63. *Against Apion*, I, 29, *Josephus*, vol. I, p. 175. See ibid., p. 174 where the editor noted that Théodore Reinach (1860–1928) thought that Josephus was wrong. In fact, neither Reinach nor the editor was aware of the passages in Chronicles cited above. It is high time to point out that Reinach's scholarship, as that of his brother Solomon (1858–1932), has been grossly exaggerated. Comically, they referred to themselves as *nous Gaulois*, prompting the French public to burst into laughter since everybody knew that their family came from Germany. Among the French intelligentsia, they were referred as *les savants Juifs* – the adjective '*Juif*' was intended as a pejorative to counter their pretense. In general, they promoted the kind of 'Jewish' scholarship designated to please their French masters by discrediting Jewish values and tradition. Their methodology still thrives in some intellectual circles in Israel and abroad where 'scholarship' is a code-name for ideas that might profit anti-Jews and anti-Judaism bigots. See A.S. Yahuda, *The Accuracy of the Bible*, p. 116. About Solomon, see A. S. Yahuda, *'Eber ve-'Arab* (New York: Ha-Histadrut ha-'Ibrit be-Ameriqa, 1946), p. 100 n. 43.
64. See the very important note in *Against Apion*, I, 154–165, *Josephus*, vol. I, pp.

the information dependable and punctilious.[65] In many cases, the inconsistencies found by modern historians are more indicative of their unfamiliarity with archival procedures than actual contradictions. The following example illustrates our point. In rabbinic tradition, and in accordance with the authoritative copies of the Talmud at the Academy in Lucena, Spain, R. David ibn Daud (12th century) recorded that the First Temple lasted 410 years, although in fact it was destroyed 23 years later. This appeared to historians as a "glaring contradiction."[66] In fact, all that this shows is the historians' unfamiliarity with the registry of public records and archival procedures that were current in Israel and in rabbinic tradition. A national 'date' is not simply the day and month on which an alleged event occurred, but the time in which said event was duly registered by the officer in charge. Therefore, as ibn Daud pointed out, since the government of Israel ceased to function in the year 410, at that time, too, the Temple ceased to exist, not in fact, but in chronology.

> The Temple was built in the year 2929. The Destruction of the Temple was 433 years (later). However, it was chronologically reckoned 410 (מנו) since from the start of the exile of (King) Jehoyakim it could no longer be regarded as a government.[67]

Jewish records were far superior to those of the Greeks on two accounts. First, it was "the original neglect of the Greeks to keep official records of current events." This was true not only of minor Greek states but, "Even among the Athenians… we find that nothing of the kind existed."[68] Second, Greek historians "were concerned

225–229.

65. See above Section III, n. 145.
66. R. Abraham ibn Daud, *Sefer ha-Qabbala,* ed. trans. and annotated by Gerson D. Cohen (Philadelphia, The Jewish Publication Society, 1967), p. 6 (ll. 20–23). For the rabbinic sources, see ed. note ad loc. and his comments, pp. 108, 192–197.
67. *Sefer ha-Qabbala* (Heb.), p. 3 (ll. 10–11), our translation.
68. *Against Apion,* I, 20–21, *Josephus,* vol. I, p. 171.

not so much to discover the truth as to display their literary ability."[69] Hence, the contradictions and indifference to method and detail plaguing Greek historical accounts.[70] By contrast, Jews kept official records since early antiquity, "and that to our own times these records have been, and if I may venture to say so, will continue to be, preserved with scrupulous accuracy."[71] An additional fact meriting special consideration: Jewish veneration for the sacred text is unparalleled in other nations.

> For, although such long ages have now passed, no one has ventured either to add, or to remove, or to alter a syllable; and it is an instinct with every Jew, from the day of his birth, to regard them as the decrees of God, to abide by them, and, if need be, cheerfully to die for them. Time and again ere now the sight has been witnessed of prisoners enduring tortures and death in every form in the theaters, rather than to utter a single word against the laws and the allied documents.
>
> What Greek would endure as much for the same cause? Even to save the entire collection of his nation's writings from destruction he would not face the smallest personal injury. For the Greeks they are mere stories improvised according to the fancy of their authors; and in this estimate even of the older historians they are quite justified, when they see some of their own contemporaries venturing to describe events in which they bore no part, without taking the trouble to seek information from those who know the facts.[72]

Such a situation could not be tolerated, not by Imperial Rome or any totalitarian regime! On the 9th of Ab 68 C.E. during the attack against the Temple of Jerusalem, Titus "gave his troops permission to burn

69. *Against Apion*, I, 24, *Josephus*, vol. I, p. 172.
70. See *Against Apion*, I, 1–27, *Josephus*, vol. I, pp. 163–173.
71. *Against Apion*, I, 29, *Josephus*, vol. I, p. 175. See appendix 26.
72. *Against Apion*, I, 44–45, *Josephus*, vol. I, p. 181. E.g. Herodotus, cf. ibid. 74, p. 193.

and sack the city. For that day they refrained; but on the next they set fire to the Archives" and other places containing Israel's national documentation and records.[73] The motivation for the destruction of the Temple was not strictly military, but was part of the ongoing psychological warfare against the *memory* of Israel. An important consideration was the obliteration of Jewish judicial autonomy. Let us remember that the seat of the Sanhedrin, or 'Supreme Court,' was at the Temple.[74] True, as a result of Roman occupation, the Sanhedrin had either lost or abdicated the right to adjudicate on political and criminal matters, especially when involving capital punishment. Nonetheless, it still was a formidable organization, commanding enormous authority throughout the Diaspora. The destruction of the Temple and national archives was intended to give a mortal blow to the Sanhedrin.

The judicial vacuum was filled by the surviving sages. A new judicial organization, the *Bet Din ha-Gadol* ('Supreme Court of Justice'), was established at Yabne (ca. 68 C.E.).[75] Deprived of government support and under the crushing weight of occupation, the *Bet Din ha-Gadol* used its office with extreme care and wisdom. An important organ of the Supreme Court was the *Yeshiba* (pl. *Yeshibot*, 'seating' from the root YShB 'to seat'), usually translated as 'academy' but actually meaning 'plenary session' (or 'sessions,' as in English law; see appendix 27). The presiding officer was the 'Prince' (*Nasi*) of the Jewish people.[76] It was a unique institution, with no paral-

73. Josephus, *Jewish Wars*, VI, 354, *Josephus*, vol. 3, p. 479. These were the annals containing the sacred documentation and books of Israel. The archives containing business and government documentation were burnt by the Jews several years before, see ibid., note a.
74. For an historical survey, see Hugo Mantel, *Studies in the History of the Sanhedrin* (Cambridge, Mass.: Harvard University Press, 1961), chapter 2.
75. See Tosefta Sanhedrin VIII: 1, p. 427. On the historical background, see *Judaism*, vol. 1, pp. 83–92; *Studies in the History of the Sanhedrin*, index; Jacob Neusner, *A Life of Rabban Yohanan ben Zakkai* (Leiden: E. J. Brill, 1962).
76. See Horayot 13b; *Sefer ha-Miṣvot*, negative precept #316, p. 326; *MT Sanhedrin* 1:3. For an historical analysis of this title, see *Studies in the History of the Sanhedrin*,

lels in either Greek or Roman educational tradition. It was first established by the Supreme Court at Yabne. These sessions were conducted in the presence of the general public.[77] Not only were actual cases adjudicated, but also theoretical controversies, as well as questions presented by the public.[78] The model for the *Yeshiba* was the *Ohel Mo'ed* (Tent of Assembly) in the Desert where the Law was formally promulgated (see appendix 28). The *Yeshiba* was a *national* institution representing the *official* views, doctrines, and traditions of Israel. Since the national records had been destroyed, one of the tasks of the *Bet Din ha-Gadol* in conjunction with the *Yeshiba* was collecting, authenticating and cataloguing the tradition lingering in the minds and hearts of the sages. It was a highly complex and arduous task. Let us consider, for the sake of illustration, the matter concerning the volume of improperly drawn water (מים שאובים) that would invalidate a ritual-pool (מקוה). There were several traditions, two of which had been previously reported by two of the most distinguished members of the Sanhedrin, Shammai (ca. 50 B.C.E.–ca. 30 C.E.) and Hillel (end of 1st century B.C.E.–beginning of 1st century C.E.). After what must have been a grueling and time-consuming investigation, the Court decided to accept the testimony of two "weavers," members of a very humble profession, living in what must have been the poorest section of town (שער

---

chapters 1 and 5, and Index *passim*.

77. See Horayot 13b; Tosefta Sanhedrin VII, 8–9, p. 426; Tosefta Soṭa VII, 9, pp. 193–194 and parallels.

78. See Berakhot 27b-28a, the parallel in Yerushalmi Berakhot IV, 1, 7a, and the eminent analysis by Louis Ginzberg, *A Commentary to the Palestinian Talmud*, (Heb.), vol. 4 (New York: The Jewish Theological Seminary of America, 1941), pp. 174–220. The questions were conducted according to strict procedure; see Tosefta Sanhedrin VII, 7, p. 426; and *MT Talmud Tora* 4:7–8. A scholar by the name of Felimo presented an actual case (מעשה, cf. Tosefta ibid.) for deliberation. Erroneously, R. Judah the Prince thought that he had presented a hypothetical case and not a מעשה (cf. Nidda 26b). Therefore, he censured him for breaking with protocol; see Menaḥot 37a. This is the reason why Maimonides did not include this case in the laws of 'excommunication' (חרם), cf. *Kesef Mishne, Talmud Tora*, 6:14 at the end.

האשפות, Mishna 'Eduyot 1:3). In this fashion, the Supreme Court endeavored to collect and authenticate the legal traditions and doctrines accumulated since the Theophany at Sinai.[79]

The heart and brain behind this project was R. 'Aqiba (50–135). Anticipating Roman intentions (see below), R. 'Aqiba and his school went forth all over Israel to collect and classify the living traditions and doctrines circulating among different schools and scholars. Before long, Rome was ready to carry out the second phase of its onslaught against Israel. Romans understood the value of 'memory' and that whoever controls the memory of a people controls their future. Soon they realized that in the case of Israel the actual archives containing the National Memory were the sages and teachers of Tora. Therefore, as long as they remained alive, Jewish memory would thrive. In line with their famous pragmatism, Roman authorities concluded that the most effective way to vacate Israel's memory was by butchering the sages together with their families, and destroying the seats of learning. To justify such an operation, they passed a series of anti-Jewish measures designed to provoke rebellion. The Talmud reports a story to illustrate the problem. The place is Judea, the year 135. The story consists of three parts (סוגיה משולשת), each containing two points to be detected by the attentive reader. The first part introduces the characters, R. 'Aqiba and Pappus ben Judah (1st and 2nd centuries, see appendix 29). Prefiguring the 'enlightened' Jew, the Greek name 'Pappus' suggests assimilation, whereas 'Judah' serves to identify his Jewish roots. The packaging is suggestive of those wishing to appear Jewish to Jews (cf. I Cor. 9:20) and 'enlightened' to the ruling authorities (cf. Acts 22:25–29). At the time of our story, the Romans had prohibited the study of Tora. R. 'Aqiba disregarded this injunction, and organized mass rallies where he alone studied Tora in their presence. (In this fashion, he was sheltering the Jewish public from

79. The principal laws collected during that period are contained in Mishna and Tosefta 'Eduyot. For an overview and general analysis of these sources, see J. N. Epstein, *Prolegomena* (Heb.), ed. E. Z. Melamed (Jerusalem: Magnes Press, 1957), pp. 424–444.

Roman retaliation, while showing defiance to the Roman authorities). In the role of 'enlightened' Jew, Pappus came to the rally to confront R. 'Aqiba. To taunt him, he addressed him as plain 'Aqiba, without the title 'rabbi.'

> "Aren't you scared of the authorities?" he asked him. By evoking dread, Pappus was introducing the most powerful tool of totalitarian regimes: intimidation and the manipulation of fear.
>
> "I shall illustrate [our case] with a parable," he answered. "A fox was walking by a riverbed, and saw a school of fish running amok from place to place. He asked them: From what are you trying to escape?"
>
> They answered: "Fishermen are casting nets over us!"
>
> "Would you like to come up to the shore," asked the fox, "and you and I will live together, just like my ancestors lived together with your ancestors?"
>
> "Do you deem yourself the craftiest of all animals?" replied the fish. "Well, to us, you are not (= your argument is not) crafty but rather dumb! If when dwelling in our life-habitat we are in fear, how much more frightened we shall be if we were to move to our death-habitat! The same applies to us. If when studying Tora about which is written, 'That is your life and the length of your days' (Deut. 30:20), we are in peril, how much more in peril we would be if we were to abandon it!?"

For our purpose, two points of the metaphor are particularly valuable. First, Imperial Rome is depicted as a fox, the symbol of shrewdness, rather than wisdom. Roman might (as the might of all forms of tyranny) hinged on the ability to launch psychological warfare. For this purpose, 'collective memory' is a 'social construction' promoted for profane purposes. A frequent tactic of the aggressor is to dumbfound the prey by constructing a past where fox and fish lived in idyllic harmony: history and historians are tools designed to promote national policy. It is by 'restaging' memory and manipulating it for political purposes that Rome dominates the vanquished.[80] Second, *Pax Romana* is not gratis (see chapter 34). The fish is required to forfeit its ethos and learn to walk on dry land, under the fox's shadow.

The second part has to do with R. 'Aqiba's imprisonment and martyrdom. Having no more use of Pappus, the Roman authorities turned against him and condemned him to death. The two met again, this time under significantly different circumstances. Surprised to see Pappus, R. 'Aqiba asked:

"Pappus! What brings you here?"

> He replied: "Fortunate are you, R. 'Aqiba, who was apprehended (for teaching) the words of the Tora. Woe unto Pappus who was apprehended for some absurdity!"

The Romans had concocted some trumped-up charge against Pappus and were getting rid of him. Let us pay attention to the following two points. One has to do with the manner in which totalitarian regimes dispose of quislings. Second, the 'enlightened' Jew ready to deal with Roman 'reality,' turns into a humane, reflective individual. He now addresses R. 'Aqiba with the title 'rabbi' and recognizes his own folly.[81]

The story ends with the martyrdom of R. 'Aqiba. At the time,

80. Hence the bullying-savants, poets, and historians at the service of the state, and the remuneration they receive for their service. For a comprehensive study of a local community defending its own memory against the official version of the state, see Ana María Alonso, "The Effects of Truth: Re-Presentations of the Past and the Imagining of Community," *Journal of Historical Sociology* 1 (1988), pp. 33–57.
81. The legend that Jesus converted a criminal impaled on a cross next to him was inspired by what had actually taken place with Pappus and R. 'Aqiba. Significantly, there is no story that Jesus persuaded any of his tormentors to join him on the cross, as with R. Ḥananya b. Teradyon; see 'Aboda Zara 18a and *In the Shadow of History*, p. 199.

he was eighty-five years old. The torture began in the early morning, at "the hour of the *Shema'*" – the prayer proclaiming that God is Israel's One and Only Sovereign. As the Romans were "lacerating his flesh with iron combs, he was acknowledging the sovereignty of the Heavens," i.e., he was reciting the *Shema'*. In astonishment his disciples asked:

> "Even here?"
> He replied: "All my life I was at pains because I had expounded the verse "(love God with all your heart and) all your life" (Deut. 6:5) to mean – 'even if He would be taking your life!' I said to myself: 'if it would come to that, I would fulfill it!' Now that it has come to me, shouldn't I fulfill it?"
> He then prolonged the (word) 'one' (אחד), until his soul departed (uttering the word) אחד.[82]

The first point that comes to mind is the responsibility of leadership. A leader, whether religious or otherwise, must ask himself in earnest whether he could personally perform what he is advocating to his followers. Second concerns the responsibility of martyrdom. It is a most solemn responsibility. A conscientious leader cannot allow his martyrdom to become an excuse for hatred and bloodshed. Rather than whine and complain (see Matt. 27:46: *Eli, Eli lama sabachthani,* the correct translation of which is: 'God, O God! Why have you *slaughtered* me?' –not as per the Authorized Version: "My God, my God! Why hast thou forsaken me?"), he should offer thanks to

82. Berakhot 61b. On the Jewish attitude towards political and intellectual bullies, see José Faur, "Of Cultural Intimidation and Other *Miscellanea*: Bar-Sheshakh *v.* Raba," *Review of Rabbinic Judaism* 5 (2002), pp. 34–50. The Berlin blockade and the 'Cuban' missile crisis during the Cold War, on the one hand, and the Berlin airlift and President Kennedy's response to this type of blackmail, on the other, come to mind. Free men and women will not allow bullies to intimidate them!

God for having given him the opportunity to 'sanctify His name,' as R. 'Aqiba did. In this fashion, his followers would be inspired to be kinder and more humane, rather than to pillage, rape, and murder in the name of 'love.'

# Chapter 40
# The Emergence of the Sword/Cross Axis

The monolinguistic mind conceives of its own linguistic and cultural apparatus as universal categories of human thought (see above chapter 2). There is only one truth, a single language capable of expressing it, and a unique form of government embodying human ideality: their own. By virtue of speaking a different language, aliens reflect inadequacy and abnormality. Monolinguistic truth is valid at all times and in all societies. The 'other' is not 'an' 'other,' but an inferior species exhibiting lesser standards of thought and culture.[83] The mission of Hellenism was to bring monolingualistic values and ideology to the barbarians – something akin to the 'white man's burden' in colonial times. There was a political dimension to this mission. Essential to despotic governments is the ability to dominate *without* consent. The principal task of a monolingualistic culture is to establish hierarchic structures that will assist the vanquished to surrender mind and soul to the victor. The task of art, literature, and philosophy is to promote the victor's superiority. Jews and Judaism interfered with this process.[84] From all the languages and cultures of the ancient world, Egyptian, Babylonian, and Persian, only Jewish culture and value continued to flourish. Humanity had to be saved

83. See *Golden Doves*, pp. 7–8, 23–37; and *In the Shadow of History*, pp. 4–7.
84. Cf. Shabbat 33b-34a and *Golden Doves*, pp. 144–145.

from this obscenity! As noted by the greatest of Roman historians, "King Antiochus endeavored to abolish Jewish superstition and introduce Greek civilization." However, "the war… prevented his improving this basest of all people."[85] It was high time to finish the job. The Theophany at Sinai resonating in the collective memory of Israel had to be silenced – we may add, for the advance of humanity. Granted, some 'errors' *may* have been made but, as all serious students of Tacitus know, the underlying principle upon which the historiography of the great master stands is that, 'One cannot expect the mighty to make an omelet without breaking some eggs.'

In totalitarian regimes, culture goes hand in hand with state policy. In the case of Imperial Rome, the purpose of civilization was to neutralize the 'other' without having to resort to physical extermination. This brings us to the second phase of the war against Israel. Warfare is easier to carry on when promising the victim something valuable. During the siege of Jerusalem, Vespasian negotiated with one of the principal Jewish leaders, R. Johanan b. Zakkai (1st century), to spare the sages and academies of learning.[86] It was designed to split Jewish public opinion, and allow Rome to deal with the sages at a later, more propitious time.[87] Vespasian never intended to honor the agreement. By the time of R. 'Aqiba, Roman authorities, in line with their famous pragmatism, concluded that the hour had come to remove Israel's frontal lobe. This could be accomplished effectively by butchering the sages and destroying the seats of learning. The privilege of performing such an operation fell upon no less an august figure than Emperor Hadrian (ruled 117–138), known for his devotion to Hellenistic culture. With this purpose in mind, he passed a series of anti-Jewish measures intended to provoke the Jews. Contrary to what historians pontificate, Bar Kokhba's 'uprising' (132–135) was schemed

85. Tacitus, *History*, V, 8, p. 662; cf. 13, p. 665; cited above n. 29.
86. For a probing and thoughtful study of this pivotal chapter of Jewish history, see Jacob Neusner, *A Life of Rabban Yohanan ben Zakkai.*\
87. This may explain the feeling of doubts and remorse expressed by R. Johanan ben Zakkai on his deathbed, see Berakhot 28b.

and nurtured by Rome – not by Jewish 'patriots.' The purpose was to provide an excuse to carry out the greatest genocide in recorded history: over 80 per cent of the Jewish population in Judea and close to 50 percent of the general Jewish population elsewhere were slaughtered.

> According to this estimate, then, in three and a half years of the war the casualties of various kinds reached a total of some 600,000 or was the magnitude of about fifty percent. This reference is to the population of the *whole* country; in Judea, it may have been ninety percent.[88]

The target was the city of Bethar (Hebrew: *Bitter*), the seat of Tora learning and scholarship. It was not accidental that on the 9th of Ab 135 (C.E.), the anniversary of the Roman destruction of the Temple and the national archives of Israel, Roman hordes broke into Bethar and proceeded to torture and exterminate the entire population. "With the exception of the Holocaust of European Jewry by the Nazis, it would seem that there was never such a catastrophe like that of Bar Kokhba, one in which so many Jews were killed at once." This assessment is correct only when measuring the catastrophe in absolute numbers. In proportionate terms, however, it was the greatest genocide ever suffered by the Jewish people. "In Judea, the Romans destroyed almost every settlement." The reason that the extermination of the Jews was not completed is not because the Romans were less determined than the Nazis, but because "the Romans did not attain that degree of technology and administrative proficiency that the Nazis later developed." In fact, it was the greatest genocide in ancient history. "No pogrom is commensurate with that which the Romans perpetrated against the inhabitants of Judea."[89] Hadrian's

88. Yehoshafat Harkabi, *The Bar Kokhba Syndrome* (Chappaqua, N.Y.: Russel Books, 1983), p. 46. Gibbon, *The Decline and Fall of the Roman Empire*, vol. 1, p. 390, justifies this massacre as "the rights of victory," although qualifying it "with unusual rigour." see appendix 20.
89. *The Bar Kokhba Syndrome*, p. 48.

accomplishments were duly appreciated. In his honor, a Temple to the Divine Hadrian was dedicated in 145. Later historians shared this view. Reportedly, Sir Edward Gibbon described his rule as "the happiest of mankind's history." Arnold Toynbee (1889–1975) – a most worthy representative of Tacitus' historiography – declared that the Jewish people and civilization were a "fossil."[90] This could exonerate any and all anti-Jewish measures – you cannot kill a corpse! (see appendix 22.)

That was not enough. To make sure that the memory of Israel would be permanently erased, it was important to intensify the psychological warfare. Roman culture and tradition were ill-equipped for this type of combat. Suddenly, an unexpected ally emerged ready to give a *coup de grace* to "vanquished Israel." To understand the niceties of this type of warfare it would be helpful to bear in mind that in a totalitarian regime 'religion,' 'truth,' 'justice,' etc. are instruments designed to promote state policy and propaganda. To gain grace in the eyes of Roman authorities, Christianity – not the Christianity of Jesus and James, but that of Paul and John – invented a new kind of foe: the religious enemy, and a new kind of war: religious war. Henceforth one could target an enemy not only on political grounds, but also on 'religious' grounds: to save the enemy's soul. The issue was first examined by R. Benamozegh (1823–1900), concluding:

> Yes, the religious enemy is a creation altogether Christian, unknown to Judaism, *impossible* even at the moment that it admits that eternal salvation is not the exclusive heritage of the Mosaic Law.[91]

90. Only specially bred bulls are dumb enough to believe that if they were to make this or that pirouette, the *toreador* would spare them the butcher's knife. This is why there is no point in arguing with bigots, regardless of religious or political denomination. See, however, the valiant efforts of R. Jacob Agus, "Toynbee's Epistle to the Jews," *Commentary* 32 (1961), pp. 239–242.
91. *Jewish and Christian Ethics*, pp. 83–84.

Roman authorities began to take notice of the tactical value of Christianity. Thus was set in motion the Christianization of Rome. See Ramsay MacMullen, *Christianizing the Roman Empire* (New Haven: Yale University Press, 1984).[92] It culminated when Constantine, called henceforth "the Great," made Christianity the religion of the State (313). His conversion, however, was not a matter of conscience, but a consequence of his *military* victory. Walter Kaufmann called attention to this revealing fact, glossed over by historians of religion:

> What is really much more extraordinary than the tale of the miraculous vision is the fact that the decisive turn in the history of Christianity was brought about by a Roman emperor who was persuaded by a huge military victory that Christianity was true and that the cross should henceforth be his emblem. For him, of course, taking up the cross did not involve turning his back on war, empire, and victory. He placed his triumphal arch in Rome next to that of Titus, which had celebrated the destruction of Jerusalem, but made it far more opulent – three arches in one – and went on to wage campaigns for the Empire.[93]

In line with pagan political ideals, the arch of the first and most important emperor in Christian history was dedicated to "Constantine as Cosmocrator" (see above chapter 33). Jesus, too, is *Rex* in the capacity of Cosmocrator (see above chapter 34). In the construction, spoils were taken from the monuments dedicated to Trajan (98–117) and Hadrian – two emperors who had gained prominence for having massacred Jews. To make the point clearer, the arch was built next to Titus' Arch, celebrating the destruction of the Temple in Jerusalem and the burning of Israel's archives. A final point: Constantine's Arch consists of three arches in one, symbolic of the Holy Trinity – the most fundamental doctrine of the religion of love which he helped establish.

92. See Ramsay MacMullen, *Christianizing the Roman Empire* (New Haven: Yale University Press, 1984).

93. *Religions in Four Dimensions*, p. 142.

Let us survey some of the points mentioned above. Christianity was incorporated into the State to carry on the psychological warfare against Israel. Its principal objective was to lobotomize Israel and deny Israel the right to remember. In the course of time, the alliance sword/cross would be more dependent on each other: the sovereign would become 'defender of the faith' and the Church would defend the empire (although, as it was shown by Gibbons et al, the Church betrayed that trust in support of what was later known as the 'Holy Roman Empire,' i.e., the *German Nation*; see appendix 20). Thus, monarchs ruled by 'the grace of God' and their subjects owed them 'unlimited subservience.' In this fashion, the axis sword/cross inaugurated a new system of socio-political control that dominated western society until the American Revolution.

About half a millennium later, another 'monotheistic' religion, in the footsteps of Christianity, accepted Tacitus' doctrine: Israel has no right to remember, her memory is fundamentally flawed. Islam was consistent. If one were to deny Israel's memory, then one would have to reject the whole Scripture.[94] Accordingly, the most fundamental principle of Islam is the doctrine of *taḥrif*, proclaiming that the Scripture is a Jewish forgery (see *Koran* 2:70; 3:64; 5:16, 45; 6:91). The *true* history of Israel is known to Islam or to Christendom, exclusively. Questions pertaining to Israel's memory could be effectively settled by the point of the sword, or the flames of the Inquisition. People wishing a more relaxed atmosphere could accomplish the same by reading the works of Gibbon or Toynbee and their disciples, springing from the most exotic points of the globe (see appendix 20).

94. I suspect that this was the guiding principle steering biblical critics, beginning with Welhausen. As a young student I used to ask, 'What about applying the same critical canons to the Gospels and the German Constitution?'

# Chapter 41
# A Crisis of Memory

The objective of the two-pronged policy was to erase Israel's National Memory. The slaughtering of Jewish sages by Rome and Christian appropriation of Scripture were intended to lobotomize Israel, as was done to all other peoples living under their axis. To accomplish this, the Church pillaged and plundered the Scripture. By cherry picking this or that verse out of context, Christianity could now defuse the message of the Scripture and use it to justify the persecution of Jews and undesirables (see above chapter 27). To validate this outrage the Church launched the most vicious campaign against the Jews. The notion of *Verus Israel* – a rephrasing of Paul's claim that Christians are "the Israel of God" (Gal. 6:17; cf. I Cor. 10:18) – ranks as the most villainous case in the universal history of infamy. (Can you imagine a people, unable to read or speak English, having contempt for the American way of life, hijacking the Constitution on the ground of being *Verus* America? see, however, appendix 20.) Having this infamy in mind, R. Johanan declared that someone "alien" to the Jewish people, i.e., a Christian, "intensely studying the Tora" equals an impostor seeking to disinherit a proprietor by robbing his identity; or a rapist seeking to violate his neighbor's wife on the pretense of being her *Verus* husband (see appendix 30).[95] Since the National Memory of a people encodes their intellectual structures and patterns of thought and emotion, the erasure of Israel's memory sought

95. Sanhedrin 59a; see *Golden Doves*, pp. 14–15, 50.

to reduce the Jews to a densely amnesiac mass, exactly like the rest of the people living under the aegis cross/sword.

To fully appreciate the depth of this crisis, some preliminary remarks are of the essence. The Law, in the quality of a *written* document, does not have the force of *law* until it is *promulgated* orally by the Supreme Court. "Although the Tora was given at Sinai," taught the rabbis, "(the people of) Israel were not legally accountable until it was promulgated orally (נתפרשה) to them at *Ohel Mo'ed* (the Tent of Assembly)."[96] In English tradition, too, a legislation is not binding until announced by 'heralds' (= 'hear ye'!). Similarly, the Supreme Court of the USA issues oral summaries of its decisions *before* they are filed. Prior to the destruction of the Temple, the legal traditions and interpretations of Israel – beginning with Moses, the head of the first Supreme Court of Israel – were filed in the national archives. The Court's records, main points of case law, as well as pertinent instructions and information concerning new legislation, were not published. As in other judicial systems, the records of the Jewish Court were not available to the general public but only to authorized personnel. Members of the Court, such as Shammai and Hillel, would take transcripts and notes from the archives, which they would then deposit in their private schools, to be subsequently used in the course of teaching the Law.[97] The records deposited in the school's archives became known as "the six orders of the Mishna, archived from the days of Hillel and Shammai."[98] They were not edited, and contained, on occasion, views

96. Shir ha-Shirim Rabba, II, iii, 4, 14d; cf. ibid. III, i, 4, 19c. See the sources cited in *Hellenism in Jewish Palestine*, pp. 200–202.
97. See *MT* Introduction, ll. 46–52.
98. This tradition was reported by R. Sherira Gaon, *Sha'are Teshuba* #187, 76a; cf. *Sefer Yoḥasin*, 18a, 62b, and below n. 113. In Hebrew, the term 'בית' associated with Shammai and Hillel, usually translated as 'school,' indicates 'housing' – a reference to the records deposited there; see II Chr. 13:22; 24:27 and above n. 62. It may be of some interest to note that in Sephardic tradition *Bet Midrash* refers to a place of study containing a private library and manuscript collection *unavailable to the general public*; see appendix 6. R. Se'adya Gaon maintained

which were not held by the sages themselves.[99] Moreover, as is often the case with the minutes taken by judges in legal proceedings, the language is terse and cryptic. (That is why, in modern law, a judge's minutes do not constitute legal evidence of the actual judgment.) Since the students of Shammai and Hillel did not always "minister sufficiently" to their teachers, occasionally they misinterpreted these file-notes, and reached unwarranted conclusions. They thus unduly increased "legal controversy in Israel."[100]

At this early stage of Jewish education, legal instruction was imparted in conjunction with the exposition of the Written Law. Accordingly, the legal material passed on in the classroom was known as *perush* 'interpretation'; a term commonly used in the sense of 'exposition' of the conceptual aspect or 'reduced gist' of the law, but having also the technical sense of 'promulgation' and 'oral transmission' (see appendix 28). The focus of *perush* is the 'conceptual gist' of the law, and it was taught as part of curriculum to advanced students of Scripture. By definition, the *perush* is not 'explicit' in the text. A measurement of the rhetorical ability of the teacher was to show how the *perush* was 'encoded' (*remiza*) in the wording of the Tora (see appendix 31). The focus of this method was grasping the *perush* conceptually, not textually. The premises and 'conceptual gist' of the Law (in contradistinction to the 'clue' or *remez* in the text of the Law), is known as the *ṭa'am* (pl. *ṭa'ame*).[101] It was reported that when

that there were *mishnayot* from Biblical times, i.e., 'official records'; see *Saadya's Commentary on Genesis*, p. 186 and the sources cited ibid. n. 103. For further references, see appendix 26.

99. See for example, Mishna 'Eduyot 1:7, 8, 11; Kelim 22:4; cf. *Tosafot* on Yebamot 117a, s.v. *bet*; *Tosafot* on Ketubot 53b, s.v. *she-'en*.

100. See Tosefta Ḥagiga 2:9, p. 384. For additional sources and parallels, see ed. notes ibid. Cf. Introduction, *Perush ha-Mishnayot*, vol. 1, pp. 20–21; *Golden Doves*, pp. 98–99; and below n. 113. A good example of this type of linguistic 'controversy' are Mishna Kil'ayim 2:6 and Shebi'it 1:1. This is why it was not uncommon to revise and amend the view of these schools, particularly when reported by sources secondary to the Mishna, e.g., Ḥolin 104b-105a.

101. See appendix 19.

R. 'Aqiba "would be arranging halakhot before the students," he would encourage those "who had heard a *ṭa'am* against a fellow student to step forward and speak."[102] A second form of legal instruction was halakha (pl. halakhot), consisting of a carefully redacted formula. Halakha was imparted after instruction of the Scriptural justification of the law, and required 'perfect memorization' (גרסא), followed by 'comprehension' (גמיר); and concluding with 'critical analysis' (סביר) at the final stage of legal training.[103]

There were advantages and disadvantages in each method. By demanding verbatim transmission of halakha, uncertainty as to what the teacher had actually taught was reduced. Nonetheless, it was occasionally impossible to determine whether halakha variations were a matter of style or of substance (see Tosefta Para 11:8, p. 640). More grievously, sometimes sages trained in different schools could not be satisfied that a halakha reported by a colleague was authentic, and would flatly reject it (see Tosefta 'Oqaṣin 3:13, p. 689), or argue that it was "flawed" (Mishna Ohalot 16:1; cf. Tosefta Ohalot 15:12, p. 613 and Shabbat 17a. For further analysis, see appendix 32). The *perush* methodology, too, was problematic. Although it permitted students to approach directly the conceptual gist of the law since it was not formally edited, variations in style and nuance might be taken as matters of substance, and thus "increased legal controversy in Israel."[104] Referring to the *perush* methodology, R. Sherira Gaon (ca. 906 – ca. 1006) noted that prior to the destruction of the Temple each sage "knew and learned" conceptually the gist of the law. At this early period, the conceptual aspects of the Law, "were clearly grasped as if they were a halakha received from Moses at Sinai," i.e., clearly, without ambiguity (cf. appendix 33). He added, "there were no [substantial] differences or disputes among them (the sages)."[105] The *perush*, we are apprised, was like notes that teachers use to "explain nowadays

102. Tosefta Zabim 1:5, p. 676. Cf. *Golden Doves*, pp. 88–89, 97–98.
103. See *Golden Doves*, pp. 95–96, and appendix 37.
104. See above n. 100.
105. *IShG*, p. 22; see *Golden Doves*, p. 97.

to our disciples, which every (teacher) knows (equally) but each (teacher) writes differently."[106]

As noted in the preceding chapter, soon after the destruction of the national archives (68 C.E.), R. 'Aqiba began a project designed to collect the archival material circulating among surviving jurists, scholars, and students. His activities are described as follows:

> To what might R. 'Aqiba be likened? – To a laborer who took his basket and went forth (to collect the produce). When he found wheat, he put some in the basket. When he found barley, he put that in; spelt, he put that in; lentils, he put them in. Upon returning home he sorted out the wheat by itself, barley by itself, beans by themselves.[107]

The results of R. 'Aqiba's labor were "the great (collections of) Mishnayot" mentioned by the rabbis.[108] After his martyrdom, the project was continued by his disciples. The task, however, was far from complete. Since the national archives had been burned, the material collected by R. 'Aqiba and his school required certification (see above chapter 38). This was not always possible, especially after the massacre of rabbis at Bethar (135 C.E.). As reported by R. Sherira Gaon:

> Upon the destruction of the Temple they (the rabbis) went to Bethar. Bethar was also destroyed. The rabbis were scattered in every direction. Because of the convulsions, persecutions, and general confusion prevalent at the time, the disciples were

106. *IShG,* pp. 18–19. This view was shared by Maimonides, *MT* Introduction, ll. 46–52; cf. *Golden Doves,* pp. 58, 109 and 191 n. 12.

107. *AdRN* A, XVIII, p. xxxiv. Probably this is the sense of '*she-hitqin*' in Yerushalmi Sheqalim V, 1, 48c. See *Golden Doves,* pp. 98–99, and below n. 144.

108. Horayot III, 8, 48c; *Midrash Ekha Rabbati, Petiḥata* XXIII, p. 18; Qohelet Rabba VI, 1, s.v. *ish,* 17a; etc. There were other collections, the most famous were those of R. Ḥiyya and R. Osha'ya, see Ḥolin 141a-b; *Ekha Rabbati, Petiḥata* XXIII, p. 18, and editor's note 6; and those of R. Osha'ya, R. Hunna, and Bar Qappara, mentioned in Y. Horayot III, 8, 48c. Cf. *MT* Introduction, ll. 68–69.

> unable to minister (to their teachers) properly, and controversies (concerning the content and meaning of legal tradition) increased.[109]

To meet these problems, R. ʻAqiba proposed "to mint the whole Tora into coins" – a project that was completed with the publication of the Mishna (see below chapter 43).

Maimonides called attention to the axis 'sword/cross' bent on destroying Israel. Before the rise of Christianity, Israel had been targeted either intellectually, by thinkers objecting to some aspects of Judaism, or by military powers. Christianity instituted a new form of warfare, involving the coordination of military might with religious polemics.

> Afterwards, there was established a new sect, which structured itself on these two methods. I mean (the continuing) military assault on the one hand, and altercation and polemic on the other. (The new sect) deemed that this (tactic) would erase the memory of the nation (of Israel) and the Tora more efficiently. [To buttress this tactic] it made a political decision to lay claim to prophecy, and that it had received a Law to substitute God's Law, and that it, too, proceeded from God and it was akin to [His] righteous word. [The purpose of this claim was] to create uncertainty and perplexity, having one [revelation] challenging the other, while attributing both to a single God.[110]

Elsewhere, the combination of military might and state-sponsored truth proved enormously successful. It dominated European policy throughout the Middle Ages and modern times, whether such truth was 'religious,' 'secular,' or 'atheistic.' The model was later adopted by Islam.

109. *IShG*, pp. 10–11; see *Golden Doves*, pp. 97–99.
110. *Iggeret Teman*, pp. 11–12.

And yet Israel survived and continued to thrive and grow. The secret of this success lies in the publication of the Mishna.

# Chapter 42
# Unmasking Spurious *Verus Israel*

The rabbinic movement emerged to meet the crisis brought about by the aegis sword/cross. Given that without a National Memory the remnants of Israel would have vanished, it was imperative to bring R. 'Aqiba's project to completion and "mint the whole Tora into coins." This meant the publication of the archival material *nationally*. Preparations began immediately after Bethar (132–135). Galilee had been spared from some of the ravages taking place in Judea. Meeting in Usha, the surviving students of R. 'Aqiba addressed "the elders of Galilee" with this call: "Whoever had learned let him step forward and teach! Whoever had not learned let him step forward and learn!"[111] The emphasis on "teaching" *and* "learning" was designed to avoid conflict and reach consensus. In this fashion, further material was collected and catalogued. The preparations were completed around the years 189–220, with the publication of the Mishna by R. Judah the Prince.[112] The national publication of the Mishna rendered all of its content *legal tender*, enjoying universal acceptability.

I would like to put forward a thesis that admittedly would require

111. Shir ha-Shirim Rabba II, v, 3, 15b-c; cf. *Sefer Yoḥasin*, p. 94a. On the historical background of this period, see *Studies in the History of the Sanhedrin*, chapter 4.

112. Hebrew 'נשיא.' On the meaning of this title, see *Studies in the History of the Sanhedrin*, chapter 1; on his offices, see ibid., chapter 5.

a full-fledged analysis, but for which I can presently venture to conjecture. I propose that the language, structure, and conceptual organization of the Mishna are archival (= *derekh qeṣara*; see appendix 34) – not 'literary.' Moreover, the classification of the legal material into six classes (*sedarim*), and further subdivision into tractates (*massekhtot*), chapters (*peraqim*) and articles (*halakhot*), follow Jewish archival standards. Geonic tradition gives some support to this thesis. It explicitly mentions, "The six orders of the Mishna that were archived (דאתגניזו) since the days of Hillel and Shammai."[113] Another medieval tradition states "that since the days of Moses and until Hillel there were 600 orders (*sidre*) of Mishna, as God had given Moses at Sinai."[114] For our purposes it should be noted that the Mishna comprises about 523 chapters. The "600 orders (*sidre*)" may be a round number for the files, later edited as chapters. The language of the Mishna, awkward by literary canons, is the standard style of minutes and legal files and records.

The six orders of the Mishna parallel human development. Zera'im, the first order, focuses on agricultural laws, 'space'– the earliest dimension in a child's cognitive development. The following order, Mo'ed examines the laws pertaining to the Jewish holidays, i.e., 'time'– a dimension that the child discovers after apprehending space. Nashim deals with 'family law' – an area that the child discovers soon after the preceding two. The fourth order, Neziqim, concerns an individual's involvement with *all* aspects of human society: torts, contracts, business transactions, social and commercial contacts with Jews and with heathens, and the organization and authority of the Judiciary. It also

113. *Sha'are Teshuba* #187, 76a; cf. above n. 98. The term 'דאתגניזו,' root GNZ, means, as translated above, 'to file,' 'to archive under seal'; see *Targum* on Deut. 32:34; and not necessarily 'to suppress,' 'to discard,' as in popular usage; see *Golden Doves*, p. 102.

114. Ḥagiga 14a; cf. R. Ḥ.Y.D. Azulai, *Ya'ir Ozen* (Leghorn, 5552/1792), s.v. Mishna (39); and the references in R. Solomon Algazi, *Yabin Shemu'a* #332. This tradition was recorded in *Sha'are Teshuba* #20; see *Iyye ha-Yam*, 9b. It is connected to the "600 or 700 *sidre Mishna*," Ḥagiga 14a. On the precise meaning of *sidre*, see appendix 36. On the sense of "from Moses at Sinai," see appendix 33.

includes aphorisms and didactic sentences designed to express basic norms of thought and conduct, which the child will need as he develops and assumes full social and personal responsibility. Conceptually, the proximity of family law to Neziqim reflects the Jewish view that society is an extended family; that ethical upbringing ought to include civic as well as personal morality. It also suggests that moral and criminal misconduct are the effect of faulty upbringing and education. The fifth order, Qadashim deals with sacramental space and the cult at the Temple, an area that should engage the individual at a later stage of spiritual development. The final order, Ṭahorot concerns ritual purity, as the individual prepares himself for a more personal and direct contact with his Maker.[115]

The Mishna is an intellectual miracle. Out of the ashes of genocide there emerged the most significant intellectual accomplishment of any nation, past or present: the official publication of the *records* containing Israel's *National Memory*. It has been noted that 'memory' consists of the capacity both to encode and to retrieve information. Thus, the Mishna not only stored the legal traditions and doctrines of Israel, but also encoded the canons of thought and emotional patterns, essential to retrieve and further develop the memory of Israel. Even when exposing the intricacies of the laws of purity at one level, the Mishna projects the ideas and principles constituting the mind of Israel. As taught by Professor Neusner:

> Discourse takes place at not one but two (or more) levels, and cases in general are meant for exemplary purposes. That is to say, the issues concern principles that transcend the subject-matter of the law and that in fact affect themselves and topics entirely unrelated to the law, physics… metaphysics… and ethics… for example…[116]

---

115. Concerning the last two orders, cf. R. Solomon Finzi, *Mafteaḥ ha-Gemara* (printed in *Temim De'im*, Venice, 1622), V, 94d-95a.

116. Jacob Neusner, *The Philosophical Mishna*, vols. 1–3 (Atlanta, Georgia: Scholars Press, 1988–9), vol. 1, p. 223. In these three volumes Professor Neusner examines

Given that without a National Memory, the remnants of Israel would have perished, the Mishna is the operational vehicle for *national* revival. At the same time, since it encodes the structures and canons of Israel, the Mishna is the matrix of Jewish dynamic thinking and intellectual creativity. The rabbis compared "the six orders of the Mishna" to the original "six mothers of Israel," including Bilha and Zilpa. Like the biblical matriarchs, the "six orders" are perennially giving life and nourishment to the children of Israel.[117] In this respect, the Mishna is something more formidable than the formal publication of Israel's national archives. It is, first and foremost, the *conveyance of the national archives of Israel from the Temple in Jerusalem to the memory of the people* (see below chapter 43). Addressing the axis 'cross/sword,' which intended to obliterate the National Memory together with the physical existence of Israel, the rabbis,

---

the basic philosophical frame of the Mishna. For a substantive discussion of the economic, political, theological, and philosophical outlook of the Mishna, see idem, *The Social Study of Judaism*, vol. 2 (Atlanta, Georgia: Scholars Press, 1988), pp. 3–125. On the Judaism of the Mishna in general, see idem, *The Social Study of Judaism*, vol. 1 (Atlanta, Georgia: Scholars Press, 1988), pp. 29–55.

117. *Pesiqta de-Rab Kahana* I, 7, vol. 1, pp. 11–12; Debarim Rabba XII, 17, vol. 2, p. 98. Some time ago, a distinguished member of *Shearith Israel*, in New York, told me that Judge Cardozo was fluent in the six orders of the Mishna. The gentleman happened to be quite learned in Rabbinics and I had no reason to doubt him. However, I do not know when he arrived in the USA, and he may have arrived after the Justice's death, in which case he must have received this information from some reliable source. Regrettably, it did not occur to me to ask him at the time for his source. Nonetheless, I believe it to be correct, and in the course of my teachings I had the opportunity to point out various traces of Rabbinics in the writings and decisions of Judge Cardozo. A case in point is *Riggs v. Palmer*, 115 N.Y. 506, which is based on a principle formulated by the rabbis. Interestingly, Judge Cardozo, in his *The Nature of the Judicial Process* (New Haven: Yale University Press, 1949), p. 41, alluded to this: "But over against these was another principle, of greater generality, *its roots deeply fastened in universal sentiments of justice* [italics added], the principle that no man should profit from his own inequity or take advantage of his own wrong." see Mishna Ḥalla 2:7; and cf. Shebi'it 9:9; Baba Qamma 39a; *MT Gezela* 2:8 and *Mekhira* 12:13.

commenting on Lev. 26:44 (where God assures Israel that He shall not renounce His "covenant with them"), explained: "… 'neither did I abandon them' – at the time of the Romans. And I instituted for them the House of Ribbi [R. Judah the Prince] and the sages in subsequent generations."[118]

At a time when the enemies of Israel fancied to have lobotomized the people who stood in solemn testimony to God's Word at Sinai, Rome through brutal genocide, and Christianity by plundering the Scripture, the survivors responded with the publication of the Mishna. To Imperial Rome, the Mishna replies that ideas cannot be butchered. To Christianity, the Mishna replies that 'God's Word,' when buttressed by the sword, equals blasphemy. The following story illustrates our point. Soon after the publication of the Mishna, R. Judah sent two sages throughout the cities of Israel with the purpose "of establishing schools [for the teaching of] Scripture and Mishna."

> Upon arriving at a town having no schools, they would say to the town people: "bring in the town's guardians."
>
> Then they would go out and bring in the town's guardians.
>
> The sages would then say: "Are these the town's guardians? These are the destroyers of the town!"
>
> "Then who may the town's guards be?" the people would ask.
>
> They would respond: "The teachers of Scripture and Mishna"![119]

A final point. The rabbis identified the Mishna with "God's mystery" (*sod*). Unlike pagan mysteries available to the enlightened elite, either in cult and or theology, the 'mystery' of Israel – in accordance with the horizontal character of Judaism – is entrusted to the memory of the people (see appendix 35). Having in mind those masquerading

118. Megilla 11a; cf. R. 'Azarya Fijo, *Bina le-'Ittim* (Jerusalem: Vagshel, 5749/1989), vol. 2, p. 82.

119. Y. Ḥagiga I, 7, 76c. Cf. *Ekha Rabbati, Petiḥata,* II, pp. 1–2; XII, p. 12; cf. pp. 64, 100, 104, 138; and Shabbat 119b.

as *Verus Israel,* the rabbis proposed that Israel's identity cannot be demonstrated by the rattling translations to an analphabetic audience incapable of nuance. The identity of Israel lies in its *unwritten* memory, which alone gives meaning to its *written* Scripture. In the phrase of the rabbis:

> Moses requested [from God] that the Mishna, too, should [be published] in writing. God, however, foresaw that in the future the nations would translate the Tora and read it in Greek and claim: "We too are Israel!"
>
> God said to Moses: "Would you want me to put into writing [i.e. 'to publish'] most of my Tora [i.e., the Mishna] – then they [i.e. Israel] would be regarded as [equal] to aliens?"
>
> "Why would it be so"?! asked Moses.
>
> "Because the Mishna is God's mystery *(sod)."*
>
> But why, we may ask, do those parading as *Verus Israel* have to be excluded? To clarify this point, the rabbis appended an important note.
>
> "God reveals His mystery *(sod)* to no one except the righteous." As it is written: "The secret *(sod)* of the Lord is for those who fear Him" (Ps. 25:14).

In Scripture, "fear of God" is recognition of God's sovereignty on *earth.* God will share His 'mysteries' only with those who recognize God's full supreme authority among men. The rabbis continue:

> "One may verify (the above doctrine) by the fact that when God was angry at Sodom and Gomorrah, on account of their evil conduct, and wished to destroy Sodom, He did not reach a verdict until He first confided in Abraham."[120]

120. *Midrash Tanḥuma, Vayyera* VI, vol. 1, p. 88; cf. Y. Pe'a II, 6, 17a; Bemidbar Rabba XIV, 10, vol. 2, 61d; see R. Judah al-Bargeloni, *Perush le-Sefer Yeṣira,* pp. 5–6. In this context, 'God's mystery,' may be an allusion to the 'circumcision,' which

The message is clear. Because Abraham 'feared God' he was *unafraid* to argue with Him in defense of sinners, even of the ilk of Sodom and Gomorrah. By implication, those who acquiesce to mass murder and preach unlimited submission to tyrants are no better than the masters they serve.

The Mishna is the apparatus designed to preserve Israel's memory, to ward off imperialistic powers, and to unmask spurious *Verus Israel.* Thus, it opens with an overwhelming question intended to distinguish between fear of God and self-indulgent moralism. About the year 180, when Jewish survivors began to rise from the ashes of Roman genocide, they turned to those who destroyed their Temple, burnt their national archives, razed their schools, massacred hundreds of thousands of innocent victims, and vilified their ethos. Confronting those trying to extinguish God's voice at Sinai, they posed a single, crushing question. It became Israel's battle cry throughout the ages. The question is: "At what moment in time does the recitation of the evening *Shema'* begin?" (Mishna Berakhot 1:1). People impervious to this question have never heard the voice of the God of Israel. At the end of the Mishna ('Oqaṣin 3:12), there is an additional note by R. Simeon ben Ḥalafta (2nd and 3rd centuries), which summarizes the preceding 523 chapters. "God has found no vessel better suited to contain Israel's blessing than *shalom.*"[121]

---

symbolizes the 'secret' covenant between God and Abraham's children; see *Yalquṭ Shim'oni*, Ps. #702, vol. 2, 451c, s.v. *sod*; cf. and appendix 22. On the relation between 'God's mystery' and 'Fear of God,' see Ḥagiga 14a.

121. See Mishna 'Eduyot 8:7 and Berakhot 64a. This addition is alluded to in Bemidbar Rabba XIII, 15 (16), vol. 2, 54b. Cf. Mishna Kelim 30:4 and Yoma 16a. For important sources on this concept, see *The Mishna of Rabbi Eliezer*, IV, pp. 65–87. Professor Daniel Sperber edited, translated, and annotated a chapter of a late rabbinic tractate, *Great is Peace* (Jerusalem: Massada Press, 1979), containing valuable insights on the subject. Cf. above Section III, n. 315.

# Chapter 43
# The Publication of the Mishna

In Jewish tradition Moses alone had the distinction to have been appointed by God as His emissary (שליח) with the authority to deliver to Israel the judicial connotations, the rules of interpretation, and the administration of the Tora.[122] Commenting on the verse, "These are the statutes, regulations, and laws that God put between Him and Israel, in the hand of Moses at Mount Sinai" (Lev. 26:46), the rabbis taught:

> *That God put between Him and the people of Israel.* – "Moses had the merit of being appointed emissary (שליח) between Israel and their Father in Heaven." *In the hand of Moses at Mount Sinai.* – "It teaches that the Tora was delivered – its *halakhot, nuances and explanations* (פרושיה) – in Moses' hand at Sinai."[123]

---

122. On this fundamental doctrine, see *Guide* II, 39; *Perush ha-Mishnayot*, Ḥolin 7:6, vol. 5, p. 212; *MT Yesode ha-Tora* 8:1–3; and *Studies in the Mishne Tora*, pp. 13–19. There is a passage in *Epistle to Yemen*, p. 78, where Maimonides refers to Moses as "the first emissary (Ar. *rasul*)." This is not because Judaism admits that there may be another such emissary, but rather because he was writing in Arabic, wherein *rasul* usually applies to Mohammed. Maimonides wanted to alert the reader to the fact that he was referring to the 'first,' i.e., Moses, not to the 'other.'

123. *Sifra, Be-Ḥuqqotai*, X, 8 (12), 122a; cf. ibid. X, 13 (8), 127b; *AdRN*, A, I, p. 1. On the 'nuances' of the Tora (דקדוקי), cf. Shir ha-Shirim Rabba I, 8, s.v. *shir*, 2c, and appendix 37.

Two national institutions, the Court and the National Academy (*Yeshiba*), were established to preserve, develop, and transmit Moses' teachings. God directed Moses, in the capacity of Chief Justice, to "gather the seventy elders" and constitute the first Supreme Court of Israel. He also charged him to "pass on" to them from "his spirit" so that they could partake in the guidance of the people (see Num. 11:16–17). As *the* Teacher of Israel he was personally responsible for the dissemination of this knowledge, and was directed to "lay down" (תשים) before them the legal norms that he received from God (see Ex. 21:1; cf. Deut. 4:44). In accordance with both the meaning and context of this term, the *Targum* rendered to "lay down" (תשים) as 'תסדר,' root SDR – connoting both the 'topics' as well as the 'order' in which the theme at hand is to unfold (see appendix 36). It meant that Moses had to convey the Law in units of information that could be grasped by the general public, both linguistically and conceptually (see appendix 37).

A society professing the rule of Law has the supreme responsibility of providing basic legal education to *all* the people.[124] Legal knowledge should not be the patrimony of a favored class or group. Legal norms and doctrines ought to be internalized and stand at the psychological foundation of the mind, to be transmitted and expanded both socially and culturally. After giving the legal instructions to the High Priest, the priests, and the elders, Moses taught these laws to the general public.[125] Before his death, Moses further "explicated" the Tora to the general public (Deut. 1:5).[126] To ensure the continuity of these institutions he instructed (צוה, see appendix 12), as supreme

124. See Deut. 31:12; Tosefta Soṭa, VII, 9, p. 194; Ḥagiga 3a; and *AdRN* A, XVIII, pp. 67–68. Cf. Deut. 29:10.
125. 'Erubin 54b. Cf. Ex. 24:1; *Midrash Tanḥuma, Va-Yaqhel,* 8, vol. 2, p. 124; and *Saadya's Commentary on Genesis,* p. 186 (Ar. p. 15). See also Introduction, *Sefer ha-Mafteaḥ,* 2b; Introduction, *Perush ha-Mishnayot,* vol. 1, p. 2.
126. See *Sifre* #4, p. 13; Temura 16a; cf. Introduction, *Perush ha-Mishnayot,* vol. 1, p. 3. Concerning the instructions that Moses delivered in the capacity of Chief Justice, Maimonides uses the verb צוה ('instructed'); see *MT* Introduction, l. 7.

political leader, "the elders *and* Joshua, *and* the rest of all Israel" to administer the Law according to the regulations and principles that he taught.[127] Second, in the capacity of teacher, Moses "conveyed (מסר) to Joshua his disciple the legal tradition; and further instructed (צוהו) him" – in the capacity of political leader – "to guard and teach it." "Joshua, too," we are apprised, "taught throughout his life [the traditions that he received from Moses] orally."[128]

R. Judah the Prince, too, held both offices. Under his leadership the Mishna was published simultaneously by both the Supreme Court and the National Academy of Israel. In the capacity of Chief Justice, he had access to all the legal records that had survived. Accordingly:

> He put together all judicial traditions, laws, clarifications, and explanations regarding the entire Law, that have been learned since our Teacher Moses, which were exposed by the Courts of Justice throughout the generations. Out of all [this material] he redacted the Book of the Mishna.[129]

As the Head of the National Academy, he was invested with the authority to explicate the Law and administer its public teaching. Commenting on the verse "The scepter shall not depart from Judah" (Gen. 49:10), the rabbis affirmed: "These are the princes [belonging to] Ribbi's (= R. Judah the Prince) dynasty, who [have the authority] to teach Tora in public" (ברבים).[130] Teaching "Tora in public (ברבים)" stands for the right to issue the authoritative expositions

---

However, when referring to those to whom Moses passed on the tradition in the capacity of teacher, Maimonides uses the verb מסר ('delivered'); see ibid., l. 12.

127. Introduction, *MT*, ll. 7–8; cf. *Mamrim* 1:1. Maimonides mentions Joshua *after* the elders, because his authority as head of the nation rested on the elders, not the other way around. Cf. Y. Horayot III, 4, 48b-c.

128. *MT* Introduction, ll. 11–13; cf. Introduction, *Perush ha-Mishnayot*, vol. 1, p. 4.

129. *MT* Introduction, ll. 52–55.

130. See Sanhedrin 5a and Horayot 11b; *IShG*, pp. 76–77, and *Genizah Studies*, vol. 1, p. 220. This tradition is reported only in Babylonian sources. The parallel in Bereshit Rabba XCVII, 10, vol. 3, p. 1219 is a later interpolation, not found in

of the Law to the *general public* and it is therefore synonymous with 'publication' (see appendix 38).

The publication of the Mishna consisted of two separate ceremonies. First, in the capacity of Chief Justice, R. Judah the Prince "recited orally" (ושיננו) the text of the Mishna "to the sages in public." 'שיננו' (root ShNH) is a technical term used exclusively for the recitation and transmission of halakha (see appendix 39). 'Mishna' (from the same root) stands primarily for 'authorized text.'[131] The publication of the Mishna involved the review and editing of the legal material. Out of the two styles used in legal instruction, halakha and *perush* (see above chapter 40), halakha was chosen. Hence the 'Mishna' became the official text of halakha. In the words of R. Sherira Gaon, "*hilkheta* (Aramaic for halakha) is our Mishna, redacted by R. Judah the Prince."[132] The ceremony, whereby the Chief Justice recited (שיננו) the Mishna in the presence of the members of the Court, served to authenticate that it was officially published with the consent and the authority of this body. Similarly, Moses had transmitted all of the legal doctrines "to the seventy elders in his Court."[133]

The second ceremony consisted of "unveiling (ונגלה) [the Mishna] to all Israel; consequently it was written by everyone and was taught everywhere."[134] To bring out the concrete meaning of this phrase, we need to recall that the unpublished material contained in various

---

Bereshit Rabba, Vat. Ebr. 30 (Jerusalem: Makor, 5731/1971), pp. 187–188. *Targum Neophyti* 1 on Gen. 49:10, vol. 1, p. 331, renders "scribes who teach the Law" in general, without any allusion to Hillel's dynasty.

131. See *Studies in the History of the Sanhedrin*, pp. 39–41, 239–240, and *passim* index. Therefore once the Talmud was officially edited, overlooking a Talmudic source renders the judgment null and void; see Sanhedrin 6a.

132. *IShG*, p. 50, and editor's note 5, on p. 7; see *Teshubot ha-Geonim*, ed. A. Harkavi (Berlin: 1887), #262, p. 135; Yerushalmi Horayot III, 7, 48c; *Golden Doves*, pp. 99–100; and J. N. Epstein, ed., *Perush ha-Ge'onim 'al Ṭahorot* (Berlin: Mekize Nirdamim, 1924), p. 3 n. 1. Cf. *Lehem Mishne* on *MT Ishut* 8:4.

133. *MT* Introduction, l. 10.

134. *MT* Introduction, ll. 52–55. The source is Sanhedrin 5a, stating that R. Judah the Prince "taught Tora in public (ברבים)," i.e., he published it. See appendix 38.

files and archives is designated *megillat setarim*, "a scroll" containing "private," i.e., unpublished material, not for general circulation (see appendix 40). In contrast, to 'publish' such material is designated *galle* ('unveiling') – a previously private text and making it available for the general public (see appendix 41). In this respect, too, the editor of the Mishna followed in the footsteps of Moses, who taught the oral traditions to the general public. Hence, he "sat" – *ex Cathedra* in the capacity of Head of the Academy – "throughout his life, and taught the Mishna in public together with his Court."[135]

Maimonides began the *Mishne Tora* by alluding to the difference between the original *perush* archived since Moses and the Oral Law:

> Each precept that was issued to Moses at Sinai was issued with its explication (בפרושן). As it is written: "And I [God] gave you (Moses) the stone-tablets, the Law, and the Precept (מצוה)." *Law* refers to the written text, whereas *Precept* refers to its *perush*. He (God) instructed us to administer the *Law* according to the *Precept*. The *Precept* is known [in rabbinic parlance] as Oral Law.[136]

Moses refrained from publishing it. "However, the *Precept* which constitutes the *perush* of the Tora was not written [i.e., published] by him (Moses), but (he, Moses) instructed the elders, Joshua and the rest of Israel" to safeguard it and transmit it.[137]

There was no precedent for the publication of the Mishna. As mentioned earlier, the records of Israel were not open to the general

---

135. *MT* Introduction, ll. 60–61; cf. *IShG*, pp. 58–59.

136. *MT* Introduction, ll. 2–4. See Introduction, *Perush ha-Mishnayot*, vol. 1, pp. 1–2; cf. *MT Teshuba* 3:8. In the course of time, however, *perush* and *Tora she-be-'al pe* became synonymous and were used indiscriminately even by as careful a writer as Maimonides; cf. *MT* Introduction, ll. 10, 12. See R. Pirqoi b. Baboi, in *Genizah Studies*, vol. 2, p. 571; R. Judah al-Bargeloni, *Perush Sefer Yeṣira*, p. 4, cf. p. 5 at the end.

137. *MT* Introduction, ll. 7–8.

public. Only occasionally, the Chief Justice would read from his minutes in public.

> From the time of Moses until the days of R. Judah the Prince, no work was redacted to teach the Oral Law publicly.[138] But in each and every generation, the Chief Justice or the Prophet [see appendix 26] of that generation would write for his personal use a memorandum of the various traditions which he had collected from his teachers, and would teach it orally in public[139] (ברבים).

A private individual, too, would occasionally "Write for his personal use, according to his own understanding, the explanations of the Law and halakhot which he had heard."[140] Hence the question: "Why did R. Judah the Prince do this [publish the Mishna] and not leave the matter as it had always been?" The answer is poignant and to the point:

> Because he witnessed the steady decline in the (number of) disciples and that increasingly new torments were regularly being devised [against Israel]. At the same time, the Empire of Evil was steadily expanding her dominion, and gaining strength throughout the world – while Israel was being pushed out, further and further to the confines (of the globe).

The Mishna was published "in order that the Oral Law should not be erased from the memory of Israel." With this purpose in mind, R. Judah the Prince "composed a treatise accessible to all," that is, formally published, "which could be learned rapidly, and not

138. Cf. *IShG*, p. 18.
139. *MT* Introduction, ll. 46–49. Cf. appendix 38.
140. *MT* Introduction, ll. 49–50. These notes were informal records with no standing in a Court of Law.

forgotten."[141] The *oral* dimension of the Mishna, demanding active and continuous rehearsal, was a decisive factor in the retention of the text: once it was learned, particularly at a young age, it would not be easily forgotten or amended.[142] Public instruction of a text rich in legal concepts and ready-made behavioral recipes internalized the system and transformed the people of Israel into a *Law* abiding society. It was a singular achievement!

In this context, I would like to call attention to the Biblical term 'תקן' (root TQN) describing the activities of *Qohelet* (Ecclesiastes, whom Jewish tradition identifies as King Solomon). It says that he "established (תקן) many proverbs" (Eccl. 12:9). There are two basic meanings attached to this term. First, it is regularly used in rabbinic literature in the sense of 'promulgation of rulings, either by the political or by the judicial authorities.' Second, these rulings are transmitted to the general public orally. Thus, according to tradition, King Solomon circulated many aphorisms among the people designed to help them govern themselves. In this precise sense the Talmud and Geonim described the publication of the Mishna by R. Judah the Prince as 'תקין' (root TQN) 'to establish, to decree', that is, in the mold of King Solomon's aphorisms. (see appendix 42).[143]

In sum: originally, the doctrines and minutes of the Supreme Court of Israel, beginning with Moses, were not published. Although basic legal instruction was offered to all, the archival material of the Court was unavailable to the general public. The enemies of Israel took advantage of this situation, first by destroying the archives and butchering the sages; then by sponsoring a coercive ideology designed to bewilder the general public. Israel resolved the crisis in a most creative manner. By conveying its national archives from the precinct of the Temple to the mind of the people, a situation of mutual interdependence was established, whereby the Mishna would structure the collective memory of Israel, and the people

141. *MT* Introduction, ll. 56–60. Cf. *Saadya's Commentary on Genesis*, p. 186.

142. See *Golden Doves*, pp. 92–94.

143. Yebamot 64b; see *IShG*, pp. 7, 50.

would give substance and meaning to these records. Rabbinic literature in general and Talmud in particular are the outcome of this unique type of symbiosis.

# Chapter 44
# Minting Tradition into Oral Law

Rabbi 'Aqiba – the intellectual and spiritual father of the Mishna – proposed "minting the whole Tora into coins."[144] The metaphor 'coin/speech' was known to the Ancient Greeks, and has been extensively discussed in modern scholarship. Reflecting Greek tradition, which associates coinage with tyranny, Jesus wanted to expel the money changers from the Temple (Jn. 2:14–15, see below).[145] Philo, on the other hand, compared Moses to "a good money changer"[146] – a metaphor later adopted by the rabbis.[147] In the rabbinic economy of ideas, 'coinage' involves seven fundamental concepts.

First, a 'coin' is a 'seal' bearing the imprint of an archetypal model.[148] What renders a piece of metal legal tender is the fact that it bears an inscription, a symbol of, and therefore guaranteed by, the political authority issuing it. In pagan political ideology, government is a

144. *AdRN*, A, XVIII, p. 67; see *Golden Doves*, pp. 98–99. Cf. above n. 107.
145. See Marc Shell, *The Economy of Literature* (Baltimore: Hopkins University Press, 1978), pp. 12–13, and 34–35. About Jesus incident with the money changers, see ibid., p. 156 and above Section III n. 106.
146. "On Sobriety," 20, in *Philo*, vol. 3, p. 455.
147. *Sifre* #13, p. 22; see *Golden Doves*, pp. 142–143.
148. The "image of God" in man is portrayed as God's currency on earth; see *Golden Doves*, pp. 140–142.

function of might (see above chapter 12). According to rabbinic tradition, a minimum requirement for *de facto* political authority, with the right to legislate, is having its currency accepted as legal tender.[149] In this consideration, minting the oral tradition and its subsequent circulation attested to the fact that although deprived of military might, Jews constituted a sovereign nation.

Second, the inscription on a coin guarantees its authenticity. Even before Bethar, the availability of sages who could certify a *perush* or *halakha* was scarce. Prior to the official publication of the Mishna, traditions circulating among the rabbis were compared to coins wanting certification. "I have many coins," bewailed R. 'Aqiba at the death of one of his teachers, "but I have no bankers who could certify them."[150] Once issued as *legal tender* the authenticity of the Mishna is guaranteed, requiring no further validation.

Third, the inscription of a coin is semantically identical to the metal bearing the inscription: the metal of the coin *is* the inscription and vice versa.[151] Similarly, the *memory* of Israel bearing the Mishna and the *inscriptions* thereof are one and the same.

---

149. *MT Gezela* 5:18. The source is Megilla 14b, stipulating that before his coronation David lacked political authority, since "his currency has not yet circulated." Cf. Nedarim 28a and Baba Qamma 113b. Bearing this rule in mind, Jews in the Sassanide empire regarded the Roman Empire as more legitimate than the Persian; see Shebu'ot 6b, 'Aboda Zara 2b, and R. Hayye Gaon's *responsum* in *Qehillat Shelomo* (Jerusalem, 5659/1899), #11, p. 16. As long as the king's currency was accepted, he could not be deposed; see Y. Sanhedrin II, 5, 20b and the parallel source in *Midrash Shemu'el* XXIII, 12, p. 59. The rabbis distinguished between a currency issued by a failed rebellion, such as Bar-Kokhba's or by a deposed king, which is no longer to be regarded as legal tender, and the currency of a previous king, which is regarded as legal tender; see Tosefta Ma'aser Sheni 1:5–6, p. 244; Baba Qamma 97a-b; Y. Ma'aser Sheni I, 1, 59d. For further reference, cf. Mishna Ma'aser Sheni 1:2, *MT Ma'aser Sheni* 4:10, and *Tosefta Ki-Fshuṭah, Zera'im*, vol. 2, p. 717.

150. Sanhedrin 68a and Mishna Nazir 7:4. See *Golden Doves,* p. 142.

151. This explains why some rabbis avoided looking at a Roman coin; see 'Aboda Zara 5a. Probably the coin in question had the image of Caesar claiming to be divine, cf. *The Economy of Literature*, p. 82.

Fourth, legal tender functions as the *measure* of value: wares are measured against it, but legal tender cannot be measured against wares.[152] Both the economic and textual aspects of coinage follow a semiotic principle, whereby the interpreter system cannot be interpreted by another system; e.g., the Braille and Morse systems are interpreted by the alphabet, but not the other way around. In Judaism, too, there is a semiological relation between the Oral Law and Scripture, wherein the Oral Law is the interpreter system and Scripture is the interpreted system. This principle acquires precision when we recall that the Oral Law is the articulation of the original *perush* or interpreter of the Law. Accordingly, Oral Law can interpret Scripture but Scripture cannot interpret Oral Law. Would the Oral Law become the subject of 'interpretation' it would cease to be an 'interpreter' system.[153] Thus *derasha* may not be applied to oral texts.[154]

Fifth, special measures must be taken against forgery. In antiquity this was the responsibility of money changers. The same applied to

152. Also, it cannot be measured against other currencies as in modern monetary systems. In light of this principle, we can understand the prohibition of interest. What renders payment of interest inequitable in Jewish law are two facts. First, payment is guaranteed; Jewish law does not recognize default of a loan. Second, Jewish law deals with 'hard currency' which, since it functions as the economic measure of value, cannot fluctuate. However, when there is a risk of loss and non-payment, as in an investment, the laws of 'interest' do not apply; see R. David Nieto, *Maṭṭe Dan* 3:135–144. In my estimation, the same logic does not apply to 'fiat money,' as with modern monetary systems, where currency is subject to government policy and fluctuation. This is particularly true in a global economy.

153. See above chapter 6, and *Golden Doves*, pp. 111–113. Given that Scripture cannot be used as 'a measure,' Baba Meṣi'a 33a describes Scripture as "a measure which is not a measure," (מדה שאינה מדה) i.e., which cannot be used to measure the Mishna, which is itself a "measure." The Mishna itself, however, is not the same as the "Talmud," which is the standard against which all other measures are reckoned: "you have no measure more authoritative than this" (אין לך מדה גדולה מזו); see Baba Batra 145b, and *'Arukh*, s.v. *midda*. R. Profiaṭ Duran, *Ma'ase Efod* (Vienna, 1865), p. 4 preserved a slightly different version: "העוסקים במקרא, מדה," rather than "מדה שאינה מדה." Cf. below n. 262.

154. See *Golden Doves*, p. 125.

the world of ideas, particularly at a time when Gnostic Christians and marginal Jews circulated all kinds of apocryphal works and dicta designed to confuse the general public. Jesus' opposition to money changers (Jn. 2:14–15, Matt. 21:12) – the bankers of antiquity – would leave the public open to hoax and deception and lead inevitably to the collapse of the monetary system (see appendix 43). In the course of this chapter we shall see that a principal concern in the instruction of Oral Law was to prevent forgery and debasement of authentic tradition.

Sixth, essentially, a monetary system functions in density and exchangeability of value. Concerning oral texts, R. Me'ir, one of R. 'Aqiba's principal disciples and the sage whose editorial labor served as the basis for the redaction of the Mishna, counseled: "Endeavor at all times to formulate the words of the Tora into comprehensive principles." This means that the wording must be as dense and inclusive as possible. "For if you were to formulate them in detail, they would wear you down, and you would not know what to do with them." To illustrate this point he offered an analogy from commerce. A businessman needs a large amount of money for his trade. If he carried it in small denominations, he would be exhausted, "and not know how to handle them." In such a situation, it would be advisable "to exchange them into golden coins that could be converted [on demand] and spent in any place that he wishes."[155] A principal characteristic of the style of the Mishna is brevity and maximum density of meaning. This is consistent with the archival character of the Mishna (see above chapter 41).

Seventh, to serve as a medium of exchange coinage must be stable. Ideally, the fiscal authorities should not modify the rate of exchange or manipulate it.[156] This may explain the fact that during his long tenure, R. Judah the Prince and his court changed some of their views, recognized new material, and approved some halakhot

155. *Sifre* #306, p. 339; see below, n. 180.
156. See *The Tyrant's Writ*, pp. 32–33.

that had previously been rejected. And yet, these changes were *not* incorporated into the text of the Mishna. Such changes would have resulted in havoc. R. Emanuel Ḥai Ricchi (1668–1743), one of the finest Talmudists of his time, noted how difficult it would be in practical terms to amend a text that had been memorized in school at an early age. In no time, conflict would have arisen as to which is the 'revised' and which is the 'original' version.[157]

The preceding considerations allow for a more precise understanding of 'written' and 'oral' Law. Let us begin by noting, at the very outset, that the expression 'Oral Law' (תורה שבעל פה) is not to be found in the Mishna, Tosefta, or any other Tannaitic source! It appears in the Babylonian Talmud, but not in the Yerushalmi (see appendix 44). The reason is obvious. Only after [a] minting the *perush* into *coins,* [b] processing them into halakhot, and [c] *imprinting* them in the *memory of the people,* could they acquire the status of [i] a 'Law' which is essentially [ii] 'Oral' and could be [iii] freely communicated and exchanged, as legal tender.

The publication of a written text is radically different from an oral text, not because one is written and the other is not, but rather, because a written text is published to be *read,* whereas an oral text is published to be *recited* (see appendix 45). In Hebrew, 'reading' involves *derasha,* i.e., *interpretation* and *subjective* understanding (see above chapter 9). An oral text involves 'recitation' and *qabbala,* i.e., *acceptance* from an official transmitter (*mashne, tanna*) and the responsibility to *authenticate* it and *faithfully transmit* it (see appendix 32). Popular wisdom notwithstanding, in no place did the sages state that it is forbidden (אסור) to write the Oral Law or to recite the Written Law orally (see appendix 45). Consequently, in no place did the rabbis provide a special 'dispensation' to 'write the Oral Law,' as commonly believed (see appendix 46). What the rabbis stipulated was that "written texts," i.e., Scripture, "you are not authorized to speak" – in the sense of 'formal conveyance' – "verbally." Accordingly,

157. See *Golden Doves,* pp. 92–94.

the Scripture is to be classified as a document that was "published to be written" (נתנה להכתב, see appendix 45). For the purpose of our present discussion this means that Scripture could only be *transmitted* from an authorized text (תאג'). Therefore, a variant reading may not be introduced on the basis of oral tradition, but only from a properly certified text[158] (.(תאג' Conversely, "an oral text" – such as the Mishna – "you are not authorized to say" – in the sense of 'formal transmission' – "in writing," but only from an official transmitter (*mashne, tanna*).[159] These texts belong to the class of documents that were "published not to be written" (לא נתנה להכתב). Thus, although put into writing, they do not have the status of a written document (see appendix 45). In short, just as the Scripture can only be copied properly from a certified scroll (תאג') and conveyed in writing, so too the Mishna (and Talmud), as an *oral* text, must be duly received from the lips of a certified instructor (*mashne, tanna*) and be transmitted orally.[160]

---

158. E.g., the Scrolls of Tora deposited at the *Sidra*; see Y. Kil'ayim III, 1, 28c. Variants in the Scripture may be accepted as long as they proceeded from duly accredited codices, such as those of the Masoret Ben-Ephraim. For reasons of history, rather than doctrine or law, Ben-Asher's version became standard because it received Maimonides' approval; see *MT Sefer Tora* 8:4.
159. In a sense, the *tanna* can be compared to a conveyancer in English law, who examines a title of real estate and certifies its authenticity; see below n. 160. That is why, to ensure that the Tora "would not be forgotten from Israel," R. Ḥiyya would have "*written* the Five Books" of the Tora and "*recited* the Six Orders" of the Mishna to six children; see Baba Meṣi'a 85b. Noticeably, each child could then "recite" to others the Order that he had learned, since he 'received' it from a *tanna*. See below n. 166.
160. Text variants were introduced and acknowledged on the basis of oral traditions from duly certified transmitters; see *IShG*, pp. 23–25; *Teshubot ha-Ge'onim* (Harkavi), #229, p. 107; *Genizah Studies*, vol. 2, pp. 58–59. Talmudic sages continuously challenged the version of the Mishna on the basis of texts which they had received from their respective certified instructors – but not from written copies. For a survey of this material, see Ezra Z. Melammed, *Essays in Talmudic Literature* (Heb.) (Jerusalem: Hebrew University, 1986), pp. 57–84. In "The Status of Jewish Real Estate outside Israel's Territory," pp. 782, 786–788, I examined one such controversy in 'Arakhin 29a. See the following note.

The following *responsum* by Maimonides elucidates this principle. A question was addressed to him inquiring why conflicts among Talmudic sages concerning the pronunciation of some words in the Mishna were not resolved by consulting an authorized codex: "isn't the [text of] the Mishna [written] before us!?" To which Maimonides replied:

> Is the [text of the] Mishna [contained] in a codex at the Temple Archive, containing neither fewer nor extra letters [= an exact number of letters]!? [So] how could it be established what R. [Judah] the Prince wrote in the Mishna?... [The accurate text of the Mishna can be established] only from certified sages – not from codices![161]

A similar position was presented earlier by R. Sherira Gaon: "The Talmud and Mishna were not written," i.e., were not given to be transmitted in writing. Therefore, "the rabbis are careful to learn the *girsa* [of the Mishna and Talmud], by heart," that is, from certified transmitters, "not from written," i.e., 'authoritatively written' "texts."[162] This is exactly the view of R. Nissim Gaon. Although the sages had "found it necessary to write (= edit) the Talmud, as they saw the poverty of [our] nation and her wanting." Nonetheless, "they would transmit its text (גורסין) by heart."[163] The fact that a text was classified as 'oral' did not mean that it was not put down in writing (see appendix 45). The fact that the tractates of the Mishna were arranged according to size, rather than theme, attests to the fact that we are

161. *Teshubot ha-Rambam*, #442, vol. 3, p. 721. Accordingly, we may understand the criticism raised by R. Sherira Gaon, *Sha'are Teshuba* #187, 75b, against the "little foxes" who "take out their books" to prove Talmudic matters; see below chapter 50. Although the Mishna may be colloquially referred as "כתבי הקודש," see *Sefer ha-Qabbala* (Heb.), p. 56 (l. 157), cf. ibid p. 33 (ll. 6–7), it never acquired the status of 'written'; see R. Joseph ibn Megas, *She'elot wu-Tshubot* (Salonika, 5546/1786), #92, 13a, cited below appendix 45, and *Golden Doves*, pp. xvii, 121.

162. *IShG*, pp. 71–72; cf. ibid., pp. 24–25.

163. Introduction, *Sefer ha-Mafteaḥ*, 3b. See appendix 45.

dealing with codices stacked up on top of one another, as practiced in oriental libraries, where smaller volumes are placed on top of larger volumes, regardless of theme.[164] Yet, since these codices contained 'oral' rather than 'written' material, they could not serve as authoritative texts (see appendix 45).

As with coinage, an important ingredient of a text is the material on which it is inscribed. In the case of the Scripture, to acquire canonical status (כשר) a scroll must be transcribed with a special ink, on specially prepared parchment.[165] The same applies to the Mishna. The transmitter (*mashne, tanna*) is the instrument transcribing the text. As with a scroll, the oral material must be transcribed onto a specially prepared material: the memory of the student. Again, just as a text that has been duly copied acquires the status of the original (תאג'), a student who received the oral text from a certified transmitter equals the transmitter.[166]

Instruction of an oral text is radically different from that of

---

164. Hence the principle establishing that "there is no order to the Mishna"; Baba Qamma 102a, 'Aboda Zara 7a; cf. *IShG*, pp. 32–33. Each pile of volumes consisted of a single order, where the particular tractates were stacked one on top of another according to size. It seems that the six orders were placed consecutively, one row next to the other, according to the six classes, *Zera'im.. Ṭahorot* ; see *Kesef Mishne* on *MT Roṣeaḥ* 9:1. This coincides with the view of R. Moses ben Ḥabib, *Kappot Temarim* (New York, 5713/1953), 56d, on *Tosafot*, Sukka 37a s.v. *kol din*, that the above-mentioned rule applies only to tractates in the same order, but not tractates in different orders. See, however, Maimonides, *Perush ha-Mishnayot*, Introduction, vol. 1, p. 24ff. where he attempted to present a theory explaining the rationale for the peculiar sequence of the tractates of the Mishna, and *IShG*, pp. 33–34.

165. See *MT Sefer Tora* chapter 10.

166. Thus, the children instructed by R. Ḥiyya, Baba Meṣi'a 85b, equal R. Ḥiyya; see above n. 158. *Shone* (= Aramaic *matne*) is the verb indicating the transmission of an oral text by a certified instructor. It is now clear why the rabbis warned not to *shone* to an improper student; see Ḥolin 133a; *Golden Doves*, p. 188 n. 9; and appendix 39. Given that the student's memory registers the collective memory of Israel, the rabbis stipulated "not to convey (מוסרים), the words of the Tora (i.e., oral tradition) to an alien"; see Ḥagiga 13a and *Golden Doves*, pp. 14–15. Officers and Treasury clerks, too, must be US citizens.

Scripture. In addition to the general sense of the written text of Scripture, available to the general public, there is a special type of instruction that Arabic speaking Jews call *talqin* (root LQN, cf. *Koran* 2:35), 'instruction and oral dictation.' It comprises three levels. The first level consists of coaching the student to memorize the text verbatim. At this stage, the student is expected to *recite the text* flawlessly (cf. *Perush ha-Mishnayot,* Berakhot 5:4, vol. 1, pp. 74, 75) – as if it were a poem – cf. R. Se'adya Gaon's translation to Deut. 31:19). As with Balaam, who was instructed to recite the "words which were placed in his mouth" in spite of his own personal sentiments against Israel (see R. Se'adya Gaon's translation of Num. 22:38, 23:3, 5, 12, and his *Perush* on Prov. 28:18, p. 232). This type of instruction is known in rabbinic tradition as *girsa.*[167] The second level is the transmission of the original *intention* of the text,[168] and corresponds to the *gamir* stage of rabbinic education. The third level involves mastering the *principles* underlying the oral text. Concerning this third level of *talqin*-instruction, Se'adya Gaon wrote: "is (the method) by which one learns the premises and principles [peculiar] to a discipline from someone preceding him."[169]

167. Traditionally, this term is associated with the Aramaic *garis* 'half a horse-bean,' and therefore connected to 'crushing, pounding' the lesson into the student; cf. *IShG,* p. 7, ed. note 9. Instead, I would like to propose the Arabic root GRS 'to plant,' in the sense of 'planting' the text in the memory of the student; see Tosefta Soṭa 7:11, p. 194; Ḥagiga 3b, cited below n. 189; and *Golden Doves,* p. 183 n. 58. The metaphor 'planting/studying' is the theme of the blessing that each reader pronounces after concluding his portion (עלייה) of the Tora. The reader gives thanks to God for the Tora that He gave us. Adding: "a true Tora, He planted (נטע) inside us." Thus, the rule comparing an incompetent teacher to a planter who blundered in his task, acquires sense and precision; see Baba Batra 21b in conjunction with *MT Sekhirut* 10:7. See also Shraga Abramson, *Ba-Merkazim wuba-Tefuṣot,* (Jerusalem: Mossad Harav Kook, 5725/1965), p. 150, ll. 3–4.

168. Cf. R. Abraham Maimonides, *Perush,* p. 229.

169. R. Se'adya Gaon, *Perush* on *Mishle,* ed. R. Joseph Qafiḥ (Jerusalem, 5736/1976), p. 16; cf. ibid., p. 232. Yefet b. 'Eli, in his *Commentary* to Prov. 2:10 used this term somehow similarly, but, given his Karraite background, not exactly the same; see Israel Gunzig's edition (Krakow, 1898), pp. xvi-xvii. Cf. *Ba-Merkazim*

This level corresponds to the rabbinic *sabir* or critical understanding of the law[170] (see appendix 37).

Instruction of a *talqin*-composition requires the assistance of a skilled teacher; as with a map or musical notations, which cannot be grasped by the uninitiated student unless tutored by a competent instructor.[171] That is why *talqin* cannot be taught in writing. The instructor is required to evaluate the intellectual make-up of the student, his knowledge of the subject at hand, and his grasp of the subject – something that could best be determined through interaction with the student. R. Sar Shalom (d. ca. 859/864), who occupied the chair of Gaon at Sura for about ten years (ca. 850), alluded to some of the vicissitudes facing the instructor of halakha. Addressing a correspondent who asked him to explain a *halakha* in detail, the Gaon wrote:

> If you could be motivated to come personally to us, then it would be possible to explain them [the niceties and details of the halakha] thoroughly, and clearly differentiate one from the other – as "a word spoken on its two axes" (cf. Prov. 25:11). Because only when a disciple is seated in front of his instructor, arguing a point of halakha, can his instructor know (for certain) in which direction his mind moves; what he does not know, what he discerns clearly, and what he has trouble in understanding. Then (the instructor) can expose (the subject)

---

*wuba-Tefuṣot*, p. 150 ll. 15–20, and *Homo Mysticus*, p. 111. This term was also used by the master of Masora in Tiberias to describe the instruction of the proper vocalization and enunciation of the Hebrew Scripture; see *Cairo Geniza*, p. 78, mistranslated by Kahle as "inspiration."

170. See *Golden Doves*, pp. 95–96.

171. See Introduction, *Perush ha-Mishnayot*, vol. 1, p. 18 in which some halakhot could not be inferred from the text of Tora, but only known through *talqin* derived from Moses (the Arabic text is faulty; instead of תלקית read: תלקין). Cf. *Golden Doves*, pp. 111–113; cf. pp. xxv, 16–17.

> to him, brighten his eyes, and point out the (various) facets of the halakha. But in writing, what can he do? Quite little![172]

This leads to one of the most fundamental aspects of Mishna and Talmudic studies: the immediacy between the intellectual processing of the texts and the method of oral transmission. There was special wisdom in this strategy. Referring to the loss of esoteric tradition in Israel, Maimonides wrote:

> You should know that the numerous disciplines that were in our nation concerning the true meaning of these matters have vanished in the course of time, and are under the domination of ignorant nations. Given that these matters were not accessible to the general public, as we have explained [see *MT Yesode ha-Tora* 2:12; 4:10], and that the only text accessible to the general public was the Scripture.
>
> You already know that originally even the legal traditions were not compiled, in compliance with the well-known doctrine of our nation: "Words that have been said to you orally you may not (אי אתה רשאי) say them in writing." This was superlative wisdom concerning the Law! Because they attempted to avert falling into what in effect happened later to it [the Law]. I mean, scores of opinions, the predominance of divisive doctrines, confusion as to the sense of the edited texts, ambiguity pertaining to it, division among the people leading to the establishment of sects, and bewilderment concerning the implementation (Ar. *al-a'mal)* of the law. Given that all these matters had originally pertained to the Supreme Court,

172. *Teshubot Ge'onim Qadmonim*, ed. David Cassel (Berlin, 1848), #46, 9a; reprinted in ed. R. Samuel ha-Cohen Weinberg, *Teshubot R. Sar Shalom* (Jerusalem: Mossad Harav Kook, 1975), #84, pp. 100–101. On the sense of "a word spoken on its two axes"; see *Golden Doves*, p. 122, cf. pp.114–116.

> as we have explained in our Magnus Opus (the *Mishne Tora*), and as it was indicated by the Tora.[173]

To be efficient, a monetary system must be stable. This implies, above all, the responsibility not to debase the coinage or manipulate it at will.[174] We can now understand why, although R. Judah the Prince and his court changed some of their views and accepted halakhot which they had previously rejected, they refrained, nonetheless, from incorporating these changes into the text of the Mishna, or to formally publish them in a different collection. This leads to a series of questions: How can further halakhic developments be duly registered? How can sages and students learn about the introduction of new sources, and judicial reexamination and reversals of the court? A further question: since the Mishna is the national coinage of Israel, what is it that could be measured and obtained with the said coin? Finally, given that the basic function of money is to facilitate trade, how effective was the Mishna in promoting the exchange of Jewish values and ideas?

The publication of the Mishna served to establish the space between national and vernacular memory. The rabbinic mind unfolds in the intellectual space created by these two memories. At the center of that space stood the *Yeshiba*, where texts and traditions were freely evaluated and exchanged.

---

173. *Guide*, I, 71, p. 121, ll. 9–19. See below the quotation from Chief Rabbi Hertz, n. 261. On the sense of *al-a'mal*, see Section V, n. 317.

174. See *The Tyrant's Writ*, pp. 32–33.

# Chapter 45
# National and Vernacular Memory

After the publication of the Mishna, Jewish authorities refrained from publishing collections circulating privately among various schools.[175] There was wisdom in this strategy.

Let us begin by pointing out that the *Sifra* and *Sifre* on Leviticus and Deuteronomy, edited by Rab (2nd and 3rd centuries) – one of the foremost rabbinic authorities of all time – were not published. These collections contain the enabling legislative justification of many of the *halakhot* in the Mishna. Similarly, the *Mekhilta* on Exodus, as well as the famous homiletic collections known as *Midrash Rabbot* on the Pentateuch and the Five Scrolls, and many other compilations, although containing material pertaining to the traditional doctrines of Israel, were not published. The official publication of exegetical material would have hampered 'reading' the Law, and restricted personal interpretation (*derasha*). 'Studying Tora' would be nothing more than an authoritarian 'instruction in the truth' (or *belehrt*) – a code term for psychological and intellectual coercion (as with the establishment of the German Empire in 1871 and Bismarck's nationalist demagoguery). This strategy was consistent with the doctrine that "matters pertaining to the heart" do not fall within the jurisdiction of the court (see above chapter 11). The tradition around the Law originating with Moses

175. Cf. *IShG*, p. 36.

that was subsequently augmented and transmitted by the Supreme Court throughout the ages pertains to the actual *implementation* of the *miṣvot*. It focuses on actions – not on matters of faith. Echoing this fundamental principle, Maimonides opened the *Introduction* to the *Mishne Tora* with this remarkable passage:

> Every precept given to Moses at Sinai was given with its explanation.... We were ordered to implement (לעשות) the Law according to the *miṣva*. This *miṣva* is designated [in rabbinic parlance] "Oral Law."[176]

Put differently, the details, clarifications, and doctrines transmitted from Moses on, concern the implementation (לעשות) of the Law – a term connected with 'action, deed' (לעשות = Ar. *al-a'mal*) under the jurisdiction of the court – not of creeds. Explicitly, Maimonides declared that matters of faith are not justiciable:

> We have already mentioned several times that whenever there are differences of opinion among the sages, which do not involve action (Ar. *'amal*), but pertain only to matters of faith, there is no way in which a halakhic decision could be rendered about it.[177]

176. *MT* Introduction, ll. 2–4; cf. ll. 95–97, 156–157. Similarly in *Mamrim* 1:1: "the *actions* of the Law," and in 1:2: "*to act* in accordance..." see quotation from *Guide* above n. 173. R. Se'adya Gaon Ex. 18:20 used Ar. *'amal* to translate Heb. מעשה. See Section V, n. 317.

177. *Perush ha-Mishnayot, Sanhedrin* 10:3, vol. 4, p. 218; cf. Soṭa 3:3, vol. 3, p. 257; Shebu'ot 1:4, vol. 4, p. 250; *Sefer ha-Miṣvot*, negative precept #193, p. 242; *Teshubot ha-Rambam* #458, vol. 2, p. 739; cf. *Iggerot ha-Rambam*, vol. 2, p. 461. Maran Joseph Caro, too, held a similar position; see his *Abqat Rokhel* (Salonika, 5551/1791), #28, 34c s.v. *ve-'od*. Similarly, Maimonides occasionally leaves out from the *MT* views that do not belong to law proper, e.g., concerning cutting of the nails, Mo'ed Qaṭan 18a; singing to the bride, Ketubot 17a (this meets the objection raised by R. Joshua Sh. Ardiṭ, *Ḥinna ve-Ḥisda*, vol. 2, [Izmir, 5633/1873], 6b-c). Therefore, Maimonides would explain a Mishna differently than the Talmud does in matters not pertaining to halakha; see Nazir 5:5, *Perush*

Before probing into the Jewish strategy of publication we must take note that halakhic collections, too, such as the Tosefta, were never published. Why?

The concept of a 'National Memory' gains resonance through syntagmatic opposition to a 'vernacular memory.' If the Mishna represents Israel's 'National Memory,' then all the unpublished material must be regarded *ipso facto* as 'vernacular memory.' To understand the interplay of these two types of memory, let us point out that contrary to what historians and rabbinic scholars teach, the Mishna is not a code of law. Jews never codified the Law or any part thereof.[178] Emphatically, the rabbis declared: "A law cannot be learned from the Mishna!" (see appendix 48). Rather, the Mishna is a collection of legal themes and questions *to be investigated* and *expanded* at the

---

*ha-Mishnayot*, vol. 3, p. 182. Occasionally, he would offer a different explanation from the Mishna itself; contrast *Guide* III, 45, p. 423 (ll. 23–25) with Middot 3:4. R. Se'adya Gaon, too, explained a Mishna differently than both the Babli and the Yerushalmi; see his Teshubot, in *Oeuvres Complete*, vol. 9 (Paris: Ernest Leroux, 1897), ed. R. Joel Muller, #14, p. 103 n. 3. The preceding will explain the fact that *Emora'im* occasionally oppose the *Tanna'im* in the field of Biblical exegeses and doctrine (*aggadot*). In the words of R. Jacob Ḥajez, *Teḥillat Ḥokhma* (Verona, 5407/1647), III, #40, p. 63: "That in subjects concerning exegeses (*derashot*) and homilies (*aggadot*) it does not matter if an *Emora* opposes a *Tanna*." Commenting on this view, R. Hezekiah David Abulafia, *Ben Zequnim* (Leghorn, 5553/1793), 13a noted: "He meant, that he [the *Emora*] had as much authority as that of a *Tanna*. Possibly, the reason for that is that *Emora'im* were more knowledgeable in questions of exegeses and matters not pertaining to law and [they proposed] more satisfying explanations." Cf. below Section V, nn. 92, 174. This is consistent with the principle upheld by the Geonim and other rabbinic authorities that a legislation passed on the basis of biblical exegesis can be abrogated by a less senior court on the basis of another biblical exegesis; see above Section II, nn. 110, 112.

178. A legal 'code' in Roman law, or in a modern Civil law system, *excludes* all legal material outside it. After Justinian promulgated *Corpus Juris Civilis*, no one in a Roman Court could quote an earlier law. Similarly, in France after the promulgation of *Code Napoleon* (1804), all preceding legislation was abrogated; see John Henry Merryman, *The Civil Law Tradition* (Stanford, CA: Stanford University Press, 1985), chapter 5. Judaism never recognized such 'codes.'

*Yeshiba,* similar to what Vico refers to as *ars topica judicalis.*[179] We mentioned earlier that the Mishna is divided into six *Sedarim,* a term denoting 'themes of oratory' – like the liturgical themes in the Siddur or 'Prayer Book' – to be expanded by the precentor at the Synagogue; or the themes of Exodus, which are to be expanded on the night of Passover by the participants at the Seder (see appendix 36). The Mishna, too, contains the legal *topics* to be expanded by the masters of rabbinic eloquence or *emora'im* (singular *emora* from the root 'AMR 'to speak,' 'to articulate,' 'to expose'), designating the Talmudic sage. The *emora* or Talmudic sage is the master of eloquence competent to develop the topics of the ancient masters of the Mishna (see appendix 49). As indicated above, the style of the Mishna is marked by brevity and density.

It would be important to point out that R. Me'ir, who advised to formulate the lessons into coins of high denomination, proposed that one "should *shone* (the lesson) to his disciples by the shorter pathway (דרך קצרה)."[180] Thus, at the conclusion of each class, the teacher would encode the gist of the lesson in a concise formula that the student could easily memorize and later, as the opportunity arose, decode. Using R. Me'ir's analogy, the student would be able to "exchange" these coins and use them "in any place he wishes." R. Ṣadoq, who served as Gaon at Sura (816–818), wrote: "Our Holy Teacher (R. Judah the Prince), further condensed the extended (style) of the previous masters." The rationale is simple: "since every single word derives from judiciary tradition (*qabbala*)," there would be no need for substantiation. "In addition," he continued, "it (the Mishna)

179. *On the Study Methods of Our Time,* XI, p. 48; cf. *The Art of Rhetoric* (Atlanta: Rodopi, 1996), XIII, p. 28. For an incisive, well-focused study, see Robert C. Miner, "Verum-factum and Practical Wisdom in the Early Writings of Giambattista Vico," *Journal of the History of Ideas* 59 (1998), pp. 53–73.

180. See Pesaḥim 3b and Ḥolin 63b, where this rule is reported in the name of R. Me'ir; cf. above n. 155 and Rashi on Zebaḥim 2a s.v. *lamma.* A principal concern of this style is maximum meaning with minimum verbosity, see *MT De'ot* 2:4; cf. *MT* Introduction, l. 158, and appendix 34.

encoded all the innovative points contained in the *barraitot*."[181] The task of the Talmudic sages was to *expand* these topics, through rabbinic rhetoric and dialectic, and 'solve' the 'clues' (*remez*) and 'short pathways' (דרך קצרה) in the Mishna (see Appendices 31, 34), by interplaying the vernacular sources in the light of the Mishna.

> The master *emora'im* who arose after Ribbi (= R. Judah the Prince) were in much need of those *barraitot*, because through them they could extract all those profound matters expressed in the Mishna succinctly (Aramaic קיטא = Heb. דרך קצרה), in cryptograms (*remez*), and in general principles. Through them (the *barraitot*) they were able to dig up stems and innovative (doctrines) and corollaries [from the root-principle]. Given that Ribbi (= R. Judah the Prince) only redacted for them (future students) root-principles, but he did not expose what can be learned from them by judicial analogy. [To accomplish this] these masters (*emora'im*) required in-depth analysis and judicial theory (*sebara*). Some also required (additional) sources (*milta*), and had to compare one source to analogous sources, and connect it with its root-principle [in the Mishna].[182]

Through the interplay of sources, both national and vernacular, the *emora'im* "could elucidate a [matter in the Mishna] expressed succinctly, from [a matter] expressed fully [elsewhere]; and [a matter] which lies deeply in one Mishna, would be made clear (by analyzing) another Mishna."[183] Thus, the principle formulated by Talmudic commentators: "The mode of the *tanna* (master of the Mishna) is to *condense*, whereas the mode of an *emora* is to *expand*" (see appendix 49).

The *Yeshiba* or National Academy was the forum where these traditions were properly evaluated and exchanged. The sage was the officer in charge of regulating and evaluating the exchange. As

181. Cited in R. Joseph ibn Verga, *She'erit Yosef* (Warsaw, 1909), p. 1.

182. *IShG*, p. 43.

183. *IShG*, p. 44.

with commerce, the exchange was effected through persuasion, not coercion. An important factor in the discussions of the *emora'im* was the unpublished material introduced in the forum (cf. appendix 50). Primary among this material were the 'external sources' (Aramaic *barraitot,* sing. *barraita*), coming from unpublished collections of *perush* and halakha. A *barraita,* however, although from trustworthy sources, could not be cited unless approved by the head of the *Yeshiba.* Occasionally, R. Johanan would reject a *barraita* flatly and instruct the *tanna*: "Go! Recite it outside" (the *Yeshiba*).[184] Sometimes, the *barraita* would be accepted, not as proposed, but with some textual or semantic emendations. These emendations were not the effect of some sort of 'scientific' editing, on the basis of more 'authoritative' texts, as fancied by some illustrious scholars, but were mostly based on rhetorical or legal considerations. The status of an external source varied. If it was accepted by all the *Yeshibot* then it was quoted as *tanu rabbanan* ('thus the rabbis recited'). If only approved by a single *Yeshiba,* then it would be quoted as *tanya* ('it was recited'). If it had been approved only by the *tanna* of the *Yeshiba,* it was quoted with the verb *tana* (the *tanna* had *tana* 'recited').[185] A source cited by a single member was introduced as *tane* ('someone recited'). Occasionally, an *emora* knew of a *barraita* which had not yet been approved, and would develop the lesson as if it were his. Later, when the lesson would be reviewed in another *Yeshiba,* which had recognized the *barraita,* the editor would note that the view expressed in the lesson could be corroborated by that *barraita* (see appendix 51). A tannaitic tradition later formulated by *emora'im* was introduced as 'it was said' (איתמר) i.e., by *emora'im.*[186] In this fashion,

184. Shabbat 106a, 'Erubin 9a, Yoma 43b, Beṣa 12a-b, Yebamot 77b, Baba Qamma 34b, Sanhedrin 62b. Or what amounts to the same, that the text in question was "erroneous" (משבשתא); see Shabbat 121b; Pesaḥim 100a; Giṭṭin 73a; Qiddushin 47b; cf. Ḥolin 141b and *IShG*, p. 39.

185. Since the *tanna* generally recited from standard collections, the verb *tana* is usually associated with the Tosefta.

186. See *Golden Doves*, pp. 99–100.

the unpublished material was introduced into the forum and freely exchanged with the Mishna. The exchanges between the national and the vernacular traditions constitute the heart and soul of the Talmud (see the following chapter). Given that the entire edifice of rabbinic thought rests on the Mishna, the rabbis said: "A pillar of iron – that is what the Mishna is!"[187]

The intellectual space of the sages is the realm of the verisimilar. It pertains to rhetoric rather than metaphysics (see the following chapter). One will fail to find in the Talmud formal and analytical proofs, proceeding, as with the Scholastics, from syllogisms accompanied by axioms, premises and conclusions. Talmudic 'proofs' are not 'demonstrative'– structured from formal deductions and inductions. Talmudic dialectics deals with probable and improbable alternatives, inferences and analogue constructs, indeterminate and statistical knowledge, variables and quantitative differences.[188] Let us note that the Talmudic lexicon does not register the words 'rational' (מושכל) or 'necessary' (הכרח). Its dialectic is expository: it proposes the 'reasonable' (סברא), not the absolute. The divergent and contradictory opinions of the *emora'im* are not classified as 'true' (אמת) and 'false' (שקר).

Fundamental to the *Yeshibot* is a doctrine enunciated by the *Emora* Samuel (2nd and 3rd centuries). He had been a member of the court of R. Judah the Prince that published the Mishna. Thus, he represented the generation of scholars bridging between the Mishna and the Talmudic period. In addition, he was the head of the famous *Yeshiba* at Nehar De'a. Referring to the numerous controversies between the schools of Hillel and Shammai, he taught:

---

187. Vayiqqra Rabba XXI, 5, vol. 3, p. 481. For additional sources, see ed. note ad loc. The expression comes from Jer. 1:18. Radaq explained: "*an iron pillar* – that no one could tilt or break."

188. See *Homo Mysticus*, p. 112; cf. ibid., pp. 102, 113, 118–119. Within this context, it would be important to consider the fact that Maimonides rejected Aristotle's concept of absolute necessity, see ibid., pp. 113–115.

> These [of the school of Shammai] and those [of the school of Hillel] [express] the words of the Living God, but the halakha [legal norm] is according to the school of Hillel.[189]

From this doctrine, two fundamental corollaries follow. First, rabbinic dialectics postulate an absolute horizontality among the dissenting parties: each expresses "the words of the Living God." Second (and as a consequence of the former), controversies are not to be resolved according to some categories of 'truth,' but through the process of halakha (legal norm), where the judicial authorities *adopt* one position instead of another. The divergent view is not false. Rather, there are specific reasons and situations which would "incline us to choose" (להטות, see chapter below) in one direction rather than the other. This is why rabbinic literature also includes dissident and minority opinions (see next chapter). The above doctrine is conceptually linked to a homily delivered by R. Eleazar b. 'Azarya (1st and 2nd centuries), at Yabne, around the year 100. The theme was a verse in Ecclesiastes (12:11): "The words of the wise are as goads. And as well fastened nails are planted (the words spoken) by people gathering in assemblies. All was given by a single Shepherd." The homily runs as follows:

> "...*people gathering in assemblies*" refers to people coming and sitting in various 'assemblies' [to examine a matter] and [after delivering] they would declare that something [proposed to be] impure is 'impure,' and that something [proposed to be] pure is 'pure.' – 'Impure': appropriately [proper procedure]; and 'pure': appropriately [proper procedure]. Lest someone tells himself: Since (those of) the School of Shammai have declared it 'impure' and those of the School of Hillel have declared it 'pure'; one [authority] has prohibited it and another [authority] has permitted it, what is the purpose that I should

189. Talmud 'Erubin 13b. Therefore, the study of Tora equals "the words of the Living God"; see Yoma 35b; Y. Berakhot I, 4, 3b; Yebamot I, 6, 3b; Soṭa III, 4, 19a; and cf. Giṭṭin 6b. Cf. below n. 221.

> study Tora?! [To meet] this objection the Scripture (instead of saying) 'words' [implying something stagnant and inert] (it said) "*the* words" (Deut. 1:1) – every single word (developed around the Tora) was given by the same Shepherd! One God has created them, a single Leader has bestowed them, the Lord of all creatures, blessed be He, has spoken it! You, too, build different rooms within your heart and store in them the words of the School of Shammai and the words of the School of Hillel, the words of those (who have declared something) impure and the words of those (who have declared it) pure.[190]

Rabbinic disagreements and arguments mostly concern areas in which either the substance of the law itself, or its application, was not sufficiently clear. As with *dinim mufla'im* (see above chapter 10), such matters are not determined on the basis of some sort of cosmic truth, known to the privileged elite. Rather, as the Law charges, the judges must "lean (להטות) towards the majority" (Ex. 23:2; see appendix 52). Law is not governed by a cosmic truth, according to which the case at hand could be resolved, once and forever, as per *modus geometrico*. The verb "to lean" (להטות) implies an 'alternative' (see Num. 20:17; 21:22; II Sam. 2:19), and therefore a subjective 'choice' (see I Sam. 14:7; I Kings 2:28).[191] It is also used metaphorically, as when "departing" from practice (Gen. 38:1, 16), or from standard procedure; especially when "leaning" prejudicially against the poor and the helpless (see

190. Tosefta Soṭa 6:11–12, p. 195. On rabbinic parallels and sources, see editor's notes and *Tosefta Ki-Fshuṭah*, vol. 8, p. 681. Probably, the expression "different rooms" in which to store memory, refers to a specific technique of memorization; see *Golden Doves*, pp. 32–33. The memorization by way of *shinnun* or *verbatim* repetition was instituted later, as a result of the publication of the Mishna. That is why, in the parallel source, Ḥagiga 3b instead of "different rooms" in which to store memory, we read: "make your ear as a funnel" – to capture the oral texts. On the semantic principle of this doctrine, see Section III, n. 130. Cf. above n. 167.

191. It could apply even when no resolution has been taken, and one is only 'wavering' about the matter at hand; see Sanhedrin 49a.

Is. 10:2; Prov. 17:23; 18:5; Job 24:4; Lam. 3:35). It could apply also to someone who had lost his 'way' and needs assistance "to lean" and focus towards his final destination (I Kings 8:58). God was displeased with King Solomon "because he leaned his hearing," that is, subjectively "away from God, (although) twice He had revealed Himself to him" (I Kings 11:9).

Although resolved by the court, the verisimilar character of laws unfolding through the process of "leaning" (להטות) remains constant. A judicial decision does not render the law unchangeable. Another court, at a different time and situation, could point in a different direction. Since each court is in fact inspired by the same Shepherd, each pronouncement, in turn, is 'the word of the living God.' The purpose of judicial dialectics is to arrive at a consensus through persuasion, and point to a *course* to follow. In this connection, it would be helpful to note that halakha suggests 'walking' and 'way,' rather than 'theory'; and it is thus semantically analogous to 'jurisprudence' (composed of *jus* and *prudentia* 'practical wisdom'). It is semantically analogous to "Tora." As noted by R. Abraham ibn 'Ezra, the word "*Tora* stems from the root YRH," in the sense of "pointing out the right path."[192] The magistrates, teachers, and society *choose* "to lean" (= להטות) towards one *path* and decide to *walk* in the direction pointed out by one of the opinions rather than the other. They don't – they cannot – transform the realm of the verisimilar into an absolute. We had the opportunity to learn that "the Tora that God revealed to Israel was revealed in [terms that express] forty-nine modes of impurity and forty-nine modes of purity." This implies the polysemic quality of the revealed Law (and therefore the essential ambiguity of legal texts). It also implies the perennial need to ascribe meaning and legal precision to these texts.[193]

192. Commentary to Psalms 19:9.

193. See above Section II, n. 104. For further reference, see José Faur, "The Legal Thinking of the Tosafot," *Dine Israel* 6 (1975), pp. L-LI. On the legal theory underlying the 'ambiguities' of the Law, see *Studies in the Mishne Tora,* p. 21; R. Nissim Gerondi, *Derashot ha-Ran* (Jerusalem: Mossad Harav Kook, 2003),

# Chapter 46
# *Meliṣa* and the Realm of the Verisimilar

To be able to *choose* "to lean towards" (= להטות) is a fundamental quality, intrinsic to the freedom of the image of God within, which unfolds in the realm of the verisimilar. The unfolding resulting from 'choosing' (= להטות) gains expression in *meliṣa* – a special type of dialectics – which allows for the exchange of ideas and the possibility of persuading and of being persuaded. Wittgenstein has an important passage concerning the western attitude towards Jews:

> In western civilization the Jew is always measured on scales which do not fit him. Many people can see clearly that the Greek thinkers were neither philosophers in the western sense nor scientists in the western sense, that the participants in the Olympian Games were not sportsmen and do not fit in to any western occupation. But it is the same with the Jews. And by taking the words of our [language] as the only possible standards we constantly fail to do them justice.[194]

---

III, p. 120; R. Raphael Joseph Ḥazzan, *Ḥiqre Leb, Yore De'a,* (part I) (Leghorn, 5554/1794), #87, 131 b-c; idem, *Ḥiqre Leb, Eben ha-Ezer* (Salonika, 5573/1813), #5, 9c-d; etc., and appendix 52.

194. *Culture and Value*, p. 16.

Greek rational idealism deals in absolute categories. Knowledge (*epistime*) reflects a cosmic truth, timeless and invariable as Euclidian geometry. Conclusions are derived from proofs (*apodeixis*) resting on well-established axioms and perfectly executed syllogisms. Like metaphysics and geometry, Greek rational idealism pertains to the necessary and universal. It excludes the probable: categorically and absolutely. This affects our concepts of ethics and morality. The *truth* that moral philosophers deal with is an objective category.[195] As the root *vir* suggests, *truth* (*veritas*) means 'might, force.' Hence, the *quantum leap* from the metaphysical (to be) to the ethical (to do): violence is a function of ethics. Greek rational idealism imposes itself. The same is true for its updated versions (such as the mathematical model of the Cartesian system): they exclude the probable and verisimilar. Consequently, there is no need for eloquence and persuasion: the medium of 'truth' is cultural and intellectual coercion.

There is a huge difference between rational idealism and Tora. One *exposes* on the basis of perfect demonstration (*apodeixis*), the other *proposes*. Rational idealism demonstrates; Hebrew Scripture persuades. Greek 'knowledge' (*epistime*) closes the subject; Hebrew 'wisdom' (חכמה) inaugurates a dialogue (like Vichian *sapienta*; see below). Rational idealism finds expression in geometry and metaphysics; Hebrew Scripture in law, dialectics, and the proper conduct of individual and society.[196] Rational idealism rejects the probable; the intellectual space of the Hebrews is the verisimilar. As an expression of disdain to Hebrew ethos and tradition, some historians are in the habit of projecting Greek rational idealism into the Hebrew Scripture as a matter of fact. "In a universe created by God," pontificates a laureate scientist, "the world and its inhabitants were neces-

195. Cf. Ch. Perleman, *Justice, Law, and Argument* (Dodrech-Holland: D. Reidel, 1980), p. 113.

196. For a thorough and penetrating analysis of the basic differences between Hebrew and Greek thought, see Thorleif Boman, *Hebrew Thought Compared with Greek* (New York: W. W. Norton, 1970), especially his conclusive summary, pp. 193–208.

sary as they ought to be."[197] If there is one thing that the Hebrew Scripture teaches it is that 'creation' is *not* necessary. The term 'created' (ברא) – the first verb in the Hebrew Scripture – is related to 'cutting, severing.' Thus, indicating the absolute and categorical distance – epistemologically and ontologically – between Creator and creation (see Concluding Reflections, Section I). The Creator exists 'necessarily' (מחויב המציאות). Creation pertains to the realm of the 'possible'[198] (.(אפשר המציאות Bearing this in mind, we can appreciate why Maimonides opened the first chapter of his *Mishne Tora* with an exposition of this fundamental doctrine.[199]

The intellectual space of the Tora is in the ambit of the verisimilar, where more than one probability is possible. Accordingly, the principles and precepts of the Tora do not admit the same methodology as mathematics and physics. R. Levi ben Gereshom explained:

> We cannot ignore the fact that concerning Tora matters, one cannot give causes which are factually necessary, as done in mathematics. Neither can we, in this [matter], propose the class of causes that are given in physics. This is in no way possible, since the realm of the Tora does not admit this type of verification.[200]

The space of the 'possible' is the distance between the 'necessary' and the 'impossible,' at both the physical and intellectual levels. Fundamental to the Maimonidean apparatus is the distinction between what is scientifically 'necessary' – something based on apodictic

---

197. Francois Jacob, in *The Possible and the Actual* (New York: Pantheon Books, 1982), p. 23; cf. below n. 203.
198. Had creation been 'necessary,' it would then have been ontologically indistinguishable, from the Creator – as with pagan and non-Hebrew theology.
199. See *Homo Mysticus*, pp. 98–101. Concerning the verb *bara*, see R. Abraham ibn 'Ezra on Gen. 1:1 and *Mikhlal Yofi* ad loc. 1a.
200. R. Levi ben Gereshom, Introduction, *Perush 'al ha-Tora* (Venice, 5307/1547), 2c-d.

demonstration (*apodeixis*) derived from scientifically demonstrable facts (Ar. *burhan*) – and what is only statistically 'probable,' but neither 'necessary' nor 'impossible.' "The impossible," wrote Maimonides "has a permanent nature."[201] The same physical rules determining that a given condition is 'necessary' exclude another as 'impossible.' At the same time, not everything that is not 'necessary' must be deemed 'impossible.' Between these two poles – the necessary and the impossible – lies the realm of the possible and statistically probable. The possible, however, cannot be apprehended apodictically, but only inferred from an 'indication' – a thing or phenomenon – functioning as a 'sign post' (Ar. *dalala*) signaling at something exterior to itself, not comprehended within the system. The construct of a 'sign post' (Ar. *dalala*) is statistically probable (על דרך הרוב), but not necessarily so.[202] We can now understand why in his criticism of Galen, Maimonides reproached him for considering apodictic proofs alone and neglecting the probable. "What is helpful in medicine as well as in most arts," he remarked, "are the probable and complex syllogisms."[203] That is, a method focusing on the space between what it is scientifically

201. *Guide* III, 15, p. 331 (ll. 25–26); cf. ibid. II, 13, p. 197 (ll. 10–21); III, 34, p. 391 (ll. 14–15).

202. See *Homo Mysticus*, pp. 111–112. Maimonides' 'possible' is somehow analogous to, but not the same as, Aristotle's *enthymeme*. Maimonides uses the Hebrew 'פלא,' generally translated as 'miracle,' as something 'unpredictable,' see *MT Roṣeaḥ* 6:3, 12; or something 'difficult to anticipate,' as an 'act of God' in common law, see *Mekhira* 19:5; or 'a statistical oddity,' *Qiddush ha-Ḥodesh* 5:2 and 9:8; or something unusual, *Mamrim* 6:3. Thus, its sense of 'omen'; see *Ṭum'at Ṣara'at* 16:10. Cf. *Targum* Ex. 3:20.

203. *Iggerot*, ed. and trans. R. Joseph Qafiḥ (Jerusalem: Mossad Harav Kook, 1972), p. 153. On the 'possible,' see *Maimonides' Treatise on Logic*, chapters 4, 8. François Jacob, in *The Possible and the Actual*, p. 31 wrote:

> Complex objects, whether living or not, are produced by evolutionary processes in which two kinds of factors are involved: constraints that, at every level, specify the rules of the game and define what is possible with those systems; and the historical circumstances that determine the actual course of events and control the actual interactions between the systems.

Cf. above n. 197.

*necessary* within a given system, and what may be *probable* in a situation arising from the interplay of diverse systems and factors. A 'sign post' (Ar. *dalala*), is a kind of anomaly, which can be detected only upon knowing the precise constraints established by 'apodictic proof' (*burhan*). Given that imagination neglects scientific constraints altogether, Maimonides rejected the notion that imagination could serve as an index of what is actually possible;[204] or what amounts to the same, "that the model of the possible need not be examined in conjunction with the actual."[205] At the same time, we should not confuse the improbable with the impossible. Something could be deemed impossible within a given system, and yet be possible or statistically probable in a situation resulting from the interplay of different systems and factors. It is a remarkable fact that Ar. *dalala*, standing for an 'index' or 'sign-post' pointing out the possible, is the first word of the two terms making up the title of Maimonides' *Guide* (*dalalat*) *for the Perplexed*.[206] In the same spirit, Vico writes: "let us regard such perceptive aids merely as *dei compitales* (i.e., merely as road signs), indicating in what direction and by what path the student should walk."[207]

The same thing applies to the world of ideas. Hebrew intellectual tradition unfolds in the realm of the verisimilar. Sephardic sages regarded the Scripture as a paradigm of "eloquence" (מליצה)[208] – a term used to translate the Greek *rhetoric*.[209] "Jews," wrote R. Solomon

---

204. *Guide* I, 73, p. 135 (ll. 8–9). This proposition is fully treated ibid., pp. 144–148; see *Homo Mysticus*, pp. 65–69.

205. *Guide* I, 73, p. 144 (ll. 13–15). Proposition 10 ibid. stands in opposition to the idea that the 'possible' can be independent from the 'necessary.'

206. See *Golden Doves*, pp. 74–76, 78; *Homo Mysticus*, pp. 50, 52, 102.

207. *On the Study Methods of Our Time*, X, p. 46.

208. See the Spanish-Hebrew bilingual edition of R. David Nieto, *Maṭṭe Dan* (London, 54741714), IV, index, fol. 97a; IV, 8, fol. 103a. R. Judah al-Ḥarizi used this term to translate the title of Aristotle's *Rhetoric*.

209. For an overview of rhetoric in the ancient world, see Werner Eisenhut, *Einfuhrung in die Antike Rhetorik und ihre Geschichte* (Darmstadt: Wissenschaftliche Buchgesellschaft, 1974). Anyone interested in rhetoric as a factor in modern humanism, should read Juan Luis Víves, *El arte retórica/De ratione dicendi* (bilingual edition, Barcelona: Anthropos, 1998). On the influence of rhetoricians

ibn Verga, "are the masters of eloquence (מליצה)," due to the fact "that their children are raised in the lap of the (Hebrew) Bible, which is the essence of eloquence (מליצה).[210] Similarly, R. David Nieto (who lived at the same time as Vico), maintained that the Hebrew Bible is the supreme paradigm of eloquence.[211] The source is rabbinic. Referring to "eloquence" (מליצה) in Proverbs (1:6), the rabbis commented: "It alludes to the Tora itself which is called 'eloquence' (מליצה). In the future it would save those who are engaged in it from the Judgment of Hell."[212] In fact, the rabbis included "the songs...puzzles...

---

on the development of Roman law, see H. F. Jolowicz, *Historical Introduction to the Study of Roman Law* (Cambridge: Cambridge University Press, 1967), pp. 576–577. On the importance of rhetoric in the schooling of modern attorneys and jurists, see James Boyd White, *Heracles' Bow* (Madison: Wisconsin University Press, 1985), chapter 2. Modern attorneys are beginning to recognize that "Rhetoric is Part of the Lawyer's Craft"; see the lively article bearing this title, by Susan McCloskey, 10 *Journal,* November/December 2002, New York State Bar Association.

210. *Shebeṭ Yehuda,* XXXII, p. 80. See *In the Shadow of History,* pp. 180–181; and José Faur, "Imagination and Religious Pluralism: Maimonides, ibn Verga, and Vico," *New Vico Studies* 10 (1992), pp. 36–51.

211. *Maṭṭe Dan,* Bilingual edition, IV, 8, 103a. Generally, Hebrew lexicographers associate "eloquence" (מליצה) with 'pleasing, enjoyable'; see *Sefer ha-Shorashim,* of R. Jonah ibn Jannaḥ and of Radaq, s.v. 'מליצה.' In this sense it is also used in Judeo-Arabic. Concerning the meaning of this term, see R. Joshua ibn Shu'eb, *Derashot* (Constantinople, 5280/1520) [no pagination], *Vayyigash,* s.v. *beni,* wrote: "Eloquence (מליצה) is the plain meaning of the Scripture, similar to 'evident'; in contradistinction to metaphors and riddles." cf. ibid. *Shemini,* s.v. *ṣaddiq;* and ibid. *Aḥaron shel Pesaḥ,* s.v. *vekhen amru.* This definition is contrary to R. Immanuel of Rome, *The Book of Proverbs* (Naples, ca. 1487, offset: Jerusalem, The Hebrew University Press, 1981), p. 6, who wrote that "eloquence (מליצה)" concerns the 'riddles' and esoteric intention of the text, rather than *peshaṭ.* For a full discussion of *meliṣa;* see R. Judah Messer Leon, *Nofet Ṣufim* (Mantua ca. 1475, offset: Jerusalem: The Jewish National and University Library Press, 1981).

212. *Midrash Mishle* I, 6, p. 43, cf. editor's note. In rabbinic literature, מליצה is associated with the 'Holy Spirit'; see *AdRN* A, XXXIV, p. 102. It is one of the ten styles used to express "God's word"; see Bereshit Rabba XLIV, vol. 1, p. 429; Shir ha-Shirim Rabba III, [4], 19c; *AdRN* B, XXXVII, p. 95, etc. Cf. *Midrash Tehillim* LXXVIII, p. 344.

metaphors and 'eloquence' (מליצה)" as part of Tora.[213] The sense of 'rhetoric' discussed by Philo when describing his intellectual formation is probably one and the same as the biblical 'מליצה.' His early education included "Rhetoric," that is,

> Rhetoric, [i] sharpening the mind to the observation of facts, [ii] and training and welding thought to expression, will make the man a true master of words and thought, thus taking into its charge the peculiar and special gift which nature has not bestowed on any other living creature. [iii] Dialectic, the sister and twin, as some have said, of Rhetoric, distinguishes true argument from false, and convicts the plausibilities of sophistry, and thus will heal that great plague of the soul, deceit.[214]

The "eloquence" (מליצה) tradition, taught ibn Verga, continued to be cultivated by Talmudic sages.[215] The ideal Talmudic student is one who has mastered the art of eloquence. It includes [i] sharpness, [ii] and fluency. Given that "the wicked, too, have eloquence (מליצה),"[216] the student must learn [iii] how to discern and confront the false ideas and deceits of sophists and the like who use rhetoric to confuse and manipulate the gullible (see below chapter 48). Commenting on the verse urging parents to "rehearse" (ושיננתם) the Tora "to your children" (Deut. 6:7), the rabbis taught:

> To "rehearse" (ושיננתם) – it means that the words of the Tora should be [i] point-sharp on your tongue, [ii] that if someone would ask you something, you would not vacillate, but answer pointedly.[217]

---

213. *Midrash Tehillim* LXXVIII, p. 344. Cf. *Homo Mysticus*, p. 168.
214. "The Preliminary Studies," 17, *Philo*, vol. 4, p. 467.
215. *Shebeṭ Yehuda*, XXXII. p. 89 (ll. 3–4).
216. See Shir ha-Shirim Rabba I, [6], 1c-d.
217. *Sifre* #34, p. 60. The purpose of this training is to have the student gain a clear and unambiguous knowledge of the matter at hand; see Sanhedrin 7b. The rabbis compare a sage who has mastered this art to an expert archer who aims

The training should enable the student [iii] "up to the point that sophists can reckon."[218] I.e., so that he could stand up to misleading rhetoricians.

Likewise, Vico associated Greek 'rhetoric' with the Latin [ii] "*fluentia* (words that flow) and [i] *dicentia* (words that speak)." Adding: "Fluency is indeed a peculiar virtue of speech from which the things that are said without prior preparation or reflection emerge by their very nature, not so much from the speaker, but seem to be speaking forth by themselves." As if echoing the rabbinic idea of "rehearsing" (ושיננתם), comprehending both 'repetition' and 'rehearsal,' Vico adds: "Fluency is the most difficult skill of this art, and therefore it is the last to be achieved and is acquired more by practice than by precept."[219] [iii] "At a later stage let them learn criticism," he advised, "so that they can apply the fullness of their personal judgment to what they have been taught.[220] Hence the perennial 'differences of opinion' (מחלוקת) crisscrossing rabbinic literature. Since the purpose of

the arrow straight into the target, without hesitation; see Qiddushin 30a-b. In this context we should point out that students who know how to reply, but do not know how to 'draw the bow,' are referred to as "those armed with a shield"; see Berakhot 27b; Bekhorot 36a, and the following note.

218. *Pesiqta de-Rab Kahana* (Mandelbaum), XII, 22, vol. 1, p. 220. Dr. Mandelbaum interpreted the Hebrew *sophists* in the Hebrew text as 'sophists.' This interpretation reflects the standard meaning of this term, as well as the context about figurative 'battles' fought against 'adversaries' discussed in the same paragraph; cf. *'Aruch ha-Shalem* s.v. *safasta*, vol. 6, p. 105. Professor Lieberman's interpretation, ibid., vol. 2, p. 474, as "*computator, calculator*," although linguistically plausible, makes no contextual sense, especially in light of the fact that this homily is regularly associated with 'battle' against 'opponents'; see Qiddushin 30b and *Midrash Tanna'im* on Deut. 6:7, p. 26. Cf. above n. 217.

219. Vico, *The Art of Rhetoric*, I, p. 3. Cf. Sanhedrin 7b.

220. *The Art of Rhetoric*, III, p. 19. Vico's theory of rhetoric had a direct impact on his idea of historical consciousness; see Umberto Galeazzi, "Vico e la conscenza storica: Sui Sapere ermeneutico della Scienza Nuova," in Antonio Quarta e Paolo Pellegrino (eds.), *Humanitas: Studi in Memoria di Antonio Verri*, vol. 1, (Lecce: Mario Congedo Editore, 1999), pp. 321-343. Cf. Fabrizio Lomonaco, "Critica storica e pirronismo: il modello olondese nell'età di Vico," *Bollettino Filosofico*, 15 (1999), pp. 213–238.

eloquence (מליצה) is persuasion and consensus, it is essential to treat different and opposing views horizontally. Referring to the Talmud's legal dialectic, Perelman observed:

> Jewish tradition, which never intended to conceive the law through a scientific model, offers a meaningful history on this point. In the Talmud two schools of Biblical interpretation are in constant struggle, the school of Hillel and the school of Shammai… One Voice from above replied that both theses expressed the word of the Living God. This lesson is clear: Two opposed interpretations can be equally respected, and it is not necessary to mark as unreasonable at least one of these interpretations.[221]

Vichian *elocutio,* too, unfolds in the ambit of the probable. Therefore, it rejects the scientific model since it fails to consider opposing views.

> This failure to concern themselves with the opinions of others has not only been a source of blame, but has proven to be extremely prejudicial, not only to private persons but to eminent leaders and great rulers as well.[222]

From the perspective of rational idealism, when two individuals arrive at two opposite conclusions, one must necessarily conclude that at least one is wrong. The *other* expresses an *erroneous* view that does not agree with the *rational.* Applied to the legal ambit, this model would lead to the absurd conclusion that a great number of our most

---

221. *Justice, Law, and Argument,* p. 165. Cf. above n. 189.
222. *On the Study Methods of our Time,* VII, p. 35. The link between the Vichian elocution and the probable has been thoroughly examined in *Sensus Communis,* chapter 3. For an in-depth analysis of this dispute see, Linda Gardiner Janik, "A Renaissance Quarrel: The Origin of Vico's Anti-Cartesianism," *New Vico Studies,* 1 (1983), pp. 39–50.

distinguished jurists are either irrational or dishonest. As Perelman has observed in his criticism of the Cartesian model:

> If the important decisions of the Supreme Court of the United States are rarely unanimous, one should accuse at least one of these respected jurists of being irrational or dishonest. Or should one perhaps conclude that disagreements in (matters of) law should be explained with specific reasons?[223]

That is why in their discussions the rabbis include the opposing view. The same applies to Vico, given "...that in the art of oratory the relationship between speaker and listeners is of the essence," someone oblivious to opposing views would fail to persuade his audience.[224]

There is an additional reason correlating Vico and the rabbis. Both rabbinic halakha and Vichian *prudentia* (see above chapter 44) seek to discover not a single truth but the circumstances which may have given rise to opposing views in connection to a single event. Vico explained:

> The difference, therefore, between abstract knowledge and prudence is this: in science, the outstanding intellect is that which succeeds in reducing a large multitude of physical effects to a single cause; in the domain of prudence, excellence is accorded to those who ferret out the greatest possible number of causes which may be produced by a single event, and who are able to conjecture which of all these causes is the true one.[225]

Finally, both rabbinic dialectics and Vichian *elocutio* are grounded on a common ground recognized by all parties: the *peshaṭ* or 'commonly accepted' of the rabbis; and 'common sense' (*sensus communis*)

---

223. *Justice, Law, and Argument*, p. 165.
224. *On the Study Methods of our Time*, III, p. 15.
225. *On the Study Methods of our Time*, VII, p. 34.

of Vico (see above chapter 7).[226] "It is a positive fact that, just as knowledge originates in truth and error in falsity," observed Vico, "so common sense (*sensus communis*) arises from perceptions based on verisimilitude."[227] We can now appreciate why the sages urged the student to always bear in mind both sides of a controversy.[228] Similarly, Vico advised that a student who intends to devote his life to "the legal profession or the judiciary, a political speaker or a pulpit orator," should not waste "too much time on those subjects which are taught by abstract geometry." Adding:

> Let him, instead, cultivate his mind with an ingenious method; let him study topics, and defend both sides of a controversy, be it on nature, man, or politics, in a freer and brighter style of expression. Let him not spurn reasons that wear a semblance of probability and verisimilitude.[229]

"The role of eloquence," as Vico tells us, "is to persuade; an orator is persuasive when he calls forth in his hearers the mood which he desires."[230] It stands to reason, therefore, that he would be able to accomplish this only when knowing the diverse views circulating among his audience.

We can better appreciate now why a student who had completed

---

226. Cf. Qiddushin 30b and *AdRN* A, I, 1, p. 1, and appendix 28. Medieval scholars referred to the common ground with the Hebrew term *'iqqar* or with the Arabic *'aṣl* ('principle'); see *Studies in the Mishne Tora*, p. 38.
227. *On the Study Methods of our Time*, III, p. 13.
228. See Tosefta Soṭa 6:11–12, p. 195, quoted above n. 190.
229. *On the Study Methods of our Time*, VII, p. 41; "ingenious" (*ingenium*) is a key-concept in the rhetoric developed by the *converso* Juan Luis Víves, in his *El arte retórica/De ratione dicendi*; see Index of Subjects. On the role of this concept in Vico, see Ernesto Grassi, *Vico and Humanism* (New York: Peter Lang, 1990). Some familiarity with rabbinic tradition, however, would reveal that *ingenium* in both Víves and Vico, is nothing more than the *ḥiddush* of Talmudic scholars, as practiced in Spain from the 13th century on.
230. *On the Study Methods of our Time*, VII, p. 38.

his education is designated 'a disciple of the *sages*' (תלמיד חכמים). The plural is of the essence. Only a student who had been exposed to more than a single school could develop a critical judgment of his own that would permit him to persuade and be persuaded. This is why "the disciples of the sages" are described as those "promoting peace in the world."[231]

231. On the plural form of 'sages,' see *Golden Doves*, pp. xviii-xix.

# Chapter 47
# Expanding National Memory

The Talmud is a collection of rabbinic *elocutio* around the classical topics (*ars topica judicalis*) of the Mishna. The exchanges and discussions conducted at different times and at different *Yeshibot* were recorded and eventually edited in the Talmud. In the Babli the *weaving* of diverse sources, views, and controversies about the topic at hand – many taken place in different *Yeshibot* over long periods of time – are laced into a single, cogent unit known as *sugya* (pl. *sugyot*), the Syriac equivalent of halakha, implying 'course,' 'flow' as well as 'structure.'[232] The *sugya* comes in various forms. The weaving and design of the *sugya* follow specific structures, conditioned by editorial strategies, rather than simple chronology. The language is dense and precise, and uses highly technical terminology. The arguments are keen, requiring enormous concentration and erudition on the

232. There are two Talmuds, one compiled in Tiberias towards the end of the 4th century. It is usually known as the Yerushalmi. The other, known as the Babli, the most authoritative one, was composed towards the end of the 5th century (see below). Both, the Yerushalmi and Babli record the discussions at their *Yeshibot*. There is, however, a major difference. In the Yerushalmi we find mostly brief notes containing the material that could *enable* an *emora* to construct the *sugya*. By contrast, generally the *sugya* in the Babli is complete and finished. Thus, although the Yerushalmi is referred to as *gemara* (see appendix 48), Maimonides was careful to point out that the redactor of the Babylonian Talmud, "compiled ... and completed it (*gemaro*)," *MT* Introduction, ll. 101–102; whereas the Yerushalmi was only "compiled," ibid. ll. 69, 92, but not 'completed.' see appendix 48.

part of both the instructor and the student. Although referred to as the interpretation of the Mishna,[233] the Talmud is not a commentary in the standard sense of the term. Here is what Maimonides has to say about it:

> ... I have seen that the Talmud makes of the Mishna what no one can ever do on the basis of a logical syllogism (Ar. *qiyas*). So (that occasionally) it (the Talmud) would introduce (new) principles and declare that it (the Mishna) was constructed upon such and such premises. Or that the (text) of the Mishna had omitted some words and it meant to say so and so. Or that this (view stated in the) Mishna actually expresses a (dissenting opinion) from a rabbi who maintained so and so. Furthermore in the course of explaining it (the Mishna), it (the Talmud) would add to its wording, subtract from it and elucidate its reasons (without positive demonstrations).[234]

Put another way, the *sugya* is a record of the dialectical and rhetorical comments carried out at the *Yeshibot* around the Mishna. The purpose is not to expose, as with a geometrical theorem, but to *expand* the topic at hand, and present the different views expressed on the matter. In this fashion, the 'coins' of the Mishna are exchanged, and the memory of Israel further developed in a dynamic and creative way. Thus, if a judge failed to notice that the case at hand was mentioned in the Mishna, his decision is void. The same is true with the Talmud. Were a judge to neglect the discussions of the "general *sugya* " of the Talmudic sages, he "had erred in a subject-matter of the Mishna" (טעה בדבר משנה), and his decision is rendered as erroneous. In Jewish law, an erroneous judgment needs not to be formally reversed and is automatically void (see appendix 48).

Before we can evaluate the strategic purpose of the Talmud we

233. *IShG*, p. 55; *Sefer ha-Mafteaḥ*, 3a; *MT* Introduction, ll. 93–94.

234. Introduction, *Perush ha-Mishnayot*, vol. 1, pp. 47–48.

must consider the process of de-bureaucratization taking place from the beginning of the first Exile (6th century B.C.E.), until the end of the Talmudic period (ca. 6th century C.E.). Ever since the destruction of the First Temple, Israel responded to military defeat by designing institutions and promoting values that would advance the people under the Law. The first Jewish Commonwealth resulted in the development and establishment of three bureaucracies: the monarchy, the priesthood, and the judiciary (see above chapter 18). The Second Commonwealth represented the erosion and eventual demise of these governing bodies. As each of these governing bodies collapsed, the vacuum was subsequently filled with the publication of national texts and the establishment of new institutions. The fall of the Kingdom of Judea (587 B.C.E.) brought to an end the old monarchy. The Jewish people lost not only military control over their land, but were not even permitted to return to their homeland. The political situation changed when Cyrus I conquered Babylonia (539 B.C.E.), and the Land of Israel fell under Persian control. The first Babylonian exiles were permitted to return to Israel thanks to an order issued by Cyrus I (538 B.C.E.), urging the Jews to come back to their homeland and build the Temple. Out of this crisis a new kind of political organization emerged: the Tora was solemnly proclaimed as the Constitution of Israel, representing the highest Law of the nation. Henceforth, the supreme sovereign of Israel would be its Constitution – the Tora – acknowledged by the Jewish people (see above chapter 21).

During the Second Commonwealth, the Hasmoneans, a priestly family, led the Maccabean revolt against the Seleucids, and assumed control not only of the Temple, but also of the throne. Whereas the early monarchs sought to dominate the Temple and the Judiciary from the throne, the Hasmoneans sought to dominate the other two bureaucracies from the Temple. The rabbis regarded them as usurpers and illegitimate. Courageously, they declared that non-Davidic kings (i.e., Hasmoneans and Herodians) may not sit in judgment (Mishna Sanhedrin 2:2), and pleaded with the Hasmoneans to separate altar from throne. The rabbis' position may be summarized as follows:

> The Hasmonean rulers rejected the Pharisee plea to separate altar and throne, and forcibly combined the sacred office of high priesthood with an aggressive policy of conquest and territorial expansion. The descendants of Aaron were no longer "doing the work of Aaron." Shemaya and Abtalion, according to Talmudic tradition, descendants of the Assyrian king Sennacherib, called themselves "descendants of the heathen, who do the work of Aaron."[235]

Hillel's emphasis on the peaceful role of the priesthood must be understood as a direct disapproval of the Hasmoneans. In particular, the sages found offensive the Hasmoneans' propensity to war and violence. Partly, their criticism was a reaction against acts of cruelty committed by some Hasmonean rulers and later on by King Herod. During the battles between the two Hasmonean princes, Hyrcanus II and Aristobulus II, Onias, a member of the association of peace-loving men (*Ḥasidim*), refused to pray for the victory of Hyrcanus' forces "since those who stand now with me are Thy people and those who are besieged are also Thy priests." For his nonintervention in this civil war, Onias paid with his life.[236] The chain of national catastrophes befalling the Jewish people at the end of the Second Commonwealth resulted in the destruction of the Temple (68 C.E.) and the collapse of the second bureaucracy of Israel.

Intelligently, the rabbis did not confuse the abuses of some within the priestly leadership with either the priesthood itself or the institution of the Temple. Not everything associated with the priesthood was negative. In fact, the earliest system of public education known to humankind was established by the High Priest Joshua ben Gamla. It was thanks to this public system that the Scripture came to be the source of values and legal instruction of Jewish society; and consequently, legal fluency and respect for the Law came to occupy a central

235. Nahum Glatzer, "Peace in Classical Judaism," in his *Essays in Jewish Thought* (Alabama: Alabama University Press, 1978), p. 38.
236. "Peace in Classical Judaism," p. 38.

place in Jewish lifestyle and ethos. Rather than vacate the priesthood altogether, the sages, in the footsteps of Ezra (the first High Priest of the Second Commonwealth), responded to the void created by military defeat by spawning the most revolutionary idea in the history of religion: the Temple would be symbolically represented by the Synagogue, and the sacramental sacrifices by the liturgy.[237] Consequently, the 'Prayer Book' became the most popular text in Judaism, outdoing in some respects the Scripture itself! Thus, out of the ashes of devastation, there emerged a fresh approach to worship that would revolutionize the concept of 'religion' in much of the world. In this context, let us consider the fact that the model for the Christian Church and Muslim Mosque is the Synagogue, not the Temple.

The destruction of the Temple eventually brought an end to the third bureaucracy, the Sanhedrin, or Supreme Court. In its place was organized the *Bet Din ha-Gadol,* acting as the Supreme Court, but with reduced power. The further constraints imposed on the *Bet Din* led to a radically new concept of authority and a new perception of the Jewish past. The authority of the great men of Israel was the effect of their teachings, not merely their office. Unlike the 'elder' (זקן) of yore who was invested with judicial right by virtue of his office, the rabbinic 'sage' (חכם) was invested with authority by virtue of his teachings. In the course of time, the sage ranked above priest.[238] This became factual with the publication of the Mishna, converting halakha into legal tender. By the end of the rabbinic period the sage began to displace the judge.[239] The sage, like the prophet of

237. See "Law and Hermeneutics," pp. 1672–1744; "Monolingualism and Judaism," pp. 1737–1739.

238. See Mishna Horayot 3:8; cf. Soṭa 4b; and *Perush ha-Mishnayot,* Giṭṭin 5:8, vol. 3, pp. 225–226. On the displacement of the priest by the pious, see Jacob Neusner, *A Life of Rabban Yohanan ben Zakkai,* pp. 33–63; idem, *A History of the Jews in Babylonia,* vol. 3 (Leiden: E. J. Brill, 1968), pp. 102–126. Cf. Mo'ed Qaṭan 16b; and *Yalquṭ Shim'oni* on II Sam. 23, vol. 2, #165, 372a.

239. On the preeminence of the scholar over the judge in Babylonia, see the incident with Samuel and Mor 'Uqba, Mo'ed Qaṭan 16b; and the confrontation between Resh Laqqish and R. Judah Nesi'a, Yerushalmi Sanhedrin II, 1, 19d-20a. On

yore, with no office and without the backing of a bureaucratic apparatus, was regarded as the living embodiment and soul of the Law. Commenting on a Talmudic passage censuring those who stand up in reverence before the Scroll of the Tora, but not before a sage, R. Saul Levi Mortera pointed out that indeed, "the *Sefer Tora* is a Law without soul." He added: "the scholar who studies and expounds it is a living, animated Law."[240]

Soon after, the Jewish people faced a new crisis inaugurated by the alliance cross/sword under Constantine (see above chapter 25). The persecution of Jews throughout the Roman Empire intensified, especially in the Holy Land. The enemies of Israel hoped that by wrenching the Jews away from their ancestral home, Judaism would be abolished, once and for all. In response, Jews began to move eastwards to Sassanide Babylonia (present Iran and Iraq), away from "the kingdom of evil." A strategic decision, resulting in the formation of the Babylonian Talmud, was the transferring of the archives from the *Yeshibot* in Israel to the *Yeshibot* in Babylonia.[241]

The Christianization of the Roman Empire was a catalyst for new and more intense conflicts. These conflicts had a ripple effect in the east, with a direct impact on the political and economic life of Sassanide Babylonia. By the middle of the 5th century, large contingents of Jews began to move away westward: to other areas in the Middle

---

the displacement of the judge by the sage, see Y. Berakhot IV, 2, 7d; the prayer excludes 'guilty and innocent,' implying, thereby, that this was not referring to a Court of Justice; see R. Samuel Ashkenazi, *Yefe Mar'e*, 17a. That was especially true in the resolution of legal problems with no immediate application; see Jacob Neusner, *A History of the Jews in Babylonia*, vol. 4 (Leiden: E. J. Brill, 1969), pp. 125–402.

240. R. Saul Levi Mortera, in Rehuel Jessurun, *Dialogo dos Montes*, ed. and trans. Philip Polack (London: Tamiesis Books, 1975), pp. 99–100. Unlike the gospels and apostles, the Jewish sage did not exploit his position for the glorification of heroes and saints, but for the celebration of the Tora; see Jacob Neusner, *Making the Classics in Judaism* (Atlanta, Georgia: Scholars Press, 1989), pp. 79–80.

241. See *Iyye ha-Yam*, 100a-102b. Christians in Byzantium were most vicious in their attempt to suppress Jewish rituals; see *'Eber ve-'Arab*, pp. 139–140.

East and Asia, to North Africa, throughout the Mediterranean basin, and to small enclaves in Byzantium and Western Europe. The end result was that Babylonian Jewry no longer constituted the "majority of the Jewish people."[242] Pagan organizations function best in a social vacuum, emotionally and intellectually insulated from the people. Jewish institutions, however, have no authority outside Jewish society. Social autonomy in Exile is possible only when the majority of the people share common educational and judicial institutions and maintain unfettered contacts with each other. With the fragmentation of the Jewish people and the ensuing isolation from one another, there was no longer an integral Jewish society, but only societies or communities of Jews. The change affected the status of the ancestral *Yeshibot*. Since they were no longer administered by an organization in direct contact with the people, they could no longer be regarded as *national institutions*. Furthermore, because of the new geographical dispersion, the *Yeshibot* were no longer accessible to the majority of the Jewish population. For that reason, these institutions could no longer represent *national* consensus. Given that the majority of the Jewish people no longer resided in the same geo-political setting, allowing free access and communication, how could there be an integral Jewish society?

The Babylonian Talmud was designed to meet the crisis of spiritual and intellectual fragmentation brought about by the collapse of Jewish society. From its incipient moment, Jewish strategy had been designed to confront political crises by creating something new in the annals of history. In what follows we shall see that the Babylonian Talmud is much more than a book. It is a virtual society, embodying the minds and voices of myriads of Jews at the *Kalla* gatherings.

242. See *MT* Introduction, ll. 111–112.

# Chapter 48
# *Kalla* and the Formation of the Babylonian Talmud

The Talmud is not the product of a cloister. Quite the contrary. It was born in the open space of the *Kalla,* of which the classroom was a part, not the other way around. According to tradition, the Babylonian Talmud was redacted under the direction of Rab Ashe (335–426), head of the *Yeshiba* and the *national* Court (*Bet Din*), together with his colleague Rabina (d. 422).[243] Primarily, the Talmud contains the material that was either developed at, or transmitted and revised by, a *national* institution: the *Yeshiba.* "All" the traditions that were deposited in the hands of the sages, "from the days of Moses and until his time," wrote Maimonides, were "redacted by Rab Ashe in the Talmud."[244] It was subsequently "concluded" (גמרו) with the formal approval of the elders (see appendix 48). A key factor for the understanding of the Babylonian Talmud is that it constitutes a formal closure of the 'oral' period: *de jure* "Rab Ashe and Rabina" are "the last two sages in the chain of oral tradition inaugurated by Moses."[245]

---

243. See *MT* Introduction, ll. 91, 108–109, 111; cf. ibid., l. 75. On the identity of this sage, see Avinoam Cohen, *Ravina and Contemporary Sages* (Heb.) (Ramat Gan: Bar Ilan University, 2001). Cf. the marginal note in Introduction, *Sefer ha-Mafteaḥ,* 3a, and *Studies in the Mishne Tora,* p. 41 n. 56.
244. *MT* Introduction, l. 104. See Introduction, *Perush ha-Mishnayot,* vol. 1, pp. 34–35.
245. See Baba Meṣi'a 86a and *MT* Introduction, ll. 108–111.

Henceforth, no sage would have the authority to introduce any further material in the name of oral tradition. Why?

The authority of the Talmud, its foundation and specific function, are organically linked to the *Kalla* institution. This institution, unique in the annals of intellectual history and education, was established in Talmudic times and continued to function well after into the Geonic period.[246] The *Kalla* was a month-long convention during which students and sages from all over the Jewish world gathered to study a Talmudic Tractate, which was assigned by the head of *Yeshiba* five-months earlier. The *Kalla* began at the end of the five-month period, when students and sages attended the classes, symposia (מתיבות) and judicial deliberations offered by the *Yeshiba* faculty. There were two *Kalla* meetings per year, one in the month of Adar (winter) and another in the month of Elul (summer). In addition to the faculty and regular student-body, the *Kalla* was attended by outside students and sages, as well as by the magistrates and highest judicial and political officials of the nation.[247] During this month Jews from all walks of life came together to exchange ideas, and learned and revised the texts, traditions, and legal concepts of the tractate at hand. At these meetings, matters of law raised by local communities all over, as well as issues of national policy, were deliberated and brought to conclusion.[248] In this fashion, Jews from most diverse backgrounds met and learned as one, fostering bonds of love and amity going all the way back to Sinai.

The Babylonian Talmud was conceived in the compactness of mind and spirit of the *Kalla*. According to Geonic tradition, Rab

246. See *Geonica*, vol. 2, p. 326 and Professor Ginzberg's comment, ibid., p. 302. Cf. Ch. Albeck, *Mabo la-Talmudim*, pp. 601–604. For a good summary of the material and different views on the subject; see David M. Goodblatt, *Rabbinic Instruction in Sasanian Babylonia* (Leiden: E. J. Brill, 1975), chapter 6. Cf. Professor Y. D. Gilat, "Kallah, Months of," in *EJ*, vol. 10, cls. 710–712.

247. For a Geonic description of some of the *Kalla* ceremonies, see *Rabbinic Instruction in Sasanian Babylonia*, pp. 161–162.

248. See Simha Assaf, *Tequfat ha-Ge'onim* (Jerusalem: Mossad Harav Kook, 5715/1955), pp. 256–260.

Ashe served as head of the *Yeshiba* for close to sixty years. Under his ministry one hundred and twenty *Kalla* conventions were organized. Each *Kalla* focused on a single tractate. These meetings were divided into two thirty-year cycles, known as *mahdora* (see appendix 53). There was "a primary" or original "*mahdora*" of the Talmud and "a final" or conclusive "*mahdora*."[249] In this fashion, every tractate was studied once in the primary cycle, and then further revised thirty years later in the final cycle. Concerning these cycles, R. Sherira Gaon wrote:

> Rab Ashe presided over his *Yeshiba* for close to sixty years. As it was said in the chapter "Someone who had passed away" (Baba Batra 157b): "In the original *mahdora* he (Rab Ashe) told us this, but in the conclusive *mahdora* he told us differently. Since the rabbis had decreed to study two tractates per year, be it small or large, it was possible to go over the entire Talmud in thirty years. Given that Rab Ashe presided for close to sixty years, there were two cycles. He (Rab Ashe) died in the year 738 [= 426 C.E.].[250]

R. Ḥanan'el explained:

> We have a tradition (*qabbala*) in our hands, that every year, they [the sages] were fully active for two months [during the *Kalla*] in the study of Talmud, and they would complete it [the curriculum] in thirty years, and then they would go over it and start all over again.

R. Nathan b. Yeḥi'el (1035-ca. 1110), author of the *'Arukh,* to whom we owe the preceding quotation, added:

249. Baba Batra 157b.
250. *IShG*, pp. 93–94.

> Rab Ashe ministered (as head of) the *Yeshiba* for sixty years, and every year he would occupy himself in the months of Elul and Adar, the months of *Kalla* [in the compilation of the Talmud]. And he completed the Talmud twice. In the first cycle he explained... and in the second he explained...[251]

A similar tradition was reported by R. Judah al-Bargeloni:

> The meaning of "original *mahdora*" and "final *mahdora*" is as follows. R. Ashe ministered (as head) of the *Yeshiba* for sixty years. The entire Talmud counts with sixty tractates. Each tractate was revised twice [at two different cycles], given that they studied two (tractates) per year, one in the month of Adar and one in the month of Elul.[252]

The Babylonian Talmud was produced at these *Kalla* meetings. The study, final approval and revision of the text were conducted in the general assembly, with the participation of all the sages of Israel and their disciples. Thus, the Talmud represents the views "of all or the majority of the sages of Israel."[253] Its authority derives from the fact that it was "approved by all Israel."[254] Alluding to the *Kalla* meetings, Maimonides added:

> ...the elders [of Israel] adjudicated (פסקו) and concluded (וגמרו) that the law is thus. Everything, from the days of Moses until his days, was compiled by R. Ashe in the Talmud.[255]

The Talmud is not a code of law. Emphatically, the rabbis declared: "one cannot learn a halakha from the Talmud" (see appendix 48).

251. *'Arukh* s.v. *hadar* (3).
252. *Sefer ha-'Ittim*, p. 247
253. *MT* Introduction, ll. 130–131.
254. *MT* Introduction, l. 129. See appendix 48.
255. *MT* Introduction, ll. 103–104.

Furthermore, unlike the Mishna, it was never officially published. Its authority rests on a single fact: it represents *national* consensus.

> ...Everything contained in the Babylonian Talmud is mandatory upon all Israel. It is incumbent upon every town and city, to follow all the policies established by the sages of the Talmud, to enforce their prohibitions and comply with their ordinances.[256]

The Talmud was the very last matter approved *nationally* by the Jewish people. Afterwards, Jews scattered all over the globe and there was no longer a unified Jewish community.

> After the Court of R. Ashe, who redacted the Talmud during the life of his son and concluded it, Israel suffered a most brutal dispersion throughout all the lands of the globe, reaching the extremes [of the world] and distant regions. Many conflicts broke out throughout the world and armies obstructed the traveling routes.[257]

Since the new socio-political conditions did not permit unfettered access to the *Yeshibot* they could no longer be regarded as *national* institutions.

> Consequently, the study of the Tora diminished, and Israel could no longer gather [during the *Kalla* months] in the *Yeshibot* and study in [assemblies] of thousands and tens of thousands as was previously done.[258]

256. *MT* Introduction, ll. 126–128. See quotation below at n. 265.
257. *MT* Introduction, ll. 111–113. This explains why previous discussions brought to a close (*setam*) in the first *Mahdora* were afterwards rejected on the basis of other authorities introduced in the second *Mahdora*; see appendix 53.
258. *MT* Introduction, ll. 114–115, see *Studies in the Mishne Tora*, pp. 41–45. Cf. *Sefer ha-Galui*, p. 195.

Dispersion also affected the status of the courts. A direct effect of fragmentation and intellectual isolation was the fact that there was no longer a single, integral, Jewish society, but rather various communities of Jews. Consequently, the post-Talmudic court could not be regarded as a *national* institution, but only as a *Bet Din shel Yehidim*, i.e., "a community court" with only regional jurisdiction.[259] The closure of oral tradition is a direct consequence of the above. The authority of the Oral Law must come from the people. The logic is clear: without a national institution there is no way to either 'accept' or 'reject' anything in the name of Israel.

The Talmud was not created in a monastery, away from the laity, where better and superior men find shelter from the 'outside world.' The opposite was true. Not only was the Talmud conceived and born at the *Kalla*, but its purpose was to also transmit the *temperament* and *personality* of the *Kalla* society, in all its facets and modalities. Just as the Synagogue is a virtual experience of the Temple, and the liturgy of the sacramental services, so the Talmud is a virtual *Kalla* experience. Through the Babylonian Talmud, students and sages from fragmented Israel have unfettered access to the *Kalla* world and hear the voices of Jews from Tiberias and Caesarea, from Lydia and from Sippore, from Nehar De'a, Fum be-Dita and Sura, and countless other seats of learning. In concert and as one, pupil and teacher, learned and commoner, disciple and sage, brilliant and mediocre, share in their discussions, reflect on their ideas, and renew their bonds with an *integral Jewish society*. That is why the Talmud is much more than a book or a landscape of things lost: it is a virtual *Kalla*, a holistic experience. Upon entering the Talmud, one and all can sit at the feet of the sages, partake in their discussions, and join the men and women standing firmly at the *berit* Sinai-Moab, set and ready to carry on the *Morasha* of Israel; not in some dingy cloister, but amidst the sound and voices of the *Kalla*. Hence the folklore, exegesis, psychological insights, esoteric and metaphysical meditations, stories and tales crisscrossing the legal

259. *MT* Introduction ll. 119–120. See *Studies in the Mishne Tora*, pp. 43–44.

principles and doctrines taught by the sages. Without the sound and voices of the *Kalla*, a Jew could no longer relate to the Scripture as a *Jew*: his perception would be *skewed* and *alien* to the *nation* of Israel.[260] Quoting "a great philologist who was also a Talmudist," Chief Rabbi Hertz (1872–1946) wrote:

> Suppose the teaching of Talmud was suddenly interrupted during the life of a generation; the tradition once lost, it would be well-nigh impossible to recover it.[261]

It is clear why in Jewish tradition the study of Talmud is the highest intellectual pursuit, higher even than the Scripture and Mishna,[262] since, borrowing an expression from Edmond Jabès (1912–1991), studying Talmud is "perforating oblivion because oblivion is the thick rind around our origins."[263] Those who engage in Talmud are much more than teachers and scholars: they are 'sages' (חכמים, singular חכם) or 'disciples of sages' (תלמידי חכמים), for they constitute the living link to the "whole Tora, handed down continuously generation after generation from our Teacher Moses."[264]

Since biblical times, Jews confronted the sword with the Book and military defeat with institutions that elevate the quality of Jewish life. Ezra responded to the collapse of biblical monarchy by proclaiming the Tora as the Constitution of Israel – the first true

260. As Vico alerted the reader in *On the Study Methods of our Time*, III, p. 13: "There is a danger that instruction in advanced philosophical criticism may lead to an abnormal growth of abstract intellectualism, and render young people unfit for the practice of eloquence."
261. "The Talmud as a Book," in his *Sermons Addresses and Studies*, vol. 3 (London: Soncino Press, 1938), p. 253. I believe that the Talmudist in question was none other than Professor Louis Ginzberg (1873–1953), one of the most illustrious Talmudists in modern times.
262. See Baba Meṣi'a 33a-b; Yerushalmi Shabbat XVI, 1, 15c. Cf. *Yerushalmi Ki-Fshuṭo*, pp. 193194. Cf. above n. 153.
263. Edmond Jabès, *Elya* (Berkeley, Ca.: Tree, 1973), p. 7.
264. See *MT* Introduction, ll. 131–132, quoted below at n. 265.

constitution known to humankind! The rabbis responded to the collapse of the Temple by proclaiming that God may be truly worshipped "in the service of the heart," rendering the Synagogue and liturgy a worthy "parallel" (כנגד) to the sacramental worship at the Temple. When the national archives were incinerated and the sages butchered, R. Judah and his Court responded by depositing the remnants of the national archives in the *memory of the people*; minting the Oral Law into legal tender, for all to use. Finally, when Jewish society was about to collapse, making *national* consensus impossible, R. Ashe and Rabina, together with the *last* national Court of Israel erected a *virtual* Jewish society, where consensus could be reached, and traditions – both national and vernacular – exchanged and negotiated through *meliṣa*.

For fifteen hundred years, the Talmud stood alone against cultural arrogance, the aggression of the mighty, the epistemology of the infallible, the conceit of the spiritual superior and the intellectually enlightened. The Talmud is the most maligned book in Christian history, and with good reason. Alone it stands for consensus rather than coercion; for dialectics and interaction in which *all* members of society have a voice, including those standing outside the fringe of Scripture – the magicians and the heretics, the agnostics and the fraudulent, and even the depraved and the demoniac. All of these, within the joyous ambiance of *Kalla*, amidst a multitude of voices in a multitude of languages, spoken by the most diverse assembly known to humankind: the Jewish crowd. Without these voices, the teachings of the sages would be empty, without a soul; Israel's memory would fade away and with it the words uttered by God at Sinai.

The authenticity of the Talmud is vouchsafed by the fact that it was "concluded" by the last *national* court of Israel. Its authority rests on a single fact: it was accepted as the living voice of God by myriads of sages and students and men and women, of all persuasions and temperaments. This, by the only people who had *actually* heard God's speech at Sinai, and could discern the resonance of His voice. In the words of Maimonides:

> Given that all the words of the Talmud were set by the common consent of all Israel, and the sages instituting, decreeing, establishing a policy, or adjudicating a case instructing that the law is thus, are all the sages of Israel or the majority, and they were the recipients of the judicial tradition (*qabbala*) pertaining to the whole Tora, in a continuous chain, one generation from the other until our Teacher Moses.[265]

Thus, to repudiate the Talmud is to repudiate the National Memory of Israel, from the last sage all the way up to Moses at Sinai.

265. *MT* Introduction, ll. 128–132.

# Concluding Reflections

National Memory is not the sum of individual memories. It is fundamentally political. In the language of Scripture: *Morasha* (Deut. 33:4), a dynamic process of the people, effected by the people, and for the people (see appendix 12). It either expands or it ceases to exist. When it falters, it cannot be 'recaptured' by historians as a function of upgraded poets, with the power to "restore a nation's memory, or that of mankind."[266] The 'past' that an individual 'discovers' in the 'present' is a poetic creation; akin to the analphabetic memory of poets transporting an enchanted audience back to a mythical past – like Ruben's portraits of biblical scenes, and the Roman fox in R. 'Aqiba's metaphor (see above chapter 39). That is why neither history nor historians can restore Israel's memory. Having this in mind, we can better appreciate a luminous passage by an outstanding Jewish historiographer:

> Yet those who would demand of the historian that he be the restorer of Jewish memory attribute to him powers that he may not possess. Intrinsically, modern Jewish historiography cannot replace an eroded group memory which, as we have seen throughout, never depended on historians in the first place. The collective memories of the Jewish people were a function of the shared faith, cohesiveness, and will of the

266. Eugen Rosenstock-Huessy, quoted by Yosef H. Yerushalmi, *Zakhor* (Seattle: Washington University Press, 1982), p. 93.

> group itself, transmitting and recreating its past through an entire complex of interlocking social and religious institutions organically to create this.[267]

Jewish Memory developed around the *Book* and the minted traditions of the nation. In quality of *Morasha*, the Memory of Israel was entrusted to the mind *of* the people, so that it must be furthered *by* the people, *for* the sake of people. Therefore, it is immune to analphabetic discourse (see above chapter 4 and Concluding Reflections Section I), and cannot be restored by an act of magic, whether philosophical, poetical or historical. The *superstitiosus* past peddled by pseudo-Jewish-historians and poets is designed to bewitch and becloud – not to instruct. By contrast, the purpose of eloquence (מליצה) around the *Book* and minted memories is to generate consensus, upon which could be erected 'sign-posts' pointing the way ahead. Once apprehended from the perspective of eloquence we realize that Jewish Memory never ceased to *expand* – sometimes tragically, at other times blissfully.

Hebrew eloquence unfolds within the perimeters of horizontality. A rabbinic law stipulates that "the teacher may not sit on a chair and students on the ground; either all sit on the ground or all sit on chairs."[268] History of Religions recorded the apotheosis of men and women ascending to heaven, seated in regal splendor, and keeping an eye on their respective faithful below. In fact, anyone can ascend to heaven, *post mortem*. More meaningful is the God of Tora who *descends* to Sinai. Significantly, He does not act as a raving demagogue, but as a loving father. When the people demanded of Prophet Samuel to appoint a king to fight their wars, because they would rather gain control of the Promised Land by the sword of the monarch than by the grace of God, God revealed to Samuel: "They have not rejected you... but Me." Nonetheless, in what constitutes the purest expression of *true* democracy, God instructs Samuel: "Now therefore hearken

267. *Zakhor*, p. 94.

268. *MT Talmud Tora* 4:2; *Shulḥan 'Arukh, Yore De'a* CCXLVI, 9. The source is Megilla 21a.

unto their voice" (I Sam. 8:7–9, see above chapter 17). One can only guess what the deity of other 'monotheistic' religions would have replied to such a demand. Later, when the sages rejected a celestial voice and proclaimed: "The Law is not in the Heavens!" He responded joyously: "My children have defeated me! My children have defeated me!" (see above chapter 7.) A hierarchic venue can structure polemics, where those in the possession of the truth pulverize their opponents, but cannot produce men and women who could climb over and stand on their leader's shoulders. The Talmud relates that when Moses was transported to the future to attend a class given by R. 'Aqiba, he could not make head or tail of the lesson. When a student asked R. 'Aqiba for his source, he answered: "it is a *halakha* that Moses taught at Sinai."[269] Can you picture members of other 'monotheistic religions' relating a similar story about their founder? For Jewish Memory to bloom, flourish and bear fruits, a Mishna environment is of the essence. Thus the sages taught: "All the exiles would not be gathered in, if not for the merit of the Mishna."[270] This warrants long and continuous *Kalla* forums – as with R. Ashe – where national and vernacular memories circulate freely, everyone gaining from the other, each and every one speaking "the words of the Living God."

The sustained and continuous denunciation of corrupt political leaders by the prophets and sages of Israel has no parallel in history. Throughout their long history, the Jewish people alone held fast to the principle that all forms of authority must be grounded in the Law and be accountable to the Law. Jewish 'inability' to 'assimilate' is a corollary of having rejected the notion that authority is the effect of power; that violence, whether by the word of *europaischen Menschentums* or the sword of the mighty, merits compliance. Plea for 'Jewish Assimilation' is a plea for exchanging the Covenant at Sinai for political demagoguery. Or what amounts to the same: "the words of the Living God" for gibberish.

---

269. See Menaḥot 29b; and "Introductory Remarks," Section V.

270. Vayyiqra Rabba, VII, 3, vol. 1, p. 155.

# Section V

# The Folly of Israel

## Introductory Remarks

"The conflict between Galileo and the Inquisition," wrote Russell, "is not merely the conflict between free thought and bigotry or between science and religion; it is a conflict between the spirit of induction and the spirit of deduction." He added:

> Those who believe in deduction as the method of arriving at knowledge are compelled to find their premises somewhere, usually in a sacred book. Deduction from inspired books is

> the method of arriving at truth employed by jurists, Christians, Mohammedans, and Communists.[1]

This interpretation is, in my view, mistaken. The cohesive element of a hierarchic apparatus is predicated on persecution of the 'other' – as when Pharaoh sought to solidify his kingdom by inventing a national enemy (see Ex. 1:8–22). Without 'an-other' targeted for persecution, hierarchic systems collapse. With the Christianization and subsequent disintegration of the Roman Empire, the central force cohering society was the persecution of undesirables. The discovery of 'an-other' to target – be they 'lepers,' 'witches,' Jews, or any such devilish creatures – was a matter of national security. In this respect, a most important contribution of Christianity was the introduction of 'heresy' as a dynamic factor in the hounding of the 'other.' In a hierarchic system the function of 'truth' is to uncover 'heresy' and identify those warranting persecution. Hierarchic 'truth' is the prerogative of Adam-*Elohim*: those standing below know it because someone above told them so. 'Knowledge' by virtue of obedience renders its possessors not only 'free' (of the possibility of 'error') but also it awards them the right to hound the 'an-other' standing below. Rejection of this 'truth' is not only 'wrong' but also an act of insubordination. The question of papal infallibility in the *Church* v. *Galileo* centered on two premises: [i] pontifical *rank*, which renders [ii] truth an *imperative*. Rationality, whether 'scientific' or 'theological,' is nothing more than an act of submission to *auctoritas*. (In atheistic regimes with shallow public education systems, too, a major purpose of drafting young men and women to the army is to break their spirit and train them to submit to rank.) Within such a system, 'truth' is a matter of status, independent of a Book or a *ketab* and *mikhtab*. A direct consequence of 'hierarchic truth' is that Galileo was the last Italian scientist until modern times.

Hebrew truth is context-bound. The judiciary is expected to consult with expert witnesses and evaluate the facts presented before them. On

1. Bertrand Russell, *The Scientific Outlook* (New York: W.W. Norton, 1962), p. 33.

one such occasion, R. Judah the Prince, Chief Editor of the Mishna and President of the Supreme Court of Israel, did not hesitate to consult with non-Jewish experts, and declared: "The gentile sages have prevailed over the Jewish sages."[2] Given that the Hebrew truth is neither abstract nor cosmic, it is continuously expanding within the dialectical context of Adam/*Adon*. The Tora revealed at Sinai was published in the collective memory of Israel, involving a dynamic act of reception/transmission, by, of, and for the people: perennially unfolding and developing within the specific historical context of Israel. When a divine voice tried to interfere in the decision making process of the court, it was dismissed on the grounds that "the Tora is not in heaven!" (see above chapter 6).

A story told by Rab (2nd and 3rd centuries) sheds light on this principle. When Moses ascended to heaven to receive the Tora, he saw God tying calligraphic ornaments on some of the letters. The purpose was to indicate that interconnection of these letters may yield some hitherto unknown principle. Curious, Moses asked: "Who impedes You?" (from fully revealing these messages *now*?) God did not reply. Instead, He told Moses that in the future there would be a sage who would unfold these messages. The intent is obvious. To be functional, a truth must be historically bound. Because the truth that the Tora teaches is continuously unfolding, people in an early historical period cannot fathom its future development and application. As if to corroborate this principle, God transported Moses to R. 'Aqiba's school. In the course of delivering the lecture, R. 'Aqiba was asked for the source of the lesson. "It is a halakha taught by Moses at Sinai," he responded. Moses, the rabbis noted, "could not understand what they were talking about."[3]

2. Pesaḥim 94b. See José Faur, "Ve-Niṣḥu," in eds. Chief Justice Aaron Barak and Menashe Shawa, *Minḥa le-Yiṣḥaq* (Tel-Aviv: Lishkhat 'Orkhe ha-Din, 1999), pp. 113–133.

3. Menaḥot 29b; see above Section IV, n. 269. In this connection it would be particularly helpful to consider a point made by Ludwig von Bertalanffy, *General System Theory* (New York: George Braziller, 1968), p. 227:

Furthermore, the symbolic world created by men gains a life of its own, as

What is unique about the *meliṣa*-truth is that it is continuously growing in ways transcending the mind of the original author. Could the genius who discovered the number zero foretell the future mathematical developments made possible by his finding? Could the Wright brothers fathom the continuous 'upgrading' made to their original invention? Another story illustrates the intellectual frame for *meliṣa*. Man must be under the direct shade of God (in terms of Adam/*Adon*, rather than under Adam-*Elohim*). God instructed Moses to appoint Bezalel as Chief Artisan in the design and manufacture of the Tent of Assembly, as well as the vessels and Ark containing the Tablets. At the time Bezalel was twelve years old. To test the acumen of this *wunderkind*, Moses changed the order of the plan. Bezalel thought the plan wrong and challenged Moses: "Perhaps God has instructed you (differently)?" and proceeded to put forward a plan that coincided with God's instructions. Astonished at his sharpness, Moses exclaimed: "Have you perhaps been under the Shadow of God?!"[4] By contrast, the truth expressed by hierarchic man must be *under* the Shadow of an Adam-*Elohim* – never under God's Shadow.

Looking at the political and intellectual map of the last millennium of Jewish history, it is nigh impossible to square it with the concept of Law and the *ketab* and *mikhtab* systems described in the preceding sections. What happened? The central thesis of this section is that Jews *chose* to escape from Reason under the guidance of "little foxes" (שועלים קטנים). In a system refusing to use might to crush opposing views, a genuine revolution is never ended. Accomplishments do not ward off future failure. Israel is the only nation that warned the people, at the apogee of their success, of the possibility of failure. Right before crossing the Jordan, Moses alerted Israel that failure of the system may result in Exile (Deut. 29:27), but *not* in the dissolution of the

---

it were; it becomes more intelligent than its creator. The symbol system of mathematics, for example, is embodied in an enormous thinking machine which, fed with a statement, produces in return a solution on the basis of a fixed process of concatenation of symbols, which could hardly be anticipated.

4. Berakhot 54b.

covenant (see Deut. 30; Neh. 1:5–11, and above chapter 5). After the inauguration of the First Temple, God warned King Solomon that deviation from the pact would lead to national catastrophe (I Kings 8:6–9; cf. II Chr. 7:19–22). Intrinsic to a dynamic scheme is not only the possibility of progress, but also of failure. As with Jacob's angels: not only do they ascend *up* the ladder but also descend; i.e., they could *fail* and *trip down* before going up again (see Gen. 28:12; cf. Mic. 7:8).

"The Folly of Israel" proposes that the collapse of the main Jewish values and institutions came about as the result of the anti-Maimonidean ideology. Three groups contributed to its development and triumph. From Talmudic times there had been circles of rabbinic learning scattered throughout the Diaspora. In the far away communities of Germany, France, and Spain, geographically and culturally distant from the Academies of Babel (Babylonia) and the Holy Land, a populist conception of rabbinic Judaism emerged, autonomous from the traditional teachings of the Talmudic Academies. Out of these circles emerged the bogus-Talmudists described by R. Sherira Gaon as "little foxes" (שועלים קטנים), who challenged the authority of the *Yeshibot* (see appendix 54). Already by the beginning of the 11th century there were Talmudists in the Iberian Peninsula who opposed the intellectual traditions and values creating what later historians would designate 'the Golden Age of Spain' (chapters 49–51). A second movement arose in Germany as a reaction to the First Crusades (1096). In response to the atrocities committed in the name of 'religion,' Jews countered with the creation of a heroic ideology, promoted by hymnologists and chroniclers under the rubric *qedoshim* (sing. *qadosh*). An essential element of our thesis is that this term, usually translated as 'saints,' actually stood for 'heroes,' with all the paraphernalia that European folklore attached to 'heroic' behavior and ethos. This ideology spread south to France. The result was a new religious conception, which came to be known as 'Qabbala' (chapter 52–53). Soon thereafter, the new religion crossed into the Iberian Peninsula. The combination of heroic ideology, Qabbala, and bogus-Talmudists gave rise to the axis 'Rabbis of France' → 'Qabbala' → 'anti-Maimonidean.'

It culminated with the triumph of the anti-Maimonidean movement (1180–1249), resulting in a series of strategic blunders that effectively prevented the emergence of a competent leadership (both secular and religious), ending with the collapse of the most important communities in France and Germany. It was followed by mass defection to Christianity, culminating in the Expulsion (1492), and the eradication of Jewish life from Spain and Portugal.

We also propose that the values associated with Maimonides were developed before, and independently of Maimonides, and that those values constituted the standards of Judaism in the communities culturally close to the Academies in Babel and the Holy Land. The 'Maimonidean controversy' was, in fact, a culture clash, peculiar to the ethos and temperament of European Jewry. This will explain why the anti-Maimonidean → qabbalistic movement never took root in the communities in Byzantium (Italy included), the Middle East and North Africa. Having preserved a modicum of contact with the traditions of the ancient Academies, these communities were immune to the anti-Maimonidean ideology.

In part, this thesis rests on a view suggested by R. Solomon ibn Verga, that Jewish tribulations are the consequence of a "natural cause" (הסיבה הטבעית); i.e., the mechanics of history – not of some paranormal 'punishment' from the realm of the supernatural. Specifically, that when faced with choices, inept Jewish leadership infallibly opted for the one leading to disaster.[5] One of the purposes of Qabbala was deflecting responsibility away from inept leadership and placing it in the realm of the mystical.

In terms of the general scheme of this work, the anti-Maimonidean/Qabbala movement was a call on behalf of heroic truth and culture, voiced by "*europaischen Menschentums*" (see Concluding Reflections Section I, and appendix 58) in opposition to humanistic discourse and *meliṣa*.

5. See *In the Shadow of History*, pp. 204–213.

# Chapter 49
# *Qabbala* and the Conveyance of Talmudic Tradition

From late Antiquity and throughout the Middle Ages, there were circles of Jews all over the Diaspora devoted to rabbinic learning. These circles were independent of the *Yeshibot*. Some of the students were merchants whose travels brought them into contact with the *Yeshibot*, and had the opportunity to become acquainted with the teachings and writings of the Geonim. Some may have actually attended the *Yeshibot*, and then returned home before completing their studies. At one time, through the *Kalla* institution, the *Yeshibot* exercised a modicum of supervision over these circles (see above chapter 48). With the waning of the *Yeshibot* from the 9th century on, these contacts weakened. Consequently, in regions culturally and geographically distant from Babel, populist conceptions of rabbinic Judaism emerged in the realms of faith, spirituality, and cult. Some of these developments had more to do with local folklore and sacrality than Tora. In his *Contra Judaeos*, Agobard (ca. 779–840), Archbishop of Lyons, noted that French Jews believed in the corporeality of God and anthropomorphism.[6] A factor in these types of beliefs was that "Jews from France... say that these, I mean all the *aggadot*, are from

6. See Bernhard Blumenkranz, *Les auteurs chretiens latins du moyen age sur les juifs et le Judaism* (Paris: Mouton, 1963), p. 165 n. 63. For an adequate understanding of the passion for anthropomorphism characterizing anti-Maimonidean ethos and culture, see *The New Science* ##180–181, p. 70; ##220–221, p. 76; ##405–406,

the mouth of the Almighty." To them, this meant that they must be interpreted in a most literal fashion (see below).[7] When meeting Jews "professing the unity of God" in their pilgrimage to the Holy Land, some French Jews felt embarrassed about their creeds.[8] In their criticism against the Rabbanites, Karraites targeted such creeds as "a Minor and a Major God," the anthropomorphic work "*Shi'ur Qoma,*" and the proclamation announcing "the abrogation of the vows..." made on the 9th of Tishri, declaring that all vows that will be made "shall be null and void."[9]

Hence, the tension between the official teachings of Israel, as articulated and transmitted by the *Yeshibot*, and the teachings evolving from those circles. In considering their significance, it is important to remember that by the end of the 8th century, Judaism was deeply divided between Karraites, denying rabbinic authority altogether, and the Geonim at the *Yeshibot* in Babel and the Holy Land, maintaining the authority of tradition, as conveyed by an uninterrupted chain of transmission, known as *qabbala* (see below). The above mentioned circles of learning represented a middle ground. On the one hand, unlike the Karraites, they recognized the authority of rabbinic texts and tradition. On the other hand, because of personal ideology, coupled with geographical and cultural distancing from the *Yeshibot*, some

pp. 129–130; and #816, p. 312. Let us note that R. Hayye Gaon, in *Teshubot ha-Ge'onim ha-Ḥadashot*, #155, 67, pp. 219–220, regarded people holding this type of belief as *minim*. Cf. appendix 55.

7. See Saul Lieberman, *Shkiin* (Jerusalem: Bamberg & Wahrman, 1939), p. 11. Cf. Rabad on *MT Teshuba* 3:7; and R. Abraham Maimonides, *Teshubot*, ed. A. H. Freimann (Jerusalem: Mekize Nirdamim, 1937), #4, p. 15, and n. 6.
8. Jacob Mann, *Texts and Studies*, 2 vols. (New York: Ktav Publishing, 1972), vol. 2, p. 38, n. 73.
9. See *Texts and Studies*, vol. 2, pp. 85–86. They associated the minor deity with the *meṭaṭron* of the Talmud; see *Shkiin*, pp. 14–15. For further reference, see *Studies in the Mishne Tora*, pp. 136–137, 184, 189 n. 68; and R. Judah al-Bargeloni, *Perush Sefer Yeṣira*, p. 21. On a 'major' and 'minor' deity, cf. *Zohar*, 3 vols. (Leghorn, 5618/1858), vol. 2, 274a. From a *responsum* by Maimonides, *Teshubot ha-Rambam* #117, vol. 1, pp. 200–201, it seems that they associated the 'deity' of *Shi'ur Qoma* with the 'minor deity' peculiar to their belief.

of the principles and doctrines that they taught were not grounded on *qabbala*. The resolution of this quandary led to two conflicting movements, which later historians would designate 'Maimonidean' and 'anti-Maimonidean.'

The background of this conflict was presented by R. Abraham ibn Daud (ca. 1110–1180), in *Sefer ha-Qabbala,* written around 1160. The plan of the book was to trace the transmittal of *qabbala* from the *Yeshibot* in Babel to the Jewish communities throughout the Diaspora. The transmittal led to the establishment of a new institution, the rabbinate, with the authority to convey and further expand the *qabbala* of Israel. The bulk of the book consists of a chronological presentation of the main echelons of Jewish tradition, from the biblical period and the destruction of the Second Commonwealth (I-II), and thence to the rabbinic period, concluding with the publication of the Talmud (III-IV). From the Talmudic period he then continued with the chronological succession of the Seboraim and Geonim (V-VI), the last recipients of the *qabbala.*[10]

Having documented the transmittal of the *qabbala* to the *Yeshibot* in Babel, R. Abraham ibn Daud then proceeded to document the transmittal of *qabbala* from the *Yeshibot* to the communities around the Mediterranean Basin. On the basis of this transmittal a new institution was established: the rabbinate (רבנות). Suddenly – or providentially, depending on your point of view – what appeared to be a random incident unfolded into a chain of events giving rise to a new period of Jewish history. The *Yeshibot,* in dire need of funds for the *Kalla* conventions, appointed four Talmudic sages to collect funds. The vessel carrying these sages was taken over by pirates from Spain. The event was recorded by R. Abraham ibn Daud, and became known as 'the story of the four captives.' Various communities around the Mediterranean Basin ransomed these sages. Given that the captives

10. See quotation from *Sefer ha-Qabbala,* below at n. 22. Cf. *Kuzari* III, 63–67. The trustworthiness of Jewish prophets is proclaimed by the faithful in the blessing preceding the recitation of the *hafṭara,* declaring that they are "the prophets of truth and justice."

were officers of the *Yeshibot,* they were invested with the authority of *qabbala*. One of the captives was R. Moses (d. ca. 965). He was ransomed by the community of Cordova, and succeeded in establishing a rabbinic school in the city. In one of the most affecting stories of the book, R. Abraham ibn Daud portrays the meeting between the ransomed captive, R. Moses, and some of the leaders of the community. The scene is lyrical, startling and magnetic – worthy of a modern stage – filled with verbal snapshots, which, as in a family album, can be fully appreciated only by those close to the original characters. Because modern scholars are unacquainted with rabbinic discourse, the main points of this scene were overlooked. Here is what R. Abraham ibn Daud wrote:

> Now there was in Cordova a synagogue that was called the College Synagogue, where a judge by the name R. Nathan, a pious man (חסיד) of distinction [rather "than R. Nathan the Pious, who was a man of distinction"], used to preside. The people of Spain were not thoroughly versed (בקיאין) in the words of our rabbis of blessed memory. Nevertheless, with the little knowledge they did possess, they conducted a school and interpreted [the traditions] more or less [i.e., by conjecture; "more or less accurately" is meaningless]. Once R. Nathan explained [the law requiring] "immersion for each sprinkling," which is found in the Tractate Yoma, but he was unable to explain it correctly. Thereupon, R. Moses, who was seated in the corner like an attendant, arose before R. Nathan and said to him: "Rabbi, this would result in an excess of immersions!" When he and the students heard his words, they marveled to each other and asked him to explain the law to them. This he did quite properly. Then each of them propounded to him all the difficulties which they had, and he replied to them out of the abundance of his wisdom.[11]

11. *Sefer ha-Qabbala*, p. 65 (Heb. pp. 47–48). For a discussion of this passage, see

The text discussed by these sages [Tosefta Yoma, III, 2, p. 241] represents a very high stage of rabbinic education. *It is so advanced that it does not form part of the standard curriculum of even the most advanced rabbinic school today*. This should alert the educated reader that the participants had received advanced rabbinic training. But where could they have received this type of schooling? Triggering a domino-like series of images in the mind of the informed reader, the question points to two overlapping traditions originating around Cordova at the end of the 8th century. First, a tradition that Prince R. Neṭruna'e b. Ḥakhina'e came to Andalusia from Babel (around the year 770), and wrote "for the children of Sepharad the Talmud by heart" (see appendix 47). Corroborating this tradition were "the elders" of the community, who were the recipients of Talmudic lessons, stemming from that solitary voyager.[12] Another tradition speaks of the Exilarch R. Isaac, buried around Cordova, who taught the people Talmud.* His teachings bore fruit. R. Samuel ha-Nagid (993–1056) reported that the people "did not neglect… even one of the Talmudic regulations that have been arranged for them by the Exilarch R. Isaac to be learned by heart."[13] As if to suggest these traditions, R. Abraham ibn Daud informed us that the historic encounter took place in Cordova, at the Synagogue named the "College Synagogue," i.e., the rabbinical school.

We shall now return to our story. The astonishment of the sages of Cordova was caused by four words: "Rabbi, this would result in an excess of immersions!" (ר' פשו להו טבילות!). A question arises:

---

*Tosefta Ki-Fshuṭah*, vol. 4, pp. 778–779. On the high level of erudition required to master this type of text, cf. *MT* Introduction, l. 152.

12. *Sefer ha-'Ittim*, pp. 255–256; see R. Judah al-Bargeloni, *Perush Sefer Yeṣira*, p. 187 (cf. ibid., pp. 107–108); and editor's note, p. 321. People in North Africa knew of him; see *Teshubot ha-Ge'onim* (Harkavi), #199, p. 90.

* Yebamot 115b.

13. *Sefer ha-'Ittim*, p. 267; cf. *IShG*, p. 104. On the Talmudic tradition in Sepharad, see Professor Shraga Abramson, "*Mi-Torato shel R. Shemu'el ha-Nagid*," *Sinai* (Jubilee Volume) 100 (5748/1988), pp. 23–24. There is no cogent reason to doubt the authenticity of this tradition, other than rabbinic illiteracy, coupled with bias, camouflaged by bogus scholarship.

Given that we are dealing with seasoned scholars, and given that the difficulty raised by R. Moses is obvious, what caused them to "marvel at each other?" Our question is particularly poignant when realizing that they "marveled" before he had the opportunity to clarify the passage! (Incidentally, the explanation itself was so unimportant that it was not recorded.) The significance of R. Moses' words becomes evident upon noticing that he spoke them in the Aramaic dialect of the *Yeshibot*. The dialect was exclusive to rabbinic discourse, which was not spoken by any community and it could only be known by special tutoring.[14] When R. Hayye Gaon dreamt of R. Se'adya Gaon and wished to ask him a question, "he asked him in the Aramaic language in use among them (the sages)."[15] Fluency in that language was the hallmark of a Talmudic sage. When R. Samuel ha-Nagid sent a letter to R. Ḥanan'el expressing grief at the death of R. Ḥushi'el his father, the preface, epilogue, as well as the poem itself were written in a flawless Rabbinic Aramaic.[16] To demonstrate rabbinic fluency, works on the Talmud had to be written in that language; e.g., the *Hilkheta* of R. Samuel ha-Nagid and the *Halakhot* of R. Isaac Alfasi. In a letter written to the Sages of Lunel, Maimonides referred to some commentaries he had on the Talmud "that I composed in the language

14. See Introduction, *MT* ll. 137–138; *Sefer ha-Miṣvot*, I, p. 11. Cf. Shraga Abramson, *Perush Rabbenu Ḥanan'el la-Talmud*, p. 120.

15. See R. Moses ibn 'Ezra, *Kitab al-Muḥaḍara wal-Mudhakara*, ed. and trans. A. S. Halkin (Jerusalem: Mekize Nirdamim, 1975), p. 126. For some examples, see R. Se'adya, *Perush* to *Daniel*, ed. and trans. R. Joseph Qafiḥ (Jerusalem: Deror, 5741/1991), p. 84. The expression "לישנא דרבנן" found in Qiddushin 2b is Seboraitic. To my mind, the reason that 'Anan, the founder of Karraism and champion of the Hebrew Scripture, chose to inaugurate his anti-rabbinic movement with an Aramaic motto (חפישו באורייתא שפיר) was to validate his credentials by demonstrating his fluency in the rabbinic dialect of this language.

16. See *Diwan Shemu'el ha-Nagid, Ben Tehillim*, ed. Dov Jarden (Jerusalem: Hebrew Union College Press, 1966), #107, pp. 256–260. His fluency in rabbinics is reflected in his poetry; see Shraga Abramson, "*Dibre Ḥazal be-Shirat ha-Nagid*," *World Congress for Jewish Studies*, I (Jerusalem: Hebrew University Press, 5712/1952), pp. 274–278; see *Hilkhot ha-Nagid*, pp. 63–64.

of the rabbis" (בלשנא דרבנן).[17] Errors were not tolerated. When the celebrated R. Joseph ibn Santas ibn Abitur (ca. 939-after 1012) was in North Africa on his way from Spain to Babel, he wrote a letter to a local sage in this dialect. The sage "replied to him, pointing out his error to him, but in a mild and tranquil tone."[18]

Thus, the four words pronounced by the ransomed stranger disclosed a most precious secret: he was a sage from one of the *Yeshibot*! We will now proceed with another question intended to reveal the enormous significance of this event: in which way was the instruction provided by R. Moses qualitatively different than what had been previously known? The answer will provide the key to unraveling the mind and concept formation of what became known as 'the Maimonidean tradition.' Before the arrival of R. Moses, the people in Sepharad had access to an authoritative text of the Talmud, properly delivered by a bona fide sage. However, as indicated by R. Abraham ibn Daud, the *interpretation* and *application* of the text they knew "more or less" i.e., by conjecture, not by *qabbala*!

R. Abraham ibn Daud knew the names of only three of the ransomed sages. Each sage managed to establish a rabbinic school at his new home, and was succeeded by his son, who further developed the intellectual tradition received from his father. These sages were: the above mentioned R. Moses, who established a school in Cordova, and

17. *Iggerot ha-Rambam*, vol. 2, p. 558. Maimonides wrote the *Mishne Tora* in Hebrew, not Aramaic, to indicate that this work was *not* intended for an academic graduate; see below, chapter 63, and *Studies in the Mishne Tora*, pp. 52–54.

18. *Sefer ha-Qabbala*, p. 67. The form 'Saṭnas' is a metathesis of *Sanṭas* (שנטאש) 'Saintes,' France, a place known for its sages; see Henry Gross, *Gallia Judaica* (Amsterdam: Philo Press, 1969), pp. 659–660. The proper spelling is found in ms. מ, at *Sefer ha-Qabbala*, (Heb.), p. 48 (l. 46) and in *Kitab al-Muḥaḍara*, p. 59. Several opinions were advanced to explain why this sage refused to return to Spain and assume the leadership of the Rabbinic Academy; see "*Mi-Torato shel R. Shemu'el ha-Nagid*," p. 24. In my view, his discovery that he did not have a perfect command of the rabbinic dialect was so traumatic that he could no longer see himself worthy of assuming the direction of the rabbinic school; see *Sefer ha-Qabbala* (Heb.), p. 51 (ll. 90–91).

was succeeded by his son Ḥanokh (d. 1014); R. Shemarya (d. 1011), who established himself in Fostat (Old Cairo), and was succeeded by his son R. Elḥanan (d. 1026); and R. Ḥushi'el (10th and 11th centuries) who established a school in Kairowan, modern Tunisia, together with his son R. Ḥanan'el. Most probably, the fourth sage established himself somewhere in Byzantine Italy, from where emerged the schools of R. Gereshom (960–1028) and R. Nathan b. Yeḥi'el (1035–ca. 1110), author of the famous Talmudic Lexicon; the school of Rashi and R. Tam (ca. 1110–1171); and the commentator on the Mishna, R. Isaac Malkiṣedeq (11th and 12th centuries). The fruits of this anonymous sage were soon evident. Mention was made "of a great scholar from France by the name of R. Paregoros," who took up residence in Cordova.[19] There were others:

> We have heard that in France there are great scholars and *ge'onim* and that each and every one of them is a rabbi who inherits the Tora appropriately, [i.e.] with the intention of passing it on. Indeed, they have been bequeathing it in the spirit of the verse: "That I may cause those who love me to inherit substance, that I may fill their treasures" [Prov. 8:21].

Ibn Daud then proceeded to enumerate some of the most prominent French scholars known to him. It is highly instructive that the last scholar mentioned by name is none other than the celebrated R. Tam. He concluded the Section with this moving passage:

> May the Holy One, blessed be He, protect and preserve their disciples and heirs and grant them the opportunity to study, teach and spread the knowledge of the Tora throughout Israel.[20]

19. *Sefer ha-Qabbala*, p. 79. Concerning Talmudic sages in Byzantine Italy, see H. J. Zimmels, "Scholars and Scholarship in Byzantium and Italy," in ed. Cecil Roth, *The Dark Ages* (New Brunswick: Rutgers University Press, 1966), pp. 177–185.
20. *Sefer ha-Qabbala*, pp. 89–90.

Maimonides, too, acknowledged the legitimacy of the Geonim of "France" (Introduction *MT* l. 134; see below chapter 63).

The school of Cordova continued to flourish. "The mastery of the Talmud now rested [exclusively] in Sepharad [i.e., Andalusia – not Spain!]".[21] An important factor contributing to this success was the arrival of R. Isaac Alfasi (1013–1103, a disciple of R. Nissim, ca. 990–1062, and R. Ḥanan'el), who established himself at Lucena, where the school of Cordova moved. Out of this school came the celebrated R. Joseph ibn Megas (1077–1141), and Maimonides's father, R. Maimon b. Joseph (d. 1165/1170).

At the end of his *Commentary to the Mishna,* Maimonides appended a chain of seven ancestors who served as judges in Cordova. A reckoning of that list will show that first in the chain, R. 'Obadya was a contemporary of R. Moses, 'the captive' who established the famous *Yeshiba* in Cordova. This implies that he must have been one of sages who, together with R. Nathan, "marveled at each other" upon hearing the stranger speak. And now a suggestion for which I have no textual evidence. Maimonides' father realized that the tradition inaugurated by R. Moses 'the captive' was coming to an end. To mark this pivotal moment he called his newborn son by the name of the founder of the Andalusian Rabbinate. If so, the purpose of the list was to hint at the connection between Moses b. Maimon, the writer, and Moses 'the captive,' founder of the *Yeshiba* at Cordova. Accordingly, the famous dictum, "From Moses till Moses there was none like Moses" – intended to compare R. Moses Maimonides with R. Moses 'the captive' – not with Moses of the Pentateuch!

21. *Sefer ha-Qabbala,* p. 78.

# Chapter 50
# "Little Foxes" – Rabbis without *Qabbala*

The purpose of *Sefer ha-Qabbala* was to record the conveyance of the original title of *qabbala,* originating with the first government of Israel at Sinai, down to a newly-founded institution: the rabbinate (רבנות). In this manner, R. Abraham ibn Daud intended to demonstrate that the new possessors were invested with the authority to interpret, transmit, and adjudicate *qabbala*. As with a chain of title in modern law, R. Abraham ibn Daud documented the successive conveyances from the original government of Israel to the new rabbinic institution, each being a perfect conveyance of the original title. In his words:

> The transmittal of the *qabbala* of the sages had proceeded from the mouths of the Prophets: from trustworthy witnesses to trustworthy witnesses, as we have presented in this work.[22]

The successive conveyances of *qabbala* passed from the *Yeshibot* of the Geonim to the newly established institution: the rabbinate (רבנות). "The generation of these three men, R. Ḥanan'el, R. Nissim, and R. Samuel ha-Levi ha-Nagid, constituted the first generation of the

22. *Sefer ha-Qabbala* (Heb.), p. 38 (ll. 33–34). Given the perfect conveyance of the rabbinic *qabbala,* there is no need for further corroboration; see R. Nissim Gaon, Introduction, *Sefer ha-Mafteaḥ,* 2b.

rabbinate[23] (רבנות)." The title passed over to R. Joseph ibn Megas and the members of his school. In total, the successive chain of *qabbala* from biblical times to the present,

> totaled thirty-eight generations, from (Prophets) Ḥaggai and Zacharias to R. Joseph ha-Levi (ibn Megas), of blessed memory. All of whom are trustworthy witnesses from the mouth of trustworthy witnesses. Neither their transmittal nor the(ir) sequence of holiness was ever broken off.[24]

By underlining the trustworthiness of the witnesses, R. Abraham ibn Daud was stipulating that the *qabbala* conveyed by the *Yeshibot* was recorded and made readily available to a bona fide public. In this fashion, the rabbinic institution established by the four sages was radically different than that of the informal circles of learning scattered through the Diaspora. The title of *qabbala* had been conveyed by officers of the *Yeshibot* to the new rabbinic institution, investing the holders with legitimate authority. Thus, unlike those who had acquired their rabbinic learning without formal *qabbala*, the instruction of the newly established rabbinate (רבנות) was authoritative – not "more or less!"

The basic elements of this doctrine were laid down by R. Nissim Gaon:

> ... And (the people of Israel) have notified [to their posterity] in good faith about God's Law, written by Moses the son of Amram, may he rest in peace, as it has been conveyed to them. And [that by virtue of such a delivery] they convey its meaning and connotation. This conveyance was made from many to many [i.e., publicly]. [The reason for making such conveyance

23. *Sefer ha-Qabbala* (Heb.), p. 58 (ll. 191–192), (Eng. p 78).

24. *Sefer ha-Qabbala* (Heb.), p. 67 (ll. 330–332). Accordingly, he specified, ibid., p. 73, that his chain of tradition includes only: "the Faculty of the Talmudic schools" (בעלי ישיבות), that is, those who had been the formal recipients of a properly conveyed *qabbala*.

> public is that] the public required such information in order to fulfill it (the Law). Said conveyance was made through an uninterrupted chain of transmission going all the way up to the period of the prophets – may they rest in peace! – which was corroborated by witnesses. Actual notice of it and its guidance are public knowledge, fully acknowledged and put into practice: one historical period in succession to another, and one generation in succession to another. Accordingly, their information admits no challenge, and no alternative tradition (Ar. *taqlid)*. The aforementioned cannot be dismissed unless fraudulent conveyance is claimed. These are our basic principles upon which we stand. Whatever queries may arise from the outward (sense of the Scripture) may be explained – an explanation conforming with these principles[25] (see Appendices 32, 33).

In order to do justice to the momentous significance of the rabbinic institution established by the four captives, it is essential to come to grips with the fact that the authority of the *Yeshibot* had been challenged – in the words of Sherira Gaon – by "little foxes" (שועלים קטנים). They were not Karraites, since they were challenging the Geonim on the basis of rabbinic texts.

> There are among us students – "little foxes" having no substance – who challenge (us) and call into question (the authority) of the Geonim, pillars of the world. Asking: 'how do they know that matter?' [In support for their challenge] they [i] take out their books (ספריהם). [ii] But they understand not the deeds of God and the making of His hands [i.e., the text that they are quoting]; and do not comprehend even a small

25. *R. Nissim Ga'on*, p. 354. A similar argument was presented by Maimonides to justify the abrogation of vows; see *Perush ha-Mishnayot, Nedarim* 10:8, vol. 3, pp. 152–153.

> fraction of what a minor student of a student of the least important of the Geonim comprehends.[26]

The fault with "little foxes" was two-fold. They [i] challenged the authority of the Geonim on the basis of *their books* (ספריהם). This meant that they did not know the Talmud orally, pointing to a deficient, unauthorized schooling. It will be recalled that although the Oral Law was put into writing, citations could be made only from properly authorized transmitters – not from codices (see above chapter 43). Furthermore, their challenge was made on the basis of unauthorized copies.[27] In addition, they [ii] were not regularly enrolled students at the *Yeshibot*, and lacked formal training. Therefore they "don't comprehend even a small fraction of what a student of a student of the least important of the Geonim comprehends." In simpler words: they had no proper training and were unaware of how the law was taught at the *Yeshiba*. The same condemnation was made by R. Pirqoi b. Baboi (8th and 9th centuries) several centuries before: there are students challenging the *Yeshibot*. They [i] use unauthorized copies of the Talmud, and [ii] base their theories on conjecture, without knowledge of the official teachings at the *Yeshiba*.

---

26. In *Iyye ha-Yam* (= *Sha'are Teshuba*), #187, 75b-76a. This *responsum* is also found at the head of *Teshubot ha-Ge'onim, Sha'are Ṣedeq* (Jerusalem, 5726/1966). The authenticity of this *responsum* has been challenged by S. D. Luzzato and others on the basis of their *a priori* ideas of 'rabbinical authority.' Its authenticity, however, was amply demonstrated in *Iyye ha-Yam*, 117a-119a; and *Studies in the Mishne Tora*, p. 36 n. 12. It was alluded to by Maimonides in *MT Talmud Tora* 5:4; see below n. 49. The expression, "a minor student" (תלמיד אחד מתלמידיו הקטנים) was used by R. Abraham Maimonides, *Milḥamot ha-Shem*, ed. R. Ruben Margaliot (Jerusalem: Mossad Harav Kook, n.d.), p. 70. The father of these 'little foxes,' is the 'Big Fox' mentioned in Berakhot 61b; see above, chapter 39.
27. Referred to as "a student's vernacular version" (שיטפא דתלמידאי תרביצאי); see appendix 41. Therefore, it was important to ascertain that the citation of the Talmud was not from "a vernacular version" (לישנא דשיטפא); see *Sefer ha-'Ittim*, pp. 245–246. In later literature, this expression was used to indicate an inaccurate quotation; see R. Moses al-Ashqar, *She'elot wu-Tshubot* (Jerusalem, 5719/1959), #22, 72a.

> [i] Some of them (the irregular students) found volumes of the Mishna, and of some (tractates of the) Talmud that were unpublished (גנוזות), [ii] and everyone occupied himself in (learning from) books and explained (the text) by conjecture (ופירש לדעתו מה שעלה בלבו) because they did not previously have sages who could instruct them how to apply the law.[28]

By "unpublished" (גנוזות) copies, texts that were not officially authorized by the *Yeshibot* was meant.[29] Given that these men were not enrolled as regular students at the *Yeshibot,* they were not privy to "previous sages" to instruct them. Consequently, their interpretation was nothing more than "conjecture" (ופירש לדעתו מה שעלה בלבו). In contemporary terms, this would be similar to a group of men studying law on their own, and then proceeding to challenge the authority of the Supreme Court and our national law schools.

A pivotal point: as shown previously, the *Yeshibot* were the legal

28. Edited by Professor Shalom Spiegel, "Le-Farashat ha-Polmos…," *Jubilee Volume in Honor of Professor Harry A. Wolfson* (Jerusalem: American Academy for Jewish Studies, 1965), Hebrew Section, p. 245. Not having "sages who could instruct them how to apply the law" is the equivalent to not knowing "standard legal procedure" (דרך המשפט) and "the process of law" (דרך ההלכה), mentioned in appendix 48.
29. On the meaning of this term, see *Golden Doves*, pp. 109–110; cf. ibid., pp. 102–103, and the quotation from R. Israel M. Ḥazzan. See however, "Le-Farashat ha-Polmos…," pp. 254–258. In Aramaic, the term *ganaz* is used to translate the Hebrew *yaḥsan* implying 'long term storage'; see *Targum* on Is. 23:18. Hence '*Bet Geniza*' in Pesaḥim 118b. Such a storeroom was used to deposit the most precious objects, see Berakhot 32b; implying special care and attention; see Shabbat 105b. The Scroll of the Tora belonging to the king was deposited in such a storeroom; see Sanhedrin 22a. The Scroll that God wrote before creating the world, too, was deposited in a similar storeroom; see Zebaḥim 116a. To ensure their preservation, objects deposited in the *yaḥsan/geniza* were especially wrapped; see Kelim 16:5, *Perush ha-Ge'onim,* p. 46; *Perush ha-Mishnayot, Kelim* 16:5, vol. 6, pp. 149–150, and the note of R. Judah ibn Bal'am, ed. M. Peretz, *Commentary to Isaiah* (Ramat-Gan: Bar-Ilan University 1992), on Is. 23:18, p. 119. Hence the custom prevalent in some Sephardic Synagogues to have the whole parchment of the Tora wrapped in a special cloth.

holders of the original title of *qabbala* at Sinai. This title awarded them the status of "Sanhedrin."

> Consequently the *Yeshiba* stands in place of Moses our Teacher, and through it the Law of Israel is executed. Whoever would challenge it, would in fact be challenging the Sovereign of the Law (i.e., God), given that it (the *Yeshiba*) is its (the Law's) seat. He is also challenging Moses, may he rest in peace, since it (the *Yeshiba*) is his chair.[30]

To defy the authority of the *Yeshibot* is rebellion against the most sacred authority of Israel. Quoting R. Sherira Gaon:

> How, then, foxes that have yet to see the light can rise, and assume to speak contemptuously against God and His inheritance?! [How could they dare] challenge those who had winnowed the entire Talmud over twelve times, and examined everything that had been conveyed from the days of Joshua the son of Nun – one in succession from the other, as if it were 'a halakha proceeding from Moses at Sinai' [i.e., trustworthy and authoritative, see appendix 33].[How could they] impute error even to a student of (even) the least important of the Geonim, [given that by virtue of succession] all of their words are the words of the living God. Even at the College of Moses, Lord of Prophets, they would not have dismissed them. Their understanding and analyses [of tradition] is what God had charged Moses with [see above chapter 45]! Even when they issue a view, citing no proof from which place [in the Talmud] it is to be found, there should be no concern, be it on a small or on a major matter. Whoever challenges any of their words is as if he would be challenging God and His Law.[31]

---

30. R. Shemu'el b. 'Eli, *Qobeṣ shel Iggerot*, ed. R. Simḥa Assaf (Jerusalem: Makor, 5730/1970), pp. 51–52. See *Studies in the Mishne Tora*, pp. 33–36.
31. *Iyye ha-Yam*, #187, 75b-76a; printed at the head of *Teshubot ha-Ge'onim, Sha'are*

This does not mean that a bona fide sage could not disagree with a decision or an interpretation of the Geonim. No one in Sepharad honored the Geonim more than R. Samuel ha-Nagid, and yet he did not hesitate to disagree with them.[32] What was meant was that a contrary opinion should not be expressed in a contemptuous manner, impairing the dignity of their *qabbala*.

Who were these "little foxes?" Since they are contrasted with "a minor student of a student of the least important of the Geonim," we know that they were not regularly enrolled students. We were told that "some of them reside (שוכנים) in the Land of Israel." Perhaps it was intended to convey that they were not part of the local communities but voyagers who stopped for some respite from their business trips. I propose that the "little foxes" were the informal students, merchants, and travelers who had acquired a modicum of rabbinic learning at home, and were now challenging the authority of the *Yeshibot*.[33] Upon returning home, some of these students would teach in the name of the Geonim, either through ignorance or malice, doctrines contrary

*Ṣedeq*.

32. See *Diwan Shemu'el ha-Nagid, Ben-Tehillim*, #27, p. 92 (ll. 51–57). The same applies to Maimonides; see for example *Teshubot ha-Rambam*, #217, vol. 2, p. 383, and many others.

33. Obviously, there also were full-fledged students from Christian Europe enrolled at the *Yeshibot*; see *Sefer ha-'Ittim*, p. 110. The expression, "they do not have on hand (אין בידם) a single halakha," *Genizah Studies*, vol. 2, p. 560, is similar to the statement by R. Yehudai Gaon, head of the *Yeshiba* in Sura (ca. 757–761), ibid., pp. 558–559: "You have never asked me a question and I responded to it unless [i] there was a source to it in the Talmud, [ii] and I learned it as *halakha le-ma'ase* from my teacher and my teacher from his teacher." The last expression is similar to "have on hand" (בידם). Thus, authoritative instruction of halakha requires: [i] fluency in Talmudic sources, plus [ii] *qabbala* in the form of *official* instruction on how to apply said halakha; see *MT Shemiṭṭa ve-Yobel* 10:6, quoted below n. 311. Let us note that a sage, i.e., a *talmid ḥakham*, has the right to ask "wherefrom" (מהיכן) is the source of a particular doctrine or legal decision; see *Genizah Studies*, vol. 2, p. 557. In certain types of litigations, the guilty party may ask the court to show the "rationale" (טעם) of a decision; see Sanhedrin 31b; *MT Sanhedrin* 6:6; *Shulḥan 'Arukh, Ḥoshen Mishpaṭ* XIV, 1, 4. Finally, in Hebrew 'to reside' (שכני) is not equal to one who 'dwells' (יושב).

to the Tora. In the introductory poem to *Hilkheta Geburata*, R. Samuel ha-Nagid alerted the reader that some people with ill intentions went as far as circulating bogus instructions in the name of the Geonim. There are "many who scattered away" (שוטטו) from the teachings of the Talmud, and "have issued instructions to the people contravening the words of the Talmud." Either to discredit the *Yeshibot* or to justify their own ideology, they would say "shocking things" (אמרות לא כשרות) "in the name of the Heads" of the *Yeshibot*. "Nowadays, they have circulated in their names (of the Geonim) *responsa* that have caused many to go astray from the right path." R. Samuel ha-Nagid, who was most familiar with the writings of the Geonim, ascertained: "They (the Geonim), did not say that. However, that is what nowadays is written in their names!" Most noticeably, he referred to these bogus-Talmudists as "sectarians" (מינים)[34] (see appendix 55).

Generally, the appellative "sectarians/heretics" (מינים) was used in reference to the Karraites, who denied rabbinic tradition altogether. However, in Andalusia they also applied this term to people not complying with standard rabbinic practice. To illustrate, R. Samuel ha-Nagid described Jews in Northern Spain (Catalonia) suspected of neglecting the recitation of the *Targum* (see below chapter 53) as a community about which, "there were rumors that they practice some secret facet of sectarianism/heresy[35] (צד מינות)." In the above poem,

---

The former indicates someone having dealings with the people of the area, but not necessarily dwelling in the same vicinity; see R. Isaac Samuel Reggio, *Be'ur Yashar*, (Vienna: 1821), on Ex. 25:8, vol. 2, 116a.

34. *Diwan Shemu'el ha-Nagid, Ben-Tehillim*, #27, p. 91 (ll. 29–37). For an overview of this poem, reflecting the standard opinions on this matter, see "*Mi-Torato shel R. Shemu'el ha-Nagid*," pp. 9–13. In my view, however, the purpose of *Hilkheta Geburata* was to focus, exclusively, on the legal areas that had been contaminated by the misinformation circulated by bogus-Talmudists. Concerning the spread of malicious misinformation in the name of the Geonim, see *Iyye ha-Yam*, 117b-118a.

35. *Sefer ha-'Ittim*, p. 267; cf. "*Mi-Torato shel R. Shemu'el ha-Nagid mi-Sfarad*," pp. 9, 11–12. The source for this judgment is a ruling issued by R. Netruna'e Gaon, cited in *Seder Rab Amram Ga'on*, ed. Daniel Goldshmidt (Jerusalem: Mossad

too, he referred to those misrepresenting the Geonim as "sectarians/heretics" (מינים). The rationale is obvious. Given that the *Yeshiba* represents the chain of tradition, defiance of its authority, either like Karraites or by proposing an alternative tradition, impairs the dignity of *qabbala* and the unity of the Jewish people.[36] Similarly, in our system of law it would make no difference whether one chooses to ignore the Supreme Court because he does not recognize its legitimacy, as with the Karraites, or because he claims that one can dispense with its interpretation of the Constitution, as with the "little foxes." This can help us solve a riddle. Repeatedly, R. Abraham ibn Daud asserted that his main objective was to combat sectarian *minim* whom he identified as Karraites.[37] At the same time, he repeatedly said that in Spain, the Karraites were numerically and intellectually insignificant.[38] If so, why write a book to disprove them? It seems to me that his actual objective was not the Karraites proper, but those who were "close to" them (קרובים למינים). This is why he goes on to explain "that unlike the Rabbanites, the *minim*," headed by 'Anan (8th century), the founder of the Karraite movement and his son,

> ... who had been disciples of R. Yehudai (Gaon) have broken away from him (the Gaon) and his *qabbala* without presenting any argument whatsoever, only because of their envy. They cannot claim (about their teachings): [i] this is a *qabbala* that we have received by the mouth of so and so, [ii] but they fabricate (בודים) [laws] out of their own mind.[39]

---

Harav Kook, 1971), p. 77. As noted by R. Joseph Qafiḥ, in his edition of *More Ha-Nebukhim* (Jerusalem: Mossad Harav Kook, 1972), vol. 1, chapter 48, p. 108 n. 4, the Karraites opposed the recitation of the *Targum*. See appendix 61.

36. See *Kuzari* III, 49, p. 134.
37. *Sefer ha-Qabbala* (Heb.), pp. 42 (l. 103); 67 (ll. 333–336); 68 (ll. 351–354); cf. 72 (ll. 401415); 74.
38. *Sefer ha-Qabbala* (Heb.), numerically: p. 67 (l. 337), and intellectually: pp. 69–70 (ll. 355368), 72 (ll. 402–405).
39. *Sefer ha-Qabbala* (Heb.), p. 67 (ll. 333–336). Likewise, in p. 38 (ll. 33–36), he charged that'Anan had broken away from [i] *qabbala*, and [ii] fabricated laws

Likewise, we are told that the head of the Karraites in Castile,

> …[i] Counterfeited (בדא) out of his own mind civil and inheritance law without giving any argument, [ii] without *qabbala*, without any source; just by declaring: 'reason has thus dictated.'[40]

The same verb was used in the Scripture in reference to King Jeroboam who had "counterfeited (בדא) an altar that he made" (I Kings 12:33). Maimonides used the same term to describe someone proposing a heretical interpretation of the Tora.[41] Accordingly, it would not be unreasonable to propose that the actual targets of *Sefer ha-Qabbala* were not the Karraites proper but rabbis without *qabbala*, who were "close to *minim*" (קרוב למינים) or who maintained only a "facet of sectarianism" (צד מינות) (see appendix 55).

In the East, these men were the focus of a poem penned by R. Elḥanan of Fostat, Egypt. We may recall that his father, R. Shemarya was one of the four captives. Both father and son seemed to have been officers of the *Yeshiba* and disciples of R. Sherira Gaon.[42] Therefore, we can be sure that they were aware of the problems created by the "little foxes." In a provocative and engaging poem, R. Elḥanan laid down the main arguments against this type of student. The language of the poem is dense – almost cryptic – expecting the reader to unravel the subtle hints and innuendos to rabbinic literature. The technique is a kind of rhythmic interlacing of praise (A) for those following the time-honored method of studying, and blame (B) for

---

out of his own mind.

40. *Sefer ha-Qabbala* (Heb.), p. 72 (ll. 413–414). Cf. ibid., p. 13 (l. 24).

41. *MT Melakhim* 11:3. The printed text בודאי is faulty and makes no sense. The correct reading is found in R. Joseph ibn 'Aqnin, *Hitgallut ha-Sodot*, ed. and trans. A. S. Halkin (Jerusalem: Mekize Nirdamim, 1964), p. 143: בדאי; cf. ibid p. 148; and *Teshubot ha-Rambam*, #440, vol. 2, p. 730 (l. 7).

42. See Shraga Abramson, *Ba-Merkazim wuba-Tefuṣot*, chapters 9–10; Jacob Mann, *The Jews in Egypt and in Palestine*, vol. 1, pp. 26–41; *idem*, *Texts and Studies*, vol. 1, pp. 199–201.

those disloyal to tradition, forming a pattern (A/B, B/A, etc.). Sixty lines of the poem have been preserved. The first 16 lines form an acrostic, spelling out the name of the author and his father. After the acrostic, every second line begins with one of the letters of the alphabet. The style is that of the ancient 'hymnologists' (פייטנים), highly dense, replete with biblical and rabbinic allusions. The main points raised in the poem are three. First, knowledge of Tora can only be acquired by pursuing the well-regimented curriculum of the *Yeshibot*. Second, the amateurish, undisciplined knowledge acquired by students outside the *Yeshibot* will lead to misconceptions and falsification of the Tora.[43] Third, irregular students should reconsider their ways and study Tora systematically, according to the curriculum of the *Yeshiba*. The poem is too complex and the variables too many to be fully treated here. To gain an insight into the mind and style of the author, analysis of the first 24 lines will suffice.

The opening 9 lines (A/B) begin with a tribute to genuine students (lines 1–4), followed by a censure of the "immature, empty (students) who betray the traditions held in the hands of their ancestors from Sinai" (lines 8–9). The following 10 lines (B/A), explain the main reasons why these students had forsaken traditional education (lines 10–14). It is neither ideological nor doctrinal, but due to a lack of dedication. The systematic study is highly regimented, demanding "grueling rehearsal, toil, physical endurance, exhaustion" (cf. Abot 6:5; Berakhot 63b; *MT Talmud Tora* 3:12). Part-time students cannot possibly carry on the program on their own. "They need to be present at the gate (of the school), in the evenings and mornings, (in the company of other) students" (lines 10–11). Consequently, the Tora will not be found among those "navigating (the sea), among sons engaging in commerce, among haughty businessmen; it will not be found among conceited and arrogant and supercilious men, whose feet run in the pursuit of evil, who rush after their profit" (lines 12–14). These

43. Maimonides, too, wished that his favorite student R. Joseph b. Judah, should learn the secrets of the Tora in "an orderly fashion"; see the Epistle at the head of the *Guide*, p. 1 (l. 21).

students are not willing to follow the *Yeshiba* program because their primary interest is commerce, not Tora. To make his point stick, the author alludes to a rabbinic homily in Deut. 30:12–13 found in *Kalla Rabbati* ("It is not in heaven... Neither is it on the other side of the sea"). The Tora "*is not in the heavens* – it will not be found among the haughty. *Neither will it be found on the other side of the sea* – it will not be found among businessmen, tradesmen, and sailors."[44] Only full-time students are bestowed with wisdom "from the beginning, when they (first ascend) towards the crest of the hill, until the end (of their schooling) when they reach the road (ahead of them), because they have persisted from morning until late" (lines 15–16). These students are immersed in learning. They "seek intelligence, (everywhere) in town, at the entrance of the gates. They pursue it as if it were silver and gold, as if they would be searching for hidden treasures. They rely (תכו, see appendix 56) on the legacy of their fathers, they wear themselves out, wandering to villages and towns" (lines 15–19). A genuine student is someone ready to cross villages and towns to reach the place of study. Here the author is paraphrasing a Talmudic homily (Baba Batra 8a) on Deut. 33:3, extolling those students "who wear out their feet, from town to town and from city to city, to study Tora." For the sake of learning, they leave the comfort of home and travel long distances to reach the *Yeshiba*. The following five lines (20–24) describe the dedicated student. He is determined to be a link in the chain of transmission, for the sake of the "words (מדברות) that were ordered to be conveyed," that is, faithfully transmitted, and "that were spoken orally (שבעל פה מדברים)" – a reference to the Geonim who convey the text of the Talmud orally. The matrix of this line is a rabbinic homily on Deut. 33:3. Playing on two of the terms: "carrying" (ישא) and "your words" (מדברתיך), the rabbis expound: "*to carry on the words of God* – these are the disciples of sages who wear out their

44. In *Massekhtot Kalla*, ed. R. Michael Higger (New York: Moinester Publishing, 1936), 5:4, p. 292; cf. 'Erubin 55a; Debarim Rabba (Lieberman), p. 119; *MT Talmud Tora* 3:8; *Perush ha-Mishnayot*, Abot 2:6, vol. 4, p. 424; 4:12, p. 447.

feet to bear (לישא) and pass over (וליתן) God's words."[45] The next line reads: "their bodies exhausted, they are sunburned, blackened, because they (seek) the laws (given) at Ḥoreb (Sinai)." The reference is to a Talmudic homily on Song of Songs 5:11, where the shepherdess describes her beloved: "His locks are curled, and black as a raven." Playing on the words "curled locks" (קווצותיו תלתלים), as if was written (קוץ תלים), the rabbis say: "on every tip [of every letter of the Tora], there are heaps upon heaps" of halakhot. Taking שְׁחֹרוֹת ('black') as if it read, שחרות ('dusks'), they went on to ask: "In whom will you find 'heaps upon heaps' of halakhot?" They answered: – "In a disciple staying up in school, from the morning-dusk until the evening-dusk."[46] To produce this type of student, "their teachers, who have guarded the words of the early sages, organize various (study) groups, (where) they implant (the teachings of the early sages) as goads and nails" (lines 23–24). Again, the context is a Talmudic homily on Eccl. 12:11.[47]

The numerous cryptic allusions to rabbinic literature make it abundantly clear that the author was addressing a public that was both knowledgeable and respectful of such literature. These allusions could not possibly impress a Karraite. The homilies alluded to in the poem are what Maimonides described as "in the manner of poetic license" –having nothing to do with the overt sense of the verse.[48] Yet, for reasons having nothing to do with scholarship, the poem is commonly interpreted as a polemic against Karraites. A Karraite, however, could not decode, let alone care, about a single line of the poem.

The preceding considerations point out the fact that in addition to Karraites denying rabbinic tradition altogether, the Geonim had to cope with "little foxes" (cf. appendix 54). It is possible to argue

45. Baba Batra 8a. Cf. R. Se'adya on Deut. 33:3.
46. 'Erubin 21b, cf. Menaḥot 29b.
47. See Ḥagiga 3b, and Section IV, n. 190.
48. See *Guide* III, 43, p. 420 (l. 3); *Perush ha-Mishnayot, Abot* 2:6, vol. 4, p. 424; R. Abraham Maimonides, *Perush*, pp. 67, 79, 89, 201; idem, *Milḥamot ha-Shem*, p. 91; cf. *Kuzari* III, 66, Arabic text, p. 142 l. 12; and *Homo Mysticus*, p. 111. See appendix 56.

that technically, they were not *minim* since they actually recognized the authority of the Talmud. However, one would have to agree that they were pretty "close to *minim*," since they arrogated to themselves the right to ignore the *qabbala* of the *Yeshibot* and adjudicate the Law "more or less," by virtue of ideas and theories fabricated out of their own mind. Maimonides took notice of this peril. After formulating the law of the Talmud prohibiting students who have not completed their studies from issuing legal opinions, he added a phrase for which there is no source in the Talmud. To enlighten the learned reader, he was careful to include the words "little foxes" – found nowhere in this sense, except for the *responsum* by R. Sherira Gaon mentioned earlier. With chilling precision, Maimonides described the activities of this new breed of 'rabbis':

> These are the minimal students who never had developed their (knowledge of) Tora suitably, and seek to aggrandize themselves among the ignoramuses and people of their town. They jump and sit at the head, to judge and instruct in Israel. They are the ones who increase discord, tear down the world, dim the light of the Tora, and destroy (מחבלים) the "Vineyard of the Lord of Hosts." About them, said Solomon in his wisdom, "We were overtaken by foxes – little foxes destroying (מחבלים) vineyards" (Song. 2:15).[49]

A concluding comment: 'little foxes' suggests that they will never grow into 'fully-fledged-foxes.' Why? This brings to mind pseudo-Jewish-intellectuals of the sort of Pappus b. Judah, at the service of 'big-fox-Rome' (see above chapter 39). For reasons too obvious to spell out, historians refrain from identifying "little foxes" with 'anti-Maimonideans.'

---

49. *MT Talmud Tora* 5:4; cf. *Guide* II, 43, at the end. His son, too, referred to the anti-Maimonideans of his time as "little foxes"; see *Milḥamot ha-Shem*, pp. 56, 76 (= *Teshubot*, #7, p. 93). See *Seforno* on Song. 2:15, and appendix 54.

# Chapter 51
# The Day of the Willow

The case of Judge R. Nathan of Cordova yielding his seat on behalf of a stranger was exceptional. The title "pious" (חסיד) by which R. Abraham ibn Daud described him was meant to be taken seriously, in its biblical sense (see appendix 60). It would be unrealistic to suppose that other men who had gained a reputation for their learning would be as gracious. (Rather, it would be more reasonable to expect that they would fight tooth and nail for fame and glory.) For these men the principles and ideas upon which 'the Golden Age' of Sepharad was built – the disciplined study of Scripture and Talmud, the cultivation of poetry and literature, the study of science and philosophy, and above all, the development of a way and values conducive to what may be described as 'religious humanism' – had to be opposed by all means. What prevented these men from declaring open war against the new graduates was the prominence they gained, not only among the centers of power, but also among the masses. We hope to show in the course of this section that when the opportunity arose (with the collapse of the Jewish communities in Andalusia), these men became the spearhead for the most powerful group in Jewish Iberian history: the 'anti-Maimonideans.'

The first recorded clash between a 'Maimonidean' and an 'anti-Maimonidean' took place early in the 11th century (ca. 1020–1027), in Andalusia. It was "the day of the willow," a ceremony celebrated on the seventh day of Sukkot, at the end of the summer. On that day, Jews perform an ancient rite with a willow branch. R. Samuel ha-

Nagid and a friend were on their way to the morning services when they heard shrieking noises coming from a Synagogue. Thinking that some people were desecrating the place, they came in. "Perhaps someone was using the sanctuary to shelter his donkey or his cattle?" they asked. "No!" they were told, "But a rabbi is giving a class in Talmud" (lines 6–9). Entering the sanctuary, they saw the teacher, attired in rabbinic robes and related paraphernalia, "fringes on the four corners of the garment, a beard, and a hat" – as if the habits would make a sage! "Teacher and students were shaking their heads," yelling the text and mispronouncing every single word. Sporadically, the teacher would interrupt their reading in the middle of a word, offering some bombastic and long-winded explanation (lines 10–14). "I greeted the rabbi respectfully. He answered me belligerently, as [if I were] a foe" (line 15) (*Diwan R. Shemu'el ha-Nagid, Ben-Tehillim*, #83, pp. 228–229).

Let us consider some of the faults that the author attributed to these bogus-Talmudists. l. 1: they regard themselves as superior. The root *RHB* in the opening line indicates 'lordship,' 'hierarchic superiority.'[50] l. 2: they are "gullible" (פתי; cf. Prov. 14:15) and "gluttons" (מתי-בטן). In our case these attributes are interrelated. Because they are naïve, they take rabbinic *aggadot* in their most literal sense, particularly the one speaking about the 'banquet' awaiting the pious in

50. The root *RHB* indicates someone assuming 'hierarchic superiority' and demanding unmerited 'lordship' over someone else; see Is. 3:5, Ḥagiga 14a. The rabbis associate *rahab* with imperial "kingdom"; see *Midrash Tehillim* XC, 15, p. 392; and R. Judah ibn Bal'am, *Perush* on Is. 51:9, p. 208. 'Raḥab,' the name of the lady who helped the Israelites invade the land, Josh. 2:1, most probably reflects the ancient pronunciation of '*rahab*' as *raḥab*, in which case, her name meant 'Lady.' (Cf. the view of R. Judah Ḥayyuj, cited in R. David Qimḥi, *Sefer ha-Shorashim*, s.v. *rahab*, p. 690.) The honorific sense of '*rahab*' is reflected in the Arabic cognate used to designate a 'nun' and 'monk,' i.e., 'lady' and 'lord' implying rank and deference. (Hence, the use of the appellative '*rahib*' in Arabic Sufi literature to designate Christian anchorites.) This is also the gist of this term in Song. 6:5, "Turn away your eyes from me, for they make me feel meek and unworthy (*hirhibuni*)" – as if in the presence of a *rahbe*; cf. Prov. 6:3. The notion of 'fear' attached to this term in Arabic is a consequence of, not the grounds for, this designation.

the beyond. For them savoring food – and with it the whole gamut of human sensuality – stands for the highest level of human experience.[51] Later, Maimonides would be attacked for proposing that the rabbis never intended a gastronomical banquet. For the anti-Maimonidean faithful, denial of a gastronomical banquet in heaven equals heresy. When you come to think about it, what could the purpose of all the earthly tribulations be without a positive assurance of the most succulent banquet you can imagine? On the other hand, for the Geonim to take the *aggadot* in their plain meaning would be like interpreting a painting by Salvador Dali or Jackson Pollock in the manner of a border inspector looking at a passport photo (see below chapter 57). By associating 'gluttons' with 'gullible' the author was pointing out their immediacy: they are gullible because their thoughts are governed by sensual gratification; and vice versa. l. 3: they are haughty (cf. l. 1). This is a reference to the arrogance peculiar to bogus-Talmudists. Because they measured themselves by the endorsement they received from ignoramuses, shaking their heads erratically, they believed themselves to be superior to R. Hayye Gaon (the greatest Talmudic authority at the time). For them, he would barely qualify as Ziba – a deceitful servant of King Saul's household.[52] l. 4: appearance is everything

51. On the authority of the *aggadot*, see above Section IV, n. 177. Because the anti-Maimonideans regarded sensory perception as the highest form of human understanding, they insisted that prophecy is basically sensory. Likewise, they maintained the angels actually ate the food that Abraham served them; see Ramban on Gen. 18:1 and my *Rabbi Israel Moses Ḥazzan*, p. 126 n. 10. There is no doubt in my mind that the main rationale for the standard version, 'Aboda Zara 65a "דידן עדיפא טפי מהאי" – implying greater sexual delight in the World to Come – was to promote the anti-Maimonidean ideology concerning sensual gratifications in general; cf. *MT Teshuba* 8:2, 6, and below nn. 154–156. The original version is found in ed. Shraga Abramson, *Tractate 'Abodah Zarah* (New York: The Jewish Theological Seminary of America, 1957), p. 112. It reads: "דידן עדיפא טפי" – without "מהאי." For an analysis of the story, see José Faur, "Of Cultural Intimidation and Other *Miscellanea*: Bar-Sheshakh *v.* Raba," *Review of Rabbinic Judaism* 5 (2002), p. 34–50. On the ms. version, see ibid., p. 41 nn. 19, 21.

52. See II Sam. 9; 16:1–5; and Shabbat 56a. He was not an officer of Saul, as sug-

(cf. l. 2). It would suffice for someone to wear rabbinic apparel to have these men believe him to be qualified to be Head of a *Yeshiba* (see Yerushalmi Bikkurim III, 3, 65d, at appendix 10). l. 12: they are insensitive to grammar, so that the 'Talmud' they 'study' is a fabrication of their gibberish. In the course of this chapter, we will see that there are other, more sinister aspects to linguistic gibberish. l. 15: the teacher is poorly mannered and bellicose. This is symptomatic of the violence peculiar to the anti-Maimonidean notion of devotion (see below chapters 56, 64). Thus, whereas the disciples of sages bring peace, not only among Jews, but also to the world (see above chapter 56), bogus-Talmudists are perennially attacking someone: *goyim*, 'other' Jews, and when no one else, each other, beginning at home.

We shall now proceed to examine some of the more subtle aspects of the poem. The "day of the willow" casually mentioned in the poem (l. 5), provides the model to tell apart a Talmudic sage growing up by the fountain-spring of the ancient *Yeshibot* from bogus-Talmudists. Concerning Sukkot, the Tora specifies to "take willows from a brook" together with a branch of a palm-tree and other plants (Lev. 23:40). The rabbis taught that there is a bogus-willow, growing wild in the mountains, which cannot be used. The Tora-willow usually grows by a brook; in our poem, suggesting the *qabbala* flowing from the *Yeshibot* (cf. Ps. 1:3; 52:10; Jer. 11:16). The bogus-willow, like the instructor and students shrieking out an imaginary text, are "like a thistle in the desert" (l. 11): solitary and unfruitful. They shake, not by their inner vigor, but by outside forces, as when the wind shakes the bogus-willow in the mountain (cf. Jer. 17:6; Ps. 1:4). The rabbis taught that one could easily identify the bogus willow by its leaves. The "mouth" (פיה) – standing in Hebrew for 'edges'– of its leaves are "rough like a saw." In our poem, they symbolize the speech and mannerisms of bogus-Talmudists. By contrast, the leaves of the Tora-willow have a "smooth mouth" (פיה חלק). An additional feature: the bogus-willow

gested by some biblical scholars, but a *slave* of "Saul's household" (II Sam 9:1). His name derives from his place of origin; see *Tosefta Shebi'it* 4:9, p. 180, and cf. *Tosefta ki-Fshuṭah*, p. 533.

usually grows on mountains, emblematic of haughtiness, whereas the Tora-willow flourishes by a placid fountain of water (cf. Ps 23:1). By way of association, the reader is reminded of a lesson given by R. El'azar b. 'Azarya (1st and 2nd centuries), about the "thistle in the desert." It was reported in Abot 3:21:

> One whose wisdom is greater than his deeds, what is he like? A tree whose branches are many and its roots few. And the wind comes and roots it up and overturns it on its face, as it is said (Jer. 17:6): "He shall be like a thistle in the desert, and would not see good coming. He shall dwell in dry lands in the desert: in salty soil, uninhabitable." But one whose deeds exceed his wisdom, what is he like? A tree whose branches are few and its roots many; so that even if all the winds that are in the world come and blow upon it they stir it not from its place, as it is said (Jer. 17:8): "He shall be like a tree planted by the water, that sends forth its roots by the river; and heat shall not come on to it; and its leaves shall be green, and it shall not be troubled in a year of drought nor cease from yielding fruit.[53]

Concerning the rite of the willow celebrated on the seventh day of Sukkot, it consists of taking a branch of willow and striking the ground

53. Except for the two quotations from Scripture, I have used the translation of Reverend Travers Hereford, *The Ethics of the Talmud: Sayings of the Fathers* (New York: Schocken, 1962), pp. 92–93. My rendition "thistle" is from R. Hayye Gaon, as reported by Radaq ad loc.; cf. *Perush ha-Mishnayot, 'Oqaṣin* 3:2, vol. 7, p. 731. 'Tamarisk' is untenable; see R. Judah ibn Bal'am, *Commentary to Jeremiah*, ed. M. Peretz (Ramat-Gan: Bar-Ilan University, 2002), ad loc., p. 76. See Mishna Sukka 3:3; Sukka 34a; *MT Sukka ve-Lulab* 7:3–4. In Talmudic times, people often confused these two classes of willow, and their names were frequently interchanged; see Shabbat 36a. According to the rabbis, Sukka 34a, Israel's misfortunes are the result of behaving as a willow on top of a mountain, when it should behave as a willow by the side of a fountain. Cf. *Kuzari* IV, 22–23, pp. 177–178.

with it three times. Significantly, this ritual requires no blessing.[54] Finally, in the last three lines of the poem (16–18) the author mentions that at the end of the class the teacher began (והחל) to recite the "Morning Blessings." I think that R. Samuel ha-Nagid wanted to point out the fact that there was no correlation between what the Talmud *teaches*, in our case that these blessings ought to be said in the course of waking up and getting ready for the daily chores, and the common practice of lumping them all together at the Synagogue.[55]

A similar description of bogus-Talmudists was given by the celebrated grammarian R. Jonah ibn Jannaḥ (11th century), a contemporary of R. Samuel ha-Nagid. There are 'Talmudists' notorious for their disdain of language, their fear of grammar, and their contempt for traditional authority. Their disdainful attitude towards language is evident in their sloppy reading, full of barbarisms [i, ii]. Obviously, someone caring little for the word spoken by God has nothing to do with the rabbis. Therefore, it would be improper to identify their views and behavior with the Talmud, which in fact they do not know [vi]. Their lack of respect extends to the Tora, as evidenced in their analphabetic reading of the text. Consequently, they are impervious to even the most basic Masoretic rules [ix]. They hate grammar [iv]. Probably, as a defense mechanism, they camouflage their meager knowledge with a high measure of abusive speech and behavior [v]. Given their derision of traditional authority, they would not study under a properly trained instructor [vii]. (In this connection it would be wise to remember the words of Professor Ginzberg, one of the great Talmudists of modern times, cited above, in Section IV, n. 261.) Their barbarous handling of the text leads them to proclaim some

54. See Sukka 44b; *MT Sukka* 7:22.

55. See *MT Tefilla* 7:9 and *Kesef Mishne* ad loc. I would like to point out that in Judeo-Arabic, *ḥafz* is identical to the Hebrew cognate; see R. Se'adya Gaon, *Tafsir Yesha'ya*, ed. and trans. Y. Ratzaby (Kiriat Ono: Makhon Moshe, 1993), on 52:12, p. 118. Therefore the term *ḥafz* in *Teshubot ha-Rambam*, #261, vol. 2, p. 491, refers to someone saying the blessing in a 'disorderly fashion,' like our bogus-Talmudist.

scandalous views [iii]. Finally, at the psychological level, they dread grammar. For them grammar is one and the same as heresy [ix]. I believe that their anxiety springs from the feeling that an accurate understanding of the text would reveal that their faith has little to do with either Talmud or Tora.

The following is a translation of what R. Jonah ibn Jannaḥ wrote on the matter:

> [i] ... So that everyone pronounces a word as he pleases and speaks as he wishes, being impervious to that (the pronunciation) and insensitive to it (the morphology and syntax of the language). As if language was not regulated by laws and had no fixed categories. They use language (only) for matters easy to apprehend, (barely) sufficient for the presentation of their exposition. [ii] However, they are careless about the roots (of words) and do not know their (morphological) derivations. [iii] They happen to hold some scandalous views and beliefs which we ought to distance ourselves from. [iv] Most of those putting down this science (grammar), and disparaging the lessons that this discipline provides, are inclined towards something relating to Talmudic studies [v]. They are arrogant with the little knowledge they have acquired, and haughty with the miniscule understanding that they have obtained (Talmudic studies). I heard about one of their famous (teachers) who [declared that] the study of grammar is worthless, that expertise in it is of no value, that it yields no profit, and that those who have researched and mastered its nuances have toiled in vain, gaining no fruit from their labor.
>
> The reason that they have come to deride this (about the study of language) is because [vi] they read the Talmudic (text) ungrammatically (Ar. *malḥuna*: 'full of barbarisms'); and the lesson which they study bursts with distorted pronunciation (Ar. *muṣaḥifa*).[56] They are impervious to this because they

56. These two Arabic terms reflect the expression גרסא וסברא in Geonic literature.

> were not privy to a genuine education, and their studies do not come from a bona fide chain of tradition (Ar. *isnad* = *qabbala*) [vii]. (A consequence of) this (contempt of language) is that most of them read Scripture sloppily, making little of the masoretic pronunciation. They do not distinguish (even) between a *qameṣ* and a *pattaḥ*, or between a grave and an acute syllable [viii]. They dread the study of morphology; (for them) to speak about it is some sort of heresy [ix].

In contradistinction to all that, R. Jonah ibn Jannaḥ pointed out that the Geonim, beginning with R. Se'adya, had labored intensely to produce grammatical and linguistic studies to enlighten and educate the general public.[57] See appendix 58.

In their criticism of bogus-Talmudists, R. Samuel ha-Nagid and R. Jonah ibn Jannaḥ called attention to their analphabetic 'reading' of the sacred texts of Israel – as if correct pronunciation and adherence to grammatical rules would contravene sacrality. The criticism

---

In a poem by R. Dunnash ibn Labraṭ in honor of R. Shemarya b. Elḥanan, published by Jacob Mann, *The Jews in Egypt and in Palestine*, vol. 2, p. 23 (l. 19) there is a reference to the correct enunciation of the Talmud (פאר גורס), through which he was "silencing thereby the cursed" [ארורים דמיים = דוממים], i.e., those who were in fact blaspheming, through their barbaric pronunciation of the text. Cf. R. Samuel ha-Nagid's poem, #83, l. 12, and cf. above n. 50. Likewise, the curse against those who "distort" the text (גורס שני), is not against the Karraites, as proposed by Abramson, *Ba-Merkazim wuba-Tefuṣot*, p. 162, but against the 'little foxes.' Traditionally, גרס, גרסא, referred to the correct 'pronunciation of a term, imparted by the instructor to his disciples.' Concerning the 'curse' befalling instructors who don't teach their disciples the correct pronunciation, see Baba Batra 21a-b.

57. Our translation comes from the Arabic original, *Kitab al-Luma'*, p. 3, in consultation with the Hebrew translation by R. Judah ibn Tibbon, *Sefer ha-Riqma*, vol. 1, pp. 11–12. Concerning the literary creations of the Geonim that directly benefited the general public, cf. *Sefer ha-Qabbala*, pp. 101–103; (Heb.), pp. 72–74. R. Jonah ibn Jannaḥ was a master Talmudist. For an assessment, see Shraga Abramson, *Mi-Pi Ba'ale Leshonot* (Jerusalem: Mossad Harav Kook, 5748/1998), pp. 193–399. I remember several occasions when Professor Lieberman would mention with great admiration some of the sharp notes on rabbinic lexicography made by this outstanding linguist.

is connected to the 'Maimonidean' opposition to recitation of 'liturgical hymns' (פיוטים) in the prayers (see below chapter 52). Opposition to these hymns was not merely a reaction against anthropomorphisms – no matter what, liturgy will contain a measure of human projections – but on the effect of these hymns on the mind and emotions of the faithful.

The most lucid presentation of this criticism may be found in R. Abraham ibn 'Ezra's *Commentary on Ecclesiastes* 5:1. In short, prayers are the closest, most intimate contact between a human and his/her Maker. The criticism focuses on the *style* – not the content of these hymns. In this type of hymn, the purpose of the author is to *challenge* the reader to discover the sense of a series of incomprehensible locutions – as with riddles, cryptograms, and complex crossword puzzles. By injecting this type of hymn into the liturgy, the worshipper is made to feel inadequate, requiring an *intercessor* to *tell* (not to explain!) her/him the sense of the hymns that *she/he* is chanting; as if saying: 'God, I am dull and brainless and don't know what I am saying, but I believe there is a *Judischen Menschentum* up there whom I trust and he will tell you what I mean.' As in pagan worship, the faithful *surrenders* his/her own mind to someone else: she/he believes because someone *told* her/him to believe. "Therefore, it is forbidden for any person to include in his prayer hymns whose basic meaning he does not know." Before reciting a hymn, an individual is duty-bound to examine it critically. "He (the faithful) should not rely on the original intention of the author," writes ibn 'Ezra, "for there is no human who does not blunder." Alluding to the fact that only a properly transmitted *qabbala* is authoritative, he added: "Or perhaps the copyists have blundered." More grievously: inserting incomprehensible hymns into the service will *prevent* the worshipper from praying with *kavvana* ('intention') – something that Professor Heschel described as "the participation of the soul."[58] At the least, it

58. Abraham Joshua Heschel, *God in Search of Man* (Philadelphia: Jewish Publication Society, 1956), p. 310.

requires, as Maran Joseph Caro codified, "focusing on the meaning of the words of the blessings."[59] To facilitate *kavvana,* the rabbis went so far as to include "the recitation of the *Shema'*, the Prayers, and the After-meal blessing" in the list of prayers that "may be recited in any language" (Mishna Soṭa 7:1).[60] The effect of a liturgy replete with incomprehensible locutions is to create a series of semantic gaps and dislocations which would render *kavvana* a psychological impossibility.[61] In this fashion, the Hebrew prayers are transformed into some sort of theurgical mumbo-jumbo, where erratic shaking counts more than *kavvana.*[62] The criticism, let it be noted, is against incorporating these hymns into the liturgy – not against the poets themselves and their original audience.[63] By way of analogy, let us imagine someone attempting to insert a poem by Walt Whitman, or better still, Ezra

59. *Shulḥan 'Arukh, Oraḥ Ḥayyim* V, 1; cf. XCVIII, 1. Often, *minhag* ('custom') is invoked as the justification to include such hymns in the liturgy. Let me point out that the identification of *minhag* with 'folklore' is another anti-Maimonidean fabrication. In rabbinics, the term stands for 'local norms enacted by the communal authorities'; see Introduction, *MT* ll. 99–102, 109-111, 125–132; cf. l. 118; and *Mamrim* 2:2. The role of folklore in law is obvious. However, blind adherence to dysfunctional folkways does not have the sanction of Law, but of coercion. In such a case, adherence to folklore is a travesty *against* the Law: as if the Law transmitted by the *national* institutions of Israel has a lower standing than folklore and could be displaced by it. In the Rabbinic Hebrew in the Holy Land, *minhag* stood for 'the practice of the Court'; see *Studies in the Mishne Tora,* p. 34 n. 11. Cf. *The Paradoxes of Legal Sciences,* pp. 14–18.

60. See Tosefta, Soṭa VII, 7, pp. 192–193; Berakhot 13a, 40b; Soṭa 32b-33a; *MT Shema'* 2:10; Berakhot 1:6; *Perush ha-Mishnayot, Soṭa* 7:1, vol. 3, p. 266; *Shulḥan 'Arukh, Oraḥ Ḥayyim* LXII, 2; cf. ibid CI, 4.

61. *Teshubot ha-Rambam, #,* vol. 2, p. 401. This is why Maimonides opposed the mixture of languages in the liturgy; see *MT Tefilla* 1:4; and R. Abraham ibn 'Ezra, in his *Commentary* to *Eccl.* 5:1, s.v. *veha-dabar ha-sheni.* This is also the reason why the Hebrew 'Aqademya' sponsors the circulation of foreign terms designed to displace perfectly clear Hebrew. See appendix 7.

62. Cf. Soṭa 22a, *tane tanna ve-la yada'.*

63. Cleverly, the central focus of the criticism was sidestepped (cf. chapter 61), and taken as if it was intended as some sort of ethnic denigration. For a survey of such responses, see Z. Malachi, "*Abraham ibn 'Ezra neged Qalir,*" *Peles* (Tel Aviv: Tel Aviv University, 1980), pp. 273–296. See appendix 58.

Pound, into our national anthem. It would be regarded as a double sacrilege: linking our *national* hymn to a *private* creation, which happens to be *unintelligible* to the common citizen.[64]

There was a purpose in transforming the language of Scripture and Talmud into an assortment of empty cacophonies. Hebrew intelligence is alphabetic, and as such is translatable into other languages and cultures. By rendering the language of Judaism into an assortment of phonetic slabs that cannot be analyzed alphabetically, the Tora was transformed into analphabetic poetry; that is, into a poem that can only be translated into another untranslatable poem (see above chapter 2). In such a semantic environment, bogus-Talmudists function as poets, not sages. A simple tune, in unison with a shaking crowd, will suffice to beguile the audience and lead it into the enchanting world of magic and myth. Shaking crowds are impervious to alphabetic discourse. They are "the masses" described by Ortega y Gasset – a description that applies with unsettling exactness to the anti-Maimonidean crowd.

> The mass crushes beneath it everything that is different, everything that is excellent, individual, qualified and select. Anybody who is not like everybody, who does not think like everybody, runs the risk of being eliminated. And it is clear, of course, that this 'everybody' is not 'everybody.'[65]

Anti-Maimonidean contempt for grammar and language was the effect of semantic assimilation to analphabetic thought and culture

---

64. R. Sabato Morais, *Italian Hebrew Literature* (New York: The Jewish Theological Seminary, 1926), p. 238 and editor's n. See the remark by R. Israel M. Ḥazzan, in my *Rabbi Israel Moses Ḥazzan*, p. 80. By way of contrast, the rabbis disallow inclusion of the attributes of God in the liturgy – even when they were used by prophets – since these terms were not properly understood by the general public; see *Guide* I, 59.
65. José Ortega y Gasset, *The Revolt of the Masses* (New York: W. W. Norton & Company, 1957), p. 18.

(see appendix 58). Traditionally, it was fluency in Scripture and the alphabetic intelligence encoded in the sacred texts that permitted the Jew to resist the trappings of analphabetic civilization (see above chapter 4). Disregard for the canons of biblical prosody, derision of linguistic studies, and the introduction of undecipherable compositions into the liturgy constituted a formal repudiation of alphabetic intelligence. Bereft of alphabetic semantics, the traditional texts of Israel no longer cohere. *Meliṣa*-discourse and politeness, once the earmarks of the rabbinic sage, were displaced by squabble and lack of manners. The end result was the hero replacing the sage. In this connection, I would like to remind the reader of what Bertolt Brecht (1898–1956) reportedly said: "Happy is the country which requires no heroes." The following chapters intend to illustrate the wisdom of his words.

# Chapter 52
# The Genesis of Jewish Heroic Virtue

Our knowledge of Jewish social and spiritual life during the Dark Ages is meager at best, so we cannot describe with any level of accuracy the factors that contributed to the rise of what became known in medieval Jewish hymnology and chronologies as *qedoshim* ('saints'). This much, however, can be ascertained: it had nothing to do with the same term in rabbinic literature. Rather, as we will try to show in the course of this chapter, it was the result of semantic assimilation to the patterns of thought and feeling of the general European society (see appendix 59).

The ideology embodied in the *qedoshim*-literature originated with the carnage of the First Crusade in 1096. Mass neurosis is contagious. The lunacy of the Crusaders, vented as 'religious devotion,' resulted in the immolation of thousands of Jews. The impact on the minds of the victims was horrendous. Traditionally, Jews were exceptionally careful not to absorb their persecutors' ideology. According to the hymnologists and chroniclers, this time things were different. If we are to believe these writers, the religious zeal of the Crusaders became paradigmatic of spiritual valor and determination in the minds of the victims. In their efforts to show that their own faith was second to none, some responded by murdering their own children to save them from apostasy and forced conversion. Instead of being commensurate, Jewish chroniclers and hymnologists portrayed these parents (as well as their children) as *qedoshim* ('saints') – models to envy and emulate, rather than assist.[66] The standard view on this matter was summarized by Bodoff:

> These communities tried to fight back, sometimes with the aid of Christian protectors, clergy and laity, sometimes without; ultimately *they* determined to trump the triumphalism of the Crusaders and to assert the supremacy of the Jewish faith, and their own loyalty to it, over that of their oppressor Crusader adversaries. So *they* killed their children and then themselves before they could be killed to avoid being forcibly converted. Not only were their actions chronicled by Jews a short time later in the most glowing terms and the martyrs described as "holy ones," but rabbis of great learning and status soon after failed to challenge the propriety of the suicides and the murders as a sanctification of God's name. And, to enshrine permanently the actions of the martyrs as a model of faith for all time, the martyrdoms were embodied in Jewish liturgy, to be recited forever in penitential *piyyuṭim* (poetry).[67]

A central thesis of the *qedoshim*-literature is that parents were inspired to immolate their children by the biblical story of God *testing* Abraham to offer Isaac as a sacrifice (Gen. 28). This is what one of the chronologists of the time wrote:

> Who has heard or seen such a thing? Ask and see: Has there ever been an *akedah* like this in all the generations since Adam? Did eleven hundred *akedot* take place on a single day, all of them comparable to the binding of Isaac son of Abraham?

66. See Salo W. Baron, *A Social and Religious History of the Jews*, vol. 4 (Philadelphia: Jewish Publication Society, 1957), pp. 144–145 and corresponding n. on pp. 309–310.
67. Lipman Bodoff, *The Binding of Isaac, Religious Murders, & Kabbala* (New York: Devorah Publishing, 2005), p. 187.

> Yet for one bound on Mount Moriah the world shook, as it is stated: "Behold the angels cried and the skies darkened." What did they do now, why did the skies not darken and the stars not dim…when on one day…there were killed eleven hundred pure souls, including babes and infants…? Wilt Thou remain silent of these, O Lord? [68]

The writers of the *qedoshim*-literature were not eyewitnesses. Yet, their compositions are taken as if they were firsthand accounts, warranting no further investigation. I disagree. In my view, their compositions are akin to the *acta* and *passiones* of martyrs, and the cult of martyrs and saints in Christian devotional tradition. It would be helpful to consider that the *Yizkor* service introduced at that period was borrowed from the Church services commemorating martyrs by reciting their names and praying for their souls. Professor Theodor Gaster (1906–1992) pointed out that the formula, too, is from the Church.

> The custom of commemorating martyrs by reciting their names and praying for their repose was borrowed directly from the Christian Church. From the fourth century onwards it was the practice of the Church, during the celebration of the Mass, to offer a special prayer for local martyrs and deceased dignitaries, their names being read out from a diptych – that is, from two wooden boards folded together like the pages of a book. The prayer, which *followed* the recitation of the names (*oratio post nomina*), originally ran as follows: "To the souls of

68. *Zakhor*, p. 38. The Hebrew original comes from ed. A. M. Haberman, *Sefer Gezerot* (Jerusalem: Sifre Tarshish, 1945), p. 32. On the literary aspects of the liturgical poems known as '*gezerot*,' see E. Fleischer, *Hebrew Liturgical Poetry in the Middle Ages* (Heb.), (Jerusalem: Keter Publishing, 1975), pp. 470–471. For a comprehensive study of this theme in the context of Jewish Martyrology, see Shalom Spiegel, "The Legend of Isaac's Slaying and Resurrection," in *Alexander Marx Jubilee Volume*, Hebrew Section (New York: Jewish Theological Seminary, 1950), pp. 471–547. See also idem, *The Last Trial* (New York: Schocken, 1969).

> all these give rest, O sovereign Lord our God, in Thine holy tabernacle." Later this was developed into a longer petition which is still part of the service and which is known from its opening word as the Momento, viz.: "Remember also, O Lord, thy servants male and female who have preceded us with a token of their faith; and may they sleep in the sleep of peace. To ourselves, O Lord, and to [the souls of] all who are at rest in Christ we beseech Thee to grant a place of repose and peace, through that same Christ our Lord, amen."

He added:

> The correspondence of this formula – apart, of course, from its purely Christian elements – with that of the *Yizkor* prayer and, in even more marked degree, with the requiem for the dead (*Hashkabah*) used in the Sephardic liturgy, is indeed remarkable. First: the names "*Momento*" and "*Yizkor*," both derived from the opening words of the prayer, are in fact identical. Second: just as the diptych lists begin with the names of generally venerated worthies of the Church, so too, as we have seen, does the Jewish *Memorbuch*. (Indeed, it is still customary in England to recite a second *Yizkor* commemorating deceased Chief Rabbis.) Third: the expressions used are virtually the same. In the Christian prayer, God is besought to grant to the souls of the deceased a place in His "holy tabernacle"; in the Jewish prayer, He is asked to grant them "abiding rest under the wings of the Divine Presence in the exalted place of the holy and pure" – where the word rendered "exalted place" really refers to a particular degree or level of heaven, and "the holy" (*kedoshim*) is the regular Hebrew term for "martyrs." In the Christian formula, God is entreated to grant that the martyrs "sleep in the sleep of peace"; while the Jewish requiem used by the Sepharadim asks that the dead "may rest in peace upon their beds" and that "peace may accompany them." Finally, the

> Christian formula invokes on the departed the blessing of eternal repose "alongside all who are at rest in Christ"; while the Jewish version entreats that they abide "with all the righteous who are in Paradise."[69]

The intention of martyrology literature is not to produce a factual report, as in modern journalism, but to veil, embellish, and inspire. Jewish law and common sense require us not to be credulous of hearsay confessions involving crime.[70] To assume that parents would murder their children on the basis of the *'aqeda* story without further corroboration, because it is so stated in the *qedoshim*-literature is to confuse a literary composition with a properly executed deposition.[71] Hyperbole aside, parents of whatever religious persuasion never took

69. Theodore Gaster, *The Holy and the Profane* (New York: William Morrow, 1980), pp. 185–187. For an overview of this literary *genre*, see *European Literature and the Middle Ages*, pp. 425-428. On the inclusion of Jewish Martyrs in the Community annals for special commemorative services, see Salo W. Baron, *A Social and Religious History of the Jews*, vol. 4, pp. 145–146 and corresponding n. A good example for interlacing myth and legend can be seen in the chansons and epic tales of the period; cf. Robert Chazan, *European Jewry and the First Crusade* (Berkeley: University of California Press, 1987), pp. 150–151, 328.
70. On the legal status of self-incrimination, as well as the possible psychological grounds motivating such a confession, see *MT Sanhedrin* 18:6. Furthermore, Judaism discounts *a priori* the possibility that parents would want to kill their children; see *MT Geneba* 9:10.
71. Just because these stories have been told and retold countless times, does not excuse modern historians from critical analysis. For the main sources on this topic, see *A Social and Religious History of the Jews*, vol. 4, pp. 285–287. As noted by Ivan Marcus in his review, "Robert Chazan, *European Jewry and the First Crusade*," *Speculum*, 64 (1989), p. 686:

    ...these texts are not documentary records to which theological comments or poems have been added. They are a highly edited, rhetorically colored, and liturgically motivated literary reworking of circular letters and oral reports, written for definite purposes. The narrators were concerned with praising and exonerating local pious Jews who felt compelled to kill their own families and commit suicide. Cf. Lipman Bodoff, "Abraham's Covenant, Chosenness, and the Binding of Isaac," *Midstream* (November/December 2006), pp. 21–26.

the *'aqeda* story as a justification for slaughtering their children. Particularly, when in the story, God explicitly commanded Abraham: "lay *not* thy hand upon the lad, neither do anything unto him!" (Gen. 22:12). Rather, I propose, it would be more prudent to assume that these unfortunate parents died fighting tooth and nail protecting their offspring, and that the hymns and chronologies were exalting their abnegation in terms of the devotional ideals *peculiar to the literary models of their time and place.* Let it be noted that the authors of the *qedoshim* -literature were *not* sages but local bards.[72]

Judaism does not recognize 'heroes' or 'heroism.' The concept of 'hero' is the result of semantic assimilation (see appendix 59). In Jewish tradition, *qadosh/qedoshim* has nothing to do with heroism. On the contrary, this status can be gained even by doing something as trifling as washing your fingertips before the after-meal blessing,[73] or by abstaining from glancing at the image of an idol on something as mundane as a coin.[74] In Jewish tradition, piety (*Ḥasidut*) must be expressed within the confines of the licit and normative (see appendix 60). Someone transcending these boundaries – the classical hero of European ethos – is described as a "stupid Ḥasid' (חסיד שוטה). Alerting one to the possibility that such 'religiosity' may be intended to deceive, the "stupid" saint is in the same list as the "sly, malevolent" (רשע, ערום) and the pervert, who "tear down the world" under the

72. The above will help solve a puzzle noted by Joseph Dan, "*Be'ayat Qiddush ha-Shem,*" in *Holy Wars and Martyrology* (Jerusalem: The Historical Society of Israel, 1967), p. 122: among the dozens of works on the liturgy, *Ḥasidut,* and mysticism written by Ashkenazic sages of the time, there is not a single hint about the tragic events depicted in martyrology hymns! It is important to note that although martyrology hymnologists wrote in a style more or less similar to that of the earlier Ashkenazic *payṭanim,* they exclusively focused, in the steps of Christian martyrologies, on tragic motifs. This can explain the fact that they did not write *qerobot,* since these hymns focus on the blissful times of the Patriarchs; see Aharon Mirsky, *Ha-Piyyuṭ* (Jerusalem: Magnes Press, 1990), pp. 689–693.

73. See Berakhot 53b, where *qedoshim* is associated with washing the fingertips after a meal (a norm conspicuously neglected by latter-day-saints).

74. 'Aboda Zara 50a and Y. Sanhedrin X, 5, 29c. See appendix 58.

pretension of religiosity (Mishna Soṭa 3:4).[75] Aware that 'devotion' may be symptomatic of mental sickness and an imbalanced personality rather than spirituality, the rabbis warned: "An illiterate man cannot be a Ḥasid!' (Abot 2:5; see appendix 60). The *qedoshim* that the *payṭanim* celebrate, however, have encroached not only on Jewish law, but also even on the most basic human feelings and sanity. In fact, the *payṭanim* were celebrating Church ideology of "salvation via penitence and martyrdom."[76] Because the terms of Judaism had been assimilated to the semantic context of the general environment (see appendix 58), the *payṭanim* were celebrating *Christian heroic virtue* rather than *Jewish Ḥasidut*. In the case of Christianity, however, given its negative attitude towards the Law, sainthood is essentially *heroic*, transcending the normative and conventional. A Christian saint cannot face martyrdom because the *Law* demands it, but only from supernatural motives. The title 'martyr' in Christendom is semantically akin to the pagan title 'hero' – celebrated for his bravery, and acting from supernatural motives, rather than for his punctilious adherence to the demands of the law. Referring to Christian martyrs, Augustine commented: "If the ordinary language of the Church allowed it, we might more elegantly call these men our heroes."[77]

The similarity between the *payṭanim-qadosh* and the hero/martyr/saint of Christian and pagan lore is deeper than semantics. Conceptually, the *qadosh* – like the hero/martyr/saint – gained rank in a primordial, mythical moment, experienced only by the privileged. As with the hero, the *qadosh*/martyr/saint "conquers immortality by his suicide-apotheosis on the pyre."[78] Each of them is moved by a supernatural force enabling him to reach a nobler and more archaic

75. Cf. Soṭa 20a-21b; Y. Soṭa III, 4, 18c-19a; *MT 'Arakhin* 8:13. The term ערום ('sly, malevolent') is used in Scripture to describe the snake deceiving Eve; see Gen. 3:1.
76. *A Social and Religious History of the Jews*, vol. 4, p. 95. See appendix 59.
77. *The City of God*, X, 22 (New York: Modern Library), p. 326.
78. Mircea Eliade, *A History of Religious Ideas*, 3 vols. (Chicago: Chicago University Press, 1988), vol. 1, p. 289.

'truth.' It is by his *will to power*, that *qadosh*/hero/martyr/saint rises above and beyond the earthly and reaches the trans-worldly, revealing a mode of existence that everyone can admire but not emulate. It is by virtue of his will, rather than by conventional means, that the *qadosh*/hero/martyr/saint gains access to a primordial, mythical moment, which he then shares with his peers, disciples and devotees. That is why, in the function of Adam/*Elohim*, the *qadosh*/hero/martyr/saint serves as an intermediary and a mediator between gods and men.[79]

The hymns glorifying heroic behavior were placed at the heart of the liturgy and recited with special pathos and fervor. To make space for their recitation, the Synagogue services were reformed. It began with the abolition of one of the most ancient rabbinic institutions: the recitation of the *Targum* version of Scripture (see appendix 61). It would not be an exaggeration to say that in the course of time, the Synagogue and Prayer Book became an ancillary tool for the recitation of these hymns (see above chapter 51 and below chapter 53).[80] In this fashion, Jewish religion, faith, and ethos were conditioned to the heroic ideology of the *payṭanim-qadosh*. The Ḥasid ('pious,' 'virtuous') and *Ḥasidut* ('piety,' 'virtue') of Medieval Ashkenaz, noted Eliade, were "a new and original creation," having nothing to do with rabbinic tradition.[81] A Ḥasid is one who *experiences* vicariously the events described in the *qedoshim*-martyrology liturgy, and is ever-ready to suffer martyrdom for the sake of 'holiness.' Christian martyrs

79. Cf. *A History of Religious Ideas*, vol. 1, pp. 284–289. On the cult of saints and martyrs in Christianity; see ibid., vol. 3, pp. 50–54. For the main bibliography on the subject, see ibid., pp. 299–300. Cf. idem, *The Myth of Eternal Return* (Princeton: Princeton University Press, 1974), pp. 35, 105. On the close spiritual relation of early Ashkenazic Jewry to Christianity, see *European Jewry and the First Crusade*, pp. 4, 134–136.
80. The Ashkenazic Synagogue adopted the liturgical tradition of *piyyutim* as practiced in the Holy Land, not Babel; see Israel M. Ta-Shma, *Early Franco-German Ritual and Custom* (Heb.) (Jerusalem: Hebrew University, 1992), pp. 74–75, 90–92, 98–99.
81. *A History of Religious Ideas*, vol. 3, p. 166. For a historic overview, see *A Social and Religious History of the Jews*, vol. 8, pp. 42–54. Cf. appendix 60.

imitate Jesus unto death. Martyrology hymns permit the Ḥasid to do the same: not only would he gladly accept agony unto death for the sake of the Tora, as Jewish martyrs in the past, but he "yearns to be martyred."[82]

Officially, Christianity disavowed the military. However, beginning with the Crusades, the Church recognized that the military could serve a sacred purpose. Therefore, it offered the "*Benedictio novis militis*" to the chevalier by blessing the sword at the altar, and the performance of a variety of rituals. In this fashion, both the military and religious forged an alliance dedicated to goodness and the pursuit of justice. We therefore should not be surprised to discover that in that semantic environment, the Ḥasid would find inspiration in the *heroic virtue* of knights and soldiers, risking limb and life for the sake of their masters. Ḥasidim, we are told, ought to think of themselves as

> … knights charging into combat, to show their valor under the command of their masters. They will not flee from the (enemy's) sword, risking limb and death. All this they do (for fear) of humiliation – because desertion (in the face of the enemy) is regarded as dishonor, and (therefore), if they would die in combat they will receive no reward from their master. How much more we ought to suffer misery and pain, and prepare our souls to die under the command of our King, the Master of all, blessed be His Name.[83]

Like a knight, the Ḥasid lived under a special Code of Chivalry. The piety that he practiced was not the prosaic piety of the rabbis, but *heroic virtue* – as displayed by soldiers in combat, fighting for the honor of their master (cf. appendix 67).*

82. R. Judah he-Ḥasid, *Sefer ha-Ḥasidim*, ed. R. Reuben Margulies (Jerusalem: Mossad Harav Kook, 5724/1964), #955, p. 514; see below n. 84. Paul also used military symbols, such as "putting on the breastplate of faith and love; and for a helmet, the hope of salvation" (I Thess. 5:8).

83. *Sefer ha-Ḥasidim*, #94, p. 134.

If one were to change the word 'Christian' for ḥasidic, the description of heroic virtue offered by Pope Benedict XIV (1675–1758) perfectly describes ḥasidic virtuous ideology:

> In order to be heroic a Christian virtue must enable its owner to perform virtuous actions with uncommon promptitude, ease, and pleasure, *from supernatural motives and without human reasoning, with self-abnegation and full control over his natural inclinations*[84](Italics added).

As with the avid reader of chivalric literature such as *Don Quixote*, the Ḥasid is always ready to sacrifice everything for his vocation.[85] Here lies the abysmal difference between the prosaic piety of the rabbis and *Ḥasidut*. By seeking to imitate the heroic deeds of heroes-*qedoshim*, the Ḥasid can find glory and gain access to the realm of the cosmic and paranormal. He, too, similar to *Don Quixote* and other legendary knights, battles the demonic forces threatening the weak and subdues them at will. In bounty and kindness, he then shares his privileged status with disciples and devotees, awarding them salvation and glory. The rank of this hero stems from his charisma and the enthusiasm generated by his devotees. He accomplishes this, primarily, through example and coaching.

At the beginning (1170–1240) of what became known as *Ḥaside Ashkenaz*, or 'the Pious of Germany,' in the Rhineland communities, the mystical element was sober, focusing primarily on the prayers and rituals.[86] This is how Eliade describes the ways of the Ḥasid:

---

* I.e. For "the rebbe."

84. Quoted by J. Wilhelm, "Heroic Virtue," *Catholic Encyclopedia*, vol. 8, p. 292.

85. See *Sefer ha-Ḥasidim* #787, p. 467, and above n. 81. 'Ashkenaz' included also Ḥasidim in France; see *Early Franco-German Ritual and Custom* (Heb.), p. 95.

86. See Israel Ta-Shma, *Ha-Tefilla ha-Ashkenazit ha-Qeduma* (Jerusalem: Hebrew University Press, 5763/2003), pp. 46–53; Philip S. Alexander, "Mysticism," in Martin Goodman, ed., *Oxford Handbook of Jewish Studies* (Oxford: Oxford University Press, 2002), pp. 710–711.

> The Ḥasids endeavor to obtain a perfect serenity of the spirit: they accept imperturbably the injuries and threats of other members of the community. They do not court power; however, they make use of mysterious magical capacities. Their penances betray certain Christian influences, except where sexuality is concerned. For as is well known, Judaism never accepted that type of asceticism. On the other hand, a strong pantheistic tendency has been noted: 'God is even closer to the universe and to man than the soul is to the body.'[87]

Later, when *Ḥasidut* crossed over into Southern France and Spain, things changed. Principally, rituals began to be perceived in terms of theurgical manipulations. To justify this perception, a new religion was created under the general rubric 'Kabbala.' It centered around the kind of cosmic sacrality still lingering among peasants in Southern Europe, as well as on folklore and other miscellanea. An important factor in the formulation of Kabbala was the belief in corporeality of God, divine anthropomorphism, etc., noted by Agobard and Karraites (see above chapter 49). According to Bodoff, the Kabbala-religion rests on the following seven tenets:

> (1) that God separated himself from the material world of Creation, and that evil was, simultaneously, a part of God and thus a part of the created world; (2) that during the cosmic catastrophe of Creation, Divine lights and sparks were scattered through the world, and that God was immanent in the world...; (3) that this mythic God was knowable in anthropomorphic ways, having various aspects, genders, physical forms, and the need for sexual unions and even biological functions; (4) that man can acquire knowledge of God and

87. *A History of Religious Ideas*, p. 166. The quote proceeds from *Major Trends*, p. 108. On the mystical literature written in Ashkenaz, see Joseph Dan, "The Vicissitudes of the Esoterism of German Hasidim," in *Studies in Mysticism and Religion* (Jerusalem: Magnes Press, 1967), Hebrew Section, pp. 87–99.

> commune and unite with Him, experiencing the 'joy' of 'annihilating the self' and mystically transcending the barrier of corporeal existence; (5) that man can and must battle and escape the evil of material existence by asceticism, poverty... and, instead, embrace the perfect life of martyrdom and the physical-spiritual bliss of mystical death through union with God, *unio mystica* – whenever man wants it and not just when God invites it – by means of prayer, ecstasy, and magic...; (6) that the true secrets of the Tora, the 'second' revelation of Judaism, can burst forth from the heart of every Jew who understands and practices Kabbala – each moment brings its own novel understanding of God's Will; (7) that the shattered Divinity – see (2) above – depends on man's mystical behavior to restore the primordial, supernal perfection and harmony.[88]

Henceforth, Jewish wisdom and holiness and blessedness were all incarnate, not in the classical rabbinic sage, but in the Ḥasid/*qadosh*. Those who were not privy to this knowledge, even if they were as eminent a sage as Rashi, could not attain the level of perfection made now available via *Ḥasidut*. The following account, in ms. 926 at the Moscow National Library, is an example. Reflecting the standards of evidence peculiar to the new ideology, we are informed about Rashi, who we are now in a position to fully appreciate. The accuracy of this account is beyond reproach, given that it was reported by an anonymous "distinguished student, who has heard it from one of the grandees [anonymous] from among the great French (sages)."

> ... A pious and austere man of great reputation ascended in a dream to the Heavenly Academy. There he saw great sages

88. Lipman Bodoff, *The Binding of Isaac, Religious Murders, & Kabbala* (New York: Devorah Publishing, 2005), pp. 194–195. See *A History of Religious Ideas*, vol. 3, p. 45, and the note on pp. 249–250. On the peculiar tendencies of sages from Europe and the Holy Land towards magic and the paranormal, see R. Judah al-Bargeloni, *Perush Sefer Yeṣira*, pp. 103–105.

> investigating Tora, together with their disciples before them. He lifted his eyes and noticed an old man seated at the Academy, head bent down, staring at the floor (in shame) – not daring to raise his eyes and look up (at his colleagues). He (the great French sage) asked the members of the Academy about him. They responded: 'This is Rashi, the Frenchman, who enlightened the Diaspora with his commentaries. However, since during his lifetime he was not meticulous about the precept of phylacteries, he feels embarrassed in the presence of his colleagues; (that is why he is) seated with much humility, head down.'[89]

It would be safe to assume that by "not being meticulous" it was not meant that Rashi neglected this precept altogether – after all the standard phylacteries are called by his name! – but, rather, that he did not observe it according to some of the trendy mystical cults then in vogue.

89. In *Newly Discovered Geonic Responsa* (Heb.) (Jerusalem-Cleveland: Ofeq Institute, 5755/1995), pp. 237–238, n. 38. One of Rashi's views that could have provoked the ire of the new ideologues is his comment on Deut. 29:19. About bogus *Ḥasidut* in general, see appendix 60.

# Chapter 53
# Heroic Knowledge

The heroic model of the *payṭanim* was exploited, resulting in transforming the concept and function of 'rabbi.' The classical rabbi was a sage and a teacher, whose authority rested on mastery of the normative interpretations of the Tora. From the point of view of *Ḥasidut*, the goal of studying 'Tora' is a mystical experience and the acquisition of supernatural power – not classical knowledge. The knowledge that the Ḥasid possesses and seeks to impart is *heroic knowledge* – a knowledge that he uses like the legendary chevalier to combat evil and promote good. This knowledge flows from a cosmic truth, awarding its possessor the ability to manipulate and subdue demonical and paranormal forces. To advance this ideology, it was necessary to re-make the past. Thus began a process designed to transfigure the past sages of Israel into heroes of quasi-divine dimensions. To facilitate kabbalistic interpretations, the text of Scripture was tampered with and rabbinic texts doctored. Glosses, interpolations, and textual changes were freely introduced into the works of celebrated authorities. Some works were abolished; others were taken out of circulation, while compositions of uncertain background were given superlative prominence.[90]

90. See Israel Ta-Shma, "*Qeliṭatam shel sifre ha-Rif, ha-Raḥ, ve-Halakhot Gedolot be-Ṣarfat wub-Ashkenaz be-me'ot ha-Yod-Alef-Yod-Bet*," *Qiryat Sefer* 55 (1980), pp. 191–201; and idem, "*Sifriyyatam shel ḥakhme Ashkenaz bene ha-Me'a ha-Yod Alef-Yod Bet*," *Qiryat Sefer* 60 (1985), pp. 298–309. The obsession with 'emendations' reached such a chaos that Rama, *Shulḥan 'Arukh, Oraḥ Ḥayyim*, CXLIII,

A major step in the promotion of kabbalistic ideologies and the mystification of Jewish texts was reforming the Synagogue. We have mentioned in the preceding chapter that to make room for the long chanting of hymns, the recitation of the *Targum* was abrogated, offhandedly, as if it were a trifle matter of little value (see appendix 61). There were decisive consequences to this reform, which deserve to be explained precisely because they remained unnoticed. If we are to come to grips with the strategic significance of this step, an adequate conception of the kabbalistic ideology is essential. Briefly and to the point, Eliade described it as follows:

> To the sanctification of life by the medium of the work and rites prescribed by the Talmud, the kabbalists add the mythological valorization of Nature and Man, the importance of mystical experience, and even certain themes of Gnostic origin. One can discern in this phenomenon of 'opening,' and this effort at revalorization, the nostalgia for a religious universe where the Hebrew Scriptures and the Talmud coexist with a cosmic religiosity, and with Gnosticism and mysticism.[91]

The *Targum* was a major obstacle to the above. (Can you name a single community where the *Targum* was recited that espoused the anti-Maimonidean ideology?) For generations, the *Targum* stood

4 concluded that their "Tora Scrolls are not very accurate," and therefore there would be no point in returning a Scroll because of a word that should have been written as plena or defective; cf. R. Arie Lieb, *Sha'agat Arye* (Warsaw, 5629/1869), #36. So it would be naïve, if not plainly disingenuous, to take their reports about what the great rabbinic authorities of the past had actually said or written without critical examination. E.g., R. Tam's view on *ḥerem hayyishub*; see L. Rabbinowitz, *The Ḥerem Hayyishub* (London: Edward Goldstone, 1945), pp. 23–24. On the mystical power of 'learning,' see Eliot Wolfson, "The Mystical Significance of Tora Study in German Pietism," *Jewish Quarterly Review* 84 (1993), pp. 43–78.

91. *A History of Religious Ideas*, vol. 3, p. 171. Cf. Joseph Dan, *On Sanctity* (Heb.) (Jerusalem: Hebrew University Press, 1997), p. 345 n. 63.

as a bulwark against masking mythological and Gnostic ideas under the rubric of 'Tora.' Without an official exposition of Scripture, it was impossible for the faithful to distinguish between blabber and 'Tora.' We have previously noted some of the analphabetic tendencies among bogus-Talmudists in Spain; particularly, their denigration of Hebrew grammar and their lack of care for the accurate reading of Scripture (see above chapter 51). Bearing this in mind, we can appreciate why canceling the public recitation of the *Targum* constituted *minut* ('heresy'). The matter was particularly serious because the abolition of the *Targum* was one of the earmarks of the Karraite Synagogue (see above n. 35 and appendix 55). The reformed Synagogue revolutionized rabbinic education. Traditionally, the textual transmission of the Scripture or Written Law, including the proper Masoretic reading and standard interpretation of the text, was the responsibility of the Synagogue. The Oral Law was the exclusive responsibility of the *Yeshiba* and *Bet Midrash*.[92] The *Targum* was the bridge between the Scripture, written in Hebrew, and the Talmud written in Aramaic. In addition to providing the standard exposition of the Tora, the public recitation of the *Targum* awarded the students fluency in basic Aramaic, and thereby *direct* access to rabbinic texts and traditions. For all practical purposes, canceling the public recitation of the *Targum* prevented the student from apprehending the rabbinic text with his own eyes. This was particularly important in order to

92. The Synagogue and the *Yeshiba/BetMidrash* were independent of each other. Accordingly, the differences between the halakha as taught by the *Yeshiba* and the *Targum* do not necessarily imply that a rift had taken place between these institutions but simply that each was carrying on its own ancestral tradition; cf. José Faur "The *Targumim* and *Halakha*," *Jewish Quarterly Review*, 66 (1976), pp. 19–26. The same applies to the text and order of the books in the Hebrew Bible and other matters pertaining to the services and liturgy. The Synagogue and the *Yeshiba* kept their own liturgical traditions, without interfering with each other. Initially, the conflict with the Karraites centered on the authority of the Oral Law, and it pertained to the *Yeshiba/Bet Midrash* – not to the Synagogue. This fundamental point, however, is systematically overlooked by modern scholars; see, for example, *The Cairo Geniza*, pp. 86–91.

shield bogus-Talmudists. We have mentioned earlier the traumatic experience suffered by R. Joseph ibn Sanṭas for some errors that he made in Aramaic (see above n. 18). By way of contrast, it would be no exaggeration to say that it is impossible to find a single sentence in correct Aramaic by bogus-Talmudists and mystics!

The preceding affected the patterns of rabbinic scholarship. Traditionally, as in the schools of Rashi and *Tosafot,* classical texts and earlier authorities were the object of critical study. Rabbinic scholarship focused on *what* the text said. The opinions of preceding authorities were examined, and then accepted or rejected on the basis of textual evidence and conceptual analyses. Given that direct access to the text was no longer possible (or desirable), critical analysis was impossible. Henceforth, the focus of rabbinic scholarship centered on *who* said this or that *about* the text. The student was at the mercy of 'experts.' Since no one could determine the sense of the text on his own, this led to the establishment of a hierarchic system of *auctores majores ad minores* (= ראשונים, אחרונים), as with Christian scholastics. According to this methodology, one can demonstrate or refute a view simply by quoting an 'authority' (see below chapter 60 and appendix 69).

A key premise of this methodology is a doctrine generally described as the 'decline of the generations.' In a nutshell, it postulates that preceding generations were inherently superior by the fact that there is a gradual falling down of souls (see below chapter 61). A kind of Paul's doctrine of the 'original sin' combined with Darwin's theory of evolution in reverse.[93] Since the interpretations given by the

93. This doctrine had been anticipated by Horace, *Odes and Epodes,* trans. and ed. Niall Rudd (Loeb Classical Library), III, 6, p. 105 who wrote: "Our fathers' age, worse than our grandfathers', gave birth to us, inferior breed, who will in due course produce still more degenerate offspring." Maimonides had nothing to do with this doctrine; cf. above, Section IV, n. 177. For a coherent discussion of the subject, see Menachem Kellner, *Maimonides on the Decline of the Generations and the Nature of Rabbinic Authority* (Albany: SUNY Press, 1996); for a shorter version, see idem, "Maimonides on the Decline of the Generations," in *Ḥazon Naḥum* (New York: Yeshiva University, 5758/1998), pp. 163–185. I disagree with Professor Kellner in two closely related details, not germane to his main thesis.

hallowed authorities did not always coincide with the text or common sense, "learned fools" or masters of "false eloquence" (paraphrasing Vico), invented a special type of casuistry, "ready to uphold either of the opposing sides of a case indifferently."[94] The 'truth' that *qadosh*/Ḥasid teaches is a heroic, integral truth, qualitatively different from vulgar truth. Objections to that truth or lack of understanding are the result of a stupid audience, incapable of grasping the realm of the cosmic and arcane. The purpose of Kabbala is to provide both illumination and redemption to the abject Jew.

Sage and hero are mutually exclusive. A sage is not infallible, and scholars may be proven to be wrong. In fact, the Geonim formulated a principle declaring: "the halakha is to be rendered according to the latter (authorities)."[95] In the capacity of hero, the truth of the *qadosh*/Ḥasid is hierarchically superior. Refusal to acknowledge it is tantamount to defiance against hierarchic authority. Bezalel could argue with Moses and make his point stick. However, casting doubts

---

First, Bilstein's interpretation of Sherira Gaon's *Iggeret* is flawed, the result of lack of familiarity with basic rabbinic terminology, coupled with the desire to attribute mystical ideology developed by later kabbalistic circles to earlier rabbinic authorities. Second, there is abundant evidence that Maimonides was thoroughly acquainted with the Gaon's *Iggeret*.

94. *The New Science* #1102, p. 423. It became known as *pilpul*. Let it be noted that Rashi on Ḥolin 81a s.v. *hatra'at safeq*, used this term in a derogatory fashion. Later, as the new ideology took roots, it was used in a positive sense to indicate someone possessing genuine knowledge; see *Sefer Ḥasidim* #296, p. 238; R. Ḥayyim b. Isaac, *Or Zarua'* (Israel, 1958) I (*Teshubot*) #752, 108b; *Ṭur Ḥoshen Mishpaṭ* VII, 3. The same applies to pseudo-Rashi, on Horayot 14a s.v. *ve-ḥad*. (We should remind the reader that the printed commentary although coming from Rashi's school, was not penned by the great master himself.) For an appraisal of the *pilpul* methodology in the later Yeshives; see Ludwig Blau, "Methods of Teaching Talmud," *Jewish Quarterly Review* 15 (1903), pp. 121–134. Concerning *pilpul* in modern Yeshives, see William B. Helmreich, *The World of the Yeshiva* (Hoboken, New Jersey: Ktav Publishing, 2000), pp. 108–113. This *pilpul* has nothing to do with either the term or the methodology of *pilpul* in rabbinic literature.

95. On this principle, see the eminent study of Professor Israel Ta-Shma, "*Hilkheta Kebatrai*."

on the omniscience of the Ḥasid/*qadosh* man of letters is insurgency against God (see below chapter 54 and cf. appendix 69). Objectors to the association 'man of letters/hero' can make some capital out of the fact that the classical hero was not a man of letters, but a warrior. This was true of places where literacy was uncommon. In literate circles, however, like the Jewish communities in the Middle Ages and European society in modern times, a man of letters could assume the role of hero. This point was the subject of a lecture delivered on May 19th 1840, "The Hero as a Man of Letters," by Thomas Carlyle (1795–1881):

> If *Hero* be taken to mean genuine, then I say the Hero as Man of Letters will be found discharging a function for us which is ever honorable, ever the highest; and was once well known to be the highest. He is uttering-forth, in such a way as he has, the inspired soul of him; all that a man, in any case, can do. I say *inspired;* for what we call 'originality,' 'sincerity,' 'genius,' the heroic quality we have no good name for, signifies that. The Hero is he who lives in the inward sphere of things, in the True, Divine and Eternal, which exists as always, unseen to most; under the Temporary, Trivial: his being is in that; he declares that abroad, by act or speech as it may be, in declaring himself abroad. His life, as we said before, is a piece of everlasting heart of Nature herself: all man's life is, – but the weak may know not the fact, and are untrue to it, in most times; the strong few are strong, heroic, perennial, because it cannot be hidden from them. The Man of Letters, like every Hero, is there to proclaim that in such sort as he can. Intrinsically it is the same function in which the old generation named a man Prophet, Priest, Divinity for doing; which all manner of Heroes, by speech or by act, are sent into the world to do.

An essential characteristic of the "*true* Literary Man, what we here call the *Hero*," writes Carlyle in the name of Fichte, is that he lives "wholly in this Divine Idea."[96] At the risk of oversimplification, I would like to suggest that the *qadosh*/Ḥasid is the early and most pristine expression of Carlyle's Hero. As in other similar cases, Medieval Jewry anticipated some of the ideas later discovered by European savants.

96. Thomas Carlyle, *On Heroes, Hero-Worship, and the Heroic in History* (New York: Chelsea House, 1983), pp. 189, 191. Vico developed this theme in an inaugural lecture; see *Il De mente heroica*,' in *Varia* (Naples: A. Guida, 1996). For a critical account of this lecture, see Josep Martinez Bibal, "*El* De Mente Heroica," *Cuadernos sobre Vico*, 15–16 (2003), pp. 101–119.

# Chapter 54
# Payback Time – the Case of the Catalonian Rabbis

Jewish Heroic ideology penetrated the Iberian Peninsula in a three-prong movement: 'anti-Maimonidean,' 'Kabbala,' and 'Rabbis of France' (usually referred to as חכמי צרפת, 'the Sages of France'; רבו־תינו הצרפתים, 'our French masters'; and גדולי צרפת, 'the Grandees of France'). Generally, these subjects are studied separately, as if disconnected from one another. Attention should be paid, however, to the fact that Spanish Kabbala [not to be confused with Lurianic Kabbala] originated in the cities of Gerona and Barcelona, the hotbed of anti-Maimonidean activities. The link connecting these two movements, neglected by contemporary historians, is the 'Rabbis of France.' "The rise of this secret lore," noted the great historian Heinrich Graetz (1817–1891), "coincides with the time of the Maimunistic controversy, through which it was launched into existence."[97] R. Jonah of Gerona

97. H. Graetz, *History of the Jews*, vol. 3 (Philadelphia: The Jewish Publication Society, 1894), p. 547. The expression "French Rabbis" did not include the lesser French Rabbis in the region of Provençe, who were not anti-Maimonideans; see the valuable study of E. E. Urbach, "The Participation of German and French Scholars in the Controversy about Maimonides and his Works," (Heb.), *Zion* 12 (1947), pp. 149–159. The first rabbis in Spain to allude to "French Rabbis" were from Ramban's circle. The earliest mention can be found in his *Ḥiddushim* on Baba Batra 55a s.v. *wu-maṣati*; 'Aboda Zara 72a s.v. *ve-khatab*; Ḥolin 37b s.v. *ve-yesh*; 53a s.v. *emar*. It is also found among commentators from the same region; see R. Solomon b. Adrete, *Ḥiddushim* on 'Erubin 89b s.v. *ella*; 90a s.v. *be-'emet*;

(ca. 1200–1263), who had the distinction to have introduced German *Ḥasidut* into Spain and was a major player in the anti-Maimonidean movement, studied Kabbala with R. Isaac the Blind (son and disciple of Maimonides' nemesis, R. David of Posquièrs).[98] In what follows, I would like to propose that 'anti-Maimonidean' → 'Kabbala' → 'Rabbis of France' constituted a single movement.

The anti-Maimonidean movement (1180–1240) came at a critical moment in Iberian Jewish history. Until the mid-12th century the Jewish Communities in Central and Northern Spain were governed, more or less, according to the values, culture, and traditions of their brethren in Andalusia. With the destruction of the Andalusian Communities by Muslim fanatics from North Africa, Jewish intelligentsia left Spain. For political, as well as cultural reasons, Jewish leadership passed over to Castile. Soon, this leadership was challenged by the anti-Maimonideans penetrating Catalonia from the North. Overtly, their intention was to combat heresy and promote Kabbala. Actually, their aim was to discredit the established institutions and leadership. To understand their motivation, let us begin by pointing out that Catalonia was never part of Sepharad (more or less like Naples and Sicily, with regard to the rest of Italy). Granted, at one time Catalonian Jewry, like other communities in the Iberian Peninsula, acknowledged some of the values and leadership of Jewish Andalusia. However, they never conceded their hegemony. Catalonian Jewry did not feel, nor in fact were they regarded as, part of Sepharad. Their liturgy was different. A disciple of R. Solomon Adrete informed us that the Catalonian Synagogue continued "to include the *piyyuṭim*

---

Beṣa 21b s.v. *wul-'inyan*; Ketubot 16a s.v. *ha*; Giṭṭin 4a s.v. *me-hadrenan*; 'Aboda Zara 51a. See also, Riṭba on Rosh HaShana 34a s.v. *ve-ha-ṭa'am*; Sukka 45b s.v. *mihu*; Ketubot 8a s.v. *rab*; Qiddushin 10a s.v. *amar*; 28a s.v. *ve-'ad*.

98. On this school of Kabbala, see Gershom Scholem, *Ha-Qabbala be-Probanṣ* (Jerusalem: Academon, 5746/1986); idem, *Reshit ha-Qabbala* (Jerusalem: Schocken, 5708/1948), pp. 99–126. On the life and ideology of R. Jonah, see the eminent study of Professor Israel Ta-Shma, "*Ḥasidut Ashkenaz bi-Sfarad: Rabbenu Yona Gerondi, ha-'ish wu-fa'olo*," in *Galut Aḥar Gola* (Jerusalem: Machon Ben Zvi, 1989).

of Yannai in its prayers."[99] Their halakhic practices, too, differed. A Catalan rabbi in North Africa explained:

> You should know that we are the (children) of those who had been banished from Catalonia, and we conduct ourselves in accordance (with the norms) followed by our ancestors, we continue these practices in the places that, because of our sins, we have been driven… And although the legal decisions [of their rabbis] are not commonly known, nonetheless, it would be improper to question the norms of their communities. Even though a particular custom may not be registered in any book we must assume that the norm had been established in accordance with the great [rabbis].[100]

Catalan Jewry, too, was independent of their brethren from Castile. While Jews in Castile continue to use Arabic (see below chapter 61), Catalan Jews translated the Scripture into Catalan, before it was translated into the Spanish of Castile.[101] Maran Joseph Caro was careful to register separately the "custom of Sepharad" and "the custom of Catalonia."[102]

Catalonian Jewry was fiercely independent. Concerning the recitation of the *Targum* they did not hesitate to confront R. Samuel

---

99. R. Joshua ibn Shu'eb, *Derashot* (Constantinople, 5282/1522), *Shemini* (n. p.).
100. R. Abraham ibn Ṭawwa'ah, *Ḥuṭ ha-Mshullash*, III, #10, in *Sefer ha-Tashbeṣ*, part IV, 3d. It seems that the Catalonian rabbinate had their own edition of the Talmud "גמרות קטלוניא"; see the quotation in *Birke Yosef, Oraḥ Ḥayyim*, XXV, 5.
101. *Ladino* was never the language *spoken* by the Jews (just like Jews never spoke the Aramaic of the *Targum*). Rather, it was the language used to translate the Scripture. Hence, the verb *ladinar*. The syntax is radically different than the spoken language, referred to as '*Judio*' – a noun synonymous with '*Yiddish*.' My grandmother used to refer to that language as '*castilla*'; i.e., the language spoken in Castile.
102. See *Bet Yosef, Oraḥ Ḥayyim*, XLVI, s.v. *katab ha-'agur*; CXLIII, s.v. *wu-ma she-pirash*; DCXIX, s.v. *wu-ma she-'amar rabbenu*; *Yore De'a* CCLXXIX, s.v. *wu-ma she-'amar ve-afillu*.

ha-Nagid, who, in turn, referred to them as holding "some aspects of *minut*" (see above chapter 50 and appendix 61). During this conflict, some of these rebels "died under the whip."[103] It is hard to believe that Catalonian rabbis would have forgotten such ignominy. Rather, it would be safe to assume that in "The Day of the Willow" they would not have flinched, and would have stood firmly on the side of the shrieking Talmudists. The collapse of Andalusian Jewry opened up a window of opportunity to pay back. The window could close quickly. There was something ominous in neighboring Toledo. As a result of the collapse of Andalusian Jewry a large influx of refugees arrived in that city. Among the refugees were Andalusian sages planning to open a Talmudic academy. R. Abraham ibn Daud, one of these refugees, reported that, since the children of R. Joseph ibn Megas

> ...were unable to maintain academies [in Lucena] and were [among] the first to flee to the city of Toledo, they have been making whatever effort they could to raise disciples, and the Holy One, blessed be He, has shown His approval of their deeds. They are the last of the Talmudic scholars of the present age.[104]

To strengthen their position, the newcomers brought with them the library of Lucena, as well as the private collection of R. Samuel ha-Nagid, containing the most prestigious copies of Talmud and Rabbinics, going all the way back to the Geonic period (see below Concluding Reflections).

Success of these sages would have marked the end of the Catalonian rabbinate. Something had to be done to discredit the newcomers and ensure that their Talmudic academy would not succeed. The decisive battle would have to be fought in Toledo – the new 'Jewish' capital of Sepharad. The first step, however, was to outlaw the

103. *Sefer ha-'Ittim*, p. 267.

104. *Sefer ha-Qabbala*, p. 88; (Heb., p. 66, ll. 314–316).

'Maimonideans' in Catalonia. With this goal in mind three separate groups were organized. To combat the sages raised in 'Sepharad,' a new brand of spiritual leadership was introduced: the 'Rabbis of France' (see the following chapter). These rabbis were credited with heroic knowledge and might. To justify their disdain for the Talmudic *qabbala* of the Geonim and Andalusia, a new, more potent alternative was proposed: 'archaic' *Kabbala* – descending in mysterious channels from Moses to the mystics of Gerona (see below chapter 57). Unlike the mundane 'philosophy' of the 'Maimonideans,' something more sublime and potent was offered: cosmic sacrality and paranormal knowledge. In place of science and logic and reason, the new creed proposed the occult, magic, and the power to manipulate the demonic forces causing havoc in the world (see below chapters 58–60). Instead of earthly sages, Israel would be guided by heroes and saints. However, a hero without a cause is a waste. Heroic logic demands a paranormal foe to confront and destroy, as with the legendary knights marching forth to slay the dragons (and *Don Quixote* charging against the windmills). Without a demoniac nemesis, heroes are useless. Hence, the imperative to find a worthy enemy. The designated foe was 'Maimonides.' As with the legendary chevaliers fighting Moors and Saracens in the *Chansons de Geste*, these heroes, too, came from France to rescue helpless Catalan damsels from the claws of perfidious Maimonideans. The shiny knights were the 'Rabbis of France.' Who were these rabbis?

# Chapter 55
# "Our Lords, the Rabbis of France"

'Rabbis of France' was a code term invented to bully the opposition. It referred to rabbis in France and Germany sympathetic to promoting anti-Maimonidean policies. They comprised the type of dysfunctional Talmudist confronted by R. Samuel ha-Nagid: in every detail (see above chapter 51). The supreme authority of the "Rabbis of France" was formally instituted by the saintly R. Moses b. Nahman (1194–1270), known by the acronym Ramban – a cousin and disciple of the magnificent R. Jonah.[105] This is how he addressed them: "Oh! *Our Lords,* French Rabbis, we are your pupils and by your words we live!"[106] These rabbis were invested with imperial authority over *all* Israel. "*Our* Rabbis of France," announced R. Joseph ben Ṭodros Abul'afya (12th and 13th centuries), one of the earliest anti-Maimonideans in Castile, are those "from whose waters we drink, and by their words live *in all the confines of the world.*" Their decisions and interpretations are binding on all parties. On their authority, R. Judah al-Fakhkhar (d. 1235) denied permission to R. David Qimḥi

105. See *Kitbe Ramban,* vol. 1, p. 397 n. 1. See below n. 124.

106. In his "Letter to the French Rabbis," in *Iggerot Qena'ot,* III, 8b. Accordingly, he proposed in his *Perush* on Lev. 19:2, vol. 1. pp. 115–117, that when the Tora urged the Jews to be *qedoshim,* it meant that they should adapt heroic virtue; see below chapter 64. In a poem, *Kitbe Ramban,* vol. 1, p. 402, he praised *qedoshim*-style martyrdom.

(ca. 1160–ca. 1235) – one of the most learned Jews in Western Europe at the time – to present a defense of Maimonides in Toledo, "in compliance with the verdict of *our* Rabbis of France."[107] There are two fundamental characteristics to this appellative. First, the rabbis are anonymous. Not only are the people not told *who* had transmitted to the anti-Maimonideans in *Spain* the verdict of the "Rabbis of France," but what is particularly revealing, no one needs to know *who* these sages are, their names, *when* and *where* they lived, in *which* communities they served, *what* they wrote, or from *whence* they acquired their judicial supremacy. Second, they have judicial supremacy in the interpretation of the Tora even on matters pertaining to life and death. Questioning their opinions, even when running against the Law and Talmud, is nothing less than blasphemy. On their behalf, Jewish Law must be put aside. An illuminating example is a note by R. Yom Ṭob as-Sibili (ca. 1250–1330; known by the acronym Riṭba) – one of the great Talmudist from Christian Spain. In a passage examining whether it is permitted to commit suicide or to speed one's own demise to avoid torture, he cited a *marginal note* that he had found *appended* to the *Tosafot*. In the note, a reference was made to a passage in Bereshit Rabba (XXXIV, 13, vol. 1, p. 324), proposing that King Saul was not guilty of suicide since he killed himself to avoid dreadful torture and dishonor (see I Sam. 31:4). This is followed by an anonymous note: "We learn from the preceding that it is permitted to slaughter children in a pogrom for (fear) that they will be forced to apostatize." The argument is unpersuasive. The view concerning King Saul's suicide is not recorded in the Talmud but in the *Midrash* – which is generally not recognized as an authoritative source of halakha.[108] More to the point, forced conversions, as deplorable as they may be, do not equal the case of King Saul, involving the certainty of ghastly torture

107. The first quotation is from "*Milḥemet ha-Dat*," ed. J. I. Kobakak, *Jeshurun* VIII (Bamberg, 1875), p. 29; and the second from ibid., p. 40. See appendix 57.

108. The bibliography on the subject is vast. For some learned insights, see *Oṣar Ḥilluf Minhagim*, ed. B. M. Lewin (Heb.) (Jerusalem: Makor, 1972), #40, p. 80; *Tashbeṣ* III, #160; R. Mal'akhi Cohen, *Yad Mal'akhi* (New York: Keter,

and national disgrace.[109] Finally, there is a huge difference between *self*-inflicted deaths, as with the case of King Saul, and murdering little babies! Riṭba was unconvinced: "These are matters requiring study and serious investigation." So far, he was following standard rabbinic reasoning. Unexpectedly, he retracted, appending this baffling remark: "However, since an elder has passed judgment (permitting the slaughtering of children) the matter is settled." The source citing the "elder" (an allusion to R. Tam) was not identified. One would think that citing a verdict by one of the most meticulous legal minds standing in glaring contradiction to the Sixth Commandment ("Do not murder") would warrant disclosing the source and argument. By the same token, one would expect that Riṭba, who never before shied away from disagreeing with R. Tam, would present a contrary position. None of this happened. As if per magic, the mind of this great Talmudist came to a full stop when confronted with the phrase 'Rabbis of France.' Submissively, he recanted: "We have heard in the name of the Grandees of France that it is permitted to carry on in practice this decision"[110] (הלכה למעשה).

Let us consider the following three points. First, the authority of the 'Rabbis of France' may not be questioned, even in matters entailing the commission of heinous crimes. Second, it is a self-justifying pronouncement warranting no corroboration. It suffices for someone

5706/1946), #72; R. Ḥayyim J. D. Azulai, *'En Zokher*, (Leghorn, 5552/1792), Alef, #42. Cf. R. Jacob Ḥajez, *Halakhot Qeṭannot* (Venice, 5464/1704) II, #34, 30c; etc.

109. See R. Samuel Ashkenazi, *Yefe To'ar* (*Bereshit*) (Venice: 5357/1597), 217a. Cf. *The City of God* I, 17, p. 22; and I, 20, p. 26. For the best and most comprehensive examination of suicide in Jewish law, see R. Israel Moses Ḥazzan, *Kerakh shel Romi* (Leghorn, 5636/1876), #15.

110. *Ḥiddushe ha-Riṭba*, 'Aboda Zara (Jerusalem: Mossad Harav Kook: 5756/1996), cl. 81. Cf. Maran, *Bedeq ha-Bayit*, 10a-b, on *Yore De'a* CLVII, s.v. *b"h*. On his behalf we should point out that some scholars abstained from expressing ideas that could be construed as 'Maimonidean' for fear of their life; see *Milḥamot ha-Shem*, p. 77. The following are some of the places in which *Riṭba* disagrees with R. Tam; *Ḥiddushe ha-Riṭba* (Mossad Harav Kook): 'Erubin, col. 490; Shebu'ot, cols.482–483; 'Aboda Zara, col. 302; Ḥolin, cols. 175, 206, 288; etc.

to utter: 'Rabbis of France,' or for an anonymous hand to write it on the margin of a text, to render their view inviolable, thus excluding nasty questions such as: *who* they are, *what* evidence is there that they actually issued such a verdict, *where* can it be found, *when* was it issued, and under *which* circumstance. Such inquiries, standard in rabbinic legal tradition, are to be put aside in deference to the 'Rabbis of France.' Third, they are inerrant. Although the Supreme Court of Israel is prone to error, 'Rabbis of France' are infallible, and standard consideration must be put aside in deference to their rank. See appendix 67.

The status of the 'Rabbis of France' acquires precision upon considering that their supremacy was not predicated on standard knowledge and authority, but on the fact that they "grew up in the fields of Kabbala, plump and fresh."[111] R. Joseph Abul'afya chided the Maimonideans for being wrathful at "*our* Rabbis of France" and for refusing to "follow in the footsteps of the sages of the Kabbala." Clear evidence of their supremacy is the fact that "all the sages of the Kabbala, whom I saw, heard their words, or read their works, follow in the paths of *our* Rabbis of France."[112] Conversely, "*our* French Rabbis" are the supreme authority over all Israel, because they are "the instructors who teach and disclose to us every [kabbalistic] mystery."[113] In stark contrast, the Maimonideans undermine "the foundations of the Kabbala," and obliquely "speak ill of *our* French Rabbis." Thus, he pleaded with them to recant, and "rely on the sages of the Kabbala… because everything that the sages of the Kabbala have planted are blooming trees, full of trustworthy seeds." To defy them is nothing

111. "Letter to the French Rabbis," in *Iggerot Qena'ot*, III, 8c. This may be an allusion to the special power granted to kabbalists; see below nn. 153, 213.
112. "*Milḥemet ha-Dat*," pp. 30, 45; cf. ibid., p. 22.
113. Ramban, Introduction, *Dine De-Garme*, printed at the end of his Commentary to Baba Batra. To soothe the fear of these rabbis, he assured them that in Spain "no one" [as of yet] has condemned or disparaged "our Kabbala"; see "Letter to the French Rabbis," in "*Iggerot Qena'ot*," *Qobeṣ Teshubot*, III, 9a.

less than insubordination against God: no one "should either rebel against the Almighty, or confront the sages of Kabbala."[114]

The anti-Maimonidean strategy will become crystal clear upon noticing that unless one accepts the theological notions of the Kabbala, there is nothing heretical about the Maimonideans. Conversely, without an *a priori* recognition of the hegemony of "our Lords, the Rabbis of France," there are no means by which to authenticate the Kabbala. To put it less ponderously: without 'Kabbala/Rabbis of France' there would be no 'Maimonideans/ heretics.' The entire anti-Maimonidean movement would then be reduced to a cluster of irresponsible assertions, backed up by neither reasoned argument nor palpable evidence. Hence the axis: Kabbala → Rabbis of France → anti-Maimonideans.

By way of conclusion let us note that during the 13th and 14th centuries, when the anti-Maimonidean movement raged in Spain, there were a large number of Jewish communities all over France. These communities were not homogenous. Each had its own religious and intellectual modality, rooted in very ancient and venerable traditions. Isn't it strange that although they were often quoted, nobody cared to identify these 'Rabbis of France,' or say who had crowned them with this title? It would certainly not be irrelevant to know *how* somebody in Castile or Catalonia knew their views. When the illustrious Chief Rabbi of Toledo, R. Me'ir Abul'afya (ca. 1170–1244), who at the time had joined the anti-Maimonidean movement, asserted that he "was writing to *all* the sages of France,"[115] are we to believe that he had taken an inventory of every single rabbi in France and forwarded the letter to them? By the same token, we cannot prevent ourselves from asking why it is that in his epistle to the 'Rabbis of France' in 'defense' of the Maimonideans, Ramban managed to omit their names and addresses. Granted that some rabbis in France were

114. "*Milḥemet ha-Dat* pp. 22, 45, 32, 46.

115. *Kitab al-Rasa'yil le-Rabbenu Me'ir ha-Levi* (henceforth: *Kitab al-Rasa'yil*) (Paris, 5631/1871), First Epistle, p. 2. The same applies to Riṭba, *Ḥiddushim*, at Rosh HaShana 34a s.v. *ve-ha-ṭa'am*.

pro-Kabbala and anti-Maimonidean; granted also that some rabbis in Spain communicated with some of their colleagues in France, but were these rabbis speaking for *the entire* French rabbinate? If so, who anointed them: *where* and *when*? Bearing this in mind I would like to suggest – provocative as it may seem – that we are dealing with a literary device used by a preachy group moved by ideological fervor. A group, unable to persuade through judicious argument, used the formula 'Rabbis of France' to bludgeon the heads of the public with hectoring assertions. Before we rush to judgment, we should consider that we are dealing with the enchanted world of heroes and devils and knights and damsels in distress. As Cervantes taught, in that world, every knight had the right to fashion a *Dulcinea* in the mythical kingdom of Toboso. The 'Rabbis of France' were the *Dulcinea* of anti-Maimonidean knights chasing windmills in Spain. Would anyone fault *Don Quixote* (I, 4) for stopping the traveling merchants and demanding that they acknowledge *Dulcinea's* supreme beauty and excellence – or else?

# Chapter 56
# Fighting Assimilation?

Commonplace among modern historians is the notion that in his endeavor to explain Judaism "philosophically," Maimonides "established principles which did not by any means bear a Jewish stamp on them, nor were they in consonance with the Bible, and still less with the Talmud." It is reasonable, therefore, to argue that those "whose learning was entirely confined to the Talmud" would oppose him. In support, it was noted that some Maimonidean doctrines, concerning 'miracles,' 'prophecy,' 'immortality,' as well as the status of the non-legal elements of the Talmud (*aggada*), were "in the eyes, not only of the strict Talmudists, but also of more educated men, a heretical attack upon Judaism, which they believed it was their duty to energetically repel."[116] To further substantiate this view, historians pointed to the high level of assimilation, heresy, and apostasy befalling Iberian Jewry. "There were many, it would seem, in Spain, who found in Maimonidean philosophy convenient support for their extreme liberalism," remarked Y. Baer, further adding: "These men accepted only a faith of reason and rejected popular beliefs." In despair, Baer noted that they also "denied the value of talmudic *aggadot*." The cause, it is freely assumed, lies in the philosophical and rationalistic

116. *History of the Jews*, vol. 3, pp. 522, 523. This assertion is the result of indoctrination and faulty Talmudic schooling. In no place in the Talmud is there to be found those "established principles" against "philosophy"; see R. Ḥiyya ha-Cohen de la-Ara, *Mishmerot Kehunna* (Amsterdam, 5508/1748), 36b. Cf. below n. 119, and appendix 57. On the authority of the *aggadot*, see above, Section IV, n. 177.

trends generated by the Maimonideans. More particularly: "secular acculturation" and "Averroism."[117]

These claims will be examined in detail in the following chapters. Here it will suffice to point out that in the ancient communities of Syria, Egypt, Yemen and throughout North Africa, where Maimonides' works and the intellectual tradition he represented reigned supreme, none of the above took place. Why? For reasons having to do with personal ideology, modern historians failed to consider the connection between the triumph of the anti-Maimonideans, the rise of Kabbala, and the decay of Jewish learning and leadership, leading to mass conversions and the Expulsion of 1492. Specifically, that mass apostasy to Christianity took place *after* – not *before* – the ban against Maimonideans. Somehow, nobody cared to notice that Petrus Alfonsi (12th century), Nicholas Donin (13th century) and Pablo Christiani (d. 1274), as well as scores of other apostates, were the product of the anti-Maimonidean schooling and tradition.[118]

Before proceeding, we must dispose of another common misapprehension. The notion that according to the rabbis all contacts with the 'nations,' are synonymous with 'assimilation,' and 'heresy' is an anti-Maimonidean fabrication. Not only did the rabbis acknowledge the "wisdom among the nations," but they also instituted a special blessing to celebrate this fact (see above chapter 25). More fundamentally, they recognized that in a situation of close proximity to other peoples and cultures, 'borrowing,' whether conscious or not, is a given. The strategy open to Jews (and other minorities) is not to pretend that they are insulated from the rest, but to make a conscious decision as to what they wish to absorb and what they wish to

117. Yitzhak Baer, *A History of the Jews in Christian Spain*, 2 vols. (Philadelphia: The Jewish Publication of America, 1961–5722), vol. 1, p. 97. See appendix 63.

118. This runs contrary to the view of John Tolan, *Petrus Alfonsi and his Medieval Readers* (Gainesville: University Press of Florida, 1993). Petrus Alfonsi was born in Northern Spain and was not 'Andalusian.' He was proficient in neither Hebrew nor Arabic, and his knowledge of Bible and Talmud proceeded from the circles described by R. Samuel ha-Nagid, above chapter 51.

ward off. The difference between the various communities of Israel depended, exclusively, on this choice. The rabbis taught: "Like those who are upright among them (the gentiles) you did not do, but like those among them (the gentiles) who are corrupt, you do!"[119] On the basis of this doctrine, R. Baḥyye ibn Faquda explained that in addition to classical biblical and rabbinic sources and Jewish sages, he would be citing also the views of non-Jews.

> Furthermore, in this (matter) I will be following in the footsteps and tradition of our predecessors, as well as (in the footsteps) of the virtuous and wise men of every generation (i.e., non-Jews) found in our language (Arabic), on those (subjects) which I found propitious for soothing the souls, and direct the hearts to study; e.g., the maxims of philosophers, the morals of ascetic men in the world and their pleasing habits. As our predecessors have taught: "One verse says: 'You have done after the laws of the nations around you' (Ezek. 11:12). While another verse says: 'neither have you done after the ordinances of the nations around you' (Ezek. 5:8). How are we to explain this? Like those who are upright among them (the nations) – you haven't done; but like those among them who are corrupt, you have done!"[120]

Consequently, rabbis chided their congregants for failing to emulate the *good* example and mores offered by their gentile neighbors.[121]

A close reading of the above passage could greatly benefit Jewish historians. When finally admitting that Kabbala had absorbed

---

119. Sanhedrin 39b. See *Genizah Studies*, vol. 1, pp. 225–226. Accordingly, the Geonim did not hesitate to consult with Christian scholars regarding difficult expressions in the Scriptures; see *Kitab al-Muḥaḍara*, p. 227; cf. below n. 311. On the limits of this collaboration, see *Golden Doves*, pp. 123–124.

120. *Ḥobot ha-Lebabot*, p. 36. See above n. 115. Cf. *'Eber ve-'Arab*, p. 138.

121. See *Gib'at Sha'ul*, p. 257; R. Israel Moses Ḥazzan, *Words of Peace and Truth* (London, Samuel Meldola: 5605/1845), pp. 13–14; etc.

important elements of Christianity, Professor Baron reasoned that Jews had also borrowed from Islamic culture. This type of reckoning is not helpful. Since times of yore, Jews have been absorbing ideas and values from other civilizations – that is a fact. What is significant is *what* they chose to absorb and *what* they chose to reject. Here is what Professor Baron wrote:

> In the process they borrowed much from their Christian environment, both orthodox and sectarian, just as their predecessors in the East had been nurtured from undying springs of pre-Christian and Christian gnosis and, to a lesser extent, of Muslim *Sufism*. But almost unconsciously they absorbed all these foreign ingredients, as their homiletical predecessors of all ages had done, and integrated them organically into the fabric of Jewish thought by constant reinterpretation and hermeneutic confirmation by words of Scripture.[122]

Oversimplifications will not do. To assess the Kabbala/anti-Maimonidean movement it would be necessary to establish *what* they had borrowed from the Christian environment. In the course of this chapter we propose that they had borrowed its worst feature: persecution of the 'other.' From its incipient moment, post-Jesus Christianity was predicated on persecuting the 'other.' In a persecuting society, the 'other' is a creation of the system. "For there must also be heresies among you," declared Paul, "that they which are approved may be made manifest" (I Cor. 11:19).[123] Persecution creates the 'other' – in religious terminology: 'heresy' – not the other way around. Responding to a mimetic impulse, the anti-Maimonidean/ Kabbala proponents went on a witch-hunt rampage in the pursuit of Jewish 'heretics,' exactly as Christians had engaged in the persecution of men of the stature of Peter Abelard (1079–1153) and Thomas

122. *A Social and Economic History of the Jews*, vol. 8, p. 51.
123. Cf. St. Augustine, *Confessions* (Oxford: Oxford University Press, 1991), p. 129.

Aquinas (1224/5–1274). The anti-Maimonideans were inspired by men like Bernard of Clairvaux (1090–1153) – the "great detective of heresy" *and* "the Father of Mysticism" – not by the sages of Israel![124] Take note of the reason given by R. Solomon b. Adrete (ca. 1235–ca. 1310) for the ban against the Maimonideans, which he pronounced in Barcelona on July 26, 1305:

> Go into the distant lands where Canaanites [a code term for 'Christians'] and all gentiles live! They would condemn them [the Maimonideans] as heretics, even for a single heresy and abomination that they had written in their books... and they would tie them up in vine branches and incinerate them until they turned into ashes![125]

A strategic decision – with horrendous consequences as of yet not fully explored by modern historians – was to approach the ecclesiastical authorities to fight Jewish 'heretics.' The anti-Maimonideans pleaded with them that in their endeavor to stamp out heresy, the ecclesiastical authorities should burn the books of Jewish heretics.[126] Consequently, they went "crying and begging" to the ecclesiastical authorities "to pass judgment" on "other," i.e., non-Christian, "works" – a reference to Maimonides' writings. R. Jonah went first to the Franciscans and then to the Dominicans. He implored: "Look, most of our people are heretics and unbelievers, because they were

---

124. See *In the Shadow of History*, pp. 2, 11–12. On the culture of violence peculiar to their time, see David Nirenberg, *Communities of Violence* (Princeton, N.J.: Princeton University Press, 1996). On the function of 'heresy' during the Inquisition, see the studies in M. Zerner, ed. *Inventer l'hérésie?* (Nice: Centre de etudes médiévales, 1998).

125. In *Minḥat Qena'ot* (Pressburg, 1838), XX, p. 61, Ramban awarded him the title *ḥasid*; see *Qobeṣ Teshubot ha-Rambam* (Leipzig, 5619/1859); henceforth: "*Iggerot Qena'ot*," in *Qobeṣ Teshubot*), III, 10d; see above n. 104. R. Adrete had the distinction of studying under R. Jonah, see below n. 136, who is credited with introducing *Ḥasidut* in Spain; see *Ḥasidut Ashkenaz bi-Sfarad*.

126. See "*Milḥemet ha-Dat*," p. 49.

duped by R. Moses of Egypt [Maimonides] who wrote heretical books. You exterminate your heretics, exterminate ours, too!"[127] The anti-Maimonideans succeeded, "and by their command they made a large fireplace" and proceeded to burn Maimonides' works.[128]

In defense of R. Jonah, R. Joseph Abul'afya argued that he had been compelled to seek assistance from the Church since his coreligionists refused to assist him, "because he had raised the flag of the Kabbala." (Parenthetically: this shows that the allegation that "the saintly Rabbis of France" fully supported the anti-Maimonideans is a fabrication). The premise of this argument is that in such a contingency it would be legitimate to ask the Church to condemn Jewish books to the fire. In a similar vein he proposed that the incineration of Maimonides' works had merely "ensued." In view of this clarification, R. Abul'afya counseled the Maimonideans to accept the facts and not defy "the sages of the Kabbala."[129] A similar account was given by R. David Qimḥi. In his zeal to promote his new ideology, R. Jonah informed the Church (a capital offense in Judaism) about

127. *Iggerot Qena'ot*, in *Qobeṣ Teshubot ha-Rambam*, III, 4c. Cf. *History of the Jews*, vol. 3, pp. 542–544. The anti-Maimonideans have the distinction of inaugurating in Europe the tradition of burning Jewish books, continuing into recent times; see Stephen J. Whitfield, "Where They Burn Books… " *Modern Judaism* 22 (2002), pp. 213–233. Thus, the tradition of violence as a genuine expression of devotion, earmarking Jewish conflicts throughout modern times. For example, the murder of a liberal rabbi and his daughter by a Ḥasidic Jew; see Simon Dubnow, *Geschichte des Chassidismus* (Berlin: Judischer Verlag, 1931), vol. 1, p. 202; cf. ibid., vol. 2, p. 223. See also Raphael Mahler, *A History of Modern Jewry* (New York: Schocken, 1971), pp. 476–80, 489–90, 492, 514; Raphael Patai, *The Jewish Mind* (New York: Charles Scribner's Sons, 1977), pp. 199, 558; and Lippman Bodoff, "The Message of the Prophet Elisha," *Midstream* (February/March 1999), p. 12 n. 9. I cannot help thinking that the sanctioning of violence as a genuine expression of devotion was a factor in the assassination of Prime Minister Rabin; see the insightful essay of Lippman Bodoff, "Religious Murders: Weeds in the Garden of Jewish Tradition?" *Midstream* (January 1988), pp. 9–14.

128. "*Milḥemet ha-Dat*," p. 50.

129. "*Milḥemet ha-Dat*," pp. 43, 46.

Maimonides' heresies. In a letter addressed to R. Judah al-Fakhkhar, R. David Qimḥi replied:

> My intention is neither to denounce nor debate you, but to let you know about the person whom you have chosen and declared to be righteous, wise, and unblemished. Whereas in fact he [R. Jonah] is wicked and unlearned, given that he had passed to the side of evil [a reference to going to the Church for assistance], perverted his ways, and became an informer and an enemy collaborator. His subsequent actions revealed the true motives of his earlier actions. May heaven expose his sin and earth rise against him! Because when he had realized that the rabbis in France had rejected him and regarded him as an unlearned person, and knew him to be the bearer of false testimony, he turned to the graven images and idol worshippers [i.e., the Church]; begged them and they consented to help him since he was denouncing the Jews. First, he went to the Franciscans, saying: 'Look, most of our people are heretics and unbelievers, because they were duped by R. Moses of Egypt [Maimonides] who wrote heretical books. You exterminate your heretics, exterminate also ours!' Thereafter, they ordered those books to be burnt, which were the *Book of Knowledge* [the first book of the *Mishne Tora*] and the *Guide*. His uncircumcised heart, however, did not rest until he repeated the same words to the Dominicans and the clergy. Finally, the words reached the Cardinal [Romanus]. Consequently, the Jews in Montpellier and those associated with them fell into grave danger, becoming the ridicule and scorn of gentiles. This heinous slanderer (Cardinal Romanus) went out from town to town, saying: 'See! The Jewish Law is over! They have become two sects! And there is no other religion except for ours!'[130]

---

130. *Iggerot Qena'ot*, in *Qobeṣ Teshubot*, III, 4c.

A similar account was given by two members of the ibn Ḥasdai family. In a letter by R. Abraham ibn Ḥasdai and his brother Judah (early 13th century) addressed to the communities of Castile, Aragon, Navarre, and Leon, it was reported that in their zeal to ban Maimonides' works, members of R. Jonah's circle approached the highest echelons of the Christian clergy, begging them "to issue a verdict on the other works, and on their orders they made a large fireplace" and burned Maimonides' books. To persuade the ecclesiastical authorities, the anti-Maimonideans argued that since they had been so diligent in destroying the works of Christian heretics, they should do the same with the works of Jewish heretics. Another contemporary, R. Samuel Saportas (13th century), gave a similar report. Although he did not mention the actual burning of Maimonides' works, he wrote that in response to Jewish appeals to the ecclesiastical authorities, the writings of Maimonides were brought before an ecclesiastical tribunal for examination.[131] R. Abraham Maimonides gave a similar account:

> It was reported in our land that the books of my father – may his memory be blessed! – the *Guide* and *Book of Knowledge* were burned by one of the [Jewish] factions in Montpellier, by the authority of [Christian] officials assisting them, given that they [the *Guide* and Book of Knowledge] prove their [Christian] religion false. Hence, Christians would surely assist them [the anti-Maimonideans] because their faith is not far removed from theirs.[132]

The anti-Maimonideans defended this course of action. In a letter addressed to R. Qimḥi, R. al-Fakhkhar explained that R. Solomon of Montpellier found himself abandoned by his colleagues [– what about the alleged support of 'the French Rabbis'?]. Therefore, he found it necessary to send his disciple, R. Jonah on a mission to the

131. "*Milḥemet ha-Dat,*" pp. 49, 50, 154.
132. *Milḥamot ha-Shem*, p. 55.

Church. The purpose was nothing less than "to avenge the vengeance of the Lord" (לנקום נקמת השם). In view of the threat posed by the Maimonideans, it was perfectly legitimate to seek the intervention of the ecclesiastical authorities. By having Maimonides' works burnt, "He (R. Jonah) saved the Holy Writings from *your* fire." Alluding to a rabbinic principle whereby an object condemned to be burned acquires the status of 'burnt,' R. al-Fakhkhar explained: "it [the *Guide*] warrants burning"[133] (לשרפה הוא עומד.) Therefore, such burning is not a sacrilege but a sacramental offering: "a fire kindling on the altar, so that the children of Israel would not whore after it (the *Guide* )."[134] In defense of R. Jonah's appeal to the Church, R. al-Fakhkhar argued that R. Solomon of Montpellier was desperate. Given that no one among his colleagues was willing to assist him (What about the 'anti-Maimonideans' → 'Rabbis of France'?!), he had to take matters into his own hands.

> And it came to pass that when he saw that all of you had conspired against him [i.e., the rabbis did not accede to his demands] and that he was almost defeated, he was much afraid of the rebels who had surrounded him, because they did not come to assist God, to assist God among the mighty.[135]

R. Adrete graced this episode with an illuminating explanation:

> ...because in that city there are found those who write iniquities about the Tora, and if there are some heretical writings, they ought to be incinerated, as if they were the books of sorcerers.[136]

133. *Iggerot Qena'ot,* in *Qobeṣ Teshubot,* III, 2c-d.

134. *"Milḥemet ha-Dat,"* p. 97.

135. *Iggerot Qena'ot,* in *Qobeṣ Teshubot,* III, 2c. This confirms R. David Qimḥi's account that when the anti-Maimonideans failed to convince the local rabbinic authorities, they resorted to appeals to the ecclesiastical tribunal; see above nn. 130, 131.

136. *Teshubot ha-Rishba,* ed. Ch. Z. Dimitrovsky, part I, 2 vols. (Jerusalem: Mossad

We should recall that this august figure not only had the distinction to study under R. Jonah,[137] but also to pronounce the ban against the Maimonideans. Therefore, we should not be surprised to find him applauding the spirit of ecumenicalism exhibited by the Church. In appreciation he penned these lovely lines:

> Could I blame people who are not of the covenant [i.e. Christians] if they would stretch their hands against this corruption and blaspheme by the people of our Law, and they [i.e. Christians] just like us, would open their mouths [against them]?[138]

The implications were horrific! The public, which was not as torpid as their religious leaders thought, recognized this for what it was: a repudiation of Jewish tradition and institutions, and a formal acknowledgement of Christian supremacy in matters of the spirit. Can one imagine the demoralizing effect on a Jewish public witnessing revered rabbis and trusted leaders gloating at the torching of Hebrew books by Christian monks? The fact that such a question never crosses the mind of our learned Jewish historians speaks for itself.

An important consideration: such an enterprise required large sums of money. The editor of one of R. Abraham Maimonides' epistles mentioned that bribes were paid to government officials, probably involving large sums. Who provided these funds? Before proposing a possible source, it would be helpful to note that there may have been some mundane factors behind R. Adrete's anti-Maimonidean fervor. Some members of the old leadership held his ministry in contempt. "We have heard from the contending parties that (some) are disrespectful (of R. Adrete)," wrote Ramban, "and have done away with all signs of compliance towards him." Adding: "They have profaned

---

Harav Kook, 1990), vol. 1, p. 361.

137. See *Ḥiddushe ha-Rishba, Shabbat,* ed. Y Bruner (Jerusalem: Mossad Harav Kook, 5746/1986), on Shabbat 50a s. v. *ve-rab*, col. 247; R. Shem Ṭob ibn Gaon, *Migdal 'Oz*, on *MT Ṣiṣit* 1:15.

138. *Teshubot ha-Rishba* (Ch. Z. Dimitrovsky), vol. 1, p. 398.

the sacred, they have abused the Tora."[139] R. Adrete acknowledged the fact. In the epistle announcing the ban, he wrote: "Everyone in the Community is holy (*qedoshim*)," i.e., they support him, "except for some of the Elected of the Congregation, who are the leaders of the people on account of their rank."[140] This is a reference to the old leadership, who were Maimonideans through and through. In accordance with standard halakha, Jews in Old Sepharad were not money lenders (see below chapter 61). There were some, among the newly arrived 'holy men' (*qedoshim*), who made their livelihood by loaning money to the general Christian population. R. Adrete had been in the business of lending money to Christians. Given that these practices will inevitably lead to anti-Jewish demonstrations, some of the old leadership must have raised objections. Others, particularly among the new 'holy men' (*qedoshim*) residents who engaged in the money lending trade, may have been eager to replace them, and could have provided the anti-Maimonideans with the necessary funds. The new leadership was well represented in Toledo. In appreciation for having persuaded the Christian authorities to burn Maimonides' works, the community of Toledo awarded R. Jonah the position of preacher, which he kept until his death.[141]

---

139. About the money paid in bribes, see "*Iggerot Qena'ot*," in *Qobeṣ Teshubot*, III, 15a. Concerning contempt for R. Adrete, see ibid. 10d. Undoubtedly, these were "the princes" (הנשיאים) ruling Barcelona who did not care for R. Adrete and his ideology. Concerning these "princes" (הנשיאים), see R. Benjamin of Tudela, *The Itinerary of Benjamin of Tudela*, Marcus Nathan Adler, ed. and trans. (New York: Philipp Feldheim, n.d.), p. 2, referred to it as a city "where there is a small holy congregation, including sages and wise men and illustrious princes (ונשיאים גדולים)" (our translation). R. Joseph b. Zabbara, *Sefer Sha'ashu'im*, ed. Israel Davidson (Berlin: Eshkol, 5685/1925), pp. 15–16. Similarly, R. Judah al-Ḥarizi, *Taḥkemoni* (Warsaw, 5659/1899), L, p. 350, described Barcelona as "the city of princes and of prominent leadership" –all of whom were Maimonideans, unsympathetic to bogus-Talmudists and newcomer kabbalists.

140. *Teshubot ha-Rishba*, vol. 1, #416, 152a. Cf. *Teshubot ha-Rishba* (Dimitrovsky), vol. 1, pp. 279280; 343–344. See below at n. 178.

141. Jewish historians have performed breathtaking acrobatics to *misread* the obvious facts. The oft-heard apology that the Jewish Communities would not have

R. Abraham Maimonides, who had followed these events in the West very closely, classified the protagonists as the proverbial "Little Foxes" (see above chapter 50) – defiant of tradition, scorning Geonic authority, and not hesitating to rend Israel asunder on behalf of their own ideology – with the assistance of the Church if warranted.

> ...They call wickedness 'good' and good 'wickedness!' They deem light to be darkness and darkness to be light. They seduced themselves with their own foolishness, and they go on to strengthen their silliness. As noted by the rabbis, concerning pagans: "They tend to reinforce their own fabrications" (*Giṭṭin* 28b). "Little foxes that destroy the vineyards" – they rose against Israel's faith, the words of the great Geonim, and distinguished sages! They hate those who love truth, those who profess God's unity in reality, (because of) what they explained out of their ignorance and their polluted faith, which is debasing them. Because they understood, in accordance with their knowledge of the *Guide of the Perplexed* and the *Book of Knowledge*, and out of their huge jealousy and arrogance, they carried on their falsehood with the power of Christians and burnt these books. We should not be astonished at that, since because of the sins of Israel, Epistemos also burnt the Tora.[142]

---

tolerated such behavior ignores the power of zeal and the marginality of halakha in the lives of ideologues; see Daniel Jeremy Silver, *Maimonidean Criticism and the Maimonidean Controversy* (Leiden: E. J. Brill, 1965), pp. 150, 154, 155.

142. *Teshubot R. Abraham b. Ha-Rambam* #75, p. 93. In a private communication, Professor Mayer I. Gruber noted an interesting characteristic of the Ashkenazic sense of tradition:

> Perhaps Rashi is reflecting a tendency among Ashkenazi exegetes to just make things up as one goes along, which, as you know, characterizes all streams in modern Ashkenazi Jewry to this day – Reform, Orthodox, and Conservative. My other parade example of this tendency to just make things up has to do with the fact that Spanish Bible mss. that include pictures of the menorah and other Temple implements seem to reflect the same artistic traditions found in

# Chapter 57
# *Kabbala* vs. *Qabbala*

To ensure anti-Maimonidean control, R. Solomon Adrete made certain that the next rabbi of Toledo would fully reflect the new ideology. This rabbi was no less a figure than the saintly R. Asher (ca. 1250–1327). He, too, was a professional money lender and represented the best that heroic ideology and sainthood had to offer (see below chapters 62 and 63). Thus, in 1305, the same year that R. Solomon Adrete announced the anti-Maimonidean ban in Barcelona, R. Asher was installed as Chief Rabbi of Spain. Henceforth, things were not quite the same.

The triumph of the anti-Maimonideans and the subsequent spread of Kabbala from Catalonia to Castile (13th-15th centuries) are yet to be properly evaluated. Because of their own agendas, historians refrain from pointing out the connection between the triumph of the anti-Maimonideans, the rise of Kabbala, the spread of pietistic doctrines, and the decay of Jewish learning and leadership, ending in mass conversions and the Expulsion in 1492. According to Baer, since Jewish apostasy was the result of 'rationalism,' the rise of Kabbala and

---

the mosaics of Byzantine period synagogues in the Land of Israel. Our oldest Ashkenazic illuminated manuscript which is Munich #5, which is also the oldest dated manuscript of Rashi's Bible commentaries, seems to just make things up without any acquaintance with the ancient artistic traditions. Now I do not know how far one may go with just two examples – but perhaps there is an insight here, which could be worked out by someone.

If we are to judge from the above, it seems quite far.

pietism should have strengthened Judaism. Yet the opposite was the case. Soon after the ban and the spread of Kabbala, Jewish leadership faltered, giving rise to antisemitic riots throughout Spain. By the time of the Black Plague (1348), the most important Jewish communities in Catalonia and Aragon had been wiped out, including Gerona, the birthplace of Spanish Kabbala, and Barcelona, where the ban against the Maimonideans was pronounced less than fifty years earlier. A short time later (1391–1412), a series of massacres decimated most of the communities in Spain. During that period many Jews were forced to convert to escape death. Some, however, converted out of sincere conviction. In this chapter we will examine the link between the spread of Kabbala and Jewish mass conversions to Christianity.

Camouflaged by theological noise and pious pretense, the aim of the Kabbala/anti-Maimonideans was to substitute the transmittal of *qabbala* of the Geonim and Old Sepharad with a Kabbala deeply entrenched in Christian and pagan lore. Anti-Maimonidean Kabbala has nothing to do with the great mystics of Israel. If there is one thing that we can ascertain about *Jewish* mysticism, it is that it was a matter of supreme privacy and subjectivity – something pertaining to matters "of the heart" – not a guiding principle to be imposed on others as a matter of public policy. The great mystical figures of Israel, such as R. Moses Cordovero (1522–1570), R. Isaac Luria (1534–1572), and R. Ḥayyim Viṭal (1542–1620) did not preach their esoteric ideas, and least of all use them to persecute dissidents and cause rifts in Israel.[143] By way of contrast, "Discord was the mother of this monstrosity" [Kabbala], noted Graetz, "which has ever been the cause of schism."[144] The appropriation of the term Kabbala (= *qabbala*) was designed to displace the traditional *qabbala* and replace

143. Concerning the latter, see the *responsum* of his son, R. Samuel Viṭal, *Be'er Mayim Ḥayyim* (Jerusalem, 5726/1966), #19, 52b-54a. See R. Israel Jacob Algazi, *Shalme Ṣibbur* (Salonika, 5550/1790), #5, 6d; and *Teshubot R. Abraham b. ha-Rambam*, #63, p. 64.

144. *History of the Jews*, vol. 3, p. 547.

it with mystical lore.[145] By changing the content of *qabbala,* the anti-Maimonideans simultaneously awarded a mantle of respectability to their doctrines in the eyes of the unlettered and vacated authentic rabbinic tradition. If this was not *minut,* in the eyes of Old Sepharad it was pretty close to it (see above chapter 51 and appendix 55). The transformation was done surreptitiously, so as not to arouse the ire of the general public.

The following *responsum* by R. Adrete illuminates both the ways and the aims of the anti-Maimonideans. It concerns a Talmudic *aggada* by R. Qaṭina (3rd century) that the world would last six thousand years and then lie "destroyed" (חרוב or חרב) for "one" thousand years. In the course of his explanation, R. Adrete formulated the principle that although one may interpret some passages of the Scripture allegorically, "the Kabbala *in our hands*" (מקובל בידנו) must be accepted in its literal sense.[146] His explanation requires some elaboration. If we were to explain that the actual world would be destroyed, then "one [thousand]" years would make little sense. On the other hand, if by 'world' it was meant 'human society' that would be in a state of cultural disarray and devastation, then there would be no difficulty in explaining 'one thousand.' Therefore, in order to explain that by the year 6000 the world would be annihilated, R. Adrete had to interpret "one [thousand] years" figuratively. "If we are to understand that by the end of the year six thousand the world would be totally

145. For a methodical (if inaccurate) defense of this term as synonymous with mysticism, see R. Abraham Shalom, *Neve Shalom* (Venice, 5335/1575), 65a-68b; cf. *Ma'ase Efod,* pp. 9–10. The form 'Kabbala' in modern scholarship is a mistransliteration of *qabbala,* and serves to express disdain for the basic rules of phonetics of both English and Hebrew. Until modern days, in the Near East, mystic lore was referred as *sod,* 'esoteric' – not Kabbala. Kabbala was only used to indicate a specific school, e. g. *qabbalat ha-'ari.*

146. *Teshubot ha-Rishba,* (Bne Brak, 5718/1958), vol. 1, #9, 4b; cf ibid #417, 170a-171b. The Talmudic passage is found in Rosh HaShana 31a and parallels. On his allegorical interpretation of Scripture, see his *Commentary* on Megilla 15a, ed. Ch. Z. Dimitrovsky, *Ḥiddushe ha-Rishba* (Jerusalem: Mossad Harav Kook, 5741/1981), col. 98.

destroyed," observed the scholar submitting the question, then "what could be the sense that the world would be destroyed (חרוב) for one thousand years?!" R. Adrete acknowledged the problem. However, for reasons that will be soon apparent, he conceded that "one" thousand is to be taken figuratively.

> Concerning your question: 'how could those thousand [years] be reckoned, since there is no time without the orbiting of the spheres?' This [question] would have been valid if we had taken the expression in a precise sense (על צד הכיוון האמיתי).[147] He argued:
>
> You may explain (the expression "one [thousand years]") as you wish [i.e., figuratively]. At any rate you must note that according to that (Talmudic) sage, the world would function in its ordinary way for six thousand years, and for "one [thousand, it would be] destroyed," which means that it would not function in its ordinary way, but in a poorer and faulty way, on account of the constitution of the material world. This is so because they (the rabbis) designate with the term 'destroyed' something which has deteriorated and has become faulty, not something that had been improved. And we find no one in the Talmud disagreeing with him (the author of the above view).

(The last point is inaccurate; see appendix 57.)

In brief, whereas "six thousand" must be taken in a literal sense, "one [thousand]" must be understood figuratively. Why? Before addressing this question, let us note that R. Adrete justified his interpretation on the basis of "Kabbala *in our hands*"[148] (מקובל בידנו), or "*true* Kabbala" (הקבלה האמיתית), which has been "received in *our* hands" (בידינו קבלה or מקובל בידנו).[149] This is a restrictive category.

---

147. *Teshubot ha-Rishba,* vol. 1 #9, 5a.
148. *Teshubot ha-Rishba,* vol. 1 #9, 4b.
149. *Teshubot ha-Rishba,* vol. 1 #9, 4a (*in fine*); #418, 162a; #423, 175b; and *Teshubot*

In a different *responsum* discussing the true mysteries of Israel, he exclaimed: "fortunate is he whom God had privileged with knowledge of their holy mystery (אשרי מי שזכהו השם יתברך לעמוד בסודן המקודש) [a reference to those sages who had access to the "Mystery of the Holy Trinity," see below chapter 60], which in R. Adrete's mind equals "the true Kabbala that was entrusted into the hands of the sages of Israel" (הקבלה האמיתית המסורה בידי חכמי ישראל), and is the exclusive patrimony of "those whom God had graced" (למי שחננו השם יתברך).[150] That is why he was careful to indicate that the Kabbala which he was proposing was not the standard *qabbala* of rabbinic tradition, but, exclusively, that "which is in *our* hands" and was entrusted "in the hands of *some* of the sages of our Tora" (מקובל ביד מקצת מחכמי תורתנו).[151] In the initial segment of his *responsum*, he specified that he was speaking on behalf of "every sage and sage of the Tora who are *Ḥasidim*" (חכם מחכמי תורתנו החסידים) – an allusion to the heroic Ḥasid/*qadosh* of Germany and France.[152] These are the celebrated heroic-*qedoshim*, standing between men and the gods. The truth that they impart is compelling. Failure to obey them constitutes rebellion against Heaven. The reason for this is because their doctrines were not transmitted by regular men, but by "prophets." R. Adrete explained, "This Kabbala, which is [exclusively] in the hands of *some* of the sages of Israel, is as if it were heard from

*ha-Rishba*, vol. 1 #9, 4b. He dealt with the same subject in #94 and #423. Cf. *Teshubot ha-Rishba*, (Ch. Z. Dimitrovsky), vol. 1, p. 28. Cf. *Kitbe Ramban*, vol. 1, p. 168.

150. *Teshubot ha-Rishba*, vol. 1 #9, 4a; #423, 175b; and similarly below, 176a: למי שחננו השם יתברך. The expression הקבלה האמיתית appears twice in that *responsum*. As we shall see in the chapter below, these are the sages privy to the mystery of the Holy Trinity.

151. *Teshubot ha-Rishba*, vol. 1 #9, 4b, or ibid: בידינו קבלה, and 5b. These are the elite, endowed with supernatural power; see appendix 67.

152. *Teshubot ha-Rishba*, vol. 1 #9, 4c. He identified himself with the Ḥasidim; see above n. 124. As attested by Ramban, these Ḥasidim had paranormal powers. This included the power to resurrect the dead, which, according to the rabbis, rests exclusively in the hands of God; see Ta'aniyot 2a, and the quotation below n. 215.

the mouths of the prophets" (שזה הקבלה ביד מקצת חכמי ישראל כמפי הנביאים).[153] At this point, a critical question comes to mind: What was the origin of that special Kabbala which was unknown to either the Geonim or the sages of Old Sepharad? An unbiased reading of R. Qaṭina's words will show that there is no clear evidence that he was actually forecasting the annihilation of planet earth or the collapse of civilization. More to the point, there is no evidence that Talmudic authorities regarded his view as a cardinal doctrine.[154]

R. Adrete was utilizing the words of R. Qaṭina to introduce to Judaism the Christian doctrine of Jesus' 'Second Coming,' where he is supposed to reign on earth for one thousand years. This is how Gibbon describes it:

> The ancient and popular doctrine of the Millennium was intimately connected with the second coming of Christ. As the works of creation had been finished in six days, their duration in their present state, according to a tradition which was attributed to the prophet Elijah, was fixed to six thousand years. By the same analogy it was inferred that this long period of labor and contention, which was now almost elapsed, would be succeeded by a joyful Sabbath of a thousand years; and Christ, with the triumphant band of the saints and the elect who had escaped death, or had been miraculously revived, would reign upon earth till time appointed for the last and general

153. *Teshubot ha-Rishba*, vol. 1 #9, 6a; cf. 4a (*in fine*). There is, however, a slight difference between them and the prophets of Israel. The title 'prophet' (נביא) in Scripture is awarded to those to whom God's word *descends*. In the case of the *qedoshim*/Ḥasidim, as with pagan spiritism, the diviner *ascends* to heaven and has direct access to the gods, angels, and the entire realm of the paranormal. Medieval Jewry was blessed with a plethora of such 'prophets' ascending heaven at will, consulting the ministering angels (מלאכי השרת), and similar entities inhabiting the yonder (see appendix 64). The felicitous events befalling these communities in the following decades corroborate the worth of that bliss.
154. See *Neve Shalom*, 184b-185a; R. Abraham Ṣabba', *Ṣeror ha-Mor* (Cracow, 5365/1605), 165c; *Keli Faz*, 18c; *Yefe To'ar*, 248b; et al. See appendix 59.

> resurrection. So pleasing was this hope to the mind of believers, that the *New Jerusalem,* the seat of this blissful kingdom, was quickly adorned with all the gayest colors of the imagination. A felicity consisting only of pure and spiritual pleasure would have appeared too refined for its inhabitants, who were supposed to possess their human nature and senses.[155]

The last point is of the essence. It coincides with the *qedoshim* eschatology that after the annihilation of the world by the year 6000, resurrection of the dead would take place, followed by a new world which they identified with 'the World to Come' (עולם הבא).* Since the pious "were supposed to possess their human nature and senses," this means that the 'banquet' promised to the pious would take place down here on earth and – contrary to the Maimonidean heresy – it would consist of very yummy delicacies of immeasurable delight (see above chapter 51).[156]

---

155. *The Decline and Fall of the Roman Empire,* vol. 1, p. 403.

* Cf. *Guide* II, 29, p. 243.

156. The most despicable aspect of the Maimonidean heresy was his denying that 'the banquet' would consist of luscious, lip-smacking food. Defiantly, Maimonides used the term 'World to Come' (עולם הבא) to designate an incorporeal world. This type of idea would surely result in a crisis of faith. What could the point of spirituality be if it were bereft of gastronomy?! For a defense of such a gastronomical banquet, see R. Baḥye b. Asher, *Be'ur 'al ha-Tora,* ed. C. D. Chavel, 3 vols. (Jerusalem: Mossad Harav Kook, 5736/1976), on Ex. 16:3, vol. 2, pp. 142–143. It has been shown that Maimonides' 'Last Will,' printed in *Qobeṣ Teshubot ha-Rambam,* III, 38a-40b, is a forgery. Most probably, it was composed by a Maimonidean who was acquainted with the ways of his son, R. Abraham. Nonetheless, his criticism of "the French", 40a-b, may in fact reflect the impression made by some anti-Maimonideans:

    ... the French don't appear to recognize the Creator – blessed be He – except when they are ingesting boiled ox meat, seasoned in vinegar and garlic – a condiment that they call 'salsa.' When the steam of vinegar and the haze of garlic go up their brains, they meditate. Then, no matter when, they imagine – through them [the condiments and food] – to be in presence of God, blessed be He! And [they also imagine] that He is near their prayers and their screaming, when reading the Talmud and other compositions by the Heads of Academies [cf.

Rather than from the chain of tradition of the Geonim and rabbis of Old Sepharad, the anti-Maimonidean Kabbala reached the *qedoshim* from an impeachable chain of Christian notables that could be corroborated by good people all over, even among the old folks (see below n. 173). Quoting Gibbons again:

> The assurance of such a Millennium, was carefully inculcated by a succession of fathers from Justyn Martyr and Irenaeus, who conversed with the immediate disciples of the apostles, down to Lactantius, who was preceptor to the son of Constantine.[157]

The Christian origin of the preceding doctrine may explain why the number "one [thousand]" should be understood figuratively. In Christian tradition, 'one thousand years' is an emblematic number designating indefinite longevity. It symbolizes a period of life that nobody, even the Patriarchs, reached outside Paradise, and it would be awarded to the pious under the reign of Jesus.[158] The view that this world would be annihilated had been formulated by the great Spanish

---

the poem of R. Samuel ha-Nagid, *Diwan R. Shemu'el ha-Nagid, Ben-Tehillim*, #83, ll. 10–14, cited above n. 50]. Also [they feel to be near God], by making of God a mat for their tongues [to step on], mentioning and speaking about God at all times in anthropomorphic terms… Generally, they have two wives. So, that their minds are invariably fixed on sex, eating, and drinking, and on other sensual pleasures. And they believe that in this fashion God is in their presence and that He is listening to them!

Cf. *Milḥamot ha-Shem*, pp. 61–64, 68; cf. *Guide* I, 5 and 31; III, 8, p. 311, ll. 19–23, and above chapter 51. Part of this 'Last Will,' is quoted in "Extracts from Joseph Sambari's Chronicle," in ed. Ad. Neubauer, *Medieval Jewish Chronicles*, part I (Oxford: Clarendon Press, 1887), p. 131.

157. *The Decline and Fall of the Roman Empire*, vol. 1, p. 404.

158. See R. Le Deaut, "Milenarismo," *Enciclopedia de la Biblia* (Barcelona: Ediciones Garriga, 1969), vol. 5, cols. 161–163. In my view the reason that Abayye, Rosh HaShana 31a, insisted that the period of "devastation" will last two thousand years, rather than one thousand, is to dispel any possible linkage between this rabbinic doctrine and Christian millennialism.

mystic Isidore of Seville (d. 636). In line with Christian millenarians, this mystic regarded the week of creation to parallel the weeks of the world. This doctrine passed on to "the hands of *some* of the sages of Israel," i.e., *qedoshim*-rabbis, from Christian millenarians, (rather than from the 'Talmud'). Enthralled by its brilliance, some kabbalists went on to develop an apocalyptic vision, along millenarian lines, when all things would "return to the mystical pure Nothingness."[159]

One may argue that there is nothing 'wrong' with such a belief, since Judaism recognizes freedom in "matters of the heart."[160] The problem, however, was not with this or that kabbalistic belief, but with the fact that anti-Maimonidean kabbalists tried to impose their ideology on everyone, in every which way. In the process they ended up de-authorizing the *qabbala* of the Geonim and Old Sepharad from whose hands the Talmud and interpretation of the Law passed to all Israel. Overtaken by zeal, the anti-Maimonidean kabbalists underrated the intelligence of the public, and failed to realize that by nit-picking on the earlier authorities, they were undermining the foundations of Jewish authority. In particular, their appeal for ecclesiastic intervention was nothing less than a public recognition of Christian preeminence in matters of the spirit. The consequence of this form

159. See Gershom Scholem, *The Origin of the Kabbala* (Princeton: Princeton University Press, 1987), p. 409. Cf. Moshe Idel, "Nahmanides, *Kabbala, Halakha,* and Spiritual Leadership," in eds. Moshe Idel and Mortimer Ostow, *Jewish Mystical Leaders and Leadership in the 13th Century* (Northvale, New Jersey: Jason Aronson, 1998), pp. 65–69. For a further elaboration of this doctrine, see R. Ḥasdai Crescas, *Or ha-Shem* (Tel-Aviv, 5723/1963), IV, 1, 85a-86a; R. Isaac 'Arama, *Ḥazut Qasha* (Sabioneta, 5312/1552), XI, 23a; XII, 27a, b; R. Isaac Abarbanel, *Mif'alot Elohim* (Lemberg, 1863), VII, 3, 48d-51b; cf. ibid VIII. It should be noted, in passing, that belief in a return to a mythical time where the faithful emerge as regenerated beings is common to some very archaic as well as modern religions. For example, the mystical death in Jesus and resurrection through baptism; see Mircea Eliade, *Rites and the Symbols of Initiation* (New York: Harper & Row, 1975), chapter 6.

160. Indeed, some venerable rabbis held such belief; see, for example, the view cited by R. Abraham ibn 'Ezra on Ex. 31:13; cf. Lev. 25:2. For a penetrating discussion of the subject, see *The Conciliator*, Part I, pp. 41–45; Part II, pp. 272–275.

of 'Jewish devotion' was mass defection to Christianity, and the end of Jewish life in the Iberian Peninsula.

There was yet another reason why R. Adrete insisted that the 'destruction of the world' must be understood literally: it could be used to discredit Maimonides.[161] First, as prognosticated by the *qedoshim*-eschatology, after the annihilation of the world by the year 6000, resurrection of the dead would take place, which would be followed by a new world that they identified with 'the World to Come' of the rabbis. In the footsteps of Christian millenarians, they could identify 'the World to Come' of the rabbis with something quite earthly – not with Heaven, as taught by Maimonides. This meant that the 'banquet' promised to the pious would take place down here on earth and it would consist of unbelievable food (see above chapter 51). By way of contrast, Maimonidean interpretation of 'the World to Come' in spiritual, non-sensory terms would surely result in a crisis of faith.[162] A pragmatic consequence of the above was that Maimonideans could now be duly charged with 'heresy.'[163] There was

161. R. Abraham Maimonides called attention to the anti-Maimonidean method to explain some elements of an *aggada* metaphorically, while at the same time insisting that other elements must be interpreted in a most literal sense – and then proceeding to charge with heresy those failing to accept that 'doctrine' *literally*; see *Milḥamot ha-Shem*, pp. 69–71.
162. See above n. 155.
163. See R. Aaron Meshullam in *Kitab al-Rasa'yil*, p. 36. For Maimonides' definition of the 'World to Come' (עולם הבא) in terms of a transcendental realm after death see *MT Teshuba* 8:2. It has nothing to do with the Messianic Age, which concerns the *political* redemption of the *nation* of Israel; see ibid 8:7; *MT Melakhim* 12:2; cf. ibid 11:1, 3; 12:1, 4. Anti-Maimonideans took advantage of the different usage of this term, and argued that by stating that 'the World to Come' (עולם הבא) is incorporeal, Maimonides was in effect denying resurrection of the dead, and he was therefore a heretic; see Rabad *MT Teshuba*, 8:2, 8; cf. *Kitab al-Rasa'yil*, pp. 37–38. To answer this accusation, Maimonides composed the *Treatise on Resurrection*. Concerning the Maimonidean heresy, ascertaining that 'the banquet' promised to the faithful does not consist of real lip-smacking food, see the sharp-witted comment of Rabad, *MT Teshuba* 8:4, cf. *Kitab al-Rasa'yil*, pp. 33, 134–135.

another 'heresy' that belief in the annihilation of the world could help expose. By teaching that the Tora did not stipulate that the world would be destroyed (see *Guide* II, 27–29), Maimonides was in fact ascertaining the stability of the laws of physics, as well as the validity of science and rationality! To make sure that the attentive reader would not miss the point, R. Adrete declared at the opening of this *responsum* that he had nothing to say to "the heretics" (הכופרים). He then proceeded to identify them as those who maintain that "the impossible has a permanent nature" – a direct quotation from the *Guide* (III, 15).[164] Elsewhere, he equated this view with those heresies "which are forbidden to be heard, even more to be uttered."[165] We can now understand why R. Adrete was unyielding in his interpretation that the "world" would be annihilated: it was imperative to demonstrate the impermanent character of the physical laws. If one were to maintain that the "destruction" of the world meant the decay of *human society*, then there would no longer be any grounds to charge the Maimonideans with 'heresy.' More grievously, "those who have been graced by God" could not hound them for refusing to submit to "the true Kabbala."[166] On the other hand, by establishing that belief in the final destruction of this world is central to the Jewish faith, it could be positively 'proven' that 'nature' is not stable,

164. *Teshubot ha-Rishba*, vol. 1 #9, 3b-4a; cf. *Teshubot ha-Rishba* (Dimitrovsky), vol. 1, pp. 161–162; 296. R. Yeda'ya Bedersi noted that this was a direct allusion to Maimonides; see *Teshubot ha-Rishba*, vol. 1 #418, 168b. By the way, R. Joshua ibn Shu'eb, *Derashot, Beshallaḥ*, a disciple of R. Adrete, wrote that in an epistle composed by his teacher, he read that there are two types of 'impossibilities,' one epistemological, in relation to man, and another ontological, in relation to God. Only the second class is branded 'heretical.' I believe that what R. Shu'eb actually saw was *Teshubot ha-Rishba*, vol. 1 #418, 168b-169b s.v. *ha-nimna'*. However, this epistle was written by R. Yeda'ya Bedersi *to* R. Adrete! see below n. 297, and "Two Models of Jewish Spirituality," p. 41.

165. *Teshubot ha-Rishba* (Dimitrovsky), vol. 1, pp. 296–297. Cf. *Derashot ha-Ran*, III, pp. 104–105.

166. See the apology R. Yeda'ya Bedersi, in *Teshubot ha-Rishba*, vol. 1 #418; and ibid 162a, s.v. *aha*.

and thereby delegitimize the basis upon which rested the apparatus of the Geonim and the sages of Sepharad. Since

> ... all of their words are construed upon [the validity of] nature; however, since the most basic element in humans is dust, they would be forcefully pulled towards nature... Truly, it is impossible to join two opposites [Tora and nature] together.[167]

The purpose in insisting that some *aggadot* must be interpreted literally was to deny the stability of the physical laws.

This view was defended by one of the greatest luminaries to have graced Western intellectual history: the saintly R. Asher. We had the opportunity to see that R. Adrete, in order to perpetuate his legacy, made sure that R. Asher would be appointed spiritual leader of Toledo. In fact, echoing R. Adrete's ideology, R. Asher reasoned that from too much knowledge perdition would surely follow, as happened to the 'other' sages: "But from so much wisdom they went off down-deep and became corrupt, and were forced to repudiate the Law of Moses"[168] (see below chapter 57.) The intellectual foundations for the denial of nature were laid down by Ramban, among the earliest kabbalists in Spain, who borrowed it from the Mu'tazila (as cited and explained in the *Guide*). Basically, he believed that the very concept of religion rules out the admission of nature as an operative force. The world is affected by mysterious powers. The premature death of an embryo, for instance, is as wondrous as any of the miracles of Scripture: in both cases the hand of God had directly intervened *against* nature. That is why belief in Tora should equal negation of nature.

> When we examine [this matter] properly we will see that no one has a portion in the Tora of Moses our Teacher, may he rest in peace, unless he believes that all of our things and

167. *Teshubot ha-Rishba* (Dimitrovsky), vol. 1, pp. 341–342.
168. *Teshubot ha-Rosh* 55:9.

> actions, all of them, are miracles – not involved with nature or the procedure of the world – since the assurances made by the Tora are absolute miracles and wonders. If one were to say that nature controls everything and is active in the world, [then we must admit] that a man did not die or live because of some merit or iniquity. However, since we believe that God is the one who destroyed this embryo before his day would have come according to nature, [we must also admit] that the hand of God produced it and changed nature, as when the Red Sea split.[169]

Thus, according to Ramban, "No one could believe in the Tora and in the validity of nature, at all."[170] The only difference between "hidden miracles" (נסים נסתרים) and the more obvious ones is that in the latter the change of nature is evident,[171] whereas with the former the miracle is not obvious. Indeed, belief in "hidden miracles" (נסים נסת־רים) pertains to "the foundation" of Judaism (מיסודי התורה).[172] (From this perspective, the difference between the natural and the wondrous is equivocal. "I am amazed at Maimonides," quipped Ramban, "who minimized miracles and maximized nature"[173] (see appendix 57).

The omission of the *qabbala* of the Geonim and Old Sepharad from the above *responsum* was deliberate. This is a pivotal point considering that the term *qabbala* and its derivatives appear no less than twenty-seven times! Not only are we appraised of the importance of "the *qabbala* held in the hands of Israel from the mouth of

---

169. *Kitbe Ramban,* vol. 1, p. 153; see *Perush ha-Tora* on Gen. 17:1, and 46:15, vol. 1, pp. 98, 254.

170. *Kitbe Ramban,* vol. 1, p. 192; see *Perush ha-Tora* on Ex. 6:2, vol. 1, p. 303. The mystical view of nature had been previously proposed by the Mu'tazila, and adequately explained in the *Guide* I, 73 (Proposition VI), pp. 140 (l. 2)-142 (l. 2).

171. *Perush ha-Tora* on Gen. 17:1, vol. 1, pp. 98–99.

172. *Perush ha-Tora* on Gen. 46:15, vol. 1, p. 253. "*Yesode ha-Tora*" here implies criticism of Maimonides for not including this doctrine in his *Yesode ha-Tora*.

173. *Kitbe Ramban,* vol. 1, p. 154.

their sages," and "the *qabbala* that was successively received from one generation to the other from our teacher Moses," but also of "the *true qabbala*" (הקבלה האמיתית) which "was received by us," and even of "the *qabbala* resting in the hands of the old men and women of our people."[174] Omitting the *qabbala* of the Geonim and sages of old Sepharad signaled that it was worthless; ranking below, "the *qabbala* resting in the hands of the old men and women of our people." The reason is obvious. According to the *qabbala* of the Geonim and sages of old Sepharad, from R. Se'adya Gaon all the way through the Geonic transmittal of tradition, including R. Sherira, R. Hayye, and their disciples R. Ḥanan'el and R. Nissim, Talmudic *aggadot* may be explained figuratively, and they could even be dismissed altogether (אין סומכין על דברי אגדה).[175] This doctrine was accepted by the highest authorities of Old Sepharad, including R. Isaac Alfasi (1013–1103), R. Judah al-Bargeloni, and R. Judah ha-Levi.[176] In a letter addressed to R. al-Fakhkhar, chief anti-Maimonidean in Toledo, R. David Qimḥi reminded him that the principle stipulating that *aggadot* may be interpreted figuratively was not formulated by a group of trouble-makers, but by the highest authorities of Israel, from whose hands the Jewish people received the entire rabbinic apparatus, including the text of the Talmud and its interpretation.

> Concerning the *aggadot* we explain them in accordance with the laws and [rational] evidence, since they are bonded to

174. *Teshubot ha-Rishba*, vol. 1 #9, 4a.

175. *Geonic Responsa* (Heb.), ed. Elazar Hurvitz (New York, 1995), p. 211. See "*Milḥemet ha-Dat*," pp. 133–138, 151–152. The authority for this doctrine was none other than R. Sherira Gaon; see *The Mishna of Rabbi Eliezer* (Heb.), pp. 28–31. Cf. above Section IV, n. 177.

176. See *Studies in the Mishne Tora*, p. 192 n. 92 and ibid., pp. 184–186. Cf. *Iggerot ha-Rambam*, vol. 2, p. 461; *Kitab al-Rasa'yil*, pp. 36, 56, 134, 138. This is the place to point out that 'metaphoric locutions' are part of human speech; only those alien to the linguistic community would fail to grasp the figurative sense of such locutions. Consider such Hebrew expressions as "a cow said… a door said" in Mishna Nazir 2:2 and Nazir 10b.

> reason and allude to wisdom, as we were taught by our predecessors the Geonim, such as our teachers Sherira, Hayye, Isaac Alfasi, and the rest of the Geonim, pillars of the world and the foundations of the earth! Concerning the [interpretation] of *aggadot,* we depend and rely on their teachings and words, not on others![177]

A similar point was made by R. Samuel Saportas. Given that Rabbinic Judaism regarded the Geonim as the highest post-Talmudic authority, and unanimously agreed that *aggadot* may be interpreted figuratively or dismissed altogether, the matter should be regarded as settled.

> Behold, all of the great Geonim of our Tora agree that there are *aggadot* that were expressed figuratively, as you saw [from the preceding quotation] from R. Nissim Gaon of blessed memory, who had stated this point clearly. In addition to him, many Geonim, the fathers of the Talmudic legacy and *qabbala* – and there is nothing higher than their words to measure them by – [confirm to this principle], particularly R. Hayye Gaon who wrote at length on this matter in his commentary on Ḥagiga.[178]

Confronting the anti-Maimonideans for rejecting the tradition of the Geonim, R. Saportas remarked:

> I am very astonished at you, O superior scholars, for you have cast these matters behind your back! What is most amazing about that is that you damned anyone who does not explain the words of our rabbis and their *aggadot* according to Rashi.[179]

---

177. "*Iggerot Qena'ot,*" in *Qobeṣ Teshubot ha-Rambam,* III, 3d.
178. See "*Milḥemet ha-Dat,*" p. 151; see ibid pp. 133–138, 152. Cf. the citation in R. Moses al-Ashqar, *She'elot wu-Tshubot* (5719/1959), #117, p. 313a.
179. "*Milḥemet ha-Dat,*" p. 152.

More critically, as noted by R. Samuel Saportas, according to the Talmud, R. Qaṭina's view was not accepted by all.[180]

We may add that demanding that *aggadot* be interpreted literally, while at the same time interpreting the *qedoshim*-hymns in the most extreme, farfetched ways does appear a bit disingenuous (see above chapter 51).[181]

R. Adrete had acknowledged Ramban as the highest rabbinic authority, and said of him: "Our Teacher, the Great Rabbi… we have nobody greater than him in wisdom, in authority, and in fear of sin."[182] Nonetheless, he discarded his advice. Appropriately, Ramban understood that an esoteric ideology – no matter what – is, and should remain, personal. Therefore, he maintained that it should not be imposed on the general public, and advocated a policy of conciliation. "It is not possible to compel all of Israel to be Ḥasidim!"[183] Under the leadership of R. Adrete, the anti-Maimonideans endeavored to prove him wrong. In a bold step, they charged ahead into battle to make heroic ideology and heroic virtue the earmark of all Israel – like Don Quixote who "sallied forth into battle." It should be a matter of some importance to note that as R. Adrete marched forth in Holy War, he borrowed the battle cry of the celebrated Korah, *verbatim*:, who charged against Moses: "that all the congregation is holy" (כי-כל העדה כלם קדושים), and therefore Moses had no right to "set himself above the assembly of the Lord" (Num. 16:3). In similar fashion, R. Adrete justified the anti-Maimonidean ban on the grounds that "the entire congregation is holy (כל העדה כלם קדושים), except for some insignificant members – the community leaders – who because of

180. *"Milḥemet ha-Dat,"* p. 151. See appendix 57; cf. R. Samuel Laniado, *Keli Faz* (Venice, 5417/1657), 18c.

181. The association of *peshaṭ* with *aggada* is an oxymoron. The term *peshaṭ* ('spread out') refers to an interpretation of the *text* of Scripture that became 'generally accepted'; see above chapter 9. Moreover, unlike *halakha*, *aggada* lacks an authoritative text, and therefore it cannot be 'transmitted'; see *Golden Doves*, pp. 89–96.

182. *Teshubot ha-Rishba*, vol. 1, #413, 145a.

183. *"Iggeret ha-Ramban,"* in *Qobeṣ Teshubot ha-Rambam*, III, 10c.

their rank stand at the head of the people."[184] Thus, as proposed by Koraḥ when challenging Moses leadership, their authority should be ignored.

184. *Teshubot ha-Rishba,* vol. 1 #416, 152a. See above nn. 138–139.

# Chapter 58
# Cult of the Occult

Belief in magic permeated ancient and medieval society. Although Scripture and the rabbis opposed magic and demonology, many Jews, even among the learned and pious, were influenced by the general trend of their times, and either rationalized or tried to circumvent these prohibitions. The rabbis endeavored to prevent the people from following pagan practices. On this basic issue, Professor Lieberman wrote:

> The mirror of Rabbinic literature reflects a continuous war between the Rabbis and the masses. The Rabbis warned the townspeople not to follow the way of the Gentiles, not to adopt the Hellenistic manner of life, but most bitterly they fought the superstitions of the ignorant country people. The history of this fight of the Rabbis against the Gentile manner of life and popular superstitions is recorded in almost every branch of Rabbinic literature.[185]

185. Saul Lieberman, *Greek in Jewish Palestine* (New York: Philipp Feldheim, 1965), p. 92. For a general overview, see MT 'Aboda Zara. For a study of this problem in Rabbinic times, see *Greek in Jewish Palestine*, pp. 97–114. Of special interest is the ancient material on Jewish magic, edited and annotated by Professor M. Margalioth, *Sefer ha-Razim* (Jerusalem: The American Academy for Jewish Research, 1966). The following anecdote may illustrate the kind of rationalization justifying the practice of sorcery. Sometime ago, I met an old man from Damascus, who told me how he and some rabbis performed a ritual known in Judeo-Spanish as *endulgado*, to cure a young man who had fallen sick. The

Prudently, some of these practices were tolerated: witch-hunting was never popular among the ancient rabbis of Israel. Again, quoting Lieberman:

> Their efforts not always bore fruit, particularly among the masses and the uneducated: But it is hardly possible that the great masses of the Jewish people in the big towns conducted themselves in conformity with the idealistic views of the Rabbis... The ignorant people... adopted their neighbors' belief in magic, astrology and all kinds of superstitions in defiance of the Written and Oral Laws.[186]

When examining how the rabbis dealt with the widespread belief in superstition and magic, Professor Lieberman showed that occasionally, when the rabbis were convinced that it would be futile to try to eradicate these practices, they changed their content and gave them a religious meaning:

> The Rabbis of Babylonia did not fight this superstition, but, on the contrary, sanctioned it by endowing it with a religious character.... The same may be said of many other ceremonies.... They may have had their origin in popular superstitions, but the Rabbis reinterpreted them until they were transformed into ceremonies with true religious content.[187]

---

man had some rabbinical knowledge, and when I pointed out to him that most authorities regarded this ritual as idolatrous, he responded: "You don't understand. Otherwise the boy would have died; we had to save his life." A similar attitude justified anti-Maimonideans for breaking the law: there are imperatives that excuse transgression of the law.

186. *Greek in Jewish Palestine*, p. 91. In this respect we should remind the reader that among Jews in the Middle East, astrologers belonged to the lowest stratum of society; see S. D. Goitein, *Religion in a Religious Age* (Cambridge, Mass: Association for Jewish Studies, 1974), p. 15.

187. *Greek in Jewish Palestine*, p. 106.

At this point a fundamental question arises: is there any cogent distinction between 'religion' and 'magic' or 'superstition?' According to the Book and *ketab* and *mikhtab* systems, Jewish rituals are propitious not because of some supernatural power within, but because God and Israel established so in a freely contracted *berit* (see above chapter 5). Other rituals are *'aboda zara*, because they are grounded on the preeminence of might and the presumed power to manipulate paranormal factors. Once halakha is subordinated to kabbalistic considerations, the difference between the realm of 'religion' and 'magic' vanishes. Put differently, outside the context of a contracted Law, 'religion' is an expression of 'violence' and it can be sustained only in a culture of might. By endeavoring to reinterpret Judaism in terms of the paranormal, Kabbala acted in the opposite direction of the rabbis.

Before addressing the nature of the anti-Maimonidean crusade, let me dispose of a misconception. Their attack on Maimonides was not based on their alleged distaste for Aristotle. Ramban himself made reference to Aristotle throughout his works. Nor was it a simplistic aversion to 'rationalism.' Ramban did not hesitate to discard the view of the Tora concerning the formation of rainbows (Gen. 9:12) in favor of the more 'rational' view of the "Greeks."[188] In fact, Ramban and his devotees were much more 'independent' and 'rationalistic' in areas

188. *Perush ha-Ramban* on Gen. 9:12, vol. 1, p. 64. Ramban acknowledged that according to Scripture the rainbow was created after the deluge. "However, we must believe in the view of the Greeks that the rainbow comes through nature from the rays of the sun on the humid air." After some discussion, he said: "whether the rainbow was [created] now [as Scripture says] or it was through nature…" Then, he goes on to discuss "the hidden mystery" that he is about to reveal. This coincides with the doctrine about the "empty" sense of the Tora, which can be discarded in favor of the "Greeks," in contradistinction to the "soul," which he would be infusing with his explanations of the Tora. See *Teshubot ha-Rishba*, vol. 1 #9, 4a s. v. *ve-da' ki kol ḥakham*, where he spells out the criterion of "the pious" (חסידים) for making this type of exegesis. On the attitude of Ramban's circle towards philosophy, see Israel Ta-Shma, "Rabbi Yonah Girondi: Spirituality and Leadership," in eds. Moshe Idel and Mortimer Ostow, *Jewish Mystical Leaders and Leadership in the 13th Century* (Northvale, New Jersey: Jason Aronson, 1998), pp. 155–177.

affecting *their* ideology – magic and the cult of the occult – than Maimonides and his school were towards Aristotle's *Physics* and *Metaphysics*.[189] Jewish law prohibits astrology. The Tora describes "astrologers, augurs, and sorcerers" as the "abominations (תועבות) of the nations" (Deut. 18:9). They are "God's abomination" (תועבת), and "because of these abominations (תועבות)" the Canaanites were expelled from the Holy Land (Deut. 18:12). Nonetheless, Ramban maintained that, "astrology and augury are not abominations, and God did not expel the Canaanites because of it, since everybody desires to know their future." After examining different techniques of augury, like the flight and cry of birds, and astrological signs, Ramban remarked: "all these are not an abomination (תועבה) among the nations." He further added that these acts "should be regarded as smart of them"[190] (see appendix 65). Belief in the validity of augury and divination conditioned his understanding of prophecy. They are more or less the same: one is operative in the Holy Land via prophets and the other outside Israel via augurs and sorcerers. Ramban maintained that the biblical injunctions against magic only apply in the Land of Israel and for Jews alone. He found support for this view in the fact that this injunction was formulated when Israel was about to enter the Promised Land (Deut. 18:9). Since they had prophets, they did not "have any need for it (magic), because [God] will send to them prophets there." However, "Gentiles needed to learn about their future from sorcerers and magicians."[191] It should follow that in the Diaspora, with the absence of prophecy, Jews are no longer forbidden to delve into necromancy and the supernatural. Concerning the use of witchcraft in self-defense against magical acts, R. Adrete wrote: "It may be

189. See *Homo Mysticus*, pp. 89–126.

190. *Perush ha-Tora* on Deut. 18:9, vol. 2, pp. 427–428. For a pilpulistic defense of this cult by a famous devotee; see R. Baḥye b. Asher, *Be'ur 'al ha-Tora*, on Gen. 15:5, vol. 1, p. 149.

191. *Kitbe Ramban*, vol. 1, p. 150. Cf. H. R. Trevor-Roper, *The European Witch-Craze* (New York: Harper Torch Books, 1967), pp. 92–93.

possible to engage in those forbidden (magical) practices to repeal an act of witchery performed by a sorcerer."[192]

The rabbis relate that a proselyte, who had been an astrologer before converting to Judaism, decided to refrain from taking a trip because the astrological signs were not propitious. "Then he backtracked, saying: 'Haven't I fastened myself to this holy nation so that I could dissociate myself from these matters?! For the sake of my Maker, I shall go!'"[193] In opposition, Ramban was an ardent astrologer. Although the Tora prohibits the manufacturing and usage of images, Ramban maintained that since astrological images can manipulate the spirits, such images are licit. He arrived at this conclusion from his general theory on magic, according to which properly manufactured astrological images have the power to divert ill omens. Quoting a kabbalist-astrologer, he ascertained that through the manipulation of astrological images it is possible to turn an astrological *NeGa'* [נגע = 'plague'] into an astrological *'oNeG* [ענג = 'delight'].[194] Given that there is a relationship between the distribution of power in the zodiac and in the human body, Ramban practiced astrological medicine. He also designed an astrological diet, which he registered in a poem.[195] He was renowned for his uncanny ability to manufacture

192. *Teshubot ha-Rishba* (Dimitrovsky), vol. 1, p. 305, cf. p. 306. See ed. Leon A. Feldman, "*Teshubat ha-Rishba le-Ḥakham me-Ḥakhme ha-Goyim 'al Emunat ha-Yiḥud*," *Sinai*, Jubilee Volume, 100 (1987), vol. 2, pp. 637–639.

193. Y. Shabbat VI, 9, 8d. On the correct version and interpretation of this passage; see *Yerushalmi Ki-Fshu⌧o*, pp. 115–116. For a further analysis, see *Greek in Jewish Palestine*, pp. 149–152; and idem, "On Adjurations among the Jews," (Heb.) *Tarbiz* 27 (1958), pp. 183184. See, however, Ramban, *Teshubot*, #104, p. 154. Incidentally, in a rabbinic source cited in *Greek in Jewish Palestine*, p. 149, astrological consultations are referred to as consulting with "the idols," cf. ibid. n. 28. This coincides with Maimonides' view, *Iggerot ha-Rambam*, vol. 2, p. 480: "…that astrology – those matters are the essence of idolatry." see R. Abraham Maimonides, *Perush*, p. 454.

194. *Perush ha-Tora* on Deut. 18:9, vol. 2, p. 427. The astrologer probably was R. 'Azriel; see his *Commentary on Talmudic Aggadoth* (Heb.), ed. Isaiah Tishby (Jerusalem: Magnes Press, 1982), p. 28.

195. See *Kitbe Ramban*, vol. 1, pp. 385–386.

zodiacal images for medical purposes. For example, an image of a lion to cure the right kidney, or of a virgin for the left kidney, etc.[196] To justify this practice, Ramban did not hesitate to mention that there were "philosophers" – i.e., necromancers – "who drew spirit into the images and [awarded them] speech."[197] A factor in his attitude toward the practice of scientific medicine was accepting the early Christian belief that sicknesses are a divine punishment, and consequently the practice of scientific medicine is nothing more than a human effort to defy God's will.[198]

In the footsteps of Ramban, there were others who practiced astrological medicine. R. Adrete made use of astrological images. Defending himself against criticism, he responded: "our teacher, the great Rabbi Ramban of blessed memory, permitted and manufactured [such images]. And there was no one like him in wisdom, seasoning, and fear of sin."[199] It should be noted, however, that the alleged "fear of sin," did not meet rabbinic standards. The rabbis reported a tradition that King Hezekiah ordered "to melt down the copper-snake made by Moses and took out of circulation a Book of Medicine" (see Num. 21:9; Mishna Pesaḥim 4:9; cf. Rosh HaShana 3:8). The rabbis explained that the reason for melting the copper-snake was because people were offering incense for healing purposes (see II Kings 18:4; Tosefta, 'Aboda Zara 3:19, p. 465; *AdRN* I, 2, pp. 11–12). According to Maimonides, the "Book" that was taken out of circulation was a treatise on astrological medicine (of the type practiced by Ramban).[200]

196. See *Teshubot ha-Rishba*, vol. 1, #167, at the end. His reputation for the manufacturing of such images was well established; see Joseph Shatzmiller, "The Forms of the Twelve Constellations: A 14th Century Controversy," (Heb.). In *Shlomo Pines Jubilee Volume*, Part II, *Jerusalem Studies in Jewish Thought* 9 (1990), pp. 400, 402–403.

197. *Perush ha-Tora* on Deut. 18:9, vol. 2, p. 426. See appendix 65; and cf. above n. 185.

198. See José Faur, "*Zekhut ha-Rofe...*" *Dine Israel* 7 (1976), pp. 79–80.

199. *Teshubot ha-Rishba* (Dimitrovsky), vol. 1, p. 282; see "Two Models of Jewish Spirituality," pp. 35–40; and "*Zekhut ha-Rofe ...* ," pp. 82–83.

200. See *Perush ha-Mishnayot*, *Pesaḥim* 4:10, vol. 2, pp. 176–179; cf. *Guide* III, 37, p.

Even anti-Maimonideans were shocked. R. Abba Mare (14th century), a leading anti-Maimonidean in southern France, replied:

> ... if one were to permit such an image, then we would also have to permit other images. For the reason that just like they manufactured this special image for constellation Aries, they also manufactured special images for all the other eleven members of the Zodiac, to cure each of the main members [of the human body]. Were we to permit this, people would neither pray to God nor go to physicians (cf. II Chr. 16:12). A wise man told me that there is a special book on the subject, which divides the celestial sphere into forty-eight images. These are: the twelve zodiacs, plus twenty-one images to the south and fifteen to the north. Out of these, are designed all of the works of witchcraft and those [astrological] images. Some of those images are made with a special metal, and they are wrapped with a cloth dyed in a particular color, and incense of musk or wax is offered to them – and there is no doubt that this is idolatry – blessed be the Lord that separated us from them! If you would permit [only] a small image from that book, then you should permit every one, since all these types [of images] are one and the same.[201]

And now a question: within the boundaries of common rationality, is there any cogent distinction between the images designed by Ramban and R. Adrete and those of the Christian liturgy?

---

402 (l. 2). R. Menahem Me'iri, *Bet ha-Beḥira* on Pesaḥim 56a, p. 204a, noted that such a practice "is forbidden according to the Tora." On the Jewish position on astrology, see *Bet ha-Beḥira* on Sanhedrin 68a, pp. 251–254. On the positive attitude of the rabbis towards the practice of scientific medicine, see "*Ve-Niṣḥu ...*," pp. 120–121, and "*Zekhut ha-Rofe ...*," pp. 80–86.

201. *Teshubot ha-Rishba* (Dimitrovsky), vol. 1, pp. 274–275.

# Chapter 59
# The Anti-Scientific Obstinacy of the Maimonideans

The fault with the Maimonideans was that they had the impudence to classify sorcery and witchcraft – and therefore the whole dynamics of spiritism and demonology (= *ruchnios*) – as "lies and falsehood."[202] That was a shameful lie, designed to hurt the feelings of good people! Referring to the Maimonideans as "those who pretend to be wise and emulate the Greek" (a code name for Maimonides),[203] Ramban ascertained that their belief could be proven false by the facts provided by "the science of necromancy" (חכמת הנגרומנסיה). Discussing the different types of idolatry among pagans, Ramban wrote:

> ... there were those who went back to worship demons (שדים), which are spirits, as I will explain later with God's help. Some of which are in charge over the nations (enabling them) to become the lords of the land, to defeat their foes and those who encounter them – as is well-known about them from the science of necromancy (מחכמת הנגרומנסיה).[204]

202. *MT 'Aboda Zara* 11:16. Cf. Introduction, *Perush ha-Mishnayot*, vol. 1, p. 5; *Iggerot ha-Rambam*, vol. 2, pp. 479–480. For background and analysis, see Shlomo Pines, "On the Concept of 'Spirits,'" (Heb.) *Tarbiz* 57 (1988), pp. 511–540.

203. On the precise meaning of this expression, see "Two Models of Jewish Spirituality," 32 n. 91.

204. *Perush ha-Ramban* on Ex. 20:3, vol. 1, p. 393. "Magic," R. Nissim Gerondi informs

Regarding the whole ambit of spiritism, Ramban explained:

> ... it is known from the science of necromancy (מחכמת הנגרו־מנסיה) and also the [incorporeal] minds. There are also hints about them in the Tora, to those who understand their mystery. I cannot explain it because then we would have to shut the mouth of those who pretend to know nature, and follow the Greek – who denies everything except what he discerns, and he and his evil disciples had the audacity to disbelieve [the Ḥasidim, see below] – that everything which he did not detect by his own acumen is untrue.[205]

The term "Greek" above does not refer to Aristotle. Ramban himself quoted Aristotle numerous times by name. Moreover, in no place did Aristotle deny the existence of demons. In fact, during the Middle Ages a work on demons attributed to him was circulated. Rather, it refers to Maimonides, who explicitly denied the existence of demons. For reasons of prudence – Maimonides was highly venerated by the people, and a blatant criticism of him could have been counter-productive – rather than consideration, Ramban chose to refer to him by innuendo.[206]

The science of necromancy is intimately connected with astrology, another science that Ramban mastered. To substantiate the merits of this science, Ramban, who had given serious thought to the matter, quoted approvingly a work of a necromancer who was also a master

---

us, "is one of the divisions of physical science," *Derashot ha-Ran*, III, p. 105.

205. *Perush ha-Ramban* on Lev. 16:8, vol. 2, p. 91.

206. On the issue of 'demons' in Maimonides, see *Studies in the Mishne Tora*, pp. 1–2; *Homo Mysticus*, pp. 127–129, 132, 151. On Aristotle's work on demons, see A. C. Pearson, "Demons and Spirits," *Encyclopedia of Religion and Ethics*, vol. 4 (Edinburgh: T. &T. Clark, 1911), pp. 193–194. Ramban used innuendo to express his criticism of those who did not believe in augury. In *Perush ha-Tora* on Deut. 18:9, vol. 2, p. 427, he referred to them as "those pretending to be saintly" (מתחסדים), and to R. Abraham ibn 'Ezra as "someone pretending to be saintly" (מתחסד).

astrologer (see appendix 65). Ramban's faith in necromancy contributed to the shaping of his beliefs in the Tora. The legible text of the Tora is marginal to the subtext composed of magical names, which constitute the very "soul" (נשמה) of the Tora. In a study penned either by him or a member of his circle, we learn that the Tora "is not only empty as in its common sense (ריקנית כפשטה), but it has also a soul (נשמה)." Regardless of what Ramban had in mind, in a dense Christian environment, this distinction will indubitably suggest Paul's distinction of "letter and spirit" (Cor. 3:6), in support of the abolition of the Tora.[207] Paul's distinction is fundamental to Ramban's theurgy: "the whole Tora in its entirety consists of names of God."[208] The subtext consists of the letters consecutively written, without spaces between them, which can be rearranged into secret formulas to conjure mysterious names of God, with super-magical power. "We have a tradition (Kabbala)… that the entire Tora, from beginning to end, consists of [magical] names."[209] The legible text was transmitted in writing by Moses to the people. The hermetic subtext, comprising holy names, was transmitted to Moses orally.[210] "In every section of the Pentateuch," he wrote, "there is the name by which that thing was created or made, or how that thing was realized."[211] King Solomon's wisdom, too, came through the possession of these names.[212] Likewise, Moses brought the ten plagues and split the sea because of a special

207. See *Ma'amar 'al Penimiyut ha-Tora*, in *Kitbe Ramban*, vol. 2, p. 468; and "Two Models of Jewish Spirituality," p. 30.

208. Introduction, *Perush ha-Ramban*, vol. 1, p. 6; *Torat ha-Shem Temima*, in *Kitbe Ramban*, vol. 1, p. 168. The same theory is found in R. 'Azriel, *Commentary on Talmudic Aggadoth* (Heb.), p. 76, ll. 19–20.

209. *Kitbe Ramban*, vol. 1, p. 168. There is no source for such a doctrine in rabbinic literature.

210. Introduction, *Perush ha-Ramban*, vol. 1, p. 7. There is no source for such a doctrine in rabbinic literature.

211. Introduction, in *Perush ha-Ramban*, vol. 1, p. 6. The same doctrine is found in R. 'Azriel, *Commentary on Talmudic Aggadoth* (Heb.), p. 76, ll. 19–20.

212. Introduction, in *Perush ha-Ramban*, vol. 1, pp. 5–6.

name that was revealed to him.[213] Knowledge of a certain name will empower an individual to resurrect the dead.[214] Another "produces the secret miracles made for the pious."[215] "It is well known to many," he solemnly declared, that these names were "used by the pious of the generations." In this fashion, the pious "knew how to kill and to resurrect, to desolate and to destroy, to demolish and to annihilate, to build and to plant."[216] Moses transmitted the secret names to superior men who managed to pass them on through unbeknownst channels to the hermetic circles in and around Catalonia.[217]

Ramban himself was personally familiar with "the science of magic and augury."[218] Through the pietistic circles in Germany

213. *Perush ha-Ramban* on Gen. 17:1, vol. 1, pp. 98–99.
214. *Kitbe Ramban,* vol. 1, p. 168.
215. *Perush ha-Ramban* on Gen. 17:1, vol. 1, p. 98; cf. *Kitbe Ramban,* vol. 1, pp. 191–192.
216. *Kitbe Ramban,* vol. 1, p. 168. See above, n. 151.
217. See, Introduction, in *Perush ha-Ramban,* vol. 1, p. 7, cf. p. 6. For some background, see Gershom Scholem, *On the Kabbala* (New York: Schocken Books, 1969), pp. 37–42. Eventually, this textuological approach affected the core concept and function of the liturgy. The prayer book was transfigured into a series of strategically placed series of conjurations, made up of the rearranged consonants of the text, designed to maneuver and control the realm of the divine. Some conjurations have a comical flavor. The following is one example. A most solemn prayer pronounced at the end of the Sephardic services (but not at the Spanish and Portuguese) in the night of Rosh HaShana, invokes the "great and holy name diacarnosa" (ולמען השם הגדול והקדוש דיקרנוסה) that is supposed to be encoded in the subtexts of two Scriptural passages. This superlative magical name is nothing more than the Spanish "dea carnosa" or "fleshy" – probably in the sense of a 'portly' – "goddess!" Let us not forget that until recently, only plump ladies were regarded as sexually attractive. Casually, I brought this point to the attention of an acquaintance. Upon realizing the gravity of the matter, he wished to request from the rabbi to remove said conjuration from the prayer. I remember telling him that since nobody, including the rabbi, had the foggiest idea of what they were saying, there was no point in removing it. On the influence of Kabbala on the Sephardic liturgy, particularly after the Expulsion, see the note of Stefan C. Reif, *Judaism and Hebrew Prayer* (Cambridge: Cambridge University Press, 1993), pp. 205–206.
218. See *Perush ha-Ramban* on Ex. 20:3, vol. 1, pp. 392–393; and "Two Models of Jewish Spirituality," pp. 35–40.

(חסידי אשכנז) he became acquainted with demonology. "I have heard that the norm in Germany is to practice demonology (לעסוק בדברי השדים), they conjure them, send them, and use them for different tasks."[219] R. Adrete, too, was privy to similar information: "I have heard explicitly that the pious from Germany (חסידי אלמנייא) practiced demonology, they conjure them, send them (to perform chores), and use them for various tasks."[220] The "handbooks on demonology" (כתבי שמושי השדים) were packed with valuable information; e.g., that the mother of the first demon was no other than Ashmedon's wife, "From whom the demons (השדים) were born."[221] There were other such valuable facts known from the "ancient and authentic sciences" of chirognomy and chiromancy, corroborating the realm of the occult. A case in point is that of a Byzantine Jew, known as "the Greek." He had been tutored on the niceties of these sciences by "the pious from Germany" (חסידי אשכנז). This Jew "could tell amazing things just by looking at someone's physiognomy."[222] Ramban was personally familiar with "the science of magic and augury."[223] Through the pietistic circles in Germany, he learned demonology, and was apprised of their various activities.[224] These sciences are not peripheral. In Ramban's mind, demonology and spiritism stand at the heart and soul of Judaism. Consider this undeniable truth: Moses was beheld as a superior master of witchcraft and necromancy. After enumerating the areas in which Moses excelled, Ramban added: "higher than all that was that he knew all

219. *Kitbe Ramban,* vol. 1, p. 381; cf. p. 146 and *Teshubot ha-Ramban,* #104, p. 157. See "Two Models of Jewish Spirituality," pp. 33–34.

220. *Teshubot ha-Rishba,* vol. 1 #413, p. 149a; *Teshubot ha-Rishba* (Dimitrovsky), vol. 1, p. 307. He probably obtained this information from scholars from Ashkenaz who had joined his school; cf. *Teshubot ha-Rishba,* vol. 1, #396, p. 140a.

221. *Perush ha-Ramban* on Gen. 4:22, vol. 1, p. 46. *Cf Kitbe Ramban,* vol. 1, p. 168, and *Zohar* I, 19b.

222. *Kitbe Ramban,* vol. 1, p. 162.

223. See Introduction, *Perush ha-Ramban,* vol. 1, p. 6.

224. See *Perush ha-Ramban* on Gen. 4:22, vol. 1, p. 46; and *Kitbe Ramban,* vol. 1, p. 146; cf. *Teshubot ha-Ramban,* #104, p. 157.

types of witchcraft, and from there he would ascend to the spheres, to the heavens and their hosts." King Solomon, too, "was expert in witchcraft, which was the wisdom of Egypt."[225]

To Ramban and his circle, spiritism (*ruchnios*), occultism, and demonology constitute the matrix of religion. By denying belief in demons and spiritism (*ruchnios*), Maimonideans were rejecting the possibility of religion. That is why their teaching represents the rankest of all heresies, something more heinous than pre-Mosaic paganism:

> In those pristine days, as were the days of Moses our Teacher, may he rest in peace, everyone knew this. Given that in those days the sciences were all (related to) spiritism (*ruchnios*), involving the entire gamut of demons and witchcraft, and the various types of incense [needed to attract] the forces of heaven. Because they were close to the time of the Creation of the world and of the Flood, nobody denied Creation of the world or rebelled against God. Although they wanted to benefit themselves by worshipping the sun, moon, and constellations, and they would build for them images to receive the heavenly power.... At any rate, at the time of Moses our Teacher, may he rest in peace! – no one was [as] wicked or heretical as to deny these (truths). The only thing that the gentile nations doubted was prophecy.[226]

Within the ordinary limits of human understanding, the esoterics of spiritism (*ruchnios*) is indistinguishable from the old cosmic sacrality, common to pagan humanity. For reasons of mental health and stability, both the rabbis and the Church resisted this. It still lingered, however, among the peasants and kabbalists in Europe. Addressing this matter, Mircea Eliade wrote:

225. Introduction, *Perush ha-Ramban*, vol. 1, pp. 3, 6.

226. *Kitbe Ramban*, vol. 1, p. 147. See "Two Models of Jewish Spirituality," pp. 30–34.

> Although in the eyes of a Puritan the cosmic religion of the southeastern European peasants could have been considered a form of paganism, it was still a "cosmic, Christian liturgy." A similar process occurred in medieval Judaism. Thanks mainly to the tradition embodied in the Kabbala, a "cosmic sacrality," which seemed to have been irretrievably lost after the rabbinical reform had been successfully recovered.[227]

In Old Sepharad, spiritism and magic were regarded as nonsense. Here is how R. Samuel ibn Tibbon (ca. 1160–ca. 1230), the Hebrew translator of the *Guide,* defined 'spiritism' – the matrix of Ramban's religion:

> *Spiritism* (רוחניות). Some heathens believed that the emanations of stars descended upon images specially built for the stars, as well as upon the *Asheroth,* which they specially planted for this purpose. They imagined that these images and *Asheroth* knew the future, as per prophecy, and that they [the astral emanations] spoke to them.[228]

Were one to accept the Maimonidean view, then it would be necessary to conclude that the pietistic teachers were gravely disturbed men, and that their kabbalistic visions and teachings were nothing more than disjointed hallucinations. Ramban was gifted with a sharp, quick wit, and understood quite well the implications that denial of demonology meant, for him personally and for the brand of spiritism (*ruchnios*) that he was promoting. Hence, his anger at Maimonides and the Maimonideans: they were heartless. Their real objective was

227. Mircea Eliade, *The Quest: History and Meaning in Religion* (Chicago: Chicago University Press, 1969), Preface (n. p.). On the notion of cosmic sacrality and its place in Kabbala, see *Homo Mysticus*, pp. 3–5.

228. In the appendix to his Hebrew translation of the *Guide*, s. v. רוחניות. For further background, see *Kuzari*, I, 79, pp. 23–24; I, 97, p. 34; IV, 23, p. 178. Cf. "A Crisis of Categories," pp. 52–53; and *Homo Mysticus*, pp. 11–13.

to hurt saintly men like him, who had witnessed demons and had kept intimate contact with them and other supernatural beings. "There are many pretending to be saints, and reject divinations," wrote Ramban alluding to the Maimonideans, "claiming that there is no truth in them. Arguing: who could have told a raven or a swallow what the future will be?!" Pointedly, he reminds these disbelievers: "We cannot disagree with facts that are witnessed by everyone."[229] Indeed, these sorts of facts were attested to by thousands and thousands of people, like night-flying witches, metamorphoses, and witches' Sabbaths, filling the late medieval and Renaissance world. These facts, as so aptly put by Trevor-Roper, could be "disbelieved only (as a doctor of the Sorbonne wrote in 1609) by those of unsound mind."[230] Thus, the anguish in Ramban's impassionate cry:

> Look here at the cruelty of the head of the philosophers [=Maimonides] and his obstinacy, may his name be blotted out! For he denies many things witnessed by many. We also witnessed their reality, and they [these realities] are fully acknowledged throughout the world.[231]

Those who investigated the psychological grounds of demonology offered the following description:

> Because it often appears as something unconscious that is independent of, and often counter to, my conscious intentions, it is experienced as something happening outside of me. That is the demon. As Paul says, they cause me not to do the good that I would do and to carry out the evil that I would

229. *Perush ha-Ramban* on Deut. 18:3, vol. 2, pp. 427–428. Cf. Rabad on *MT 'Aboda Zara* 11:4; *Teshubot ha-Rishba*, vol. 1, #413, 146b. On the mental process peculiar to divination, see *Homo Mysticus*, pp. 59–60. For a bird's eye view of some of their main doctrines and ideas, see *History of the Jews*, vol. 3, pp. 547–558.
230. *The European Witch-Craze*, p. 92.
231. *Kitbe Ramban*, vol. 1, p. 147.

> not (Rom. 7:19). Since they often thwart my will, I experience them as alien to my ego. Thus there is a strong tendency to set them up outside myself. The danger there, of course, is that they then elude my ability to deal with them. In that case, they can easily transform into my neighbor.[232]

A similar insight was offered by Eliade:

> The conception of the enemy as a demonic being, a veritable incarnation of the powers of evil, has also survived until our own days. *The psychoanalysis of these mythic images that still animate the modern world will perhaps show us the extent to which we project our own destructive desires upon the "enemy"*[233] (Italics added).

Many Jews in Antiquity and throughout pre-modern times, even among the pious and learned, espoused some of the beliefs prevailing in pagan society. However, unlike Christians, Jews indulging in magic and demonology did not maintain that spiritism was a cardinal principle of Judaism. In this respect, the difference with Christianity is profound. One can be a good Jew and not believe in spiritism, but one cannot accept Christianity unless he is willing to acknowledge the validity of magic and demonology, upon which Jesus' ministry rests. "In the New Testament," writes a renowned psychiatrist, "Jesus is the conqueror of demons, the exorcist, who at the end of time will render the Devil and his demons powerless (I Jn. 3:8)."[234] When

232. Alfred Ribi, *Demons of the Inner World* (Boston & London: Shambala, 1990), p. 192. These demons are related to the 'traces' roaming throughout the unconscious mind, discussed by Maimonides; see *Homo Mysticism*, pp. 132–137.

233. Mircea Eliade, *Images and Symbols* (Princeton: Princeton University Press, 1991), p. 38.

234. *Demons of the Inner World*, p. 25. For an historical analysis of this subject, see the studies of F. C. Conybeare, "Demonology of the New Testament," *Jewish Quarterly Review* 8 (1896), pp. 576–608; *idem*, "Christian Demonology," *Jewish Quarterly Review* 9 (1897), pp. 59–114.

"the Council wishes to present the Church as God's kingdom," we are taught, "it appeals to the miracles of Jesus and specifically to his exorcisms."[235] In fact, "it was precisely with reference to exorcisms that Jesus made the well-known statement: 'The kingdom of God is upon you.' [Lk. 11:20; see Matt. 12:28]." Modern Catholic theologians confirm this belief. At the Vatican Council II, the Sacred Congregation for Divine Worship, pointed out that to deny demonology is

> ... to admit that at these critical moments of the consciousness of Jesus, despite its evident lucidity and self-mastery in the face of the Jews, was in fact, subject to delusions and that his world lacked all consistency.[236]

What was truly revolutionary about the anti-Maimonidean kabbalists was not merely their indulgence in magic and demonology, but their commitment to the Christian principle that these beliefs are crucial to 'religion.' In this manner, they promoted beliefs and modes of thought that placed Judaism in a position of strategic vulnerability in respect to Christianity. Because the kabbalistic ideology brought the Jewish population very close to the thinking patterns and demeanor of the Christian population, it facilitated Jewish acculturation to the social majority, and acceptance of Christian canons of truth and thinking. This will become more apparent upon recalling that for the Church, the mass with all of its paraphernalia was the greatest magic act ever: "the mass, with its music, words of consecration, incense, lights, wine, and the supreme magical effect – transubstantiation." This is the reason that the Church condemned magic, "the Church has her own magic" – the mass – and "there is no room for any other."[237]

235. The source for this reference is cited in S. C. D. W. "Christian Faith and Demonology," in ed. Austin Flannery, *Vatican Collection Volume II* (Collegeville, MN: The Liturgical Press, 1982), p. 484 n. 106.

236. "Christian Faith and Demonology," p. 472, and pp. 459–460.

237. D. F. Walker, *Spiritual and Demonic Magic* (Notre Dame: University of Notre Dame, 1975), p. 36.

# Chapter 60
# The Five Pillars of Anti-Maimonidean Kabbala

In the following five segments we will examine five areas in which anti-Maimonidean teachings contributed to apostasy from Judaism to Christianity, particularly within the dense and oppressive environment of Medieval Spain.

## First: Instituting the Kabbala as the Supreme Theology of Israel

Traditionally, matters not directly connected with the judiciary – designated "matters of the heart" – including *aggadot* and *derashot*, were not imposed by the fiat of authority, but dialogued through the process of *meliṣa* (see above chapters 44–45). Intelligently, the rabbis confined esoteric topics and ideology to the realm of the subjective and personal, best negotiated between an individual and his or her Maker. The establishment of a rigid, esoteric theological system, whose basic fundaments – by definition – transcend the grasp of the 'unprivileged,' relegated the Jewish man and woman to a situation of hierarchic submission, as with the Christian *fidelis subditus*. Within this structure you must believe *in*, because you are first and foremost, a *fidelis subditus* (faithful subject), as with Christianity (see below, and above chapters 13, 28, and 53). This posed a dilemma: given that the faithful must remain in a state of hierarchic ignorance, and given that the standard *qabbala* of the Geonim and Old Sepharad is without merits, by which means could the Jewish *fidelis subditus* distinguish between the hierarchy of the kabbalists and that of the Christian clergy? (see below).

## Second: Subordination of Halakha to Kabbala

Although professing the abolition of the Law and spiritual freedom, the Church soon discovered that human society couldn't be properly organized without a legal system. Canon law differs from other legal systems (including the Jewish) because it posits a theological apparatus to which juridical matters are subordinated. By contrast, in Judaism (as in all modern legal systems), the law is not subordinated to another, hierarchically superior system. Jewish theology is the *consequence*, not the grounds, of law.[238] Thus, halakha is an autonomous system that cannot be manipulated by extraneous ideologies (see appendix 10). A principal objective of the anti-Maimonideans was to subordinate halakha to a theological system generated *outside* Jewish canonical texts and rabbinic tradition. Since in Judaism theology is only implicit in the classical texts – never explicit as with Christianity – for all practical purposes, the submission of halakha to theology meant the abrogation of the Law to whatever whimsical 'theological' explanation may be supplied. Consider the doctrine taught by R. 'Azriel (13th century), one of the fathers of anti-Maimonidean Kabbala, that "the Mishna" – the highest authority of Jewish law – represents

238. Therefore, Maimonides included the basic theological and ethical principles of Israel in his legal code *MT Yesode ha-Tora* and *De'ot,* under the title of twenty-one *biblical precepts*. That was the principal reason that the anti-Maimonideans burnt that section of the *MT*. Prudently, Maran decided to avoid getting embroiled in this problem by omitting the subject altogether. A consequence of this decision is the fact that some of his disciples were the teachers of Shabbetai Zvi devotees.

"the darkness"[239] (שהחושך זו המשנה). Echoing the Christian doctrine that the Law is dead, the kabbalists proclaimed that the Mishna equals Moses' sepulcher: "his sepulcher is the Mishna"[240] (וקבורה דיליה משנה איהי). Thus, they endorsed the fundamental Christian doctrine that the 'Old' Law is dead. In the same line, Ramban proclaimed that the Law *per se* does not save. He graced this doctrine with an insightful thesis: one may be depraved within the confines of the Law (נבל ברשות תורה). In the long list in which he enumerated the matters essential for salvation *omitted* by the Law, some concern moral and spiritual edification, noting, appropriately, that those were recommended by the rabbis. At the same time, he maintained that "abstention from the pollution (הטומאה) that was **not** forbidden to us by the Law," is essential for salvation.[241] In this fundamental principle, Ramban rejected the Jewish concept of "sanctification through the performance of the precepts" (see appendix 4) in favor of a theurgical approach to religion. Within this context it will be well to bear in mind that, as Professor Idel has incisively argued, "The significance of such a close relationship between theosophy and theurgy is… crucial for understanding the dynamics of the main trend of *Kabbala.*" It means that there is no split "between Nahmanides the kabbalist and Nahmanides the halakhist." That is why, "certain mystical elements can also be found in his conception of *halakha.*"[242] At this juncture,

239. *Commentary on Talmudic Aggadoth* (Heb.), p. 111. For a highly informative and substantive study, see J. Katz, "Halakha and Kabbala – First Contacts," (Heb.), in *Yitzhak F. Baer Memorial Volume* (Jerusalem: The Historical Society of Israel, 1980), pp. 148–172. On the supremacy of the Talmud over mystical lore in Old Sepharad, see R. Judah al-Bargeloni, *Perush Sefer Yeṣira*, pp. 186–187.

240. *Zohar*, vol. 1, 27b; cf ibid., vol. 3, 244b.

241. *Perush ha-Ramban* on Lev. 19:2, vol. 1, pp. 115–117. See *In the Shadow of History*, p. 222 n. 23. On the relation between 'pollution' and 'sacredness,' see *Teshubot ha-Rishba* (Dimitrovsky), vol. 1, p. 173.

242. "Nahmanides, *Kabbala, Halakha,* and Spiritual Leadership," pp. 68, 69. A good example is Ramban's belief that wine which is not red is unacceptable for *Qiddush*. There are no rabbinic sources for this view. On the contrary, according to rabbinic sources a good white wine is preferable to red; see Maran Joseph Caro, *Bet Yosef, Oraḥ Ḥayyim* CCLXXII, s.v. *garsenan*. A major consequence

it would be opportune to note that he maintained that since the destruction of the Temple in Jerusalem, the Jewish Court has lacked biblical authority (see appendix 66).

## Third: Hermeneutics Displaces the Text of the Tora

A cornerstone of Kabbala is that hermeneutics reveals the 'true' meaning of the Scripture, thus displacing Scripture. In their view, the thirteen rules of hermeneutics of the rabbis are not part of a *meliṣa*-process, but the method by which 'authorial intention' is revealed. Therefore, there can be no difference between the *text* of Scripture and the *interpretation* of Scripture. Thus, although the rabbis stipulated the principle that hermeneutics cannot displace the *peshaṭ* or *sensus communis* of Scripture (see above chapter 6), Ramban argued that since the 'truth' is one, what difference would it make whether something is explicit or was learned from hermeneutics?[243] (see appendix 66).

Kabbala-hermeneutics is Platonic. It assumes a *theory*, postulating an *a priori* knowledge of the 'ideal' sense of the text. In this case, as Julia Kristeva pointedly observed, "... one does not interpret something outside theory but rather that theory harbors its objects within its own logic."[244] The interpreter's agenda is to 'un-cover' the text and 'reveal' the 'ideal forms' within. Thus, projecting concepts developed *outside* the text *into* the text. In this fashion, the 'ambiguity'

---

of the marginalization of halakha was the emergence of the charismatic leader. Since the text could no longer serve as an objective criterion, there was a need for a charismatic leadership that could determine the content and meaning of Judaism. On this topic, see "Inspiration in the Middle Ages," pp. 175–208. One of the most successful models of this type of leadership was Shabbetai Zvi and his disciples, in both religious and antireligious apparel. Cf. The Reform Movement.

243. *Hasagot ha-Ramban*, in *Sefer ha-Miṣvot le-ha-Rambam*, ed. Ch. Chavel (Jerusalem: Mossad Harav Kook, 1981), II, s.v. *ve-'akhshav*, p. 31. See quotation from *Guide* III, 43, p. 420, ll. 1–6, in appendix 52.

244. Julia Kristeva, "Psychoanalysis and the Polis," in ed. W. J. T. Mitchell, *The Politics of Interpretation* (Chicago: The University of Chicago Press, 1983), p. 85.

intrinsic to alphabetic reading is replaced by an interpretation that simultaneously explains the text and de-alphabetizes it; as with Christian literary theory, whereby the Christian Scripture simultaneously interprets the 'Old Law' and displaces it by interpreting it. R. Asher acknowledged this principle. Hence, he proposed that the precept to write a Scroll of the Tora should "nowadays" be reformed: "instead, one should write each of the five books of the Tora separately, the Mishna, Talmud, and commentaries, so that he and his children could use them for studying" (see appendix 62).

## Fourth: Preeminence of the Hermetic Subtext of the Tora

A fundamental idea of Pauline antinomianism is the distinction between the "letter" and "spirit" of the Law (Cor. 3:6). A bit less elegantly, anti-Maimonidean Kabbala, too, distinguished between the "empty" sense of the evident tenor (*peshaṭ*) of the Tora and the "soul" (נשמה). The Tora, we are apprised, "is not only empty as per its common sense (אין תורה ריקנית כפשטה לבד), but it also has a soul that I [i.e. God] blew into the Tora, and that is what in fact is the most important" (אבל יש לה נשמה שנפחתי אני בתורה, והוא העיקר).[245]

The "soul" (probably identical to "God's theurgic names") is encoded in the subtext of the Tora, made up of the Hebrew consonants. By re-combining the consonants it would be possible to unravel God's theurgic names. We should recall that according to this system, "the whole Tora is made up of God's names," awarding the possessor theurgic power. That was how Moses produced the ten plagues and all kind of miracles, and Solomon acquired his uncanny

---

245. *Ma'amar 'al Penimiyut ha-Tora,* in *Kitbe Ramban,* vol. 2, p. 468; cf. *Zohar,* vol. 3, 152a. See *Torat ha-Shem Temima,* in *Kitbe Ramban,* vol. 1, p. 142. R. David ibn Abi Zimra, cited in *Golden Doves,* p. 136, espoused a similar doctrine. A corollary of this thesis is that the Oral Law that Moses transmitted publicly to Israel (see 'Erubin 54b), pertains to the "empty" aspect of the Tora. This is consistent with other similar views suggesting that the *revealed* Tora does not save.

wisdom.[246] Possession of a certain magical name bestows power to resurrect the dead.[247] Another "produces the secret miracles made for the pious."[248] "It is well known to many," he declared solemnly, that these names were "used by the pious of the [various] generations." It is through the manipulation of these divine names that the Ḥasidim "knew how to kill and how to resurrect, how to desolate and how to destroy, how to demolish and how to annihilate, how to build and how to plant."[249] This is consistent with the doctrine advanced by R. 'Azriel that "whatever is derived from reason is called Tora."[250] By 'reason,' he probably meant the 'spirit' or 'soul' of the text 'revealed' through their peculiar brand of hermeneutics.

## Fifth: Dismantling a Word into Its Consonants And Rearranging the Consonants to Form a New Word, Revealing Thereby a Hitherto Unknown Theological Doctrine Developed Outside the Tora and Rabbinic Tradition

One of Kabbala's methods was to dismantle a word into its consonants and rearrange them to create a new word. On the basis of the reconstructed term, a dogma developed *outside* the Scripture and rabbinic tradition is 'revealed.' An illuminating example is the Trinitarian doctrine espoused by R. Adrete.[251] The discussion appears in a *responsum* in which he presented "the true mystical traditions which are in the hands of the sages of Israel," i.e., the anti-Maimonideans

246. See above notes 205–206.
247. *Kitbe Ramban*, vol. 1, p. 168. See below n. 248.
248. *Perush ha-Ramban* on Gen. 17:1, vol. 1, p. 98; cf. *Kitbe Ramban*, vol. 1, pp. 191–192.
249. *Kitbe Ramban*, vol. 1, p. 168. See above nn. 151, 215.
250. *Commentary on Talmudic Aggadoth* (Heb.), p. 77.
251. This doctrine may be connected to the belief that God's secret name, consisting of seventy-two letters, is to be divided into segments of three letters each; see Introduction, *Perush ha-Ramban*, p. 7; cf. *Teshubot ha-Rishba*, vol. 1 #220.

in the regions of Catalonia, France, and Germany. This doctrine is supposed to elucidate "the mystery" (הסוד) of the prayer addressing God as "the God of Abraham, the God of Isaac, and the God of Jacob." Already by the first third of the 13th century, Jewish apostates interpreted this doxology as a Jewish manifesto of the Christian Holy Trinity.[252] The explanation discussed by R. Adrete centered on the three Hebrew consonants B-R-K (ב-ר-ך), making the word *BaRuKh* (ב-רו-ך 'blessed'). Following a technique used by Ramban and similar authorities in Gerona, the consonants were rearranged to read *RoKheB* (רו-כ-ב 'mounted') – for God as "Provident and Savior" (משגיח ומציל); *BeKhoR* (ב-כו-ר 'First Born') – for God's "dominion and greatness over all" (ממשלה והגדולה על הכל); and *KeRuB* (כ-רו-ב) – for the "intellect onto which one ought to cleave" (שכל שראוי להדבק בו). All three personas are one in "*BaRuKh*"[253] (ב-רו-ך). In similar fashion, R. Adrete sided with Christian exegetes – against Maimonides – and proposed a Trinitarian interpretation of the first verse of the *Shema'* (Deut. 6:4).[254] Similarly, R. 'Azriel proposed that God had created the universe, "with three names of His great name."[255] In the same theological mood, he explained that *'amen*, consisting of three consonants '-M-N (א-מ-ן), could be rearranged

252. See Américo Castro, "Disputa entre un Cristiano y un Judío," in his *De la España que aún no conocía*, vol. 3 (Mexico: Finestere, 1972), p. 204, ll. 25–27. The language is early 13th century Castilian, cf. ibid., p. 205. The famous Dominican Priest Raymudo Martyn, addressed R. Adrete on this matter; see *Teshubat ha-Rishba*, pp. 636–637.

253. *Teshubot ha-Rishba*, vol. 1, #423, 176a.

254. *Teshubot ha-Rishba*, (Ch. Z. Dimitrovsky), vol. 1, pp. 213–214. Maimonides' interpretation of this verse is to be found in *Maimonides' Treatise on Resurrection*, ed. Joshua Finkel (New York: American Academy for Jewish Research, 1939), Hebrew/Arabic texts, p. 1. See editor's n. 2, p. 93; R. Abraham ibn 'Ezra, Gen. 18:1; and *In the Shadow of History*, p. 15, and p. 223 n. 37. In a *responsum* addressed to Raymudo Martyn, R. Adrete rejects the Trinitarian interpretation proposed by the Christian priest; "*Teshubat ha-Rishba...*," pp. 636–641. It seems, however, that this was a matter of prudence, rather than of substance.

255. *Commentary on the Talmudic Aggadoth* (Heb.), p. 87, this was probably an allusion to the first three *sefirot*, see ibid., p. 108 and cf. p. 109.

as *'aMeN* (א-מ-ן), *'uMaN* (או-מ-ן), and *'iMuN* (אי-מו-ן), paralleling 'reason' (שכל), 'rational' (משכיל), and 'reasoned' (מושכל) – "three names of a single essence"[256] (שלושה שמות של מהות אחת). Within this context, "names" are not divine appellations, but real persona within the divinity.[257] R. 'Azriel referred to God as *Rokheb* (רוכב), and identified *Kerub* (כרוב) with the *Shekhina* ('Divine presence').[258]

In the semantic context of the time, it would be impossible not to identify *RoKheb* (רוכב) with the 'Father,' *BeKhoR* (בכור) with the 'Son,' and *KeRuB* (כרוב) with the 'Holy Ghost': these three personas becoming One in *BaRuKh* (ברוך). Indeed, Christian Scripture refers to Jesus as "the first born" (Rom. 8:29; Heb. 1:6; Col. 1:18), and "the First born of all Creation" (Col. 1:15). In similar fashion, Ramban proposed that the first three words of the Tora (בראשית ברא אלהים) "At the beginning/ God/ created" should be rearranged to read, "At the beginning/ God/ was created"[259] (בראש יתברא אלהים). To sustain this doctrine, Jewish apostates changed the vocalization of the Hebrew *bara* ('created') – the second word of the Tora – to Aramaic, rendering it *bera* ('the son'); resulting in: "At the beginning the son of God (ברא דאדני) completed the heavens and earth."[260] To his

256. *Commentary on Talmudic Aggadoth* (Heb.), pp. 24–25; cf. pp. 45, 81. This triad comprises the first three *sefirot*; see ibid., p. 54, and are the object of prayers, ibid., p. 56. On the plurality of the divinity, see ibid., pp. 17, 56–57. On the relation of the plurality to the divinity itself, see ibid., p. 16 and *Tiqqune ha-Zohar* (Leghorn, 5646/1886), XVIII, 34b.

257. This may be gathered from a close reading of *Commentary on Talmudic Aggadoth* (Heb.), p. 91 (ll. 17–21).

258. See *Commentary on Talmudic Aggadoth* (Heb.), p. 9. The reference to *Bekhor* is on p. 11. It is also possible that *Bekhor* here alludes to the "primeval light that emanated from God … before the creation of the world" from which the other two *sefirot* were generated; see ibid., p. 110 and cf. pp. 20, 25.

259. Introduction, *Perush ha-Ramban,* vol. 1, p. 6; see *Kitbe Ramban,* vol. 1, p. 168. Gershom Scholem, in *The Origin of the Kabbala,* p. 409 n. 201, shows that Ramban quoted the Christian Scripture and used Christian sources in his development of Purgatory.

260. Aramaic version of the Pentateuch, *Neophyti* 1, Gen. 1:1. Belief in the Divine Trinity was an important factor among Jewish heretics and mystics, particularly

credit, later in life Ramban sensed the perils involved in some of his kabbalistic doctrines and tried to dissociate himself from some of them. That is why, in opposition to the other mystics of Gerona, at the end of the Introduction to his *Commentary to the Pentateuch*, he stipulated that the actual meaning of the "secrets of the Tora" cannot possibly be learned by reading his book, and they could be taught only orally:

> Behold, here I am faithfully assuring and properly counseling whosoever is looking at this book, not to apply the views, or to further develop the concepts concerning any of the allusions about the secrets of the Tora that I am writing. I am thereby letting him know, in earnest, that my words will not be understood at all by any mind or intelligence, except from the mouth of a kabbalist sage to the ear of a receiver who can understand.* On [this matter] opinions are an iniquity, and ideas a harmful sacrilege that prevent any benefit.[261]

Trinitarian doctrines continued to flourish among Iberian Jews and later among pseudo-Lurianics, followers of Shabbetai Zvi (1626–1676). A most forceful exponent of the doctrine of the Holy Trinity was the heretic Neḥamya Ḥayyon (ca. 1655–ca. 1730).[262]

Concerning the divine name 'E-Lo-H-Y-M ('God'), R. Baḥye b. Asher (13th century), a distinguished disciple of R. Adrete, explained:

---

after the Expulsion, see "A Crisis of Categories," p. 57.

* One may then be forgiven for asking what the purpose of publishing these words was.

261. Introduction, in *Perush ha-Ramban*, p. 6. Most probably, the criticism of R. Nissim of Gerona against Ramban's Kabbala concerned the pluralities of divinities, which one could infer from his writings; see *In the Shadow of History*, p. 15. In a private conversation, Professor Idel brought to my attention that whereas other kabbalists from Gerona counted with disciples furthering their ideas, it is not known of any kabbalist that regarded himself as a pupil of Ramban.

262. He was confronted and refuted by R. David Nieto, in his *Esh Dat* (London, 1715), 13a-15a, 17b-23b.

"according to the Kabbala" this name "comprises two words: 'EL + HM [א-ל + הם = 'They' <are> 'God'], and these ['They'] are encoded in the Y(י)" – the *Yod* of 'E-Lo-H-Y-M, which in Hebrew stands for the number ten.[263] R. Abraham Abul'afya (1240–after 1291), in my view the most serious mystic of the time, reproached R. Adrete for sponsoring such a doctrine:

> Accordingly, let me point out to you, that the masters of Kabbala [and] *sefirot,* believed to profess monotheism, and (tried) to elude the Trinitarian doctrine. [In fact] they ended making Him ten. Just like the gentiles professing: 'He is Three and the Three are One,' some kabbalists say: 'the divinity is Ten *sefirot* and the Ten are One.'[264]

The point made by a rationalist – probably a Maimonidean – is abundantly clear: "(Whereas) the Christians believe in the Trinity, the mystics believe in the Tentary (= ten *sefirot*)."[265]

In Spain there circulated a treatise from Ashkenazic kabbalistic circles claiming that the Holy Trinity represents the most genuine form of monotheism. Apostates used this argument to persuade Jews of the preeminence of Christianity. R. Solomon ibn Verga put these words in the mouth of a Christian sage:

---

263. R. Baḥye b. Asher, *Be'ur,* on Gen. 1:1, vol. 1, p. 15. Cf. editor's note ad loc. In Ex. 17:16, vol. 2, p. 158 he explained: ביו"ד לחבר השם; that is: אל+הם. See Samuel David Luzzato, *"Vikkuaḥ 'al ha-qabbala,"* in idem, *Meḥqare Yahdut* (Warsaw, 5673/1913), pp. 140–141. For the kabbalistic rationalization of the Holy Trinity, see R. Joseph Chicatilla, *Sha'are Ora* (Warsaw, 5643/1883), pp. 28–33, the commentary ibid on p. 31, n. 3. It is worthy of attention that R. Baḥye b. Asher, in his *Be'ur* on Deut. 29:9, vol. 3, p. 430, ascertained that as a consequence of Israel's sin, the Covenant at Sinai was abrogated, and there was a need for a second Covenant. Thus, confirming the Christian claim against Israel. See below n. 290.
264. In ed. Adolph Jellinek, *Ginze Ḥokhmat ha-Qabbala* (Leipzig, 1853), p. 19.
265. *Teshubot ha-Ribash,* #157.

> The Trinity is not polytheism but simple monotheism to those who understand. I saw three great Ashkenazic sages (ושלשה גדולים מחכמי אשכנז), and learned from them in the books of Kabbala, and discovered that the Trinity is monotheism. On the basis of these words I asked them (the Jews): 'Who then are better, you or your forefathers?'[266]

Responding to their own spiritual bent, modern historians refrain from pointing out the connection between the triumph of the anti-Maimonideans, the rise of Kabbala, and mass conversions to Christianity.

266. *Shebeṭ Yehuda*, VII, p. 37; see *In the Shadow of History*, pp. 14–15. Cf. Harvey J. Hames, *The Art of Conversion* (Leiden: Brill, 2000), chapter 4.

# Chapter 61
# The Problem with 'Philosophy'

The recognition of a 'rationality' based on humanistic values by the Maimonideans was intended to create an attitude: the Tora should not be merely feared but understood and respected. The matrix of this rationality is a *meliṣa*-culture, based on the Book and the *ketab* and *mikhtab* systems as exemplified in Talmudic discourse. The operational idea in a heroic-culture is the supremacy of might. 'Truth' is a matter of status. Refusal to accept the 'truth' is *insubordination*. By contrast, in a *meliṣa*-culture, resolution of conflicts is advanced by fostering an environment permitting horizontal discourse. Referring to the *meliṣa*-truth (= אמת or 'mutual trust'), the psalmist noted that "it springs out from the earth." As when planting a tree (cf. Jer. 1:10; 31:27): it will take time and labor. The participants themselves may not live to enjoy the fruits. Counseling for patience, the psalmist concluded: "While righteousness looks down from heaven" (Ps. 85:12) – at the truth planted below. In a heroic environment the truth *triumphs*. It imposes itself on the 'other,' confirming thereby the logic of might. Victory is achieved through violence; compliance through intimidation. In a culture of violence, the supreme responsibility of the authorities is to protect the people from error, either 'spiritual' or 'intellectual.' 'We should do this,' or 'abstain from that,' 'lest this perhaps' (= שמא) *may* occur. Without intimidation, neither government nor resolution of conflicts is viable. (Similarly, without Hell none of the 'monotheistic religions' could sell their Paradise.) Thus, the excellence of the anti-Maimonideans is proven by the fact that they managed to silence the 'other.'

A most powerful tool in the anti-Maimonidean arsenal was the term 'philosophy' – semantically akin to the 'grammar' of bogus-Talmudists. In principle, they maintained "that anyone who studies science is a heretic and rejects the Tora. And that in case anyone had learned the science of philosophy, his belief in the doctrines of the Tora will be contrary to the faith."[267] (Similar to the argument about grammar made by bogus-Talmudists; see above chapter 51). Thus, 'philosophy' was used as a tool to delegitimize each and every disagreeable view, regardless of content. A case in point is the use of this term in a *responsum* issued by R. Asher. In assessing the implications of his position, it would be important to recall that although he sympathized with the anti-Maimonideans' ideology, he was relatively moderate and judicious.[268] The good rabbi never read a line of philosophy in his life.

In a *responsum* written when he first came to Spain, he acknowledged: "that I am lacking any proficiency in these writings (philosophy)." That is why, he acknowledged, people failed to "consult him on matters of faith because they believed that they pertain to philosophy." And yet, although he had never laid an eye on any of Aristotle's works, he could ascertain that Maimonides "was steadfastly (committed) to each of Aristotle's words." He then went on to compare Maimonides

> ...to a child being carried on the bosom of a nursing-father (see Num. 11:12), following him in every step. Every one of his judgments and principles are stamped with his (Aristotle's) stamp.[269]

Likewise, in the case we are about to examine, R. Asher declared:

---

267. Cited in *Milḥamot ha-Shem*, p. 59. Cf. above n. 115.

268. See his well-balanced *responsum* in *Besamim Rosh* #240, 75b, bearing his signature.

269. *Besamim Rosh* #251, 76b. At the end of the *responsum*, 77c, he initialed his signature אבה"רי, standing for אשר בן ה"רב יחיאל.

> And although I do not know your secular knowledge, blessed be the Lord who saved me from it! And the sign and proof came [that it] had apostatized man from the fear of God and from His Law![270]

The case he was addressing took place in the year 1321, a short time before his death. A dispute arose about the meaning of a pre-nuptial agreement registered in the by-laws of the Community of Toledo in classical Arabic, a language that R. Asher did not know. There was no official Hebrew translation. R. Israel de Toledo, secretary of the Court and one of those who had worked hard to secure R. Asher's position as Chief Rabbi of Toledo, made a translation for his benefit. On the basis of the translation, R. Asher rendered a decision. The translator (as an expert witness) argued that R. Asher's interpretation of the translation violated the *semantic* connotations of the original Arabic.[271]

---

270. All quotations and references are from *Teshubot ha-Rosh*, 55:9. R. Asher's thesis was incorporated in *Zohar*, vol. 2, 124a. The illustrious Gaon of Vilna, too, was privy to the same type of illumination. Although he acknowledged that he had never studied 'philosophy,' nonetheless, he could ascertain that "the cursed philosophy had seduced him [Maimonides] with her perfidious cunning"; see his note on *Yore De'a* CXXIX, 14. For a long and valiant effort to exculpate this type of language; see Israel Dienstag, "*Ha-Im Hitnagged ha-Gra le-Mishnato ha-Pilosophit shel ha-Rambam*? *Talpioth* 4 (1949), pp. 253–268. I don't think it is necessary to make excuses. Men of good faith would agree that the best way to put some fear of God in the thick skulls of people is by using a harsh tone. In fact, the distinguished Gaon used a much harsher tone to express his disagreement with *his own mentor* and *maternal grandfather*, on a relatively minor point of law; see his note on *Yore De'a* CCXCIII, 2. Concerning his attitude to 'secular' studies in general, see the heroic defense by Aaron M. Schrieber, "*Hashqafato…*" *BaDaD* 9 (5759/1999), pp. 5–28.
271. The view of R. de Toledo appears in *Teshubot ha-Rosh*, 55:9. The underlying thesis is that the *text* of a *private agreement between two parties* ought not to be interpreted according to Talmudic hermeneutics and rabbinic linguistic connotations, but according to the semantic field of the particular *language*, as well as the *place* and *time*, in which the document was written. The requirements for the proper interpretation of such a document are two: 'common sense' (סברא), which is familiarity with the syntactical and semantic apparatus of

R. Asher responded that he had based his decision on the translation furnished to him by R. Israel de Toledo. The point of the translator, however, concerned the *semantics,* not the lexical translation. In the position of presiding judge, R. Asher could have either rejected the translator's objection, or examined the legal status of translations in rabbinic jurisprudence. He chose neither. Instead, he raised the issue of 'philosophy.' R. Asher was a master at sidestepping questions. His tactic was to *impute* to the 'other' some untenable views, and thus be able to digress into tangential issues, nothing to do with the subject at hand. In our case, he deflected what was a purely judicial issue (see below), to a confrontation of 'philosophy *v.* the Law of Moses.' Shrewdly, he branded R. Israel's 'reason' (שכל) 'philosophy.' As Tora incarnate, he would be defending the Law. His first line of assault was to deprecate the Geonic and Sephardic traditions by attacking the personal integrity of those sages.

> Shall we prove or confirm, in rendering a guilty or innocent verdict, or a prohibition or permission, from the science of *your* logic [the linguistic analysis presented by the translator], which was denounced by all the Tora sages? Isn't it true that those who instituted it did not believe in Moses and in the righteous judgments and injunctions that were given in writing and by tradition? Then, how could those who draw from

---

the speaking-community; and proficiency in classical Arabic, the language in which the pre-nuptial agreement was written. To substantiate his argument, R. de Toledo pointed out that the basic terms of the pre-nuptial agreement in question, such as 'marriage,' 'wife,' 'inheritance,' have a semantic field of their own (within the speaking-community), *independent* of the peculiar legal lexicon (of both the Jewish and non-Jewish communities), which is more restrictive and specialized. Forgetting with whom he was dealing, the poor rabbi made the fatal mistake of employing the term 'reason' (שכל) to indicate the syntactical relations determined by the linguistic apparatus. Cleverly, R. Asher grabbed this term and associated it with infamous 'philosophy' – something akin to 'communist/capitalist' in some political quarters – and used it to launch a devastating attack on the poor translator.

> its waters bring from it a proof for the injunctions and judgments of our Teacher Moses, may he rest in peace! Or [how could they] judge a case with parables used in the science of *their* logic? It shall not be so! No! Would in my days and in my place a case be judged with parables?!

R. Asher knew that he was Tora incarnate, with supreme mastery of the Law (see appendix 67). Despite his ingrained humility (typical of heroic-*qedoshim*), he had to publicly announce for all to know, once and for all: "Thank God, as long as I live, there is still Law in Israel, to bring proofs from the Mishna, and the Babylonian Talmud and Yerushalmi, and you have no need to bring parables to render a judgment." Lamentably, in our case, the good rabbi failed to document his position from either the Babylonian Talmud or Yerushalmi. He also failed to refer to the views made by other halakhic authorities on the subject (see below). In fact, he seemed to have been clueless about the *legal* issues pertaining to the case. At any rate, he continued:

> Since the science of philosophy and the science of the Law and judgments do not follow the same path – because the science of the Law is the tradition received by Moses at Sinai, the sage would expound it according to the hermeneutics that could be used to expound it, comparing one item to another. Although these things do not concur with physical science, we still will follow tradition. But the science of philosophy is natural, and they were very wise, and determined every item according to its nature.

In an exemplary mood, the good teacher warned against too much wisdom: it leads to perdition. That is what happened to the 'other' teachers:

> But from so much wisdom they went deep down and they became corrupt, and were forced to repudiate the Law of Moses, because all the Law is not natural, but tradition…

Anticipating *Church* v. *Galileo*, the saintly rabbi concluded with this ruling:

> Whoever would enter from the beginning into this science [philosophy], will never escape from it and will be incapable to bring to his heart the science of the Law, because he would not be able to recant from the natural science to which he was accustomed, because his heart will always be attracted to it. Therefore, he will never grasp the wisdom of the Law, which is the path of life, since his heart will always be with the natural science. He would wish to compare these two sciences, bring proof from one onto the other. As a result he would twist the Law, because they are mutually exclusive and are not compatible with one another.[272]

One can only wonder, given that the good rabbi had never studied philosophy, what the basis was for such a judgment. Modern Jewish historians, hopelessly ignorant of both philosophy and law – Jewish and otherwise – reiterate R. Asher's view, identifying the case as one of 'philosophy *v.* the Law.'[273] In fact, it is a purely legal matter. Early in its history, the Jewish Court recognized the value of expert testimony, regardless of whether said expert was a Jew or a Gentile.[274] Talmudic

---

272. *Teshubot ha-Rosh* 55:9. To the best of my abilities, I was unable to confirm his claim about knowledge of 'Yerushalmi.' Invariably, his quotations from the Yerushalmi come from *secondary sources* – the works of Talmudic scholars who, in the course of their comments and explanations, happened to quote it. Were it not for his claim, one could have concluded that the saintly rabbi never laid an eye on a volume of the Yerushalmi. Cf. below n. 346.
273. See *A History of the Jews in Christian Spain*, vol. 1, pp. 318–319. For a detailed analysis of this case, see Israel Ta-Shma, "*Shiqqulim Pilosofim be-Hakhra'at ha-Halakha bi-Sfarad*," *Sefunot* 18 (1985), pp. 99–109.
274. While it is within the authority of the court to *consult* with an expert witness or with the *opinion* of a non-Jewish court, it is not permissible to ask a non-Jewish court to certify or approve of a halakhic decision since this would compromise the autonomy of the Jewish judiciary. This basic point was overlooked by R. Ḥayyim Palaggi, *Ḥuqqot ha-Ḥayyim* (Izmir, 5632/1872), #1, 5d-6a. On the status of expert witnesses in Jewish law, see "*Ve-Niṣḥu …*," pp. 113–133. Obviously, in

sages did not hesitate to consult heathens to learn the nuances of foreign terms.[275] This type of consultation is permitted even when pertaining to the text of the Scripture. R. Hayye Gaon would consult with the local head of the Syrian Church about biblical lexicography.[276] According to the Talmud, when the court does not know the languages of the litigants it is required to use the services of an expert translator.[277] Maimonides summarized this rule:

> It would not be proper for a judge to try a case where he does not know the language of the litigants. If he understands the subject [in general terms] but does not speak (the language), it is sufficient. However, to discharge his duty before Heaven, he should have an expert in that language to assist him to judge between the parties.[278]

The same principle should apply to a document or a by-law presented to the court in a foreign language. The issue raised by the translator was a legitimate one: it pertains to the extent that a judge is bound to take into consideration the semantic connotations of the original document, which were not reflected in the translation, especially when the expert witness claims that the decision of the court violates the connotation of the document. Se'adya Gaon discussed the matter.[279]

---

such a case, the final authority rests with the judge either to accept or reject an expert opinion. Nonetheless, it would not be regarded an affront to the court for an expert witness to argue his point, as in the case of R. Israel de Toledo.

275. See Y. Baba Batra VIII, 8, 16c. Cf. *Greek in Jewish Palestine*, p. 26 n. 76.
276. See *Golden Doves*, p. 124.
277. Makkot 6b; see *Ḥiddushe ha-Riṭba*, ad loc. This requirement was codified in *MT Sanhedrin* 21:8; cf. 2:6; and *Shulḥan 'Arukh, Ḥoshen Mishpaṭ* XVII, 6; cf. XXVIII, 6. In *Perush* R. Ḥanan'el ad loc., it was explained that the case concerned the litigants (דאתו לקמי דרבא בדינא) – not the witnesses. For a detailed discussion, see *Birke Yosef*, on *Ḥoshen Mishpaṭ* XVII, 6.
278. *Teshubot ha-Rambam*, #322, vol. 2, p. 591. Cf. Rabad on *MT Shebu'ot* 6:9. In Rosh HaShana 26a-b, there is a report about a rabbi who recused himself from a case, because he did not know the *semantic* sense of a term.
279. *Teshubot*, ed. Joel Muller, in *Ouvres Completes de R. Saadia…*, vol. 9 (Paris: Ernest Leroux, 1897), p. 133.

As the presiding judge, R. Asher had the authority to overrule the translator's testimony. That is a given. Instead, he preferred to muzzle the translator by crying 'Philosophy!' and imputing the personal integrity of the Geonim and sages of Old Sepharad! The fact that neither the saintly rabbi nor our learned historians had the foggiest idea about the halakhic issues and sources of the case speaks for itself.

The position advanced by R. Asher about the incompatibility of the 'Law' and natural sciences appears a bit disingenuous in light of the fact that on a different occasion he had asked the same R. Israel de Toledo to explain to him a Mishna in Kil'ayim (having to do with a law bearing on plane geometry, a subject far too complex for the knowledgeable rabbi to manage on his own) and help him decide between two conflicting interpretations.[280] Indeed, there were outstanding halakhic authorities, among both Sepharadim and Ashkenazim, who in their halakhic decisions took into consideration facts provided by the scientific community of their times. R. Envidal de Toledo (14th century) did not hesitate to base halakhic decisions on the basis "of the science of optics."[281] R. Moses Isserles (1525/30–1572), the Rama, one of the most respected halakhic authorities in both Sephardic and Ashkenazic traditions, *rejected* a Talmudic decision, "since it is contradicted by common experience."[282]

A most serious matter was R. Asher's condemnation of 'philosophy.' In one sweep, the saintly rabbi was disposing of the Geonic tradition – from Se'adya to Hayye, as well as the entire Sephardic Golden Age – as corrupt and illegitimate! We should not be surprised to find out that some sages regarded that demeanor inappropriate,

---

280. Quoted in full by Maran Joseph Caro, *Kesef Mishne, Kil'ayim* 6:2. Other inerrant scholars, too, were somehow uncomfortable with the same Mishna; see Rabad ibid 6:2, and below n. 341.

281. *Maggid Mishne* on *MT Sukka* 5:15. This view was cited approvingly by Maran Joseph Caro, *Bet Yosef, Oraḥ Ḥayyim* 631 s.v. *sekhakhah*. Similarly, R. Jacob Ḥajez, *Halakhot Qeṭannot*, part I, #218 substantiated a halakhic decision from chemistry; cf. ibid. #282 and R. Menaḥem de Lonzano, *Shete Yadot* (Jerusalem, 5730/1970), 80b, etc.

282. *Shulḥan 'Arukh, Eben ha-'Ezer* 156:4. The source for this view was cited by Maran Joseph Caro, *Bet Yosef, Eben ha-'Ezer* 156 s.v. *katub bi-tshubat*.

particularly for someone claiming to incarnate "Law in Israel." The celebrated R. Eliyahu ha-Levi b. Benjamin (15th and 16th centuries), from the old Ashkenazic Community in Turkey and one of the great Talmudic scholars of the time, addressed the halakhic implications of such a diatribe.[283] The case he adjudicated concerned someone who called a fellow Jew "a heretic and an atheist" for studying Aristotle (and presumably other philosophical works). One of the points raised by R. Eliyahu ha-Levi was that by insulting that individual,

> He was also offending the past saints, deprecating the Geonim and sages who studied sciences, such as R. Se'adya Gaon, R. Hayye Gaon, and after them other sages such as ibn Gabirol, R. Judah ha-Levi, R. Abraham ibn 'Ezra, Maimonides, and the sages of every generation who have built a fortress to counter those who attack our Holy Tora.

Members of other religions have praised Maimonides for his philosophical contributions and the development of central concepts in areas of faith. "There is no doubt," R. Eliyahu ha-Levi pointedly observed, "that whoever deprecates some science in general, is also deprecating those who studied it – and they were great sages, now defunct." Those who attacked philosophy claimed that these works might contain errors and give credence to ideas contrary to Judaism. "This," however, "does not warrant censuring someone who studies their words," he replied. Bearing in mind that philosophical and scientific works "deal not in faith, but in demonstrations," he rightfully

283. All the quotations come from his *Zeqan Aharon* (Constantinople, 5494/1734), #25, 30a-31a. Unaware of this publication, S. Assaf, "*Me-Ginze Bet ha-Sefarim …*," in *Minḥa le-David Yellin* (Jerusalem: Ruben Mass, 5695/1925), pp. 228–233, published the same responsum in the name of R. David b. Abi Zimra. As common among rabbis, the *responsum* must have been sent to R. Abi Zimra for endorsement. His signature was probably intended to express approval and not authorship. The reverse is also possible, namely that the R. Abi Zimra's *responsum* reached R. Levi and was put in his collection of *responsa*. An inspection of the actual manuscript published by Professor Assaf could settle the matter.

noted that in such matters, "Authentic tradition" suffices. By implication he suggested that those who criticize philosophical endeavor might be short of confidence in the Tora. In support, he quotes a rabbinic adage: "Let our wonderful Tora not be," in your mind, "like their empty chatter!" Meaning: there is nothing to fear from ideas contrary to our faith. According to R. Eliyahu ha-Levi such verbal abuse constitutes injury, warranting the intervention of the court.

The position of R. Asher was also rejected by the celebrated R. Moses Isserles (Rama). In what was an obvious allusion to R. Asher's view, he noted that the ban issued against 'philosophy' never included the study of physical sciences. They may have intended to prohibit only some Aristotelian works:

> They never intended, however, to prohibit the study of the works of scholars and their investigations concerning the material world and its nature (במהות המציאות וטבעיהן). On the contrary, through [this type of investigation] the greatness of the Creator becomes more manifest.

In support of his thesis, Rama reminded the reader that the Talmud had declared: "Whoever pronounces a word of wisdom, although from the nations (i.e., a gentile) he should be entitled 'sage' (חכם)."[284] Furthermore, even those claiming that the philosophical works of heathens may be somehow perilous would have to concede that it couldn't apply if their ideas are learned,

> From the works of the sages of blessed memory, from whose waters we do constantly drink. In particular, from Maimonides, of blessed memory! No one has ever thought to prohibit this! We could state with absolute certainty that nothing pernicious can be found in any of his works.

284. Megilla 16a.

To let us know that he was aware of the events surrounding Maimonidean works, he added:

> Although some sages disagreed with him and burnt his works, nonetheless his works have spread among all the later authorities of blessed memory! Everyone placed them [Maimonides' works] as a crown over their heads, and brings proof from them as if they would constitute 'a *halakha* received from Moses at Sinai' (כהלכה למשה מסיני).[285]

Attesting to his conviction, he began his famous *Mappa* on *Shulḥan 'Arukh* with a quotation from the *Guide*.[286]

---

285. *She'elot wu-Tshubot R. Moshe Isserles* (Amsterdam, 5471/1711), #7, 4c.

286. Similarly, Maran Joseph Caro, *Bet Yosef, Yore De'a* CLXXXI s.v. *haqafat*, rejected a disparaging remark against Maimonides made by R. Jacob, in the *Ṭur* (for dealing with the reason for one of the Scriptural Precepts, in the *Guide*). It is pertinent to our discussion that Maran began his reply by rejecting the view that R. Jacob *imputes* to Maimonides a classical anti-Maimonidean tactic: "It is unworthy [to suggest] that Maimonides held this!" Then Maran proceeded to challenge him with this fundamental question: "Who had actually cared for the honor of the Tora and precepts, more than him?" Finally, it is important to recall the scientific activities of R. David Gans (1541–1613) – a worthy disciple of Rama! By the way, if we are to judge the Rama's approach to the study of Talmud by the commentary on Tractate Ḥolin by his disciple, R. Eli'ezer Ashkenazi, *Dammeseq Eli'ezer* (Lublin, 5407/1607), which I had the privilege to study – one would have to admit that his methodology is very close to that of R. Menaḥem Me'iri – having nothing to do with the pilpulistic hodgepodge of bogus-Talmudists.

# Chapter 62
# A Reflective Response to R. Hayye Gaon's Call

Common opinion notwithstanding, the anti-Maimonideans did not represent a more 'genuine' version of Judaism. The view that some of the Maimonidean doctrines constitute 'heresy' is the result of assimilation and deficient Talmudic schooling, whereby zeal displaces halakha. Because modern historians are the product of an education grounded on anti-Maimonidean concepts of 'religion' and 'Judaism,' they fail to realize that their notions are not measured by the standards of the Rabbinic Schools of Andalusia and the Geonim. Studying the anti-Maimonidean writings today from the vantage of contemporary scholarship, one wonders whether any of them possessed the tools to pass a critical judgment on the *Guide*. It was written in Arabic, a language foreign to them, about topics demanding a high level of intellectual discipline and sophistication. The Hebrew translation of the *Guide* could not help this type of reader any more than a modern translation could help one of these historians make head or tail of Wittgenstein's *Tractatus* or Whitehead and Russell's *Principia Mathematica*.

In a letter addressed to R. Judah al-Fakhkhar, R. Meshullam of Lunel (ca. 1175–ca. 1250) stressed the fact that those who support Maimonides' *Guide* observed the Law meticulously, "And if their heart follows the *Guide*, as they were inspired by heaven to do, they are God fearing and do uphold His Law."[287] A similar point was made by R. David Qimḥi. The anti-Maimonideans were not more punctilious in the observance of the Law.

> We are the ones who strengthen the Law, who rely on the teachings of the rabbis of blessed memory, and who give aid without deceit. [We are the ones] who rise early in the morning and stay late at night in the House of the Lord, and stand with awe and reverence as it is [fit] for Israel to do. [We are] punctilious in the words of the Scribes, and we are those who [actually] teach the Law, unlike the bogus accusations of [those] rebels.

He added:

> We are heirs to our Patriarch Abraham' legacy, about whom the Lord testified, "In order that he should direct his children and family [to practice charity and justice]." Our houses are wide open for travelers and those in need of respite. We toil in [the study of] Tora day and night. We support the poor secretly. We distribute alms at all times and hours. Among us there are some who have consecrated books for [the benefit] of the poor in need [of books], and they disburse the fee to study Scripture and Talmud.

Here, R. Qimḥi was appealing to the rabbinic principle that someone conforming to "the Tora and precepts" ought to be regarded as "your comrade," regardless of personal ideology.[288] Assuming a minimum of rabbinic integrity, R. Qimḥi concluded with this overwhelming question: "Are those to be called 'transgressors of the Law?'"[289] Giving

287. *"Milḥemet ha-Dat,"* p. 92.
288. Shebu'ot 30a. Cf. *Besamim Rosh* #240, 75b; *Zeqan Aharon* #25, 30d.
289. *Iggerot Qena'ot*, III, 3d. For some background literature, see *Maimonidean Criticism and the Maimonidean Controversy*, pp. 175–182.

vent to their own religious prejudices, historians answered with a resounding: 'Yes!' In what follows, I will try to show that the question raises foundational issues and deserves to be taken seriously.

Among the alleged reasons justifying the condemnation of Maimonides was the danger of 'heresy.' And yet, in spite of all the accusations hurled against the Maimonideans there is no documentation substantiating these charges. One has yet to find a single Maimonidean who can serve as a counterpart to such apostates as Abner de Burgos (1260/70–ca. 1347) and Jerónimo de Santa Fe (d. ca. 1419), reared in the anti-Maimonidean schools. It has been documented that kabbalistic doctrines have influenced the famous apostate Abner de Burgos. Although he was well acquainted with the philosophical literature of the time, he shared in matters of religion the views of the anti-Maimonideans, "that philosophy... is forbidden to those who believe in the Tora."[290] His personal ideology, as well as his language and style, conform to those who had rejected the role of philosophy in spiritual matters.[291] Not only did he quote approvingly from "the sages of the Kabbala,"[292] but his Trinitarian ideologies are a spin-off of the Trinitarian doctrines of Gerona and the Castilian kabbalist R. Joseph Chicatilla (1248–ca. 1325).[293]

The same applies to the alleged religious laxity of Maimonideans. Other than historians' prejudices, not a single accusation can be supported by record. The case of the Maimonidean sage R. Levi ben Ḥayyim (b. ca. 1250) from Provençe, gives credence to our view. The anti-Maimonideans had battled him mercilessly for alleged heresies

---

290. See Y. Baer, "The Kabalistic Doctrine in the Christological Teaching of Abner of Burgos," (Heb.) *Tarbiz* 27 (1958), pp. 278–289. The quotation is from his *Teshubot la-Meḥaref,* photocopy of Parma Ms. in the appendix of Shoshana G. Gershenzon, *A Study of* Teshuvot la-Meḥaref *by Abner of Burgos,* Ph. D. Thesis (New York: The Jewish Theological Seminary of America, 1984), p. 303a.

291. This point had been overlooked in the very fine analysis *Teshubot la-Meḥaref,* pp. 64–66. What Gershenzon designates as "anti-Averroistic tendencies within the Church," is nothing more than "anti-Maimonidean tendencies among Jews."

292. *Teshubot la-Meḥaref,* p. 307b.

293. *Teshubot la-Meḥaref,* pp. 95–108. Cf. above n. 261.

and laxity. No less a figure than the late Professor Abraham Halkin (1903–1990) investigated these allegations. On the basis of a careful study of all the documentation available, he showed that the opposite was the case. Concluding with these touching lines:

> Statements of this sort, in my humble opinion, prove conclusively that a grave injustice has been done to Levi ben Abraham ben Ḥayyim in branding him a heretic, a seducer and a subverter. His love of his faith, coupled with his admiration of philosophy, impelled him, as it did his fellow intellectuals, to strive zealously to demonstrate that Judaism contains all wisdom, nay, that it is the mother of all learning, which is now the proud possession of others.[294]

Psychologically, antisemitism, ethnic hatred, and all forms of bias and persecution are nothing more than demonic projections by one segment of the population onto the 'other.' Significantly, in spite of the rich documentation of the period, not a word of the anti-Maimonidean allegations can be supported by record. It seems to me that just as Christians were projecting their *own* demons onto the 'other' (the Jews), the anti-Maimonideans, in mimetic response, projected their demons onto their *own* 'other': the Maimonideans. Often, R. Adrete accused the Maimonideans of "heresy and abomination that they had written in their books," and made reference to their "heretical writings" which, in his view "ought to be incinerated"; and accused their authors of personal "corruption" and "blaspheme" (see above nn. 124, 135, 137). However, not a single word of their abominations and alleged heresies is spelled out! Until the laxity and heresy of a *single* 'Maimonidean' is properly analyzed and documented, it would be safe to say that the demons combated so heroically by the anti-Maimonideans lived deep inside their own psyche and nowhere else.

294. Abraham Halkin, "Why was Levi ben Ḥayyim Hounded?" *Proceedings of the American Academy for Jewish Research*, 34 (1966), p. 76. Cf. *The European Witch-Craze*, chapter 3.

The *Guide* is a follow-up to the guideline set by R. Hayye Gaon, properly described as "the last Gaon in time and the first in eminence." We will be focusing on a *responsum* that he addressed to R. Samuel ha-Nagid, the principal architect of what became known as "the Golden Age of Spain." The question itself is not extant, but from the answer it is evident that it had to do with the permissibility of secular studies, 'philosophy' in medieval and premodern parlance. The answer appears in two versions. The original version was cited by Ramban, in his epistle to the "Rabbis of France," urging them to show moderation.[295] There is also a bogus version, variously published from a manuscript found in Catalonia.[296] The bogus version was revised by the anti-Maimonideans to buttress their position. The first part of the answer is the same in both versions. It reads as follows:

> For physical, as well as spiritual welfare, and for proper human guidance, intense study of Mishna and Talmud is (required). That is certainly good for Israel! Since by studying Tora (an individual sage) will benefit himself and other sages; he also will be benefiting the general public, by providing them with useful guidance in the path of the Tora and precepts.

The bogus version continues:

> However, if someone would distance his heart from this, and occupy himself in the matters that you have mentioned [i.e., philosophy], he would be taking himself away from the fear

295. All subsequent translations from the 'original version' proceed from the Hebrew text in *Qobeṣ Teshubot*, III, 10c. This version also appears in *Kitbe Ramban*, vol. 1, pp. 349–350.

296. Our translation of this version is from the *'En Ya'aqob* on Ḥagiga, II, 11, s.v. *qarob*. An identical version is found in *Teshubot ha-Ribash* #45; R. Simon and Solomon Duran, *Yakhin wu-Bo'az* (Leghorn, 5542/1782) vol. 1 #134; *Oṣar ha-Ge'onim*, Ḥagiga, pp. 65–66. Cf. below n. 340. For a discussion of these two versions, see *Iyye ha-Yam*, #5, 2b-3b.

> of God, and will go astray in those matters, for the reason that he would be disconnecting himself totally from all the words of the Tora. Out of this disconnection, people are prone to become confused, and would not care to forsake the prayers and the rest of the precepts.

The blank condemnation is puzzling. Particularly, since R. Samuel ha-Nagid had publicly acknowledged the supreme authority of R. Hayye Gaon.[297] Not only did R. Samuel ha-Nagid and his circles engage vigorously in secular matters, but R. Hayye Gaon himself, as well as his father in-law, R. Samuel Ḥofni Gaon, and the celebrated R. Se'adya Gaon, pursued philosophical studies. More to the point: why would someone who studies secular subjects be "disconnecting himself totally from all the words of the Tora?" Upon reading the original text published by Ramban, we discover that pious hands had deleted one word! The original text reads: "However, if someone would distance his heart from this, and occupy himself *exclusively* (בלבד) with the matters that you have mentioned, he would be taking himself away from the fear of God." The bogus version continues: "and go astray in those matters, for the reason that he will be disconnecting himself totally from all the words of the Tora." The sense is unclear: why would such a person "go astray?" In the original text we read: "and go astray *in those matters found written in sectarian books* (באותן הענינים הכתובים בספרים החיצונים)." The term "sectarian books" (ספרים החיצונים) is a reference to the large Karraite and sectarian material (including those by 'little foxes') written *against* Rabbinic Judaism. This type of literature can bewilder a Jew conversant in secular studies but bereft of Jewish learning. In the end, such an individual could end up "disconnecting himself totally from all the words of the Tora." The Gaon explained further: "As a result of this disconnection, people are prone to become confused, and will not care to forsake

297. See *Diwan R. Shemu'el ha-Nagid, Ben-Tehillim*, #27, pp. 91–92 (ll. 42–46). On his dependence on R. Hayye Gaon, see *Sefer ha-Qabbala* (Heb.), p. 57 (ll. 179–180).

the prayers and the rest of the precepts." The next paragraph, out of place in the revised version, follows naturally in the original text. The bogus version continues:

> On the other hand, individuals finding (ימצאו) themselves on the side of Tora and the fear of God, would – as a result (of their studies) – be guiding the people towards the fear of God and repentance, without any hesitation, and they would have no doubts in the Holy One, blessed be He!

The original text is about the same, with two minor variations.

> On the other hand, individuals *dedicating* themselves (ימסרו) to Tora and the fear of God, would – as a result of this (their studies) – be guiding the people, *undoubtedly towards a happy end* (לאחרית טובה), and they would have no doubts (בלי פקפוק) in the Holy One, blessed be He!

The last few words ("they would have no doubts in the Holy One, blessed be He") may be a critical reference to the polytheistic and anthropomorphic doctrines embraced by some anti-Maimonideans.

The variations in the concluding paragraph are most revealing. The bogus version reads:

> If you would encounter people engaged in those matters, ascertaining that (theirs) is a smooth pathway, and through it they would attain knowledge of God – don't listen to them and don't believe them! Be sure that they are lying to you! And you will not find fear of sin, diligence (in the fulfillment of the precepts), humility, purity, and holiness except among people occupying themselves in the study of the Mishna and Talmud.

These are the words of the Gaon. Our Teacher Hayye, Father of Israel, may his memory be blessed!

In the original version we read:

> If you would encounter people engaged in those matters [= the ספרים החיצונים or "sectarian books" mentioned previously] *and in philosophical methodology* (ודרכי הפילוסופיא), ascertaining that (theirs) is a smooth path, and through it they will attain knowledge of God – don't listen to them and don't believe them! Be sure, they are lying to you! And you will not find fear of sin, humility, and holiness except among people occupying themselves in the study of the Mishna and the Talmud *together with science, not with science alone* (ובחכמה יחד, לא בדברי חכמה בלבד).

At the end of the bogus version there is a note by the editor, R. Israel b. Ḥabib:

> This text I copied from a book which I have found in the house of a [God]-fearing and blameless sage, from the Kingdom of Catalonia, which from ancient times had a multitude of sages and elders. May their memory be blessed!

The detail informing the reader that he had copied the text from a Catalonian manuscript is most revealing. The original *responsum* was quoted by Ramban. He was from Catalonia and must have deposited the original in one of the rabbinic libraries in town. Catalonia was also the bedrock of anti-Maimonideans kabbalists. Moved by pious zeal, some anti-Maimonidean doctored the text. The Bar-Sheshets and Durans quoting the bogus version came from Majorca, a place with close ties to Catalonia. Both families settled in Algiers. At least one of them must have brought the bogus version to their new home. This explains why their bogus version is the same as the one cited in *'En Ya'aqob*. The integrity of the rabbis quoting the bogus version is beyond question. Rather, they (like many others) were the victims of one of those pious forgeries characterizing ideologues of all persuasions, believing that the end justifies the means. None of these rabbis could have known that the version that they were quoting had been adulterated by someone, believing that zeal excuses integrity, both religious and intellectual (cf. above chapter 26 and appendix 55).

Maimonides' *Guide* is a follow up to R. Hayye Gaon's guideline. A close reading of the epistle to his disciple, at the head of the *Guide*, will show that he was dedicating his book precisely to a student who had followed the Gaon's instruction, and mastered his Talmudic *and* scientific studies. As a result, such an individual was *perplexed*. To that specific class of student Maimonides dedicated the *Guide*.[298]

Reading the original text of R. Hayye can help us value the integrity of the anti-Maimonideans and understand why, in presenting their arguments, they avoided mentioning the *qabbala* of the Geonim. It can also explain why they barred sages such as R. Qimḥi from presenting a defense of Maimonides.[299] If by chance a careless editor would overlook a contrary view, as it was with the defense presented by R. Bedersi, it would be left unanswered: R. Adrete never deigned it with a reply.[300]

298. The annotated text and variations of the dedicatory epistle had been the subject of a very fine study by D. H. Baneth, *Iggerot ha-Rambam* (Jerusalem: Mekize Nirdamim, 1947), pp. 3–9; cf. the Hebrew version, ibid., pp. 9–16.

299. See quotation above in n. 106 and appendix 57.

300. *Teshubot ha-Rishba*, vol. 1 #418. The first editor, too sluggish to analyze the content, thought that it was written by R. Adrete (see above n. 158). That is why he did not eliminate it altogether! Violence and zeal, both intellectual and emotional, are supreme testimony of religiosity according to the Islamic-Christian concept of *ijtihad*, but it was flatly rejected by the Maimonideans and the Andalusian school; see "Two Models of Jewish Spirituality," pp. 7–17, 19–23. On the legal and judicial implications of 'violence,' see José Faur, "Law and Hermeneutics in Rabbinic Tradition," *Cardozo Law Review* 14 (1993), pp. 1662–1666.

# Chapter 63
# The *Mishne Tora*

Studying the anti-Maimonidean readings of the *Mishne Tora* – a work based on a meticulous examination of the Talmud and juridical traditions of the Geonim – one cannot help but wonder whether they had any idea of what halakha is or if they actually cared about it. They were unfamiliar with the rudiments of Semitic grammar and philology, knew not rabbinic rhetoric and jurisprudence, and they were not conversant with the major halakhic and hermeneutic principles developed in the Academies of the Geonim and Old Sepharad. If one were to judge their level of comprehension by the grammar of their writings – I have failed to find a perfect topic sentence in any of their works – one would have to admit that textual analysis and cohesiveness were not part of their mental apparatus. In addition, the texts they studied, including the Scripture and Talmud, had been subjected to whimsical 'doctoring' by careless and semi-lettered scribes.[301] Generally, their objections rest on faulty texts, analphabetic readings, and unfamiliarity with Geonic scholarship.

With the dispersion of the Jewish communities and subsequent loss of central authority, the Mishna and Talmud, set by the last national authority of Israel, became the statutory law of the Jews (see above chapters 43–48). An important consideration in determining which of the numerous legal views proposed and discussed in the Mishna and Talmud are to be included in the set of statutory laws

301. See above n. 89.

are the judicial interpretations and applications in the daily life of the people (הלכה למעשה). Another consideration approaches something analogous to 'settled law' (הלכה קבועה, etc., see appendix 68). These are laws that had been contested, both in substance and meaning, but were later interpreted and applied by the judicial authorities without any substantial challenge. We should recall that Judaism does not recognize the separation of the legislative from the judiciary, and the judiciary is not constricted by an independent legislative body. In a Civil law system, a judge is basically an expert clerk. When facing conflicting interpretations or an unclear legislation, the judge is expected to refer the matter to the legislature for authoritative interpretation. In the Jewish legal system, the court cannot refer the matter to a 'superior' authority for clarification. Thus, the application of the law (הלכה למעשה) is left to the discretion of the judiciary. Consequently, the rabbis were particularly sensitive to what Justice Cardozo referred to as the tension between the 'inconstancy' of society and the 'constancy' of the law.[302] This is why there isn't – there couldn't be – a full congruence between the law as taught in school and the case at hand. The Mishna (Berakhot 2:5–7) cites three cases where Rabban Gamli'el (1st and 2nd centuries) acted differently than what he taught his disciples (see appendix 69). For that reason, when a law is examined in terms of the circumstances at hand, it is never 'clear.' Anticipating human lethargy, even among judges, the first counsel that the Men of the Great Assembly (4th century B. C. E.) wished to pass on to the future sages of Israel was "to be cautious in judgment" (Abot 1:1). Only torpid minds could perceive a law in absolute terms. "The certainty of the laws," wrote Vico "is an obscurity of judgment backed only by authority."[303] A similar point was made in a lecture delivered by Justice Holmes (1841–1935). Essentially, a lawyer engages in "prediction, the prediction of the incidence of the public force through the instrumentality of the courts."[304] In reference to Jewish

302. *The Paradoxes of Legal Science*, pp. 10–11.

303. *The New Science*, CXI #321, p. 93.

304. Oliver Wendell Holmes, "The Path of the Law," *Harvard Law Review* 10 (1897),

law, Maimonides observed: "The laws of the Tora express the general and usual. The rabbis spoke according to the current."[305] To render a fair judgment, the rabbi and judge must take into account the *uniqueness* of the case at hand. Even when the same case comes before you, don't say: "This case has already appeared before me, and I went over it, over and over and over, but be cautious as you judge."[306] We can illustrate this process from the realm of aesthetics: "Art is opposed to general ideas, it describes only the individual, desires only the unique. It does not classify: it *de*classifies."[307] The task of the rabbi (and judge), too, is to *de*classify, by articulating the tension between the generality expressed in the law and the specificity of the case at hand. Only then could he proceed to bridge the tension in a quantum jump. That is why every halakhic decision is a new and fresh analysis of the law. Since a legal decision is not a 'purely objective' discipline, an important factor in the application of the law is the mood of the judge at *the time* of judgment. Commenting on the rabbinic principle, "A judge must follow what his eyes show him," R. Gereshom, speaking in the first person, explained: "According to what appears to *me* at the moment that *I* rendered [the judgment]. At a different moment it may have appeared to *me* differently."[308] Given that the mood-factor is unknown, we can ascertain that while the judicial interpretations and applications of rabbis and judges (הלכה למעשה) in various cases and communities differ, rigorously speaking, we can actually never be sure that they are really conflicting with one another. That is why, except for anti-Maimonidean ideologues, the various practices and

---

p. 61. Cf. appendix 48.

305. *Teshubot ha-Rambam*, #224, vol. 2, p. 399; cf. ibid #252, vol. 2, p. 461; *Perush ha-Mishnayot*, 'Eduyot 2:9, vol. 4, p. 299; *Studies in the Mishne Tora*, p. 57 n. 75. R. Abraham Maimonides, *Perush*, p. 98, noted that the Hebrew 'כל' ('all') serves to indicate the 'general and preponderant' – not the absolute 'all' and 'each and every one.' cf. *The Paradoxes of Legal Science*, pp. 6–9.

306. *Sifre*, #16, p. 25. Cf. *MT Sanhedrin* 20:8.

307. Marcel Schwob, *The King in the Golden Mask* (Manchester: Carcanet, 1982), p. 115.

308. *Perush R. Gereshom*, Baba Batra 131a.

standards of the communities throughout the Diaspora, although diverse, were not regarded as 'in conflict' (מחלוקת) with the other.

The *Mishne Tora* is a follow up to the guidelines of classical Jewish education – something about which the anti-Maimonideans were clueless. The purpose was to produce a work reflecting a consensus understanding of the law, which could be used as a textbook for the second stage of education. To this effect, Maimonides stipulated that he was giving a presentation of the law of the Talmud, "as it was taught by the Geonim in all of their works" (Introduction to the *MT*, ll. 165–166; cf. Sh. Abramson, *Perush R. Ḥanan'el la-Talmud*, p. 110). That other scholars could challenge these interpretations and propose a different view either in the construction or application of the law – goes without saying. This point gains clarity upon noting that the term 'Gaon' (Excellency), used by Maimonides, included *all* rabbinic sages, regardless of geography. 'Geonim' or 'sages qualified to render an exposition of the law' are "those who rose in the Land of Israel, Babylonia, Sepharad and France" (Introduction to the *MT*, ll. 133–134). 'France,' in the language of the time, included Germany and (some regions in) Italy. Therefore,

> If one of the Geonim taught that the path of the law (דרך המשפט) is in this direction, and another court coming after him understood that this is not the path of the law (דרך המשפט) written in the Talmud, they need not abide by the early one but by the one whose words make more sense, regardless of whether he is an earlier or later [authority] (Introduction to the *MT*, ll. 122–125).[309]

309. Cf. *MT Mamrim* 1:5; and "*Shelosh Teshubot le-R. Hayye Gaon*," *Ginze Kedem* 2 (1923), p. 19. Maimonides rejected the notion that the title 'Gaon' was exclusive to Babylonia, or that a scholar could be disqualified on account of geography or cultural background; see Introduction, (ll. 132–135); *Teshubot ha-Rambam*, #310, vol. 2, p. 576. On the term 'France,' see *Texts and Studies*, vol. 2, p. 39, n. 74. In this connection we would like to point out that Maimonides appointed to the position of judge a scholar who was most probably 'French,' and sympathetic to

This logic was the guiding principle adopted by many Jewish communities throughout history: to respect the halakhic autonomy of other communities. A corollary of this principle was disallowing a rabbi to try to impose his views or authority on a rabbi of another community. The principle was clearly formulated by R. Samuel de Medina (1506–1589), rabbi of Salonika, one of the largest and most influential communities at the time.

> A sage has no right to intrude into the area of another colleague, although he may be most excellent among the excellent – like Rabban Gamli'el – and the other most simple among the simple.[310]

In essence, in the *Mishne Tora* Maimonides was acting as a lawyer giving guidance, rather than anointed beatific issuing decisions *ex Cathedra*. As such it is a learned legal treatise, embodying mainstream understanding of Jewish law, according to the halakhic traditions to which Maimonides was privy.[311] Nonetheless, even Maimonides himself did not regard his legal conclusions as superlatives. A good

---

some of the anti-Maimonidean ideologies; see below n. 318. More significantly, Maimonides protected him against the attack of some influential men in the area; see *Iggerot ha-Rambam*, vol. 2, pp. 336–350. Likewise, Maimonides treated respectfully R. Meir, a disciple of his nemesis Rabad; see Jacob Mann, *Texts and Studies*, vol. 2, p. 397 n. 10. Similarly, his son R. Abraham did not permit local men to treat French rabbis disrespectfully; see *Milḥamot ha-Shem*, p. 53; and even less to delegitimize their halakhic opinions; see ibid., p. 59. On the expression "the path of the law" (דרך המשפט); see appendix 48, and cf. above n. 303.

310. R. Samuel de Medina, *Teshubot Meharashdam, Ḥoshen Mishpaṭ* (Salonika, 5358/1598), #12, 8a; cf. ibid., #7. The principle applies to every community, none can exercise authority over the other; see R. David ha-Kohen, *Teshubot ha-Radaq* (Constantinople, 5297/1537), #XIII, 104b-105b; cf. ibid., #XXII, 15, 165c-166a. For a critical appraisal of some Talmudic and rabbinic sources on the subject, see Professor David Weiss Halivni, "The Role of the *Mara D'atra* in Jewish Law," *Proceedings of the Rabbinical Assembly* (1976), pp. 124–129.

311. See *Sefer ha-Miṣvot*, pp. 1–3; cf. *Iggerot*, vol. 2, p. 454 (l. 15). His task was to 'expose' not to 'explain' the law; see ibid., pp. 440–442; 445 (ll. 14–15); and *Kesef*

example of his legal thinking is his ruling concerning the computation of the Sabbatical year (שמיטה). His own computation differed from the standard practice. Nonetheless, he ruled in favor of the computation by the "Geonim and inhabitants of the Holy Land." He justified his ruling as follows:

> On that [the tradition of the "Geonim and inhabitants of the Holy Land"] we place our trust, and in accordance to their computation we issue instruction concerning the [computation of the year of the various] tithes, the Sabbatical (laws), and the abolition of loans. Given that the *qabbala* and judicial practice (מעשה) are the principal pillars in the instruction of the law. And on them we should rely.[312]

The style of the *Mishne Tora* is that of a scholarly recapitulation or "transcript" (דרך קצרה, Introduction, *MT* l. 158; see appendix 34) of the law that could provide a pivotal point of argument, but is not, and never was intended to be, a code as in a Civil law system which the judiciary *must* follow. Clearly and unambiguously, he wrote in the Introduction (l. 160) that the laws he was formulating were "approximate" (קרובים) – not final! Not only does the *Mishne Tora* contain laws and regulations impossible to apply in practice (הלכה למעשה), but Maimonides himself did not hesitate to depart from the *Mishne Tora* in the application of the law (הלכה למעשה). To alert the attentive reader to this effect, he noted that some of the procedural norms are not observed by the courts, "... since we do not have the

---

*Mishne* on Kelim 6:2. This is why occasionally he retracted from a position he held in *Perush ha-Mishnayot*, for instance Giṭṭin 5:8, vol. 3, p. 225, on behalf of "the standard practice today," as instituted by the Geonim; see *MT Tefilla* 12:18.

312. *MT Shemiṭṭa ve-Yobel* 10:6. The term '*qabbala*' here stands for authoritative instruction as imparted by the Geonim, not by conjecture "more or less"; see above, chapter 49, and n. 33. The term "judicial practice (מעשה)" is equivalent to the Arabic *'amal*; see *Perush ha-Mishnayot Bekhorot* 4:4, vol. 5, p. 242. Cf. Section II, nn. 123, 127; Section IV, nn. 173, 176; and appendix 48.

means to execute the law to the hilt."[313] A few examples may help clarify his position. Maimonides registered the biblical prohibition to "never take up residence in Egypt" (Deut. 28:68; see Deut. 17:16 and Ex. 14:13)."[314] Yet he himself, as well as countless Jews, lived in Egypt. Some rabbinic sages tried to justify this practice in terms of the law, in my view unsuccessfully. Most instructive is the fact that Maimonides himself did not find it necessary to apologize or to give an explanation. Another is a rabbinic regulation designed to prevent promiscuous relations between a female slave and her master. To this purpose, an injunction was passed stipulating that a man *suspected* of licentious relations with his female slave, [a] must free her, [b] and in punishment, he is prohibited to marry her. In view that in the present social situation, point [b] may result in injury to her, as she could find herself unprotected in an alien environment, on several occasions Maimonides issued decisions to the effect that the owner "should free her and marry her," in order to protect her thus from further abuse.[315] In another case, Maimonides registered a rabbinic regulation prohibiting a woman who was widowed twice to remarry. Nonetheless, he permitted this (הלכה למעשה) when the need arose to wed again.[316] An illuminating example concerns a Talmudic ruling. Maimonides registered a Talmudic law prohibiting teaching Tora to a non-Jew. Nonetheless, he issued a decision that "it is permitted to teach Tora to Christians" since they believe "in the integrity of the text of Scripture."[317] Finally, Maimonides registered the ruling that a Scroll of the Tora that had not been written accord-

313. *MT Sanhedrin* 21:5. The same expression appears in *Perush ha-Mishnayot, Megilla* 1:1, vol. 2, p. 344.
314. *Sefer ha-Miṣvot*, Negative Precept #46, p. 205; *MT Melakhim* 5:7–8.
315. *MT Gerushin* 10:14; *Teshubot ha-Rambam* #211, vol. 2, pp. 374–375.
316. See *MT Issure Bi'a* 21:1, and *Teshubot ha-Rambam* #15, vol. 1, pp. 22–24.
317. See *MT Melakhim* 10:9; *Teshubot ha-Rambam* #149, vol. 1, pp. 284–285. The source for this ruling is Shabbat 116a, concerning Samuel's visit to Be-Abidan. According to R. Ḥanan'el, this was a place attended by Christian scholars. In particular, Jews appreciated the insight of Syriac scholars in Hebrew lexicography; cf. R. Abraham b. Maimonides, *Perush*, p. 422; and above n. 118.

ing to the ten specifications laid down by the rabbis "cannot be used for public reading." Nonetheless, Maimonides, in accordance to the standard practice in Andalusia, issued a decision permitting the use of such a Scroll for public reading.[318] In general, we may say that an important factor in the 'contradictions' between the *Mishne Tora* and Maimonides' *responsa* is the failure to distinguish between the judicial application of a rule (הלכה למעשה) and the law as taught in school.

Some objected to the *Mishne Tora* on the grounds that it might allow unqualified people to render legal decisions[319] (הוראה). According to this line of reasoning we should prohibit medical and pharmacological treatises on the grounds that unqualified people may use them to practice the trade clandestinely, etc. The basis of this objection is an analphabetic notion of 'knowledge.' In the footsteps of the scholastics, anti-Maimonideans believed that a quotation from an authority by a non-scholar had merits. Citations from halakhic authorities had standing only when transmitted by sages to bona fide disciples of sages, or if their citation had been submitted to, and subsequently approved by, judicial authorities. The notion that by virtue of having attended some classes of a sage a student may claim to be a disciple of said sage has no standing in the Talmud.[320] Simply put: 'knowl-

318. See *MT Sefer Tora* 10:1; *Teshubot ha-Rambam* #294, vol. 2, pp. 552–553. For further background, see *Studies in the Mishne Tora*, pp. 181–182, nn. 32–33. The position of Maimonides has been explained by Maran, *Kesef Mishne* on *Sefer Tora* 10:1.

319. See the quotation of R. Phineas in Maimonides' *Iggerot*, vol. 2, p. 438 (ll. 14–21). It is not clear whether R. Phineas was from France or from Byzantium. Cf. Maimonides, *Qobeṣ Teshubot Ha-Rambam*, part 1, 27a, where Maimonides tried to dissuade R. Phineas from "returning to Romania," i.e., Byzantium. However, in fol. 26c, Maimonides seemed to include him with the "people of France." In the fragments of a work by a pupil of Maimonides, published by Abraham S. Halkin, "In Defense of Maimonides' Code" (Heb.), *Tarbiz* 25 (1956), p. 427, R. Phineas is referred to as one "of the scholars of France." R. Phineas may have been a Byzantine Jew who went to France to study, or most probably a French Jew who spent some time in Byzantium before taking up residence in Alexandria.

320. See Zebaḥim 96b. For a comprehensive analysis of the status and definition of

edge' of halakha by an unqualified student (תלמיד שלא הגיע להוראה) is *non*-knowledge.[321] In this connection we should recall that the rabbis had declared that in such a case one cannot render halakha even from the Talmud (see appendix 48). To assume that judicial authorities would accept a decision simply because it comes from the *Mishne Tora*, or any other source, without proper development and argumentation, is preposterous (see appendix 69). This is the place to remind the reader that the *Mishne Tora* was written in Hebrew, i.e., *for the general public*. This should have sufficed for anyone with a minimal rabbinic training to realize that it was composed for a public *not* conversant with "לישנא דרבנן," or the Aramaic dialect of rabbinical discourse proper (see above chapter 49). Therefore it could not award the reader authority to render "a legal decision."

We can now proceed to examine the principal argument put forward to de-legitimize the *Mishne Tora* – repeated *ad nauseam* by modern historians. In the same intellectual mood of the 'little foxes' challenging the Geonim by asking, "How do they know that matter" (see above chapter 50), anti-Maimonideans sought to delegitimize the *Mishne Tora* because it does not cite its sources. Characteristically, no one thought to ask these critics for *their* source that a legal decision – whether in Jewish or in general jurisprudence – is not authoritative unless it validates its sources. The argument is malicious and erroneous: a 'source' is worthless to a public not fluent in rabbinics. Ultimately, such a public would have to *rely* (לסמוך) on one authority or another (or on the supposed evidence and substantiation of the alleged 'source'), but such an individual could not pass a critical judgment on the matter.[322] The information can be helpful

---

a 'disciple,' see *Yad Mal'akhi* #663. In this connection it would be important to consider the fact that a report made by an 'elder' (סבא), i.e., someone regularly attending the *Yeshiba*, but not a faculty member, has no standing; see Nidda 8b and the note by Maran Joseph Caro, *Kesef Mishne* on *MT Shemiṭṭa ve-Yobel* 7:19.

321. See Horayot 2b and pseudo-R. Ḥanan'el, ad loc.; *MT Shegagot* 13:5. Cf. *MT Talmud Tora* 5:4; Sanhedrin 20:8.

322. See R. David 'Arama, *Perush 'al ha-Rambam* (Salonika, 5330/1570), 2c; *Studies in*

only to a scholar with a partial knowledge of the subject. The rabbis, however, barred passing on such information. Explicitly, they taught: "it is not to be explained to a scholar" (חכם); that is, either the rationale (טעמא) or the source of the halakha under discussion (cf. appendix 19). Moreover, if a scholar did not catch the halakha the first time, a request to repeat it should be denied: "...it is not [even] to be repeated to a scholar"[323] (.(חכם The sense of this rule is simple: someone unfamiliar with *all* relevant sources, or having an attention span requiring hearing the halakha more than once is not qualified to participate in an intelligent discussion of the subject. Accordingly, when writing a legal decision, the rabbis abstained from specifying the 'rationale' (טעמא), i.e., the source and or logic of their decision. Raba, head of the *Yeshiba,* issued a judicial instruction to two of his disciples who had been appointed to the bench:

> When you find an objection against a judicial decision (פיסקא דדינא) of mine brought before you, do not declare it 'invalid' until you have consulted with me. If I could offer the rationale (טעמא), I would present it to you, and if not I would retract it. After (my) death you should neither tear it nor should you rely on it: do not tear it, since if I would have been present I

---

*the Mishne Tora,* p. 55 n. 66. It may be a point of some interest that Thucydides did not indicate his sources. As noted by A. D. Momigliano "Historiography on Written and Oral Traditions," in *Studies in Historiography* (New York: Harper & Row, 1966), p. 214: "He assumes the responsibility for what he says, and feels no need to leave a choice to the reader." It would be safe to assume that in such a case, *pseudo*-Jewish intellectuals would not dare raise any objections!

323. *Sifra, Meṣora',* Par. III, 5, 11, 75c, as cited in ed. Joshua Finkel, *Maimonides' Treatise On Resurrection* (New York: The American Academy for Jewish Research, 1939), p. 37. The same text appears in ed. Louis Finkelstein, *Sifra* (New York: The Jewish Theological Seminary, 5717–1956), p. 324; in R. Aaron ibn Ḥayyim, *Qorban Aharon* (Venice: 5369/1609), 153c, and in his commentary ad loc. The text in *Sifra* (Vienna, 5622/1862) 75c is slightly different, but it amounts to the same: "it is not to be repeated to a sage (חכם)... it is not to be explained to a sage (חכם)."

> might have been able to give the rationale (טעמא), but do not rely on it, since a judge must follow what his eyes show him.[324]

Obviously, in his decisions, Raba did not specify the rationale (טעמא) of his judgment; otherwise there would be no need to consult with him. On the basis of Raba's principle, Maimonides formulated the following rule:

> In general, let me tell you. Any statement that comes before us that belongs to one of the Geonim who are acknowledged for their legal decisions (הוראה), and for whom we do not have any clear evidence (for their decision = טעמא), we will neither rebuff it, nor ought we to declare it erroneous. Rather, we should say, there might be some basis (to it). However, it would be wrong for us to rely on it, and we should not carry it out until we know its rationale.[325]

In Talmudic times there were collections of 'plain halakha ' (הלכה פסוקה), formulating the law without any explanation, and no one raised the objections raised by the anti-Maimonideans.[326] More significant is the fact that in the formulation of the law Maimonides generally retained a key-term indicating to a master in rabbinics – scholars of the rank of R. Envidal de Toledo and Maran Joseph Caro – the source from which the halakha derived.

The anti-Maimonideans did not bother with any of the above. Their criticism was a matter of expediency. Before the publication of the *Mishne Tora*, the general public had no access to the law of Israel. In Toledo, for example, rabbis refused to teach the public not only

324. Baba Batra 130b-131a; see appendix 48. The source of Raba is Tosefta Sanhedrin 3:8, p. 419, cited below n. 332. For further background on טעמא, see appendix 19.

325. *Teshubot ha-Rambam*, #310, vol. 2, p. 576; cf. #138, vol. 1, pp. 266–267.

326. See Berakhot 31a; cf. Sanhedrin 106b; *Kalla Rabbati*, ed. Michael Higger (Brooklyn: Moinester Publishing, 1936), 5:4, p. 287; 6:4, p. 305.

Talmud, but, also, such basic work as R. Isaac Alfasi's *Halakhot*. The public was at the mercy of the clergy. Referring to R. Me'ir Abul'afya, Chief Rabbi of Toledo (and at the time an active anti-Maimonidean), the president of the community wrote: "[He] would render judgments on his own, according to his whim. Nobody could challenge him because they did not know what the law was." The publication of *Mishne Tora* changed all this. For the first time, the public could assess the decisions rendered by the clergy in the light of a work fully accessible to them. Again, referring to the Chief Rabbi, the head of the community made this valuable observation:

> Upon seeing this [the *Mishne Tora*], the above-mentioned judges, of whom this conceited idiot, speaking arrogantly, is one of them, their envy grew. Their anger kindled and they tried to allure those who support the 'Law of Moses' [the *Mishne Tora*]... to depart from the right path. They are now further sinning, speaking slanderously (about Maimonides) to the ignoramuses, as what that idiot wrote in a book. Many more things were [added later to the slander] *in order that they* [the public] *should obey him* [the chief rabbi] *and not depart from his words.*[327]

A *sine qua non* for anti-Maimonidean criticism is an analphabetic public shaking and shrieking at an imaginary text. They, however, did not dare to present their criticism to a rabbinic sage. We had the opportunity to note that they refused permission to R. David Qimḥi to come to Toledo and present a defense of Maimonides (see above chapter 55 and appendix 57). To take their criticism at face value is to treat ideologues more seriously than they deserve.

---

327. *In the Shadow of History*, pp. 16–17. R. Me'ir Abul'afya was an honest man, and when he realized that he had been manipulated by unscrupulous individuals, he fully recanted, see ibid.

# Chapter 64
# Hierarchic Truth

A telling detail of anti-Maimonidean speech is its lack of civility. It attained a level of invective unprecedented in Jewish literary history. The term 'strictures' (השגות; singular השגה), designed to 'prove' Maimonides wrong, implies 'seizing' a victim in hot pursuit (see Ex. 15:9, Deut. 28:45). It involves *persecution* of, and passing the sting onto, the 'other.'[328] In this connection we should point out that anti-Maimonideans gained their reputation not for their teachings, but for their attacks. Rabbis were seen as gladiators or pugilists seeking to find the contender's weak points and bringing him to his knees. The purpose was not simply to destroy, but to humiliate and coerce the subject into a state of hierarchic submission (see Ps. 7:6, and the commentaries of R. Abraham ibn 'Ezra and R. David Qimḥi). The mood was that of contending knights, rather than Talmudic sages engaged in *meliṣa* discourse (see appendix 67). The master of this style was the celebrated R. Abraham b. David of Posquièrs (ca. 1125–1198), known by the acronym Rabad.[329] To understand the function of this style, it is important to recall that anti-Maimonidean truth is hierarchic. In quality of *europaischen Menschentums,* anti-Maimonideans possess a higher truth – nobler, and more archaic than that of the vulgar. It must be

328. A more benign nomenclature is 'emendation' (הגהה), a term referring to a scroll of the Tora that is 'ritually void' (פסול), and cannot be kept unless 'amended.'

329. For an impassioned panegyric of this towering figure, by a most worthy representative; see I. Twersky, *Rabad of Posquières* (Cambridge: Harvard University Press, 1962).

acknowledged by those standing below, not because it is true – those of lesser rank are too stupid to understand – but because a superior man told them so (see quotations below at notes 356–357). Truth is a matter of personal status: *who* says it is of the essence. In sharp contrast, Maimonides left out the names of the rabbinic authorities who had originally taught the laws and doctrines of Israel. "Your work enlightens the world," said an early critic in reference to the *Mishne Tora*, "but only to someone who had occupied himself in the Talmud and knows the names of the sages who occupied themselves in the Talmud."[330] In response, Maimonides pointed out that the compilers of classic rabbinic works, too, tended to omit the names of the authors. It is true that the Mishna cites the names of the rabbis, but that was to serve as reference, not to prove a point.

> Lest one who fails to understand will say: Didn't the Mishna mention the names of the sages? thinking that that is the proof. That is not the proof! The proof would be to expose *why* this rabbi said 'this' and *why* the other rabbi said 'that!' That would be proof![331]

In this, Maimonides was following in the footsteps of one of the great rabbinic eminences of all time. As noted by Joel Muller, the learned editor of Se'adya's *Treatise on Inheritance*:

> Another distinction: He (Se'adya Gaon) did not mention a rule or law in the name of its authors. Rather, he spoke of the laws of the Tora as a legislator, and did not mention (the laws in reference to) the Mishna, the Tanna'im and Emora'im, as he did not mention the verses of the Tora... In this fashion he was the model and trailblazer to Maimonides afterwards.[332]

330. R. Phineas, cited in *Iggerot ha-Rambam*, vol. 2, p. 438.
331. *Iggerot ha-Rambam*, vol. 2, p. 441.
332. Joel Muller, ed. R. Se'adya Gaon, *Traité de Successions* (Paris: Ernest Leroux, 1897), p. x.

At the center of this debate stands an overwhelming question. Granted that in matters of governance and law, compliance and deference to authority are of the essence. The question arises in the field of ideas. What constitutes knowledge: submission to an authority or rational understanding? (cf. *Church* v. *Galileo,* and Introductory Remarks above.) It is axiomatic for the anti-Maimonideans that knowledge is a matter of rank. Therefore, a principal factor in determining the merits of an idea is *who* says it. In a long stricture at the Introduction to the *Mishne Tora,* Rabad made known why he attacked this work:

> ... Because they [all other authors] brought proof to their words, *and* [in the sense of *namely*] cited the words of others by name. There was a great advantage to this since many a time a judge may think to prohibit or permit (something), and has proof from a place. Nevertheless, if he had known that someone greater than him had developed the theme in a different direction, he would have changed his mind. Now, I don't know why I should change my mind, (or) sway off from my tradition, (or) from my evidence on account of this author's work. If the party disagreeing with me would have been greater than I – fine! But if I am greater than he – why should I call off my view because of his view? Furthermore, sometimes there are differences of opinion among the Geonim, and this author chose one and registered it in his work. Why should I rely on his choice – since I don't agree with it? Not knowing if the party I disagree with (Maimonides) is worthy of disagreement.

The view that a judge knowing "that someone greater than he" had expressed a contrary opinion "would have changed his mind" runs contrary to the Talmudic principle: "A judge must follow what his eyes show him" (Baba Batra 131a and parallels). According to the rabbis, the Tora disallows a judge to reason: "'It would be sufficient for me if I propose [a view] similar to my teacher's' – but you should say what is on your mind."[333] In accordance to this principle, Maimonides proposed that if there is a conflict among legal experts, one should follow the view that makes more sense, "regardless of whether he is an earlier or later (authority)" (Introduction *MT* ll. 124–125; see above chapter 59). As a matter of rank, Rabad expected others to accept his views, and not to quibble about sources. "You must accept my view without any investigation, on account that I am older and wiser than you," he wrote in the preface of one of his *responsum*. He would make an exception, however and "disclose the rationale (הטעם = טעמא) so that others may learn from it, and also to protect myself from rabble-rousers who rise up" against their superior.[334]

The purpose of strictures is to establish rank: hence the need for intimidation and incivility. Rabad belonged to the elite of the "upright" (ישרים), and it was incumbent on him to impose rank as a matter of principle. In one of his strictures he explained:

> The way in which he (Maimonides) wrote is far-distant from me! 'Much has shined upon me' [cf. Ps. 102:4], and [I concluded] that it [Maimonides] is not privy to the wondrous mystery that is kept for the *upright*[335] (מן הסוד המופלא הצפון לישרים) (see appendix 67).

A privilege awarded to the elite is the experience of a glorious epiphany that awards access to the supernatural. In gratitude, after appending one of his strictures, Rabad thanked God for having "revealed His mystery (סודו) to those who fear Him; and the wisdom that He keeps for the upright (לישרים)" [cf. Prov. 2:7].[336] The truth that he

333. Tosefta Sanhedrin 3:8, p. 419; cf. R. David Pardo, *Ḥasde David*, ad loc., vol. 2 (Leghorn: 5650/1790), 61a; *MT Sanhedrin* 10:1; *Sefer ha-Miṣvot*, negative precept #283, pp. 312–313.

334. *Teshubot wu-Psaqim* (Jerusalem: Mossad Harav Kook, 5724/1964), #20, p. 65.

335. *MT Ṭum'at Okhalin* 15:1.

336. *MT Mishkab wu-Moshab* 7:7.

conveyed belongs to a higher realm: "It had been revealed to me, from the Mystery of God which [He discloses] to those who fear Him!"[337] The view that he was proposing must be accepted forthwith: "Since the Holy Spirit has already appeared in our school, and we concluded that..."[338] He belonged to a privileged family. His father, his son and himself – all three – were known to have witnessed prophet Elijah revealing himself to them.[339] Rank excused him from reading the entire paragraph that he was disparaging, or to check the authenticity of the text of the Talmud that he was quoting.[340] A hero-sage has the supreme duty to defend his devotees, no matter what. This will explain why, even when conceding that anthropomorphism is contrary to Jewish faith, he admonished Maimonides for registering corporeality as 'heresy,' since people *superior* and *worthier* than him, that is, of higher rank (i.e., Rabad's devotees), believed that the deity was corporeal:

> Why should *he* call that 'heretic' when greater and better (people) than him [cf. I Kings 2:33] have followed that course of thought [corporeality], because of what they saw in Scripture, and more because of what they saw in the *aggadot* that confuse the mind.[341]

---

337. *MT Bet ha-Beḥira* 6:14; cf. Ps. 25:14.
338. *MT Lulab* 8:5; cf. his *Teshubot wu-Psaqim*, #211, p. 263. See R. Joseph ibn Leb, *Teshubot* (Amsterdam, 5446/1686), part III, #116, 59b; *Petaḥ 'Enayim* (Leghorn, 5550/1790) on Baba Mesi'a 86a.
339. Reported in "Extracts from Joseph Sambari's Chronicle," p. 125.
340. See *Maggid Mishne* on *Ḥameṣ wu-Maṣṣa* 3:7, etc.; and idem on *Love wu-Malve* 15:1, etc.
341. *MT Teshuba* 3:7. The source for Maimonides is R. Hayye Gaon, in *Teshubot ha-Ge'onim ha- Ḥadashot*, #155, 67, p. 220. See R. Abraham b. Maimonides, in *Qobeṣ Teshubot*, III, 15d-16b. Shocked by his tone, and the harm in terms of public relations that it may cause to the anti-Maimonidean crusade, pious hands rewrote these words; see *Sefer ha-'Iqqarim* I, 2 and *Kesef Mishne*, ad loc. Cf. above n. 295.

As a matter of personal status Rabad had the right – more precisely: the duty – to treat those who disagreed with him with contempt. Although from the days of Abraham, people were urged to excel in hospitality and kindness to the traveler and stranger, R. Zeraḥya ha-Levi was prevented from entering the city in the heart of winter because he had been critical of some of Rabad's views. Consequently, he had to spend the night in the open where he subsequently died. There was a genteel, softer, and friendlier side to Rabad, if just a bit patronizing. After dismissing one of Maimonides' views, he added: "Were it not for the fact that he had made a great labor in gathering the words of the Talmud, the Yerushalmi and Tosefta, I would have summoned against him the people, elders, and sages…"[342]

Although the rabbis taught that "someone who honors himself by deprecating others has no portion in the world to come,"[343] the purpose of heroic criticism is to identify the weak points of the adversary and bring him to his knees. Since this type of swordplay necessitates a semi-lettered audience, points are gained by deprecating the 'other.' Thus the rude behavior, accepted as normal in heroic rabbinic argument (see appendix 67). It may not be irrelevant to add that, invariably, heroic rabbis are monolinguistic.[344] A note of some interest: this august figure continues to be the source of inspiration for some of the most forward-looking rabbinic minds of our time. His preeminence is axiomatic. To ascertain this fact, the *Mishne Tora* is the only book among the thousands and thousands of works in the CD of "The Responsa Project," Bar-Ilan University, which is

---

342. *MT Kil'ayim* 6:2. The halakha has to do with plane geometry, a subject where epiphany, for mysterious reasons, was inactive. Rabad misunderstood the whole issue. R. Asher, too, had problems with plane geometry; see above n. 279. Maimonides' view was explained to him by R. Israel de Toledo, quoted in *Kesef Mishne*; see also Radbaz ad loc.

343. Y. Ḥagiga II, 1, 77c; see *MT De'ot* 6:3; *Teshuba* 3:7, 14; 4:4, and above Section III, n. 233.

344. See *MT Qeri'at Shema'* 2:10; and *Maggid Mishne* on *Berakhot* 1:6.

only available with the strictures of his nemesis, Rabad. With all due respect to Maimonides, it would be wise to have a real rabbi keeping a vigilant eye on his writings.

# Chapter 65
# The Inerrant Saint

In one of his frequent digressions in praise of "the pious of Ashkenaz," the author of a critically acclaimed study on the history of Sepharad wrote this curious passage:

> The pietists of Germany, like their forefathers who had founded the communities and academies in the Rhineland, still drew vigor from the vitalizing fountains of talmudic lore. And even though they were influenced by theological ideas and popular beliefs current among their Christian neighbors, these simple men understood the fundamental principles of the lore of our sages better than any other generation in the history of the Diaspora.[345]

In Jewish tradition, the Supreme Court of Israel, the High Priest, the Political Sovereign, and even prophets, not to mention earthly rabbis, are prone to error (see above chapter 10).[346] A principal objective in delegitimizing the *Mishne Tora* was to fill the ensuing vacuum with an inerrant ministry. The most successful representative of this class of ministry was none other than the saintly R. Asher. We had the opportunity to mention that in 1305, Heaven rewarded Iberian Jewry for their anti-Maimonidean zeal. They succeeded

345. *A History of the Jews in Christian Spain,* vol. 1, pp. 98–99.
346. See Introduction, *Perush ha-Mishnayot,* vol. 1, pp. 31; *Iggerot ha-Rambam,* vol. 2, p. 450.

in installing R. Asher as the rabbi of Toledo, and as such, as the supreme spiritual authority of all Jews in Christian Spain. Throughout their ministry he and his children brought to bear 'the spirit of inerrant piety' – commonly known as '*Ḥasidut*'– into Spain. He was Tora incarnate. "As long as I am alive," he wrote, "there is Tora in Israel."[347] R. Asher was aware of his excellence. No one could vie with him either in wisdom or sanctity and, we may add, humility: "Thank God, God has graced me, and I possess all that which pertains to the true reasoning of the Law of Moses our Teacher, as [good] as all the present sages of Sepharad today." The rabbis preceding him in Toledo were illegitimate, because they derived their authority from "the authority invested in them by the king."[348] The scribes and notaries were untrustworthy, since they did their work "to increase their profit."[349] For all practical purposes, this meant that one could refer neither to the early decisions of the court nor check with community clerks about legal practices and procedures. It goes without saying that he would not recognize the right to refer to Maimonides by anyone "who is not thoroughly conversant with the Mishna and Talmud"[350] – thus excluding anyone not approved

347. *Teshubot ha-Rosh* 55:9, cited above at n. 269. The rabbis censured self-indulgence and boasting for alleged knowledge; see Ta'aniyot 20a-b; *Eliyahu Zuṭa* XVI, 75b; and *Midrash Mishle* XX, 9, p. 89. Particularly illuminating are the words of R. Abraham Maimonides, *High Ways of Perfection*, ed. and trans. Samuel Rosenblatt, vol. 2 (Baltimore: John Hopkins Press, 1938), p. 57. Concerning the offense of conceit for someone in a position of leadership, see ibid., pp. 81–85. Cf. above n. 271.

348. His appointment, too, came from the king, not from Heaven. In *Teshubot ha-Rosh*, 21:9 cited below n. 350, he refers to the authority invested in him by the king. Nonetheless, 'other' rabbis lacked divine authority and legitimacy. In a series of queries presented by R. Asher to R. Adrete, *Teshubot ha-Rishba*, vol. 1 (##461–523), he consulted with him about the permissibility of verbally abusing rabbis appointed by the king (#475). For a halakhic discussion on the authority of such a rabbi, see R. Isaac bar Sheshet, *Teshubot ha-Ribash*, #271; and R. Simon bar Semaḥ Duran, *Tashbeṣ*, I, ##158–159.

349. See *In the Shadow of History*, p. 18.

350. *Teshubot ha-Rosh*, 31:9.

by him. "Damned be (תיפח רוחם) those who judge on the basis of the books and writings of great [scholars] and do not know Mishna and Talmud at all."[351] Differing from him was an affront to the Law of Moses and formal apostasy. Take, for example, the case of R. Jacob de Valencia. Following standard halakhic practice among the Geonim and Old Sepharad, he prohibited in his own hometown the use of a public throughway (מבוי מפולש) on the Sabbath, unless a real door was appended to one of its entrances. R. Asher disagreed. Consequently, he threatened R. Jacob with excommunication: "I am excommunicating you. If you would have lived at the time of the Sanhedrin they would have put you to death."[352] To make sure that he would comply, he wrote to some of his confidants, "...you and others should persecute him." He then issued the following judgment:

> I am warning you and all the community to excommunicate that madman, Jacob the son of Rabbi Moses... And there is a religious commandment to excommunicate him throughout all the Communities of Sepharad. And also that he should be condemned to death, as with the law of a rebellious judge.

If he would not recant, he would impose on R. Jacob de Valencia, "by the authority invested in me by our lord the king (בכח המלך), the fine of a thousand coins to be paid to the governor of the city."[353]

The following case taking place in a small town in Castile in the year 1320 is indicative of the level of the zeal that his ministry inspired. A young widow fell in love with a Christian and maintained extramarital relations with him. R. Judah b. Waqar, a leading anti-Maimonidean,

---

351. *Teshubot ha-Rosh*, 43:12.

352. *Teshubot ha-Rosh*, 21:8.

353. *Teshubot ha-Rosh*, 21:9. See "Two Models of Jewish Spirituality," pp. 25–26. We should recall that at one time, R. Asher had dismissed the judicial authorities before him in Toledo as illegitimate, because they had acted "by the authority of the king"; see above n. 345.

took charge of the investigation. "I found no Jew who could offer a clear testimony on the matter," he admitted. Nonetheless, he decided to punish her by cutting off her nose and leaving her permanently disfigured. To this effect he asked permission from R. Asher. The saintly rabbi answered:

> To the honorable sage R. Judah b. Waqar, may God Guard him! You have acted beautifully to punish her by the law, so that she would be repulsive in the sight of her adulterers. Do this at once, so that she would not behave impudently. It would be proper to impose on her a fine according to her wealth. Peace be on you and yours, heartily![354]

Later, the case came before R. Adrete. Addressing R. Judah b. Waqar, he wrote: "Many people grumble against you, but you have acted according to the verdict of R. Asher, may God Guard him!" However, R. Adrete went on to show that on legal grounds, the decision was erroneous.[355]

An important tool in the ministry of inerrant rabbis was to make the public feel guilty and stupid and hollow and discombobulated. The following doctrine formulated by R. Asher aimed at installing in the Jew the pathos of guilt and helplessness and unworthiness.

> A most important doctrine for the time is to acknowledge that we are wretched before the Most High. And that this is the reason why He had left us in this harsh exile. And that when we would repent and do what is right in His eyes, He will in turn have mercy on us.

This is a cardinal doctrine. Someone rejecting it must be classified as heretic:

354. *Teshubot ha-Rosh* 18:13.
355. *Besamim Rosh* #192, 65b-c.

> However, someone disagreeing with the preceding is an atheist and a heretic, because he implies that God is unjust, prevaricating justice and acting deceitfully with His servants. [By implication, such an individual would be] desecrating His names gratuitously in the presence of everyone. [Such an individual] is rejecting the entire Tora. In general the Tora cannot be effective without a deeply ingrained faith that we have gone astray from the (right) path.[356]

The excellence of the inerrant ministry is above reproach (see appendix 67). It stands to reason, therefore, that everyone should remain in a state of submission, and not question his verdict. The source of this doctrine is not to be found in the Talmud, but in a doctrine formulated by Pope Gregory the Great (6th century): "The verdict of the superior – no matter whether just or unjust – had to be obeyed by the inferior subject." Emulating the *fidelis christianus,* the Jew, too, must express his faith through *obedience*: "because the subject has faith in the superior's institutions."[357] A rabbi is 'inerrant' because those who owe him *obedience* (in modern parlance: *emunas ḥokhomim*) may not challenge him. The basis for this doctrine is a bull issued by Pope Boniface, a contemporary of our saintly rabbi, who in 1302 formulated the principle that, "If the supreme power errs it can be judged only by God and not by man."[358]

An important innovation introduced by the inerrant ministry was lending money to Christians with interest. Popular opinion notwithstanding, the Talmud prohibits this practice, except in some limited circumstances. "I do not know what the legal basis is for our practice to lend them [the Christians] money," wrote R. Nissim of Gerona (ca 1310–ca. 1375).[359] Jews in old Sepharad did not indulge in money

---

356. *Besamim Rosh,* #251, 76d.

357. Quoted in *In the Shadow of History,* p. 33.

358. Quoted in Jeffrey Burton Russell, *A History of Medieval Christianity* (New York, 1968), p. 168. Cf. "One-Dimensional Jew," pp. 44–46.

359. *Teshubot ha-Ran* (New York: Publishing Corporation, n.d.) #56, 47b; see

lending. The rationale is quite simple. Although the Tora permits lending money with interest "to the alien" (לנכרי), members of the host country should not be regarded as "aliens." The fact that a Jew receives favors from the host country establishes a civil, as well as an ethical obligation, to treat the non-Jewish population as 'brothers' – not as aliens! A Jew is forbidden to lend money to another Jew with interest, explained R. David Qimḥi, as a matter of civic fellowship. Now, generally, there is no civic fellowship between Jews and gentiles. That is why the Tora does not prohibit loaning money to a gentile with interest. However, when gentiles have extended their fellowship to us, permitting us to dwell with them, there is a *civic fellowship* (= תיקון העולם, דרכי שלום), and it would be incumbent upon the Jew to reciprocate and treat them accordingly. In his words:

> Certainly, if a gentile had done favors and goodness to the Jew, a Jew is duty bound (חייב) to reciprocate in kind and to benefit him. Extending loans without interest is a greater favor than giving (him) a gift, as many are more embarrassed to accept a gift than to borrow.[360]

R. Asher had been a professional moneylender in his native Germany. Generally, business transactions are prohibited during the festive days (חול המועד) between the first and last days of Holidays. Consequently, it was the custom in Germany among "those who feared the Lord," to prohibit such transactions during these festive days. Assuming that other Jews would surely not be among "those who feared the Lord," R. Asher recounted that he had allowed members of his household to lend money with interest even during that period, for fear that the gentile might go to another Jew, and they would lose a client. In keeping with his altruistic standard, he offered this highly principled justification.

---

*Teshubot ha-Ge'onim, Sha'are Ṣedeq*, IV, 2, #20, p. 90; *MT Love wu-Malve* 5:2; cf. Makkot 24a.

360. *Commentary on Psalms* 15:5, p. 37.

> And I permitted in my house lending money with interest to a gentile, who was used to coming regularly to my house to borrow, because if they would not lend him, he would go to the house of another Jew who would lend him, and (he would) lure him to become his client, and that will constitute a loss.[361]

Jewish practice of usury bordered on the pathological and self-destructive. It was not only against halakha and common sense, but the most powerful reason for hatred against Jews. Since all that a gentile had to do to cancel his loan was to charge the Jew with some anti-Christian activity, money lending promoted such accusations, followed by anti-Jewish riots and countless massacres.[362]

R. Asher's son, R. Judah (1270–1349), shared the same outlook and policies of his father. After R. Asher's death (1321) the anti-Maimonideans succeeded in appointing his son as a worthy successor. He, too, belonged to the inerrantly pious. As a mark of humility he was known as 'pious' (חסיד). Aware of the special lineage, in his last will he requested from his children that they, too, "should become pious (להיות חסידים)."[363] Nonetheless, there were complaints about his ministry.[364] The incident we are to examine took place about the year 1345. Some had expressed concern about the numerous halakhic conflicts dividing the community under his ministry (see below). R. Judah denied these allegations. On the contrary, in the last forty years "there never were fewer conflicts among judicial experts." The second complaint concerned the circulation of "malicious slander" about the rabbi. Addressing the officers of the community, he offered this eloquent defense:

361. *Hilkhot ha-Rosh, Mo'ed Qaṭan* I, 24.

362. For further discussion of the subject, see *In the Shadow of History*, pp. 22–23.

363. In his last will, published by S. Schechter, "*Ṣavva'a*," *Bet-Talmud* 4 (5645/1885), p. 345.

364. All the following quotations and references proceed from R. Judah ben ha-Rosh, *Zikhron Yehuda*, eds. J. Rosenberg and D. Cassel, (Berlin, 5606/1846), #54, 9a.

> (Occasionally) when (people were) incensed (at the rabbi's behavior), you declare that you don't believe it (the accusation) in your hearts, since you are my witnesses and also the community, that from the day that you have chosen me to sit on my father's chair, I showed favor to no one in a judicial process. It is possible, however, that unknowingly I blundered: "Surely I am brutish, unlike a man, and have not the understanding of a man" (Prov. 30:2). However, if rebelliously, or with impunity, or maliciously I have committed any grievance to anyone, may God never forgive me! This is why it gives me great pain that they are suspicious of me in any of those matters. Therefore, if an important person whom no one in this land can judge, either says or does anything with the intention of defaming me among the public, let God judge between me and him and repay him for his ill!

From the preceding one may wrongly conclude that, unlike his father, R. Judah was not inerrant. That was not the case. The above was expressed as a conciliatory remark for public relations purposes. In reality, he, too, was inerrant. This may be gathered from the explanation he gave for dismissing the Community's petition to adopt Maimonides' *Mishne Tora*. To quell the controversy surrounding him, some proposed to adopt the *Mishne Tora* as their Community Code of Law, as it had been done throughout Sepharad. To this end, a preliminary accord (הסכמה) was drafted. For reasons that the good rabbi did not care to divulge, he rejected the petition. "There are reasons," replied R. Judah, "that exclude approving their accord, which I do not wish now to spell out." Instead, he offered this curious argument: "You should not learn from [the policies of] others in Sepharad! On the contrary, others should learn from you because the city of Toledo is the metropolis of Israel, and its grandees are the grandees of the Diaspora of Ariel!" (The term 'Ariel' is an allusion to himself Judah = Ariel). The gist of this remark will be obvious upon considering that early in the same *responsum* he had argued that although most of Maimonides' decisions were correct, some were not. By inference, one may conclude that his decisions were free from error. We can now appreciate the snide remarks and impatience with those daring to disagree with him.

The following case permits a glimpse at the grounds for some of the rumors surrounding the rabbi. The particulars also illustrate the type of ministry that the anti-Maimonideans fought so hard to establish. The case pertains to a decision issued by the rabbinic court in Segovia, presided by R. Ḥayyim ha-Arukh (14th century).[365] The case revolved around three witnesses of dubious character, testifying on behalf of a certain Moses 'Aṭias that he had contracted matrimony with a certain lady. In the process of collecting these testimonies, the court discovered that in a previous case one of the witnesses had been found guilty of willfully committing perjury in a judicial proceeding (שבועת שקר). The court also determined that the second witness had been found guilty of giving false testimony (שהעיד עדות שקר). The third witness was known to have desecrated the Sabbath willfully (שחילל את השבת במזיד). Since these witnesses were unqualified to testify in a Jewish Court of Law, and since the alleged bride denied that the ceremony had taken place, R. ha-Arukh issued a decision declaring the alleged wedding null and void, and the presumed bride free to marry without need of a bill of divorce. R. Judah disagreed and declared the decision illegitimate and the marriage valid.

Halakhic disputes are common. What makes this case worthy of note is the patronizing, dismissive vein with which the presiding rabbi of the Court is treated. We shall call attention to three aspects of R. Judah's response. First, R. ha-Arukh wrote a legal decision on the

---

365. All of the following quotations and references proceed from *Zikhron Yehuda*, #89, 36a-38a. As indicated by the ed., our R. ha-Arukh was the father of R. Menaḥem, who maintained halakhic correspondence with R. Isaac bar Sheshet, *Teshubot Ribash*, ##229–233, at Salamanca; and #312, at Zamora. There are numerous families in the Eastern Mediterranean communities bearing this name; see, for instance, the case examined by R. Moses b. Ḥabib, *She'elot wu-Tshubot Moharam ben Ḥabib* (Jerusalem: 5687/1927), #5, 35b-48c.

case. Except for an alleged slur made by R. ha-Arukh, R. Judah was careful *not* to quote from it. Rather, he sidestepped it, declaring that he would not "address himself to all the nonsense (דברים בטלים) that he [R. ha-Arukh] wrote in his decision." Stated crudely, this means that the reader would not be permitted to consider the merits of the case, but he would have to rely solely on R. Judah's *conclusions*. Without even a window of insight, R. Judah resolved to act on the basis of hearsay (שמענו מפי מגידי אמת) and rumor (שיצא קול) – most probably stemming from the party of the groom – that the court's verdict was illegal. Second, he *assumed* that the members of the court, including the presiding judge, were unqualified. Without presenting a shred of evidence, he argued: *perhaps* (אם) the witness did not commit perjury in a judicial procedure, but only had failed to fulfill a promissory oath (שבועת ביטוי); *perhaps* (אם) the other witness had not committed the kind of crime that would disqualify him (לאו שיש בו מלקות); *perhaps* (אם) the third witness only transgressed a rabbinic prohibition. To *impute* such gross errors to a court of law, on the basis of hearsay, without first instituting a formal judicial investigation, is so malicious a slander that it might be regarded as defamation.[366] Third, rather than hold judgment and invite the court to rebut these charges, he issued a series of invectives against the presiding judge: "he deserves to be banned under excommunication, and to be cursed and punished by incarceration and death"; "he had never studied nor he had read"; "we will not address ourselves to the sources which he brought to prove the case from the Talmud, tractates Yebamot, Giṭṭin, and Baba Meṣi'a. It is not worthy of reply because even a chick that did not yet open its eyes could not have written what he wrote; and furthermore he does not deserve to receive a response" etc. On the basis of these invectives, he issued the following ruling:

To the Holy Congregation, the Congregation of Segovia (may God protect them):

366. Cf *MT 'Edut* 6:5.

> You are hereby warned! This letter or a copy should be sent immediately to that R. Ḥayyim ha-Arukh, (notifying him) that we are rendering a judgment (against him) and (issuing an) excommunicatory sentence, that on the day that he shall see this letter or a copy of it certified by witnesses, that he should immediately renounce his above-mentioned verdict and decision, and declare it void. Furthermore, that he should send it therewith to [the Community of] Segovia within a period of eight days, so that it would be read (in the presence) of the Community.

Fortunately, the authorities in Segovia managed to preserve a sense of humor, and did not react in kind. At the end of the *responsum* the scribe appended a note, stating that R. ha-Arukh withdrew his decision. Thereupon, the Community of Segovia arranged a meeting between him and the representatives of R. Judah, at the Rabbinic Court in Seville (a city where anti-Maimonideans did not roam freely). At the meeting, R. ha-Arukh presented his written decision and was given an opportunity to reply to the rabbis of Toledo. The matter was fully debated, "And the rabbis of Seville agreed with the aforementioned judgment of R. Ḥayyim ha-Arukh" (see appendix 63).

# Chapter 66
# Israel's Fourth Miracle

The same ideologues who applauded parents murdering little children – "for the sake of the Heavens" – perceived the Judaism of the Golden Age as a heretical monstrosity. R. Judah (d. 299), one of the fathers of the Babylonian Talmud, taught that Jerusalem was destroyed because "in her midst," that is publicly, "students of sages were affronted." To indicate his source, he followed his statement with a doctrine taught by his teacher Rab. It says: "Whoever affronts a student of sages will find no cure for his affliction."[367] There is logic to this – a "natural consequence" (הסיבה הטבעית) – borrowing from R. Solomon ibn Verga (see above, Introductory Remarks). A community permitting rabble-rousers to treat sages with impudence would be unable to secure proper guidance in time of danger. The same applies to individuals in the habit of treating men of wisdom with contempt. They would fail to find intelligent counsel when facing dilemma and personal crisis. Sepharad, too, was destroyed because the people allowed heroic devotion to muzzle wisdom; cosmic sacrality to displace halakha; and dysfunctional mysticism to substitute the Scripture and Talmud. Thus, persecution and suppression of critical thinking brought an end to the 'Golden Age of Spain.' By the fourteenth century, magic and the occult became integral to Jewish life. Even among the intellectual circles in Castile, Moses was depicted

367. Shabbat 119b. See *MT Talmud Tora* 6:11; and cf. *De'ot* 2:1; *Teshuba* 6:3; *Ṭum'at Ṣara'at* 16:10; *Iggeret Teman*, p. 74.

as a master magician. Rabbis such as Samuel ibn Ṣarṣa, Solomon ibn Ya'ish, Ezra Gategno, Shem Ṭob ibn Shapruṭ, Solomon Franco, Joseph Ṭob 'Alem, Shem Ṭob ibn Mayor, Solomon Alconstantin, and others, applied Neo-Platonic lore, magic, and the occult, to 'explain' Jewish religion: from astrology, augury, and demonology, to spiritism, chiromancy and chirognomy.[368] Anti-Maimonidean Kabbala endowed meaning to these beliefs. If, as Professor Lieberman taught, occasionally the rabbis would modify a pagan practice among the masses, too difficult to eradicate, and give to it a Jewish meaning (see above chapter 54), anti-Maimonidean Kabbala worked in the opposite direction. It endeavored to endow every Jewish symbol and ritual with notions and beliefs from the realm of theurgy and pagan sacrality.

The spirit of inerrancy affected the object and method of the rabbinic academies. With this purpose in mind, R. Asher composed 'Glosses to the Talmud' (*Tosafot ha-Rosh*). One of the purposes was to control the flow of ideas and shield students from other commentaries and methodologies. Concerning this point his son, R. Jacob, wrote to a colleague who was about to come to Spain: "you need not bring the (works of) *Tosafot*, since we only study the notes of my father, of blessed memory."[369] As for the approach to the traditional institutions of Israel, let us consider, by way of illustration, the *explanation* given by R. Asher for abolishing the recitation of the *Targum* at the Synagogue (an institution that the rabbis attributed to Ezra the Scribe), because "what advantage is there (מה תועלת יש) to the *Targum* since they don't understand it?" What made such reasoning

368. For an in-depth study of this material, see Dov Schwarts, "*Ṣurot Shonot shel Magia*," (Heb.) *Proceedings of the American Academy for Jewish Studies*, 57 (1990–1991), pp. 17–46. On the depiction of Moses as a master magician, see ibid., p. 35 n. 50. There is much valuable information and insight on these types of activities in Norman E. Frimer and Dov Schwarts, *The Life and Thought of Shem Tov ibn Shaprut* (Heb.) (Jerusalem: Ben-Zvi Institute, 1992).

369. For a detailed study of his methodology; see José Faur, "*Tosafot ha-Rosh le-Massekhet Berakhot*," *Proceedings of the American Academy for Jewish Research* 33 (1965), (Hebrew Section), pp. 41–65. For the citation of the letter, see ibid., p. 65. Cf. *Teshubot ha-Rosh*, #51:2.

disturbing is that, at the same time, the good rabbi claimed that the *Targum* "was established by the Holy Spirit!"[370] Were we to follow this line of reasoning, we would end up vacating the entire Prayer Book, since "they" – whoever *they* happened to be – "don't understand it!" The principal argument, "what advantage is there (מה תועלת יש) to the *Targum*," is mind-boggling. In fact, it could be used to call off many, if not all, Jewish ceremonies and religious precepts. R. Asher used this course of reasoning (מה תועלת יש), to clinch other legal decisions (see appendix 61).

The results of this type of ministry were catastrophic. Not a single commentary pertaining to the Scripture, the Talmud, or even a single collection of *responsa* from the Castilian rabbis of the period was published at the time. Under the tutelage of that rabbinate, the new graduates further contributed to the dissolution of Jewish values. Here is how R. Solomon Al'ami (ca. 1370–1420), himself a foe of philosophical studies, described the new ministry produced in Spain:

> Some of our recent sages lost their way in the wilderness! They erred [even] before the most palpable! Because they hate and are jealous of each other; and they put up the Tora for sale and for presents. The objective of their curriculum is to know how to read [the Tora] meticulously, so that they could expand their own innovations. [Also wanting] is the study of Talmud and other works; since they concentrated on every minute detail of the law, and the various views and opinions [not with the substance of the law]. They thrust aside the humility of the virtuous, temperance and holiness. What [one rabbi] instructs the other casts in doubt; what [one rabbi] permits, the other prohibits. Through their quarrels, the Law had become two! They knit [their views] on a spider's web, embarrassing themselves and exposing their wickedness. Their eyes are closed and they cannot see; their hearts fail to understand. They

370. *Hilkhot ha-Rosh, Megilla* III, 6. See appendix 61.

> show favor [when issuing legal decisions] in the Law, and fail to tell the people their disgrace since God had poured over them a spirit of foolishness and had closed their eyes. This is what brought disgrace to the Tora in the eyes of all those who saw and heard [them].[371]

The introduction of the *pilpul*-methodology reduced Talmudic studies to casuistry and hair-splitting conjectures; far removed from real life-situations and the application of the Law. Consequently, the people had little regard for these graduates. R. Joseph Jabès (d. 1507), who was an eyewitness to the Expulsion, commented on the deplorable situation of the Talmudic Academies in Castile. As a result of the *pilpul*-methodology, the students

> …wasted all of their days, they never were able to grasp the intent of the Law. One need not mention that they never attained the ultimate goal (of studying Tora), which is [proper] behavior, and (basic) knowledge of the laws needed in the conduct of daily affairs.[372]

The result of this leadership was the promotion of strife, the dissolution of communal and family ties, and personal hatred and animosity. In an imaginary dialogue between Jew and foe, R. Solomon ibn Verga put these words in the mouth of the antisemite: "For every one of you that the enemy kills, you kill a thousand of yourself."[373]

Erroneously, some, particularly among "the best and the wisest," who could not accept incoherent blathering as a substitute for 'Tora,' chose to defect and decided to escape from the madness reigning

371. R. Solomon Al'ami, *Iggeret Musar*, ed. A. A. Haberman (Jerusalem: Sifriyat Meqorot, 1946), pp. 40–41. On his opposition to philosophical studies, see ibid., pp. 32–33, 41–42.

372. Introduction to *Or ha-Ḥayyim* (Ferrara, 5314/1554), n. p. See *In the Shadow of History*, p. 20.

373. *Shebeṭ Yehuda*, XXXII, p. 81. Cf. *In the Shadow of History*, pp. 204–207.

in the *Juderías* (see appendix 70). This is how R. Moses Arragel described the situation in Spain in 1422, a little over one hundred years after the establishment of the infallible ministry.

> In the past the Jews of Castile prospered and were the crown and garland of all the Jewish Diaspora... Now our best and wisest children have left us. Nothing remains of our science... and at the riverbed whose waters once carried ships, there cannot be found today even small brooks. Our science has thus vanished.[374]

The final unfolding of this type of ministry took place in 1492, when the last Chief Rabbi of Spain chose to convert, rather than join his brethren in the Expulsion.

Modern historians, dumbfounded by the analphabetic tune of *qedoshim*-hymnologists, failed to see the nexus between heroic madness and the collapse of Iberian Jewry. There is something terribly wrong with a scholarship that keeps on asking why so many Jews fell short at the time of the Expulsion, while perversely ignoring the behavior of the most celebrated rabbis. A more meaningful question would be why, after 250 years of spiritual and intellectual pandemonium, so many brave souls chose to leave Spain and Portugal rather than convert.

This brings us to what I designate the Fourth Miracle of Israel, unfolding from the Middle Ages to our own days: Jewish achievements, growth and excellence, *in spite* of a thoroughly inept leadership. Jews alone can boast of the fact that regardless of time and location, given two choices, their leaders will invariably opt for the less propitious one. Thus, I propose that Jewish survival and success constitute the most portentous of all Miracles, past and present. With all due respect to other religions, resurrection and transubstantiation, and

374. In *Biblia de la Casa de Alba* (Madrid: Imprenta Artistica, 1920), p. 13. Cf. *In the Shadow of History*, pp. 2, 19.

even ascension to paradise on a prodigious mount pale to naught when we contrast the turpitude of Jewish leadership with the feats and triumphs of Jews, both collectively and individually.

# Concluding Reflections

Basically, the anti-Maimonidean Kabbala, fed by heroic madness, was a subversive movement where *appearances* were of substance. With this purpose in mind, key-terms such as *qabbala,* Tora, halakha, *barukh,* etc., were emptied of their *original* sense and their shell incubated with connotations fundamentally contrary to Judaism and common sense. A *sine qua non* for the anti-Maimonidean success was addressing a public with little access to Jewish fundamentals. We can now appreciate the motivation for discrediting Maimonidean texts and Maimonidean scholars. The literary *genre* associated with the anti-Maimonidean crusade bears this thesis. Instead of writing their *own* books, anti-Maimonideans preferred to append their views onto the creation of others. This is in line with a fundamental aspect of their ethos: they acquired their reputation not for their teaching but for their attacks. Accordingly, they used popular works, such as the *Halakhot* of R. Isaac Alfasi and the *Mishne Tora* as conduits (in 'aggressive' editing, by appending glosses, 'commentaries' and digressions, or by introducing slight changes that would not be noticed by the unsuspecting reader). Why? It is true, these rabbis did not feel comfortable expressing themselves in correct Hebrew, and would avoid exposing themselves to a public who was still familiar with basic grammar. There may have been, however, another more substantive reason. It pertains to the *subversive* character of their ideology. By packaging their ideologies in works that had gained the confidence of the public, they were able to gain circulation among the semi-literate audience, silencing at the same time the opposition. Anti-Maimonideans *dreaded* confronting *real* Maimonideans. It was imperative not to allow the 'others' to express their *own* beliefs in their *own* words. The success of this strategy depended on a public ready to follow rather than think.

Anti-Maimonideans of all brands, old and new, often brag about their steadfast loyalty to 'tradition': how punctiliously they practice it, and how faithfully they have preserved it. Boasting aside, they did not manage to preserve even three phonetic sounds in the names of the three Patriarchs of Israel: the '*he*' (ה)of Abra(ה)am, the '*ḥet*' (ח)of Is(ח)aac, and the ''*ayin*' (ע) of Ja(ע)cob.[375] (Can you imagine a great band of 'true Americans' sloppily pronouncing the *sh* of Washington, the *m* of Adams, and the *J* of Jefferson?) Anti-Maimonideans neglected even the consonantal text of the Tora! According to halakha, certain words in the Tora must be written with a defective (חסר) spelling and others with full (מלא) spelling. In the case of a mistake, the Scroll of the Tora is void (פסול) and should be substituted with an accurate (כשר) Scroll. By the 16th century, uncertainty was so great that Rama declared: "Our Scrolls of Tora are not so exact as to warrant the substitution of one for another (Scroll) that could be more correct."[376] (That would be equivalent to a group claiming exclusive legitimacy of constitutional interpretation, yet unsure how to spell it!)

Anti-Maimonideans were *not* motivated by concern for the preservation and promotion of 'Tora' and 'Talmud.' Their alleged zeal should be carefully reviewed in light of the fact that they were directly responsible for the burning of the Talmud in 1242. One need not be particularly bright to have realized that bribing the ecclesiastical authorities to burn Maimonides' works established a dangerous precedent. It should be a matter of interest to note that those instigating the Christian authorities were apostates who, like Donin and Pablo Christiani, had obtained their spiritual formation at the feet of

---

375. See *The Itinerary of Benjamin of Tudela*, p. 21.

376. *Mappa* on *Shulḥan 'Arukh, Oraḥ Ḥayyim*, CXLIII, 4. See appendix 62.

bogus-Talmudists preaching anti-Maimonidean ideologies. The disappearance of the famous library of Lucena gives substance to our thesis. It contained the oldest and most valuable collection of Talmud and Rabbinic literature. It included some of the oldest and most reliable copies of the Talmud and Rabbinic literature from the Geonic period and the private collections of R. Samuel ha-Nagid and R. Joseph ibn Megas. After the collapse of the Jewish communities in Andalusia, the library was transported in its entirety to Toledo. The last known scholar to have had access to it was R. Me'ir Abul'afya, chief Rabbi of Toledo. As a result of the anti-Maimonidean victory, the library totally vanished. Since the copies of the Talmud and Rabbinical works it contained were at variance with anti-Maimonideans' texts, 'Andalusian' copies became a rarity. The library had been the depository of works reflecting the long and rich traditions of the Golden Age of Sepharad – values that were not congruent with the new ideologies. It would be no exaggeration to say that from the point of view of Jewish intellectual tradition, the disappearance of that library parallels the destruction of the library of Alexandria for classical Antiquity (see appendix 70). The fact that the text of both the Babylonian Talmud and Yerushalmi were sloppily edited (it is impossible to find a single page in either of these works free from error) by two apostates, Felix Pratensis and Jacob ibn Adoniah (ca. 1470–ca. 1538), and published by a Christian printing house, speaks loudly about the merits of these self-appointed 'guardians' of the 'Talmud.' If we add to the above the *pilpul* methodology – precluding any intelligent comprehension of the text – it would be difficult not to associate their unbridled devotion to 'Tora' with deeply unresolved oedipal impulses.

The triumph of the *Church* v. *Galileo* marked the end of Italian scientific activity until recent times. Anti-Maimonideans were not less successful. Their triumph marked the end of Jewish creative thought. It was not until modern times, when European universities opened their doors to Jews that Jewish genius flourished: invariably, *outside* the Jewish quarters. Jewish inspectors of truth – or the 'little foxes' –would not have permitted a Freud or an Einstein to flourish in their midst. Rabbis who dared to think suffered vicious persecution; e.g., Israel Moses Ḥazzan, Elie Benamozegh, Isaac Abul'afya, Aaron b. Shim'on, et al. In his own way, R. Sherira Gaon alluded to the destructive ways of bogus-Talmudists. By relating them to "little foxes *destroying* (מחבלים) the vineyards," he was signaling that they caused damage for its own sake. The purpose was to demolish "vineyards" – symbols of the traditions and values built by Israel over the centuries – not to make use of the grapes! 'Little foxes' affected the mode of Jewish scholarship. The objective of learning was not to enlighten and expand, but, as best expressed by the term of *hasagot*, to 'prove *the other* [Jew] wrong' (see appendix 67). This philosophy was reflected among *pseudo*-Jewish scholars, whose emphasis was to discredit the hallowed texts of Israel, and thrust them aside as meaningless and irrelevant. Or what is worse, packaging the "empty shell" of the Tora with ideas regurgitated by anti-Judaism ideologues.

# Epilogue

The rabbis prescribed that every morning, no matter how sinful or wicked an individual may be, she/he should inaugurate his/her day with gratefulness and unbridled buoyancy for goodness:

> My God, the soul that You have bestowed on me is pure! You have created it, You have shaped it, You have breathed it into me, You are safeguarding it within me. And You will take it away from me, and return it to me in the days to come. So long as the soul is within me, I avow before You, O My God and the God of my fathers, that You are the Sovereign of all creation, Ruler of every living being, Lord of every soul, Living and Existent forever! Blessed are You that returns souls to their dead bodies!

One of the objectives of our long journey is to question the lofty contempt which the *europaischen Menschentums* of all creeds and persuasions profess towards the Hebrew Scripture and Rabbinic tradition. It is easy to mock the Tora and the Talmud and the rabbis and Jews, especially when addressing an analphabetic crowd, under the protection of a Rex, serving the sword of might; it is even easier when camouflaged under concepts appropriated from Jewish tradition. But, can these men create a society where the common person can greet the morning with the words, "My God, the soul that You have bestowed on me is pure…?" The rabbis did their best to create a horizontal society *under* the Law. If some other religions have a law (be it canon or *shari'a*), in Judaism *Law* is *the* religion. Rather than freedom *under* the Law, openly contracted by the people in the presence of God, as per the '*Old* Testament,' *europaischen Menschentums* propose a hierarchic organization governed by the elite Adam-*Elohim* standing *above* the Law. In a society ministered under the auspices of *europaischen Menschentums* dreams are banned. Humanistic voices are silenced by the deafening preaching of godless scientists, soulless academicians, and brainless artists speaking all at once, in microphonic tones. Children of a heartless society grow up to be dummies. They could clone other dummies and march together to the beat of some analphabetic slogan, but they cannot be fathers and mothers and brothers and sisters and aunts and uncles and cousins and neighbors. The Tora opens with a simple proposition: "In the beginning God created the heavens and the earth." In plain words, it means that only He, by virtue of being the absolute Creator, is absolute Sovereign, and He has given you a pure soul. Now, let us see what you can do with this precious gift! Bent on proving the seven-blessings of the rabbis wrong, *europaischen Menschentums* propose an alternative: "At the end a dummy, or bunch of dummies, will destroy all of the above." Godless technology, under the direction of Adam-*Elohim*, makes the anti-dream proposition a poignant alternative.

A final point. Those who came to America and helped it grow, from the first settlers till the most recent refugee, are/were victims of Adam-*Elohim*, the spiritually haughty and epistemologically infallible. Guided by the Hand of God, the Founding Fathers provided the intellectual and moral principles that will prevent the ideologies of *europaischen Menschentums* from taking root. That is why I believe that being a good American makes you a better Jew, and vice versa.

# The Horizontal Society

## Understanding the Covenant and Alphabetic Judaism

### Volume II

# Contents

# Contents

# 1. Vocalization of the Scroll of the Tora

A Scroll of the Tora that has been vocalized is 'ritually invalid' (פסול), even if one were to erase the vowels. The authority for disallowing a vocalized *Sefer Tora* is a work attributed to R. Judah al-Bargeloni, ed. Elkan Adler, *An Eleventh Century Introduction to the Hebrew Bible* (Heb.) (Oxford: Private Circulation, 1897), p. 38:

> It is forbidden to vocalize a Scroll of the Tora; a vocalized Scroll is ritually invalid. As we were instructed concerning Scrolls: 'One cannot read from a vocalized [Scroll]. Even if he were to erase the vowels [still] it [the Scroll] cannot be used [for liturgical] reading.' R. Yehudai Gaon (8th century) of blessed memory said: 'One may not put a colon [used in Hebrew as a period] at the end of the verse; if one puts it, then he should erase it. R. Hayye Gaon sent the following *responsum* to R. Nissim's Academy (of blessed memory), in Arabic: Concerning a Scroll of the Tora that had been vocalized ... we have written on this matter in [our work] *Rules for Scribes*: "A vocalized Scroll of the Tora may not be read in public, even if

> the vowels had been erased. If it was taken out (to be read in public) it must be returned and another Scroll must be taken out in its place. It should not be kept, since with this blemish it had forfeited the status of Scroll of the Tora."

Before proceeding further we must call attention to the expression 'heads of the [Scriptural] verses' ('ראשי פסוקים'), found in rabbinic literature. It is generally understood to refer to the 'beginning' of the verse, as in *Midrash Zuṭa, Ruth* (Buber) II, 8; in which case this would be an ellipsis for ראשי תיבות של פסוקים "the first letters [or words] of the verses," cf. *Midrash Tanḥuma* ([Warsaw] Lublin, 1913), *Ha'azinu* V, 5, p. 213; and cf. *Tosafot* Yoma 37b, s.v. *be-sirrugin*. (A similar ellipsis is found in Shabbat 12b: "ראשי פרשיות" for ראשי תיבות של פרשיות.) In my view this expression is not always an ellipsis. In the case of "ראשי פסוקים" it stands for "the superlinear punctuation at the head of the verses" – a reference to the punctuation in vogue in Babel and Israel. See Bereshit Rabba, Ms. Vatican Ebr. 30, Facsimile (Jerusalem: Makor, 5731/1971) XXXV, 41b: אלו ראשי פסוקים; Bereshit Rabba, eds. Theodor-Albeck, 3 vols. (Jerusalem: Wahrman Books, 1965), p. 342. In Y. Megilla IV, 1, 74d, the rabbis associated "ראשי פסוקים" with the verse "**and they understood** the Scripture" (Neh. 8:8). Support for this interpretation is to be found in the parallel version, Megilla 3a, as quoted by R. Baḥye b. Asher, *Perush*, vol. 1, p. 169, which reads: "**and they understood** – this is ניקוד," i.e., 'vocalization.' Accordingly, the rule in *Massekhet Soferim* III, 7, ed. Dr. Michael Higger (New York: Debe Rabbanan, 1937), pp. 125–126, disallowing a Scroll "שעקרו ראשי פסוקים" refers to a Scroll that had been vocalized after which "the superlinear vocalization was erased," which then remains ritually invalid, and "one should not read from it." (For parallel sources and bibliography, see ed. note ad loc.) This rule was recorded in *Maḥzor Viṭry* #524 and thereof in *Haggahot Maymoniyot* on *MT Sefer Tora* 10:1 (b); see *Bet Yosef* and *Shulḥan 'Arukh Yore De'a* CCLXXIV, 7.

The above rule in *Massekhet Soferim* coincides with the Geonic decision cited above in two fundamental points. First, the Scroll is ritually void (פסול). Second, it retains the status of ritually void (פסול) even if the vowels were to be erased. It is generally assumed that vocalization renders the Scroll void because the Tora should bear no 'marks.' This explanation cannot be accepted for the following two reasons. First, according to scribal tradition some consonants of the Tora are occasionally marked with a point on top; see, for example, Berakhot 4a, Nazir 23a, Horayot 10b, etc.; *AdRN*, A, XXXIV, p. 100. Furthermore, a Scroll with errors may be amended. Accordingly, why should a vocalized Scroll retain the status of ritually void (פסול) after the vowels have been erased? As we shall see, the theory for disallowing such a Scroll pertains to the Hebrew concept of 'lettering' and 'reading.'

The Hebrew 'letter' (אות) stands for a 'distinctive' mark or sign. God is referred to "as 'letter'" (אות) – in the sense of being 'absolutely distinctive and unique' – even "among myriads (of heavenly angels)"; see *Midrash Tanḥuma* (Buber), vol. 2, p. 39 and *Golden Doves,* p. 83. A 'letter' is not only different from all other signs of the alphabet, but it must be inscribed within a blank, *writable* space, from all its sides. The blank-space is not merely to ensure that one letter does not touch another: it pertains to the very *action* of writing. In Hebrew, 'to write' is an intransitive verb. Therefore, you don't write *a* book but you write *in* a book or *on* a parchment (see below appendix 2). However, once a letter has been inscribed in a suitable blank-space it retains its 'written' status even when there is no longer any space around it. Consider the following rule: if a letter was written around a punctured parchment, so that the perforation is contained within the letter or between two letters, the Scroll is void (פסול), although the perforation does not affect any letter. However, if the perforation within a letter, or between two letters, or between two words, occurred *afterwards,* the Scroll is valid, providing that the perforation had not expunged a letter. Borges, too, included blank spaces in his definition of writing; see *Golden Doves,* p. 116.

Hebrew reading warrants *successive synthesis*; see *Golden Doves,* pp. 30–35. A vocalized Tora is void because, in effect, vocalization links the letters and words *semantically* to one another, canceling, thereby, the blank space between the letters. A vocalized text allows only for *simultaneous synthesis*; the reader plays a passive role, 'picking up the sound from the page.' In this case, someone would be 'reciting from memory,' rather than 'reading.' Moreover, vocalization would limit the countless interpretations comprehended in the consonantal text of the Tora; see *Golden Doves*, pp. 136–137, and would exclude the possibility of successive 'reading'; see *Golden Doves*, pp. 118–123. According to this theory, even Maimonides, who in extreme circumstances permits the use of a void Scroll (ספר פסול) for liturgical services, would disallow the use of a vocalized Scroll, since in such a circumstance, the text would be 'recited' rather than 'read'; cf. *Homo Mysticus*, pp. 186–187. It should be noted, in passing, that apophasis and the entire realm of negative theology pertain to *successive synthesis*. A Hebrew letter it *is* not. Rather, by synthesizing it successively to the next, the reader creates something fundamentally different than each letter in isolation; see *Homo Mysticus*, part I. (This coincides with the syntagmatic character of the Hebrew Alphabet: a 'letter' (אות) signifies in that it is *different* than all other letters; see *Golden Doves*, pp. xxiv-xxv.) Finally, vocalized writing would function as an 'idol' standing between God and his creatures; like with hieroglyphics a vocalized text would border on idolatry, by making openness to God and a reciprocal relationship impossible.

Halakhic scholars debated whether it would be permissible to vocalize a bill of divorce. The standard practice among Sephardic scribes is to use diacritic marks (as an apostrophe or a dot) to transliterate a foreign *consonant* into Hebrew; see R. Moses b. Ḥabib, *'Azarat Nashim* (Leipzig, 5619/1859), 101b-103a, but not to vocalize the text; see R. Ovadiah Yosef, *Yabbia' Omer*, vol. 7 (Jerusalem, 5753/1993), *Eben ha-'Ezer*, #22, p. 380, contrary to *Shulḥan 'Arukh, Oraḥ Ḥayyim* DCXCI, #9.

# 2. Hebrew 'Writing' and 'Reading'

Jewish law interprets 'to write' (כתב) as an intransitive verb, as if it were a 'complete' action needing no direct object. The expression "he shall write a *sefer*" (Deut. 24:1) in reference to the bill of divorce does not contain a preposition indicating the object of the verb. Accordingly, it is taken to mean to 'write in a precise wording or formula' specifying the divorce (in which case *sefer* is an adverb of 'write') not a 'parchment' or a 'scroll!' – see Giṭṭin 21b; cf. Soṭa 16a and R. Abraham ha-Levi, *Ginnat Veradim*, vol. 2 (Constantinople, 5476/1716), *Eben ha-'Ezer* I, #5, 3d-4d. Thus, 'writing' may take on an existence of its own, independent of the parchment or material on which it was written. (This may explain the rationale for permitting, in extreme cases, writing the Tora on a parchment which was not prepared adequately; see Saul Lieberman, *Shkiin* [Jerusalem: Bamberg & Wahrman, 1939], p. 25.) Consider the following rule. One who executes a work on the Sabbath with the intention of damaging an object is exempt. And yet, if one were to write on a parchment with the intention of damaging the parchment he stands guilty, since with writing, the "infraction is not because of the place on which the writing took place [= the parchment], but because of the writing (itself)" (*MT Shabbat* 11:9). Therefore, on witnessing a scroll of the Tora burning, one must rend his garment twice, once because of the destruction of the parchment and once because of the destruction of the writing; see Mo'ed Qaṭan 26a. Similarly, R. Ḥanaya ben Teradyon (2nd century), while burning at the stake together with the Scroll of the Tora, "saw [only] the parchment burning, while the letters flew away"; see 'Aboda Zara 18a. cf. Roland Barthes, "To Write: An Intransitive Verb?" in eds. Richard Macksey and Eugenio Donato, *The Structuralist Controversy* (Baltimore: Johns Hopkins University Press, 1972), pp. 134–155.

The preposition 'on' (על-, ב) can be used to render 'to write' as a transitive verb, as the rule stipulating that the king "shall write (כתב) for himself a summary of this Tora *on* a scroll (על-ספר)... and he shall read *in it* (קרא בו)..." (Deut. 17:18–19; cf. Section III, n. 129). As noted by the commentators, the masculine preposition *in it* (קרא בו) clearly indicates that the object of the verb is the actual Scroll, which is masculine, rather than the 'Tora' which is feminine; cf. Rashi on Deut. 29:20. That is why the Talmud interprets the clause "Someone reading (קורא) from (ב-) the Tora" (Mishna Berakhot 2:1) as an ellipsis for the clause "Someone who was reading from *the Scroll* of the Tora"; therefore, concluding that the reference is to "Someone reading from [*the Scroll* of the Tora] for the purpose of proof-reading (בקורא להגיה) it; see Berakhot 13a and Section I, n. 2. For the meaning of the expression "summary of this Tora," see *Golden Doves*, pp. 53–54.

'Book' is a Jewish invention (see above chapter 7). This will help us understand why Arabic-speaking Jews used the term *kuttab*, root KTB 'writing' – having to do with the *ketab* system discussed in Section I – to designate 'elementary-school.' There was a good reason for this choice. The classical designation of the Hebrew primary school (*Talmud Tora* and *Bet ha-Sefer*) has to do with 'book.' However, when Jews began to settle in the Arabian Peninsula (particularly from the 2nd century on to escape Roman persecution, see chapter 40), 'writing' was unknown in the region. Before the advent of Islam (7th century), native pagans were referred to as *jahiliya*, 'analphabets.' The root KTB ('writing') was unknown in Arabic, and it is one of the many key-terms from Hebrew and Aramaic introduced by Jews to the Arabic lexicon; cf. A. S. Yahuda, *'Eber ve-'Arab* (New York: Ha-Histadrut ha-'Ibrit be-Ameriqa, 1946), p. 138, n. 6; and p. 152 n. 2. [For a penetrating analysis of this early period, see Charles Cutler Torrey, *The Jewish Foundation of Islam* (New York: Jewish Institute of Religion Press, 1933). On the impact of rabbinic thought and terminology on the formative period of Islam, see Abraham I Katsh, *Judaism in Islam* (Heb.) (Jerusalem: Kiryat Sepher, 1957); and A. S. Yahuda, *Al-Hidaja* (Leiden: E. J. Brill, 1912), pp. 82–91. cf. appendix 27.] Instead of KTB, the Arabic root ZBR (sing. *zabar*; pl. *zubur*), 'engraving,' 'embellishment,'* has to do with the Greek *gramma* used for 'letter,' but actually meaning 'lines of drawing,' and 'picture'; and the Greek *graphes* used for 'writing,' but actually meaning 'drawing,' 'delineation,' and 'picture' (= Heb. *roshem*). This root – rather than *ketab* (see Section I, n. 5) – was used in Arabic to designate 'writings' and 'books' in general (more specifically the Psalms; see *Koran* 26:195). Briefly, if one is to understand 'book' in its Hebrew connotation, that is, *writing* made of *letters* (rather than 'drawings' made of 'pictures'), composed for *reading*, then the Arabic language *does not* have a term for 'book.' (Arabic-speaking Jews use *sifr*, from the Hebrew *sefer* to designate the Scroll of the Tora; and Arabic *maṣḥaf* from *ṣaḥifa* 'page' of a 'notebook,' to designate a 'volume.' This term indicates the outer form of a codex; that is, 'pages written on the recto and verso, bound into a single volume' – not its content). Arabic *kitab* (pl. *kutub*) stands for *writing*, not for *book*; that is the term used by Muhammed to describe the Tora (see *Koran* 2:41, 50, 79, 81, 83, etc.). Again, the word *Qur'an* used to designate the Muslim Holy Scripture is an Arabization of the Hebrew *miqra* (root QR'), which Jews introduced to the Arabic language; it has to do with 'reading' – not with 'book.'

In such an environment, a 'book' is nothing more than a paranormal object, which one may want to possess for aesthetic or magical purposes, like an amulet; as with Kien, in Canetti's *Auto da Fé*; see *Golden Doves*, pp. 4–7, 9; and cf. Section I, n. 65. Accordingly, the

---

* Cf. The Hebrew, *ḥarut 'al ha-luḥot*, Ex. 32:16.

purpose of Jewish elementary education was *kuttab,* instruction in the *ketab* system, so that the children would grasp the concept of 'book.' Thus Jews identified themselves as *Ahlu-l-Kitabu,* usually translated as 'people of the book,' but actually meaning 'people of the writing.' The term *kuttab* in modern Arabic came from the Jews. Another term having to do with education, *madrasa* 'religious school' and the corresponding verb *daras* 'to study,' were introduced by Jews; they are Arabizations coined, respectively, from the Hebrew *midrash* and *darash*. For the Arabic source, see Abraham Shalom Yahuda, "A Contribution to Qur'an and Ḥadith Interpretation," in *Ignace Goldziher Memorial Volume,* part I, p. 290.

# 3. Alphabetization and *Masora*

Hebrew writing warrants an alphabetic script, rather than hieroglyphics; otherwise, writing would border on idolatry; cf. José Faur, "God as a Writer: Omnipresence and the Art of Dissimulation," *Bible and the Intellectual Life* 6 (1989), p. 32; and above appendix 1. Eventually, Egyptian scribes learned to write in alphabetic script, but it was not used systematically; see Cyrus H. Gordon, *The Ancient Near East* (New York: W. W. Norton, 1965), pp. 54–55. For some insights on the Hebrew Alphabet, see idem, *Before Columbus* (New York: Crown Publishers, 1971), pp. 99–100.

An index of Jewish alphabetization is the *Masora* appended to the Hebrew Scripture – unique in textual history – where even minute orthographic irregularities, odd letters, as well as unusual morphological and phonological phenomena, including vowels and accents, are minutely accounted for and catalogued. For an excellent overview of this highly complex subject, see A. Dothan, "Massorah," *EJ* vol. 16, cols. 1402–1482. This apparatus is a fundamental condition for registering the text of Scripture; see *Golden Doves*, p. 108. Of course, to the analphabetic and monolinguistic mind these are nonsensical notes. For the sake of illustration, let us consider the case of Richard Simon, the father of textual criticism of the Christian Scripture. He did not know a word of Hebrew. And yet, at the end of *The Preface* to his *A Critical History of the text of the New Testament* (London, 1689), he chided Christian Hebraists for their admiration of the *Masora,* and wrote: "It is a Vanity in the admirers of the Hebrew Text of the Jews, to bestow such great praises on the Massoreth, a good part of which consists in Trifles or superstitious Observations."

# 4. Precept, Monolatry, and Sanctity

The Tora includes a series of teachings, instructions, prescriptions, and prohibitions known as 'precepts' (מצוות, sing. מצוה). A 'precept' is a contractual commitment – *not* a 'command' (see below appendix 12). The term *azhara* (pl. *azharot*) used in Rabbinic Hebrew to indicate something disallowed by the Law, is not semantically equivalent to a 'prohibition' issued by a menacing force. As noted by R. Abraham b. ha-Rambam, *Perush*, p. 298, the root of this term is ZHR, standing for 'brilliance' and 'enlightenment.' It means 'to instruct' someone about his or her responsibilities, cf. II Kings 6:10; by "illuminating the intellectual perception, which resembles light, [just as its opposite] ignorance is compared to darkness; cf. Eccl. 2:13." Therefore, *azharot* stand not only for what the Tora outlaws, but also for what it prescribes; as per the liturgical compositions bearing this name, which include both negative as well as positive precepts.

A 'command' is an order issued by a superior force *imposing* its will on those below; see *Crowds and Power*, pp. 351–355. God did not *impose* the Law. The objective of a 'command' is 'obedience.' The Hebrew lexicon contains no term for 'obedience.' The Hebrew term comparable to 'obedience,' שמע means not only 'to hear' but also 'to understand' and 'to acknowledge'; see *Golden Doves*, pp. 29–30. Fulfillment of a 'precept' involves [i] recognition of the *contractual commitment* at Sinai-Moab and [ii] *compliance*. In a state of 'compulsion'

(אונס), there cannot be either 'compliance' or its opposite 'transgression' (עברה); see Yebamot 53b-54a; *MT Yesode ha-Tora* 5:4; *MT Sanhedrin* 20:2; *Sefer ha-Miṣvot,* negative precept #294; cf. *Maggid Mishne* on *MT Sukka ve-Lulav* 8:15. The subject of a precept is at a perennial 'crossroad,' free to choose one path and reject the other; see Deut. 30:15, 19; and cf. 11:26–28; *MT Teshuba* 3:4; 5:1–2. Hence, freedom of choice is "the great principle upon which the Law and precept (מצוה) stand" (*MT Teshuba* 5:3; see *Golden Doves,* pp. 66–69). [Here Maimonides uses *miṣva* in its double sense of 'Oral Law, instruction' and a 'duty to be performed'; see the quotation in Section IV n. 179.] On the other hand, the subject of a command is in a state of perennial *submission* and is excluded from any decision-making. He "can never stand at a crossroad, for, even if he did, it is not he who decides which road to take" (*Crowds and Power,* p. 361). Only man, in quality of being created in God's image can be subject to a מצוה, see below appendix 24.

*Miṣva* involves consent and personal accountability. Therefore, although Judaism is universal and open to one and all – the first system in history to accept proselytes – it is not Catholic; i.e., it cannot be *imposed.* More accurately, pried from consent and volition, a *miṣva* equals a command. Protological man dwelt within the realm of myth, where 'reality' is the effect of a series of mental projections and displacements. At this level of consciousness, people are incapable of distinguishing between their feelings and emotions, and the outside world. A case in point is that of Adam and Eve after eating the forbidden fruit and taking refuge "inside" (בתוך) the Tree of Knowledge (Gen. 3:8, see *Homo Mysticus,* pp. 58–69), thus evading accountability and responsibility by initiating a process of 'guilt' and 'guilt displacement' to 'another.' Adam blames Eve. In mimetic response, Eve blames the snake (Gen. 3:12–13; see *Homo Mysticus,* p. 80). Protological man, too, by sequestering himself into the realm of myth, evades responsibility by denying accountability: invariably, an-other is the 'responsible.' A prerequisite for Judaism is personal accountability and responsibility. People inhabiting the realm of myth and fiction cannot grasp the distinction between a contracted duty and a command imposed by a despot. At this level of consciousness, all lines of division between a *miṣva* and a command vanish. Invariably, *miṣvot* will be misread as *commands*, and participation in the Sinaitic covenant would be pointless.

Formally, there are 613 'precepts' (מצות). Each is a kind of 'general system principle' unfolding into a variety of fields of interests, distinct levels of consciousness, and different strata of opportunities. Together, the precepts comprise a *total system* (see chapter 24), and could be fulfilled only collectively by "the Congregation of Jacob" (Deut. 33:4). Thus, the Jewish people ought to serve Him in unity and harmony, as a close-knit crew, for no individual could possibly fulfill every single precept; see the remarks of R. Moses di Ṭrani, *Qiryat Sefer* (Venice, 5311/1551), Introduction, chapter 7. Given that fulfillment of a precept presupposes acknowledgment of the *berit*, the rabbis taught that someone who had complied with a single precept – no matter whether by 'honoring one's parents,' or 'sending a bird away before taking her nestling,' etc. – "has a portion in the World to Come," since that individual has in fact partaken in the *berit*. According to the rabbis, the diversity of precepts was intended to offer an opportunity to every Jew to partake in the fulfillment of the Tora. Since it would be difficult to find a single Jew who, in the course of his or her life, had not fulfilled at least a single precept, the rabbis taught that "every single [member] of Israel has a portion in the World to Come" (Mishna Sanhedrin 10:1), i.e., she or he had *merited* salvation. This doctrine was formulated by R. Ḥananya ben 'Aqashya (2nd century), and is contained in a most popular Mishna (Makkot 3:17), usually recited before the *Qaddish*, when concluding the study of Abot. It proclaims that the great variety of precepts contained in the Tora was given because God wished "to warrant merit to Israel" (לזכות את ישראל). In *Perush ha-Mishnayot*, ibid, vol. 4, p. 247, Maimonides explained:

> It is one of the Law's fundaments of faith, that if an individual had executed [even] one of the 613 precepts of the Law, in a proper and satisfactory manner, without associating with it

> some mundane designs at all, but did it for its own sake, as [an act of] love…that person has gained the rights to the life in the World to Come. R. Ḥananya teaches that the great variety of precepts ensures that during the entire course of one's life one would have had the opportunity to perfectly fulfill [at least] a single [precept].

Since a precept is, by definition, a contractual requirement, it stands to reason that an individual who is "required to fulfill a precept and executes it has more merits than one who is not required to fulfill the precept and nonetheless executes it" (גדול המצווה ועושה יותר ממי שאינו מצווה ועושה; Qiddushin 31a; see *Ḥiddushe ha-Riṭba*, ad loc. cols. 346–347). Conversely, someone who is not required to fulfill a precept cannot be faulted for not fulfilling that precept. Thus, the principle formulated by R. David ha-Kohen, *Teshubot ha-Radak* (Constantinople, 5297/1537), #XVII, 9, 119b: "A gentile fulfilling the seven Noahide precepts, and a woman fulfilling the [specific] precepts incumbent upon her, equal [the sanctity of] a High Priest"; cf. Baba Qamma 38a, and *The Mishnah of Rabbi Eliezer* (Heb.), VI, p. 121. Similarly, the rabbis taught that the Patriarchs "fulfilled the entire Tora," see Yoma 28b, because they fulfilled whatever God asked of them; see Tosefta Qiddushin 5:20, p. 299; *Tosefta Ki-Fshuṭah*, p. 986. cf. R. Abraham Maimonides, *Perush*, p. 120. The same applies to a 'transgression' (עברה). Someone who is not a subject of the covenant cannot be charged with 'transgression' (עברה). In this respect Judaism distinguishes between 'reward and punishment,' relating exclusively to precepts (שכר מצוה), and 'recompense and chastisement' (= Ar. 'עוץ') that relate uniformly to all (אין הקב"ה מקפח שכר שום בריאה; Pesaḥim 118b; Baba Qamma 38b; etc.); see R. Hayye Gaon, in *Gaonica*, ed. S. Assaf (Jerusalem: Darom, 1933), # XV, pp. 155–156; and the comments of Professor Zucker, "*'Iyyunim*," pp. 102–104.

A major consequence of the concept of fulfilling a *miṣva* is that it cannot involve the transgression of a law. Hence the rabbinic rule that "a precept which was fulfilled via a transgression" (מצוה הבאה בעברה)

is without merit; see Sukka 30a and *MT Issure Mizbeaḥ* 5:9. There is a lively discussion in Y. Shabbat XIII, 3, 14a among 3rd century rabbis, concerning someone who "ate a stolen *maṣṣa*" on the night of the Seder, "has not fulfilled his requirement." "R. Jonah explained: A transgression (עברה) cannot constitute a precept (מצוה)." The same idea was expressed differently by his colleague, R. Yose: "A 'precept' (מצוה) cannot be constituted via a transgression (עברה)." The root of this doctrine is that God can be worshipped only according to the rules established at Sinai-Moab. Therefore, someone sinning within the Law cannot have fulfilled a precept! In the words of R. Ila, "[It is written:] '*These* are the precepts' (מצוות; Lev. 27:34; Num. 36:13) – if you fulfill them as they were prescribed they are precepts (מצוות), and if not they are not precepts (מצוות)." cf. *Mekhilta de-R. Shim'on b. Yoḥai*, p. 139, cited below, and *Maggid Mishne* on *MT Ḥameṣ wu-Maṣṣa* 6:7.

The preceding bears directly on the Hebrew concept of 'sanctity' (קדושה): it can be acquired only by fulfilling the precepts. Thus, "to be holy unto your God" (Num. 15:40), means that "holiness is acquired through [the fulfillment] of each one of the precepts" (קדושת כל המצוות; *Sifre Bemidbar* #115, p. 127). "What does the sanctity of the precepts (קדושת המצוות) mean?" asked the rabbis. "That every time that God adds another precept to Israel, He is adding sanctity to them" (*Mekhilta de-R. Shim'on b. Yoḥai*, p. 139); cf. *Guide* III, 33, p. 390, ll. 1–8.

Belief in the 'sanctity of the precepts' (קדושת המצוות) constitutes a repudiation of the notion of cosmic sacrality, common to pagan humanity. "To be sacred" (Lev. 20:7), taught the rabbis, "this is the sanctity of all the precepts" (קדושת כל המצוות). Sanctity cannot be acquired through pagan rituals. Pondering on the apparent redundancy of the verse, "and you shall become sacred and will be sacred" (Lev. 20:7), the rabbis explained: "This [the apparent redundancy, comes to teach] abstention from an alien cult. Lest you may say, 'this refers to the sanctity of all the precepts' (קדושת כל המצוות) [and is not a repudiation of pagan cult]! Since it had already stated "you shall be sacred" (Lev. 19:2) – the sanctity of all the precepts (קדושת כל המצ־וות) was already stipulated. Then, what are you to learn from "and you shall become sacred and will be sacred? This is abstention from alien worship." (*Sifra Qedoshim* X, 2, 82b. Concerning 'alien cult,' see below appendix 11, and Introductory Remarks, Section III). Accordingly, Maimonides concluded that there is no semantic difference between God exhorting Israel to "be sacred" and His saying "fulfill my precepts." The same applies to terms such as 'purity' and 'impurity'; they are semantically identical to 'observe my precepts and don't transgress my ordinances'; see *Sefer ha-Miṣvot,* IV, pp. 18–19; *Guide* III, 33 and 47; and *Kuzari* III, 49. cf. R. Abraham b. ha-Rambam, *Perush,* p. 302.

Consequently, Judaism also repudiates *jihad*-devotion, whether against others or against ourselves; see below appendix 59. Or what amounts to the same, Judaism repudiates the *minut* ideology whereby the end justifies the means; see Prov. 3:17 and below appendix 55.

We can now proceed to examine a fundamental dimension of Jewish monolatry. It not only means that God is to be worshipped exclusively according to the precepts of the *berit,* but that said precepts are to be fulfilled according to the norms stipulated by halakha ('Rabbinic law') – not by intuition and pious impulse! R. Judah ha-Levi explained that this postulates that the precepts are not some sort of indeterminate articles to be executed according to one's whims, but that "they have known and precise definitions" (*Kuzari* III, 49; Ar. p. 129, l. 13). The Tora is "exact" (Ar. מצ'בוטה), with precise demarcations (*Kuzari* II, 50; Ar. p. 70, l. 14). Thus, religious devotion cannot be grounded on "your personal feeling and sagacity" (*Kuzari*; III, 49; Ar. p. 130, l. 19; cf. I, 99; III, 53), and it must be expressed within the boundaries of the precepts, i.e., "according to their definitions and stipulations" (*Kuzari* I, 79; Ar. p. 20, l. 17). This means that "diligence and fervent zeal" are not valid criteria for religion and spirituality. In fact, the sin of the golden calf (Ex. 32:1–8) was not because the children of Israel worshipped another deity or worshipped an image, but because they gave free rein to religious fervor and worshipped the God of Israel with a ritual which was not specified in the covenant (see *Kuzari* I, 97; cf. ibid I, 79 and IV, 14 and 23. For a full examination of the subject, see José Faur, "The Biblical Idea of Idolatry," *The Jewish Quarterly Review* 69 [1978], pp. 1–26).

Thus, a major difference emerges between Judaism and other spiritual systems ('monotheistic religions' included) concerning the place and function of religious zeal. In Judaism, fervor and personal endeavor alone do not equal 'religion'; rather, religious fervor must operate within the strict confines of halakha. Were one to admit that personal endeavor could serve as a spiritual criterion, then there would no longer be any grounds to differentiate between heathenism, magic, and 'religion'; see José Faur, "Two Models of Jewish Spirituality," *Shofar* 10 (1992), pp. 7–11; and *Studies in the Mishne Tora,* pp. 126–132. The main purpose of this doctrine is not to exclude pathos and feelings from worship, but to make sure that religious devotion is confined to the perimeters of the Law.

Let us point out, by way of conclusion, that the rabbis distinguished between a 'precept' (מצוה) and a 'mandatory action' that one is compelled to do under pressure (חובה); e.g., washing the fingertips after a meal, which is done for hygienic reasons; in contradistinction to the ritual of the washing of the hands (נטילת ידים) done as a 'precept' (מצוה); see Ḥolin 105a; cf. *Tosafot* on Giṭṭin 90b s.v. *'im*. Because the rabbis (Shabbat 25b) referred to the lighting of the Sabbath candles as 'mandatory' (חובה), it was debated whether it also required a 'blessing.' For a learned analysis of this debate, see R. Raṣon 'Arusi, "*Birkat Hadlaqat ...,*" *Sinai* 85 (5739/1979), pp. 55–91. Occasionally, the term 'precept' (מצוה) is used in the sense of 'a good' or 'preferred action'; see, for example, Maran, *Shulḥan 'Arukh, Oraḥ Ḥayyim* ##XXIV, 2; XC, 12; CXC, 4; etc.

# 5. Defilement of the Hands

Concerning the rule that upon touching a Scroll of the Hebrew Scripture the hands are ritually defiled, the Mishna Yadayim 4:6 explains: "לפי חבתן היא טומאתן"; that is, "their impurity is a function of their high esteem" in which the Scrolls of Scripture are held; cf. ibid. 3:5; Mishna Kelim 15:6. To grasp the sense of this legislation, it is necessary to consider the obsession with 'sacred' objects peculiar to the protological mind. The subject has been examined by Mircea Eliade, *The Sacred and the Profane* (San Diego: Harcourt Brace & Company, 1987). Let me quote one of the pertinent passages, pp. 11–12:

> The modern Occidental experiences certain uneasiness before many manifestations of the sacred. He finds it difficult to accept the fact that, for many human beings, the sacred can be manifested in stones or trees, for example. But as we shall soon see, what is involved is not a veneration of the stone in itself, or a cult of the tree in itself. The sacred tree, or the sacred stone are not adored as stone or tree; they are worshipped precisely because they are *hierophanies,* because they show something that is no longer stone or tree but the *sacred,* the *ganz andere* [wholly other].

A pivotal point in Scripture and Rabbinic tradition is that sanctity may be acquired only through the fulfillment of God's precepts (see appendix 4). Through touching one can acquire 'ritual impurity'

(טומאה), but not sacrality! It appears that some believed that one could draw in the 'sacrality' from a 'sacred object' by touching it; see R. David Qimḥi on Ezek. 44:19 and R. Abraham ibn 'Ezra on Ex. 28:2. When the sacred object was afar, as with the moon and other heavenly bodies, the worshipper would stretch his hand towards it, as if to kiss it, and draw in its sacrality unto himself, cf. Job 31:27 and R. Se'adya Gaon's *Commentary*, ad loc. It was alleged that Babylonian Jews would pull the hair off the scape-goat on its way to the desert on the Day of Atonement, and say to it: "Seize [my sins] and go away! Seize [my sins] and go away!" Mishna Yoma 6:4; see Saul Lieberman, *Tosefta Ki-Fshuṭah*, 10 vols. (New York: The Jewish Theological Seminary of America, 1955–2001), vol. 4, p. 794. Tosefta Kippurim 3:13, p. 245, reports that the people committing this sacrilege were Alexandrian Jews – an accusation that they vehemently rejected; see Y. Yoma VI, 4, 33d. On their part, Babylonian Jews replied that they were not the culprits, but the victims of Alexandrian slander, see Yoma 66b.

To discourage this type of devotion, the Tora declared that [even] priests engaged in preparation of the red heifer and purification water – basic elements for the purification ritual – are themselves ritually impure (see Num. 19:7–10, 21). Likewise, the rabbis taught that ashes of the red heifer, as well as the sprinkling-water used in the purification-rite, are ritually impure; see Mishna Kelim 1:1, 2; cf. Tosefta Para 10:1, p. 638; Mishna Para 4:4 and *MT Para* 5:1–7. Indeed, to make sure that the people would not believe that the priest preparing the red heifer was something of a 'pure icon,' the rabbis demanded that the priest should be in a state of (minor) impurity; see Mishna Para 3:6 and *MT Para* 1:14. With this purpose in mind, the Tora declared that the person leading the scape-goat into the desert – an essential procedure in the atonement ritual – is ritually impure; see Lev. 16:26, Mishna Yoma 6:6. Moreover, the rabbis stipulated that he could perform the ritual while in a state of impurity; see Yoma 66b and *MT 'Abodat Yom ha-Kippurim* 5:21. A similar rule applied to all other sacrifices burnt outside the Sanctuary (and therefore exposed to abuse by the uneducated public); see *MT Para* 5:1–7. To dissuade the people from touching the sacrifices, it was taught that coming in contact with a sacrifice would render the person ritually impure – something that caused dread to pagans as well as Jews. This seems to have been the context of the query that the priests submitted to Prophet Ḥaggai, whether food that came in contact with the meat of a sacrifice is 'sanctified,' see Ḥaggai 2:12 – a euphemism for 'prohibited,' see *Targum* ad loc.; cf. *Targum* on Deut. 22:9, and R. Abraham ibn 'Ezra on Ex. 30:29. Some visitors, particularly during the holidays, were tempted to touch the sacred objects at the Temple, especially the table containing the shewbread (see Ex. 25:23–30), representing material abundance and sustenance. To discourage this practice, the authorities at the Temple warned the public: "Beware, lest you touch the (shewbread) table"; see Mishna Ḥagiga 3:8; Ḥagiga 26b; Y. Ḥagiga III, 8, 79d. The explanation offered by the Talmudic commentators, that the warning was intended to prevent the people from defiling the table (see Ḥagiga 26b and commentaries), is elusive. People ritually impure were prohibited from entering the sanctuary – a rule strictly observed during the holidays by *everyone* – even those habitually lax about ritual purity; see Mishna Ḥagiga 3:6. Indeed, during the holiday season, "all of Israel have [the status] of colleagues (חברים)" – individuals known for their punctilious observance of purity laws; see Ḥagiga 26a and *MT Ṭum'at Mishkab wu-Moshab* 11:9. Therefore, there could be no reason for assuming that someone would defile the Temple's objects. Moreover, these objects were zealously guarded by the priests, and virtually impossible to touch. It seems to me that the intention was to warn the people that *they* would be defiled by the sacred objects! Evidence for this thesis is the textual variant and reading preserved in R. Ḥanan'el, Ḥagiga 27a, that the Menorah was immersed *at night* for purification purposes. According to the standard explanation it makes no sense to 'purify' the Menorah at the time that it is supposed to be lit! This is why R. Ḥanan'el's reading had been rejected; see Professor Lieberman *Tosefta Ki-Fshuṭah*, vol. 5, p. 1336. In fact, the text *is* authentic, not only because it was transmitted by R. Ḥanan'el, but also because it is supported by the Tosefta

Ḥagiga 3:35, p. 304, edited by Lieberman himself! According to the Tosefta, the Zadokites criticized the rabbis for prescribing that the Menorah should undergo a purification ritual, crying: "Look! They are immersing the Light of the Moon!" Reference to the Menorah as the "Light of the Moon" clearly indicates that the purification rite took place at night, not during the day. That makes perfect sense if one were to assume that the purpose of 'purifying' such objects was to debunk the popular belief that these objects had some sort of magical power; cf. Radaq on Zech. 4:2; and R. Abraham ibn 'Ezra on Num. 3:8; 4:20.

A similar strategy underlined the legislation stipulating that touching a Scroll of the Scripture would result in 'defilement' of the hands. The purpose was to contest the belief that a volume of Scripture is some sort of magical totem, and one could draw in 'sacrality' by touching it (or by dancing with it in frenzy) rather than by studying it. The justification offered by the rabbis that touching a volume of Scripture renders the hands impure, "לפי חיבתן היא טומאתן" (Mishna Yadayim 4:6; Tosefta Yadayim, 2:19, p. 684) means: 'their impurity is a function of the affection' professed for these objects by the unlettered public. Since the actual volumes of Scripture (rather than the content) are particularly prized by the unlettered public (see the frenzy-dance by the analphabetic-crowds during Simḥat Tora), it could become the object of adoration (as in cosmic religiosity). Therefore, the rabbis declared that touching them would defile the hands. Accordingly, that legislation did not apply to the scrolls read at the Temple; see Mishna Kelim 15:6. In my view, the purpose of the rule stipulating that *teruma* that has touched a volume of the Scripture becomes impure, Mishna Zabim 5:12; Shabbat 13b, 14a (cf. Megilla 7a), was to contravene those who believed that by 'bonding together' two sacred objects their respective sacrality would be augmented.

The rabbinic strategy declaring that the above items were impure was systematically challenged by the Zadokites. Concerning the red heifer, see Mishna Para 3:6; and *MT Para* 1:14. Regarding the Menorah, see Tosefta Ḥagiga 3:35, p. 304. The same applies to the 'defilement' of hands by way of touching a volume of Scripture, see Mishna Yadayim 4:6–7; Tosefta Yadayim, 2:19, p. 684.

# 6. 'Depositing a Text' for Publication

The root NWH, 'depositing,' is frequently used for 'placing' something in a ceremonial way; see Ex. 16:34; Num. 17:19; Deut. 14:28; II Chr. 4:8; cf. Makkot 18b, and Menaḥot 61b. Thus, the priest "placed" (והניחו, root NWḤ) the first-fruits next to the altar (Deut. 26:4). The noun טנא describing the 'receptacle' containing the first-fruits is found as a verb in Phoenician and other Northwestern Semitic languages, and it denotes 'setting up a votive offering'; see Cyrus H. Gordon, *Evidence for the Minoan Language* (Ventnor, N.J.: Ventnor Publishers, 1966), p. 28. Likewise, "blessing" (Ezek. 44:30) and "wisdom" (Prov. 14:33) are metaphorically "deposited" by God. In the same tenor, God settled His presence (מנוחתי, root NWḤ) at the Temple forever; see Ps. 132:14, cf. Is. 66:1. Since God 'placed' His presence in the Land of Israel, it is referred to as מנוחתי, see Ps. 95:11. Moses, too, "deposited" (הניח, root NWḤ) in the Ark, the Tablets containing the Decalogue (I Kings 8:9). According to the rabbis these Tablets, "laid deposited (מונחים, root NWḤ) in the Ark" together "with the fragments of [the first] Tablets," Baba Batra 14b. Rather than 'resting,' the expression בית מנוחה (I Chr. 28:2), in reference to the Temple, has to do with 'placing,' and 'depositing' "the Ark containing God's covenant"; see I Chr. 28:2, cf. I Sam. 6:18; I Kings 8:56; Ps. 132:8, 14. On the basis of this connotation, the rabbis taught that the requirement to "place there" (והניחם, root NWḤ) the High Priest's ceremonial garments at the conclusion of the Day of Atonement's ceremony (Lev. 16:23), meant that they must be *deposited away* in a protected area (גניזה); see Pesaḥim 26a and *MT Kele ha-Miqdash* 8:4.

Articles which were 'deposited' were to remain in place indefinitely. In the language of the rabbis: "until Elijah comes"; see Baba Meṣi'a 3a. Therefore, it was used for 'burial,' see I Kings 13:31. Since articles placed in 'deposit' were not expected to be moved to another location, the rabbis taught that a vessel "that was designed to stay down" (העשוי לנחת, root NWḤ), did not have the status of a movable object, and therefore could not become defiled, Ḥagiga 26b; see *MT Kelim* 3:1. Similarly, the Scriptural prohibition against removing an object from one premise to another on the Sabbath, applies only when said object had been first 'placed' (הנחה, root NWḤ) on that premise, and then removed (עקירה) and 'placed' (הנחה) on another premise; see Mishna Shabbat 1:1; *MT Shabbat* 13:1. [This meets the objection against Rashi raised by *Tosafot*, Sukka 43a s.v. *ve-ya'birennu.*] In the same tenor, out of deference, one should not 'place' other books on top of a Scroll of the Tora; see Megilla 27a, *MT Sefer Tora* 10:5 – not simply 'put' or 'left' casually, as commonly thought. Because things 'placed in deposit' enjoy 'protection' (מנוחה, root NWḤ), this term is used to convey a sense of inner 'tranquility,' and 'security'; see Ruth 1:9; Jer. 45:3; as well as 'peace,' see I Chr. 22:9. This is why the Land of Israel, as the promised home of the Jews, is designated מנוחה, see Deut. 12:9; cf. Is. 28:12; Mic. 2:10.

From the preceding, it is clear why the flask of oil found after the Temple was recaptured at the end of the Maccabean revolt was assumed *not* to have been defiled, since it had been "deposited" (מונח) and "under seal"; see Shabbat 21b. On the specific connotation of the term 'להניח' in connection to phylacteries, see below appendix 9.

# 7. An Academy to Police the Hebrew Language

See Section II, n. 24, Vico's *The New Science*, #936, p. 342. It is for the reason given by Vico, namely that a free people ought to exercise "sovereignty over languages and letters," that I oppose the establishment of a National Academy in Israel with the authority to impose meaning and to regulate the linguistic apparatus of a people, while at the same time, perversely denying legitimacy to their linguistic and literary tradition. As a regulatory body, the *Aqademya* cares little about the language that it is supposed to watch over. Let me point out that it is hardly possible to find a single member of the *Aqademya* who could read a section of the Scroll of the Tora without making capital errors. In fact, they consistently confuse about one-third of the consonants of the alphabet, not to speak of grave and acute syllables, all forms of *dagesh*, etc. Children exhibiting similar reading impediments in a French or English primary school are sent to remedial schools. Such an agency can acquire Orwellian dimensions when motivated by political ideologies, as in modern Israel, particularly when important segments of the media are state-sponsored. [A special tax called '*igra*' used to be *imposed* on every house owning a radio or TV apparatus, to pay for the state-sponsored-media – regardless of whether the owner wishes to watch the state-sponsored media or not. As with the 'Church-tax' levied in Germany and in other Christian countries on members of communities, regardless of whether they attended

Church or not.] On the danger of an agency with authority to manufacture words, see Martin Buber, "To Create New Words?" in Martin Buber, *A Believing Humanism* (New York: Simon and Schuster, 1967), p. 31. The rabbis noted that when people do not exercise linguistic autonomy, justice and law are inoperative. Given that the people in the Eastern Roman Empire were not fluent in the legal and political language of the state, the rabbis (Mishna Giṭṭin 8:5) designated the Roman government an "unfair empire" (מלכות שאינה הוגנת). The reason for this is because the people of the area "have neither [their own] writing (*ketab*) nor [their own] language" (Giṭṭin 80a; cf. 'Aboda Zara 10a). In such an environment, 'law, justice, etc.,' are objects of linguistic manipulation, rather than substance; see the humorous story in Shabbat 116a-b.

Let us consider, for the sake of illustration, one of the new terms sponsored by the *Aqademya*. For reasons having to do with psychology rather than linguistics, it discarded the traditional nomenclature of personal pronouns, in favor of *guf* (גוף). Believing that this term is equivalent to 'person,' we have 'first *guf*,' 'second *guf*,' etc. Hebrew *guf*, however, is not a 'person.' It serves to indicate *inanimate objects*, such as 'land,' see Baba Meṣi'a 96a; 'fruits,' see Ḥolin 114b; 'a beast,' see Menaḥot 14b, Temura 9b; and an 'amorphous fetus,' see Tosefta Nidda 4:15, p. 645, Nidda 23a, b, 24a, b. In Medieval Hebrew, *guf* stood for 'substance' and 'matter' in general. A popular hymn sung at the Synagogue proclaims that "God is not a *guf*" – in the sense that He is not corporeal. The 'oversight' may be related to the anti-humanistic ideology dominating the Israeli elite, according to which, 'human' is a misnomer for a certain mass of chemical substances meant to serve the social and political machinery of the State; see appendix 24. Another monstrosity, pointing to the dark and murky creeds lurking beneath the mind of this august institution, is using the Hebrew 'קרבן,' standing for 'a sacramental or votive sacrifice offered to God at the Temple,' to designate a 'victim' of a crime or an accident. It takes a profoundly sick psyche to confuse the fatality of a crime or accident with an offering presented to God.

These points aside, it does not seem too much to expect that a minimal requirement to qualify for membership in such an august body would be to know how to say 'Academy' in Hebrew – rather than *aqademya* – a term never before used in Hebrew sources. Let us note that it does not appear in the first, and to a large extent still the best, *Modern Hebrew Lexicon,* by Eliezer ben Yehuda (1858–1922) – and for good reason! Cf. Section V, n. 61. An English reader may best appreciate the linguistic elegance of this august body, by considering that the exact translation of their title is, "The Academy to the Hebrew Language." In fact, the title is nothing less than a linguistic oxymoron. *Aqademya* being a Greek term unknown in Hebrew, used to designate a 'Hebrew' institution for the purpose of promoting Hebrew! That would be equivalent to something like, "The English *Midrashiya* for the study and promotion of English" – in an English speaking country! Rhetoric aside, the main purpose of this august institution is to *alienate* Israelis from the Scripture: people speaking Modern Hebrew cannot understand a single sentence from the Hebrew Scripture.

# 8. Reciting a Text for Publication

When Jeremiah attempted to publish an elegy on the future destruction of Jerusalem, the first step consisted of reciting the text to his trusted scribe Barukh ben Neriya (Jer. 36:1–4). Then, he instructed him to recite it publicly at the Temple (Jer. 36:6, 8–9). Barukh ben Neriya did this from the office of "the scribe, at the upper hall, from the entrance of the new gate ... in the ears of all the people" (v. 10). Jeremiah's elegy was banned and not allowed to circulate, see Jer. 36:11–26. In my view, its publication was banned not merely on account of the content, but also because Barukh ben Neriya affronted the king by bypassing the authorities and by publishing the text directly to the general public. It is worthy of note that when the officer who permitted Barukh ben Neriya to read the text in public became aware of the content, he immediately reported the matter to the officials "sitting at the Scribe's Hall" (v. 12). The officers requested Barukh ben Neriya to withdraw the text, and advised him that he, as well as Jeremiah, had better hide (v. 19, cf. v. 26). Finally, the text was brought to the king himself, who condemned it to the flame. The removal of the text from circulation was carried out in a special ceremony. An officer read before the king three or four verses at a time, and then the king would "cut it out with a scribe's razor" and throw the piece to the flames (vv. 21–23).

Let us conclude with three additional notes. First, some officers disapproved of the king's action (see v. 25). Second, God ordered Jeremiah to write the text again. This time, however, Jeremiah did not publish the text but passed it privately to Barukh ben Neriya (vv. 28–32). According to the rabbis the text in question was *Ekha*. Since it was not published by the higher authorities of Israel, this work was included neither in the *Prophets* nor in the *Hagiography*, but as one of the "Five Scrolls," indicating later and lesser rank publication. The authorities did not forgive his behavior. That is why Jeremiah is not mentioned in the *Books of Kings*; see Joseph Klausner, "Why was Jeremiah Ignored in the Book of Kings?" In *Alexander Marx Jubilee Volume*, Hebrew Section (New York: Jewish Theological Seminary, 1953), pp. 189–203.

# 9. Wearing Phylacteries

A fundamental act of Jewish devotion consists of 'wearing' (Hebrew: לבש; Judeo-Arabic: *libs*; Judeo-Spanish: *vestir*) the 'phylacteries' (תפלין, singular תפלה) every weekday. One is placed on the arm and another on the forehead; see Berakhot 14b and *Sha'are Teshuba* #153, p. 16b. The phylactery of the arm is designated אות 'sign' (Ex. 13:9, 16). This is not the place to launch a full-fledged analysis of biblical semiotics. Within the limits of our subject, it would suffice to note that in Hebrew semiotics a 'sign' conveys both 'difference' and 'meaning.' More precisely: meaning through difference; see *Golden Doves*, pp. xxiv-xxv, 83. A 'sign' is either recognized or not, and it cannot be subjected to analysis or division; see *Golden Doves*, pp. 77–78. (Hence, the four sections of the Tora it contains are written on a *single* parchment, and its folder is *not* divided; see below.) The phrase לאות ('for a sign') appears with regard to three different precepts throughout Scripture. The function of these signs is to identify the Jew to *others*, (the circumcision, Gen. 17:11; the phylactery on the arm Ex. 13:9, 16; Deut. 11:18; and the Sabbath, Ezek. 20:12, 20); cf. R. Se'adya Gaon, *Commentary on Exodus*, ed. and trans. Y. Ratzaby (Jerusalem: Mossad Harav Kook, 1998), pp. 187–188. Cyrus Gordon, *Adventures in the Near East*, (London: Phoenix House, 1957), p. 78, noted that the 'seal' was used for identification purposes. Notably, לאות of the phylactery of the arm parallels the 'ensign' that the Jewish monarch wore attached to his arm; see Sanhedrin 21b and the quotation from Philo in Section III, n. 126.

The focus of this appendix is the second phylactery, to be placed on the forehead. It is designated זכרון (Ex. 13:9), *Targum*: דוכרן – a 'memorandum.' As we hope to show in the following, its significance is its connection to the inner dynamics of Jewish memoranda and national archives. The forehead phylactery is designed as a 'folder,' containing four separate compartments or wallets (בתים), in each of which is stored a different 'file' (see below). Each file must be rolled from left to right (*MT Tefillin* 2:1, 3:7, 5:6), so that one wishing to examine it could read it from beginning to end. Each roll is then tied with a leather strip, and the strip bound over with a string of hair (*MT Tefillin* 3:1, 8). [There is a picture of an ancient file from Jewish Elephantine of the 5th Century BCE: see 'rolled and sealed,' in the *Encyclopedia Judaica*, vol. 3, p. 374.] The file is then stored in one of the assigned compartments (בתים; see *MT Tefillin* 3:5). The letter *Shin* (last letter of *Qadosh* 'Holy') on the right side of the folder serves to indicate that it contains sacred memoranda – not commercial or diplomatic documentation. The four-armed *Shin* on the left side (*MT Tefillin* 3:1, 2) indicates that there are four interconnected files (something that could not be made with either the letter *Qof* or *Dalet* of *Qadosh*). The term 'אחמתא' in Ezra 6:2 serves to designate a royal file. This is how it is described in *Midrash Daniel wu-Midrash 'Ezra*, p. 122: "It is a type of a file where they keep letters and books." Cf. Radaq, *Sefer ha-Shorashim* on Ezra, cl. 838. I take this term to be a metathesis of 'אמתחת' Gen. 44:1, 2, (root MTḤ 'to stretch') which is a 'sack of leather'; see R. Jonah ibn Jannaḥ, *Sefer ha-Shorashim*, p. 276, and Radaq, *Sefer ha-Shorashim*, cl. 406.

The nuances peculiar to the phylacteries conform to the norms regulating the writing and filing of sacred archives. Some of the divergences between these norms and those regulating a Scroll of the Tora (see *MT Tefillin* 1:16; 4:15) are clearly understood upon recalling that the Tora is a *book* designed for circulation – not an archived document. Because a duly archived file cannot be amended, neither the tefillin nor mezuza can be corrected; see *MT Tefillin* 1:16, 2:2. On the other hand, a Scroll of the Tora is a *book* for reading, and faults can be rectified; see Ketubot 19b, and *MT Tefillin* 1:16; *Sefer Tora* 7:12–13. Therefore, unlike the tefillin and mezuza (see *MT Tefillin* 1:6–9), the Tora must be written on a different type of parchment, with wide margins, *MT Sefer Tora* 7:4–7; and in a special format, *MT Sefer Tora* 9:1–12, etc; cf. Mishna Megilla 1:8. Although the mezuza, too, is an archived file, unlike the tefillin it is exposed to the outside and needs to be periodically examined, see *MT Mezuza* 5:9, whereas the tefillin do not need to be periodically examined; see *Mekhilta de-R. Yishma'el*, p. 69; *Sha'are Teshuba* #153, 16c; *MT Tefillin* 2:11; cf. *Teshubot R. Neṭruna'e Gaon*, ed. Robert Brody (Ofeq Institute: Jerusalem-Cleveland, 1994), vol. 2, pp. 405–406. This explains why it must be written differently, and on a different material than the tefillin; see *MT Tefillin* 1:8–9, 12, etc.

The four files of the tefillin are a memoranda of the *whole* Tora. The first file (Ex. 13:1–10) records the *salvation* of Israel from Egypt. The second file (Ex. 13:11–16) registers the *connection* between the Exodus and the Land of Israel: the significance of the former must be carried onto the latter. The third and fourth files establish, respectively, the cornerstone of Judaism: first, *faith* in and *love* of God (Deut. 6:4–9); and second, *fulfillment* of His precepts (Deut. 11:13–21). There is *nothing* in the whole Tora which is not comprehended in these memoranda. In the words of the rabbis, Qiddushin 35a: "The whole Tora has been placed side by side (הוקשה) with the tefillin." Similarly, we find in *Sha'are Teshuba*, #153, 16b (quoting the *Mekhilta*, see below): "Whoever wears tefillin it is as if the whole Tora is (active) on his lips"; including the Oral Law, see ibid., 16c, and *Yalquṭ Shim'oni, Bo*, #222, s.v. *lema'an*, vol. 2, 69c. [This source was overlooked by R. Isaac Berakha, *Berekh Yiṣḥaq* (Venice, 7523/1763), 38c.] To stress the parallel between the Tora and the phylacteries, both are to be sewn similarly; see Makkot 11a and *Yalquṭ Shim'oni, Bo*, #222, s.v. *lema'an*, vol. 2, 69c. The rabbis did not intend an exact parallel between the Tora and phylacteries, but to point out a kind of symmetry between them, where one synthesizes or symbolizes the other. This critical idea was instituted in law. Judicial procedure requires that in the administration of certain oaths (שבועת הדיינים), the defendant should hold a Scroll of the Tora. If this key element is omitted, the oath is invalid and must be administered again. Could the tefillin be used instead? The law varies. In a case in which the defendant is *not* a learned individual, judicial procedure requires him to hold an actual Scroll of the Tora; the tefillin would be accepted only in case of an oversight. However, if the defendant is learned, judicial procedure requires him to hold only the tefillin – not the Tora (see Shebu'ot 38b, *MT Shebu'ot* 11:11–12). The underlying principle is clear. The symmetry Tora/phylacteries is approximate; ultimately, it depends on the individual making the synthesis.

The preceding will elucidate a number of regulations about the tefillin. Let us point out that the tefillin may not be worn at night, on holidays, and on the Sabbath. This regulation makes good sense upon realizing that archives were accessible during daylight and on weekdays only. As with archives, the files of the phylactery are positioned in reference to someone *facing* them, as if that individual would want to open and examine them – not in reference to the person wearing them; see *MT Tefillin* 3:5, cf. 3:7. Consistent with the preceding, the act of placing on the phylacteries is designated, להניח (root NWḤ) – a term standing for 'placing' or 'depositing' a valued object in a sacred place for safe-keeping, see above appendix 6. Most appropriately, the blessing *for* this act is להניח, see *MT Tefillin* 4:5, and cf. *Bet Yosef, Oraḥ Ḥayyim*, XXV, 7. By depositing the phylacteries on himself the Jew becomes a national archive incarnate. Thus, the most important memoranda of Israel are secured. We can now appreciate the regulation stating that the head phylactery acquires its special status *after* it is duly placed on the forehead; see *MT Tefillin* 3:17. It is the individual Jew, in function of 'archive,' who is the reason for the tefillin's special sanctity – not the other way around. Because the actual *body* [hence the concept of 'wearing' – *labash/libes/vestir tefillin*] is archive incarnate, the fulfillment of this commandment requires the highest level of personal hygiene (see Shabbat 130a, *MT Tefillin* 4:15) and mental focusing (see *MT Tefillin* 4:14) – something not required in the performance of any other ritual. Lest the tefillin be taken to be some sort of amulet, the rabbis stipulated that it is *incumbent on the individual wearing it* "to protect" it; see Tosefta Ḥagiga 1:2, p. 374–375; Sukka 42a; 'Arakhin 2b; and *Tosefta Ki-Fshuṭah,* vol. 5, p. 1269 – rather than expect to be protected by it! (Although, I heard of butchers wearing tefillin to ensure that they would incur no harm when cutting the meat.)

Circular phylacteries and amulets on the forehead were used in Ancient Egypt for magical protection, particularly among 'theosophists.' In Elias Bickerman and Morton Smith, *The Ancient History of Western Civilization* (New York: Harper & Row, 1976), after p. 50, #79, there is a picture of the bust of a theosophist from the 3rd century with a circular phylactery. (A 'circular' headgear is still worn by the Japanese 'Yamabushi' priests.) Given that this type of headgear was used for magical protection, the rabbis referred to them as *amagoza, magos* ('of' or 'pertaining to,' a 'magician'); see Mishna Megilla 3:8; and Talmud Megilla 24b. Regarding head ornaments used for decorative purposes, see *Sha'are Teshuba* #153, 16c.

The preceding considerations explain the original matrix of the *bar miṣva* ceremony. It celebrates the child assuming personal responsibility as a depositary of Israel's sacred treasures. In the Sephardic tradition the ceremony is designated *libes at-Tfillin* in Judeo-Arabic, and *vestir el Tefillin* in Judeo-Spanish – rather than '*bar miṣva.*' Usually, senior members of the family will assist the child in the task of placing the tefillin for the first time, thus symbolizing transmittal of tradition. Those refusing to "deposit" (מניח, root NWḤ) tefillin on their "cranium" – an allusion to the head phylactery – have failed to permit their *bodies* to act as the living archive of Israel. Therefore, in a sense, they have "executed a transgression [against the Tora] *with their own body*" (פושעי ישראל בגופם); see Rosh HaShana 17a. Connected to this symbolism is the custom that those directly participating in the circumcision ceremony (father, *mohel* and *ṣandaq*) are to wear tefillin; see R. Joseph Ḥayyim David Azulai, *Mar'it ha-'Ayyin,* (Leghorn, 5564/1804), 127c.

The details surrounding the meaning and execution of duly filed memoranda are to be supplied by the archivists (see Est. 6:1–3); in our case, the individual wearing the phylacteries. Therefore, the phylactery of the head is symbolically associated with learning and scholarship; see Ex. 13:9, Yoma 86a, cf. Shabbat 13a. Some maintain that as a sign of humility, it would be appropriate for a student to wear a smaller phylactery than that of a sage; see *Teshubot ha-Ge'onim*, ed. R. Jacob Musafia (Jerusalem, 5727/1967), #3, 6a-b, cf. Matt. 23:5. Some rabbinic authorities argued that it may be construed as conceit for someone who is not a sage to wear phylacteries altogether; see *Newly Discovered Geonic Responsa*, #161, pp. 233–237. Following this trend of thought, others proposed that since a scholar is in fact a living Tora (see *Homo Mysticus*, pp. 7–8), he should not be required to wear phylacteries altogether! In evidence, a paragraph was cited from *Mekhilta de-R. Yishma'el*, p. 68. That may have been the reason why some rabbis from the Holy Land did not wear tefillin; see *Newly Discovered Geonic Responsa*, #161, pp. 234–235. The authenticity of the citation from the *Mekhilta* was rejected by the *Ṭur* and *Bet Yosef, Oraḥ Ḥayyim*, XXXVIII, 6 and all subsequent authorities. On juridical principles alone, R. Samuel ben Ḥofni Gaon (d. 1013) rejected the citation; see Abraham E. Harkavi, *Zikhron la-Rishonim*, I (Petersburg, 1880), p. 38. In fact, it is contradicted by the Y. 'Erubin VI, 1, 26a, establishing the principle that, "whoever is required to [study] Tora is required to put on tefillin." Finally, as pointed out by R. Israel Moses Ḥazzan, *Iyye ha-Yam*, 61a, the citation from the *Mekhilta* is faulty. The original text read: "Whoever wears tefillin it is as if the whole Tora is (active) on his lips."

Historical circumstances following the Destruction of the Second Temple brought about the momentous significance of tefillin. The Romans were bent not only on the physical genocide of Israel, but also on the eradication of the Tora. With this purpose in mind, after authorizing his troops "to burn and sack" Jerusalem, "on the next day," Titus "set fire to the Archives" (Josephus, *Jewish Wars*, VI, 354; vol. 3, p. 479). The Jews made a strategic decision: Roman brutality would be met with the tefillin. Thus, every Jew would become the symbolic archive of Israel. It should not be surprising to discover, therefore, that the tefillin became a target of Roman persecution. With special reference to the phylactery of the head, they decreed: "Whoever places (מניח) tefillin, (we shall) prick out his brain" (Shabbat 49a; cf. Megilla 24b).

There is a beautiful symbolism in the rabbinic doctrine that God, too, wears the phylactery of the head (Berakhot 6a-b; cf. *Teshubot ha-Ge'onim,* ed. R. Jacob Musafia, #115, p. 35). The memoranda attesting to God's miracles and precepts are guarded by each Jew in his own person. Reciprocally, He, too, guards the deeds and wonders wrought by Israel throughout her long and torturous history in His 'personal archive.' That is why the verse in God's tefillin reads: "Who could compare to Israel, Your nation, a people unique in earth" (I Chr. 17:21).

The preceding could shed light on the syntax underlying the concept of Rosh HaShana. In the Tora this holiday is referred to as זכרון תרועה מקרא קודש (Lev. 23:24). Here, too, the *Targum* rendered זכרון as דוכרן, 'a memorandum.' The next term (תרועה) is rendered יבבא, a 'trumpet' or 'proclamation' made at the sound of a shofar. The last two terms מקרא ('a call') and קודש ('to the sanctuary') specify that this is a 'summons' to appear at the קודש, 'sanctuary.' Before exploring the sense of the verse we should note that the prosodic marks (טעמים) connect זכרון-תרועה as one syntactical unit, and מקרא-קודש as a second syntactical unit. Accordingly, the sense of מקרא-קודש, intersects and complements זכרון-תרועה, as follows: A1–B2 = B1–A2 = A1+B2. Thus: מקרא/תרועה = זכרון/קודש. The exact translation is [A1] "a memoranda" [B2] "at the Sanctuary"; i.e., [A2] "a summons" [B1] "with a trumpet". In plain terms: 'A summons to be executed with a trumpet, calling to appear at the Sanctuary where the memoranda (pertaining to each individual) will be reviewed.' Precisely and to the point, the rabbis interpreted this to mean that on Rosh HaShana we are summoned to appear at the Sanctuary, where the memoranda registering our actions (see Mal. 3:16; Est. 2:23, 6:1) will be examined before the Divine Tribunal. As with all memoranda, the archivists will be called on to supply the details (see above). Hence, the motifs of 'Divine Judgment,' and 'Books of Life and Death' (see Rosh HaShana 16b), peculiar to the liturgy and pathos of the day.

# 10. The Autonomy of the Law

Belief in the autonomy of the Law underlies much of biblical and post-biblical Jewish history. Throughout the ages, the political, ecclesiastical, and judicial authorities were challenged by the people – in the name of the Law.

The episode of Ahab and Nabot (I Kings 21) illustrates how in Ancient Israel, even tyrants did not claim eminent domain and recognized the supreme authority of the Law. When Nabot refused to sell his vineyard, Ahab fell into despair, not knowing what to do. The idea of using trumped up charges against Nabot came from his wife, the pagan queen Jezebel, who herself (the daughter of a Syrian king) was well acquainted with the art of judicial manipulation. Remarkably, even under those circumstances, meticulous procedure was observed. More importantly, the eventual usurpation of Nabot's property was denounced for generations as a most heinous crime (see II Kings 9:21–26); see below appendix 13. The Rabbinic doctrine of 'the kingdom of heaven' (מלכות שמים), Mishna Berakhot 2:2, usually explained in theological terms, is a *political* doctrine. It postulates that the "kingdom," i.e., the sovereignty, "of heaven," i.e., the Law, is supreme (see chapter 19). From this doctrine two legal principles emerge: "there cannot be a fiduciary relation in matters involving a transgression' of the Law" (אין שליח לדבר עברה), and "the orders of a superior authority and the orders of an inferior authority, whose orders shall we obey?" (דברי הרב דברי התלמיד, דברי מי שומעים); See Qiddushin 42b and parallels; *MT Melakhim* 3:9; *Sefer ha-Miṣvot,* positive precept, #173, p.

146; cf. *MT Me'ila* 7:2. The first formula rejects the notion that there could be a duty to act on behalf of another person in matters involving an illegal act. Therefore, neither the king nor any other authority may be obeyed in matters involving the breaking of the Law. The second formula establishes that an individual is responsible for his own actions, and cannot claim immunity on the basis that he was acting as an agent of a 'higher authority.'

The same standards apply to the ecclesiastical authorities: they, too, are under the absolute mandate of the Law. When acting outside the confines of the Law, the priesthood has no authority. The conflict between Amos and the high priest Amaziah (Am. 7:7–17) illustrates this fundamental principle: the office of high priest was challenged at the royal sanctuary, by Amos – a common individual with no office. The point is clear: the eminence of the priesthood is the effect of the Law, and it must be measured accordingly. (This episode has been the subject of a brilliant analysis by Professor Shalom Spiegel, "Amos vs. Amaziah," in ed. Judah Goldin, *The Jewish Expression*, New Haven: Yale University Press, 1976, pp. 38–65. cf. Mal. 2:5–7.)

A similar incident took place during the period of the Second Temple in Jerusalem. The rabbis reported a clash between the people and the high priest, who was also the king, when he deviated from a prescribed ritual (see Mishna Sukka 4:9). Josephus, *Jewish Antiquities*, XIII, 372, vol. 7, p. 413, described the incident as follows:

> As for Alexander, his own people revolted against him – for the nation was aroused against him – at the celebration of the festival, and as he stood beside the altar and was about to sacrifice, they pelted him with citrons, it being a custom among the Jews that at the festival of Tabernacles everyone holds wands made of palm branches and citrons – these we have described elsewhere; and they added insult to injury by saying that he was descended from captives and was unfit to hold office and to sacrifice; and being enraged at this, he killed some six thousand of them, and also placed a wooden

> barrier about the altar and the temple as far as the coping (of the court) which the priests alone were permitted to enter, and by this means blocked the people's way to him. He also maintained foreign troops of Psidians and Cilicians, for he could not use Syrians, being at war with them.

For the feeling of disgust that the people had for this type of high priest, in contrast to the reverence that they had for two proselytes, teachers of the Law, see Yoma 71b, and *In the Shadow of History,* p. 201.

The authority of the judiciary, too, depends on the Law. We have seen that if the Supreme Court of Israel issues a decision contrary to the Law, it is not to be obeyed (see chapters 10, 20, etc.; and *Studies in the Mishne Tora*, pp. 20–24). Maimonides codified the rule that if the Jewish authorities appoint an unqualified person as judge, the appointment is worthless (*MT Sanhedrin* 4:15; cf. *MT Melakhim* 1:7). The following passage, Y. Bikkurim III, 3, 65d, offers a glimpse into the rabbis' view on this matter:

> [1] R. Mane (3rd century) would deprecate those [judges] who were appointed because of money. [2] R. Amme (end of 3rd century) applied to them the verse "Gods of silver and gods of gold do not make for yourselves" (Ex. 20:23). [3] R. Joshia (3rd century) said, his *ṭallet* (mantle) is to be regarded as a donkey's back strap. [4] R. [A]shyan (3rd and 4th centuries) said: Whoever is appointed because of money, one cannot stand up [in reverence] before him or call him 'Rabbi,' and his mantle is to be regarded as a donkey's back strap. [5] R. Ze'ira (3rd and 4th centuries) and a rabbi were seated, when one of those who was appointed because of money passed. Said that rabbi to R. Ze'ira: 'Let us pretend that we are studying, so that we would not need to stand up before him.'

The reason that the mantles of these judges are compared to a donkey's back strap is that, as a matter of distinction, the judges used a thick mantle, see Lieberman, *Tosefta Ki-Fshuṭah, Shabbat*, pp. 70–71. The point here is that just as a donkey, because of the back strap, does not feel its rider, this type of judge is not aware that he is being driven by those who invested him with the mantle of authority.

In the matter of incompetent judges duly appointed by the Exilarch, R. Hayye Gaon (939–1038) issued the following decision:

> Concerning your query about judges who impound the beds of the poor and other objects, not in accordance with the law of the Tora, and [consequently] the creditors come and rob their houses and loot their beds and utensils which cannot be [legally] impounded, and you have no power to constrain them. Let the spirit of those judges be accursed! They are judges of Sodom! Ye Robbers and Thieves! Concerning them it is written: "You have looted the vineyard; the loot of the poor is in their houses" (Is. 3:14). Therefore, you must disseminate the word among all your neighbors and nearby places, and disgrace them and remove them from office, since they do not care about the Tora and the words of our rabbis of blessed memory. And you, who know the law of the Tora and rabbinic statutes, organize, take council, deliberate, and bring forth from among you God-fearing men and scholars who care for the honor of the Tora, and appoint them over you. You should have no second thoughts about this matter. (*Sha'are Teshuba* #86.)

The same principle was applied to the political authorities. As per the following Geonic decision (*Newly Discovered Geonic Responsa*, #96, p. 88; cf. p. 274 [iv]):

> A king, governor, or tax-collector who sends [agents] to the Community to excommunicate for his own private needs and endeavors either to punish or to seize Jewish money – and it is impossible not to excommunicate because of [his] coercion.

> All excommunications that were issued are worthless, and no one should pay any attention to them. Likewise, if an Israelite who had deposited money with a friend, and was denounced, and the king ordered that he [who received the deposit] should be excommunicated, and the confidant does not want to disclose [the deposit he received in trust] except to the heirs [as required by the law] in order to pay [i.e. the debts incurred by the deceased]: Blessing shall descend on him, and the baseless curse will not come! No one should heed that ban and excommunication. And we must acknowledge him [the confidant] for the good [that he did], and bless him because he persisted in his faithfulness, and he is compassionate with the heirs. Concerning this man it is written, "My eyes are on the faithful of the earth" (Ps. 101:6).

Concerning judges appointed for money, see below appendix 58.

Throughout their long history the Jewish people remained steadfast to the principle that all forms of authority must be grounded on the Tora.

Let us review some the principles pertaining to the interpretation and application of the Law discussed in the preceding sections. The "Tora" – comprising the total value-system of Israel – is the result of a *berit* (covenant), freely contracted between God and Israel. Specifically, the Pentateuch or Written Law is the Constitution, while the Oral Law is the *perush* representing the interpretation of the Jewish Constitution by the Supreme Court. The Mishna contains the halakhot, 'regulations,' pertaining to the Jewish Constitution, as formulated by R. Judah ha-Nasi and the Supreme Court of Israel. To apply these regulations, however, we need a "Court Ruling" (see Baba Batra 130b; Horayot 2a; *MT Shegagot* 12:2; 13:1; and below appendix 48). The Talmud contains the Court Rulings of the last National Court of the Jewish people. Since after the Talmudic period there were no National Courts, there was a need for the expert opinion of *posqim* "rabbinic jurists." Although technically lacking the authority of a National Court, their codes and responsa were a kind of "General Counsel Memoranda," reflecting, but not representing, what the opinion of the National Court was (or would have been if the issue had come before them).

A good model for the Rabbinic System is the Internal Revenue Code of the USA. The Code itself is drafted by the Congress, the legislative branch of government. In this sense, it parallels the Written Law. All income tax rules must ultimately find a source in the Code and apply the rules by its authority. In applying the Code we need to consult the "Treasury Regulations," paralleling the Mishna. The regulations, however, are not drafted by the Congress, but by the Department of Treasury (nobody knows for sure, but it is probably a part of the Executive). As with the Mishna, the "Regulations" constitute the official *perush* of the Code. To apply the Code one must consult with the "Regulations," just as one must consult the "Regulations" of the Mishna, before applying the law of the Pentateuch. In addition, there are "Court Rulings," issued by the Judiciary (not the Executive). They are similar to the Rabbinic Court of the Talmud reviewing the regulations of the Mishna. Generally, a Court will not disagree with a "Regulation," and will limit itself to resolving specific issues brought before it. For instance, "Treasury Regulations" require the taxation of "income." The Court could decide if a particular item constitutes "income" for tax purposes, but it would not rule on what is not income. For our purpose, there are also "Revenue Rulings" by the IRS (treasury) that, like the Talmudic Court, will adjudicate on specific questions submitted before it, e. g., whether an entity is a corporation or a partnership. Finally, there is the "General Counsel Memoranda" issued by the attorneys of the Internal Revenue Service. Although technically lacking authority, the memoranda, like the decisions issued by the *posqim*, are practically binding, in the sense that they are an accurate description of what the Internal Revenue Service ruling will be. (In this context it would be opportune to remember that as noted by Justice Holmes, lawyering is a form of "prediction" of what the court may decide; see above Section V, n. 303.)

Given that the Tora was entrusted "to the community of Jacob" (Deut. 33:4), 'law' is not simply what the Supreme Court – or the political and ecclesiastical authorities – dictate. Thus, the Jewish Supreme Court can be found in judicial error. On this key-issue the Jewish legal system differs from other systems. By way of contrast, although the Supreme Court of the US may occasionally decide that a prior opinion was 'erroneous,' it could never be 'in error'; see "Law and Hermeneutics in Rabbinic Jurisprudence," pp. 1670–1672. Rhetorical noise aside, the Constitution is what the US Supreme Court says it is. This point was elucidated by Chief Justice Charles Evans Hughes (1862–1948) – one of the most brilliant minds to grace the Court. "We are under a Constitution," he declared – "but the Constitution is what the judges say it is." (Cited by Joseph W. Bishop, Jr., *Justice Under Fire: A Study of Military Law* [New York: Charterhouse, 1974], p. 175). A corollary to this doctrine is that although the Supreme Court may be theoretically 'erroneous,' it cannot commit a judicial mistake. Given the absolute discretion of the Supreme Court, "the people," as argued by Jefferson, "will have ceased to be their own rulers, having to that extent practically resigned their government in the hands of that eminent tribunal" (see Section II n. 137). It is true that the U.S. constitutional system with its checks and balances, designed to make sure that the court does not overstep its boundaries, offers a sense of stability. However, even well-accepted constitutional principles could – at least at the theoretic level – be subject to broad change and abrogation.

Therefore, Constitutional Law pertains more to the realm of the ethical than to the legal. Here is what Jolowicz, *Lectures on Jurisprudence*, p. 25 writes:

> *Constitutional Law* also, in so far as it relates to the composition of the sovereign, is no law. For whether a particular man, or particular body or composition of bodies is habitually obeyed by the bulk of a society, is a question of fact. Moreover, what is commonly called 'constitutional law' – meaning the principles

> upon which the sovereign should act – is really only positive morality, for sovereign power cannot be limited.

Modern states, too, uphold the same ideal. The objective of legal and judicial institutions is to express, and thereby uphold and defend, the wishes of the 'sovereign.' True to the ideal that might equals right, litigation is in essence a *battle* between two parties. In Rome, the source and inspiration of Western legal tradition, a trial is "in its substance a struggle, a battle in a closed arena... a shock of contending forces." Rather than justice, the task of the court is to serve as the arena of "a just duel fought out between them [the parties] in the full light of day under certain rules, which the umpire is present to enforce." (Both quotations come from M. Car Ferguson, "A Day in Court in Justinian's Rome: Some Problems of Evidence, Proof, and Justice in Roman Law," *Iowa Law Review* 46 [1960–1], p. 740.) To a large extent, this is still the case in modern judicial systems, where equality before the law is not readily attainable. Invariably, the legal system will end up protecting established inequality and hierarchies; cf. "Repressive Tolerance," pp. 116–117. (The classical portrayal of this type of justice is Albert Camus, *The Stranger*, see chapter 3 in particular.) Appropriately, one may argue that modern constitutions guarantee basic human rights. Indeed they do. However, since these constitutions are neither 'eternal' nor 'divine' – as with the Jewish Law – they may be changed at the wish of the sovereign. Thus, even in the best of democracies, we must recognize the possibility of disenfranchising national minorities and undesirable individuals in a strictly constitutional manner. More to the point, since there is no formal covenant articulating the specifics of the law, in fact the Constitution is nothing more than "the persons and bodies who can amend the Constitution." Thus, the actual sovereign is the person or persons who could alter and interpret the Constitution. Clearly, the Preamble of the Constitution proclaiming, "We the People of the United States do ordain and establish this Constitution," presupposes an authoritative body ("We the People") anteceding the legal system. This offers unlimited constitutional powers to "the People." At the same time, since the Supreme Court cannot be in judicial error, "We the people," is in fact a circumlocution for what five out of nine judges dictate.

There is one major difference between Tora – as the basic constitutive document of the Jewish Nation – and the US Constitution. The Judicial authority to interpret and review the Tora by the Supreme Court is explicitly authorized by a provision *in* the Tora (Deut. 17:8–13). The authority of the US Supreme Court to interpret and review the Constitution is not enumerated in the Constitution, but, rather, derives from its own ruling, *Marbury v Madison,* in which it assumes judicial supremacy in constitutional interpretation and the authority to impose its constitutional interpretations on other branches of government. The difference is huge.

The inability of Jews to assimilate into other political, religious, or legal systems is a corollary of having rejected the notion that authority is the effect of power; that is, violence.

# 11. Alien Cult

The Hebrew idea of monolatry – in the sense of worshipping God according to the specific terms prescribed in the covenant – stands at the basis of the Scriptural prohibition of *'aboda zara* ('alien worship'). It includes not only the prohibition against worshipping images or other deities, but also worshipping God with an 'alien worship,' i.e., with cults and rituals not prescribed in the covenant; see above appendix 4. From this perspective, it is irrelevant whether one worships God with images or with an unprescribed cult. The rabbis stipulated that worshipping Michael, the 'ministering angel of Israel,' constitutes *'aboda zara*; see Tosefta Ḥolin 2:18, p. 503; 'Aboda Zara 42b; Ḥolin 40a; etc. Similarly, Talmudic law classifies Christianity as *'aboda zara* not because it worships images – images were introduced into Christianity after the Talmudic period – but solely because it worships with a cult *not* stipulated in the Sinaitic covenant; see *Studies in the Mishne Tora*, pp. 230–238.

The concept of 'alien deities' was instituted by Patriarch Jacob, who referred to pagan idols as "alien deities," (אלהי נכר; Gen. 35:2, 4); see Se'adya's translation ad loc. The sense of this term will be clear upon considering that a married woman is described as 'alien' (זרה, נכריה), i.e., forbidden, not because she is evil but because she is *not* your wife; see Prov. 2:16; 7:5. Therefore, worshipping other deities is compared to adultery; see, for example Hosea (chapter 1). Although an Israelite is permitted to marry a priest's daughter, he is referred to as 'alien' (זר) to indicate that he is *not* a priest (Lev. 22:12). Similarly, the two sons of Aaron were punished because they offered an "alien incense" (אש זרה), i.e., which God "had not ordered them" (Lev. 10:1; cf. Num. 3:4; 26:61); see R. Se'adya Gaon, "Fragments," ed. M. Zucker, *Sura* 2 (1955–1956), pp. 337–338. The same term is used to proscribe priests in general from offering an "alien incense" (קטרת זרה; Ex. 30:9). In the same vein, a 'ritual' (עבודה) which is 'alien' (זרה) is forbidden, not because it is necessarily 'evil,' but, simply, because it is 'alien' to Judaism. In the words of R. Elie Benamozegh, *Em la-Miqra*, vol. 3 (Leghorn, 1863), 41b:

> ...That truly, any type of deviation or change from the prescribed rituals and required conditions [stipulated in the Tora] is designated "*'aboda zara*," because it is in fact 'alien' (*zara*), constituting not 'worship' (*'aboda*) of the God of Israel, but worship of an alien god, or to what was fabricated (by the worshippers).

The term 'alien cult' (עבודה זרה) used by the rabbis to designate other religions (including Christianity) has been misconstrued to mean 'idolatry.' The excuse for such an interpretation is semantic assimilation (see appendix 58), coupled with rabbinic illiteracy. Simply put, an 'alien cult' is any form of worship not prescribed by the Law. Therefore, it applies exclusively to Jews. The rabbis (Megilla 9b) noted that after translating the prohibition against worshipping "other gods ... the sun, or the moon, or any host of heaven," the Septuagint added: "which He did not command you to do" (Deut. 17:3). The English translation of the Septuagint "which he commanded not to do" is incorrect. Cf. *Homo Mysticus*, pp. 9–13.

Jewish regulations of *'aboda zara* don't apply to gentiles outside the Land of Israel. According to the Mishna (Berakhot 9:1), someone witnessing a place where idols were removed, should say: "Blessed is God, Sovereign of the Universe that *'aboda zara* has been removed *from our land*." Cf. *Sifre* #61 (3), p. 127; *Sefer ha-Miṣvot*, positive precept #185, p. 153. Let us point out that Maimonides registered the status of a pious gentile in two places. In *MT Teshuba* 3:5 he codified the rabbinic doctrine that a "pious from among the nations of the world" has a portion in the World-to-Come, i.e., he would be saved (just like a Jew), but refrained from defining 'pious.' This is consistent with the view that Judaism, although open to *all*, is *not* Catholic like Christianity and Islam; i.e., it cannot and will not impose its ideas of sanctity and devotion on the rest of the world. Therefore, Maimonides was careful *not* to define what constitutes a 'sin' for a gentile; cf. *MT Teshuba* 3:2. He defined a pious gentile in terms of the seven Noahide *miṣvot* in the section about Jewish governance and territory, concerning the status of non-Jewish residents in the Holy Land (*MT Melakhim* 9:2). The sense is obvious. An alien residing in Israel must respect Jewish standards and regulations as it would be expected from every alien to respect the laws and regulations of the host country. Support for this thesis is the fact that Maimonides included as one of these seven *miṣvot* establishing a judicial system to try capital cases (*MT Melakhim* 10:11, cf. 8:7; 9:1, 14). This could hardly be feasible outside the Land of Israel. I don't share the view of R. Abraham b. ha-Rambam, *Perush,* p. 302; cf. editor's n. 14.

The preceding is in line with the thesis that we proposed in chapter 25, that idols and rituals branded by the rabbis as *'aboda zara* are state-sponsored (mostly representing imperial dominance over Israel). Explicitly, the rabbis excluded from *'aboda zara* "someone worshipping an object out of love or fear." (For a detailed analysis of the sources and opinions on this subject, see *Studies in the Mishne Tora*, pp. 219–230. Cf. *Homo Mysticus*, p. 10.) We should note that in Antiquity the worship of alien deities was regarded as a 'civil,' rather than a 'religious' offense, in the modern sense of this term; see Albert Barnes, *The Book of Job*, vol. 1 (New York: Leavitt, Trow, & Company, 1845), pp. xxviii-xxix. In this connection I would like to quote a passage from Reverend Jonathan Mayhew, in *Seven Sermons,* reprinted in *Religion in America* (New York: Arno Press, 1969), pp. 68–69:

> It is to be remembered that Judaism was at least as much a *political* as a *religious* institution. The *Jews* had God for their

> immediate *king* and *lawgiver,* both in *church* and *state.* Their *civil* and *ecclesiastical* polity were blended together; and being derived from the same source, every violation of the law of *Moses* might be considered and punished as an offence against the state, in a greater or less degree: And *idolatry* being in these circumstances equivalent to *high treason,* it is not strange that a capital punishment should be annexed to it.

# 12. *Morasha*

*Morasha* is the Hebrew term for 'National Memory' (see Introductory Remarks, Section IV). It is mentioned twice in the Tora, once in relation to the *territory* of Israel (Ex. 6:8; cf. Ezek. 11:15; 25:4; 33:24; 36:5), and again in relation to the *Law* of Israel (Deut. 33:4). Although related to 'succession' it is not synonymous with 'inheritance' (*yerusha*). "In a common succession," explained the rabbis, "the living inherit the dead, but here [concerning the Land of Israel], the dead inherit the living," Baba Batra 117a. An heir may dispose of his inheritance as he or she wishes. *Morasha* is akin to the 'fee tail estate' in feudal England, that an heir receives with the special responsibility of keeping the estate in the family. This explains Nabot's refusal to sell his vineyard to King Ahab; see I Kings 21 and above, appendix 10.

We are now in a position to properly evaluate the semantics of *Morasha* with respect to the Law (Deut. 33:4). It involves transmission of said Law in perpetuity, from one generation to the other; see *Targum* ad loc. Commenting on this verse, R. Abraham ibn 'Ezra pointedly noted that the preposition ל- ('for') in 'for us' ["Law instructed ל-נו," i.e., 'for us,' rather than 'to us'] should apply also to the terms '*morasha*' and '*qehillat*.' Accordingly, the verse is to be rendered: "A Law was instructed (צוה) for us (לנו), for (ל-) *morasha*, for (ל-) the Congregation of Jacob." He explained: "It means that it [the Law] should be conveyed in succession from one generation to the other, (each) conveying (to the next): 'This is what we have received from our Teacher Moses as heritage in our hands.'" For a comprehensive analysis of this passage, see R. Isaac Shrem, *Be'er Yiṣḥaq* (Leghorn, 5624/1864), 152b, note #14. There are some obvious errors in the printed text of R. Abraham ibn 'Ezra's note. In my opinion the correct text should read:

> תורה צוה לנו משה – זהו שישא, ויאמר דור לדור: כך העתקנו מפי משה ירושה בידינו. ויהיה למ"ד לנו מושך עצמו ואחר עמו, וכן היא: מורשה לקהלת יעקב... ויהי: מורשה – למורשה לקהלת יעקב.

Cf. Ms. Vat. Ebr. 38. Ed. Prof. Etan Levine, *Abraham ibn Ezra's Commentary to the Pentateuch*, (Jerusalem: Makor, 1974), p. 212]. A similar syntactical construction (צוה לי, rather than 'אותי'), in the sense 'he instructed me *to say*,' is found in I Sam. 20:29.

To fully appreciate the niceties implicit in '*Morasha* of the Law,' let us begin by noting that the verb צוה is not semantically identical to 'command.' 'To command' implies rank and authority and the power to compel, as in a hierarchic system, when a superior officer issues an order to a subaltern. In this sense it is found only occasionally; e.g., when the *pagan king* of Aram instructed (צוה) his captains to target King Ahab (I Kings 22:31), or when King Ahasuerus issued an order (צוה) that everyone should prostrate himself to Haman (Est. 3:2; cf. 3:12 and 8:9). In the latter case, government officials asked Mordecai why he was "transgressing the command (מצות) of the king" and refusing to prostrate himself to Haman (Est. 3:3). Generally, however, it appears in the sense of 'instruction,' implying 'trust and confidence' that the recipient would comply, rather than 'obedience' (cf. above appendix 4). As with parents expecting their children to comply with their instruction. Bearing the sense of 'trust,' it appears as the 'last will' of a father (see Gen. 18:19; 50:16; Jer. 35:6, 14, 18; 39:11); or as a 'request" from a relative (Est. 2:10, 20), or a friend (I Sam. 20:29), or a teacher to his disciple (Jer. 51:59) – implying *hope and expectation* that the will or request will be fulfilled. In the same vein, it also denotes 'instruction' offered by a mentor to his disciples; see Deut.

4:14; 6:1; Tosefta Sanhedrin 4:7, p. 421; Nedarim 37a and cf. Jer. 51:59. In rabbinic literature, this verb is used for 'instructions' from father to children regarding how they should conduct their affairs after he passes away; see Pesaḥim 112a, b; 113b; Baba Batra 147a. Since these kinds of instructions were usually given at the deathbed (see Gen. 49:29; II Sam. 17:23; I Kings 2:1; II Kings 20:1; Is. 38:1; cf. *MT Qeri'at Shema'* 1:4), in rabbinic literature this verb is also used in conjunction with a gift by a donor contemplating death (*causa mortis*); see Gittin 66a; Baba Batra 151b; *MT Zekhiyya* 8:2, 5, 23, etc. It appears also as a noun, in the form צוואה, for a 'deed' or a 'last will' in which the testator declares how he wishes to dispose of his properties; see *MT Sanhedrin* 24:1; *Shulḥan 'Arukh, Ḥoshen Mishpaṭ* CCCLIII, 32; etc. In reference to the territory of Israel, God, as the Executor of the heritage "instructs" (צוה) how the territory should be parceled and passed in succession; see Num. 34:29; 36:2; Josh. 1:13.

In light of the preceding, it seems appropriate to render צוה as 'conveyance' and 'transmission,' implying therefore, to 'delegate' and 'entrust' the recipients – rather than the usual rendering 'to command.' Consider, for example, the people's request "to bring the *Scroll* of the Law which Moses צוה Israel" (Neh. 8:1; cf. ibid. 8:14). One may *command* the Law, but not the *Scroll* of the Law! A more appropriate rendition would be 'to bring in the *Scroll* that Moses had *entrusted* Israel with,' i.e., the Scroll of the Law that Moses had deposited in the national archives of Israel (see above chapter 7). The same applies to the "precepts that Moses צוה to the children of Israel" (Lev. 27:34). It means: "the precepts that Moses had 'conveyed,' thus 'entrusting' Israel" – rather than 'commanding'; cf. Deut. 4:13; Judges 3:4; I Kings 11:10; II Kings 17:34. Similarly, on the basis that God "ויצו" Adam (Gen. 2:16), Maimonides concluded that Adam, as the recipient of 'the image of God' was an intelligent being, "given that one cannot convey an instruction to a beast or to someone who lacks intelligence" (*Guide* I, 2, p. 16, ll. 13–17; cf. *Saadya's Commentary on Genesis*, p. 274 and editor's n. 363). However, one can certainly give a 'command' to a beast or a machine; see above chapter 24, and "Performative and

Descriptive Utterances in Jewish Law," pp. 112–114. That is why God did not 'ויצו' the "big fish" to swallow Jonah (Jonah 2:1).

If we are to come to grips with the full sense of 'צוה' it would be important to take note that, together with the sense of 'trust,' this verb denotes also 'the responsibility incumbent upon the recipient to fulfill the trust and to convey it further' to the nation of Israel. About Joshua it was written: "There was not a word that Moses had entrusted (צוה), which Joshua did not read (קרא) before the Congregation of Israel" (Josh. 8:35). Joshua did not "read" something "commanded" to him, but something which Moses had *entrusted* him to 'convey' to the people. In this manner, the Scripture teaches that Joshua was a trustworthy executor of whatever Moses had entrusted (צוה) him; see Josh. 8:31; 11:15; and cf. Deut. 34:9. R. Abraham ibn 'Ezra's interpretation is clearly stated in Ps. 78:5: "For He established a testimony in Jacob, and a Law He appointed in Israel, which He entrusted (צוה) our fathers, that they should make known to their children." The double sense of 'trust/conveyance' of 'צוה' is fundamental to the Hebrew concept of 'Law': it factually depends on *conveyance* to, and *trust* in, future generations, rather than the might of an army or a police force. Thus, the responsibility incumbent upon each generation not to betray the trust of their parents, see II Kings 21:8.

To sum up, *Morasha* is a *national* pledge by Israel with respect to their *territory* and their *Law*. Specifically, it implies the solemn responsibility of keeping this double trust in the domain of Israel, and *conveying* it in *trust* to the next generation as fiduciaries of the original *Morasha*, in perpetuity. Hence, the double sense of the verb 'צוה.'

# 13. Becoming a Single Body

Halakha regards a husband and a wife as a single body; see Berakhot 24a; *MT Qeri'at Shema'* 3:18; cf. Bekhorot 35b. "A man," the rabbis taught, "should love his wife [at least] as his own body"; Yebamot 62b and Sanhedrin 76b. They are also regarded as a single person. Therefore a man cannot testify against his wife for the same reason that he cannot testify against himself, given that this would constitute self-incrimination; see Sanhedrin 9b-10a. Conversely, the bill of divorce is designated כריתות (see Deut. 24:1, 3), 'cutting' – as if 'tearing a single body' and rendering it into two parts. At a corporeal level, sexual relations establish a special link between the parties; e.g., a man having sexual relations with a woman in a state of menstrual impurity will acquire the woman's status; see Lev. 15:24 and Mishna Kelim 1:5. Consider also Soṭa 3b, where sexual contact involves after death communion between the parties. It should be noted that the verb דבק is *not* connected with sexual activity, see Deut. 4:4; 10:20; 11:22; 30:20; Ruth 1:14, etc. Eventually, this type of pathos evolved into what Judah described as two souls "attached" (קשורה) to each other; see Gen. 44:30 and *Targum* ad loc. It culminated in the principle expressed in Lev. 19:18 to love our fellow-human as ourselves. (This is not to be confused with the narcissistic love expressed by inquisitors, missionaries, and preachy lunatics of both religious and secular persuasions.)

The Jewish people, too, are regarded "as a single body and a single soul." Therefore, if "one of them were to sin, all of them are chastised" (*Mekhilta de-R. Shim'on b. Yoḥai*, p. 139), cf. Section III, n. 152.

# 14. Gideon and Washington

'Apotheosis' and the 'deification' of rulers pose the greatest danger to political freedom and democracy. There is little doubt that the concept of sovereignty, reflected in the monarchy and modern dictatorships, whether from the left or the right, involves the deification of the ruler. Concerning the deification of rulers, see *Mekhilta de-R. Yishma'el, Massekhta de-Vayyassa'*, p. 17, where it proposes that the rebels wishing to appoint a "chief" to guide them back to Egypt (Num. 14:4), were seeking a leader who could eventually appropriate the spirit of the idol and act as a deity. The rebels reasoned: "It seems to us that no one remained alive in Egypt. Let us take on a chief, and we will make for ourselves an idol and it [i.e., the spirit dwelling in the idol] will come down and rest over [i.e., incarnate] our chief, and we will return to Egypt." Cf. *Mekhilta de-R. Shim'on b. Yoḥai*, p. 102; Rashi and *Em la-Miqra* on Num. 14:4, vol. 4, 43a-b; R. Se'adya Ga'on, *Perush* to Daniel, p. 70.

In a question addressed to R. David b. Abi Zimra, *Teshubot Radbaz*, 2 vols. (Warsaw, 5642/1882), Part IV, vol. 2 (#187 = 1258), a case was presented to him concerning a preacher who maintained that those who worshipped the golden calf had previously worshipped Moses as a god. The rabbi concluded that the preacher was wrong but nonetheless he did not warrant excommunication. With all due respect, I believe that the preacher was making a valid point, particularly in light of the rabbinic sources cited above. Only people believing that Moses incarnated the spirit of God would believe that the same spirit could be transferred and incarnate a statue and then another leader. The Pope, as *incarnation* of God's Word when acting *ex Cathedra,* is the most powerful exposition of this political ideology – certainly, much more successful than the institution that the late Emperor Hirohito (1901–1989) represented. Rev. Jonathan Mayhew, too, saw the close relation between belief in the "divine right of kings" and the "fabulous and chimerical" doctrine of "transubstantiation." see Section III, n. 301.

The danger of these ideas was clearly perceived by Washington and the Founding Fathers. It was their spiritual fortitude that prevented this sort of ideology from taking root in America. I believe that the reason that George Washington had such strong reservations about accepting the presidency was his concern that the office of the presidency might be linked to his military victory. Many thought that Washington was the 'logical' candidate, simply because he defeated the English. Washington, who was a profoundly religious man with deep roots in the Hebrew Scripture, needed to be convinced that his military victory was *not* the principal reason for his election as president. The "Brumidi's Fresco" illustrates how real the danger of apotheosis was.

# 15. The Concept of *Galut*

The four constitutive points underlying the *concept* of *Galut* were developed by the Prophet Ezekiel. They are: [a] the corruption of Jewish political leadership. The misery befalling Israel was not the result of some recondite fate lying in the realm of the mysterious (as mystics and corrupt politicians preach), but the consequence of incompetent leadership (see chapters 8, 13, 19, 22, 34). [b] In such a situation, there is a need to assume *individual responsibility* for one's fate, adhere to the requirements of the Law (see chapters 18, 20, 22), and ignore the counsel of a fundamentally boorish leadership. [c] This will result in the national redemption of the people (see chapters 11, 36–39). [d] In the end, this strategy will culminate in the rebuilding of the Temple in Jerusalem and the full restoration of the nation of Israel (see chapters 40–48).

# 16. By Virtue of Conquest

The right of the 'English Crown' to possess territories by virtue of conquest is fully acknowledged by the US Supreme Court, and serves as the basis for American sovereignty over the territories and lands previously occupied by Native Americans. Cf. *Em la-Miqra*, vol. 1, p. 158a, on Gen. 48:22, s.v. *be-ḥarbi*, and the term *beni della lancia*.

In a decision rendered on March 10, 1823, "Johnson and Graham's Lessee *v.* William McIntosh," 21 US 543, 5L.Ed. 681, 8 Wheat. 543 (1823), at 12–13, we read:

> Thus has our whole country been granted by the crown while in the occupation of the Indians. These grants purport to convey the soil as well as the right of dominion to the grantees. In those governments which were denominated royal, where the right to the soil was not vested in individuals, but remained in the crown, or was vested in the colonial government, the king claimed and exercised the right of granting lands and of dismembering the government at his will.... In all of them, the soil, at the time the grants were made, was occupied by the Indians. Yet almost every title within those governments is dependent on these grants.... It has never been objected to this, or to any other similar grant, that the title as well as possession was in the Indians when it was made, and that it passed nothing on that account.

Cf. ibid. 21 US 543 at 592–605.

In the US, the Congress is the Sovereign, and therefore the absolute owner of the land. In a ruling, The Tee-Hit-Ton Indians *v.* United States 348 US 272, 75S. Ct. 313, 99 L. Ed. 314, 1955. at 279, we read:

> After conquest they were permitted to occupy portions of territory over which they had previously exercised "sovereignty," as we use the term. This is not a property right of occupancy which the sovereign grants and protects against intrusion by third parties but which right of occupancy may be terminated and such lands fully disposed of by the sovereign itself without any legally enforceable obligation to compensate the Indians.

For our purpose it is significant to note the view of Senator Plumb, cited ibid at 293:

> I do not know by what tenure the Indians are there nor what ordinarily characterizes their claim of title, but it will be observed that the language of the *proviso* I propose to amend puts them into very small quarters. I think about 2 feet by 6 to each Indian would be the proper construction of the language 'actually in their use or occupation.' Under the general rule of occupation by a white man, that would be a tolerably limited occupation and might possibly land them in the sea.

It is worthy of note that this decision was rendered *after* the landmark decision (Brown *v.* Board of Education) on February 7, 1955 barring racial discrimination in Public Education.

The theory of 'conquest,' awarding European nations the right to take possession of the territories of Native Americans, is grounded on the theory of *occupatio* (and 'discovery') in Roman law. In a nutshell, it means that something which was never the subject of ownership (*res nullius*) belongs to the first person taking possession; see

Henry Maine, *Ancient Law*, pp. 144–147. Native Americans were not regarded as fully human, and therefore America was regarded as unpopulated; see my "Jews, Conversos, and Native Americans: The Iberian Experience," *Review of Rabbinic Judaism* 3 (2000), pp. 95–121. For an extensive and well-documented study, see Steven T. Newcomb, "The Evidence of Christian Nationalism in Federal Indian Law: The Doctrine of Discovery, *Johnson v. McIntosh,* and Plenary Power," *New York University Review of Law and Social Change* 20 (1992–1994), pp. 303–341. A more or less similar doctrine was put forward by Henry Wheaton, *Elements of International Law*, ed. with notes by George Grafton Wilson (Oxford: Clarendon Press, 1936). According to this illustrious legal scholar, the Native Americans were a "dependent nation," and must be regarded as a "ward" incapable of managing their personal affairs. By a "dependent nation," I presume that he meant that, "A tribe is not a 'foreign State,' within the meaning of the Constitution, for the purpose of suing in the Federal Courts." Here is what he writes in #38 p. 50:

> They were a domestic dependent nation; their relation to us resembles that of a ward to his guardian; and they had an unquestionable right to the lands they occupied, until that right should be extinguished by a voluntary cessation to our government.

His position is not clear. A ward retains title of his property, but cannot make any contracts respecting said property. Accordingly, it would be instructive to learn, by which legal theory could the Native Americans have "extinguished by a voluntary cessation" their rights? Elsewhere, Henry Wheaton, *International Law* (literal reproduction of 8th ed., 1866, London: Humphrey Milford, 1936), p. 587 wrote: "That discovery gave an exclusive right to extinguish the Indian title of occupancy, either by purchase or by conquest." Rhetoric aside, since their human status was not actually acknowledged, their ancestral lands were in fact never theirs. The purpose of dislodging or purchasing land from Native Americans was to "extinguish," i.e., 'to absorb' the 'title' from their lands. Again, quoting Wheaton, p. 51:

> Whenever the republic has bought out an Indian tribe, and induced it to remove from a section of country, the act has always been 'extinguishment of the Indian title' upon the lands of the United States.

This is what he wrote, p. 51:

> The Indian tribes have only a right of occupancy. Their possession was held to be so nomadic and uncivilized character as to amount to no more than a kind of servitude or lien upon the land, chiefly for fishing and hunting: the absolute title being in the republic.

This view is reflected in a Supreme Court ruling, *The Tee-Hit-Ton Indians v. United States* 348 US 272, at 293, citing 15 Long. Rec. 530, that, "Permissive Indian occupancy may be extinguished by Congress in its own discretion without compensation." However, "Generous provision has been willingly made to allow tribes to recover for wrong, as a matter of grace, not because of legal liability." (cf. ibid. at 279). *The Tee-Hit-Ton Indians v. United States* 348 U.S. 272, 75 S. Ct. 313, 99 L. Ed. 314 (1955), p. 293:

> It is to be presumed that in this matter the United States would be governed by such considerations of justice as would control *a Christian* people in their treatment of an *ignorant and dependent race* (Italics added).

It has been generally assumed that extinction of the Indian title required an act of Congress. This, however, was not to be the case. In 1986, some members of Missiquoi Abenaki Tribe in Vermont were fishing without a license. In their defense, they argued that since they were fishing in their ancestral home, they were not required to obtain a license. Moreover, their rights were never extinguished by Congress. The local judge decided in their favor. However, the decision was appealed by the State of Vermont, and the State Court overturned the lower court's decision, ruling in favor of the State (*County of Oneida v. Oneida Indian Nation*, 470 U.S. 226, 247 (1985); (*State v. Elliot* 616 A. 2d 210 [Vt. 1992], *cert. denied*. 113 S. Ct 1258 [1993]). See Joseph William Singer, *Entitlement* (New Haven: Yale University Press, 2000), pp. 181–190.

Two other doctrines derive from the preceding: (i) 'Eminent Domain,' according to which the Fifth Amendment is interpreted as a tacit recognition of the Government's power to take private property for public use; and (ii) 'Sovereign Immunity,' establishing that no suit can be instituted against the Sovereign without its consent. The latter is predicated on the logic that the 'King can do no wrong,' or what amounts to the same, that there can be no legal rights against the authority that makes the law. In simpler words: might is right and not the other way around. See the following appendix.

# 17. Private Property

The idea of private property as an institution *immune from government intervention* is exclusively Jewish. It was proclaimed by God at Sinai, when He declared: "Thou shall not steal" (Ex. 20:13). It is of paramount importance to note that it was proclaimed in the desert, *outside the perimeters of government and settled society.* Therefore it is not a *privilege* awarded by the Sovereign to his faithful subjects, a privilege that the Sovereign could withdraw or condition. The standard idea of 'property' as ultimately dependent on the sovereign renders "Thou shall not steal" meaningless. In fact, 'sovereign' and 'private ownership' are two mutually incompatible concepts. John Locke was quite aware of this pivotal point. The following is a quotation from his "Second Treatise of Government," *Two Treatises of Government*, #194, p. 395:

> Their *Persons* are *free* by a Native Right, and their *properties,* be they more or less, are *their own, and at their own dispose*, and not at his; or else it is not property. Supposing the Conqueror gives to one Man a Thousand Acres, to him and his Heirs for-ever; to another he lets a Thousand Acres, for his life, under the rent of *l.* 50 or *l.* 500 *per Ann*. Has not the one of these a Right to his Thousand Acres for ever, and the other during his Life, paying the said Rent? And hath not the Tenant for Life a *property* in all that he gets over and above his Rent, by his Labour and Industry, during the said term, supposing it be

> double the Rent? Can anyone say, The King, or Conqueror, after his Grant, may by his Power of Conqueror, take away all, or part of the Land from the Heirs of one, or from the other, during his Life, he paying the Rent? Or, can he take away from either the Goods or Money they have got upon the said Land, at his pleasure? If he can, then all free and voluntary *Contracts* cease, and are void in the World; there needs nothing to dissolve at any time but Power enough: And the *Grants* and Promises of *Men in power*, are but Mockery and Collusion. For can there be anything more ridiculous than to say, I give you and yours this forever; and that in the surest and most solemn way of conveyance can be devised: And yet it is to be understood, that I have Right, if I please, to take it away from you again to Morrow?

Concerning the doctrine that the Sovereign has absolute dominion over the lands of the country by right of Conquest, Locke wrote in the "Second Treatise of Government," *Two Treatises of Government*, #193, p. 395:

> But granting that the *Conqueror* in a just War has a Right to the Estates, as well as Power over the Persons of the Conquered; which, 'tis plain, he *hath* not: Nothing of *Absolute Power* will follow from hence in the continuance of the Government. Because the Descendants of these being all Free-men, if he grants them Estates and Possessions to inhabit his Country (without which it would be worth nothing) whatsoever he grants them, they have, so far as it is granted, *property* in. The nature whereof is, that *without a Man's own consent it cannot be taken from him.*

On the relation of 'property' to 'sovereignty,' see Morris R. Cohen, "Property and Sovereignty," *Cornell Law Quarterly* 13 (1927–1928), pp. 8–30. For some valuable insights on the concept of 'property,' see

Laura S. Underkuffer, "On Property: An Essay," in Elizabeth Mensch and Alan Freeman eds., *Property Law: International Library of Essays in Law and Legal Theory* (New York: New York University Press, 1992), vol. 1, pp. 414–417. See above appendix 16.

# 18. Equality before the Law

Early in human history, tribal organization consisted of people living under the same chief. Sir Henry Summer Maine, *The Early History of Institutions* (Port Washington, N. Y.: Kennikat Press, 1966), p. 69 writes: "In some cases the Tribe can hardly be otherwise described than as the group subjected to one chieftain." A more common form of tribal organization, centering on families, was based on the belief that all members of the Tribe descended from a common ancestor. Roland de Vaux, *Ancient Israel,* vol. 1, p. 4 writes: "A tribe is an autonomous group of families who believe they are descended from a common ancestor. Each tribe is called by the name or surname of that ancestor." And ibid. p. 5: "What unites all the tribesmen, then, is this blood relationship, real or supposed; they all consider themselves 'brothers' in a wide sense." This element was particularly dominant in the Indo-European world. Maine, ibid. p. 66, wrote: "If a man was not of kin to another there was nothing between them. He was an enemy to be slain, or spoiled or hated, as much as the wild beasts upon which the tribe made war, as belonging indeed to the craftiest and cruelest order of wild animals. It would scarcely be too strong an assertion that the dogs which followed the camp had more in common with it than the tribesmen of an alien and unrelated tribe."

In the Near East, tribal organization widened to include people not thought of as physically descendent from the same ancestor. De Vaux, p. 6, noted: "Individuals, too, can be incorporated into a tribe either by adoption into a family... or through acceptance by the sheikh or the elders." Eventually both notions of tribe and family blended. Links could be established through blood and obedience.

Concerning the *alien,* the *enemy,* and the *guest,* we read in *Indo-European Language and Society,* p. 294: "In short, the notions of enemy, stranger, guest, which for us form three distinct entities – semantically and legally – in the Indo-European languages show close connections. This cannot be understood except by starting from the idea that the stranger is of necessity an enemy and correlatively that the enemy is necessarily a stranger. It is always because a man born elsewhere is *a priori* an enemy that a mutual bond is necessary to establish between him and the EGO relations of hospitality, which would be inconceivable within the community itself. In the same way, in the early history of Rome, the stranger becomes a *hostis,* enjoying *pari iure cumpopulo Romano,* legal rights equal to those of the Roman citizen."

Outside of Israel, the idea of *ethnical* equality before the law came late, even among advanced societies, enjoying a progressive judicial system. This could be shown from the "Chinese Exclusion Act," promulgated in the not too distant past. "The USA Act of Congress, Chinese Exclusion Act," May 6, 1882. *U. S. Statutes at Large,* vol. XXII, #14, p. 58 says:

> That thereafter no State court or court of the United States shall admit Chinese to Citizenship; and all laws in conflict with this act are hereby repealed.

For the above and other comparable cases see the valuable monograph of Milton R. Konvitz, *The Alien and the Asiatic in American Law* (Ithaca, N.Y.: Cornell University, 1946).

In the year 1839, the schooner, 'Amistad,' carrying a cargo of slaves recently brought from Africa, dropped anchor on the coast of Connecticut. The Spanish government argued that since the slaves were Spanish property they should be returned to Cuba. President Van Buren agreed. However, in February 1841 the US Supreme Court ruled that they had been kidnapped and had been transported illegally, and were therefore free. Let it be noted that the rights of runaway slaves seeking asylum were already stipulated in Deut. 23:16. It is worthy of attention that at the same time, in the Dred Scott decision of 1857, the Supreme Court ruled that no black – whether a slave or free – could be a US citizen since his ancestors were brought into the country as slaves. As a non-citizen, Scott did not have the right to sue in a Federal Court and was to remain a slave.

# 19. Ṭ'M

In Aramaic, the Semitic root Ṭ'M stands for an executive order; see Dan. 3:29; 4:3; 6:27, and the corresponding translation of R. Se'adya Ga'on, *Perush* to Daniel, pp. 72, 76, 119; see also Ezra 4:19; 5:3, 17 and *Midrash Daniel wu-Midrash 'Ezra*, pp. 41, 43, 121. In Hebrew, the usual sense of this root is 'taste' and 'food'; although, as noted by R. Jonah ibn Jannaḥ, *Sefer ha-Shorashim*, s.v. *ṭa'am*, p. 182, it is also used in the sense of 'counsel' and 'deliberation'; see Ps. 34:9, Prov. 31:18, Job 12:20. Both senses of 'taste' and 'deliberation' indicate a primary, conclusive knowledge.

The Aramaic טעמא is widely used in the Talmud. When applied to halakha it stands for the basic premises and 'conceptual gist' of the law. The טעמא of a halakha was not explicit. Rather, it was expected that students and scholars would construe on their own the טעמא of the halakha. We are informed that as part of training his students, R. 'Aqiba would encourage them to step forward and present a different טעם for the halakha under discussion; see Tosefta Zabim 1:5, p. 676 and the quotation in Section IV, n. 102. The ability to construe the טעמא of the halakha is an absolute prerequisite to pass a legal opinion on the subject under consideration. Explicitly, the rabbis barred disclosing the טעם of a halakha under discussion; see *Sifra* 75c, quoted above in Section V, n. 320. This is why, when issuing a legal decision, the court did not disclose the טעם of its decision, unless it was requested by the guilty party, see Sanhedrin 31b. The upshot of this rule is that someone not knowing the טעם of a legal decision cannot use it as a precedent and apply it to a new case; see Baba Batra 130b-131a, quoted in Section V, n. 321. For that reason, R. Abraham Maimonides disqualified a decision given by a judge, since he failed to demonstrate that he had understood the conceptual gist of the halakha; see *Teshubot R. Abraham b. ha-Rambam,* #98 quoted below, appendix 65. This is exactly what Maimonides meant when he wrote that legal demonstration (ראיה) consists in knowing "to expose **why** a legal authority concluded thus"; see *Iggerot ha-Rambam,* vol. 2, p. 441, quoted above Section V, n. 328. See below Appendices 48 and 69.

# 20. Malicious Erudition

Edward Gibbon was heir to the learned studies of the antiquarians and the philosophic historians of the Enlightenment, such as Jean-Baptiste D'Alambert (1717–1783) and Voltaire. From some of them he also learned how "to blend malice and erudition"; see A. D. Momigliano "Gibbon's Contribution to Historical Method," in his *Studies in Historiography* (New York: Harper & Row, 1966), pp. 40–55, especially p. 43. He was also heir to the virulent anti-Jewish and anti-Judaism mood of classical antisemites, from Apion, Tacitus, and Cicero in Antiquity (see above chapter 37), to Voltaire, Rousseau and the rest of the Enlightenment's *philosophes* (cf. chapter 12 and the quotation from Maine, Section III, n. 23). Here are a few examples taken from *The Decline and Fall of the Roman Empire*, XV, vol. 1, p. 383: "The Jews, who, under the Assyrian and Persian monarchies, had languished for many ages the most despised portion of their slaves." They are "an ungrateful race" (p. 385), and "unsocial people" (p. 386). Indeed, they are so hateful, that they constitute a distinct human species:

> The sullen obstinacy with which they maintained their peculiar rites and unsocial manners seemed to mark them out a distinct species of men, who boldly professed, or who faintly disguised, their implacable hatred to the rest of human-kind (p. 384).

Concerning Christian misanthropy, see below Appendices 21 and 24. However, as Gibbon kindly explained, Christian intolerance is no fault of its own. Although it managed to overlook upwards of ninety-eight percent of Judaism, unfortunately, "The inflexible and, if we may use the expression, the intolerant zeal of the Christians, derived, it is true, from Jewish religion" (p. 383). Jewish history (in contradistinction to the civilized societies of *europaischen Menschentums*) is nothing but a "sanguinary list of murders, of executions, and of massacres, which stain almost every page of the Jewish annals" (p. 392). Jewish resistance to Hadrian was "desperate fanaticism" (p. 390), and consequently, illegitimate. By contrast, Hadrian's massacre of almost the entire Judean population, including women and children – the biggest known genocide in human history – (see chapter 40), was nothing more than "the rights of victory"; although, Gibbon had to admit, these rights were exercised "with unusual rigor" (p. 390). Jewish faithfulness to the Tora is the effect of their peculiar "obstinacy" (pp. 384, 388). Their rituals consist of "useless and obsolete ceremonies" (p. 389). By opposition, the Christian rite – I presume he had in mind the Eucharist where the faithful consume the flesh and blood of their Savior – is "a pure and spiritual worship" (p. 388), see below appendix 23. With the power of a *superstes* (see Introductory Remarks, Section IV, n. 2), Gibbon *knew* exactly how people all over felt about Jewish rituals. Here is what he writes in p. 387:

> They still insisted with inflexible rigour on those parts of the law which it was in their power to practice. The peculiar distinction of days, of meats, and a variety of trivial though burdensome observances, were so many objects of disgust and aversion for the other nations, to whose habits and prejudices they were diametrically opposite.

By way of contrast, let us see what Philo wrote on the same topic in *Moses* II, 13, *Philo*, vol. 6, p. 459–461:

> We may fairly say that mankind from east to west, every country and nation and state, shew aversion to foreign institutions,

> and think that they will enhance respect for their own by shewing disrespect for those of other countries. It is not so with ours. They attract and win the attention of all, of barbarians, of Greeks, of dwellers on the mainland and islands, of nations of the east and west, of Europe and Asia, of the whole inhabited world from end to end. For, who has not shewn his high respect for that sacred seventh day, by giving rest and relaxation from labour to himself and his neighbours, freemen and slaves alike, and beyond these to his beasts? For the holiday extends also to every herd, and to all creatures made to minister to men, who serve like slaves their natural master. It extends also to every kind of tree and plant; for it is not permitted to cut any shoot or branch, or even a leaf, or to pluck any fruit whatsoever. All such are set at liberty on that day, and live as it were in freedom, under the general edict that proclaims that none should touch them.

Philo also mentioned the fact that multitudes of non-Jews came to celebrate the translation of the Septuagint together with the Jews; see quotation in Section IV, n. 24. One only can wonder why the people in Colonial America, as well as in India, Africa, etc., did not make similar celebrations for the Magna Carta?

One could argue that Gibbon's 'malicious erudition' was tactical. Since he had blamed the spread of Christianity for the collapse of the Roman Empire, he had to malign Jews and their religion lest he be accused of being 'pro' Jewish – a blemish too heavy to bear in the enlightened society of 18th century Continental Europe. On his anti-Christian views, see Shelby Thomas McCloy, *Gibbon's Antagonism to Christianity* (London: William & Norgate, 1933). I propose that his malice was rather substantive. A major point of Gibbon's was the link between the spread of Christianity and the collapse of the Roman Empire. In our terms, the "Two-Realm Governance" solution proposed by Christianity and accepted by the Caesars (see chapter 26) suffered a sudden reversal. This was fundamental to Gibbon's ideology, "that history changes by revolutions rather than by slow evolution" ("Gibbon's Contribution to Historical Method," p. 49). In our case, the revolution was brought about by Christianity. "At the same time, Gibbon brought into special prominence, as Voltaire had done, that the Christians joined hands with the Barbarians to destroy the Empire," wrote Momigliano, ibid. p. 48. This was a brilliant move, destined to further expand Christianity and consolidate Church power.

As those experienced in the art of commerce know, a key element in negotiation is the availability of alternative suppliers to force your provider to acquiesce to your terms. The triumph of the Barbarians and the subsequent fragmentation of the Roman Empire into countless and deeply antagonistic territories provided the Church with a large number of suppliers. By contrast, once Judaism was declared unfit for human consumption, Caesars of all denominations found themselves lacking alternative suppliers with whom to negotiate. (Julian's 'universal toleration' was an attempt to find new suppliers. It was, however, too little, too late; see *Decline and Fall*, XXIII.) 'Secularism' – and all forms of political and intellectual ideologies – are intended to provide alternative suppliers to the Caesars of the world. Gibbon understood this well. Rather than presenting an 'objective' picture of the past, Gibbon presented a 'history' designed to promote a peculiar ideology close to his own mind and ethos. Again, quoting Momigliano, p. 49:

> Thus his *Decline and Fall* is both a complex and vivid picture of the Middle Ages from a *certain point of view and unique self-portrait of the eighteenth century mind* (Italics added).

Lest some may want to consider the legal and political system of the Hebrew Scripture and the Jews, as in Colonial America at the time (see chapter 36), it was imperative to repeat the same antisemitic litany for all to hear. 'Jewish' danger was greater in England where, as shown by W. B. Selbie, "The Influence of the Old Testament on Puritanism" was supreme. It was incumbent upon Gibbon, in quality of *europaischen Menschentums* (see Momigliano, pp. 44–48), to defame the Jews and their religion in the name of honor and common decency.

A marginal note. For the sake of fairness, let us note that Christian betrayal of Roman Caesars on behalf of barbarians is perfectly legitimate according to *minut* ethics where the end justifies the means; see below appendix 55. In simple terms: if the Church could be *Verus Israel*, why could barbarians not become *Sacrum Romanun Imperium Nationis Germanicae*? cf. appendix 30.

# 21. Why We Should All Strive to Be Illiterate

The Pauline ideal is for all to be illiterate, "for the letter killeth, but the spirit giveth life" (II Cor. 3:6). According to *minut* hermeneutics, Moses' veil symbolizes the blurred, obscure character peculiar to the written text: "Even unto this day, when Moses [i.e., the Tora] is read, the veil is upon their heart" [i.e., of the readers] (II Cor. 3:15, cf. vv. 7, 13–14). To free humanity from writing, Jesus was nailed to the cross. Thus, "Blotting out the handwriting of ordinances that were against us [= the Scriptural precepts], which was contrary to us, and took it out of the way, nailing it to his cross" (II Col. 2:14). The "veil" covering Moses' face remained "untaken in the reading of the Old Testament [*diatheke,* i.e., the Tora]," but was "done away in Christ" (II Cor. 3:14), allowing, as per Greek ideality, for the truth to shine forth (cf. II Cor. 3:16–18). Jesus' truth is superior to the Tora because it "is written not with ink, but with the Spirit of the living God; not in tables of stone, but in the fleshy tables of the heart" (II Cor. 3:3). This posits, as per Greek analphabetic ideality (see chapter 2), that the written word hinders 'the truth.' Since this surreal 'truth' is not easily communicated to people in a different psychological mood, misanthropy enables its possessor to dismiss 'the others' as inferior beings questioning 'the obvious' (leading, thus, to the dehumanization of the 'other,' see appendix 24). Without hatred, this brand of truth would turn into a harrowing nightmare of self-delusion. See appendix 22.

The "illiterate people" (עם הארץ) constituted a class unto themselves based not on birth or economic status, but on their attitude towards education and lifestyle; see the learned work of George F. Moore, "The Am-ha-Arez (The People of the Land) and the Haberim (Associates)," in F. J. Foakes-Jackson and Kirsopp Lake eds., *The Acts of the Apostles* (*The Beginning of Christianity*), vol. 1 (London: Macmillan, 1920), pp. 439–445. The "illiterate people" discussed in Pesaḥim 49b, are not merely unlettered men, but people repudiating the Book on behalf of theological analphabetism. "Greater is the hatred that illiterate men (עמי הארץ) profess towards the disciples of sages," remarked the rabbis, "than what the (pagan) nations profess against Israel." In my view, they were the early Judeo-Christians forming Jesus' Crowd.

# 22. Purloining an Ass for Christ: Freedom *without* Law

There is something more than symbolic in the fact that the Christian Messiah is portrayed as entering Jerusalem on a purloined ass, to show his fulfillment of the prophetic vision of 'a just and righteous' Savior. Matthew 21:2–3 relates how Jesus sent two of his disciples to dispossess an ass on his behalf, in his capacity as 'King' of the Jews'; see *Leviathan*, XX [106], p. 259. This is in line with Jesus' doctrine to "Render unto Caesar the things which are Caesar's" (Matt. 22:21), thus validating the tax-collectors' practice to dispossess property from the legitimate owner without due process; see below appendix 60, p. 919. As with Jesus, donkeys were seized by tax-collectors without much ado; see Mishna Baba Qamma 10:2. Compare this with Moses, Num. 16:15, who would not "seize" a single donkey from anyone; see *Targum*, R. Se'adya, and Rashi ad loc.; cf. I Sam. 12:3. In defense of Jesus' behavior, we may argue that since "the Son of man hath the power on earth to forgive sins" (Matt. 9:6), he could surely exercise His prerogative of mercy on Himself and His followers and relieve Himself and His followers of any crimes and disabilities – as a pagan Rex would; see above chapter 26. According to the doctrine that "the Son of man hath the power on earth to forgive sins," salvation is a matter of personal whim, rather than justice. To this we should add Jesus' temperament, always in ire, cursing and threatening with dire consequences those who would not concur with him. An obvious reference to this kind of behavior is a passage in Abot 5:19 contrasting "the disciples of Abraham" with "the disciples of Balaam, the wicked." Balaam, too, was a prophet, but in contradistinction to Abraham, his 'blessings' were valued mainly because of the magical threat of his curses, see Num. 22:6. (Indeed, it is difficult not to gain the impression that the public that Jesus addressed was more affected by fear of his curses than by the bliss of his blessings.) On the association 'Balaam/Jesus,' see the version of Sanhedrin 39b cited by R. Ḥanan'el, ad loc. I believe that the passage in *Mekhilta de-R. Yishma'el*, p. 221, that upon hearing of the Theophany at Sinai "all the kings of the nations of the world went up to consult with Balaam," is an allusion to Paul who furthered the strategy of threats and curses in the promotion of spiritual salvation. Surely, his doctrine about the 'Law' was balsam to pagan authorities, since by abrogating the Tora Paul was in fact giving free rein to totalitarian governments. On the identification 'Balaam/Jesus,' see *Christianity and the Talmud*, pp. 64–78.

Concerning the Paulian doctrine of Freedom *without* Law, see chapter 12. It equals Freedom *via* Submission. In Eph. 5:21–25 we read:

> Submitting yourselves one to another in the fear of God. Wives, submit yourselves unto your own husbands, as unto the Lord. For the husband is the head of the wife, even as Christ is the head of the church: and he is the saviour of the body. Therefore as the church is subject unto Christ, so let the wives be to their own husbands in every thing. Husbands, love your wives, even as Christ also loved the church, and gave himself for it.

The incarnate *logos* is the Spirit, that is, freedom *from* the Law: "and where the Spirit of the Lord *is*, there *is* liberty" (II Cor. 3:17). Those who are "led" by the Spirit, Paul assured his audience, "are not under the Law" (Gal. 5:18). Accordingly, the *logos* displaces – in legal terminology, abrogates – the Law: "For the Law came through Moses," explained John, "but grace and truth came through Jesus" (Jn. 7:18). Cf. "The Rich Man's Salvation," in *Clement of Alexandria* (Loeb

Classical Library), VI, 939 P., pp. 283–287. The abrogation of writing came with Jesus' death, "Blotting out the handwriting of ordinances that were against us [= the Scriptural *miṣvot*], which was contrary to us, and took it out of the way, nailing it to his cross" (Col. 2:14; cf. 1:13–14). The blood 'blotting' writing was that very blood that would "deliver" mankind "from darkness," i.e. *alphabetic* reasoning, and thereby bring "redemption" and "forgiveness of sins" through analphabetic spirituality (Col. 1:13–14). According to this theory, the purpose of Jesus' death was *analphabetic* freedom or, what amounts to the same, freedom from the alphabet. By abrogating the circumcision, Paul was in fact urging a renunciation of the covenant that God made with Patriarch Abraham (Gen. chapter 17), thus formally breaking all ties with the alphabetic God of Israel. See Gal. 5:1–5 and Section III, n. 275.

# 23. Ingesting Jesus

There is some irony in the fact that Jewish dietary laws are derided by the rationale that "Not that which goeth into the mouth defileth a man" (Matt. 15:11; see ibid. 12–20; Mk. 7:15; cf. Acts 10:10–16; *I* Cor. 8:8). At the same time, salvation is gained by ingesting "that which goeth into the mouth," i.e., the Eucharist. No wonder that Reverend Mayhew regarded "transubstantiation" as "fabulous and chimerical"; see above appendix 14, and Section III, n. 301. The whole idea of 'swallowing' another and of being 'swallowed' by another is typical of sado-masochist tendencies, common to individuals who have lost self-esteem; see *Escape from Freedom*, p. 180. On the magical character of the Eucharist, see Morton Smith, *Jesus the Magician*, pp. 122–123. For a modern testimonial on the subject, see Pope John Paul II, "On the Mystery and Worship of the Eucharist," in ed. Austin Flannery, O. P. *Vatican Council II* (Collegeville, MN: The Liturgical Press, 1982), pp. 64–92. cf. Section III, n. 67.

In Eccl. 10:12, King Solomon points to two different approaches in which an individual may address another person. "The words of a wise man's mouth (פי) are gracious (חן)," that is, they generate mutual cordiality and sympathy – essential for carrying on a *meliṣa*-discourse, in which both parties stand horizontally *vis a vis* the other; see chapter 46. By way of contrast, "the lips (שפתות) of a deceitful person will swallow him up," thus, excluding the possibility of speech between two subjective parties; see chapter 3. Within such a context, the only possible relationship is that of superior/inferior, whereby the superior incorporates the other into his body. Or what amounts to the same, the inferior must annihilate his/her own personality to be swallowed by the superior. There is a minor linguistic detail worth noting. The words of the wise-man are uttered by his "mouth," in the singular. By contrast, the words of a deceitful speaker come out of his "lips," in the plural. Implying duplicity; see above Section I, notes 92 and 131.

# 24. Extreme Dichotomy

The Christian doctrine of "Two-Governances" is a spin-off of the "Splitting of the *Logos,*" inaugurating Greek philosophical thought; see Jose Faur, "Splitting of the *Logos,*" *New Vico Studies* 3 (1985), pp. 85–103. In turn, the 'Splitting of the *Logos*' is a spin-off of the polytheistic *Weltanschauung* peculiar to *europaischen Menschentums,* where the universe is divided into neatly compartmentalized sections, having absolutely nothing to do with one another. At the intellectual level, this led to what Ortega y Gasset called "The Barbarism of Specialization"; see *Golden Doves,* p. 153 n. 81. By positing the doctrine of "Two-Governances" at the center of Western intellectual and spiritual life, Christianity was in fact sanctioning a course of thought which, at the very least, disallowed for humanism, biblical or otherwise; see *In the Shadow of History,* pp. 33–34. An example of this sort of extreme dichotomy is the philosophy that views the human 'other' as void of spirituality and individuality; see *In the Shadow of History,* pp. 4–8. This is conceptually connected to the materialistic ideology positing man as a cog in the large political and social machine of the State. Concerning this philosophy, very real in our own times, Ludwig von Bertalanffy, *General System Theory,* pp. 52–53, wrote:

> Man is not only a political animal; he is, before and above all, an individual. The real values of humanity are not those which it shares with biological entities, the function of an organism or a community of animals, but those which stem from the

individual mind. Human society is not a community of ants or termites, governed by inherited instinct and controlled by the laws of the super ordinate whole; it is based upon the achievements of the individual and is doomed if the individual is made a cog in the social machine. This, I believe, is the ultimate precept a theory of organization can give: not a manual for dictators of any denomination more efficiently to subjugate human beings by the scientific application of Iron Laws, but a warning that the Leviathan of organization must not swallow the individual without sealing its own inevitable doom.

# 25. Erasing the Memory of 'Amaleq

A fundamental dimension of Israel is its National Memory. It is on this basis that political judgments are achievable. When National Memory is discarded or fails to elicit a response, Israel ceases to function as an autonomous political entity, and national disasters follow. The role of Jewish National Memory is evident in the case of 'Amaleq, Israel's political arch-enemy. They were the earliest terrorists on record. What made their attack particularly heinous was that, (a) it was unprovoked, since Israel was passing through the desert and not through their territory; (b) it was sudden, against unsuspecting travelers; and, (c) it was carried out against the "weak and infirm" who could not defend themselves, rather than against the army (Deut. 25:17–18). As we shall see in what follows, these facts, rather than mere 'ethnicity' are the defining elements of 'Amaleq.

The Tora did not specify the atrocities perpetuated by 'Amaleq; rather, they were entrusted to the National Memory of Israel. Jews are required to "remember" what 'Amaleq did (Deut.. 25:17), and to "erase the remembrance (זכר) of 'Amaleq" (Deut. 25:19; cf. Ex. 17:14). The conflict must be carried on from generation to generation (Ex. 17:16). Usually, this is understood in ethnical terms. This understanding is unacceptable. Clearly and unambiguously the Tora mentions "the *remembrance* (זכר) of 'Amaleq!" According to the rabbis, after King Sennacherib invaded the Near East, the original natives of the region were deported and replaced with others. Therefore, the present inhabitants of these areas could no longer be identified with the national entities mentioned in Scripture. See Mishna Yadayim 4:4; Tosefta Qiddushin 5:4, pp. 295–296; Tosefta Yadayim 2:17, pp. 683–684. For additional sources and an in-depth discussion of the subject, see *Tosefta Ki-Fshuṭah*, Nashim, pp. 972–974. Therefore, it is impossible to identify the ethnicity of any of the ancient inhabitants of the region. (Maimonides applied this principle to *all* people of the region, see *MT Issure Bi'a* 12:25; *Melakhim* 5:4, and Radbaz's note ad loc.) Thus, on technical grounds alone it would be impossible to identify any one person or people with the original inhabitants of the region. If so, how could Jews be expected to keep on fighting the 'Amaleqite enemy "from generation to generation?" The question is particularly poignant in light of the fact that after having lost contact with 'Amaleq for over 500 years, Jews in Persia were able to identify Haman – the proverbial 'Jew-hater' – with 'Amaleq (see Esther 3:1, 10, etc.). What was the basis for this identification?

The correct meaning of the "remembrance" was given by R. Isaac Abul'afya (1824–1910), *Pene Yiṣḥaq*, vol. 6 (Jerusalem 5668/1908), *Shabbat Zakhor*, 41a. He called attention to the fact that the Scripture charged Israel to erase "the *remembrance* (זכר)" – never the *seed* (זרע) – of 'Amaleq! What was intolerable about 'Amaleq was their inhumanity against unsuspecting travelers; particularly, marking the weak and infirm as the preferred target. The remembrance of 'Amaleq has little to do with ethnicity, but with a level of inhuman behavior that cannot be tolerated, no matter what. This type of threat faces Israel "from generation to generation." Because Israel had registered in her National Memory the atrocities committed by 'Amaleq, she is charged with the double responsibility of identifying and erasing *the remembrance* of 'Amaleq. The Jews in Persia were able to identify Haman with their proverbial enemy because in their National Memory his activities and ideology reminded them of 'Amaleq: it was a matter of behavior, not merely genealogy or nationality. After a detailed analysis of the sources, R. Abul'afya, concluded:

> From the preceding we have learned that a people who became infamous (because of the manner in which they conducted their attack against the Jewish people) were designated 'Amaleq. This (identification) may take place even in our own days, when people who are ethnically mixed (and cannot be identified ethnically as 'Amaleq) .... At any rate, once they are identified as 'Amaleq, because of their behavior they are one and the same with 'Amaleq, and to eradicate them will constitute, in fact, erasing the name of 'Amaleq.

This point is implicit in the rabbinic tradition declaring that the descendants of Haman taught Tora to the Jewish people (Giṭṭin 57b). If 'Amaleq is a matter of genealogy, the rabbis should have put them to death, rather than give them teaching positions; cf. *In the Shadow of History*, pp. 200–201.

The preceding could help us resolve a halakhic puzzle. An absolute stipulation to classify a Scriptural assignment as a precept (*miṣva*) is that, at least in theory, it could be fulfilled in perpetuity (*Sefer ha-Miṣvot*, III). To wit, although sacramental sacrifices are not offered today, nonetheless they qualify as precepts (*miṣvot*) since they could be offered when the Temple is rebuilt. Now, if to erase "the remembrance (זכר) of 'Amaleq" meant some sort of 'ethnic cleansing,' then once executed, it could never be fulfilled again. (Maimonides attempts to cope with the problem, in my view unsuccessfully, see *Sefer ha-Miṣvot*, positive precept #187. The same problem applies to the precept to destroy the seven Canaanite nations – once it is properly fulfilled, it could not be fulfilled again.) On the other hand, identification of 'Amaleq in terms of behavior and the memories that it evokes, rather than ethnicity, permits the fulfillment of this *miṣva* in perpetuity.

A final note: there may be several valid interpretations on how to identify and proceed to erase the "memory of 'Amaleq." 'Ethnic cleansing,' however, is not one of them.

# 26. 'Prophets/Scribes' and the National Archives of Israel

The *Targum* to the *Prophets* translates 'prophet' (נביא), when not accompanied by a personal name, as 'scribe, scribes' (ספר ספריא); see I Sam. 10:11; 19:20; II Kings 17:13; Is. 3:2; 9:14; 29:10; Jer. 29:1. The same applies when it appears together with *kohen, kohanim*; see II Kings 23:2; Is. 28:7; Jer. 14:18; 23:11; 26:16; Zech. 7:3; Lam. 2:20. Support for this tradition may be seen in the frequent association of 'prophet' (נביא) with 'writing' in the book of Chronicles, see I Chr. 29:29; II Chr. 9:29; 12:15; 32:32; cf 13:22; 26:22. It is in this connotation that 'prophet' (נביא) is used in Abot 1:1: "Moses ... conveyed the Tora to Joshua ... and the elders to the prophets (נביאים)." As I proposed in *Golden Doves*, pp. 14–15, 124, 'Tora' in the above passage is a reference to the legal tradition kept in the national archives. In my view, the original sense of the title 'prophet' (נביא) that in medieval Ashkenazic tradition was given to some of the sages, was not that of the biblical 'prophet,' as commonly understood, but of 'scribe,' 'archivist'; i.e., 'guardian of tradition'; see, however, Abraham Heschel, "Inspiration in the Middle Ages," in *Alexander Marx Jubilee Volume*, Hebrew Section (New York: The Jewish Theological Seminary of America, 1950), pp. 175–236. Maimonides, too, in his "*Introduction*" *MT*, ll. 47–48, stated that "the head of the court or the *prophet* of that generation would write for himself a summary of the legal traditions, which he had learned from his teachers, and then teach them orally"; see above chapter 30.

Similarly, R. Se'adya Gaon wrote that before the exile these traditions were "supervised and safeguarded by the king and priests, particularly at the time of the prophets"; *Saadya's Commentary on Genesis*, p. 186 (Ar. p. 15). Professor Zucker's translation, "kept in their memory" is inaccurate. Although the Arabic root ḤFẒ could be used in the sense of 'remembering,' ḤRS conveys 'to watch, to safeguard,' as per archives, rather than to remember.

I would like to translate here a passage of R. Elie Benamozegh about the National Archives of Israel and their relation to the Oral Law. Commenting on Ex. 18:13, in *Em la-Miqra* vol. 2, 51a, he wrote:

> There is little doubt that prior to the appointment of judges, Moses judged alone, as mentioned in the Tora. Thereafter, Moses would sit to adjudicate only difficult cases. The same applied to all the judges who came throughout the generations; as with Deborah to whom the children of Israel would come for judgment. In general, it was the same with all the laws and rules that our judges adjudicated throughout the ages [those difficult cases that would be resolved by the highest judicial authority]. It is unwarranted (to assume) that some record would not have been kept in the midst of the nation. Where would you find a nation that would not register the legal decisions of its judges in every single case, in addition to its written history? Rather, it would be safe to assume that when (a new) case which had not been adjudicated previously, came before Moses, and which in turn he had to present before God, as was the case of Zelophehad's daughters [see Num. 27:1–11], (that the case had been properly recorded by the Court). Many more such cases came up in every generation, [i.e.] new questions about which there were not to be found a clear statement in the Scripture [= *Dinim Mufla'im*], and which were resolved by the prophets and elders [of the

time] according to accepted procedures – these constitute the Oral Law. Thus, one may learn about the existence of (the Oral Law), as with as much validity and reasonable evidence, as with *mores geometrico*.

# 27. *Yeshiba*

In its original sense, *Yeshiba* stood for a 'session' of the judicial authorities. (The name *Yeshiba* ('seating') reflects the fact that at these meetings the 'seating' arrangements were regulated by strict procedure; see Tosefta Sanhedrin VII, 8–9, p. 426; Horayot 13b; cf. Baba Batra 120a and Pesaḥim 119a.) It is one of the principal National Institutions of Israel. Members of the *Yeshiba* were duly appointed with the consent of the public; see *Sifre Bemidbar* #92, p. 93; *Sifre Debarim* #13, p. 22. Because the school was an integral part of the court, sometimes it is difficult to ascertain whether '*Yeshiba*' refers to the court proper or to the school; see for example, Mishna Yadayim 3:8; 4:2; *Sifre* #321, p. 370. Another institution of higher learning was the *Bet Midrash*. However, unlike the *Yeshiba*, it was not attached to the court and was not a national institution. On the relation of the *Yeshiba* to 'ordination,' see *Studies in the History of the Sanhedrin*, pp. 208–212. For *Yeshiba* in the sense of 'School of Higher Learning,' see Ta'aniyot 8a; Mo'ed Qaṭan 16b; Nidda 70b; and Derekh Ereṣ 2:8, p. 94. The term *Yeshiba* was also used to designate a special 'session' arraigned to deliberate some scholarly matters; see 'Erubin 26a, Ketubot 103b, Baba Qamma 16b; or public policy; see Yoma 28b, and *Perush ha-Mishnayot, Bekhorot* 4:4, vol. 5, p. 245. This term passed into the *Koran* in the form *majlis* (58:12) from the root *jalasa* ('to seat') – an exact translation of Hebrew *Yeshiba*; see Abraham Shalom Yahuda, "A Contribution to Qur'an and Ḥadith Interpretation," in *Ignace Goldziher Memorial Volume*, part I (Budapest, 1948), pp. 290–292.

# 28. *Perush*, *Be'ur*, and *Peshaṭ*

In Qiddushin 49b, 'Tora' is associated with מדרש תורה, i.e., 'exegesis.' There were several styles and various functions attached to exegesis. *Be'ur* stands for 'elucidation,' 'clarification'; see *Sifre* #5, p. 13. This term is connected to באר ('well'), from where water flows (unlike בור ('pit'), which collects water from the rain; see *Yalquṭ Shim'oni, 'Eqeb* #873, vol. 1, 298d; and R. Abraham ibn 'Ezra on Lev. 11:36). Since to tap water from a well one needs 'to dig,' this term was associated with 'perforating' a hard surface. By association, it was also used for 'engraving' an inscription on stone (Deut. 27:8; Hab. 2:2); see J. L. Palache, *Semantic Notes on the Hebrew Lexicon* (Leiden: Brill, 1958), s.v. *be'er*, p. 9. On the semantic association of באר to the act of 'inscribing/chiseling' on stone, see Soṭa 35b. Given that 'digging' (to make a well) and 'chiseling' (a stone) involves perforating a hard surface to bring up its contents (water, law), and given that legislators 'engrave' the new rules on stone, the *Targum* to Num. 21:18 associated 'באר' in "a well (באר) was dug by the princes, it was perforated by the nobles of the nation, with their scepter and with their staves" – with 'legislation.' Thus, it rendered *with their scepter and with their staves*, as "*the scribes* (ספריא) *with their staves*"; cf. R. Se'adya Gaon ad loc. In the same vein, the *Targum* rendered the verb באר (Deut. 1:5) as "explaining the teaching of the Tora" (אולפן אוריתא); cf. R. Se'adya ad loc. and Sanhedrin 34a. In this precise sense Maimonides uses this term at the head of each Section (הלכות) of the *MT*. After giving a list of the biblical precepts to be examined he concludes with the following sentence: "And the *be'ur* of all these precepts (will be presented) in the following chapters."

For some interesting insights into this matter, see R. Elie Benamozegh, *Mabo le-Tora she-be-'al Pe,* ed. R. E. Zini (Jerusalem, 5762/2002), pp. 28–42.

*Perush* stands for something 'separate' from the common and the general, warranting, therefore, 'specification' and 'notification'; see *Targum* to Deut. 21:17. Accordingly, to be binding, a *perush* warrants 'judicial instruction,' see *Targum* on Deut. 17:8; and 'promulgation'; see Vayyiqra Rabba, I, 10, vol. 1, pp. 24–25; Shir ha-Shirim Rabba II, 1, 4, vol. 2, 14d; III, 1, 4, vol. 2, 19c. cf. *Tosefta Ki-Fshuṭah,* vol. 8, pp. 699–702; *Hellenism in Jewish Palestine,* pp. 200–202; and *A Dictionary of Greek & Latin Legal Terms,* s.v. *diatagma,* pp. 79–81.

*Perush* is construed on the basis of the *general* sense of the phrase; see Mishna 'Aboda Zara 1:5; cf. Tosefta Demai 1:8, p. 63; Baba Qamma 11:1, 2, p. 58; Baba Meṣi'a 1:19, p. 66; Baba Batra 9:2, p. 160, etc. Therefore, one would need to say: "I heard explicitly" (שמעתי בפרוש), Mishna Shebi'it 6:5, 6; 'Orla 1:7, etc. to indicate that although he was not repeating the words verbatim, he was transmitting the actual sense of the phrase. Invariably, *perush* refers to a *formulated* text. To place the locus of a *perush,* the sages (*Sifre* #40, pp. 83–84) would ask: "Where is it to be found, the explicated text of this matter (פרושו של דבר)?" Although it mostly concerns Scripture, occasionally *perush* is used in connection to oral texts; see Mishna Nedarim 2:4 and Sanhedrin 7:5. On the identification of 'Oral Law' with the *perush* of the 'Written Law'; see the Geonic *responsum,* in A. E. Harkavi, *Ḥadashim gam Yeshanim* (Jerusalem: Karmiel, 5730/1970) (II, p. 72), p. 368.

On *peshaṭ,* see Shabbat 15a; 'Aboda Zara 8b; Ḥolin 135a; Y. Sanhedrin I, 1, 18a, etc. where *peshaṭ* involves 'familiarity,' 'general consensus.' Hence the expression "a prohibition that was accepted [*pashaṭ*] throughout Israel" (פשט איסורו בכל ישראל); see 'Aboda Zara 36a; Ḥolin 135a. This root appears in the sense of 'usual,' 'frequent,' 'habitual'; see *Midrash Tanḥuma* (Constantinople, offset reproduction by Makor: Jerusalem, 1971), 30b. The association of *peshaṭ* with the 'plain' or 'grammatical' sense of the text was introduced by medieval commentators of Scripture. The rabbis, however, were not concerned with grammar or philological data. In fact, the rabbis classified as *peshaṭ* explanations that have nothing to do with the 'literal' sense of the verse; see, for example, 'Erubin 23b; Yebamot 24a; Ketubot 111b; Sanhedrin 100b; Zebaḥim 113a; 'Arakhin 8b, 32a, etc. Rather, *peshaṭ* has to do with "stretching" (*pashaṭ*) the scroll containing the text to be expounded (see appendix 41). Thus the expression "whereto is this text *pashuṭ*?" – in the sense: "where does [the verse] apply"; see Vayyiqra Rabba, XVI, b, vol. 2, p. 351. Occasionally, when an explanation had been thoroughly assimilated into the text, the verb 'read' (קרא) is used; see *TY Berakhot* III, 1, 6c.

The term *peshiṭa,* in the Babylonian Talmud refers to "the explanations given by teachers (in the classroom) to their students – the type of explanations that every [student] was not required to learn by heart and to include in the *gemara*" [lesson, see below appendix 48], but later on, the teachers found it necessary to incorporate [that explanation] into the *gemara*" (*IShG,* p. 63). Although the term *peshiṭa* is frequently used in seboraitic editorial notes, the expression itself originated in the tannaitic expression *pashuṭ hu lan,* in Vayyiqra Rabba, XI, 6, vol. 1, p. 227; cf. *pashṭa lan,* Baba Qamma 47a, 62a.

For further material and analyses, see *Golden Doves,* pp. xvii, 12, 136137; José Faur, "Basic Concepts in Rabbinic Hermeneutics," *Shofar* 16 (1997), pp. 1–12; idem "Retórica y hermenéutica: Vico y la tradición rabínica," in ed. E. Hidalgo-Serna, et al, *Pensar Para el Nuevo Siglo,* vol. 3 (Napoli: La Citta del Sole, 2001), pp. 917–938; and above Section IV, n. 226.

# 29. Pappus b. Judah

He was a Jewish sage flourishing in the 1st century C.E. and variously cited in Tannaitic and Talmudic sources. Although his name is spelled in a variety of forms (פפיס, פפייס, יהודה בן פפוס, פפוס בן יהודה), they all allude to the same Pappus b. Judah, the protagonist of the story we examined in chapter 39; see *A Commentary on the Palestinian Talmud*, vol. 1, p. 410. He testified before the rabbis on an assortment of halakhic issues; see Mishna ʻEduyot 7:5 (= Nazir 3:2), and Nazir 16a. In one case, he testified about the ritual meal of a sacrifice in which he participated together with his family at the Temple, see ʻEduyot 7:6 (= Temura 3:1), and cf. Rosh HaShana, 6a. He also testified together with R. Joshua, Mishna ʻEduyot 7:6; Tosefta ʻEduyot 3:1, p. 459; Sanhedrin 2:13, p. 418; and with R. Judah b. Betera, see Beṣa 29b. The fact that a view which he reported (שמעתי) is duly registered in Mishna Sheqalim 4:7, confirms that his reputation was well established among the sages.

His behavior, however, was considered eccentric and unbecoming; see Y. Berakhot II, 9, 5d. (The same story, however, is attributed in Baba Qamma 81b to R. Judah b. Qanusa.) The manner in which he treated his wife served as an example, "Of someone who saw a fly standing inside his cup [but not touching the drink] threw it, and (refused) to drink from it. Like Pappus b. Judah, who shut the door before his wife and left" (Tosefta Soṭa 5:9, pp. 178–179; cf. *Tosfeta Ki-Fshuṭah*, vol. 8, p. 661). More to our point, he seemed to share some of the Gnostic ideology peculiar to early Christians, positing some kind of Primeval Adam (or *Protanthropos*); see *Mekhilta de-R. Yishma'el,* pp. 112–113; Bereshit Rabba XXI, 5, vol. 1, pp. 200–201, and editor's n. ibid. cf. Shir ha-Shirim Rabba I, 9, 10d; and *AdRN,* A, XXVII, 42a. At the same time, he was critical of Moses and Israel, while commending the gentiles; see *Mekhilta de-R. Shim'on b. Yoḥai,* p. 131; cf. *Mekhilta de-R. Yishma'el,* p. 194 and Sanhedrin 94a. This may explain his policy of seeking accommodation with the Romans.

# 30. *Verus Israel*?

See above chapter 42, and *Golden Doves*, p. 15. Cf. R. Saul Levi Mortera, *Gib'at Sha'ul*, II, p. 13; and R. 'Azarya de Fijo, *Bina le-'Ittim*, vol. 2, p. 82. A person who has been the victim of identity theft could empathize with Jewish agony over the Christian claim of *Verus Israel*. The rabbis compared this to a man who witnesses someone impersonating him and then on the basis of the pretended identity proceeds to rape his wife; or that he claims ownership over his property and then proceeds to expel him from his domicile. Similarly, *cristianos viejos* would rape Native American women while their husbands were tied under the bed; see José Faur, "Jews, Conversos, and Native Americans: The Iberian Experience," *Annual of Rabbinic Judaism* 3 (2000), pp. 95–121. On the psychological process whereby the murderer usurps the personality of the victim and appropriates his name, see Jorge Luis Borges, "La forma de la espada," *Ficciones*, pp. 491–495, a beautiful metaphor for *Verus Israel*. In *converso* tradition the 'sword' is a code-term for 'the cross,' given that both have the same form.

To properly understand the Church's claim of *Verus Israel*, and its subsequent attitude towards Jews and Judaism, we should bear in mind that theological blabber aside, the Church was organized as a *corpus* or 'corporation of Christ' or *Christi*, in the model of Roman commercial corporations (see chapter 29). The success of the Church is the result of its excellence in the art of hostile takeover. The claim *Verus Israel* was part of its bid to take over 'Israel.' The bid, however, was rejected by the 'board': the shareholders preferred to suffer agony and martyrdom than accept the new management. As a result, even the Judeo-Christian communities originally formed around Jesus and his disciples were ignored by the new corporation: the Church Fathers regarded Jesus' original disciples, their companions and families, as heretics! There was a good reason for that. By rejecting the original bid, Jews proved themselves 'perfidious,' i.e., unwilling to submit to hostile takeovers. Therefore, it would be wise not to trust a Judeo-Christian as well; only those of pagan background could be *Verus Israel*! That will explain the preeminence of Paul over James and Peter, and the Church's efforts to *erase every trace* of the *early* Christian Community in the Holy Land. This could explain the fact that *St Peter's Basilica* was not built upon the Apostle's tomb, as claimed by the Church, but over a pagan cemetery. Accordingly, it would be unrealistic to expect the Church to try to become *Verus* Judeo-Christian – by honoring the original Judeo-Christian communities in the Holy Land – before pretending to be *Verus* Israel. As those acquainted with the art of hostile takeovers will tell you, there would be no remission of sins, earthly or otherwise, for the board and shareholders who have refused to cooperate fully with the new management.

A marginal note. The attitude of the Church towards the original Judeo-Christian communities was similar to its attitude towards the Roman Empire. As historians teach us, Christians joined forces with the Barbarians to destroy the Empire. In its place was created the *Sacrum Romanun Imperium Nationis Germanicae*, bringing enlightenment, liberty and peace to European society until modern times. Cf. above appendix 20.

# 31. *Remez*

*Remez*, a term widely used in rabbinic literature, stands for a 'gesture' or non-verbal 'sign' made to communicate. For example, signals made to a deaf-mute person, see Mishna Giṭṭin 5:7, Tosefta Yebamot 13:7, p. 49; or by a husband unable to speak, 'signaling' that he wishes to divorce his wife; see Tosefta Giṭṭin 5:1, p. 263; Yebamot 120b, etc. It is commonly (but not exclusively) used to indicate a gesture made in visual contact by the eyes (for example, 'winking' at someone, as in Arabic); see Yoma 19a. It also stands for an 'encoded' term or a word used not as a linguistic symbol, but in the place of a non-verbal 'signal,' suggesting something outside the semantic field of the sentence. Accordingly, a *remez* may be suggested by a full or defective spelling of a word; see Shabbat 103b; cf. *Teshubot Ge'onim Qadmonim* #79, 23b and *Kelale Shemu'el*, 5d; or by the general impression, gained from a peculiar style or construction of a verse; see 'Aboda Zara 25a; Zebaḥim 115b; Menaḥot 76b; etc. *Remez* cannot be treated as speech. Although 'written,' it functions as an *extensional* sign, outside its semantic field. Like a non-verbal 'riddle' or 'cryptogram,' it requires 'decoding' and 'unraveling,' rather than linguistic 'interpretation.' Therefore, it should not be taken as a kind of word-puzzle (as per 'כל שמות הנרמזים באותיותיו ובפסוקיו').

Given the non-linguistic character of a *remez*, it cannot, by definition, be linguistically explicit; see Sanhedrin 10a, Ḥolin 42a, etc. Consequently, since the 613 *miṣvot* were "said" (נאמרו) to Moses (Makkot 24a), implying speech and verbal communication, a *remez* cannot be in and of itself a *miṣva* (but at most, a *detail* in a *miṣva*); see *Sefer ha-Miṣvot,* III, p. 16 (contrary to Ramban ibid.). Neither could it be decoded on the basis of *sebara* (which is essentially linguistic); see Yebamot 54b, but only via rabbinic promulgation. Thus, we find that rabbis enacted a series of halakhot on the basis of a *remez* in Scripture; see Mo'ed Qaṭan 5a, Yebamot 21a, Nedarim 39b, Qiddushin 80b, Sanhedrin 21b, 46b, 83b; etc. We can understand now why, if a sage reports a law that is not explicit in Scripture, it is assumed that it has been 'suggested' somewhere by a *remez.* In such a case, the sages proceed to ask where in Scripture it was 'suggested' (היכא רמיזא); see Megilla 2a, Sanhedrin 81b, etc. The Geonim, too, justified certain rituals on the basis of a *remez* preserved in their tradition; see *She'iltot, Bereshit,* I, vol. 1, p. 12; *Sha'are Teshuba* #31, 13a. *Remez* pertains to *dinim mufla'im.* Since its resolution is not based on linguistic considerations, it is up to the legislative authorities to determine whether the law or rule promulgated on the basis of a *remez* is to be regarded as 'rabbinical' or 'scriptural.'

The keys and general system of the *remez*-technique were taught by the sages during the Second Temple period to advanced students. For our purpose, let us point out that the *derashot,* or homilies, in *Sifra* and *Sifre* were designed to identify the *loci* in Scripture encoding (רמיזא) some of the halakhot contained in the Mishna. Concerning this fundamental aspect of rabbinics, R. Sherira Gaon, *IShG,* p. 39 reported:

> *Sifra* and *Sifre* are the *derashot* of Scripture and (pointing) to the *hilkheta* (Aramaic for *halakha*) is encoded (רמיזא) in the Scripture. Originally, during the Second Temple, (and) in the rabbinic period, they would teach (תני, i.e., via oral tradition) this method to them (their disciples).

See *Golden Doves,* p. 97.

The famous thirteen rules of rabbinic hermeneutics, widely discussed but rarely understood, are the principal keys designed to unravel the *remez.* Referring to the *curriculum* of the traditional rabbinic academies, Maimonides (*MT Talmud Tora* 1:11) wrote that it included three sections: the study of Scripture, the study of oral tradition, and a special section, 'Talmud' whose purpose was to train the student, to

> ... understand and comprehend the relation between the final conclusion of a subject [as promulgated by the rabbis] to its beginning [the *remez*], and (learn how) to draw one thing from the other, and match up one thing to the other, and understand the rules of hermeneutics that expound the Tora, until he could grasp the foundation of these rules of hermeneutics, and how such matters, as 'prohibited and permitted,' that he had previously learned from oral tradition, were derived. This process is what is designated 'Talmud.'

According to Maimonides, the above three-part curriculum should be followed in the formative stages of education. However, after having mastered the system, a scholar should devote his efforts "only to Talmud, in accordance with his mental scope and intellectual maturity" (*MT Talmud Tora* 1:12).

Finally, we should note that *remez* can allude to halakhic material, see *Sifre* Bemidbar #116, p. 132; or to some basic doctrine; see *Sifre* Debarim #329, p. 379. It may also encode esoteric material, in which case its identification and development follow a special methodology (see *Homo Mysticus*). Given that the original connotation of *remez* is a 'gesture,' at times certain stories in the Talmud (or Scripture) must be understood not as a *linguistic narrative* but in terms of *imagery*, functioning as a 'signal'; see *Teshubot ha-Ge'onim* (Harkavi) #244, p. 121; *Teshubot ha-Ge'onim* (Musafia) #115, 35a. To gain a better appreciation of the *remez*-methodology, it would be helpful to consider what Cyrus H. Gordon wrote about the usage of language among the ancients, *Riddles in History* (New York: Crown Publishers, 1974), pp. 53–54:

> Our contemporaries have split the atom, reached the moon, and brought color TV to the common man. The ancients, all through

> historic times (i.e., since 3000 B.C.), were not less talented than today's population, but they often expressed their intelligence in different ways. They manipulated language so deftly that it often takes the modern scholars a long time to grasp the presence, let alone all the subtleties, of ancient riddles.

In particular, ancient man indulged in the design of clever cryptograms and riddles. The Scripture may serve as a good model for this usage of language. In the words of Professor Gordon, *Riddles in History*, p. 55:

> To understand how the ancients actually felt about the sophisticated uses of language, we must turn to the old texts themselves. The Proverbs of Solomon 1:6 states that the function of an education is "to understand a proverb and clever saying: the words of the wise and riddles." For the sages it was not enough to handle plaintext. Plain language is for plain people. The elite must also master riddles and cryptograms, and grasp the deeper meaning subtly concealed beneath the surface meaning.

See *Guide*, Introduction and I, 31. On the rabbis' predilection for riddles, see Yerushalmi Demai VII, 7, 26c, and the comment of R. Jacob Ḥajez, *'Eṣ Ḥayyim* (Verona, 5408/1648), Introduction, 5a.

In a well-researched and beautifully written book, Marcel Danesi, *The Puzzle Instinct: The Meaning of Puzzles in Human Life* (Bloomington: Indiana University Press, 2002), thoroughly examined what he described as "the puzzle instinct" in man.

> The puzzle instinct is, arguably, as intrinsic to human nature as are humor, language, art, music, and all the other creative faculties that distinguish humanity from other species (*The Puzzle Instinct*, p. 208).

Of particular interest for the understanding of the *remez* methodology in rabbinic literature and in Maimonides' *Guide*, is the fact that puzzles "are solved primarily by a form of insightful thinking that the philosopher Charles Peirce called *logica utens*" (ibid.). Danesi concluded his work with these powerful words:

> Hopefully, I have shed some light on how the puzzle instinct, in its own miniature way, has guided us, and continues to guide us, in our search for an answer, whether real or imagined, to the most vexing puzzle of all – the meaning of life (ibid. p. 235).

Summing up some of the ideas discussed above. The rabbis believed that in addition to *peshaṭ* or *sensus communis,* the Scripture and rabbinic literature contain encoded messages, the *remez*. As it were, in addition to the divine message conveyed from the mouth of the Almighty as *qabbala,* there were special points communicated via His Divine Countenance, which those closer to Him could discern and eventually unravel. The solution (rather than the method) is rendered in a *derasha,* introducing the halakha or legal rule to the general public. Some of the clues, however, contain *sod* or esoteric material. The methodology by which to identify this material and unravel its content is a principal concern of Maimonides' *Guide.*

On the difference between *remez* and *asmakhta,* see appendix 33 – contrary to the view proposed in *Yad Mal'akhi* #202 and *Ohel Yesharim,* '*He*' #44. On the difference with *Derekh Qeṣara,* see appendix 34. For a learned study on Midrash, see Mayer Gruber, "The Term *Midrash* in Tannaitic Literature," in ed. Rivka Ulmer, *Discussing Cultural Influences* (Lanham: University Press of America, 2007), pp. 41–58.

# 32. *Qabbala* and *Halakha*

To gain a proper understanding of these terms it would be necessary to consider three principles connected with halakha. First, it depends on *qabbala* ('authoritative transmission'); see Mishna Pe'a 2:6; Giṭṭin 6:7; Abot 1:1; 'Eduyot 1:6; 8:7; Tosefta Pesaḥim 4:13–14, p. 165; Sanhedrin 6:2, p. 424; Yadayim 2:16, p. 683. The root QBL is common to other Semitic languages. Principally, it connotes 'frontal, face to face,' 'opposite to one another.' In Arabic it is used to designate the direction in which the faithful faces in prayer (for Moslems: Mecca; for Jews: Jerusalem), and also for 'kissing.' In Aramaic it stands for 'confrontation,' and therefore 'complaint.' It appears in Scripture as 'opposite' (in space: Ex. 26:5; 36:12; etc.; but in rabbinics also in time, see Bekhorot 57b); for 'greeting' (I Chr. 12:19), and 'in the presence of' (II Kings 15:10). It also denotes 'acceptance' (Job 2:10). It is used for formal 'acceptance,' involving understanding and commitment (Prov. 19:20; Est. 9:23, 27). In this latter sense, *qabbala* of halakha involves 'frontal reception' from an authority, as Moses at Sinai (Abot 1:1). In the process of *qabbala* the student was expected to face and pay close attention to the teacher's lip movements in order to make sure that he was hearing correctly; see Horayot 12a, cf. Ḥolin 137b. When R. Dime, Shabbat 145a, wanted to reassure Abayye that the report he was transmitting was authentic, he invoked Job 19:27: "My eyes saw and not a stranger." He added: "from the lips of R. Jeremiah I heard," the report in question; i.e., he saw it coming out of his lips. Accordingly, "When someone is transmitting an authoritative lesson (שמועה) … he should picture in his mind the image of the author of that tradition as now standing before him" (Y. Sheqalim II, 7, 47a), cf. *Golden Doves*, p. 87. When a student recited the lesson before his teacher, the teacher moved his lips in harmony with the student, signifying consent; Y. Berakhot II, 1, 4b, etc. [In Judeo-Arabic the verb *qarri*, from Hebrew QR', denotes this type of supervision.] That is why, even after death, "Every disciple of the sages, when an authoritative lesson (שמועה) is pronounced in his name in this world, his lips move smoothly in the tomb," Yebamot 97a. For a glimpse on the faithfulness and tenacity with which the students guarded the lessons they heard from their teachers, see Nidda 36b-37a. cf. *Yad Mal'akhi* #663, 169a-b.

Not all students were qualified to face the teacher. Some were only permitted to stand behind the teacher (see 'Erubin 13b, reporting that R. Judah the Prince only saw "the back of R. Me'ir.," R. Ḥanan'el ad loc., explained that at the time he was not qualified to sit in a front row).

The connotation of *qabbala*/'kissing' (as in Arabic), is evident in the *Targum* to Song. 1:2, rendering "He (God) would kiss me with the kisses of His lips," as: "... and [God] taught the Six Orders of the Mishna and Talmud." This idea was encoded in a point raised by R. Joshua, that "דדיך" in Song. 1:2 is to be read in the plural, not in the singular (Mishna 'Aboda Zara 2:5). Accordingly, the standard translation, "For thy *love* (דדיך) is better than wine," is wrong. If "דדיך" is in the plural, as per R. Joshua's teaching and the Masora reading, then we should translate it as: "For *those who love* Thee are better than wine" – being an allusion to the teachings of sages and scribes in charge of conveying the oral tradition. Hence the homily stressing that the teachings of sages and scribes are more beloved "than the wine of Tora" or Scripture itself; see 'Aboda Zara 35a; Y. Berakhot I, 4, 3b, and parallels. Cf. also 'Erubin 21b and Sanhedrin 88b. For a different interpretation, see Sh. Na'e, "*Ṭobim Dodekha Mi-Yayyin*," (Heb.), in *Studies in Talmud and Midrashic Literature in Memory of Tirzah Lifshitz* (Jerusalem: Bialik Institute, 2005), pp. 411–434.

Therefore halakha stands for authentic tradition (Tosefta Ḥagiga

3:33, p. 393; Ketubot 6:6, p. 76; Qiddushin 5:4, p. 295; Zebaḥim 1:8, p. 480), indicating 'an accepted norm' (see Mishna 'Erubin 4:8, Baba Meṣi'a 5:8, Sanhedrin 11:6, Menaḥot 4:3; Tosefta Ta'aniyot 2:5, p. 331; Yebamot 1:9, p. 2; Baba Qamma 6:5, p. 22; Sanhedrin 3:9, p. 420; 'Eduyot 2:7, p. 458). The status of a halakha, however, is not a matter of history but of law, to be awarded by the judiciary, not by historians; see *MT Mamrim* 1:1.

A legal position may be put forward as a *din* – 'a view arrived at through judicial analysis,' or as a halakha – 'authoritative transmission.' A duly acknowledged halakha must be accepted, whereas a *din* could be challenged (see Mishna Yebamot 8:3; Keritot 3:9; cf. Nazir 7:4). Whether a legal position is a halakha or a *din* is a matter to be decided by the judiciary. Prior to being settled, there could be controversy on the subject (see Tosefta Ṭebul Yom 1:10, p. 685), and it could be treated as a regular *din* (see Tosefta Nazir 5:1, pp. 141–142; Ohalot 4:14, p. 601). When the status of a legal view is challenged, the case may be submitted to a vote and the majority opinion prevails (see Mishna 'Eduyot 1:5, 6; Tosefta Ḥagiga 2:9, pp. 383–384; cf. Mishna 'Eduyot 5:7). However, once the matter has been settled by the court and awarded the status of halakha, it cannot be challenged on the basis of *din* (cf. Mishna Pe'a 4:1, 2; Giṭṭin 6:7; 'Eduyot 8:7). That is why halakha is often used in the sense of 'established norm' (see Mishna Pe'a 3:6; Shebi'it 9:5; Yebamot 4:13; Baba Qamma 3:9; cf. *Targum* on Gen. 40:13 and *Pseudo-Jonathan* on Gen. 40:13, 43:33 and Deut. 12:27, etc.).

It is clear now why rejecting a halakha equals 'heresy' (כפירה); see Tosefta 'Oqaṣin 3:13, p. 689. The following incident illustrates the gravity of the matter. Once, R. 'Aqiba challenged his teacher, R. Eleazar, while the latter was in the process of transmitting a halakha. The incident is depicted as follows: "his [R. 'Aqiba's] teacher, R. Eleazar, was in the process of teaching him a halakha … and he [R. 'Aqiba] dissented with him (כפר בו) during the argument (דין)" and was "admonished for it" (see Y. Pesaḥim VI, 4, 35c; *Sifre Zuṭa*, Numbers, #XII, p. 243; Pesaḥim 69a; and *Yerushalmi Ki-Fshuṭo*, p.478; cf. 'Aboda Zara 46b and Mishna Nazir 7:4).

To question the integrity of the transmission of a halakha is tantamount to rejecting the authority of the sage who transmitted it. When the rabbis decided to call for a special session to settle a matter which had been previously transmitted by R. Eleazar as *halakha le-Moshe mi-Sinai,* it was with the intention of publicly repudiating his authority (Mishna Yadayim 4:3); see Ḥagiga 3b and *Perush* R. Ḥanan'el ad loc. On one occasion, after a legal dispute, one of the parties discovered that the view he was proposing was in fact a halakha, and therefore reported it as such; see Baba Meṣi'a 23a. By contrast, a *din* could always be challenged and a dissenting opinion would be duly noted.

Since the status of a halakha depends on the court, sometimes this term is used in the sense of 'legal decision' (see Tosefta Sanhedrin 6:6, p. 424; 7:1, p. 425; 'Eduyot 1:4, p. 455; Para 7:4, p. 636; cf. Miqva'ot 4:6, p. 656); or for 'the strict legal meaning,' in contradistinction to the moral aspect of a precept; see Tosefta Baba Meṣi'a 3:14, p. 76. Not every halakha would be implemented; see Rab in Shabbat 12b; 'Erubin 7a; Beṣa 28b; Baba Qamma 30b; 'Aboda Zara 37b; Menaḥot 36b. (For further analyses, see R. Judah Rozanes, *Mishne la-Melekh* on *MT She'ar Abot ha-Ṭum'a* 19:1, s.v. *ve-khen ha-shereṣ veha-ṣefardea'.*) Samuel maintained that the entire last chapter of tractate Nidda was *la-halakha* but not for *ma'ase* ('to be implemented'); see Y. Berakhot II, 6, 5b. (Conversely, some rules were put into practice as *halakha le-ma'ase* although not formally halakhot; see Ketubot 56a.) This is why the sages distinguished between halakha and *halakha le-ma'ase*; see Baba Batra 130b; Y. Giṭṭin V, 4, 47a; cf. Horayot 2a.

For the purpose of the present discussion it is important to emphasize that the authenticity and dependability of *qabbala,* and its corollary, halakha is not a matter of 'memory.' Rabbis, whether in their initial educational stages or as advanced teachers, were prone to memory lapses and distortions; see Rabban Yoḥanan b. Zakkai, Tosefta Ohalot 16:8, p. 614. On occasion, two outstanding sages would report contradictory accounts of the same lesson that they heard together from their teacher, each ready to take an oath that his version was correct, and not that of his colleague. Later sages would attempt to reconcile between them and try to find some justification for their disagreement; see, for example, Yebamot 32a-33b; Ketubot 57a and Rashi ad loc. s.v. *amar*. The fullest account and justification of most such cases is found in *Yad Mal'akhi* #663. However, no justification for forgetfulness and memory lapses is really necessary. Consider the following passage in Shebu'ot 26a:

> When R. Kahana and R. Ase stood up from the lesson given by Rab, one would say: 'I swear: This is what Rab said.' And the second would say: 'I swear: This is what Rab said.' When they would come to Rab he would agree with only one of them. Then the second would say: 'Did I swear falsely?' (And Rab) would reply: 'Your heart coerced you!'

See below appendix 45. What makes *qabbala,* and its consequent halakha, 'infallible' is that it was recognized as such by the judiciary. Occasionally, a testimony reporting a tradition would be accepted as authentic, in so far as it makes legal sense, but not as *qabbala*; as per Yebamot 67a:

> זו עדות העיד ר' יוסי מפי שמעיה ואבטליון, והודו לו. אמר רב אשי: מי קתני וקבלו? 'והודו לו' קתני: דמסתבר טעמיה!

Concerning memory inexactness and misrepresentation, see the articles edited by Daniel L. Schacter, *Memory Distortion* (Cambridge, Mass.: Harvard University Press, 1995), particularly in part IV. On the different connotations of this term, see chapters 49, 57.

# 33. *Halakha le-Moshe mi-Sinai*

There is a special group of halakhot classified by the rabbis as 'A halakha of Moses from Sinai' (הלכה למשה מסיני); see Mishna 'Eduyot 4:3; 8:7, Tosefta Sukka 3:1, p. 266; Yadayim 2:16, p. 683. It is a major rabbinic concept. In a sense, "the entire Tora," including the oral tradition, is "halakha of Moses from Sinai"; see Nidda 45a; and cf. *'Arukh*, s.v. *mad* (1); R. Judah ha-Levi, *Kuzari* III, 21, pp. 128–130; Introduction, *Perush ha-Mishnayot*, vol. 1, p. 16. Not all of these halakhot were originally designated as such. An opinion could have been registered in the Mishna as a halakha without any qualifications (see Mishna 'Orla 3:9), and upon consideration the Talmudic authorities would classify it as 'A halakha of Moses from Sinai' (הלכה למשה מסיני); see Baba Batra 12b; Y. 'Orla III, 7, 63b; Qiddushin 37a; *MT Ma'akhalot Asurot* 10:10; *Perush ha-Mishnayot, 'Orla* 3:9, vol. 1, p. 415. In the Introduction to *Perush ha-Mishnayot*, vol. 1, pp. 18–19, Maimonides recorded a list of most of the cases that were classified as 'A halakha of Moses from Sinai.' According to Maimonides, these halakhot have two characteristics. First, they have no legislative basis in the text of the Tora, i.e., they were neither 'encoded' (*remez*; see appendix 31) in the text, nor can they be justified by judicial reasoning (דין), or rabbinic exegesis. Therefore, they could not be included in the lesson on the Tora. For purposes of mnemonics, a teacher would 'append' (אסמכתא) these halakhot to a term of the Tora; see Introduction, *Perush ha-Mishnayot*, vol. 1, pp. 18–19; R. Isaac Bar-Sheshet, *Teshubot ha-Ribash* #294. However, since these attachments would not be included in the lesson, they could not be disseminated through regular channels. Rather, they 'floated' around and were occasionally forgotten; see Yoma 80a; Y. Pe'a II, 6, 17a, cf. Shabbat I, 4, 3d. Ideally, if one could, "then one should string a tradition (שמועה) up to Moses, but if one cannot (then he should) confirm either the earlier [source] or the later [source]"; see Y. Shabbat I, 2, 3a. Because the halakhot that were 'floating' around could be easily dismissed as unimportant, R. Johanan warned scholars: "If you come in contact with a halakha and you do not know its source (= 'טיפוס'-*typos*; cf. Mishna Ketubot 1:9), don't dismiss it. Many halakhot that were given to Moses at Sinai, were thereafter placed in the Mishna" (Yerushalmi Pe'a II, 6, 17a; Ḥagiga I, 8, 76d). Hence, the need to corroborate these types of halakhot and reinforce their status.

The halakhot that were designated as 'of Moses from Sinai' are those that although [i] they have no connection with the text of Scripture, and [ii] their chain of tradition cannot be fully determined, were, nonetheless, confirmed by the rabbinic authorities as authentic. Once established as 'of Moses from Sinai,' it would be improper for a later sage to try to find some 'support' for it in Scripture; see Zebaḥim 110a. Maimonides maintained that once a halakha had been classified as 'of Moses from Sinai,' the matter was settled and its status could not be contested. We have seen above (appendix 32) that the status of a halakha is a judicial matter. This applies also to a *halakha le-Moshe mi-Sinai*. Its status is a matter of law – not of 'history!' Prior to gaining the status of *le-Moshe mi-Sinai*, a halakha could be contested (see for example Y. Pe'a I, 1, 15a; Ḥagiga I, 2, 76b; etc.). We should note that Maimonides distinguished between two classes of traditions attributed to Moses. One "about which there could not be any controversy at all" (Introduction, *Perush ha-Mishnayot*, vol. 1, p. 20; cf. *MT Melakhim* 12:2), or what amounts to the same: "about which there never was [registered] a controversy" (*MT Mamrim* 1:3). Second, a *halakha le-Moshe mi-Sinai* "about which there is no controversy" (Introduction, *Perush ha-Mishnayot*, vol. 1, p. 16) – in the present tense! Before the court renders a decision, a halakha has no standing. The rabbis reported that when a party presented a view not derived from Scripture, but claimed "thus I have received (קבלתי) from my teachers," the matter had to be submitted to the Supreme Court for a decision (see Tosefta Pesaḥim 4:13–14, p. 165; Sanhedrin 7:1, p. 425; Sanhedrin 88b; *MT Mamrim* 4:1; cf. Mishna 'Eduyot 5:7, *Perush ha-Mishnayot,* vol. 4, pp. 322–323).

The status 'of Moses from Sinai' does not imply that the halakha in question had been pronounced by Moses, but, rather, that although the chain of transmission cannot be fully traced, it has been confirmed as authentic, as if it were a halakha given by Moses at Sinai; see Shraga Abramson, *Perush R. Ḥanan'el la-Talmud,* p. 120. Consider, for example, the law about levying tithes from lands in Moab and Amon, having the status *halakha le-Moshe mi-Sinai* (Mishna Yadayim 4:3). The law itself is actually rabbinic; see *Kesef Mishne, MT Mattanot 'Aniyyim* 6:5. Therefore, as proposed by R. Shimshon (12th century), it means that the law is authentic "as if it were a halakha given by Moses at Sinai" (*Perush* ad loc.); cf. *Perush ha-Mishnayot, 'Eduyot* 8:7, vol. 4, p. 336. Similarly, according to the original version in 'Erubin 4a-b (preserved in *MT Miqva'ot* 1:12 and R. Menaḥem Me'iri, *Bet ha-Beḥira* ad loc., p. 21), a rabbinic rule establishing "that a tarnish, covering most of the body, constitutes a legal impediment" for a ritual bath, "even though (the person in question) is not troubled by it," was reported as a *halakha le-Moshe mi-Sinai.* R. Ḥanan'el on Sukka 6b referred to that particular *halakha le-Moshe mi-Sinai* as "a rabbinic decree" (גזרו). In fact, the expression *halakha le-Moshe mi-Sinai* is used in Geonic literature as synonymous with 'authentic, reliable,' and 'lucid and unambiguous'; see R. Ḥanan'el on Berakhot 64a (*Perush,* p. 145); *'Arukh,* s.v. *mad* (1); *Oṣar Ḥilluf Minhagim,* ed. B. M. Lewin (Jerusalem: Makor, 1972), p. 32; R. Ḥanan'el in his *Perush* to Berakhot, p. 145a, etc. In sum, as explained by Maimonides, *Teshubot ha-Rambam,* vol. 2, p. 632:

> ... that even a matter which is *halakha le-Moshe mi-Sinai* is designated 'from the Scribes,' given that nothing is 'from the Tora,' unless it is explicit in the Tora ... or something that the

> sages have declared to be from the Tora, of which there are only three or perhaps four cases.

The preceding meets the objections raised by R. Solomon Rafael Judah Leon Templo, *Massekhet Halakha le-Moshe mi-Sinai* (Amsterdam, 5494/1734), 3a, 5a, etc.; see the response of R. Ḥiyya ha-Cohen de la-Ara, *Mishmerot Kehunna* (Amsterdam, 5508/1748), 56b-57b; and *Studies in the Mishne Tora*, p. 32.

In conclusion, for Maimonides, the Geonim, et al, *halakha le-Moshe mi-Sinai* is a special type of tradition, which cannot be verified by standard procedure. Nonetheless, it has the status of settled law and it is legally binding; e.g., *MT Qiddush ha-Ḥodesh* 5:1–2; cf. *Mishmerot Kehunna*, 56a. The same applies to Scriptural texts; e.g. such as the 'Scroll of Esther' that is "from Sinai," see Y. Megilla I, 5, 70d; and Ruth Rabba IV, 5 (33d); and cf. *Golden Doves*, p. 190 n. 28. Put in contemporary terms, *halakha le-Moshe mi-Sinai* is somehow analogous to a Constitutional amendment (e.g., the Bill of Rights in the U.S.), added to the Constitution by the Court, and not subject to repeal by any subsequent panel of the Court.

The same applies to the expression "Truly, it was said" (באמת אמרו) in rabbinic literature (see Mishna Kil'ayim 2:2, etc., etc.), which is usually treated as a *halakha le-Moshe mi-Sinai*; see Rashi on Nazir 54b, s.v. *be'emet*. It is an authentic tradition, whose chain of transmission could not be verified by standard procedure. It is nevertheless authentic, as "if it were a *halakha le-Moshe mi-Sinai*"; see *Perush*, R. 'Obadya, on Terumot 2:1.

# 34. *Derekh Qeṣara*

*Derekh Qeṣara* or 'succinct style' refers to the 'concise' and elliptical 'style' of the Mishna in which density (rather than clarity) is a major concern; see *Golden Doves,* pp. 90–94. Originally, this expression meant 'a shorter path' than the ordinary; see Mishna Ketubot 13:7; Shebu'ot 2:3; Rashi on Shebu'ot 14b s.v. *o she-ba*; or a shorter astronomical orbit, Rosh HaShana 25a; Y. Rosh HaShana II, 6, 58b; *MT Qiddush ha-Ḥodesh* 17:23. It is one of the hermeneutical rules applied metaphorically to the text of Scripture; see *Yalquṭ Shim'oni, Noaḥ #55,* vol. 1, 14c; *Shemini* #537, vol. 1, 158c, s.v. *ve-el ha-ḥasida*; cf. *Sifra, Emor,* X, 13, 5, 95b, where it is stated that the Scripture spoke "succinctly" (בקצרה). This principle has been recognized by the great biblical commentators. On a 'shortened idiom' (קיצור דיבור), see Rashi on Ezra 42:2; R. Abraham ibn 'Ezra on Ps. 52:2. For the more common 'succinct style' (לשון קצרה), see Rashi on Gen. 29:14; 39:14; Ex. 10:5; Ezek. 27:14; R. Abraham ibn 'Ezra on Eccl. 10:18. On דרך קצרה, see Rashi on 37:1; R. Abraham ibn 'Ezra on Gen. 3:17; 6:16; 18:25; etc., etc.; Radaq on Josh. 9:21; I Sam. 12:8; I Kings 7:15; II Kings 7:2; Ps. 21:13, etc., etc. For 'a shortened verse' (מקרא קצר), see Rashi Gen. 41:13, 49; 48:1; Ex. 22:22; 32:32; Num. 14:21; 22:32; etc.; Radaq Josh. 9:21; 20:6; Judges 2:3; I Sam. 10:21, etc. In *The Mishnah of Rabbi Eliezer* (Heb.), I, 9, pp. 20–21, 'succinct style' is counted as one of the hermeneutical rules to be applied in the development of Aggada, particularly to those elements requiring expansion and further elucidation. Some Talmudic passages were regarded as elliptic, and were interpreted accordingly; see R. Isaac Alfasi, *Teshubot* #286; Rashi on 'Aboda Zara 9a s.v. *ve-'i*; *Shebu'ot* 5b s.v. *mi*; Riṭba on Sukka 2a s.v. Sukka; cf. *Perush ha- Mishnayot*, Abot 5:14, vol. 4, p. 463.

A fundamental principle in Geonic tradition is that the Mishna was redacted in a 'succinct style' (דרך קצרה); see *IShG*, pp. 28–29; and cf. ibid. pp. 17, 26–27, 36, 58. Maimonides, too, alluded to the 'succinct style' of the Mishna; see Introduction, *Perush ha-Mishnayot*, vol. 1, p. 34. This style was adopted by him in the redaction of the *MT* (see Introduction, l. 152, cf. *Iggerot*, vol. 2, pp. 441, 442, 448) in his *responsa*, see *Teshubot ha-Rambam*, vol. 2, p. 634; and in his correspondence, see *Iggerot*, vol. 2, p. 454.

# 35. God's Mystery (סוד)

The Hebrew term for 'mystery' (סוד) stands for 'assembly'; as with a 'forum' where a deliberative group convenes to examine matters of common interest; something akin to the 'assembly' of canon law and legislative bodies. The discussions held within the *Bet Midrash* were confidential and treated as *sod*, closed to the general public. Pupils violating this confidence were expelled; see Sanhedrin 31a. and cf. Mishna Sanhedrin 3:7; R. Isaac Alfasi, on Sanhedrin 31a; and the comments of R. Joseph Al-Ashqar, *Mirkebet ha-Mishne*, ed. Jacob Shpigel (5753/1993), on Abot 6:4, p. 318.

Teachers were cautioned to exercise discretion when exposing delicate matters; see Y. 'Aboda Zara II, 4, 41d (the printed text is faulty), the correct text is quoted by R. Ḥanan'el on 'Aboda Zara 35a. It admonishes the teacher: "You may immerse yourself in the words of the Tora only before upright and honest students." On the association *sod/halakha*, see Tosefta Yadayim 2:16, p. 683 and Ḥagiga 3b. Obviously, the statement by R. Johanan, that "God contracted the covenant with Israel only on account of the oral matters," Giṭṭin 60b is aimed at contravening the Christian notion that a 'covenant' with God could be established merely by appropriating the text of the Scripture without regard for the oral tradition of Israel; cf. Section IV, n. 120. For the association *qabbala*/'kissing,' see appendix 32.

# 36. *Seder*

In Jewish literature the Aramaic root SDR may include legal topics, e.g., the six *SeDaRim* of the Mishna. It may also include liturgical themes, as in *SiDduR* or 'Prayer Book,' to be developed by the precentor at the Synagogue; see, for example, Berakhot 13a, 34a; Rosh HaShana 35a. Hence, we have the Passover *SeDeR* where the participants gather to develop the theme of the Exodus; see Section III, n. 21. The term SiDRa which is commonly used to designate the weekly portion of the Tora, probably included the Aramaic version (as *Neophyti* 1) or similar exegetical material (otherwise, it would not have made any sense to have Rab repeat the *sidra* so many times; see Yoma 87a-b, and cf. 'Aboda Zara 19a). The Arabic *tatlawaha'a,* root WLY, 'to adjoin, to place next,' used by R. Se'adya Gaon to translate the biblical term *tasim* (Ex. 21:1), has a similar connotation; cf. *Targum* and R. Se'adya on Deut. 4:44. Maimonides, too, used this Arabic term in the same technical sense; see, for example, Introduction, *Perush ha-Mishnayot,* vol. 1, p. 2. On the association of the Hebrew *sima* with the Aramaic *sedura,* see 'Erubin 54b.

Talmudic Academies counted with a special instructor, *sadrana;* see Pesaḥim 105b and cf. Y. Horayot III, 8, 48c (cf. below appendix 41). His task was to *meSaDdeR,* 'expose the halakhot in their proper order and sequence'; see Tosefta Zabim 1:5, p. 676. The same applies to the *SeDaRim* of the Mishna, see Beṣa 16b and Ta'aniyot 8a; the Gemara, see Yoma 14b; and the Aggada, see Megilla 27a, Berakhot 10a, 'Erubin 21b, etc. (In the Arabic of the Jews from Syria, *sidr al-ḥammam* indicates the ceremonial arrangement made for the bridal ritual bath. In contemporary synagogues of congregations from Damascus and Aleppo, the *mesadder* is the official in charge of designating who will lead in the various sections of the services, and who will go up to read the Tora.) Part of the responsibilities of the Talmudic *sadran* was to invite students to attend the lecture; see *Kalla Rabbati* IV, 14, p. 263. He would also repeat the class to the students, see Yoma 15a. The "head of the *sidra*" occupied an important position, once held by no less a figure than Rab; see Ḥolin 137b. In the Yerushalmi, *sidra* stands for the building containing the 'synagogue' or 'place of study'; see Shabbat VI, 2, 8a; IX, 2, 12a; XIX, 1, 16d; Pesaḥim I, 1, 27b; Sheqalim V, 4, 49b, etc. In Samaritan dialect, *sidra* stands for "assembly"; see *Yerushalmi Ki-Fshuṭo,* p. 104. Concerning the title *resh sidra* in the Talmud (Ḥolin 137b) and in Geonic literature, see Abramson, *Ba-Merkazim,* p. 107. Maimonides, Introduction, *MT*, l. 170, expressed the hope that the halakhot in his *Mishne Tora* would be "*SeDuRim* fluently by heart." For an extensive discussion of the different connotations of this term, see Moshe Assis, "On the *Sidra,*" (Heb.) *Annual of Bar-Ilan University* 30–31 (2006), pp. 353–372.

# 37. The Four Levels of Instruction

In *Mekhilta, Mishpaṭim,* p. 246 we read:

> *These are the laws* (Ex. 21:1). R. ʿAqiba asked: what is the purpose of *These are the laws*? – because elsewhere it was written [i] "*Speak* to the people of Israel, and *say* to them." One may think that it would suffice to *say* [these laws] to them only once. How can it be known that one is to repeat them twice, thrice and four times until they learn them? To clarify this point the Scripture teaches: [ii] "And *teach* it [the Law] to the children of Israel" (Deut. 31:19). May one assume that it would be sufficient to learn [these laws] (once) and not to go over them again? To clarify this point the Scripture teaches: [iii] "*put it in their mouths*" (Deut. 31:19). May one assume that it would be sufficient if they knew how to repeat [these laws] without understanding them? To clarify this point the Scripture teaches: [iv] *These are the laws* (Ex. 21:1) – present [these laws] to them as a well-set-out-table (שלחן ערוך), accessible to all! Similarly, it says: "You were *taught* so that you would *know*" (Deut. 4:35).

Cf. "Hebrew Introduction," *Perush ha-Mishnayot,* vol. 1, p. 1; Rashi on Ex. 34:32; and R. Abraham Maimonides, *Perush,* pp. 304, 486.

The above exegesis is developed around the pronoun 'these' (אלה), which is interpreted as a deictic pronoun, pointing at something standing right in front of the speaker. On this type of pronoun, see José Faur, "*Ma ben ḥamor ze la-ḥamor ha-hu,*" *Sinai* 76 (1975), pp. 189–192.

In *Sifra, Be-Ḥuqqotai,* X, 8 (12), 122a we read:

> ... *That God put between Him and the people of Israel.* – Moses had the merits of being appointed emissary (שליח) between Israel and their Father in Heaven. *In the hand of Moses at Mount Sinai.* – It teaches that [i] the (text of the) Tora was delivered – (together with) [ii] its *halakhot,* [iii] *nuances* (דקדוקיה) [iv] *and explanations* (פרושיה) – to the hands of Moses at Sinai.

Cf ibid. X, 13 (8), 127b; and *AdRN* A, I, p. 1.

The above exegeses reflect the fact that Rabbinic Academies conducted classes at *four* levels, see 'Erubin 54b. At the first level, the instructor taught the students the 'order' (סדר), that is, the string and progression of the text, ("and ***say*** to them"); cf. Introduction, *Perush ha-Mishnayot,* vol. 1, p. 2. Probably, the סדרנא was the tutor in charge of this program, see above appendix 36. At level two ("and teach it") the student was expected to 'know' (see Maimonides, ibid. Ar. תעלים 'be familiar'). The purpose of the third level was for the student to become fluent in the subject ("put it in their mouth") and acquire a scholarly comprehension of the subject (Maimonides, ibid. Ar. תדריס 'study'). The fourth level concerned critical understanding ("You were taught so that you should know"). According to Maimonides, ibid. this refers to the Ar. תפסיר 'explanation,' which is equivalent to the Heb. פרוש, see above appendix 28. Such an "explanation should include all the elucidations" (Maimonides, ibid.).

These four levels correspond to knowledge [i] of the text of the Tora together with "[ii] its *halakhot,* [iii] the *nuances* [iv] and the *explanations* (פרושיה)" mentioned in the *Sifra*; see Section IV n. 123 and cf. Introduction, *Perush ha-Mishnayot,* vol. 1, p. 7. Similarly, *Sifre*

#335, pp. 384–385 advised the student that after hearing [i] "the words of the Tora" – the exposition of the Oral Law – one should [ii] "put his heart" in the lesson, as well as [iii] "his eyes," [iv] "and his ears"; cf. appendix 32 and Introduction, *Perush ha-Mishnayot*, vol. 1, p. 2. The rabbis associated 'nuances' of the Tora (דקדוקי תורה) with the need to employ metaphors in the classroom; see Shir ha-Shirim Rabba I, 8, s.v. *shir*, p. 4.

# 38. Teaching Tora in Public

Teaching the Tora in public is equivalent to publishing a judicial tradition. Accordingly, only faculty members were authorized to teach "Tora in public"; see Rosh HaShana 25b; Giṭṭin 57b; cf. Megilla 6a, Sanhedrin 96b and *AdRN* A, VI, p. 29; *Midrash Tehillim* I, 18, p. 18. On the merits of teaching Tora "in public" (ברבים), see Shir ha-Shirim Rabba I, 9, vol. 2, p. 4. This type of instruction is different than someone "gathering an assembly in public" and teaching Tora before them, 'Aboda Zara 18a; or conveying to them "a word about Tora"; see Shir ha-Shirim Rabba I, 8, vol. 2, p. 4; IV, 1 (11), p. 55; *Midrash Mishle*, VIII, 35, p. 60. Only ordained scholars could deliver "instructions" (הוראה) about laws and regulations; see Sanhedrin 5a-b; Nidda 24b; *Perush ha-Mishnayot, Bekhorot* 4:4, vol. 5, pp. 242–245.

The Mishna is the first composition dealing with the Oral Law for the explicit purpose of "teaching it in public" (*MT* Introduction, ll. 46–47).

# 39. *Shone*: Rehearsing and Conveying Halakha

This verb stands for 'rehearsing a formulated text.' Occasionally, it may refer to the text of Scripture; see Tosefta Shabbat 13:1, p. 57; or the *perush* of the Tora, cf. Qiddushin 49a and Riṭba ad loc. s.v. *'al menat*. The expression "*shone* two books," *Sifre*, Debarim #306, p. 339, may allude to the *Sifre* (pl. Aramaic for 'books'), i.e., the *perush* of two books, Numbers and Deuteronomy, rather than the text of Scripture. Mostly, however, this verb is used for the recitation of halakha. See Mishna Ta'aniyot 4:4; Abot 3:7; Tosefta Berakhot 2:12, p. 8; Shebi'it 2:13, p. 173; Kil'ayim 1:2, p. 203; Baba Qamma 7:13, p. 32; Zebaḥim 2:17, p. 483; Ḥolin 2:9, p. 502, etc.; cf. *AdRN* A, XVIII, p. 67; Megilla 28a; Sanhedrin 68a; etc. *Shone* was used to denote both the conveyance and the study of halakha; see *Sifre Debarim* #127, p. 185–186; Megilla 26b, 28b; Soṭa 22a; cf. Sanhedrin 68a. It may apply to the recitation of a halakha from the Mishna, see Ḥagiga 9b, etc.; or from the Tosefta, see *Midrash Tanḥuma, Teṣavve*, VI, vol. 2, p. 99. Mastering halakha, involved intense training; see Tosefta Ohalot 16:8, p. 614 and Para 4:7, p. 633. This is why *shone* is associated with 'sitting'; see Megilla 21a and *Golden Doves*, pp. 186–187. This type of instruction was usually conducted at the *Bet Midrash*; see Shabbat 30b; Pesaḥim 107a; *AdRN* B, III, p. 14, etc.

On *shone*, in contradistinction to *qore* ('to read from Scripture'), see Berakhot 4b; and cf. *Massekhet Derekh Ereṣ* 4:5, ed. Michael Higger (Brooklyn, N.Y.: Moinester Publishing, 1935), p. 115.

# 40. *Megillat Setarim*

On *megillat setarim*, see Shabbat 6b, 96b; Baba Meṣi'a 92a. This term has been mistranslated as 'a secret scroll,' in which case it should have been *megillat seter* or *megilla nisteret*; see *Iyye ha-Yam*, 113a-114b and *Golden Doves*, p. 109. Rather, *setarim* means 'private,' 'confidential,' e.g., *ṭum'at setarim*, in Pesaḥim 85a, etc. *Megillat setarim* is nothing more than a 'private file, not for general circulation'; see *Golden Doves*, pp. 108–111 and Section IV n. 108. This is exactly the sense of the Geonic *responsum*, *Geonica*, vol. 2, p. 319 that "*megillat setarim* contains legal decisions (הלכות פסוקות) as if it was a book of halakhot, but is not like the Talmud that is available to all" (i.e., a published work,) "and that is why it is called *megillat setarim*." (With all due respect, Professor Ginzberg's interpretation, ibid. p. 295, is not accurate.) These scrolls were found in the archives (*be* = *bet*, cf. IV n. 98) of R. Ḥiyya, a scholar famous for the quality of the archival material in his possession, see *Iyye ha-Yam*, 114b; Shir ha-Shirim Rabba VIII, 1 [2], p. 77; Qohelet Rabba II, 1 [8], 7c; VI, 1 [2], 17a; XII, 1 [7], 30b.

# 41. The Publication of Oral Texts

In rabbinic literature the verb *galle* (גלי) stands for "removing a seal and uncovering" (גלי) a hidden object; see Giṭṭin 68a; *Midrash Tehillim* LXXVIII, 12, p. 352. In the same vein, it is also used for 'divulging' (גלי) something to a friend, see Nidda 66a; or expressing formal consent to a neighbor for usage of the premises on the Sabbath, see 'Erubin 26b. A familiar expression in the Babylonian Talmud, "God had elucidated" (גלי רחמנא), means 'exposing' an ambiguous feature or a factor in the law, rather than leaving it to inference; see Pesaḥim 75a, etc. Therefore, I propose that *galle* (גלי) in Horayot 13b, stands for the 'publication' of a text, which hitherto had circulated privately; cf. above appendix 40. The rabbis (Horayot 13b) recount that two members of the *Yeshiba* planned to show that R. Simeon ben Gamliel was not fit to serve as president. According to the standard text they planned to challenge his leadership by requesting of him "to publish" (גלי) 'Oqaṣin – a tractate unknown to him. To prevent a public humiliation, a sage "went" to the archives, found said tractate, sat under R. Simeon ben Gamliel's study, *pashaṭ* ("stretched" it [the tractate], i.e., opened up the scroll), *garas* (chanted, i.e., in a fast pace used to memorize the text; cf. *Golden Doves*, p. 183 n. 58), and then *tane* (a longer chant used to examine and ponder about the meaning of the text). To alert R. Simeon ben Gamliel that he was trying to convey an urgent matter, the sage went on and again "*garas*" and then "*tane*" the text for a second time. By the following morning, when an official request was presented to R. Simeon ben Gamliel to "to publish" (גלי) said tractate, he was ready. The verb *pashaṭ* ('to stretch') was used to denote the opening and unfolding of a 'scroll'; see Y. Shabbat XVI, 1, 15c; *Ekha Rabbati,* IV, 20, p. 53; *Midrash Tanḥuma, Ki-Tissa,* XIX, p. 119; and *Yad Rama* on Baba Batra 160a, s.v. *geṭ*. It should be noted, that the sage alerting R. Simeon ben Gamliel, *garas* and *tane* the text twice, but he only "stretched" it (*pashaṭ*) once, since, as mentioned, this verb refers to the opening of the scroll, which he had to open only once.

The reading 'גלי' in the standard edition of the Talmud is not found in some manuscripts, e.g., *Paris* 1337; or in Levine's edition, *IShG,* p. 25; instead of which they read: 'פתח תנא/פתח תני.' This reading is also found in *Teshubot ha-Ge'onim,* ed. R. Nathan Coronel, p. 15. However, in ms. *Munich* 95, and in the Constantinople ed. of *IShG,* noted by Levine ibid, n. 11, we find 'גלי.' I am inclined to believe that the standard edition bears the original version. To begin with, the expression 'פתח תנא/פתח תני' is *not* Talmudic and is found nowhere else in rabbinic literature. Probably, a later copyist of *IShG* thought that 'גלי' would be difficult for the average reader to understand, and changed it for the easier 'פתח תנא/פתח תני.' Support for our interpretation is the statement, 'Erubin 53a: "Because Judeans published the tractate (גלו מסכתא), their studies (תורתן) stay solid in their hands." Namely, the fact that they published the text that was taught, making it available to everyone to further study and review it, made it possible to master the tractate and not to forget it in the course of time; see *R. Nissim Ga'on,* ed. Shraga Abramson (Jerusalem: Mekize Nirdamim, 1965), pp. 133–134, and below appendix 58.

The idea of *publishing* the text, before proceeding to analyze it, underlies the method for teaching Talmud at the traditional *Yeshiba.* As it was reported by R. Sherira Gaon, *IShG, Liqquṭim,* V, p. xxviii:

> (Before) every *Kalla* meeting we assemble the teachers (אלו־פים) and sages (of the *Yeshiba*) and enunciate (גורסים) [that is with the correct pronunciation and intonation] the tractate

> (to be studied) at the *Kalla*. And we further publish (מגלים) another tractate [that will be studied in the next *Kalla*] (see appendix 53).

The purpose of publishing (מגלים) in advance the tractate to be studied at the *Kalla* meeting, was to ensure that the prospective students would be learning the correct text, see section V, n. 56; rather than memorizing a faulty "student's vernacular version" (שיטפא דתלמידאי תרביצאי), see Section V, n. 27. On these sort of versions, see *Teshubot Ge'onim Qadmonim*, ed. David Cassel (Berlin, 1848), #78, 23b (= *Oṣar ha-Ge'onim*, Berakhot, #318, p. 113); #81, 26a; *Teshubot ha-Ge'onim ha-Ḥadashot*, #97, p. 98; and the editor's note ad loc., citing ibid #98, pp. 101–102; #149, p. 205; *Oṣar ha-Ge'onim*, Berakhot, #244, p. 88; *Ba-Merkazim*, p. 131, etc.

I would like to mention, in passing, that a similar method was used in Sephardic and Oriental *Yeshibot* until recently. The teacher would first enunciate (גורס) the text of the lesson. Next, the text would be repeated by an advanced student acting as his assistant (equal to the Talmudic *sadrana*? Cf. above appendix 36). After that, it would be recited over again and again by the entire class, until all the nuances of pronunciation and intonation were mastered. Only then would the teacher begin to explain and analyze the text. That was the method by which the writer of these lines was initiated into the study of Talmud. Later on, I had the opportunity to learn that the same method had been used in other such schools (with the exception of *Porat Yosef*, which was never representative of the Sephardic tradition, Talmudic or otherwise. Their contempt for the study of Scripture may serve as an indicator). For a glimpse on the traditional Sephardic *Yeshibot*, see José Faur, "*Hora'at ha-Talmud ba-Masoret ha-Ḥinnukhit ha- Sfaradit*," *Shebile Ḥinnukh*, 35 (1975), pp. 177–178.

The root GLH in the sense of 'publication' is found in Jer. 32:11, 14, in reference to an "open bill of sale" (*sefer ha-galui*) certifying the purchase of land by Prophet Jeremiah. On the basis of Baba Batra 160b, Rashi ad loc. explains *ha-galui* as a bill,

> ... which had been certified by the Court, on the basis of [having verified the signature] of the witnesses. Moreover, the judges wrote and signed an authorization, which in effect was the certification of the bill. Unveiling (*galui*), and thereby publishing, the matter in case the witnesses would die.

R. Se'adya Gaon used *Sefer ha-Galui* as the title of one of his works (ed. Abraham E. Harkavi, St. Petersburg, 1892), standing for "Open Letter," i.e., a work that may be read and quoted by all. (The same applies to *IShG, Liqquṭim*, IV, p. xxvii: אגרת פתוחה; and "שתי אגרות פתוחות" in *Ba-Merkazim*, p. 98: see ibid. pp. 43, 95, 96, 174.) R. Joseph Qimḥi (ca.1105–ca. 1170), too, entitled one of his works *Sefer ha-Galui* (Berlin, 5247/1877). In the sense of "official publication," *galui* is used in Est. 3:14; 8:13 (LXX: *ekthentes*). The document in question was an official "edict" (Aramaic version: *diatagma*, a loan term from the Greek; see *A Dictionary of Greek and Latin Legal Terms in Rabbinic Literature*, pp. 79–81, 210), requiring 'oral promulgation' to become effective; see above appendix 28. It should be pointed out that the *Targum Sheni* on Est. 3:14 has *itgele*. Finally, in Megilla 3b, when God reproached Jonathan ben 'Uzziel for publishing the *Targum* to the *Prophets*, He said to him: "Who *gilla* my secrets to the public."

For a different interpretation of *galle*; see Professor Shraga Abramson, *Perush R. Ḥanan'el la-Talmud* (Jerusalem: Vagshal, 5755/1995), p. 114; and *R. Nissim Ga'on*, p. 134 n. 7.

# 42. TQN (תקן)

Scripture states that King Solomon "*TiQqeN* (תקן) many proverbs" (Eccl. 12:9). This verb is commonly used in rabbinic literature in the sense of 'instituting' a statute; see Baba Qamma 82a, etc. Consequently, a properly instituted 'ordinance' or 'statute' is designated *TeQaNa* (תקנה). Occasionally the verb is used for 'establishing' a public institution, Shabbat 33b. More significantly, and in the light of its Scriptural sense, it was used for 'establishing' an 'authoritative text'; see for example, Berakhot 48b. God, too, *TiQqeN* the Tora for Israel; see Bemidbar Rabba, XIV, 11, 61d. According to *Midrash Tehillim* XIX, 2, 82b, Moses did the same with respect to the liturgy. The rabbis (Yebamot 64b) report that R. Judah ha-Nasi *TaQqiN* "the Mishna" (תקין מתניתין). A similar expression (תקין הא מתניתא) was used in Horayot 13b. R. Sherira Gaon used the same verb to indicate the 'authoritative text' of the Mishna; see *IShG*, pp. 17, 36, 41, 50; cf. Introduction, *Sefer ha-Mafteaḥ*, 3a. For *TiQqeN* in the sense of 'editing, publishing,' see the *responsum* in *Geonica*, vol. 2, p. 28. Liturgical expressions, such as '*le-TaQqeN* (לתקן) the world with the Kingdom of God,' do not mean 'to fix,' as per popular wisdom, but 'to organize, to establish firmly'; cf. Dan. 4:33. I would like to call attention to the fact that in the Yemenite liturgy we have: *le-TaKkeN* (לתכן), 'to be firmly established,' as in I Sam. 20:31; Ps. 96:10, etc.

The Hebrew *mashal* (root MShL), usually translated as 'metaphor,' and 'proverb,' is connected to *moshel*, 'ruler, legislator,' because the ideal government, as per Eccl. 12:9, governs by issuing 'aphorisms' (including both the idea of 'metaphor' and 'proverb') to guide the people. In this sense, *mashal* is an 'analogy that governs,' best understood in the light of Justice Cardozo's remark concerning the two forms of legal analogies, *The Paradoxes of Legal Science*, p. 8:

> The one searches for the analogy that is nearest in point of similarity, and adheres to it inflexibly. The other, in its choice of the analogy that shall govern, finds community of spirit more significant than resemblance of externality.

"This process of reasoning from the sample to the whole species," noted Justice Cardozo, ibid. p. 9, "is induction." Given that the halakha of the Mishna, too, serves as an 'analogy that governs,' this was, precisely, the method applied by the rabbis in their interpretation of the Mishna. We can now better appreciate the fact that R. Sherira Gaon used this verb not only in reference to the authoritative text of the Mishna, but also to indicate the *norms* that were 'established' by the editor of the Mishna by which to decode the text of the Mishna; see *IShG*, pp. 52, 53. It may be of some interest to note that Spanish speaking Sepharadim translate *halakha*, when referring to a paragraph of the Mishna, as 'aphorism' and 'apothegms.' The proximity *tiqqen*/aphorism-apothegms/*mashal* may explain the traditional 'chanting' of *halakha* (as chanting a *mashal* and an edict or *teqana* when proclaimed by the herald), see Tosefta Ohalot 16:8, p. 614; Para 4:7, p. 633; Sanhedrin 99b; Megilla 32a, etc. This is the place to remind the reader that the Mishna was chanted with a special melody; see *Golden Doves*, p. 96. This tradition was preserved in some communities in the Sabbath services, and in the recitation of Abot in the weeks between Passover and Shabu'ot.

# 43. The Introduction of the Monetary System in Rabbinic Tradition

The rabbis attributed the introduction of the monetary system to Patriarch Jacob; see Shabbat 33b; cf. *Em la-Miqra*, vol. 1, 71b-72a; 108b-109a. It is important to take note that the rabbis, Shabbat 32b used the verb *TiQqeN* to describe the establishment of the monetary system, the same verb used for the publication of the Mishna; see appendix 42. In this respect, for the rabbis, as with Aristotle, banking and bank transactions were architectonic models for the exchange and evaluation of knowledge and ideas; see *Golden Doves*, pp. 142–145.

Both conceptually and linguistically, Hebrew 'coin' (*maṭbea'*, root ṬB') is connected to a 'signet' used to 'impress' on wax or clay (cf. Mishna Sanhedrin 4:5: טובע... מטבעות). On the relationship of 'signet' to 'coins,' see George Macdonald, *Coin Types* (Glasgow: James Maclehose and Sons, 1905), pp. 43–45. In the Ancient Near East, seals were used as early as the fourth millennium; see Cyrus H. Gordon, *Adventures in the Nearest East*, p. 78, which were "tantamount to its owner's signature." Cylinders were pierced down the middle and suspended on a cord around the neck, see ibid. p. 79. Attention should be drawn to the fact that the signet served to identify the party in question; see *The Economy of Literature*, p. 33, and provided the 'symbol' of a transaction, ibid. p. 34 – as we find with "the seal and thread" in the story of Judah and Tamar, Gen. 38:18, 26.

Therefore, 'coin' (מטבע) stood for 'pattern, structure'; see *Golden Doves*, pp. 138–142. In rabbinic tradition, the human soul is God's "seal" (Mishna Sanhedrin 4:5); cf. "Allegorical Interpretation," I, 43–55, *Philo*, vol. 1, pp. 177–183; "The Posterity and Exile of Cain," 98, vol. 2, p. 383; "On the Giants," 66, vol. 2, p. 479; "Noah's Work," 18–20, vol. 3, p. 223, etc. For some background literature, see Wolfson, *Philo*, vol. 1, p. 75. Hence, the idea of archetypes in Philo and rabbinic tradition. Finally, it should be pointed out that according to both the rabbis and Philo, God's seal equals "truth," see Shabbat 55a; Philo, "Noah's Work," 18, vol. 3, p. 223. Therefore, it is subject to forgery and falsification; see 'Aboda Zara 54b; Philo, "The Worse Attacks the Better," 35–40, vol. 2, pp. 227–233, etc.

# 44. Oral Law

See Shabbat 31a; Yoma 28b; Berakhot 5a. On the differences between *Tora she-bi-Khtab* and *Tora she-be-'al Pe*, see R. Moses di Ṭrani, *Qiryat Sefer*, vol. 1 (New York, 1953), Introduction, chapter 2; *Iyye ha-Yam*, 8d-10a; Saul Lieberman, *Hellenism in Jewish Palestine*, pp. 83–99. On their legal status, see *Golden Doves*, pp. xxv-xxvi. For an overview of their content and general history, see *Judaism*, vol. 1, pp. 234–280.

The expression *Tora she-be-'al Pe* is not found in the Yerushalmi. It appears only three times in the Babylonian Talmud: in Yoma 28b, Giṭṭin 60b, and Qiddushin 66a. The *barraita* in Shabbat 31a is Babylonian; see *AdRN*, A, XV, p. 60, from whence this tradition originates. The expression 'two Toras' (שתי תורות) in *Sifra*, *Be-Ḥuqqotai*, X, 8 (12), 122a and *Sifre* #351, p. 408, connoting one written Law and another oral Law, is late. It would be well to remember that both these works were edited by Rab (see Introduction, *MT* l. 66) and brought to the Holy Land by one of his disciples; see Yebamot 72b, cf. Shebu'ot 41b. In the citation from R. 'Aqiba (Shebu'ot 29a), 'תורות' stands for the plural of 'precepts' – not of 'Law.' In Tosefta Ḥagiga 2:9, p. 384 and Soṭa 14:9, p. 238, 'שתי תורות' stands for 'dissension' – not 'two Laws.'' cf. Y. Sanhedrin I, 4, 19c.

In Giṭṭin 60b, the idea of 'two Laws,' one written and another oral, is associated with R. Johanan's circle, Tiberias late 3rd and beginning 4th century; see appendix 45. It was introduced by R. Judah b. Naḥmani in a homily, referred to as '*darash*,' 'exposed.' The sense of this term is 'presentation to the general public,' rather than to members of the *Yeshiba*; see R. Jonah ibn Jannaḥ, *Sefer ha-Shorashim*, p. 114 in the name of R. Samuel ben Ḥofni Gaon; cf. Harkavi, *Zikhron la-Rishonim* III (1880), p. 25. This may explain why this idea was not recorded in the Yerushalmi. There is an allusion to this concept in Y. Pe'a II, 6, 17a; again, connected to R. Johanan's circle. The references to 'two Laws' in the Midrash are late, most probably coming from R. Johanan's circle. Let us point out that the homily in Giṭṭin 60b and Temura 14b about the "two Laws," reported as from '*Debe R. Yishma'el Tana*,' are *not* from R. Ishmael. As noted in *Kelale Shemu'el*, s.v. *masoret*, 10a, a tradition reported as *Debe R. Yishma'el Tana* is not authoritative. It means: '*someone* from the school of R. Ishmael has reported.' (In contradistinction to *Tana Debe R. Yishma'el*, meaning: 'it was reported by the school of R. Ishmael. This meets the objections raised by *Tosafot*, Pesaḥim 5a s.v. *dibre*; cf. *Yad Mal'akhi*, p. 164.)

The preceding runs contrary to the view of Abraham Rosenthal, "Tora she-'al pe," in eds. Moshe Bar-Asher and David Rosenthal, *Meḥqerei Talmud*, vol. 2 (Jerusalem: The Hebrew University, 1993), p. 448 n. 5.

# 45. Writing the Oral Law

The sources and principal ideas on the subject were developed by R. Israel Moses Ḥazzan, *Iyye ha-Yam*, 76a-119b, to which this study is much indebted. For reasons too painful to be spelled out here, many distinguished scholars writing on the subject 'borrowed' most of their material and ideas from this sage, without due acknowledgement. There is one worthy exception; see Professor Y. Sussman, "*Tora she-be-'al Pe*," *Meḥqerei Talmud*, vol. 3, part I (2005), pp. 209–384.

The 'prohibition' against writing the 'Oral Law' is the invention of medieval commentators and modern scholars, with no basis in rabbinic texts. It would suffice to point out that *none* of the early codifiers registered such a prohibition. (Maran, refers to it casually in *Shulḥan 'Arukh, Oraḥ Ḥayyim* #49:1 and #53:14; cf. *Kesef Mishne* on *Tefilla* 12:8.) In this regard, attention should be called to R. Ḥayyim Abul'afya, *Miqra'e Qodesh* (Izmir, 5482/1722), 124a-b, who concluded that this 'prohibition' could not possibly be Scriptural. (In his *Yishrash Ya'aqob*, Izmir 5489/1729, 91b, he registered the view that it is indeed a Scriptural prohibition, and accordingly raised a question which was left unanswered. Although this work was printed seven years later, it does not necessarily represent the later views of this sage. A careful reading of both these works will show that they were written more or less at the same time. It is rather obvious that the view proposed in *Miqra'e Qodesh* is a *consequence* of the question that he posed in *Yishrash Ya'aqob* and it therefore represents his final conclusion.)

We may therefore ask: what could the rationale of such an

injunction be within the cultural perimeters of the 'People of the Book?' The question is particularly poignant upon noticing that the possibility of memorizing the entire rabbinic corpus belongs to the realm of myth (see *Iyye ha-Yam,* 101a; and above appendix 32). It was designed to beguile the credulous, rather than instruct. The Chief Editor of the Talmud, referring to mortals like himself and his colleagues, noted how difficult it was to retain the sacred texts: "[Our efforts] in regard to forgetfulness is like pressing down mustard seeds with a finger" ('Erubin 53a). R. Ḥanan'el, ad loc. (*Perush,* p. 117b) explained:

> As when someone presses his finger on mustard seeds and the like and makes a dimple, but upon lifting his finger the dimple fills up immediately. The same applies to us, no sooner do we complete a (Talmudic) Tractate and commence another that we forget the previous (tractate) (cf. *'Arukh* s.v. *eṣba'*).

See above, appendix 32.

In the long history of Jewish scholarship, there is only one single individual about whom it is possible to verify on the basis of his writings – not on the basis of fables by legendary pundits – that he had a total mastery of the entire rabbinic corpus. That individual is Maimonides, who represents the finest rabbinic memory in history. (This view was confirmed to me by the finest rabbinic memory known to me, the late Professor Saul Lieberman.) Here is what Maimonides had to say about the likelihood of knowing the Talmud by heart, in his Introduction, to *Perush ha-Mishnayot,* vol. 1, p. 48: "It is not within human faculty for any man to know the entire Talmud by heart." In a letter addressed to R. Pineḥas, a judge in Alexandria, Maimonides disallowed the possibility of knowing the rabbinic corpus by heart, *Iggerot,* vol. 2, p. 444:

> ... since there is no man on earth with the power to remember the entire Babylonian Talmud and the Yerushalmi as well as

> the three *Barraitot* [Tosefta, *Sifra*, and *Sifre*; see *Golden Doves*, p. 96] which are the bases of the law.

Cf. *MT Talmud Tora* 1:10.

Ḥagiga 3a reports a story about two mute students at the time of R. Judah ha-Nasi. Upon their recovery, it was discovered that they had mastered the major rabbinic collections, including "Talmud." It should be recalled, however, that at the time our 'Talmud' had not yet been compiled (see below appendix 48). Even if conceding, for argument's sake, the possibility of a legendary mastermind surpassing the Chief Editor of the Talmud and his colleagues, how could a non-genius memorize what Maimonides declared to be humanly impossible? There is no evidence that Talmudic students were gifted with supernatural memory. To ensure that the Tora "would not be forgotten from Israel," R. Ḥiyya would "recite the Six Orders" of the Mishna to six children, probably because it would have been difficult to find a single student who could remember the entire Mishna; see Baba Meṣi'a 85b. Students and scholars had to work hard to prepare the Mishna, see Ta'aniyot 8a and cf. Ḥagiga 9b, and memorize the lecture; see Berakhot 28a, Pesaḥim 72a, Megilla 7b, Baba Qamma 117a. The lessons they studied needed to be reviewed periodically, lest they would be forgotten; see Berakhot 38b, Pesaḥim 68b, Ḥolin 86b, Keritot 27a; cf. *Golden Doves*, p. 96. Failing to review regularly, the student would forget his studies, see Shabbat 147b. Finally, the public was not impressed by someone who could rattle off by memory a rabbinic text and not know what he was saying; see Soṭa 22a. R. Johanan, Shabbat 114a, said that a young scholar "who could respond to any question that he was asked, even in the tractate [that was being studied presently] in the *Kalla* session (see above chapter 48) may be appointed as a public leader. If only in a single tractate, [he could be appointed] to a local position; if in the entire curriculum, [he could be appointed] to the *Yeshiba*'s Faculty." (For an analysis of that passage, see *Sefer ha-'Ittim*, pp. 246–248.) Remarkably, such a scholar was not required to know by heart the entire rabbinic corpus! Similarly, what sages of the rank of R. Isaac Alfasi expected from students was to be familiar with basic rabbinic texts and ideas. With this goal in mind, sages throughout the ages produced different compendia of the Oral Law to help students become conversant with the laws. See Maimonides, Introduction, *MT* l. 170, where he expressed the hope that his work could help the students to have the halakhot sufficiently well "organized" (סדורים), so that they could be easily cited – not quoted – by heart. The correct translation of the Introduction, *Sefer ha-Miṣvot*, p. 3, is: "to facilitate the memorization by heart, some of it [the *MT*] to someone who so wishes."

More to the point, the rabbis never declared that it was 'forbidden' (אסור) to write the Oral Law. We read in two places in the Babli (but not in the Yerushalmi!): "written words you may not (אי אתה רשאי) say them by heart; oral words you may not (אי אתה רשאי) say them in writing." Before proceeding to analyze the content of this statement, let us point out that "you may not" (אי אתה רשאי) is not synonymous with 'forbidden' (אסור). Rather, it stands for 'improper' (אינו רשאי; see Mishna Berakhot 7:4); 'inappropriate' (Mishna Berakhot 1:4; cf. Mishna Berakhot 5:4; see Yebamot 7a, Nazir 34b, Sanhedrin 53a, Zebaḥim 49a, etc.) – but it does not denote a formal 'prohibition' (אסור). Often it appears as an instruction given by a higher authority (God, the Law, the judiciary) when addressing members of the court; see Tosefta Sanhedrin 1:8, p. 415, Sanhedrin 6b-7a, Y. Sanhedrin VII, 4, 24c; or in a judicial directive addressed by the court to the general public, Tosefta 'Aboda Zara 2:1, p. 462; *Mekhilta, Mishpaṭim,* (*Massekhta di-Nziqim*) I, p. 248; III, p. 259; (*Massekhta di-Khaspa*) XIX, p. 319; *Mekhilta de-R. Shim'on b. Yoḥai*, p. 146; Pesaḥim 51a, Giṭṭin 88b; Nedarim 15a , Qiddushin 18a, etc. We hope to show that the meaning of 'אי אתה רשאי' in our case is the same as in the rule concerning the status of a parchment on which was "written the *Hallel* or *Shema'* for a child to study, (that) although he is not permitted (אינו רשאי) to do (so), (nonetheless) they defile the hands," i.e., they have the status of a canonically valid text; see Tosefta Yadayim 2:11, p. 683 and *MT She'ar Abot ha-Ṭum'a* 10:9.

We will now proceed to examine the above statement. Let us begin by noting the symmetrical construction of the sentence: [a] "written words you may not say them by heart, [b] oral words you may not say them in writing," whereby a/b stand parallel to one another. Thus, if from [b] one were to conclude that it is forbidden to write oral words, then by symmetric logic it should follow [a] that it would be forbidden to quote Scripture unless read from a canonically written text – a patent absurdity! To circumvent this and similar difficulties it has been suggested that this 'prohibition' applies only "when officiating for others so that they could fulfill their religious obligation" (*Tosafot,* Temura 14b s.v. *Debarim*). It would then follow that if someone *is* officiating in the Synagogue on behalf of the congregation, he should recite the *Shema'* prayer, as well as other material coming from Scripture, from a canonically written scroll (see Ta'aniyot 28a). However, the rabbis reported that the High Priest at the Temple on the Day of Atonement recited orally a section of the Tora (Mishna Yoma 7:1). Likewise, during the *Ma'amadot* Services carried on by laymen at the Temple, portions of the Tora were recited by heart; see Mishna Ta'aniyot 4:3. For a brief description of these services, see Henry Malter, *Treatise Ta'anit* [Philadelphia: The Jewish Publication Society, 1978], p. 210, n. 230).

In the light of these and similar problems, exceptions were proposed (and further exceptions to the exceptions), with no textual basis; thus rendering the above rabbinic statement a case of whim, rather than a principle. In truth, this matter involves a fundamental methodological question. The attitude of offering offhand, dysfunctional explanations to avoid challenging texts, prevalent in some rabbinic and scholarly circles, is not helpful. The result is general disorientation, rather than instruction. For a rundown of the standard 'explanations,' see *Tosefta Ki-Fshuṭah,* vol. 3, p. 202. The presumption of a personal 'obligation' to read or to hear the reading of the Scroll of the Tora is without basis either in the Talmud or the classical codifiers; see José Faur, "*'Aliyat Qaṭan li-Qro ba-Tora,*" *Studies in Memory of the Rishon le-Zion R. Y. Nissim,* vol. 1 (Jerusalem: Yad ha-Rab Nissim,

5745/1985), pp. 123–133. There is, however, a *miṣva* to read the Megilla, which is part of Scripture. Explicitly, the Mishna Megilla 2:1 stipulates that if someone had recited it by heart and not from a properly written scroll, he had not fulfilled the *miṣva*. Yet, when the rabbis inquired what the justification for such a rule was, they were offered some exegesis (Megilla 18a). Now, if there was in fact a 'prohibition' to recite the Scripture by heart, why did the rabbis not justify the above rule by citing the principle, "written words you may not (אי אתה רשאי) say them by heart?"

It is an indisputable fact that rabbinic material was written and studied. The *tanna* was proverbially known for "spelling the words in full"; see 'Aboda Zara 9a, b and *'Arukh* s.v. *sefer* (2). In the *Sifra* (Codex Assemani LXVI), with super linear vocalization (the copying of it was completed in the year 1123), the copyist registered: 'end of *megilla*' (pp. 66, 128, 250, 287, 311, 335, 413; occasionally he also registered the end of one *megilla* and the beginning of the next (see pp. 335–336, 468), indicating, thereby, that the text was copied from scrolls. R. 'Aqiba, too, rehearsed (*shone*) the lessons by the light of a fire, *AdRN*, A, XII, p. 29, indicating, thereby, that he was reading from a written text. Likewise, the rabbis taught "that the moon was specially created for *girsa*," 'Erubin 65a, indicating that students rehearsed their lessons from written material. We have mentioned before (appendix 41) the case in which a sage obtained a copy of a tractate 'Oqaṣin and "stretched" (פשט) it before he recited it, indicating that the tractate was written in a scroll. In addition to *Megillat Setarim* (see above appendix 40), and *Megillat Ta'anit* (see *Golden Doves*, pp. 102–103), we are informed about a scroll known as *Megillat Ḥasidim* quoted favorably by the rabbis (Y. Berakhot IX, 5, 14d; *AdRN* B, XXVI, p. 52). The rabbis reported about private "notebooks" (פינקס) written by sages; see Shabbat 156a; Y. Ma'aserot II, 3, 49d, and *Iyye ha-Yam*, 114b. Jewish authorities sent epistles from Israel to their coreligionists in Babylonia, informing them about judicial decisions; see Shabbat 115a, Baba Batra 41a, Sanhedrin 29a, Shebu'ot 48b, and *IShG*, pp. 89–90. Rab penned a question to R. Judah ha-Nasi, "between the threadstitches" of a scroll, Ketubot 69a; see *Iyye ha-Yam*, 79b. By specifying that the threads were made of cotton (חיטי), the rabbis were teaching that the scroll did not contain Scripture (cf. Megilla 19a-b), but rabbinic material. Moreover, as noted in *Iyye ha-Yam*, 114a, the Talmudic expression, "he went out, he searched, and found" (נפק, דק ואשכח) describes a sage finding a hitherto unknown tannaitic text (Zebaḥim 58a, Ḥolin 6a, 31b). Likewise, the expression, "he came [to the *Yeshiba*] bringing in hand a tannaitic text" (אתא ואתי מתניתא בידיה; see Shabbat 19a, 145b; Baba Qamma 42a; 'Aboda Zara 50a, b; etc.), indicates that there were reliable archives containing rabbinic material. Occasionally, a sage finding a reliable tannaitic text would certify it before presenting it at the *Yeshiba*. Thus, the expression, "he arrived (at the *Yeshiba*) holding a tannaitic text in his hand" (אתא, ואייתי מתניתא בידיה), Shabbat 19b, 145b, Sukka 54a, Beṣa 26b, Yebamot 57a, 58a, Soṭa 24b, Baba Qamma 42a, 'Aboda Zara 50a-b, Ḥolin 68b, Bekhorot 17a, Nidda 5b, 21a-b.

The rule "written words, you may not (אי אתה רשאי) say them by heart; oral words, you may not (אי אתה רשאי) say them in writing," is first mentioned in Giṭṭin 60b. It appears at the head of a three-string homily (a/b/c) [= דרשה משולשת] on the verse "…Write for thee **these** (אלה) words, for on the basis of **these** (אלה) words, I am contracting a covenant with you" (Ex. 34:27). The three homilies were brought together to highlight the pre-eminence of oral tradition. Homily (a) –which is the main subject of this analysis – was said by R. Judah b. Naḥmani (3rd and 4th centuries): "written words, you may not (אי אתה רשאי) say them orally; oral words, you may not (אי אתה רשאי) say them in writing." Homily (b) is a *barraita* reported by someone from the school of R. Ishmael. By focusing on the deictic pronoun "[write for thee] **these** (אלה) words" (Ex. 34:27), as if God were actually pointing at the Scroll of the Tora, homily (b) proposes that **these,** i.e., the words of the Tora, and only **these**, may be put in writing, "but you may not write halakhot" (as to the specific meaning of halakhot, see below). Homily (c) by R. Johanan is directed against Christians, who appropriated the Scripture but discarded the oral tradition of Israel; see Section IV n. 120. The Talmud does not indicate the context of R. Judah b. Naḥmani's homily (on the original context, see below). From *Midrash Tanḥuma, Vayyera*, VI, vol. 1, pp. 87–88, we learn that this rule was applied to the *Targum* (Aramaic translation of the Tora). Specifically, that " … oral words," i.e., the *Targum* (which has the status of 'Oral,' see appendix 61), should not be recited from a written copy. (R. Joseph, who was blind and could not read the Tora, was renowned for his expertise on the *Targum*, a text that had to be recited orally, see Baba Qamma 3b (the comments by Rashi and *Tosafot* ad loc. s.v. *ki-dmetargem* are unintelligible to me). Conversely, "written words," i.e., the text of the Tora, "should not be recited by heart" (see editor's notes ibid.). Connected with this homily is a case mentioned in Y. Megilla IV, 1, 74d (cited by R. Isaac Alfasi, *Halakhot, Megilla* 14a), concerning "a scribe who was *copying* the *Targum* from a book" (the standard interpretation that the scribe was *reciting* the translation from a book, is wrong; cf. *Iyye ha-Yam*, 114b-115a). The scribe intended to produce a copy of the *Targum* to be used at the services. Since this contravened R. Judah b. Naḥmani's rule, the scribe was reprimanded. In this connection, we should point out that R. Isaac ibn Ghayyat and Maimonides expanded this principle to include the *qere* and *ketib* versions of Scripture, where some words are 'written' (הכתיב) one way but are to be 'recited' (והקרי) in another way. Therefore they ruled that in such cases, "written words," i.e., the 'כתיב' should not be said instead of the oral version 'הקרי'; and conversely, the oral version 'הקרי' should not be written in the scroll in place of the standard 'כתיב'; see *Golden Doves*, pp. 101–102.

The second source citing R. Judah b. Naḥmani's rule is Temura 14a-b. It concerns a passage dealing with what appeared to be two contradictory sources, as to whether or not libations and other sacramental paraphernalia (מנחת נסכים) could be offered at sunset. Unable to resolve the contradiction, R. Joseph, head of the *Yeshiba*, instructed: "erase מנחת נסכים" from one of the sources. (It should be noted that the verb 'erase' (סמי) used in this conjunction indicates that the text was indeed written; cf. *IShG*, p. 56.) On a visit to the Holy Land one of the participants in the discussion learned of another source according to which the emendation would be unnecessary. He said: "If I had an epistle (at hand) I would have mailed it to R. Joseph, saying: you don't (need to) erase מנחת נסכים." The Talmud then asks a question based on a string of three statements (see *Iyye ha-Yam*, 78b-79a), concerning the permissibility of writing an epistle notifying about an oral text. The first, in the name of R. Johanan, stipulates that those "writing halakhot are as if they burn the Tora, and whoever learns from them will have no reward." To further corroborate this point, homilies (a) and (b) mentioned above are cited. The answer is revealing: "A new matter is different." In support for this distinction the rabbis called attention to the fact that both R. Johanan and Resh Laqqish, "were in the habit of perusing a scroll of Aggada on the Sabbath."

The reply was right on target. R. Johanan's criticism was directed against scribes writing halakhot for students who preferred to learn this material from codices, rather than from certified transmitters (*mashne, tanna*). The rationale for this criticism is evident once we realize that *halakhot* is synonymous with 'Mishna.' (On the identity *halakhot*/Mishna, see Section IV, n. 132. The chapters of the Mishna are divided into *halakhot*; see standard editions of Yerushalmi, *Perush ha-Mishnayot*, etc. The current division of the Mishna into 'Mishna' (*sic*) is another index of the high acumen of the legendary masters of Talmudic lore.) As mentioned earlier, the Mishna, in quality of *oral publication*, required that the text be (i) conveyed orally by official transmitters, and (ii) thereafter by their certified students who, in turn, had learned the lesson by heart; see chapter 33. What R. Judah b. Naḥmani was saying is that just as the text of Scripture can only be conveyed and corroborated from an authorized codex (*taj*), the text of the Mishna, too, must be conveyed and corroborated from authorized transmitters (*tanna, mashne*) and their students. Put in precise formulation, this rule states: "Written words," i.e., the text of Scripture, "you may not say them," in the sense of authorized transmission, "by heart" but only from authorized codices. Conversely, "Oral words," that is the Mishna (and later on, the Talmud), "you may not say them in writing." The reason is obvious. Prior to the destruction of the Temple, a work could be published by depositing (*manḥa*) an authorized copy in the National Archives; like *Megillat Ta'anit* that was "deposited" (*manḥa*) for all to read, to copy and cite; see 'Erubin 60b, *Iyye ha-Yam*, 80a and *Golden Doves*, p. 102. Post-Temple Jewry did not have such archives. Through a strategic decision, having enormous impact on the intellectual and political development of Israel, the publication of the Mishna instituted a new class of National Archives: the memory of the Jewish people. Hence R. Johanan's censure of scribes who produced codices designed to help students wishing to circumvent the official transmission of the *mashne* and *tanna* and learn the Mishna 'on their own.'

The concern was imminent in the light of Christian appropriation of Scripture and their subsequent claim to be *Verus Israel*; see above chapter 31. If the Mishna could be corroborated by a 'book,' in no time it would be appropriated by Israel's foes, who would then claim it as their own. R. Abin (3rd and 4th centuries), a distinguished disciple of R. Johanan, showed what could happen if the memory of Israel were canonized in a written text. In Y. Pe'a II, 6, 17a we read:

> If I (God) would have written most of my laws (= the Mishna), then you (Israel) could not be distinguished from impostors. 'What would the difference between you and the nations' be? These (the Jews) would put forward their Scroll (of the Tora) and these (the nations) would put forward their Scroll (of the Tora)! These (the Jews) would put forward their written notes [for the Mishna], and these (the nations) would put forward their written notes [for the Mishna]!

This passage should be read in conjunction with the passage from *Midrash Tanḥuma* cited in Section IV n. 120.

R. Johanan's criticism was balanced. He only rebuffed the conveyance and study of *halakhot* (= Mishna) from written codices, but not of other material. Evidence of this is the fact that he and Resh Laqqish would read from a scroll of Aggada on the Sabbath. This was also the legal basis for mailing an epistle to R. Joseph about 'מנחת נסכים': R. Johanan had only censured the transmission of a halakha! However, since the epistle was about "a new matter," not a halakha, "it is different" and not included in R. Johanan's censure; see *Iyye ha-Yam*, 81a. Accordingly, there were scholars who regularly used written material for Aggada, see Y. Kil'ayim IX, 3, 32b. And yet, R. Johanan and Resh Laqqish felt the need to excuse themselves for using a scroll of Aggada, by quoting Psalms (119:126). Why?

The need to find some justification lies in the fact that in their time there were scholars, like R. Joshua b. Levi (2nd and 3rd centuries), who opposed, totally and unequivocally, the teaching and study of Aggada from a written text. In Y. Shabbat XVI, l fol. 15c, we read:

> R. Joshua b. Levi said: Whoever writes an aggada has no portion in the world to come. Whoever comments upon it [the written text], will churn [in Hell, another version: מתברך 'is to be excommunicated']. Whoever hears it will receive no reward. R. Joshua b. Levi said: Except for once, I never looked at a book of Aggada. I looked at it and found it written and learned…, And yet, I am frightened at night. R. Ḥiyya b. Abba saw a book of Aggada, and said: 'If what is written is correct, let the hand that wrote it be cut off!' Someone [in the audience] told him: 'It was the father of that man [himself] who wrote it [and nothing happened to him!]' He replied: 'So, I said: Let the hand that wrote it be cut off! And so it came to pass [that that individual lost his hand], just "like an error which proceeded from a ruler" (Eccl. 10:5).

The opposition was not against the study of Aggada per se, but against the study of Aggada from a written text. Evidence of this is the fact that R. Joshua b. Levi is depicted as a master of Aggada; see Baba Qamma 55a. The reason, again, was motivated by the threat posed by the rise of heresy and ideologies bent on destroying Judaism. A 'book,' among the analphabetic and semi-literate, is a mighty amulet with magical – not literary – power. Thus, the opposition to *books* of Aggada, containing esoteric material that could be manipulated by unscrupulous ideologues. The following story in Y. Pesaḥim V, 3, 32a illustrates our point:

> R. Simlai came to R. Jonathan. He asked him: 'Teach me Aggada.' He answered him: 'I have a family tradition not to teach Aggada to either a Babylonian or to a Southerner, because they are arrogant and have little knowledge of Tora. And you are from Nehar De'a, and live in the South.

Finally, some sages believed that the study of Aggada in general was a waste of time. In Y. Ma'aserot III, 10, 51a, we read:

> Once, R. Ze'ira, R. Abba b. Kahana, and R. Levi were seated (studying Tora). R. Ze'ira was teasing those [who were studying] Aggada, and shouted at them: 'Books of Witchcraft!' R. Abba bar Kahana asked him: 'Why are you teasing them? Ask [them anything] and they will answer you [adequately]!'

R. Ze'ira asked a question to one of the students and a discussion ensued. At the end of the discussion, R. Ze'ira said to him:

> – 'Your explanation has spun over and over and it will keep on spinning,' i.e., 'there is nothing conclusive that one can learn from it [Aggada]!'

Turning to his son, he told him:

> – 'Jeremiah, my son, keep on studying (the rule) about 'Two figs on one stick' [a halakhic question that was being discussed at the *Yeshiba*] – which is more valuable than anything else!'

By reading Aggada from a *scroll*, R. Johanan and Resh Laqqish were defying their colleagues. Hence the need to offer some justification for teaching this material, particularly on the Sabbath (i.e., in public). For the critical text and notes on this passage, see Yehuda Felix, *Tractate Ma'aserot* (Heb.) (Ramat-Gan: Bar-Ilan University Press, 2005), pp. 173–174, and ibid, p. 7 n. 4.

In the area of contracts, rabbinic law distinguishes between two kinds of documentation, one intended 'to be written' (ניתנה להכתב), and a second 'not (intended) to be written' (לא ניתנה להכתב), see Harkavi, *Teshubot ha-Ge'onim*, #346, p. 175. There are some important differences between them. For our purposes, the principal difference is in the latitude of interpretation given to the court. A contract intended 'to be written' can be the object of wide interpretation, whereas if it was 'not (intended) to be written' it is to be strictly interpreted. [On the basis of this the theory, Maimonides distinguishes between certain declarations of the testator made orally, which must be strictly interpreted, and a written will that could be interpreted differently than the testator's intentions; see *MT Naḥalot* 6:2; cf. *MT Zekhiyya* 6:2.] The status of these documents is not affected by whether the contract was in fact put down in writing or not. Putting in writing a document that belongs to the 'not to be written' class will not affect its status, and vice versa; see *Golden Doves*, pp. 102–105. The same principle applies to the 'written' and 'oral' texts of Israel. Thus, we read in *The Mishnah of Rabbi Eliezer* (Heb.), VI, p. 122:

> ומפני מה נתנה התורה ממשלה לחכמים כל זאת? לפי שדברי נבואה נתנו להכתב ודברי חכמים לא נתני להכתב, אלא חכמים מורין אותן לתלמידיהן ולתלימידי תלמידיהן הלכה למעשה.
>
> How is it that the Tora vested the sages with (interpretive) authority? – Because the words of Prophecy [i.e. Scripture] are given to be written (ניתנו להכתב), whereas the words of the sages were not given to be written (לא ניתנו להכתב).

With this understanding in mind, R. Judah Almadari (13th-14th centuries) explained an enigmatic passage in Sanhedrin 99a, condemning someone who is "not attentive" (משגיח) – in the sense of not being sufficiently respectful – "of the Mishna." According to R. Almadari this passage addresses people "who belittle it (the Mishna), as if it would not be fundamental, since it was given orally and was not given to be written (לא ניתנה להכתב), while in fact it is the Word of God," *Sanhedre Gedola*, vol. 2 (Jerusalem: Makhon Harry Fischel, 5729/1969), p. 273; cf. *Shiṭṭa Mequbbeṣet* on Temura 14b n. 3.

Given that the Mishna and Talmud were not published 'to be written,' they retained their status of a non-book even when they were put in writing. In a *responsum* (*Teshubot* #92, 13a) addressing the status of written copies of the Talmud, R. Joseph ibn Megas wrote:

> …the Talmud is the explication and interpretation of the Tora – not the true [i.e., pristine, original] Tora. Can't you see that it (the parchment where the Talmud is written) does not have traced lines [the earmark of a 'book' in Jewish tradition] as the true Tora has? From this (fact) you can learn that its sanctity (of the text of the Talmud) does not compare to the sanctity of the Tora itself, or even to the sanctity of the other books of Scripture. Therefore, considering the facts that (such a volume) does not render the hands of those who touch it impure [see above appendix 5]; and furthermore, it does not require traced lines, [we may conclude] that one may not deposit it either on top of (a volume containing) the Hagiography, or on top of the Prophets, and of course not on top of the Tora.

Cf. R. David b. Abi Zimra, *Teshubot Radbaz,* 2 vols. (Warsaw, 5642/1882), vol. 1, Part II, #771; and Section IV, n. 161.

Concerning the status of portions of the Scripture that were not written in accordance with canon rules, matters are a little more complicated. There were Talmudic sages who regarded a scroll containing the *Haftaroth* (the portions of the Prophets to be read on the Sabbath), as a non-book. In their view, such a scroll cannot be used on the Sabbath, since "it was not given to be written" (לא ניתן להכתב). The final decision, however, was to uphold the dissenting opinion, and permit the usage of such a scroll (Giṭṭin 60a). This was not due to a special 'dispensation' (as per Catholic Canon law, see below appendix 46). Rather, this decision was in line with the ruling concerning the status of a small parchment containing a portion of Scripture, such as the "*Hallel* or *Shema'* written for a child to study, (that) although not permitted (אינו רשאי), nonetheless they defile the hands," i.e., they have the status of a canonically valid text; Tosefta Yadayim 2:11, p. 683; cf. *MT She'ar Abot ha-Ṭum'a* 10:9. I would like to point out that ancient inscriptions and documents from rabbinic times are not germane to the questions of whether the Mishna and Talmud were regarded as 'written.' The issue is a matter of *legal status,* not of historical fact.

In conclusion, the Mishna, and later on the Talmud, belong to the class of documents that were 'not given to be written.' This means, first and foremost, that unlike the text of Scripture that is to be conveyed and authenticated from certified copies (*taj*), the text of the Mishna and Talmud can be conveyed only from official oral transmitters (*mashne, tanna*); cf. Section IV, n. 159. This understanding can help us appreciate R. Johanan's strong words against those "writing *halakhot*," i.e., the Mishna. Since such students would be relying on written copies, these scribes were in essence "burning the Tora." The sense of R. Johanan's charge is clear upon realizing that the whole strategy against the Christian challenge rested on the principle that *Verus Israel* is to be identified through her National Memory – not through books. The scribes facilitating written copies of the Mishna were in fact thwarting rabbinic strategy. Students availing themselves of such codices were undermining the very basis upon which the Mishna rests: the link *halakha* → *qabbala* 'authoritative conveyance,' which is to be effected by a frontal, direct reception from teacher to student; in the same manner as when God 'kissed' Israel at Sinai and gave them the Oral Law (see above Appendices 32, 35). Thus,

R. Johanan added: "whoever learns from them [Mishna codices] will not receive reward." The rabbinic system of education was scrupulously maintained in the Geonic *Yeshibot*. In *IShG*, pp. 71–72 we read: "The Talmud and Mishna were not written," i.e., were not published to be transmitted in writing. Therefore, "the rabbis are careful to learn the *girsa* [of the Mishna and Talmud] by heart," that is, from certified transmitters, "not from written," i.e., pseudo-authoritative codices. In support of this tradition, R. Sherira Gaon cited the Talmud in Temura quoted above. This tradition was standard throughout the Near East, and it was followed in the *Yeshiba* established by R. Moses and his son R. Ḥanokh in Cordoba, see chapters 49, 51. In Sepharad, the text of the Talmud had been originally delivered by R. Neṭruna'e Nasi "by heart, not from writing"; see Section V, nn. 12–13. This tradition reflects the principle that the text of the Talmud ought to be conveyed by heart, from an authoritative transmitter, rather than from codices copied without the authority of the *Yeshibot*. That was the case in Sepharad, at least until the triumph of the anti-Maimonidean revolution when the sense of *qabbala* was vacated to make room for 'Kabbala' (see chapter 57). The change was only a first step in a process designed to transform the Tora into an amulet of super-magical power (see Section V). A few consequences resulting from this swap were noted by Maimonides in the *Guide* (see quotation in Section IV n. 173). We should call attention to the ancient institution of *Mishmara*, conducted every Sabbath afternoon, when the faithful gather to read a portion of the twenty-four books of the Hebrew Scripture and the Mishna. In this fashion, the text of the entire Hebrew Scripture and the Mishna is properly registered and transmitted to the community every single year. It is still scrupulously observed by some communities throughout the Middle East. The text of the *Mishmara*, and the sections to be read each Sabbath, have been recently edited in a work under the title, *Ḥoq le-Ya'aqob*, 2 vols. Jerusalem, 5755/1995.

# 46. Was there a 'Dispensation' to Write the Oral Law?

A consequence of the notion that it is forbidden to write the Oral Law is the view that a special dispensation was issued to sanction the writing of the Mishna, Talmud, and similar texts. This pivotal point was proposed by Rashi (Giṭṭin 60b s.v. *wu-dbarim*): "that it is not permitted to write the Talmud, but for the fact that otherwise the Tora would be forgotten." Obviously, Judaism, as all legal systems, recognizes that under special circumstances the authorities may issue exemptions or release someone from a legal obligation. Such exemptions, however, must be issued by either the political (*MT Roṣeah* 2:4; Sanhedrin 18:6) or judicial (*MT Roṣeah* 2:4) authorities – they cannot be inferred by an interested party! Moreover they must be temporary (*MT Sanhedrin* 24:4. For a survey of the principal sources and views on the subject, see *Encyclopedia Talmudit,* vol. 8, s.v. *hora'at sha'a*). Otherwise, they would be regarded as an 'abrogation' of the Law, and would contravene one of the fundaments of the Sinai-Moab *berit* (see *MT Mamrim* 2:4; and *Studies in the Mishne Tora,* p. 16). What is especially disturbing about such a claim, from the point of view of traditional halakha, is that such a 'dispensation' is not explicit anywhere in rabbinic sources. One would expect that license to break the law, particularly in such an exact system as rabbinic halakha, would warrant a clear statement on the subject, either by the Talmud or the Geonic authorities. The justification advanced by Rashi (Temura 14b s.v. *'et*), based on his interpretation of Ps. 119:126, that "when they do the thing for the sake of the sanctity of His Name, it would be worthy to annul Thy Tora, and it is better that it should be uprooted," sounds antinomian: through and through. In spirit, if not in fact, the notion that extenuating circumstances due to assumed mental and spiritual decay with the passing of time suffices, *ipso facto*, to abolish a law, seems to be modelled on the idea of 'dispensation' as per Church law, rather than anything remotely halakhic.

We shall now proceed to examine the alleged authorization to write the Oral Law. It is justified on the basis of Ps. 119:126: "It is time to act for God, (because) they have voided Thy Law." According to Rashi ad loc. this means: "that they transgress the words of the Tora in order to make a fence and boundary to Israel." See also R. Menaḥem Me'iri, *Perush Tehillim*, p. 247, etc., and subsequently Rashi on Giṭṭin 60a s.v. *'et*; *Tosafot* on Shabbat 115a s.v. *lo*; R. Zeraḥya ha-Levi, *Ha-Ma'or ha-Qaṭan*, ibid, s.v. *itmar*; etc. In his Introduction to *Megillat Ester* (Venice, 5352/1592), R. Isaac de Leon reiterated the often repeated litany that R. Judah the Prince "expounded" (דרש) the above-mentioned verse to justify "writing the Mishna." Such a *derasha* is an invention of commentators found nowhere in the Talmud. Similar 'justifications' to transgress a law for 'a good cause' was extended to other cases; see pseudo-Rashi on Keritot 8a s.v. *nikhnas*; Rabad on *MT Mamrim* 2:9; Riṭba on Yoma 69a, s.v. *wuba-medina*, and on Baba Meṣi'a 29b s.v. *tanu*; etc. So convinced were later commentators of the soundness of this doctrine, that they did not hesitate to apply it, as a matter of fact, to 'explain' some 'difficult' passages in Maimonides; see *Kesef Mishne* on *MT Talmud Tora* 3:10; *Maggid Mishne* on *MT Shabbat* 23:26; and *Leḥem Mishne* on *MT Meḥussare Kappara* 1:10.

Respectfully, I submit that the above interpretation is unacceptable on two grounds. First, as pointed out above, it is fundamentally antinomian. The idea (Rashi, Berakhot 54a s.v. *'et*) "that occasionally they abrogated (מבטלים) the words of the Tora to act on God's behalf" (cf. Rashi ibid. 63a s.v. *'et*, and Giṭṭin 60a s.v. *'et*) would make it possible to disrupt any legal system under the claim that one was acting for the "sake of Heaven," or for the "Sanctification of the Name of God," or to "safeguard" the Tora (see Rashi on Temura 14b quoted above). Who, exactly, is authorized to make such a claim is – to say the least – problematic. Second, this interpretation of Ps. 119:126 runs contrary to both its traditional interpretation as well as the literal sense of the verse; see *Targum* ad loc.; *Midrash Tehillim* CXIX, 57, p. 501; as well as R. Se'adya Gaon and R. Abraham ibn 'Ezra ad loc. For a concise summary of the various interpretations, see Radaq on Psalms, pp. 276–277. With all due respect, we will see that not only is the above interpretation not justified by rabbinic sources, but it actually runs contrary to what the Talmud explicitly taught about the subject.

The above verse was first cited in Mishna Berakhot 9:7 to justify why, at a time when Israel was in one of the bleakest periods of her history, almost to the point of extinction, the rabbis instituted a rule urging the use of God's name when greeting a friend. To justify this enactment, the rabbis cited the above verse to teach that precisely at a moment of crisis, when God seemed to have abandoned Israel, we should show courage and trust in Him (see Introductory Remarks, Section IV). Thus we should mention His name repeatedly in our daily greetings. The Mishna reads as follow:

> ...They (further) instituted that one should greet a friend with the Name (of God). As it is written: "and Boaz arrived from Beth Leḥem, and said to the harvesters: 'May God be with you" (Ruth 2:4... In addition it was said: "Do not feel embarrassed because your mother has aged" (Prov. 23:22). It is also written: "It is time to act for God; they have made Thy Law void" (Ps. 119:126). R. Nathan said: '(Have) they have made Thy Law void? (Then) it is time for God to act!'

Commenting on the Mishna and the addition brought in the name of R. Nathan, Raba, Berakhot 63a, remarked that this verse may be interpreted in either direction. "From beginning to end," as interpreted by the Mishna, in which case it means: "It is time to act for

God – right now! Why? – Because they have voided Thy Law!" Or "from end to beginning," as interpreted by R. Nathan, in which case it means: "They," [we shall give details later] "have voided Thy Law"; i.e., have declared Thine Law null and void. Therefore, "It is time for God to act," that is: He shall punish them. See *Midrash Tehillim* CXIX, 57, p. 501 and Radaq on Psalms, pp. 276–277.

To clarify the context of Raba's remarks we should note that the previous paragraph in the Mishna reports a rule instituted by the rabbis to contravene the *minim* ('heretics'). Our rule, too, was instituted with the same purpose in mind. According to a tradition transmitted by R. Hayye Gaon, these *minim* were antinomian heretics who regarded the Tora as null and void. R. Hayye Gaon knew the details. To make public their view, the *minim* were in the habit of publicly invoking the Holy Trinity in their daily greetings. In response to this challenge, the rabbis instituted that we should mention *God's* Name in our greetings.

> When the heretics (*ha-minim*) faltered, they (the rabbis) instituted that one should greet his friend with the Name (of God). The reason for (having instituted such a rule) is the sorry situation (confronting the Jews, to be specified in what follows). Accordingly, the rabbis wanted that God's name should always be on the lips of the people. [The rule was instituted] because in their greeting, the heretics (*ha-minim*) would say: 'May you be blessed by the Father, the Son, and the Holy Ghost!' (ברוך מר! לאבא, וברא, ורוחא דקודשא!). In response, the rabbis instituted that we should say: 'May God bless you!' (יברכך! ייי) – thus distinguishing our [mode of greeting] *'shalom'* [from that of the *minim*].

Quoted by R. Zachariah Aghamati, *Sefer ha-Ner* on *Berakhot* (British Museum, ms. 11361), fol. 50b. The attribution to R. Hayye Gaon is found ibid. fol. 51a.

Maimonides, *Perush ha-Mishnayot, Berakhot* 9:7, vol. 1, p. 91, further elucidated the purpose of citing Prov. 23:22:

> It comes to teach that one should not disregard the rules instituted by the sages, although a (particular) rule may be old and dated. To illustrate this point, they cited Solomon's proverb ("Do not feel embarrassed because your mother has aged," i.e., don't be disrespectful to the ancient Law of Israel simply because it is 'old'!).

This point addresses the claim that the 'Old' Testament is voided by a 'New' one simply because one is 'old' and the other is 'new.' Concerning the interpretation of Ps. 119:126 in Giṭṭin and Temura, see appendix 45.

# 47. Hebrew *Ḥibber* and Arabic *Tadwin*

For psychological, rather than intellectual reasons, Professor Abramson, *R. Nissim Ga'on,* p. 29 n. 2, failed to grasp the passage in *Sefer ha-Mafteaḥ,* 3b. There is no ambivalence or contradiction in the above, once we remember that Arabic speaking Jews used the Hebrew KTB not only in the general sense of 'writing,' but also as the semantic equivalent of the Arabic *tadwin,* 'to redact, to compile, to officially register.' See, for example, *Perush ha-Mishnayot,* Megilla 1:1, vol. 2, p. 344: *tadwin al-talmud*; cf. Bekhorot 4:4, vol. 5, p. 249. [In this sense, this term was used by R. Se'adya Gaon, in *Perush Mishle,* p. 194 (the Hebrew translation is faulty).] Similarly, according to a tradition recorded in *Sefer ha-'Ittim,* pp. 255–256, an illustrious sage, Prince R. Neṭruna'e b. Ḥakhina'e, who came to Spain from Babel around the year 770), "wrote (כתב) for the children of Sepharad the [text of the entire] Talmud by heart, not from a written [codex]." Here, the sense of the Hebrew 'writing' (כתב) is *tadwin* ('official compilation'). By emphasizing that it was transmitted "by heart, not from a written [codex]," the author was signaling that the conveyance of the text was done according to the proper procedure, and its authority derived from an authorized sage – not from a written codex! A more accurate translation of *tadwin* would be the Hebrew *ḥibber*; see *MT* Introduction, ll. 54–55, where Maimonides states that R. Judah the Prince "compiled [*ḥibber* = *tadwin*] ... the book of the Mishna."

Obviously, *ḥibber* here means 'redacted, officially registered,' since, as we have seen in Section IV n. 161, Maimonides disallowed such a [written] codex. Concerning the sage coming to Spain mentioned above, see Mordecai Margalioth, *Hilkhot Hannagid* (Heb.) (Jerusalem: The American Academy for Jewish Research, 1962), pp. 1–3.

# 48. *Gemara* and *Talmud*

The rabbis (Baba Batra 130b; Nidda 7b) established the following principle:

> One cannot learn a halakha either from the Mishna or from the Talmud or from a judicial act (מעשה) unless one had been instructed: 'implement (מעשה) [this]!' [cf. *Eliyahu Zuṭa* XVI, *Tana Debe Eliyahu*, part II (Lublin, 5657/1897), p. 132.]

This doctrine was codified by R. Isaac Alfasi (*Halakhot, Yebamot* 17a; cf. ibid. *'Erubin* 11b; *Baba Batra* 58b), who stipulated that this principle is valid even when the Mishna has explicitly declared that the halakha is like a particular opinion. The same view had been expressed earlier by *Halakhot Gedolot*, ed. R. E. Hildesheimer, vol. 2. (Jerusalem: Mekize Nirdamim, 1980), p. 56; vol. 3, p. 352. It was subsequently accepted by other authorities, see *Perush R. Ḥanan'el la-Talmud*, p. 319; Maimonides, *Perush ha-Mishnayot, Shebi'it* 9:5, vol. 1, p. 259; R. Joseph b. 'Aqnin, *Mebo ha-Talmud* (Jerusalem: 5727/1967), p. 5; cf. *Studies in the Mishne Tora*, p. 39 n. 46. A good example of this principle is Menaḥot 37b, where R. Judah transmits the halakha in the name of Samuel, and it is rejected without the citation of a single authority (ולית הלכתא כותיה)! Notably, it was dismissed by Saboraitic, i.e., post-Talmudic, authority. (For further analysis of this source, see appendix 53.)

There is, however, a responsum by the saintly R. Solomon b. Adrete, vol. 1, #335 explaining that the rabbis meant only to limit the authority of the Mishna when it contradicts a rule

> ... stipulated by the *Gemara* (= Talmud); e.g. if they [i.e., the Mishna] would have said: 'the law is like the minority opinion,' or 'the law is like R. Eleazar *v.* R. Joshua.' However, when it does not contradict an accepted rule, why should we not learn [the halakha] from it [i.e., the Mishna]?

That sort of explanation does not provide useful guidance. R. Me'ir Abul'afia, in his *Yad Rama* on Baba Batra 130b, called attention to the judicial principle that a judgment that "overlooks a matter in the Mishna, is reversible" (Sanhedrin 6a), implying thereby, that the Mishna is indeed authoritative. With reference to this, I would like to point out an important passage in *Sifra, Emor* VII, 9:3, 93b (cited by Rashi on Lev. 22:31; cf. ibid. *Aḥare Mot* VI, 12:10,74b; and *Sifre* #59, p. 125), on the verse "And you shall guard my *miṣvot*, and implement them" (Lev. 22:31). It runs as follows:

> *And you shall guard* (ושמרת) – these are the Mishna; *and implement them* – these are the implementation (of the *miṣvot*): Whatever is not in the Mishna is not (subject to) implementation.

The sense of this passage is that the execution of *miṣvot* requires adequate knowledge of the specific rules and regulations (see appendix 4), and that these rules are contained in the Mishna. Therefore, "Whatever is not in the Mishna is not (subject to) implementation," thus establishing the fact that the Mishna is the most authoritative source of halakha! Incidentally, as is often the case in Hebrew, *you shall guard* (ושמרת) is here interpreted 'to remember' – alluding to the fact that we must *guard* (ושמרת) the text of the Mishna by constant rehearsal and memorization.

One would like to know if there is substance – beyond R. Adrete's invocation – to the proposition that a later rabbinic rule could supersede the authority of a document published by the Supreme Court of Israel. The question is particularly poignant in view of the fact that the rabbis themselves taught that rules concerning the resolution of conflicts are not categorical; see ʿErubin 29a; Qiddushin 34a; and *Yad Mal'akhi* ##23–24. (Concerning the difference of opinion between Maimonides and Rabad on this matter, see *MT ʿArakhin* 1:6 and *Kesef Mishne* ad loc.) Finally, R. Adrete failed to address the rest of the passage stating that one may neither learn halakha from the Talmud!

To resolve the quandary posed by the principle, "One cannot learn a halakha either from the Mishna or from the Talmud …" some erased the 'ת' from תלמוד, rendering it למוד 'study'; see the commentaries of Rashbam, ad loc. s.v. *wu-mor sabar*; R. Zachariah Aghamati, *Tractates Baba Kamma …* (London: British Museum, 1961), 293a; and *Yad Rama*, ibid. To make this amendment consistent, other texts were also doctored; see *Halakhot Gedolot*, ed. R. E. Hildesheimer, vol. 3 (Jerusalem: Mekize Nirdamim, 1988), p. 352, and editor's note on *Halakhot Gedolot*, vol. 2, p. 56 n. 5. This permitted the commentators to establish such differences as 'before' and 'after' the Talmud was "written" (sic), etc. The doctored version, however, is not corroborated by early manuscripts; see Ch. Albeck, *Mabo la-Talmudim* (Tel-Aviv: Dvir, 1969), pp. 599–601. Rashi on Nidda 7b s.v. *ha*, proposed that "Talmud" in the above passage alluded to tannaitic material, and did not refer to *our* Talmud; cf. *IShG*, pp. 48–50. This view was accepted by other commentators; see Riṭba on Baba Batra 130b; etc.

R. Joseph ibn Megas (in his *Commentary to Baba Batra* 130b) proposed that "Talmud" in the preceding quotation alluded to the "Talmud" *before* it was edited by R. Ashe and his Court.

> Our Talmud constitutes a legislative pronouncement (הלכה למעשה). In view of the fact that it was edited after close reading and analysis, and [after] several redactions [see appendix 53], it is as if they would have said: 'it is a legislative pronouncement' (הלכה למעשה) – given that it was edited to be implemented!

This view was adopted by R. Zachariah Aghamati, on Baba Batra, ibid, 293 a; R. Joseph b. 'Aqnin, *Mebo ha-Talmud*, p. 5; *Yad Rama*, ibid, etc.

To bring out the concrete meaning of this statement, it would be helpful to bear in mind that in the Introduction to the *MT* (ll. 111–112), Maimonides wrote that R. Ashe not only "edited" (חיבר) the Talmud but also "concluded it" (גמרו, root GMR). In Jewish law, *GeMaR ha-din* stands for the [i] 'deliberation process' when the evidence and arguments are weighed (*MT Sanhedrin* 22:9); [ii] followed by the voting of the judges (*MT Sanhedrin* chapters 8–10; cf. 12:3); [iii] and concluding with the pronouncement of the verdict (*MT Sanhedrin* 21:3; 22:9; see *Kesef Mishne* on Sanhedrin 3:3; and ibid. 7:2, 11:8). After enumerating the different classes of law and judicial traditions edited in the Talmud (ll. 93–103), Maimonides emphasized (ll. 103–104) that R. Ashe edited the judicial determinations and traditions,

> which were adjudicated in the Court of that time, in accordance with the hermeneutical rules by which the Tora is explicated, and were decided by the elders [= members of the court], and concluded (גמרו) that the law is thus, all (of the preceding material) – from the days of Moses until his day – were edited (חיבר, see appendix 47) by R. Ashe in the Talmud.

See Introduction, *Perush ha-Mishnayot*, vol. 1, pp. 34–35, cited below. Maimonides' view stems from the tradition concerning the two revisions of the entire Talmud, conducted in the general assembly; see chapter 37 and below appendix 53. (The same applies to R. Joseph ibn Megas' statement quoted above, concerning the "several redactions" of the Talmud.)

The key term in the above quotation is 'גמרו,' root GMR. From the Aramaic translation of Job 22:22, we learn that 'גמר' stands for a 'lesson learned orally from an authorized instructor.' The verse reads: "**Receive, I pray thee, the Tora** from His (God's) mouth (קח-נא תורה מפיו)." The *Targum* rendered the first three words (קח-נא תורה), as

"*Gemar* thus the Law" (גמר כדון אוריתא). It would appear that a more literal translation would have been *qabbel* (קבל) – as it has been preserved in the more ancient *Targum to Job from Qumran Cave XI,* ed. Michael Sokoloff (Ramat-Gan: Bar-Ilan University, 1974), p. 40. [For a very valuable overview of the traditional *Targum* to Job, see Pinkhos Churgin, *The Targum to Hagiographa* (New York: Horeb, 1945), pp. 87–116.] I believe that the choice of *gemar* was intended to convey a fundamental aspect of 'oral transmission.' Namely, *gemar* does not merely refer to 'instruction,' but, specifically: 'instruction of the Law by the highest authority.' In this manner, the end of the verse, "and lay up His words in your heart," can be taken as exemplary of the classical rabbinic classroom, where the student was expected to memorize the lesson by heart. There is another aspect to this root. We had the opportunity to learn that "גמיר" in Ezra 7:12 parallels "עד תמם" in Deut. 31:24. For that reason, it also conveys the sense of being 'complete' and 'thoroughly redacted'; see Section II, n. 6. We can now appreciate the rabbinic expression "learned the lesson from the mouth" of an authorized teacher (גמר שמעתתא מפומיה דרביה כרחבה דפומבדיתא), Pesaḥim 52b, to indicate that the sage in question had been the recipient of 'an authoritative and thoroughly redacted lesson'; cf. Pesaḥim 104b; Beṣa 27a; Mo'ed Qaṭan 22a; Ḥagiga 15b; Ḥolin 50a, 124a; Nidda 48a. Finally, some sages associated *gemara* in the Talmud with the abovementioned *gemir* in Ezra 7:12; see *Midrash 'Ezra,* p. 128. In effect, in the Talmud, *gemara* stands for [i] a thoroughly edited lesson, which was [ii] formally approved by the *Yeshiba.* Its authority derives from the fact that thereafter it was [iii] 'instituted' (קבעו) in the official program of study, and therefore was known by academic tradition. Consequently, it was important to ascertain whether or not a lesson had been 'instituted in the *gemara*' (קבעיתו בגמרא, 'Erubin 32b). See 'Erubin 19a, 38b; Pesaḥim 115a; Yebamot 86a; Qiddushin 53a; Shebu'ot 12a; Makkot 23b; cf. Berakhot 12b. For further background, see *IShG,* pp. 41, 62–64; Rashi on Yoma 33a s.v. *Abayye; Perush ha-Mishnayot, Nazir* 1:2, vol. 3, p. 165; cf. p. 166.

Given that the authority of *gemara* stems from the fact that it was incorporated into the official curriculum of the *Yeshiba,* a view that had been originally derived from biblical exegesis acquires *ipso facto,* by virtue of having been incorporated into the *gemara*-lesson, the status of *gemara,* even when the exegesis was originally intended as a mnemonic device (אסמכתא). Accordingly, said exegesis is to be treated as substantive; cf. quotation of R. Ḥanan'el, in Shraga Abrahamson, *Perush R. Ḥanan'el la-Talmud,* p. 66; cf. Yoma 71b, Ta'aniyot 17b. The same applies to a view originating in *sebara* (judicial reasoning). Once it had been incorporated in the *gemara-* lesson, it should be regarded, [as if it were] "*halakha le-Moshe mi-Sinai*"; see R. Ḥanan'el on Sanhedrin 53a. cf. the note of R. Moses Zacuto, *Qol ha-Remez* (Amsterdam, 5479/1719), 133d: "גמרא ... והיינו דתנן נמסרו"; [the new edition, Jerusalem 5754/1994, p. 389, has an *erratum*]; *IShG,* pp. 22 and 23; and appendix 33. Therefore, although a *gemara*-lesson may have originally been derived from 'judicial analogy' (Ar. *qiyas,* see *Perush ha-Mishnayot,* vol. 2, p. 10), its authority is higher than 'legal opinion' (סברא). To illustrate, if one were to contest a 'legal opinion' (סברא) on the basis of an authoritative text, the dissenting party would surely retract it. However, "if he [the dissenting party] had received it as *gemara*-lesson, he would not retract it" (Nazir 38b-39a, see *Tosafot* s.v. *Amar Rab Papa*; and cf. Baba Qamma 61a, Ta'aniyot 2b, Ḥolin 44b, Nidda 2b; and the story with R. Isaac b. Judah and Rame b. Ḥama, Zebaḥim 76b). Accordingly, R. Ḥanan'el ('Erubin 60a); R. Isaac Alfasi, (*Halakhot, 'Erubin* 18a); and Maimonides (*MT 'Erubin* 5:20) codified the view of the *gemara*-lesson. On the authority of *gemara* over *sebara,* see *IShG,* pp. 43–46, and ibid. appendix 7, pp. vi-vii; cf. Rama on *Yore De'a* #242:31; and José Faur, "On Martyrdom in Jewish Law," (Heb.) *Annual of Bar-Ilan University,* 30–31 (2006), pp. 401–403. The preceding will explain why Abayye ('Erubin 60a) inquired whether a legal view was a 'legal opinion' (סברא) or a *gemara*-lesson. When asked what difference that would make, he replied: "one who has become proficient in a *gemara*-lesson – should he be treated as if he were chanting a song?" (Concerning 'singing a song,' see Ta'aniyot 32a, and *Kelale Shemu'el* 8a.) Consequently, he demanded from his teacher to be thorough when delivering to him a *gemara*-lesson; see Shabbat 106b and parallels. (On Abayye's predilection for the *gemara*-lesson, see Yoma 14b, 33a.) The description of Abayye's lessons as "chewing bones" in comparison to Raba's "juicy meat," in Baba Batra 22a may have been due to the fact that Abayye preferred to organize the teaching material as a *gemara*-lesson, while Raba preferred to develop his class on the basis of 'legal opinion' (סברא); cf. 'Erubin 53a. The comparison of Abayye's lesson to "chewing bones" is an interplay of גמר – lesson/ גרם – bone.

The study of *gemara* demanded arduous work; see Baba Batra 145b, cf. ibid. 121a; Berakhot 38b; Nedarim 41a; and Abayye's statement in 'Erubin 53a. It also required a special method of instruction; cf. *IShG*, pp. 26–27. Some schools were renowned for the instruction of *gemara* and others for *sebara*. To take advantage of the situation, R. Me'ir learned *gemara* in the school of R. Ishmael and *sebara* in the school of R. 'Aqiba ('Erubin 13a). (This is why R. Sherira Gaon, *IShG*, pp. 26–27, found it necessary to clarify that the method used by R. Me'ir in redacting the Mishna – a method emulated later by R. Judah the Prince – was not the product of "his own mind (מלבו)," i.e., *sebara*, "but according to the *gemara*-method that he learned from his teachers.") There were teachers in Talmudic times who managed to include both methods of study. Thus, after R. Ḥisda's lesson, some students "would first run through the *gemara* together" to commit it to memory, "and then examine the *sebara*" (Sukka 29a). Given that *gemara* is grounded on academic tradition, it can be neither construed from nor inferred on the basis of judicial reasoning; see Giṭṭin 6b. Furthermore, since *gemara* is a thoroughly redacted lesson, a student is not authorized to expand it; see 'Erubin 38b; Ḥolin 103b. For the same reason, neither is he required to defend it; see Rosh HaShana 4a. Knowing a text at the *gemara* level presupposed a solid knowledge of the subject. (The term *gemara* in the standard version of 'Erubin 78a is not found in R. Ḥanan'el, Riṭba and other sages; cf. *Diqduqe Soferim* ad loc.) Therefore, although one may not begin to learn chanting (= *girsa*) of the Book of Esther on the Sabbath, if he had already mastered (*gamir*-knowledge) the text, he may study its *girsa* on the Sabbath; see R. Yehudai Gaon, *Halakhot Pesuqot,* ed. R. S. Sassoon (Jerusalem: Mekize Nirdamim, 1950), p. 38 (ll. 2–4); and the Hebrew version, in *Hilkhot Re'u,* (Versailles: Cerf et fils, 1886), p. 11.

The "masters of *gemara*" occupied a special position, second only to the "masters of Mishna" (Baba Batra 8a), and were compared to "flourishing pomegranates" of Song. 7:13; see 'Erubin 21b. R. Sherira Gaon, *IShG,* pp. 43–44, explained that the high esteem enjoyed by sages with wide *gamir* knowledge was due to the fact there were revealed "to them the *ṭa'ame* of the Tora." Elsewhere, (Tosefta Qiddushin 5:21, p. 299) we are advised that at the end of the Patriarch Abraham's life, there were revealed to him "the *ṭa'ame* of the Tora"; cf. *IShG,* pp. 22 and 23. On the merits of a sage "teaching *ṭa'ame* of the Tora in public," see *Midrash Tanḥuma,* (Warsaw), *Teṣavve,* IX, 9, p. 86. The importance of this type of knowledge will be evident upon recalling that knowing the *ṭa'ame* of a law is an absolute requirement for qualifying to express an opinion on the subject; see above appendix 19. Hence those who have mastered *gemara* are duly compared to "flourishing pomegranates" – ready to yield fruit.

A consequence of the preceding is that someone who is *gamir* but not *sabir* is better qualified than someone who is only *sabir*. R. Sherira Gaon, *IShG,* p. 44, explained:

> Given that one who is *gamir* can issue an authoritative instruction (הוראה) about those topics which he has learned, and issue a legislative pronouncement (הלכה למעשה). However, one who (only) knows a legal theory (סביר) cannot. What is the reason? – Because, how could someone having no *gemara* develop (his views) from a theory (סברא)?! However, someone knowing the *gemara* (about the law), the ruling would conform to what he has transmitted, and his judgment cannot be rejected on the basis of a theory (סברא)!

In line with R. Sherira Gaon, R. Joseph ibn Megas and Maimonides maintained that the editing of the Talmud, as finally redacted by R. Ashe's Court through two *mahdorot* (see appendix 53), awarded it the status of *gemara*. It is pertinent to note that in Geonic and oriental tradition, the Babylonian Talmud was commonly referred to as '*gemara*.' (In the Maimonidean school [as well as in other regions of Spain] and in some oriental communities, the Talmud was known as *gemar* ('conclusion'). Karraites, too, referred to the 'Talmud' as *gemar*; cf. the quotation in *Cairo Geniza*, p. 81. Since the text of the Talmud was conclusively edited (*gemar, gemara*), "we may neither add nor subtract from it"; Introduction, *Perush ha-Mishnayot*, vol. 1, p. 46; see *Studies in the Mishne Tora*, p. 41.) Together with the Mishna, the *gemar/gemara* stands for "the formulated tradition" (Ar. *al-manqul al-manṣuṣ*) of Israel, *Perush ha-Mishnayot, Bekhorot* 4:4, vol. 5, p. 242. It would be of interest to note that according to the Geonim, *Sha'are Teshuba*, #61, etc., and R. Isaac Alfasi on Berakhot 34a, etc., some early commentators and Maimonides twice, once in *Shemona Peraqim* IV, *Perush ha-Mishnayot*, vol. 4, 385 and another in Bekhorot 4:4, vol. 5, p. 242, the Talmud Yerushalmi is referred to as "גמרא דבני מערבא."

*Talmud* (Hebrew root LMD) is not synonymous with *limmud* ('study'). Its grammatical form is rare, and it was examined by R. Solomon Finzi, *Mafteaḥ ha-Gemara*, IV, 93c. In my view, this grammatical form, like *tarbut* (Num. 32:14, see *Targum* and R. Se'adya ad loc.), implies 'continuity, resolution,' as well as 'constancy,' and 'perseverance,' like with a devoted *talmid* (I Chr. 25:8) 'disciple.' The same applies to the analogous structure *tagmul* (see ***tagmul**ohi*, Ps. 116:12) in the sense of 'constant and stable' reward. The same also applies to rabbinic idioms such as *taḥrut, tanḥum,* etc. In this vein, *talmud* stands for a 'lesson,' either taught or learned, demanding 'constancy, unrelenting learning, and further inquiry.' It involves critical methodology; see Rashi cited by R. Isaac Abarbanel, *Naḥalat Abot* on Abot 4:16; cf. *IShG* p. 51 and *MT Talmud Tora* 1:11–12. In this context it is important to note that the rabbis associated *talmud* with the weights of a scale; see *Midrash Shemu'el*, p. 82. This supports the view that originally *talmud* stood for a *method*, rather than a particular subject or text; cf. Berakhot 11b, and Albeck, *Mabo la-Talmudim*, pp. 102–103. Probably that is the sense in which it appears in *Sefer ha-'Ittim*, p. 289.

*Talmud* stands for a session of intense study, when matters are critically analyzed and debated; see *'Arukh*, s.v. *mad* (1) and *MT Talmud Tora* 1:11–12, cited above, appendix 31. The conclusions are tentative, and do not equal 'legal instruction' (הוראה), cf. *Kesef Mishne* on *Issure Bi'a* 10:10, and *Ma'aser* 4:8. Therefore, although someone who has drunk an alcoholic beverage during the Sabbath and Holidays is forbidden to impart legal instruction (הוראה), he nonetheless could teach *Talmud*; see Keritot 13b. [The printed text has been doctored; see, however, *Babylonian Talmud, Codex Florence* (Jerusalem: Makor, 1972), vol. 1, p. 271; *Sifra* (Codex Assemani LXVI, New York: Jewish Theological Seminary, 1956), p. 200 where *Talmud* is excluded from 'legal instruction' (הוראה).] In the final account, whether a lesson is הוראה or *Talmud* would depend on the instructor's intention, not on the text. This point was made abundantly clear by R. Gereshom, in his *Perush* on *Keritot* 13b (= 15a). If the instructor used a text, whether of Scripture, Mishna, or Talmud, as a medium to impart a legal instruction, the lesson would be regarded as הוראה, and he would be forbidden to teach it in case he had drunk an alcoholic beverage, such as on the Sabbath or Holidays. There is one exception. If the instructor regularly uses his lectures to impart הוראה, he should not teach at all after drinking, since the students would assume that he was imparting a legal instruction, rather than an academic lecture; see R. Gereshom, ibid. and *MT Bi'at ha-Miqdash* 1:4.

Finally, the sages differentiated between Talmud and 'a (thoroughly) edited Talmudic lesson' (תלמוד ערוך); see Shebu'ot 40b; Zebaḥim 19a; Menaḥot 66b; Me'ila 17a. Such material is somehow analogous (but since it was not instituted in the official curriculum, not identical) to *gemara*. According to Maimonides, "תלמוד ערוך" stands for "an authentic tradition, which he [the author/transmitter] does not validate with exegesis and it does not originate from judicial analogy (Ar. קיאס)," *Perush ha-Mishnayot, Menaḥot* 2:2, vol. 5, p. 109; cf. Rashi, Menaḥot 14b s.v. *she'en*. This is the basis for the halakhic principle: "one should not discard it (תלמוד ערוך) because of a legal opinion (סברא)"; see R. Isaac Alfasi, *Halakhot, Yebamot* 29b; cf. ibid, *Ketubot* 63b; *Teshubot ha-Rambam* #345, vol. 2, p. 618; *Iggerot ha-Rambam*, vol. 2, p. 507, and cf. ibid, p. 443.

According to Maimonides, Introduction, *Perush ha-Mishnayot*, vol. 1, pp. 34–35, the final redaction of the Talmud included four objectives:

> To authenticate and explain the various and conflicting views around the Mishna.
>
> To adjudicate conflicts concerning: (a) the text of the Mishna, (b) its legal definition, (c) and the principles deduced from it on the basis of judicial analysis. (Similarly in his *Iggerot*, vol. 2, p. 442, Maimonides wrote: "The Talmud has adjudicated each halakha, either specifically, or in general by [establishing] rules according to which the halakhot could be decided." cf. *Studies in the Mishne Tora*, p. 39.)
>
> To record new laws and rulings by the sages, as well as newly enacted statutes. (cf. Introduction, *MT* ll.93–104.)
>
> To transmit, register, and set down hermeneutic and esoteric material concerning matters of faith and spirituality.

We have mentioned before that although a lesson may have been derived from exegesis, once it was given the status of *gemara* it could no longer be challenged either by faulting the exegesis or by offering an alternative explanation. The same applies to a lesson originally derived from a legal opinion (סברא). Once it had been awarded the status of *gemara*, it must be regarded [as if it were] "*halakha le-Moshe mi-Sinai*"; see R. Ḥanan'el on Sanhedrin 53a. In his *Perush* on Baba Meṣi'a 33a (Jerusalem: Mossad Harav Kook, 1988), p. 73, R. Ḥanan'el wrote:

> However, someone who scrutinizes the Talmud, instructing and explaining the *miṣvot* correctly, imparting legislative pronouncement (הלכה למעשה) – there is no measure higher than

> that (i.e., the Talmud)! Given that in the Talmud is to be found the interpretation of the Mishna and the Precept(s) known through tradition, as *halakha le-Moshe mi-Sinai.*

Accordingly, ignoring a Talmudic source constitutes "committing an error in a matter (exposed) in the Mishna," i.e., an authoritative text. That is the reason why if a judge or a scholar issued a legal decision, and "forgot said text, or [in the printed Arabic text and translation there is an *erratum*, read: *'o* (או)) instead of *'an* (אן)] did not know it – then he had actually 'overlooked a matter in the Mishna'" (and the judgment is reversible); *Perush ha-Mishnayot, Bekhorot* 4:4, vol. 5, p. 242; see Sanhedrin 6a. The same applies to a *barraita*; see Baba Qamma 117a. Here the term 'Mishna' stands for 'authoritative text.' Conversely, a faulty or unreliable text is a 'non-Mishna' (אינו משנה); see, for example, Berakhot 36b; Beṣa 12b; Yebamot 43a; Ketubot 81b; Ḥolin 82a, etc.

We can now proceed to examine the statement, "One cannot learn a halakha either from the Mishna or from the Talmud or from adjudication (מעשה), unless he had been instructed: 'implement [this]'!" What the rabbis were saying is that rabbinic texts, including the Mishna, Talmud, etc., are not codes of law that would permit a student or an incompetent judge to declare what the halakha is because he 'had learned' thus from an authorized text. As a matter of fact, after citing the source proscribing "learning halakha" from the Talmud etc., three substantive notes were appended.

First, the exclusion is categorical only in the case of a 'sick' animal unfit for ritual slaughtering. In other cases, legal matters and authoritative texts could be generally cited to help gain knowledge of the matter at hand, as is customary in juridical studies.

Second, even when a court renders a decision, it could not be used as a legal precedent unless the court had explicitly instructed: implement [this]! Cf. Horayot 2b.

Third, Raba, head of the *Yeshiba*, instructed two of his disciples who had been appointed to the bench not to rely on his decisions if they did not know the טעמא, but, rather, they should follow what their eyes showed them; Baba Batra 130b-131a, quoted in Section V n. 321. The court's decisions were regularly signed by the judges; see Yebamot 22a; Giṭṭin 19b; Y. Qiddushin III, 12, 64d. Nonetheless, a halakha cannot be determined merely by quoting an 'authority' even as important as Raba, unless the judge is a competent sage *concurring* with the decision; cf. appendix 69. The same ruling is applicable to a tannaitic source. A judicial decision rendered without knowledge of an authoritative source (or the general practice of the courts) could be reversed; see Baba Qamma 117a, and cf. Sanhedrin 6a. It is clear now why even a sage of the rank of R. Papa had to consult first with Raba before basing a legal decision on a rabbinic text unknown to him, which had been brought to his attention; see Nidda 12a-b. However, as pointed out by R. Mane, an authority who is *sebar*, i.e., a sage (see *Targum* to Lev. 19:32), may derive the halakha from the Mishna, etc.; see Y. Pe'a II, 6, 17a.

Granted that the study of Talmud represents the highest form of legal studies (see Baba Meṣi'a 33a-b; Y. Shabbat XVI, 1, 15c; Horayot III, 5, 48c), nonetheless, neither the Mishna nor the Talmud are 'codes of law' authorizing a student or an incompetent judge to impart halakha. Only someone competent, preferably in both "the final conclusions (*gamir*, from *gemara*) and in the legal theory (*sabir*, from *sebara*) of the entire Tora," or at least competent in "the final conclusions (*gamir*) of the entire Tora," is authorized to declare what the halakha is; see Horayot 2b; cf. Sanhedrin 5b, 7b; and *Perush ha-Mishnayot, Bekhorot* 4:4, vol. 5, p. 244. Rather than codes of law, the Mishna and Talmud contain authentic legal traditions that point to "the path of the law" (דרך המשפט), which includes both judicial procedure and substantive law; see *MT* Introduction, ll. 116, 123, 124; cf. *Iggerot*, vol. 2, p. 438. Maimonides used the same expression to translate the rule prohibiting the appointment to the bench of someone who "is not *gamir*"; see Sanhedrin 7b, and R. David ibn Abi Zimra, on *MT Sanhedrin* 3:8. In two places in the *MT*, in the section containing the 'Classification of the *miṣvot*' according to subject matter, *Sefer Shofeṭim*, Sanhedrin, (*MT* Introduction, l. 495, #2), and in the 'Register of the *Miṣvot*' #2, at the head of Sanhedrin, Maimonides reiterated the prohibition to appoint a judge who does not know "the path of the law" (דרך המשפט). In *Sefer ha-Miṣvot* (written in Arabic), negative precept #284, p. 313, Maimonides defined this prohibition as appointing to the bench someone who is not "fluent in the knowledge of Tora" (*shari'a*). [For both Muslims and Jews, this term stands for knowledge of the *legal apparatus of the 'Law'* (*'ilm shar'i*); cf. Introduction, *Sefer ha-Miṣvot,* p. 2.] Since such an individual does not qualify as an "expert" (מומחה), his appointment to the bench is invalid; see *Perush ha-Mishnayot, Bekhorot* 4:4, vol. 5, pp. 242–243, and *MT Sanhedrin* 4:15. The qualification to be appointed to the bench varies. Maimonides, *Perush ha-Mishnayot, Bekhorot* 4:4, vol. 5, p. 244, referred to Tractate Horayot (most probably 2b) as the source for the rule stipulating that a judge must be "*gamir* in the entire Tora." This level of expertise, however, is not required for all judicial appointments; see ibid. pp. 244–245.

The concept of "the path of the law" (דרך המשפט) was basic to the intellectual background of the area. It was taken for granted that to qualify to adjudicate a halakhic case, one would need not just fluency in rabbinic sources, but also in the "the path of the law" (דרך המשפט). That is why one is not authorized to derive halakha from the Talmud, unless one is fluent "... in the principles according to which it is correct to adjudicate the halakha from the Talmud," *Perush ha-Mishnayot, Soṭa* 2:4, vol. 3, p. 253. Therefore, in addition to mastery of "the Babli, Yerushalmi, *Sifra, Sifre,* and Tosefta" to conclude the halakha, a sage should have

> ... an extensive mind, a judicious spirit, and lengthy time. Only then can it be known from them [the above-mentioned sources] the proper method concerning matters that are forbidden and that are permitted, and what the rest of the laws of the Tora are (Introduction, *MT* ll. 151–154).

(About the four sources – Babli and Yerushalmi count as one, see *Golden Doves,* p. 96, and n. 83, pp. 185–186.)

I would like to call attention to two questions submitted to Maimonides (probably appealing to the decision of a local judge), where it was specified that they were seeking to know the "the path of the law" (דרך המשפט) of the case in question; see *She'elot ha-Rambam,* #7, vol. 1, p. 10; and #66, p. 106. A similar term, "the path of the halakha," (דרך ההלכה) was used by his son R. Abraham Maimonides, *Milḥamot ha-Shem,* pp. 50, 60, 67. Finally, I would like to point out that Justice Holmes delivered a lectured entitled, "The Path of The Law," see Section V, n. 303.

The Talmud represents settled law (see appendix 68) as practiced in the various courts (= Ar. *al-'amal*) of Israel; see *Perush ha-Mishnayot, Bekhorot* 4:4, vol. 5, p. 242 (cf. *Perush ha-Mishnayot,* Introduction, vol. 1, pp. 22, 48; Ketubot 9:2, vol. 3, p. 94; Soṭa 2:4, vol. 3, p. 254; 'Eduyot 7:6, vol. 4, p. 329; etc.). Its authority rests on a single fact: the people accepted it as the supreme judicial authority. On the meaning of *'amal* in Islamic jurisprudence, see Joseph Shacht, *Introduction to Islamic Law* (Oxford: Oxford University Press, 1964), pp. 61–62. See Section V n. 317.

There is a learned discussion by W. Bacher, "Gemara," *Hebrew Union College Annual* (1904), pp. 26–36, but in a completely different direction.

# 49. *Emora*

Generally, *emora* (pl. *emora'im*) serves to designate a Talmudic sage from after the period of the Mishna (second half of 3rd century) until the redaction of the Talmud by R. Ashe and his Court (second half of 5th century). The name derives from 'AMR, 'to say,' 'to make public'; see R. Eliahu Bahur, *Meturgeman* (Izna, 5301/1541), s.v. *emora'a,* 6b. In rabbinic literature it stands for a 'sage skilled in the art of elocution and persuasion.' There were exercises specially designed to train the student in dialectics, where the teacher would assign one group to argue on behalf of one view, and another group to argue on behalf of the contrary view. These arguments would be [i] anonymous and [ii] prefaced with the expression 'אמר לך' usually mistranslated 'he said/maintained,' but actually meaning 'he *could* have argued.' Accordingly, they cannot serve as evidence about the merits of the case, or the actual position of those arguing on its behalf; see *Kesef Mishne, MT Ma'ase ha-Qorbanot* 15:7. That it is why they are generally disregarded by the classical jurists, such as R. Isaac Alfasi and Maimonides. However, when the party proposing 'אמר לך' is named, it can serve as evidence that the party in question actually concurred with the position he was proposing; see *Kesef Mishne, MT Shebu'ot* 3:8. This point was overlooked by *Yad Mal'akhi* #35. There are many expressions peculiar to rhetorical discourse, and it was incumbent upon teacher and student to distinguish between a rhetorical and a strictly legal discourse; see for example, R. Menaḥem Me'iri, on 'Erubin, pp. 244b; 245a, b; 246b, etc.

Semantically, *emora* is connected to the verse "Today you have declared (*he-'emarta*, root 'AMR) that the Lord is your God" (Deut. 26:17). The *Targum* rendered *he-'emarta* as '*ḥaṭabat*.' As in Arabic, this Aramaic voice stands for 'persuasive and eloquent speech'; (see *Targum* to Ps. 73:7 where *ḥoṭabehon* stands for 'articulation,' 'wording'; cf. *Midrash Tehillim* LXXIII, 3, p. 335; the note of R. Se'adya Gaon ad loc., and Radaq *Perush*, p. 169). This is how the rabbis interpreted this verse, *Mekhilta*, *Shira* III, p. 126. Israel says:

> (God) made me into a verse (*'imra*), and I, too, made Him into a verse (*'imra*).
> He made me into a verse, as it is written: "And God declared unto you (*he-'emirekha*)" (Deut. 26:18). I too made him into a verse, as it is written: "Today you have declared (*he-'emarta*) that the Lord is your God" (Deut. 26:17).
> But don't the nations of the world, too, offer their praises to God?
> Yes, but mine are sweeter and more pleasant to Him!
> (See Tosefta Soṭa 7:10, p. 194.)

The relation *he-'emarta* → *'imra* → *ḥaṭiba* is evident upon realizing that the Aramaic *ḥaṭiba* (which has nothing to do with the Hebrew homonym) means the same as its Arabic cognate *khaṭaba*, 'to deliver a public speech, to address someone.' In Judeo-Arabic this term is used exclusively for a 'formal proposal of matrimony' (it passed onto the Judeo-Spanish *apalabrar* 'to give your word in solemn promise of matrimony,' 'to be engaged'). Expanding on the *Targum* the rabbis (Berakhot 6a) taught:

> Said God to Israel: You have made me into a single *ḥaṭiba* in this world, i.e., you have declared My Uniqueness, as it is written 'Hear, O Israel, the Lord our God, the Lord is One' (Deut. 6:4). I, too, shall make you into a single *ḥaṭiba* in this world, as it is written, 'Who is like Thine people Israel, one people in the world' (II Sam. 7:23).

As it were, God and Israel exchanged vows of mutual love and commitment, as a groom and a bride. (This is precisely what R. Judah ha-Levi, cryptically quoted by R. Abraham ibn 'Ezra on Deut. 26:17, had in mind; cf. *Kuzari* 2:55–56.) Similarly, the expression "ומחטבי ברכות" from a Geniza fragment, in *Ba-Merkazim*, p. 166 stands for "the *formulators* or *reciters* of blessings."

Hebrew commentators overlooked the fact that the term *ḥaṭiba* in the above Talmudic passage comes from the *Targum*. Instead, it was assumed that it was a Hebrew word, failing consequently to grasp the sense of the sentence; see *Tosefta Ki-Fshuṭah*, Soṭa, p. 680. With all due respect, the term 'חטבות' in Prov. 7:16 has nothing to do with the *Targum* '*ḥaṭiba*'; see ed. Frank Talmage, *The Commentaries on Proverbs of the Kimhi Family* (Heb.) (Jerusalem: Magnes Press, 1990), pp. 36, 192, 365. Rather, the correct meaning is found in R. Se'adya Gaon's translation, that rendered 'חטבות' by the Aramaic 'ארוכא' – as per Rabbinic Hebrew 'ארוכות המטה' (Mishna Sukka 1:8, Kelim 19:6), that is "bedsteads' or two long boards resting on the four corners of the bed; see *Perush ha-Mishnayot, Kelim* 19:6, vol. 6, pp. 177–178. 'חטבות' are the corners (cf. Ps. 142:12) where the two boards rest on top of the legs of the bed (cf. *Perush ha-Mishnayot, 'Eduyot* 7:7, vol. 4, pp. 329–330). There was a special quilt that "affluent people made (around) their bed strides" for decorative purposes; see *Perush ha-Ge'onim le-Seder Ṭaharot*, p. 52. According to R. Se'adya Gaon, the verb "adorned" (רבדתי) in the first part of the verse, also applies to the second part. So that it reads, "I have adorned (רבדתי) my bed with tapestry; the bed strides (resting) at the corners (חטבות) (I covered up, 'רבדתי' with quilt) stuffed (with padding) from Egypt"; see Arabic text, p. 69; the Hebrew translation is not exact. In a similar sense, 'חטבות' was used by the celebrated Talmudist R. Elḥanan (d. 1026), in an epistle, expressing the hope that God would "attire" the recipients as if they were "חטבות" or bed-posts, i.e., with 'stuffed tapestry' as prosperous men used to be dressed in. The letter was published by Prof. Abramson, *Ba-Merkazim wuba-Tefuṣot*, p. 176 (l. 11).

Intimately connected with the preceding is the fact that, according to the rabbis, 'AMR (in contradistinction to *dibber*) denotes 'placid, temperate speech'; see *Mekhilta de-R. Yishma'el, Yitro, Beḥodesh*, II, p. 207; and *Midrash Tanḥuma, Vayyiggash* 7, vol. 1, p. 206 – a point that passed to the *Vulgate*; cf. Cyrus H. Gordon, "Rabbinic Exegesis in the Vulgate and Proverbs," *Journal of Biblical Literature* 49 (1930), p. 391. The *emora*, too, like the Arabic *khaṭib*, was an 'orator' skilled in the art of eloquence and persuasion. His specific function had to do with the *Yeshiba* method of instruction. At the *Yeshiba*, the teacher conceptualized his lesson into a highly dense formula, and did not fully expound the lesson directly to the students. The task to expose and develop the lesson was left to the *emora*. His duty was twofold: to further explain, expand and develop the subject matter, and to serve as a kind of loudspeaker, enunciating the material, clearly and loudly, to the students. The teacher remained seated and the *emora* would stand, bending down to hear *directly* from the mouth of the master the kernel of the lesson (see Mo'ed Qaṭan 21a, and the comic incident reported in Sanhedrin 7b). Generally, the classroom consisted of eight rows of students (see Menaḥot 29b; probably comprising eight students each. Thus the rule, Soṭa 5a, that an advanced student should only have "one eighth of one eighth" of self-pride; i.e., that he should bear the level of self-esteem tolerated of a novice). Depending on the row where the students were seated they would discuss the material with the *emora* and between themselves. Those seated in the front row would finally engage the teacher in an in-depth discussion of the lesson, witnessed by the entire student body; see Ḥolin 137b. The number of *emora'im* required for a given lesson would therefore depend on the number of students attending the class; see Ketubot 106a. Many distinguished sages, among them Rab, acted occasionally as the *emora* of another sage, see Yoma 20b.

A similar practice was adopted in the public *derasha*. The teacher or lecturer sat and the *emora* would stand and transmit the lecture; see 'Erubin 16b, 104a; Ta'aniyot 8a; Giṭṭin 43a; Baba Batra 127a; Sanhedrin 44a; Zebaḥim 18a, 94b; Ḥolin 100a; Keritot 13b; Nidda 68a. The rabbis relate the *emora* institution to Moses and Aaron. According to *Midrash Tanḥuma, Va'era*, 10, vol. 2, p. 24, when Moses said to

God that he could not possibly speak before Pharaoh because he "was not a man of words" (Ex. 4:10), God assured him that Aaron would assist him, "In the same manner that one who is delivering a public homily, the *emora* says before him" – the teacher, and then proceeds to expand and clearly enunciate the homily to the audience. "You (Moses) too, speak whatever I prescribe to you, and your brother Aaron will say it to Pharaoh."

The post-Mishna sage is designated *emora* because, as it were, he was expanding and enunciating the voice of the ancient masters to the classroom. There is a substantial reason for that. As we are reminded by R. Sherira Gaon, *IShG*, p. 36, the Mishna contains mainly "root-principles" redacted "in a concise style" (Aramaic *qeyaṭa* = Heb. *qeṣara*), as well as cryptic expressions (*remez*, see appendix 31; and Section IV, notes 180, 181. The task of the Talmudic *emora'im* is to expose these matters to the future generations of students. Their authority was supreme. To wit, on the basis of their teachings, the sages would choose to depart from standard canons and rules in favor of the minority opinion; see *IShG*, p. 55; and *Teshubot ha-Ge'onim*, Harkavi, #439, p. 232. Hence, the rule of Rashbam on Pesaḥim 101b s.v. *leqib'e*, "that the [Talmudic] *emora* routinely expands"; cf. *Tosafot*, Beṣa 25a, s.v. *kan*. Obviously, it was intended only as a *general* – not a categorical – rule; this meets the objections raised by *Yad Mal'akhi* #53.

In my view, the post-Talmudic *emora*, too, was also in charge of *expanding* the lesson taught at school, regardless of subject; as per *Targum* on Job 3:18: "the schoolchildren would no longer hear the voice of the *emora*.

# 50. National Publication for Use in Constitutional Interpretation: The Jewish and the US Systems

In the Jewish legal system the Tora is both the Constitution of Israel and its primary legal code (see above chapters 6, 10 and appendix 10). In Rabbinic times, to be quoted in the legal interpretation of the Tora or Constitution of Israel, a source or view had to be formally published, e.g., either as the Mishna, published by R. Judah the Prince (see chapters 43–44), or the Talmud, published by the last National Court of Israel (see above appendix 48). Sources and opinions that were not published by a national institution, such as *Sifra*, *Sifre*, and various collections of *barraitot*, although proceeding from respected sources, needed to be certified by the *Yeshiba* or *Bet Midrash* to qualify as a source of constitutional interpretation (see chapters 45, 57). The Jewish Supreme Court dealt directly with constitutional interpretation, in contrast to only analyzing prior judicial decisions or authorized statements of the Law as being correct or 'constitutional,' as is often the case in modern Western jurisprudence.

The US legal system does not have a mechanism by which the national documentation and sources that could serve as authoritative material for constitutional interpretation are published. The values and collective mind frame (or *Mental Law*) that produced the US Constitution have not been officially recorded in a *national* volume. While US statutes and appellate opinions are in fact published, they are never officially conveyed (*nimsar*) to the general public. Even the US Constitution is not conveyed (*nimsar*) to the people, and thus there can never be a *hora'ath ṭa'ut,* or Constitutional reading that is objectively wrong"; see José Faur, "Law and Hermeneutics in Rabbinic Tradition," *Cardozo Law Review* 14 (1993), pp. 1657–1679. Thus 'publication' does not confer the same rights on US citizens that official publication confers on Israelites. A case in point is *The Federalist Papers,* whose value as a source of constitutional exegesis continues to be vigorously debated among constitutional scholars; for a critical and highly informative overview, see Dan T. Coenen, "A Rhetoric for Ratification: the Argument of *The Federalist* and its Impact on Constitutional Interpretation," *Duke Law Journal* 56 (2006), pp. 469–543. In this respect, the American legal system lacks an identifiable 'Mental Law' or National Memory. Rather, statutes seem to be self-executing and no publication is required for them to be effective. Once the governor or president, as appropriate, signs the law, it is effective.

In brief, our modern legal systems have neither a national depository of the legal decisions and opinions, parallel to the Mishna and Talmud, nor an equivalent to the *miṣva* to write a *Sefer* of the US Constitution, to be read and cherished (see below appendix 62), nor a public forum 'to proclaim the Constitution,' as per the weekly reading of the Tora (see quotation from Josephus, in Section III, n. 343). In fact, modern civic education does not provide the general student the necessary learning to properly understand and appreciate the Law of the land. And yet, as the ancient jurists taught: *Ignorantia non excusat lex.*

# 51. *Tanya Kevatteh* (תניא כוותיה)

This phrase means there is 'a *tanya* that corroborates *his* view' (תניא כוותיה). It is used in the Babylonian Talmud when in the course of examining a thesis developed by a sage in the Holy Land, it was discovered that there was some tannaitic material supporting that thesis. The term appears in connection with lessons developed by R. Johanan, see: Rosh HaShana 3a; Soṭa 46b; Giṭṭin 87a; 'Aboda Zara 53b; etc.; by R. Ḥiyya bar Abba, see: Baba Batra 82b; and by R. Amme, see: Nedarim 75a. Sometimes, however, a tannaitic source is mentioned not to corroborate, but to insinuate that the *emora* may be plagiarizing; see Yebamot 91a; Ketubot 19a; Baba Batra 133a. Our point meets the objection raised by Rashbam on Pesaḥim 101b s.v. *hakhi garsennan*. Quite often, this expression is used also to support a dissenting *emora* by quoting a *tanya* (תניא כוותיה); cf. Sanhedrin 21b as cited in *Midrash Daniel wu-Midrash 'Ezra*, p. 127 and editor's n. 11.

# 52. Leaning Towards the Majority

From its incipient moment, the Jewish legal system recognized areas requiring judicial discretion and interpretation – the whole area of *Dinim Mufla'im* (see above chapter 8) – or legislative action, to be resolved by a majority vote. (In Judaism both the legislature and judiciary are the prerogative of the Sanhedrin or Supreme Court.) The justification for this procedure is Ex. 23:2. This verse comprises three segments. First, it prohibits "following the majority to do iniquity (לרעות)." As per the *Targum* (לאבאשה), Hebrew 'לרעות' is a transitive verb. It addresses a judge convinced that the majority is erroneous. In such a case, the judge holding a minority opinion should not say, 'Since anyhow the majority view will prevail, I might as well vote with them, so that the verdict of the court will be unanimous.' Thus the Tora instructs the judge: "Do not follow the majority opinion, to do [what in your view is] an iniquity." The second segment reads: "and do not argue (תענה) in a litigation, to sway (לנטות)." Hebrew לנטות, is also a transitive verb; see R. Se'adya's translation. It applies to a judge either arguing just for the sake of departing from the established procedure; cf. Deut. 27:19, and the *Targum*'s and R. Se'adya's translation; as well as to a judge deliberately *refraining* from raising an issue that could have pointed out to the court another aspect of the case; see *Targum* ad loc. The third segment instructs a judge holding a minority opinion to accept the verdict of the court, although in his view it is erroneous. Later (Ex. 23:6–7), the Tora addresses a judge who is convinced that the accused, who appears "innocent and righteous," is actually guilty. The judge is instructed not to twist either the law or the facts, for the sake of 'fairness.' Concerning a criminal who had either manipulated the judicial process or was unfairly exonerated by the court, God promises: "I will not regard as righteous, someone who is guilty"; i.e., his punishment is to be meted out by God, not men. If a judge is convinced that one of the witnesses is fraudulent, or that one of the plaintiffs is fooling the court, he should excuse himself (*MT Sanhedrin* 24:3), but should not twist either the law or the facts.

New cases without legal precedent were debated and decided by a majority vote; see Mishna Yadayim 3:5; 4:1, 3; cf. Tosefta Sanhedrin 7:1, p. 425; Sanhedrin 88b; Introduction, *Perush ha-Mishnayot,* vol. 1, p. 4. The same applies to judicial uncertainties, where the law is not explicit or sufficiently clear; see *MT Ishut* 12:18; 18:19; *Zekhiyya* 3:8, 6:14; *Shekhenim* 12:1; *She'ela wu-Fiqqadon* 4:4; *Malve ve-Love* 14:3, 25:14; *Ṭo'en ve-Niṭ'an* 3:14, 5:10, 9:5.

The Jewish legal system excludes lawyers. The justices must fully conceptualize both sides of the case and simultaneously play the role of attorney and judge. Therefore, is not sufficient for a member of the court to show that his view conforms to the law, but he has to show that he had also taken into account the contrary opinion. This attitude helps create an environment in which both sides of the case express "the words of the Living God." The final vote is the result of persuasion, not mere formal correctness. The rabbis acknowledged that members of the School of Shammai were sharper in their legal reasoning (Yebamot 14a). Nonetheless, the halakha was decided in favor of the School of Hillel because they were more courteous and understanding: taking into account the opposite view ('Erubin 13b). In this fashion the halakha is established on the basis of consensus and practical reasoning, rather than rigorous formalism.

Legal argumentation and rhetorical discourse presuppose a common foundation accepted by all parties. For the Hebrews, this is the Scripture, serving as the common ground, with a *sensus communis* or meaning of the text shared by the entire nation: sage and ordinary, traditional or sectarian (see Sanhedrin 33b and Horayot 4a, b). Therefore, it was incumbent upon jurists and judges to express their views through Scripture and appeal to the *sensus communis* of the public, more or less, as we expect the decisions of our judges today to reflect public reasoning. There is an important aspect to be considered. Argumentation and modes of interpretation are not in themselves sources of authority, but only means to *persuade* the public by appealing to their cultural setting. Concerning the homilies (דרשות) of the rabbis, Maimonides explained that the methodology "is understood among those who comprehend their (the sages') words." Namely, "that for them (the sages) this is a form of poetic license (Ar. *nawadir al-sha'riya*), not the actual meaning of the text" (*Guide* III, 43, p. 419, ll. 24–26; cf. *Perush ha-Mishnayot, Sheqalim* 1:4, vol. 2, p. 207; there is an error in the Arabic text and it should read: *al-nawadir*). Erroneously, some Jewish scholars "imagine that [the *derashot*] intend to convey the actual meaning of that verse" (ibid. ll. 26–28). Consequently,

> ...they struggled to demonstrate and defend what they imagined to have been the correctness of the *derashot*. Since they believed that it was the actual meaning of the text, and that *derashot* were equal in rank to the legal tradition [that they conveyed]; failing to grasp the dissimilarity between them (legal tradition) with what (merely) was poetic license. In those days that (peculiar) methodology was popular and commonly used by everyone, as poetry is used nowadays by poets (Ibid. p. 420, ll. 1–6).

Cf. Introduction, *Perush ha-Mishnayot,* vol. 1, pp. 35–41. On 'poetic license,' see *Homo Mysticus*, p. 111.

A good model for *dinim mufla'im* is Quantum Mechanics, where a particle has many possible coordinates simultaneously (as provided by Schroedinger Equations). However, once you actually look at the particle via experiment/observation, the multiple possibilities coalesce into one – and only one – set of co-ordinates. In this fashion, the 'multivalent potentiality' of a particle becomes confined to one state, post-observation. Similarly, the various possibilities to execute a *miṣva* coalesce into one and only one, post-*perush* of *dinim mufla'im*, via the thirteen rules of rabbinic hermeneutics; see quotation in Section II, n. 104.

By way of conclusion let me point out the following three principles, intimately bound to the above. First, the perennial ambiguity intrinsic to *dinim mufla'im*. Simply put, there are aspects in the Law that escape a final, permanent and unexceptional definition. The Law cannot be executed by applying a certain code, as per classical mechanics. Rather, the court is charged to "lean" (להטות) in the direction pointed to by the majority, but it does not have the authority to restructure the Law, eradicate all vagueness, and render the text univocal, for all time to come. Second (and as a consequence of the preceding), although a superior court should not overrule a statute that was enacted by a previous court, unless it regards itself more knowledgeable and competent, if said statute was promulgated on the basis of a homily, the Geonim, Maimonides, as well as other rabbinic authorities, maintain that a later court may overrule it; see *Studies in the Mishne Tora*, pp. 31–32, 49. Finally, the authority of the court is to be expressed through rhetorical discourse, based on the foundations of Scripture, as rooted in the collective consciousness of the people. Thus, it would be incumbent upon the court to appeal to these values, rather than invoke violence or the threat of violence, celestial or otherwise.

For some insights on this subject, see R. Ḥayyim Alfandari, *Esh Dat*, 23d-25d; and *Justice, Law and Argument*, chapter 14.

# 53. *Mahdora*

In Scripture and rabbinic literature, the root HDR stands for 'splendor,' 'glory'; see Dan. 4:15. Hence the sense of *meHaDdeRin,* or praising God's 'splendor and glory' in the liturgy; see *Mekhilta de-R. Shim'on b. Yoḥai,* XIV, 14, p. 56; Mishna Pesaḥim 10:5; and cf. Dan. 4:34. In a similar vein, we find 'beautifying (*HiDduR*) a *miṣva*'; see Baba Qamma 9b and Shabbat 21b; and cf. Shabbat 133b and Sukka 11b. [The use of *mehadderin* to indicate a 'higher' standard of *permitted* food is another illustration of the caliber of Tora-knowledge and intellectual honesty of those involved in the packaging and marketing of Judaism.] There is a homonym, from the root DWR 'circle' and 'serpentine,' as in a winding road; see Is. 45:2 and R. Se'adya Gaon, *Tafsir,* p. 100; R. Judah ibn Bal'am, *Perush Yesha'yahu,* p. 189; R. Jonah ibn Jannaḥ, *Sefer ha-Shorashim,* s.v. HDR p. 117. Radaq, *Sefer ha-Shorashim,* s.v. HDR pointed to Ḥolin 113a where this root appears in the sense of 'serpentine,' as in 'coiled intestine' (*HaDRa*). In rabbinics, this root is also used in the sense of 'reverting' (your opinion, i.e., 'changing your mind!'), e.g., *HaDuR bakh,* in Baba Meṣi'a 49a, 51a, etc. or: *aHDaR bakh,* Baba Batra 111a, etc. The Aramaic expression *le-'ahdure* in Qiddushin 22a stands for the Hebrew "go around [begging] from door to door"; see Mishna Ketubot 13:3, Baba Batra 9:1; Shabbat 151b; cf. Rashi on Qiddushin 22a s.v. *le-'ahdure* in Qiddushin 22a; and R. Solomon Farḥon, *Maḥberet he-'Arukh,* ed. S. Gottlieb Stern (Pressburg 5604/1844), 16b, s.v. HDR.

In our case, the term *maHDoRa* stands for the thirty-year program 'cycle,' encompassing the entire Talmud. It is semantically close to the Latin *curriculum*, 'running course'; *curro* ('to move quickly'), and finally a 'program of study.' R. Jonah ibn Jannaḥ, *Sefer ha-Shorashim*, s.v. HDR, p. 117, registers a rabbinic expression (which I was unable to locate) *HoDRana di-qarta*, 'the path encircling a city' (could it be an *erratum* for: הדורא דכנתא, at Ḥolin 113a?) – somehow akin to *mahdora* encircling the entire study program. In Talmudic Aramaic *medorta* [= *mehdorta*] means 'to reach and catch someone'; see *Teshubot ha-Ge'onim* (Harkavi), #330, p. 158.

The fact that there were two such cycles explains why a view presented as conclusive (סתם) in the first *Mahdora* is rejected in the second *Mahdora*, on the basis of new evidence; see Section IV, n. 257. (This is why Maimonides decides in favor of the authority mentioned *afterwards*, since it represents the second and final *Mahdora*; cf. "Concerning the Term *Qore be-Iggeret*," p. 27 n. 39.) A good example of this procedure is found in Menaḥot 37b, where R. Judah transmits in the name of Samuel that the halakha is like R. Ishmael. Yet, without citing a contrary opinion, the Talmud rejects it! The contrary opinion is never formulated. Rather, it may be *inferred* from an incident with Rabina and Mor b. Rab Ashe, mentioned ibid. To my mind, this indicates that the incident was brought to the attention of the *Kalla* sages at a later point, and there was not sufficient time to redact it. Another example is Yebamot 105b, where the view of Ribbi et al. is rejected by הלכתא, without any explanation; cf. Yebamot 61b.

Generally, the expression *HaDRakh 'alan ve-HaDRan 'alakh*, found at the end of the Talmudic tractates, is explained as 'return': "You shall *return* to us and we shall *return* [or 'we have come back'] to you." I am not certain, but I think that the late Professor Lieberman explained it in the sense of 'beauty,' as when bidding farewell to a friend, or as when bidding farewell to the altar, see Mishna Sukka 4:5 and *Hellenism in Jewish Palestine*, p. 11 n. 46. In the same manner, when completing a tractate, we bid farewell to it: 'Let your *beauty* be upon us and our *beauty* be upon thee!' These parting words, said when completing an entire tractate, intend to convey that we shall remember only thy beauty, rather than the toil we encountered when learning that tractate. At the same time, we beg the tractate to overlook our errors and faulty interpretations and remember our good will, etc. [There is either a scribal error or a misprint in the text of R. Judah ibn Bal'am, *Perush Yesha'yahu*, p. 189 cited above. From the Arabic text, it is evident that he intended to explain the rabbinic expression *HaDuR bakh* ('revert!') – not, as per the Hebrew: *hadran 'alakh*!] I would like to suggest another explanation. Occasionally, as a form of poetic license (cf. above appendix 52), the senses of these roots are applied to each other; see Sukka 31b, 35a; and Shir ha-Shirim Rabba VII, 1, [9], p. 75. Accordingly, the parting words: *HaDRakh 'alan ve-HaDRan 'alakh*, stand for: 'Thy *splendor* is upon us and we shall *return* to Thee!'

For a detailed study of the root HDR in rabbinics; see *'Arukh ha-Shalem*, s.v. *hadar* (3) and s.v. *hadura*.

# 54. "Little Foxes"

Poorly trained rabbinic students and bogus rabbis were a disrupting factor in Jewish life throughout the ages; see chapter 63. Because Israel was never organized hierarchically as the Catholic Church, with the power to regiment and impose its will on the clergy, it was relatively easy for unqualified rabbis and students to fool the faithful. Even outstanding rabbinic figures had to cope with the "little foxes" sowing havoc and discord in their respective communities; see R. Eliahu Mizraḥi, *She'elot wu-Tshubot Re'em* (Jerusalem, 5698/1938), #15, 33a; #66, 215a; R. Moses al-Ashqar, *She'elot*, #112, pp. 180–182; R. Levi b. Ḥabib, *She'elot* (Venice, 5325/1565) #31; R. Samuel de Medina, *Teshubot Meharashdam, Eben ha-'Ezer* (Saloniki, 5358/1598), #43, 37a; etc.; cf. *Shulḥan 'Arukh, Ḥoshen Mishpaṭ*, I #1. This problem was further exacerbated by the 'rabbinic ordination' (סמיכה) awarded in the Ashkenazic rabbinate; see R. Isaac bar Sheshet, *Teshubot ha-Ribash* ##270–271, 74b-76c. As in all systems, 'ordination' was occasionally awarded to unworthy pupils; see R. Moses Isserles, *Teshubot ha-Rama*, #55, 34a. For an overview of the problem, see Professor Meir Benayahu, 'Introduction,' R. David ha-Kohen, *Teshubot ha-Radak* (Jerusalem: Yad ha-Rab Nissim, 5748/1988), pp. 33–36. It goes without saying that in such circumstances the 'ordination' is worthless; see *MT Sanhedrin* 4:15 and below appendix 69. In this context, it is worth noting that the Sephardic rabbinate did not award ordination at all; see R. Isaac Abarbanel, *Naḥalat Abot*, on Abot 6:1, p. 376; R. Jacob Castro, *'Erekh Leḥem* (Constantinople, 5478/1718), *Yore De'a*,

CCXLII, 6, 47d-48a. On the Ashkenazic Ordination, see M. Broyer, "The Ashkenazi Semikha," (Heb.) *Zion* 33 (1968), pp. 15–46. On the ordination and the rise of the professional Rabbi, see Irving A. Agus, *Responsa of the Tosaphists* (Heb.), (New York: Talpioth, Yeshiva University, 1954), pp. 18–28. cf. below appendix 67.

# 55. *Minim* and *Minut*

The rabbis classified *minim* (sin. *min*) as "those who have rejected (one) of the principles" (כופר בעקר) of the Jewish faith; see R. Ḥanan'el and Rashi, on Shabbat 75a; *'Arukh* s.v. GDF; and cf. Rashi on Deut. 1:12. Similarly, Maimonides, *Teshubot ha-Rambam,* #263, vol. 2, p. 499, defined *min* "as someone who rejects one of the principles of the Tora; e.g., someone postulating that the Tora is not from Heaven"; see ibid., #449, p. 730; *Perush ha-Mishnayot, Berakhot* 9:7, vol. 1, p. 90; cf. Sanhedrin 10:1, vol. 4, pp. 209, 217; *Guide* II, 19, p. 215, l. 12; III, 17, 335, ll. 8–16. According to Maimonides there are five such principles; see above chapter 25. In the rabbinic mind, a *min* is the most shameful type of 'heretic' – more wretched and evil than even the infamous epicurean (the *apiqoros* of rabbinic literature). What makes the *minim* particularly odious is their methodology of deception. They are perfidious: they use Scripture not to teach but to mislead the naive. They beguile the gullible, exposing a single aspect of their doctrines in order to block the prey's judgment, thus driving him/her to do things that he/she will lament for the rest of his/her life. Their manifest reliance on the Tora and their use of Jewish terms and sources are gimmicks intended to take in the dull-witted. In spite of their pretentious religiosity, they are cynics who believe in no religion. In brief, for them the end justifies the means; see quotation from Jung at Section III, n. 225. This is how Maimonides, in his *Iggeret ha-Shmad, Iggerot ha-Rambam,* vol. 1, p. 37, described them:

> ...*Minut* is more heinous than idolatry, because the *minim* – may God cut them off! – poke fun at (all) religions, and say: 'Those who propose them are wicked. Those who study them are crazy.' In fact, they deny prophecy altogether.

Cf. *Perush ha-Mishnayot, Ḥolin* 1:2, vol. 5, p. 175; Yadayim 4:6, vol. 7, p. 717, and Section III n. 209.

Through a peculiar type of 'hermeneutics' a metamorphosis takes place whereby the Tora is not only 'dead' but also 'deadly.' On this point, see José Faur, "Don Quixote: Talmudist and *mucho más*," *Review of Rabbinic Judaism* 4 (2001), pp. 143–144. Appropriately, the rabbis compared *minut* to "toxic waters," which appear crystalline and placid, but are fatal to any and all who drink from them; see Abot 1:11 and *Perush ha-Mishnayot*, vol. 4, p. 414; cf. *Perush ha-Mishnayot, Nedarim* 10:8, vol. 3, p. 153. *Minim* are perfidious through and through because they use the Tora as a ploy to dupe the innocent. Therefore, a Scroll of Tora written by a *min* ought to be incinerated together with the names of God that it contains; see *MT Yesode ha-Tora* 6:8 [the standard version 'אפיקורס' is wrong, instead read: 'מין ישראל']. The underlying theory is that even the Tetragrammaton, representing the Holy of Holies, is contaminated with their idolatrous schemes. Addressing this rule, the rabbis, Shabbat 116a, cited the verse: "and behind the entrance at the door-post (mezuza) you (i. e. the *minim*) have placed your remembrance" (Is. 57:8) – that is, your idolatrous fabrications. Meaning: you use the mezuza – a sacred Jewish object – as a ploy to ensnare the innocent! see the note of R. Jacob ibn Forna, cited by R. Ḥayyim Algazi, *Bene Ḥayye* (Orta-Kivvae, 5479/1719), 64a; cf. *Keli Faz*, 217d-218a. In Judaism, context is of the essence. Thus, the texts of the Tora that were not written with the proper sanctity (קדושה) have no standing. Similarly, to study Tora and reflect about it has no merits in an environment which is not clean; see R. Jacob Ḥajez, *Halakhot Qeṭannot*, Part 1, #15, 3d. For the same reason it is not appropriate to teach Tora to an unethical student; see *MT Talmud Tora* 4:1.

The motivation behind the *min* and *minut* pertains to the morbid and pathological; 'theology' is but a cover to camouflage their abnormal impulse to pervert the innocent. (Accordingly, this type of immorality is referred to in Judeo-Spanish as "*pecado de padre*".) The rabbis associate *minut* with sexual aberrations and political collaboration with the *enemies* of Israel; see 'Aboda Zara 17a-b, *Homo Mysticus*, pp. 37–38, and the corresponding note on p. 203. They are sick, "and beyond healing"; see Maimonides, *Perush ha-Mishnayot, Abot* 2:17, vol. 4, p. 429. Let us note, in passing, that the sex of *minut* has nothing to do with the "dynamic call" discussed by D. H. Lawrence, or the "erotic" excitement involved in the "unveiling of the truth," by Roland Barthes; see *Golden Doves*, p. 115. Rather, it is the gruesome, sinister sex, described by D. M. Thomas, *The White Hotel* (New York: Viking Press, 1981). The purpose of this type of 'sex' is to agonize the victim, like the Spanish conquistador raping a Native American woman while the husband is tied under the bed; see "Jews, *Conversos* and Native Americans: The Iberian Experience," p. 106. On the pathological aspects of the *min*-mentality, see my "De-authorization of the Law: Paul and the Oedipal Model," *Journal of Psychiatry and the Humanities* 11 (1989), pp. 222–243.

Consequently, whereas all types of sinners may be accepted back into the fold after 'repenting' (תשובה), see *MT Teshuba* 3:7, 14, "Jewish *minim* are not Jews in any matter whatsoever, and can never be accepted as repentant," *MT 'Aboda Zara* 2:5. Maimonides, *Teshubot ha-Rambam*, vol. 2, pp. 501–502 explained that if their contrition is sincere, God would surely forgive them, just as He forgives every penitent. However, since *minut* is grounded on make-believe and deception, only God can know whether a *min* had actually repented. Plain humans, however, can never be sure that "the piety that they show is not because of fear or to take in the people." The Geonic decision, *Sha'are Ṣedeq*, III, vi, 11, p. 56, accepting an inveterate offender back into the fold after undergoing proper repentance, concerns an entrenched sinner – not an ideological *min*.

The status of *min* applies to someone who practices *minut* because of his own personal ideology, see *MT 'Edut* 11:10; however, someone who denies a principle of Jewish faith because he was raised in a community disparaging some of the fundamental principles of Israel is not a *min*; see *MT Mamrim* 3:3. This distinction was widely accepted by other legal authorities; see *Besamim Rosh* #240, cf. ibid. #251; *Teshubot Radbaz,* IV, #187 (= 1255); and R. Joseph Albo, *Sefer ha-ʿIqqarim* I, 2.

In later rabbinic parlance *min/minut* were used to designate a Jew or group of Jews who because of personal ideology and/or behavior caused rifts in Israel. That is why R. Samuel ha-Nagid classified bogus-Talmudists as *minim*; see Section V, n. 34. The same designation was applied to communities that did not observe the standard norms of Israel; see *Shaʿare Ṣedeq,* III, vi, 7, pp. 54–55; ibid. 10, p. 55. cf. the question presented to Maimonides, *Teshubot ha-Rambam,* #263, vol. 2, pp. 495–498. It was on this basis alone that congregations that no longer recited the *Targum* at the Synagogue were described as having a "facet of *minut*" (צד מינות); see Section V, n. 35; or as R. Judah al-Bargeloni, *Perush Sefer Yeṣira,* p. 5 wrote that, they were "close to *minim*" since they were departing from accepted standards. The matter was graver when a community chose to depart from standard rabbinic practice and adapt a more 'stringent' position in compliance with Karraite custom; see *Teshubot ha-Rambam,* #320, vol. 2, pp. 588–589. One of the distinguishing features of *minim* was that they "fabricated" (בדו) their ideology "out of their hearts"; see *Teshubot ha-Rambam,* #449, vol. 2, p. 730; cf. ibid. #242, p. 437; and Section V, nn. 39–40. In this aspect, they emulated the ancient Zadokites who fabricated their laws "out of their own minds, not from tradition" (שמורים מהעולה על רוחם, לא מן הקבלה), *MT Para* 1:14. Maimonides classified departure from standard ritual in compliance with Karraite practice as *minut*; see *Teshubot ha-Rambam,* #242, vol. 2, p. 436: (מנהג מינות, (מינות גמורה)) and (אמונת המינים); p. 437: (מינות), and (מעשה המינים); p. 439: (מינות גמורה); and (שמחזיקין במינות זו); p. 441: (דרכי המינים). Thus, the gravity of abrogating the *Targum* – a practice first initiated by the Karraite Synagogue; see Section V, n. 35 and below appendix 61.

# 56. *Tukku* (תכו)

*Tukku* (תְּכּו) is a homonym appearing twice in Scripture. First, the root NKH (נכ"ה), Is. 1:5; and second, from the root TKhKh/TKK (תכ"כ) Deut. 33:3. In Judeo-Arabic, 'תכא' [*dagesh hazaq*] stands for a 'cushion' used for reclining on the floor; e.g., the small pillow that the faithful bring to the Synagogue to rest on; see A. S. Yahuda, "A Contribution to Qur'an and Ḥadith Interpretation," *Ignance Goldziher*, part I, pp. 293–295; hence the verb 'יתכא,' see *Perush Mishnayot, Berakhot* 8:4, vol. 1, p. 84. Among Jews from Syria it is used metaphorically in the sense of 'reclining' and 'resting' (אנ-תכא) on a sofa or divan; cf. *Perush Mishnayot, Berakhot* 1:6, 7, vol. 1, p. 72. This may be the gist of Raba's statement, Berakhot 63b, playing on the term 'הסכת' (Deut. 27:9); as if it were written 'כת'+'הס,' he expounded: "At all times, one should learn Tora (= 'הס') and then 'reflect' (= 'יהגה' כת' or ככת, reclining on a sofa). I was informed that Moroccan Jews use 'תכא' [no *dagesh*] for a 'small table' or 'tray' put before the guest. In this sense it mostly appears in the Talmud; see Berakhot 46b; Pesaḥim 100b, 110b, 115b; Giṭṭin 67b, etc.

People were in the habit of reclining on the 'תכא.' Hence the expression, Berakhot 42a: "I am reclining on the 'תכא' of the Exilarch," to explain that although the attendants have removed the tray from before the guests, the meal was not formally over until the 'תכא' was removed from before the host. Having many 'תכא' [no *dagesh*] in one's home to accommodate guests and friends – be they 'cushions' or 'trays' – was a sign of wealth and influence. Accordingly, we read in Prov. 29:13: "A poor man and a man having (many) pillows/trays (תככים) met, the Lord enlightens the eyes of both of them," i.e., God cares about the wealthy and the poor equally.

In sum, whether in the sense of 'cushion' or 'tray,' the root TKhKh/TKK indicates an object serving as the 'seat,' 'base,' or 'venue' whereon something rests or stands. In this precise sense, R. Se'adya Gaon interpreted "תכו" Deut. 33:3, cf. *Targum,* Rashi and R. Abraham ibn 'Ezra. Accordingly, the English rendition of this verse should be, "(Although) He loves the people," that is humanity in general, "all His holy ones" – a reference to Israel – "are in Your hand," that is, they enjoy special providence. The second half of the verse explains why Israel merits such privilege: "And," which in Semitic languages has the gist of 'since,' "they are the recipients (תכו) of your footsteps, the transmitters of your instructions." In the style of homilies made 'in the manner of poetic license,' see Section V, n. 48, R. Joseph (Baba Batra 8a) interpreted our "תכו" here, root TKhKh/TKK (תכ"כ), in light of the homonym in Is. 1:5, root NKH (נכ"ה), and lectured: "These" – the recipients (תכו, root תכ"כ) of your footsteps, the transmitters of your instructions – "are the disciples of sages, hurting (תכו, root נכ"ה) their feet, traveling from town to town and from city to city to learn Tora" – a reference to the end of the verse – to be tutored by the transmitters of your instructions.

# 57. About "Strict Talmudists"

According to R. Adrete, the view proposed by R. Qaṭina that after the year 6000 the world shall be 'destroyed' (two versions: חרוב, and another: חריב; see below) for one thousand years (Rosh HaShana 31a and parallels), is a cardinal principle of Judaism (cf. *Targum* to Deut. 32:12). It ought to be accepted *verbatim*, since "we find no one in the Talmud disagreeing" with it (*Teshubot ha-Rishba,* vol. 1 #9, 5a, cited in Section V, n. 146). Before proceeding with an analysis of the text, let us point out that this is the most important rabbinic source in the anti-Maimonidean arsenal. It provided a strategic argument: if this view had indeed been accepted by *all* the Talmudic sages, it could then be argued that the Maimonidean and Geonic view about the stability of the physical world and the laws of nature is untruthful and heretical. It could also be argued, as maintained by Ramban and other anti-Maimonidean mystics, that "No one could believe in the Tora and in the validity of nature, at all" (cited above Section V, n. 169). It would then follow that to confine the interpretation of the aggadot to the restraints of nature and common sense, as per Geonic and Maimonidean scholarship, is a denial of Jewish faith.

A close reading of Rosh HaShana 31a, however, makes it abundantly clear that the anti-Maimonidean interpretation is untenable, and that it was construed for argumentative purposes, not for instruction. The Talmudic passage centers on the rationale for each of the seven psalms recited by the Levites at the Temple, one on each of the corresponding days of the week (see Mishna Tamid 6:7).

R. 'Aqiba explained that the first six psalms celebrate the Six Days of Creation, while the seventh psalm celebrates the future Sabbath, "a day which (will be) thoroughly Sabbath" (ליום שכולו שבת), i.e., the Sabbath which God will institute at the end of days. Let us point out that the text before R. Ḥanan'el read: "ליום שעתיד להיות כולו שבת." R. Ḥanan'el explained:

> On the Seventh Day (the Levites sang), "A Song for the Sabbath Day" (Ps. 92:1) – to a Day that in the future shall be thoroughly Sabbath. That is 'one thousand years,' which is 'God's Day' [cf Sanhedrin 97a], and it will be followed by the Resurrection of the Dead.

Two major points emerge from the above. The world *will not* be destroyed, and after the year 6000 there shall be a millennium of bliss, symbolized by the Sabbath. This is a reference to the Hebrew concept of palingenesis which will occur at the end of days; see Introductory Remarks, Section III and *Kesef Mishne on Teshuba* 8:2, 8. On the connection between Resurrection and the future Sabbath, see below.

The explanation reported in the name of R. 'Aqiba was contested by R. Neḥemya (2nd century). In his view, just as the first six psalms celebrate the Days of Creation, the seventh psalm, too, comes to celebrate the Sabbath of Creation, when God "ceased" creating (see R. Ḥanan'el ad loc. and *Golden Doves,* pp. 51–52). At this point, the Talmud introduces R. Qaṭina's view, with an important remark: "And the preceding controversy (between R. 'Aqiba and R. Neḥemya) concerns R. Qaṭina's view (וקמיפלגי בדרב קטינא), that the world will last for six thousand years, and (for) one will be destroyed." The remark "and the preceding controversy concerns the view of…" (וקמיפלגי בדרב…) is a technical term, common in Talmudic literature. It proposes that a view expressed by *one* of the contesting parties mentioned earlier, in our case R. 'Aqiba, is conceptually linked to a view independently proposed by another sage, in our case R. Qaṭina. It would follow, then, that R. Qaṭina *does not* concur with R. Neḥemya, who ascribes the seventh psalm to the Sabbath of Creation and not to the future Sabbath at the end of times. Patently, this seems to rebut the claim that, "we find no one in the Talmud disagreeing with him," (*Teshubot ha-Rishba*, vol. 1, #9, 5a, cited Section V, n. 146). Support for R. Adrete's view may be found in Rashi ad loc. s.v. *ve-qa*, stating that *both* R. 'Aqiba and R. Neḥemya concur that the psalm of the Seventh Day refers to the Sabbath at the end of time. (I would like to point out that Rashi's style is awkward. Also, at least one line is missing from the corresponding passage in R. Ḥanan'el. Could it be that pious hands doctored the text so as not to offend an overly zealous public?) R. Adrete proposed that both R. 'Aqiba and R. Neḥemya were alluding to the future Sabbath at the end of the year 6000, and they only disagreed on the length of the future Sabbath: R. 'Aqiba maintained that it will last for one thousand years, whereas R. Neḥemya maintained that it will last for two thousand years. According to this line of thought, R. Neḥemya held a view later introduced in the name of Abayye, namely, that the future Sabbath will last two thousand years (אמר אביי: תרי חרוב).

There are two technical difficulties with this explanation, both of which concern the rules of citation. When the Talmud wishes to connect two independent controversies with one another, it *first* cites both controversies, and *then* it stipulates that the second controversy is somehow related to the first. In our case, after introducing the controversy between R. 'Aqiba and R. Neḥemya, the Talmud should have cited the alleged controversy between R. Qaṭina and Abayye, and *then* it should have stipulated that these two controversies are somehow related (וקמיפלגי בפלוגתא דרבי עקיבא ורבי נחמיה, ר' קטינא כרבי עקיבא ואביי כרבי נחמיה); see, for example, Ketubot 88b; Qiddushin 69b; Sanhedrin 9a; Bekhorot 25b, etc. In our case, however, the Talmud states: וקמיפלגי בדרב קטינא, "and the preceding controversy is relevant to the view of R. Qaṭina" alone – not to R. Qaṭina **and** Abayye! Furthermore, when citing two authorities, if the second authority *does not* oppose the first, the Talmudic formula is "אמר" and then the name of the authority. However, if the second authority *opposes* the preceding authority, first it cites the name of the authority, and then "אמר." Thus, if Abayye had opposed R. Qaṭina, the Talmud should have said: "אביי אמר." (Concerning this rule, see "On Martyrdom in Jewish Law," p. 398.) However, ancient editions and mss. read: "אמר אביי" – not "אביי אמר!"

There is a more substantial problem. The term "חריב/חרוב" in connection with R. Qaṭina's millennium *does not* mean 'annihilated' – as assumed by R. Adrete – but to 'lie in waste.' E.g., as with the Temple "that is חריב," that is, 'in ruins'; see Sanhedrin 96b; cf. Giṭṭin 57a; etc. The same applies with the form 'חרוב.' It means 'devastated by war'; see Megilla 4a; Giṭṭin 55b; 'Aboda Zara 50a; 'Arakhin 12a, b; etc. For example, the *Targum* on Hos. 4:3 rendered "Therefore doth the land **mourn**," as תחרוב ארעא. Accordingly, the sense of R. Qaṭina is that this "world" (עלמא), standing for pagan dominion and civilization, would last for a period of six thousand years. This period would be followed by a millennium of bliss, during which pagan civilization and dominion would collapse (חריב/חרוב). (On this type of celebration, see Berakhot 57b and Yebamot 17a.) This millennium alludes to the Messianic Age (see Mishna Berakhot 1:5), preceding the Resurrection of the Dead and the recognition of the Kingdom of God by the entire world. In keeping with this line of thought, the Talmud cites the view of Abayye that the world will "lie in waste for two (thousand years)." In support, Abayye quotes Hos. 6:2: "After **two days**, He will revive us on the third day. He will raise us up, that we may live in His presence" (as cited in full by R. Ḥanan'el). The *Targum* interpreted this verse as a prayer: "May (God) revive us in the Days of Solace, which will come in the future, on the Day of the Resurrection of the Dead. He will raise us up, and we shall live in His presence." Having the *Targum* in mind, Abayye proposed that the Messianic Age would be followed by the Resurrection of the Dead. Thus, Resurrection will be the link bridging the collapse of pagan civilization, forecasted by R. Qaṭina, and the future Sabbath of R. 'Aqiba that will come to pass at the end of time. Hence, the 'two-millennia' of Abayye: one for the collapse of paganism and the other for Resurrection.

In short, the interpretation offered by R. Adrete suffers some serious shortcomings. Conceptually, it is somehow problematic to see how the Talmud could have linked R. Qaṭina's view that the world will be destroyed with R. 'Aqiba's Sabbath suggesting heavenly bliss (cf. *AdRN, Hosafa* II, p. 152, s.v. *bayyom*). Of course, we can always point in his defense to Rashi. But, what about those who follow the text of the Talmud and the explanation offered by R. Ḥanan'el? Are we to dismiss them as heretics? Can we perhaps reconsider the plea submitted by R. Saportas to the anti-Maimonideans? It seems eminently sensible:

> I am very astonished at you, O superior scholars, for you have cast these matters behind your back! What is most amazing about that is that you damned anyone who does not explain the words of our rabbis and their aggadot according to Rashi (Quoted in Section V, nn. 178–179).

The idea that rabbinic scholarship and punctilious adherence to the Talmud were the decisive sources underlying anti-Maimonidean zeal needs to be carefully examined. See Section V, n. 115.

The preceding may help one understand why the anti-Maimonideans were determined to prevent sages of the rank of R. David Qimḥi from presenting a defense of Maimonides in Toledo; see Section V nn. 106, 298.

# 58. Semantic Assimilation

We had the opportunity to notice that in the intellectual tradition of Israel a semiotic relationship prevails between the text of Scripture and the Mental Law, whereby the Mental Law functions in the capacity of interpreter and the Scripture as the interpreted system. This relationship cannot be inverted; functioning as the interpreter system, the Mental Law cannot be interpreted by another system, just as we cannot interpret mathematics in terms of chemical phenomena or language in terms of the Morse code (see chapter 6). A major consequence of the bogus-Talmudists' unawareness of Scripture (see chapter 51) was that the Mental Law could no longer function as the *interpreter* system of Scripture. Rather, the Talmud and the entire corpus of rabbinic literature comprising the Mental Law became the *interpreted* system! The *interpreter* system was the analphabetic environment that bogus-Talmudists shared with their less sophisticated neighbors. Thus the twaddle and gabble peculiar to their 'dissertations': they hardly make sense!

The rabbis were sensitive to the dangers of semantic assimilation. A word severed from the 'signified,' e.g., as in incomprehensible liturgical pieces, is void of meaning; see Section V, n. 61. In such a situation the 'signifier' could be attached to whatever 'poets' and unscrupulous leaders wish to connect it; see chapter 4 and above appendix 7. Worse than this, the text of Scripture could be used as the *signifier* to a *signified* absorbed from antagonistic cultures and value-systems alien to Judaism. We have previously observed that in Judaism context is of the essence, and that the Tora and even the Tetragrammaton have no standing in a tainted environment, see appendix 56. The same applies to the Semantics of the Law. Since the meaning of an expression and its syntactical combinations are conditioned by, and interpreted within, the linguistic context of the community, without semantic autonomy, the traditional texts of Israel, Talmud included, can be reduced to a string of incoherent cacophonies, as with the 'Talmudists' in "The Day of the Willow" (see above chapter 51). At worst, the sacred texts could be used as tools to undermine the Tora and promote discord in Israel, as with 'Heroic Virtue,' see chapter 52.

Jews preserved semantic autonomy through the study of the text and language of Scripture. Therefore, the rabbis prescribed that as soon as a child "can speak, his father must teach him the **language** of the Tora"; see Y. Sukka III, 12, 54a; cf. Tosefta Ḥagiga 1:2, p. 375; *Sifre* #46, p. 104; Sukka 42a; and *Tosefta Ki-Fshuṭah,* Mo'ed, p. 1269. This foundational duty is registered in the major codes of law; see *MT Talmud Tora* 1:6; *Shulḥan 'Arukh, Yore De'a* CCXLV, 5. It consists of mastering the *Hebrew* text of Scripture. In this respect, translations – including the official Aramaic *Targum* – do not equal 'Scripture'; see Nedarim 36b. Someone reading a translation of the Bible has not discharged this foundational responsibility; see *MT Shabbat* 23:26 and below appendix 60. Biblical commentaries, too, do not equal 'Scripture'; see *MT Talmud Tora* 1:12. Therefore, the parental responsibility consists in having children master the proper "reading of the entire Scripture"; see *MT Talmud Tora* 1:7; *Shulḥan 'Arukh, Yore De'a* CCXLV, 6; cf. Qiddushin 30a, *Bayit Ḥadash* on *Ṭur Yore De'a* CCXLV, s.v. *haya*; and *Be'ur Ha-Gra* on *Shulḥan 'Arukh,* ibid. #14. Often, to justify biblical illiteracy, bogus-Talmudists cite R. Tam's view, *Tosafot* Qiddushin 30a s.v. loc. This 'proof' illustrates the level of appraisal and the reading evaluation peculiar to Scriptural-illiterate 'Talmudists.' R. Tam, himself an accomplished poet and Hebrew grammarian, was not referring to the foundational duty of mastering the text of the Hebrew Scripture, incumbent upon every Jew. Rather, he was referring to the daily requirement to study Tora incumbent upon everyone, including accomplished scholars. Obviously, when R. Tam said that "*we* (אנו) rely on..." the study of the Babylonian Talmud alone, he was including in the first person plural, seasoned scholars like himself – not illiterate students unfamiliar with the rudiments of Scripture. Incidentally, R. Tam's view was shared by Maimonides, *MT Talmud Tora* 1:12. (Respectfully, I don't agree with the interpretation of *Leḥem Mishne*, ad loc.)

Hebrew 'reading' comprises not only correct diction, but also mastery of Hebrew prosody (*ṭe'amim*); see Nedarim 36b and "Concerning the Term *Qore be-Iggeret*" (Heb.), p. 23. Their importance can be seen in the fact that the rabbis associated the prosody (*ṭe'amim*) with King Solomon; see 'Erubin 21b. On the supreme importance of mastering the vocalization *and* prosody of the Scripture, see *Kuzari* II, 72–73; III, 30–31.

Given that Jews lived in a hostile cultural environment, 'studying Tora' could amount to little if the hallowed texts and values are processed according to the linguistic and logical syntax of pagan society. The rabbis ('Erubin 53a-b) reported that unlike Galileans, Judeans did not assimilate because they were "punctilious" (הקפידו) about their language. To ensure this, they appended [vocalization] signs (ומתנחי להו סימני). R. Jonah ibn Jannaḥ, *Kitab al-Luma'*, p. 2 ll. 11–13, translated this expression to mean: "וצע אלאעראב ואלתדקיק ואלתעליל." In Judeo-Arabic, 'אלאעראב' stands not for 'grammatical inflection,' etc., as in classical Arabic, but for the punctuation appended to the text to signal the vocalization of the Hebrew wording. The term "וצ'ע" is an exact translation of "מתנחי," 'to place,' cf. Baba Batra 14b. Accordingly, "וצ'ע אלאעראב" are the vocalization marks *placed* on the text, designed to ensure the correct pronunciation of a word. The second term "תדקיק" stands for 'precision.' In Arabic, *mudaqqiq,* as per its Hebrew cognate, is someone who pronounces (see Mishna Berakhot 2:3) or acts (see Y. Berakhot II, 1, 4b) with 'precision.' In our context, it probably refers to the accurate enunciation of the word, as per tonic and atonic syllables, *dagesh*, etc., as well as the rules of prosody. The third term means 'to know or to examine the operative causes' of something. Since the topic is grammar, R. Jonah ibn Jannaḥ probably had in mind the morphologies of the language. Finally, on the basis of parallels from rabbinic texts, he explained the verb 'הקפידו' as to be 'conscientious,' 'scrupulous,' and 'demanding.' According to this explanation, the rabbis said that because "Judeans were punctilious about their language," they developed a system by which to transmit its proper vocalization and linguistic nuances. Therefore, "their Tora stood firmly in their hands." Let us note, that the three-fold division proposed by R. Jonah ibn Jannaḥ ("וצ'ע אלאעראב/ואלתדקיק/ואלת־עליל") is implicit in Neh. 8:8; see Megilla 3a; Y. Megilla IV, 1, 74d; Nedarim 36b; and cf. *Midrash 'Ezra*, p. 150. In addition to correct speech, Judeans learned from a single teacher. This awarded them semantic consistency and standardization. Finally, they published the text of the tractate that they taught, thus authorizing review and formal transmission of the material. In this fashion, they avoided long and contentious divisions. In contrast, the Galileans neglected all these; they failed to preserve their intellectual heritage (לא נתקיימה תורתן בידם), and ended up assimilating. Jewish sages in the Middle Ages too, beginning with R. Se'adya Gaon (882–942), called attention to the dangers of linguistic neglect, taking place all the way from the late biblical period; see his *Ha'egron*, ed. N. Allony (Jerusalem: The Academy of the Hebrew Language, 1969), pp. 158–160.

Throughout the Diaspora, the Scripture was Israel's virtual Temple. Upon opening the hallowed text, the faithful – no matter where and when – unlocked the Gates of Heaven and entered hallowed ground. Thus, the Jew could hear the voices of the Patriarchs and Moses and the Prophets; David's sweet songs, Job and his friends' dissertations about the Ways of the Lord, and multitudes of men and women speaking to God and hearing His words. On occasion, she/he discovered that God was in fact talking to her/him at that very moment. This essential point was made by R. Isaac Profiaṭ Duran (died ca. 1414), *Ma'ase Efod*, p. 11.

> ... Just as the Temple was the ground of God's continuous presence (שכינה) in the bosom of Israel ... so this Sacred Book (=

> the Hebrew Scripture) is the operational vehicle by which the Divine Providence is manifest within the Nation (of Israel): when intensely studying it with the proper attitude, and further penetrating its precious pronouncements. It (the Scripture) is the means by which (the Jewish) continuity is preserved, for the ability (of the Jewish people) to overcome (adversity) and gain success.

Scripture is also the means by which Israel will obtain atonement for her past follies and regain national redemption.

> Just as at the Temple, the Nation's sins ... were atoned through the performance of the solemn sacramental rituals, studying this Sacred Book, with the appropriate attitude, keeping it always in mind, and retaining it in the hearts (of the people), will be the grounds for God's pardoning the Nation's sins and her failings.

To give coherence to his argument, R. Duran went on to show that both Scripture and Temple were structured into three parallel sections.

> This Sacred Book has properties similar to those of the Temple. It is (also) divided into three sections. [1] The Temple comprised the Holy of Holies, where the Ark containing the Scroll of the Law was placed. [2] Then the Sanctuary, where the table, the menorah, and the golden altar stood. [3] And the Hall or Yard containing the altar of the holocaust... Similarly, this Sacred Book contains [three sections]. [First] the Divine Law, conveyed by God to Moses our Teacher, may he rest in peace, Lord of the Prophets, whose prophecy is categoric unlike that of any other prophets, God having spoken to him face to face. The second section consists of the *Prophets* that although proceeding from God were conveyed through angels ... The third section contains the *Hagiography* which

> was pronounced by the Holy Spirit, a [prophetic] class lower than Prophecy.

Cf. Dov Rafel, "*Haqdamat Sefer 'Ma'ase Efod' le-Profiaṭ Duran,*" *Sinai,* Jubilee Volume, 100 (1987), vol. 2, p. 756.

R. Raḥamim Menaḥem Miṭrani (d. 5627/1867), author of *Me'am Lo'ez* on Joshua, put forward a similar thesis. The book was written in Judeo-Spanish and translated into Hebrew by Samuel Yerushalmi (Jerusalem: H. Vagshal, 5732/1972). In the author's Introduction, p. 10, we read:

> ... The Twenty-four [books comprising the Hebrew Scripture] were called by our sages 'Sacred Books' – in analogy to God's Sanctuary [see above Section II, n. 70]. Given that presently we have no Sanctuary, the Sacred Books shielded us just as the Temple had previously shielded Israel. It is thanks to these Twenty-four Sacred Books that we are able to survive this brutal Exile. Thus, in the same fashion that the sacramental sacrifices atoned for us (at the Temple), the Sacred Books, too, atone for us ... since the Twenty-four Sacred Books parallel the Temple. They are divided into three sections: the *Law, Prophets,* and *Hagiography,* similar to the Temple that contained three sections: the Holy of Holies, the Sanctuary (*Hekhal),* and the Hall. For this reason they were called 'God's Sanctuary.' The Twenty-four Books [comprising the Hebrew Scripture] parallel the twenty-four Priestly Guards serving at the Temple.
>
> When Israel went into Exile to Babylonia, they were eventually saved because they studied the *Law,* and sought to understand it. As it is written: "And they read the Scroll of God's Law, distinctly, and they gave the sense [of the text], and caused them to understand the reading" (Neh. 8:8) – since they would read from the Scroll of the Law and explain the text with great acumen and rationale and understanding of what they studied. Because of this good habit they had the merits

> to have the Second Temple built in their own days. Later, after they went once more into Exile, they repented and again began to study the *Law, Prophets,* and *Hagiography*. And God gave us grace in the eyes of the nations, and evil decrees (against Jews) were called off. (The Jews of) France and Germany, however, were the exception, and many misfortunes befell them because they were lax and did not set daily classes to study the *Law, Prophets,* and *Hagiography*. The Expulsion from Sepharad, too, came about for the same reason: the people of Sepharad had neglected this [see above chapter 66]. The people of Aragon, however, were the exception, and they were saved because they studied the *Law, Prophets,* and *Hagiography*. Among us in the Ottoman Empire, where the majority (of Jews) came from the Expulsion from Sepharad, they are still lax in their study of the *Prophets* and *Hagiography*. Even the few souls who study them, do not study their explanation properly. What are we to respond in the Celestial Court when they ask us why we have neglected to study them?

Sigmund Freud, too, sensed something similar. When referring to the dispersion of Israel he wrote, *Moses and Monotheism,* trans. Katherine Jones (New York: Vintage Books, 1955), p. 147: "From now on, it was the Holy Book, and the study of it, that kept the scattered people together." We can now appreciate the feeling of disgust by men of the ilk of R. Samuel ha-Nagid and R. Jonah ibn Jannaḥ at the analphabetic reading of bogus-Talmudists. Indeed, if you believe that the Scripture *is* God's Sanctuary, reading the Tora with contempt for basic Masoretic rules is no less offensive than someone stepping all over the Holy of Holies trashing it under his feet and knocking it down with rude indifference. See above chapter 51.

The purpose of Maimonides' definition of key-biblical terms in the first part of the *Guide* was to expose the semantic assimilation that these terms underwent as a consequence of analphabetic interpretation. On the propensity of the persecuted to absorb the mental norms of the persecutor, see *In the Shadow of History*, pp. 9–12; a good example of this phenomenon is the identification of *'aboda zara* with 'idolatry' (see appendix 11). On the assimilation of 'theological' doctrines proposed by hostile religions, see *Homo Mysticus*, pp. 96–98. An important characteristic of semantic assimilation is the fact that the victim is never aware that the ideas and values which he has absorbed will end up devouring him from within; see *Homo Mysticus*, pp. 130–131 and above chapters 56, 57. One of the most harmful forms of Jewish assimilation is the notion of monolingualism, according to which 'Hebrew' is the equivalent of some sort of superior language with magical power. It would be of some interest to note that Johann Gottlieb Fichte (1762–1814), whom Russell regarded as the spiritual father of Nazism, maintained that, "The purity of the German language makes the German alone capable of profundity." Therefore, "to have character and to be German undoubtedly means the same"; cited by Bertrand Russell, "The Ancestry of Fascism," (1935), in idem, *Let the People Think* (London: Watts & Co., 1941), pp. 68–69. See Fichte, *Addresses to the German Nation*, trans. R. F. Jones and G. H. Turnbull (Chicago: Open Court, 1922); and idem, "On the Linguistic Capacity and the Origin of Language," in trans. and ed. Jere Paul Surber, *Language and German Idealism: Fichte's Linguistic Philosophy* (Atlantic Highland, N.J.: Humanities Press, 1996). For further thoughts on the subject, see above chapter 2.

# 59. Heroes and Heroism

'Heroism' and 'heroic action and behavior' are pagan concepts; see *The New Science*, ##610–611, p. 225–226; cf ibid. ##637–641, pp. 239–242. The identification of 'martyrdom' (מסירות נפש) with 'heroism' is another instance of semantic assimilation. Judaism does not recognize heroism as a virtue – the highest form of personal endeavor – whereby an individual offers his life for the sake of a belief or ideal. What Scripture applauds is a high level of magnanimity and virtuous *behavior* towards fellow human beings; see C. Gancho, "Heroísmo Religioso," *Enciclopedia Biblica*, vol. 3 (Barcelona: Ediciones Garriaga, 1964), cols. 1212–1213.

Maimonides was particularly sensitive to the dangers of mental assimilation affecting some Jewish scholars as well as the general public; see *Guide* II, 11, p. 192, ll. 17–29. In an important passage in *Shemona Peraqim* IV, *Perush ha-Mishnayot*, vol. 4, 384, where he criticized Jews who had adopted certain ascetic ideals, he wrote:

> ...Those members of our religion who mimic the nations have postulated – and I am addressing myself specifically to them – that (the reason) they inflict pain onto their bodies and repress their bodily pleasures (Ar. מן אשקא אג'סאמהם וקטע לד'תהם), is to prepare the bodily faculties (to worship God)... they are wrong, as I shall explain.

Cf. ibid, p. 383 n. 22; cf. above, Section III p. 106, n. 51. In *Shemona Peraqim* VI, *Perush ha-Mishnayot,* vol. 4, 392, Maimonides referred to "some of our later scholars who have contracted the sickness (Ar. מרצ'וא) of theologians (Ar. מתכלמין)." About these theologians, see *Homo Mysticus,* pp. 94–98. One of the symptoms "is a sickness which they find in their souls (Ar. מרץ' יג'דונה פי אנפסהם), and which they can neither articulate nor express." That is their belief that the precepts of the Tora have no rationale; see *Guide* III, 31, p. 382, ll. 23–24; cf. ibid. 32, p. 385, l. 19.

The association *qadosh*/hero is the effect of semantic assimilation. The notion that 'sanctity' (קדושה) can be obtained outside the fulfillment of a 'precept' (מצוה) contradicts the rabbinic doctrine stipulating that "holiness is acquired through [the fulfillment] of each one of the precepts" (קדושת כל המצות); see appendix 4. For that reason, Maimonides classified heroism as wrongdoing, not a virtue. When discussing the 'golden rule' of balancing two extreme tendencies affecting the individual's behavior, *Shemona Peraqim* IV, *Perush ha-Mishnayot,* vol. 4, 381, he observed:

> Many people are in error about these actions, supposing that one of these extremes is 'good' and constitutes a 'moral virtue' of the soul. Sometimes, they suppose the former extreme to be 'good' – as when they suppose 'heroism' to be a moral quality, and call the heroes 'brave.' And when they see someone behaving with extreme daring and intrepidness, challenging danger and purposely putting himself in harm's way, and perchance he is saved, they praise him and say: 'this is a brave person!'

Cf. *Homo Mysticus,* p. 156. The *converso* writer, too, was anti-hero, for example, *Lazarillo de Tormes* and *Don Quixote*; see *In the Shadow of History,* pp. 62, 69–70. Let us note that no lesser a thinker than Luis Vives espoused what may be properly described as an anti-hero ideology; see ibid. p. 240 n. 75.

The preceding bears directly on the concept of 'martyrdom.' For

Judaism, 'Sanctification of the Name [of God]' (קדוש השם), or 'martyrdom,' is not a reworked version of Christian 'heroism'; see above Section V n. 75. As with all precepts, this, too, is regulated by precise legal definitions. Therefore, although martyrdom is commendable under the circumstances defined by the Law, it is sinful if done when not required by the Law. Rather, such an individual is responsible for his own death, and would have to render account for his folly before his Maker; see *MT Yesode ha-Tora* 5:1. For a detailed analysis of this precept in Jewish Law, see "On Martyrdom in Jewish Law: Maimonides and Nahmanides," pp. 373–407.

The place of 'religious fervor' in Judaism was the focus of a dispute between Maimonides and an anonymous rabbi urging North African Jews to martyrdom rather than confess Muhammad's mission; see *Iggeret ha-Shmad* in *Iggerot ha-Rambam*, vol. 1, pp. 30–59. Maimonides' point was that only when a Jew is coerced to worship in a manner specifically defined by Jewish law as *'aboda zara* is martyrdom commendable. On the halakhic issues involved, see "Two Models of Jewish Spirituality," pp. 11–17. The real concern, however, pertained to assimilation. Inspired by Christian (and Muslim) religious fervor, the anonymous rabbi argued that since Christians would "rather die than confess his [Muhammad] mission," Jews, too, should choose martyrdom. To which Maimonides retorted, "Is it that there is no God in Israel that we have to learn about our faith from Moslems and Christians?" If one were to accept the notion that pious fervor is a true expression of religiosity, then, Maimonides reasoned, "we would have to burn ourselves and our children in the service of God," as heathens practiced in biblical times. Maimonides concluded that the rabbi was espousing "the view of heretics (*minim*; cf. ibid. p. 37 and above appendix 55) and Christians," ibid. p. 33. Maimonides' argument coincides with the position of R. Judah ha-Levi, *Kuzari* III, 23, rejecting the role of 'religious fervor' from Judaism. Otherwise, we would have to adopt the practices of "believers in dualism, in the eternity of the world, in [the conjuration of] spirits, in the ways of hermits dwelling in seclusion in mountains, and those who burn their children in fire [as a religious service], given that they, too, are also striving (*mujtahidun*) to draw near God." See above Appendices 4 and 51.

Let us note, in conclusion, that the whole idea of 'heroism' involves the notion of 'triumph' and 'war' and 'violence.' Thomas Carlyle (1795–1881), who was a great admirer of Fichte, and was the author of *On Heroes and Hero Worship* (1841), believed that, "There is no objective criterion of 'nobility' except success in war"; cited by Russell, *Let the People Think*, p. 70. See Jorge Luis Borges, "Dos Libros," in *Obras Completas* (Madrid: Ultramar, 1977), pp. 723–726.

# 60. *Ḥasid* and *Ḥasidut*

There is a concerted effort among modern historians, both 'religious' and 'secular' to discredit Maimonides and the Maimonidean tradition by claiming that, on the one hand, he was 'too' rationalist, and on other hand, that his son was 'too' mystical. Their primary intent is to validate current models of Judaism, of either a soulless, absurd rationalism, or a brainless piety. Both these models are the effect of semantic assimilation, see above appendix 58, and have nothing to do with either the Hebrew Scripture or the Talmud. A principal consideration of my *Homo Mysticus* was the centrality of a genuine mystical experience in Maimonides' intellectual apparatus, and consequently, of the importance of exposing brainless *ḥasidut*. Thus the need to further develop and expose the meaning of *Jewish* piety, something about which our modern historians know nothing.

Let me point out the extraordinary fact that Maimonides' descendants for six generations composed works on *ḥasidut*. His son, R. Abraham, wrote *The High Ways to Perfection*, and thus did his children and children's children! The last descendant known to us – Maimonides' sixth generation – R. David Maimon, penned *al-Murshid*, ed. and trans. P. B. Fenton (Jerusalem: Mekize Nirdamim, 1987). Before embarking upon an exposition of this topic, let us make it clear that the prevailing definition of *ḥasidut* as doing *more* than what the Tora requires, as per heroic-*qedoshim* virtue, is incorrect. If we are to come to grips with the Jewish concept of *ḥasidut* we must remember that although the fulfillment of a single *miṣva* suffices for salvation, see above appendix 4, it is still incumbent upon everyone, if and whenever possible, to try and fulfill every single *miṣva*. In light of this doctrine, it would be presumptuous for any individual to boast of having done *more* than what the Tora has required; that somehow he *never* missed an opportunity to do what was incumbent upon him and that in no way has he ever erred. There is a remarkable passage, in *The High Ways to Perfection*, vol. 2, pp. 65–69, addressing this common fallacy:

> Now it is necessary that we call thy attention also to the fact that just as some of the scholars err by being conceited about their knowledge until they return to the correct point of view to the principles and general (outlines) to which we have called attention, thus some pious err by being conceited about their religiosity and their piety until they return to the correct point of view to the principles and general (outlines) to which we shall call attention. And that is that thou must know that we are commanded by Him, exalted be He, (nay) held accountable, for the performance of *all* "The commandments of the Torah," its (positive) commands as well as its prohibitions – and thou knowest the multitude of their numbers and what is specified for thee to perform of them, and no one in Israel may content himself with the performance of some of them to the exclusion of certain others that are specified for him. He said, exalted be He: "Oh that they had a heart like this always, to fear Me, to keep all My commandments always" (Deut. 5:26). Mark (well) His statement "all my commandments" and "always." And such (statements) are numerous in the Bible – "In all the ways which the Lord your God hath commanded you, shall ye walk" (Deut. 5:30). "And ye shall do all my commandments" (Num. 15:40)...
>
> If, then, we were to assume (the existence of) a person who obeys all that is incumbent upon him of the "positive commandments" not being remiss in anything that is incumbent

upon him thereof, (and who at the same time) refrains from (transgressing) all "negative commands" not perpetrating anything thereof except one "commandment," that would be a defect in (his observance of) "he did not keep all His commandments," but overstepped or transgressed some of them; and even if we were to assume that he be safe from all that, always, for the (entire) length of his life except one time, as for example that he trespass in the (matter of the) "love of a neighbor" on some day or he transgress (the prohibition of) "keeping (a grudge)" for some time, that would be a defect in (his observance of) religion because "he did not keep (the commandments) always" as God, exalted be He, had commanded.

... And in accordance with this observation Solomon stated categorically and publicly saying: "For there is not a righteous man upon earth who doeth good and sinneth not" (Eccl. 7:20). How, then, is it conceivable that a human being should pride himself on religiosity? ...

Moreover is it necessary to remember the expressed statement of the Torah that cautions the adherent of the Law against thinking that he possesses complete piety and he is deserving of His salvation.

If, now, thou beest of those who are externally religious, how, then, canst thou be vain thereof, when before thee is inward religiosity which is the aim of the external (type)? If, again, thou art of those who serve (God) with inward religiosity, how then, canst thou be vain thereof, when thou art held accountable for errors, as they (Yebamot 121b) have said: "The Holy One Blessed Be He deals with those around Him strictly, even to a hair's breadth?"

The following anecdote about Maimonides, ibid. p. 71, is an illuminating example of his opinion of those believing themselves to be faultless.

> It was said in his (Maimonides) presence that one of the religious said on the night of (the Day) of "Atonement": "I do not know what sin I should repent from." Said my father and teacher, the memory of the righteous is blessed, when he heard that: "Poor fellow! If he had (only) known what he ought to know, he would have repented from thinking within himself that he has no sin to repent (cf. *The High Ways to Perfection*, vol. 1, p. 54).

We now return to *ḥasid* and *ḥasidut*. German *ḥasidut*, tells us Professor Marcus:

> ... is centered on the premise that God's will consists of more than what was explicitly revealed in the Torah and mediated by rabbinic law. Infinite in scope, the will of the Creator is required of the Pietist. Complementing that idea is the infinite obligation which the Pietist has of being "forever resourceful in fearing God," of engaging continuously in a search for the hidden will by striving to discover new prohibitions, make new safeguards, new ways of serving God by "fearing Him," by loving Him selflessly, sacrificially, totally. But the total process of this search requires that the Pietists experience divinely arranged trials expressed in the power of evil impulse in oneself and in society. Those trials are designed to provide opportunities for the Pietist to earn reward and to make it possible for a righteous person to appear. Finally, the soteriological basis for the Qalonides' [a distinguished rabbinic family flourishing in Ashkenaz] pietistic ideal is expressed as a reinterpretation of the maxim that "reward is proportional to pain" (Ivan G. Marcus, *Piety and Society*, Leiden: E. J. Brill, 1981, p. 35).

This view, however, has nothing to do with either the Hebrew Scripture or Talmud, but with the tendencies of submission and domination discussed in *Escape from Freedom*, chapter 5. Concerning the term *ḥasid,* it should be noted that in Jer. 3:12 God depicts Himself as *ḥasid,* a term which in Ps. 145:17 is used to depict the exquisite and wondrous workings of the Lord; cf. *Guide* III, 53, p. 465, ll. 9–18. *Ḥasid* may also apply to individuals, see II Sam. 22:26, Mic. 7:2, Ps. 12:2; as well as to nations, Ps. 43:1. The rabbis regarded *ḥasidut* and *middat ḥasidut,* 'norm of *ḥasidut*' as an exemplary conduct, not required by halakha but that one should try to do as a kind of *noblesse oblige*; see Baba Meṣi'a 52b, Ḥolin 130b, etc., in contradistinction to *middat din,* 'legal norm'; see Y. Shebi'it X, 4, 39d, etc. In the Golden Age of Spain, *ḥasid* was used to depict an individual 'sensitive' to the exquisite providence exhibited by God. The title was given to gentiles; see *MT Teshuba* 3:5; cf. *Sefer Sha'ashu'im,* p. 7 n. 3 (cf. however, *Sefer ha-Kuzari* II, 49). In this respect, we should note that the rabbis extended this term metaphorically to indicate gracious habits among animals; see Ḥolin 63a, *Midrash Tehillim,* CIV, 14, p. 444; cf. *Abot de-R. Natan,* A, VIII, p. 38. In my opinion, biblical *ḥesed,* too, indicates a behavior reflecting exquisite attention and care. (Occasionally it is used as a euphemism for 'shame,' 'abomination,' e.g. Lev. 20:17.) For a different understanding of this term, see Nelson Glueck, *Ḥesed in the Bible* (Cincinnati: Hebrew Union College, 1967).

Not everything exceeding the strict requirement of halakha qualifies as *ḥasidut*; see Y. Berakhot II, 9, 5d; *Perush ha-Mishnayot, Soṭa* 3:3, vol. 3, p. 256. There must be a rationale to 'devotion.' On one occasion, upon examining the merits of some 'devotional' act, the individual in question was censured for the nonsense he was doing, instead of being commended for it, see *Abot de-R. Natan,* A, XII, p. 56 and cf. Tosefta Soṭa 15:11–12, p. 243–244. An example of senseless *ḥasidut* would be someone becoming destitute as a result of squandering all of his assets for charity; see *MT 'Arakhin* 9:13. Similarly, Mishna Soṭa 3:3 denounces "a foolish *ḥasid*."

A *ḥasid* is much more than a *ḥakham* ('sage'), as we will now demonstrate. The latter is someone who had acquired a measure of both intellectual and ethical qualities; see *Perush ha-Mishnayot, Abot* 5:6, vol. 4, p. 458, and *Guide* III, 54. A *ḥasid* is an individual who, in addition to having developed his intellectual and ethical faculties (see *Perush ha-Mishnayot, Abot* 2:10, vol. 4, p. 425), is committed to a life-long process of spiritual edification and excellence. Given that the forces and impulses within an individual are not perfectly calibrated, see *MT De'ot* 1:1, a *ḥasid* is someone who in the process of harmonizing these forces within, tilts one of these impulses slightly in one direction in such a manner that results in spiritual development and enhancement; see *Perush ha-Mishnayot, Abot* 5:11–13, pp. 460–463; cf. ibid. 4:4, p. 440 and *Sefer ha-Kuzari* II, 50; III, 4. We should note in this context that in Nedarim 32b the "good tendency" in man (יצר הטוב) is likened to "a wise, but frail individual." Although having "wisdom," this individual needs to struggle to contravene the "bad tendency" (יצר הרע) – who is a "mighty king," implying cunning and physical power. In this manner, man's inner conflicts are likened to a struggle between wisdom and might. Maimonides dedicated the bulk of *Shemona Peraqim, Perush ha-Mishnayot,* vol. 4, pp. 372–407, as well as *MT De'ot* chapter 1, to explaining how to proceed with this type of intellectual and ethical calibration. Accordingly, *ḥasidut* involves a continuous process of introspection and evaluation; cf. Mo'ed Qaṭan 5a and Baba Batra 78b.

Before presenting an outline of Maimonides' general theory of *ḥasid* (Ar. פאצ'ל), it would be helpful to examine a few key Arabic terms that he used in developing this subject. These terms are well known from Sufist literature. Nonetheless, to bring out their concrete meaning, a few notes would be helpful. The first term, 'אנקטאע,' conveys the general sense of 'dedication' and 'consecration,' and this is how it is rendered by Jewish translators. There is a fundamental aspect to this term that could be lost in translation. The root of 'אנקטאע' is 'קט"ע,' which means 'to excise,' 'to cut,' and 'break off.' In our case, it involves a *psychological process* by which the individual 'dissociates himself from his surroundings' by mentally 'excising himself' from the mundane and daily routine. E.g., Israel's "אנקטאע" from the worldly by journeying into the Desert, and putting her faith in God's providence; see Ps. 78:52 and *Guide* III, 24, p. 362, l. 24; cf. R. Abraham, *Perush*, p. 379. (Hence the term *ḥesed* in Jer. 2:2; see *Homo Mysticus*, p. 163, and cf. ibid. pp. 156, 158.) The second term, 'כ'לואת', root כ'ל"ו, is commonly found in Sufist literature in the sense of 'solitude.' Let us note in passing that this is one of the many Hebrew and Aramaic key theological and legal terms brought into the Muslim world by Arabic speaking Jews. It appears in Jer. 32:2: "כלוא"; root 'כל"א,' cf. Num. 11:28: "כלאם," denoting 'imprisonment,' 'detention'; see *Targum* and R. Se'adya Gaon ad loc.; cf. Gen. 23:6; and cf. II Kings 17:4; Ps. 88:9, etc. The form 'כלא' (cf. Jer. 37:4) is used in Modern Hebrew to designate 'jail' and the 'penitentiary' in general. In our context, it refers to the 'boundaries' that an individual resolves to set *upon* himself, to shelter himself from a specific lure lurking 'outside,' affecting one of his weak points; cf. Ḥolin 6a. Maimonides' son, R. Abraham, dedicated an entire chapter to explaining and analyzing the niceties of this facet of *ḥasidut*; see *The High Ways to Perfection*, vol. 2, pp. 382–425; and cf. his *Perush*, pp. 109, 307. The third term, 'אנפראד,' root פר"ד, means 'to be alone in seclusion.' It also implies 'uniqueness' and 'singularity.' In our case, the individual seeks 'seclusion' to be 'alone in the Presence of God.' The fourth term, 'תסעי,' root סע"י, has the general meaning of 'to endeavor.' In our context, however, it stands for 'journeying' and 'marching' towards a given destination. The Hebrew cognate is used in the Scripture to describe Israel's journey through the Desert; see Ex. 13:20; 14:15; Num. 30:28; Ps. 78:52, etc.; and *Homo Mysticus*, p. 245 n. 246. Maimonides used this term to describe the 'journey' ahead, challenging those who had the grit to cross the threshold of the Heavenly Palace; see *Guide* III, 51, p. 455, l. 4; p. 456, l. 26; p. 457, l. 8; p. 459, l. 27; p. 463, ll. 15–16.

The first three terms are found in a passage where Maimonides discussed the special "kind of worship" that comes "after" the individual "formed an intellectual conception" of God:

> It was thus explained that the object of [the intellectual] conception [of God] is to be able to excise oneself (אנקטאע) [from the mundane] for Him, and drive the intellect towards His love, always. This could best be accomplished in solitude (כ'לואות) and retreat (אנפראד). That is the reason why every

> *hasid* (Ar. פאצ'ל) favors retreat (אנפראד), and shuns human contact except for necessity (*Guide* III, 51, p. 457, ll. 12–15).

The fourth term appears in a passage proposing that the special type of worship is possible only after the individual has perceived God in rational terms:

> However, one ought to endeavor to proceed towards this class of worship only after having formed an intellectual conception [of God]. Then, when one is able to conceive of God and His works according to what reason determines, one should proceed and endeavor to excise oneself (אנקטאע) [from the mundane] and advance in His direction (Ar. ותסעי, root סע"י) towards His nearness. Also, one should strengthen the link between oneself and God, which is the mind. (*Guide* III, 51, p. 456, ll. 24–27.)

I take the 'intellectual conception of God,' 'breaking off' with the mundane, and then 'journeying' towards the ultimate quest, as an inner dynamic process in which each step is predicated on the other. Cf. *MT Teshuba* 10:6:

> ליחד עצמו (= כ'לואת), להבין ולהשכיל בחכמות ותבונות (= אנקטאע) המודיעים לו את קונו כפי כח שיש באדם להבין ולהשיג (= אנפראד).

Maimonides alerted the reader that in his quest, the individual would have to "persist constantly" (Ar. אלחץ' אבדא) and conceptualize God mentally, "not on the basis of social convention or imagination"; *Guide* III, 51, p. 457, ll. 10–11. It is in this state of mind that the faithful can attain what the rabbis designated

> ... worship of the heart (Heb. עבודה שבלב), which means to me to direct the mind towards the First Intelligence and to with-

> draw (Ar. אנפראד) according to his faculties. This is the reason why at his deathbed, David instructed Solomon and stressed these matters (to him). I mean, to journey (Ar. אלסעי) towards His perception, and advance (Ar. אלסעי) towards worshipping Him after (rational) discernment (*Guide* III, 51, p. 457, ll. 5–9).

The rabbinic source is Mishna Berakhot 5:1, where it is reported that before prayers (= עבודה שבלב), "the ancient *ḥasidim* would withdraw for one hour." Maimonides, *Perush ha-Mishnayot*, vol. 1, p. 74 explained that these men "would discontinue (Ar. יקטעון, root קט"ע) conversation and thought and then get ready to pray." cf. *MT Tefilla* 4:16 and R. Abraham Maimonides, *Teshubot*, #62, pp. 62–65. For some insight and background, see *Homo Mysticus*, pp. 168–180. Thus, God's "praise" may be found only "in the community of *ḥasidim*" (Ps. 149:1).

Although we should all strive to adopt some norms of *ḥasidut*, particularly acts of compassion towards others, see *MT 'Abadim* 9:5 and *Mattanot 'Aniyyim* 10:1–3, not everyone can actually be a *ḥasid*. In fact, the rabbis ranked *ḥasidut* as one of the highest degrees of human development; see Mishna Soṭa 9:5, 'Aboda Zara 20a, Y. Sheqalim, III, 3, 47c, etc. Maimonides ranked *ḥasidut* to be only one step below prophecy; see 'Introduction,' *Shemona Peraqim, Perush ha-Mishnayot*, vol. 4, p. 372; cf. Introduction, *Perush ha-Mishnayot*, vol. 1, pp. 42–43. In the course of time, genuine *ḥasidut* became a rarity; see Tosefta Soṭa 15:5, p. 240 and Y. Soṭa, IX, 16, 24c.

Summing up our discussion so far, although an ignorant person could and should adopt some of the *norms* peculiar to *ḥasidut*, either as a matter of social habit or personal disposition, see *Perush ha-Mishnayot, Abot* 2:6, vol. 4, p. 424; 5:6, p. 457, he cannot possibly be a *ḥasid*.

Having the bogus-*ḥasid* in mind, Maimonides wrote that to believe that "an illiterate person could be a *ḥasid* is not only a flat denial of what the rabbis have categorically rejected (see Abot 2:5), but also of reason" (Introduction, *Perush ha-Mishnayot*, vol. 1, p. 43). On the reasons moving some people to pretend to be a *ḥasid*, see *Ḥobot ha-Lebabot*, IX, 3, pp. 391–393. Not only is it that an illiterate person (עם

הארץ) could not be a *ḥasid*, but close contact with such people would hinder mental and spiritual edification. This is why, although the rabbis cautioned not to be anti-social, see *Perush ha-Mishanyot, Soṭa* 3:3, vol. 3, p. 256, and urged all to be courteous to everyone, see Abot 4:1 and cf. Mishna Berakhot 2:2, nonetheless, one should not fraternize in the company of illiterate people (עמי הארץ); see *The High Ways to Perfection*, vol. 2, p. 79. And least of all, one should not eat and consort with them, see Pesaḥim 49a. The reason is that this level of fraternization would hinder the kind of internal solitude essential for *ḥasidut*. For this reason the *ḥasid* "will avoid human contact except for necessity" (*Guide* III, 51, p. 457, ll. 10–15). Bearing this in mind, the Pharisees, Heb. 'פרושים' – a term that in Judeo-Arabic linguistic tradition is synonymous with 'asceticism' (Ar. *zuhd*) – avoided fraternizing with ill-bred and ignominious people; see *MT Ṭum'at Okhalin* 16:12. (As was pointed out by A. S. Yahuda, *'Ereb ve-'Arab*, p. 159 n. 8, 'Pharisees' have nothing to do with the '*Mu'tazila*'.)

The anti-Pharisee diatribe in Matt. 23:1–39, etc. needs to be critically examined. Obviously, there were bogus-Pharisees, see Mishna Soṭa 3:3; Soṭa 22a; Y. Berakhot IX, 5, 14b; *Abot de-R. Natan*, A, XXXVII, p. 109; B, XLV, p. 124 and the editor's notes ad loc.; cf. *Guide* III, 33, p. 390, ll. 11–20, etc. – just as there were bogus-*ḥasidim*; see *Ḥobot ha-Lebabot*, IX, 3, pp. 391–393. Conceit and phony religiosity are not exclusive to Jews and Judaism (with the minor difference that Jews do their utmost to expose their own religious impostors, whereas in other systems they do their utmost to conceal them). Abominations of all kinds are not strange to the Christian clergy. Spanish speaking Sepharadim used the expression *Pecado de padre*, 'A sin of a Christian-priest,' to designate 'a repulsive outrage.' Rather, the Pharisees were maligned because they disclosed something highly sensitive about Jesus' background and lifestyle. Contrary to popular myth, Jesus did not belong to the 'unprivileged' class. In some circles, he gained a reputation as a lover of food and wine.

"The Son of Man came eating and drinking and they say, 'Look, a glutton and winebibber, a friend of tax-collectors and sinners!'" (Matt.

11:19). This alone should suffice to dispel the myth about Jesus' poverty and frugal habits. His family tomb, recently discovered in Talpioth, between ancient Jerusalem and Beth Lehem, proves beyond the shadow of a doubt that the image of 'helpless-baby in the manger,' as portrayed in Lk. 2:7, pertains to the Jesus of myth, not to the Jesus of history. Concerning his family's tomb, see Simcha Jacobovici and Charles Pellegrino, *Jesus Family Tomb* (San Francisco: Harper, 2007). I propose that the main rationale for the anti-Pharisee diatribe is because they dared censure Jesus for consorting with "tax-collectors and sinners"; see Matt. 9:9–13; 10:3; cf. Lk. 18:9–14, etc. The Pharisees did not censure Jesus' disciples, but, as per Matt. 9:11, *only* Jesus himself. (The fact that this point went unnoticed by specialists on the subject is indicative of the level of intellectual integrity peculiar to those involved in explaining the Christian Scripture.) The following is the translation of the passage in Matt. 9:10–11, as rendered in *Pocket Interlinear New Testament*, Jay P. Green, Sr. Editor (Grand Rapids, Michigan: Baker Book House, 1982), p. 19:

> And it happened as he [Jesus] reclined in the house, Behold many tax-collectors and sinners coming, *they* were reclining with Jesus and his disciples. And seeing, the Pharisees said to his disciples, Why does your teacher eat with tax-collectors and sinners?

Let us pay close attention to two remarkable details casually overlooked by specialists. First, the expression "reclined in the house" reminds us of the triclinium, peculiar to Roman luxury homes, commonly used by the upper classes for reclining at the *coena,* or dinner. This ties up with an important custom connected to the triclinium: the "washing of the feet" – but not the hands, see below – mentioned in connection to Jesus (Jn. 12:2–4) and his disciples (Jn. 13:2–4). As we learn from numerous paintings and brass relief, people reclined barefooted for fear of soiling the triclinium. We can now understand the need for washing the feet before reclining. Usually, the washing was performed by servants standing ready to minister to the guest. In the case of Jesus (Jn. 12:2–4) and his disciples (Jn. 13:3–16) it was done by someone important, as a sign of affection. The fact that Jesus did not seem to mind that Mary "anointed his feet" with costly oil (Jn. 12:1–3), rather than, as proposed by Judas (the prototype 'Jew'), distributing the money among the poor (cf. Jn. 12:8), indicates that he was not a stranger to these types of amenities. From the fact that after washing the feet of his disciples, Jesus "reclined" (Jn. 13:12, as accurately translated in the *Pocket Interlinear New Testament*, p. 263: "reclining again"), we learn that the participants in the Last Supper were lying on a triclinium, as peculiar to Roman luxury dinners. Second is the fact that "tax-collectors" – the *publicans* of the Vulgate – dined at a place frequented by Jesus and his disciples. Tax-collectors were men of great wealth, who paid large amounts of money to purchase from the Roman authorities the right to extort taxes from the people. They were greedy and predatory and evil. One does not need to be particularly perspicacious to realize that "tax-collectors and sinners" would not share their triclinium with penniless preachers and lily-white youths. A most telling detail is that *they* came to Jesus and *they* reclined with him, indicating that *they* cherished him. Why?

Jesus was the darling of tax-collectors – and for a good reason! His famous dictum: "Render unto Caesar the things which are Caesar's" (Matt. 22:21), gave these thugs a mantle of respectability. This was consistent with his theory that in the mode of Roman tax-collectors it was permitted to seize property on his behalf without due process; see Matt. 21:2–3 and above appendix 22. From the sumptuous tombs of the early Christians in the Talpioth area, it is obvious that these mausoleums belonged to very affluent families, who could not possibly have made their fortunes as shop-keepers, laborers, and artisans. Our point is supported by the uncensored version of the Talmud (mss. original of Sanhedrin 43a, Yad ha-Rab Herzog; Firenzi, III, 7–9; etc.). Concerning Jesus' trial, it says: "the case of Jesus' [trial] was idiosyncratic because he was close to the ruling circles" (שאני ישוע הנצרי שקרוב למלכות היה). How? We propose that these were the tax-collectors with whom he shared the triclinium. One such individual was Joseph of Arimathea, described as a "rich man," who was "a disciple of Jesus." In the idiom of the rabbis, he must have been quite 'close to the ruling circles.' Evidence to this is the fact that he had direct access to Pilate, and could walk straight into him and ask "for the body of Jesus." At once, Pilate complied, and "commanded the body [of Jesus] to be given to him." (People acquainted with the ways of 'the ruling circles' – then and now – know that tyrants and bully autocrats are extremely accommodating and pleasing with those who provide them with sustenance. In our case, tax collectors.) It is highly symbolic that before being moved to his family mausoleum, Jesus was laid to rest in the "new tomb which he (Joseph of Arimathea) had hewn out of the rock" for himself (Matt. 27:57–60); thus sharing with tax-collectors, something much more symbolic than the triclinium.

A point of some interest: We have mentioned that in deference to the habits of the wealthy and mighty, Jesus and his disciples would wash their feet before reclining at the triclinium. At the same time, they treated with contempt and derision the washing of the hands before eating, as prescribed by Jewish tradition. Because it was the habit of the well-to-do and haughty to poke fun at the poor for washing their hands, the rabbis taught that "whoever sneers at the washing of the hands, (המזלזל בנטילת ידים) will himself become destitute"; see Shabbat 62b. Such an individual, "will be pulled-up from the world" (נעקר מן העולם), i.e., violently; see Soṭa 4b. In fact, it was considered so grave an offense that such an individual merited excommunication; see Berakhot 19a. And yet, as we read in the Christian Scripture, Jesus defended such a conduct:

> Then the Pharisees and some of the scribes came together to Him, having come from Jerusalem. Now when they saw some of His disciples eat bread with defiled, that is, with unwashed hands, they found fault. For the Pharisees and all the Jews do not eat unless they wash *their* hands in a special way, holding

> the tradition of the elders. *When they come* from the marketplace, they do not eat unless they wash. And there are many other things which they have received and hold, *like* the washing of the cups, pitchers, copper vessels, and couches. Then the Pharisees and scribes asked Him, "Why do Your disciples not walk according to the traditions of the elders, but eat bread with unwashed hands?" (Mk. 7:1–5).

The question seems eminently sensible. It would certainly not be entirely irrelevant to ask why washing the feet with costly oil in the manner of the lavish and opulent is preferable to the washing of the hands as practiced by Israel? It should be noted that the Pharisees and scribes addressed Jesus respectfully. In response, Jesus allegedly retorted with a barrage of insults (see Mk. 7:6–23). (I personally don't believe that Jesus actually uttered any of these insults. Note that when R. Eli'ezer, who had contact with Jesus' disciples, was asked if "פלוני" – an obvious allusion to Jesus – "has a portion in the World-to-Come," he refused to answer; see Yoma 66b. If Jesus had actually acted as described in Mark and other similar passages in the Christian Scripture, their question and his declining to answer would make little sense.)

Summing up all of the above: As per Judeo-Arabic tradition, the Pharisees represented true *ḥasidut*. Because they had succeeded in freeing themselves (אנקטאע) from 'the ruling circles,' they dared to confront those preaching spirituality to the poor while sharing the triclinium with heartless tax-collectors and depraved sinners. Hence, the close, intimate relationship between *minut, minim*, and the *rashut*, or 'ruling circles'; see chapter 26, and the texts cited in Section III, nn. 321–323; and cf. appendix 55. Thus, the imperative of maligning the Pharisees, and all those daring to disturb the *coena* of the mighty: old and new.

# 61. The *Targum*

The term *Targum* has two distinct connotations. Generally, in rabbinic parlance it refers to the Aramaic versions of the Tora and Prophets, used in the liturgical services (Megilla 3a), and still practiced in the Yemenite Synagogue; see R. Raṣon 'Arusi, "*Qeri'at Tirgum ha-Tora veha-Hafṭara be-Ṣibbur,*" *Sinai* 89 (5742/1982), pp. 219–238. For a reason that will become clear in what follows, these versions were not regarded as 'translations' but as a *perush,* 'commentary.' (Hence, the wealth of exegetical material found in these 'translations'; e.g. *Targum Neophyti* 1.) The sages associated these versions with Neh. 8:8, where the term "explicit" (מפורש) is identified as *Targum*. Therefore, these translations are to be treated as *perush* ('explanations') of the Scripture (see Nedarim 37b), and are consequently classified as 'oral texts'; see Y. Nedarim IV, 3, 38c; *Sefer ha-'Ittim,* p. 244; *Studies in the Mishne Tora,* p.179 n. 28; *Golden Doves,* p. 54, and above appendix 58. The sages in Megilla 3a described the publication of the Aramaic *Targum* to the Tora as recited "from the mouth (מפי) of R. Eli'ezer and R. Joshua." This expression is found in all Babylonian sources. In the parallel source in Y. Megilla I, 9, 71c, when referring to Aqila's Greek translation, it is said that it was recited "before (לפני) R. Eli'ezer and R. Joshua." There is no substantial difference between these expressions, and they stand for 'reciting under the supervision and authority,' or 'with the approval of.'

*Targum* is also used in the sense of 'literal rendering' of Scripture; see R. Ḥanan'el cited in *Tosafot* Soṭa 33a, s.v. *kol.* R. Judah al-Bargeloni,

*An Eleventh Century Introduction to the Hebrew Bible,* p. 22, observed that there are three views on the status of these translations. First is the early position, representing the majority view, "that all the books of Scripture may be written in all languages" (Mishna Megilla 1:8). This position is reflected in Mishna Shabbat 16:1 establishing that "every sacred writing (i.e., Scripture) is to be rescued on the Sabbath in the case of fire ... Although written in any language, it still requires proper storage (*geniza*)." For some valuable notes and clarifications, see Professor Abraham Goldberg, *Commentary to the Mishna Shabbat* (Heb.) (Jerusalem: Jewish Theological Seminary, 1976), pp. 285–286. Second is the opinion reported in Mishna Yadayim 4:5, that all the books of Scripture must be "written in square [Hebrew] script, on a parchment and with ink." Third, is the view of Rabban Simeon b. Gamliel that "all the Books of Scripture can only be written in Hebrew; with the exception of the Tora (which may be written in Greek). When they gave permission to write the Scripture in Greek, they only permitted (the writing of) the Scroll of the Tora" (Mishna Megilla 1:8).

The basis for this exemption was the translation of the Septuagint; see Megilla 9a-b. An important precedent was the scroll of the *Targum* to Job, which was brought to the attention of Rabban Gamliel the elder (1st century), and he ordered that it should be "stored away" (*geniza*), i.e., to be removed from circulation. The details and context of that decision were contested (Tosefta Shabbat 13:2–3, p. 57). Eventually, as stipulated by the Mishna Yadayim 4:5, only Scriptural texts written in Hebrew, in the traditional square script, on a parchment and with ink, "defile the hands," i.e., they carry canonical status; see *MT Sefer Tora* 10:1[9]; cf. *Ma'ase Efod,* p. 10. Later Talmudic authorities, in Shabbat 115a debated whether or not such translations could be rescued on the Sabbath in case of fire. For the textual basis of this conflict, see *Golden Doves,* p. 184. R. Ḥisda argued that they should be rescued since to let them burn may be construed as a "disgrace of sacred writings." In the end, the view of R. Hunna prevailed that these translations have no canonical status; see *MT She'ar Abot ha-Ṭum'a* 9:6–7. Consequently, they may neither be rescued from fire on the

Sabbath, nor should they be read even during weekdays; see *MT Shabbat* 23:26. Why?

Here again, we are dealing with the Christian appropriation of the Scripture. Principally, the *minut* strategy of displacing the Hebrew Scripture with tendentious and fraudulent 'translations,' the purpose of which was to mislead the credulous, the analphabetic, and the semi-literate. R. Judah noted that a 'translation' might be tendentious and disingenuous even if verbally accurate. "Whoever translates a verse literally," he remarked, could occasionally be "a counterfeiter"; and conversely, "whoever adds to it [the text] may be a blasphemer," Tosefta Megilla 3:41, p. 364; see *Oṣar ha-Ge'onim, Qiddushin*, vol. 9, p. 129; and the note of R. Benjamin Musafia, *'Arukh* s.v. *Targum*. In *Sha'are Teshuba* #330, 29c we read: "The *Targum* to which the sages refer is that which is in our hands, but other translations do not carry the same sanctity as does the *Targum*.... Thus, the distinction between "*our Targum*" (Qiddushin 49a), which is legitimate, and 'their' *Targum* which by implication is not; cf. *Tosefta Ki-Fshuṭah*, p. 1223.

We can now appreciate the wisdom of assigning to the official *Targum* the status of *perush* 'commentary.' Thus, not only may it not displace the original Scripture, but it is conditioned by it. By denying the *Targum/perush* the status of a 'written text' and classifying it as 'oral,' the rabbis were making sure that it could not be used to challenge the Scripture itself. Furthermore, not only did the rabbis prohibit the use of written copies of the *Targum* in the Synagogue services, but they further prohibited the reader of the Tora "to assist the translator, lest they should say that 'the *Targum* is written in the (scroll) of the Tora,'" Megilla 32a. See appendix 45.

In sum, the *Targum* that the rabbis prohibited is a "written *Targum*" (כתובין תרגום) or "a Scroll containing the *Targum* of Job," as per Tosefta Shabbat 13:2, p. 57; i.e., translations intended to substitute and eventually displace the Scripture itself – not *our Targum* functioning as *perush*. To ensure that the public would know that such translations had nothing to do with the Jewish Scriptures, the rabbis instructed that one may not rescue them on the Sabbath. To further emphasize this point, Maimonides, *MT Shabbat* 23:26 declared that even "on weekdays it is prohibited to read them." The distinction between the common translations referred to by Maimonides, and "our *Targum*" was overlooked by his grandson, R. Joshua Maimonides, *Teshubot R. Joshua ha-Nagid*, ed. and trans. R. Y. Ratzabi (Jerusalem: Makhon le-Ḥeqer Mishnat ha-Rambam, 5749/1989), #25, pp. 73–74. A final point must be made here. Arabic-speaking Jews designate the translations made by R. Se'adya Gaon and others, *sharaḥ* 'analysis' –never *naqal* 'translation.' Likewise, Spanish-speaking Jews referred to the Judeo-Spanish rendition as *ladinar*, not as a *tradución*. To my knowledge, the first Spanish *tradución* made by Jews was for the specific use of *conversos* returning to Judaism. According to R. Menaḥem Me'iri, *Bet ha-Beḥira, Berakhot* (Jerusalem: Makhon ha-Talmud ha-Israeli, 5725/1965), p. 40, studying the Scripture in translation suffices to fulfill the *miṣva* of 'studying Tora.' See, however, *Halakhot Qeṭannot*, Part 1, #15, 3d. Both these sages overlooked *MT Shabbat* 23:26 mentioned above. We should also note that translations of Scripture would render the Jewish reader captive to the semantic nuances and developments of a foreign linguistic environment; see appendix 58. That may be the reason why "the Land of Israel trembled" when the Scripture was translated; see Megilla 3a.

The oral presentation of the *Targum* at the public reading of the Tora is an institution which according to the rabbis went all the way back to Ezra the Scribe; see Megilla 3a. The Karraites were the first ones to eliminate the recitation of the *Targum* from the Synagogue services; see Section V, n. 35. Others soon followed, and the recitation of the *Targum* was abrogated; see chapters 53–54. Failing to take account of the ruling of R. Neṭruna'e Gaon on behalf of the recitation the *Targum*, registered in *Seder Rab 'Amram Ga'on*, p. 77, R. Asher, *Hilkhot ha-Rosh*, Megilla III, 6, justified the abrogation of the *Targum* as follows:

> It seems that they would recite the *Targum* to explain it to this public, because this public spoke Aramaic. But to us, what

> advantage is there (מה תועלת יש) to the *Targum* since they don't understand it? One should not say, "Let us emulate them [i.e., the rabbis who endeavored to render a version of the Tora in the language of the public], and consequently that [someone] should explain [the Tora portion] in a language that they understand." Since we can say, "The *Targum* is different because it was established by the Holy Spirit!"

The explanation is problematic. The *Targum* was not composed for "the illiterate people who did not know Hebrew," as proposed by R. Asher; see also his *Tosafot ha-Rosh,* on Berakhot 8b, s.v. *afillu,* in *Berakha Meshulleshet* (Warsaw, 5623/1853), 6b; *Hilkhot ha-Rosh, Berakhot* I, 8. Rather, it was composed in the official literary Aramaic; see Paul Kahle, *The Cairo Geniza,* pp. 192–195. One does not need to be an expert in Semitic philology to realize that the language of the *Targum* was not the Aramaic spoken by Jews in Talmudic times, and yet, it continued to be recited and understood by the educated public. (Just as the King James Bible continues to be read and studied although its dialect of English is no longer spoken.) R. Joseph, an expert in the *Targum,* pointed to its usefulness even for seasoned scholars; see Megilla 3a, Mo'ed Qaṭan 28b, Sanhedrin 94b; and cf. *Tosafot* on Baba Qamma 3b, s.v. *ki-dmetargem.* This point had been the focus of a highly persuasive and thoughtful study by Samuel David Luzzatto, *Philoxenus* (Heb.) (Cracow, 1895), see especially, pp. v-23. Thus, the argument that since "**they** don't understand" the *Targum,* it should be eliminated from the services does not cohere. The fact that the *Targum* of the Passover and Shabu'ot *hafṭarot* continued to be recited in the Synagogue (see *Tosafot* on Megilla 24a s.v. *ve-im*), although "**they**" could not understand a word of it, undermines this argument. Let us consider, in passing, that according to the Talmud, Shabbat 12b, Aramaic was regarded to be particularly suitable for liturgical purposes, and therefore the *Qaddish* is recited in that language; see *Ṭur Oraḥ Ḥayyim* LVI. Then, should the *Qaddish* also be eliminated because "**they**" don't understand Aramaic? Were one to pursue this logic, it would be necessary to dismiss the entire Prayer Book, since "**they**" – the same folks who supposedly don't understand the *Targum* – would surely not understand the Hebrew prayers.

If one were to take seriously the alleged concern for the general public, it would be expected to recite in its place a translation of the weekly portion of the Tora in "a language that they understand" (cf. R. Neṭruna'e Gaon, in *Seder Rab 'Amram Ga'on*, p. 77). Anticipating this point, R. Asher countered that no translation could parallel the *Targum*, since it "was established by the Holy Spirit!" (*Hilkhot ha-Rosh, Berakhot* I, 8; *Tosafot ha-Rosh* s.v. *afillu*, 8b; cf. *Tosafot R. Yehuda he-Ḥasid* on Berakhot 8a, s.v. *shenayim*, in *Berakha Meshulleshet*, 1a; *Tosafot* on Berakhot 8a s.v. *shenayim*). The argument is unclear. To begin with, at no place did the rabbis state that the *Targum* "was established by the Holy Spirit." At the same time, it seems awkward to dismiss a liturgical piece supposedly "established by the Holy Spirit," simply because "**they** don't understand it?!" It should be of some interest to note that R. Asher, *Hilkhot ha-Rosh, Berakhot* I, 8; *Tosafot ha-Rosh* s.v. *afillu*, 8b, maintained that "by reading a *perush* (commentary) to the Tora" at home, "one had fulfilled the duty of reading the *Targum*" together with the weekly portion of the Tora, "since it contains the explanation of every single word." R. Asher did not care to identify which *perush* (commentary), although it would be safe to assume that it *was not* the one penned by R. Abraham ibn 'Ezra; cf. *Bet Yosef, Oraḥ Ḥayyim* CCLXXXV, 2. Curiously, in the case of the *perush* (commentary), "the Holy Spirit" was no longer a factor. Moreover, if there were any substance to the concerns about the welfare of the general public, then some efforts should have been made to instruct the public who "don't understand it." Significantly, this argument was made by R. Neṭruna'e Gaon, *Seder Rab 'Amram Ga'on*, p. 77. Addressing those who wanted to eliminate the *Targum* from the services because they did not understand it, he replied: "Let them learn the *Targum*!" Sadly, even rabbis of formidable reputation could no longer come to grips with relatively simple words; see R. Solomon b. Adrete, *Teshubot*, vol. 1, #164, and the note of R. Yaḥya

Qoraḥ, *Marpe Lashon* on Gen. 25:27. Hence the introduction of *pilpul,* ending with the total disarray of Talmudic studies; see Section V, nn. 93 and 371.

The other point advanced by R. Asher for the elimination of the *Targum*: "What advantage is there (מה תועלת יש) to the *Targum*?" – is mind-boggling! It was introduced by Paul to denigrate the circumcision, Rom. 3:1: "What advantage then hath the Jew? On what profit is there for circumcision?" To appreciate the catastrophic implications of this argument it would be important to consider the semantic connotations of "what advantage is there (מה תועלת יש)." It appears only once in the Talmud (Pesaḥim 108b), in connection to whether it would be better to give children nuts (and other such goodies) to eat to celebrate the Passover Seder, or to serve them wine. According to the rabbis, it would be better to give children special goodies for the holiday rather than the ceremonial wine, since, "What advantage is there in serving wine to infants?" (מה תועלת יש לתינוקות ביין). In this sense it was also used by R. Asher, *Hilkhot ha-Rosh, Baba Batra* I, 29. Medieval authors used this expression for a 'purposeless action'; see Rashi on Ketubot 69b s.v. *ve-khi*; Baba Meṣi'a 39b s.v. *amar*; *Tosafot,* Shabbat 78b, s.v. *tanna qamma*; and Ketubot 56a, s.v. *keshe-shobartah*; *Hilkhot ha-Rosh,* 'Erubin IV, 3; Mo'ed Qaṭan III, 36 (= Ketubot I, 6); Baba Batra V, 4; 'Aboda Zara V, 36; *Teshubot ha-Rosh,* XIII, 20; CVIII, 2; etc., etc. It was also used to indicate something that is spiritually meaningless. In a medieval midrash, ed. J. D. Eisenstein, *Ozar Midrashim,* 2 vols. (New York, 1915), vol. 1, p. 5, Abraham said to an old woman worshipping an idol: "It is of no benefit (אין בו תועלת) either for itself or for someone worshipping it." According to Rashi, Yoma 67b s.v. *ha-saṭan,* Satan attempted to persuade Israel "that the Tora is not true, since what is the benefit in all these?" (שהתורה אינה אמת, כי מה תועלת בכל אלו). R. Tam, too, quoted by R. Asher, *Hilkhot ha-Rosh,* Rosh HaShana, I, 5, used this expression to denote something religiously meaningless. In this exact sense, R. Asher used this idiom in *Teshubot ha-Rosh,* IV, 22; XIII, 14, etc.

A subordinate, but significant issue is whether or not there is any rationale, other than bias, to insist on the recitation of impenetrable and inexplicable hymns (פיוטים), which *nobody* understands, in many cases penned by anonymous writers, and yet casually dismiss an institution established by Ezra (and "the Holy Spirit"!), because "what advantage is there?" (מה תועלת יש), and also since "they don't understand it?!" Cf. chapter 53.

# 62. Writing a *Sefer Tora*

The proposal to substitute the precept to write the Tora was made by R. Asher, "*Hilkhot Sefer Tora,*" #1, *Halakhot Qeṭannot* (printed at the end of Talmud Menaḥot). The justification for this reform was the doctrine "What advantage is there?" (מה תועלת יש); see *Teshubot ha-Rosh,* #13:14 and above appendix 61. This is also the position of his son R. Jacob, in *Ṭur, Yore De'a* CCLXXX, at the beginning; see *Perisha* ad loc., *Shakh* n. #v; *ha-Gra* n. #iv; R. Aharon Kotler, *Mishnat Aharon.* Vol. 1 (Jerusalem: Makhon Yerushalayim, 5745/1985), #32, p. 152. It is pertinent to our discussion to recall that R. Arie Leib, *Sha'agat Arye,* #36 had shown that the *miṣva* to write the Tora has nothing to do with the *miṣva* to study Tora. Because the hermeneutic theory underlying R. Asher's position was not fully understood, some insisted that R. Asher meant to say that in *addition* to writing a Scroll of the Tora one should also write the commentaries, etc.; see Maran Joseph Caro, *Shulḥan 'Arukh, Yore De'a* CCLXXX, 2. For a summary discussion of this view, see R. Ḥayyim Palaggi, *Birkat Mo'adekha le-Ḥayyim,* vol. 1 (Izmir, 5628/1868), 50a ff. For some additional notes, see *Studies in the Mishne Tora,* p. 181 nn. 36 and 39. Recently, the view of R. Asher was brought to bear on the following question. In sickness, a lady made a vow to donate a Scroll of the Tora to a synagogue. Upon her recovery a formal question was submitted to the late R. Aharon Kotler as to whether she could renounce her vow and instead donate the sum to assist a rabbinic student to continue his studies. An important factor in the decision to permit her to do that was R. Asher's thesis; see *Mishnat Aharon,* vol. 1, pp. 152–159; and cf. *Teshubot ha-Rosh,* #13:14.

# 63. The Sorrowful Scholarship of Professor Baer

When I first met Professor Baer on a visit to Israel in 1961, I remember asking him if he could name a single Jewish Averroist who converted to Christianity; see *In the Shadow of History*, p. 235 n. 55. In earnest, I don't think the good professor read a line of Averroes in his life, and if he did, I doubt that he could understand a word. As in most of his research, he relied on secondary sources; in this case, on Ernst Rénan's classical work, *Averroès et l'Averroism* (Paris: Calman-Lévy, 1852). Baer's reasoning is impeccable. What Rénan said about Christians in Italy during the 15th and 16th centuries must surely apply to Jews in Spain in the 12th and 13th centuries. Any further investigation would only have hampered the methodology developed by this celebrated historian.

An example of his methodology may be found in his *Toledot Hayyehudim bi-Sfarad ha-Noṣrit* (Tel Aviv: Am Oved: 5719/1959), pp. 519–520 n. 71. Without a single insight into the legal issues between R. Judah and R. ha-Arukh examined above in chapter 65, he disposed of the decision of the Court of Segovia simply by *imputing* to the members of Court the *views* assigned to them by R. Judah. Pointing an accusing finger at the Court of Seville (for siding with R. ha-Arukh) Baer intoned this grave sentence: "It means that they decided against clear-cut halakha and against the view of the preachers of the generation in Toledo," i.e., R. Judah. Incredibly, this remark was made by an individual who could not read a single *halakhic responsum* on his own!

An example of Baer's competence pertains to a remark made by R. ha-Arukh concerning an opinion held by R. Moses de Coucy. Apparently, there were some conflicting views concerning the status of one of the witnesses, in which case there would have been only a single witness testifying to an alleged wedding. De Coucy believed that a marriage performed in the presence of a single witness has some validity (חוששין לקדושיו). Since this view had been rejected by most authorities, including R. Judah's father, R. Asher (see *Hilkhot ha-Rosh, Qiddushin* III, 12), R. ha-Arukh, in accordance with standard halakhic practice in Sepharad (*Bet Yosef, Eben ha-'Ezer* XLII, s.v. *ha-meqaddesh*), dismissed that view. It is pertinent to add that in the case at hand, where the alleged bride denied having consented to the marriage, even those authorities upholding R. de Coucy's view considered the case without merits (see *Bet Yosef* and R. Moses Isserles, *Darke Moshe* ibid., n. ii). Accordingly, R. ha-Arukh dismissed de Coucy's view with the remark "לית דחש לקימחיה" ('no one cares about his flour'), i.e., no one accepts his view; see *Zikhron Yehuda*, 37a. This is the *only* quotation of R. ha-Arukh made by R. Judah! Why? Since he could not find something substantive with which to assail him, he found a pretext to abuse him personally by alleging that this was an offensive remark. To this effect, he wrote: "In order that not even a single letter (of what R. ha-Arukh wrote) would be regarded as true, we have to be extensive and discredit him by citing his own words." R. Judah, who was an expert in diversionary tactics and name-calling, jumped at the opportunity to heave against the rabbi a series of invectives: "This alone suffices to excommunicate you, for you have spoken ill of the world luminaries and slurred them [in the plural]. [Scholars who are] greater than you and your teachers upheld and apply his decisions" (namely himself – not a single legal authority in Spain shared this view! His younger brother, R. Jacob, simply *mentions* this opinion, without declaring that the halakha is according to this view. How could he? Especially since his father and mentor decided against de

Coucy!). There is nothing remotely offensive about the expression "לית דחש לקימחיה" ('no one cares about his flour'). It is found in the Talmud (Sukka 54a and parallels), and means 'heedlessness' (see Rashi ad loc., s.v. *de-la*). In fact, Maran Joseph Caro used it to dismiss a view held by R. Jacob b. ha-Rosh; see *Ṭur* and *Bet Yosef, Yore De'a,* CCCXL, s. v. *ve-shi'ura* (*in fine*). A similar expression, "*let de-ḥash lah,*" is found in Baba Meṣi'a 110b, Bekhorot 3b, etc. In Nedarim 7b it was used to dismiss a view held by no lesser a figure than R. 'Aqiba! (לית דחש להא דר' עקיבא). Hoping for a rabbinically illiterate reader, R. Judah grabbed the opportunity to assail his opponent and create a diversionary tactic. On the basis of prejudice, and without having the foggiest idea of the meaning of these words, Baer repeats the same gibberish about "לית דחש לקימחיה"; see ibid. Cautioning against this type of historiography, scholars from Graetz to Baron warned about historians acting as theologians; in our case, of preaching rather than teaching. Incidentally, R. Isaac bar Sheshet, *Teshubot ha-Ribash* #230, *in fine,* addressed the son of our R. Ḥayyim as "the wise and learned Rabbi, our teacher Menaḥem, may God guard him, the son of the honorable Rabbi, our teacher Ḥayyim, may he rest in peace, ha-Arukh." A similar formula is found at the end of #233.

For a detailed discussion of the halakhic issues of this particular case, see Y. Shiber, "The status and confirmation of witnesses at wedding ceremonies in Jewish law," Ph.D. thesis presented at Bar Ilan University, Fall, 2002, pp. 126–129.

# 64. Medieval Jewish Prophets

On these superior men, see the magisterial essay by Abraham Heschel, "Inspiration in the Middle Ages," in *Alexander Marx Jubilee Volume*, Hebrew Section (New York: The Jewish Theological Seminary of America, 1950), pp.175–208. On the title *nabi*, see ibid. pp. 180–190. For a description of the method by which the "early *ḥasidim*" and "prophets" reached prophecy, see R. Adrete, in ed. R. Sh. M. Weinberger, *Ḥiddushe ha-Rishba 'al Aggadot ha-Shas* (Jerusalem, 5726/1966), pp. 81–82; *Zohar*, vol. 2, 144b. This has nothing to do with the expression "as I was shown from Heaven," etc., in Geonic literature, which is nothing more than 'I was inspired to say that'; in contemporary idiom: 'it is my considered opinion.' See "Inspiration in the Middle Ages," pp. 192–193. Access to the supernatural excuses faulty scholarship. When faced with a difficult query, all that a rabbi was required to do was to formulate the question in his dreams (*she'elat ḥalom*), and promptly and without delay would receive an authoritative reply from heavens. One such an individual was R. Jacob de Mervaise [or Marvege] (12th and 13th centuries). He published his questions and answers, *She'elot wu-Tshubot min ha-Shamayim* ('Queries and Replies from Heaven'), ed. R. Reuben Margoliot Jerusalem: Mossad Harav Kook, 1957. All these men were in possession of *Ruwaḥ ha-Qodesh* ('Holy Spirit') and were thus infallible. How else could one explain that every stroke of their pen contained such wondrous wisdom? See "Inspiration in the Middle Ages," pp. 193–195; and Israel Ta-Shma, "Tosafot Gornish," *Sinai* 68 (1971), pp. 85–86. It would not be surprising to discover that in this tradition, the occult is a fundamental dimension of 'rabbinic wisdom.' Hence, the function of conjurations, mystical lore, and the occult in general among these rabbis, cf. "Inspiration in the Middle Ages," pp. 190–208.

# 65. The Science of Necromancy

About the flight and cry of birds, the following story in Josephus, *Against Apion*, I, 192–194, *Josephus*, vol. 1, p. 241, may be instructive. It was witnessed by Hecataeus of Abderas (ca. 300 BCE) in a campaign around the Red Sea. The soldiers were going back and forth, following the instructions given to them by a seer. When a Jewish soldier inquired about the strange behavior, the seer pointed to a bird that he was watching.

> The Jew, without saying a word, drew his bow, shot and struck the bird, and killed it... Taking the bird in his hands, continued, 'Pray, how could any sound information about our march be given by this creature, which could not provide for its own safety? Had it been gifted with divination, it would not have come to this spot, for fear of being killed by an arrow of Mosolamus [משולם] the Jew.'

Concerning the rational basis of necromancy and its relationship to astrology, Ramban, *Perush ha-Tora* on Deut. 18:9, vol. 2, p. 427, explained:

> And now learn and understand the subjects of witchcraft! The Creator blessed be He, when creating everything out

of nothing, made that the higher should rule over the lower beneath it. He placed the power of the earth and all that is in it (the earth) under the stars and constellations, in accordance with their trajectory and their view of them [on the earth], as it is demonstrated in the science of astrology (בחכמת האיצטגנינות). He also appointed rulers, angels, and ministers over the stars and constellations, which are their soul. Behold, their rule, from the moment that they came to be and forever, must be according to the decree of the superior which (God) had appointed over them. However, it was part of His mighty wonders that He put into the potency of the superior rulers types of images and powers that could invert the ruling of what lies underneath them. That if in the sight of the stars ahead, facing earth, is good or bad to the earth, or to a nation, or to a person, those superior faces could be inverted by altering that very sight [i. e. through astrological images]. As they [kabbalist astrologers] said: the inversion of *NeGa'* [נ-ג-ע plague] will turn into *'oNeG* [ע-נ-ג delight]. [cf. R. 'Azriel, *Commentary on Talmudic Aggadoth*, p. 28.] He did so because He Himself, blessed be His Name, "Changes the seasons and the times" (Dan. 2:21)...without changing the nature of the world, and that the stars and constellations would make their trajectory according to their order. The author of *Sefer ha-Lebana* ('The Book of the Moon') – who was an expert in necromancy – instructed that when the moon, for example, which is called 'the sphere of the world' is at the head of Aries, and there is such and such a zodiac sign, to make an image of such and such material, engrave on it [the image], and [mark] the name of the [astrological] time and the angel appointed over it [the zodiac sign], according to the names mentioned in that book. And if one were to offer such and such incense, in such and such a manner, then it [the zodiac sign] would look upon it [the object] for evil, to uproot and to destroy, to demolish and to ravage. However, when the moon is in another

> constellation, [he prescribes to] make an image and (offer) incense in a different manner for all good, to build and to plant.

For magic and witchcraft among Jews in late Antiquity, see Mordecai Margalioth, *Sepher ha-Razim* (Heb.) (Jerusalem: The American Academy for Jewish research, 1966).

Concerning Deut. 18:12, stating that all sorts of divination and magic are "abominations" (תועבות), Ramban, *Perush ha-Tora*, vol. 2, p. 427, argued:

> The Scripture said: "For all who do these (כל־עשה אלה) things are an abomination (תועבת) unto the Lord" – but it did not say, "Anyone who does any of these" (עושה כל־אלה)! Because the Scripture was [only] referring to most of these [witch works], since a soothsayer and enchanter are not an abomination (אינה תועבה).

Hebrew syntax does not allow for such a hermeneutical option. If the text would have said, "Who does all of these" (עושה כל־אלה), as suggested by Ramban, then it would have meant that only doing *all* of the above would constitute an 'abomination' (תועבה)! Another consideration, to make head or tail of this argument, the verse has to be read *kol, 'ose elle*. However, in the Masoretic text *kol* and *'ose* are joined by a *maqqaf*: *kol-'ose*! More fundamental, such an interpretation would have to ignore the particle *ki* ('because,' 'since,' 'that'), the most powerful conjunction in the Hebrew language, joining vv. 9–12. Specifically, v. 9 begins with *ki*, introducing the prohibition of doing any of the "abominations" of the Canaanites; vv. 10–11, enumerate the magical practices of the Canaanites, including augury and astrology. These are followed by v. 12 beginning with *ki*, thus including all the terms first introduced by the same conjunction in v. 9. Let us point out that in the introductory v. 9, we have "abominations" (תועבות) in the plural; meaning: all of the following cases to be enumerated in vv. 10–11. However, in the concluding v. 12, we have "abomination"

(תועבת) – in the singular; meaning: each of the above mentioned! Finally, the rabbis, *Sifre* #173, p. 220, taught:

> "For it is an abomination unto the Lord whosoever does any of these things." – Perhaps (you would say) that he is not guilty unless he would transgress all of them (abominations)? Therefore the Scripture taught: "whosoever does any of these" – even one of these!

Cf. Makkot 24a.

It seems that there were people prior to Ramban who explained "abominations" in a similar vein. To alert the public that such a view runs contrary to the rabbis, Rashi on Deut. 18:12 quoted the abovementioned *Sifre*.

# 66. The Mandate of the Jewish Court According to Ramban

Concerning the mandate of the Jewish Court, the Scripture states: "Throughout your generations, in all your dwellings" (Num. 35:29) – that is, even after the destruction of the Temple and throughout the Diaspora. Nonetheless, Ramban, *Perush ha-Tora,* vol. 2, p. 339, declared: "After the destruction of the Temple it [the Jewish Court] has no mandate either in the Land of Israel or the Diaspora." (Contrary to Rashi on Ḥolin 52a s.v. *ella.*) He further elaborated this thesis in *Hasagot ha-Ramban,* in *Sefer ha-Miṣvot le-ha-Rambam,* ed. Ch. Chavel (Jerusalem: Mossad Harav Kook, 1981), *Miṣvat 'Ase* #153, pp. 212–226; see *Studies in the Mishne Tora,* p. 43 n. 72. This means that the entire rabbinic apparatus and institutions, including the Mishna, Talmud, and Calendar establishing the Jewish Holidays, have no legal mandate. We should remind the reader that Ramban also rejected Maimonides' position that the authority of the rabbis (including the Mishna and Talmudic periods) to legislate new statutes is from the Tora; see his *Hasagot ha-Ramban, Sefer ha-Miṣvot le-ha-Rambam*, I, and *Studies in the Mishne Tora,* pp. 14–15, 19–25. Later on, this doctrine was exploited by Spinoza to argue that rabbinic authority was null and void.

# 67. The Ministry of Luminous Rabbis: Unerring and Inerrable

Ramban rejected the doctrine that the Tora awarded the rabbis authority to legislate and promulgate new ordinances, see above appendix 66. At the same time, he maintained that rabbinic interpretations of the Tora equaled Tora; see Section V, n. 240. Thus presupposing a Cosmic Truth, reachable only to self-selecting elites, such as the heroic-*qedoshim-ḥasidim* (later displaced by the secular *europaischen Menschentums* in the realm of Jewish political and communal leadership), standing between the vulgar and the godly; see Section V, n. 333. A consequence of this view was the validation of a hierarchic system of governance and truth, stipulating that those standing above 'know best' and those below ought to obey by virtue of a truth that they are too stupid to understand, ever.

Essential to Ramban's doctrine described above, appendix 66, is the belief that the rabbinic sages derived their authority, not from the national institutions of Israel (the Rabbinic Academies and the judiciary), but because, like the ancient prophets, they had access to the Holy Spirit; cf. appendix 64, and "Nahmanides, *Kabbalah, Halakha,* and Spiritual Leadership," pp. 69–70. There are no rabbinic sources to support this doctrine. In an unpublished paper, R. Josh Yuter, "Ramban," located this doctrine in Tertullian, *De Pudicita*, 21, trans. Henry Bettenson, *The Later Christian Fathers: A Selection from the Writings of the Fathers from St. Cyril of Jerusalem to St. Leo the Great* (Oxford: Oxford University Press 1977), p. 113:

> For the Church is properly and primarily the Spirit, in whom is the trinity of the one divinity, the Father, the Son, and the Holy Spirit. The Spirit makes the assembly of the Church, which the Lord established in three persons. And thus, the whole number of those who have leagued together in this faith is given the status of the Church by the Church's author and consecrator… For the right of judgment belongs to the Lord, not to the servant; to God himself, not to the priest.

In line with the foregoing, the author of *Sefer ha-Ḥinnukh*, ed. R. Ch. Chavel (Jerusalem: Mossad Harav Kook, 5729/1969), #492 (a member of Ramban's circle) proposed the radical view that the biblical precept to submit to the decisions of the Supreme Court is now to be fulfilled by obeying "the great sages among us during our days." The submission must be total, whoever does not "… obey the counsel of the great Tora sages of the time *in everything that they command* is disregarding a positive precept and his penalty is very grave." He arrived at this view by surreptitiously introducing two revolutionary ideas. First, the authority of the Supreme Court includes the power to determine "what is the mystery of the Tora" (סוד התורה). Second, he redefined the term 'judge' (שופט) to mean 'sage.' Thus, when paraphrasing the Scriptural precept establishing the judicial authority of the Supreme Court (Deut. 17:10), *Sefer ha-Ḥinnukh*, #508 [4], p. 627, he declared:

> Included in this precept is the obligation to obey and execute at all times, what was ordered by the judge, that is, *the greatest sage among us in our time*. As our rabbis of blessed memory taught, "Jephtah was in his time as Samuel was in his."

This idea was the result of combining Ramban's view that after the destruction of the Temple the authority of rabbis was a consequence of their superior knowledge (and not of their judicial office), with Rashi's view (Ḥolin 52a s. v. *ella)* that even in post-Talmudic times a judge (that is, a member of the community's *Bet Din*) had Scriptural mandate. Accordingly, the author of *Sefer ha-Ḥinnukh* reinterpreted the rabbinic principle, "Jephtah was in his time as Samuel was in his" (Rosh HaShana 25b), to mean that the *sages* of one generation [although not members of the *Bet Din*], were equivalent to Prophet Samuel and must be equally obeyed, regardless of how insignificant they appeared in the eyes of their contemporaries. This interpretation runs contrary to Scripture (I Chr. 9:20) and the rabbis, who maintained that Pinehas, Aaron's grandson, was alive during Jephtah's time; see Bereshit Rabba, LX, 13, vol. 2, p. 643. And yet, the rabbis recognized the authority of Jephtah – the presiding Judge – and not of Pinehas! It follows that the interpretation of the Law rests in the hands of the judiciary, not the 'sages!' Rather, as taught by R. Se'adya Gaon and Maimonides, the principle "Jephtah was in his time as Samuel was in his," comes to establish *parity* between the Supreme Court at different historical periods, e.g., the Court Presided by Prophet Samuel and the Court Presided by Jephtah have equal rank and should be equally acknowledged; see *Studies in the Mishne Tora,* p. 36 n. 28.

There are several consequences to the above-mentioned view. First, given that the author failed to outline how it could be determined who in fact is "the greatest sage among us in our time," conflicting views, for all practical purposes, could only be resolved through strife and violence. Thus, the strategy of faultfinding, misinformation, and intimidation accepted as standard norms of 'rabbinic discourse' (past and present). Second, the 'sage' as personified by anti-Maimonidean ideology, was possessed by "the Holy Spirit" and therefore was unerring and inerrable; see Section V, nn. 333–336. God Himself acts through these judges, and He "is the real factor that decides and, accordingly, a court cannot fail to decide justly" ("Nahmanides, *Kabbalah, Halakhah,* and Spiritual Leadership," p. 71).

The best model and inspiration for this kind of ministry was the celebrated R. Abraham of Posquièrs, who, thanks to his being possessed by "the Holy Spirit" enjoyed total clairvoyance in matters earthly and divine – with the exception of plane geometry; see above chapter 64. Some maintained that the same status should be extended to the local rabbi: he must be obeyed as if he were "the Supreme Court having authority over (the people) of their generation." He, too, was inerrant and his decisions could not be appealed:

> …Although all the city's sages and notables may surpass the community rabbi in wisdom and expertise, they are irrelevant in regard to him. Since his authority was appointed over them, he has the legal status of royalty, ranking as the Supreme Court of Jerusalem, in regards to which all sages are irrelevant.

Quoted in *She'elot wu-Tshubot Re'em*, #57, p. 185.

Some rabbis in France believed that their authority should extend to other communities, including Spain. One such rabbi was Moses ha-Levi who on his own promulgated a decree which on account of his rank must be obeyed by other communities. To whom, R. Isaac bar Sheshet (1326–1408), *Teshubot ha-Ribash* #271, responded:

> Indeed, our teacher R. Moses ha-Levi is superb in wisdom and is superb in expertise. However, he is not yet a Prince standing over the members of our Nation in place of our Teacher Moses, as the head of the Superior Court (סנהדרי גדולה), with the authority to promulgate decrees over all Israel, and prohibit that which is permitted. Furthermore, even a Prince could not pass decrees on his own but with the unanimous or majority consent of the Court (סנהדרין).

After extensive documentation on this point, R. Isaac bar Sheshet added: "No individual scholar, however, promulgated prohibitions upon all Israel, but only upon the residents of his city and precinct. Others, however, need not accept his prohibitions."

According to legal tradition, the new regulations promulgated by Joshua were made in conjunction with "his [Supreme] Court," *MT Nizqe Mamon* 5:3 (יהושע ובית דינו). The same applied to King David, see *MT Issure Bi'a* 22:1 (דוד ובית דינו); and his son Solomon, see *MT 'Erubin* 1:2; *She'ar Abot ha-Ṭum'a* 8:8 (שלמה ובית דינו); Ezra, see *MT Qeri'at Shema'* 1:7; 4:8; *Tefilla* 1:4; *Berakhot* 1:5 (עזרא ובית דינו); Rabban Gamli'el, see *MT Tefilla* 2:1 (רבן גמליאל ובית דינו); et al. In his own mind, however, the new rabbi felt that he was in fact *superior* to the Supreme Court of Israel at the Temple in Jerusalem. The latter is subject to error, in which case the Court must bring an expiatory sacrifice; see Lev. 4:13, Num. 15:24, Mishna Horayot, Tosefta as well as Talmud Babli and Yerushalmi (two versions); see "Law and Hermeneutics," pp. 1670–1672; "One-Dimensional Jew," pp. 34–36.

Talmudic sages, too, were prone to error and did not hesitate to announce their blunders publicly; see 'Erubin 16b, 104a; Zebaḥim 94b; Ḥolin 56a; Nidda 68a. (The term *darash* found in these sources, except for Nidda 68a, stands for a *public* announcement; see R. Jonah ibn Jannaḥ, *Sefer ha-Shorashim*, p. 114. The reason that *darash* is absent from the passage in Nidda 68a is that the sage in question could not make his retraction personally and had to send his retraction through a messenger.)

Disagreement between jurists, as reflected in every line of the Talmud, is quite common, and neither party was necessarily 'wrong'; see above chapter 45. Traditional rabbis, too, did not hesitate to admit error; Rashi confessed that he "did not know"; see his Commentary to Gen. 28:5, 35:13, Ex. 22:28. On the other hand, luminous rabbis, having gained their privileged position through some sort of revelatory experiences, could not possibly be 'wrong' or 'not know.' Since they were acting by and through the 'Holy Spirit,' to presume or infer that they could be in error would be nothing less than heresy. In the words of R. Josh Yuter, this allowed privileged rabbis to enjoy "a greater creativity in the domain of halakha." R. Yuter also showed that the submission of halakha to luminous interpretation meant that there were no legal norms that could not be manipulated by theological considerations. In such a system 'Tora' is nothing more than a rhetorical tool designed to justify the rabbi's whims. As argued by R. Yuter: "This allows for almost limitless subjectivity regarding what is considered to be the Law." It meant that "rabbis cannot be held accountable to an objective source," simply because "there is no objective source which could not be manipulated to reach any desired conclusion" ("Nahmanides, *Kabbalah, Halakha,* and Spiritual Leadership," p. 71). The net result was unrestrained manipulation of halakha for either theological or political ideologies. For all practical purposes this equaled the abrogation of the whole institution of halakha and its substitution by a system to be justified by pointless casuistry and mystical noise. In contemporary circles this ideology is known as "*daas* Tora"; see "One-Dimensional Jew," p. 45; and *The World of the Yeshiva*, pp. 68–69. A more effective and less pompous expression, used in similar circles, is "the spirit of halakha." This allows privileged rabbis halakhic clairvoyance without the need to know a single *iota* of Jewish law.

In sum, in Old Sepharad, rabbinic authority was centered on the judicial institutions established by the local communities. A principal objective of the anti-Maimonideans was to undermine their authority. Toward this end, it was crucial to delegitimize the *Mishne Tora* and to discredit the values of Israel formulated by the Geonim and the sages of the Golden Age. The anti-Maimonidean rabbis would fill the ensuing vacuum.

Not all *qedoshim*-rabbis claimed to be inerrant. Consider the *responsum* penned by R. Moses Sofer (1762–1839), *Ḥatam Sofer, Qobeṣ Teshubot* (Jerusalem: 5733/1973), #65, 76b. He was the spiritual leader of Hungarian Jewry, one of the most important communities at the time. His standing and reputation for sanctity, wisdom, and leadership were unique. See the learned study by Aaron M. Schreiber, "The Ḥatam Sofer's Nuanced Attitude Toward Secular Learning, Maskilim, and Reformers," *The Tora u-Madda Journal* 11 (2002–2003), pp. 123–173. And yet, he freely admitted that during the forty years of his ministry he was erroneous twice. To be precise, not quite so; rather, he acknowledged that twice he wrongly admitted that he had been in error. (Whether to be erroneous for having wrongly admitted that one had committed a blunder is to be regarded as 'error' is a matter too subtle to be examined by the writer of these lines.) To appreciate the nuanced position of this illustrious rabbi it would be important to remember that in the *qedoshim* environment, rabbinic discussions and arguments are grasped in terms of a combat between knights; see Section V, n. 82. In the *hasagot*-mood, the contenders' main concern, as per heroic combat, is victory, rather than prosaic 'truth' or 'justice' (see chapter 64). No greater humiliation could befall a hero than having to apologize or admit error. Therefore, it would be best to view queries and answers as clever stratagems, designed to trap the opponent and win victory. As the author of our *responsum* explained, the rabbis submitting questions to him were quite familiar with the usual views on the matter, and expected that

> ...perhaps he [i] could offer a fresh aspect (לחדש דבר), different than what the standard authorities [had exposed]. [ii] Or would differ from them (לחלוק עליהם), [iii] or to say that one should rely on the opinion of such an authority, etc.

In view of such a situation, the highest concern of a rabbi issuing a reply was to parry any possible attack, in case the party in question decided to investigate the subject and find a flaw in the rabbi's reasoning. In which case, he would be forced to admit error, since everyone could make a mistake.

> Therefore, I necessarily have to let him know the reason for having decided (the matter) differently than the opinion of the rabbi submitting the question. So that he should not scrutinize after me and find that I made a mistake, and (then) I would have to apologize and declare: 'What I have submitted to you was in error'– given that every human can err! That is why I have to make known [to those who submit a query before me] the grounds [for the decision I am making] and my rationale.

The query that our learned rabbi was examining was a criticism to a previous reply. Our rabbi realized that the rabbi submitting the question had investigated his reply and was raising some valid objections.

> Now, upon receiving his query again, censuring me, [inquiring] if I still maintained my original position, I see, however that his demonstrations are without merit. I have realized that he had scrutinized after me, but having not found [any contrary argument] except for a number of objections having no merits. Why should I have to reply to him and justify myself? Why should I bother with that?! Either way: if he would comply with my decision – that would be fine! – and if he would not comply – that would be even better – so that I would no longer be responsible! Since I fulfilled my responsibility and I have replied to him, and am no longer obliged to clarify the matter more!

Having dismissed the objections raised by the rabbi, he would no longer risk the possibility of admitting error and having to retract publicly. It is in this context that our rabbi disclosed that he had a spotless – or quasi spotless – record.

> However, if I am in error I would have to retract. Thank God, in the last forty years I have not [committed an error], except twice. Once, I was corrected by the erudite rabbi … and I concurred with him. However, I have now studied … and examined [the matter], and realized that I was mistaken for concurring with him … The other time [that I acknowledged error] … the erudite rabbi … [corrected me] and I concurred with him. However, [another] erudite rabbi … summarized my *responsum,* and concluded that I was mistaken in concurring [with the contender rabbi and to acknowledge error], but that the law was according to my original decision. Thank God, except for these [two cases] I don't know [of any error that I committed].

In a census taken in 1941 in Hungary, 61,548 Jews had converted to Christianity; by 1944 the number was 100,000. We should also note that 69,400 Jews had passed over to the Russian Orthodox Church. In the year 1854, the number of Jews who passed over to the Russian Orthodox Church was 4,439; see William O. McCagg, Jr., "Jewish Conversion in Hungary in Modern Times," in Todd M. Endelman, ed. *Jewish Apostasy in the Modern World* (New York: Holmes & Meier, 1987), pp. 142–164. It is true that the ministry of this celestial rabbi had taken place some 100 years earlier. What is truly baffling is that in spite of having been privileged with such a splendid stewardship, when the opportunity arose, a large number of Jews chose to convert to Christianity. Facing this mystery, even the most rationalistic mind would have to confess how recondite and inexplicable the ways of history are!

# 68. Settled Law

See *Studies in the Mishne Tora,* pp. 47–60. There is a concept in rabbinic legal discourse akin to 'settled law' in American legal tradition. It refers to a law assumed to have been settled by the courts in one way, but within the power of the court to change. In this sense, for example, it was used by John G. Kester in an oral argument before the Supreme Court, on October 4, 2006, p. 17: "This case came as a shock in 2004. And, in fact, the judges below, in this series of cases, all said, 'We thought it was settled law the other way.'"

A similar idiom is "קבעו ... הלכה לדורות," Tosefta Berakhot 5:2, p. 25; Berakhot 11a; Pesaḥim 100a; Ketubot 50b; *Teshubot ha-Rambam,* #310, vol. 2, p. 577 (in contradistinction with "הוראת שעה," which is a legal decision that *cannot be cited as precedent,* cf. *MT Sanhedrin* 24:4). The same applies to "הלכה רווחת," Yebamot 14b; Ḥolin 57b; Y. Yebamot I, 6, 3a; *The Mishnah of Rabbi Eliezer* (Heb.), IX, p. 169; *Teshubot Rab Neṭruna'e Ga'on,* 2 vols. (Jerusalem: Ofeq Institute, 5754/1994), #223–224, vol. 2, p. 350; #329, vol. 2, p. 490; *Teshubot Ge'one Mizraḥ wu-Ma'arab,* #72, 18a; *Teshubot ha-Ge'onim ha-Ḥadashot,* #153, p. 210; #179, p. 253; R. Isaac Alfasi, *Halakhot, Ketubot* 44a. The same is the case with "קבע הלכה," Tosefta Berakhot 1:4, p. 2; 5:2, p. 26; cf. Demai 5:24, p. 93 and Ḥolin 57b; Ta'aniyot 2:5, p. 331; Ḥagiga 2:11, p. 385. An analogous expression is "הלכה קבועה," see *Teshubot Rab Neṭruna'e Ga'on,* #223, vol. 1, p. 219; #321, vol. 2, p. 476 (= *Sha'are Ṣedeq* IV, 4, #56, p. 149). In R. Abraham ibn 'Ezra, Introduction, *Commentary to the Pentateuch,* s.v. *Ha-Derekh Ha-Rbi'it,* we find: "ויש שהוא כהלכה שאינה קבועה." A good example of 'settled law' is the note of R. Ḥanan'el on Shabbat 92b, cf. Shraga Abramson, *Perush Rabbenu Ḥanan'el la-Talmud,* p. 110.

To say that the anti-Maimonideans were not acquainted with any of the above is nothing less than a gross euphemism.

# 69. Relying on Legal Sources and Authorities

No reliable halakhic expert (סביר וגמיר בכל התורה כלה) would deem a quotation from a 'source' – any source – to constitute in and of itself a legal decision (פסק, הוראה). The trajectory from a source or sources to a legal decision (הלכה למעשה) is what Maimonides refers to as "the *path* of the law" (דרך המשפט); see appendix 48 and Section V, n. 303. In this connection, it would be highly instructive to examine a few key-passages in a *responsum*, *Teshubot R. Abraham b. ha-Rambam*, #98, pp. 143–149. The case concerned a decision issued by a local judge. The issue was complex, and the case was submitted to Maimonides' son for review. What makes this case particularly significant is the fact that the sitting judge rendered the verdict on the basis of the *Mishne Tora*. The first point of concern was that fluency in and familiarity with legal texts were not sufficient to render a judgment without a proper conceptualization of the law and proficiency in "the path of the law" (דרך המשפט). Here is the passage in question:

> In particular, cases requiring judicial analysis and study (Ar. נט'ר ותפקה) require the exercise of sharp judicial investigation and impeccable procedure (Ar. חד'ק אלפקיה וחסן תצרפה = Heb. דרך המשפט) in (the interpretation) of the written text (of the law). It is because of cases like this, that (the Tora) stipulated that judges must be "wise and intelligent" (Deut. 1:13) – since

> in the adjudication of the law, one (qualification) without the other is of no use. 'Wisdom' stands for knowledge of what was previously said (on the matter), and 'intelligence' is excellence in (legal) conceptualization and procedure (Ar. חסן אלתצור ואלתצרף, p. 144).

Turning to the quotation from the *Mishne Tora* (p. 147), R. Abraham Maimonides remarked: "The judge who based his view on the text of the work (*Mishne Tora*) has, doubtlessly read only the first half (of the paragraph) ... and skipped the end." In law, a quotation is meaningless unless it is accompanied by solid judicial analysis. To accomplish this, the judge had to show the "conceptual gist" (טעם) of the edict that had been argued; see appendix 19. In the case brought before R. Abraham Maimonides, the sitting judge failed to show how it was applicable to the case at hand (p. 146). Again, a quotation "from the work" (*Mishne Tora*) is no substitute for judicial analysis. The pivotal point to be asked is: "Did (the judgment) rendered conform to the best judicial analysis and judicial process (Ar. חסן אלפקה ואלתצרף) of the halakhot (involved in the case before us)?"

It follows that a case cannot be resolved on the basis of legal citations without taking into consideration the specific circumstances present in the case at hand. Objectors to this view may want to make reference to the rabbinic principle that a "statement should not be quantified differently" (נתת דבריך לשיעורים, Shabbat 35b, etc.); i.e., it should be interpreted uniformly. Anticipating this argument, R. Abraham Maimonides explained the enormous difference between formulating a law or legal principle in the abstract [as when explaining a law in class; cf. Mishna Berakhot 2:5–7], where precision and consistency are of the essence, and a judge "sitting in judgment or rendering a judicial instruction on a specific case (Ar. בחסב וקאעה ג'רת)." Concerning the latter, he offered the following outline:

> In general, let me say that a judge who bases his decisions only on the literal reading of the text is weak and pathetic. This

> attitude, in fact, runs contrary to (what the rabbis instructed): "A judge must follow what his eyes showed him!" (p. 147).

In simple terms, this means that quoting the law will not suffice when rendering a legal decision! Rather, the text of the law should serve as the *basis* upon which a legal theory is construed.

> The manifest tenor of a legal text (Ar. אלאמור אלמסטורה) should function as the judicial doctrine (Ar. אצל of the case at hand). However, it is incumbent upon the judge, either adjudicating or giving judicial instruction, to analyze (the doctrine or doctrines) in light of each of the circumstances pertaining to the case before him. The judge must relate the judgment that he is rendering to a (legal) concept, which he construes on the basis of derivations (Ar. פרוע) stemming from those judicial doctrines. The numerous stories mentioned in the Talmud about legal decisions, were not brought for naught, neither were they cited in order to rely [uncritically] on them, but to educate the judge so that he should learn from them about the power of judicial analysis and the best judicial procedure (Ar. קוה פקה וחסן תצרף; pp. 147–148).

On the imperative for the judge to consider the specificities of the case at hand, rather than rely on generalities, see R. Joseph b. Susan quoted by R. Samuel de Oceda, *Midrash Shemu'el* (Amsterdam, 5627/1867), on Abot 1:18, 19b.

In essence, judicial reliance on the view of legal authorities, without proper analysis, is a form of advocacy which no competent judge would cite as a source of textual meaning. I would like to call attention to a halakhic method developed in recent years. Rather than examining the legal issue according to the traditional sources and judicial procedure, always taking into account the distinctiveness of the case at hand, as it was practiced in both the Sephardic and Ashkenazic rabbinate (I am thinking of the late R. 'Uzziel and R. Herzog, respectively, the first Chief Sephardic and Chief Ashkenazic Rabbis of the State of Israel), it has become acceptable for unlearned rabbis to render halakhic decisions by rumbling 'sources,' without proper analysis of either the law or the case. (In the footsteps of scholastic 'proof' consisting of 'quoting' an authority; see above chapter 53.) According to the new methodology, a 'judicial decision' is rendered simply by tallying the views expressed by different authorities in the course of time, and then 'relying' (לסמוך) on the 'majority view' (דעת הרוב), i.e., 18 *vs.* 17. If the number is the same on both sides, then if the prohibition is biblical, it is forbidden and if rabbinical it is permitted. To my mind, this is like someone who is not a certified physician prescribing a medical procedure by tallying medical opinions on the matter – without checking the patient! The method is fundamentally flawed. First, it is practically impossible to tally the total number of opinions on any given issue, particularly if one were to take into account manuscripts and rare editions, as well as views issued on the matter that for a number of reasons never reached major libraries and publications. Moreover, to augment the 'total' number of authorities 'consulted,' these rabbis include writers citing or making reference to one another. Furthermore, in the process of listing and classifying the various views, they are portrayed monochromatically, without examining either the nuance of the ruling or its specific context. Its principal shortcoming, however, is the failure to offer a critical appraisal of the views in question. Given that conclusions are reached on the basis of 'majority view' (דעת הרוב), the analysis is superficial and trite, as the rabbi attempts 'to explain' his decision through the use of lame analogies. Key issues are overlooked. Contrary opinions are often sidestepped in a dismissive vein (אין כאן מקום להאריך, etc.). To assume a posture of self-assurance and mask lack of knowledge, the tone varies from condescension to irreverence and unabashed disrespect, interrupted here and there by irrelevant digressions. Because these rabbinic authorities are halakhically incompetent and intellectually insecure, often, when they decide in favor of a more lenient position, they go on to counsel adoption of the stringent view (והמחמיר תבוא עליו ברכה). Concerning this type of semi-literate halakhists, see the penetrating remarks of R. Ḥayyim D. Sh. Zurafa, *Sha'ar Shelomo* (Leghorn, 5638/1878), 165c–166b. R. Israel Moses Ḥazzan called attention to the enormous damage that bogus-halakhists cause. In particular, how their halakhic decisions promote division and turn their supporters into superstitious fanatics, rather than into men and women of faith; see my *R. Israel Moses Ḥazzan* (Heb.) (Haifa: Academic Publishers, 1978), pp. 79–82.

There is nothing wrong with someone who does not know a halakha 'relying' (סומך) on the opinion of an expert, just as we do when we file our tax returns; see above appendix 10. Indeed, R. Joseph ibn Megas maintains that someone who is not a thoroughly competent Talmudist fully acquainted with the interpretations and ruling of the Geonim, and "relies on the Geonic responsa" (מי שמורה מתשובת הגאונים וסמך עליהם) is preferable to someone "who thinks he knows Talmud and relies on himself" (שחושב שהוא יודע בתלמוד וסומך על עצמו), *She'elot wu-Tshubot* #195, 29d; cf. *Studies in the Mishne Tora*, pp. 39–40. Some of the great legal minds of Israel – among them the celebrated Maran Joseph Caro and the Rama – would 'rely' (לסמוך) on the 'majority view' or on the local authorities and traditions. However, they were, first and foremost, eminent legal scholars (גמיר וסביר בכל התורה כולה), and they knew how to bring into play the whole gamut of sources, as well as legal precedent and legal theory, to bear upon their own analyses and conclusions. Hence, the incisive, highly informed insights characterizing their writings. By way of contrast, contemporary rabbis tallying opinions are not consummate scholars (גמיר וסביר בכל התורה כולה). My dissatisfaction with their halakhic conclusions is not because they are *necessarily* wrong – indeed, many times they happen to be right! But because these rabbis act as if they were issuing a judicial decision (הוראה), when in fact they may only be *counseling* to rely (לסמוך) or not to rely (לסמוך) on this or that authority. In which case, their counsel may not be necessarily better (or worse) than a similar counsel advanced by any other such rabbi, and it would not warrant stirring up strife and contention among various Jewish communities and congregants. That is why, like the classical anti-Maimonideans, these rabbis make sure that their audience is made up of a halakhically illiterate or semi-literate (תלמיד שלא הגיע להוראה) public, unable to realize that what they promote as a judicial ruling (פסק, הוראה)is nothing more than an advocacy position, motivated in some cases by ideology and politics, rather than halakha.

For some sobering remarks on those who are not proficient in all legal sources (גמיר וסביר בכל התורה כולה) issuing decisions on the basis of ideology, rather than halakha, see *Birke Yosef, Ḥoshen Mishpaṭ*, XV, 3.

# 70. The Library of Lucena

Concerning the Library of Lucena, see R. Abraham Zacuto, *Yoḥasin ha-Shalem,* eds. Herschell Filipowski and A. H. Freimann (Jerusalem, 5723/1963), 214 a-b. On R. Abul'afia's ancient manuscripts of the Talmud, cf. R. Mordechai Sabato, *A Yemenite Manuscript of Tractate Sanhedrin* (Heb.) (Jerusalem: Yad Izhak Ben-Zvi, 1998), p. 217. On the collection of Talmud from the Geonim, and the private library of R. Samuel ha-Nagid and R. Joseph ibn Megas, see *Kitab Al-Rasa'yil,* pp. 79–80; cf. ibid, p. 68. From the substantial quotations of Geonic and early sources, it is evident that Ramban had some knowledge of these materials. However, it is not clear whether he had direct access to the library or only to some material circulating freely among the learned. The incunabula fragments of the Talmud printed in Spain, edited by H. Z. Dimitrovski, *S'ridei Talmud,* 2 vols. (New York: The Jewish Theological Seminary, 1977) are to be carefully examined. I only studied the fragments of 'Erubin. Although they contain significant variants, many are consistent with later 'French' readings, rather than what is known as 'Andalusian.'

# Bibliography

## Biblical Literature


*Biblia Rabinica = Miqra'ot Gedolot.* 4 vols. Venice, 5308/1548.

*The Bible in Aramaic.* 5 vols. Ed. Alexander Sperber. Leiden: E. J. Brill, 1962.

*Targum Anqelos = Targum Onqelos.* In *Miqra'ot Gedolot.*

*Targum to Job from Qumran Cave XI.* Ed. Michael Sokoloff Ramat-Gan: Bar-Ilan University, 1974.

*Targum Neophyti* 1. Ed. Alejandro Díez Macho. 6 vols. Madrid and Barcelona: Consejo de Investigaciones Científicas, 1968–1979.

*Targum Pseudo-Jonathan.* Ed. M. Ginsburger, *Pseudo-Jonathan.* Berlin: S. Calvary, 1903.

*Sharaḥ.* Arabic version. R. Se'adya Gaon. Ed. J. Derenbourg, *Version Arabe du Pentateuque.* Paris : Ernest Leroux, 1893.

## Jewish Hellenistic Literature

*Book of Maccabees.* In *Apocrypha.* Ed. R. H. Charles. Oxford: Clarendon Press, 1978.

*Eupolemus.* In ed. J. Freudenthal. *Hellenistische Studien.* Vol. 2. Breslau, 1875.

Josephus. *Complete Works.* Loeb Classical Library.

Philo. *Complete Works.* 10 vols. and 2 Supplements. Loeb Classical Library.

## Rabbinic Literature

### Tannaitic and Talmudic

*Abot de-R. Natan. Ed. Salomon Schechter. Vienna, 5647/1887.*

*Babylonian Talmud. Codex Florence. Jerusalem: Makor, 1972.*

*Diqduqe Soferim. Raphael N. N. Rabbinovicz. 15 vols. Jerusalem, 5720/1960.*

*Masechet Derech Eretz and Perek Ha-Shalom (Heb.). Ed. Daniel Sperber. Jerusalem: Sur-Ot, 1994.*

*Massekhet Soferim. Ed. R. Michael Higger. New York: Debe-Rabbanan, 1937.*

*Massekhet Kalla Rabbati. Ed. Michael Higger. Brooklyn: Moinester Publishing, 1936.*

*Mishna. In Maimonides' Perush ha-Mishnayot. Ed. and trans. R. Joseph Qafiḥ. 7 vols. Jerusalem: Mossad Harav Kook, 1967.*

*Mishna Shabbat. In Abraham Goldberg. Commentary to the Mishna Shabbat (Heb.). Jerusalem: Jewish Theological Seminary, 1976.*

*S'ridei Talmud. Ed. H. Z. Dimitrovski. 2 vols. New York: The Jewish Theological Seminary, 1977.*

*Talmud Babli. Standard Edition. 18 vols. Vilna: Re'em, 5668/1908.*

*Talmud Yerushalmi. Venice, 5283/1523.*

*Talmud Yerushalmi Fragments of the Genizah. Ed. Louis Ginzberg. New York: The Jewish Theological Seminary, 1909.*

*Tosefta. Ed. M. S. Zuckermandel. Jerusalem: Wahrman Books, 5735/1975.*

*Tosefta. Ed. Saul Lieberman. Zera'im-Neziqin. New York: Jewish Theological Seminary, 1955–2001.*

*Tractate Abodah Zarah. Ed. Shraga Abramson. New York: The Jewish Theological Seminary of America, 1957.*

*Tractate Ma'aserot (Heb.). Ed. and comm. Yehuda Felix. Ramat-Gan: Bar-Ilan University Press, 2005.*

*Treatise Ta'anit. Ed. Henry Malter. Philadelphia: The Jewish Publication Society, 1978.*

*A Yemenite Manuscript of Tractate Sanhedrin (Heb.). Ed. R. Mordechai Sabato. Jerusalem: Yad Izhak Ben-Zvi, 1998.*

*Yerushalmi Qiddushin. Constantinople, 5514/1754.*

## Midrashim

*Aggadat Ester*. Ed. Salomon Buber. Cracow, 5657/1897.

*Bereshit Rabba*. Ms. Vatican Ebr. 30. Facsimile. Jerusalem: Makor, 5731/1971.

*Bereshit Rabba*. Eds. J. Theodor and Ch. Albeck. 3 vols. Jerusalem: Wahrman Books, 1965.

*Debarim Rabba*. Ed. Saul Lieberman. Jerusalem: Wahrman Books, 1974.

*Ekha Rabbati*. Ed. Salomon Buber. Vilna, 1899.

*Great is Peace* (Heb.). Ed. Daniel Sperber. Jerusalem: Massada Press, 1979.

*Mekhilta de-R Yishma'el*. Eds. H. S. Horovitz and I. A. Rabin. Jerusalem: Wahrmann Books, 1970.

*Mekhilta de-R. Shim'on b. Yoḥai*. Eds. J. N. Epstein and E. Z. Melamed. Jerusalem: Mekize Nirdamim, 1955.

*Midrash Aggada*. Ed. Salomon Buber. Vienna, 1894.

*Midrash ha-Gadol. Bereshit*. Ed. Mordecai Margulies. Jerusalem: Mossad Harav Kook, 5727/1967.

*Midrash ha-Gadol. Deuteronomy*. Ed. S. Fisch. Jerusalem: Mossad Harav Kook, 1972.

*Midrash Mishle*. Ed. Salomon Buber. Vilna: 5653/1893.

*Midrash Rabba* [*'al ha-Tora ve-Ḥamesh Megillot*]. 2 vols. Vilna. Reprinted: Jerusalem, 5735/1975.

*Midrash Shemu'el*. Ed. Salomon Buber. Cracow, 5653/1893.

*Midrash Tanḥuma*. 2 vols. Warsaw, 5611/1851.

*Midrash Tanḥuma*. Ed. S. Buber. 2 vols. Vilna, 5645/1885.

*Midrash Tanna'im, Debarim*. Ed. David Z. Hoffman. Berlin, 5668/69–1909.

*Midrash Tehillim*. Ed. Salomon Buber. New York: Om Publishing, 1947.

*Midrash Zuṭa*. Ed. Salomon Buber. Berlin, 1894.

*Mishnat R. Eli'ezer*. Ed. H. G. Enelow. New York, Jewish Theological Seminary, 1933.

*Ozar Midrashim*. 2 vols. Ed. J. D. Eisenstein. New York, 1915.

*Pesiqta de-Rab Kahana*. Bernard Mandelbaum. 2 vols. New York: The Jewish Theological Seminary, 1962.

*Qohelet Rabba*. In *Midrash Rabba* [*'al ha-Tora ve-Ḥamesh Megillot*].

*Shir ha-Shirim Rabba*. In *Midrash Rabba* [*'al ha-Tora ve-Ḥamesh Megillot*].

*Sifra*. Codex Assemani LXVI. Ed. Louis Finkelstein. New York: The Jewish Theological Seminary, 5717–1956.

*Sifra*. Ed. Isaac Hirsch Weiss. Vienna, 5622/1862.

*Sifre Bemidbar*. Ed. H. Horovitz. Jerusalem: Wahrman Books, 1966.

*Sifre Debarim*. Ed. Louis Finkelstein. New York: The Jewish Theological Seminary of America, 1969.

*Sifre Zuṭa*. Ed. Menaḥem Kahana. Jerusalem: Magnes Press, 2002.

*Tana de-Be Eliyahu*. Lublin, 5657/1897.

*Vayyiqra Rabba*. Ed. Mordecai Margulies. 5 vols. Jerusalem: American Academy for Jewish Research, 1960.

*Yalquṭ Shim'oni*. 2 vols. Jerusalem: Ch. Vegshel, n.d.

*Zohar*. 3 vols. Leghorn, 5618/1858.

*Tiqqune ha-Zohar*. Leghorn, 5646/1886.

## Geonic Literature

R. 'Amram Gaon. *Seder Rab 'Amram Ga'on*. Ed. Daniel Goldshmidt. Jerusalem: Mossad Harav Kook, 1971.

*Gaonica*. Ed. S. Assaf. Jerusalem: Darom, 1933.

*Genizah Studies*. Ed. Louis Ginzberg. 2 vols. New York: Jewish Theological Seminary, 1928–1929.

*Geonic Responsa* (Heb.). Ed. Elazar Hurvitz. New York, 1995.

*Geonica*. Ed. Louis Ginzberg. 2 vols. New York: Jewish Theological Seminary, 1909.

*Ḥadashim gam Yeshanim*. Ed. Abraham E. Harkavi. Jerusalem: Karmiel, 5730/1970.

*Halakhot Gedolot*. Ed. Ezriel Hildesheimer. Vol. 1. Jerusalem: Mekize Nirdamim, 1971.

*Halakhot Pesuqot*. Ed. R. S. Sassoon. Jerusalem: Mekize Nirdamim, 1950. Hebrew version, *Hilkhot Re'u*. Versailles: Cerf et fils, 1886.

R. Ḥanan'el. *Perush*. In *Talmud Babli*. Vilna: Re'em, 5668/1908.

*Pesaḥim. Jerusalem. Makhon Leb Sameaḥ, 5751/1991.*

Harkavi, A. E. *Ḥadashim gam Yeshanim*. Jerusalem: Karmiel, 5730/1970.

Ḥazzan, R. Israel Moses. *'Iyye ha-Yam*. Ed. and annotated by Leghorn: 5629/1869.

*Hilkhot Re'u*. See *Halakhot Pesuqot*.

Mann, Jacob. *The Jews in Egypt and in Palestine*. 2 vols. Oxford: Oxford University Press, 1969.

*Texts and Studies. 2 vols. New York: Ktav Publishing, 1972.*

*Newly Discovered Geonic Responsa* (Heb.). Eds. S. Emanuel and A. Shoshana. Jerusalem – Cleveland: Ofeq Institute, 1995.

R. Nissim Gaon. *Sefer ha-Mafteaḥ*. Ed. J. Goldenthal. Vienna, 1847.

*R. Nissim Ga'on. Ed. Shraga Abramson. Jerusalem: Mekize Nirdamim, 1965.*

*Oṣar ha-Ge'onim*. 13 vols. Ed. B. M. Lewin. Jerusalem, 1928–1943.

*Oṣar ha-Ge'onim. Sanhedrin*. Ed. R. Ch. Z. Tobias. Jerusalem: Mossad Harav Kook, 1966.

*Perush ha-Ge'onim 'al Ṭahorot*. Ed. J. N. Epstein. Berlin: Mekize Nirdamim, 1924.

*Qehillat Shelomo*. Ed. R. Solomon A. Wertheimer. Jerusalem, 5659/1899.

R. Se'adya Gaon. *Commentary on Exodus*. Ed. and trans. Y. Ratzaby. Jerusalem: Mossad Harav Kook, 1998.

*"Fragments." Ed. M. Zucker. Sura 2 (1955–1956).*

*Ha'egron. Ed. N. Allony. Jerusalem: The Academy of the Hebrew Language, 1969.*

*Perush. Daniel. Ed. and trans. R. Joseph Qafiḥ. Jerusalem: Deror, 5741/1991.*

*Perush. Mishle. Ed. and trans. R. Joseph Qafiḥ. Jerusalem, 5736/1976.*

*Saadya's Commentary on Genesis (Heb.). Ed. Moshe Zucker. New York: Jewish Theological Seminary, 1984. See Zucker, Moses. Rav Saadya Ga'on's Translation of the Torah.*

*Sefer ha-Galui. Ed. Abraham E. Harkavi. In Zikhron la-Rishonim, vol. 5. St. Petersburg, 1892.*

*Tafsir Yesha'ya. Ed. and trans. Y Ratzaby. Kiriat Ono: Mekhon Moshe, 1993.*

*Teshubot. Traité de Successions. In Oeuvres Complète, vol. 9. Ed. R. Joel Muller. Paris: Ernest Leroux, 1897.*

*Sha'are Ṣedeq*. Jerusalem, 5726/1966.

"*Shalosh Teshubot le-R. Hayye Gaon.*" *Ginze Kedem* 2 (1923).

R. Sherira Gaon. *Iggeret*. Ed. B. M. Lewin. Haifa,1921.

*Teshubot Ge'onim Qadmonim*. Ed. David Cassel. Berlin, 1848.

*Teshubot ha-Ge'onim*. Ed. R. Jacob Musafia. Lyck, 5624/1864.

*Teshubot ha-Ge'onim*. Ed. Abraham E. Harkavi. Berlin, 1887.

*Teshubot R. Neṭruna'e Ga'on*. 2 vols. Ed. Robert Brody. Jerusalem – Cleveland: Ofeq Institute, 1994.

*Teshubot R. Sar Shalom*. Ed. R. Samuel ha-Cohen Weinberg. Jerusalem: Mossad Harav Kook, 1975.

*Zikhron la-Rishonim*. Ed. Abraham E. Harkavi. Petersburg, 1880.

## Jewish and Rabbinic Writers

R. Aaron ibn Ḥayyim. See Ibn Ḥayyim, R. Aaron.

Abarbanel, R. Isaac. *Mif'alot Elohim*. Lemberg, 1863.

*Naḥalat Abot. New York, 5713–1953.*

Abendana, R. Isaac. *Discourses on the Ecclesiastical and Civil Polity of the Jews*. London, 1706.

Abi Zimra, R. David b. *Teshubot ha-Radbaz*. 2. vols. Warsaw, 5642/1882.

R. Abraham b. David (of Posquières). *Teshubot wu-Psaqim*. Jerusalem: Mossad Harav Kook, 5724/1964.

R. Abraham ibn 'Ezra. See Ibn 'Ezra, R. Abraham.

R. Abraham ibn Ṭawwa'ah. See Ibn Ṭawwa'ah, R. Abraham.

Abrahams, Israel. *Studies in Pharisaism and the Gospels*. Second Series. New York: Ktav Publishing House, 1967.

Abramson, Shraga. *Ba-Merkazim wuba-Tefuṣot bi-Tqufat ha-Ge'onim*. Jerusalem: Mossad Harav Kook, 5725/1965.

*"Dibre Ḥazal be-Shirat ha-Nagid." World Congress for Jewish Studies. I. Jerusalem: Hebrew University Press, 5712/1952.*

*Mi-Pi Ba'ale Leshonot. Jerusalem: Mossad Harav Kook, 5748/1998.*

*"Mi-Torato shel R. Shemu'el ha-Nagid." Sinai (Jubilee Volume) 100 (5748/1988).*

*Perush R. Ḥanan'el la-Talmud. Jerusalem: Vagshal, 5755/1995.*

*Tractate Abodah Zarah. Ed. Shraga Abramson. New York: The Jewish Theological Seminary of America, 1957.*

Abulafia, R. Hezekiah David. *Ben Zequnim*. Leghorn, 5553/1793.

Abul'afya, R. Isaac. *Pene Yiṣḥaq*. Vol. 6. Jerusalem, 5668/1908.

Abul'afya, R. Ḥayyim. *Miqra'e Qodesh*. Izmir, 5482/1722.

*Yishrash Ya'aqob. Izmir 5489/1729.*

Abul'afya, R. Me'ir ha-Levi. *Kitab Al-Rasa'yil le-Rabbenu Me'ir ha-Levi*. Paris, 5631/1871.

*Yad Rama on Baba Batra. New York: Da'at, 5712/1952.*

Adrete, R. Solomon. *Ḥiddushe ha-Rishba 'al Aggadot ha-Shas*. Ed. R. Sh. M. Weinberger. Jerusalem, 5726/1966.

*Ḥiddushe ha-Rishba. Megilla. Ed. Z. Dimitrovsky. Jerusalem: Mossad Harav Kook, 5741/1981.*

*Ḥiddushe ha-Rishba. Rosh HaShana. Ed. Z. Dimitrovsky. Jerusalem: Mossad Harav Kook, 5741/1981.*

*Ḥiddushe ha-Rishba. Shabbat. Ed. Y. Bruner. Jerusalem: Mossad Harav Kook, 5746/1986.*

*Teshubot ha-Rishba. Vol. 1. Bne Brak, 5718/1958.*

*Teshubot ha-Rishba. Ed. Ch. Z. Dimitrovsky. 2 vols. Jerusalem: Mossad Harav Kook, 1990.*

Aghamati, R. Zachariah. *Sefer ha-Ner. Berakhot* (British Museum, ms. 11361).

*The Tractates Baba Kamma... London: British Museum, 1961.*

Agus, R. Jacob. "Toynbee's Epistle to the Jews." *Commentary* 32 (1961).

Al'ami, R. Solomon. *Iggeret Musar*. Ed. A. A. Haberman. Jerusalem: Sifriyat Meqorot, 1946.

Al-Ashqar, R. Joseph. *Mirkebet ha-Mishne*. Ed. J. Shpigel 5753/1993.

Al-Ashqar, R. Moses. *She'elot*. Jerusalem, 5719/1959.

Albeck, Ch. *Mabo la-Talmudim*. Tel Aviv: Dvir, 1969.

Albelda, R. Moses. *Darash Moshe*. Venice, 5363/1603.

Albo, R. Joseph. *Sefer ha-'Iqqarim*. Ed. and trans. Isaac Husik. Philadelphia: The Jewish Publication Society, 1946.

Alexander, Edward. *The Jewish Wars: Reflections by One of the Belligerents*. Carbondale: Southern Illinois University Press, 1996.

Alexander, Philip S. "Mysticism." In Martin Goodman, ed. *Oxford Handbook of Jewish Studies*. Oxford: Oxford University Press, 2002.

Alfandari, R. Ḥayyim. *Esh Dat*. Constantinople, 5478/1718.

Algazi, R. Ḥayyim. *Bene Ḥayye*. Orta-Kivvae, 5479/1719.

Algazi, R. Israel Jacob. *Shalme Ṣibbur*. Saloniki, 5550/1790.

Algazi, R. Solomon. *Yabin Shemu'a*. Leghorn, 5552/1792.

Al-Ḥarizi, R. Judah. *Taḥkemoni*. Warsaw, 5659/1899.

Almadari, R. Judah. Ed. R. Y. ha-Levi Kuperberg. In *Sanhedre Gedola*. Vol. 2. Jerusalem: Makhon Harry Fischel, 5729/1969.

Almosnino, R. Moses. *Tefilla le-Moshe*. Israel: Hamakhon le-Ḥeqer Yahdut Saloniki, 5748/1988.

Amram, David Werner. *The Jewish Law of Divorce.* London: David Nutt, 1897.

'Arama, R. David. *Perush 'al ha-Rambam.* Saloniki, 5330/1570.

'Arama, R. Isaac. *Ḥazut Qasha.* Sabioneta, 5312/1552.

Ardit, R. Joshua Sh. *Ḥinna ve-Ḥisda.* 3 vols. Izmir, 5633/1873.

Arragel, R. Moses. In *Biblia de la Casa de Alba.* Madrid: Imprenta Artistica, 1920.

'Arusi, R. Raṣon. "*Birkat Hadlaqat...*" *Sinai* 85 (5739/1979).

*"Qeri'at Tirgum ha-Tora veha-Hafṭara be-Ṣibbur." Sinai 89 (5742/1982).*

Asher, R. *Hilkhot ha-Rosh.* Standard Edition.

*Teshubot ha-Rosh. Constantinople, 5277/1517.*

*Tosafot ha-Rosh. Berakhot. In Berakha Meshulleshet. Warsaw, 5623/1853.*

Assaf, S. "*Me-Ginze Bet-ha-Sefarim...*" In *Minḥa le-David Yellin.* Jerusalem: Ruben Mass, 5695/1925.

*Tequfat ha-Ge'onim. Jerusalem: Mossad Harav Kook, 5715/1955.*

R. 'Azriel. *Commentary of Talmudic Aggadoth* (Heb.). Ed. Isaiah Tishby. Jerusalem: Magnes Press, 1982.

Azulai, R. Ḥ.Y.D. *Birke Yosef.* Leghorn, 5534–36/1774–76.

*Mar'it ha-'Ayyin. Leghorn, 5564/1804.*

*Petaḥ 'Enayim. Leghorn, 5550/1790.*

*Ya'ir Ozen. Leghorn, 5552/1792.*

Baḥur, R. Eliahu. *Meturgeman.* Izna, 1541.

R. Baḥye b. Asher. *Be'ur.* Ed. C. B. Chavel. 3 vols. Jerusalem: Mossad Harav Kook: 5737/1977.

Baer, Yitzhak. *A History of the Jews in Christian Spain.* 2 vols. Philadelphia: The Jewish Publication of America, 1961–5722.

*"The Kabalistic Doctrine in the Christological Teaching of Abner of Burgos" (Heb.). Tarbiz 27 (1958).*

Baron, Salo W. *A Social and Religious History of the Jews.* Vols. 3, 4, 8. Philadelphia: Jewish Publication Society, 1957.

Belkin, Samuel. *In His Image.* New York: Abelard-Schuman, n.d.

Benamozegh, R. Elie. *Em la-Miqra.* 5 vols. Leghorn, 1862–1865.

*Jewish and Christian Ethics. San Francisco: Emanuel Blochman, 5633–1873.*

*Mabo le-Tora she-be-'al Pe. Ed. R. E. Zini. Jerusalem, 5762/2002.*

R. Benjamin of Tudela. *The Itinerary of Benjamin of Tudela.* Ed. and trans. Marcus Nathan Adler. New York: Philipp Feldheim, n.d.

Benveniste, R. Joshua. *Sede Yehoshua'*. Constantinople, 5514/1754.

Berakha, R. Isaac. *Berakh Yiṣḥaq*. Venice, 5723/1763.

Berkovitz, R. Eliezer. *Essential Essays on Judaism.* Jerusalem: Shalem Press, 2002.

*Besamim Rosh*. Ed. R. Isaac de Molina. Berlin, 5553/1793.

Bickerman, Elias. *From Ezra to the Last of the Maccabees.* New York: Schocken Books, 1962.

*The God of the Maccabees. Leiden: E. J. Brill, 1979.*

*The Jews in the Greek Age. Cambridge, Mass.: Harvard University Press, 1988.*

*"The Maccabean Uprising: An Interpretation." In ed. Judah Goldin. The Jewish Expression. New Haven: Yale University Press, 1976.*

*Studies in Jewish and Christian History. 3 vols. Leiden: E. J. Brill, 1986.*

Blau, Ludwig. "Methods of Teaching Talmud." *Jewish Quarterly Review* 15 (1903).

Blumenkranz, Bernhard. *Les auteurs chretiens latins du moyen age sur les Juifs et le Judaism*. Paris: Mouton, 1963.

Bodoff, Lipman. "Abraham's Covenant, Chosenness, and the Binding of Isaac." *Midstream*. November/December 2006.

*The Binding of Isaac, Religious Murders, & Kabbalah. New York: Devorah Publishing, 2005.*

*"The Message of the Prophet Elisha." Midstream. February/March 1999.*

*"Religious Murders: Weeds in the Garden of Jewish Tradition?" Midstream. January 1988.*

Boṭon, R. Abraham de. *Leḥem Mishne*. In *Mishne Tora*. Standard Edition.

Broyer, M. "The Ashkenazi Semikha" (Heb.). *Zion* 33 (1968).

Buber, Martin. "To Create New Words?" In Martin Buber, *A Believing Humanism*. New York: Simon and Schuster, 1967.

Cardoso, Isaac. *Las Excelencias de los Hebreos*. Amsterdam, 1679.

Caro, Maran Joseph. *Abqat Rokhel*. Saloniki, 5551/1791.

*Bedeq ha-Bayit. Standard Edition.*

*Bet Yosef. Standard Edition.*

*Kesef Mishne. In Mishne Tora. Standard Edition.*

*Shulḥan 'Arukh. Standard Edition.*

Castro, R. Jacob. *'Erekh Leḥem*. Constantinople, 5478/1718.

Chazan, Robert. *European Jewry and the First Crusade*. Berkeley: University of California Press, 1987.

Chicatilla, R. Joseph. *Sha'are Ora*. Warsaw, 5643/1883.

Churgin, Pinkhos. *The Targum to Hagiographa*. New York: Horeb, 1945.

Cohen, R. Abraham. *Sabbath Sermons*. London: Soncino Press, 1960.

Cohen, Avinoam. *Ravina and Contemporary Sages* (Heb.). Ramat Gan: Bar Ilan University, 2001.

Crescas, R. Ḥasdai. *Or ha-Shem*. Tel-Aviv, 5723/1963.

Dan, Joseph. "*Be'ayat Qiddush ha-Shem*." In *Holy Wars and Martyrology*. Jerusalem: The Historical Society of Israel, 1967.

*On Sanctity (Heb.). Jerusalem: Hebrew University Press, 1997.*

*"The Vicissitudes of the Esotericism of German Hasidim." In Studies in Mysticism and Religion. Hebrew Section. Jerusalem: Magnes Press, 1967.*

R. David ha-Kohen. *Teshubot ha-Radak*. Constantinople, 5297/1537.

De la-Ara, R. Ḥiyya ha-Cohen. *Mishmerot Kehunna*. Amsterdam, 5508/1748.

Dershowitz, Alan M. *The Genesis of Justice*. New York: Warner Books, 2000.

Dienstag, Israel. "*Ha-Im Hitnagged ha-Gra le-Mishnato ha-Pilosophit shel ha-Rambam?*" *Talpioth* 4 (1949).

Dubnow, Simon. *Geschichte des Chassidismus*. Vol. 1. Berlin: Judischer Verlag, 1931.

Duran, R. Isaac Profiaṭ. *Ma'ase Efod*. Vienna, 1865.

Duran, R. Simon b. Ṣemaḥ. *Tashbeṣ*. Amsterdam, 5498/1738.

*and R. Solomon Duran, Yakhin wu-Bo'az. Leghorn, 5542/1782.*
R. Eli'ezer Ashkenazi. *Dammeseq Eli'ezer*. Lublin, 5407/1647.
R. Eliyahu ha-Levi. *Zeqan Aharon*. Constantinople, 5494/1734.
Elitzur, Yehudah. *Israel and the Bible* (Heb.). Ramat-Gan: Bar-Ilan University Press, 1999.
Epstein, J. N. *Prolegomena* (Heb.). Ed. E. Z. Melamed. 2 vols. Jerusalem: Magnes Press, 1957.
Fano, R. Menaḥem 'Azarya di. *Teshubot*. Venice, 5360/1600.
Farḥon, R. Solomon. *Maḥberet he-'Arukh*. Ed. S. Gottlieb Stern. Pressburg 5604/1844.
Faur, José. "*'Aliyat Qaṭan li-Qro ba-Tora.*" In *Studies in Memory of the Rishon le-Zion R. Y. Nissim*, vol. 1. Jerusalem: Yad ha-Rab Nissim, 5745/1985.
*"Basic Concepts in Rabbinic Hermeneutics." Shofar 16 (1997).*
*"The Biblical Idea of Idolatry," Jewish Quarterly Review 69 (1978).*
*"A Crisis of Categories: Kabbalah and the Rise of Apostasy in Spain." In eds. Moshe Lazar and Stephen Haliczer. The Jews of Spain and The Expulsion of 1492. California: Labyrinthos, 1997.*
*"Concerning the Term Qore be-Iggeret" (Heb.). Alei Sefer 15 (1988–1989).*
*"David Nassy: On Prejudice and Related Matters." In eds. Lea Dasberg and Jonathan N. Cohen. Neveh Ya'akov: Jubilee Volume Presented to Dr. Jaap Meijer. Assen, The Netherlands: Van Gorcum, 1982.*
*"Delocutive Expressions in the Hebrew Liturgy," Ancient Studies in Memory of Elias Bickerman (The Journal of the Ancient Near Eastern Society) 16–17 (1984–1985).*
*"Don Quixote: Talmudist and mucho más." The Review of Rabbinic Judaism 4 (2001).*
*"El pensamiento Sefardí frente a la iluminación Europea." In Pensamiento y Mística Hispanojudía y Sefardí. Cuenca: Ediciones de la Universidad de Casilla-La Mancha, 2001.*
*"Esoteric Knowledge and the Vulgar: Parallels between Newton and Maimonides." Trumah 12 (2002).*
*"Francisco Sánchez's Theory of Cognition and Vico's verum/factum." New Vico Studies 5 (1987).*

*"God as a Writer: Omnipresence and the Art of Dissimulation." Religion & Intellectual Life 6 (1989).*

*Golden Doves with Silver Dots: Semiotics and Textuality in Rabbinic Tradition. Bloomington: Indiana University Press, 1986.*

*"The Hebrew Personal Pronoun." In Perspectives on Jews and Judaism. New York: Rabbinical Assembly, 1979.*

*"The Hebrew Species Concept and the Origin of Evolution: R. Benamozegh's Response to Darwin." Rassegna Mensile di Israel 63 (1997).*

*"Hora'at ha-Talmud ba-Masoret ha-Ḥinnukhit ha-Sfaradit," Shebile Ḥinnukh, 35 (1975).*

*Homo Mysticus. Syracuse: Syracuse University Press, 1999.*

*"Idolatry." Encyclopedia Judaica.*

*"Imagination and Religious Pluralism: Maimonides, ibn Verga, and Vico." New Vico Studies 10 (1992).*

*In the Shadow of History. Albany, N.Y.: SUNY, 1992.*

*"Jews, Conversos, and Native Americans: The Iberian Experience." Annual of Rabbinic Judaism 3 (2000).*

*"The Jewish Mentality of Francisco Sánchez," Mentalities 7 (1992).*

*"Law and Hermeneutics in Rabbinic Tradition." Cardozo Law Review 14 (1993).*

*"The Legal Thinking of the Tosafot." Dine Israel 6 (1975).*

*"The Limits of Readerly Collusion in Rabbinic Tradition." Soundings 76 (1993).*

*"Maimonides' Starting Precept" (Heb.). In ed. Shamir Yona. Or le-Mayer: Studies in Bible, Semitic Languages, Rabbinic Literature, and Ancient Civilizations. Beer Sheva: Ben-Gurion University, 2010.*

*"On Martyrdom in Jewish Law" (Heb.). Annual of Bar-Ilan University, 30–31 (2006).*

*"Monolingualism and Judaism." Cardozo Law Review 14 (1993).*

*"Newton, Maimonidean." Review of Rabbinic Judaism 6 (2003).*

*"Of Cultural Intimidation and Other Miscellanea: Bar-Sheshakh v. Raba." Review of Rabbinic Judaism 5 (2002).*

*"One-Dimensional Jew." Review of Rabbinic Judaism 2 (1999).*

*"Performative and Descriptive Utterances in Jewish Law" (Heb.). In ed. Arye Edrei. Studies in Jewish Law in Honor of Professor Aaron Kirschenbaum (Dine Israel 20–21, 5760–5761).*

*"Person and Subjectivity: A Linguistic Category." Mentalities 6 (1990).*

*Rabbi Israel Moses Ḥazzan: The Man and his Works (Heb.) Haifa: Academic Publishers, 1978.*

*"Retórica y hermenéutica: Vico y la tradición rabínica." In ed. E. Hidalgo-Serna, et al. Pensar Para el Nuevo Siglo. Vol. 3. Napoli: La Cittá del Sole, 2001.*

*"Sephardim in the Nineteenth Century: New Directions and Old Values." Proceedings of the American Academy for Jewish Research 44 (1977).*

*"Sir Isaac Newton – 'a Judaic Monotheist of the School of Maimonides.'" In eds. Gorge K. Hasselhoff and Otfried Fraisse. Moses Maimonides (1138–1204). Germany: Ergon Verlag, 2004.*

*Studies in the Mishne Tora (Heb.). Jerusalem: Mossad Harav Kook, 1978.*

*"The Splitting of the Logos: Some Remarks on Vico and Rabbinic Tradition." New Vico Studies 3 (1985).*

*"The Status of Jewish Real Estate outside Israel's Territory" (Heb.). In Honour of Prof. Avner H. Shaki. Ed. Chief Justice Aharon Barak, Law Review Netanya Academic College, 4 (2005).*

*"The Targumim and Halakha." Jewish Quarterly Review 66 (1976).*

*"The Third Person in Semitic Grammatical Theory and General Linguistics." Linguistica Biblica Bohn 46 (1979).*

*"Tosafot ha-Rosh le-Massekhet Berakhot." Proceedings of the American Academy for Jewish Research 33 (1965).*

*"Two Models of Jewish Spirituality." Shofar 10 (1992).*

*"Ve-Niṣḥu Ḥakhme Ummot ha-'Olam et Ḥakhme Yisrael." In Minḥa Le-Yiṣḥaq. Eds. Chief Justice of Israel Supreme Court Aharon Barak and Professor Menashe Shawa. Jerusalem: Lishkat 'Orkhe-Din, 1999.*

*"Vico, el Humanismo Religioso y la Tradición Sefardita." Cuadernos sobre Vico 7 (1997).*

*"Zekhut ha-Rofe..." Dine Israel 7 (1976).*

Feldman, Leon A. "*Teshubat ha-Rishba...*" *Sinai.* Jubilee Volume, 100 (1987).

Fijo, R. 'Azarya de. *Bina le-'Ittim.* 2 vols. Jerusalem: Vagshel, 5749/1989.

Finzi, R. Solomon. *Mafteaḥ ha-Gemara.* In *Temim De'im.* Venice, 1622.

Fleischer, Ezra. *Hebrew Liturgical Poetry in the Middle Ages* (Heb.). Jerusalem: Keter Publishing, 1975.

Friedman, M. A. "*Ve-Khatab lo...*" *Sinai* 84 (5739/1979).

Frimer, Norman. See Schwarts, Dov.

Gaster, Theodor H. *Festivals of the Jewish Year.* New York: William Morrow and Company, 1952.

*The Holy and the Profane. New York: William Morrow, 1980.*

R. Gereshom. *Perush R. Gereshom.* In *Talmud Babli.* Vilna: Re'em, 5668/1908.

Gershenzon, Shoshana G. *A Study of* Teshuvot la-Meḥaref *by Abner of Burgos.* Ph.D. Thesis. New York: The Jewish Theological Seminary of America, 1984.

Gilat, Y. D. "Kallah, Months of." In *Encyclopaedia Judaica.*

Ginzberg, Louis. *A Commentary to the Palestinian Talmud* (Heb.). Vols. 3–4. New York: The Jewish Theological Seminary of America, 1941.

Glatzer, Nahum. "Peace in Classical Judaism." In his *Essays in Jewish Thought.* Alabama: Alabama University Press, 1978.

Glueck, Nelson. *Ḥesed in the Bible.* Cincinnati: Hebrew Union College, 1967.

Goiten, S. D. *Religion in a Religious Age.* Cambridge, Mass.: Association for Jewish Studies, 1974.

Goldberg, Abraham. *Commentary to the Mishna Shabbat* (Heb.). Jerusalem: Jewish Theological Seminary, 1976.

Goodblatt, David M. *Rabbinic Instruction in Sasanian Babylonia.* Leiden: E. J. Brill, 1975.

Gordis, Robert. "Democratic Origins in Ancient Israel – the Biblical

*'Edah.*" In *Alexander Marx Jubilee Volume* (English Section). New York: The Jewish Theological Seminary of America, 1950.

Graetz, Heinrich. *History of the Jews*. Vol. 3. Philadelphia: Jewish Publication Society, 1894.

Gruber, Mayer I. "The Term *Midrash* in Tannaitic Literature." In ed. Rivka Ulmer, *Discussing Cultural Influences*. Lanham: University Press of America, 2007.

*"God, Image of." In Encyclopaedia of Judaism, Supplement #1.*

Ḥabib, R. Israel Jacob. *'En Ya'aqob*. Standard Edition.

Ḥabib, R. Levi b. *She'elot wu-Tshubot*. Venice, 5325/1565.

Ḥabib, R. Moses b. *'Azarat Nashim*. Leipzig, 5619/1859.

*Kappot Temarim. New York, 5713/1953.*

*She'elot wu-Tshubot. Jerusalem: 5687/1927.*

Ḥajez, R. Jacob. *'Eṣ Ḥayyim*. Verona, 5408/1648.

*Halakhot Qeṭannot. Venice, 5464/1704.*

*Tehillat Ḥokhma. Verona, 5407/1647.*

Halkin, Abraham. "In Defense of Maimonides' Code" (Heb.). *Tarbiz* 25 (1956).

*"Why was Levi ben Hayyim Hounded?" Proceedings of the American Academy for Jewish Research, 34 (1966).*

Harkabi, Yehoshafat. *The Bar Kokhba Syndrome*. Chappaqua, N.Y.: Russel Books, 1983.

R. Ḥatam Sofer. *Qobeṣ. Teshubot*. Jerusalem: 5733/1973.

R. Ḥayyim b. Isaac. *Or Zarua'*. Israel, 1958.

Ḥazzan, R. Raphael Joseph. *Ḥiqre Leb. Eben ha-'Ezer*. Saloniki, 5573/1813.

*Ḥiqre Leb. Yore De'a. Part I. Leghorn, 5554/1794.*

Ḥazzan, R. Israel Moses. *Iyye ha-Yam*. Leghorn, 5629/1869.

*Kerakh shel Romi. Leghorn, 5636/1876.*

*Words of Peace and Truth. Ed. Samuel Meldola. London, 5605/1845.*

*Hellenistic Views on Jews and Judaism*. Jerusalem: Zalman Shazar Center, 1974.

Heinman, I. "*Midrash.*" *Encyclopaedia Miqra'it*. Jerusalem: Bialik, 1988.

Helmreich, William B. *The World of the Yeshiva*. Hoboken, New Jersey: Ktav Publishing, 2000.

Hertz, Chief Rabbi J. H. *The Pentateuch and Haftorahs*. London: Soncino Press, 5758/1997.

*Sermons, Addresses and Studies*. 3 vols. London: Soncino Press, 1938.

Heschel, Abraham Joshua. *God in Search of Man*. Philadelphia: Jewish Publication Society, 1956.

"Inspiration in the Middle Ages." In *Alexander Marx Jubilee Volume (Heb. Section)*. New York: The Jewish Theological Seminary of America, 1950.

*The Prophets*. New York: The Burning Bush Press, 1962.

*The Sabbath*. New York: Harper & Row, 1952.

*Ḥoq le-Ya'aqob*. 2 vols. Jerusalem, 5755/1995.

Ibn 'Aqnin, R. Joseph ben Judah. *Hitgallut ha-Sodot ve-Hofa'at ha-Me'orot*. Ed. and trans. A. S. Halkin. Jerusalem: Mekize Nirdamim, 1964.

*Mebo ha-Talmud*. Jerusalem, 5727/1967.

Ibn 'Aṭṭar, R. Ḥayyim. *Or ha-Ḥayyim*. Warsaw, 5671/1911.

Ibn Bal'am, R. Judah. *Commentary to Isaiah*. Ed. M. Peretz. Ramat-Gan: Bar-Ilan University, 1992.

*Commentary to Jeremiah*. Ed. M. Peretz. Ramat-Gan: Bar-Ilan University, 2002.

Ibn Daud, R. Abraham. *Sefer ha-Qabbalah*. Ed. trans. and annotated by Gerson D. Cohen. Philadelphia, The Jewish Publication Society, 1967.

Ibn 'Ezra, R. Abraham. *Commentary* to *Ecclesiastes*. In *Miqra'ot Gedolot*.

*Commentary to the Tora*. In *Miqra'ot Gedolot*. Ms. Vat. Ebr. 38. Ed. Prof. Etan Levine. *Abraham ibn Ezra's Commentary to the Pentateuch*. Jerusalem: Makor, 1974.

*Yesod Mora ve-Sod Tora*. Eds. Joseph Cohen and Uriel Simon. Ramat-Gan: Bar- Ilan University Press, 2002.

Ibn 'Ezra, R. Moses. *Kitab al-Muḥaḍara wal-Mudhakara*. Ed. and trans. A. S. Halkin. Jerusalem: Mekize Nirdamim, 1975.

Ibn Faquda, R. Baḥye. Arabic original: *Kitab al-Hadaya ila Fara'iḍ al-Qulub*. Ed. A. S. Yahuda. Leiden: E.J. Brill, 1912. Hebrew trans.

and Arabic original, in *Ḥobot ha-Lebabot*. R. Joseph Qafiḥ. Jerusalem, 5733/1973.

Ibn Gaon, R. Shem Ṭob. *Migdal 'Oz*. In *Mishne Tora*. Standard Edition.

Ibn Ḥayyim, R. Aaron. *Qorban Aharon*. Venice: 5369/1609.

Ibn Jannaḥ, R. Jonah. *Kitab al-Luma'*. Ed. Joseph Derenbourg. Paris: F. Vieweg, 1886. Hebrew translation, R. Judah ibn Tibbon, *Sefer ha-Riqma*. Ed. M. Wilensky. Berlin: Akademie-Verlag, 1930. Facsimile edition. 2 vols. Jerusalem: Academy for the Hebrew Language, 5724/1964.

*Sefer ha-Shorashim. Hebrew trans. R. Judah ibn Tibbon. Berlin: Mekize Nirdamim, 1896.*

Ibn Leb, R. Joseph. *Teshubot*. Amsterdam, 5446/1686.

Ibn Megas, R. Joseph. *She'elot wu-Tshubot*. Saloniki, 5546/1786.

Ibn Shu'eb, R. Joel. *Nora Tehillot*. Saloniki, 5329/1569.

Ibn Shu'eb, R. Joshua. *Derashot 'al ha-Tora*. Constantinople, 5283/1523.

Ibn Verga, R. Joseph. *She'erit Yosef*. Warsaw, 1909.

Ibn Verga, R. Solomon. *Shebeṭ Yehuda*. Eds. Azriel Shochet and Y. Baer. Jerusalem: Mossad Bialik, 5707/1947.

Ibn Ṭawwa'ah, R. Abraham. *Ḥuṭ ha-Mshullash*. In *Sefer ha-Tashbeṣ*. Amsterdam, 5498/1738.

Idel, Moshe. "Nahmanides, *Kabbalah, Halakha,* and Spiritual Leadership." In eds. Moshe Idel and Mortimer Ostow, *Jewish Mystical Leaders and Leadership in the 13th Century*. Northvale, New Jersey: Jason Aronson, 1998.

R. Immanuel of Rome. *The Book of Proverbs*. Naples, ca. 1487. Offset: Jerusalem, The Hebrew University Press, 1981.

R. Isaac b. Sheshet. *Teshubot ha-Ribash*. New York, 5714/1954.

Isserles, R. Moses. *Mappa*. In *Shulḥan 'Arukh*. Standard Edition.

*She'elot wu-Tshubot. Amsterdam, 5471/1711.*

Jabès, Edmond. *Elya*. Berkeley, Ca.: Tree, 1973.

R. Jacob Castro. See Castro, R. Jacob.

Jellinek, Adolph. *Ginze Ḥokhmat ha-Qabbala*. Leipzig, 1853.

Jessurun, Rehuel. *Dialogo dos Montes*. Ed. and trans. Philip Polack. London: Tamiesis Books, 1975.

R. Joel ibn Shu'eb. See Ibn Shu'eb, R. Joel.
R. Jonah ibn Jannaḥ. See Ibn Jannaḥ, R. Jonah.
R. Joseph ibn 'Aqnin. See Ibn 'Aqnin, R. Joseph.
R. Joseph ibn Leb. See Ibn Leb, R. Joseph.
R. Joseph ibn Megas. See Ibn Megas, R. Joseph.
R. Joseph ibn Verga. See Ibn Verga, R. Joseph.
R. Joseph b. Zabbara. *Sefer Sha'ashu'im*. Ed. Israel Davison. Berlin: Eshkol, 5685/1925.
R. Joseph Jabès. See Ya'beṣ, R. Joseph.
R. Joshua ha-Nagid. See Maimonides, R. Joshua.
R. Joshua ibn Shu'eb, see Ibn Shu'eb, R. Joshua.
R. Judah al-Barceloni. See R. Judah al-Bargeloni.
R. Judah al-Bargeloni. *Sefer ha-Sheṭarot*. Ed. S. J. Halberstam. Berlin: Mekize Nirdamim, 1898.
*Perush Sefer Yeṣira. Berlin: Mekize Nirdamim, 1885.*
*Sefer ha-'Ittim. Cracow, 5660/1900.*
R. Judah ha-Levi. *Kuzari*. Arabic original, *Kitab al-Radd wal-Dalil fi al-Din al-Dhalil*. Ed. H. Baneth. Jerusalem: Magnes Press, 1977. Hebrew version: *Kuzari*. Ed. and trans. Yehuda Even Shmuel. Tel Aviv: Dvir Publishing, 1994.
*The Liturgical Poetry of R. Yehuda ha-Levi (Heb.). Ed. Dov Jarden, vol. 1. Jerusalem, 1978.*
*Selected Poems of Jehudah Halevi. Philadelphia: Jewish Publication Society, 1928.*
R. Judah b. ha-Rosh. *Zikhron Yehuda*. Eds. J. Rosenberg and D. Cassel. Berlin, 5606/1846.
R. Judah he-Ḥasid. *Sefer ha-Ḥasidim*. Ed. R. Reuben Margulies. Jerusalem: Mossad Harav Kook, 5724/1964.
R. Judah he-Ḥasid, Sir Leon. *Tosafot Berakhot*. In *Berakha Meshulleshet*. Warsaw, 5623/1853.
R. Judah ibn Bal'am. See Ibn Bal'am, R. Judah.
R. Judah Messer Leon. *Nofet Ṣufim*. Mantua ca. 1475. Offset: Jerusalem: The Jewish National and University Library Press, 1981.
Kasher, Rimon. "The Interpretation of Scripture in Rabbinic

Literature." In ed. Martin Jan Mulder, *Mikra*. Philadelphia: Fortress Press, 1988.

Katsh, Abraham I. *Judaism in Islam* (Heb.). Jerusalem: Kiryat Sepher, 1957.

Katz, J. "Halakhah and Kabbala – First Contacts" (Heb.). In *Yitzhak F. Baer Memorial Volume*. Jerusalem: The Historical Society of Israel, 1980.

Kellner, Menachem. *Maimonides on the Decline of the Generations and the Nature of Rabbinic Authority*. Albany: SUNY Press, 1996.

*"Maimonides on the Decline of the Generations." In Ḥazon Naḥum. New York: Yeshiva University, 5758/1998.*

*"A New and Unexpected Textual Witness." Tarbiz 75 (2006), pp. 565–566 (Hebrew).*

Kimḥi (Qimḥi), R. David. *Hebrew Grammar (Mikhlol)*. Trans. and annotated by William Chomsky. New York: Bloch Publishing, 1952–5713.

Kimḥi (Qimḥi). *The Commentaries on Proverbs of the Kimhi Family*. Ed. Frank Talmage. Jerusalem: Magnes Press, 1990.

Klausner, Joseph. "Why was Jeremiah Ignored in the Book of Kings?" In *Alexander Marx Jubilee Volume*. Hebrew Section. New York: Jewish Theological Seminary, 1953.

Konvitz, Milton R. *The Alien and the Asiatic in American Law*. Ithaca, N.Y.: Cornell University, 1946.

*"Conscience, Natural Law and Civil Disobedience in the Jewish Tradition." In Of Law and Man. Ed. Shlomo Shoham. Sabra Books: New York and Tel Aviv: 1971.*

*"A Philosophy of Human Rights." In eds. Abraham I. Katsh and Leon Nemoy. Essays on the Occasion of the Seventieth Anniversary of the Dropsie University. Philadelphia: Dropsie University, 1979.*

*Religious Liberty and Conscience. New York: Viking Press, 1968.*

Koppel, Moshe. *Seder Kinnim*. Israel: Aluma Publishing, 1998.

Kotler, R. Aharon. *Mishnat Aharon*. Vol. 1. Jerusalem: Makhon Yerushalayim, 5745/1985.

*La Nazione Ebrea a Livorno e a Pisa* (1591–1700). Edited and annotated by Professor Renzo Toaff. Florence: Leo S. Olschki, 1990.

Laniado, R. Samuel. *Keli Faz*. Venice, 5417/1657.

Leib, R. Arie. *Sha'agat Arye*. Warsaw, 5629/1869.

Lieberman, Saul. *Greek in Jewish Palestine*. New York: Philipp Feldheim, 1965.

*Hellenism in Jewish Palestine. New York: The Jewish Theological Seminary of America, 1950.*

*"How Much Greek in Jewish Palestine?" In Biblical and Other Studies. Cambridge, Mass.: Harvard University Press, 1963.*

*"On Adjurations among the Jews" (Heb.). Tarbiz 27 (1958).*

*Shkiin. Jerusalem: Bamberg & Wahrman, 1939.*

*Tosefta Ki-Fshuṭah. 10 vols. New York: The Jewish Theological Seminary of America, 1955–2001.*

*Yerushalmi Ki-Fshuṭo. Jerusalem: Darom, 5695/1935.*

Leiman, Sid Z. *The Canonization of Hebrew Scripture*. New Haven: The Connecticut Academy of Art and Sciences, 1991.

Leon, R. Isaac de. *Megillat Ester*. Venice, 5352/1592.

Lerner, Meron B. "The Simple Meaning..." (Heb.). *Annual of Bar-Ilan University* 30–31 (2006).

R. Levi ben Gereshom. *Perush 'al ha-Tora*. Venice, 5307/1547.

R. Levi b. Ḥabib. *She'elot*. Venice, 5325/1565.

Levi, R. Abraham ha-. *Ginnat Veradim*. Vol. 2. Constantinople, 5476/1716.

Levi, R. Judah ha-. See R. Judah ha-Levi.

Levine, Étan. *Heaven and Earth, Law and Love: Studies in Biblical Thought*. Berlin: Walter de Gruyter, 2000.

Levy, Hans. "Cicero on the Jews in his Speech for the Defense of Flaccus" (Heb.). *Zion* 7 (1942).

*Studies in Jewish Hellenism (Heb.). Jerusalem: Bialik Institute, 1969.*

*"Tacitus on the Origin and Manners of the Jews" (Heb.). Zion 8 (1943).*

Lonzano, R. Menaḥem de. *Shete Yadot*. Jerusalem, 5730/1970.

Luzzato, Samuel David. *Commentary to the Pentateuch* (Heb.). Tel Aviv: Dvir, 1965.

*Philoxenus (Heb.) Cracow, 1895.*

*"Vikkuah 'al ha-qabbala." In his Meḥqare Yahdut. Warsaw, 5673/1913.*

Ma'arabi, Pereṣ. "*Ledarko...*," *Sinai* (Jubilee Volume) 100 (5748/1988).

Mahler, Raphael. *A History of Modern Jewry*. New York: Schocken, 1971.

Maimonides, R. Abraham. *Milhamot ha-Shem*. Ed. R. Ruben Margaliot. Jerusalem: Mossad Harav Kook, n.d.

*The High Ways to Perfection. Ed. and trans. Samuel Rosenblatt. Vol. 2. Baltimore: John Hopkins Press, 1938.*

*Perush. Ed. Sh. Wiesenberg. Letchworth, 1959.*

*Teshubot. Ed. A. H. Freimann. Jerusalem: Mekize Nirdamim, 1937.*

Maimonides, R. David. *Al-Murshid*. Ed. and trans. P B. Fenton. Jerusalem: Mekize Nirdamim, 1987.

Maimonides, R. Joshua. *Teshubot R. Joshua ha-Nagid*. Ed. and trans. R. Y. Ratzabi. Jerusalem: Makhon le-Ḥeqer Mishnat ha-Rambam, 5749/1989.

Maimonides, R. Moses. *Epistle to Yemen* (= *Iggeret Teman*). Ed. Abraham S. Halkin. Trans. Boaz Cohen. New York: American Academy for Jewish Studies, 1952.

*Guide for the Perplexed. Arabic original, Dalalat al-Ḥa'irin. Ed. Issachar Joel and Solomon Munk. Jerusalem, 1931.*

*Iggeret Teman. See Epistle to Yemen.*

*Iggerot. Ed. and trans. R. Joseph Qafiḥ. Jerusalem: Mossad Harav Kook, 1972.*

*Iggerot ha-Rambam. Ed. D. H. Baneth. Jerusalem: Mekize Nirdamim, 1947.*

*Letters and Essays of Maimonides (Heb.). Ed. and trans. Isaac Shailat. 2 vols. Maaleh Adumim: Maaliyot Press, 5748/1988.*

*Mishne Tora. Standard Edition.*

*Perush ha-Mishnayot. Ed. and trans. R. Joseph Qafiḥ. 7 vols. Jerusalem: Mossad Harav Kook, 1967.*

*Qobeṣ Teshubot ha-Rambam. Leipzig, 5619/1859.*

*Sefer ha-Madda'. Eds. M. H. Katzenelenbogen and Saul Lieberman. Jerusalem: Mossad Harav Kook, 1964.*

*Sefer ha-Miṣvot. Ed. and trans. R. Joseph Qafiḥ. Jerusalem: Mossad Harav Kook, 1971.*

*Teshubot ha-Rambam. Ed and trans. J. Blau. 4 vols. Jerusalem: Mekize Nirdamim, 1975–1986.*

*Treatise on Logic. Ed. and trans. Israel Efros. New York: American Academy for Jewish Research, 1938.*

*Treatise on Resurrection. Ed. Joshua Finkel. New York: American Academy for Jewish Research, 1939.*

Malachi, Z. "*Abraham ibn 'Ezra neged Qalir.*" *Peles*. Tel-Aviv: Tel Aviv University, 1980.

Mal'akhi, R. Jacob. *Yad Mal'akhi*. New York: Keter, 5706/1946.

Malter, Henry. *The Treatise Ta'anit*. Ed. Philadelphia: The Jewish Publication Society, 1978.

R. Manasseh ben Israel. *The Conciliator*. London: 5602/1842.

Mantel, Hugo. *Studies in the History of the Sanhedrin*. Cambridge, Mass.: Harvard University Press, 1961.

Marcus, Ivan. *Piety and Society*. Leiden: E.J. Brill, 1981.

*"Robert Chazan, European Jewry and the First Crusade." Speculum, 64 (1989).*

Margalioth, M. *Sefer ha-Razim*. Jerusalem: The American Academy for Jewish Research, 1966.

Masnut, R. Samuel. *Midrash Daniel wu-Midrash 'Ezra*. Eds. I. S. Lange and S. Schwartz. Jerusalem: Mekize Nirdamim, 1968.

Medina, R. Samuel de. *Teshubot Meharashdam. Ḥoshen Mishpaṭ*. Saloniki, 5358/1598. Melammed, Ezra Z. *Essays in Talmudic Literature* (Heb.). Jerusalem: Hebrew University, 1986.

R. Menaḥem Me'iri. *Bet ha-Beḥira, Pesaḥim*. Jerusalem: Yad ha-R. Herzog, 5726/1966.

*Bet ha-Beḥira, Sanhedrin. Ed. A. Sofer. Jerusalem: Qedem, 5734/1974.*

Mervaise [or Marvege], R. Jacob de. *She'elot wu-Tshubot min ha-Shamayim*. Ed. R. Reuben Margoliot. Jerusalem: Mossad Harav Kook, 1957.

*Milḥemet ha-Dat*. Ed. J. I. Kobakak. *Jeshurun* VIII (Bamberg, 1875).

*Minḥat Qena'ot*. Pressburg, 1838.

Mirsky, Aharon. *Ha-Piyyuṭ*. Jerusalem: Magnes Press, 1990.

Miṭrani, R. Raḥamim Menaḥem. *Me'am Lo'ez,* on *Joshua*. Trans. to Heb. by Samuel Yerushalmi. Jerusalem: H. Vagshal, 5732/1972.

Morais, R. Sabato. *Italian Hebrew Literature*. New York: The Jewish Theological Seminary, 1926.

Morais, Vamberto. *A Short History of Anti-Semitism*. New York: W.W. Norton: 1972.

Mortera. R. Saul Levi. In Rehuel Jessurun. *Dialogo dos Montes*. Ed. and trans. Philip Polack. London: Tamiesis Books, 1975.

*Gib'at Sha'ul. Brooklyn, N.Y., 5751/1991.*

*Providencia de Dios con Yisrael. Ms. Etz Hayyim 48C 20. Hebrew University Library.*

Na'e, Sh. "*Ṭobim Dodekha Mi-Yayyin.*" (Heb.). *Studies in Talmud and Midrashic Literature* in *Memory of Tirzah Lifshitz*. Jerusalem: Bialik Institute, 2005.

Nahmanides, R. Moses. *Hasagot ha-Ramban*. Ed. C. B. Chavel. In *Sefer ha-Miṣvot le-ha-Rambam*. Jerusalem: Mossad Harav Kook, 1981.

*Kitbe Ramban. 2 vols. Ed. C. B. Chavel. Jerusalem: Mossad Harav Kook, 1963.*

*Perush ha-Tora. 2 vols. Ed. C. B. Chavel. Jerusalem: Mossad Harav Kook, 1962.*

*Teshubot. Ed. C. B. Chavel. Jerusalem: Mossad Harav Kook, 1975.*

Nassy, David. *Lettre politico-theologico-morale sur les Juifs*. Paramaribo, ca. 1789.

R. Nathan b. Yeḥi'el. *'Arukh*. *Aruch Completum*. Ed. Alexander Kohut. 8 vols. Vienna and Berlin: Menora, 1926.

Neubauer, Ad. *Medieval Jewish Chronicles*. Oxford: Clarendon Press, 1887.

Neusner, Jacob. "The Constitutions of Judaism in Ancient Times: The Pentateuch and the Mishnah." *Journal of Reform Judaism* 36 (1989).

*A Life of Rabban Yohanan ben Zakkai. Leiden: E. J. Brill, 1962.*

*A History of the Jews in Babylonia. Vols. 3–4. Leiden: E. J. Brill, 1968–1969.*

*Making the Classics in Judaism. Atlanta, Georgia: Scholars Press, 1989.*

*The Philosophical Mishnah. 3 vols. Atlanta, Georgia: Scholars Press, 1988–89.*

*The Social Study of Judaism. 2 vols. Atlanta, Georgia: Scholars Press, 1988.*

*Understanding seeking Faith. Vol. 3. Atlanta, Georgia: Scholars Press, 1988.*

Nieto, R. David. *Esh Dat.* London, 1715.

*Maṭṭe Dan. Spanish-Hebrew. London, 5474–1714.*

R. Nissim Gerondi. *Derashot ha-Ran.* Jerusalem: Mossad Harav Kook, 2003.

*Teshubot. New York: Publishing Corporation, n.d.*

Oceda, R. Samuel de. *Midrash Shemu'el.* Amsterdam, 5627/1867.

*Otzar Ḥilluf Minhagim.* Ed. B. M. Lewin. Jerusalem: Makor, 1972.

Palache, J. L. *Semantic Notes on the Hebrew Lexicon.* Leiden: Brill, 1958.

Palaggi, R. Ḥayyim. *Ḥuqqot ha-Ḥayyim.* Izmir, 5632/1872.

*Re'e Ḥayyim. Vol. 2. Izmir, 5624/1864.*

Pardo, R. David. *Sifre Debe-Rab.* Saloniki, 5559/1799.

*Ḥasde David. Vol. 2. Leghorn: 5650/1790.*

Patai, Raphael. *The Jewish Mind.* New York: Charles Scribner's Sons, 1977.

Perrot, Charles. "The Reading of the Bible in the Ancient Synagogue." In ed. Martin Jan Mulder, *Mikra.* Philadelphia: Fortress Press, 1988.

Pines, Shlomo. "On the Concept of 'Spirits'" (Heb.) *Tarbiz* 57 (1988).

Qimhi, R. David. *Commentary on Psalms.* (Heb.) Ed. Abraham Darom. Jerusalem: Mossad Harav Kook, 1971.

*Sefer ha-Mikhlol. See R. David Kimḥi (Qimḥi). Hebrew Grammar (Mikhlol).*

*Sefer ha-Shorashim. Eds. J. H. R. Biesenthal and F. Lebrecht. Berlin, 1847.*

Qimḥi, R. Joseph. *Sefer ha-Galui.* Berlin, 5247/1877.

Rabad (of Posquières). See R. Abraham b. David.

Rabbinowitz, L. *The Ḥerem Hayyishub.* London: Edward Goldstone, 1945.

Radaq. See Qimḥi, R. David; Kimḥi, R. David.

Rafel, Dov. "*Haqdamat Sefer 'Ma'ase Efod' le-Profiaṭ Duran,*" *Sinai.* Jubilee Volume, 100 (1987).

Rama. See Isserles, R. Moses.
Reggio, R. Samuel Isaac. *Be'ur Yashar*. 5 vols. Vienna, 5581/1821.
*Thora et Philosophia (Heb.). Vienna, 1827.*
Reif, Stefan C. *Judaism and Hebrew Prayer*. Cambridge: Cambridge University Press, 1993.
Reviv, Hanoch. *The Elders in Ancient Israel* (Heb.). Jerusalem: The Magnes Press, 1983.
Riṭba. See R. Yom Ṭob as-Sibili.
Rosenthal, Abraham. "*Tora she-'al pe.*" In eds. Moshe Bar-Asher and David Rosenthal, *Meḥqerei Talmud*. Vol. 2. Jerusalem: The Hebrew University, 1993.
Rozanes, R. Judah. *Mishne la-Melekh*. In *Mishne Tora*, standard edition.
Sabato, R. Mordechai. *A Yemenite Manuscript of Tractate Sanhedrin* (Heb.). Jerusalem: Yad Izhak Ben-Zvi, 1998.
Ṣabba', R. Abraham. *Ṣeror ha-Mor*. Cracow, 5365/1605.
Salvador, Joseph. *Paris, Rome et Jerusalem*. Vol. 1. Paris: Michel Lévy Frères, 1860.
R. Samuel Ashkenazi. *Yefe To'ar*. *Bereshit*. Venice: 5357/1597.
R. Samuel b. 'Eli. *Qobeṣ shel Iggerot*. Ed. R. Simḥa Assaf. Jerusalem: Makor, 5730/1970.
R. Samuel ha-Nagid. *Diwan Shemu'el ha-Nagid*. *Ben Tehillim*. Ed. Dov Jarden. Jerusalem: Hebrew Union College Press, 1966.
*Hilkhot Hannagid (Heb.). Ed. Mordecai Margalioth. Jerusalem: The American Academy for Jewish Research, 1962.*
R. Santob de Carrión. *Don Sem Tob Glosas de Sabiduría*. Ed. Agustin García Calvo. Madrid: Alianza Editorial, 1974. Ed. trans. and annotated by T. A. Perry. *The Moral Proverbs of Santob of Carrión*. Princeton: Princeton University Press, 1987.
Schechter, Salomon. *Aspects of Jewish Theology*. New York: Schocken, 1961.
*"Ṣavva'a." Bet-Talmud 4 (5645/1885).*
Scholem, Gershom. *Ha-Qabbala be-Probanṣ*. Jerusalem: Academon, 5746/1986.
*Major Trends. New York: Schocken Books, 1961.*
*On the Kabbalah. New York: Schocken Books, 1969.*

*The Origin of the Kabbalah*. Princeton: Princeton University Press, 1987.

*Reshit ha-Qabbala*. Jerusalem: Schocken, 5708/1948.

Schrieber, Aaron M. "The Ḥatam Sofer's Nuanced Attitude Towards Secular Learning, Maskilim, and Reformers." *The Tora u-Madda Journal* 11 (2002–2003).

"*Hashqafato...*" *BaDaD* 9 (5759/1999).

Schwarts, Dov. "*Ṣurot Shonot shel Magia...*" *Proceedings of the American Academy for Jewish Studies*, 57 (1990–1991).

*and Frimer, Norman E. The Life and Thought of Shem Tov ibn Shaprut (Heb.). Jerusalem: Ben-Zvi Institute, 1992.*

Scott, Robert E. See Schwartz, Alan and.

*Sefer Gezerot*. Ed. A. M. Haberman. Jerusalem: Sifre Tarshish, 1945.

*Sefer ha-Ḥinnukh*. Ed. R. C. B. Chavel. Jerusalem: Mossad Harav Kook, 5729/1969.

*Sepher ha-Razim* (Heb.). Ed. Mordecai Margalioth. Jerusalem: The American Academy for Jewish Research, 1966.

R. Sforno. *Be'ur 'al ha-Tora*. Warsaw, 5617/1857.

Shalom, R. Abraham. *Neve Shalom*. Venice, 5335/1575.

Shatzmiller, Joseph. "The Forms of the Twelve Constellations: A 14th Century Controversy," (Heb.). In *Shlomo Pines Jubilee Volume. Jerusalem Studies in Jewish Thought* 9 (1990).

R. Shem Ṭob ben Isaac Arduṭiel. See R. Santob de Carrión.

Shepard, Sanford. *Shem Tov: His World and His Words*. Miami: Ediciones Universal, 1978.

Shiber, Y. "The status and confirmation of witnesses at wedding ceremonies in Jewish law." Ph.D. thesis presented at Bar Ilan University, Fall, 2002.

R. Shimshon. *Perush ha-Mishnayot*. In *Talmud Babli*. Standard Edition. 18 vols. Vilna: Re'em, 5668/1908.

R. Shimshon of Chinon. *Sefer Keritut*. Warsaw, 5645/1885.

Shrem, R. Isaac. *Be'er Yiṣḥaq*. Leghorn, 5624/1864.

Silver, Daniel Jeremy. *Maimonidean Criticism and the Maimonidean Controversy*. Leiden: E. J. Brill, 1965.

R. Simḥa b. Samuel. *Maḥzor Viṭry*. Berlin, 5642–5657/1882–1897.

Sofer, R. Moses. *Ḥatam Sofer, Qobeṣ Teshubot*. Jerusalem: 5733/1973.

R. Solomon b. Melekh. *Mikhlal Yofi*. Amsterdam, 5445/1685.

Speiser, E. A. "The Biblical Idea of History in Its Common Near Eastern Setting." In ed. Judah Goldin. *The Jewish Expression*. New Haven: Yale University Press, 1976.

*"'People' and 'nation' of Israel." Journal of Biblical Literature 79 (1960).*

Sperber, Daniel. *A Dictionary of Greek & Latin Legal Terms*. Ramat Gan: Bar-Ilan University, 1984.

Spiegel, Shalom. "Amos vs. Amaziah." In ed. Judah Goldin. *The Jewish Expression*. New Haven: Yale University Press, 1976.

*"The Legend of Isaac's Slaying and Resurrection." In Alexander Marx Jubilee Volume. Hebrew Section. New York: Jewish Theological Seminary, 1953.*

*The Last Trial. New York: Schocken, 1969.*

*"Le-Farashat ha-Polmos..." In Jubilee Volume in Honor of Professor Harry A. Wolfson. Hebrew Section. Jerusalem: American Academy for Jewish Studies, 1965.*

Stein, Leopold. *Untersuchungen uber die Proverbios Morales*. Berlin: Mayer & Muller, 1900.

Stern, Menahem. *Greek and Latin Authors on Jews and Judaism*, 3 vols. Jerusalem: The Israel Academy of Science and Humanities, 1974–1984.

Straus, Oscar S. *The Origin of the Republican Form of Government in the United States*. New York: G. P. Putnam's Sons, 1885.

*Roger Williams. New York: D. Appleton-Century, 1936.*

Sulzberger, Mayer. *The Polity of the Ancient Hebrews*. Philadelphia: Julius H. Greenstone, 1912.

Sussman, Y. "Tora she-be-'al Pe." *Meḥqerei Talmud*. Vol. 3, Part I (2005).

Ta-Shma, Israel M. *Early Franco-German Ritual and Custom* (Heb.). Jerusalem: Hebrew University, 1992.

*"Ḥasidut Ashkenaz bi-Sfarad: Rabbenu Yona Gerondi, ha-'ish wu-fa'olo." In Galut Aḥar Gola. Jerusalem: Machon Ben Zvi, 1989.*

*Ha-Tefilla ha-Ashkenazit ha-Qeduma. Jerusalem: Hebrew University Press, 5763/2003.*

*"Hilkheta Kebatrai" (Heb.). Shenaton ha-Mishpaṭ Ha-Ivri 6–7 (1979–1980).*

*"Qeliṭatam shel sifre ha-Rif ha-Raḥ, ve-Halakhot Gedolot be-Ṣarfat wub-Ashkenaz be-Me'ot ha-Yod-Alef-Yod-Bet." Qiryat Sefer 55 (1980).*

"Rabbi Yonah Girondi: Spirituality and Leadership." In eds. Moshe Idel and Mortimer Ostow. *Jewish Mystical Leaders and Leadership in the 13th Century*. Northvale, New Jersey: Jason Aronson, 1998.

*"Shiqqulim Pilosofim be-Hakhra'at ha-Halakha bi-Sfarad." Sefunot 18 (1985).*

*"Sifriyyatam shel Ḥakhme Ashkenaz bene ha-Me'a ha-Yod Alef-Yod Bet." Qiryat Sefer 60 (1985).*

*"Tosafot Gornish." Sinai 68 (1971).*

Tcherikover, Victor. *Hellenistic Civilization and the Jews*. Philadelphia: Jewish Publication Society, 1961.

Templo, R. Solomon Rafael Judah Leon. *Massekhet Halakha le-Moshe mi-Sinai*. Amsterdam, 5494/1734.

Toaff, Professor Renzo. See *La Nazione Ebrea a Livorno e a Pisa*.

Tolan, John. *Petrus Alfonsi and his Medieval Readers*. Gainesville: University Press of Florida, 1993.

Torre, R. Lelio della. "Quelques mots sur la peine de mort et la séparation de pouvoirs chez les anciens Juifs." In his *Scritti Sparsi*, vol. 2. Padova: P. Prosperini, 1908.

*Tosafot*. In *Talmud Babli*. Vilna: Re'em, 5485/1725.

*Responsa of the Tosaphists (Heb.). Ed. Irving Agus. New York: Talpioth, Yeshiva University, 1954.*

Ṭrani, R. Moses di. *Bet Elohim*. Venice, 5311/1551.

*Qiryat Sefer. New York, 1953.*

Twersky, I. *Rabad of Posquières*. Cambridge: Harvard University Press, 1962.

Urbach, E. E. "The Participation of German and French Scholars in the Controversy about Maimonides and his Works" (Heb.). *Zion* 12 (1947).

Viṭal, R. Samuel. *Be'er Mayim Ḥayyim*. Jerusalem, 5726/1966.

Weiss Halivni, David. *Peshaṭ and Derash*. New York: Oxford University Press, 1991.

*"The Role of the Mara D'atra in Jewish Law." Proceedings of the Rabbinical Assembly (1976).*

Whitfield, Stephen J. "Where They Burn Books..." *Modern Judaism* 22 (2002).

Wolfson, Elliot. "The Mystical Significance of Torah Study in German Pietism." *Jewish Quarterly Review* 84 (1993).

Wolfson, Harry A. *Philo*. 2 vols. Cambridge, Mass.: Harvard University Press, 1948.

Ya'beṣ, R. Joseph. *Or ha-Ḥayyim*. Ferrara, 5314/1554.

Yafe Ashkenazi, R. Samuel. *Yefe Mar'e*. Berlin, 5485/1725.

Yahuda, A. S. "A Contribution to Qur'an and Ḥadith Interpretation." In *Ignace Goldziher Memorial Volume*. Part I. Budapest, 1948.

*'Eber ve-'Arab. New York: Ha-Histadrut ha-'Ibrit be-Ameriqa, 1946.*

*The Language of the Pentateuch. Oxford: Oxford University Press, 1933.*

Yefet b. 'Eli. *Commentary to Proverbs*. Ed. Israel Gunzig. Krakow, 1898.

Yerushalmi, Yosef H. *Zakhor*. Seattle: Washington University Press, 1982.

R. Yom Ṭob as-Sibili. *Ḥiddushe ha-Riṭba*. Jerusalem: Mossad Harav Kook, 1985–1996.

Yosef, R. Ovadiah. *Yabbia' Omer*. Vol. 7. Jerusalem, 5753/1993.

Yuter, R. Josh. "Ramban." Unpublished.

Zabbara. See R. Joseph b. Zabbara.

Zacuto, R. Abraham. *Sefer Yoḥasin ha-Shalem*. Eds. Herschell Filipowski and A. H. Freimann. Jerusalem, 5723/1963.

Zacuto R. Moses. *Qol ha-Remez*. Amsterdam, 5479/1719.

Zahalon, R. Jacob. *A Guide for Preachers*. Ed. and trans. R. Henry Adler Sosland. New York: The Jewish Theological Seminary of America, 1987.

Zimmels, H. J. "Scholars and Scholarship in Byzantium and Italy." In ed. Cecil Roth, *The Dark Ages*. New Brunswick: Rutgers University Press, 1966.

Zucker, Moses. "'Iyyunim." *Proceedings of the American Academy for Jewish Research* 49 (1982).

*Rav Saadya Ga'on's Translation of the Torah. (Heb.). New York: Philipp Feldheim, 1959.*

Zurafa, R. Ḥayyim D. Sh. *Sha'ar Shelomo*. Leghorn, 5638/1878.

## Western Sources and Writers

Albright, W. F. "The Reform of Jehoshaphat." In *Alexander Marx's Jubilee Volume*. New York: The Jewish Theological Seminary, 1950.

Alonso, Ana Maria. "The Effects of Truth: Re-Presentations of the Past and the Imagining of Community." *Journal of Historical Sociology* 1 (1988).

Amoroso, Leonardo. "Vico e l'antichissima sapienza degli Ebrei." In ed. Giovanni Matteucci. *Studi sul "De antiquissima Italorum sapientia di Vico."* Bologna: Quodlibet, 2002.

Arieti, Sylvano. *Creativity*. New York: Basic Books, 1976.

Assmann, Jan. *Moses the Egyptian*. Cambridge, Mass. Harvard University Press, 1997.

Augustin, St. *The City of God*. New York: Modern Library.

*Confessions. Oxford: Oxford University Press, 1991.*

Bacon, Francis. *Proficiency and Advancement of Learning*. Oxford: Oxford University Press, 2000.

Barnes, Albert. *The Book of Job*. Vol. 1. New York: Leavitt, Trow, & Company, 1845.

Barthes, Roland. "To Write: An Intransitive Verb?" In eds. Richard Macksey and Eugenio Donato. *The Structuralist Controversy*. Baltimore: Johns Hopkins University Press, 1972.

Bauckham, Richard. *The Bible in Politics*. Louisville, Kentucky: John Knox Press, 1989.

Bauval, R. G. "The seeding of the Star Gods: A Fertility Ritual inside the Cheops's Pyramid?" In *Discussions in Egyptology* 16 (1990).

Beckwith, Roger T. "Formation of the Hebrew Bible." In ed. Martin Jan Mulder, *Mikra*. Philadelphia: Fortress Press, 1988.

Benveniste, Émile. *Indo-European Language and Society.* Coral Gables, Florida: University of Miami Press, 1973.

*Problems in General Linguistics. Coral Gables, Florida: University of Miami, 1971.*

Berlin, Isaiah. *Vico & Herder*. New York: The Viking Press. 1976.

Bertalanffy, Ludwig von. *General System Theory*. New York: George Braziller, 1968.

Bishop, Joseph W. Jr., *Justice Under Fire: A Study of Military Law*. New York: Charterhouse, 1974.

Blackstone, Sir William. *Commentaries on the Laws of England*. Facsimile 1765 edition, Chicago University Press, 1972.

Boman, Thorleif. *Hebrew Thought Compared with Greek*. New York: W. W. Norton, 1970.

Borges, Jorge Luis. *Obras Completas*. Madrid: Espasa-Calpe, 1982.

*"Borges on Life and Death." Interview with Amelia Barili. New York Times Review, July 13, 1986.*

*Borges, Oral. Buenos Aires: Emecé Editores, 1979.*

*"El arte narrativo y la magia." In his Discusión. Buenos Aires: Emecé, 1964.*

*Nueve Ensayos Dantescos. Madrid: Ultramar, 1977.*

Borkowski, A. *Textbook on Roman Law*. Oxford: Blackstone, 1997.

Bryer, Anthony and Herrin, Judith. Eds. *Iconoclasm.* Birmingham: University of Birmingham, 1975.

Burkert, Walter. *Creation of the Sacred*. Cambridge, Mass.: Harvard University Press, 1996.

Camus, Albert. *The Stranger*. Vintage Book, 1946.

Canetti, Elias. *Crowds and Power*. Middlesex, England: Penguin Books, 1973.

Cardozo, Benjamin. *The Nature of the Judicial Process*. New Haven: Yale University Press, 1949.

*The Paradoxes of Legal Science. New York: Columbia University, 1928.*

Carlyle, Thomas. *On Heroes, Hero-Worship, and the Heroic in History.* New York: Chelsea House, 1983.

Cassin, René. "From the Ten Commandments to the Rights of Man." In ed. Sh. Shoham. *Of Law and Man: Essays in Honor of Haim H. Cohn*. New York: Sabra Books, 1971.

Cassirer, Ernst. *Language and Myth*. New York: Dover Publications, n.d.

*The Philosophy of Symbolic Forms. Vol. 3. New Haven: Yale University Press, 1957.*

Castro, Américo. "Disputa entre un Cristiano y un Judío." In his *De la España que aún no conocía*, vol. 3. Mexico: Finestere, 1972.

*La Realidad Histórica de España. Mexico City: Editorial Porrua, 1975.*

Chatterjee, Ranjit. "Before and Beyond Linguistics: The Case of Professor Nietzsche, Philologist." In eds. Colin E. Nicholson and Ranjit Chatterjee. *Tropic Crucible: Self and Theory*. Singapore: University of Singapore, 1984.

*Wittgenstein and Judaism. New York: Peter Lang, 2005.*

*Cicero*. Loeb Classical Library.

*Clement of Alexandria*. Loeb Classical Library.

Coenen, Dan T. "A Rhetoric for Ratification: the Argument of *The Federalist* and its Impact on Constitutional Interpretation." *Duke Law Journal* 56 (2006).

Cohen, Morris R. "Property and Sovereignty." *Cornell Law Quarterly* 13 (1927–1928).

Cohn, Haim H. "Religious Human Rights." *Dine Israel* 19 (1997–1998).

Conybeare, F. C. "Christian Demonology." *Jewish Quarterly Review* 9 (1897).

*"Demonology of the New Testament." Jewish Quarterly Review 8 (1896).*

Costa, Gustavo. "Fantasia y Magia Diabólica en Vico." *Cuadernos sobre Vico*, 15–16 (2003).

Cowley, A. *Aramaic Papyri of the Fifth Century B.C.* Oxford: Clarendon Press, 1932.

Crone, Patricia and Cook, Michael. *Hagarism*. Cambridge: Cambridge University Press, 1977.

Cuffel, Victoria. "The Classical Greek Concept of Slavery." *Journal of the History of Ideas* 27 (1966).

Curtius, Ernst Robert. *European Literature and the Middle Ages*. Princeton: Princeton University Press, 1973.

Daly, Mary. *Beyond God the Father*. Boston: Beacon, 1973.

Derrida, Jacques. "The Supplement of the Copula: Philosophy *before* Linguistics," *The Georgia Review* 30 (1976). [Reprinted in ed. Josué V. Harari, *Textual Strategies* (Ithaca, New York: Cornell University Press, 1979)].

*Writing and Difference. Chicago: Chicago University Press, 1978.*

Detienne, Marcel. *The Masters of Truth in Archaic Greece*. New York: Zone Books, 1996.

Devereux, George. "Charismatic Leadership and Crisis." *Psychoanalysis and the Social Sciences* 4 (1955).

Driscoll, James F. "Theocracy." *The Catholic Encyclopedia*. New York: Robert Appleton, 1910.

Dukeminier, Jesse. *Property* (Gilbert Law Summaries).

*and Krier, James E. Property. Boston: Little, Brown, and Company, 1988.*

Eliade, Mircea. *A History of Religious Ideas*. 3 vols. Chicago: Chicago University Press, 1988.

*Images and Symbols. Princeton: Princeton University Press, 1991.*

*Myth and Reality. New York: Harper Torchbooks, 1975.*

*The Myth of Eternal Return. Princeton: Princeton University Press, 1974.*

*The Quest: History and Meaning in Religion. Chicago: Chicago University Press, 1969.*

*Rites and the Symbols of Initiation. New York: Harper & Row, 1975.*

*The Sacred and the Profane. San Diego: Harcourt Brace & Company, 1987.*

Eliot, T.S. "The Three Voices of Poetry." In his *On Poetry and Poets*. New York: Farrar, Strauss and Cudahy, 1957.

Eisenhut, Werner. *Einfuhrung in die Antike Rhetorik und ihre Geschichte.* Darmstadt: Wissenschaftliche Buchgesellschaft, 1974.

Finley, M. I. "Was Greek Civilization Based on Slave Labour?" In *Slavery in Classical Antiquity: Views and Controversies.* Cambridge: Cambridge University Press, 1960.

Frankfort, Henry. *Kingship and the Gods.* Chicago: Chicago University Press, 1948.

Freud, Sigmund. *Civilization and its Discontents.* New York: Doubleday, 1958.

*Moses and Monotheism. New York: Vintage Books, 1955.*

Fromm, Eric. *The Anatomy of Human Destructiveness.* New York: Holt, Rinehart, and Winston: 1973.

*Escape from Freedom. New York: Avon Books, 1965.*

*The Heart of Man. New York: Harper & Row, 1964.*

*Man For Himself. New York: Henry Holt and Company, 1947.*

*Psychoanalysis and Religion. New Haven: Yale University Press, 1950.*

Forsythe, David P. "The Politics of Efficacy: The United Nations and Human Rights." In ed. Lawrence S. Finkelstein. *Politics in the United Nations System.* Durham and London: Duke University Press, 1988.

Galeazzi, Umberto. "Vico e la conscenza storica: Sui Sapere ermeneutico della Scienza Nuova." In eds. Antonio Quarta e Paolo Pellegrino. *Humanitas: Studi in Memoria di Antonio Verri.* Vol. 1. Lecce: Mario Congedo Editore, 1999.

Gancho, C. "Heroísmo Religioso." *Enciclopedia Bíblica.* Barcelona: Ediciones Garriaga, 1964.

Gardiner Janik, Linda. "A Renaissance Quarrel: The Origin of Vico's Anti-Cartesianism." *New Vico Studies,* 1 (1983).

Gesenius, Wilhelm. *Hebrew and English Lexicon.* Oxford: Clarendon Press, 1907.

Gibbon, Edward. *The Decline and Fall of the Roman Empire.* 3 vols. New York. The Modern Library, n.d.

Gómez de Lino, Ignacio. *Mundo, Magia, Memoria.* N.p.: Taurus, 1981.

Goodenough, E. R. "The Bible as Product of the Ancient World." In

*Five Essays on the Bible*. New York: American Council of Learned Societies, 1960.

*The Politics of Philo Judaeus. New Haven: Yale University Press, 1935.*

Gordon, Cyrus H. *Adventures in the Near East*. London: Phoenix House, 1957.

*The Ancient Near East. New York: W. W. Norton, 1965.*

*Before Columbus. New York: Crown Publishers, 1971.*

*Evidence for the Minoan Language. Ventnor, N.J.: Ventnor Publishers, 1966.*

*"Rabbinic Exegesis in the Vulgate of Proverbs," Journal of Biblical Literature, 49 (1930).*

Grassi, Ernesto. *Vico and Humanism*. New York: Peter Lang, 1990.

Hames, Harvey J. *The Art of Conversion*. Leiden: Brill, 2000.

Harris, Sam. *Letter to a Christian Nation*. New York: Alfred A. Knopf, 2006.

Hart, H. L. *The Concept of Law*. Oxford: Clarendon Press, 1994.

Heelan, Patrick A. "Perception as a Hermeneutical Act." In eds. Hugh J. Silverman and Don Ihde, *Hermeneutics and Deconstruction*. Albany: State University of New York Press, 1985.

Heidegger, M. *Early Greek Thought*. San Francisco: Harper & Row, 1975.

*" ...Poetically Man Dwells..." In his Poetry, Language, Thought. New York: Harper & Row, 1975.*

Hengel, Martin. *Jews, Greeks and Barbarians*. Philadelphia: Fortress Press, 1980.

*Judaism and Hellenism. Philadelphia: Fortress Press, 1974.*

Hertford, R. Travers. *Christianity in Talmud and Midrash*. London: Williams & Norgate, 1903.

*The Ethics of the Talmud: Sayings of the Fathers. New York: Schocken, 1962.*

Hobbes, Thomas. *Leviathan*. London. Penguin Classics. 1984.

Holmes, O. W. "The Path of the Law," *Harvard Law Review* 10 (1897).

Horace. *Odes and Epodes*. Trans. and ed. Niall Rudd. Loeb Classical Library.

Husserl, Edmund. "The Crisis of European Man." In his *Phenomenology and the Crisis of Philosophy*. New York: Harper Torch Books, 1965.

*Iliad of Homer*. Trans. by Richmond Lattimore. Chicago: Chicago University Press, 1951.

Illich, Ivan and Sanders, Barry. *ABC: The Alphabetization of the Popular Mind*. San Francisco: North Point Press, 1988.

Jacob, François. *The Possible and the Actual*. New York: Pantheon Books, 1982.

Jacobovici, Simcha and Pellegrino, Charles. *Jesus Family Tomb*. San Francisco: Harper, 2007.

Jolowicz, H. F. *Lectures on Jurisprudence*. London: University of London, 1963.

*Historical Introduction to the Study of Roman Law. Cambridge: Cambridge University Press, 1967.*

Joyce, James. *A Portrait of the Artist as a Young Man*. New York: Modern Library, 1928.

Jung, C. G. *The Undiscovered Self*. New York: A Mentor Book, 1957.

Kahle, Paul. *The Cairo Geniza*. Oxford: Blackwell, 1959.

Kantorowicz, Ernst H. *The King's Two Bodies*. Princeton: Princeton University Press, 1957.

Kaufmann, Walter. *Religions in Four Dimensions*. New York: Reader's Digest Press, 1976.

Kockelmans, Joseph J. "Language, Meaning, and Ek-sistence." In his *On Heidegger and Language*. Evanston: Northwestern University Press, 1972.

Korey, William. "Human Rights at the U.N.: Illusion and Reality." In ed. Sh. Shoham. *Of Law and Man: Essays in Honor of Haim H. Cohn*. New York: Sabra Books, 1971.

Kristeva, Julia. "Psychoanalysis and the Polis." In ed. W J. T. Mitchell. *The Politics of Interpretation*. Chicago: The University of Chicago Press, 1983.

Le Deaut, R. "Milenarismo." *Enciclopedia de la Biblia*. Barcelona: Ediciones Garriga, 1969.

Lerner, Daniel. "The Coercive Ideologists in Perspective." In *World Revolutionary Elites*. Eds. Harold D. Lasswell and Daniel Lerner. Cambridge, Mass.: M.I.T. Press, 1966.

Levin, David Michael. "The Living Body of Tradition." *Religious Tradition* (University of Sidney), 5 (1983).

Locke, John. *Two Treatises of Government*. Cambridge: Cambridge University Press, 1988.

Lomonaco, Fabrizio. "Critica storica e pirronismo: il modello olondese nell'età di Vico." *Bollettino Filosofico*, 15 (1999).

Luzzatti, Luigi. *God in Freedom*. New York: Macmillan Company, 1930.

MacMullen, Ramsay. *Christianizing the Roman Empire*. New Haven: Yale University Press, 1984.

Maine, Henry. *Ancient Law*. New York: Dutton, 1965.

*Lectures on the Early History of Institutions. Port Washington, N.Y.: Kennikat Press, 1966.*

Maitland, F. W *The Constitutional History of England*. Cambridge: Cambridge University Press, 1950.

Marcuse, Herbert. *An Essay on Liberation*. Pelican Books.

*One-Dimensional Man. Boston: Beacon Press, 1964.*

*"Repressive Tolerance." In ed. R. P Wolff et al. A Critique of Pure Tolerance. Boston: Beacon Press, 1969.*

Martinez Bibal, Josep. "*El* De Mente Heroica." *Cuadernos sobre Vico* 15–16 (2003).

Matteo, Ignazio di. "Il 'Tahrif' ad alterazione della Biblia secondo I musulmani." *Bessarione* 38 (1922).

Mayhew, Rev. Jonathan. *Discourse, Concerning Unlimited Submission and Non-Resistance to the Higher Powers*. Reprinted in *Religion in America*. New York: Arno Press, 1969.

*Seven Sermons. Reprinted in Religion in America. New York: Arno Press, 1969.*

McCagg, William O. Jr. "Jewish Conversion in Hungary in Modern Times." In ed. Todd M. Endelman. *Jewish Apostasy in the Modern World*. New York: Holmes & Meier, 1987.

McCloskey, Susan. "Rhetoric is Part of the Lawyer's Craft." 10 *Journal,* November/December 2002. New York State Bar Association.

McCloy, Shelby Thomas. *Gibbon's Antagonism To Christianity*. London: William & Norgate, 1933.

Merryman, John Henry. *The Civil Law Tradition*. Stanford: Stanford University Press, 1985.

Miner, Robert C. "*Verum-factum* and Practical Wisdom in the Early Writings of Giambattista Vico." *Journal of the History of Ideas* 59 (1998).

Momigliano, Arnaldo. *Alien Wisdom*. New York: Cambridge University Press, 1975.

*Essays in Ancient and Modern Historiography. Middletown, Conn.: Wesleyan University Press, 1982.*

*Studies in Historiography. New York: Harper & Row, 1966.*

Moore, George F. "The Am-ha-Arez (The People of the Land) and the Haberim (Associates)." In F. J. Foakes-Jackson and Kirsopp Lake eds., *The Acts of the Apostles* (*The Beginning of Christianity*). Vol. 1. London: Macmillan, 1920.

*History of Religions. 2 vols. Edinburgh: T. & T. Clark, 1920.*

*Judaism. 3 vols. Cambridge: Harvard University Press, 1966.*

Morgan, Prys. "From a Death to a View: The Hunt for the Welsh Past in the Romantic Period." In eds. Eric Hobsbawm and Terence Ranger. *The Invention of Tradition*. Cambridge: Cambridge University Press, 1992.

*The Nag Hammadi Library*. Ed. James M. Robinson. New York: Harper & Row, 1977.

Newcomb, Steven T. "The Evidence of Christian Nationalism in Federal Indian Law: The Doctrine of Discovery, *Johnson v. McIntosh,* and Plenary Power." *New York University Review of Law and Social Change* 20 (1992–1994).

Newton, Isaac. *Principia*. 2 vols. Berkeley and Los Angeles: University of California Press, 1962.

Nicholls, William. *Christian Antisemitism*. Northvale, N.J.: Jason Aronson, 1993.

Nietzsche, Friedrich. *Beyond Good and Evil.* Penguin Books.
*Why I am so Wise. Penguin Books.*
Nigg, Walter. *The Heretics: Heresy Through the Ages.* New York: Dorset Press, 1962.
Nirenberg, David. *Communities of Violence.* Princeton, N.J.: Princeton University Press, 1996.
Nunes Carvalho, David. *Forty Centuries of Ink.* New York: Banks Law Publishing, 1904.
Ortega y Gasset, José. *The Revolt of the Masses.* New York: W. W. Norton & Company, 1957.
*Pagan Monotheism in Late Antiquity.* Eds. Athanassiadi, Polymnia and Frede, Michael. Oxford: Oxford University Press, 1999.
Paz, Octavio. *Claude Lévi-Strauss: An Introduction.* New York: Dell Publishing, 1978.
Pearson, C. "Demons and Spirits." *Encyclopedia of Religion and Ethics.* Vol. 4. Edinburgh: T&T Clark, 1926.
Pellegrino, Charles. See Jacobovici, Simcha.
Perleman, Ch. *Justice, Law, and Argument.* Dodrech-Holland. D. Reidel, 1980.
Plato. *Collected Works.* Trans. by B. Jowett. New York: Greystone Press, n.d.
Pope John Paul II. "On the Mystery and Worship of the Eucharist." In ed. Austin Flannery, O. P. *Vatican Council II.* Collegeville, MN: The Liturgical Press, 1982.
Ribi, Alfred. *Demons of the Inner World.* Boston: Shambala, 1990.
Ricoeur, Paul. *Interpretation Theory.* Fort Worth, Texas: Texas Christian University Press, 1976.
Robinson, Theodore H. *Prophecy and the Prophets in Ancient Israel.* London: Duckworth, 1923.
Romilly, Jacqueline de. *Magic and Rhetoric in Ancient Greece.* Cambridge, Mass.: Harvard University Press, 1975.
Rousseau, Jean-Jacques. *Social Contract.* In ed. Charles M. Andrews, *Famous Utopias.* New York: Tudor Publishing, n. d.

Rudnick Luft, Sandra. *Vico's Uncanny Humanism*. Ithaca, N.Y.: Cornell University Press, 2003.

Russell, Bertrand. "How to Read and Understand History." In his *Understanding History*. New York: Philosophical Library, 1957.

*Let the People Think. London: Watts & Co., 1941.*

*The Scientific Outlook. New York: W.W. Norton, 1962.*

*Why I am not a Christian. New York: Simon & Schuster, 1957.*

Russell, Jeffrey Burton. *A History of Medieval Christianity*. New York, 1968.

S. C. D. W. "Christian Faith and Demonology." In ed. Austin Flannery. *Vatican Collection Volume II*. Collegeville, MN: The Liturgical Press, 1982.

Sánchez, Francisco. *Quod nihil scitur.* In *Opera Omnia.* Ed. Joaquim de Carvalho. Coimbra: Universidade de Coimbra, 1955.

Schneider, N. "Die Unkundenbehalter von Ur III und die archivalische Systematik." *Orientalia* N.S. 9 (1940).

Schwartz, Alan and Scott, Robert E. "The Law and Economics of Preliminary Agreements," *Harvard Law Review* (2007).

Schwob, Marcel. *The King in the Golden Mask*. Manchester: Carcanet, 1982.

Seeskin, Kenneth. *Dialogue and Discovery: A Study in Socratic Method.* Albany, N.Y.: SUNY, 1987.

Selbie, W. B. "The Influence of the Old Testament on Puritanism." In eds. I. Abrahams et al. *The Legacy of Israel*. Oxford: Clarendon Press, 1928.

Shell, Marc. *The Economy of Literature*. Baltimore: Hopkins University Press, 1978.

Simon, Richard. *A Critical History of the text of the New Testament.* London, 1689.

Singer, Joseph William. *Entitlement.* New Haven: Yale University Press, 2000.

Slater, Philip. *The Pursuit of Loneliness*. Boston: Beacon Press, 1976.

Smith, Morton. *Jesus the Magician*. San Francisco: Harper & Row, 1978.

*Palestinian Parties and Politics that Shaped the Old Testament. New York: Columbia University Press, 1971.*

*The Secret Gospel. New York: Harper & Row, 1978.*

*Studies in the Cult of Y. 2 vols. Ed. Shaye J. D. Cohen. Leiden: E. J. Brill, 1996.*

Steiner, George. *Martin Heidegger*. New York: Viking Press, 1978.

Tacitus. *The Complete Works of Tacitus*. Ed. Moses Hadas. New York: Modern Library, 1942.

Tarn Steiner, Deborah. *The Tyrant's Writ*. Princeton: Princeton University Press, 1994.

Tillich, Paul. "The Decline and the Validity of the Idea of Progress." In ed. Jerald C. Brauer, *The Future of Religions*. New York: Harper & Row, 1966.

*Dynamics of Faith. New York: Harper & Row, 1958.*

Thomas, D. M. *The White Hotel*. New York: Viking Press, 1981.

Thomas Aquinas. *Summa Theologicae.* English version, by Timothy McDermott. London: Eyre and Spottiswoode, 1989.

Torrey, Charles Cutler. *The Jewish Foundation of Islam.* New York: Jewish Institute of Religion Press, 1933.

*Treaties and other International Acts of the United States of America. Volume 2, Documents 1–40; 1776–1818*. Ed. Hunter Miller. United States Government Printing Office, Washington: 1931.

Trevor-Roper, H. R. *The European Witch-Craze*. New York: Harper Torch Books, 1967.

Ullmann, Walter. *The Individual and Society in the Middle Ages*. Baltimore: John Hopkins Press, 1966.

*Law and Politics in the Middle Ages. Ithaca, N. Y.: Cornell University Press, 1975.*

Unamuno, Miguel de. "Cómo se hace una novela?" In *Obras Completas*. Ed. M. Garcia Blanco. Madrid: Afrodisio Aguado, 1958.

*"The Word and the Letter." In his The Agony of Christianity. Princeton: Princeton University Press, 1974.*

Van Buren, Douglas. "The *Ṣalme* in Mesopotamia in Art and Religion," *Orientalia*, n.s., 10 (1941).

Vaux, Roland de. *Ancient Israel.* Vol. 1. New York: McGraw-Hill, 1965.

Vico, Giambattista. *The Art of Rhetoric.* Atlanta: Rodopi, 1996.

*The First New Science. In Vico Selected Writings. Ed. and trans. by Leon Pompa. Cambridge: Cambridge University Press, 1982.*

*Il 'De mente heroica.' In Varia. Naples: A. Guida, 1996.*

*The New Science of Giambattista Vico. Trans. by Thomas Goddard Bergin and Max Harold Fisch. Ithaca, N. Y.: Cornell University, 1968.*

*On the Study Methods of Our Time. Ithaca, New York: Cornell University Press, 1990.*

Vinning, Joseph. *From Newton's Sleep*. Princeton: Princeton University Press, 1995.

Víves, Juan Luis. *El arte retórica/De ratione dicendi.* Barcelona: Anthropos, 1998.

Walaskay, Paul W. *'...And so we came to Rome.'* Cambridge: Cambridge University Press, 2005.

Walker, D. F. *Spiritual and Demonic Magic.* Notre Dame: University of Notre Dame, 1975.

Weber, Max. *The Protestant Ethic and the Spirit of Capitalism.* New York: Charles Scribner's Sons, 1958.

Weiler, Gershon. *Jewish Theocracy.* Leiden: E. J. Brill, 1988.

Wengst, Klaus. *Pax Romana.* Philadelphia: Fortress Press, 1987.

White, James Boyd. *Heracles' Bow*. Madison: Wisconsin University Press, 1985.

Wilhelm, J. "Heroic Virtue." *Catholic Encyclopedia.* New York: Robert Appleton, 1910.

Williams, Joshua. *Principles of the Law of Real Property.* London: Hodges, Smith and Co., 1865.

Wittgenstein, Ludwig. *Culture and Value.* Chicago: Chicago University Press, 1984.

*"Lecture on Ethics." Philosophical Review 74 (1965).*

*Tractatus Logico-Philosophicus. Trans. D. F. Pears and B. F. McGuinness. London: Routledge and Kegan Paul, 1961.*

*Worterbuch fur Volkess Schulen.* Vienna: Holder-Picher-Tempsky, 1977.

Wolin, Richard. *The Seduction of Unreason*. Princeton, N.J.: Princeton University Press, 2004.

Wood, Forrest G. *The Arrogance of Faith*. New York: Alfred A. Knopf, 1990.

Yoshino, Kenji. "The City and the Poet." *Yale Law Journal* 114 (2005).

Zerner, M. Ed. *Inventer l'hérésie*? Nice: Centre de etudes médiévales, 1998.

# Text and Society

## History of the Revealed Text

# Contents

# Introduction

*Joseph Faur*

Before Ḥakham Faur's passing, I had the privilege of acquiring his laptop, which contained a significant portion of his written corpus, including personal letters and notes written by himself. Perusing the material, I fortuitously discovered an English version of a book called *Text and Society*.[1] Until then, I was only aware of: *Texte et société: histoire sociale du texte revele*, the French version of this monograph. In fact, upon further investigation, I discovered that there exist multiple versions of this work.

The discovery of multiple versions of the work on the Hakham's laptop left my co-editor, Eli Shaubi, and I in a state of perplexity. We consulted with Aharon Haleva, who is an insightful student of Faur's writings, and he helped us unravel this mystery. Haleva kindly provided us with two English versions of this work (which he previously

1. Published in *La Société Juive a Travers les Ages*, vol. 1 (Paris: Librairie Fayard, 1992), pp. 43–113; notes pp. 691–705.

obtained), alongside a concise explanation suggesting that the book was likely originally written in English, and that it served as a prototype for the more expansive composition, *The Horizontal Society*.

Further examination confirmed Haleva's conclusions. Shaubi identified three distinct stages in Faur's compilation of *Text and Society*. In the first stage, the work consisted of 13 chapters, and we had two slightly varying files of this version, albeit with minor changes. Faur then added an additional chapter to Section III, and two more chapters to Section IV, resulting in a total of 16 chapters. Finally, Faur introduced another chapter to Section I and made modifications to certain chapter headings. We used this final edition as the basis for the work presented to you.

These findings shed light on the evolutionary stages of Faur's work, illustrating the incremental growth and refinement of *Text and Society,* which would eventually become Faur's well known composition: *The Horizontal Society*.

This begs the following question: why publish *Text and Society* in the first place if it is simply an earlier and less complete version of *The Horizontal Society*?

First, we discovered that while many of the ideas presented in *Text and Society* were later expounded upon in *The Horizontal Society,* there were numerous insights that found expression exclusively in *Text and Society*. In and of themselves, these insights would compel us to publish this important work.

However, there is a second consideration. *Text and Society* elucidates its subject matters with a unique clarity and concision – being characteristic of the Hakham's gift for organizing and teaching difficult topics – making them uniquely accessible to the reader. Consequently, this work must be given its proper place and role in the *Collected Works,* as it serves as a valuable gateway to those embarking on the study of *The Horizontal Society*.

*Text and Society* contains four sections:

Section I focuses on the literary principles associated with the concept of Tora and its connection to Jewish society. It explores how

Rabbinic Judaism is built upon the reciprocal relationship between the people and the Book, encompassing the ideas of revelation, authoritative publication of texts, and hermeneutics.

Section II examines Jewish autonomy and the process of de-bureaucratization in Jewish history. It covers the period from the destruction of the First Jewish Commonwealth to the end of the Talmudic era, with Talmudic society constituting the last autonomous Jewish society in exile before the rise of Islam.

Section III delves into the impact of the collapse of Talmudic society on the relationship between the people and the Book. It investigates the Rabbanite-Karaite conflict, as well as the question of whether a text, such as the Talmud, can function as a substitute for certain social or national institutions. This section also explores the different strategies adopted by Babylonian Jewry, Sepharad, and Ashkenaz to navigate their respective historical and socio-political contexts.

Section IV delves into the relationship between text and society in modern times. It argues that traditional Judaism, both Sephardic and Ashkenazic, continued to uphold the values and ideas developed during the Middle Ages. However, modern Jewry was influenced by Spinoza, who emphasized the incompatibility between the Jewish ideal of "the Book" and the pagan notion of the "State." Spinoza's ideas prompted the transformation of *the Book* into *a book,* together with the concomitant acceptance of the modern State. Movements within modern Judaism revolved around the acceptance or rejection of Spinoza's ideology.

Upon reading this work, and for that matter, all of Hakham Faur's works, it is strongly encouraged to pay close attention to the footnotes and sources. Educated readers stand to benefit greatly by drawing comparisons between the ideas presented in the current work and their counterparts in *The Horizontal Society.*

It is my sincere hope that all readers of this previously unpublished work will duly recognize and value the profound wisdom and erudition offered by Hakham Faur. While embarking upon the intellectual voyage through the pages of this remarkable piece, it is my prayer that the readers gain substantial benefits and insights from its contents.

Sivan 18, 5783,
June 7, 2023.

# Prologue

Text and society are the two dimensions of Israel. Because Judaism perceives the meaning of a text in terms of its factual implementation (see below chs. 3, 6), the Jewish society is the 'commentary' on the text. Thus, historiography is the interpretation of human events – not in terms of some atextual categories – but according to the Book; outside the perimeters of the Book, there is no history. Conversely, the meaning of a text is not to be determined on the basis of philological and literary canons alone, but, specifically, on the way it is reflected in the life and institutions of the people who have accepted the Book. If the Book is the text of a people, then the people are the commentary – without the people of Israel, the Book of Israel does not have meaning. From this perspective, the only way to understand properly the difference between the Jewish Book and the writings of other people is by examining how the particular texts are reflected in their concrete lives and histories.

This study comprises four sections. In order to grasp the perimeters of the 'Jewish-people/Jewish-text' complex, the first section (chs. 1–6) examines the literary principles encompassed by the idea of "Tora" and its relation to Jewish society. These principles are developed by assuming the main constituents and foundations of Rabbinic Judaism. The primary thesis of this section is the close relationship between the people and the Book. All the literary categories – from belief in revelation to the intricacies of the publication of authoritative texts, including the perimeters of hermeneutics – are grounded on the relationship 'people/Book.' This relationship is reciprocal. Not only do the people affect the Book through their peculiar readings and hermeneutics, but also the Book affects the people by producing a unique polity governed by literary principles.

The second section (chs. 7–8) examines the concept of Jewish autonomy and the process of de-bureaucratization that is distinctive of Jewish society. As the Jewish people were losing their national bureaucracies, they filled the vacuum with a special class of literature. This section covers a long period, from the destruction of the First Jewish Commonwealth (586 B.C.E.), until about the end of the Talmudic period (6th century C. E.). The Talmudic society represented the last autonomous Jewish society in Exile. It ended before the rise of Islam.

The third section (chs. 9–12) examines the impact of the collapse of the Talmudic society on the people/Book relationship. Could this relationship have survived in such a social vacuum? The Rabbanite-Karaite conflict was directly connected with this issue: can a text, in our case the Talmud, function in place of a society? (ch. 9). Medieval Judaism produced three distinct traditions designed to overcome this vacuum and meet the challenge of an alien environment: one was in Babylonia, and the other two flourished in Western Europe; one in Sepharad (the Iberian Peninsula and Southern France) and the other in Ashkenaz (Northern France and Teutonic countries). Although they all shared the same spiritual and literary tradition, their strategies for survival were conditioned by their historical and socio-political contexts. Babylonian Jewry developed strong bureaucracies, designed to maintain its political and spiritual autonomy. Responding to their specific situations, Sepharad and Ashkenaz developed two opposite strategies. The difference pertains to semiotics and semantics. Semiotically, their strategies concerned the relation of the outer structure of a symbol to the values it conveys. Sephardic tradition developed in a pluralistic society, where it was 'one of several minorities' – not the 'only' minority. Tolerance demands reciprocity. Not only must the majority be willing to accept the minority, but the minority must also learn to express its individual values and concerns in terms and symbols intelligible to the rest of society. To survive, the minority must learn how to use the symbols of the society to convey its own specific tradition. In turn, because the Sephardic communities developed in pluralistic societies, they were more tolerant of different Jewish cultures and traditions. The emphasis was on *Kelal Yisra'el* (The Totality of the [Jewish Communities] of Israel), rather than on ethnicity and regionality.

Ashkenazic tradition developed in monolithic societies, where Jews were 'the only minority.' In these areas, ethnic and regional differences were of the essence. In such societies, minorities are conditioned to be semantically dependent on the majority. It will be seen that whereas in Sepharad the cultural symbols of the non-Jewish society were used to convey Jewish values, in Ashkenaz, Jewish symbols were used to convey the ideas and institutions of the outside world. A pivotal consequence of this difference concerns semantic solvency. Sephardic communities, even when using non-Jewish symbols and language, continued to be semantically autonomous. On the other hand, Ashkenazic communities, even when using Jewish symbols, were semantically dependent on the non-Jewish environment. An index of semantic autonomy are the *conversos* ('Iberian Jews coerced to accept Christianity'). Although bereft of all Jewish symbols, thanks to their semantic solvency they were able to maintain their own identities for centuries – a unique phenomenon in religious history.

The last section (chs. 13–16) examines the relation of text-society in modern times. The principal thesis of this section is that whereas traditional Judaism, both Sephardic and Ashkenazic, continue to consolidate and formulate the values and ideas developed during the Middle Ages (ch. 13), modern Jewry is spiritually dependent on Spinoza. He, better than anybody else in modern history, understood that the Jewish ideal of the 'Book' (with a capital B) is incompatible with the pagan notion of the 'State' (with a capital S), and that conversely, the Hebrew ideal of the 'state' (with a lower case s) is incompatible with the pagan concept of 'book.' Spinoza's revolutionary idea consisted of transforming the 'Book' into *a* book, thereby preparing the ground for the transformation of the 'state' into the modern State (chs. 14–15). For the Jews, the transformation Book ⊠ book implied forfeiting the national dimension of the Jewish people. We will see that in Spinoza's economy of ideas, 'Book' minus 'Jewish political dimension' equals 'book' plus 'full acceptance of the modern State.' All subsequent movements within modern Judaism concern either acceptance or rejection of Spinoza's ideology (ch. 16).

# Section I

## Chapter 1
## Authoritative Texts: Scripture and the Oral Law

Judaism possesses a corpus of written literature: the Hebrew Scripture, known as *Tora she-bi-Khtab* ('Written Law'), and a corpus of oral tradition known as *Tora she-be-ʿal Pe* ('Oral Law').[1] Together, they constitute the body of Jewish authoritative texts.

1. See Shabbat 31a; Yoma 28b; Berakhot 5a. On the differences between *Tora she-bi-Khtab* and *Tora she-be-'al Pe*, see Moses di Ṭrani, *Qiryat Sefer*, vol. 1 (New York, 1953), Introduction, ch. 2; R. Israel Moses Ḥazzan, *Iyye ha-Yam* (Leghorn, 5629/1869), 8d-10a; Saul Lieberman, *Hellenism in Jewish Palestine* (New York: The Jewish Theological Seminary of America, 1950), pp. 83–99. On their legal status, see my *Studies in the Mishne Tora* (Heb) (Jerusalem: Mossad Harav Kook, 1978), pp. 18–19; and my *Golden Doves with Silver Dots: Semiotics and*

The 'Books of the Scripture,' or *Tora she-bi-Khtab*, are divided into a threefold hierarchical group. The first and most authoritative book is the 'Pentateuch,' or 'Five Books' of Moses, known by the generic term Tora ('Law'). The second group is the *Nebi'im* ('Prophets'). The third is the *Ketubim* ('Hagiographa').

The Pentateuch is at the head of the hierarchical scale. It is the 'Law,' or more precisely, the 'Constitution' of the People of Israel.[2] It was written by Moses himself acting as God's amanuensis and is the source of all political, judiciary and ecclesiastical authority. Therefore, it is hierarchically superior to all other books.

Next comes the *Nebi'im*, containing the books relating to the ecclesiastical history of Israel, from the conquest of Canaan until the fall of Jerusalem (597 B.C.E.) and its destruction (586 B.C.E.) by the Babylonians. This group also contains the literature of the major prophets of Israel. In these books, God addresses the people, hence their 'prophetic' character.

Last, are the *Ketubim*. Here, *man* is addressing God or his fellow humans. Therefore, these represent the 'wisdom literature' of Israel. This group also contains the entire chronological history of the Jewish people, from its very beginning until and including the return of the Jewish people to the Land of Israel after the first Exile (538 B.C.E.). In Rabbinic literature, both the *Nebi'im* and *Ketubim* are known by the generic term *Qabbala* ('Tradition'), in contradistinction to the Tora, or five books of Moses.

The threefold division of the Scripture is ancient. It was explicitly

---

*Textuality in Rabbinic Tradition* (Bloomington: Indiana University Press, 1986), pp. XXV-XXVI. On their content and general history, see George Foot Moore, *Judaism*, vol. 1 (Cambridge, Mass.: Harvard University Press, 1927), pp. 234–280.

2. For Philo's views on this matter, see Harry Austryn Wolfson, *Philo* (Cambridge, Mass.: Harvard University Press, 1948), vol. 2, pp. 374–395. For a modern perspective on this issue, see Jacob Neusner, "The Constitutions of Judaism in Ancient Times: The Pentateuch and the Mishna," *Journal of Reform Judaism* 36 (1989), 55–63; and idem, *Understanding seeking Faith*, vol. 3 (Atlanta, Georgia: Scholars Press, 1988), pp. 145–162.

mentioned by the year 130 B.C.E.[3] The canon of the Scripture was closed circa 100 C.E.[4] Henceforth, no further writings would be incorporated into the Scripture. The closing of the canon is related to the political situation of Israel. In Judaism, a canon text is a *national* text. The publication of such a text requires national approval and the participation of a properly constituted authority (see below ch. 4). Hence, shortly after the destruction of the Second Temple (68 C.E.) and the loss of political autonomy, the Rabbis at Yabne closed the canon and no further books could be accepted as part of the Scripture. Henceforth, writing would be a surrogate for the spoken word. It would belong to the 'Oral Law,' i.e., it would be regarded as a 'commentary' to the Scripture and lack textuological dimensions.[5]

The books included in the Scripture have a special status. The Rabbis decreed that all the books contained in the Scripture defile the hands.[6] Therefore, they had to be handled with care. These texts were marked externally by a special cover designed to prevent defilement of the hands. All of these books must be read according to the rules of biblical prosody (*ṭe'amim*).[7] Such reading was reserved for the *holy books*. It was particularly prohibited to read Christian sectarian works with *ṭe'amim*, as this could be misinterpreted to mean that they are part of the Scripture.[8] Externally, the different status was marked by the prohibition to lay a copy of *Nebi'im* or *Ketubim* on top of the Tora, or a copy of *Ketubim* on top of *Nebi'im*. Also, there is a special obligation to stand before a scroll of the Tora and to treat it with reverence. Internally, these books were distinguished by the fact that the Tora was to be read publicly in the synagogue every Sab-

---

3. See Roger T. Beckwith, "Formation of the Hebrew Bible," in ed. Martin Jan Mulder, *Mikra* (Philadelphia: Fortress Press, 1988), p. 51.
4. See ibid., pp. 58–61.
5. Cf. *Golden Doves*, pp. 132–133.
6. Mishna Yadayim 3:5. See Aaron Demsky and Meir Bar-Ilan, "Writing in Ancient Israel and Early Judaism," *Mikra*, pp. 36–37.
7. See *Golden Doves*, p. 10.
8. See my "Concerning the Term *Qore be-Iggeret*," (Heb), *Alei Sefer*, 15 (1988–89), p. 27.

bath morning in a forum of no less than ten men by at least seven readers, and three times a week (including Sabbath afternoon) by three readers. The *Nebi'im* were to be read publicly only on Sabbath morning, after the seven readers completed the reading of the Tora.[9] Although large portions of the Psalms were incorporated into the liturgy, there was no obligation to publicly "read" the *Ketubim* (i.e. from a properly inscribed scroll). Moreover, a Rabbinic legislation prohibited the private readings of *Ketubim* on Sabbath afternoon, at the time of the public homily.

The authoritative works containing the Oral Law are the Mishna (ca. 189), compiled by the ethnarch R. Judah the Prince (ca. 160–220), and the Babylonian (ca. 499) and Jerusalem (fourth century) Talmuds. Principally, these works deal with the judicial and political institutions of the Jewish people, as well as with all legal issues under public and private law. These matters are known by the generic term halakha ('law'), i.e., they are "authoritative" and may be enforced by the judiciary (see below ch. 5).

The bulk of Rabbinic hermeneutics of the Scripture, both in its legal and exegetical aspects, is contained in special collections known as Midrashim (singular Midrash). These are generally divided into *Midrash Halakha* ('Legal Hermeneutics') and *Midrash Aggada* ('Exegetical Hermeneutics'). The former concerns the hermeneutic apparatus used in determining the legal elements of the Scripture, and issues falling into the perimeter of public right. The *Mekhilta* (on Exodus), *Sifra* or *Torat Kohanim* (on Leviticus), and *Sifre* (on Numbers and Deuteronomy) are the most authoritative collections of this material. The *Midrash Aggada* is contained in numerous collections. The best known are *Midrash Rabba* and *Midrash Tanḥuma*, on the Pentateuch and "The Five Scrolls" (Song of Songs, Ruth, Ecclesiastes, Lamentations, and Esther). To elaborate, matters falling outside the jurisdiction of the court are known by the generic term *aggada*

---

9. See Charles Perrot, "The Reading of the Bible in the Ancient Synagogue," in *Mikra*, pp. 127–159.

('narrative').[10] Correspondingly, the material in the *Midrash Aggada* collections pertains to the private realm, and thus falls outside the perimeter of public right (see below ch. 5).

10. On the formal distinction between *halakha* and *aggada,* see *Golden Doves,* pp. 89–96.

# Chapter 2
# The Horizontality of the Covenant: The Grid 'People/Book'

The Jewish people are the only horizontal society in history. Judaism rejects the notion of hierarchy, in relation both to God and to man. The function of the 'Book' is to maintain absolute horizontality between man and man and between man and God.

Jewish texts and the Jewish People have a syntagmatic relationship and are defined in terms of one another. The Book is the text that was given to the *Jewish* people, and the *Jewish* people are the people to whom the Book was given. Their mutual task is to perpetuate one another by means of transmission: the people perpetuate the Book by passing it from one generation to the other, and the Book perpetuates the people by producing a generation capable of carrying on the transmission process.

The Jewish concepts of 'Book' and 'people' are unique. The interaction 'people/Book' results in a special, non-hierarchical realm: the text. The text is "holy" because it establishes a horizontal relationship between God and man and between man and man. A "holy" text must exclude hierarchical categories and reduce the participating parties to a level of absolute parallelism. This text is known as Tora.

The Tora itself is the result of a bilateral, that is, horizontal, covenant between God and Israel. It is grounded on the *berit* or bilateral 'covenant' established between God and the people of Israel at the foot of Mount Sinai. Although the notion of 'covenant' was common in the ancient Near East, it was only enacted between people, not between man and a deity. The uniqueness of the Sinaitic covenant rests on the fact that it alone is a *bilateral* alliance between God and "an entire nation." Previously, God had made a unilateral covenant with Noah not to upset the forces of nature (Gen. 9:8–17). He had also instituted a covenant with the Patriarchs to give their children the Holy Land and to make them "His" people, i.e., to make a bilateral *berit* with the entire nation. When the children of Israel cried to the Lord because of their enslavement, God's first act was to 'remember,' i.e., to acknowledge, the covenant that he had contracted with the Patriarchs (Ex. 2: 24). Never, however, neither before the Sinaitic covenant nor after it, did God establish a *bilateral* covenant with *an entire nation.*[11]

The *berit* between God and Israel was established at Mount Sinai. It was executed in four steps:

1. **Proposal of the Pact**. At God's request, Moses offered Israel the establishment of a bilateral covenant with the Lord. The terms of the covenant were as follows: Israel, on her part, would accept God's Law as binding; God, on His part, would recognize Israel as a kingdom of priests and a holy nation. The Jewish people accepted the proposal. Moses thereupon relayed their decision to God (Ex. 19: 3–6).
2. **The Theophany at Sinai**. Three days after Israel accepted God's proposal, God revealed Himself amidst thunder, lightning, and turmoil "before the eyes of all Israel," and spoke to them the Ten Commandments (Ex. 19:16–20, 25) "face to face" (Deut. 5:4).
3. **Moses' Ascension to the 'Arafel (thick darkness)**. After God's Theophany, Moses ascended to the *'arafel* to receive representative commandments of the Law – a series of religious, moral,

11. For a thorough discussion of this fundamental concept, see my "Understanding the Covenant," *Tradition* 9 (1968), pp. 33–55.

and judicial legislations. Upon descending from the *'arafel,* Moses transmitted these commandments to the people. The people replied: "All the words which God had spoken we shall do." During the night, Moses put these commandments into writing. This document is known as "the book of the *berit*" (Ex. 20:21–24:4).

4. **Ratification of the Pact**. On the following morning, the pact was ratified. Moses ordered the erection of twelve pillars, representing the tribes of Israel, and an altar, representing God. Then, Moses sent the young men of Israel to offer sacrifices. Half of the blood of the sacrifices was poured into basins; the rest was sprinkled onto the altar. Thereupon, Moses proceeded to read to the people "the book of the *berit*." God was conspicuously absent. The morning was quiet and serene; there was no thunder, lightning, or anything that could coerce, frighten, or intimidate the people. Freely and in unison, the people broke the stillness of the morning with the words: "All that God will tell us we shall execute and obey." Then, Moses took the rest of the blood and sprinkled it on the people saying: "Behold the blood of the *berit* that God made with you, on all these words" (Ex. 24: 4–8).

Thus took place an event with no parallel in history: a bilateral covenant between God and an entire people. The Scripture records revelations and covenants between God and individuals, but only at Sinai did God speak to an entire people and establish a covenant with them. Before leaving the Sinai Desert, the blessings and penalties of the covenant were stipulated (Lev. 26: 3–46). God transmitted the rest of the commandments to Moses throughout the forty years of wandering in the desert. At the fields of Moab, before crossing the River Jordan into the Promised Land, Moses and the people ratified the commandments that they received during these forty years with another pact (Deut. 28:69).

The covenant Sinai-Moab was thus formally sealed: neither God nor the people may add, subtract, or introduce modifications (Deut.

13:1).[12] The Hebrew idea of monolotry means that the *only* God must be worshipped *only as prescribed* by the covenant. In this specific sense, halakha, or the legal definition of the commandments, is intrinsic to Jewish worship. All other forms of worship constitute *'aboda zara* ('alien worship'). This term, mistranslated under Christian influence as 'idolatry,' does not merely indicate the prohibition to worship images or *another* deity. It also forbids worshipping God with an 'alien worship,' that is, with a ritual not prescribed by the covenant.[13] From the perspective of Scripture, it makes no difference whether one worships God with images, worships with an unprescribed cult, or worships an angel or intercessor, etc. In all these cases, the worshipper is guilty of *'aboda zara*. To worship God with an alien, that is, unprescribed, cult is a violation of the covenant as either adding to or subtracting from it.[14] The Rabbis noted that after the Septuagint translated the prohibition to worship "other gods… the sun, or the moon, or any host of heaven," it added (to the masoretic text): "which He did not command you to do" (Deut. 17:3).[15]

Outside the *berit*, a relationship with the divine is predicated on *violence*. It sanctions the logic that the will of the deity *must* be accepted, by the fiat that an inferior *must* submit to the will of a superior. Except for the Tora, all religions, including the so-called 'monotheistic' ones, are models sanctioning the right of the mighty to impose their will on the weak. The idea of a bilateral covenant with God rejects the notion of vertical authority. This idea of a covenant projects the belief that authority is the effect of mutual agreement and horizontality. According to this view, the divinity is not to be obeyed by the fiat of a prophetic oracle or miracle (= proof of

12. See Megilla 2b; *Mishne Tora, Yesode ha-Tora* 8:2–3; 9:1–2.
13. See my "The Biblical Idea of Idolatry," *Jewish Quarterly Review* 69 (1978), pp. 1–26; and my *Homo Mysticus: A Guide to Maimonides's Guide for the Perplexed* (Syracuse: Syracuse University Press, 1988), pp. 10–11.
14. See *Studies in the Mishne Tora*, p. 209 n. 92.
15. See Megilla 9b. The English translation of the Septuagint "which he commanded you not to do" both misses the point and is incorrect.

might), but solely as the result, and within the strict framework, of a freely negotiated covenant. That is why, rather than 'obedience' to God in the abstract, Judaism recognizes 'fulfillment (*qiyyum*) of the *miṣvot*,' i.e., the terms of the covenant. Thus, 'obedience' to God is the effect, not the cause, of the *berit*. Accordingly, the Rabbis taught that commandments revealed before Sinai are not binding.[16] Similarly, the miracles of Moses are regarded as authentic because they were performed "before the eyes of *all* Israel" (Deut. 34:12), i.e., they were accepted as authentic *by the people*, rather than *imposed* by the fiat of ecclesiastical authority.

A covenant that does not eliminate verticality, binding both parties equally, functions on hierarchical principles, whereby the superior party exercises dominion over the inferior one. Therefore, in Jewish thought, God, too, is bound by the covenant. Unlike a human sovereign, who is hierarchically superior to his subjects and above the law, God is bound to the *berit*. Quoting a Greek proverb, "That the law is not written for the king," i. e., it is not binding, the rabbis said:

> "Ordinarily, when a human king issues a decree, if he chooses, he obeys it; otherwise, [only] others obey it. But when the Holy One, blessed be He, issues a decree, He is the first to obey it."[17]

Since God Himself is bound to the covenant, and He can neither abrogate, reinterpret, nor introduce any additions to it, the *berit* is eternal. The Tora is the official document containing the *berit* between God and Israel.

---

16. Y. Mo'ed Qaṭan III, 8, 82c. See *Studies in the Mishne Tora*, p. 14 n. 5, and pp. 148–151.
17. Y. Rosh HaShana I, 3, 57b. The correct version is found in Louis Ginzberg ed., *The Yerushalmi Fragments of the Genizah* (New York 1909), p. 145. For the correct interpretation of this passage, see Saul Lieberman, "How Much Greek in Jewish Palestine?" in *Biblical and Other Studies* (Cambridge, Mass.: Harvard University Press, 1963), p. 128.

# Chapter 3
# Reciprocity: Oral Law as Mental Law

The function of the Oral Law and its relation to the Written Law is best understood within the context of horizontality. Horizontality involves a general linguistic principle governing the act of speech and communication.

In Western tradition, "reading is the counterpart of the act of writing."[18] For the Hebrews, 'writing' is not structurally connected with 'reading.' In Hebrew, *qara* designates not only 'reading,' but also purely atextual oral activities, such as 'calling' and 'summoning.' This is why 'reading' also stands for 'calling up for signification' and '*understanding* the text.'[19] In Rabbinic literature, 'to read' (*qara*) implies also 'understanding the plain sense of the Scripture (*miqra*).'[20] In the Hebrew tradition, 'writing' is structurally connected, not with 'reading,' but with 'interpretation.' The process of interpretation is based on an *unwritten* frame of reference that gives the written text textuological dimension and meaning. The structure 'writing/interpretation' follows a principle of general linguistics whereby writ-

18. Paul Ricoeur, *Interpretation Theory: Discourse and the Surplus of Meaning* (Fort Worth: The Texas Christian University, 1976), p. 71.
19. See *Golden Doves*, p. 134.
20. See TY Berakhot I, 3, 4, c-d, the story with R. Ḥiyya and R. Jonathan. For the contrast between *qore* and *doresh* see Mishna Yoma I, 3, and *Golden Doves*, p. XVIII.

ing – any kind of writing – necessarily involves a mental, unwritten context. "My work consists of two parts," wrote Ludwig Wittgenstein (1889–1951), "the one present here plus all that I have not written. And it is precisely this second part that is the important one."[21] Similarly the *Zohar* – a book that is traditionally associated with R. Shim'on ben Yoḥai (second century) and which modern scholars attribute to Moses de Leon (ca. 1250–1306) – declared in the name of R. El'azar: "My silence built a Sanctuary above and a Sanctuary below. Truly (it is commonly said), 'If a word is worth one coin, then silence is worth two.'"[22] Accordingly, for every written text there must be an oral counterpart – a *Tora she-be-'al Pe*.

Formally, the Oral Law is the *perush* ('interpretation') of the Written Law.[23] Among Spanish-speaking Sepharadim, the Oral Law is designated '*Ley Mental*' or 'Mental Law.' Indeed, the Oral Law not only transmits the actual interpretation of the Written Tora, but also includes the mental canons by which the Israelites standing at the foot of Mount Sinai processed God's speech and gave it meaning.[24] It is this *initial* comprehension, and not the bare text empty of sense, that constitutes the Sinai-Moab *berit*. Rabbi Johanan (ca. 180-ca. 279), one of the great masters of the Talmud, formulated this basic principle: "God did not contract [the] covenant with Israel, but on account of the oral words," that is, the Oral or Mental Law.[25] As it were, God formulated His message, not in abstract terms, but in accordance with the specific linguistic apparatus of the children of Israel. It follows, therefore, that the actual covenant is not the written text, severed from the mental context of the participants, but the Oral Law, as processed by, and recorded in, the mind of the people. From this point of view, the question 'what does the text mean?' – is inconsequential. What matters is: 'how was the text understood by the participants of the

21. *Worterbuch fur Volkess Schulen* (Vienna: Holder-Picher-Tempsky, 1977), p. XVII.
22. *Zohar* (Leghorn, 5618/1858), vol. 1, 2a.
23. See *Golden Doves*, p. 111.
24. See *Golden Doves*, pp. XVII, 54; cf. ibid. pp. 12, 136–137.
25. Giṭṭin 60b.

covenant?' In Judaism, the purpose of the interpretation is not, like in pagan hermeneutics, to 'discover' the mind of the author and the original sense' of the text. Rather, as is indicated by the Hebrew term *perush,* the purpose is 'to unfold' the sense of the text in a forward direction. The book of Deuteronomy is regarded as the 'commentary' to the first four books of the Pentateuch because it shows the further development and the actual implementation of the Tora. Similarly, the Mishna and Talmud are the *perush* of the Written Law because they show how it was understood and implemented. Hence, *perush* also means promulgation and legislation.[26]

The theory behind this doctrine is that meaning is not a fiat imposed by the first person, but the effect of a hermeneutic process generated by the second person. This follows a general linguistic principle whereby all verbal formulations and subsequent communications, both written and oral, are conditioned by the decoding system of the second person. In contracts, this principle is known as "offer and acceptance." Thus, linguistic communication is grounded on the absolute horizontality of the first and second persons. Horizontality necessitates linguistic reciprocity. The act of speech is not determined by the first person. The first person only puts forward the linguistic symbols of the utterance. Although language and culture demarcate the semantic perimeters of the utterance, its actual meaning is determined by the active participation of the second person (and his decoding system). There is another aspect to linguistic reciprocity. 'I' can be addressed only to a 'you' who in turn can utter 'I,' thereby transforming the original first person into a 'you.'[27] Thus, the act of speech cannot take place unless the first person accepts the decoding system of the second person and the principle of reciprocity.

---

26. See *Hellenism in Jewish Palestine*, p. 200 n. 5. For the root P.R.Sh. in the sense of "to bring out," "to make publicly known," see R. Abraham ibn 'Ezra on Prov. 13:16 and David Yellin, "Forgotten Meanings of Hebrew Roots in the Bible, in *Jewish Studies in memory of Israel Abrahams* (New York: The Jewish Institute of Religion, 1927), p. 454.
27. See *Golden Doves*, pp. 42–43.

It follows, therefore, that every bilateral agreement rests on the mental understanding of the parties. Hence, the Rabbinic doctrine: "God revealed two *Torot* to Israel, one written and one oral,"[28] that is, the written text expressing the mind of the first person, and the oral law expressing the mind of the second person. By positing that both these *Torot* are divine, Rabbinic doctrine postulates the absolute horizontality of the Sinai-Moab covenant.

One implication of this is that God, the other party of the covenant, does not invade the mind of the second party, Israel, and dictate the meaning of the covenant. If it is God who provided the written layer of the covenant, then it is the Jews who provided the linguistic and mental apparatus by which the terms of the covenant acquire meaning. Hence, the principle, formulated by Rabbi Joshua (1st and 2nd centuries), excluding divine intervention (either in the form of oracles or miracles) from influencing the interpretation of the Tora. The axiom upon which this principle is based is that the "Tora is no longer in the heavens!" Namely, that it was already given at Mount Sinai, and the pact was sealed.[29] At the literary level, too, meaning, or the "aesthetic fact," in the words of Borges (1900–1986),

> …necessitates the conjunction of the reader and the text; and only then does it exist. It is absurd to suppose that a volume is much more than a volume. It begins to exist when a reader opens it. Then the aesthetic phenomenon exists; it is similar to the moment in which the book was conceived.[30] Horizontality and the conjunction of the 'author/reader' lead into the Hebrew concept of publication.

28. *Sifre*, ed. Louis Finkelstein (New York: The Jewish Theological Seminary of America, 1969), # 351, p. 408. Cf. *Sifra*, ed. Isaac Hirsch Weiss (Vienna, 5622/1862), *Be-Ḥuqqotai* 2 (Lev. 26:46), 112c. Shabbat 31a and Berakhot 5a.
29. Baba Mesi'a 59b; cf. *Golden Doves*, pp. 13–14, 119.
30. *Borges, Oral* (Buenos Aires: Emecé Editores, 1979), p. 66.

An essential element of the Hebrew concept of publication is the formal surrendering of the text by the author to a specific public – thus, breaking the grid 'text/author,' and establishing the semantic perimeters of the text. A 'published text' is no longer under the control of its author: it belongs to the public to whom it was surrendered.[31] In the case of the people of Israel, there is a reciprocal relationship. To stress this relationship, Arabic speaking Jews identified themselves as *Ahlu-l-Kitabu*. By possessing the Tora, the people of Israel not only become 'the people of the Book,' i.e., who possess the Book, but also the people who belong to the Book.

31. Cf. *Golden Doves*, pp. 2, 13, 119–120.

# Chapter 4
# The Publication of the Hebrew Scripture: Surrendering and Certification

The Hebrew idea of publication reflects the special relationship between the people and the text. Since the Tora is a legal document, binding the people of Israel in the eyes of God, 'publication' of a text carries on the responsibility to safeguard it from possible forgeries and interpolations. At the end of the Pentateuch, we are told that Moses delivered a copy of the Tora to the priests to be deposited in the Ark of the Covenant (Deut. 31:9). In this manner, the text of the Tora was formally published.[32] Authorized copies of the Tora were preserved and supervised in the Temple's archives.[33] A similar process was used among Oriental and Sephardic communities throughout the ages, where an authorized copy of the Tora, known by the Arabic term *taj* ('crown'), was deposited in the synagogue's archive. In this way, copies of the Tora were checked for possible blunders and authorized reproductions issued.[34]

---

32. See *Hellenism in Jewish Palestine*, p. 86. Similarly, the Rabbis maintained that the Oral Law was not legally binding until it was publicly promulgated, that is, published, see ibid. pp. 200–202, and below, chapter 6.
33. See "Formation of the Hebrew Bible," pp. 40–45.
34. See Maimonides, *Perush ha-Mishnayot*, vol. 1, pp. 3–4, where it is said that Moses gave a copy of the Scroll of the Tora to each tribe *liqtadi biha* ("to be regulated

The specific process of publication in Jewish literary tradition, as well as its function, has been neglected by modern scholars. In accordance with Christian doctrine, Jewish scholars assume that in Judaism the sole constituent of 'sacred writings' is whether they "were written by prophets, that is by men who had the holy spirit."[35] This assumption is incorrect. Although Jews believe that their sacred books were inspired by the Holy Spirit,[36] not all text inspired by the Holy Spirit acquired the status of a sacred writing. There was a process of publication, without which no text could be regarded as part of the Scripture. Indeed, a close reading of Rabbinic sources will show that the 'holiness' of a text was the result, not the cause, of publication.

In Jewish tradition, the Theophany at Sinai is designated as *mattan Tora*, the 'giving' or 'presentation' of the Tora to Israel. It includes two distinct procedures: its formal 'presentation' by God (*natan*), and *qabbalat ha-Tora*, the formal 'acceptance of the Tora' by Israel. The same term *natan* also described Moses' deliverance of the scroll of the Tora to the priests (Deut. 31:9) for the purpose of publication. Intimately connected with the 'presentation' and 'acceptance' of the Tora is *mesira* ('surrendering'). One aspect of this term is the act of 'surrendering' a document by its legal holder to a Court of Justice, thereby empowering the Court to interpret and execute it.[37] The same term is used to describe the transmission of the Tora by Moses. Each generation of Jews accepts the Tora from its predecessors and then surrenders it to the next generation.[38] The process of *accepting* a composition with the express commitment of *surrendering* it to the next generation is the publication of a text. Therefore, the text was

---

by it"), that is, to control future copies of the Tora.

35. *Judaism*, vol. 1, p. 238. This view is generally followed by Jewish writers, see for example, Rimon Kasher, "The Interpretation of Scripture in Rabbinic Literature," *Mikra*, pp. 548–549.

36. See Tosefta Yadayim 2:14; Megilla 7a; Y. Megilla I, 1 70d and its explanation in *Golden Doves*, pp. 105–106.

37. See *Golden Doves*, p. 88.

38. See ibid., pp. XXV-XXVI, 13–14.

safeguarded in a sacred place, first at the Temple, and later at the synagogue. This specific form of publication is a condition *sine qua non* of the Jewish text.[39]

From the preceding, it follows that a text, in addition to (i) intrinsically denoting divine inspiration, (ii) and exhibiting evidence that the author was the recipient of divine inspiration (rather than a forger or plagiarist), it must (iii) be formally published. An essential feature of publication is *acceptance* of the text by the public with the specific commitment of surrendering it to subsequent generations. These three basic elements of the Holy Scripture were spelled out by Se'adya Gaon (882–942):

> The constitutives of prophetic Writings are three. One of them is that it should include some mention of prophecy, for example, "And God said…," or the teaching of some [previously] unknown matter [thereby indicating divine inspiration], as with Proverbs, Ecclesiastes, and Esther. The second is proof that the author of that book is indeed a prophet… And the third is that the Nation accepts that book [in the collection of] the Sacred Books, and collectively transmits it. If these three [conditions] are not met, but only one [or two], that book is not a prophetic book.[40]

In Rabbinic tradition, a text is said to have been inspired by the Holy Spirit only upon being formally published, that is, collectively accepted by the people as a sacred text, and certified as such by the proper authorities. The consequence of such a procedure is *derasha* ('exposition') of the text. A text is said to form part of the 'holy writings' when it is 'consigned to be written' (*nittan le-hikkateb*) and a certified copy is accessible to the public. Only such a text is *nittan le-hiddaresh,* that is, it may be the subject of *derasha* ('authoritative

39. See *Hellenism in Jewish Palestine*, pp. 85–86, 200.
40. *Sefer ha-Galui*, in *Zikhron la-Rishonim*, vol. 5, ed. Abraham E. Harkavi (St. Petersburg, 1892), p. 163.

exposition' of the Law). *Derasha* is exclusive to canonized writings. Other books, although containing valuable data, e.g., Ecclesiasticus, may not be formally expounded because they were not published.[41]

This procedure parallels that of a legal document that must be "surrendered" (*nimsar*) to the judicial authorities, in order to be properly interpreted and executed. With the act of *mesira,* the author surrenders the text, and it is thereby "consigned to be expounded" (*nittan le-hiddaresh*) by the Rabbinic Court.[42]

An instance of some of the subtleties involving publication may be found with the Book of Esther. Although it now forms part of the Hebrew canon, its status was debated until the third century, and continued to be disputed through the Middle Ages.[43] A close reading of the Rabbinic discussions on the status of Esther shows that the basis for designating it as written by the Holy Spirit is the verse stating that it had been "accepted" (*qibbel*[*u*]) and "certified" (*ve-qiyyemu*) (Est. 9: 27). The two greatest Talmudic masters of Babylonia, Rab and Samuel (2nd and 3rd centuries), disputed whether it was "certified" by the earthly authorities or by Heaven. It should be noted that 'certification' is a technical term referring to the process of judicial certification (*qiyyum sheṭarot*) – a legal prerequisite for formal interpretation and execution of a legal document.[44] Samuel, following the order of the verse, maintained that it was first "accepted" by the people and then "certified" only in the Heavens, implying that it was not properly certified: "They certified above [i.e., in the Heavens] what was accepted below," i.e., by the people. Rab maintained that first, Esther was *certified* by the people, that is, by the proper authorities, and then approved (*hiskim*) by God.[45] Pointing out the defective spelling of *qibbel*[*u*] in the singular, Rab remarked: "it is written *ve-qibbel,* it was

41. See *Golden Doves,* pp. 100–110.
42. See *Golden Doves,* pp. XXV, 109, 123–124.
43. See "Concerning the Term *Qore be-Iggeret,*" pp. 24–26.
44. See *Golden Doves,* pp. 107, 143.
45. Megilla 7a.

the Lord of the Jews (i.e. God) who accepted it!"[46] His view agrees with the Talmudic authorities who declared that Esther "was from Sinai,"[47] in the sense that it was properly certified and had acquired the status of a canonical text. This view, which was subsequently accepted by all Rabbinic authorities, endorses the position that Esther *nittena le-hiddaresh*, i.e. "is a text that may be the subject of *derasha*."[48]

Samuel's position, although rejected by later authorities, is more revealing of the complexity of publication. On the one hand, Samuel admitted Rabbinic legislation requiring the reading of Esther on the day of Purim.[49] Furthermore, he also believed that it was inspired by the Holy Spirit. On the other hand, although 'holy,' since he maintained that it was never properly certified as a written document, it had the status of an 'oral' document. The Talmud presented his views as follows:

> [The scroll of] Esther does not defile the hands [i.e. it is not canonical]. Shall we then assume that Samuel maintains that [the scroll of] Esther was not pronounced by the Holy Spirit? But Samuel has said: "[The scroll of] Esther was pronounced by the Holy Spirit!" – it was pronounced for reading, but it was not pronounced for writing (*ne'emara liqrot ve-lo ne'emara le-hikkateb*).[50]

This position is consistent with his aforementioned view that, although the people had in fact "accepted" (*qibbel*[*u*]) Esther, it was only "certified" (*ve-qiyyemu*) in the Heavens – not by the earthly authority. Therefore, although "written with the Holy Spirit," Esther "was consigned for reading, but was not consigned for writing" (*ne'emara liqrot ve-lo ne'emara le-hikkateb*).

46. Ruth Rabba IV, 5 (33d).
47. Y. Megilla I, 7, 70d.
48. Y. Megilla I, 1, 70a; cf. *Golden Doves*, pp. 103–108.
49. See *Golden Doves*, p. 104.
50. Megilla 7a.

Samuel's view reflects the tradition of the Academy of Neharde'a, of which he was its most celebrated head, that rather than a 'book' (*sefer*), with full textuological dimensions, Esther has the status of an 'epistle' (*iggeret*).[51] The legal model for the 'epistle' of Samuel's Esther is to be found in the official documents of ancient Persia. In Persian chancelleries, an official decision was recorded and filed under its own heading and arranged either chronologically or according to subject matter. It was designated by the Aramaic *dikhrona* ('memorandum'), paralleling the Greek *hypomnematismos*.[52] The *dikhrona* was usually recorded in a *megilla* ('scroll') (see Ezra 6:1). Generally, the memoranda were destined for different government departments and were not made public. Diplomatic and official correspondence were sent in 'epistles' (*iggera, iggerta*) (see Ezra 4:8, 11; 5:6; Neh. 2:7–9; 6:19), whose actual text was *not* available to the general public. Government decisions that needed to be made known to the public were proclaimed *orally* by heralds, from 'epistles' (*iggerot*) (see II Chr. 30:6).[53] These epistles were only read, and written copies of the text were not available to the general public. Samuel and members of his Academy at Neharde'a maintained that Esther was an *iggeret* (see Esther 9:29). Following the model of the Persian chancelleries, Samuel contended that Esther was an *iggeret,* and therefore only consigned to be read, like heralds proclaiming official news, but not to be written, i.e., its text was never officially published. To highlight this point, in the feast of Purim, the communities that had accepted Samuel's view modeled their reading of Esther on the proclamations of heralds. Imitating heralds, they first unfolded the scroll of Esther, and only then proceeded to read it, *without the traditional cantillation*

---

51. See "Concerning the term *Qore be-Iggeret,*" pp. 25–26.
52. On this type of document, see the very illuminating discussion by Elias Bickerman, "The Edict of Cyrus in Ezra 1," *Studies in Jewish and Christian History*, vol. 1 (Leiden: E. J. Brill 1976), pp. 72–76.
53. On the oral proclamations by heralds, see ibid., pp. 74–76.

*of the Scripture,* and duplicating the intonations of heralds making their proclamations.[54]

The source for Samuel's view was R. Joshua, who contended that Esther was not part of the Hebrew canon. Significantly, R. Joshua maintained that Esther was a *zikkaron* ('memorandum') – the Hebrew equivalent of the Aramaic *dikhrona* – rather than a 'book' – a published text accessible to the public.[55] The reason for associating the term *zikkaron* in the Pentateuch with the *dikhrona* of Esther lies in the fact that Moses was ordered to write a "*zikkaron* and place in the ears of Joshua" (Ex. 17:14). Moses, however, did not read it to Joshua. Moreover, the object of the verb "place" is not the *zikkaron* – it does not say "place *it*" (*ve-simo,* cf. Deut. 31:19), but *ve-sim.* Moses was not ordered to "place in the ears of Joshua" the text of the memorandum. Rather, the second half of the verse states that God will blot out the memory of 'Amaleq. In other words, Moses was to treat the *zikkaron* as a diplomatic memorandum, whose written text is kept in the archives, and its gist is transmitted orally.

The dispute concerning the status of Esther concerns historical facts: was the text certified by the proper authorities? And if so, was it certified as a written text, or only for reading purposes? Consequently: could it serve as the basis of *derasha*? There was no disagreement, however, on the literary principles: only a text that was properly certified and consigned for the general public was to be included in the Holy Scripture and could be used for *derasha.* For the purposes of the present discussion, it is important to take note that the book of Chronicles was published for *derasha* purposes alone.[56]

---

54. See "Concerning the Term *Qore be-Iggeret,*" p. 26.
55. See Megilla 7a. The printed text is corrupt, see *Diqduqe Soferim* ad loc., and *Golden Doves,* pp. 108–109.
56. See Vayyiqra Rabba I, 3, ed. Mordecai Margulies (Jerusalem: American Academy for Jewish Research, 1960), 5 vols., vol. 1, pp. 7–8, and editor's note. See the valuable note of R. Israel Moses Ḥazzan, *Iyye ha-Yam* (Leghorn, 5629/1869), 99b-100.

# Chapter 5
# Oral Tradition and Hermeneutics

In Rabbinic literature, the expression Oral Law (*Tora she-be-'al Pe*) is often used in a generic sense, comprising all doctrines not explicit in the Scripture, including Rabbinic statutes and homilies. This oral tradition, however, is not homogenous. It comprises three different classes:

First is the original interpretation of the covenant, as understood by the children of Israel – the Mental Law of the people – transmitted from generation to generation by an uninterrupted chain of transmission going all the way to Sinai (*de-'oraita*). According to the Rabbis, this Oral Law was formally published in the 'Tent of the Gathering' (*Ohel Mo'ed*) during the forty years in the desert.[57] The publication of the Oral Law corresponds to the *promulgation* of the commandments contained in the Written Law, thus making them binding. Since written texts are subject to diverse interpretations, the Rabbis regarded the text of the Written Law without a formal interpretation, as unpromulgated and unenforceable: through the Oral Law, its official *perush* ('interpretation') (see ch. 3), the Tora acquires the force of law and may be implemented by the judiciary.[58]

Second are the homilies interpreting the 'ambiguous elements' in

57. See 'Erubin 54b; Maimonides, *Perush ha-Mishnayot*, vol. 1, pp. 1–3.
58. See Vayyiqra Rabba, I, 10, vol. 1, pp. 24–25; Shir ha-Shirim Rabba II, 1, 4, vol. 2,

Scripture, i.e. those elements that were not defined by the original Oral Law. The Geonim (heads of the Talmudic Academies in Babylonia) and Maimonides refer to these elements as *dinim mufla'im* ('undefined laws'). Through judicial exegesis (*derasha*), these elements acquire definition and the force of law. A distinctive mark of judicial exegesis is the 'thirteen modes' (*shelosh 'esre middot*) used in the development of the *derasha*. Since these modes of exposition are not conclusive, conflicting interpretations are to be resolved by a majority vote (*'omedim le-minyan*). At the theoretic level, these definitions too function as the promulgation of the law.[59]

Lastly are the statutes, legal doctrines, and adjudications transmitted through the centuries by the Jewish authorities (*de-rabbanan*).[60]

The Oral Law at Sinai forms the nucleus of the covenant (*de-'oraita*). As the Mental Law of the covenant, it conditions all readings and subsequent interpretations. Indeed, the act of *qabbala* ('acceptance') of the Law means, first and foremost, that the people accept, and are thereby conditioned by, the traditions of their predecessors. Departure from this original understanding constitutes a breach of the covenant. Even the high priest, the supreme court, and the monarch have no authority to depart from the Mental Law in their interpretation of the Law. The fact that the Tora stipulates an expiatory sacrifice for the High Priest (Lev. 4:1–12), for the Supreme Court of Israel (Lev. 4:13–21; Num. 15:22–26), and for the political sovereign (Lev. 4:22–26), when sinning or issuing a faulty legal decision, clearly shows that all forms of authority must submit to an objective, unalterable Law that is not subject to interpretation and manipulation.[61]

---

14d; III, 1, 4, vol. 2, 19c. Cf. Saul Lieberman, *Tosefta Ki-Fshuṭah*, vol. 8 (New York: The Jewish Theological Seminary of America, 1973), pp. 699–702; *Hellenism in Jewish Palestine*, pp. 200–202.

59. See *Studies in the Mishne Tora*, pp. 20–21, 25–32.

60. See *MT Mamrim* 1:2.

61. See José Faur, "Law and Hermeneutics in Rabbinic Jurisprudence," *Cardozo Law Review* 14 (1993), pp. 1664–1669; idem, "One-Dimensional Jew," *Annual of Rabbinic Judaism* 2 (1999), pp. 34–38.

Were the authorities to render a decision deviating from this original nucleus, it would be illegal and must be disobeyed. Referring to this fundamental aspect of the Law, the Rabbis taught:

> Could it be that if they [the Supreme Court] would tell you that the right is the left, or that the left is the right, that you should obey them? – That is why the Scripture states: "Do not depart from the statement that they tell you [the Supreme Court's verdict] either to the right or to the left" (Deut. 17: 11) – only when they tell you that the right is the right and the left is the left, [then] you must obey them![62]

At the same time, the rabbis conceived of the Tora as a polysemic text that is capable of endless interpretations and variations. Concerning this aspect of the Scripture, the Rabbis state:

> A single verse may unfold into many senses… [Someone] from the school of R. Ishmael transmitted: "[Is not My word like fire, said the Lord] and like a hammer that shatters the rock?" (Jer. 23: 29). Just as each blow of a hammer strikes forth many sparks, likewise a single verse unfolds into many senses.[63]

Indeed, a Rabbinic tradition teaches that there are "seventy faces to the Tora," that is, seventy modes of interpretation, corresponding to the seventy nations making up humankind. Furthermore, within each mode there are as many variations as individuals. Indeed, the mystics taught that there are six hundred thousand faces to the Tora, equal to the number of individuals standing at the foot of Mount Sinai.[64] A consequence of this doctrine is the belief in the parity of

---

62. Y. Horayot I, 1, 45d. See *Studies in the Mishne Tora*, pp. 21–24. This doctrine has been upheld by post-Talmudic authorities, see the sources in "Law and Hermeneutics in Rabbinic Jurisprudence," pp. 1668–1669.
63. Sanhedrin 34a. See *Golden Doves*, pp. xiii-xiv.
64. See *Golden Doves*, p. 120.

conflicting opinions. "These and these, are the words of the living God," ascertained the Rabbis.[65] Moreover, the term *mesira* ('surrendering'), describing the transmission of the Tora from one generation to the next, implies the right of interpretation (see ch. 4).

The apparent contradiction between the right of interpretation, on the one hand, and the absolute validity of the Mental Law, on the other, is resolved upon considering that the right for *derasha* of the Law applies, exclusively, to *dinim mufla'im*, i.e., those elements in the Scripture not defined by the Mental Law.[66] Since there is a constant appurtenance between the formulation of the text by God (first person), and its perception by the children of Israel (second person), there always will be elements in the Scripture that are not defined by the Oral Law. These elements may be expanded through exegesis or legislation. Commenting on the Scriptural verse stipulating the authority of the Supreme Court to interpret the *undefined* elements of the Tora (Deut. 17:8–11), the Rabbis taught:

> Even when the right does appear in your eyes to be [the] left and the left to be [the] right, you must obey them.[67]

From the preceding, it follows that the legal interpretation of the Written Law is the prerogative of the Court, and therefore a *judicial* right. Two very important principles ensue: First, interpretation is binding only in areas that fall within the jurisdiction of the Court, what is commonly known as public law, not matters of belief and dogma; second, even when issued by the Supreme Court of Israel, interpretation does not *reveal* the meaning of the text, but rather *institutes* its judicial sense.

The fundamental principle that the jurisdiction of the Supreme Court pertains to the realm of public law was formulated by Baḥye ibn Faquda (eleventh century), one of the great Rabbinic figures of

65. 'Erubin 13b.
66. See *Studies in the Mishne Tora*, pp. 21–24.
67. *Sifre* #154, p. 207.

Iberian Jewry. He observed that the Scripture (Deut. 17: 8–11) grants authority to the Supreme Court on purely legal matters, what he designated 'duties of the limbs,' i.e., external obligations – not on matters of personal faith, or 'duties of the heart.' On these matters, tradition and judicial authority do not suffice:

> The [Tora] did not say, when you have some doubts concerning the unity of God, or [the meaning] of God's names and His attributes, or on one of the doctrines of religion, which man can arrive at through intelligence and reason, that you must accept them on the authority of the sages of the Tora, and that you should rely on mere tradition.[68]

This is why, outside the realm of the purely legal, or public law, there is a wide scope for freedom of Scriptural exegesis. In this regard, it is important to point out that Rabbinic tradition does not regard exegesis itself as binding.[69] More precisely, only the purely legal aspect of exegesis is binding, not the actual exegesis of the verse: as long as the law itself is upheld, the verse may be interpreted differently.[70]

This leads to the second principle of Rabbinic hermeneutics, that interpretation does not 'discover' the original sense of the text, but, rather generates meaning.

In Greek literary theory, interpretation displaces the original text,

---

68. *Kitab al-Hadaya ila fara'iḍ al-Qulub*, ed. A. S. Yahuda (Leyden, 1912), p. 16. This is obvious from the Mishna Sanhedrin 10:1 dealing with heretical views, that states: "… he who **says** (*ha-'omer*)" –not "he who believes." A similar formula was adopted by Maimonides, *Mishne Tora, Teshuba* 3:7–8 who refers to heretics as those "who say (*ha-'omer*), implying, thereby, that in Judaism 'heresy' does not concern private beliefs, but **the public manifestation** of views offensive to the Community of Israel.
69. See *Studies in the Mishne Tora*, pp. 183–186.
70. This is particularly evident in Maimonides who quite often cites as a source of the law a different verse than that quoted by the Rabbis. See, for example, *Kesef Mishne* on *Mishne Tora, Ma'ase ha-Qorbanot* 5:3; *Leḥem Mishne* on *Temura* 4:3 and *Melakhim* 1:1, etc.

becoming *the* text. The original ambiguity of the text, necessitating explication, is supplanted by the interpretation –which in effect functions as *the* text, displacing the original. Likewise, in Christian tradition the New Testament explains the Hebrew Scripture, thereby displacing it. This view stems from the notion that the purpose of interpretation is to 'uncover' the 'original' mind of the author and the pristine sense of the text. Intimately connected with this view is the belief that texts are unisemic: once 'deciphered,' all alternative interpretations are spurious.

In Rabbinic tradition, interpretation *generates* – but does not discover – meaning. This is why, although conditioning the *law* of the Scripture, the exegetical definitions of *dinim mufla'im* do not *displace* the text and its intrinsic ambiguity. The authority of these definitions is not the text of the Scripture itself. Rather, it is the *judicial* authority of the Court to interpret the terms of documents under its jurisdiction. Therefore, interpretation of the Scripture never acquires the status of Scripture. Regarding a Scriptural verse that was the subject of interpretation, the Rabbis declared: "A verse cannot be unbound from its accepted sense (*peshuṭo*),"[71] i.e. it cannot be displaced by exegesis.[72] Similarly, Joseph ibn Megas (1077–1141) – one of the foremost Rabbinic authorities from the Iberian Peninsula – taught concerning the Oral Law and its explanations of the Written Law: "It does not equal the true [i.e., the original text of the] Tora."[73] Underlying this

71. Shabbat 63a; Yebamot 11b, 24a. See R. Joseph ben Judah ibn 'Aqnin, ed. and trans. A. S. Halkin *Hitgallut ha-Sodot ve-Hofa'at ha-Me'orot* (Jerusalem: Mekize Nirdamim, 1964), p. 143.
72. This point may bear on the issue raised by Se'adya Gaon (and others) concerning commandments whose plain meaning is different from what was established by judicial exegesis. Are they also binding according to their *peshaṭ*? For example, the prohibition "not to put a stumbling block before a blind person" (Lev. 19:14) was explained by the Rabbis as an injunction against aiding someone to transgress the law, see 'Aboda Zara 6a-b. See Moshe Zucker, *Saadya's Commentary on Genesis* (New York: The Jewish Theological Seminary of America, 1984), (Heb) [Introduction], pp. 53–54. See note 74.
73. *She'elot wu-Tshubot Ribbi Yosef ibn Megas* (Salonika, 5546/1786), #92, 13a.

principle, Maimonides declared that all legal definitions which were not part of the original Mental Law, but generated by exegesis (*dinim mufla'im*), are not Scriptural (*de-'oraita*).

Paradoxically, the notion that interpretation displaces the text negates the right of interpretation. The claim that interpretation 'discovers' the original sense excludes all further interpretations. In order to preserve the right to interpretation, and reject the notion that interpretation supplants the text, the Rabbis regarded the *judicial* status of laws generated through interpretation as *lower* than those promulgated as Rabbinic enactments.[74] This fundamental point becomes obvious when considering that, according to Rabbinic jurisprudence, a legislation promulgated by a Court can only be abrogated by a higher Court. However, if the legislation was the result of Scriptural interpretation, it may be abrogated even by a lower Court.[75]

Accordingly, there are two distinct elements in the Scripture: one which was defined by Mosaic tradition, and is not subject to further interpretation or revision, and another, the *dinim mufla'im* that were never defined by the original Oral Law and may be expanded and redefined by subsequent authorities through exegesis and legislation.

As mentioned earlier (ch. 3), the original Mental Law is the *perush* ('interpretation') of the Written Law. As a *perush*, it has a semiotic relationship with the text that it explains. In this type of relationship, the interpreter system cannot be interpreted in terms of the interpreted system. For example, the Morse and Braille systems are interpreted

---

74. We must distinguish between the **juridical** effect of exegesis and its **judicial** status. Juridically, the exegesis of *dinim mufla'im* may, in fact, condition a Scriptural law. Judicially, however, their status is not Scriptural and they can be limited or abrogated by another Court, see *Studies of the Mishne Tora*, pp. 25–32.

75. See *Golden Doves*, pp. 15–16. The source for this view is Y. Shebi'it I,1, 33a. The printed text is corrupt. In the correct version cited by R. Shelomo 'Adani, *Melekhet Shelomo*, on Mishna Shebi'it I, 1, an injunction had been abrogated by an inferior Court, because it had been promulgated by the higher Court "on the basis of a verse, and it was abrogated (by the lower Court) on the basis of a verse."

in terms of the alphabet, but the alphabet cannot be interpreted in terms of the Morse or Braille systems. Similarly, in modern science, we interpret physical and chemical phenomena in mathematical terms, but we cannot interpret mathematics in terms of physical and chemical phenomena.[76] This is why the relationship 'Mental Law/Written Law,' is not reversible: the Mental Law may not be understood in terms of the Written Law. Accordingly, the Rabbis established that the Oral Law cannot be the object of hermeneutics.[77]

As a distinct system, reflecting the intellectual apparatus of a people, the Mental Law cannot be 'deduced' from the text of the Scripture, or from any other text: it must be known through oral transmission and instruction. Indeed, without a prior Mental Law providing the textuological dimensions of writing, there is no text. Arabic-speaking Jews designate with the term *talqin* the type of instruction required for the interpretation of Jewish texts. Without *talqin*, every reading becomes, necessarily, a misreading – a deviation from the Mental Law of the participants in the Sinai-Moab covenant. It is now clear why the Geonim insisted that *talqin* could not be imparted in writing but only orally. The instructor of *talqin* must supply the student with the linguistic and intellectual apparatus needed to grasp the text in its original sense.[78] This follows a semiological principle whereby the interpretation of one system must be made, necessarily, in terms of another system. Consider a map or a musical composition: they cannot be explained in terms of themselves. A second map or another rendering of the music composition could expand the original version, but it would not explain it.[79] Through *talqin*, the new generation becomes the generation of the Exodus and directly participates in the Sinai-Moab covenant (see Deut. 29: 13–14).

The right to hermeneutics and exegesis of the Scripture is implicit in the term *mesira*, whereby the document in question is surrendered

76. See *Golden Doves*, pp. 111–112.
77. See ibid., p. 88.
78. See ibid., pp. XXV, 16–17, 111–112.
79. See ibid., pp. 111–112.

to the judgment of the Court. Unlike the Sadducees, who rejected the right to interpret the Scripture, the Pharisees and their followers, the Rabbis, recognized the right to apply exegesis to the text of the Tora. According to the Rabbis, "The Tora itself had granted the sages the right to interpret" the Scripture.[80] For the Rabbis, 'interpretation' is not exclusive to a divinely revealed text; it is the privilege of the Court to interpret documents under its jurisdiction. This is why the Court may apply *derasha* to secular documents.[81] In the case of the text of the Scripture, however, the act of *mesira* by the preceding generation is predicated upon the initial act of *qabbala* ('acceptance') of the oral tradition. Therefore, the right to apply hermeneutics to the Tora, is the exclusive patrimony of the *ḥakham* ('sage') – one who had become a master of the Mental Law and the cumulative wisdom of Israel.[82]

In sum, in Jewish tradition, hermeneutics is conditioned on a previous acceptance of the Mental Law – the original connotations and thinking apparatus peculiar to the participants of the Sinai-Moab covenant. Without mastering this Mental Law, all readings of the Scripture are misreadings. Further textuological or hermeneutical developments can neither displace nor acquire a status similar to the Mental Law of the Israelites at Sinai. This is why, at the legal level, the *derasha* is confined to the *dinim mufla'im* – those elements not explicitly defined by the Oral Law: the *derasha* cannot displace the text or acquire the status of the text.

A *derasha* contradicting any of these two radical principles constitutes a betrayal of the people of Sinai-Moab, as either subtracting from or adding to the covenant. The Rabbis classified individuals indulging in this type of exegesis as engaging "in faltering interpretations" (*derashot shel dofi*), that is, 'explanations' designed to undermine authority, and "exposing faces in the Tora" (*megalle panim*

80. *Sifre Bemidbar*, ed. H. Horovitz (Jerusalem: Wahrman Books, 1966), # 134, p. 179; cf. variants. See *Studies in the Mishne Tora*, pp. 21–24.
81. See *Golden Doves*, pp. 123–124.
82. See ibid., p. XVIII.

*ba-Tora*) in malicious ways.[83] As the illustrious Simeon b. Semaḥ Duran (1361–1444) showed in his book *Qeshet wu-Magen* (Leghorn 5523/1763), with these classifications, the Rabbis intended to characterize the Christological and antinomian *derashot* in the Christian Scripture and Patristic literature.

83. Sanhedrin 99b. See *Golden Doves*, p. XXI. There are two different versions of *megalle panim*. In Abot 3:14 Maimonides reads *megalle panim ba-Tora*; see *Perush ha-Mishanyot* on Abot 3:14, vol. 4, p. 433. Maimonides incorporated this version into *MT Teshuba* 3:11. Most probably, this was the version that he had in Sanhedrin 99b. In the specific sense of 'defiance,' this expression is used in 'Erubin 69a. In *Teshubot ha-Rambam* #149, vol. 1, p. 285, Maimonides used this expression in the sense of 'malice' and 'intellectual perversion'; cf. *Hitgallut ha-Sodot ve-Hofa'at ha-Me'orot*, p. 143. The more popular version in Abot and Sanhedrin is *megalle panim ba-Tora she-lo ka-halakha*, "unveiling in the Tora directions contrary to the law," i.e., subversive exegesis designed to undermine a particular law. See "Law and Hermeneutics in Rabbinic Jurisprudence," pp. 1676–1677; and my "Monolingualism and Judaism," *Cardozo Law Review* 6 (1993), pp. 1739–1740.

## Chapter 6

# The Literal and Exegetical Dimensions of the Text

Rabbinic tradition recognizes two modes of textual interpretation: one refers to the 'literal sense' (*peshaṭ*), and the other to the 'canonical exegesis' (*derasha*) of the text.[84] These modes of analysis inform one another and are meaningful in contrast with each other. 'Exegesis' (*derasha*) necessarily implies a 'literal sense' (*peshaṭ*) accessible to all members of the linguistic community. The traditional opposition of *derasha/peshaṭ* reflects the principle that *derasha* is meaningful only when standing in paradigmatic opposition to *peshaṭ*, and vice versa. 'Interpretation' presupposes an intentional process and a deliberate methodology. What are the precise perimeters of these methodologies? It would be seen that, here again, the semantic boundaries are determined by the public, rather than by the text or the method.

The oldest Rabbinic expression standing for 'literal sense of the text,' is "Something on which the Sadducees agree" [with the Pharisees], that is, a settled matter.[85] Since this expression was used in

84. I have dealt extensively with this matter in "Basic Concepts in Rabbinic Hermeneutics," *Shofar* 16 (1997), pp. 1–12.
85. Sanhedrin 33b; Horayot 4a, 4b. It should be noted that, according to Maimonides, the legislation agreed upon by the Sadducees and Pharisees was not grounded on the actual literal sense of the Scripture, but on a *derasha*, see *Mishne Tora, Sanhedrin* 10:9; cf. pseudo-R. Ḥanan'el on Horayot 5b.

a judicial context, it must have been operative in the Court of law, reflecting a period in history when the Pharisees and Sadducees served within the same judicial system (probably before their expulsion from the Sanhedrin during the reign of John Hyrcanus [135–104 B.C.E.], or at the latest during Salome Alexandra's reign [76–67 B.C.E.]). Before examining the specifics of *peshaṭ*, it is worth noting that the very idea that the concurrence between dissenting parties (i.e. Sadducees and Pharisees) constitutes a literary category, proves that there was a nationally acknowledged nucleus of Scriptural interpretation, transcending party politics. More importantly, this expression shows that, for the Rabbis, 'literal sense' was analogous to 'consensus.' This is contrary to the common view, assuming that *peshaṭ* is grounded on the recognition of an absolute meaning of the text, known through some mode of objective analysis. Although the notion of *peshaṭ* as the 'literal' meaning of the text was prevalent among some biblical commentators in the Middle Ages, this was not the case in the Rabbinic period. For the Rabbis, the 'objective' meaning of the text – like the meaning of all signs and semiotic compositions – is known conventionally. The principal difference between *peshaṭ* and *derasha* is one of conventionality: whereas the *peshaṭ* meaning is generally accepted, that of *derasha* is not.

*Peshaṭ,* usually translated as 'literal sense,' actually means 'commonly accepted,' 'spread out,'[86] and it involves 'general consensus.'[87] The same root also appears with the sense of 'usual,' 'frequent,' 'habitual.'[88] Analogously, it may mean 'reviewing a lesson,' in the sense of 'familiarizing oneself with a text.'[89] A similar expression *pashaṭ* or

86. See Shabbat 15a; 'Aboda Zara 8b; Ḥolin 135a.
87. Hence the expression *pashaṭ issuro be-khol yisra'el* ('a prohibition that was generally accepted [*pashaṭ*] throughout Israel'), see 'Aboda Zara 36a; Ḥolin 135a.
88. See *Midrash Tanḥuma* (Constantinople ed., offset reproduction by Makor: Jerusalem, 1971), 30b.
89. See Shemot Rabba, XLVII in *Midrash Rabbot* (Venice, 5364/1604), 113a.

*pashiṭ* is used to mean 'reviewing.'[90] Therefore, rather than 'objective' analysis, *peshaṭ* reflects 'consensus,' 'familiarity,' and 'general agreement.' Since the Rabbis were not concerned with grammar or philological data, the opposition of *derash/peshaṭ* must be understood in terms of 'personal interpretation/general consensus.' This view is confirmed by the fact that the Rabbis classified as *peshaṭ* explanations that have nothing to do with the 'objective,' or 'literal' sense of the verse.[91]

Since the *peshaṭ* represents the conventional meaning of the text, it is a constructive process, helping shape and structure the logical and psychological factors binding the collective mind of the community.[92] In this precise sense, *peshaṭ* is a universal phenomenon: the *sensus communis* of every linguistic community.[93] *Derasha* represents a deliberate interpretation – independent of the conventional sense or the intention of the author.[94] These two types of textual interpretations correspond to two types of perceptual processes. On the one hand, there is the processing of data conditioned by cultural, psychological, and linguistic factors peculiar to every linguistic community. This process shapes the sense of 'reality' perceived by the members of the community, without a deliberate methodology on the part of the interpreter.[95] The result is the type of 'absolute experience' whose grounds transcend analysis and interpretation. From this perspective,

---

90. Y. Berakhot III, 1, 6c.
91. Consider, for example, 'Erubin 23b; Yebamot 24a; Ketubot 111b; Sanhedrin 100b; Zebaḥim 113a; 'Arakhin 8b, 32a.
92. Therefore, it essentially corresponds to the horizontal axis of language, see *Golden Doves*, pp. XIV-XV.
93. See "Basic Concepts in Rabbinic Hermeneutics," pp. 3–8.
94. See ibid., pp. XVIII, XXV, 2, 122–124.
95. See Patrick A. Heelan, "Perception as a Hermeneutical Act," in eds. Hugh J. Silverman and Don Ihde *Hermeneutics and Deconstruction* (Albany: State University of New York Press, 1985), pp. 43–54. Nietzsche, too, rejected the distinction 'literal/figurative,' and concluded that all words were metaphors. On this point, see the valuable study of Ranjit Chatterjee, "Before and Beyond Linguistics: The Case of Professor Nietzsche, Philologist," in eds. Colin E. Nicholson and Ranjit Chatterjee *Tropic Crucible: Self and Theory* (Singapore: University of Singapore, 1984), pp. 25–35.

'perception' is a kind of 'reading' (in a special sense) of a 'text' (in a special sense), somehow analogous to the reading of a literary text, and is consequently hermeneutical.[96]

This type of perception parallels the *peshaṭ*, whereby the text is subjected to a process shared by all the members of the linguistic community. This process takes place without a deliberate methodology on the part of the interpreter.

On the other hand, there are methods of interpretation, developed through creative thinking and acquired through education, whereby an individual processes a specific set of data in a mode which is different from that of the general society, occasionally using a sub-code available only to a segment of the speaking community. This process is analogous to the *derasha*.

There is a constant tension between *derasha* and *peshaṭ*, corresponding to the tension between the individual and collective views. This tension subsides when the individual view is accepted by the linguistic community and becomes the conventional view of society. Thus, *peshaṭ* evolves from *derasha*: *derasha* precedes *peshaṭ*. This is particularly evident with the *Targum* (plural *Targumim*), or Aramaic versions of the Scripture, representing the conventional sense of the text, which has absorbed many of the *derashot*. Consider the verse, "Don't cook a kid in its mother's milk" (Ex. 23:19). Reflecting Rabbinic exegesis, it is rendered by the *Targum*: "Don't eat meat cooked in milk." Likewise, the verse "an eye for an eye" (Ex. 21:23) is rendered by the *Targum*: the "monetary value of the eye." The absorption of *derashot* is particularly abundant in the *Targumim* that were in vogue in Israel. The same linguistic phenomenon took place in the Middle Ages, when the *peshaṭ* of the Pentateuch became identified, among Arabic-speaking Jews, with Se'adya's translation of the Pentateuch, and later on in many European communities, with Rashi's commentary.

The semantic evolution of a text is not exclusive to Scripture. It pertains to all texts read throughout the ages. Interpretation breaks

96. See "Perception as a Hermeneutical Act," p. 52.

the grid 'author/text,' thus displacing its original sense. In a lecture on "The Book," Borges noted the fluid state of semantics of literary texts:

> Heraclitus said (I had mentioned this several times) that since the waters change, no one goes down to the same river twice. Much more terrible is [the fact] that we are no less fluid than the river. Each time that we read a book, the connotation of the words have changed… *Hamlet* is not exactly the *Hamlet* that Shakespeare had conceived at the beginning of the XVII century, *Hamlet* is the *Hamlet* of Coleridge, of Goethe and Bradley. *Hamlet* had been reborn. The same is the case with *Don Quixote*… The readers had enriched the book.[97]

There is a radical difference between the *derasha* ⊠ *peshaṭ* evolution taking place in general literature and in that of the Scripture. In general literature, the original language of the text continues to be spoken. Consequently, the semantic changes are first assimilated linguistically and then projected onto the text. The reading community is unaware that its own *peshaṭ* is in effect a *derasha*. Since evolutionary changes go undetected, the *derasha* appears disguised as *peshaṭ* – as part of a collective reality imposing itself on the text.

According to Rabbinic tradition, *derasha* was first introduced by Hillel (d. ca. 20 B.C.E.), when Hebrew had ceased to be a spoken language. By then, Hebrew had been reduced to *leshon haqodesh*, or more precisely, *lishana debe qudsha* ('the language [spoken at] the Temple'). Later on, it was reduced to the language of scholars, and became known as *leshon ḥakhamim* ('the language of the sages').[98] Since there no longer was a linguistic community where the language of the Scripture could reflect the semantic changes, the new linguistic connotations had to be made first in the text, and only later on could they be projected onto the reading public. Whereas in general

97. *Borges, Oral*, p. 24.
98. See *Golden Doves*, p. XX.

literature, semantic fluidity is projected from the linguistic community onto the text, in Rabbinic tradition it passes from the text onto the reading public: the new interpretations alter the linguistic and intellectual horizon of the community.

In sum, the *derasha/peshaṭ* opposition follows principles present in general linguistics. What the linguistic community absorbs into its present linguistic and cultural horizon corresponds to *peshaṭ*. 'Interpretation' is the linguistic and cultural elements that have not yet been absorbed by the general public. As those elements are incorporated into the horizontal axis of the community, they become a new *peshaṭ*. These semantic changes, in turn, would affect the processing and understanding of all literary texts and create new *derashot*. Generally, these changes go unnoticed, and the linguistic community at large is unaware of the process *derasha* → *peshaṭ*. Because of historical reasons, when Hebrew ceased to be the spoken language of the Jews, the fluctuations and flow of ideas could no longer be registered in the language of the Scripture, and then projected onto the text. The process had to be inverted: first the *derasha* was applied onto the text, and then it was projected onto the reading public. One of the effects of this process was a greater awareness, on the part of the educated public, of the *derasha* origin of later formed *peshaṭ*.

# Section II

## Chapter 7
## Literary and Political Autonomy

The most singular aspect of the Jewish people is the idea of a two-dimensional autonomy. The Jewish people regard themselves as a fully autonomous entity: politically, in regard to other nations, and spiritually, in regard to other value systems. This idea is grounded on the literary theory underlying the Jewish concept of text and the Book.

Autonomy is a principal Jewish concept. It means self-government according to one's own laws and criteria. A society is autonomous when the ordering of human conduct and the adjustment of human relations are relative to its own criteria and interests. Autonomy presupposes a Law, independent of bureaucracies, whether political, religious, or judicial, that is recognized as the sole source of authority.

Such a Law was realized only once in history: in the covenant between God and Israel (see above ch. 2). Unlike 'freedom' – an abstract concept with negative connotations (e.g. freedom from oppression, or coercion, or hunger, or need) – the Exodus from Egypt resulted in 'autonomy' (*ḥerut*) – the affirmation of certain inalienable rights contracted with God. The function of the Law is to guarantee both national and personal autonomy. Without the Law, autonomy is not possible. As the rabbis taught, "No one is autonomous (*ben ḥorin*) unless he is deeply-engaged (*'oseq*) in the Tora."[1] Political and personal autonomy is guaranteed by the Sinai-Moab covenant. As an autonomous entity, the individual owes allegiance to the Law, rather than to a sovereign or body politic. Rather than a 'subject' subservient to a superior being, be it the deity, a man, or a group of men, the participants of the Covenant – including God and the earthly authorities – are equally bound to the Law (see above ch. 3).

Autonomy came about after the Exodus. Emancipation from the bondage of Egypt did not merely produce 'freedom,' but full autonomy. The Exodus involved two distinct elements: "journeying three days into the desert," and "worshipping" God (Ex. 5:3). It is a remarkable fact that Moses did not ask Pharaoh to 'free' the people, but to let them worship God in the "desert" (Ex. 5:3). Moses rejected Pharaoh's offer to worship God in Egypt (Ex. 8:21), insisting that He must be worshipped in the desert (Ex. 8:23). Why? In Hebrew, the primary meaning of 'desert' (*midbar*) is not 'arid' or 'barren,' but a territory that is not under the sovereignty of any political authority. Both Moses and Pharaoh clearly understood that once outside the boundaries of Egypt, the Jewish people would no longer be under Egyptian sovereignty. To ensure that no Egyptian claim would be lingering, they would be journeying for a period of "three days into the desert" (Ex. 5:3, 8:23), thus proclaiming the forfeiture of any Egyptian claim over the people of Israel. The second element, "worshipping God," meant that the Jewish people would formally accept God as

1. Abot 6:2.

their supreme sovereign. God's sovereignty is not confined to the realm of the 'spiritual.' In biblical thought, God is the King of Israel, ruling them according to the Tora. This doctrine has overwhelming political consequence: it rejects the pagan notion of absolute sovereignty, whereby the people are the subjects of the State, owing absolute obedience to the sovereign or body politic. Thus, whereas in the pagan mind the king is God, in Judaism God is King.

The formal acceptance of God's sovereignty took place during the Theophany at Sinai. Sinai was in the 'desert' – a site that was not under the authority of any sovereign. Only at such a site would God give the Tora to Israel and would the people acquire freedom to worship Him.[2] Henceforth, God declared that the people of Israel were to be *His* slaves (Lev. 25: 42, 55). As the Rabbis explained, this means principally that the Jews *would not be* "slaves to slaves."[3] In this fashion, Israel, unlike other people, would not be under the authority of a human or fall under the jurisdiction of a sovereign, either politically or individually.[4] The political subjection of Israel or the judicial subjection of Jews constitutes a challenge to God's sovereignty.[5]

The uniqueness of the Jewish political system rests, primarily, on this pivotal point: whereas the freedom offered by all political systems, ancient and modern, is predicated on personal unfreedom and the unconditional subjection of the individual to a man or group of men constituting the sovereign body politic, allegiance to the Law as the sole source of authority frees the Jew from obedience to man. From this perspective, all political systems, except for Judaism, are

---

2. See *Mekhilta de-R. Yishma'el*, eds. H. S. Horovitz and I. A. Rabin (Jerusalem: Wahrman Books, 1970), p. 205. Cf. *Mekhilta de-R. Shim'on ben Yoḥai*, p. 137.
3. Baba Meṣi'a 10a.
4. In the *Sifra* on this verse, *Behar*, Par. VI (Warsaw, 1866), 106b, it says: "My jurisdiction (*shiṭri*) over them (the people of Israel)," declared God, "precedes (any other jurisdiction)." Accordingly, if the king were to order a Jew to do something against the law, such an order should be disregarded as unlawful, see *MT Melakhim* 3:9.
5. Cf. the disputation between Turnus Rufus, the Roman governor of Judea and R. 'Aqiba, Baba Batra 10a.

a form of enslavement, as the rights of an individual depend on the sovereign or body politic – a man or a group of men – rather than on an eternal and immutable Tora.

This political theory bears directly on the Hebrew concept of nationhood. In pagan thought, national integrity is linked to territory and the violence that this concept entails. With the loss of national territory, the people lose the right to self-governance and national autonomy. In Hebrew thought, nationhood is the effect of Law. A people are a nation, with the right for self-governance, by virtue of the Law. Israel became a nation before conquering the Holy Land (Deut. 27:11). Therefore, even after losing control of their territory, the Jewish people remain an autonomous nation. The Jewish idea of Exile means that, even with the loss of territory, the Law is valid and fully recognized by the Jews as the only source of political and personal authority. Being in a state of exile, rather than accepting the local host as the supreme political authority, is a political manifesto ascertaining that the Jewish people have not forfeited their rights over their national territory: they intend to again take possession of it and establish themselves as a nation in their ancestral home. Two thousand years of ignominy and persecution lay bare the fortitude of this will.

The preceding political theory is intimately connected with the theory of the Book. In the Jewish mind, the Book must be an absolute autonomous literary entity. It cannot depend on any other system, in any detail or aspect. Even the system in which it was inscribed and transmitted was fully autonomous. The Jewish historian Eupolemus (second century B.C.E.) ascertained that Moses, when writing the Tora, first introduced alphabetic script.[6] The prohibition against graven images necessitated alphabetic script, where the letters stand for sounds – in contradistinction to hieroglyphics, where symbols stand for things. Otherwise, writing would have been idolatry.[7]

6. See *Golden Doves*, pp. 10, 120.
7. Cf. My "God as a Writer: Omnipresence and the Art of Dissimulation," *The Bible and the Intellectual Life*, 6 (1989), p. 32.

The Tora itself is independent of the physical world. As the Rabbis taught, the Tora antecedes creation.[8] By contrast, neither the Christian nor Moslem Scriptures are an autonomous literary entity. They are contingent on the Hebrew Scripture, from which they draw support and against which they proclaim their own superiority and doctrinal instructions. By way of contrast, the Tora never refers to another source from which it draws authority. This crucial point was made by R. Saul Levi Mortera (ca. 1596–1660). Drawing on the fact that one of God's designations in the Hebrew Scripture is *Shadday* ('Autonomous,' 'Omnipotent'), R. Mortera illustrates that the Tora, too, is an autonomous literary composition, independent of any other book:

> The Law of Moses (is autonomous in respect to others) and [thus] it is similar and bears a resemblance to God, blessed be He, in that respect. This is not the case with other laws [i.e., religions] claiming to be divine, because only the Law of Moses declares to be the effect of God's work. It is proven so, because the Law of Moses is autonomous in respect to others, since it does not appropriate either its spirit or its principles from any of the other earlier laws [i.e., religions] or writings, but derives only from God Himself, the cause of all beings. This is not the case with other laws [i.e., religions] since they all take their principles and foundations from the Law of Moses, so much so, that if one were to imagine that the Law of Moses is spurious, then all the laws would be spurious. On the other hand, if one were to imagine that those laws are spurious, it [the Law of Moses] would not be affected. The same correspondence [prevails] between [God] the Omnipotent and Autonomous and all other entities, because in the same manner that God, blessed be He, was the infinite eternity before anything had come to be, the Law of Moses was from its beginning what

8. Pesaḥim 54b. Cf. R. Saul Levi Mortera, *Providencia de Dios con Yisrael*, Ms. Etz Hayyim 48C 20 (Hebrew University Library), pp. 120, 138–139.

> it is now – before there were any of the laws [i.e., religions] claiming today to be divine.[9]

Literary autonomy leads into full personal and political autonomy. The Tora is a total system, encompassing all aspects of political and personal life. Other systems, whether political or spiritual, do not concern man in his *totality* but only some of his aspects.

> … [T]he Law that He gave them provided them with everything they needed for the government of their soul, their body, their domicile, the police, the morality, and all what was required and indispensable for the education of the human mind. Having no need to consult in any situation of their republic, to the counsel of any, but the divine Law. In no content do they need either other sciences, or other Philosophies, or other documents in the world, but the Law of which God, blessed be He, is the author, [and] had provided everything needed for human happiness.[10]

By contrast, the Christian and Moslem Scriptures do not offer a total system by which the nation and the individual could gain full autonomy of their political and personal lives.[11] To govern themselves, both as individuals and as a nation, the members of these religions need to appeal to other systems, in the realm of the political, military, economic, and philosophic. Thus, the individual is in a state of trustful dependence on the source of power and authority, upon which he or she has no say. In the Hebrew mind, this is to be in a state of perennial unfreedom. To celebrate his autonomy, every morning the Jew not only blesses the Lord in thanks for not being born a 'gentile,' but also for not being born a 'slave.'

9. Ibid., ch. 2, fol. 3a. cf. Judah ha-Levi, *The Kuzary*, I, 4–10.
10. Ibid., ch. 63, fol. 159b.
11. See ibid., chs. 65–66. Cf. Josephus, *Against Apion* (Loeb Classical Library), II, 168–174, pp. 359–363.

## Chapter 8

# Rabbinic Literature and the De-Bureaucratization of the Jewish People

The literary history of the Jewish people substantiates the special relationship between the literary autonomy of the Book and the political and personal autonomy of the people. It became manifest as the bureaucracies governing the Jewish people ceased to exist. In order to preserve a modicum of personal and political autonomy, the vacuum was filled with literary compositions and institutions. Accordingly, to understand the function of literature in Israel, it is essential to understand the process of de-bureaucratization that took place within the Jewish people, from the beginning of the first Exile until the end of the 16th century with the publication of the *Shulḥan 'Arukh* (1565) (see below ch. 13).

During the first Commonwealth, the Jewish people were governed by three bureaucracies: the monarchy, the priesthood, and the judiciary.

The monarchy represented the political power that strongly influenced, and sometimes plainly dominated, the two other bureaucracies. The fall of the Kingdom of Judea (587 B.C.E.) brought to an end the first bureaucracy. The vacuum resulting from the collapse of the monarchy was filled by the Tora, which the Jewish people acknowledged as their supreme authority, with control over the two other bureaucracies. This was formalized by a national covenant (*amana*), circa 458 B.C.E., whereby the Tora was proclaimed as the only source of authority (Neh. 10:1–37, especially verses 1, 29–30; cf. chapter 13).[12] Thus, the Tora was formally proclaimed the Constitution of the Jewish people, representing the highest Law of the people. Indeed, Philo conceived of the Pentateuch as "the ideal Constitution."[13]

The second bureaucracy was the Temple at Jerusalem. The Temple represented the presence of the divine amidst Israel. The priests, who were in charge of the services and the Holy precinct, administered it and were headed by the high priest. During the Hellenistic period, this bureaucracy suffered a drastic change with the ascendancy to the throne of the Hasmoneans, a priestly family. This priestly family had successfully led the Maccabean revolt against the Seleucids. With their victory, they became not only the rulers of the Temple, but also the monarchs of Israel. They reversed the role of the monarchs in biblical times: whereas the early monarchs sought to dominate the Temple and the judiciary from the throne, the Hasmoneans dominated the other two bureaucracies from the Temple. The Rabbis regarded them as usurpers and illegitimate. Emphatically, they declared that non-Davidic kings (i.e. Hasmoneans and Herodians) could not sit in judgment.[14] Specifically, they pleaded with the Hasmoneans to

12. See my "Some Observations on the Character of Classical Jewish Culture," *Journal of Jewish Studies* 28 (1977), pp. 36–37. The term *amana,* root 'AMN, means 'to bind,' 'to fasten,' 'to join permanently separate items,' see *Mishna* 'Oqaṣin 2:6; *Perush ha-Mishnayot* ad loc, Ṭahorot, vol. 2, pp. 726–727; cf. *MT Ṭum'at Okhalin* 6:11.
13. See Harry Austryn Wolfson, *Philo* (Cambridge, Mass.: Harvard University Press, 1948), vol. 2, pp. 374–395. For a modern perspective on this issue, see Jacob Neusner, "The Constitutions of Judaism in Ancient Times: The Pentateuch and the Mishna," *Journal of Reform Judaism,* 36 (1989), pp. 55–63; and idem, *Understanding seeking Faith,* vol. 3 (Atlanta, Georgia: Scholars Press, 1988), pp. 145–162. See also Elias Bickerman, *The Jews in the Greek Age* (Cambridge, Mass.: Harvard University Press, 1988), chapter 6.
14. Mishna Sanhedrin 2:2.

confine their activities to the altar and to relinquish the monarchy. Their position was summarized as follows:

> The Hasmonean rulers rejected the Pharisean plea to separate altar and throne, and forcibly combined the sacred office of high priesthood with an aggressive policy of conquest and territorial expansion. The descendants of Aaron were no longer "doing the work of Aaron." Shemayah and Abtalion, according to talmudic tradition, descendants of the Assyrian king Sennacherib, called themselves "descendants of the heathen, who do the work of Aaron."[15]

Hillel's emphasis on the peaceful role of the priesthood must be understood as a direct criticism of the Hasmoneans. More obvious was the Rabbis' confrontation with Antipater. They found particularly offensive the propensity of these monarchs for war and violence:

> This negative attitude towards war is, partly, rooted in the prophetic view of the messianic future. Partly, however, the increasing emphasis on peace on the part of classical Judaism in its early development is to be understood as a reaction against acts of cruelty committed by some Hasmonean rulers and as an answer to King Herod's ruthless administration. During the battles between the two Hasmonean princes, Hyrcanus II and Aristobulus II, Onias, a member of the association of peace-loving men (Hasidim), refused to pray for the victory of Hyrcanus' forces 'since those who stand now with me are Thy people and those who are besieged are also Thy priests.' For his non-intervention in this civil war Onias paid with his life.[16]

15. Nahum Glatzer, "The Attitude Towards Rome in the Third-Century Judaism," in *Essays in Jewish Thought*, p. 38.
16. Ibid., p. 38, see p. 39.

The chain of national catastrophes befalling the Jewish people at the end of the second Commonwealth resulted in the destruction of the Temple (68 C.E.) and the collapse of the second bureaucracy of Israel. The outcome was a pivotal moment in the history of religion, whereby the synagogue replaced the altar and the liturgy replaced the oblations and sacramental offerings at the Temple. Unlike the Temple, the synagogue is a lay institution. Over the course of time, the 'Prayer Book' became one of the most popular writings in Judaism, outdoing in some respects the Scripture itself.

The destruction of the Second Temple seriously eroded the judiciary, the third bureaucracy of Israel. Although in one way or another this bureaucracy continues to function until this very day, it underwent significant changes. The vacuum that resulted from the destruction of the Temple generated a revolutionary idea in the history of religion, whereby the role performed by Priest-Temple and Elders-Sanhedrin would be replaced by the Sage-Tora.

In the biblical period, the judiciary was represented by the elders, the judges, and the Levites.[17] Later, in Hellenistic times, the Sanhedrin, or 'Supreme Court,' seated at one of the Temple's chambers represented the highest judicial authority of Israel.[18] By the end of the second Commonwealth, the Sanhedrin had either lost or abdicated the right to adjudicate on political and criminal matters, especially when involving capital punishment. It came to an end with the destruction of the Temple.

The vacuum was filled by the *Bet Din ha-Gadol* ('Supreme Court of Justice') established at Yabne (ca. 70).[19] On the one hand, the power of this institution was severely curtailed. Deprived of any government

17. On the judiciary functions of the 'Elders,' see *The Polity of the Ancient Hebrews*, pp. 48–81; Hanoch Reviv, *The Elders in Ancient Israel* (Heb) (Jerusalem: The Magness Press, 1983).
18. For a general historical survey, see Hugo Mantel, *Studies in the History of the Sanhedrin* (Cambridge, Mass.: Harvard University Press, 1961), chapter 2.
19. See Tosefta Sanhedrin VIII: 1, p. 427. For some background literature on the subject, see George Foote Moore, *Judaism* 3 vols. (Cambridge, Mass.: Harvard

support and under the crushing weight of Roman occupation, the *Bet Din ha-Gadol* could no longer fully exercise its authority and used its office with extreme care and wisdom. Significantly, its members were no longer designated the title of *zaqen* ('elder'), as the members of the Sanhedrin had been, but simply as *ḥakham* ('sage'), or *ribbi* ('master' or 'teacher'). On the other hand, this Court of Justice became the depository, as well as the center of study and dissemination, of the Oral Law, containing the traditions and doctrines accumulated by the people of Israel since the Theophany at Sinai. The *Bet Midrash* ('School of Higher Learning') and *Yeshiba* ('Academy') – where the Oral Law was properly studied and taught – became an indispensable institution for the proper functioning of the Court.

The peculiar state of the Jewish Court spawned a new concept of authority in the history of legal thought. Rather than base their authority on the office they occupied, the members of this Court (and of all subsequent Rabbinic Courts)[20] linked their authority to the traditions and doctrines they represented. Unlike the *zaqen,* who was invested with authority by virtue of his office, the sage drew his authority by virtue of the traditions and doctrines he was teaching. This led to a radically new concept of legal authority and a fresh perception of the Jewish intellectual past: the authority of the great men of Israel derived from their teachings, not from their office. A consequence of this view was that anyone transmitting an authentic tradition or doctrine was as worthy of approval as if he were occupying the highest office of Israel. On this fundamental point the Rabbis taught:

> If one hears a statement from the lowliest Israelite, he must consider it as if he had actually heard it from a great sage… and it should be considered not only as if it were heard from

University Press, 1966), vol. 1, pp. 83–92; *Studies in the History of the Sanhedrin,* index; Jacob Neusner, *A Life of Rabban Yohanan ben Zakkai* (Leiden: E. J. Brill, 1962).

20. See Maimonides, *Mishne Tora, Sanhedrin* 4:15; and the Geonic responsa in *Sha'are Teshuba,* # 86 and # 195.

> a single sage, but as if it were heard from all the sages ... and not only as if it were heard from all the sages, but as if it were heard from the Sanhedrin ... and not only as if it were heard from the Sanhedrin, but as if it were heard from Moses, the Shepherd ... and not only as if it were heard from Moses the Shepherd, but as if it were heard from the mouth of God, blessed be He.[21]

A subsequent national catastrophe further eroded the authority of the Court, accelerating the de-bureaucratization process, namely the destruction of Bitter (mispronounced *Bethar*), on the 9th of Ab 135, at the end of the Bar Kochba uprising (132–135). As a result, the text, rather than the living sage, became the most authoritative source of tradition. The Geonim viewed this catastrophe as the beginning of the Rabbinic movement leading to the compilation of the Mishna and the formation of the Palestinian and Babylonian Talmuds.[22]

Originally, although there was agreement and consensus among the sages as to the substance of the Oral Law, it was not formulated in a uniform text. Rather, each sage and school formulated and taught the Oral Law in its own words and according to its own pedagogical schemes. Since the sages recognized that the different formulations of the doctrines and traditions were matters of style, and not content, there were very few substantive controversies. With the collapse of the Bar Kochba revolt, culminating in the destruction of Bitter, this situation changed abruptly. The Judean population was crushed with unprecedented cruelty and terror. Rome perpetrated the greatest known genocide in ancient history. About ninety percent of the Jewish population in Judea, and upward of fifty percent of the Jews throughout the Roman Empire were exterminated.[23] The centers of

21. *Sifre* #41, p. 86.
22. See *Golden Doves*, pp. 84–86. Modern historic research confirms this view, see Yehoshafat Harkabi, *The Bar Kokhba Syndrome*, trans. Max D. Ticktin (Chappaqua, N.Y.: Rossel Books, 1983), pp. 45–53.
23. See *The Bar Kokhba Syndrome*, p. 48.

Jewish study were destroyed and the majority of the sages killed. This situation further eroded the judiciary in two ways. First, most of the sages transmitting the Oral Law were killed. The few survivors were scattered, and unable to coordinate their teaching in a systematic fashion. Second, there arose many controversies among the surviving students concerning their traditions and doctrines. The reason for this was that many of them had not sufficiently matured at the feet of their teachers. Consequently, they failed to understand that the various formulations of the Oral Law did not signify differences in substance.[24]

In order to preserve the Oral Law, and give to it a final text, it was imperative to compile all the known traditions and edit them in an authoritative frame with an officially approved text, thus producing a national record of the Oral Law. The principal figure behind this project was R. 'Aqiba (50–135) and his school. To accomplish this task, he collected, authenticated, classified, and redacted all the traditions and doctrines circulating in the different schools. His activities were described as follows:

> To what might R. 'Aqiba be likened? To a laborer who took his basket and went forth (to collect the produce). When he found wheat, he put some in the basket; when he found barley, he put that in; spelt, he put that in; lentils, he put them in. Upon returning home, he sorted out the wheat by itself, the barley by itself, the beans by themselves.[25]

This project was completed several generations later (ca. 189–220) by Judah the Prince, who had adopted the methodology of R. Me'ir (2nd century), R. 'Aqiba's most distinguished disciple. This work is known as the Mishna ('authoritative text'). It is divided into six orders or sections, and comprises all the legal formulations and doc-

---

24. See *Golden Doves*, pp. 97–98.
25. *Abot de-R. Nathan*, XVIII, p. xxxiv.

trines transmitted by the Jewish authorities, throughout history. It was immediately acknowledged by all the sages of Israel as the most authoritative formulation of the Oral Law.[26]

The Mishna constitutes the greatest literary miracle in history. Out of the dark shadows of the worst genocide in history, there emerged the most significant intellectual accomplishment of any nation: the *official record* of its *national* tradition.

The vacuum resulting from the loss of sages who had direct access to the chain of tradition, gave rise to the compilation of the Mishna. Thus, Jewish legal tradition was preserved. The Mishna guaranteed the autonomy of the judiciary system, governing the whole gamut of Jewish life, from the political and judicial to the ritual and sacramental. In a deeper sense, the Mishna not only perpetuated the legal traditions and doctrines of a people, but also the peculiar canons of thought and patterns of feelings peculiar to the ethos of Israel. Even when exposing the intricacies of the laws of purity, or sacrilege, at one level, the Mishna is projecting principles and ideas pertaining to a basic Jewish 'philosophy,' at another level. Concerning the multi-level discourse of the Mishna, Professor Neusner remarked:

> Discourse takes place at not one but two (or more) levels, and cases in general are meant for exemplary purposes. That is to say, the issues concern principles that transcend the subject-matter of the law and that in fact affect themselves and topics entirely unrelated to the law, physics … metaphysics … and ethics … for example.[27]

26. See ibid., pp. 84–100.
27. Jacob Neusner, *The Philosophical Mishnah*, vols. 1–3 (Atlanta, Georgia: Scholars Press, 1988–9), vol. 1, p. 223. In these three volumes, Professor Neusner examines the specific philosophical frame of most of the *Mishna*. For a substantive discussion of the economic, political, theological, and philosophical outlook of the Mishna, see idem, *The Social Study of Judaism*, vol. 2 (Atlanta, Georgia: Scholars Press, 1988), pp. 3–125. On the Judaism of the Mishna in general, see idem, *The Social Study of Judaism*, vol. 1 (Atlanta, Georgia: Scholars Press, 1988), pp. 29–55.

Because the Mishna had encoded the structure and canons constituting the 'mental Law' of Israel, rather than merely recording laws, it is the source of intellectual, as well as judicial and political autonomy. Thus, as long as there is a Jew studying the Mishna, Israel is alive and redemption is possible. As the Rabbis taught: "all the exiles would not be gathered in, if not for the merit of the Mishna."[28]

The publication of the Mishna served to charter the future literary output of the Jews. The Tosefta, compiled by R. Ḥiyya shortly after the publication of the Mishna, contains material pertaining to the topics of the Mishna that were not included by Judah the Prince. The *Sifra* and *Sifre* (but not the *Mekhilta* on Exodus) edit exegetical material respectively around Leviticus and Numbers-Deuteronomy, serving as a background to the Mishna. The famous *Midrash Rabbot* is a compilation of the homiletical material on the Pentateuch and the Five Scrolls. Numerous other such collections, many of which have not reached us, were produced. They all had the same purpose: the preservation and study of the traditional doctrines of Israel.

By far the most vital literature produced around the Mishna are the two Talmuds, composed respectively in the Holy Land and in Babylonia. The latter Talmud became the pattern of normative Judaism. Officially, the Talmud is the commentary of the Mishna, but it is not a *commentary* in the standard sense of the term. Its material is a record of the discussions carried out around the topics of the Mishna at the national academies (*Yeshibot*). It comprises the distilled wisdom of the greatest minds in Judaism for over half a millennium. Since by that time, the Academy functioned as the *Bet Din ha-Gadol* or 'Supreme Court,' its legal discussions reflect the highest and most sophisticated analysis of juridical materials in Jewish tradition. Throughout these discussions, manifold other topics – bearing on economics, politics, psychology, philology, history, etc. – are cited, analyzed, and debated. In addition, scores of sources not contained

28. Vayyiqra Rabba [ed. Margulies], vol. 6, VII, 3, p. 155.

in the Mishna are studied and recorded. There is also material bearing on the theological, magical, and folkloric.

The literary unit of the Talmud is the *sugya*, the Syriac equivalent of halakha, implying 'course,' 'flow' as well as 'structure.' The *sugya* comes in various forms. Its essential feature is the weaving together of diverse sources, views, and controversies about the topic at hand – many of which had taken place in different schools and in different circumstances, over long periods of time – into a single, cogent unit. The style is dense and precise, using highly technical terminology. The arguments are keen, requiring enormous concentration and erudition on the part of both the teacher and the student. Judaism has always regarded the mastering of the Talmud as the highest form of education, even higher than the mastering of Scripture.[29]

With the Talmud, the process of de-bureaucratization resulted in the displacement of the priest by the pious, and the judge by the sage.[30] Indeed, the sage, occupying no office, became the true representative of the wisdom of the Tora, and was held in higher regard than an individual occupying any of the aforementioned three bureaucracies. The Rabbis referred to the three bureaucracies governing Israel as the "three crowns." The "crown of the Tora," includes the professional clergy, especially the members of the Court, as well as the scholar without an office, who only has his "good name." Addressing

29. See Baba Mesi'a 33a; *Mishne Tora, Talmud Tora* 1:12.
30. On the displacement of the priest by the pious, see Jacob Neusner, *A Life of Rabban Yohanan ben Zakkai* (Leiden: E. J. Brill, 1962), pp. 33–63; and idem, *A History of the Jews in Babylonia*, vol. 3 (Leiden: E. J. Brill, 1968), pp. 102–126. Cf. Mo'ed Qaṭan 16b; and *Yalquṭ Shim'oni* on II Samuel 23 (165). The preeminence of the scholar over the judge in Babylonia is explicit in the incident between Shemu'el and Mor 'Uqba in Mo'ed Qaṭan 16b; cf. Y. Sanhedrin II, 1, 19d-20a, the incident between Resh Laqqish and R. Yehuda Nesi'a. On the displacement of the judge by the sage, see Y. Berakhot IV, 2, 7d. It should be noted that the prayer excludes 'guilty and innocent,' implying thereby that it was not a Court of Justice, see R. Samuel Ashkenazi, *Yefe Mar'e* (Berlin, 5509/1749), 17a. Especially, legislative matters with no immediate application passed from the Court of Justice to the *Bet Midrash*, see Jacob Neusner, *A History of the Jews in Babylonia*, vol. 4 (Leiden: E. J. Brill, 1969), pp. 125–402.

the merits of these crowns, R. Shim'on (2nd century) commented: "There are three crowns: the crown of Tora, the crown of priesthood, and the crown of royalty – but the crown of a good name exceeds them all." The last two crowns are hereditary, whereas concerning the crown of the Tora, "anyone who wishes to take it on may come and do so."[31] Since the Law is the source of all authority, it follows that "the crown of the Tora" is above the other two.[32]

As the process of de-bureaucratization gained momentum, the scholar became the living symbol of the Tora. Through him the Tora is animated, and he becomes the embodiment of the Tora. Commenting on a Talmudic passage that censures the Babylonians for not standing up before the sages, R. Saul Levi Mortera commented:

> [The] dictum of the great R. Jochanan: These stupid Babylonians, who stand up before the *Sefer Tora* and do not stand up before the scholars. This scholar was right to call them stupid, because they were trying to uphold a good custom introduced into Israel and were not upholding what God in his Law expressly commands: Thou shalt rise before the hoary head and honor the face of an old man – the man, that is to say, who is old through his great understanding, acquired by means of the amount of Law he had learned; he reveals this himself, for the *Sefer Tora* is Law without soul, but the scholar who studies and expounds it is a living animated Law.[33]

---

31. Abot 4:12.
32. See Yoma 72a; *Mishne Tora, Talmud Tora* 3:1. This fundamental idea was first developed by R. Israel Moses Ḥazzan, cf. my *Rabbi Israel Moses Ḥazzan: The Man and His Works* (Heb.) (Haifa: Academic Publishers, 1978), pp. 64–65; and "The Character of Classical Jewish Literature," pp. 36–40. It was borrowed and further developed by Stuart A. Cohen, "The Concept of the Three *Ketarim*," *AJS Review*, 9 (1984), pp. 27–54.
33. In Rehuel Jessurun, *Dialogo dos Montes*, ed. and trans. Philip Polack (London: Tamiesis Books, 1975), pp. 99–100.

It should be noted at this juncture, that unlike the gospels and apostles, the Jewish sage did not use the Tora as a means for self-glorification into a hero or saint. Rather, the Jewish sage was a resolute *instrument* for the celebration and aggrandizement of the Tora – never the other way around.[34]

34. Cf. Jacob Neusner, *Making the Classics in Judaism* (Atlanta, Georgia: Scholars Press, 1989), pp. 79–80.

# Section III

## Chapter 9
## The Post-Talmudic Period: Text without a Society

The end of the Talmudic period came about as a result of new demographic changes that profoundly affected the character of the Jewish society and its relation to the text. According to medieval authorities, the compilation of the Talmud took place in Sassanide Persia, at about or after the year 499. This era was followed by that of the *Sebora'im* or 'disciples' (of the *Emora'im*). Very little is known about them. Their main literary activities consisted of proofreading and editing the Talmud. They finished and edited *sugyot* that were not adequately completed. They also provided critical and explanatory notes, adding material still circulating in the Academies in oral form. Occasionally, they appended marginal notes and brief comments to the text and even published new *sugyot*. According to some, this period ended with Simuna, who died in the year 540, while others maintain that it ended with Sheshna in 689. The Seboraitic sages were followed by the *Geonim* ('Eminences'), or Heads of the Talmudic Academies, who flourished in Babylonia under the early Caliphs, from about the 8th until the beginning of the 13th centuries. This was one of the most productive times in Jewish intellectual history, rivaled only by the period of the Jews in Moorish Spain (see below chs. 10, 11). It was punctured by two major crises that would have deep and lasting effects on the Jewish people and their perception of themselves and of text. Both these crises revolved around the 'text-society' relationship, specifically around the nature of the post-Talmudic society.

How did the Talmudic period come to an end? More precisely: what were the reasons adduced for the termination of that period and the beginning of a new epoch? Only Maimonides (1135–1204) addressed this problem directly. The Talmudic period concluded with the end of the Jewish society. The reason was demographical. Persecutions, as well as political and economic turmoils, resulted in the dispersion of the Jewish Community from ancestral Babylonia, and thereby signaled the end of Jewish society. The underlying thesis is that social autonomy in Exile is possible only when the majority of the people share common educational and judicial institutions. With the fragmentation of the Jewish people and the ensuing isolation from one another, Jewish society ceased to exist:

> And after the Court of Rab Ashe, who finished the Talmud during the life of his son and completed it, Israel was dispersed throughout all the lands, a severe dispersion, and reached the extremes [of the world], and distant islands. Many conflicts broke out throughout the world, and the routes were obstructed by armies. Thus, the study of the Tora diminished,

> and Israel did not gather as before to study in their Academies, in thousands and tens-of-thousands.[1]

Consequentially, there no longer was *a* Jewish society, but multiple societies or communities of Jews. This change affected the status of the ancestral *Yeshibot.* Since they were no longer accessible to the majority of the Jewish population and were no longer administered by an organization under the auspices of the *nation* of Israel, they could not be regarded as *national* institutions, representing national consensus. The same was the case with the old Courts of Justice of Talmudic times. The demographic changes affected their jurisdiction, transforming them from national to regional institutions:

> Every Court of Justice, in every city, that was established after the Talmud and legislated a prohibition, promulgated a statute, or established a custom for the people of its city or of many cities, its decisions did not disseminate throughout Israel, because of the distances and poor road conditions. And because the court of justice of that city was local, whereas the Supreme Court of Seventy-One [members] had ceased to function many years before the compilation of the Talmud.[2]

This theory is grounded on the principle that authority stems from the people. Therefore, no public authority could have standing without a society sanctioning it. The Talmud is binding on all Israel because it represents the will of the last autonomous Jewish society:

> ... [E]verything contained in the Babylonian Talmud is mandatory upon all Israel. It is binding upon every town and every

1. Introduction to the *Mishne Tora,* ll. 111–5. (The numeration of the lines corresponds to *Sefer ha-Madda'*, eds. Katzenelenbogen-Lieberman [Jerusalem: Mossad Harav Kook, 1964].)
2. Ibid., ll. 117–121.

> city to follow all the policies established by the sages of the Talmud, to enforce their prohibitions and to comply with their ordinances. Since all the words of the Talmud were set by the common consent of all Israel, and the sages instituting, decreeing, establishing a policy or adjudicating a case teaching that the law is thus, are all the sages of Israel, or the majority.[3]

As a result of the demographic fragmentation of the post-Talmudic society, there could no longer be *national* sages and institutions, representative of the *nation* of Israel. Hence, the fundamental distinction between the law of the Talmud and that of the post-Talmudic era. The Talmud comprises the views and opinions "that were agreed upon by all Israel," embodying thus the views and traditions "of all or of the majority of the sages of Israel."[4] Thus, it represents *national* consensus and *public authority*. Its ultimate basis is socio-political: its authority derives from the nation of Israel (in Exile). Hence, it has binding jurisdiction over all Israel. On the other hand, post-Talmudic authorities lack a *national* political basis and do not represent Jewish *public authority*. Their authority is strictly local, limited to the communities that accept them.

Since the Talmud encompasses all the values, mores, and traditions of the last autonomous Jewish society, it constitutes the highest form of Jewish *Paideia*, even higher than the Scripture.[5] The Talmud provided the post-Talmudic Jew with the possibility of transcending his fragmentation and partaking in *Kelal Yisra'el*. Here, the text comes to replace not an institution, but *the Jewish Society in Exile*. Hence, the folklore, exegesis, psychological insights, esoteric and metaphysical meditations intersecting the judiciary decisions and opinions rendered by the highest legal minds of Israel. The Talmud is not a book: it is a living, dynamic and *autonomous Jewish Society*. Without the intellectual, psychological, and social apparatus of the

3. Ibid., ll. 126–31.
4. Ibid., ll. 130–131.
5. See Baba Meṣi'a 33a, *Mishne Tora, Talmud Tora* 3:11–12.

Talmud, the Jew could no longer relate even to the Scripture: he would be perceiving the Scripture with an alien perspective. This is why for the Jew the study of Talmud is much more than pure scholarship. It is the means by which to transcend the alien environment and gain a Jewish identity. It is through the study of Talmud that the student overcomes the social and intellectual fragmentation in which he dwells, and inhabits a world that is really his. In this fashion, the student absorbs and assimilates the patterns of thought and feeling of the last Jewish society. To borrow an expression from Edmond Jabès, the study of Talmud is "perforating oblivion because oblivion is the thick rind around our origins."[6]

The preceding represents the position of post-Talmudic Rabbinical authorities, who regarded the Talmud as the most authoritative depositary of the Oral Law and tradition. This position was challenged by the Karaites. Usually, the conflict between Rabbanites and Karaites is depicted as one concerning the validity of the "Written" versus the "Oral" laws. Although essentially correct, this view misses the profound issues underlying this controversy. Common opinion notwithstanding, the Karaites did not deny the validity of the Oral law and tradition. Like the Rabbanites, they recognized the same three sources of authority, namely: Scripture, tradition, and *qiyas* (an Arabic term meaning 'judicial analogy' and implying 'personal judgment and opinion').[7] The conflict pertained to the hierarchy of these sources. For the Rabbanites, tradition, as reflected in the Talmud, is the highest *legal* authority: Scripture and personal judgment must be contextualized within the accumulated experience of the Talmudic society. The theory underlying this position is that the society, rather than national and political institutions, is the source of authority and the supreme guarantors of Jewish values. For the Karaites, Jewish national institutions came to an end with the biblical period. Without national institutions, specifically the monarchy and

6. Edmond Jabès, *Elya* (Berkeley, Ca.: Tree, 1973), p. 7.

7. See *Studies in the Mishne Tora*, pp. 80–86.

the Temple, oral tradition (and thereby the entire Talmudic apparatus) has a marginal role. Therefore, it must be scrutinized and evaluated in light of Scripture and *qiyas*. The underlying theory is that the political institutions – not society – are the source of authority and the only trustworthy guarantors of tradition. Since in many cases the Talmudic traditions appear to contradict personal *qiyas*, they must be dismissed as peripheral and inauthentic.[8]

This controversy touches upon another fundamental issue: could a text, in our case the Talmud, be an adequate substitute for a society? For the Rabbanites, the Talmud is a bridge, effectively connecting the post-Talmudic societies throughout the Diaspora with the autonomous Jewish society of Sassanide Babylonia, and thereby with the biblical society of Israel. In this fashion, the societies of Jews constitute *the* Jewish Society in Exile; more precisely, the Israelite society. To the Karaites, the chain with the biblical past was irrevocably broken. Social and spiritual fragmentation is terminal and intrinsic to the post-Exilic Jew, specifically the post-Talmudic Jew. It should be noted, in passing, that the Karaite movement failed at the social level. The dwindling of their large communities to a trickle was not the effect of pogroms and persecution, but simply of assimilation, either to Islam or to the Rabbanite communities, thus demonstrating the intimate relation of text-Book: without an autonomous Jewish society, the biblical text is ineffective. It is because the Talmud provided the constitutive of the autonomous Jewish society, that the relation of Jew-Scripture survived.

8. See ibid., pp. 86–99.

# Chapter 10
# Cultural Challenge: Social and Intellectual Implications

The special bond 'Jewish-society/text' was directly challenged by Islamic culture. Unlike Christianity, the challenge of Islam was generally on cultural grounds. When addressing itself to the elite of the non-Moslem minorities, Islam preferred not to impose its religion by force, but through its culture. It believed its culture to be so superior that it expected these minorities to accept Islam in order to fully participate in Arabic culture. There is a profound cultural dimension to the Moslem faith. Islam claims that the Koran is the most perfect book in the Arabic language. So perfect that only Allah Himself could have composed it. Essential to this argument is the belief that Arabic is the most perfect language, pointing to its poetry and narrative as evidence. At the same time, the 'Abbasid Caliphs promoted an atmosphere of enlightenment and universality that wrought havoc among the religious minorities. They could no longer shelter themselves behind the walls of linguistic or cultural separatism and ethnicity. The effect of this policy was the mass defection of the non-Moslem elite to Islam, and the ensuing religious and cultural collapse of the non-Moslem minorities. This is how two modern historians describe Islamic policy:

> When the 'Abbasid enlightenment lured the non-Muslims from their ghettoes to take part in an inter-confessional

> discussion of truth conducted in the international language of philosophy at the court of Baghdad, the effect was unsurprisingly a renewed attack of the vertigo of relativity: on the one hand the rival truths were no longer insulated by physical segregation, and on the other they could no longer be kept apart by intellectual segregation. The common language deprived the traditional explanations of religious diversity of their old unthinking plausibility, with the new and unsettling consequence that both the explanations and the truths were put in perspective and so ceased to be supreme.[9]

It was a highly effective policy. All non-Moslem urban elites, Christians in particular, succumbed to Islam. Bereft of their intellectual and religious leadership, these minorities languished in cultural and spiritual stagnation. The only exception was the Jewish elite. Only Jews preserved their elite and continued to thrive under Islam.[10] Why?

The answer to this puzzle lies in the special relationship 'text/society' characteristic of Judaism. Generally, the attention of the Jewish sage was directed toward the interpretation and exposition of the text. The challenge from Islam brought about a radical change in orientation: from text to society. For the bond text-society to survive, the sages would have to address themselves directly to the society and interpret the people in light of the new socio-cultural situation. Since the frame of reference contained in the collective memory of the Talmudic society was not readily present in the mind of the student, the task of the instructor was to first supply the student with the frame of reference required to understand the text. Arabic-speaking Jews designated the oral instruction required to teach such a text as *talqin*. *Talqin* cannot be made in writing. It must be delivered per-

9. Patricia Crone and Michael Cook, *Hagarism* (Cambridge: Cambridge University Press, 1977), pp. 84–85.
10. See ibid., pp. 83–91.

sonally by oral instruction (see above ch. 5).[11] To accomplish this aim, the Jewish sage, first and foremost, needed to be bi-cultural. His task was to interpret both the text and the student in light of the new circumstances, and serve as a bridge between the autonomous Jewish society of the Talmud and the intellectual environment of the student. The new literary activities flourishing throughout the Jewish world were designed to fill the gap between the contemporary Jew and the Jewish texts.

The Geonic period (8th to 13th centuries) that flourished in Babylonia was momentous for its creative quality. The aim was the preservation of Jewish autonomy. The *Geonim's* literary activities may be divided into six areas. First are the numerous responsa they issued, ranging in the thousands, about law, religious doctrines, and the interpretation of the Talmud and other Rabbinic sources. Second, the composition of monographs on specific legal issues, as well as commentaries on some sections of the Talmud. These works were specifically designed to elucidate Jewish law and Rabbinic literature. Some of these works reached monumental proportions, such as R. Samuel ben Ḥofni's (d. 1013) famous "Introduction to the Talmud." Third, biblical exegesis and translations. These works were particularly important in view of the fact that Hebrew was not known to the masses. Moreover, many of the traditional Scriptural themes and values needed to be reinterpreted in light of the new cultural and intellectual environment. Intimately connected with these activities was the growth of the philological and grammatical study of Hebrew. Fresh knowledge of Hebrew led to the composition of poetry, liturgy in particular. Fourth, polemical works. Although some of these works were directed against other religions, most were directed against Jewish sectarians, particularly the Karaites. The significance of this type of literature lies, principally, in the fact that the arguments were drawn from the common values of the general culture, rather

11. See also my "Some General Observations on the Character of Classical Jewish Literature," p. 36.

than from authority. Fifth, philosophical works. In Antiquity, Jewish philosophical activity had ceased with Philo. It was introduced again in the Middle Ages by Se'adya, in his book *Beliefs and Creeds*. Again, the significance of such a work lies in the approach, whereby Jewish heritage and values were to be reasoned by common intelligence, rather than by the fiat of authority. Sixth, a renewed interest in traditional Jewish mystical works. Se'adya wrote a commentary to the *Sefer Yeṣira*, a book originating in Talmudic times. These Academies also produced works on the *Merkaba* ('Chariot') and *Hekhalot* ('Palaces') literature. These works contain the mystical itinerary of the soul, ascending through different celestial spheres or 'palaces,' leading to mystical ecstasy. Although these mystical works did not directly contribute to Jewish autonomy, they served to validate Jewish tradition, and thus,` obliquely, the sources of Jewish autonomy.

# Chapter 11

# Textual Strategies and Cultural Autonomy: The Golden Age of Sepharad

The culture and society developed by Jews in Moorish Spain departed in three fundamental points from that of Babylonian Jewry.

First, the authority of the Talmud was to be limited to the legal aspects of Judaism. Keenly aware of its own *social individuation,* Sephardic Jewry realized that the Talmud could not be a *full-scale model* for their own contemporary setting. At the same time, the Talmud was the source of the Oral Law, and the link with the chain of tradition going all the way to Sinai. Hence, the fundamental distinction between public and private authority. Whereas the legal and judicial elements of the Talmud (halakha) are the Law of Israel and binding on all Jews, all other elements not pertaining to public authority (*haggada*), are not equally binding.[12] This principle was first formulated by one of the most revered figures of the Sephardic Golden Age, R. Baḥye ibn Faquda. Himself a *dayyan* ('judge') and member of the judiciary, he formulated the principle that Judaism recognizes judicial

12. On this fundamental distinction, see *Studies in the Mishne Tora,* pp. 183–193.

authority only in areas which he designated "duties of the limbs," that is, public law (see above ch. 5).[13]

A similar position was formulated by Maimonides. The obligation to obey the Supreme Court of Israel is "on the *execution* [italics added] of the law."[14] Accordingly, only those aspects of the Talmud concerning the *execution* of the commandments, that is, the "duties of the limbs," are binding. Furthermore, what are ultimately binding in the Talmud are the judicial decisions and the formulation of the laws, not the discussions and reasonings of the Talmudic sages; hence, the codification of the Talmud characteristic of Sephardic Jewry. The first codification of Talmudic law was produced in the Academy of Lucena, by the renowned scholar R. Isaac Alfasi (1013–1103). This effort culminated in the *Mishne Tora* by Maimonides, the only codification of the entire corpus of the Rabbinic legal system ever produced. We may now understand the remarkable fact that Andalusian Jewry, the cradle of Sephardic intellectual life and tradition, did not produce a single commentary to the Talmud.[15]

This led to a second and more fundamental step: the limitation and restriction of clerical authority. Unlike the communities in Babylonia (and Ashkenaz), the ultimate source of authority was the legal code, not the clergy. The relation 'society-text' would have

13. Cf. above n. 60.
14. *Mishne Tora, Mamrim* 1:1. The same position is maintained in *Sefer ha-Miṣvot*, ed. R. Joseph Qafiḥ (Jerusalem: Mossad Harav Kook, 5731/1971), positive commandment #174, p. 147, where he limited the authority of the Supreme Court to matters of "prohibitions and authorization," i.e., matters involving a specific behavior and action. Similarly, ibid., in negative commandment #312, p. 325, he again emphasized that the prohibition to disobey the Supreme Court is "in the execution of the Tora."
15. The notes on the tractates Baba Batra and Shebu'ot by R. Joseph ibn Megas are late recensions of marginal annotations compiled by his disciples. The first commentaries to the Talmud were written in the 13th century, after the destruction of Andalusian Jewry. They were produced primarily in Northern Spain, as a direct result of French influence, and were totally dominated by the school of *Tosafot*. The only commentaries not to have been totally dominated by these schools are those of R. Meir Abul'afya.

to be effected directly by the individual, without clergy functioning as mediators between the reader and the Book. In this context, it is important to underline that in the Sephardic tradition, the Rabbi is usually addressed as *ḥakham* ('sage'), a reference to his knowledge, rather than as *rab* or *ribbi* ('master'), implying authority: it is due to his superior knowledge, rather than his office, that he is to be respected and obeyed.

Finally, and as a consequence of the preceding, there was a revival of biblical studies. The relation people-Book standing at the center of Jewish life not only requires awareness of social individuation, but also a direct, *personal* relationship with the Scripture. If at the legal level, the Jew in Sepharad identified with the Talmud, he identified with the Scripture *personally*, that is, linguistically, emotionally, and ideologically. In order to have direct access to the Book, it is not sufficient to 'know' Hebrew. One must penetrate the structures and shades of the language and discover its most recondite secrets. In fact, as long as a reader does not make it the instrument of his most intimate thoughts and emotions, he would be reading the language of the Book in 'translation' as an outsider. Thus in Sepharad, Hebrew became a means for literary composition and was recognized as the depository of the ultimate values and ideals of Israel: Hebrew blossomed into its most beautiful and creative period since biblical times.

By the 10th and 11th centuries, the Jewish communities in Moorish Spain were eclipsing the ancient centers in the East. These communities reached their apogee in the 12th century. Their attitude towards the text resulted in the most glorious chapter in Jewish intellectual history: "the Golden Age of Sepharad." The culture that they developed around the text was grounded on the strategy of bi-culturalism initiated by Se'adya. It involved a fundamental change in the formulation and presentation of Judaism. Generally, religious minorities justify their own idiosyncrasies on the bases of (superior) ethnicity and (exceptional) authority. Bi-culturalism rests on 'universal' values transcending and encompassing both cultures and populations. Therefore, it could not invoke ethnicity or the fiat of authority. The appeal of the Sephardic tradition stems precisely from its ability to express Judaism in terms and structures transcending ethnical and regional boundaries. Since the Talmud was not perceived as a total model, the "Talmudic society" of Sassanide Babylonia could not be a complete paradigm for Sepharad. There was a need to cement the building blocks of society in light of the intellectual and spiritual concerns of the communities and the challenges of the Moorish culture and civilization. Essentially, the strategy of bi-culturalism is to utilize key-symbols of contemporary culture and civilization to express the values and traditions of Israel. Therefore, instead of demanding cultural segregation from their society, or acquiescing to cultural assimilation and disintegration, Sepharad responded to the Moorish challenge by capturing its key-symbols and then transforming them into instruments serving Judaism. Explaining to a French Jew his involvement with secular studies, Maimonides wrote that he had used them as handmaids to the Tora, "to show to the nations and princes her beauty, for she is indeed very beautiful."[16] In this way, it was possible to produce something that was part and parcel of the general and cultural climate, and at the same time to be distinctly Jewish. Thus, the very key-symbols designed to bring about the defection of the Jewish elite and the collapse of communities, became the means to further cement the bond of the society with the Book. Bi-culturalism also allows for a better appreciation of both cultures. Consequently, the Sephardic Jew never felt alienated from either his Jewish or non-Jewish environment. We shall proceed to examine some of the results.

In order to prove the preeminence of Arabic and of the Koran, Moslem scholars developed some of the most comprehensive and profound grammatical and philological studies ever known. Rather than ignore this monumental accomplishment or lose their identity by immersing themselves in the study of Arabic, Jewish scholars in

16. Letter to R. Jonathan of Lunel, in Isaac Shailat ed., *Letters and Essays of Moses Maimonides* (Heb), (Maaleh Adumim, Israel: Maaliyot Press, 5748/1988), vol. 2, p. 502.

Moorish Spain initiated a line of Hebrew linguistic inquiry as yet unparalleled. It began with the works of Menaḥem ibn Saruq (10th century), who composed a lexicon of the entire Bible. His disciple, Judah Ḥayyuj (ca. 945–1000), discovered the most important principle governing Semitic languages: words derive from a triliteral root. This discovery revolutionized the study of language in general and grammatical theory in particular. Dunnash ibn Labraṭ (10th century), a brilliant grammarian who sat at the feet of Se'adya, settled in Spain, bringing with him the invaluable knowledge of his teacher. Judah ibn Qurayyish (9th century), from North Africa, introduced the study of comparative philology. This type of inquiry was pursued in Spain by Abu Brahim Isaac ben Barun (ca. 1100), the author of *Kitab al-Muwazana* – a lexicographical study of Hebrew and Arabic. Linguistic research, culminated in the works of Samuel ha-Nagid (933–1055), Moses ibn Chiqatilla (11th century), Judah ibn Bal'am (11th century), and above all the great master of grammatical theory, Jonah ibn Jannaḥ (11th century).

Linguistic research led to an impassioned study of the Hebrew Scripture, as well as to the composition of highly sophisticated exegetical works. Islam asserted that its Scripture was written in the most perfect literary style. The challenge was accepted. In order to respond intelligently to this challenge, there was a need to subject the Scriptural text to a rigorous linguistic analysis. No aspect of Hebrew escaped their attention: from phonology to lexicography, and from syntax to rhetoric. By applying the newly discovered linguistic principles to the text of the Scripture, they demonstrated that the language of the Scripture was second to none. The commentaries produced are yet to be surpassed. Prominent among these biblical exegetes were ibn Bal'am, ibn Chiqatilla, the renowned Abraham ibn 'Ezra (1089–1164), and Joseph (ca. 1105-ca. 1170), Moses (d. ca. 1190), and David Qimḥi (ca. 1160-ca. 1235).

Islam substantiated its claim of linguistic superiority by pointing to its literary monuments, in particular its poetry. This sense of linguistic superiority permeated all segments of society and exercised a strong influence upon both the upper classes and the masses. Jews in Moorish Spain accepted this key cultural symbol. However, rather than passively 'borrowing' it and assimilating, they succeeded in transforming it into an effective vehicle of Jewish ideology. To appreciate the subtlety of this response, it should be noted that Arabic poetry was primarily concerned with form (rhyme, meter, rhythm, and imagery), not with substance and ideas. The Jews accepted the poetic forms current in Moorish Spain. However, they did not write in Arabic, but in Hebrew. Unlike his Arab counterpart, the Hebrew poet was concerned with poetic substance (aesthetic, theme development, and ideas). In this fashion, rather than assimilating into the general culture or refusing to respond to the challenge of the outside world, the Jews had the creative genius to adapt the literary forms of the society to the specific needs of their community.

This strategy resulted in two of the most precious monuments of the Sephardic tradition: poetry and rhymed narrative. Sephardic poetry was inaugurated by ibn Labraṭ. He adapted the metric of Arabic poetry to the Hebrew language. This technique was further perfected in the poems of Samuel ha-Nagid, Moses ibn 'Ezra (ca. 1055–1135), Judah ha-Levi (ca. 1075–1141), and above all Solomon ibn Gabirol (ca. 1020-ca. 1057). An illustration of the number and variations of themes and metrics is the poetry of Samuel ha-Nagid. One thousand eight hundred and eighteen poems of his, in nearly seventy metric variations, have survived. Other Hebrew writers adapted the Arabic narrative style known as *maqama*. This literary genre is best exemplified in the works of Joseph ibn Zabbara (b. ca. 1140), Judah al-Ḥarizi (1170–1235) and Abraham ibn Ḥasdai (13th century). Because this form of 'Jewish' expression did not insulate the Jew from the surrounding culture, poetry penetrated all levels of life and society: at the synagogue, as part of the liturgy, in the intimacy of the home, and at festive and sad occasions.[17]

17. The best illustration of this procedure is the practice throughout the Sephardic world to sing some of the liturgy and devotional hymns (*baqqashot*) to the music of popular Christian and Moslem songs. Like most of the customs of the

The same strategy and creative gift was applied to the works of philosophy and theology. Taking as a point of departure Hellenistic rationalism and some ideas from the Judaic tradition, the great Arab thinkers were able to produce a philosophy that threatened the whole notion of religious diversity so fundamental to Judaism. The Jewish classics of the time, such as *Duties of the Heart* and *The Kuzari*, served as a response to the cultural challenges of this type of philosophy. A more subtle response came with Maimonides' *Guide for the Perplexed*. Traditional Jewish philosophy, from Se'adya onward, took its main arguments and methodology from Moslem theologians, mainly the Mu'tazila, and applied them to Judaism. This school developed a type of reasoning according to which religious and philosophical thoughts were irreconcilable. Obliquely, it intimated the need to submit to religious authority and suppress critical thinking. Rather than identifying Judaism with the authoritarian ideology of the Mu'tazila (making the Jew vulnerable to the arguments of Islam and Christianity), Maimonides identified Judaism with rationalism and critical thinking. By demonstrating that rational truth and revelation cannot possibly be contradictory, Maimonides was allowing for the application of critical thinking to the study of religion, thus rejecting authoritarianism and setting the foundation for the religious humanism characteristic of Sepharad. It

---

Sephardic Synagogue, this practice, too, originated in Spain. Here, the melody ('outer structure') is disconnected from its inner structure or song, and then it is linked to a Hebrew composition. Remarkably, the same melody that in the non-Jewish society is used to raise concupiscence and romance, is associated by the Jewish sub-group with religious fervor and devotion. There are many advantages to such a procedure. To begin with, the general public is usually gratified to have the Jew adopting such a symbol in the Synagogue, thus compensating for their feelings of inferiority and inadequacy. Consequently, they do not regard the Synagogue and Jewish services as something ominous and intimidating. Furthermore, it spared the Jew the need to frequent the places where those popular songs were played or to sing their words, and be exposed to their values and mores. Finally, it demanded that the Jew grasp a symbol semantically, that is, in terms of its content, rather than semiotically, in terms of its outer structure.

is by developing the humanistic aspects of Judaism, rather than by invoking the authority of faith, that Jews would be best protected from the authoritarian religions of Islam and Christendom, which demanded suppression of personal reason and submission to clerical authorities as the price for salvation.

Western civilization does not allow minorities to participate in its culture or to borrow any of its key-symbols. This was particularly true of Christian Spain, which perceived the entire gamut of its culture in religious terms. Accordingly, Jews in Christian Spain were unable to effect the same cultural response as their coreligionists in Andalusia. The only instances of cultural transformation that took place on Christian soil were the Sephardic ballads known as *Romances*. This process was not effected by scholars, but by the common folk. They excellently illustrate how a popular key-symbol of Western society could effectively be used to transmit Jewish values and ideas. *Romances* are folk songs, and in both Christian and Jewish tradition, they belong to the uneducated masses. Rather than remain culturally isolated, the Jewish masses in Castile adapted the *Romances* from their Christian counterparts to express their feelings, hopes, and concerns. The Jewish *Romances* are anonymous and were transmitted orally. Women participated to a large degree in the transmission and composition of these ballads. Music was an important element of the *Romances,* and their verses have a melodic fluency. Their language was the vernacular Spanish of the Jews. These ballads dwell on traditional Jewish themes, e.g., the sacrifice of Isaac, the birth of Abraham and Moses, Haman's persecution of the Jews, and scores of biblical and Jewish themes. They also dwell on both personal incidents and historical events. One of the most significant aspects of these ballads is that they do not express the scholarly view of 'normative' Judaism, but the view of the uneducated folk. In the *Romances,* the masses found a key-symbol independent of the establishment, thus presenting their own perception of Judaism. Since these ballads were aesthetically appealing, they exercised considerable influence in molding the character of the average man and woman.[18]

Another important key-symbol of Western culture adapted by the Sepharadim was the drama. This took place outside the Iberian peninsula, mostly during the 17th and 18th centuries. Jews in Amsterdam and other cities in Western Europe wrote and produced plays designed to express Jewish identity and values.[19]

In sum, in a pluralistic environment such as Sepharad, the society-text relationship cannot function in a cultural vacuum. It requires a direct response to the specific challenges of the general environment. Within this context, rather than address themselves to the Book, the sages must address themselves to the people of the Book. In doing this, they have to utilize the key-symbols of the general society. To be effective, it is necessary to recognize social and intellectual individuation within the Jewish community. The acceptability of drama and ballads, reflecting both extremes of the social spectrum, as valid means of *Jewish* expression, clearly shows that no social group may be precluded from choosing its own key-symbols. The literature produced in such an environment is a commentary on the society, not on the text. This is why, within the Sephardic tradition, commentaries and books about the Book do not displace the Book. They function as a kind of *talqin* designed to help the people address the Book on their own. The Book, however, remains unexplained.[20] Interpretation takes place only at the moment that the reader opens the Book and reads it as a writer.

---

18. Since modern investigators of *Romances* are conspicuously ignorant of Judaism, they have neglected to examine the pedagogical function of these ballads.
19. For a detailed study of Sephardic drama in Spanish, see Henry V. Besso, *Dramatic Literature of the Sephardic Jews of Amsterdam in the XVIIth and XVIIIth Centuries* (New York: 1947).
20. This is why Sephardic writers never produced commentaries of the type of Rashi.

# Chapter 12
# Ashkenaz: Idealization of the Talmudic Society

Ashkenazic Jewry flourished in the monolithic societies of Northern France and Teutonic countries that defined themselves in terms of ethnicity and regionality. Jewish minorities, too, were defined and perceived themselves in those terms. As in all Christian societies, the people were hierarchically structured and rigorously segregated, both socially and culturally. Members of one social stratum were prohibited from borrowing any of the key-symbols of another stratum. Since Jews were precluded from participating in the general culture of the land, their situation was radically different than in Sepharad. In Moorish Spain, minorities had to interact with Arab civilization. In Ashkenaz, they were excluded from such participation. Within this context, the Talmud had to become a *total* and *complete* model. It was not only a source of law and jurisprudence, as in Sepharad, but a paradigm to be followed and emulated in all its aspects, including those of doctrinal, exegetical, and folklorish nature. This is why Ashkenazim never attempted to codify the Talmud. Unlike their counterparts in Sepharad, Ashkenazic sages regarded Talmudic argumentation and its peculiar mode of reasoning not as rhetorical devices used in Academic discussions, but as models of thinking to be duplicated in daily life by every Jew. Curbed from interacting with the outside environment, Ashkenazic Jewry internalized the Talmudic society. Geography and history collapsed: the Jewish society in

Ashkenaz and that of the Talmud were perceived as one and the same. This identity became the *raison d'etre* of Ashkenazic society and the source of spiritual autonomy and religious inspiration throughout some of the darkest and most painful periods in Jewish history.

At the same time, like all minorities, Ashkenazic Jewry was deeply affected by external and internal factors. Cultural, as well as social, economical, and political conditions, precluded a total and absolute identity with the Talmud. No matter what, Jewish society in medieval France and Germany, was *not* and could *not* be the Talmudic society of Sassanide Babylonia. This tension was heightened by semantic infiltration from the majority. Exclusion from the key-symbols of society foster – not prevent – semantic assimilation. The values of the majority penetrate the key-symbols of the segregated minority and alter their content and function.[21] The minority loses its semantic

21. An excellent example of semantic assimilation is the 'ordination' (*semikha*) of Rabbis. According to Rabbinic legislation, *semikha* may be issued only by the proper Rabbinic authorities in the Holy Land and ceased to be awarded before the end of the Talmudic period. This sense was lost in Ashkenaz. As in Christian society, *semikha* came to mean a 'diploma' issued by a teacher to a student. Contrasting the Ashkenazic practice with the prohibition to award 'Rabbinic ordination,' Isaac Abarbanel (1437–1508), *Naḥalat 'Abot* (New York: D. Silberman, 5713/1953), VI, 1, p. 241, remarked:

> This was also the case throughout Sepharad: when the communities were established there, ordination was awarded to no one. However, upon my arrival in Italy, I discovered that this practice was widely spread, to be ordained one by another. And I found that the origin [of this practice] was from the Ashkenazim, among whom everyone ordains and is ordained and [they bear the title of] 'Rabbis.' I do not know what their grounds are for this authority, if not that they imitate the ways of the gentiles who make doctors, and they do likewise. I wish that at least they would ordain as Rabbis worthy individuals. Because the Geonim have written that in our times one who is a master in the three orders [of the Talmud], Mo'ed ['Festivals'], Nashim ['Family Law'], and Neziqim ['Civil Law'], is designated *ḥakham* ['sage']. If in addition to these he is a master in Qadashim ['Sacrificial Law'], he is designated *ribbi* ['rabbi']. If in addition to these he is a master in Zera'im ['Agricultural Law'] and Ṭahorot ['Purity Law'], he is designated *ga'on* ['eminence']. How then can they ordain people who have not mastered even a single Talmudic tractate?

solvency, depending on the majority for their mental and emotional lexicon. Thus, although using different 'signifiers,' both the majority and the segregated minority share similar 'signified.'[22] In such a situation, basic ideas from the general environment penetrate the minorities, affecting their values and patterns of thought and feelings. One such penetration was the place of *minhag* ('custom') in Jewish life. According to Talmudic jurisprudence, custom is merely an ancillary element, subsidiary to law and legislation. In accordance with the legal tradition peculiar to Teutonic communities, Ashkenazic Jewry, particularly in the 11th and 12th centuries, regarded custom – not Talmud and Rabbinic legislation – as the most authoritative source of law.[23] Reflecting the legal beliefs of the environment, they, too, regarded ethnicity and regionality as the ultimate source of authority and the most authentic seal of Jewish bond.[24] This clashed with the standard view upholding the Talmud and Rabbinic tradition as the supreme legal authority.

The clash between ideality (Talmud) and society (Franco-German) resulted in a fundamental tension characteristic of the spiritual

---

Unlike the Church, Judaism does not recognize a priesthood outside the Temple in charge of religious life, such as prayers and funerals. The *semikha*, however, came to be analogous to the 'ordination' in the Christian church, whereby one takes the holy order and is consecrated to the priesthood. See M. Broyer, "The Ashkenazi Semikha," (Heb) *Zion* 33 (1968), pp. 15–46. On the ordination and the rise of the professional Rabbi, see Irving A. Agus, *Responsa of the Tosaphists* (Heb), (New York: Talpioth, Yeshiva University, 1954), pp. 18–28.

22. An essential element of all monolithic societies is that symbols must be perceived semiotically – in terms of their outer structure – never semiologically, in terms of their meaning and function. In this fashion, although sharing the same semantic apparatus, the majority and the minority could share the illusion of being perfectly insulated from one another.

23. On this fundamental issue see the magistral monograph of Israel Ta-Shma, "*Halakha, Minhag, wu-Masoret be-Yahdut Ashkenaz ba-me'ot ha-yod alef-yod bet*," *Sidra* 3 (1987), pp. 85–161. On the extent of the authority of custom in Ashkenazic tradition, see R. Joseph Colon, *Sefer ha-Shorashim*, IX and LIV. Cf., my "The Legal Thinking of the Tosafot," *Dine Israel* 6 (1975), LXIV.

24. See preceding note.

and intellectual life of Ashkenaz. It was resolved via a special type of casuistry known as *pilpul.*[25] Paradoxically, to reconcile these views it would be necessary to posit that somehow, standard Rabbinic sources are wanting. Through *pilpul,* the sources are supplemented and recast to reflect the social and cultural realities of the particular region and times. An index of the tension ideality-society may be seen in the position of Professor Agus (1910–1984), one of the most respected historians on the subject. Although his view is not openly acknowledged by all, it illustrates the level of tension between ideality and the actual, particularly when one is not predisposed to yield to the reconciliations affected by the *pilpul* methodology:

> ...I pointed out that the scholars of Babylonia of both the Talmudic and Geonic periods...were not acquainted with Jewish public law, a branch of the Oral law in which the Franco-German scholars of the Middle Ages were great experts. Moreover, in this book...I attempt to prove on the basis of significant evidence that this body of public law, so clearly known to the above-mentioned Franco-German scholars, was an integral part of the Oral Law as it was studied by the most advanced scholars of the pre-Bar-Kochba period [i.e. before 132–135 of the common era]. Here, therefore, we possess undeniable evidence of the fact that among the captives of war carried away to the West, or among the Jews who came to settle in Italy before the revolts, there were scholars of the Oral Law who had a greater and more profound knowledge of Judaism and of Jewish law, than the *Tannaim* who were the members of the Sanhedrin of Usha and whose teachings were eventually incorporated in Talmudic literature.[26]

25. Itself the result of semantic assimilation, see below.

26. *The Heroic Age of Franco-German Jewry,* pp. 5–6.

Ashkenazic literary creativity pursued two major objectives: the preservation of regional lore, and the neutralization of different sources and traditions. It comprised three periods.

The first period began at about the end of the 10th century, coming into full bloom in the 11th and 12th centuries.[27] The objective of these works was twofold: to preserve the local customs and peculiar views, such as evidenced in *Ma'ase ha-Ge'onim* written by members of the Machir family in Germany, or *Sefer ha-'Ora* and *Maḥzor Viṭry*, in France; and to shield their local customs and views from criticism, either from classical texts or from more recent works. With this purpose in mind, classical texts, from the Scripture to the Talmud and Midrash, were subjected to what Professor Ta-Shma describes as "aggressive" editing, whereby the authoritative texts of Judaism were purged from any element that could impugn local views and customs. This resulted in a new recension of Jewish classical texts, displacing the originals.[28] The same method was applied to more recent works representing the Oriental and Sephardic traditions, such as *'Iggeret Sherira Ga'on, Halakhot Gedolot, Perush Rabbenu Ḥanan'el,* and *Hilkhot ha-Rif.*[29] When a work had wide circulation and the text could not be revised, then it would be accompanied by *haggahot* ('emendations') designed to adapt it to the local customs.[30] Occasionally, to curb a popular work, it would be subjected to 'hostile criticism' (*hasagot*) designed to discredit the author. Both of these methods were applied against Maimonides' famous code *Mishne Tora*. The best known *hasagot* are those of the Rabad (R. Abraham ben David [ca. 1125–1198]) – one of the most saintly and revered figures.[31] A major

27. See the very important work of Avraham Grossman, *The Early Sages of Ashkenaz*.
28. See Israel Ta-Shma, "*Sifriyyatam shel Ḥakhme Ashkenaz bene ha-Me'a ha-Yod Alef-Yod Bet,*" *Qiryat Sefer* 60 (1985), pp. 298–309.
29. See Professor Israel Ta-Shma, "*Qeliṭatam shel sifre ha-Rif, ha-Raḥ, ve-Halakhot Gedolot be-Ṣarfat wub-Ashkenaz ba-me'ot ha-Yod-Alef-Yod-Bet,*" *Qiryat Sefer* 55 (1980), pp. 191–201.
30. In its original connotation, *haggahot* refers to 'emendations of mistakes' that render the scroll of the Tora 'unfit' for reading (*pasul*).
31. Invariably, these *hasagot* are based on the Ashkenazic recension of the Talmud

criticism of the Rabad, repeated by many others, was that Maimonides did not disclose his sources.[32] Obviously, as in modern jurisprudence, when a judge writes an opinion or a lawyer presents a memorandum to a judge, citations and precedents are of the essence. This, however, is not the case with a *code* of law. Indeed, ever since Yehudai Gaon, head of the Academy of Sura (ca. 757–761), there had been published codes of law without reference to sources.[33]

Intimately connected with the need to protect local customs and views was the methodology applied to the study of Talmud. The most successful work to come out of the Ashkenazic tradition, affecting Judaism till the present, is a commentary to the Talmud known as *Tosafot* ('Glosses'). Ludwig Blau (1861–1936), one of the most eminent Rabbinic scholars of recent times, noted, "About the twelfth century flourished in France the *glossatores* of Roman law, and the Tossaphists, who were the *glossatores* of Talmudic law. The same spirit prevails in either school."[34] Applying the standard methodology used by French

---

and the interpretations circulating in those communities – unlike Maimonides who based his legal decisions on the original text of the Talmud and the traditional interpretations coming from the schools of the Geonim. See my book, *Studies in the Mishne Tora*, pp. 1, 5.

32. See Rabad's *Hasagot* at the end of the Introduction to the *Mishne Tora*. Invariably, a close reading of the *Mishne Tora* will reveal, to those who are familiar with the entire output of Rabbinic tradition, the specific source of Maimonides. As I indicated in my *Studies in the Mishne Tora*, the problems concerning Maimonides' sources stem from the fact that some have not been preserved, and the current versions of the Talmud and other Rabbinic sources correspond to the late recensions made in Ashkenaz.

33. Significantly, Rabad did not disclose *his* source for ascertaining that a code of law is unworthy unless it specifies the source of every item. See *Teshubot ha-Rabad* #XX. It is well known that in many of his *hasagot* the Rabad does not disclose *his* sources, assuming, like Maimonides had assumed, that the critical reader would be acquainted with the traditional literature on the subject; cf. *Studies in the Mishne Tora*, p. 55 n. 66. More striking is the fact that he himself refrained from citing many of the sources in his books of codes, see his *Sefer Ba'ale ha-Nefesh*.

34. Ludwig Blau, "Methods of Teaching the Talmud," *Jewish Quarterly Review* 15 (1903), p. 125.

jurists and glossators (hence '*Tosafot*': 'Glosses') to accommodate Roman law to the new economical and social situation of medieval France, their Jewish counterparts sought to accommodate Talmudic law to their local views and customs. The strategy of this type of casuistry is to detach the key-terms from their original context, thus neutralizing the text. In this fashion, the link with the original connotation is dissolved, and they can now be associated with new values and functions.[35] It revolutionized the study of Talmud in two highly significant ways. First, paralleling Christian colleges and universities, Jewish studies shifted from the objective analysis of the text to dialectics and argumentation.[36] Second, it inverted the semantic orientation of the student. Originally, an interpretation would be evaluated in terms of the text that it was supposed to explain. With the *Tosafot*, this relationship was inverted. As with Western literary tradition, interpretation here displaced the text (see above ch. 5). An absolute condition for the study of *Tosafot* is that it cannot be tested in terms of the actual text of the Talmud. As was noted by the anonymous author of *'Alilot Debarim*, this approach demands that the student validates the Talmud in terms of *Tosafot*.[37] This peculiar

---

35. See "The Legal Thinking of the Tosafot," L-LXXII.
36. See the incisive remarks of Israel Ta-Shma, "The Practice of *Talmud-Torah* as a Social and Religious Problem in *Sefer Haḥassidim*," (Heb.) *Bar-Ilan* 1415 (1977), pp. 106–108. An excellent example of this type of casuistry is the work described by Israel Ta-Shma, "*Tosafot Gornish*," *Sinai* 68 (1971), pp. 153–161.
37. "*'Alilot Debarim*," *Oṣar Neḥmad* 4 (1863), p. 183. Cf. Israel Ta-Shma, "*Hekhan Nitḥabbar Sefer 'Alilot Debarim?*" *Alei Sefer* 3 (1977), p. 44; and idem, "*Yedi'ot Ḥadashot 'al 'Tosafot Gornish' ve-'Inyanan*," *Alei Sefer* 2 (1976), p. 80. This approach still dominates contemporary *Yeshibot*. As noted by Ludwig Blau, "Methods of Teaching the Talmud," p. 126:

    In reality it is not the Talmud which is taught, but the Talmud is employed as a text to the history of its exegesis. In the higher special tuition the Talmud does not form the principal subject-matter of the lecture, but it only affords the indispensable basis to illustrate to the audience, more or less completely, the attempts of a large number of commentators, *glossatores*, writers of *novellae*, etc., in their exegetical, codifying, or other pursuits. No special school of modern times has been able to rid itself entirely of these evils.

form of casuistry became known as *pilpul*. Although the term *pilpul* is Talmudic,[38] as with other Jewish key-symbols, it lost its original semantic connotation.[39] Thus, any possible tensions between the Talmud and local views and customs were eliminated. Ludwig Blau noted that as a result of this methodology, "The Talmud, in the way in which it is generally taught, has neither object, nor material, nor method."[40] Contrasting the *Tosafot's* methodology with that of the older Academies in the East and Moorish Spain, he remarked:

> In spite of the admiration due to the piety and diligence of these scholars and of the Talmudic heroes of the German-Polish period, it must be admitted that most of them were unable to uphold the comprehensiveness of view which distinguished the Talmudic scholars of the earlier periods.[41]

The second literary period flourished from the 12th to the 14th centuries. Applying the methodology of the *Tosafot*, these works attempted to blend and harmonize the pietistic ideals of *Sefer ha-Ḥasidim*, with the local customs and views of the Ashkenazic communities. Some of these works are *Sefer ha-Raban* by R. Eliezer ben Nathan of Mainz (ca. 1090-ca. 1170), *Sefer Yere'im* by R. Eliezer ben Samuel of Metz (ca. 1115-ca. 1198), *Sefer ha-Teruma* by R. Barukh ben Isaac of Worms (12th and 13th centuries), *Sefer Rabya* by R. Eliezer ben Joel ha-Levi of

38. On the precise meaning of this term, see my "*Hora'at ha-Talmud ba-Masoret ha-Ḥinnukhit ha-Sefaradit*," *Shebile ha-Ḥinnukh* 25 (1975), p. 183 n. 28.
39. For an in depth study of its development and principal elements, see Chaim Zalman Dimitrovsky, "On the Pilpulistic Method," *Salo Wittmayer Baron Jubilee Volume*, Hebrew Section (Jerusalem: American Academy for Jewish Research, 1974), pp. 111–181. Unfortunately, scholars have abstained from comparing this type of casuistry with that of the scholastics. For instance, there is little doubt that the famous '*chiluk*' ('distinction'), one of the essential terms of *pilpul*, is nothing but *distinction* – a basic term in scholastic dialectics borrowed from classical rhetoric.
40. "Methods of Teaching the Talmud," p. 123.
41. Ibid, p. 125. On the way the Talmud was taught in the East, see ibid., p. 129.

Bonn (1140–1225), *Sefer 'Or Zarua'* by R. Isaac ben Moses of Vienna (ca. 1180-ca.1250), and *Sefer Miṣvot Gadol* by R. Moses ben Jacob of Coucy (13th century).

The last period, from the 14th century till the end of the Middle Ages, focused on the composition of specialized works to assist the professional clergyman. These works collected the local customs and views on such diverse topics as circumcision, the writing of a scroll of the Tora, permitted and prohibited foods, and the preparation of legal contracts.[42]

A major consequence of the relativization of the text was the emergence of the charismatic leader. Since the text could no longer serve as an objective criterion, there was a need for a special type of leadership which could determine the content of Judaism. These were men endowed with supernatural powers. They had direct access to God, the angels, and the entire gamut of the supernatural.[43] Some bore the title *nabi* ('prophet'). These men could ascend to heaven and consult with the ministering angels (*mal'akhe ha-sharet*) and all types of supernatural beings.[44] One such *nabi* was the celebrated R. Jacob Tam (1090–1171), who would ascend in a dream to heaven and deliberate with celestial beings. On one occasion, he summoned Moses himself, who appeared to him and conceded the argument.[45] This power was shared by some of his disciples. One of them was the celebrated R. Isaac ben Samuel of Dampierre (d. ca. 1185), known as 'Isaac the Elder,' who would ascend to heaven and confer with the 'ministering angels' (*mal'akhe ha-sharet*).[46] There were many who formulated legal queries in their dreams (*she'elat ḥalom*), and received

42. See Israel Ta-Shma, "*Qavvim le-'Ofyah shel Safrut ha-Halakha be-Ashkenaz ba-Me'ot ha-Yod-'Alef-Yod-Gimal,*" *Alei Sefer* 4 (1977), pp. 20–41.
43. On this topic see the magistral essay by Abraham Heschel, "Inspiration in the Middle Ages," *Alexander Marx Jubilee Volume*, Hebrew Section (New York: The Jewish Theological Seminary of America, 1950), pp. 175–208.
44. See ibid., pp. 180–190.
45. See ibid., pp. 182–184.
46. See ibid., p. 184. For other similar cases, see ibid. ff.

authoritative replies from heaven. One such individual was R. Jacob de Mervaise [or Marvege] (12th and 13th centuries). He published these questions and answers in a book, *She'elot wu-Tshubot min ha-Shamayyim* ('Questions and Answers from Heaven'), (ed. R. Reuben Margoliot Jerusalem: Mossad Harav Kook, 1957). All these men were in possession of *Ruwaḥ ha-Qodesh* ('Holy Spirit'), and thus were infallible. How else can one explain that every stroke of their pen could contain such a precise and wondrous wisdom as was attributed to their writings?[47] Indeed, the acclaimed Rabad proclaimed "that the Holy Spirit appeared in our School," and therefore he was incapable of error.[48] Hence, the function of incantations, mystical lore, and the occult in general.[49]

In sum, Ashkenazic communities totally identified with the ideal Talmudic society. Consequently, their literary efforts were directed toward the accommodation and fitting of this ideal to the actual circumstances of their region and times. The relation society-text was to be made via the ideal society of Talmudic times. No efforts were needed to directly address the reality behind the ideal, or to understand the people as they really were. Instead, the text of the classical sources was relativized and made to fit the new circumstances. Relativization of the text involves suppression of critical knowledge. Submission to a higher authority, preferably in the form of a charismatic leader, rather than critical knowledge or a humanistic interpretation of the text, became the essential ingredient by which the individual could partake in the awe-inspiring power of the Book.

---

47. Cf. ibid. pp. 193–195; and "*Yedi'ot Ḥadashot 'al Tosafot Gornish,*" pp. 85–86.
48. *Lulab* 8:5; cf. *Bet ha-Beḥira* 6:15; and his *Teshubot wu-Psaqim*, # 211, p. 263. See "Inspiration in the Middle Ages," pp. 192–193.
49. Cf. "Inspiration in the Middle Ages," pp. 190–208.





# Section IV

## Chapter 13

## After the Middle Ages: Consolidating Old Values and Ideas

After the Middle Ages, Jews did not develop new cultural and literary strategies. The basic two strategies forged in Sepharad and Ashkenaz continued to dominate Jewish intellectual and spiritual life. The flurry of literary and religious activities in the 16th and 17th centuries, by both Sepharadim and Ashkenazim, were offshoots of basic ideas, premises, and systems current in medieval times. As a result of the numerous Jewish expulsions from Western Europe, beginning with France and Germany and culminating in the final edict of Expulsion from Spain in 1492, the ancient Jewish communities were destroyed. A demographic change thus took place whereby most of the Jewish population moved from West to East (Poland, Hungary, as far as Russia, and the Ukraine in Europe; North Africa and the Ottoman Empire in the Orient). This situation brought together Jews from different regions and cultural temperaments. Through the Mediterranean basin, North Africa, and the Middle East, the newcomers settled in ancient and venerable communities, some of which were the bearers of different traditions and customs. Hence the need for consolidation, characterizing Jewish intellectual activity from the 16th century on, in which the major ideas, trends, and institutions of the Middle Ages were finally shaped and formulated.

An important development during this period was a new codification of the Law by the Sephardic communities. The encounter of disparate traditions and methodologies, brought about by the different expulsions, had the potential to result in social unrest and discord. To avoid this danger, there was a need to establish a supreme criterion that could serve as the ultimate legal canon for all Israel. This goal was accomplished by Maran Joseph Caro (1488–1575) – one of the most brilliant legal minds in Jewish history. In the *Shulḥan 'Arukh* (Venice, 1565), he codified all the laws that the Jewish Nation in Exile needed for self-government. Rather than imposing a peculiar regional view or a local tradition, he established a symbolic 'Jewish High Court' representing the supreme legal criteria of *Kelal Yisra'el* ('the Community of Israel'), including both Sepharadim and Ashkenazim. He chose as members of this 'Court' R. Isaac Alfasi, whose code was the highest authority in North Africa, Maimonides, whose code was the law in the Middle East and many regions in Sepharad, and R. Asher, whose code was the highest authority in Ashkenaz and some circles of Sepharad. Whenever they coincided, Maran would codify the law accordingly. In cases of conflict, he would follow the opinion of the majority. Whenever there was no majority, as when one of these authorities did not formulate an opinion, the views of other legal masters were considered. Soon, the *Shulḥan 'Arukh* was recognized as the supreme legal authority by all Sephardic Jewry. Written in a lucid and unambiguous style, it was directly accessible to the people and became the staple of Sephardic education. Thus, the process of judicial de-bureaucratization which began in antiquity was brought to a final conclusion. In conformity with the anti-clerical and anti-authoritarian trends of old Sepharad, direct access to such a code freed the people from the arbitrariness and authoritarianism of the clergy and communal bureaucracies.[1] Accordingly, Sephardic Jewry never experienced anti-religious feelings or exploded into schismatic movements. As a result of the firm theoretical and institutional basis of the judiciary system, legal writings and institutions continued to flourish till the present.[2]

The codification of Jewish Law by the *Shulḥan 'Arukh* ran contrary to the legal traditions and ideologies of Ashkenaz on two closely related points. First, the idea of a uniform law, equally binding on all, clashed with the notions of regional and ethnic variety, folklore, and usage, developed over the centuries. Second, direct access to the law on the part of the faithful would severely curb the power of the religious authorities. Three of the most eminent rabbis of Ashkenaz, each making use of a different literary style, responded to the challenge of codification. R. Moses Isserles (1525 or 1530–1572) – the most distinguished legal mind produced in Ashkenaz since medieval times – appended a large number of *haggahot* ('emendations') to the

1. This did not mean that legal experts could not challenge a decision of Maran; they often did. It meant, however, that it could not be done arbitrarily, on flimsy or authoritarian grounds. This compelled the legal expert to expose his reasoning and formulate the legal theory and precedents warranting such a departure. Thus, the enormous volume and high quality of legal literature generated by Sepharadim. On the judicial basis of the *Shulḥan 'Arukh* and its subsequent acceptance, see my "*Yaḥas Ḥakhme ha-Sefaradim le-Samkhut Maran ke-Poseq*," *R. Yosef Qaro* (Jerusalem: Mossad Harav Kook, 5739/1979), pp. 189–197. For a further exploration of this subject, see the very valuable articles by Meir Benayahu, in *Asufot* 3 (1989).
2. On the quality of this literature in modern times, see my "Lessons for our day from Sephardic Halakhic Sources," *Proceedings of the Rabbinical Assembly*, 1978, pp. 57–73.

*Shulḥan 'Arukh*. In this manner, he simultaneously registered the local customs and views and de-authorized the *Shulḥan 'Arukh*. R. Solomon Luria (ca. 1510–1573) used his commentaries to the Talmud as a stage to argue against the methodology and legal opinions of Maran. The most successful approach to de-authorize the *Shulḥan 'Arukh* was perfected by R. Shabbetai Cohen (1621–1663) – an outstanding jurist. In his critical notes, known as *Shakh* (the *Sifte Kohen*), he examined some of the controversies between Maran and R. Isserles, as well as other legal views and opinions, and concluded with his own decisions. Soon, scores of similar works appeared, designed to question, criticize, and pass comment on the *Shulḥan 'Arukh*. In Ashkenazic literary tradition, interpretation displaces the text. The numerous commentaries, notes, and emendations succeeded in de-authorizing the *Shulḥan 'Arukh* – necessitating thereby submission to local authorities on all matters related to ritual, law, and custom. Never again was the *Shulḥan 'Arukh* reprinted alone. It is now printed surrounded on all sides by incisions, emendations, and critical notes, stifled and de-authorized by 'commentaries.' Very few commentaries, however, were attached to the *Bet Yosef*, a previous work written by Maran which was the basis for the codification of the *Shulḥan 'Arukh*. It is the work *par excellence* on Rabbinic jurisprudence, and a must for all those seriously interested in the codification of Jewish law. In that work, all legal sources and opinions were meticulously analyzed and catalogued. The fact that these 'commentaries' were not published separately but were attached to a code of law, where in depth discussion of the subject is impossible (rather than to the *Bet Yosef*, a work conducive to legal analysis), is indicative of the tendency to de-authorize codes of law.

The consolidation and reformulation of medieval institutions and ideas continued in Ashkenaz during the 18th century. The Hasidic movement, founded by the legendary R. Israel Ba'al Shem Ṭov (ca. 1700–1760), known affectionately as the Besht, came to emphasize and reformulate the pietistic and mystical elements first developed in Medieval Germany. As had their medieval counterparts, they, too, saw in the charismatic leader the highest expression of religious authority. By emphasizing these elements over those of a strictly legal nature (halakha), they further expanded de-authoritarian tendencies to include the realm of the juridical, rather than codification *per se*. Hence, the fierce opposition that they elicited from the local Rabbinic establishment.[3]

New directions in the Jewish world came as a direct result of Spinoza. He was eminently the most anti-Book Jewish thinker in modern times. As we will see in the following chapters, his major objective was the elimination of the Book and its substitution by the State. In his *Theologico-Political Treatise* (1670) he denied the claims for divine authority based on the text of Scripture and religious tradition. Overtly, the aim was to break the grid 'theology-philosophy' initiated by Philo, and later appropriated by the Church fathers. In reality, it was to break the grid 'Church-State' and to accomplish the secularization of Western man – an ideal finally realized with the French Revolution.[4] In this way, new possibilities opened for the Jew, where the society-text relationship could now be replaced by the relationship society-State.

3. The Hasidic movement generated an enormous amount of literature, comprising about 3,000 items. More importantly, basic elements of their teachings were interpreted and incorporated into mainstream Jewish thought by two of the most outstanding thinkers of our generation, Martin Buber (1878–1965) and Abraham J. Heschel (1907–1972).
4. On the impact of Spinoza on the French Revolution, see Daniel Mornet, *Les origines intellectuelles de la Révolution Française* (Paris: Armand Colin, 1933); and Paul Vernière, *Spinoza et la pensée Française avant la Révolution*, 2 vols. (Paris: P. U. F., 1954).

# Chapter 14
# From Book to book: Spinoza and Subversive Hermeneutics

Essentially, the biblical criticism of Spinoza is the transformation of the Book (an absolute text) into *a* book (a relative text). The strategy deployed in the development of biblical criticism and the collapse of the Book consisted in switching from a synchronic analysis of the text to a purely diachronic analysis.[5] Ferdinand de Saussure (1857–1913) observed that all value systems (economics, law, linguistics, etc.) may be studied diachronically, that is in terms of the development of some of its elements through successive stages, or synchronically, in terms of its actual states. Diachrony corresponds to the vertical axis of the system, and it is concerned with the individual elements as they successively unfold through time. Synchrony corresponds to the horizontal axis of the system, that is, to those static aspects at any one time "that bind together the coexisting terms and form a system in the collective mind" of those directly participating in it. (For example, one may either study the *history* of the law of evidence, or its actual *state* and application in the Court of Justice.) One of the most important conditions of these two axes is that they are mutually irreducible, and cannot be introjected into the other. Thus, when examining an element diachronically, one must totally suppress synchrony, and vice

5. And then proceed to project the elements of the diachronic axis onto the study of the synchronic axis, see below.

versa. For example, when using the French negation *pas,* one must suppress its historical identity with the substantive "step."[6] Structurally, the flaw with the type of criticism generated by Spinoza is the application of the values and notions peculiar to the diachronic axis to the synchronic axis of the text. As with grammarians of the type of Franz Bopp (1791–1867), this methodology involves constant straddling between the specific states of a system (synchronic axis) and its successions (diachronic axis).[7] It is an absolute condition for the reader of the Book – of *any* book, whether Dante's *Inferno* or Dumas' *The Three Musketeers* – to approach the system synchronically: as a static structure whose coexisting terms form a total pattern. The projection of the diachronic axis onto the static aspects of a text, a la Spinoza or a la Bopp, is disruptive: it functions as anti-Book, transforming it into an atextual oxymoron. Once removed from its synchronic apparatus, the elements of the text could be subjected to subversive hermeneutics, i.e., they could be used to assail the static structure of the text as it coexists in the collective mind of the reader. This leads into one of the most significant aspects of Spinoza's literary theory: the relation of hermeneutics to power.

Consistent with the view that a text ought to be interpreted in agreement with the mind of the author, Spinoza maintained that the legal texts of a nation can only be interpreted by the duly appointed authority. To permit individuals or self-appointed bodies to interpret these texts would result in the termination of the state.[8]

At the same time, Spinoza maintained that he could interpret the Hebrew Scripture 'objectively,' that is, outside the structure binding together the coexisting terms of the system in the collective mind of the Jewish people. Assuming the possibility of absolute objectivity and neutrality, Spinoza claimed that he could examine the Hebrew

---

6. See *Golden Doves*, pp. xiv-xv.
7. See ibid., p. xv.
8. See his *A Political Treatise*, trans. R. H. M. Elwes (New York: Dover Publications, 1951), III, 3, 4, 7.

Bible "in a careful, impartial" fashion,[9] regardless of the professed beliefs of the authors. This view posits the possibility of a total 'innocent reading.'[10] Anticipating nineteenth century Jewish scholarship (*Wissenschaft des Judentums*), Spinoza maintained that Jewish texts could be interpreted on the basis of purely objective data, as natural phenomena in the physical sciences.[11] Negating the synchronic axis of value-systems, he declared that the "method of interpreting Scripture, does not widely differ from the method of interpreting nature – in fact, it is almost the same."[12]

We can now proceed with a critical question: On what grounds can there be a distinction between texts such as those written by Spinoza, that must be interpreted in agreement with the professed views of the author, that is, synchronically, and biblical texts, which are to be interpreted on the basis of 'objective' data alone? The question is compounded by the fact that Spinoza recognized that the Scripture was the legal text of the Jewish nation. In accordance with Jewish tradition, he maintained that the Bible constituted "the law of the individual Hebrew state" and it was binding only on the Jews.[13] The reason for this was that it was "revealed and ordained to the Jews only."[14] Since the Scripture is the national text of the Jew, it should follow that it may be interpreted by the Jewish authorities alone. Accordingly, we may ask: On what grounds can one distinguish between national texts, which may be interpreted only by the duly appointed

9. *A Theologico-Political Treatise*, 'Preface,' p. 8.
10. On this type of reading see *Golden Doves*, p. xiii.
11. Obviously, even 'empirical' data and scientific observations are conditioned by purely subjective factors. See Jeremy Campbell, *Grammatical Man* (New York: Simon and Schuster, 1982), p. 49.
12. *A Theologico-Political Treatise*, VII, p. 99. Professor Strauss, (*Persecution and the Art of Writing*, p. 146) remarked that for Spinoza, "understanding the Bible consisted not in understanding the Biblical authors exactly as they understood themselves but in understanding them better than they understood themselves." He never explained, however, in what way, precisely, it was 'better.'
13. *A Theologico-Political Treatise*, 'Preface,' p. 8.
14. Ibid., III, p. 47.

authority, and those of the Jewish people that could be interpreted by a self-appointed philosopher or Church?

Spinoza's theory of biblical hermeneutics is premised on the belief that might is right. Projecting traditional Christian doctrine, he maintained that since the Jewish people have no might, as was amply demonstrated by countless pogroms and expulsions, they ceased to constitute a nation. Therefore, unlike other national texts, Jewish texts need not be interpreted by a duly constituted authority. Spinoza made clear in the Preface to the *Theologico-Political Treatise* that for him the Jewish nation had ceased to exist. The Law, he declared, is no longer binding "even on Hebrews after the downfall of their nation."[15] Therefore, in accordance with Christian doctrine, Spinoza put forward the thesis that the election of Israel was 'temporal,' and that it had ceased to exist as a nation.[16] To make sure that no one would regard Jewish survival as a sign of divine providence towards Israel, he deliberately altered Spanish history,[17] arguing that Jewish survival was the effect of gentile hatred.[18]

Spinoza's literary theory constitutes a repudiation of Hebrew political thinking. For Spinoza, it is the nation – a people with the *power* to control their public and private government – that transforms *a book* into *the Book*. For Jews, right, in the form of a bilateral covenant – not power – is might: the Book gives the people their national status (see above chs. 2, 7). Therefore, as long as there is a Book, there is a nation of Israel, with full political authority and intellectual autonomy. Were one to consider this view, then the whole premise of the *Theologico-Political Treatise* and the *Ethics* collapses.

15. Ibid., 'Preface,' p. 8.
16. See ibid., III, pp. 54–56.
17. I have developed this point in my forthcoming book, *In the Shadow of History: Iberian Jews and Conversos at the Dawn of Modernity* (New York: SUNY Press), chapter 9, sect. X. Cf. Y. H. Yerushalmi, "*Dibre Spinoza 'al Qiyyum ha-'Am ha-Yehudi,*" *Ha-'Aqademiya ha-Le'ummit ha-Yisra'elit le-Madda'im*, vol. 6, fas. 10 (Jerusalem, 5743/1983), pp. 189–190.
18. *A Theologico-Political Treatise*, III, pp. 55–56.

All the ancillary concepts developed by Spinoza, such as the identity of God and nature, the superiority of Jesus over Moses, the impossibility of miracles, the mortality of the soul, etc., would be reduced to inconsequential views surreptitiously masked as 'innocent' readings of somebody else's Book.

The validity of Spinoza's theory of hermeneutics hinges on whether the Jewish people are a nation. Only by conceding that there is no longer a people of the Book does *the* Book become *a* book. The function of (subversive) hermeneutics is not to bring about the downfall of the Book – the transformation Book-book is a purely political process – but merely the recasting of the elements of the Book in terms of the new political reality.

# Chapter 15
# The Place of the State in the Bookless Society

The alternative to the people-Book relationship is people-State. Since Spinoza conceived of the 'State' as an absolute autonomous entity, rather than in terms of some transcendental structure of values (otherwise it would be reducible to a Book and not be absolutely sovereign), he postulated the belief that sovereignty and right are the effect of power. He who has power has sovereignty, and vice versa.[19]

Power has cosmological value.[20] Consistent with this view is his belief that power and virtue are synonymous, "By virtue and power I understand the same thing."[21]

The preceding bears directly on Spinoza's concept of the origin of the state. To form the state, each individual must cede his natural right.[22] The state is the effect of either the implicit or historical transference by the people of their natural rights to the sovereign. Spinoza took the Jewish concept of *berit* ('covenant'), contracted by God

---

19. Even God is absolutely sovereign because He is absolutely powerful; cf. *A Theologico-Political Treatise*, XVI, p. 200.
20. See Gilles Deleuze, *Spinoza: Practical Philosophy*, trans. Robert Hurley (San Francisco: City Lights Books, 1988), p. 102. On this basic concept, see the enlightened discussion by Harry A. Wolfson, *Spinoza* (Cambridge, Mass.: 1934), vol. 2, pp. 195–208.
21. *Ethics*, IV, def. 8, p. 191.
22. *Ethics*, IV, n. 2, pp. 216–217. Cf. *A Political Treatise*, III, 3.

and the Jewish people, as the paradigm of democratic transference of power by the people to the sovereign. Therefore, the ideal form of transference is that of a democracy: "A body politic of this kind is called a Democracy, which may be defined as a society which wields all its power as a whole."[23] 'Democracy' concerns the *transference* of power, not the *actual* government, by the people. Since *A Political Treatise* is incomplete, it is not known what Spinoza meant by 'democracy,' or how he intended to organize it.[24] There is little doubt, however, that within his 'democratic' state, there was no absolute equality, and that power continued to play a determining role. Hierarchical differentiations are intrinsic to the Bookless society. Horizontality is the function of the Book (see above ch. 2). Evidence to this is the position he allotted women. Since might is right, Spinoza regarded women as inferior, insisting that they were objects of lust and unfit for political life. Projecting deeply anti-feminine prejudices, he reasoned:

> But if by nature women were equal to men, and were equally distinguished by force of character and ability, in which human power and therefore human right chiefly consist; surely among nations so many and different some would be found, where both sexes rule alike, and others, where men are ruled by women, and so brought up, that they can make less use of their abilities. And since this is nowhere the case, one may assert with perfect propriety, that women have not by nature equal right with men: but that they necessarily give way to men, and that thus it cannot happen, that both sexes should rule alike,

23. *A Theologico-Political Treatise*, XVI, p. 205.
24. For his definition of democracy, see *A Theologico-Political Treatise*, XVI, p. 205; *A Political Treatise*, II, 17, p. 292. He believed it to be "the most natural, and the most consonant with individual liberty," *A Theologico-Political Treatise*, XVI, p. 207. There are fewer than one hundred lines on democracy, see *A Political Treatise*, XI, pp. 385–387. Probably because of his particular relationship with de Witt, he was on the side of republicanism and aristocracy, see ibid., VIII, 44, pp. 367–368.

> much less that men should be ruled by women. But if we further reflect upon human passions, how men, in fact, generally love women merely from the passion of lust, and esteem their cleverness and wisdom in proportion to the excellence of their beauty, and also how very ill-disposed men are to suffer the women they love to show any sort of favor to others, and other facts of this kind, we shall easily see that men and women cannot rule alike without great hurt to peace.[25]

Spinoza's idea of the 'state,' will become evident upon considering his notion of sovereignty, and the power that he arrogated to the above mentioned 'body politic.'[26] Spinoza maintained that whereas the people are subjected to the absolute power of the sovereign,[27] the sovereign remains in the state of nature and is bound to no laws. Because his power is unlimited, his rights, too, are unlimited: the sovereign is free to compel his subjects to do whatever he wants. Since power is the ultimate basis for all political right, it is absolutely immaterial whether the people transferred their natural rights to the sovereign willingly or under coercion. In all cases, the right of the sovereign is commensurate with his power: "Sovereigns only possess this right of imposing their will, so long as they have the full power to enforce it."[28] It makes absolutely no difference how the power was obtained.[29]

Sovereignty is unlimited and indivisible.[30] The sovereign cannot be bound by the people or by any law.[31] Since the sovereign is above the law he can do no wrong, either to others or to the people whom he governs. Therefore, there cannot be any justification for opposing

25. *A Political Treatise*, XI, 4, p. 387.
26. On this fundamental concept in Spinoza, see Louis Adelphe, *De la notion de la souveranité dans la politique de Spinoza* (Nancy: Crepin, 1910).
27. 'Sovereign' is understood here as the person or body of people exercising supreme authority, see *A Political Treatise*, III, 1 and IV, 1.
28. *A Theologico-Political Treatise*, XVI, p. 205.
29. Ibid., pp. 204–205.
30. see *A Political Treatise*, III, 3.
31. *A Theologico-Political Treatise*, XVI, p. 205. Cf. ibid., II, 15 and III, 2.

the sovereign: "I recognize no difference whether such an attempt should be followed by public loss or by public gain."[32] A consequence of Spinoza's concept of sovereignty is that civil obedience is identical to military obedience. A soldier who abandons his post, even to defeat the enemy, must be put to death because he had "infringed the rights of his commander."[33] Similarly, if anyone attempts without the sovereign's

> consent, to execute any public enterprise, even though the state might (as we said) reap benefit therefrom, such person has nonetheless infringed the sovereign's right, and would be rightly punished for treason.[34]

Since the sovereign is above the law, it is impossible for him to do anything wrong: "Wrong is conceivable only in an organized community: nor can it ever accrue to subjects from any act of the sovereign, who has the right to do what he likes."[35] Any attempt, for whatever reason, to wrest power away from the sovereign is an act of treason, providing that it *failed*. Concerning the punishment due to those who attempted to overthrow the sovereign, he wrote: "I say, *has attempted*, for if punishment were not to overtake him till he had succeeded, it would often come too late, the sovereign rights would have been acquired or transferred already."[36]

Within Spinoza's political system there is no room for individual conscience. The subject is duty bound to violate his individual conscience and to act according to the dictates of the sovereign, "And

32. Ibid., p. 209.
33. Ibid.
34. Ibid.
35. Ibid., p. 208. The sovereign can do 'wrong' only in the order of the pragmatic, see, *A Political Treatise*, IV, 4–6.
36. *A Theologico-Political Treatise*, XVI, p. 209.

so, however iniquitous the subject may think the commonwealth's decisions, he is nonetheless bound to execute them."[37]

The rulers remain in the state of nature even in relation to Divine law and "they may do whatever they like."[38] The only limits to the sovereign's authority is the fear of armed insurrection.[39] The limits of authority are a matter of prudence, rather than law, lest they turn the people's natural fear of the sovereign "into indignation and the civil state into a state of enmity."[40]

One may object that the citizens of such a State are reduced to total slavery and abjection. Spinoza addressed this issue. *Real* 'freedom' consists, precisely, of obeying what the state orders: "He alone is free who lives with free consent under the entire guidance of reason."[41] By "reason" the dictates of the state are meant.[42]

---

37. *A Political Treatise*, III, 5, pp. 302–303.
38. *A Theologico-Political Treatise*, XVI, p. 210.
39. See *A Political Treatise*, IV, 4–6; and cf. VII, 2. This is a consequence of Spinoza's view that sovereignty rests on power. Similarly, there is a symmetric relationship between the sovereign and the people: the people *fear* the sovereign, see ibid. III, 3, and the sovereign *fears* the people. Madeleine Francès, "La libertè politique, selon Spinoza," pp. 317–337, misinterpreted these passages to mean that, somehow, Spinoza is thus requiring the approval of the people and the submission of the sovereign to the consent of its citizens; or that somehow he favored peoples' revolutions. Nothing could be further from the truth. His close association with de Witt would preclude such sympathies. All Spinoza was saying is that since the sole basis of political authority is power, if the sovereign abuses his *actual* power, he may provoke the people to revolt against him and wrest away his power. It is for the same reason –and not because he believed that the sovereign should share his authority with the people – that he counseled the authorities not to force on the people those beliefs and actions that would cause them to rebel, see *A Political Treatise*, III, 8; IV, 6.
40. Ibid., IV, 4, p. 311; cf. 6, p. 312.
41. *A Theologico-Political Treatise*, XVI, p. 206. Cf., *A Political Treatise*, II, 7, 11; VII, 2. For some interesting insights into Spinoza's notion of freedom, see Robert Misrahi, "Le droit et la liberté politiques chez Spinoza," *Mélanges de Philosophie et de Littérature Juives*, 1–2 (1956–7), pp. 153–169.
42. *A Political Treatise*, III, 6, pp. 303.

# Chapter 16
# Judaism without a Book

Eighteenth century Europe was marked by major political turmoil that resulted from the collapse of the ecclesiastical society lingering from medieval times. The result was the rise of secularism and the separation of Church and State. These events affected the thought patterns and feelings of all Europeans, Jews included.

Moses Mendelssohn (1729–1786) ranked among the most erudite and sophisticated thinkers of his time. Better than anyone else, he realized that the political dimension of Israel was an obstacle for the integration of the Jew into the secular State. Tacitly accepting Spinoza's view concerning the demise of the Jewish nation, he sought to transform *the Book* into *a book*, thus allowing the Jew to integrate into the emerging Society/State. In his epoch-making *Jerusalem* (1783), he laid down the foundations for the distinction between the political elements of Judaism, which he surrendered, and those of a religious nature, which he upheld.[43] When Mendelssohn relinquished all political dimensions, such as the right to excommunicate and to appoint judges, and recognized the State as the supreme political authority of the Jews, he effectively expelled the God of Israel from the realm of the political: Judaism would now become another religion of the

43. On the political ideas of this work, see Nathan Rotenstreich, "Mendelssohn's Political Ideas," *Mordecai M. Kaplan Jubilee Volume*, Hebrew Section (New York: The Jewish Theological Seminary of America, 1953), pp. 237–247.

State.[44] This was precisely what Napoleon sought from French Jewry in his famous *Sanhedrin* on May 30, 1806.[45]

Judaism without a Jewish nation is a religion without a Book, and vice versa: Jews without a Book are only an ethnic group. In the process of divesting Judaism from its political elements, the Jewish people become a community with no national bonds. Within the context of the State, the Book becomes a book. Thus, whereas traditionally the people of the Book had a relation with a state, a folk with a book would be integrated by the State. Biblical criticism subsequently advanced by Protestant theologians, and enthusiastically acclaimed by Jewish literati, brought about the de-textualization of the Hebrew Scripture. In this fashion, the Tora became un-book: an unreadable jumble of fragmentary scribbles whipped together by witless clerks. 'Revelation' replaced 'prophecy,' and in this fashion could be reduced to general principles that may serve as tools of manipulation. The de-textualization of the Tora put an end to the people-Book relationship. From now on, the State would be recognized as the only absolute and autonomous entity. In this specific sense, by advocating that Judaism become a religion of the State, Mendelssohn was confirming Spinoza's ideal of a Book-free society where the State could dominate solely and absolutely. One of the effects of this vision was the mass participation of Jews in all political movements crisscrossing the European horizon.

Mendelssohn's writings gave birth to two intimately related movements: Reform and *Haskala*. Although Mendelssohn himself was

---

44. This is the ideology adopted by the extreme-right *ḥaredi* movement. By relegating the national and political institutions of Israel to eschatological times and refusing to recognize Jewish national institutions, they renounced the political dimensions of Israel, becoming a religion just like Christianity, etc. Thus, the function of anti-Zionism among these Jews.

45. See "Early Zionist Ideals Among Sepharadim in the Nineteenth Century," *Judaism* 25 (1976), p. 1365. Israel Jacobson saw in Napoleon's *Sanhedrin* a fulfillment of Mendelssohn's vision of Judaism. There are grounds to believe that he was the one who inspired Napoleon to form the *Sanhedrin*, see Jacob Rothschild, "Jacobson, Israel," *Encyclopaedia Judaica*, vol. 9, cls. 1240–1241.

an observant Jew, Israel Jacobson (1768–1828), Samuel Holdheim (1806–1860), Abraham Geiger (1810–1874), and others recognized him as the founder of Reform Judaism, and their spiritual leader and mentor. By conceding the political dimension of Israel, the Book became a book, opening thereby the possibility of change and revision on the basis of ideology [=גדול הדור], rather than communal institutions. Their methodologies varied. The common agenda was to speed up the process of de-authorization and de-textualization of the Law.[46] The *Haskala* (Ashkenazic 'Enlightenment') movement, too, was initiated by Mendelssohn and his circle. Its objective was to establish the 'scholarly' bases that could advance the process of Jewish disintegration. This was accomplished by applying to Judaism the methods, theories, and terminologies developed in the Christian secular world, specifically in the anti-humanistic monolingualism of German idealism. Originally, these writers chose Hebrew to express and develop their new ideology. Although originating in Germany, this movement soon spread to Austria, Russia, and Poland. Their achievements, however, were wanting even by their own standards.

By 1819, there arose a more orderly approach to the study of Judaism, known as *Wissenschaft des Judentums* ('Jewish Science'). Unlike the writers of *Haskala*, these scholars wrote in German. Modern Jewish scholarship owes much of itself to this movement. Among its more distinguished representatives were Leopold Zuns (1794–1886), R. Solomon Judah Rapoport (1790–1867), Moritz Steinschneider (1816–1907), and Abraham E. Harkavi (1835–1919). Scores of scholars contributed to all branches of Jewish studies. Some initiated groundbreaking research that opened up new areas of investigation. Nonetheless, some of their ideas and methodology were flimsy. The confusion stemmed from the fact that they did not have a firm grip on either Western culture or their own Jewish tradition. An index of

46. Some sought to justify the new changes with classical sources, pointing to Jewish scholars in the Middle Ages. Others upgraded the old *pilpul* methodology by borrowing new 'scientific' terminology, such as 'evolutionary' and 'revolutionary.'

their intellectual orientation was their obsession with German idealism, particularly Hegel's, the most Christian and most anti-Jewish of all modern philosophers.[47] This obsession was one of the elements preventing them from appreciating other aspects of Western tradition, and from realizing the kind of cultural transformation made by Sephardic Jewry.[48]

In both methodology and aim, the *Haskala* and *Wissenschaft* movements were directly dependent on Spinoza. Not only did they approach their subject diachronically, but they also proceeded, *a la* Spinoza (and *a la* Bopp), to project those views onto the synchronic axis of Judaism.[49] Because they never understood the synchronic states of Judaism, they failed to have any clear understanding of the Tora as a total system. Ingenuously, they believed that they were dealing with "empirical facts."[50] The term *Wissenschaft* ('Science') came to express their conviction that they were studying the humanities as scientists do natural phenomena. Credulously, they believed that they were surveying uniform laws – universal and categorical –determining the cultural development of all humanity, regardless of geography and time. The 'facts' that fit these categories were 'essential' – whereas all the rest must be regarded as 'peripheral' and 'unimportant.' Societies failing to exhibit this type of 'progress' must be classified as 'backwards' and 'unrepresentative' of the 'true spirit' of Judaism.

Orthodoxy and Zionism are direct reactions to Reform Judaism

47. For many of them, particularly historians like Krochmal and Gudemann, to be 'scientific' meant simply to borrow some of Hegel's terminology. In the minds of many, Judaism would attain its greatest achievement if it only could be processed in Hegelian terms and categories.

48. Cf. *Golden Doves*, pp. xi-xvi.

49. Similarly, in our days, there are those who want 'to prove' the legitimacy of patrilineal descent in Judaism by interpreting some vague source in antiquity to this effect. This would be similar to someone arguing on behalf of slavery on the basis of legislation passed before 1864.

50. On one occasion, a distinguished Talmudic scholar confided in me, "I never deal in theory, only in empirical facts!" Out of charity, I refrained from pointing out to him that "empirical facts" are also grounded on theory.

and *Haskala*. Essentially, the issue dividing Orthodoxy from Reform and Conservative Judaism is the Book/book question, with its concomitant state/State (or vice versa). State/Book are mutually exclusive: the choices are either Book/state or State/book. Reform and Conservative Judaism reject the notion of a Book as a national text, in favor of a book as a religious (in the strict pagan, monolinguistic connotation) text. This choice permits full integration into the hierarchical apparatus of the State. Orthodoxy insists that the Book, as an absolute and total text, is the *sine qua non* of Judaism. It is this special type of horizontal society, possible only within the context of the Book, that marks the Jewish people apart. Because the Book society cannot integrate into a State, Jews are in existential Exile, i.e., longing for the Messianic Age in which a full national entity will be established in the Land of Israel. The difference between the Messianic state and all other States lies in its relation to the Book. The Messianic state must be circumscribed to the Book. The Book in its categoric textual dimension will encompass the political authorities as well as the national and social institutions. In this condition, it will be a *state* (lower case *s*), never a *State* (capital *S*); and a horizontal, never a hierarchical, society.

Originally, Zionism emerged as a response to the surrendering of the political dimension of Israel.[51] Subsequent events bitterly showed the consequences of entrusting the fate of the Jewish people to a State, or of integrating the hierarchical society of the modern State. Zionism is the most successful movement in modern Jewry. Aside from its immense political accomplishments, Zionism brought about one of the most profound social and intellectual revolutions in modern

51. Baron, Salo W. ed., *Freedom and Reason: Studies in Philosophy and Jewish Culture*. Elazar, Daniel J. "American Political Theory and the Political Notions of American Jews: Convergences and Contradictions," *Jewish Journal of Sociology*, 1967, pp. 5–24. Hadas, Moses "Recent Work in Ancient Politics," *Journal of the History of Ideas* 13 (1952), pp. 110–119. J.A.M. Meerloo, "The Crime of Menticide," *American Journal of Psychiatry*, 107 (1951), pp. 594–598: people need to be trained to political servitude, either by religion or through the family structure.

history. It was the catalyst for the revival of Hebrew, both as a literary language and as a means of communication throughout the Jewish world. It also resulted in the emergence of a Jewish press and periodicals in Hebrew as well as in local languages, promoting contact and cohesiveness throughout the Jewish world. It also produced a new literary movement. Modern Hebrew, from Bialik (1873–1934) to Agnon (1888–1970), is one of Zionism's most outstanding accomplishments.

At the ideological level, however, Zionism failed to realize the significance of the political dimension of Judaism. Because Zionism itself was the product of anti-Book States and highly hierarchical societies (Marxism and Socialism), it failed to understand the meaning of a state and society within the perimeters of the Book. Therefore, it could not articulate a Jewish political ideology. Dominated by notions of ethnicity and regionality, it confused the political philosophy of Jews with Jewish political philosophy.[52] Since it never developed a vision of Jewish national identity and social horizontality embracing *Kelal Yisra'el* ('the totality of Israel'), it was unable to provide the people intellectual and personal autonomy. At the organizational level, it never overcame the old notions of ethnical and regional hierarchy. Within that system, it is more relevant whom one knows than what one knows, and whether one came from Pinsk or Minsk, than his educational and professional qualifications. Instead of fostering autonomy and self-sufficiency, Zionistic ideology promoted Jewish dependency on the non-Jewish environment – semantically, economically, politically, and psychologically. It involved a constant looking over the nation's shoulder to find out "what gentiles would say of this?" (*ma yomeru ha-goyim*). The consequence of this behavior was that

52. Paradoxically, Zionism expected to foster Jewish identity by drawing on the values and ideologies of State-societies. Even when using Jewish symbols such as *Ṣion* ('Zion'), *Ge'ulla* ('Salvation'), *Shibat Ṣion* ('Return to Zion'), and *'Am Yisra'el* ('the People of Israel'), they were in fact conveying the partisan ideologies of Socialist and Marxist societies, furthering discord and division. Thus, it pitched non-religious against religious, left against right, Hebraists against Yiddishists and Bundists, etc., etc.

soon, the new State was treated by the nations of the world with the same type of deference with which Jews were treated in the Ghetto.

In sum, the anti-Book, pro-State, hierarchical ideology developed by Spinoza illustrates the alternative to the traditional Jewish text-society. This ideology became the point of contention for all subsequent Jewish movements.

# Forbidden Meditations

## Popular Essays on Unpopular Subjects

# Contents

# Introduction

*Joseph Faur*

I can't exactly determine the year, but it was sometime in either 2016 or 2017 when I first discovered a manuscript of *Forbidden Meditations* in my father's small *bet midrash* located in the basement of our home in Ra'anana. Upon finding this manuscript, written by my grandfather and previously unknown to the general public, I was exhilarated and immediately read it from cover to cover. At the time, I was a young man in my first or second year of pre-military *yeshiba* in Israel, and was accustomed to reading my grandfather's highly academic works. However, *Forbidden Meditations* was different, and stood out to me due to its simpler language and style, easily accessible to even the average reader.

After reading the manuscript of *Forbidden Meditations*, I had several questions for my grandfather. Firstly, I wanted to understand why he had never published it, especially considering that he had published so many other highly academic works. Secondly, I wanted to know if he would be open to the idea of publishing it at some point in the future. I knew that this would be a significant undertaking, but I was deeply interested in sharing this important work with a wider audience.

Regarding the unpublished status of *Forbidden Meditations,* I received various responses, the most convincing of which was that he had become occupied with other important projects. However, I suspect that the political conflict leading to his immigration to Israel in the fall of 1993, a difficult year for my grandfather, also played a role in his decision not to publish the book (which he first completed in December 1993). Interestingly, in 2009, the Ḥakham revisited the work, reorganized it, and added more content, making efforts to publish it. But for reasons unbeknownst to me, it ultimately remained unpublished.

As to my second question, whether my grandfather would be open to the possibility of publishing *Forbidden Meditations* in the future, he told me that he would be more than happy to see it published. At that time, however, we were working on getting three other unpublished works of his out into the world, so publishing *Forbidden Meditations* would just have to wait.

I am pleased and grateful that this waiting period has finally ended, and, after a huge amount of collaborative work and effort, we can now present *Forbidden Mediations* to the general public.

*Forbidden Meditations* may be seen as a manifesto that summarizes the key ideas and themes present throughout the Ḥakham's entire edifice of works, such as *The Horizontal Society, Homo Mysticus,* and *In the Shadow of History*. Each chapter of the book serves as somewhat of a condensed version of the subjects he delves into more deeply in his other works. (He previously even included a chapter titled "The Gospel According to the Jews," which he removed in the book's later edition, seemingly because he later decided to publish it as a separate book in 2012.) *Forbidden Meditations* is a holistic guide to Ḥakham Faur's worldview, providing readers with an overarching understanding of his ideas and how they relate to contemporary issues. By reading *Forbidden Meditations*, readers may gain a solid foundation in the

Ḥakham's thought, and be able to explore his other works with a deeper understanding and appreciation.

The style of *Forbidden Meditations* is unique in several ways when compared with the Ḥakham's other works. Firstly, as the Ḥakham himself noted, it is "written in a popular style," making it more accessible to a wider audience. Additionally, the book is "chock-full of anecdotes and autobiographical musings"[1] from throughout the Ḥakham's life, offering the reader a more comprehensive understanding of the Ḥakham's personal journey and his experience as a Sepharadi living in the modern world.

While the book delves into some of the seminal ideas presented in the Ḥakham's other works, it also has a more ambitious purpose: to give Jews and gentiles "the opportunity to understand what Judaism is all about." The book does so by proposing the following question: "Only recently did the West have the courage to look into 'archaic' cultures. Will it also have the courage to look into more progressive systems, namely Judaism?"[2]

Like his other works, *Forbidden Meditations* was ahead of its time. Its political ideology and philosophical ideas were not meant for the Jewish people of 1993. In my opinion, its ideas should be of great relevance and interest to the Jewish people of 2023.

While reading *Forbidden Meditations,* it was difficult for me to just overlook the distinct stylistic differences compared to the Ḥakham's other works. I delved into the book and sought to understand the motivations behind the Ḥakham's decision to make it more prosaic and easily understandable for a wider audience. I then came across the following paragraph:

> The Judaism I believe in and live by is the Judaism of my grandfather, Joseph Faur (ca. 1865–1950) … For centuries, the Judaism of my grandparents was the Judaism of Sephardic

1. Preface, page 1146.
2. Preface, p. 1137.

> Jewry in the Ottoman Empire. It barely survived the dawn of the 20th century... The first religious experience I remember was going with my grandfather to attend the *Seliḥot* services... Just imagine, a boy of about four getting up an hour and a half before dawn, quietly washing and dressing up, careful not to disturb the rest of the family... Outside, it was pitch black, the street lights having been long off. **Holding firmly onto my grandfather's hand**, we proceeded into the darkness toward the Synagogue, while I was jumping up and down all over, cheerful and unperturbed. It was during these walks that a special bond was forged between us. Many years later, when I was going for *Seliḥot* to the Synagogue *'Ole Suriya ve-Lebanon* in Haifa, with David Faur, my wife's grandfather, I recalled the times when my grandfather and I had ventured into the darkness of the night to pray.[3]

As I read this paragraph, tears came to my eyes as I was transported back to one of my own first religious experiences.

During my childhood, my grandfather often invited me to spend Shabbat at his house without my parents. As a child, I was not accustomed to spending Shabbat away from my family and it was not easy to persuade me to come, but I ultimately agreed to spend a Shabbat, and then more *Shabbatot*, with my grandparents.

My grandparents loved having me over for *Shabbatot* and pampered me with all kinds of delicious foods, taking warm care of me on each of my visits. Among the highlights from those *Shabbatot* were the delicious cooking of my grandmother, and the long walks on the beautiful beach boardwalk in Netanya with my grandmother and grandfather.

One Shabbat stands out in my memory. I was around seven or eight years old, and my grandfather excitedly told me that it was *Perashat Mishpaṭim* and that he was going to teach me the laws of *Neziqin*.

---

3. The Judaism of My Grandfather, p.1167.

His excitement and devotion in imparting this knowledge naturally made me, his grandson, eager to learn with him.

As my grandfather and I walked the lengthy route to the synagogue, he engaged me in a conversation about life, school, and my friends. But then he switched the conversation to the laws of *Neziqin*, reciting the *Mishnayot* of the first chapter of Tractate *Baba Qamma* by heart, and then asking me to repeat after him. In this way, he was fulfilling the commandment, "And tell them to your sons and your sons' sons" (Deut. 4:9), as well as the commandment to study Tora while "walking on your way" (Deut. 6:7).

Upon arriving at the synagogue of R. David Chelouche, a close friend of my grandfather, we first went over to kiss his hand. Then, my grandfather pulled out his Livorno book of *Mishnayot* and continued to instruct me in the *Mishna* by heart, as was customary in the Sephardic Jewish tradition.

As a child, I was an aspiring *ḥazzan*, so I was pleased when Rabbi Chelouche requested that I chant *Bamme Madliqin* (from chapter two of Tractate Shabbat, recited by Jews of most traditions every Friday night during *Qabbalat Shabbat*). I distinctly remember successfully chanting the first and second *Mishnayot*, but then surprisingly starting to fall asleep before getting to the third *Mishna*. At the time, I was puzzled by my sudden fatigue and felt embarrassed. In retrospect, I now understand that I was mentally drained from the intense Tora study in which my grandfather had engaged me during our walk to the synagogue and up until the start of the *tefilla*.

It was my grandfather who had initiated to forge the bond between us, a bond very much like the one that was forged between him and his own grandfather, Joseph Faur. As I reflect on the passage from *Forbidden Meditations* in which my grandfather describes holding firmly onto his grandfather's hand, I realized that even at a young age, he was clinging tightly to his grandfather's hand as a way to forge an eternal link with the traditions of the Judaism of Sepharad. In turn, by holding my hand tightly when I was a child, my grandfather was forging a similar eternal link between myself and the ancient traditions of Sephardic Jews.

I believe that the primary aim of *Forbidden Meditations* is to establish a connection or link between you, the reader, and those same traditions of the Judaism of Sepharad. Through the ideas and meditations presented by my grandfather in the book, readers will be able to connect with this chain of tradition and, as importantly, to explore and gain a deeper understanding of these traditions. In reading this book, I hope that each reader is not only given the opportunity to forge personal links with these beautiful traditions, but would also then be inspired to read and delve further into some of my grandfather's more technical works.

Tebet 15, 5783
January 8, 2023

# Preface

Use it or lose it. Well before their ingress into Western society, Jews heard praises of Western civilization, its culture, and its value system. Discursively, and at times directly, these praises projected a negative perception of Judaism. The notion that acceptance into the political and cultural body of the West is an act of 'Jewish Emancipation' is a harsh reminder that even enlightened gentiles regarded Judaism as a kind of serfdom. No wonder. For nearly two thousand years, Western society has heard about the 'perfidious' Jews, the 'ghastly' Pharisees, and the 'harshness' of the Law. 'Rabbinics' evokes something morbid and squalid. And the Tora – the 'Old Testament' in the parlance of Christianity – is perceived as an oppressive and heartless system, not only dead but deadly. Jews were muzzled. Adequate response was impossible. Not only did they not have the means to communicate their views, even if properly disseminated, it would result in further hatred – antisemitism, expulsion, and extinction.

Now, for the first time in two thousand years, Jews can speak freely about Judaism. They can either use this opportunity or lose it. Absence of response in a free society is tantamount to forfeiture. Conditioned to mental servitude, some secular Jews regard the questioning of Western values as an act of subversion, moral ingratitude, and the breaching of good taste. In fact, Jewish silence – that is, refraining to apply the *Jewish* value system and tradition to contemporary issues, rather than merely Jews expressing opinions as members of the general society – means surrendering the right to define the 'Jewishness' of the Judeo-Christian dimensions of modern society. Within such a context, Western culture becomes prescriptive and one-dimensional.

Jewish silence affects Jewish perception of Judaism. A characteristic of contemporary Jewry is the acceptance of popular Western culture and values as a given. Whether deliberately or unintentionally, Judaism is processed to conform to current Western ideology. The elements that cannot be properly processed are overlooked, or simply discarded as unimportant. From this perspective, Judaism appears marginal and haphazard: Everything that Judaism is purported to teach has already been developed more coherently in paperback literature. The outcome of this methodology is a 'Judaism' that does not conform to Jewish sources and traditions, and lacks both emotional resonance and genuine intellectual satisfaction, thus robbing both Jews and gentiles of the opportunity to understand what Judaism is all about.

This book is an idiosyncratic work. A principal taboo dominating Jewish thinking today is the prohibition to question the ultimate superiority of current Western ideology.

As the title of this book indicates, the essays presented here are of a forbidden nature – themes which are banned from discussion because complacency with basic Western doctrines might be disturbed and, worst of all, because they may show Jewish traditional thought in a positive light. Hence the subtitle. Those familiar with my works know that I don't write haphazardly; there are no random terms or inconsequential paragraphs. Although written in a popular style, chockfull of anecdotes and autobiographical musings, both the vocabulary and the style of this work are exact. The essays presented here focus on unpopular subjects – subjects that some would bar from polite conversation, especially Jews living in a gentile society. Ultimately, this book proposes the following question: "The West has only recently mustered the courage to look into 'archaic' cultures. Will it also have the courage to look into more progressive systems, namely Judaism?"

Some of the points raised in this book may seem harsh to Christian readers. Their forbearance is appreciated. I thought it wiser to let a note of anguish escape through some of these pages, than to try to conceal the pain of two thousand years of forced silence. The purpose is to initiate a dialogue and elicit a response – not to close, but rather begin a discussion.

Unless otherwise noted, all translations are mine.

J. F.
The First Night of the Feast of Lights
Kislev 25, 5754
December 8, 1993
Brooklyn, New York

# Introduction*

A fundamental premise of this work, already developed in my *Golden Doves With Silver Dots: Semiotics and Textuality in Rabbinic Tradition* (Bloomington: Indiana University Press, 1986), is that diverse cultures and languages think differently: What may appear as 'logical' and 'sensible' within one system, may be 'incomprehensible' and 'absurd' in another system. To understand a given culture from within means not only to know its language, basic key-concepts, and institutions, but, more importantly, its patterns of thought and feelings. Otherwise, we process that culture in terms alien to itself. The result is an oxymoron, incomprehensible to those living and participating in the culture we are trying to 'interpret' and 'illuminate.'

The central concern of this collection of essays is Jewish *mental* assimilation: the application of Western canons of thought to Jewish

* Editorial Note: The present work was first written by Ḥakham Faur in 1993, along with this introduction. In the "Introduction," he discusses the primary objective of each of the book's chapters, one by one, in the order in which the book was written at the time, as set forth herein. In 2009, he revisited the work and reorganized the order of the chapters. However, he never rewrote the introduction with the new chapter order in mind. We have chosen to publish the chapters of this book as Hakham Faur intended in his most updated version. Nevertheless, we chose to keep the Introduction in its original language, pointing out the chapter discrepancies as they are mentioned.

life, tradition and literature, and the inability to think in terms of Jewish patterns of thought and feeling. To illustrate, I have shown in the aforementioned book, that, unlike the Greeks who thought visually – 'seeing *is* believing' – the Jews thought primarily in auditory terms: '*Listen*, O, Israel.' Although there are casual references to appearances, the Hebrew Scripture and the Rabbis were not interested in the outer aspect of reality. For the Jewish people, 'seeing' is *not* 'believing.' People were not measured by the way they looked, but according to their actions and words. The Scripture and Rabbis elaborated on some of the most intimate details of Abraham and Sarah, and yet nobody thought it important to tell us the color of their eyes, or whether they were tall and slender or short and obese. For Jews, these were totally irrelevant details. The same applies to other visual aspects. The Rabbis did not prescribe a canonical uniform for the Jewish clergy. A rabbi was distinguished by his scholarship, manners, and moral behavior, not by his attire. The present notion that, 'the habit makes the rabbi,' is relatively modern. As will become evident from one of the essays that follows, the present trend to express 'Jewish identity' in terms of visual appearance is, in and of itself, the result of mental assimilation. This type of assimilation, more than anything else, impedes genuine comprehension of Judaism, affecting the quality of Jewish life and institutions.

The first essay, "Pomp and Pageantry,"* focuses on the peculiarities of Jewish thought and feelings. I designate the Jewish system of thought 'holistic,' meaning that, rather than extracting a single aspect of reality and examining it in isolation, Jews view things within their complete context. In mythical thinking, a given aspect of a culture or natural phenomenon is extracted and then transformed into something imperious and supernatural. This means that one cannot choose a single aspect of a culture or a human being and simply love it or hate it without taking into consideration the entire civilization and

* Editorial Note: In the presently published version, "Pomp and Pageantry" appears as chapter 5.

person. To take one obvious example: The Jewish mind cannot sing the praises of Greek art or Roman architecture without considering those civilizations' views on human rights, slavery, and their treatment of the alien and the destitute. I designate the ability to divorce one aspect of reality from the rest – like art and architecture from other facets of society – 'mythical thinking.' In such cultures, dissected reality is projected and, thereafter, manipulated to fit some archetypal model. Things are never perceived as themselves, but are transformed mythically into something else. Levi-Straus denoted this process "bricolage." In the same manner that a handy man "detaches the cogwheels of an old alarm clock, and *they can be used again* either for the same purpose or for a different one," archaic thought can 'detach' certain aspects of reality and incorporate them into a myth.[1]

An essential property of Jewish thought and feelings is individuation. Humans do not develop merely as individuals, separate but basically identical to everyone else, but rather each person individuates, becoming something different and unique. Thus, Jews are not only different from gentiles, but, more importantly, from each other. Because every human being is absolutely different and unique, no one is either superior or inferior to anyone else. According to this view, no single individual on his or her own can have total knowledge and fully understand the 'whole truth.' The welfare of society does not depend on a superior individual – as saintly and wise as he may be – but on *collective* efforts. It is only through team effort that 'truth' is grasped; and the welfare of humankind realized. This leads to a most revolutionary idea: "People of the Covenant" – a topic fully explored in the second essay.* There are two critical features to that society: equality before the Law, and the absence of social hierarchies. It will be seen that both these features are intimately related to each other.

A fundamental principle developed in my book *In the Shadow*

1. Claude Levi-Strauss, *The Savage Mind* (Chicago: Chicago University Press, 1970), p. 35.

* Editorial Note: This chapter, originally called "The Horizontal Society," was renamed "People of the Covenant," and was ultimately moved to chapter 3.

*of History: Jews and Conversos at the Dawn of Modernity* is the propensity to mimic the enemy. There is a special relationship between the persecutor and the persecuted whereby the persecuted absorbs some of the persecutors' personality and ideology. Maimonides (1135–1204) called attention to what I designate 'mental assimilation': "Our nation," he wrote, "is a wise, wholesome nation." However, as a result of our subjugation to "evil, ignorant people" who destroyed "our sages and books," we "became ignoramuses… we mixed with them, and we assimilated their views just like we assimilated their temper and demeanor."[2] This was particularly true in the European Middle Ages. Originally, Jews viewed other people horizontally. As a result of persecution and ensuing mental assimilation, some of the enemy's attitude was assimilated, and Jews began to view 'the other' in negative terms. At first, this negative attitude was restricted to 'gentiles'; Jewish perception of the *goy* was a mirror image of gentile perception of the *Juden*. Soon, it was passed on to 'other' Jews, who either 'thought' or 'looked' different. A 'different' view of Judaism than 'ours' is 'heresy' or 'illiteracy,' whereas other lifestyles are a sure sign of 'inauthenticity.' Within this hierarchical system, not all Jewish traditions are 'genuine,' or to be more precise, there are those which are more 'authentic' than others. 'Ours,' of course, is the most 'authentic.' The problems associated with this type of demeanor are examined in the third essay, "When Different is the Same and the Same is Different."*

The fourth essay, "The Iberian and German Experience,"** is an illustration of Jewish histories viewed horizontally. The major thrust is to show that some of the peculiarities of Sephardic history, including that of the *converso,* may be found in the history of modern Austrian and German Jewries. Many of the problems facing the Iberian *converso* trying to integrate into Christian society were met by assimilated Jews trying to integrate into the Secular world. There

2. *Guide,* II, 11. The translation is our own.

* Editorial Note: This is chapter 4 in Ḥakham Faur's updated edition.

** Editorial Note: Although this chapter was seemingly omitted in Ḥakham Faur's final version, in this edition we denoted it chapter 7.

are also parallels to the Christian/Secular strategies of antisemitism in medieval and modern times. Analogously, there were coinciding responses by the Jewish communities in both situations. This essay appeared in a shorter form in *Midstream*, June-July 1992.

What about the enemy? Unlike hierarchical societies, Judaism does not identify the 'alien' or the 'other' with the enemy. Unlike Christianity, and notwithstanding all the antisemitic rhetoric to the contrary, Judaism does not recognize the *religious* enemy. The only enemy that Judaism recognizes is the *political* enemy – specifically, one threatening the territorial integrity of the nation of Israel, or the physical wellbeing of the Jewish people. In this regard, it is important to remember that Judaism is a two-dimensional system: one theological and another political. Both dimensions are not analytically discrete, and are mutually conditioned by each other. Consequentially, the military victories of Israel are regarded as the victories of the Lord, the ultimate Savior and Protector of Israel. Since the Jewish political leader is not considered hierarchically superior, he has no right to forgive the political enemy. Forgiving the political enemy means incorporating his values and *becoming* him. It is a kind of *collaboration* with the enemy that may result in spiritual assimilation: Those who forgive the enemy will absorb their values and become them. Two examples come to mind: the metamorphosis of Saul becoming an 'Amaleqite king, and the metamorphosis of Ahab becoming a Syrian despot. The Jewish position on political enemies and its further implications are the subjects of the fifth essay, "Forgiving the Enemy, Loving the Enemy, Becoming the Enemy."*

Jews have been expecting the Messiah for over 2,000 years. To this end, they were exhorted to be more punctilious in their fulfillment of the Tora. Sinful behavior – perhaps the desecration of a commandment, or the collective oversight of some horrendous transgression – may be hindering the full redemption of Israel. What could that be? Maybe the *kosher* meat is not *kosher* enough? Perhaps some

* Editorial Note: In the present edition, this chapter is chapter 8.

wording in the liturgy became corrupt with the passing of time and needs to be amended? Could it be that there is some sort of mystical ritual that, if properly executed, would end the Exile and conjure the Messiah? For centuries, Jewish preachers and exegetes tried to pinpoint the precise offense that, if corrected, will precipitate the Messianic Age. The principal thesis of the sixth essay, "My Grandmother's Trunk Or What about Political Repentance?"* is that the above is the view of the anti-Maimonideans – those zealot Jews who condemned Maimonides for all kinds of reasons, and succeeded in having his books burned and his followers branded as heretics. As I demonstrated in my book *In the Shadow of History,* that pattern of Jewish devotion was the result of assimilation to the Gentile patterns of thought and feelings. Specifically, the anti-Maimonideans absorbed the *persecuting* dimension of Western society. The triumph of the anti-Maimonideans resulted in a total revamping of Jewish fundamentals. It also affected the Messianic concepts of Israel. For the anti-Maimonideans, the Messiah is primarily an eschatological figure closer to Jesus and Shabbetai Zevi than to Bar Kochba. According to the Maimonidean tradition, *Galut* ('Exile') is the effect not of a *theological* or *cultic* sin, but of *political* folly. As mentioned, Judaism is a two-dimensional system – one religious and the other political. Only individual salvation, expressed in the Rabbinic concept of *'Olam ha-Ba* ('World to Come'), depends on the individual observance of the Tora. Thus, the doctrine of *individual teshuba* (repentance) concerns the status of the person in the World to Come. Simultaenously, the *national* welfare of Israel is affected by the collective – the *political* behavior of the people. The Messianic Age is principally a *political* redemption, affecting the status of the people not in the hereafter, but in *this* world. A principal consequence of this view is that just like the *Galut* is the result of *political* folly, the Messianic Age will be the result of *political teshuba.* By projecting Christian eschatology onto Judaism, the anti-Maimonideans succeeded in displacing the

* Editorial Note: This chapter remains chapter 6 in the present edition.

Jewish Messianic conception of redemption in *this* world with future redemption in the *next*.

Christianity and Judaism represent two categorically distinct concepts of human spirituality.* A Jew cannot merely accept Christianity any more than a gentile can accept Judaism without undergoing a radical transformation in their intellectual and psychological apparatus. Essentially, Christianity lies in the realm of the mythical: It is only within the confines of mythological thinking that the spiritual may be grasped. "Christianity as understood and practiced during the nearly two thousand years of its history," writes Mircea Eliade (1907–1986), "cannot be completely separated from mythical thinking."[3] The protagonists are not to be viewed in historical terms, but as transcending the realm of the ordinary. Ultimately, neither the *real* Jesus nor the *real* Pharisees are important in and of themselves, but only in what they represent within a definite mythical scheme. Therefore, both the historical Jesus and Pharisees must be displaced in order to make room for mythical characters. This is why Christianity does not begin at an historical time, the birth of Jesus, but at a mythological time, the resurrection. Quoting Mircea again:

> In Origen's systematic treatment of inspiration and exegesis he tells us that where spiritual truths did not correspond to historical events, 'the scripture wove into the historical narrative what did not take place – at some points what cannot take place and at others what can take place but did not.' Instead of 'myth' and 'fiction' he uses 'enigma' and 'parable';

---

* Editorial Note: Ḥakham Faur ultimately decided to remove this chapter, "The Gospels According to the Jews," from the current book, because he subsequently expanded the chapter into an entire book by the same title. That book will be published in a different volume of this series. Nevertheless, we chose to retain the next several paragraphs of the "Introduction" describing this chapter.

3. Mircea Eliade, *Myth and Reality*, trans. Willard R. Trask (New York: Harpers & Row. 1975), p. 164.

> but there is no doubt that for Origen the terms are equivalent.[4]

Thus, to accept Christianity, one must first be willing to accept the categories of mythical thought. In this specific sense, Christianity is a faithful heir of Paganism, rather than Judaism. It is a remarkable fact that little is known of the popular pagan religion in Central and Western Europe prior to Christianity. Until such studies are made, no one can ascertain for sure how much 'Christian' and how much 'pagan' Christianity really is. Therefore, no one can dismiss nonchalantly the view that Christianity did with the popular pagan rituals and beliefs what the Stoics had previously done with the mythologies of the military and feudal hierarchies – namely, give them allegorical significance in a more sophisticated system. In such a case, there may not be such a thing as a 'Christian' religion, but only a 'Christianized' version of pagan myths and rites.

Mythical thought is only operative within hierarchical systems made up of 'superiors' and 'inferiors.' Christian universality is a dimension of hierarchical thinking: because it is hierarchically superior to all, it is universally binding on all. Individuals must obey the Church for the same reason that all subordinates must obey those who are hierarchically superior. The function of theology is to show in what way Jesus and the Church are hierarchically superior (or in what way the Law and the Pharisees are hierarchically inferior). Once this premise is accepted, it *naturally* follows that all must subordinate themselves to them.

In Judaism, even if Jesus was the son of God – an absolute oxymoron within a non-mythical system – and this son of God, who was conceived without human intervention, was simultaneously the biological descendant of King David – another oxymoron for non-mythical people – he still would have no authority to impose himself on anybody. To begin with, unlike pagans, Jews did not conceive

4. Ibid., p. 166.

of a cosmic Messiah – a kind of imperial cosmocrator, *a la* Caesar, with authority over everyone everywhere. Within a horizontal system, hierarchical considerations are inoperative. Even God Himself did not impose His will on Israel. Judaism is the result of a bi-lateral covenant *negotiated* by God and Jews at the foot of Mount Sinai; not by the *fiat* of a cosmocrator obliging lowly humans to accept his authority, or else.[5] Furthermore, for Jews, the spiritual unfolds within the realm of history, not myth. The merits of a given system are to be measured in terms of history: What concrete changes were brought about, in *real* non-mythological times and circumstances? What kind of impact did that system have on people's lives? Is there less violence and oppression because of it? Jewish theologians have tried to come to terms with the problems that the Holocaust presents to Judaism. These problems are important. But I believe that not enough attention has been paid to the problems that the Holocaust presents to Christianity. After the Holocaust, how can it be explained – in non-mythical terms –that societies that were regimented by Christianity for centuries have produced the largest number of mass-murders in *real* history? The great political dictators of the West – Hitler, Stalin, Mussolini, and others – viewed themselves as cosmocraters, or universal saviors. Is there a link between that archetype and the Christian archetype of a universal savior giving mythical rebirth to a decaying cosmos? Again, after the Holocaust, how can a system that tolerated the total collapse of human values speak in the name of morality and human salvation?

Christians and Jews live in two different realms. Christians live in mythical times. Their concept of the spiritual, their symbols, archetypes, and interpretation of the Hebrew Scripture, are unacceptable to a people transcending mythical thinking. Jews refuse to view Jesus and Christianity – as well as Judaism and their own political and spiritual leaders – outside of historical time. Accordingly, they were

5. On this pivotal concept, see my study "Judaism and Monolingualism," *Cardozo Law Review* 14 (1993), pp. 1713–1744.

hated and persecuted. In the seventh essay, "The Gospel According to the Jews," the grounds and consequences of such a view are explored.

The appendix, "De-Authorization of the Law: Paul and the Oedipal Model," studies the psychological bases of Christian antisemitism. This an expanded version of an article published in *Psychoanalysis and Religion* (Baltimore and London: Johns Hopkins University Press, 1990).*

I am often asked by friends, students, and associates about my early education and formative period growing up in Buenos Aires. I have therefore included the last two essays, "From Buenos Aires to Barcelona: Some Notes on My Educational Background" and "The Judaism of My Grandfather,"** which contain plenty of biographical data. The first of these appeared earlier in Joseph Papo, *Sepharadim in 20th Century America: In Search of Unity*.

As mentioned above, I am seriously concerned with the problem of mental assimilation, specifically the metabolization of Judaism according to pagan and mythical categories. In "The Judaism of My Grandfather," I look back into my early childhood and my first glimpses at Jewish life. I still believe that at that time Judaism was more human-oriented than the more cultic approach being propagated today.

* Editorial Note: This appendix seems to have been removed from Ḥakham Faur's final version of this work. He eventually converted this chapter into a book, which will be first published in a later volume of this series.

** Editorial Note: In the present edition, these two chapters open the work, as chapter 1 and chapter 2 respectively.

# 1. Remembering Things Past: Notes on My Educational Background

I was born and educated in Buenos Aires, Argentina. My family belonged to the Sephardic Community of Damascus, which consisted of several large synagogues. We prayed in a small synagogue founded, and entirely supported, by my father's first-cousin, Jaime Salmún. Although many congregants were from Damascus, there were also Jews from Tetuán, Melilla, Istanbul, Izmir and Rhodes. In this fashion, important elements of both the Arabic and Spanish Sephardic traditions were incorporated into the services. A good example of the intertwining of traditions was the reciting of the *Songs of Songs* on Friday night, when each chapter was chanted in different melodies by one of the congregants. More pertinent, we came to realize that underneath the plurality of detail and variation, there lay a common tradition and religious outlook that we identified as 'Sephardic.' That is why we saw ourselves as 'Sepharadim,' rather than in geographical terms (Moroccan, Greek, Syrian, etc.). Only upon coming to the United States, and then Israel, I discovered how rare and precious this outlook was. Since our home was located in a non-Jewish neighborhood, the synagogue was the only place we could play and make friends with children of 'our own' (*de los muestros*). In those days, everyone attended public school. The atmosphere was heavily Catholic and most unsympathetic to anything remotely Jewish. Quickly, we had to learn to survive in an adverse cultural environment, at times highly offensive to Jewish children. Some of us felt that we were reliving the stories that our grandparents had told us about Jews in Spain. Later, I came to realize that this early experience helped me preserve my Jewish identity while studying at the University of Barcelona.

There were several Sephardic Schools (*Talmud Tora*) in Buenos Aires that offered instruction to Jewish boys in the afternoon, after the public-school day ended. I think that my Jewish education was better than average *because* we lived far from these schools. Accordingly, my father had to provide me with a private teacher. For reasons that I regard as providential, he decided to hire an Ashkenazic man of letters. His last name was Konstantinovski. I think (but I am not absolutely sure) that his first name was Moshe (his brother's name was Menashe). He was a scholar and a gentleman. Not only did he teach me the correct Hebrew pronunciation and diction according to the Sephardic tradition, but also – at my father's request – how to write and read the Sephardic script.

My more 'advanced' Jewish education came later, through classes sponsored by local communities, where there were a number of men who had grown up in the old Sephardic schools, some with a solid knowledge of rabbinic literature. Most impressive was their joviality, unassuming nature and, above all, their impeccably good manners, which indeed are the earmark of the true *ḥakham* ('sage'). This was in glaring contrast to the arrogance, somber temperament, and rudeness that I found among other teachers and educators.

An important factor in my intellectual and spiritual formation was R. Eliyahu Suli (d. 1966). He was born and educated in Damascus in accordance with the 'old' Sephardic tradition that lingered throughout the Ottoman Empire. He was the spiritual head of a very important Synagogue, Or Tora, in a section of town called Barracas. On Shabbat, I would walk the hour and a half it took to get to his afternoon class.

The same synagogue sponsored some classes on weeknights, too.

I attended the classes given by R. Jamil Harari of Aleppo, whose specialty was the legal code of Maran Joseph Caro, the *Shulhan Arukh.* My principal teacher, however, was R. Eliyahu Freue (1880–1957), the spiritual head of the Community of Damascus in Argentina, who taught me the fundamentals of Talmud, Jewish law, and rabbinics. Occasionally, I also studied with R. Aharon Ha-Kohen 'Ajami (d. 1978) from Aleppo, a pupil of the illustrious sage R. Isaac Dayyan. R. Aharon Ha-Kohen was a close friend and study companion of my maternal grandfather, Jacob 'Arukh Joli (1874–1927). When my maternal grandfather first arrived in Argentina, he lived in Rosario, a small town north of Buenos Aires. There was a small group of Jews consisting of his friend R. Aharon Ha-Kohen, Nissim Sabban, and Jacob* Shaufan. They would meet every morning in my grandfather's attic and study together before heading to synagogue to pray, and then afterwards to work. (Later on, I received a "Rabbinic Ordination," *semikha,* from R. Aharon Ha-Kohen.)

The most outstanding feature of their system of education was the attitude of the teachers and sages. Although some were accomplished scholars, they never assumed an arrogant attitude toward their students or anyone else. They were accessible to all and encouraged contrary views and free discussions.[1] The 'truth' was the result of a *collective* effort in which everyone had equal access and an equal share, rather than being imposed by an individual of a 'superior'

* Rabbi Abraham Faur: In the original manuscript, my father left a question mark next to this name. It is not clear what the question mark indicated. Apparently, there was some ambiguity as to the name of this individual.

1. On one an occasion, I was about twelve and had finished reading Darwin's *The Descent of Man.* I waited for an opportunity, when studying with R. Aharon Ha-Kohen, and managed to divert our discussion to Adam and Eve, and asked him whom Cain had married. R. Aharon Ha-Kohen gave me the standard answer that he had married one of his sisters. I was displeased with his reply since the Scripture made no mention of any such sisters. "Then what is *your* explanation?"he replied. I mentioned to him that Darwin believed that monkeys were man's original ancestors. He smiled and answered: "Let us continue with our class. Let me hear how you read." I cannot imagine a better response!

mind. Subjects were taught systematically, in a gradual fashion: from the general and basic to the specialized and esoteric. Thus, before approaching the study of Talmud, the student was expected to have a solid knowledge of Scripture, *Mishnayot,* and the famous rabbinic anthology *'En Ya'aqob*. The scope of the curriculum was wide and universal, beginning with basic Hebrew grammar. The object was to give as broad an outlook to the student as possible, by making the student familiar with the Jewish classics. There was also some effort to introduce the student to a few classical texts dealing with Jewish ethics and philosophy, such as *Ḥobot ha-Lebabot* of R. Bahye ibn Faquda and *Menorat Ha-Ma'or* of R. Isaac Aboab.

We were isolated from the Ashkenazic Community. All we knew about them was that they were Jews with different customs and traditions. Occasionally, we discovered that a schoolmate was 'Jewish,' but rarely did these contacts develop into a serious friendship. My first contact with the Ashkenazic tradition was as a teenager in the early 50's, when I met an Ashkenazic rabbi who told me about the great rabbinic academies in the United States. I felt that my Jewish education in Argentina had come to a standstill and made up my mind to go abroad to study in one of these academies. My teachers were not pleased with the idea; their moral code, however, prevented them from expressing any direct criticism of other educational systems. I remember R. Suli saying to me that on one occasion one of these famous rabbis came to visit him. Soon he discovered that the discussion centered on a few topics. When R. Suli introduced other topics or tried to examine the subject in-depth, he realized that the rabbi was not as well-learned as he had thought.

Nevertheless, I left Argentina, and after a bit of travelling, I arrived in New York. Following some research, I decided to apply to the most prestigious rabbinic academy at the time, the Beth Midrash Gavoah, under the direction of the renowned talmudist, R. Aharon Kotler (1891–1962). After an intense exam, I was accepted and entered the school in September 1955. It was quite an experience. Many of the students were married. Some were born in Eastern Europe and had been trained by rabbis of legendary dimensions. Everyone had been studying Talmud since they were six or seven. And here I was, still in my teens and the youngest student in the entire school. Not only had I embarked on Talmud study rather late in life, I had barely devoted it more than a few hours a day.

The first lesson I heard from R. Kotler sounded like a revelation. He spoke rapidly in Yiddish – a language I didn't know but was able to understand because I knew German. He quoted a large number of sources from all over the Talmud, linking them in different arrangements and showing the various interpretations and interconnections made by later rabbinic authorities. I was dazzled. Never before had I been exposed to such an array of sources and interconnections. Nevertheless, there were some points that didn't jibe. I approached R. Kotler to discuss the lesson. He was surprised that I had been able to follow. When I presented my objections, he reflected for a moment and then replied that he would give a follow-up lesson where these difficulties would be examined. This gave me an instant reputation as some sort of "genius" (*'illuy*), and after a short while, I was accepted into the inner elite group.

My years in Lakewood were pleasurable and profitable. Some time before my arrival, Providence had arranged that a small but excellent Judaic Library belonging to a German doctor would end up at the school. Since these books were not deemed fit for rabbinic students (they were mostly Sephardic books, from the Golden Age of Spain – a favorite period for German Jewry), they were put in a closet in a residential building, away from the main place of learning. I would spend hours pouring over these books, quite undisturbed.

At the same time, the lessons of R. Kotler and my contacts with fellow students made me aware of some fundamental methodological problems. Basically, that the desire to catapult into the Talmud without a systematic knowledge of Scripture and Mishna rendered the analysis of Talmud messy. On another, more personal level, I found the religious attitude disturbing. The type of dialectics that were freely applied to the study of Talmud were not only making shambles out of the text, but – what was more disturbing – they were circumventing the very concept of halakha and replacing it with what, ultimately, was the whim of a superior authority. Accordingly, the only possibility of law and morality was for the faithful to surrender his mind and soul to a superior authority, to be obeyed because it is incumbent on the faithful to obey the superior. In other words, given that their peculiar system of dialectics permits for the total manipulation of halakha, it was the privilege of the authority to make special dispensations to some, and impose new strictures upon others. To me, this was indistinguishable from Orthodox Christianity.[2]

In Lakewood, I always felt a member of the inner circle. Everyone, R. Kotler in particular, had been extremely kind and helpful. My decision to leave that world and continue my secular education was painful and costly. Nevertheless, I was determined to pay my dues and pursue a different road. Eventually, I was accepted to the University of Barcelona, where I studied under Professors Millás Valicrosa and Alejandro Díez-Macho. I received my Ph.D. in 1964 in the Semitic Philology field. I was the first Jew to have received such a degree since the Expulsion in 1492. A few months before receiving my degree, I was in Jerusalem where I happened to meet R. de Sola Pool (1885–1970), whom I greatly loved and respected. I discussed with him the possibility of obtaining a post-doctorate fellowship at the Jewish Theological Seminary of America. He wrote on my behalf, and by the time I obtained my Ph.D., I received official confirmation of a three-year fellowship. During these three years, I was able to make use of the enormous resources of the library, both printed and manuscript material, pertaining to *all* the areas of Sephardic studies. At the same time, I was in contact with some of the great Jewish minds of our generation. It was a time of growth and fulfillment.

When the fellowship ended, I was invited to join the faculty. Professor Boaz Cohen (1899–1968), who occupied the Chair of Jewish

2. See my *Horizontal Society: Understanding the Covenant and Alphabetic Judaism*, 2 vols. (Boston: Academic Press, 2008), vol. 1, chapter 28.

Codes, had retired and I could teach his course. Before accepting, I consulted with *Ḥakham* Matloub ʿAbadi, whom I met during my first stay in the United States, while still involved with Lakewood. A former disciple of R. Isaac Dayyan (the same teacher of my teacher R. Aharon Ha-Kohen ʿAjami), R. ʿAbadi was the most illustrious Sephardic *Halakhist* I had ever met. He represented Sephardic scholarship and spirituality at its highest and most authentic level. He was my mentor (I received my ordination of *Dayyan,* "Rabbinic Judge," from him), and I did not want to take such a decision without his consent. He was positive about the whole issue. When discussing the possibility of perhaps joining a more traditional institution, he responded that those institutions are plagued by politics which interfere with and cripple one's intellectual and spiritual development. He added: "If I would have had such an opportunity, I would have grabbed it!" I joined the faculty of the Jewish Theological Seminary in 1967, where I remained until 1984. I was the first Sephardic faculty member since its foundation in the days of R. Sabato Morais (1823–1897) and Henry Pereira Méndes (1852–1937).

The decision to leave the Seminary in 1984 concerned women's ordination. Professor Gerson D. Cohen (1924–1991), who was the Chancellor of the Seminary (1972–1986), was determined to have women ordained. I saw the problem in procedural terms. At the time, I occupied the Chair of Jewish Codes (that had been previously occupied by Professor Boaz Cohen). Shortly before his death, Professor Saul Lieberman (1898–1983) issued an opinion concluding that the ordination of women contradicted halakha. When the issue was first presented for a vote, the rabbinic faculty voted against it. To circumvent this problem, Chancellor Cohen included in the administrative faculty (e.g., accountants, etc.) and teachers of modern Hebrew literature. I objected to this approach on the bases of the following three problems, all of which were of a procedural nature. First, Professor Lieberman, ranking among one of the greatest sages of Israel, had issued a contrary decision. As professor of Jewish Codes, I maintained that the decision merited to be debated by rabbinic authorities, rather than to be voted out by a faculty including accountants and general administrators, who, both intellectually and personally, had little to do with halakha. Second, the principal difference between the seminary and Reform Judaism was in its commitment to halakha. By rendering halakha a matter to be decided by such a faculty, the seminary was in fact relinquishing, and thus betraying, the purpose and ideals of its founding fathers, beginning with Rabbis Morais and Pereira Méndes. In such a case, it would be both deceptive and immoral to present itself as a halakhic institution. Finally, I thought that the issue of ordaining women deserved a serious and honest discussion, where different views could be presented and examined in a spirit of civility, without demonization of contrary opinions. Erroneously, I had thought that the Jewish Theological Seminary could have been the forum for such a discussion.

# 2. The Judaism of My Grandfather

The Judaism I believe in and live by is the Judaism of my grandfather, Joseph Faur (ca. 1865–1950). He was the son of Moshe (ca. 1810–1914), known affectionately as 'Abu-Bekhor.' My grandfather was the youngest of four brothers, Bekhor (Abraham), Ezra, Eliyahu, and Selim, and two sisters, Gilsom and Esther. Before dying, my great-grandfather asked his children to bring him prunes and peaches from his favorite orchard. He then invited all his children, grandchildren, and great-grandchildren to come and share his preferred fruits with him and celebrate the fact that, throughout his life, he never suffered any ill experience. He died shortly afterwards, a very happy and fulfilled man. I don't think that nothing bad ever happened to him, but more so that – looking back at the nooks and crannies puncturing his long life (according to family tradition, he well passed his one-hundred-year birthday) – he concluded that everything turned out to have been good.

For centuries, the Judaism of my grandparents was the Judaism of Sephardic Jewry in the Ottoman Empire. It barely survived the dawn of the 20th century. By the time my grandfather had decided to leave his ancestral home in Damascus in 1914, it was almost extinct. A major factor in his decision was the prospect of being drafted into the Turkish army. It was not that Jews were afraid to serve in the military – two generations later, their descendants served with distinction in the

Israeli army – but rather they had been convinced that Turkey was wrong, and that to fight for such a cause was both senseless and wasteful. I don't know why my grandfather chose to come to Argentina. It could be because of the language. Although Arabic was the language of the Jews of Damascus, there were some, particularly among those engaged in business, who spoke the Judeo-Spanish of the Ottoman Empire. It had been the lingua franca of the Jews for centuries, and both of my grandparents spoke it as a first language.

When my grandfather arrived in Buenos Aires there was already a well-established Sephardic Community, mostly comprised of Jews from Tetuan (Spanish Morocco) who had their own synagogue. For many years, he attended their daily services, until 1946 when he had a stroke and was confined to his bed. Around 1939, one of his nephews (the son of his sister Esther), Jaime Salmun, established a synagogue that my grandfather attended on the Sabbath and holidays. For daily services, however, he continued to pray at the Tetuan Synagogue, except during *Seliḥot*, when he would pray at Salmun's synagogue.

In the Sephardic liturgy, this period lasts for forty days. It begins the first of the month of Elul and culminates on Yom Kippur, the most solemn day of the year according to Jewish liturgy. It was during this period that Moses ascended to Mount Sinai anew to ask God for forgiveness on behalf of Israel after they worshipped the golden calf. It is a time of introspection and spiritual edification, designed to prepare worshippers for the Days of Awe: the days of Rosh HaShana – in which every human is judged before the Almighty – and Yom Kippur, when the verdict is issued by the Divine Tribunal.

The first religious experience I remember was accompanying my grandfather to *Seliḥot* services. In Argentina, this period falls right before spring, when the weather is pleasant and flowers and trees begin to bloom. There was nothing as exciting as my grandfather telling me to get ready for the next morning when we would go to *Seliḥot* together. Just imagine, a boy of about four getting up an hour and a half before dawn, washing up and getting dressed quietly, careful not to disturb the rest of the family. I remember leaving my room and facing two enormous patios separating our quarters from my grandparents' quarters, followed by the silence of the night and the starry sky, the silhouettes of the trees and the fragrance of the garden flowers. There was an eerie, uncanny sensation upon seeing the familiar surroundings of the day in different shapes and colors, fearing the sudden appearance of ghosts and bizarre creatures, camouflaged in the contours of darkness. My first impulse was to run as fast as I could, but instead I would walk at my regular pace, and take a long look at the places where monsters lying in ambush might hide. Soon, I discovered that no monsters were behind those unnerving shadows, but newly-shaped silhouettes and moods of old, familiar things. Nonetheless, I was scared. Our home was separated from my grandparents' home by a door made of a green metal frame and stained glass. Upon opening that door, I felt a great sense of relief, knowing that I had reached safe grounds. The absence of plants and trees from my grandparents' patios and, thus, the absence of scary shadows greatly contributed to my peace of mind. My grandfather would be waiting in the kitchen, ten or fifteen yards further down. Together, we would cross another patio until we reached the main door (*la puerta de calle*). Outside, it was pitch black, the street lights having been long off. Holding firmly onto my grandfather's hand, we proceeded into the darkness toward the synagogue, as I jumped up and down, cheerful and unperturbed. It was during these walks that a special bond was forged between us. Many years later, on my way to *Seliḥot* services at the *'Ole Suriya ve-Lebanon* synagogue in Haifa with David Faur, my wife's grandfather, I recalled the times when my grandfather and I had ventured into the darkness of the night to pray.

Sepharadim love their *Seliḥot* services. Even those who don't pray regularly, come to *Seliḥot* for spiritual edification and renewal. Many regard these services as the most inspiring part of the liturgy. The *Seliḥot* service is made up of a special type of poetry and melody in which worshippers voice contrition for their faults and supplicate God's compassion. A special theme of this liturgy is God's unbounded mercy, and the hope for a better and more meaningful life. The liturgy is old, some from late antiquity, and many pieces coming from Old Sepharad. Their tunes are heart-rending. Each poem is chanted in a particular melody and sung by the entire congregation with passion. As my grandfather and I would approach the synagogue, we could hear the chanting. After taking our seats, the sexton would come with a tray containing little cups of Turkish coffee and glasses of tea. Within a few moments, we were immersed in the services, pouring our hearts in fellowship to the God of Israel. It was during those services that I first experienced holiness: a sense of awe and trepidation overcoming the worshipper when in the presence of the Lord of Israel. This feeling was soon followed by a spirit of buoyancy and good will. Many years later, when I was attending *Seliḥot* services at Congregation Magen David in Brooklyn, New York, my son Abraham confided that it was during those services that he felt the *Shekhina* – the divine presence of the God of Israel.

By the time we left the synagogue in the early hours of the morning, our spirit had been recharged, our vision was clearer, and our determination stronger. We were more congenial, and anticipated a beautiful day ahead.

***

A defining characteristic of Jews is their love for books and wisdom, or more precisely, for the wisdom extracted from books or for books that generate wisdom. In Damascus, my grandfather belonged to a circle of friends where, in turn, each member would bring a book unbeknown to the rest and speak about it during the traditional *Seuda Shelishit* meal on Sabbath afternoons. For the people of the book, 'truth' is a literary concept – something that a reader extracts from a sacred text and then articulates into their own words and shares with others. That is why, for the people of the book, the purpose of reading is not entertainment, but ecstasy.

As children, we simply could not understand my grandfather's passion for books and reading. It even affected the way he did business.

When he was old and semi-retired, he had a tiny shop where he would sell all types of laces. It was a known fact, witnessed by us and commented on by our parents and uncles, that when engrossed in one of his books, he would not pay attention to any of his customers. Committing the equivalent of a capital offense in the world of business, he would tell the customers to choose their own merchandise, and more painfully, let them use the yard-stick on their own to measure the laces. When I asked him about this strange behavior, he responded with the breezy self-assurance of a fortunate man: "It does not pay to interrupt the study of Tora for such a trifle. One must always know what is really important and what is only convenient. Money is important if you don't have it. If you have it, it is only convenient." To the utter exasperation of his sons, his business thrived. Women just loved to shop at his place. In addition to his business policy, there were other reasons for his popularity. He was dark, tall, very well built, and exuded enormous vigor. He had a perfect set of immaculate white teeth, a disarming smile, and sported a most handsome moustache. He knew how to dress well, and I was told that when he walked the streets of Buenos Aires, women would turn around to look at him. "Your grandfather is an Apollo," a nanny once whispered in my ear. I don't think he took this seriously.

The earmark of the well-educated Sephardic men of yore was fluency in the Scripture and rabbinic lore. Their speech was interlaced with a continuous flow of biblical and rabbinic references. The whole world, as it were, was viewed from the prism of Jewish literary tradition: Nothing was so unimportant as not to merit a passage from Scripture, a saying from the Talmud, or one of those stories transmitted by the Rabbis. In this way, they actually fulfilled the biblical commandment "and you shall speak in them" (Deut. 6:7). Even a casual conversation with these men was an intellectual adventure. For us children and other members of the family, speaking to my grandfather was a source of spiritual edification.

An important aspect of Sephardic folklore was storytelling. It was customary in Damascus to gather at a neighbor's house after dinner on

Friday nights and spend the rest of the evening telling stories. Already in his native town, my grandfather had gained the reputation of a master storyteller. There was nothing as stimulating as when the whole family gathered to hear him recount one of his famous stories. These were the classical stories of Sephardic Jewry, covering a whole gamut of topics and themes: from fully elaborated biblical narratives – in the style of *Me'am Lo'ez* – to the way in which some rabbi outsmarted an enemy of Israel and saved his community. In Jewish storytelling, the audience is never passive. Questions and objections fly right and left. This was particularly true in our case, where my mother, who had heard the same stories from her father in a slightly different version, would challenge my grandfather's version. Essential to the art of story-telling was to add this or that new tidbit, making the story new and exciting. Gifted with a phenomenal memory – a gift passed down to me and to two of my sisters – he would weave into the stories the most intricate and marvelous designs, always enhancing a new point and bringing forth a twist unforeseen by the audience.

Through these stories, the audience actually participated in, and was shaped by, the collective experiences and memories of the Jewish people. For me, these sessions were defining moments: genuine spiritual adventures, joining the present with a people and a time transcending the here and now.

My grandfather was directly involved in my education and intellectual orientation, particularly after he was confined to bedrest because of a stroke. Invariably, as I passed through his quarters on the way back from school, he would call to me and ask about my homework and studies. I owe my love of books and study to him. It was during these conversations that I learned about the great intellectual tradition of Sephardic Jewry, gained unique insight into the lives and minds of the great luminaries of Israel, and, above all, came to understand the importance of studying and having access to books.

My grandfather was directly responsible for my rabbinic studies. When I was just thirteen, he insisted that I should take up my talmudic studies seriously. He was the foe of the semi-educated rabbis who peddled their ignorance as the eternal values of Israel. In particular, he abhorred the rabbis who piled on the faithful stringency upon stringency, making the lives of those around them bleak and miserable. On top of his list of undesirables were the spurious talmudists who brought bewilderment and perennial chaos to the poor souls who happened to be their students. This is why he saw to it that I study Talmud with a proper instructor. To him, the best talmudist around was R. Eliyahu Freue (1880–1957), the spiritual leader of the community of Damascus. He had been a member of the rabbinic court in Damascus, and had the distinction of having studied under R. Isaac Abul'afia – one of the great luminaries of Israel. At the time, R. Eliyahu Freue had acquired a legendary reputation for his extraordinary erudition, his depth, and his clarity of mind. People would literally tremble in awe when in his presence.

A few months earlier, I had been invited by a group of boys from another neighborhood to go out on a Saturday night. Someone suggested: "Let's go to El Balneario," a beautiful park and promenade at the shore of the River Plate. "No, Palermo would be nicer," responded another, referring to a magnificent woodland and garden in the northern section of Buenos Aires. After some deliberation, we decided to attend a Mishna class that R. Freue was giving that night at the Agudat Dodim Synagogue. The decision was prompted by hedonistic considerations. We reasoned that it would be more pleasurable to attend R. Freue's class than to go to any other place. Not because those places were not fun, but because we could visit them another time, whereas this was a unique opportunity to listen to a great mind. We attended the class, and no one was disappointed. In my eyes, this continues to be the supreme test of a great educator: teenage boys, on a Saturday night in spring, choosing to attend a class rather than to have fun at El Balneario or in Palermo. When my grandfather told me to ask R. Freue to teach me Talmud, I responded that I was not qualified. In the Sephardic tradition, no one dared study Talmud unless they were fluent in the Scripture and Mishna. I simply shuddered at the prospect of having to be examined by such an imposing figure. "Tell him that you are my grandson. He is my friend," responded my grandfather.

One Sunday afternoon in November 1947, I took the bus to Flores, the neighborhood where R. Freue lived. A large room in the house, full of rare books and manuscripts, served as the synagogue. It was hot and humid, not uncommon in Buenos Aires at this time of year, and the congregation prayed outside on the patio. I felt awkward asking such an eminent scholar to teach me Talmud, so I waited for everyone to leave before approaching him. He was reading inside the synagogue. He was short and robust, well-shaven, and dressed in European fashion. Like all of the rabbis and teachers that I knew, he did not believe in calling attention to himself, or trying to impress the public on the basis of cosmetics. After all, the beard and other rabbinic paraphernalia of the old country were nothing more than the fashion of the region, and it made no sense to superimpose it on anywhere else. I introduced myself and told him the purpose of my visit. He directed me to take out a copy of the Pentateuch and a copy of the Mishna and wait for him outside by a table. I sat down knowing that soon would be the moment of truth.

After a few minutes, he came and told me to begin reading that week's section of the Tora (*Vayetzeh*). Never in my life did I focus so much on a text. I knew that if I made the slightest mistake, mispronounced a vowel or put a secondary accent on the wrong syllable, it would all be over. I concentrated so intensely, that until this day I know that section of the Tora by heart, without having had the need to review it! He then told me to read a small section of the Mishna and explain it. In the Sephardic tradition, there is a special melody marking the reading of the Mishna, so that in addition to proper pronunciation, I was expected to read it in accordance with the rules of prosody peculiar to that text. Apparently, he was satisfied with my performance, because before I could finish with the explanation, he instructed his daughter to bring me a cup of Turkish coffee and a biscuit. That was the sign that I had passed the test and that he had accepted me as a student. The following day I began studying Talmud with him.

The Talmud is a text that focuses on the legal discussions that took place in the ancient academies and courts of justice during the rabbinic period. It is a highly technical text, structured in extremely complex and exact pericopes. For instance, there are "three-fold pericopes", where the material is organized in patterns of three, and "two-fold pericopes", where the material is organized into two parallel sections, and so on. Without a clear understanding of the structure of the pericope, it is impossible to recognize the textual strategy of the editors and the organization of the different sources and arguments. Like all legal texts, the language of the Talmud is technical. For instance, the Talmud uses different terms to mark Tannaitic traditions (תנו רבנן, תניא, תנא, תני, תנא דבי ר' ישמעאל, דבי ר' ישמעאל תני, אמר ר' פלוני, ר' פלוני אמר etc.), or to support an opinion (כדר' פלוני, משום דר' פלוני etc.). The first task of the student is to master the technical terminology and then proceed to identify the different structures of the Talmud (צורתא דשמעתא).[1] Without mastering this basic level, it is impossible to grasp the subtleties of the arguments or the views of earlier commentators and codifiers.

R. Freue demanded absolute precision in the analysis of the terminology, structure, and legal theory discussed in the pericope at hand. Nothing could be added to, or subtracted from, the text. The teacher was responsible for unfolding the pericope to the student, teaching him to appreciate the softest shades and the minutest filigrees of the text, and instructing him how to integrate these diverse elements into a coherent picture. There was no need for those onerous explanations, torturing the text of the Talmud and mind of the student. Through the analysis of the text, the student participated in the deliberations and exchanges of the talmudic authorities as if he were present in the discussions. Thus, the text of the Talmud acquired the level of intimacy of a direct, intellectual experience witnessed by the student himself – crystalline and absolutely distinct.[2]

1. See *Golden Doves*, p. 180; pp. 105–107, and my "*Ha-Sugya ha-Kefula*," Asufot 3 (1989), pp. 467–473.
2. R. Freue's classes attained this level of study and intimacy.

Some time ago, I had to undergo a CAT scan that required me to remain motionless in a narrow tube for about 45 minutes. The noises and flashes during the test can sometimes be nerve racking and produce a feeling of claustrophobia. The technician alerted me to this possibility and advised me to put my mind at ease by concentrating on something. I followed his advice, and once inside the tube, I reviewed the first pericope of the Talmud that I studied with R. Freue. Like everything else I studied with him, it was clear in my mind and I could mentally review it at will. I only began to appreciate his skills as a talmudist and a teacher years later when I encountered the more typical Talmudic schools. What a joke! Many of these great 'talmudists' are ignorant of the most basic elements of the Talmud and cannot make head or tail of the text at hand. Their explanations never cohere into an organic scheme in any conventional sense. Miserably, they are confined to peddling their nonsensical conjectures to witless and moronic students – their 'wisdom' is a function of the ignorance of the audience. As the Rabbis said,[3] "In the land of the blind, people call a one-eyed person insightful."

One might think that sages imbued in talmudic studies and rabbinic tradition would lead an austere life. Quite the contrary: they loved people and took pleasure in living well. Because Sephardic tradition does not foster feelings of guilt, these men lacked a sense of gloom and foreboding. The vicissitudes of life and personal misfortunes were not perceived in tragic terms. Even after my grandfather was incapacitated – no longer able to move around freely – he had an optimistic attitude toward life and a carefree, buoyant sense of humor. They enjoyed life too much to let 'small' inconveniences interfere. Above all, they enjoyed human fellowship and were happy to converse with everyone, everywhere – Jews and gentiles, rich and poor, religious and secular. My grandfather associated with some of the wealthiest and most successful men of the community. At the

3. *Bereshit Rabba*, XXX, 9, eds. Theodor-Albeck, 3 vols. (Jerusalem: Wahrman Books, 1965), vol. 1, p. 275.

same time, he counted among his pals not only gentiles but, to the shock of my father and uncles, common workers at the bottom of the economic scale. To my grandmother's chagrin, he would sponsor a certain coffee shop where he played domino with his pals. To soothe her fears, he would bring me or one of my sisters along with him, order an orchata de chufa drink for us, and expect not to be interrupted until the end of the game.

What was most striking about the Judaism of that generation is that those who were more observant were not pretentious about their religiosity; they were neither dogmatic nor authoritarian. Some, although quite punctilious about their religious duties, did not behave as if they were better than anyone else, and certainly did not harass those who happened to behave differently. Jews were not classified as 'religious' or 'secular.' The key-concept underlying their attitude towards others was the Hebrew concept of *kabod* – honor or dignity. Good upbringing is reflected, first and foremost, in treating others with *kabod,* that is, deference and consideration. People, all people, were treated horizontally – that is, neither as superiors nor inferiors, but as equals. In turn, they were leery of those who treated them as superiors – for them, only wimps resorted to flattery – and they surely did not tolerate anyone treating them as inferiors. Since they treated everyone with *kabod,* they expected the same from others. When they could not treat someone respectfully, or when their dignity was impugned, relations were discontinued, regardless of whom or why.

Today, Judaism is becoming more and more cultic. 'Tora' has been reduced to an obsessive repetition of a few slogans. Spirituality is used to promote some and persecute others, and expressed in the pedantic practice of certain rituals that are flaunted. Thus, ceremonies and interdictions are removed from their original meaning and are imbued with fetish notions, strange to the Tora and the teachings of the Rabbis. In some circles, spirituality is measured by the level of stringencies – often observed with pathological scrupulosity – with which the faithful restrict themselves, particularly in the area of dietary laws. The harsher the assumed position, the more meritorious it is, regardless of its basis in Jewish law. This is particularly true of the *ḥaredi* ideology dominating 'religious' life today. An essential element of this ideology is disdain for Jews who do not adhere to their idiosyncrasies (resulting from early psychological fixations on family experiences). According to that ideology, the actual Tora contracted by Israel at Sinai is irrelevant; what really matters are the petty differences – most of which accumulated through centuries of exile and persecution – separating Jews from one another.[4] Variation in lifestyle, appearance, and politics account for most of these difference. In their eyes, this trivia is more important than monotheism, circumcision, *kashrut*, or any of the 613 miṣvot stipulated in the Tora. Thus, a Sabbath-observant Jew, who happens to dress according to another fashion code, sport a distinctive hairstyle, or support a different political ideology, may be regarded as second-rate. Conversely, their cronies may be excused for even the most flagrant violations of Jewish law and common decency. This goes to show that what ultimately matters to them is their own petty eccentricities: 'Tora' is just a means by which they peddle their habits and attack 'the other.'

The Judaism that my grandfather and his peers practiced maintained that devotion and spirituality are expressed not by imposing new restrictions and instituting new rituals, but primarily by performing acts of goodness and kindness (*gemilut ḥasadim*) to others, like the patriarch Jacob, who expressed his special thanks to His Maker by establishing institutions that would benefit others.[5] Today, we conceal human suffering through social techniques or by writing an impersonal check for a 'good cause.' But in my grandfather's Judaism, religious devotion was expressed by personally caring about someone in need.

For instance, a man by the name of Marcos Gomel, originally from Izmir, Turkey, lived down the block from my grandfather We all admired him. He was wealthy and had deep religious convictions.

---

4. For other aspects of the *ḥaredi* ideology, see "Monolingualism and Judaism," *Cardozo Law Review* 14 (1993), pp. 1713–1744.
5. See Shabbat 33b.

Sometimes, he could be so punctilious about some detail of Jewish law or synagogue service that he would get on my grandfather's nerves. His wife Rachel always miscarried, and they were childless. When someone in the community passed away and left two orphan girls, Marcos Gomel vowed to support them until the day of their marriage. He brought them to his home and they were raised as his own daughters. After a few years, they both got married and left his home for their new ones. In that very year, his wife Rachel became pregnant and did not miscarry. I have some vague memory of the circumcision of their son, Moreno, who is a few years younger than me. We were friends, and at the request of his father, I taught him the first Hebrew letters. What was more remarkable about Marcos Gomel was his sensitivity to the plight of others. When someone fell ill, he would fulfill the obligation to visit the ailing (*biqqur ḥolim*) in the old fashion way: by personally taking care of the needs of the sick. Multiple times, I saw him remove his jacket, pull up his sleeves, sweep and scrub the floor, and do other household chores for the sick. Sometime ago, when I was operated on and had difficulty taking care of my own body, I remembered how Marcos Gomel would clean and wash the private parts of the old and feeble. Within the context of his time, seeing a wealthy man minister to the ill with such devotion was a moving experience.

The Jewish concept of performing acts of goodness and kindness (*gemilut ḥasadim*) includes alleviating psychological distress. High on this list is to effect reconciliation between friends and relatives (שלום בין אדם לחבירו), particularly between husband and wife (שלום בין איש לאשתו). The image of a man and his wife entering my grandparents' home is still frozen in my memory: My grandmother scolded the husband as if he were a child, ordering him to bend down and look her straight in the eyes; the husband obeyed and covered his face, afraid to receive a whack at any moment, and promised not to do it again; and my grandfather consoled the sobbing wife. I also remember them leaving with cheerful faces. I saw that couple many more times on happy occasions. Some twenty years later, I had the pleasure of inviting them to my son's circumcision.

For my grandfather's generation, the highest Jewish precept was giving to the poor. They could not conceive of anything more sacred and sublime than taking care of the needy. Their devotion to charity knew no limits. Nathan Salmun, the father of the Salmuns of Argentina, was married to my grandfather's older sister, Esther. He was a man of modest means, but he loved to help those who were in greater need than himself. Whenever he heard about someone destitute he would run to the *gabba'im* (charity collectors) and give them all his money. Many a time, he would not realize that he was left with no funds to take care of his own family. Accordingly, the *gabba'im* would hide from him so as to not be forced to accept his charity. Even in my day, humorous stories circulated about their stunts to avoid his pursuits. When he died, his sons decided to immigrate to Argentina, but they had no money to buy tickets. The only thing that their father had left them was a quilt. Out of dire need, his wife – my great-aunt Esther – decided to sell it. When she opened the quilt to clean it before putting it for sale, she found five golden coins. It was not known whether these coins were hidden by a previous owner, or by Nathan Salmun himself, as an inheritance for his children. Each of the children took a coin to purchase a ticket. Four of them became extremely wealthy. Those who knew them believed that their success was in recompense for their father's benevolence to the poor.

Occasionally, miracles occurred that facilitated giving charity. I know of one such case that took place in New York during the depression. It concerned Jack Arama (1895–1980), from Taroudant, Morocco. His wife, Ledescia, was the daughter of Asher Levi (1856–1927), a distinguished member of the Spanish and Portuguese Synagogue in New York. He organized, and then became the president of, the first congregation of Jews from Aleppo in the United States, located in the Lower East Side. Once, when Mr. Arama was in France, he heard about a Jewish girl who, due to financial needs, was working in a house of ill repute. He paid her debts, found her a husband, and took care of the wedding. Because of adverse circumstances, Jack Arama lost his money during the depression. Eventually, he became the sexton of

Magen David Congregation in Brooklyn. He was an upright and religious man in the old Sephardic style. There were some poor families that depended on him, and he continued to provide for them even after he had lost his money. A few days before Rosh HaShana, things turned very sour, and Jack Arama realized that he could not scrape any money to help these families. He knew that they would be coming to his house that evening, expecting him to help them with the holiday's expenses. He did not know what to do. Standing in a jam-packed subway on his way home, he began to pray: "Please God, help me help these people. Next year I'll try harder, but right now there is nothing more I can do." Suddenly, there was a commotion. A man standing by him screamed, "Pickpocket! Someone just robbed me!" A policeman who was standing nearby came to the scene. People were questioned. One man standing next to Jack Arama was frisked and nothing was found. When the policeman asked the victim whether he wanted him to report the incident, the victim responded that it was useless. The next stop was Jack's. As he walked home, he noticed something in his pocket. He looked and found a brown bag full of money. Apparently, the thief was afraid to be caught and slipped the bag into his pocket. It was full of large denomination bills with slips containing names and numbers. The man who was robbed was probably collecting money for a bookie, and that was why he refused the police report. Jack Arama told me the story to illustrate how God takes care of the poor in strange ways.

A much smaller miracle once happened to me in Haifa. I used to go to a certain synagogue for evening services. There were several poor men who attended the services, and I would give some money to my son Abraham to give to them. Once, I forgot to bring money and we both felt horrible. As we walked out of the synagogue, my son noticed a few bills on the street. We believed that the money was heaven-sent. Immediately, he picked up the money and ran back to the synagogue to give it to the poor.

In those days, people were not bombarded with all kinds of sociological and psychological theories about poverty, and acted on the basis of kindness alone. The poor were not viewed as 'different,' nor were they discriminated against; they were regarded the same as everyone else, and people understood that they had become destitute because of adverse circumstances. An essential element in attending to the poor was the *kabod* with which they were treated. Because paupers came to people's houses asking for food, women were directly involved in fulfilling this supreme task. Jewish folklore has it that occasionally Elijah the Prophet disguised himself as a pauper to test the benevolence of housewives. Women took this challenge assiduously – feeding the poor was a supreme assignment.

By the time I grew up, there were no longer Jewish beggars knocking on the door for food as there were during the Ottoman period. Obviously, the socioeconomic situation of the Sephardic community in Buenos Aires had changed. Nonetheless, I was told that occasionally a Jewish beggar would knock on our door for food. I think I remember one such case, though I am not certain; the image in my mind is blurry, as if I were in a dream or in a surrealistic flight of fancy. I asked my mother about it, and she confirmed the basic points of my recollection. I also asked my wife Esther, who's from Israel – where poverty still compelled people to beg – and she recounted similar stories. Nonetheless, I am not sure whether I actually witnessed such an event at a very early age, making my memory of it blurry, or whether I constructed a memory on the basis of stories I heard. At any rate, this is what I remember, or, at the very least, think I remember: Late one sunny morning someone knocked on the door, and then I heard a whisper – "'*Ani*!" ('a beggar') –reverberate throughout the house. The women in the house became excited, as if a distinguished visitor had just arrived, and the children were instructed to be quiet and behave properly. Rapidly, two women set the table. I saw one of them take out a fresh tablecloth from a closet and spread it over the table. The other woman set the silverware. Meanwhile, the man was seated. After some exchange, he removed his shoes, and they were given to one of the girls to polish. Someone brought out a basin with a towel and soap, and helped the man clean himself. He washed his feet and tried on a new pair of shoes. One of the ladies brought him a small basin for the ritual washing of the hands (*neṭilat yadayim*), while another tied a napkin around his neck. The table was brought to him and he ate. By the time he finished eating, two packages were waiting for him – one with food and another with clothing. Some money was put in one of his pockets; he acquiesced without saying a word. Right before he left, a few words were exchanged. He exited the house, and I never saw him again.

I left Argentina a few years after my grandfather's death. To commemorate the death of a relative, Sepharadim have a ceremony called *me'ad* ('anniversary') in Arabic, and *meldado* ('study-session') in Judeo-Spanish. It consists of three elements: prayers, the study of the Tora (Mishna, Zohar, etc.), followed by a meal, to which the family of the deceased invite their friends, as well as the poor and the needy. These are, precisely, the constitutive elements of my grandfather's Judaism.

# 3. People of the Covenant

I grew up speaking several languages. And yet, in the lexicon of my childhood, 'religion' was never applied to the system of beliefs and practices peculiar to the Jewish people. Rather, we (*'am yisrael*) believed in the Tora; practicing certain precepts and adhering to certain rules that made us different from our Christian neighbors. People who were particularly scrupulous in the fulfillment of their devotional duties were 'observant' (*shomer miṣvot* in Hebrew, and *nas malaḥ* in Arabic).[1] Later, I discovered that neither the Hebrew Scripture nor the Rabbis have a term equivalent to the term 'religion.' In fact, the Tora establishes rules and regulations concerning the conduct of warfare, the installation of a sovereign, judicial procedure, etc. – matters having nothing to do with what is generally understood as 'religion.' In school, our Christian teachers taught us that 'religion' comes from the Latin *ligare* ('to tie, to bind'), i.e., the link broken by Adam's original sin, and *re*-tie it again through Jesus. Thus, 're-ligion' is a Christian invention.[2]

1. Terms such as *relijyoso, relijyosidad* in Judeo-Spanish are some of the many neologisms that penetrated the language of the Jews in the Ottoman Empire via the French, particularly with the establishment of the *Alliance Française Israelite*.
2. See José Faur, *The Naked Crowd: The Jewish Alternative to Cunning Humanity* (Ft. Lee, N.J.: 2009), pp. 22–23. For a full analysis of this term in Indo-European languages and institutions, see Émile Benveniste, *Indo-European language and Society* (Coral Gables, Florida: University of Miami Press, 1973), pp. 516–528. Cf. *Horizontal Society*, vol. 1, pp. 131–3.

It would be also wrong to characterize Judaism as a 'political system.' Although the establishment of the Jewish State in the land of Israel and various precepts dealing with public and national welfare are essential for the total fulfillment of the Tora, the Tora is not 'a political system.' Many precepts have little to do with anything 'political' in the normative sense of the term.

The West does not have a term equivalent to 'Tora.' If we wish to render 'Tora' into concepts current in Western thought, then it must be described as a two-dimensional system, one spiritual and the other political.[3] In Judaism, these dimensions intercross and are structurally connected: together they form a single, operative system.[4]

The Tora is the official articulation of this two-dimensional system. The validity of the Tora has nothing to do with either 'philosophy,' 'theology,' or 'religion.' Rather, it is the effect of the *berit,* or bilateral 'covenant,' contracted by God and Israel at the foot of Mt Sinai.

* * *

The first time that I had to explain the concept of 'Covenant' in Judaism to a well-educated Jew was at Harvard in 1957. At the time, I was interested in doing some graduate work in the field of Jewish Philosophy, and was searching for a suitable place for graduate work. Perhaps something to do with Judeo-Arabic texts, since I knew the language… or perhaps editing a text by Averroes? It was during that period that I met Morris Y. He was a philosophy major and was taking some graduate courses in German idealism. We loved discussing philosophy, particularly Kant (1724–1804) and Hegel (1770–1831). Invariably, our discussions led to Herman Cohen (1842–1918) and Franz Rosenzweig (1887–1929) and to their interpretations of Judaism. He had been recently married and I was a steady guest in his home. It was during one of those long discussions that I came to realize

3. Hence, Spinoza's 'theologico-political' system.
4. See *Horizontal Society,* vol. 1, chapter 24.

that the ultimate basis of Judaism was not – it could not possibly be – philosophical. Otherwise, it should be binding on everyone! Its basis was the Covenant contracted at Sinai.

The simple truth, as told by the Hebrew Scripture, is that Jews left Egypt and contracted a *berit* ('covenant') with God at the foot of Mt Sinai. The fact that the *berit* was bilateral, the result of mutual negotiations and agreement, and not unilaterally imposed by 'God,' or by a man, or a group of men acting on behalf of 'God' as per 'monotheistic' religions, indicates the absolute horizontality of the covenant God-Israel.

At God's initiative, Moses proposed to the people to contract a pact with God (Ex. 19:3–6). Subsequently, God descended upon Mt. Sinai and spoke the Ten Commandments to the entire people, "face to face" (Ex. 19:15–20). In this respect, it should be noted that in the mind of the other 'monotheistic' religions, it is the prophet, leader, etc. who ascends to Heaven. The case of Israel is unique because *God* descends to the people, not in an amorphous epiphany, but with a concrete alphabetic message, the most important document of *rational humanity*: the Ten Commandments. (We should note, in passing, that in this pivotal point, both Christianity and Islam follow a pagan religious model: their deity does not descend to the people, but rather their prophet ascends to Heaven, we should add, *post mortem*. Said 'fact,' however, is *not* witnessed by the people). Moses ascended, not to Heaven, but to the thick darkness where God was, and received from Him a series of precepts.[5] Upon descending from the thick darkness, Moses transmitted these precepts to the people. The people responded: "All the words that the Lord spoke we shall do." On that night, Moses put these words into writing. This document is known as "the book of the *berit*" (Ex. 20: 21–24). Early next morning, Moses ordered the erection of an altar (representing God) and twelve pillars (representing the tribes of Israel), and the offering of sacrifices, half the blood of which was poured onto the altar. He

---

5. See Sukka 5a.

then proceeded to read the "book of the *berit*." At the end of the reading, the children of Israel, freely and in unison, replied: "All that the Lord had spoken we shall do and we shall hear." Then, Moses took the rest of the blood and sprinkled it on the people, saying: "Behold the blood of the *berit* which the Lord had made with you, upon all these words" (Ex. 24:4–18). Because the *berit* is a bilateral agreement, God Himself is bound to the covenant, and neither party may add, subtract, or reinterpret any of its terms.[6]

Finally, it is important to note that at Sinai God spoke equally to each and every Jew, according to his or her specific mindset. Building on this thought, the Rabbis taught that when God spoke to the people "frontally" (*panim be-fanim*; Deut. 5:4) at Sinai, His every word came separately to each individual and asked:

> 'Do you accept me? Such and such precepts are implicit in me! Such and such laws are implicit in me! Such and such decrees, such and such ordinances, such and such *a fortiori* [reasonings] are in me! Such and such reward there is in me!' And he would respond: 'Yes and yes!'[7]

Because in the Hebrew mind, the human face represents uniqueness and individuation,[8] "frontally" (*panim be-fanim*) means that God spoke to each individual according to *his* or *her* specific mindset. So that everyone registered the same message, because God's utterance descended to his or her mindset and delivered the message accordingly. If God would have articulated His message uniformly to all, each individual would have interpreted the message differently. It is by addressing each person according to his or her own individual

---

6. For an extensive account of this fundamental doctrine, see *Horizontal Society*, vol. 1, chapter 5.
7. *Shir ha-Shirim Rabba* I, 2 (Venice, 5364/1604), 22d; cited in *Golden Doves*, p. 119.
8. See "Pomp and Pageantry," p. 1231.

mindset that the same message was equally registered in the collective consciousness of Israel.[9]

Thereafter, the people went on to build what may be properly described as a 'Covenantal Society.' Appropriately, the Rabbis used the expression "Children of the Covenant" (*bene berit*) to designate "Jews" (see Mishna *Baba Qamma* 1:2–3).

* * *

The collective experience at Sinai – an experience that could have been a mere episodic recollection in the subconscious of a few – became a phenomenological aspect in the collective consciousness of Israel. This was because the Hebrews, in the footsteps of Patriarch Abraham, attained individuation. They alone discovered that they were different, not only from the Egyptians, but, even more importantly, from each other.[10] The Hebrew precept, "And you shall love the other (*re'akha*) as you love yourself (*kamokha*)" (Lev. 19:18) – often quoted but rarely understood – means, first and foremost, that it is incumbent upon *you* to respect the individuality of the 'other' (*re'akha*) with the same intensity with which *you* defend your own.[11] A consequence of this sort of individuation is the realization that *you* cannot survive alone, that *we* are interdependent and connected to a *whole* transcending its individual parts, and that members of the Jewish society are like members of an orchestra, where no single person could perform the entire musical score.[12]

In fact, without individuation, progress and civilization are impossible. To underline this central idea, the Rabbis taught that upon seeing a contingent of 600,000 Jews, as during the experience at Sinai, one should say: "Blessed is He… who knows the undisclosed (*ha-razim*; cf. Dan. 4:6)." The meaning of this blessing is that just

9. Cf. below, "When Different is the Same and the Same is Different."
10. See *Crowds and Power*, p.208.
11. See *In the Shadow of History*, pp. 6–7.
12. See *Horizontal Society*, vol. 1, p. 121.

like "their faces do not resemble one another, so also their minds do not resemble one another."[13] God alone knows the intimate, unique "undisclosed" personality of every single individual. The basis of civilization and the possibility of social progress rest on the wise organization of this type of diverse personalities. In support of this view, the Rabbis mentioned that when Ben-Zoma (2nd century) would see a contingent of 600,000 Jews at the Temple Mount, he would say: "Blessed (is He) who created all these to serve me." Ben-Zoma explained: "How much work did Adam have to do to savor a morsel of bread... or to wear a garment... and I wake up in the morning and find all these before me."[14]

A social organization where individuation is encouraged, rather than crushed by the might of authority, requires wise political leadership. Taking on the fact that a society made up of individuals different from one another requires wise political leadership, the Rabbis taught that before dying, Moses said to God:

It is perfectly clear before Thee the mind of each and every one, and that the minds of Thy children are dissimilar from one another. I beg of Thee that when I depart from them, that Thou should designate for them a leader that would relate to each and every one of them in accordance with his mind.[15]

Thus, King Solomon requested from God "an understanding heart to judge Thy people, that I may discern between good and evil; for who is able to judge this great (*kabed*) people of Thine?" (I Kings 3:9). "Great" (*kabed*) refers to the quality of excellence peculiar to a society made up of diverse individuals. Hence, the strong relationship between individuation, progress, and wise political leadership capable of managing individualistic talent. Accordingly, the Hebrew

---

13. Tosefta Berakhot 6:2 (S. Lieberman), p. 33. See Berakhot 58a; *MT Berakhot* 10:11; *Shulḥan 'Arukh, Oraḥ Ḥayyim,* CCXIV, 5.
14. See Tosefta Berakhot 6:2–3, pp. 33–34; and Saul Lieberman, *Tosefta Ki-Fshuṭah,* vol. 1 (New York: Jewish Theological Seminary, 1955), pp. 104–106.
15. *Bemidbar Rabba,* XXI, 2 in *Midrash Rabba 'al ha-Tora ve-Ḥamesh Megillot,* 2 vols. (Jerusalem, 5735/1975), vol. 2, 88d.

idea of 'unity' (*aḥdut*), so vital for Jewish survival and far from entailing homogeneity, involves cooperation with, and appreciation of, the dissimilar other (=*re'akha*).

* * *

The preceding will help us understand Moses' strategy in the building of the *Mishkan*. Previously, while Moses was up at Mt Sinai receiving the Tablets of the Ten Commandments, a mob "assembled" (*vayyiqqahel*) and demanded that Aaron should build for them a golden calf (Ex. 32:1). Thereafter, *before* proceeding with the building of the *Mishkan,* Moses "assembled (*vayyaqhel*) all the various groups or congregations (*kol ha-'eda*) of the children of Israel" (Ex. 35:1). The verb "to assemble" stems from *QHL,* the same root as in *qahal* (or *qehilla*), 'assembly,' serving to designate the 'communities' of Israel. To demystify the collective consciousness from the negative consequences of a mob demanding a 'golden calf,' it was imperative to first "assemble" *all* the constitutive members (*kol ha-'eda*) of Israel and do something positive together. The purpose of involving the *various* groups of artisans in the production of the vessels and parts of the *Mishkan* was to have the people experience collectively the *Shekhina* "within themselves" (*betokham*), and not merely within the precincts of the *Mishkan.* (By contrast, Pagan Temples, including those built by 'monotheistic religions,' permit the faithful to experience the divine within the sanctuary, but not within themselves, after exiting the holy precinct). In this fashion, God fulfilled His promise, namely, that upon realizing the terms of the Covenant, "Ye shall be unto Me a kingdom of priests and a holy nation" (Ex. 19:6). Concerning this fundamental article, R. Abraham Maimonides explained that every member of the nation of Israel, and not just the clergy as is the case among the nations, has direct access to God.[16] Later, Moses

16. R. Abraham Maimonides, *Perush,* ed. and tr. Sh. Wiesenberg (Letchworth, 1959), p. 302.

ascertained that Israel had in fact partaken in this phenomenological experience: "And you that have cleaved unto the Lord your God are alive: every one of you this day" (Deut. 4:4). In Hebrew, to 'cleave' means a *direct* relationship between two parties, without the intervention of mediators.

The purpose of the *Mishkan*-Temple, and later on of the Synagogue, is for the *Shekhina* to inhabit in the "midst" of the people: directly, without intermediaries.

In sum, the covenant at Sinai-Moab is the matrix of Israel's collective consciousness. The *Shekhina* is the Divine Presence, manifesting every time and every place Jews come together to *fulfill* the covenant. This is how I interpret a remarkable passage penned by the remarkable scholar, Émile Durkheim:

> Collective thought is possible only through the coming together of individuals; hence it presupposes the individuals, and they in turn presuppose it, because they cannot sustain themselves except by coming together. The realm of impersonal aims and truths cannot be realized except through the collaboration of individual will and sensibilities; the reason they participate and the reasons they collaborate are the same. In short, there is something impersonal in us because there is something social in us, and since social life embraces both representation and practices, that impersonality extends quite naturally to ideas as well as to actions.[17]

Individuals, too, can reach the collective thought of Israel. As the Rabbis taught, even a solitary Jew can experience the Divine Presence every time that he "sits and studies Tora" (*Abot* 3:2 cf. ibid. 3:6).

* * *

17. Émile Durkheim, *The Elementary Forms of Religious Life*, tr. Karen E. Fields (NY: The Free Press, 1991), p. 447.

Pagan societies, including those commonly designated 'monotheistic religions', are organized hierarchically.[18] The relationship between individuals and the various social and political elements of a people is determined by a vertical system. Human society is conceived of as a scale of superiors and inferiors: those below owe obedience to those who stand above and exercise authority over them. At the top of the scale stands the political or ecclesiastical rulers exercising absolute authority; at the bottom stand the common folks, whose principal duty is obedience to those standing above them.[19] The ultimate basis for political authority is monopoly of violence. A national entity is deemed 'legitimate' when it has the ability to control and generate violence within its own borders. The purpose of terrorism is to show that the ruling authorities do not have a total monopoly of violence. Terrorists and revolutionary movements succeed when they can generate more violence than the government. Proper authority and international recognition are awarded when the insurgent forces can prove that they can generate and control violence. Regardless of revolutionary slogans and ideology, the system itself, however, remains unchanged: those in the lower echelons owe absolute obedience to those in the higher echelons – or else.

That is why the Hebrew Scripture describes Egypt as a "house of slaves" (Ex. 20:1). The greatest of all miracles, without which no other miracle could ever have taken place, was when the people of Israel realized that they were in bondage and cried to God for help, "and their supplication ascended to God from their enslavement" (Ex. 2:23–25). To understand this miracle, one could imagine Egypt as in Plato's famous parable, where everyone is chained to a cave with no light other than what was provided by a few meager torches. In Plato's parable, the truth is discovered when someone manages to break loose and exit the cave, seeing a new and beautiful world lying outside under the sun. However, people inside the cave could not

18. See *Horizontal Society*, vol. 1, chapter 28.

19. See *Horizontal Society*, vol. 1, chapter 13. Cf., "Forgiving the Enemy, Loving the Enemy, Becoming the Enemy," note 175.

fathom a world of light and shadows, unless they first climbed out from the cave into the open world. But the Jews in Egypt did! They discovered their own enslavement, while enchained in a "house of slaves" (Ex. 20:1)![20]

Ever since Christianity, gentiles have loved to speak and write about freedom. But Jews and Jews alone know the meaning of freedom, because they alone felt its yoke. Before experiencing freedom, people need, like the ancient Hebrews, to realize that they are living in a "house of slaves." Generally, when gentiles 'know' that they are slaves, it is because someone (in the upper echelons of humanity) told them so! Not so with Israel! Neither God nor Moses revealed to Israel that they were in bondage.

"And it came to pass in the course of those many days that the king of Egypt died" (Ex. 2:23). It is a curious fact that pagans lament the demise of their oppressors. A good example is the grief felt by the Russian people over the death of Stalin, one of the most brutal dictators of modern time. It was estimated that at least 20 million people were killed during Stalin's Purge. And yet, when Joseph Stalin died on 5 March 1953,

> ...the outpouring of public grief when Stalin's death was announced was remarkable ... a bearded Russian with no legs [who] had lost them during the war [and whose] body rested on a wheeled trolley ... looked up at me with a sadness in his eyes and tears streaming down his cheeks. Waving his arms, he cried 'What are we going to do? What will happen to us now that the great Joseph Vissarionovich [Stalin] has gone?' The man's mutilation and grief was such that I was lost for an answer.[21]

The Egyptians, too, lamented the death of Pharaoh. Not so with Israel! Rather, they seized the moment and gathered to lament their

---

20. See *Horizontal Society*, vol. 1, pp. 191–3; pp. 223–225.
21. Robert Conquest, *The Great Terror: Stalin's Purge of the Thirties* (New York: Macmillan 1968), p. 12.

enslavement. "And the children of Israel came to weep over their bondage, and they cried; and their supplication ascended to God from their enslavement" (Ex. 2:23).[22] Only when Israel acknowledged their bondage, did God "remember His covenant with Abraham, with Isaac, and with Jacob," and send Moses (Ex. 2:24). In Israel, the people create their leader, not the other way around! (Similarly, the people, and not merely 'those in charge,' are responsible for the crimes committed by their leaders.)

People too 'tough' to cry or too 'dense' to grasp their bondage need not the assistance of the God of Israel – there always will be someone ready to give them a 'helping hand' *gratis*, without having to bear the onus of a Law or any responsibilities![23]

Hierarchical societies depend on the political fear that they generate, thus chaining both master and slave. Because Jews are aware that bondage/freedom are part of the same political game, it is incumbent upon every Jewish man and woman to offer thanks every morning to God, not only because He did not make him or her "a slave," but also for not being born a "gentile," that is, a member of a system where 'freedom' is predicated on the enslavement of 'the other'.

* * *

For a Jew, slavery need not include iron shackles and heavy chains; it pertains to all hierarchic systems, whereby those above oppress those below. The following incident expresses the Jewish view on this matter.[24] The place is the residence of the Persian governor Bar-Sheshakh,

22. My friend Benny Dweck raised this point in a conversation we had decades ago.
23. See *Horizontal Society,* vol. 1, pp. 200.
24. *'Aboda Zara* 65a. The printed text is faulty. Our translation proceeds from the manuscript edited by Professor Shraga Abramson, *Tractate 'Abodah Zarah* (New York: The Jewish Theological Seminary of America, 1957), p. 112. For a fuller treatment of this incident, see José Faur, "Of Cultural Intimidation and other *Miscellanea*: Bar-Sheshakh vs. Raba," *Review of Rabbinic Judaism* 5 (2002), pp. 34–50. See also: https://www.youtube.com/watch?v=8ZthuraHdJA

in one of the capitals around Maḥoza, a large walled city on the west bank of the Tigris. The city was one of the most important commercial centers in the area, with a population of about 20,000 inhabitants, all of whom were Jewish. The time is sometime after 323, after Raba (d. 352) had established a famous Talmudic school in Maḥoza. The event was depressingly familiar. Raba, who had experience in backhanding Persian officers,[25] was charged with the mission of bringing an 'offering' (*qorbana*) or gift to Bar-Sheshakh. The Talmud cites this incident to illustrate a point of law. Generally, it is forbidden to bring a gift to a pagan on the occasion of a personal holiday. The Talmud proposes that if it is positively known that said pagan does not worship idols, it is permissible to do so.[26] To substantiate this view, the Talmud cites an incident in which Raba brought a present to Bar-Sheshakh on a private holiday, because he knew that "he did not worship idols." The story is divided into three parts. The first part [i] describes the setting of the meeting. The second [ii] contains the exchange between them. The last part [iii] recounts a mishap that took place at the end that served to clinch Raba's argument.

[i] The meeting took place at the governor's residence, where Bar-Sheshakh received Raba while immersed in a pool filled with rose water. Naked prostitutes around the governor were attending his wants. 'Rose water' was regarded as some sort of aphrodisiac, supposedly enhancing sexual potency.

[ii] After going through the formalities of presenting an offering to the governor, the governor turned to the Rabbi and asked him: "Do you have something like this in the world to come?" The governor was teasing the rabbi. He *knew* that *his* condition *now* was infinitely superior to that of any Jew. For the sake of amusement, rather than to spark a dialogue, he asked Raba about the *future*: would the ultimate reward which the Jew hopes to enjoy in the "world to come" match

---

25. See Ḥagiga 5b.
26. *Be-Yom Edo* in the singular, as in the manuscript text and in *MT 'Aboda Zara* 9:2. This basic point escaped the attention of the commentators; see the Katzenelenbogen-Lieberman's edition ad loc.

what Bar-Sheshakh was enjoying *right now*? Raba dared to accept the challenge. The *present* condition of the Jew was superior to that of Bar-Sheshakh, *right now*! "Ours is superior to *this* and to *this*," he said. 'This' is a deictic pronoun standing for a motion signaling an object standing before the protagonists *here* and *now*: in our case, the prostitutes attending Bar-Sheshakh. Pointing (at least linguistically) to the ladies in question, Bar-Sheshakh retorted: "But what could be superior to *this* and to *this*"? Raba replied: "Upon you stands the dread of the empire (*emata de-malkhuta*), [but] upon us does not stand (*havya 'alan*)[27] the dread of the empire (*emata de-malkhuta*)."

*Emata* ('dread') is not a fear motivated by immediate physical danger, but anxiety designed to intimidate and permit psychological coercion and manipulation.[28] The association '*emata*/empire' suggests that we are talking about a type of anxiety designed by the governing authorities to facilitate management and policy implementation. Raba was arguing that a simple Jew, *here-now* enjoyed a higher standard of living than the Persian governor, simply because the Jew is immune from the frenzy and madness of pagan civilization. Maimonides, and then Freud at the end of his life, addressed the dynamics of hysteria intrinsic to pagan civilization.[29] For a people living outside the boundaries of *emata de-malkhuta*, the seductive visions and delights enjoyed by Bar-Sheshakh and his associates are very close to what a cage of chimpanzees has to offer to a normal human being.

Raba's answer concerns the mind and heart of pagan humanity. Fear, more precisely *emata*, in the form of psychic tension and apprehension, is the matrix of pagan humanity. Without dread, pagan civilization, including its political and religious institutions, from A to Z, would collapse.[30] *Emata* is the element fueling the inner dynamics of

27. This is the text preserved in the ms, in the present tense. The standard text *tihve*, in the future tense, makes no sense.
28. See Ex. 15:16; Mishna Soṭa 1:4; Sanhedrin 4:5, Shabbat 77b.
29. See José Faur, *Homo Mysticus: A Guide to Maimonides' Guide for the Perplexed* (Syracuse, N.Y.: Syracuse University Press, 1999), pp. 11–13.
30. In all hierarchical systems, 'order' is the result of intimidation: it permeates

the political, cultural, and social machinery of pagan civilization. It shapes the consciousness and structures the patterns of thought and feeling *from within*. In our days, too, coercive ideologies, as well as intellectual and cultural intimidation, are accepted as civil modes of discourse. The Aramaic version of the Tora translates the term 'god' when referring to pagan deities, *deḥalta* ('psychological terror') *de-'amamin* ('of the gentile peoples'). It means that the principal aim of pagan religion is to instruct man how to placate the gods and avoid their rage.[31] Epicureanism is born out of the same matrix. By postulating that the gods have no interest in human affairs, Epicureanism hoped to free man from fear (of the gods) and thus help him reach *eudaimonia* ('true, full happiness'), that is, a pure pleasure *free* from pain and fear.[32]

*Emata,* particularly *emata de-malkhuta,* or the fear generated by the ruling authorities, is anxiety designed to justify government policy: without *emata*, many *malkhuta* programs could not be implemented! Put differently, Raba was telling Bar-Sheshakh: "Some, like yourself, may have overcome the fear of gods, but all of you, including those in the production and management of fear, live under the menace of the empire's *emata*."

The governor conceded Raba's point. However...

The more repressive a regime is the greater its dependence on

---

every fiber of the individual, the general society, and the government. See José Faur, "One-Dimensional Jew, Zero-Dimensional Judaism," *Annual of Rabbinic Judaism* 2 (1999), pp. 31–50. According to Hobbes, the father of modern political thought, 'fear' plays a decisive role in the formation of the state. For some glimpses, see Leo Strauss, *The Political Philosophy of Hobbes* (Chicago: Chicago University Press, 1963), chapter 5.

31. In this pivotal point 'religious cults,' which are principally motivated by fear and anxiety, differ from 'totemic cults,' which are not; see *The Elementary Forms of Religious Life*, pp. 225–226. For a different distinction between 'religious' and 'totemic' cults, see José Faur, *Studies in the Mishne Tora* (Heb.), (Jerusalem: Mossad Harav Kook, 1978), pp. 219–230; *Horizontal Society*, vol. 2, pp. 754–756.

32. This subject is discussed by Leo Strauss, *Spinoza's Critique of Religion* (New York: Schocken Books, 1965), chapter 1.

elites to run the affairs of the state and mediate between masters and dependents. Bar-Sheshakh conceded the supremacy of *emata*, but there were exceptions, especially among the elite in charge of the production and management of *emata*. One would think that Bar-Sheshakh, a major player in the art of manipulation, would be aware that he, too, could become the victim of the very machine he helped design and refine. To prevent thought of this nature, the ruling authorities provide various levels of pleasure and different codes of conduct for the elites. These 'privileges' are intended not merely to reward, but mainly to control, to block introspection and create the illusion of euphoria and invulnerability. It would not be surprising, therefore, to find Bar-Sheshakh confident that the *emata de-malkhuta* that he had so wittingly designed for others would not touch him. Thus, he snapped back at Raba: "I, however, how could the empire's *emata* be upon me?"

[iii] This type of controversy can only be resolved existentially. Unexpectedly, "While they were seated in conference," presumably discussing matters related to Jewish affairs, "a courier of the emperor came and told [Bar-Sheshakh]: 'Stand up! The Emperor has summoned you!' As he was coming out [of the pool] to leave, he told [Raba]: 'May the eye that wishes to see you (the Jewish people) hurting, split open!' Raba responded: 'Amen!' [At that moment, he slipped, probably on the wet floor, and] Bar-Sheshakh's eye split open."

There are two further points to consider. First, under the pretense of nakedness, Bar-Sheshakh wished ill on the Jews. (Nudity is a superb camouflage; that is why naked ruffians are harder to spot.) Raba knew this when he said "Amen!" Shocked that the rabbi saw through his nakedness, the governor lost his poise, slipped, and lost an eye on his way out. Raba's timing was brilliant. Having to rush to see the emperor, Bar-Sheshakh would not have the chance to retaliate, especially with a patched eye.

Second, there is no truth to the view promoted by anti-religious Jews that hatred of Jews has to do with 'religion.' Bar-Sheshakh himself was a hedonist, with little care either for the gods or for the people he governed. Rather, the matrix of antisemitism is envy: resentment against a group of people enjoying a superior quality of life, not because they are mightier, but because they manage to keep away from the traps of pagan civilization and the *emata de-malkhuta* that it engenders. For those indoctrinated in the belief that *might* is right, the sight of a happy Jew is unbearable. The rage intensifies upon realizing that *emata de-malkhuta* cannot reach those refusing to partake in the sweet delights displayed at the chimpanzee cage. The ire burst out into pandemonium upon discovering that the governor is nothing more than another monkey in the cage that he himself had contributed to building. And worst of all, that the meek rabbi knew this all along. Can anyone fault the good governor for making a Freudian slip and losing an eye on the way to the emperor?

> Although free from political fear, the Jew recognizes that by virtue of living in the bosom of a pagan political system, his freedom is inadequate. On the night of Passover, when Jews celebrate the Exodus from Egypt, there is a special declaration to be said *before* reciting the *Haggada*. Let us note that, whereas the *Haggada* is in Hebrew, this declaration is to be said in Aramaic, the colloquial language of the Jews in Talmudic times, so that it would be understood by everyone. It continues to be pronounced by Jews everywhere: "This year, here, slaves; next year, in the land of Israel, free."

A note: In Antiquity and through the ages, only Jews were conscious of the *emata de-malkhuta*-system controlling the people. Living in *Galut,* or 'Exile,' is having the guts to admit the facts of oppression. 'Emancipated' and 'enlightened' Jews are individuals too dense to realize that.[33] They are also too weak to resist the delights offered at Bar-Sheshakh's monkey-cage: they are so cute!

---

33. See *The Naked Crowd,* pp. 24–31.

* * *

In Judaism, "idolatry" and all forms of "alien worship" (*'aboda zara*), requiring the intercession of an object, a man, or a deity between the worshipper and God, are abominations since they disallow the phenomenal consciousness of *all* the members (*kol ha-'eda*) of Israel (Ex. 35:1): namely, that God makes His Presence manifest *within* the people, and not within the building of a sanctuary or an image (Ex. 25:8). *'Aboda Zara* also repudiates the doctrine that every human being is created "in the image of God" (Gen. 1:27).[34] Indirectly, and with cunning, it also presupposes the notion of a hierarchic 'humanity' arranged in a scale of 'superior/inferior,' i.e., the 'inferior' can only approach God via the 'superior.'

For a people having experienced God's voice at Sinai and, thereafter, His Presence directly "within themselves" (*betokham*), this is another instance of pagan "hubris" (*ge'ut, gebah leb, gassut ruwaḥ*). As the Rabbis taught, hubris and the God of Israel are mutually exclusive.[35] Accordingly, upon seeing a pagan Temple or a Church, Jews are instructed to recite the verse, "The house of the haughty the Lord shall obliterate" (Prov. 15:25)."[36] Not only is hubris the matrix of "idolatry," but, more precisely, it itself *is* "idolatry." "Whoever has a haughty spirit," taught the Rabbis, "equals those who worship idols," and it is "as if he had denied the existence of God," and "as if he has debauched himself with every form of sexual perversion," and "as if he had built (for himself) a sacrificial table."[37] Consequently, men with a haughty spirit "will go down to hell"[38] and "will not resurrect with

34. That is why Pauline theology, requiring the intercession of Jesus between the worshipper and God the Father, posits the corruption of the image of God within via the original sin.
35. See Soṭa 5a, 'Arakhin 15b.
36. See Berakhot 58b; *MT Berakhot* 10:19; *Shulḥan 'Arukh, Oraḥ Ḥayyim*, CCXXIV, 11.
37. Soṭa 4b.
38. Baba Batra 78b.

the dead."[39] By contrast, the Tora "is compared to water... to teach you: just like water will not gather in an elevated place, but will roll down away and gather at a lowly place, the same is with the words of the Tora."[40] Thus, the Tora will not be found among the haughty.[41] As a result, "A haughty man (*mityaher*), if he would be a sage, he would lose his wisdom; and if he would be a prophet, he would lose his prophecy."[42] For this reason, conceited scholars, regardless of affiliation or religious persuasion, have nothing meaningful to say about either Tora or Judaism.[43]

The preceding may shed light on the strange fact that Jews are unimpressed with pagan pageantry, and least of all with their ostentatious sanctuaries and smug clergy.

* * *

Antisemites understood quite well the two-dimensional character of the Tora. Specifically, once one of its dimensions is hindered, the entire system is in peril. Their strategy was/is to target a single dimension of Judaism, and thus render the entire system dysfunctional. In the Middle Ages and later on through modern times, when 'religion' was a matter of concern, Jewish rituals and core beliefs were viciously attacked.[44] In more recent times, when religious arguments had little resonance, the *political* dimension of Israel was/is targeted. Hence, the strategic value of the 'anti-Israeli' and 'anti-Zionism' line of assault. Once divested from their political dimension, Jews become easy prey, as in the 'good old days,' when 'enlightened' Jews entrusted their lives

39. Baba Batra 5a.
40. See *MT Talmud Tora* 3:9, paraphrasing *Ta'aniyot* 7a.
41. 'Erubin 55a.
42. Pesaḥim 66b. In my opinion this is a reference to Paul and his followers; see *Horizontal Society*, vol. 1, chapters 28–30.
43. See *Naked Crowd*, chapter 6.
44. See below, "Iberian Experience," p. 1279.

and possessions to the kindness of the 'Fatherland.' These Jews, ready to betray the most sacred values of Israel, did not fare particularly well.[45]

Because 'enlightened' Jews renounced the 'political' dimension of the *berit,* they failed to comprehend the demonic aspects of the Nazi movement. In 1930, one of the Warburgs said of the Nazis: "One finds among a large part of them valuable, typically German strengths, which are indeed incredible in a political connection, but show strong feeling for social and national duties."[46] Regrettably, even after they had been victimized by the 'Fatherland,' some fiercely hung onto the belief in the absolute superiority of their adopted systems. Assimilated German Jews believed that the Nazi phenomenon were just 'aberrations' of the 'true spirit' of Western culture.[47] When reading the vicious attacks made by pseudo-Jewish intellectuals against Israel, I think of Einstein's definition of 'stupid.' This is someone who keeps on making the same mistake over and over again, self-assured, however, that *this* time the result would be different.

* * *

The difference between polytheism and Hebrew monotheism is deeper than arithmetic. In the economy of pagan ideology, the various deities ruling the world are always fighting with one another. Every occurrence, whether in the realm of nature or in the affairs of man, is the triumph of one force over the other. As such, violence stands at the foundation of the cosmos. Translated into socio-political terms, this means that might is right, and that those with access to violence ought to be more authoritative than those having no access to violence. In a monotheistic universe there is no room for violence: everything that is, is by the will of God. The different creatures and forces of the universe are part of a cosmic ecological system, in which each part contributes to the well-being of the whole system. This

45. See *The Naked Crowd,* chapter 5. Cf. below, "Iberian Experience," pp. 1287–9.
46. Quoted in "The Warburgs," p. 3.
47. Cf. below, "Iberian Experience," pp. 1288–9.

basic doctrine is expressed in a blessing to be pronounced after consuming certain drinks and foods: "Blessed be He… who has created diverse beings, and their individual requirements are (found) in all what He created, bringing thus life through them to every living soul." The purpose of the Law, too, is to bring the individual and human society to a harmonious life with one another and with the rest of the world. Accordingly, the ultimate purpose of the Law is *Shalom* ('peace, harmony').

Given that the polytheistic mind views the universe in terms of power and violence, the relationship between the political power and the deities is one of control and manipulation. Pharaoh, the supreme political leader of Egypt, dreamt that he was standing *on* the Nile (Gen. 41:1), one of the principal gods of Egypt. "My Nile is for me," declared another Pharaoh, "and I made myself" (Ezek. 29:3).[48] Balaam, the highest gentile prophet in the Hebrew Scripture, tried to manipulate God; at the end he was manipulated by Him (see Num. chapters 22–24). Pagan rituals are instituted not by the gods but by the religious hierarchies with the power to determine what is propitious and what is not propitious for the deity. In spite of all the theological rhetoric, there is no place in either the Jewish or Christian Scripture that prescribes the Eucharist. As per pagan religious practice, rituals are *imposed* onto the deity by a clergy who knows what is 'best' for the gods. In this fashion, the ritual is an act of violence against the divinity.

That is why the classification 'monotheistic religions' is fallacious – another effort to blur the difference between the Hebrew and the Christian Scripture. It is as lumping together Picasso's *Matador Luis Dominguín* with a kindergartener's scribble, on the basis that in both cases pencil on paper was used. Unless you define in precise terms what the supposed 'deity' is, 'monotheism' is as valid a standard for the classification of religion as 'paper money' in the field of economics. The fact that the communist and capitalist

48. See *Horizontal Society*, vol. 1, p. 218.

economic systems use paper money does not make them 'similar.' Whatever the notion of 'God' in Christianity may be, it has nothing to do with the God of Sinai, who came *down* and *spoke* "face to face" to the *entire* community of Israel. The Christian Scripture never registers a dialogue between 'Father/God' and 'Jesus/Son.' Unlike the God of the Hebrew Scripture, the God/Father of the Christian Scripture is mute and blind and deaf to whatever is going on in the world below. Jesus chose to reveal his divinity *post mortem*, up there in Heaven, but never down on earth to the *entire* Christian community, as God did in Sinai. At any rate, by the time you can reconcile the arithmetic of the Trinity with the number '1,' there would be no point in engaging in a critical dialogue about 'monotheism,' 'religion,' or anything else.

The fact is that pagan religions, whether of the 'monotheistic' persuasion or not, are governed by hierarchic societies. There is a story in the Talmud[49] bearing on a significant aspect common to all hierarchic societies. It concerns a dispute between R. 'Aqiba (50–135), the foremost authority in the rabbinic period, and Turnus Rufus (Tinneius Rufus, the Roman governor of Judea at the time). The dispute centered on the merits of charity. In a hierarchic system, the aim of those in authority is to maintain the *status quo*. Therefore, to help someone climb up the socio-economic ladder is both rebellious and dangerous. According to this point of view, charity should be regarded as immoral and subversive. The dispute took place during one of the most critical periods of Jewish history, when thousands of Jews were being butchered by the Roman authorities and many more displaced from their ancestral homes. The working principle of Imperial Rome was the pagan belief that might is right.[50] In response to Roman atrocities, Jews mobilized all of their resources to assist the needy.

49. Baba Batra 10a.
50. This doctrine established the political legitimacy of the Conqueror. Christianity applied this doctrine to religion; hence the Holy Wars crisscrossing much of Christian Europe.

"If your God loves the poor, why does He not support them?" asked Turnus Rufus.

"In order that we should save ourselves through them from the judgment of hell" replied R. 'Aqiba.[51]

"On the contrary! You will deserve to go down to hell because of it" replied Turnus Rufus. He added: "Let me illustrate [my point] with a parable. Suppose a king was angry at one of his slaves, put him in jail, and issued an order that no one should give him food or water. And then somebody came along and gave him food and water. When the king finds out about it, wouldn't he be angry at him? And you were called 'slaves,' as it is written, "To me are the children of Israel slaves" (Lev. 25:55).

To which R. 'Aqiba responded:

"Let me illustrate (my point) with the (another) parable. Suppose a king was angry at his son, put him in jail, and issued an order that no one should give him food or water. And then somebody came along and gave him food and water. When the king finds out about it, wouldn't he send him gifts? And we are called 'sons,' as it is written, 'You are the sons of the Lord your God'" (Lev 14:1).

(Turnus Rufus) replied:

"You were called 'sons' and you were called 'slaves.' When you behave in accordance with God's will, you are called 'sons,' but when you don't behave in accordance with God's will, you are called 'slaves.' At the present [as Israel's misfortunes prove], you are not behaving in accordance with God's will."

R. 'Aqiba:

"Behold it was said: 'Hey! Break your bread with the hungry and bring the impoverished persecuted (to your) home' (Isa 58:7). To what (kind of situation) does (the expression) 'impoverished persecuted' refer? To (a situation like that of)

---

51. On the meaning of this sentence, see "Pomp and Pageantry."

> the present! (And about such a situation) it was said: 'Hey! Break your bread with the hungry.'"

There are several points brought up in this discussion relating to our subject. As a member of the ruling circles, Turnus Rufus regarded the relation of the people to God in terms of slaves to their master. Adverse circumstances are to be interpreted as the result of a mechanism that no one has the right to change. As per Greek drama, at the end, we all must submit to the devices of fate. A direct result of this view is the survival of the mightiest and the moral evil of offering assistance to the destitute.[52] For Jews, however, God's relation to the people is to be regarded as that of father to son: the son owes respect to the father, but, as per father and son, the relation is inviolable.[53] Even when warranting penance and retribution, the people are still God's beloved children, meriting whatever assistance could be offered to them. Turnus Rufus conceded that under optimal conditions, one can conceive God's relation to a people as like that of a father and a son, but this would be predicated upon a son's perfect submission; however, once the son slips, the relationship changes to that of master-slave.

Turnus Rufus' concept of society as a rigid, inviolable system continued to prevail throughout the Middle Ages and Modern times. Let us hear what the leading psychologist, Erich Fromme, had to say on this subject: "The social order was conceived as a natural order, and being a definite part of it gave a feeling of security and of belonging."[54] Because in the world of Turnus Rufus everyone is a 'slave,' scrupulously limited to the pigeon-hole assigned to him by the establishment, there is no possibility of change or progress. The following description of medieval man and society illustrates this point:

52. Such theories flourished in 19th century England in connection to Herbert Spencer's doctrine of the survival of the fittest.
53. Jewish law does not allow parents to dissolve the right of their children to inherit.
54. Eric Fromm, *Escape from Freedom* (Avon Books, 1965), p. 58.

> What characterizes medieval in contrast to modern society is its lack of individual freedom. Everybody in the earlier period was chained to his role in the social order. A man had little chance to move socially from one class to another, he was hardly able to move even geographically from one town or from one country to another. With few exceptions he had to stay where he was born. He was often not even free to dress as he pleased or to eat what he liked. The artisan had to sell at a certain place, the market of the town. A guild member was forbidden to divulge any technical secrets of production to anybody who was not a member of his guild and was compelled to let his fellow guild members share in any advantageous buying of raw material. Personal, economic, and social life was dominated by rules and obligations from which practically no sphere of activity was exempted.[55]

The one and single exception was the individualistic Jew. That is why he was/is furiously hated and envied, past and present.

* * *

Assimilation is the great danger haunting Jews. It is tricky and sneaky, and hard to detect. It penetrates the individual from within, taking hold of his patterns of thought and feelings. Once his inner mechanism is overtaken by the pagan world around him, the Jew retrogresses to mythical thinking, and is unable to detect the metamorphosis going on within, and least of all to realize that what he imagines to be 'Jewish' has nothing to do with the Tora. In such a situation, one may sport the longest beard, dress in flowing canonical robes, shake in all forms and directions, ramble ancient authorities, and yet, under all the puffing and muffing, you will find a man whose core spiritual values and concepts of devotion are rooted in pagan religiosity. One

---

55. *Escape from Freedom*, pp. 57–58.

of the most noticeable aspects of pagan ideality is "arrogance" (*ge'ut, gebah leb, gassut ruwaḥ*). Quite often, Jewish leadership, both religious and lay, try to hide their clumsiness and compensate for their incompetence by pretending to be better and wiser than everyone else. The Rabbis were quite aware of this problem. Referring to King Jerobam, the archetype of corrupt Jewish political leadership, the Rabbis remarked: "Jerobam's arrogance (*gassut ruwaḥ*) pestered him (away) from the world."[56] The Messiah, too, will not come "until the arrogant (*gasse ha-ruwaḥ*) will be eliminated from Israel."[57]

Under the aegis of the arrogant (*gasse ha-ruwaḥ*), difference of opinion equals insubordination. By contrast, the Talmud and classical Jewish literature are zigzagged with disagreement and alternative views. Unlike totalitarian systems where the truth is grasped by a single person (the Pope, the Secretary of the Party, *et al.*), in Judaism the truth is grasped collectively. Given that each human is created in God's image, it follows that everyone has something unique and outstanding to contribute.[58] Thus the truth in its totality cannot be grasped by any single person, but only collectively.[59] Jews regard Moses as the greatest of all men, and yet he was required to act collectively with the seventy elders (Ex. 24:1; Num. 11:16, 24, 25). As we learn from Maimonides' Introduction to the *Mishne Tora*, the Tora was entrusted not to Moses the individual, but "to Moses and his court," i.e., the seventy elders representing the people of Israel. Differences of opinion are encouraged. To ensure that judges could freely express their own opinion and not feel embarrassed to disagree with a more experienced judge, Jewish legal procedure requires that voting should begin with

---

56. Sanhedrin 101b.
57. Sanhedrin 98b. Maimonides' thesis, that precepts and rituals have a rationale, comes to negate the notion that the Tora is grounded on the *fiat* of authority alone. Conversely, the anti-Maimonideans – and there are plenty of them in both the 'religious' and 'secular' camps – conceive 'religion' as a system that was *imposed* on the people by the *fiat* of authority alone.
58. See "Pomp and Pageantry."
59. Cf. R. Menaḥem Me'iri, *Bet ha-Beḥira 'al Berakhot* (Jerusalem: Makhon ha-Talmud ha-Yisra'eli, 5725/1965), on Berakhot 58a, p. 206b.

the more junior members of the court.[60] Because disagreements are not viewed as acts of insubordination, but as honest men trying their best to understand the Law, the Rabbis declared: "These and these are the words of the living God."[61] The fact that normative Judaism followed one school rather than the other, does not mean that the other is 'wrong,' but, simply, that for a variety of reasons – none of them metaphysical or theological – the judicial authorities decided to adopt one system over the other. Sepharadim and Ashkenazim, for instance, follow different legal traditions, and yet, they freely quote, examine, and adopt the legal opinions of one another.[62]

As a result of assimilation, whereby 'Judaism' is measured by clothing and party associations, things have changed. Differences of opinions, whether of a religious or secular nature, are regarded as a kind of 'heresy' and 'insubordination.' Consequently, it is nay impossible to have a meaningful dialogue between members of different movements and political ideologies. When encounters between members of different groups occur, generally accidently, the conversational mood is that of 'superior/inferior.' Good manners are regarded as some sort of intellectual or psychological failing.

But this was not always the case. R. Israel Moses Ḥazzan (1807–1863), scion of one of the most prestigious rabbinic families in Jewish history, who had been appointed to the supreme rabbinic court in Jerusalem at the age of twenty-three, recognized the literary and intellectual accomplishments of R. Moses Mendelssohn (1729–1786). When someone pointed to him some of his mistakes, he replied: "Fortunate is he whose errors can be counted."[63] Moses Picciotto (1806–1879) of Aleppo, Syria, a member of a diplomatic family whose members had served in some of the most prestigious cities of Europe, had a similar attitude. Eventually, he moved, together with his son James

---

60. Mishna Sanhedrin 4:2; see *MT Sanhedrin* 10:6.
61. 'Erubin 13b.
62. See below, "Where Different is the Same and the Same is Different."
63. See José Faur, *Rabbi Israel Moses Ḥazzan: the Man and his Works* (Heb.) (Haifa: Academic Publishers, 1978), p. 23 note 63.

(1830–1897), to England, and soon after, he became the president of the Bevis Marks Synagogue. Because of his religious upbringing and ideology, he had an enormous influence on the life of the community. In his *Sketches of Anglo-Jewish History*, his son James wrote how his father spared no effort to bring about a measure of unity between the Orthodox and the Reform congregations.[64] Israel Finestein, the editor of the second edition, remarked that "Picciotto underestimates the ideological divisions between the Orthodox and the Reform."[65] I do not believe that either Ḥazzan or Picciotto had a lesser grasp of the differences between Reform and Orthodox, or that in any away they underestimated the significance of their respective ideologies. Probably, they understood the differences better than those who directly participated in the conflict. (After all, what were some of the extreme Orthodox positions if not Reform to the right?) What divided Finestein from Ḥazzan and Picciotto was their mutual perspectives. Finestein conceived of 'religion' in terms not dissimilar from that of the Catholic and Anglican Churches; accordingly, the division between Reform and Orthodox is insurmountable. Consequently, it would be pointless to try to find some common ground between the parties to serve as the basis for dialogue. My daughter Aura pointed out to me that the root of the Hebrew word *maḥloqet* ('controversy') is *ḥeleq* ('part, portion'), implying that both parties are clutching at only a segment of the subject, and thus failing to look at the total picture.

Let me give you a different approach to 'controversies.' The late R. David de Sola Pool (1885–1970) told me that he once received a query from a synagogue in Venezuela concerning the 'correct' position* of the podium (*teba*) from where the cantor chants the prayers.

---

64. In Aleppo there was an attempt to establish a 'Reform' Synagogue, see Yaron Harel, "A Spiritual Agitation in the East: The Founding of a Reform Community in Aleppo in 1862," (Heb.) HUCA (1992), pp. 19–33. Although out of focus in some areas, it presents solid points about the religious and intellectual background of the time. Picciotto may have been involved in some of the negotiations that brought an end to this schism.

65. *Sketches of Anglo-Jewish History* (London: The Soncino Press, 1956), p. 482.

His answer is exemplary and to the point: if there is a *minyan* (forum of ten men) for daily prayers, it really does not matter where the podium stands, and if there is no daily *minyan,* then it really does not matter where the podium stands.

There is a story involving Joḥe, a famous folklore hero from the Middle East, suggesting a more relaxed approach to 'religion.' Jews had their own versions of Joḥe's stories and escapades. Some of these stories are known to me only in Arabic, others only in Judeo-Spanish, and some in both. The following story I know only from Judeo-Spanish tradition. The participants are Joḥe, representing extreme simplicity bordering on the moronic, and a *Ḥakham* ('rabbi'), who was an emissary from Israel, representing extreme wisdom and piety. One day, on Yom Kippur, Joḥe decided to attend the services. However, instead of saying, "God is *eḥad* ('one')," he said, "God is *aḥer* ('another')." The person sitting next to him was scandalized and went on to tell the rabbi. The rabbi called Joḥe, and asked: "My beloved son, how do you say, "God is ... ?" –*Aḥer*! –responded Joḥe. The rabbi explained to him the difference between these two terms, and told him that from now on he must say "God is *eḥad*." Joḥe was happy because he had been instructed by such an illustrious rabbi, and all the way back home he was repeating "God is *eḥad*!" However, as soon as he entered his home, he forgot. Next day, he went back to the synagogue, and asked the rabbi, did you teach me yesterday, "God is *aḥer?*" "No, my son," he replied, "God is *eḥad, eḥad, eḥad!*" Joḥe was now happy because he knew the right way to pray, and to whomever he would see, he would shout: "*Eḥad*! *Eḥad*!" A few days later, he forgot. Again, he went to the rabbi who instructed him the right way to pray, and again Joḥe forgot. This was repeated many times. Finally, one day upon arriving at the synagogue, he was told that the rabbi had just embarked to return home to Israel. Joḥe did

---

* Rabbi Abraham Faur: The query was about the *position* of the podium, not its *direction,* which must be towards Jerusalem. The intent behind R. David de Sola Pool's response is that such a query is about nonsensical minutiae.

not give up hope. With all his might he ran to the harbor. But alas! The ship had just pulled away from the harbor. In a desperate effort, Joḥe jumped into the water and waded towards the ship. Somehow, the waters opened up, and he was able to reach the ship. He saw the rabbi on board and from below he shouted at him, "What have you taught me: *aḥer* or *eḥad*?" The rabbi answered: "Joḥe, continue praying as best as you can. Since your *aḥer* comes from your heart, it is better than the *eḥad* of many."

* * *

As the saying goes, 'The habit does not make the monk,' just like not everyone wearing a Stetson Grant hat and Durango boots is a cowboy. This view, somehow, does not seem to apply to the 'rabbinic world.' For reasons better not discussed in public, analphabetic rabbis, or rabbis without Tora, roam freely, enjoying much fame and popularity, particularly among politicians and the semi-learned. Alerting about the fact that age and appearance are not good indicators of knowledge, the Rabbis said: "Look not at the jug but at that which is in it. There may be a new jug full of old wine and an old jug which has not even new wine in it."[66] Given that bogus-rabbis are always in some sort of a mud-sling contest, perennially fighting against something or someone, the Rabbis taught: "Rabbinic Scholars (*talmide ḥakhamim*) increase peace in the world."[67] Rather than by looks and clothing, a sage is distinguished by his high moral standard, impeccable manners, and personal habits.[68] Those disregarding moral standards and civil discourse don't fit the bill – no matter how 'rabbinic' they may appear. This situation was noted by an illustrious rabbinic leader, a Holocaust survivor and a man of vast knowledge, R. Jechiel Jacob Weinberg (1882–1966). In a letter from Switzerland, 1953, he wrote:

66. Abot 4:20. See *Abot de-R. Natan,* XXXIV, B, 38a.
67. Berakhot 64a. See *Horizontal Society,* vol. 1, p. 538.
68. For an account of the sage's code of life, see *MT De'ot,* chapter 5.

> There is something that I find particularly distressing: the collapse in ethics among us, and the extreme tolerance to fraud camouflaging itself as piety (*ḥasidut*) and as concern for the dishonor of the Tora. Fraud is on the increase. It acts with cunning and gall, laughing at the innocence of those who believe in them. Were we permitted to disclose the cunning and trickery of those hypocrites the world would have been astonished and shocked; but those crooks bring fear and fright on everyone, using as weapons tale-telling, defamation, prevarication and [exposing the victim to] public humiliation. There are some that perceive and detect [the situation], but they are 'controlled' by flattery and the dispensation of false honors. At any rate, fraud prospers, and its prosperity poisons the air and causes despair to grow, with the conviction that this is the way of the world: the righteous having it bad and the wicked having it good. I am convinced that the survival of our people and the survival of our state [the State of Israel] depend on spiritual purification and the raising of our moral standards. Those who are so punctilious about the dietary laws, the mixture of wool and linen, synagogue customs, and the like, and openly transgress human ethics and morality, cause the young generation to further themselves away from religion and [the fulfillment of] the commandments. The worst problem is that the occupation in the promotion of the Tora and the observance of religion had become a source of income, and a ladder to climb up to a higher social position. In our midst are to be found men that only through this occupation had acquired fame.[69]

Bogus rabbis in rabbinic gowns feel uncomfortable in the presence of 'other' rabbis. Some time ago, I went to pay my respects to a friend

69. In ed. Abraham Beck, *Be'ayot Aqṭualiyot le-Or ha-Halakha* (Jerusalem: Mossad Harav Kook, 1993), pp. 58–59.

who lost his father. There were a number of people, among them one of those individuals associated with a religious organization supported by the deceased. He had a white beard and was wearing one of those double breasted, long black jackets. He was not pleased with the fact that people addressed me as 'Rabbi.' He asked permission to speak, and for about fifteen minutes he lectured on the evils of assimilation, particularly of those rabbis who dress like *goyim*. It was obvious to all that he was referring to me. He was kind enough, however, not to point an accusing finger at me, probably because it may have proven to be a poor strategy for fund-raising. At the end of the sermon, he sat down. I waited until he was alone and came to him. "I assume that you are an outstanding Talmudist," I said. He smiled softly as to acquiesce to the indisputable, but not so obviously as to appear conceited. "Can you tell us how you say 'lapel' in Hebrew?" The poor man was startled. He was not familiar with Modern Hebrew, and was trying frantically to fish for an equivalent term from rabbinic literature. "Well," I said, "what about 'double-breasted?'" Again, the poor man remained speechless. He could neither utter the words 'I don't know,' nor explode in a fit of ire, as this would be a poor public relation tactic. In order not to prolong his agony, I said, "One last question: Do you know how to say 'jacket' in Hebrew?" Before he could answer, I added, "The truth is that these words do not exist in Rabbinic Hebrew, simply because Jews never used such garments. What you are wearing is also gentile clothing. Now let me ask you, why is it all right for you to wear clothing according to the fashion of the late 19th century, but it is forbidden for others to dress according to the fashion of their own country and time?" Somehow, he managed to mumble something about the special clothing of a rabbi. "Do you know how Jewish law defines the rabbi's attire?" I asked. He did not have the foggiest idea. In his boundless ignorance, he fancied that the way he and his peers dressed must be the proper rabbinic code of dressing. "Well, Maimonides used two terms to define a sage's garment:

'comely' (*na'e*) and 'clean' (*naqi*)."[70] I stopped for a second, and then added, "Although some may deem your attire 'comely,' few would argue that a jacket full of greasy spots is 'clean.'"

Except for 'professional Jews' – those who make a living by being 'Jewish,' i.e., by working for political or religious organizations – most members of the Jewish faith treat others horizontally: neither as superiors nor as inferiors, but as equals. In return, they expect reciprocity, and unless he/she happens to be one of those 'professional Jews,' she/he will treat no one either as an inferior or as a superior. Many 'professional Jews,' whether 'religious' or 'secular' – especially politicians – are not aware of this simple fact: Jews, as well as non-Jews, don't care for people in the habit of speaking down to the 'other.' In the words of R. Weinberg, I think that "spiritual purification and the raising of our moral standards" would be a positive first step for Jewish success, both in Israel and abroad. After all, if God came down to Mt Sinai to speak to the people, why should it be that men and women who are supported *by our taxes and contributions* cannot do the same?

70. *MT De'ot* 5:9.

# 4. When Different Is the Same and the Same Is Different

Jewish love is unlike pagan love. For a pagan, love is essentially narcissistic, that is, love of self. Others are loved as much as they can be incorporated into the self: whatever is not similar to 'us' cannot be the object of love. This explains why deities have human features. Ultimately, to be meaningful, a deity must be fully integrated with those who worship it. The ritual of the Eucharist, whereby the deity is gastronomically digested by its worshipper, serves to express the pagan view of love.[1] This type of love is violent. When the object of love does not allow for narcissistic incorporation, it becomes the object of hate and violence. 'Christian love' kills, with countless victims of every age, race, and religion, over centuries.

I am reminded of a tragi-comic instance of this kind of love when a priest approached a victim of the Inquisition in the Auto-de-Fe held in Valladolid on June 29, 1654. As the victim was being burnt, the

1. It is in reference to this ritual that the Rabbis stated that "Jesus is condemned [to be] in fiery feces" (צואה רותחת) (Giṭṭin 57a). The Rabbis do not believe in transubstantiation, whereby the bread and wine of the Eucharist is miraculously transformed into the flesh and blood of Jesus. Therefore, as it was pointed out by R. Simon b. Semaḥ Duran, *Qeshet wu-Magen* (Leghorn, 5523/1763), 4b and 26b, the Rabbis were merely describing the Eucharist according to the mind of the Christian believer, whereby Jesus' blood and flesh become gastronomically united with the worshipper. Hence, the expression "fiery feces," i. e., hot, while still in the intestines of the worshipper, before defecation.

priest asked him whether he was truly repentant. Looking at the priest, the victim replied: "Father, do you think that this is time to joke?"[2]

A teacher of mine in Spain, who was a priest, explained to me that "the Inquisition was the highest manifestation of biblical love, and if they incinerated the Jewish bodies in fire, it was to save their souls from the fire of eternal damnation." Later, I learned that he came from a family of 'New Christians;' some of the local people, lay teachers, and prelates taunted him because of it. They must have drilled this argument into him so many times that the poor man could not stop repeating it whenever the occasion arose.

Jewish love is not narcissistic. God – whom the Hebrew Scripture instructs us to "love" (Deut. 6:5) – is "the wholly other," completely different from anyone or anything we can imagine. We can now properly understand the principle formulated by Maimonides, stating that God should not be described using positive attributes. Even the ignorant folk must learn that God has no human attributes. Otherwise, 'love of God' would become a massive exercise in narcissism. Instead of learning how to love the other, this type of love would teach how to hate the other – those who are unlike 'God and us.' Christian 'love' does not tolerate rejection. "Once the apostle Paul had laid down universal love between all men as the foundation of his Christian community," noted Freud, "the inevitable consequence in Christianity was the utmost intolerance towards all who remained outside of it."[3] In contrast, Jews did not understand the biblical precept to "love your fellow human," (Lev. 19:18) narcissistically; we must love the other precisely because they are completely different from us.[4] There are two aspects to this precept. One is positive and concerns the way people should view others: Instead of looking at the other critically – with the purpose of finding fault or blame – love involves discovering what is positive and worthy in others. This must result, in

2. Cited in *In the Shadow of History*, p. 194.
3. Sigmund Freud, *Civilization and its Discontents* (New York: Doubleday, 1958), p. 65. See *In the Shadow of History*, pp. 6–7.
4. On this fundamental point, see *In the Shadow of History*, pp. 6–7.

the words of Maimonides, in "recounting [their] worthiness" (לספר בשבחו) and recognizing the merits and accomplishments – or in other words, individuation – of the other. The second aspect is negative: It is caring and protecting the possessions and dignity of the other as if they were our own.[5] In this manner, love of Israel is the most basic and cohesive bond of the people.

Because of mental assimilation and exposure to pagan ideology, some Jews associate 'different' with 'abnormal' and 'antagonistic.' For them, everything is to be measured vertically; what is not equal must either be 'superior' or 'inferior.' Since 'others' can hardly be 'better' than 'we' are, there is a propensity to regard what is 'different' as faulty and undesirable. Therefore, Jews often feel 'culture shock' when they encounter coreligionists who have other traditions; their rituals, cuisine, and, above all, lifestyle, seem 'inauthentic.' I remember in my own case – I must have been about fifteen years old – when in my native Buenos Aires I was persuaded by a friend to attend evening services at an Ashkenazi synagogue. I grew up in a neighborhood where there were scarcely any Jews, and the few Jews we knew were all Sephardic. I attended a non-Jewish school, and there was only one boy, a war refugee, who had a 'Jewish last name.' There were some Ashkenazi shopkeepers, but we hardly had any contact with them. When, out of curiosity, I once asked who the Ashkenazim were, I was told in a solemn voice: "They are the Jews from the tribe of Benjamin." At any rate, on one Sunday afternoon, this friend and I took a bus for Villa Crespo, where there was a thriving Ashkenazi community made up mostly of war refugees and survivors. We arrived at the synagogue just before the services began. The place was enormous and well attended. Suddenly, a man pounded at the podium and said something in a Hebrew I could not understand. At once, the public responded, with a loud, piercing cry. Everyone was shaking. Some were pounding at their tables, wailing. Others were moving their heads right and left. All were praying with an intensity

---

5. *Mishne Tora, De'ot* 6:3.

which I had never witnessed before. When, a few minutes later, they stood up to recite the silent prayer, my friend and I exited the premises. I was emotionally and intellectually shocked. For about half an hour as we were riding the bus home, I could not say a word. It took some time for me to appreciate the pathos and fervor underlying this religious experience.

Fortunately, in most cases, this initial shock is quickly substituted by friendship and understanding. Generally, people realize that each tradition developed in different contexts and that every community tried to express its Jewishness according to the circumstances at hand. Occasionally, because we are prone to think in platonic terms, we imagine that there is only one single, 'genuine' form of Judaism. Just recently, I was asked by a colleague which tradition, the Sephardic or the Ashkenazic, was more authentic. I responded, "It depends on whether you define 'authentic' and 'Judaism' according to the Ashkenazic or Sephardic tradition." Our point could be illustrated with an example from the world of physics. Let's suppose that someone releases a ball from their hands and it falls to the ground. Obviously, we would consider this to be a natural phenomenon and a confirmation of Newton's law of gravity. Now, let us imagine a second scenario in which, upond being released, the ball rises. After a third time, the ball floats in a straight line. An unsophisticated observer might immediately assume that the two latter cases contradict the law of gravity. However, upon considering the *circumstances* more carefully, they would discover that in fact the last two cases confirm Newton's law of gravity. When the ball went up, it did so because it was at the bottom of a pool full of water, and when the ball floated in a straight line, it did so because it was in outer space. It is precisely because the ball was following the same law of gravity in each of the three different circumstances that it acted as it did. Indeed,

* Rabbi Abraham Faur: Buoyancy depends on the gravity of displaced water to provide upward pressure on an object placed in it. In the case of the ball in the bottom of the pool, the displaced water is being pulled down by gravity resulting in upward pressure on the ball.

if the ball would have fallen in outer space or at the bottom of the pool*, *that* would have contradicted the law of gravity.

Applied to our case, if communities living in different geographical areas and cultural centers would have developed identically, the guiding principle underlying these communities would be totally different. Imagine discovering a Jewish community that had lived in the same region in the heart of the French Alps from time immemorial, but that somehow also spoke the Arabic dialect of the Jews of Mosul, dressed in the same clothing, and ate exactly the same cuisine. This community would be *radically* different than its counterpart in Mosul. To begin with, the Arabic of the Jews of Mosul is the product of a specific linguistic tradition, affected by many *local* factors, for example, the Aramaic dialect that at one time was peculiar to the Jews of that region, Persian influence due to their geographical proximity to Iran, etc. More importantly, like most Judeo-languages, that dialect had a special double effect: it allowed Jews to communicate, albeit on a lower level, with their non-Jewish neighbors, and still insulated them linguistically. The same applies to their clothing and food. If there were such a miracle as a community of Jews in the Alps identical to the Jews of Mosul, not only would their language be a total puzzle to linguists and anthropologists, but it would also be *totally different* from that of the Jews in Mosul, since it served none of their functions. The same would apply to their cuisine and apparel. While it is perfectly normal for a Jew in Mosul to indulge in all forms of foods made with okra and eggplants, this would not be the case for a people living in the heart of the French Alps. The same would apply to a hypothetical group of Jews living high in the Atlas Mountains who spoke Yiddish, ate gefilte fish, and occasionally indulged in potato latkes with sour cream and apple sauce.

The notion that our local tradition represents 'genuine Judaism' is not exclusive to a single group. It was a phenomenon once peculiar to Jews who had grown up insulated from the rest of world Jewry, but it is no longer excusable in our days. For a long time, my paternal grandmother believed that no one could possibly be Jewish unless they spoke either Arabic or Judeo-Spanish. The following anecdote is a comical instance of this attitude: In a visit to Israel in the early sixties, I went to a grocery store with a friend to buy a few items. For reasons that only God knows, out of all the variety of languages that we knew, at that moment we were speaking Judeo-Spanish. I soon noticed that a lady in her late seventies was looking at us. She then approached me and, pulling my sleeve, asked me in a secretive tone: *Judio* ('a Jew')?

The preceding is necessary because some Jews still indulge in the fantasy of some platonic form of Judaism (preserved exclusively by their own specific tradition) which ought to serve as a paradigm for all other communities. As ridiculous as it sounds, in 1978 I received a call from a professor teaching at one of the well-established Jewish institutions of higher learning gracing New York. His name was familiar, and after exchanging some pleasantries, he asked me the most amazing question I had ever heard from anyone engaged in Jewish education: "I understand that you are familiar with the history and culture of Aleppo. Do you know whether any families still speak Yiddish?" I explained to him that during World War I a few Jewish soldiers from Austria and Germany deserted and took refuge in the community. Eventually, some of them married local girls and lived in the community. I knew one of these families. In fact, I even once met one of these soldiers. I exchanged some words with him, and it was quite possible that he still spoke some Yiddish or perhaps German. There also were some Ashkenazi families that took refuge during the Crimean war, but all of them had totally assimilated into the community. "No!" the professor answered emphatically. "I am referring to families that have been speaking Yiddish in Aleppo since the Middle Ages." After pausing for a brief moment, he added: "I believe that the community in Aleppo originally spoke Yiddish and only later switched to Arabic. I heard that some of these families continue to speak Yiddish to this day. Do you know any of them?" Seeing no purpose in this kind of conversation, I suggested the name of a rabbi – a total ignoramus who could not write in any language – who happened to be associated with the same institution where that professor taught. "If there is anyone who could assist you in this matter, he is the one." We said goodbye, and I never heard from that professor again.

This form of parochialism is not merely restricted to linguistics. Occasionally, it affects patterns of thought. Because of some Jews' own narrow view of what the 'truth' is and what the proper method is for arriving at it, they consider other Jews intellectually 'inferior.' Accordingly, they regard the literature of these people as 'gibberish' and unworthy of serious study. A distinguished scholar of Talmudic history wrote that once, while delivering a lecture, he quoted a passage from the Mishna. A Yemenite Jew sitting in the audience corrected him. The professor admitted his error and told him sarcastically, "What about you teaching us also the meaning of that passage?" "It is not my place," responded the Yemenite Jew. "You are the lecturer and I am a simple Jew who knows the text of the Mishna." The professor referred to this case as an illustration of inferior thinking and faulty education. I do not agree. It seems to me, that the Yemenite Jew showed better manners and more intellectual sophistication than the professor. On the one hand, because of his deep belief in the sacredness of the text, and the basic principle of horizontality whereby every Jew has equal access to the Law,[6] it was proper to have corrected the professor. On the other hand, it was improper for the professor to challenge him to give an interpretation of the passage. Obviously, whatever interpretation he would have given, it would have been considered wrong and would have served as an excuse to embarrass and ridicule him. Moreover, the professor's conclusion that the education and thinking process of his interlocutor was unwarranted. Elias Canetti refers to this attitude as "the passing of the sting."[7] Sometimes, we do onto others precisely the offenses and injuries that others have done to us. Cowards are the great practitioners of this art. When they suffer injury or abuse from someone too powerful to

6. See the Rabbinic quotation from *Sifre* #41, in my *Golden Doves*, p. 86.
7. See *Crowds and Power*, pp. 66–71, 354–355.

confront, they extract vengeance from an innocent victim who is too weak to retaliate. This is why oppressed mobs have always attacked Jews, and why that professor chose to attack his Yemenite student. Incidentally, by "passing the sting" onto the weaker man, the original situation is replicated, yet the roles are inverted – the persecuted is now the persecutor. There is some of this going on among Jews. Centuries of persecution and ignominy have embittered some to the extent that they find it difficult to see anything positive in other Jews and recount their "worthiness."

The Jewish people were blessed with a great variety of traditions. We normally speak of Sephardic ('Iberian') and Ashkenazi ('German') Jewries. But there are many more traditions that have survived till our very days: Byzantine ('Greek-speaking Jews' from Corfu, Janina and the vicinity), Italians (who are neither Sephardic nor Ashkenazi), Yemenite, Bukharian, Afghan, Persian, etc. Even within a single tradition, there are divisions and subdivisions, each developing according to its own historical circumstances. I remember once asking a friend, the late R. Jacob Elmaleh, about the tradition of Aleppo concerning Ninth of Ab prayers. "There is no such a thing as an [homogeneous] Aleppo tradition on prayer," he said. "Each synagogue had its own tradition." Then he proceeded to explain that some synagogues had preserved a Sephardic tradition, another was influenced by the *musta'rab* liturgy dominating Aleppo before the expulsion from Spain. Some of this influence stemmed from a now extinct tradition of an 'Israeli' (מנהג ארץ ישראל) community living in that city since late antiquity. Still others followed, more or less, the liturgical tradition of Jerusalem (מנהג ירושלים).

* * *

How are we to relate to the diversity of traditions and outlooks that make up the totality of the Jewish experience? To begin with, we should not look at Jewish traditions as ethnical. The identification of Jewish traditions with ethnicity is itself another instance of mental assimilation. Jewish tradition has nothing to do with 'ethnicity.' Ethnicity involves two aspects, both of which are unacceptable in Judaism. First, it refers to ancestry and race in their anthropological sense. This is abhorrent in Judaism, which maintains, as the Hebrew Scripture teaches, that all humans were created in the image of God (Gen. 1:26). Insofar as Jews are concerned, every member of the covenant, including proselytes, are "the children of Abraham, Isaac, and Jacob."[8] The second aspect of ethnicity relates to place of birth and nationality. For Judaism, these factors are irrelevant. All Jews, regardless of place of birth or citizenship, are equal members of the People of Israel.

It would be sinful and erroneous to associate Jewish traditions with 'ethnicities.' In fact, some of the great Sephardic scholars were of French background, such as R. Menaḥem b. Zeraḥ (ca. 1310–1385) and the famous scientist R. Abraham Zaccuto (1452- ca. 1515). The *Rishon le-Ṣion* [Chief Rabbi], R. Jacob Shaul Elyashar (1817–1906), was Ashkenazi. R. David de Sola Pool, by far the most successful Sephardic congregational rabbi in the U.S., once told me that his father's family was Ashkenazi, "Pool" meaning "Polish" in Dutch. I remember that when I was a child in Buenos Aires, there was a teacher known as Ḥakham ('Rabbi') Shemen. He was famous for having the most perfect Hebrew pronunciation. He still preserved the tradition of long and short vowels, and was regarded as the supreme master of biblical prosody; printed editions of the Bible were corrected on his authority. One day, during a casual conversation, he told me that he was born in Russia and that his parents escaping (though not certain, what I believe to have been) the Crimean war had finally settled in Damascus, where he grew up. Suspecting that I was unconvinced, the next day he brought me his passport on which "Russia" was denoted as his place of birth. Would anyone believe that these men are less Sephardic because of their place of birth? Indeed, the most Sephardic men that I encountered – individuals that dedicated their

8. See Maimonides, ed. J. Blau, *Teshubot ha-Rambam*, 3 vlms. (Jerusalem: Mekize Nirdamim, 1969), vol. 2, #293, p. 549; cf. *Sifra, Dibbura di-Ndaba Parsh.* II, 3.

lives to promoting the highest standards of the Maimonidean tradition – were *not* Sepharadim by birth. Men like Professors Harry A. Wolfson (1887–1974) and Steven S. Schwarzschild (1924–1989). But there were and are many, many more... too many to enumerate. By contrast, some of the most obscurantist men whom I crossed paths with – men who stood against everything that the 'Sephardic Golden Age' represented – bore Sephardic surnames. The simple truth is that educated Jews view the traditions of Israel as cultural systems, created by different communities throughout their long histories. 'Sepharad' and 'Ashkenaz,' for instance, are not geo-political entities. Rather, each represents distinct educational and legal models, diverse methodologies for the study and development of Jewish values, and unique visions of Judaism and lifestyles. Their purpose is to inspire, illuminate and assist the Jew to chart new paths and strategies for the future; not to imprison him in a mythical Ghetto of idyllic dimensions. It is no exaggeration to say that the greatest admirers of the Sephardic tradition are Ashkenazi scholars. In fact, almost the entire output of Jewish research and scholarship in modern times concerns Sephardic thought, history, languages, and literature. Many of these works are the life-long product of great Ashkenazi scholars who dedicated their lives to the discovery, preservation, and transmission of the Sephardic tradition.

Horizontality is the key for a full appreciation of the traditions of Israel. Rather than to view Jewish variety vertically, in terms of 'better/worse,' 'superior/inferior,' etc., we must learn how to view Jewish diversity horizontally; that is, as 'different' but 'equal': each representing the crowing efforts of a defined group of people struggling to implement the same sacred Law of Israel within its own specific historical circumstances. Due to family history, place of residence, and numerous other factors, one may find that they feel more comfortable in one tradition than in the other. But this should not prevent them from enjoying and appreciating the other traditions that Judaism has to offer. In a deeper sense, all the traditions of Israel belong equally to every Jew, just like every Jew belongs to each of these traditions: we should all learn about them and try to support and promote them. A significant positive aspect of the State of Israel in recent years is the deep sense of 'inter-traditional' attitude, particularly among the young. Military service and marriage help dispel some of the old notions about 'better' and 'worse' communities. Not only do people freely 'borrow' from other traditions, but more importantly, many would find offensive any disparaging remarks about 'other' Jews. One of my favorite synagogues in Jerusalem is Zahore Ḥamma, on Jaffa Road in Maḥane Yehuda. There are always several *minyanim* going on at the same time. What is particularly remarkable is that anyone can stand up and lead services in either tradition. No one seems to care one way or the other, because they all believe that all the liturgies of Israel are equally sacred. Some Ashkenazi communities in the US have special programs dedicated to incorporating – through lectures, exhibitions, and musical programs – some of the history and traditions of other communities into their congregations. On these occasions, part of the Sabbath services are conducted according to the liturgy of that tradition, and some of their typical foods are served at the *Qiddush*. These are beautiful practices that ought to be emulated all over. Many Sepharadim never attend Ashkenazi services. It would be highly instructive for Sephardic congregations to have similar arrangements. There could be special Sabbaths, during which their services would be conducted according to Ashkenazi liturgy. Part of the program should include songs, lectures, and even typical Ashkenazi foods. I once proposed (surprise: with no results!) that "Jewish Appreciation Programs" should be developed and incorporated in elementary and high school curricula – programs that explore the variety of contributions made by different communities throughout the Diaspora. These programs should not be restricted to folklore, but rather include the study of literature, history of ideas, diplomatic and commercial feats, and general accomplishments of these communities. These programs should foster an appreciation for the accomplishments of communities in distant lands and daring circumstances.[9] The more one knows their

9. *Mishne Tora, De'ot* 6:3.

own tradition, the more prone they are to appreciate other traditions. This explains why Jewish scholars, in particular, know how to value the worth and contributions produced by the Jewish people throughout their long history all over the Diaspora.

Rabbis and sages tend to admire, rather than resent, the scholarship produced within other intellectual traditions. I will never forget one of my teachers from Argentina, R. Nissim Freue (1895–1985), originally from Damascus. He was one of the most skillful Talmudists I ever met. He had been a businessman and was fortunate enough to spend all of his long life studying and teaching the one subject he loved most: Talmud. In his methodology, he followed the tradition of Damascus, which was that of the rest of the Ottoman Empire. For geographic reasons, works printed in North Africa were not generally known in that circle. When he came for a visit to New York, I showed him my library, one section of which contained Talmudic commentaries written by North African rabbis. "Ah!" he sighed with envy, as if feeling his own inadequacy in comparison to these masters, and adding with admiration, "חכמי המערב!" ("The sages of the West!"), a reference to North African Rabbis in Sephardic parlance. Then he sat down and proceeded to devour their notes on one of the most difficult pericopes in the Talmud ("סוגיה דמראות נגעים", *Shebu'ot* 5b-6b).

The profound admiration and respect that the great men of Israel had for other traditions is best demonstrated by the following encounter between the protagonists R. Maṭloub 'Abadi (1889–1970) and Professor Saul Lieberman (1898–1983). The event took place in November 1966. By then, I had known them both for a long time. When I left my native Buenos Aires, I had been initiated in only two levels of Talmudic studies (גרסא and עיון). Although I continued to pursue the study of Talmud intensely, I never had the opportunity to be initiated in the third and final level, which centers around decisional law (פסק הלכה). R. Maṭloub 'Abadi, scion of a distinguished rabbinic family of Aleppo, was an extraordinary teacher and a *dayyan* ('rabbinic judge'). Some of the great Sephardic Talmudic masters of this generation were his pupils. During World War II, he went into business. He was successful and was soon able to organize his affairs in such a way that allowed him to do that which he loved most: study rabbinic law and jurisprudence, and write decisional law. From him, I learned the traditional methodology of decisional law, and I regarded him as one of my rabbinic teachers. To say that Professor Lieberman was recognized as the greatest Talmudist in modern times is an understatement. There was not a single field of Talmudic studies – whether in the intricacies of Semitic philology, Greek and Latin lexicography, history, archaeology, law, and textual analysis – in which did not make substantial contributions. In fact, his scholarship was so overwhelming that it would take at least one generation of scholars just to properly evaluate his contributions.

One of my secret projects was to have R. 'Abadi and Professor Lieberman meet. I believed that each represented his own tradition at its finest. It would be fascinating to see them react to each other. I knew that such an encounter was fraught with perils – no one could foretell how such great men would interact. At any rate, I could not resist the temptation. I spoke to Professor Lieberman about R. 'Abadi. He was surprised that such a man existed in Brooklyn, or anywhere. As an act of courtesy, Professor Lieberman sent him the early volumes of his *Tosefta Ki-Fshuṭa,* one of the great modern masterpieces of rabbinic studies. A few days later, R. 'Abadi told me that he had received these books and thanked me for them. I did not think that the time was ripe to have them meet, and I waited for the right opportunity. A few months later, we were discussing something concerning a liturgical tradition of Aleppo. R. 'Abadi expressed interest in examining the famous *Siddur Aram Ṣoba* (Venice, 1545). "There is a copy at the JTS Library. Would you like me to arrange for you to see it?" I asked. He agreed. I then suggested that we also pay R. Lieberman a visit and R. 'Abadi happily welcomed the potential meeting. A week or so later, when everything was arranged, I drove R. 'Abadi to the JTS library. Professor Louis Finkelstein (1923–2000), who was the Chancellor of the Seminary at the time, personally received him. They exchanged greetings and a few comments on R. David Pardo's

(1718–1790) commentary to the *Sifre* with which both were familiar. In the years following their encounter, Professor Finkelstein would ask me to convey his personal regards to R. ʿAbadi. After examining the *Siddur Aram Ṣoba* and taking the necessary notes, we proceeded to Professor Lieberman's office.

As always, Professor Lieberman's desk was full of open books. We all sat. After spending about thirty seconds in social amenities, they began to discuss some Rabbinic topic. Quotations, corrections, interpretations, and counter-interpretations flew in all directions at the speed of light. Neither of them had to open a book to check a quotation, nor did they flinch for a second to issue a counterquotation. Finally, the whole discussion centered around Maimonides' view on a rabbinic measure (סיט). After discussing the subject for a few minutes, they concluded to consult the first edition of Maimonides' Commentary to the Mishna (Naples, 1492). Professor Lieberman owned a copy of this edition, famous for the handwritten notes and corrections made on the basis of early manuscripts. They opened the pertinent passage in *Kelim* 13:2/4. It read אצבע in the singular, thus confirming Professor Lieberman's view. The matter seemed settled. It was the first time that I had seen R. ʿAbadi lose an argument, but the evidence was clear. Professor Lieberman left the book open on top of a bookstand near the door. They sat for a few more minutes exchanging greetings. Professor Lieberman proceeded to escort us to the door. At the time, R. ʿAbadi was over seventy-seven years old and walked with the aid of a cane. Suddenly, as they were shaking hands by the door, R. ʿAbadi emitted a sound of jubilation and jumped towards the bookstand. Professor Lieberman and I were astounded and did not know what to make of it. "I was right!" said R. ʿAbadi smiling. "The correct reading is two 'אצבע'!" What happened was that as they were standing by the door, R. ʿAbadi had the opportunity to glance at the Naples edition laying open a few feet away and noticed that on top of the letter "ע" of אצבע, there was a dot written by hand 'ע, signaling that it was an abbreviation of the plural form. With the passing of time, the dot turned yellow, like the color of the paper, and it was almost imperceptible.[10] "I would like to ask you for a favor," told Professor Lieberman to R. 'Abadi. "Would you please bless me?" R. 'Abadi complied and laid his two hands over Professor Lieberman's head in prayer. Professor Lieberman escorted R. 'Abadi and me to the elevator leading to the main entrance. We walked the long hallway without saying a word. We arrived at the elevator, and I pressed the button. At this moment, R. 'Abadi turned to Professor Lieberman and told him, "Now, I would like to ask you a favor. Would you please bless me?" Professor Lieberman complied. As the elevator arrived and I held the door open, they shook hands and bid each other *shalom*. For many years, they both would ask me to convey their respective greetings to one another.

Today – more than at any other time in history, and throughout the four corners of the diaspora – the Jewish people are in dire need of leaders and sages seeking to be blessed by the collective wisdom that has accumulated over the centuries.

10. See R. Maṭloub 'Abadi, *Magen Ba'adi* (Brooklyn, N.Y. 5730/1970), p. 40.

# 5. Pomp and Pageantry

Jewishness is grounded on individuation. Individuation is something different than individuality and individualism. 'Individuality' is the feeling that everyone has of being separate and independent from everyone else. It begins to develop as soon as one knows how to say 'I' to a 'you.' By 'individuation,' I mean the realization that one has the right to see the truth with his or her own eyes. It is a more advanced stage than simple individuality, and it comes about upon the discovery not only of our own subjectivity, but also of everyone else's. That is why people who have reached individuation are not prone to subject themselves to an authoritarian system, or to accept a popular view simply because 'they' happen to say so. Although at the theoretical level, ancient Greece recognized the existence of the individual, "a true view of individual as a person, with personal rights and personal responsibilities," was unknown to the Greeks.[1] In the Middle Ages too, the idea of individuality had not yet emerged in gentile society:

> Medieval society did not deprive the individual of his freedom, because the 'individual' did not yet exist; man was still related to the world by primary ties… He did not yet conceive of any other persons as 'individuals' either… Awareness of one's individual self, of others, and of the world as separate entities, had not yet fully developed.[2]

1. E. R. Dodds, *The Greeks and the Irrational* (Berkeley & Los Angeles: University of California Press, 1968), p. 34.
2. Erich Fromm, *Escape From Freedom* (New York: Avon Books, 1969), p. 59.

The same prevailed in the Renaissance; writers did not have the vocabulary for describing the 'inner self.'[3] At this stage of human development, people were not viewed as individuals, but as members of a class or group.

This attitude attained the rank of supreme truth with the rise of Christianity: the 'other' is not to be viewed as an individual but as a member of 'another,' i.e., inimical 'group.' This basic principle, conveniently overlooked by teachers and preachers of the 'Holy Faith,' becomes abundantly clear upon considering that the Church was organized along the lines of corporation (Latin *corporatio*) in Roman law.[4] 'Salvation' is awarded to members of the corporation and to no one else, for the same reasons that dividends are awarded to shareholders and not to non-members. The corporation (or *corporatio*) awarding salvation is known as '*corpus Christi*,' not in the sense of 'body of,' but in its specific sense of 'corporation of Christ.' The Church is the executive body of said corporation. 'Salvation,' as it was brilliantly explained by Augustine of Hippo (354–430), is exclusively awarded to members of 'the corporation of Christ,' or *corpus Christi*. Outside this corporation, salvation and the Holy Spirit are inoperative. That is why those who are not bonafide members of the Church cannot receive the benefits of the Holy Spirit or become an instrument for the salvation of others.[5] Within this corporation, the absorption of the individual is total. Augustine saw in the bread and wine of the Mass a symbol of Christian unity. This unity is attained through a process of de-individualization: Just like the individual grains and grapes are crushed, becoming one in the bread and wine of the Eucharist, the faithful Christian, too, must lose his specific

---

3. See *Escape From Freedom*, p. 63.
4. On this pivotal point, see Arnold Ehrhardt, "Das Corpus Christi und die Corporation im spat-romischen Recht," *Savigny Zietschrift Roman Abt.* 70 (1953) and 71 (1954).
5. See my *In the Shadow of History: Jews and Converses at the Dawn of Modernity* (Albany: SUNY, 1992), pp. 28–29.

individuality by integrating into the *corpus Christi.*[6] This concept determined the legal status of the faithful Christian. *Incorporatio* ('incorporation') into the *corpus Christi* is achieved through baptism. In this way, the individual Christian loses, in the words of a distinguished historian of canon law, his "autonomous character." Thus, the faithful "became absorbed in the corporation itself, by the Church." A consequence of this view is that, within Christianity, the individual has no legal status. Legally, he is as non-person: he "not only had no rights, but also had no autonomous standing within the Church itself or within society."[7] Because the Church did not recognize the status of individuals, the supposed participation of some Jews in the crucifixion of Jesus[8] must be imputed to the Jewish *corporatio,* that is, on all Jews, regardless of individual participation. This logic justified the Expulsion of Jews from Spain (1492). On the pretext that *some* Jews were trying to persuade *some conversos* (Jews forcibly converted to Christianity) to return to the Jewish faith, *all* Jews were expelled from Spain. This was explained in the Edict of the Expulsion, by the Catholic monarchs Ferdinand and Isabella, as follows:

Because when a grave and horrendous crime is committed by a member of a college or university [corporation], it is reasonable that the [said] college or university should be dissolved and annihilated, and that the young should be punished on account of the old, and some on account of the others; and that those who pervert the well-being and honest living of the cities and villages, and who, by their contamination, may harm others, must be expelled from the country.[9]

Mass-murder, racial bigotry and all forms of social and religious

6. See *In the Shadow of History,* p. 44 and p., 231 n. 10.
7. Walter Ullman, *The Individual and Society,* pp. 9, 11. See further, *In the Shadow of History,* pp. 32–33.
8. On the falsehood of this accusation, see Hakham Faur's "The Gospel According to the Jews."
9. In ed. Luis Suárez Fernández, *Documentos acerca de la Expulsión de los Judíos* (Villadolid: Consejo Superior de Investigaciones Científicas, 1964), p. 393.

discrimination are the effect of looking at the 'other' not as an individual, but as a member of a different group or corporation.

* * *

The first person in recorded history to have achieved individuation is the Patriarch Abraham, the father of the Jewish people. He was born in a polytheistic world. His belief in monotheism, contravening the political and religious establishments of the time, rested on the assumption that an individual has the inalienable right to see the truth with his own eyes. Thus, the fact that 'they' had proclaimed a different view did not necessarily mean that they were right. Significantly, when God told Abraham to undertake the journey to the land of Israel, the expression ("go into yourself") was used (Gen. 12:1). The first term of this expression is the imperative "go," depart. The second term, "into yourself," is problematic. At the grammatical level, this is taken to be an idiomatic term, still common among the Jews of Damascus. At the exegetical level, there is another interpretation offered by R. Samuel Laniado (d. 1595). It suggested to Abraham the need to journey into himself and discover his own identity.[10] Accordingly, the last term of the verse, "to the land that I shall show *you*," may be translated to, 'to the land where I shall show *you to yourself*.' This means that Abraham's journey to the land of Israel will prompt him to travel into his own self and discover his uniqueness, so that he could achieve the ultimate goal of his life. The rabbis taught, "The actions of the Patriarchs are the symbols of the(ir) children."[11] Applied to the Patriarch Abraham, this means that individuation must be one of the earmarks of the Jew. Accordingly, Jews are not only different from gentiles, but, as Elias Canetti (1905–1994) observed, "in reality, they are most different from each other."[12]

Jewish individuation was properly noted by the Rabbis. Referring

10. See his *Keli Ḥemda* Venice (5355/1595), *ad loc.*
11. Mishna Soṭa 34a.
12. *Crowds and Power* (Penguin Books, 1973), p. 208.

to a prayer offered by Moses before his death, the Rabbis alluded to Jewish individuation and the special type of political leadership that it warrants:

In the same fashion that one face does not resemble another, their minds, too, do not resemble one another. Rather, every single one has his own mind…. Know that this is the case, because when Moses was about to die, he asked God: 'It is known before Thee the mind of each and every one [every member of the Jewish people], and [therefore it is known to Thee] that the minds of your children do not resemble one another. I beg Thee that when I will be taken away from them, that you appoint for them a leader who will be tolerant of them, [and treat] each and every one according to his own mind.'[13]

Accordingly, the Rabbis prescribed a blessing to be pronounced when witnessing a Jewish crowd of six hundred thousand, as it was during the forty years of wandering through the desert: "Blessed are Thou the Lord, our God, King of the Universe, who discerns what is concealed." The expression "who discerns what is concealed," alludes to the fact that even in a Jewish crowd of such dimensions, no two minds are the same: "Their minds do not resemble one another, [just like] their faces do not resemble one another."[14]

* * *

Jewishness involves the realization of individuation at its highest level. How? Jewishness entails a unique thinking process, pushing the individual not merely to be 'another' person like everyone else, but to discover their own absolute uniqueness and distinctiveness. This is achieved when the individual discovers "the image

13. *Midrash Rabba, Pineḥas* 21:2 (Vilna, reprinted Jerusalem, 5735/1975), 2 vols., vol. 2, 88d.
14. Mishna Berakhot 58a, see ibid. 58b. For a full discussion of the subject, see Saul Lieberman, *Tosefta Ki-Fshuṭa,* Mishna Berakhot (New York: Jewish Theological Seminary of America, 1955), p. 104. The source for this idea is found in the Greek and Aramaic translations of *Prov* 27:19.

of God" (Gen. 1:26) within. Translated in terms of Hebrew monotheism – where God is not only absolutely one but also absolutely unique – this means that every human being has, within him or herself, something absolutely singular and distinctive.

Christianity is anti-individuation. The doctrine that Adam's sin destroys the image of God within each human being, together with the demand that ingression to the *corpus Christi* is predicated upon crushing one's individuality – like the individual grains and grapes crushed to become one in the bread and wine of the Eucharist – prohibit the individual from discovering and realizing themselves. It is now clear why, except for Jews, people rarely attained individuation during the Middle Ages. Conversely, Jews could not remain Jewish if they did not individuate; assimilation was equated with a desire to get rid of one's unique 'I' and become like everyone else.

I shall illustrate: Imagine a Jew in Rome leaving *La Scuola Spagnola* – or any other synagogue, for that matter – and on his way home, passing by one of those magnificent cathedrals built at the turn of the 15th or 16th century. Suppose that, at the same time, there was a procession, led by the higher echelons of the Christian hierarchy – cardinals, bishops, and prelates – enrobed in splendid raiment, approaching the church. Unexpectedly, a choir of angelical voices is heard, chanting one of the many sublime songs composed by Bach or Mendelssohn, followed by a group of men and women in their finest garb. As the procession approaches, the people standing by the *piazza*, right in front of the church, respectfully withdraw, clearing a path for the procession to advance towards its final destination. Everyone stands in awe and admiration. Suddenly, a consecrated image emerges from the church, carried by a group of prelates. Instantly, everyone eases down on their faces, worshipping in veneration – except for the Jew on his way home, bypassing the crowd unperturbed. This scene was repeated countless times throughout the Jewish Diaspora. On their way to and from the market, our grandparents' generation – whether in Western or Eastern Europe, the Ottoman Empire or North Africa – had to pass splendid churches and mosques and dismiss their pageantry and pomp as insignificant. Otherwise, the Jew could not survive as a Jew. And yet, in comparison to the church and mosque, even the finest synagogue and the most exquisite Jewish service appear shabby and gray.

I myself once experienced such a situation. The place was San Just Desvern – a small town about a half-hour ride from the University of Barcelona – where I was a graduate student. It was a Sunday in April '63. I just married and was eager to show Esther, my wife, the town. I knew the place quite well, and most of the people in town were friendly. Leaving our home late in the morning, we meandered from street to street until we reached the plaza. At this time of year, Spain is simply beautiful. The weather is impeccable, not a cloud in the sky. The sun shines a brightly, and trees and plants blossom everywhere in a friendly light. The church stood on one side of the plaza, the *Ayuntamiento,* or municipality, was on the other, and a few stores and coffee shops lined the laterals. I noticed that there was an unusually large number of people, as if they were expecting something important. Unconcerned, we continued our walk to the fountain at the center of the plaza. Suddenly, there was a hush. Everyone stood still and silent. From one of the corners of the plaza, a chant was commenced. A moment later, we could see a procession carrying an image that was recently consecrated to the church. Because of religious and personal scruples, I had never set foot in a church nor witnessed Christian services. I knew that Spain was a country of extremes, but this was quite a sight. As the image advanced through the square, people threw themselves on the ground to worship it. By the time the image reached the church, the plaza transformed into a sea of heads. Everyone was facedown on the ground. That is, everyone except for Esther and me, standing at the center of the plaza admiring the fountain. People must have sensed that we were not worshipping with them. At once, they all turned their faces to look at us from the ground with both fury and amazement – they simply could not understand how one could resist partaking in such a sublime ceremony. For an instant, we could feel a thousand pairs of indignant eyes fixed upon us. A few minutes later, as the procession entered the church, everyone stood up, and Esther and I continued our promenade, happy and undisturbed.

* * *

Here is a question: What is the thinking process that enables Jews to dismiss the pomp and pageantry that other religions exhibit in favor of the dingiest of synagogues and the drabbest of Jewish services? It cannot be mere insensitivity to the beautiful and the aesthetic. Jews have always excelled in all forms of visual and auditory art. To answer this riddle, we must touch upon the peculiar thinking process underlying Jewishness.

Because of its polytheistic heritage, where the universe is conceived in terms of disparate and unrelated things, pagan thinking tends to abstract an object and analyze it as a separate entity, as if it were totally disconnected from all the rest. Given that the pagan mind can abstract an object from its context and behold it as if it were an autonomous entity, it is easy for people to project their own imagination onto the object and transform it into anything they wish. This involves transference of meaning, whereby one thing is associated and identified with something else. In this manner, things are no longer perceived *per se*, but 'as' something else. The 'as' is never a part of the object itself, but it 'represents' something outside itself.

This process is peculiar to all mythical thinking: through reflexive associations, the object *per se* is displaced and perceived 'as' something beyond the sensory experience.[15] A piece of stone or wood just carved by an artisan can be seen as a god with wondrous powers. A black cat curving its spine and raising its fur as someone walks by it, the sudden flight of an owl, the howling of a lonely dog into the night – all these could be perceived as satanic instruments. In this

15. See my "Maimonides on Imagination," *The Solomon Goldman Lectures* 6 (1993), pp. 90–91.

fashion, the ancient man in Greece and Rome perceived the sea and the rivers filled with nymphs, he saw dryads in the plants and trees, satyrs in the fields, and every type of demon and spirit swarming all over. Every natural phenomenon – a storm, the wind, a thunderbolt, the blossoming of a tree – was perceived as a disparate phenomenon, the direct manifestation of a different god.

By contrast, because the Jew believed that the whole universe is the product of one single and omnipotent Creator, everything is interrelated to everything else. Things are organically interconnected, forming a part of a total system. Therefore, a Jew does not contemplate things in isolation, but as part of a system. This leads to what I term 'holistic thinking.' According to this thought process, an object is not to be beholden in isolation, but rather considered as one part of a broader system. A man, for instance, may appear to be wonderfully kind. Our interpretation of his "kindness," could be dangerously faulty unless he is viewed within the system in which he functions and operates. It should make some difference whether he is a member of a terrorist organization, an extortionist gang or a group of swindlers preying on the elderly, on the one hand; or if he is a shopkeeper, a university professor, or a scientist dedicated to eliminating suffering and improving the quality of human life, on the other. The best compendia of holistic thinking are the Talmud Yerushalmi, composed in the land of Israel (ca. 4th century), and the Babylonian Talmud, composed in Babylonia (ca. 5th century), in which every matter in question is analyzed in terms of the larger context. Thus, holistic thinking stands in opposition to the process of further abstraction and division, leading to what José Ortega y Gasset (1883–1955) described as "the barbarism of specialization."[16] By way of contrast, the Talmud, as with a cubist painting, examines each and every subject from all of its various perspectives.

* * *

16. See my *Golden Doves with Silver Dots* (Bloomington, Indiana: Indiana University Press, 1986), p. 153 note 81.

The Tora instructs us to think holistically. Concerning Canaanite cultic practices, we read: "Take heed… lest you inquire about their gods, saying: 'How do these people worship their gods, so that I, too, shall do so?' Do not do this for the Lord your God; because all of God's abominations which He abhors, they do for their gods, for even their sons and daughters they burn in fire for their gods" (Dt 12:30–31). The plain sense of this injunction is not to worship the God of Israel with pagan rituals.[17] However, the explanation offered for this injunction ("for even their sons and daughters they burn in fire for their gods") is not clear. Obviously, the Israelites wanted to incorporate only those rituals that appear fitting for the worship of God – not child sacrifice! The question, therefore, arises: what is the rationale to prohibit their admirable rituals because they *also* sacrifice children for their gods?

A reflective response to this question provides valuable insight into the Hebrew mind. The Tora teaches that you cannot properly evaluate the merits of a single element of a culture or civilization without factoring in all other aspects of the system. What appears as 'beautiful' and 'sublime' in the eyes of a people may in fact be a ruse to hide some sinister and hideous practices. In simple terms: cultures or civilizations cannot be properly evaluated by abstracting some of their aspects and overlooking others. Rather, they must be evaluated in a holistic manner. Applying this principle to our case, it follows that to properly evaluate one aspect of a system one must factor in all of its other elements, such as human sacrifice and the incineration of children to please their gods.

Jewish assimilation takes place when one abandons holistic thinking and concentrates on certain aspects of a culture or religion while failing to notice others. The Israelites exemplified this in their enthrallment with pagan rituals while remaining oblivious to the the very same system's demand for the immolation of children.[18] As long

17. See R. I. S. Reggio, *Be'ur Ḥadash, ad loc.*, vol. 5 (Vienna, 1831), 68b.
18. Cf. R. Solomon le-Bet ha-Levi, *Dibre Shelomo*, Part I, (Venice, 5356/1596), 286c-d.

as Jews perceived gentile pomp and pageantry in terms of their total system, they could not be impressed by what their neighbors had to offer. What could the meaning of 'universal love' or 'human redemption' be for someone thinking in holistic terms, considering the fact that the 'Holy Inquisition' tortured and incinerated thousands upon thousands of mothers and children, of men and women, of old and young? However enchanting and sublime the angelical voices of the church choir may be, how could it quench the cries of these victims? People living in Catholic societies need not look to the far past of the Spanish and Portuguese Inquisitions to recognize the appalling, brutal sadism that was practiced and sanctioned by the highest echelons of the Church. When I was a young student in Spain, one could pass by sumptuous cathedrals and see the poor anguishing in hunger, while the worshippers passed by without batting an eye. When I mentioned this to a fellow student, he responded, "They are gypsies." When I retorted, "But they are also Catholics and human beings," he looked at me as though I was a strange creature who had just dropped on earth from some exotic galaxy. I heard the same type of response in Latin America: "They are Indians," or, "They are lazy and don't want to work." And when you point out to them the swollen stomach of little children, they cut the conversation short with some profanity. What is particularly painful are some of the sermons given by the clergy to console the poor and the hungry. I heard them many times on the radio on Sundays. They fostered, roughly, the following trope: "Your home may be squalid, and surely, you are destitute and famished, your children uneducated and sick. But you all are rich and free in spirit because you believe in Him." How pathetic! How 'rich in spirit' can those wretched creatures be if they could look impassively as their children starve, knowing that if, somehow, they manage to survive, they will have to endure hunger and discrimination? 'Free' to do what?! These poor people are not even free to disagree with their priest! It must be remembered that the Church had an absolute monopoly throughout Europe on spirituality and moral values for over a thousand years! Many Nazis (Hitler and Boremann, for example) were raised in "good Catholic homes." (Goering and Eichmann were Protestants.) Hitler became a choirboy at the age of six and served at mass. Reminiscing about that early period in his life, Hitler remarked that he had had "the excellent opportunity to intoxicate [him]self with the solemn splendor of the brilliant church festivals."[19] When dealing with the tragedy of the Holocaust, we often think of those who were dispossessed, displaced and murdered in concentration camps. But there were other, less obvious victims, whose number surpasses 6,000,000. I am thinking of the millions and millions of European children who were burnt at the altar by an ideology that metamorphoses human beings into perfidious fiends, torturers, bigots, thieves and mass murderers.

The Church saw nothing wrong when *Cristianos Viejos* – the 'good' Christians who had not been contaminated even partially with Jewish blood – used 'religion' as an excuse to justify their insatiable rapacity and mass murder. Reflecting on the carnage of 1391, when most of the ancient *Juderías* were wiped out by the mob in the name of Christianity, Don Pero López de Ayala (1332–1407) wrote: "And all this was a thirst for robbery, it seemed, more than devotion."[20] This strategy became the basis of the official policy of the Spanish Crown. Machiavelli (1469–1527), too, concluded that 'religion' was a subterfuge for rapacity. Concerning the policies of King Ferdinand, he observed:

> [A]nd always under the pretext of religion, he had recourse to a pious cruelty, driving out the Moors from his kingdom and despoiling them. No more miserable or unusual example may be found.[21]

The same *Cristianos Viejos* that butchered Jews and *conversos* hounded Native Americans. An Italian writer, Pedro Mártir (1459–1525), author

19. Hanns Kung, *Judaism* (New York: Crossroad, 1992), p. 237.
20. *Crónicas,* (ed. Llaguna), vol. 2, p. 391, cited in *The Structure of Spanish History,* p. 508 note 83.
21. *The Prince* (New York: Mentor Books, 1952), p. 120.

of the first chronicle of the Americas, described how these good Christians treated Native Americans as follows:

In the midst of such an abundant plenty, there is something that gives me no small anguish. These [Native Americans] so simple and naked, were used to working little; now many perish as a result of the great exhaustion in the mines, and they are desperate to the point that many kill themselves and do not care to raise children. They tell that the pregnant mothers take medicine to abort, seeing that they would give birth to slaves for the Christians. Although a royal decree had declared that they are free, nonetheless, they are forced to serve more than what would please a free man. The number of these wretched had diminished immensely; many say that a census was once made of one million two hundred thousand. How many there are today, it causes me horror to say. Let us change the subject.[22]

Not a single soul of the native population of Jamaica, Bermuda, St. Thomas, Puerto Rico, Panama, Cuba, etc. survived. Todorov demonstrated how, over the course of fifty years, the Iberian conquerors managed to reduce the population of Native Americans from eighty million to ten million. By the year 1600, the original population of Mexico had been reduced from twenty-five million to one million. This is the greatest genocide in recorded history, in both absolute and relative terms.[23]

Consider, in the name of sanity, the common practices of the *Cristianos Viejos* in the Americas: snatching children from their mothers' arms and tossing them to be devoured alive by dogs, or smashing them against rocks and leaving them to die in the mountains. The usual way to kill native leaders was in groups of thirteen, in honor of Jesus and the twelve apostles! To prolong their agony, they would burn them in a slow fire. Occasionally, the executioners would insert sticks in their mouths to prevent their screams from disturbing the

---

22. Pedro Mártir de Anglería, *Libros de las Décadas del Nuevo Mundo* (Buenos Aires: Editorial Bajel, 1944), Dec. III, Lib. VIII, chap. I, p. 273.
23. Tzevetan Todorov, *La conquete de l'amérique* (Paris: Editions du Soleil, 1982), pp. 138–139.

captain's *siesta*. Their sexual mores deserve special attention. It was a common practice to tie the hands and feet of the husband *under* the bed, while having sex with the wife *in* the bed. When a young Native American wife explained to a Spanish captain that she could not have sex with him because she had promised to be faithful to her husband, the captain unleashed the dogs and had them devour her alive.[24] Miguel de Monsalve (16th century) reported that it was common for the Spaniards to:

> Take not only the properties of these wretched [Native Americans], but also their daughters, taking them by force and raping them; if they do not give consent of their own will, they tie them, and torture them, lash them and punish them with great cruelty.... Their [Native American] women if they would find out that someone had had relations with her [Native American] husband, they burn them, mistreat and torture them, lash them and bring them before their eyes in irons, stripped, exposed, abused, dog-bitten and very hurt.[25]

On June 4, 1559, Fernando de Santillán reported how common it was for Spaniards in Chile to "unleash their dogs against some [Native Americans], burn others, in addition of mutilating them, cutting their noses, arms, or breasts, and inventing a thousand other ways how to tear them into pieces."[26] It was customary that, for reasons of work distribution, a few Spaniards would parcel a native family among themselves. Thus, one would take the wife, another the husband, and a third the children, "in the same manner as if they would have been pigs."[27] In addition to those dying of sickness, exhaustion,

24. See *In the Shadow of History*, pp. 4–5.
25. Quoted in Henry Méchoulan, *El Honor de Dios* (Barcelona: Editorial Argos Vergara, 1981), p. 49.
26. Quoted ibid., p. 41.
27. Quoted ibid., p. 51.

ill treatment, and abuse, we must consider those who were "buried alive in the mines."[28]

The crimes perpetuated by the Spaniards against Jews, *conversos*, and Native Americans were crimes against humanity. And yet, not a bleep of condemnation was uttered by the Church. In the name of human decency, what is the rationale to absolve a system with total control over the ethics and spirituality of a people, of the crimes against humanity committed under its stewardship?

A parallel situation to 'the religion of love' is to be found in 'the religion of peace.' Despite all the verbosity about 'brotherhood,' etc., no one has a worse lot than the poor in Muslim countries. You could see them wallowing in their own filth, hungry and in pain, without a single hand ever stretching to help. There must be something wrong with a system in which the same people that spend billions of dollars on all types of weaponry fail to feed their starving coreligionists living in under-developed countries, or down the block in the same neighborhood in which they live. It is simply outrageous to speak about a 'brotherly society' made up of men who regularly beat their wives and children within an inch of their lives, or to have any respect for the class of families in which everyone, male and female, participates in the orgiastic slaughtering of young girls, kindly misnamed 'honor killings.' Children raised in such an environment grow up in frustration and anger, believing that violence is the most effective means of communication. It is a sad fact – not dissimilar to the heathen incineration of children in religious ceremonies – that Muslim children are raised with a fire of hatred kindling inside of them, first and foremost against Jews and 'colonial' or 'imperialistic' regimes, and then against other forms of pan-Arabism that differ from their own peculiar brand. In their wars, Iranians and Iraqis used children to fight on the front lines. No one in the 'brotherly society' raised a voice in protest. To protect terrorists attacking Israelis, Arab mothers encourage their own children to stand in the foreground, either to

28. Quoted ibid., p. 53.

shield the terrorists or to provoke Israeli soldiers, with the hope that the media will accuse Israel of murdering innocent children. These mothers know quite well that their children might die or be severely wounded. As a matter of fact, fixed sums of money are allocated by Arab organizations to these mothers, depending on the wound the children receive, or in case of death. Isn't this another form of burning children for the gods? These mothers are applauded as the heroines of the Arab world. You could be sure that if it weren't for the money they receive, they would not have permitted their children to risk their lives and limbs. And yet, no one in the Arab world had raised a simple question: What about the children? And perhaps a more pertinent question: What about *our* media?

* * *

Because Jews thought in holistic terms, they shrugged off heathen pomp and pageantry as irrelevant and insignificant. Usually, when people want to show off their cities to strangers, they begin by taking them to the nicest sections of town. From the Hebrew perspective, the first place to visit is the neighborhoods where the poor and destitute live. It is only by knowing how the needy are treated that we can gain a real insight into the system of governance of a people. Thus, the first legislation that Moses received after the Decalogue is the laws establishing the rights of the slave (Ex. 21:1–6).

Holistic thought presumes both personal and collective responsibility. A 'good' system cannot be excused for the ill side effects that it produces. When the biblical prophet upbraided the entire people of Israel for the crimes and anomalies committed by some of the rulers and priests, he was in fact formulating the principle that evil, as minor and confined as it may seem, is symptomatic of the failure of an *entire* system. The truly prosperous society, as the psalmist sang, is not one in which the young flourish or in which there is superabundance of plant and grain, of sheep and cow, but one that manages to prosper without causing destitution and suffering to any of its members. Therefore, after enumerating all the elements of the successful society (Ps 144:12–14), the psalmist added: "and there is no crying in our streets." According to this perspective, 'side effects' are not haphazard incidents, but symptomatic of the nature of the system. We can now understand why aid to the needy is not merely a matter of altruism and benevolence. A failing system of wealth distribution causes misery. It follows, therefore, that upon transitioning out of a skewed system, it is incumbent upon those who benefited from it to aid those who were aggrieved by it. As R. 'Aqiba (50–135) taught, we must aid the poor to "save ourselves from the judgment of hell."[29] The term "judgment" implies that simple justice would demand that people that benefitted from a system should assume responsibility for its negative side-effects. In this context, it is important to remember that, as indicated by Maimonides (1135–1204), the Hebrew term *ṣedaqa*, 'charity,' comes from *ṣedeq*, 'justice.'[30]

* * *

Those who cannot think in holistic terms will never attain individuation, for the simple reason that they would not be able to grasp the uniqueness of their own specific situation. Since their minds perceive things as unrelated to one another, and they cannot synthesize the particulars of life into a total system, their thinking process is shaped by myth. Those who think in mythical terms cannot distinguish between a thing and the word designating it. In a debate with Socrates, Gorgias argued that speech affects the mind of the hearer like magic and witchcraft. Similarly, Arabs refer to speech as *siḥr al-ḥalal*, meaning 'licit' or 'white magic.'[31] Since, at this stage, people cannot distinguish between word and reality, by manipulating speech one can manipulate reality. Myth is the world created by this type of speech. At this level,

29. Baba Batra 10a.
30. *Guide* III, 53.
31. See my "Splitting of the *Logos*," *New Vico Studies* 3 (1985), pp. 87–89; and my *Horizontal Society*, pp. 111–4.

words control the mind and cast a spell upon their audience, creating illusion and deception. Myth not only creates its own world, but it displaces reality. Those who think in mythical terms are incapable of processing reality on their own; their values and opinions depend on the 'authority' of others.[32]

Myth is a powerful force in contemporary culture. It displaces reality and compels the audience to perceive reality on their terms. The purpose of advertisement is not to inform, but – as with Gorgias – to cast a spell upon the audience and create deception and illusion. Similarly, the media and entertainment companies are dedicated to the formation and circulation of myths. In moments of crisis, when faith in the system is imperiled by political, economical, or social factors, myth can fire the collective imagination of a people, 'lift the heart' and 'nourish the soul.' The preeminence of contemporary American culture resides precisely on the universal myths that it produces. As Marshall Blonsky writes: "Don't look to us for intellect – look, instead, to the blind, nearly hysteric way we live, producing a myth of global attractiveness."[33] Nothing escapes the mythologization process: from the way we eat (fast food or gourmet), to the way we dress (high or low fashion), to the cars we drive. Every minute detail is packed with heavily charged symbols, carefully controlled by myth.

These myths are also operative at the personal level. People evaluate and relate to each other according to the symbols promoted by myths. When reality fails to correspond to the myth, disillusionment takes place. A factor in the failure of the family in contemporary culture is that the basis for the initial relationship between husband and wife is a myth, whose ultimate function is the displacement of reality. Escapism, whether in the form of drugs, promiscuity, religious fundamentalism, or political terrorism, is the effect of failed mythologies. Quoting Blonsky again:

---

32. See *In the Shadow of History*, Chap. 6; and below "My Grandmother's Trunk."
33. *American Mythologies* (New York: Oxford University Press, 1992), p. 9.

> Ask the question, what you want, really want. To last in eternity; that was the religious feeling. To last by your heirs, giving your name to someone else. But if a fundamental value is to last, and yet society day by day builds an apology for something which is not lasting; if the civilization of ephemera destroys family, destroys names, destroys the very future, then men and women will desire to escape that civilization and find somewhere else to last.[34]

* * *

Jews understood well this aspect of gentile culture and did not permit mythological thinking and rhetoric to displace reality. There is a precious passage in rabbinic literature depicting an exchange between Israel and Rome. Using "daughter of Babel" as a code name for 'Rome' (it was dangerous to be explicit in this subject), the rabbis represented Imperial Rome as an old whore trying to pass herself for a youthful and innocent virgin: "Thus said Jerusalem to the daughter of Babel: 'O thou! Old and awfully evil whore! You fancy yourself to be a virgin, but you are an old wreck! Sit on the floor; (you) no longer have a throne!'"[35] It was the ability to process reality holistically, rather than to succumb to the magic of pomp and pageantry, that permitted Jews to see Imperial Rome for what it actually was. There is a passage in the Tora warning not to be dazzled by the craftsmanship and beauty of idols and not to forget what they stand for: "You have seen their abominations and ignominies: wood and stone, silver and gold which are with them," (Deut. 29:16). Now, "abominations and ignominies" cannot be directly seen in an object. Rather, they are *projections* that a culture *associates* with activities that are deemed "abominations and ignominies." To illustrate, the reason that the swastika is an abomination for Jews is not because of its intrinsic shape. The same swastika

34. *American Mythologies*, p. 504.
35. *Shir ha-Shirim Rabba* 3:4.

in a Hindu environment would not be seen as an abomination! What the Tora is teaching is that the symbols of pagan humanity should be processed holistically, as integral to a culture sponsoring "abominations and ignominies." When appraising these symbols, one should not lose sight of the fact that the very culture which sponsors their 'beauty' also sponsors the incineration of children as an act of supreme religious devotion. Let us not forget that in a culture dominated by a mythological system, it is possible to sanitize each and every symbol. In such an environment, it would be possible to imagine that within certain types of cultures, artists could devote their best talent to sanitizing such symbols. The media and artistic community could one day sanitize the swastika and Nazi atrocities, just like it sanitized Christian symbolism and atrocities.[36] Within such an environment, it would be easy to imagine beautiful swastikas incorporated in jewelry; they could even adorn a royal crown or a tiara. It is precisely in such a context that the Tora instructs that these symbols should be perceived holistically, as integral to the system that produced them. The moment a Jew suppresses this understanding and perceives them as objects of splendor and beauty, they have forfeited the covenant and their alliance with the people of Israel and God (see Dt 29:17–27).

A fundamental characteristic of myth is denial of responsibility. Myth imputes guilt (in the same way that it assigns grace), but it does not recognize responsibility. When myth does not function according to expectations, it must be due to some external reason. The integrity of the myth, however, should not be questioned. Those who are hurt are 'victims,' and their only recourse is to complain, as in contemporary America.[37]

Modern society, with its symbols and myths, creates a highly complex system of pomp and pageantry. Not only in parades, sports, and musical events, but also by charging key cultural symbols (romantic love, personal exploits, etc.) with a dense mythological connotation.

36. See my book *The Gospel According to the Jews.*
37. See Charles J. Sykes: *A Nation of Victims: The Decay of the American Character* (New York: St. Martin Press, 1992).

Only those who think holistically will not fall prey to the world of myth. Jewish disintegration comes about when holistic thinking is abandoned in favor of mythological thinking.[38] Since reality is secondary in mythological thinking,, there is always room to make apologies for the failures and ill side effects of the system. Whatever does not correspond with the myth is an oddity that in no way impugns the myth itself. It is only by retrogressing from holistic to mythological thinking that a Jew can maintain such an illusion.[39]

* * *

What about the spiritual progress taking place in the pagan world, first through Christianity and then through Islam? Could it be possible that gentile society has not yet transcended its heathen roots? According to Maimonides, both Christianity and Islam represent a foreword movement towards genuine spirituality. Thus, Maimonides writes that both Jesus and Mohammed brought humankind closer to the Messianic Age and the ways of the Tora.[40] A similar view was expressed by R. Judah ha-Levi (ca. 1075–1141).[41] R. Israel Moses Ḥazzan (1807–1863), one of the most illustrious rabbis in modern times, explained that the spiritual progress effected by these religions can be properly appreciated when comparing the present gentile

38. Invariably, synagogues that introduced pomp and pageantry into their services have failed to maintain continuity and have their grandchildren join them in worship. The failure of the Spanish and Portuguese synagogues (Orthodox), as well as Reform Temples, for member continuity is reflected in the fact that very few of their congregants are grandchildren of the people who worshipped in the same congregations. This may be directly linked to the pomp and pageantry of their services. As soon as that pomp and pageantry is acknowledged as a valid criterion of preeminence, the door to assimilation is opened. Sooner or later, the worshippers will be bored with the 'Jewish pomp' and opt for the more exciting mythical symbols of the gentile world.
39. See "Maimonides on Imagination," pp. 89–93.
40. *Mishne Torah, Melakhim* 11:4.
41. *Kuzari* 4:13.

society with the heathen society prior to Christianity and Islam. Although acknowledging the progress brought about by Christianity and Islam, R. Judah ha-Levi maintained that they remained pagan, preserving much of their original structures: "They retain the same rituals of their ancient services, as well as their festivities and holidays. They only changed the shapes – that is what they eliminated – not their [ancient] religion."[42] He recognized that with Islam, there was good will among the original founders. Simultaneously, he insisted that they had failed in their objective: "the more that they intended to draw near, the more they went astray."[43] Recent history confirms R. Judah ha-Levi's view.

In conclusion, it is upon embodying individuation – the fact that each person has something unique and precious to contribute to the benefit of all humankind – that one can feel 'chosen' and the 'crown of creation.' To ascertain this point, every morning Jews bless the good Lord for "being chosen from among all people." In 1978, I was invited to give a series of lectures on Jewish subjects at the Pontifical University of Salamanca, Spain. That was likely the first time that a professing Jew received such an invitation. The first lecture I gave dealt with theological subjects and was open only to faculty members. I understood their concern: being the foremost Catholic institution in the Spanish-speaking world, they had a particular responsibility towards their constituency. Therefore, before offering my lectures to the general student body, they had to be sure that what I was about to say would not offend the sensitivities of the public. In a sense, the first lecture was a test. In fact, at the end of that lecture I was subjected to a series of questions, mostly designed to expose my position on several critical matters. The last question concerned the Jewish concept of 'chosen.' What about other religions [read: Christianity], can't they also be chosen? I first proceeded to explain that 'chosen' in Judaism has no negative connotation: Aaron and his children were chosen to

---

42. Ibid. 4:11.
43. Ibid. 4:13.

serve at the Temple, and David and his children were chosen to be the kings of Israel. This does not mean that other peoples are inferior, but simply that they were not selected to carry out those particular missions. I then added: "To be chosen means to be willing to accept responsibility. Therefore, only those who choose to be chosen are chosen by God." Looking at them straight in the eye, I asked: "We chose to be chosen. Why did you not choose to be chosen?" Incidentally, the next morning I was informed that the faculty had unanimously voted to open my lectures up to the general student body.

# 6. My Grandmother's Trunk
# or
# What about Political Teshuba?

The first generation of Sephardic young men and women who migrated from the Ottoman Empire to Buenos Aires around World War I found paradise in the New World. Before them laid a beautiful country whose language they knew, and a friendly society that they could penetrate at will. The financial opportunities were endless. For the first time in their long history, they were free from any kind of family and communal authority. New pleasures never dreamt of in the old country were awaiting at every corner. What a picnic! The result was that most of my Jewish friends with whom I grew up or went to school assimilated. I always believed that the reason that I retained my Jewish identity was because our grandparents lived with us. My father was the first born, and as was customary among Sephardim, it was the eldest son's responsibility to provide living quarters for his parents. We lived in an enormous house, seventy meters long, in the heart of Buenos Aires. My grandparents had their own separate quarters within the house: two patios, two bedrooms, and a very large kitchen. The house was so large and so well protected with high walls that it was a world onto itself. You could not hear even the slightest sound from the outside. The walls surrounding the patios were so tall that the only place you could gaze at was either inside or up at the sky. I was fortunate to have been born in the pre-TV era, so after finishing my homework, I would spend some time playing on one of the patios, and then run to my grandparents. What a joy! My grandmother had a small chair for me, and as I sat next to her, she would tell me the most marvelous stories. There were always some delicacies for me, all made with her own hands. She had lost her father when she was a young girl, and as was customary in those days among Sepharadim, a wealthy family took her in. This was the Lisbona family, the wealthiest and most prestigious family in Damascus. My mother told me that the reason that my grandmother had such extraordinary culinary abilities was because she had learned to cook at the Lisbonas'. I knew that when she married my grandfather, she traveled from their home to her new home. My uncle Moses kept contact with this family throughout his life, long after they had lost their fortune. Like all the ladies of old Sepharad, my grandmother was the embodiment of cleanliness. For people who never saw the quarters of these women, it is impossible to imagine, but there was never a single spot that was not gleaming with cleanliness. Everything was always in its place. Their clothing was impeccably neat. No one ever raised their voice, ever. For these ladies, idleness was the worst agony. If you ever saw one of them inactive, it was either because she was sick, or in the last stage of her life. As was customary among those ladies, my grandmother would begin her day before dawn, in time to have the coffee ready before my grandfather left for morning prayers. My grandfather was very tall, about 6'3, and I remember how, before leaving the house, he would have to bend down to pass my grandmother's inspection. She would stand, brush in hand, and make sure that no speck of dust was on his clothes. My grandmother's mother's name was Lela. She would save every penny she could and, right before the market closed on Fridays, she would buy the remnant fruits and vegetables at a bargain price, and distribute the produce among the needy.

The time that I spent in the company of my grandparents was the most cheerful and edifying time I experienced. Of course, like all grandchildren, I was unable to fully appreciate who they were and what they were doing for us back then. I still cannot conceive of a greater joy than being able to kiss their hands and tell them how much I appreciate what they did for us.

Next to one of the walls in my grandmother's bedroom lay an enormous trunk that she had hauled from Damascus. It was old and rusty. She kept her most precious valuables in it: some jewelry, clothing and accessories from her wedding, a long braid of black hair from her youth, documents, and items that were especially dear to her. She never visited Israel, but she always voiced the hope to go and settle in what she would refer to as "our land." "You see," she would tell me, "no matter how beautiful and spacious the neighbor's house is, it can never be as comfortable as your own. Here, we are living in our neighbor's house." I remember how excited she – more than any other of my family members, including my Zionist uncle – was when, in May 1948, the State of Israel declared its independence. It happened late in the afternoon, around five, and she called me to her bedroom. She was particularly solemn, and began to speak about the land of Israel and about all the places we had lived and from which 'they' expelled or murdered us. Pointing at the trunk, she said: "This trunk was brought by our family from Sepharad. And we made a promise that one day we will bring it to the Land of Israel. One day you must fill it up and fulfill that promise." For me, these words enclose the essence of Jewish political *teshuba* ('repentance').

* * *

Judaism recognizes political sins. In order not to confuse these transgressions with regular sins, Maimonides referred to them as "evil actions" (*ma'asim ra'im*). The national catastrophes of Israel were the result of this type of iniquity. When describing the four days set in the Jewish calendar to mourn for the national disasters of Israel, Maimonides wrote:

> There are days in which every Jew must fast because of the catastrophes that had taken place in them. The purpose is to awaken the hearts and open up the ways for repentance. They should be a remembrance of our evil actions and of the actions of our ancestors that were as evil as our own actions today. So that by remembering these matters we shall repent and act favorably.[1]
>
> To underscore that those evil actions do not pertain to 'religious' transgressions, Maimonides associated those actions with those of "our ancestors" and "our own actions today," which obviously could not have been of a ritualistic or religious nature. The outcome of these actions are the "national catastrophes" (*ṣarot*) befalling the Jewish nation. For Maimonides, *every* national catastrophe (*ṣara*) is the effect of our "evil actions" (*ma'asim ra'im*).[2] So that the *national catastrophes* befalling Israel have little to do with 'religious' transgression; rather, they are the direct effect of our "evil" (*ra'im*), i.e., politically irresponsible, "actions" (*ma'asim*).[3]

The idea of political sin was further developed by R. Solomon ibn Verga (d. Flanders ca. 1520), author of *Shebeṭ Yehuda*.[4] The national catastrophes puncturing Jewish history since the destruction of the First Temple (586 B.C.E.), and the long, uninterrupted chain of exiles, massacres, and oppression suffered by the Jews, are not the result of 'religious' transgression. The Jewish people are certainly not less religious or more immoral than any other people to deserve such penalties.[5] The fault of Israel lies elsewhere. Thus, R. Solomon ibn Verga proposed that Jewish suffering is the result of what he designates "natural cause" (*ha-sibba ha-ṭib'it*). By 'natural,' ibn Verga meant

1. *Mishne Tora, Ta'aniyot*, 5:1.
2. *Mishne Tora, Ta'aniyot* 1:2.
3. *Mishne Tora, Ta'aniyot* 1:3.
4. On this book and author, see *In the Shadow of History*, pp. 176–180.
5. See *In the Shadow of History*, p. 205.

to *exclude* 'religious' or 'divine' punishment. Unlike the aftermath of ethics and religion, which will take place in a distant, transcendental realm of the 'World to Come,' the effect of irresponsible political behavior is *immediate* and *necessary*. The realm of the political is regulated by the principle of causality, just like in the world of physics: hence the term "cause" (*ha-sibba*). The catastrophes peculiar to the Jewish people are the result of poor political judgment, moronic and corrupt leadership, and social bickering and disunity promoted by fraudulent religious teachers.[6]

A similar position was maintained by the Rabbis: The collapse of the Second Commonwealth came about because the Courts of Justice, in charge of supervising the social and political institutions of Israel, were corrupt. On the basis of *Micah* (3:9–12), the principle was formulated that every national misfortune befalling Israel, "comes because of the corrupt judges of Israel."[7] Simarily, R. Yoḥanan (ca. 180-ca. 279), the most distinguished figure of the Talmudic period, taught "that Jerusalem was destroyed because [the courts] based themselves on [the strict] words of the Tora, and did not act beyond the boundaries of jurisprudence (*lifnim mi-shurat ha-din*)."[8] It should be noted that failure to act "beyond the boundaries of jurisprudence," was defined as the inability to consider the socio-political aspects of the law. Elsewhere, R. Yoḥanan recounted three stories illustrating how three major centers of power (Jerusalem, Ṭur-Malka, and Bitter [commonly mispronounced 'Betar']) were destroyed.[9] As understood from the perspective of the narratives, the incidents appear to be trivial. However, each illustrates the utter incompetence of Jewish leadership precisely because of their inability to consider the future implications of these incidents and take adequate political measures.

The first story concerns the case of a guest who is mistakenly

---

6. See *In the Shadow of History*, pp. 205–207.
7. Mishna Shabbat 139a.
8. Baba Meṣi'a 30b.
9. Mishna Giṭṭin 55b-58b.

invited to a party hosted by a personal enemy.[10] The guest is forcefully expelled by the host, causing him untold humiliation. The guest notes that "since the Rabbis were present and they did not censure [the host], they assented with him." The attitude of those Rabbis illustrates what was meant by refusing to act "beyond the boundaries of jurisprudence." Rigidly adhering to the law, the host was within his rights to expel any unwanted guest. However, the Rabbis failed to realize the social and political consequences of the case at hand. Their failure is further illustrated when, later in the story, the offended guest carries out a sacrifice in name of the Roman authorities. He deliberately blemishes the sacrifice in a manner considered acceptable according to Roman sacramental law, but inadmissible according to Jewish law. The story depicts how, due to legal considerations, the rabbinic authorities fail to handle the situation politically. In sum, at the beginning of the story we see how the Rabbis' nonchalant attitude about the humiliation of the expelled guest escalates interpersonal animosity into an international crisis, and the story later relates how internal strife between different Jewish factions – rather than the Roman army – was the determining factor in the military collapse of Israel. A similar point is made by the second and third stories. Israel is doomed because of inept political leadership.[11] We thus learn that, although at the time of the second Temple "they were engaged in the [study of] Tora, practice of the precepts and of charity," the Temple was destroyed "because gratuitous hatred ranked among them."[12]

Judaism recognizes the area of collective, i.e., political, *teshuba*. Maimonides wrote that the purpose of fasting during the days of national mourning is "to open up the ways of repentance."[13] Likewise, when discussing the scriptural precepts to cry before God when facing a national catastrophe, Maimonides explained, "and this matter

10. Mishna Giṭṭin 55b-56a.
11. Mishna Giṭṭin 57a-58a.
12. Mishna Yoma 9a.
13. *Mishne Tora,Ta'aniyot* 5:1.

pertains to the ways of repentance."[14] Both political and individual sins require confession.[15] However, since the ills of political sins operate within the realm of causality, it stands to reason that repentance for those sins must also operate within the same realm. This is why Maimonides was careful to point out that this type of repentance means "to act favorably" (*leheṭib*)[16] – a transitive verb that must be understood in the sense of "to remedy," "to mend." In the additional *Musaf* prayer recited on the Sabbath, it says: "And because of our sins we have been exiled from our country and we have been removed from our land." These sins were political. Accordingly, political *teshuba* must involve a specific course of action designed to bring about a concrete change in the political situation of the people. R. Judah Bibas (1780–1852), the actual father of modern Zionism,[17] understood this quite well when he called for the actual *return* of the Jewish people to the land of Israel as a first step in breaking the yoke of Exile (*galut*).[18] The reasoning is clear. If the end-result of Jewish political sins was Exile *from* their land, then it stands to reason that the first step in amending this situation would be to *return* to the Land of Israel. In our terminology, this means that political *teshuba* requires that every Jew should have a trunk ready to be filled at a moment's notice, when the first window of opportunity to return home opens.

* * *

There are two areas of merits and failings. The first area pertains to the *personal* fulfillment of the Tora, such as the abstention from

---

14. *Mishne Tora, Ta'aniyot* 1:2.
15. Concerning confession of personal sins, see *Mishne Tora, Teshuba* 1:1; 2:2. For the confession of political sins, see *Mishne Tora,Ta'aniyot* 5:1.
16. *Mishne Tora, Ta'aniyot* 5:1.
17. Shamefully ignored by modern historians on the premise that 'Zionism' must be based on atheistic considerations, and come from 'enlightened' opportunistic 'Jews'; see my "Early Zionist Ideals among Sepharadim in the Nineteenth Century," *Judaism* 25 (1976), p. 1365.
18. See "Early Zionist Ideals among Sepharadim in the Nineteenth Century," p. 1365.

prohibited foods, and the performance of prayers and of other Jewish rituals. The second area concerns the nation or community of Israel as a *political* entity, and it includes the establishment of courts of justice (*batte din*), protection of the poor and the infirm, the physical security of the nation, and similar precepts instituted by the Tora. These include decisions taken by the governing bodies affecting the welfare of the people and their relations with other nations and communities.

The ultimate objective of the first area is *personal* salvation, or what the Rabbis designate "the world to come" (*'olam habba*). Sins and merits in this area pertain to the spiritual and thereafter, and concern individual salvation. Repentance is achieved *instantly*, upon taking three steps: refraining from sin, a change of heart, and confession.[19] The laws connected with the second area are known as *mishpaṭim*, a term associated with 'civil laws,' but also including the proper *judicial procedure* required for arriving at a valid legal or political decision. The Tora is explicit as to the "consequence" (*'eqeb*) of fulfillment *mishpaṭim*: public health, as well as the economic and political welfare of the nation (Deut. 7:12–16). R. Judah ha-Levi (ca. 1075–1141) referred to the political precepts of the Tora, as "the rational laws" (*al-nu'amis al-'aqliya*). They represent a necessary stage in the organization of the community, and must naturally precede other precepts, "since without observing them the political organization (*sayasa*) of any human society is impossible." Adding: "Even a gang of outlaws could not subsist unless they are internally ruled by justice." The "rational political laws" (*al-shara'i' al-'aqliya al-sayasiya*) prescribed by the Tora are as fundamental to a society "as food, drink, movement, rest, sleep, and awakening" are to an individual. Therefore, he concluded, the religious and ritual precepts of the Tora "cannot be accomplished until the political and rational (*al-sayasiya wal-'aqliya*) laws are first established."[20]

Unlike repentance for personal sins, which occurs instantly,

19. See *Mishne Tora, Teshuba* 2:2.

20. *Kuzari* II, 48. Our translation proceeds from the original Arabic, eds. David H. Baneth, *Kitab al-Radd wa-'l Dalil fi'il Din al-Dhalil* (Jerusalem: Hebrew University Press, 1977), p. 75.

political repentance requires a long process involving a concrete set of actions designed to mend (*leheṭib*) the situation.

In the same spirit, R. Judah Bibas maintained that an indispensable step for the national redemption of Israel is the study of basic science and humanities, referred to him as "the seven wisdoms":

> The seven wisdoms or sciences, such as music, astronomy, etc., are meant. When a man is well, if he takes medicine, it will do him harm; but if he is ill, he must put away bread and take the medicine. Now, the law is bread; but the Jews are sick, they are ignorant and degraded. You must therefore lay aside the study of the law and take the medicine, which is the seven wisdoms or sciences spoken of here.[21]
>
> R. Bibas' position is consistent with the view proposed by R. Judah ha-Levi; namely, that an indispensable first step for the proper fulfillment of the personal precepts is the establishment of a society guided by "rational political laws." Given that the Jew had lost the basic criteria required for the establishment of a healthy political entity, the study of these subjects should take precedence over the study of Tora.

With the destruction of the First Temple, the final objective of the political precepts is the full restoration of the Jewish Nation to the Land of Israel. According to Jewish tradition, this would be accomplished in the Messianic Age under the leadership of the Messiah. Again, since political *teshuba* is to be accomplished by a concrete set of actions specifically designed to mend the present situation, R. Bibas maintained,

> That the Jews must be instructed in science and in arms, that they may wrest the land of Palestine from the Turks under the leadership of the Messiah, as the Greeks wrested their country.[22]

21. Cited in "Early Zionists Ideals among Sepharadim," p. 1365.
22. Cited in "Early Zionists Ideals among Sepharadim," p. 1365.

Echoing this view, a prominent member of his community declared that Jews ought to acquire "a knowledge of arms, so that they may defend their land when they get possession of it."[23] R. Bibas' position expresses the *traditional* Jewish view. As clearly spelled out by Maimonides, the last Messiah approved by the sages of Israel was Simon bar Koziba (Kokhba), on the basis of his *military* and *political* abilities.[24] Thus, although bar Koziba failed as the Messiah of Israel, *he* remains the *model*, officially recognized by the sages of Israel. To repudiate *that* model is to repudiate the authority of the sages of Israel.[25] Dismissing those who maintained that the Messiah is some sort of a wonder-maker as "fools," Maimonides wrote:

> Do not think that the King Messiah has to perform miracles and wonders, or change the [physical aspect of the] world, or resurrect the dead, and similar things as the fools say. This is not the case! Behold: R. 'Aqiba ranked among the highest sages of the Mishna, and he ministered to ben Koziba, the king, and declared that he was the King Messiah. He, as well as all the sages of his generation, deemed that he was King Messiah.[26]

The preceding coincides with the Maimonidean view that "the world to come" and "the messianic age" refer to two distinct realms, one pertaining to the thereafter and the other to the establishment of a just society on earth.[27]

---

23. Cited in "Early Zionists Ideals among Sepharadim," p. 1365.
24. *Mishne Tora, Melakhim* 11[:3]; cf. *Mishne Tora, Ta'aniyot* 5:3. All reference and quotations of *MT, Melakhim* proceed from the Constantinople 1509 edition.
25. Therefore, those who reject the model instituted by the sages of Israel, on behalf of their own model, are in fact denying the coming of the Messiah and fall in the category of *kofrim ba-'iqqar*; see *Mishne Tora, Melakhim* 11:1.
26. *Mishne Tora, Melakhim* 11:3.
27. See *Mishne Tora, Melakhim* 12:1–2; *Teshuba* 8:1; 8:7. The authority of Maimonides' view that the Messianic Age will not result in a change in the physical world, is Samuel cited in Shabbat 63a, etc. This opinion is introduced with the term *wu-fliga* ("and he contends") – a term that in the traditions of the *Ge'onim* and

Under the spell of mental assimilation, the Jewish model of the Messiah was abandoned in favor of a Jesus-Shabbetai Zvi model, whose main task concerns the realm of the supernatural. This is another instance of the anti-Maimonidean view identifying the Messianic Age with the world to come, that for them was conceived in terms of the paranormal and mystic. The ultimate source for this view is Christianity, where Jesus is identified as a Super-Cosmocrator.

It stands to reason that if spiritual edification and salvation are accomplished through the fulfillment of the *personal* precepts, then national salvation ought to be effected through the fulfillment of the *political* precepts of the Tora. It is impossible to imagine a more pious society than the Jewish community in the Middle Ages. And yet, as R. Solomon ibn Verga pointed out, their call for the Messiah was unheeded, because they neglected the precepts dealing with human relations. In a fictional dialogue with the king of Spain, he said:

> My Lord should know that the sins between man and man are much more severe than those between man and God, because they concern the urban stability and world peace. And behold, Christians are very meticulous about robbery, cheating, usury, and similar sins. But they are not particularly observant about their [duties] towards God. There are some gentiles who do not pray more than once a year. The opposite is with the Jew. Can you find a Jew that would skip even a single prayer? However, they are not [as] meticulous with [the laws of] larceny, cheating, and robbery. Therefore, God,

Old Sepharad serves to introduce the authoritative opinion. In our editions of the Talmud, the same term appears also when introducing Samuel's opinion in Berakhot 34b following the presentation of R. Yoḥanan; implying, thereby, that Samuel was disputing R. Yoḥanan. This term does not belong in Mishna Berakhot 34b, but is a later interpolation taken from Shabbat 63a, etc. Evidence to this is the fact that in *Mishne Tora,Teshuba* 8:7, Maimonides recorded R. Yoḥanan's view, whereas in *Mishne Tora, Melakhim* 12:1 he recorded Samuel's view. If R. Yoḥanan's opinion and Samuel's would have conflicted, Maimonides would not have codified both of them.

> who hates robbery, punished them, and their exile is prolonged and they have no Messiah, although the uneducated call him every Saturday night.[28]

Piety and devotion are effective at the *spiritual* level. Call for repentance of *personal* sins, and spiritual rebirth, may affect the status of the individual in the world to come. Only *political teshuba* – that is, a concrete set of actions designed to mend the political misfortunes of Israel – will bring about the Messianic Age.

* * *

Today, the most serious handicap for political *teshuba* is mental assimilation, affecting world Jewry at all levels: from the secular and agnostic to the diehard zealot. The Talmud[29] reports a story that may help us understand the situation of the Jew under foreign domination. The place is Judea, before the year 135 CE. The protagonists are R. 'Aqiba- – the champion of Jewish freedom in rabbinic times – and Pappus ben Judah, a rabbinic scholar. The latter's name expressed the symbiosis peculiar to Jews wanting to represent two conflicting systems: 'Pappus' – a Greek name – suggests assimilation, whereas 'Judah' points to his Jewish roots.[30] In this manner, he could present himself as a Jew to Jews and as an acculturated Roman to the authorities. Pappus – and this is typical of assimilated Jews – believed that he would be rewarded by the Roman authorities for championing their interest. The Talmud relates that eventually Pappus met a tragic end at hand of the Romans.[31] At the time, the Roman authorities had prohibited the study of Tora. Disregarding this law, R. 'Aqiba organized

---

28. Cited in *In the Shadow of History*, p. 22.
29. Mishna Berakhot 61a.
30. In Hebrew *ben*, 'son of,' may stand for 'derivative of,' 'distantly related to,' e.g., *ben-adam* for 'human.' Thus, whereas 'Pappus' denotes a well-established identity, 'son of (*ben*) Judah,' is somehow ambiguous.
31. Mishna Berakhot 61b.

mass rallies and studied Tora in their presence. In this way, he was exposing himself to danger, while showing his defiance of the Roman authorities. Pappus came to the rally with the express purpose of confronting R. 'Aqiba.[32] "'Aqiba, aren't you afraid of the government?" It is worth noting that to taunt him, Pappus omitted the title "Rabbi." His argument is particularly significant as it appealed to the instinct of self-preservation. It expresses the technique by which totalitarian regimes govern, instilling fear in the population. By employing this argument, Pappus reveals himself not as an impartial observer, but as one who is actively collaborating with the Roman authorities. Over the course of the story, R. 'Aqiba comes to grips with this argument. "I shall illustrate [our situation] with a parable," responded R. 'Aqiba. "A fox was walking by the shore of a river and saw a school of fish moving from place to place. He asked them, 'What are you trying to elude?' They responded, 'Fishermen are throwing nets over us.' He then asked them, 'Why don't you come out to the dry land, so that we could live together as our ancestors did?' 'Are you regarded as the craftiest of all animals?!' responded the fish. 'You are not crafty but stupid! If when dwelling in the place of our life we are afraid, how much more afraid we would be if we were to go to the place of our death.' The same is with us. If when we are studying Tora, which is our life, as it is written, 'Because it is your life and the length of your life' (Deut. 30:20), we are afraid, if we were abandon it, in how much more [danger] shall we be?"

There are four points worth noting. First, Rome is depicted as a fox, not a lion. Its strength lies in her cunning, not in her physical strength. It is the ability to manipulate the fear of the intended victim that makes Rome such a formidable enemy. The fox is unable to catch the fish. It is by exploiting the fear of the fish that the fox hopes to persuade them to abandon their strategic place of defense and come out to the surface. Second, to disorient the victim and sooth its fears,

32. Probably backed by Jews sharing Justice Cohn's theory of law. See above, "Forgiving the Enemy, Loving the Enemy, Becoming the Enemy."

Rome appeals to a fictional past of peace and harmony between fox and fish – a patent absurdity based on misinformation and deceit. The purpose of Western historiography is political: by controlling historical knowledge, Rome could further daze its prey. Third, the protection offered by Rome does not come free. It requires total surrender and loss of political autonomy: the fish must learn how to walk on dry land under the fox's shadow. Finally, R. 'Aqiba seems to be arguing that concern for outside danger is something that all organized societies, such as a school of fish, must face. Therefore, the choice 'fear' versus 'non-fear' suggested by Pappus is unrealistic and deceptive. It could only appeal to those who think in mythological terms,[33] and are therefore vulnerable to the utopian dream of fox and fish living together in peace and harmony. The only realistic choice for an autonomous society is the kind of fear it wants to face. Hence R. 'Aqiba's argument that a better strategy for survival can be planned in a natural habitat, preserving political autonomy, than by losing political autonomy under the 'protection' of a natural enemy.

* * *

Jews have long abandoned their political autonomy and now rely on the protection of foxes.[34] What distinguishes one historical period from another, in modern times, are the types of foxes chosen by Jews under the leadership of their new Pappus ben Judah. Referring to this kind of leadership, the late Professor A. S. Yahuda (1877–1951) used to say that some of our famous leaders would not hesitate to sell their own mothers for an invitation for tea with the Queen at St. James's Palace.

Intellectually, the most serious obstacle for Jewish political *teshuba* pertains to the very nature of political knowledge. The methodology and theoretical basis of political knowledge today is medieval.

---

33. See above, "Pomp and Pageantry."
34. See "The Iberian and German Experience."

Medieval knowledge was grounded on "authority" (*auctoritas, authoritas*); it conceived of the truth as essentially hierarchical. Whether in the realm of nature or the spiritual, the truth must be determined by 'authors' (*auctores, authores*), i.e., men invested with 'authority.'[35] This truth needs to be processed through a hierarchical set of 'truths.' "Medieval reverence to *auctores* went so far," writes Curtius, "that every source was held to be good. The historical and critical senses were both lacking."[36] According to this doctrine, the subject at hand should not be investigated directly, but through a *hierarchy* of authorities that controlled, *a priori*, the final outcome of the investigation. This doctrine was not only applied to religious and theological matters, but also to secular subjects, such as Aristotle in physics, Galen in medicine, and Orosius in universal history. Conceptually, modernity is inaugurated with the liberation of truth from 'authority.'[37] This came about with Francisco Sánchez's (or Sánches) (1550/51–1623) epoch-making *Quod Nihil Scitur* ('That nothing is known') (Lyons, 1581). He was the son of *conversos* and a cousin of Montaigne (1533–1592). Sánchez was the first thinker to introduce the concept of "scientific methodology" (*modus sciendi*), inaugurating a new period in Western intellectual history. His objective was to discredit the notion of *authoritas* in the realm of scientific investigation, to demonstrate the futility of Aristotelian and Scholastic methodology, and to establish the grounds for the development of a scientific methodology. All these goals are intimately linked with one another: once the notion of *authoritas* is

35. On the history of this term, see *Horizontal Society*, vol. 1, p. 566.
36. Ernst Robert Curtius, *European Literature and the Latin Middle Ages*, (Princeton, New, Jersey: Princeton University Press, 1973), p. 52. The distinction '*rishonim/aḥaronim*' current among many rabbinic circles is a direct effect of the above doctrine and its derivative '*auctores majores/minores*.'
37. A note from my late friend Dr Chatterjee: "In postmodernism, 'modernity' in your terminology, it is of course inaugurated with the 'liberation of the signifier from the signified,' traced back to the Talmud and certainly to Maimonides the Talmudist."

dismissed, it becomes possible to show the futility of Aristotelian thinking, and to propose a *modus sciendi* or "scientific methodology."[38]

Before Sánchez, objects were viewed through the accumulated interpretations of those invested with *authoritas*.[39] Thanks to Sánchez, the concept of *authoritas* in the realm of science was dismissed in favor of a scientific methodology.

Our knowledge of political truth today is grounded on *authoritas* – assuming the same theoretical principles of 'the scientific knowledge' in the Middle Ages: we know that a given fact has taken place or that a given interpretation is right because somebody with *authoritas* told us so. Except for a few select groups, no one has direct access to raw political data. Even in the most open of democratic societies, vital political information is routinely withheld from the public. The data reaching the masses are processed and distributed through the journalistic and media establishments. This process involves, necessarily, the shaping and reformulation of the raw details by the media establishments. Therefore, 'facts' presuppose faith in the *authoritas* of the agency entrusted with the gathering, distribution, and *interpretation* of political data – essentially, as per medieval 'knowledge.' On the rare occasion that private individuals, not associated with the agencies endowed with *authoritas*, offer data or information incongruent with standard policy, they can be discredited by 'citing' – precisely as per scholastic learning – some known *authoritas*. In the realm of political knowledge, the world has yet to produce a Sánchez that could develop a scientific methodology by which raw political data can be directly examined and distributed *without* the aid of the established *authoritas*. Sánchez designated scholastic knowledge as a "labyrinth of words." Addressing himself to those who regard this type of knowledge as valid, Sánchez said: "You are building a labyrinth in which you've imprisoned yourselves and other wretched people like you, lacking sharpness of reason."[40]

---

38. See *In the Shadow of History*, pp. 91–105.
39. See "Maimonides on Imagination," pp. 90–91; and above, "Pomp and Pageantry."
40. Cited in "Maimonides on Imagination," p. 99.

Contemporary journalistic and media establishments function as the clergy in medieval Christian society. They are the intermediaries, as per Christian theology, between the masses and a truth inaccessible to the masses. The transmission of such truth involves, necessarily, a processing by which the 'truth' is made accessible to the masses. Again, the general perception is that the intermediaries are a bastion of morality, above corruption and unaffected by mundane considerations, exactly as with the priesthood. One can expect corruption among government officials, members of the medical profession, and even the educational system, but not among those entrusted with the processing and transmission of truth. It goes without saying that if any impropriety would have been noted, these bastions of truth and righteousness would have reported to their superiors, exactly as with the priesthood. Let us note that the ombudsmen and other such dignitaries involved in the supervision of the formulation and distribution of truth are not accountable to the masses, exactly as with the clergy. For all practical purposes, particularly as it was lately defined by the courts, freedom of the press means that the members of this august profession are beyond the pale of the law.

* * *

Given that political truth flows from sources hostile to Jewish political interest (in contradistinction with the political interest of Jews), political *teshuba* cannot be accomplished on the basis of the truth accessible to the masses. A first step for political *teshuba* is the development of independent political criteria. How can this be accomplished? Here is where Jewish education, in general, and the *validation* of Jewish national memory, in particular, can play a vital role.[41] In the farewell song recited by Moses to Israel before his death (Deut. 32:1–43), there is a passage that specifies the process by which one should make a

41. See above, "Forgiving the Enemy, Loving the Enemy, Becoming the Enemy," note 9.

political judgment. The verse is made up of three sections: [i] a general preamble: "Remember the days of humankind, understand the years of each generation;" and two exhortations: [ii] "ask your father, and he will report to you; [iii] your elders, and they will tell you" (Deut. 32:7). The first section is a call for the validation of Jewish national memory. The second and third sections describe the process required to reach a proper political criterion. Each of these three sections is further subdivided into two segments. The first segment of section [i] alludes to the ancient, remote past, or "days of humankind," which can only be known in general terms – a reference to the period before the Patriarchs. The second segment is a call to "understand the years of each generation"– a reference to the various periods of the Jewish past; e.g. the bondage in Egypt, the Exodus, etc. With this general background in mind, section [ii] summons, first: "ask your father, and he will report to you," and then: "your elders, and they shall tell you." At first sight, the order seems problematic. One would expect, as with the first section, that those who are more ancient should be mentioned first. Therefore, consultation with the elders should have preceded consultation with the father. The problem vanishes as soon as we remember that in the Tora "elders" (*zeqenim*) stand for *political* leaders, not necessarily for elderly men. Thus, the second section of the verse is a prescription for political judgment. After considering early history, as recorded in the collective memory of the people, one is to consult his "father" – the generation preceding him – and receive pertinent information concerning the immediate past. It is only then that the elders are to be approached, and a valid political judgment can be rendered. I call this process "historical rationality."[42]

* * *

A 'kosher' Jew is someone who has the faculty to swim against the current. The Rabbis taught that if one sees a bird falling into a river

---

42. See *In the Shadow of History*, pp. 205–207.

and it swims against the current, one can be sure that it has suffered no fatal injuries and that the bird is 'kosher.' If the bird is carried by the stream, we must assume that it has suffered fatal injuries and is 'un-kosher.'[43]

A Jew that cannot swim against the current will be swept away by the contemporary flood of mass values. The ultimate purpose of Jewish education is to teach young boys and girls to listen and see on their own, and if the requirement arises, to swim against the current. This explains the vital role of education for Jewish continuity. It is also essential for Jewish *political* welfare, in both the Diaspora and Israel. Without a solid Jewish education, it is impossible to develop the kind of historical rationality and political criteria that would allow one to swim against the mass media – particularly at a time when elements hostile to the State of Israel are engaged in a constant anti-Israel barrage. When antisemitic propaganda began to take ground in Austria, Germany, and other countries in Western Europe, some Jews believed that these attacks were directed at the *Ost-Juden* – their Jewish brethren recently arrived from Eastern Europe – not at them, the *Westens-Juden*. Future events proved them tragically wrong. A most important role of Jewish education is to instruct the student about the perils implied in the dichotomy 'Diaspora/Israel,' and warn against treating Jews in Israel with the same cavalier attitude with which *Westens-Juden* treated their *Ost-Juden* brethren in the not-too-distant past. History has a funny way of repeating itself.

There is another point worth considering. Today, antisemitism is camouflaged as anti-Israel sentiment. Israel's foes point out wrongs allegedly committed by the Jewish State, the army, etc. Certainly, no state or human society is flawless, Israel included. However, these accusations involve a foundational issue. Invariably, those making the charges against Israel do so on behalf of hardened terrorists and mass murderers. It is true that, as in every war, innocent civilians are killed and maimed. What is peculiar in the case of Israel is not only

43. See Ḥolin 51b; *Mishne Tora, Sheḥiṭa* 9:15.

that these casualties are unintended, but that the same cutthroats attacking Jews do the same – and worse – to their own people. Not only do they deprive their own citizens of the most basic human rights, but they brutalize and inflict against them the most horrendous and vicious crimes with impunity. And yet, the 'humanitarian' groups taking their causes against Israel overlook what is being done to their own people in their own backyards! It is high time to point out that when the opportunity arose, many of the countries pointing an accusing finger at Israel were culpable of similar and worse crimes, both in times of war and in times of peace.[44]

Israel is not, nor pretends to be, lily-white. Errors are freely admitted and corrected. The question is not whether Israel may be criticized. From time immemorial, prophets, sages, and common folk did not shy from censuring Israel nor the Jewish establishment and society. Rather, the question is whether there is any ethical ground for joining the chorus of phony moralizers who manage to overlook every evil in the world, while standing firmly on the rights of cold-blooded murderers that terrorize Israel. The level of hypocrisy brings to mind an ancient Jewish maxim. Responding to hypocrisy, the Jew shouted: "As you preach to me: 'Cast away a speck from before your eyes'! I reply: '(You first) cast away the beam from before your eyes!'"[45] I believe that the Christian version of the same maxim better fits 'humanitarian' cynicism against Israel: "Thou hypocrite, first cast out the beam out of thine own eye: and then shall thou see clearly to cast out the mote out of thy brother's eye" (Matt. 7:5; cf. Lk. 6:41). Or, as Luke (4:23) reports in the name of Jesus: "Physician, heal yourself!" One can only wonder about the moral bearings of organizations

44. The doctrine of 'proportionate response,' a rather ambiguous rule, is arbitrarily applied to Israel when responding in self-defense. It was not applied, past or present, to other nations defending their citizens and territory.

45. 'Arakhin 15b; cf. Baba Batra 15b. The same maxim is found with a slight variation: "Improve yourself, and then try to improve others," Baba Meṣi'a 107b; Baba Batra 60b; Sanhedrin 19a.

embarked in the defense of heartless assassins and pay no attention to the cries of their victims.

And now, a simple question: Is there any moral justification for decent men and women to join hands with such organizations even when levying what they believed to be a legitimate criticism against Israel? Shouldn't it behoove them to express their criticism in a forum *not contaminated* by hypocrisy and cynicism? Don't you know that when you do business with the Devil you will be the junior partner? Regarding this issue, Jewish law can be helpful. The Hebrew Scripture formulates the following rule: "Put not your hand with the wicked to be an unrighteous witness" (Ex. 23:1). The Rabbis interpret this rule to mean that a witness of good standing should not attest before a court together with another witness known to him (but not to the court) to be a crook, although the crook is actually saying the truth.[46] "Because," as Maimonides explained, "[the honest witness] is bonding with him, and thereby, [the honest witness] is joining hands with the corrupt [witness], causing his testimony to be accepted."[47] The rationale is quite simple: By testifying together with a corrupt witness, the honest witness is enhancing the crook's reputation – a reputation that the crook will surely use to further enhance his fraudulent activities. In my opinion, the same applies when we join our voices with two-faced organizations whose sole standing is outright hostility against the Jewish people. Because these groups camouflage their hatred as 'compassion,' they are more dangerous than the classical antisemitic groups. I heard somewhere that Einstein defined 'stupid' as someone who continuously makes the same mistake, but thinks that the next time the result will be different. Put another way, national amnesia is the greatest political danger facing the Jewish people in the past and now, in Israel and abroad.

* * *

46. Mishna Shebu'ot 30b.
47. *Mishne Tora*, *'Edut* 10:1.

Jews are the only people who endow chairs at prestigious universities that are designed to knock down their own Jewish tradition and delegitimize Jewish values. Scholars supported by these chairs use their position to undermine the foundations that give shape and unity to the Jewish people – all in the name of a superior 'truth.' Consider the school of High Biblical Criticism initiated by Wellhausen (1844–1918), dominating the 'scientific' study of the 'Old' (rather than the 'New') Testament. In a short time, they managed to reduce the Hebrew Scripture to a hodge-podge of nonsensical expressions. The people involved in this type of scholarship are as uncompromising regarding their own ideologies as fanatic monks in the Dark Ages. Significantly, while those pathetic 'scientists' do not hesitate to tear the Tora into pieces on the basis of their theories, they would not dare do the same with other texts. The reason is simple: They are quite aware that their theories are not based on verifiable data, but on propositions and assumptions that can be 'corroborated' (just like astrology and witchcraft) but not scientifically demonstrated, and that, in fact, their so-called 'critical' apparatus resembles the proverbial colossus with clay feet. The following story illustrates the warped perspective developed by a colleague, famous for his expertise in this type of 'scientific' acrobatics.

I was friendly with a professor, now deceased, who had an international reputation as a biblical scholar. He had great knowledge of the vocabulary and grammar of ancient Semitic languages. However, he was under the grip of some sort of intellectual aphasia and could not properly connect the various terms of a sentence. Thus, he could offer a meticulous analysis of a particular word in *a* sentence, but not *of* the sentence. (Interestingly, he was unable to read fluently even the simplest text of the Scripture. An acute ear could sense a slight stuttering between word and word.) Simultaneously, he was totally unaware of modern linguistics, semiotics, and critical literary theory. (His methodology was that of the German school of comparative philology initiated by Franz Bopp [1791–1867], discredited by modern linguistics.) At any rate, we loved to speak about all kinds of matters related to Semitic philology, and many times we would drop into each other's offices or hold long telephone conversations on some obscure point that only philologians could find interesting. Once, I came to his office to discuss a particular explanation that he had suggested. It was a short conversation, and both of us were in a talkative mood. I knew that he was firmly convinced of the validity of Wellhausen's School of High Biblical Criticism. I had been told that he once faulted Professor Yechezkel Kutscher (1909–1971) for not amending the text of the Tora on account of being orthodox. Professor Kutscher responded that he did not amend the text because he was a scientist, not because he was orthodox: "The task of a scientist is to interpret the facts, not to change them." I was curious to probe his mind. Politely, of course, I inquired whether he had any notion of what 'scientific' was. His knowledge of mathematics was miserable and he did not have the foggiest idea of any of the exact sciences. "Since you know very little about science or scientific methodology," I asked, "how can you be sure that Wellhausen is 'scientific?' Have you ever discussed this matter with a member of the scientific community." I don't remember exactly what he told me, but it was something to the effect that he did not see the need to discuss this methodology with a scientist, since *he knew* that the methodology was scientific. I understood that it was useless to further discuss this point. I said to myself that by the same token, astrology and witchcraft should be regarded as 'scientific.' I continued: "Anyhow, are you aware that Wellhausen's historiography is based on Hegel's notion of progress and that no historian, except for Protestant theologians and anti-Bible [read: 'Old' Testament] Jews, take him seriously? Have you studied Hegel's works?" I knew that his knowledge of Hegel was less than his knowledge of mathematics. Without waiting for an answer, I proceeded: "I happen to think highly of Wittgenstein's school of logical-positivism, according to which Hegel's entire intellectual apparatus is gibberish. Do you mean to say, that for a proper understanding of Judaism, one would need to discard every philosophical school, except for that of Hegel?" I knew that I was getting on his nerves. Either out of conviction or just to spite me, his reply was in the affirmative. One could have expected such an answer perhaps from Herman Cohen (1842–1918), but it is difficult to see how someone who had no grasp of philosophy could make such an assertion, even in jest. I was now ready for the final thrust. "If you are so convinced of the validity of your methodology, would you apply it to the text of the American Constitution?" He thought for a minute, and then replied: "No." "Then why," I asked, "do you not hesitate in applying it to the text of the *Jewish* Constitution?" Again, he thought for a while. Almost whispering he said: "I cannot treat the American Constitution as if it were a Jewish text. Jewish texts are different." "But the whole point of your investigation is to demonstrate that Jewish texts are *not* different, that they are just like any other texts", I replied, adding "It's getting late. Perhaps we should continue with this discussion some other time."

Yes, Jewish texts are different! And they must be judged by standards applied to no other text! The Jewish people, too, are different and must be judged by standards applied to no other people! The State of Israel, too, is different and must be judged by standards applied to no other nation! Traditionally, this was called antisemitism. Today, it is called Jewish scholarship, enlightened Jewish leadership, and human rights! Any wonder why over fifty percent of American Jews choose to assimilate?

The next account took place around 1978, when the City of New York decided to fix Ocean Parkway, a major avenue in Brooklyn, and a street along which I used to jog. New York does not have a spring (or a fall), but after the harsh winter, before its suffocating heat and unbearable humidity are unleashed, the city has a few days which can only be described as splendorous. On one of those days, around noon, I went jogging to Church Avenue and back, as per usual. A block or so before my destination, there was a group of workers fixing the street who were sitting on the benches, resting from their hard labor. As I passed them, I noticed that they were speaking Portuguese. On my way back, I stopped for a minute to talk to them. It was an opportunity to practice my Portuguese and rest. They were very polite, and soon they told me that they were from Lisbon and had come to this country in search of work. I asked them for their names. "Pinto," told me one. "Nunes, Carvalho, Costa, Silveira, and Soares," responded the others. For an instant, I thought I was in the *Etz Hayyim* Synagogue in Amsterdam, in the seventeenth century. "Where did you live," I inquired. "We are from Bellmonte," they responded. That used to be a Jewish neighborhood, inhabited by *conversos* throughout the centuries. They must be of *converso* descent, I thought to myself. I tried to see whether I could discover anything 'Jewish' in them. Nothing in their looks, mannerisms, or way of thinking appeared 'Jewish' to me. When they asked about me, I told them that I was Sepharadi, a descent of Iberian Jews. There was no reaction. Assimilation had erased every Jewish trace from them. They were no different than any other Portuguese person belonging to the mass of the unemployable. After a few moments, we bid our farewells. As I was jogging back home, I thought that they were probably the descendents of Jews who, in a moment of crisis, decided to trust their fate to Portugal, rather than to the Commonwealth of Israel. Some of them, perhaps, looked condescendingly upon their brothers and sisters who had left their homeland to secure a Jewish future for their children. I knew that every Jew, somehow, had received a special trunk from his or her ancestors to fill and with which to return to Israel at a moment's notice. Those of us who had chosen to remain Jewish were fortunate to have a historic trunk to pass onto our children. But that is not enough. Not in *our* days. Today, we must build new trunks for our children to fill up. It is only in this way that we will fulfill the promise we made on that black day in history, when we were uprooted from the Land of Israel, *our* land. Otherwise, how could our children ever realize political *teshuba*?

# 7. The Iberian and German Experience

Underneath the variety of Jewish experience, there is a basic unity of purpose. Although they were geographically and linguistically separated, diverse Jewish communities in many instances followed paths that led to common goals and achievements. In those cases, the experiences accumulated by Jewish communities throughout dissimilar historical periods integrate into a total picture, as pieces of a jigsaw puzzle. Here, I would like to show how the Iberian and the German experiences, peculiar to the histories of Sephardic and Ashkenazic Jewries, combine, creating a full image of Western religious and political attitudes towards Jews.

It is wrong to view Judaism as either a religion or as a political system.[1] If we wish to render 'Tora' into concepts current in Western thought, it must be described as a two-dimensional system, one religious and the other political.[2] Both of these dimensions are structurally connected and cannot function separately from one another. Together, they form a single operative system. Antisemites understood this quite well. Accordingly, their strategy was to attack a single dimension: once one of these dimensions collapses, the whole system becomes inoperative. This helps us understand some

1. See above, "People of the Covenant," p. 1184.
2. Hence, Spinoza's 'theologico-political' system.

of the most important events marking the Jewish Middle Ages and the Modern period.

During the 14th and 15th centuries, various internal and external factors prompted many Iberian Jews to forfeit their religious dimension. At the time, Jews were attacked solely for their 'religion.' Thus, hundreds of Jewish communities in Spain and Portugal were decimated in the name of Christian love. Some resisted and paid with their lives. Others escaped death and managed to continue their lives as Jews. But there were also those who converted to escape death and ignominy. These are the *conversos* (Jewish 'converts') who adopted Christianity, entrusting their fate to the religious institutions of the West. Some *conversos* became devout Christians and champions of their new faith. An important element in Christian devotional life is to turn the faithful into the persecutor of those who are blinded and do not see the true light. It is not surprising, therefore, that we find some of these *conversos* expressing their new faith by harassing and oppressing Jews. Moved by their new religion, underprivileged *conversos* would take advantage of the situation and blackmail their wealthy relatives. Samuel de Usque (16th century) reported how they would go "to the houses of their richer brothers to ask for a loan… If any refused them, they accused him of Judaizing with them."[3] Inspired by Christian love, some *conversos* became rabid antisemites.

Racism is one of the many contributions made by Christian Europe. Spain always regarded herself as a paragon of Christian virtue and devotion. Displaying genuine Christian 'love,' the local population 'welcomed' all *conversos* to their bosom by establishing a distinction between *cristianos viejos* ('Old Christians'), representing genuine Christendom, and *cristianos nuevos* ('New Christians'). Although the formal excuse was 'heresy,' and the charges were cloaked in religious rhetoric, the real reason for this distinction was racism. Professor Israel Salvator Revah (1917–1973), who studied this phenomenon better than anyone else, wrote: "in the midst of the Spanish Catholic

3. Cited *In the Shadow of History*, p. 45.

community a distinction was established that must be qualified as racist."[4] This is also admitted by Christian scholars. A modern Spanish antisemite, Nicolas Lopez Martinez, professor of Theology at the Seminario Metropolitano de Burgos, devoted the first chapter of his much-acclaimed book *Los Judaizantes Castellanos* (Burgos: Publicaciones del Seminario Metropolitano, 1954), to demonstrating the "Racial Incompatibility" of *conversos* with Old Christians.

The New Christians were at once suspected of treachery and heresy. Ironically, they were more hated and despised as Christians than as Jews. The first massacre of *conversos* in Toledo in 1449 made this point quite clear. The Old Christian population descended upon their new coreligionists, indiscriminately butchering thousands of men, women, and children. To underscore the racist dimension of their hatred, the massacre was followed by a famous legislation known as *Sentencia Estatuto*, promulgated on June 5, 1449. In essence, this legislation stipulated that all *conversos*, because of their Jewish blood, were unfit for public and ecclesiastical office, and could not bear testimony against Old Christians. It is a puzzling, although true, fact, that Jewish intelligentsia throughout the ages had failed miserably to understand the Jewish situation and the nature of gentile society. There is something about Jewish intellectuals that makes them blind and dumb about anything that concerns the gentile world. Characteristically, some of the *conversos*, particularly when attaining some recognition among the Christian intelligentsia, failed to comprehend the nature of the Old Christian establishment.[5] One such individual was Alonso de Cartagena (1385–1456), Bishop of Burgos. His father, the apostate Pablo de Santa Maria (ca. 1350–1435), had been a rabbi before converting. Upon embracing Christianity, Pablo became an enemy of Jews and Judaism. Some of this hatred passed to his son Alonso. Alonso wrote his famous *Defensorium unitatis christianae* ('A Defense of Christian Unity') to show that the sins imputed by

4. Cited *In the Shadow of History*, pp. 41–42.
5. See *In the Shadow of History*, pp. 48–49.

Christianity to Jews are not racial. Accordingly, he proposed that those sins should also not be imputed to New Christians. Naively, he believed that Christian hatred was the effect of some misconstrued theological doctrine – an intellectual aberration of 'true' Christianity. To the racist insult made by Old Christians, "Go, go! That's a *marrano* ['piglet'], he is lower than dust!" Alonso de Cartagena offered this pathetic response: "They are contradicting the evangelical truth, saying that the true light cannot illuminate those who come to it."[6]

A few years later, in 1480, Pope Sixtus IV issued the bull authorizing the establishment of the Inquisition. Shortly thereafter, the Inquisition was established in Spain with the purpose of stamping out heresy from the *converso* population. The Expulsion of Jews in 1492 came as the 'final solution' to the *converso* problem. The Edict of 1492, signed by the Catholic Monarchs, claimed that the expulsion was necessary to prevent Jews from contaminating the New Christians. It opened with a declaration "that in our kingdom there are some bad Christians [i.e., *conversos*] who were Judaizing and apostatizing from our holy Catholic faith, of which the cause was the communication of Jews with Christians [i.e., *conversos*]."

The nature of the Expulsion from Spain is yet to be properly understood. So long as there were Jews in Spain, the *converso* population would find protection from the wrath of the Old Christian population. Jews were expelled from Spain to enable the Old Christians to do with the *conversos* as they saw fit. Strategically, the Expulsion was designed to thwart any possible cooperation between *conversos* and Jews. Thus, by failing to protest against the Expulsion, and by acquiescing to this savagery made in the name of 'religion,' the *conversos* left themselves open to the 'kindness' of their new brethren in faith. A short time after, on October 23, 1493, Ferdinand and Isabel were forced to issue an order restraining the local population from further harassing and abusing *conversos*. Mention was made that these New Christians "are very much persecuted, that they are called Jews and

6. Cited *In the Shadow of History*, pp. 45–46.

turncoats and many other injuries, and consequently neither they nor their servants dare walk or go out from their houses."[7]

Racist attitudes continued to thrive. Racial antisemitism was given legal force by a series of statutes known as *pureza de sangre* ('purity of blood'). To illustrate, in 1547, a new decree excluded Christians with even partial Jewish ancestry from holding office in the Cathedral Chapter of Toledo. This type of legislation persisted until 1860, demanding documentary proof of "purity of blood" (*pruebas de limpieza*) to hold public office or join *colegios mayores* (the equivalent to our exclusive clubs) and universities. Even immigration to the New World required such documentation. Partial Jewish blood, or having suckled milk from a nurse with partial *converso* ancestry, was sufficient to contaminate with 'heresy' an otherwise good Catholic.[8]

Christians love to speak about Christian love. They would do well to see how this love was implemented in real historical situations, particularly in Spain and Portugal. As a result of the racist policies, ten of thousands of New Christians were forced to flee the Iberian Peninsula to escape Christian persecution. Their new coreligionists, both in and outside the Iberian Peninsula, watched impassively as these new Christians were being persecuted and dispossessed from even the most basic elements of human dignity. Thus, the Iberian experience proved that Jews could not trust the religious institutions of the West. Convinced of the endemic insolvency of Western institutions, there arose a new determination to strengthen Jewish religious life. The following two centuries were a pivotal period in Jewish history. Popular opinion not withstanding, the break with the West (both culturally and demographically) and the ensuing Ghettoization of the Jew came in the 16th and 17th centuries. It was precisely at that period of history that Sephardic and Ashkenazic Jewries gave final

7. Cited *In the Shadow of History*, p. 42.
8. See the valuable study of Yosef Yerushalmi, "Assimilation and Racial Anti-Semitism: The Iberian and the German Models," *Leo Beck Memorial Lecture* 26 (Leo Beck Institute, 1982).

shape to the great mystical, legal, and ethical systems that regulate Jewish life to the present.

* * *

A parallel period developed during the 18th and 19th centuries. Moved by internal factors similar to those that affected Iberian Jewry, as well as by new historical circumstances, Jews began to forfeit their political dimension. In the footsteps of Paul, R. Moses Mendelssohn (1729–1786) proposed a purely religious system, with no political dimensions, or to be a bit more accurate, a system that recognizes the full and unlimited authority of the political sovereign, like the Church. Many others also followed suit on this crucial point, among them Mendelssohn's vociferous enemies in the ultra-orthodox camp (חרדים), claiming that Judaism is a religion void of any political dimension. Even when professing Messianic hope, the ultra-orthodox camp conceived of both the person and the mission of the Messiah either as a Cosmocrator-Jesus, fuming fire and brimstone (see *Book of Revelation* 19: 11–21),[9] or as a happy-go-lucky Shabbetai Zvi (1626–1676), rather than as a Simon b. Kochba (d. 135), R. 'Aqiba's protégée.[10] The net result was that Jews relinquished their own (limited) internal autonomy as a separate community within the state and entrusted their fate to the *political* institutions of the West. Under the guise of 'emancipation' and the promise of participation as full citizens of the state, ancient communities forfeited their judicial and semi-autonomous status. To facilitate full integration in the state, many converted or assimilated into all kinds of political and exotic ideologies.

Américo Castro (1885–1972) and his students have shown that one of the most remarkable results of *conversos* entering Christian society was the enormous contributions they had made in all scientific and intellectual fields: from medicine and botany, to literature,

9. See *Horizontal Society*, vol. 1, chapter 34, p. 362.
10. See above, "My Grandmother's Trunk. Or: What about Political *Teshuba*?" p. 1254.

jurisprudence and philosophy. Indeed, there is not a single creative work produced in either Spain or Portugal at the time that was not penned by a *converso*. Something similar took place in modern times when Jews entered Western society. Political integration of Jews into Western society resulted in an unprecedented intellectual flurry in all areas of human endeavor: from the scientific and political to the literary and artistic. It would be no exaggeration to say that Jewish entrance into Western society directly contributed to the most important scientific and intellectual revolution known to history. As with the *conversos*, assimilated Jews soon discovered that Western society was not ready to accept them. Despite the rhetoric to the contrary, the truth of the matter is that Western man was too petty and too provincial to fully accept the Jew. Because the Jew saw things differently (individuation), assimilation into Western society was particularly difficult. This is why, even when trying to assimilate, the German Jew was perceived as 'different,' and could not possibly be regarded as an 'equal.' In a recent book, Marcel Reich-Ranicki argues that Jews wrote differently because they were able to perceive some dark aspects of German culture that were not disclosed by other writers. This is why they were branded as "troublemakers" and "agitators."[11] Like the *converso* writers, Jews in modern times – whether they had formally converted or not – had to learn to camouflage their own Jewishness, and encode their most important ideas to an elite reader, or for future generations. In an unguarded moment, Sigmund Freud (1856–1939) gave us a glimpse into his most intimate feelings. In the "Preface to the Hebrew Translation," of *Totem and Taboo*,[12] he expressed "the emotional" impact of seeing his work in Hebrew. Although admittedly "completely estranged from the religion of his fathers," he "feels that he is in his essential nature a Jew and has no desire to alter that nature." If the question were put to him:

---

11. Marcel Reich-Ranicki, *Uber Ruhestoerer: Juden in der Deutschen Literatur* (Berlin: Deutscher Taschenbuch Verlag, 1993).
12. Printed in the *Standard Edition*, vol. 13, p. XV.

> 'Since you have abandoned all these common characteristics of your countrymen, what is there left to you that is Jewish?' he would reply: 'A very great deal, and probably its very essence.' He could not now express that essence clearly in words; but some day, no doubt, it will become accessible to the scientific mind.

This calls for a new approach in the study of the works produced by secular and assimilated Jews. Since they were not free to express their ideas openly, their works need to be decoded from a perspective similar to that which I developed for the study and analysis of *converso* literature in Spain and Portugal.[13]

There is an eerie parallel between the old statutes of *pureza de sangre* and the promulgation of racist legislation in Italy, France, and Germany.[14] As with the establishment of the Inquisition, the triumph of Nazism throughout Europe and the stripping of basic rights from Jewish citizens constituted a formal betrayal of all those Jews who had entrusted their fate to the political institutions of the West. In both cases, antisemitism was enthusiastically supported by the masses.[15] Just like in the past, when Christians watched impassively as 'other' Christians, i.e., the *conversos*, were being systematically destroyed, European citizenry watched impassively as 'other' citizens were systematically stripped of all human rights and exterminated, paradoxically, by the State, the very organization entrusted with the protection of their rights. As with the Expulsion, the extermination of European Jewry constituted the 'final solution' to the problem of the 'other.' Let us note: in both cases the instrument by which the

13. See *In the Shadow of History*, chapters 4–6.
14. On some parallels between the racist policies in the Iberian Peninsula and those of the Nazis, see Cecil Roth, "Marranos and Racial Antisemitism: A Study in Parallels," *Journal for Jewish Studies* 2 (1940) 239–248; and Yerushalmi, "Assimilation and Racial Anti-Semitisim: The Iberian and the German Models."
15. "For the role of the masses in Spain, see Solomon ibn Verga, *Shebeṭ Yehuda*, eds. Azriel Schochet and Y. Beer (Jerusalem: Mossad Bialik, 5701/1941), VII, p. 30; on the masses' support of Nazi policies, see Erich Fromm, *Escape from Freedom* (New York: Avon Books, 1965), p. 235.

Jews were exterminated was the very institutions with which they had entrusted their protection.

The parallels between the Iberian and German experiences go further. As a result of the Holocaust, many Jews quickly learned that they could not trust their fate to the political institutions of the West. Hence, the establishment of the State of Israel. In this sense, the Iberian and German experiences parallel and complement each other, one in the realm of the religious dimension of Western society and Judaism, and the other in the realm of the political dimension.

There are further parallels. Both the *converso* and the assimilated Jew in Austria and Germany were betrayed by the very system of values and people whom they trusted and identified with. Referring to the assimilated German Jew, a contemporary writer noted:

> In all the Jewish tragedy of the first half of this century, there is nothing quite so poignant as the story of the German Jews. Numerically few compared with the Jews of Eastern Europe (or, in time, of the United States), they had played after the granting of civil rights in the 19th century a quite disproportionate role in German culture and commerce; and for the most part they were passionately attached to what they believed was their Fatherland. Their love was unrequited. Germany turned on these Jews, reviled and ostracized them, in the end expelled and killed them. The millions of murdered Jews in Poland and Russia were spared one last moral torment: unlike the German Jews, they were not killed by a nation and a culture that they had dearly loved and to which they had passionately wanted to belong.[16]

The Jewish intelligentsia, in particular, failed to understand the nature of the new culture that was being developed in Europe. The 'Frankfurt

16. Geoffrey Wheatcroft, "The Warburgs," *The New York Times Book Review*, October 3, 1993, p. 3.

School' of philosophy (made up almost totally of Jews), flourishing around the 20's and 30's, is a classical example of how blind Jewish intellectuals were as to what was going on in their own backyard. More regrettably, even after they had been victimized by the new adopted system, there were elements in both traditions who fiercely clung onto the belief in the absolute superiority of their adopted systems.

This was particularly true of some intellectuals who came to fully identify with the values and institutions of the persecutor. The classical case in Spain is of the famous Juan Luis Víves (1491–1540), one of the great Christian thinkers of the time. His father had been burnt alive by the Inquisition in 1524, the bones of his mother unburied and burned, and all their property confiscated, and he himself had been the victim of racist discrimination. And yet, his faith in Christianity remained unshaken. Even after escaping Spain as a victim of racist persecution, he did not shrink from singing the praises of Christendom and taunting and attacking his former coreligionists. To top it all off, he managed to write his own *Adversus Judaicus* (*Against the Jews*).[17]

Some of the victims of Iberian racism, upon taking refuge in *converso* communities in southern France, not only refused to return to their ancestral religion, but also went out to denounce their friends and relatives for 'relapsing' into Judaism. One such case was the *converso* community in Rouen, where, in 1613, the more Catholic members actively helped in the apprehension and punishment of their relatives and friends.[18] In parallel fashion, even after the Holocaust, many Jews continued to believe in the very system that had brought about their total demise. Even after the Nuremberg laws, one of the Warburgs toasted a cousin at his bar mitzva: "Always remember that you are a German."[19] As with Alonso de Cartagena, assimilated German Jews believed that the Nazi phenomenon was just an 'aberration' of the 'true spirit' of Western culture (which, of course, only they

17. See *In The Shadow of History*, p. 45; cf. pp. 44, 89–90.
18. See Cecil Roth, "Les Marranes à Rouen," *Revue des Etudes Juives* 88 (1929), pp. 125–31.
19. Quoted in "The Warburgs," p. 24.

knew, and which one day – not in the distant future – they will reveal to the gentile masses, precisely like Jesus and Paul did).

I once asked my friend, the late Professor Steven S. Schwarzschild (1924–1989) about Ernst Cassirer (1874–1945) – a philosopher whom we both admired – how a great thinker like Cassirer could still believe in the superiority of the German culture in light of the Holocaust. Professor Schwarzschild had known Cassirer personally. He was convinced that in his heart of hearts Cassirer believed that the 'true' German ethos was what he had captured in his books, Nazism being an 'aberration' of the 'true' German ethos. More pathetic was the relation between Hannah Arendt (1906–1975) and Martin Heidegger (1889–1976), a Nazi ideologue if there ever was one. Abe Katzman had recently referred to a letter that Herbert Marcuse (1898–1979) sent after the war to his Nazi teacher Heidegger in 1947. The letter was accompanied by a package. In that letter, Marcuse addressed his teacher with the hope that he would publicly disassociate himself from the Nazis. Heidegger, "the inveterate Nazi, responds to Dear Mr. Marcuse, thanks him for the package that he had sent him, tells him that he had distributed its content among students who in the past have not been associated with the Party, thanks him for his assistance, and refuses to come with a public confession."[20]

In fact, structurally, there was no difference between the thinking process of those intellectuals and that of the Nazis. Their assimilation process consisted in abandoning Jewish holistic thinking in favor of mythical thinking (see above, "Pomp and Pageantry"). Like their mentors, assimilated Jews abstracted a single aspect of reality, which they regarded as absolutely 'true,' and displaced all the rest as marginal and trivial. We know that at the beginning, some of these Jews did not see the Nazi movement with alarm. In 1930, one of the Warburgs said of the Nazis, "one finds among a large part of them valuable, typically German strengths, which are indeed incredible in a political connection, but show strong feeling for social and national

20. In *Ha'aretz* (7/21/1993), "Book Review," p. 15.

duties."[21] Thus, a most overwhelming question, best left unanswered: Were it not for the fact that these Jewish intellectuals themselves had been the victims of Nazism, would they have condemned Nazism? A similar question was posed by Katzman: "The difficult question is: Would Dear Marcuse and his colleagues have acted differently than Dear Heidegger, Dear Jasper, Dear Carl Gustav Jung and their colleagues, if they would not have been Jewish?"[22]

Like Luis Víves, who felt the need to write one more *Adversus Judaicus* to assure his Christian friends that in no way did he identify with his former brethren, many assimilated Jews vigorously objected to the establishment of an autonomous Jewish state. Like the faithfully Catholic *conversos*, they, too, clung onto their unswerving faith in the political institutions and ideology that once watched impassively as millions of Jews were exterminated. For them, the establishment of a Jewish autonomous state was nothing else than a direct affront to their belief in the absolute superiority of Western political institutions. As with the Iberian experience, some would not shrink from taunting and attacking the men and women that devoted their lives and energies to strengthening the political dimension of Israel. In doing so, these assimilated Jews chose to join the persecutors.

Let me explain: Regardless of cultural background and religious orientation, traditionally, the Jew processed reality from the perspective of the persecuted. Hence, the radical difference between Jews and other victims: Jews alone developed an apparatus capable of processing and transmitting their suffering from the *perspective of the persecuted*. What distinguishes the extermination of Jews in Spain and Portugal from that of Native Americans, or Nazi genocide of Jews from the extermination of other minorities, is the responses that they elicited: only the Jews refused to join the persecutor and chose to transmit their laments to future generations. As such, Jews are the sole witnesses to the dark side of humanity. The religious response

21. Quoted in "The Warburgs," p. 3.
22. In *Ha'aretz* (7/21/1993), "Book Reviews," p. 15

of Sephardic and Ashkenazic Jewries after the Expulsion, as well as the political response embodied in the establishment of the State of Israel, represent the cries of the persecuted refusing to acquiesce to the religious and political institutions of the persecutor. From this perspective, our modern political counterpart of the Alonso de Cartagena, Víves, and the fanatic Judeo-Catholics of Rouen, raised against Israel, are another instance of those bent on clinging onto the ideology of the persecutors and further hindering the voice of the persecuted.

# 8. Loving the Enemy, Forgiving the Enemy, Becoming the Enemy

Judaism is often maligned because of its supposed attitude towards 'the enemy.' In contrast, Christianity is presented as 'the religion of love,' extending limitless charity to all, and the foe in particular. This is a favorite argument used by secular antisemites to taunt their Jewish friends. "Love thine enemy," (Matt. 5:43) is taken as one of the most formidable principles, proving Christian pre-eminence over all religions, especially Judaism. Is there any truth behind this claim, or is Christian's claim of moral superiority simply a diversionary tactic designed to conceal its own immoral behavior with the enemy?

Judaism distinguishes between personal and political enemies. Concerning the personal enemy, we are commanded not to hate or to take any form of revenge. If one is offended or personally hurt by another, they should confront them rather than hold a grudge.[1] We must also assist others in moments of crisis; if both friend and foe need help, Judaism teaches to first help the foe and only then the friend.[2] Indeed, a fundamental principle of Rabbinic ethics is the special duty to forgive and assist one's personal enemy.[3] Moreover,

1. See *Mishne Tora, De'ot* 6:5–6; 7:7–8.
2. See *Mishne Tora, Roṣeaḥ* 13:13–14.
3. See Elie Benamozegh, *Jewish and Christian Ethics*, trans. Emanuel Blochman

gentiles are not the *personal* enemies of Israel.[4] Since, for Judaism, a virtuous gentile has a portion in the world to come, there is no religious enemy. The only foes that Judaism recognizes as political enemies are those bent on harming the Jewish people, attacking their national institutions, or infringing upon their right to establish a sovereign state in the national territory allotted to them by the Hebrew Scripture. R. Elie Benamozegh (1823–1900), one of the most brilliant and learned Jewish thinkers in modern times, explained this fundamental principle:

> The Jew, who loved his country dearly, was the natural enemy of all who conspired against it. For such, there would be no truce, no peace, no pardon, as long as danger was imminent. Against these were the exceptional measures, the martial laws, the terrible decrees, of which we read in the law of Moses or in the books of the Rabbis, attesting one thing only – *danger* – having but one object – *public safety* – recognizing but one right – *defense* – a right not only lawful, but obligatory above all when it has reference to one's country.[5] [Italics in original]

Christianity used this last point to malign Judaism. It intentionally suppressed the fact that Judaism recognizes only the political enemy and fabricated the notion that Judaism teaches hatred towards all types of enemies, including the personal and the religious foe. To prove its moral superiority, Christianity had no qualms in misrepresenting the Scripture and the Rabbis, and then to contrast Jewish hate with Christian love. In fact, both Christianity and Judaism teach forgiveness of the personal enemy.[6] They differ on the political and religious enemy. Since Christianity is a religion with no political dimension, by definition it cannot recognize a political foe. Thus, it

(San Francisco: Emanuel Blochaman, 5633/1873), chapter 8.

4. See *Mishne Tora, Roṣeaḥ* 13:14.
5. *Jewish and Christian Ethics*, p. 83. Cf. *In the Shadow of History*, pp. 196–197.
6. See, however, *In the Shadow of History*, p. 198.

disclaims the very notion of political enemies. On the other hand, precisely because Judaism has a political dimension, those who threaten its political welfare are its foes. This point was forcefully made by R. Elie Benamozegh:

> Easy for Christianity – that knows no country or nationality – to dispute a religious nation's, a sacerdotal kingdom's, right to existence and the consequences of that right: To be scandalized whenever the preservation of Israel demands a restriction of that limitless charity which is the final object of that restriction. Israel, with erect head and calm heart, shall never blush for its political character, given it by the God of Christians, nor for the exercise of the right appertaining thereto.[7]

Conversely, since for Judaism a virtuous gentile has a portion in the world to come, it cannot recognize a religious enemy.

In place of the political enemy, Christianity was first to introduce a new kind of enemy – the religious enemy. Significantly, when teaching about the universal love that it professes to humankind, Christianity suppressed the fact that this love does not extend to the *religious* enemy. Again, quoting R. Elie Benamozegh:

> But has Christianity itself no enemies? ... Christianity, that would not have a political enemy, was obliged to have – as soon as it encountered the world – *a religious enemy*. Yes, the religious enemy is a Christian creation altogether, unknown to Judaism – *impossible* even – the moment it admits that eternal salvation is not the exclusive heritage of the Mosaic Law. So, this charity that with the Jew is stopped only by the political enemy, the Christian cannot entertain towards the religious enemy. And let it not be said that this refers only to posterior

7. *Jewish and Christian Ethics*, p. 83.

> abuses and alterations. The Gospel is there to attest that the genius of Christianity is true to itself from the most remote times. Jesus, who knew so well how to pray for his personal enemies, who would have the Jew love the Samaritan[8]... has neither love nor prayer for those not of his church. "I pray not," he says, "for the world, but for those whom thou hast given me" (Jn. 17:9); and elsewhere, "Who is not for me is against me" (Matt. 12:30; Lk. 11:23).[9]

Because Christian love and morality do not extend to the religious enemy, Christian leaders never felt any misgivings in maligning Jews and Judaism.

* * *

A fundamental dimension of Israel is its national memory.[10] It is on the basis of Israel's national memory that political judgments are made. When national memory is discarded or fails to elicit the appropriate response, Israel ceases to function as an autonomous political entity, and national disasters follow. The role of national memory is central regarding the identification of 'Amaleq – Israel's archenemy. The 'Amaleqites are the first terrorists on record. They attacked the Jewish people upon their Exodus from Egypt. What made their attack particularly hideous was the fact that [a] it was unprovoked – the Israelites were passing through the desert, and not through 'Amaleqite territory; [b] the attack was sudden, launched against unsuspecting travelers; and [c] it focused on the "weak and infirm" (*'ayef ve-yagea'*), who could not defend themselves (see Deut. 25:17–18). The Tora does not specify the particulars of this episode. Rather, they were entrusted to the memory of Israel. Accordingly,

8. I.e., his political enemy. On the significance of this point, see *In the Shadow of History*, p. 198.
9. *Jewish and Christian Ethics*, pp. 83–84.
10. On this basic idea, see *Horizontal Society*, vol. 1, chapter 37.

Jews are urged to "remember" what 'Amaleq did to us (Deut. 25:17), and then proceed to "erase 'Amaleq's remembrance (*zekher*)" (Deut. 25:19; cf. Ex. 17:14). The battle must be carried on "from generation to generation" (Ex. 17:16).

There is some confusion concerning the meaning of this precept. Usually, it is understood to be a war against the *people* of 'Amaleq. This explanation is unacceptable on both legal and linguistic grounds. One of the conditions to classify a scriptural assignment as a 'precept' (*miṣva*) is that it could, at least in theory, be executed at all times.[11] Now, once the people of 'Amaleq have been "erased from under the heavens," this precept could never be fulfilled again! We have shown elsewhere* that 'Amaleq is not merely a matter of genealogy. The Scripture exhorts Israel to eliminate the "remembrance" (*zekher*) – not the "seed" (*zera'* ) – of 'Amaleq (Ex. 17:14; Deut. 25:19). Haman was deemed "'Amaleqite" because of his behavior, not because of his genealogy. It was on this basis alone that the Jews of his time applied to him the appellation "Agagite," that is, a 'member of 'Amaleq's royal family (see Est. 3:1). This point is implicit in the Rabbinic tradition that Haman's descendants taught Tora to the Jewish people.[12] Had the Rabbis defined 'Amaleq on the basis of genealogy or ethnicity, they should have executed them, rather than giving them teaching positions.[13]

* * *

The personal sins of an Israelite sovereign may be forgiven, as with King David who sinned variously before the Lord. However, a ruling

11. E.g., the precepts pertaining to the Temple, that although incapable of being carried out in practice, are still theoretically binding. See Maimonides, *Sefer ha-Miṣvot, Shoresh* III.

* Rabbi Abraham Faur: R. Yiṣḥaq Abul'afya's explanation of *zakhor* is discussed in my father's "Remember What 'Amaleq Did Unto You," *Rabbinics Today,* Vol. 2 No. 5 (1994), pp. 1–2.

12. Mishna Giṭṭin 57b.

13. For a full treatment of this subject, see *Horizontal Society,* vol. 2, appendix 25.

sovereign's political sin is beyond redemption. A close reading of the passage where Moses hits the rock (Num. 20:1–13) will show that he lost the right to lead the people to the Promised Land upon committing a political sin. The incident took place at the end of the Forty Years of Wandering, when the people were thirsty, "and fought with Moses" (Num. 20:3). This was not the first time that the people had fought with Moses (Ex. 17:2). What was unique about this incident was the fact that in this confrontation, "Moses and Aaron went from the presence (*vayyabo mippene*) of the assembly unto the door of the Tent of Meeting and fell upon their faces" (Numbers 20:6). The expression "*vayyabo mippene*" denotes fear (cf. Gen. 7:7). As accurately translated by R. Se'adya Gaon (882–942), their going "from the presence (*vayyabo mippene*) of the assembly," actually means that they "ran away from the assembly," taking refuge in the Sanctuary.[14] Such behavior is unbecoming of a political leader and beyond repair. Once a leader panics before their public, they become unable to lead effectively. Hence, God's ruling: "Because ye believed not in Me," by panicking before the people, "to sanctify Me in the eyes of the children of Israel," with proper behavior, rather than seeking protection in the Sanctuary; "therefore ye shall not bring this assembly into the land which I have given them" (Num. 20:12).

Saul, the first king of Israel, lost the monarchy because he yielded to the demand of the people and forgave the 'Amaleqite king (I Sam. 15:9–33). To understand the significance of this episode, some words on the nature of the Jewish monarchy are helpful. The institution of the monarchy was sanctioned by the Hebrew Scripture (Deut. 17:14–20). And yet, the people's request to install a king was regarded as subversive (I Sam. 8:4–8). Why? A close reading of Deuteronomy 17:14–20 shows that the monarch was to be installed *after* the conquest and settlement of the Land of Israel, not before: "When you will come to the land which the Lord your God has given you, and

14. A similar interpretation is to be found in the *Commentary* of R. Abraham ibn 'Ezra, *ad loc.*

you have inherited it and settled on it, and you will say, 'I shall install over me a king like all the nations who are around me'" (Deut. 17:14). The expression "you have inherited and settled on it" refers to a period when the land has already been conquered and well populated, and the people are not facing a military threat.[15] Before such a period, Israel should have no monarch. In the pagan world, conquest is the basis of all political authority. By virtue of his sword, the Conqueror becomes the lawful proprietor and absolute ruler of the territory he conquered, as with William the Conqueror of Normandy who, after defeating King Harold, claimed England as his own. Later on, he parceled his territory to his lieutenants in reward for their service. In turn, they parceled their lands to others, creating a feudal system, on top of which stood the king holding absolute power.[16] Such a system rests upon a hierarchical society, disallowing equality before the law, and making everyone, save the king, subservient to someone else. A similar system was established by William the Conqueror:

> The underlying social principle was that fighters and priests should govern society, supported by a large mass of laborers. A central feature of the system was land tenure; each person's position was defined in terms of relationship to land. Each person, save the king, was deliberately made subservient to another, his landlord. And all were subservient to the crown, from whom all land titles derived.[17]

The recognition of the conqueror as the ruler of the land explains the logic in appointing George Washington as the first president of the United States.[18]

Judaism does not recognize the right of a conqueror over the

15. See *Horizontal Society*, vol. 1, p. 235.
16. See *Horizontal Society*, vol. 1, p. 279.
17. Jesse Dukeminier and James E. Krier, *Property* (Boston: Little, Brown and Company, 1988), p. 146.
18. See *Horizontal Society*, vol. 2, pp. 760–1.

conquered territory. The conquest of the land of Canaan is the effect of [a] God's promise to the patriarchs, [b] executed by Him and through His might (Deut. 8:7–18; 9:1–3). A consequence of this doctrine is that the Nation of Israel may not have a peace treaty with "any of the inhabitants" of the Land of Israel, since this would presuppose that they – and not God – had actually defeated the enemy (Ex. 34:10–16). The wars carried out by the Israelites against the Canaanites were not 'conquest,' but rather comparable to when lawful heirs take possession of their legal "inheritance" (Josh. 1:11). Given that Israel's territory *does not belong to the king*, the status of real property in Israel is different than in pagan territories. The case of Ahab and Nabot illustrates this point (see I Kings 21:1–24). The purpose of the Sabbatical and Jubilee laws (Lev. 25:1–55) is to preclude the concentration of real property and feudalism, indentured servitude, etc. that often results therefrom.

Accordingly, Judaism rejects the concept of unlimited sovereignty.[19] Since no one can claim to be the Conqueror and legal proprietor of the land, the authority of the sovereign (whether constituted as a monarch, an elected official, an elected body, etc.) has only limited authority. This follows from the principle positing that the Law is the supreme authority. By stipulating that the monarchy has to be established *after* the land has been secured and settled, the Tora was in effect precluding a future monarch from claiming the right of sovereignty by virtue of having conquered the land. Similarly, given that God Himself "fights" the enemies of Israel (Ex. 34:10–16), no one can claim the right to rule in order to defend neither the people nor the Land of Israel. Accordingly, a Jewish monarch does not enjoy sovereign immunity nor eminent domain – prerogatives of all pagan conquerors.[20] The people demanding a monarch at the time of Samuel sinned because they asked for a king that "would go ahead

---

19. On this fundamental principle, see the remarkable essay by Rabbi J. H. Hertz, "Monarchy and Freedom in Israel," in his *The Pentateuch and Haftorahs* (London: Soncino Press, 5724–1964), pp. 926–930.
20. See *Horizontal Society*, vol. 1, chapter 19.

of us, and fight our wars" (I Sam. 8:20). Such a king would end up claiming unlimited sovereignty and putting himself above the Law.[21]

We can now proceed to examine Saul's political sin. Yielding to the people's cry, King Saul pardoned the 'Amaleqite king, Agag. In this respect, Saul acted like a pagan king, above the law, with the right to dispose of the enemy as he saw fit. Consequently, Prophet Samuel censured Saul and declared his monarchy unacceptable (I Sam. 15:14–26). Remarkably, Saul's thoughts on a similar issue precede this episode (I Sam. 14:24–45). Saul, as ruler of Israel, made an oath on behalf of the people to fast during the battle against the Philistines (I Sam. 14:24). His son Jonathan, fighting the Philistines in another place, was unaware of this oath and ate some honey (I Sam. 14:27). Upon confirming this fact, Saul pronounced a death sentence against Jonathan. It took the strenuous objection of the people, accompanied by a distinctive ritual whereby they "redeemed" Jonathan, to save his life (I Sam. 14:44–45).

Saul and David represent two fundamentally different views on the relationship between Law and state. David and the Kingdom of Judah believed in a government *under* the Law, and as such of *limited* sovereignty. For Saul – and in this pivotal issue he was simply following pagan political practice – the 'Law', any law, must be subservient to the will of the sovereign. 'Monarchy,' or whichever other name may be used to designate the ruling power, cannot be limited by a 'law.' Consequently, sovereignty cannot be restricted by any institution or legislation: essentially and fundamentally, sovereignty *is* both unlimited and illimitable. That was the political philosophy governing the Northern Kingdom of Israel, founded by Jeroboam (ca. 922-ca. 901 BCE). The establishment of sanctuaries for the worship of the golden calves (I Kings 12:28) proclaimed that the Law is conditioned upon the sovereign's will, not the other way around. The forerunner of this

21. This is the meaning of Samuel's warning, see I Sam. 8:11–17. It will become obvious upon considering that the term *mishpaṭ* (I Sam. 8:11) stands for 'procedure' and not only 'right.' Accordingly, what Samuel was announcing to the people was the way that the monarch should act, and not merely what his rights were.

view was Saul, who regarded the law enacted by him as absolutely binding, and the Law of Israel as conditioned by the will of the king.

* * *

Given that the enemies of Israel are God's enemies, the victories are not Israel's. Therefore, no one, including the sovereign in conjunction with the people, has the right to pardon a national enemy. (This does not mean that vengeance or retribution must follow, but specifically, that the victor has no mandate to pardon the enemy). Those who feel "empathy" (*vayyaḥmol*) for the enemy (I Sam. 15:9) will end up becoming the enemy (see below). Jews are the only victims in recorded history that refused to efface their own personality and surrender to the enemy. The people of Israel are the first (and perhaps last) to tell the story of the persecuted from the perspective of the *persecuted*. As Jews discovered when they were slaves in Egypt, and, later on, while being deported to Babylonia, crying prevents enemy personalities from invading victims and grabbing them from within. The cycle of grief and lamentations peculiar to the Jewish calendar expresses the collective cry of Israel, the victim. For all practical purposes, the moment that the victim ceases to lament, it has capitulated; it joins the ranks of the persecutors and the "New World Order."[22] We can now gain better insight on the function of 'loathing the enemy': it serves to shield the victim from succumbing to the personality of the aggressor. By forgiving the enemy, the people assent to him, imbibe his values and reject the principle that certain actions are categorically evil and categorically inexcusable. By forgiving the enemy, the people are declaring that the victims died for naught. In my mind, a victor who is moved by psychological fear of a vanquished aggressor – and thus lets the aggressor go under the pretense of kindness – is doubly a coward: first, for betraying the victims on behalf of the aggressor; and second, by covering up his cowardice under the pretense of kindness

22. See *In the Shadow of History*, pp. 192–193.

(*vayyaḥmol*; I Sam. 15:9, see below). The psychological roots of this fear lie in the victor's awareness that *he* was not a factor in the victory; that the victory was God's, and in a pathological revolt against God, he would rather let the enemy go on the pretext of kindness than offer thanks to God, "Who Fights the Wars of Israel."

In accordance with the principle of retribution peculiar to the Hebrew Scripture, those who forgive the enemy inevitably become the enemy, for example, the Christian Church mimicking the actual murderers of Jesus, the Roman Empire, and becoming the *Roman* Catholic Church and the guardian of the *Holy Roman Empire*.[23] Citing King Saul's cruel behavior towards his own people, and his ultimate defeat at the hands of the enemy, the Rabbis formulated the following rule:

> Whoever is compassionate with the cruel will end up being cruel with the compassionate.... Whoever is compassionate with a cruel people will end up falling under them.[24]
>
> We have no description of the 'Amaleqite king. The Scripture says that Saul and the people felt "empathy" (*vayyaḥmol*) for the defeated king (I Sam. 15:9). But what kind of a person was he? The answer can be found in the abrupt personality change overtaking Saul soon after that incident. Early in his career, "the spirit of God" had come into Saul (I Sam. 10:10; 11:6). Following the incident with 'Amaleq, however, "an evil spirit" (I Sam. 16:14–16; 18:10; 19:9, 20) overtook King Saul and made him behave in odd and malicious ways. I submit that the "evil spirit" grabbing King Saul from within, was no other than the personality of Agag, King of 'Amaleq! This explains Saul's fixation with slaying David, his attempt to kill his son Jonathan, and his constant suspicion that his own people were secretly plotting against him. In the end, the man that felt

23. See *In the Shadow of History*, pp. 29, 199–200; and *Horizontal Society*, vol. 1, p. 322.
24. *Midrash Shemu'el*, ed. Salomon Baber (Cracow, 5653/1893), p. 100, n. 8.

> "empathy" for 'Amaleq, issued an order to execute the entire priestly city of Nob in cold blood: "Men and women, children and sucklings, and oxen and asses and sheep, with the edge of the sword" (I Sam. 22:19). It is highly instructive that King Saul ended up begging a young 'Amaleqite to finish him off (II Sam. 1:6–10), thus confirming the Rabbis' doctrine that, "Whoever is compassionate with a cruel people will end up falling down under them."
>
> The final outcome of a conflict is not decided on the battlefield, but afterwards in the minds of the participants. By forgiving 'Amaleq Saul became 'Amaleq and was ultimately crushed by 'Amaleq.

* * *

As a result of cultural assimilation, 'enlightened' Jews are unable to understand the issue of limited sovereignty that divided Saul and Samuel. Jewish assimilation consists of taking the worst that pagan humanity has to offer, in our case, the claim of unlimited authority. As the rabbis taught, "Like those who are upright among them [the gentiles] you did not do, but like those among them [the gentiles] who are corrupt, you do!"[25] We should not be surprised to discover, therefore, that in their entrenched battle against Judaism, enlightened Jewry adopted some of the worst elements of the enemies of Israel, beginning with Nimrod and Pharaoh. The following is a painful example of the appalling intellectual standards peculiar to the 'enlightened' elites crowning the Jewish establishment.

Unquestionably, the most respected institution of modern Israel is its Supreme Court. Its members are iconic figures, bastions of truth and righteousness, and known for their rare ability of combining superb legal knowledge with a profound sense of compassion. Their primary concern is supreme respect for the law and utmost respect for the

---

25. Sanhedrin 39b; cf. *Horizontal Society*, vol. 1, pp. 582.

people that will be affected by their decisions. And yet, at times, one cannot help pondering whether they have any notion of what it means to be a part of a *Jewish* State. I will be examining some pivotal issues discussed by the late Justice Haim H. Cohn (1911–2002), a member of Israel's Supreme Court, relevant to this discussion. I myself had the privilege of hearing him lecture on more than one occasion and have greatly benefited from studying his works. Let me preface my criticism by quoting from Cohn's "Introduction" to his classic *The Trial and Death of Jesus*. Referring to the fact that his analysis of the *New Testament* account of "Jesus' Trial and Crucifixion" clashes with basic tenets of Christian tradition and historiography, Justice Cohn writes:

> There is no shred of disrespect in an investigation of this kind: Even the greatest genius, even the holiest of men, in undertaking the interpretation of reported facts, implicitly invites a critical assessment of his views; it was only later that some such books were elevated to the rank of untouchability and indisputability.[26]

In examining the reasons why the modern State of Israel did not adopt Jewish law as its legal system, Justice Cohn offered this strategic argument:

> Since in a democratic state, it would be impossible to apply Jewish law, or any other law, without legislation, the legislator who awards authority to the divine law would ultimately give authority to himself both to change it and abrogate it. This authority is nothing more than an encroachment upon the territory of the divine legislator.[27]

Here, Justice Cohn was alluding to the fact that, in Judaism, the 'Law' contracted by the people of Israel at Sinai in a

26. *The Trial and Death of Jesus* (London: Weidenfeld and Nicolson, 1972), p. xxiv.
27. Haim H. Cohn, *The Law* [Heb.] (Jerusalem: Bialik Institute, 1991), p. 10.

solemn covenant with God, and as ratified at Moab, became the *Constitution* of the people of Israel at Sinai.[28] Accordingly, it requires no further promulgation, and thereby cannot be abrogated by any authority, whether civil, judicial, or divine. A principal consequence of this doctrine is that all forms of authority, civil, judicial, and religious, are *limited* by the Law.[29] Justice Cohn rejected this view in favor of unlimited sovereignty. He thus argued that no law can be binding without the sanction of the sovereign, and therefore every law is subject to abrogation; whereas recognition of the Law contracted by Israel in the Presence of God would limit the sovereign.[30] In a section that Justice Cohn entitled "The Supremacy of the Law" – but which in fact is a euphemism for "The Supremacy of the Sovereign," or, more precisely, "An Apology on Behalf of the Unlimited Sovereignty of the Supreme Court" – we read:

The word of the legislator overrides law and justice.... But the principle is that there is nothing after the word of the legislator – the legislator is 'sovereign' – no obligation of self-control can apply to him, at any rate, not by any law, and he has the power to turn everything upside down. In England it was said that he has the power to make males, females and females, males.[31]

Justice Cohn is echoing the view of Hobbes (1588–1679) and Spinoza (1632–1677) that sovereignty is indivisible and unlimited.[32] In the dispute between King Saul and Prophet Samuel, Justice Cohn is firmly on the side of Saul and the kings of Northern Israel, proclaiming that the sovereign is above the Law. Thus, without flinching an eye, Justice Cohn dismissed

28. See *Horizontal Society*, vol. 1, chapter 5.
29. See *Horizontal Society*, vol. 1, chapter 18.
30. See *Horizontal Society*, vol. 1, chapter 25.
31. *The Law*, p. 26.
32. See *Horizontal Society*, vol. 1, chapter 13; and *In the Shadow of History*, pp. 169–172, 184.

the entire history of the Jewish people, and embraced a theory of law which served as the basis of every totalitarian system; I am thinking of King Ferdinand's Edict of the Expulsion and the promulgation of the Nuremberg laws by the Third Reich.[33] The prophets of Israel and subsequent Jewish history stood for the principle that the ruler, whether Jewish or gentile, has only limited sovereignty. Countless Jewish martyrs – for example, the three youths that refused to bow down to the idol (see Dan. 3) – paid with their lives to uphold this principle: the earthly sovereign is denied obedience in the name of a superior law. Jewish commentators – among them R. Samuel Valerio (16th century), himself a victim of the Inquisition – found the basis for the Jewish doctrine of limited sovereignty in this episode. Quoting a rabbinic source, he surmised the view of the three youths as follows: "We recognize you as a sovereign concerning taxes and tariffs, but on matters concerning worship we do not recognize you as a sovereign but, simply, as Nebuchadnezzar."[34] For reasons that will become clear below, Justice Cohn is firmly on the side of Nebuchadnezzar, who condemned the three youth to the fire for following the divine commandments rather than the law of the State. Concerning this fundamental issue, Justice Cohn wrote:

If the fulfillment of a divine commandment constitutes a transgression of the law of the state, it is the duty of the citizen to follow the law (of the state), regardless of what his religious duty concerning the fulfillment of that commandment may be.[35]

An unintended consequence of this doctrine is that in the case of 'Patriarch Abraham *v.* King Nimrod,' Nimrod was right

---

33. See *In the Shadow of History*, pp. 169–175.
34. *Ḥazon la-Mo'ed* (Venice, 5346/1586), 40b. The Jews formulated this doctrine to Muhammad ibn Tumrat, for having refused his order to embrace Islam; see *In The Shadow of History*, p. 185.
35. *The Law*, p. 11.

> and Abraham was wrong.[36] Likewise, the Jewish midwives should have followed Pharaoh's command and killed the Jewish male babies (Ex. 1:15).[37] Principally, my disappointment with Justice Cohn is about *legal* theory: once we accord the legislator with the authority "to make males, females and females, males," what would be the *legal* grounds to disallow the legislator of making citizens non-citizens and sending them to concentration camps? I have often wondered what Justice Cohn's response as a jurist would have been if asked about the legality of the Nuremberg laws and regulations beginning on September 15 and November 14 (1935). According to his thesis – previously developed by Spinoza[38] – that every citizen is bound to suppress his personal views and submit to the dictates of the 'legislator,' the State of Israel should reprimand the pious gentiles who disobeyed the State and saved Jews, rather than honor them for their illegal activities.[39] Were Eichmann and other war criminals wrong when they claimed that they were just obeying orders from the 'legislator'?

In the case of the Tora, Cohn's argument is fallacious. "Religious duty" is borrowed from Christian theology; its semantic field is *not* a Jewish concept, and it has nothing to do with neither Law nor *miṣva*. At any rate, the notion "divine command" becomes irrelevant once the Law was ratified as the Constitution of Israel at Moab. By arrogating the authority to recast Hebrew *miṣva* to himself, Justice Cohn is in fact denying the Jewish people the right to define their Tora. (On the basis of Justice Cohn's logic, we should disallow the circulation of the U.S. Dollar as legal tender, since "In God We Trust" is a theological

---

36. For a full examination of this subject, see "Preface," in my *The Naked Crowd: The Jewish Alternatives to Cunning Humanity* (Fort Lee, N.J.: Derusha Publishing, 2009), pp. iii-vi.
37. See *Horizontal Society*, vol. 1, pp. 219.
38. See *In the Shadow of History*, pp. 169–172.
39. Cf. *In the Shadow of History*, p. 175.

doctrine.) His moral standing is doubly perplexing given that he does not believe in the Tora, and given that the Tora – as defined by the Jewish people – is the only document that can define the 'Jewish people' and their right to the Promised Land. By awarding himself the right to define Tora, Justice Cohn is in fact putting himself *above* the Tora and the Jewish people who define themselves by it. The judiciary is therefore acting as absolute monarch, *à la* Henry VIII.[40]

Regarding England… I think that it was Prime Minister Henry Palmerstone (1784–1865) who once said, "England does not have eternal enemies or eternal friends; it only has eternal interests." Here, the power of the English legal system "to make males, females and females, males" comes in quite handy.

* * *

Justice Cohn's reference to England was not haphazard. It pertains to the heart of the matter. For some dark psychological reasons too complex to be treated here, Justice Cohn is in effect proposing that Israel *must* embrace the spirit of the foe and make it its own, as with Saul. To attain this goal, the Law covenanted at Sinai must be set aside. On behalf of this bizarre theory, he argued that "we have inherited (*sheyarashnu*) the doctrine of decisional law and the vast majority of the principles of justice" from England.[41] The term "inherited" used by such an eminent jurist is bewildering. Did he mean to say that we, the Jewish people, and thereby the State of Israel, are somehow *legally* bound to England, and therefore we are no longer bound to the Law contracted at Sinai? How has the Jewish State "inherited" British law? By virtue of which ceremony did England convey her legal system to Israel? With all due respect, Justice Cohn's obsession with England has nothing to do with law; it borders on the pathological, as when Saul succumbed to the spirit of defeated 'Amaleq! To justify that in some

40. On the psychological roots of this type of hubris, see below n. 55.
41. *The Law*, p. 17.

instances Israeli law departs from British law, Justice Cohn found it necessary to devote a long paragraph. In an apologetic, yielding tone, he explained that they were not really departures, but technical adjustments: "It is mainly a technical need; it is as if one would need to translate foreign laws to the language of the land."[42]

Enlightened Jews never cease to believe in Sinai. They only get their geography mixed up, attributing to different regions and cultural realms what Judaism attributes to Sinai and the covenanted Law. Evidently, for Justice Cohn, British law acquired all the attributes of the Tora, as when he was a young man studying 'Torah.' After repudiating the Tora as the "inheritance" of the Jewish people (Deut. 33:4), he went on to claim that "we have inherited" (*sheyarashnu*) British law. Implied in this claim is that justice, morality, and law may not be found in the Hebrew Scriptures, Rabbinic literature, and Jewish writings throughout the ages. The lives of our ancestors, the countless men and women that dedicated themselves to the ideals of equity, right, and the rule of law, and paid with their blood to uphold their values, are no longer valid. It is only in English tradition that law and morality are to be found. Justice Cohn did not use the expression *Verus Israel* to describe England. This may be a bit offensive to the British. If anything, the Jewish people should strive to become *Verus Anglia*. The total transference 'Torah ▸ British law' means that the absolute superiority of British law need not be proven by rational arguments; to question that God-given-truth would be nothing less than heresy – a deed no decent person would dare commit. Here is a remarkable passage, bearing on Justice Cohn's commitment to British law:

> Nobody ever thought to shamelessly challenge (*le-ha'iz*) and say that a law that is fitting for the English people and that binds English Judges is not fitting for the people living in Israel,

42. *The Law*, p. 18.

> and should not apply to its judges because it is not just, or not ethical, or that it lacks sufficient precedent.[43]

Can you imagine an American or French judge expressing similar views?

Jewish law prohibits appointing a foreigner to the position of monarch (Deut. 17:15). The same is true with regards to magistrates and other dignitaries.[44] Arguably, this prohibition would also include dignitaries who bully people into capitulating to alien values and ideologies.[45] It should follow that people entrenched in an ideology fundamentally inimical to Jewish doctrines and traditions should abstain, as a matter of simple decency, from serving in positions affecting the wellbeing of Jews. Leaders that snicker at the legal traditions of the people – in our case the longest legal tradition from pre-Biblical days to the present – are not a great source of inspiration. Prophet Isaiah said: "No weapon that is formed against you shall succeed, and every tongue that shall rise against you in judgment you shall condemn" (Is. 54:17). That is, God will shield Israel from all weapons launched against her, *on condition* that Israel does her part and defends herself against the slander spread by her enemies.[46] With leaders continuously undermining the traditional rights and values of the people, it is not easy to quote Isaiah, or for that matter, any other passage of the Hebrew Scripture.

* * *

Once, in 1973, I was visiting Israel. It was during the Yom Kippur War, and I needed to take a bus from Jerusalem to Haifa. It was late, and the last direct bus was leaving in the next few minutes. I ran as fast as

43. *The Law*, p. 18.
44. *Mishne Tora, Melakhim* 1:4.
45. Cf. *MT Sanhedrin* 26:7.
46. I recall reading this explanation in one of the works of R. Jacob Algazi (1680–1756), but unfortunately, I could not locate it.

I could and managed to catch the bus as the door was about to close. There was one empty seat, right behind the driver. I was exhausted. I sat down and took a deep breath. Just as the bus was pulling out, a soldier carrying an enormous bag knocked on the door. The bus driver stopped and let him in. I closed my eyes and was ready for a nap. Suddenly, the bus driver and the soldier began to argue. The bus driver was agitated. "I am telling you, this bus ticket is invalid," he shouted. "You must get off, otherwise I will not drive." In vain, the soldier tried to explain to him that the reason that one line was missing from the ticket was because it was wiped out when he folded it. "Look! You still can see some of the letters," argued the soldier. "I don't care! You either bring me your supervisor, or else I will not move," replied the bus driver. It was right after the war. The soldier was returning home from active duty, probably from the front. Without saying a word, he put the bag under his head and lay down to sleep in the middle of the bus. The bus driver announced that he was not moving until the soldier left. None of the passengers paid him any attention. Wanting to help this poor soldier I suggested, "Let me pay for the solider! How much is it?" The driver rejected my offer. A minute or so later, he began to drive. As he was pulling out, he confided in me, "It was a matter of principle." Noting that I was wearing a *kippa,* he added: "You are religious. You'll understand what I mean. Suppose that today is a New Month (*Rosh Ḥodesh*), and you forget to add the special prayer. It does not matter why you forgot; the prayer is no good. The same thing applies with the bus pass. There was a missing line. Who cares why?"

Contrary to what the enlightened elites claim, ideological zealotry is not exclusive to the religious mindset. Rafael Cansinos-Assens (1882–1964) called attention to a special kind of Jew, ready to betray every issue concerning the national and historical interests of his people, on behalf of 'humanity.' In his youth, Cansinos-Assens discovered that he came from a *converso* family. Interested in meeting a 'real' Jew, he undertook the long journey from his native Seville to Madrid to meet a Jewish German doctor residing in Spain. He turned out to be one of these enlightened Jews. Upon entering the doctor's premises, Cansinos-Assens was shocked to see two pictures of Jesus. When inquiring about his beliefs, the doctor replied that he "only cared about humanity," adding, "humanity is superior to a people or a race!" Describing the incident in the third person, and referring to himself as a young man, Cansinos-Assens wrote:

> In his love for Humanity, he was negating, losing, his love for Israel. All ancient memory of his sect or tribe was cancelled: the walls of the ghettos collapsed, and large doors were being opened towards a universal joy. Israel was being confused with the other peoples of the Earth, disappearing like Earth itself when contemplated from a superior [perspective of the entire] Universe. That was very beautiful; but the young man was listening to the old man with a certain feeling of disillusionment. He thought that in his [the doctor's] hands the chosen people were fading, that in this fashion they would lose all their singularity and the significance of a nation apart among the nations, which have conferred upon it countless martyrs. It was beautiful and sweet as the healing of a wound. But by confusing itself among the other peoples in that era of brotherhood, [Israel] would lose its right to claim a compensation for its wounds and a halo for its torment. And the countless dead who had perished for confessing its faith became now dead without sense or hope for whom no apotheosis was promised, since that faith was now ancient, and also without sense.[47]

You must have guts to love. That is why cowards cannot love. They are also afraid to hate. The 'love' they profess to 'humanity,' 'justice,' 'truth,' etc., is a pathetic subterfuge designed to camouflage self-hatred, like the German doctor in Cansinos-Assens' story. In this respect,

47. Rafael Cansinos-Assens, *Las Luminarias de Janucá* (Buenos Aires: Editorial Candelabro, n. d.), pp. 45–46.

'enlightened' Jews are the worst cowards. To camouflage their self-hatred, they find some 'altruistic' cause to support, particularly if at the same time it can serve the *political* interest of Israel's foes. Their pretended 'Jewishness,' too, is plain, unadulterated cowardice. If they would convert or totally assimilate, their gentile friends would regard them as plain antisemites. Cowards are fearful of that. It is easier to pretend to be 'enlightened' than to be a bigot.

* * *

The process of mental assimilation by which Justice Cohn came to reject limited sovereignty in favor of absolute sovereignty is clear. The first step consisted of "inheriting" the legal system from England; that is, mimicking the one power that instigated Arab animosity against the Jews, and fought with all its cunning to prevent the forming of a Jewish State. Justice Cohn lived in Israel beginning in 1930 and experienced British anti-Jewish activity first-hand, in particular their efforts to deport Jewish immigrants and prevent the transfer of Holocaust survivors to Israel. His unflinching support for the British legal system has nothing to do with 'democracy,' but rather, with its opposite: thwarting the will of the duly elected representatives of the people – the Knesset – by unelected members of the judiciary acting as Orwellian Big Brothers, empowered to turn everything "upside down."[48] In this respect, I don't think Justice Cohn was acting as a legal scholar, but as a victim possessed by the "evil spirit" of the persecutor.[49] The second step consisted in barring critical judgment by declaring that the "legislator" – not those duly elected by the voters, but the judiciary, acting as some sort of truth enforcement brigade – "is 'sovereign' – no obligation of self-control can apply to him, at any rate, not by any law."[50]

48. Citation above n. 31.
49. On the propensity of assimilated Jews to mimic the persecutors of Jews, see *In the Shadow of History*, pp. 198–202.
50. Citation above n. 31.

In short, Justice Cohn endowed British law with all the attributes of the Tora, except, of course, for the restrictions that the Tora imposes on the lawmakers and judges.[51] That is why, after repudiating the Tora as the "inheritance" of the Jewish people (Deut. 33:4) on behalf of a fictitious "inheritance" from England – whose principal asset is to endow those in power "to make males, females and females, males," he goes on to proclaim that "we have inherited" (*sheyarashnu*) British law. One can only wonder what could be the moral authority of someone embarking on an "apology tour" on behalf of a legal theory that had empowered every tyrant in history to commit the most horrendous crimes against Jews, to speak in the name of the Jewish people.

People often refer to Justice Cohn's 'Jewish learning' as a young *Yeshive* student as his most formative period. Respectfully, I disagree. I believe that his formative period, both intellectually and spiritually, was as a law student at Frankfurt University (1932–1933), where he absorbed a philosophy of law that permitted the abuse of legal interpretation by the practitioners and administrators of justice during the Third Reich (i.e., successor to the Holy Roman Empire). For expediency, rather than ideology, Justice Cohn opted for 'English' rather than 'German' law; he simply chose the victor.

* * *

Justice Cohn's principal argument against incorporating Jewish Law in the legal system of the State of Israel is because it is incompatible with "a democratic state."[52] Is that so? As we will see, 'democracy' – or what Chief Justice Barak calls "substantive democracy" – is a euphemism for unlimited and illimitable judicial power; in fact, said 'democracy' is the anti-thesis of democracy, permitting a few unelected officials – the members of the Supreme Court – to void the duly elected representatives of the people. In this respect, the

51. See *Horizontal Society*, vol. 1, chapter 18.
52. Quoted above, n. 27.

Supreme Court is a philosophical replica of the Religious Court, or *Bet Din,* of the extreme-right fanatics where anything the *rebbe* says is *law,* with one major difference: Whereas the *Bet Din* would never attempt to thwart the will of the legislators (Tora, Talmud, *Posqim,* etc.), the Supreme Court sets itself above the laws passed by the duly elected representatives of the State of Israel. This version of 'democracy' conforms to extreme authoritarian systems, rather than to anything remotely close to a modern democratic state.

At this point, a fundamental question comes to mind: Could it be that rejection of the Law is motivated by judicial hubris rather than respect for 'democracy'? This issue was forcibly argued by the renowned legal scholar Robert Bork. In a review of Chief Justice Barak, *The Judge in a Democracy* (Princeton University Press), he wrote:

> Judicial vetoes of majority decisions may or may not be proper in a given case, but one thing they are not is a form of democracy. *They are a check* on democracy. Barak's assertion that both the people's decisions and the frustration of those decisions are "democracy" obliterates the distinction between rule by elected representatives and rule by judges. This, in turn, serves to justify ever-increasing judicial power [Italics in the original].[53]

In fact, the so-called 'constitutional rights' claimed by these enlightened jurists are a fiction designed to hide the unlimited power that the unelected officials of the court arrogate for themselves. The purpose of such a fiction is to allow the judiciary to override the will of the people and usurp the authority of the Knesset. Addressing this fictitious claim, Bork writes:

> The duty to protect the constitution and democracy, the second role assigned judges by Barak, turns out to be something

53. All the quotations of Robert Bork, come from his review, "Barak's Rule," *Azure* 27 (5767/2007), pp. 125–132.

> very different: A claim of judicial power to create a constitution the people did not choose, and then protect the judge-written charter against the legitimate claims of democracy. "The Israeli Supreme Court," he writes, "held that the two Basic Laws passed in 1992, Basic Law: Human Dignity and Basic Law: Freedom of Occupation, are the supreme law of the land and constitute part of Israel's constitution." … Yet as Evelyn Gordon has written, the assertion that the Basic Laws had constitutional status empowering the Israeli court to strike down contradictory legislation is "dubious in itself, given that the Basic Laws underwent no constitutional ratification process and were approved by a mere quarter of the Knesset." (The small vote is probably accounted for by the fact that it was taken in the middle of the night, and nobody suggested that the revolutionary change of giving the power to override both legislative and executive acts to the courts was in fact taking place.)

Because they see themselves as intrinsically superior to mere humans, they take enforcing their ideology on the people as a given. As accurately noted by Bork:

> Despite this, Barak is at pains to assure us that "It is not his own subjective values that the judge imposes on the society in which he operates." Rather, he must balance various conflicting interests objectively and come to a conclusion. "The question is not what the judge wants but what society needs." Since voiding a statute requires overriding the will of the people as expressed through their elected representatives, what a judge thinks "society needs" is almost certainly what a majority of the people in that society do *not* want.

In view of the preceding, it is high time to correct the erroneous view that the enlightened elitists are rank atheists. Quite the contrary: as per Adam's first sin, they *are* "as God, knowing good and evil" (Gen. 3:5).[54] In fact, they enjoy absolute omniscience. This is on account of having the rare gift of *really* knowing what the people *really* need but being too stupid to *really* know that in a *real* democracy the judiciary own the moral and, we may add, legal authority to override the duly elected representatives of the people. Against this formidable logic, Bork replied:

> It is, in any event, incorrect to suppose that a society's "need" is a fact that can be determined by an objective balancing of interests. In truth, the most important interests are likely to be conflicting value judgments. How, for instance, does a judge know whether a society "needs" freedom of abortion, some degree of regulation, or a prohibition of abortion altogether? How can a judge determine whether his or her society "needs" a constitutional right to homosexual marriage? How does he decide "objectively" whether religious education in state-supported schools should be required, made optional, or prohibited? The answer, of course, is that the judge does not, and cannot, "know" any of these things, though he may have strong feelings about them. Because the judge is, by definition, operating without guidance from positive law, it is almost certain that his personal opinions will turn out to be what society "needs."

The guiding force for the anti-Tora strategy has nothing to do with democracy. It has to do with unrestricted hubris, grounded on psychological history, rather than on concern for a society whose will is not worth considering.[55] In the end, judicial hubris ends up not only isolating the judiciary from critique, but also protecting it from critically examining their own personal situation and their negative

54. See *Horizontal Society*, vol. 1, p. 123.
55. For an acute analysis of the psychological roots of this type of hubris, see Alfred Adler, "Advantages and Disadvantages of the Inferiority Feeling," in *Superiority*

impact on the rest of society. We may sum up our discussion so far with Bork's concluding remark:

> In a word, Barak's court can turn ordinary legislation into a constitution, force it on the nation, and then announce that it can prevent any democratic amendment. In this, Barak surely establishes a world record for judicial hubris.

A similar conclusion was reached by Richard Posner, a distinguished legal scholar who also serves as a judge in the Seventh Court of Appeals for the Seventh Circuit in Chicago. Although the differences between the legal philosophies of Bork and Posner are vast, they both recognize that Chief Justice Barak's strategy is nothing more than "judicial hubris." In a review of the same book, entitled "Enlightened Despot," Posner writes:

> But only in Israel (as far as I know) do judges confer the power of abstract review on themselves, without benefit of a constitutional or legislative provision. One is reminded of Napoleon's taking the crown out of the pope's hands and putting it on his own head.[56]

Commenting on Bork's assessment, Posner remarked:

> When Robert Bork attributes "judicial hubris" to Barak, he is using as his benchmark the American system. Many Israelis think Barak hubristic, but whether he is or is not in the Israeli setting is irrelevant to Bork's judgment. All Bork means is that a judge who thinks like Barak is playing outside the boundar-

*and Social Interest*, eds. Heinz L. Ansbacher and Rowena R. Ansbacher (New York: W.W. Norton, 1979), pp. 50–56; and idem, "Complex Compulsion as Part of Personality and Neurosis," ibid., pp. 71–82.

56. All subsequent quotations of Richard Posner come from his review "Enlightened Despot," *New Republic*, April 2007.

> ies within which American judges operate. Not that there are no hubristic American decisions, of course; but their authors make some effort to tether them to orthodox legal materials, such as the constitutional text. The tether is long and frayed when, for example, a judge decides that criminalizing abortion, or refusing to grant a marriage license to a homosexual couple, is a deprivation of liberty without due process of law. Such decisions could be thought lawless in the sense that the judge is making a discretionary judgment that owes nothing to an authoritative text and everything to the judge's personal values. So there is a sense in which Barak merely carries to its logical extreme a tendency discernible in our courts. It is a matter of degree, but at some point a difference in degree can rightly be called a difference in kind.

Posner also coincides with Bork in his assessment of the so-called "Basic Laws," serving to justify judicial hubris:

> It has "Basic Laws" passed by the Knesset, Israel's parliament, which Barak has equated to a constitution by holding that the Knesset cannot repeal them. That is an amazing idea: Could our Congress pass a law authorizing every American to carry a concealed weapon, and the Supreme Court declare that the law could never be repealed? And only one-quarter of the Knesset's members voted for those laws!

This leads to what may be properly called the undemocratic interpretation of separation of powers, permitting the judiciary the willful flouting of the elected authority.

> In Barak's conception of the separation of powers, the judicial power is unlimited and the legislature cannot remove judges. (And in Israel, judges participate in the selection of judges.) Outfitted with such abstractions as "democracy," "interpretation,"

> "separation of powers," "objectivity," "reasonableness" (it is "the concept of reasonableness" that Barak would have used to adjudicate the "package deal" for the release of the terrorist), and of course "justice" ("I try to be guided by my North Star, which is justice. I try to make law and justice converge, so that the Justice will do justice"), a judge is a law unto himself.

This explains the constant meddling of the court in what normative democracies regard as the realm of elected representatives of the people – in our case the Knesset:

> Among the rules of law that Barak's judicial opinions have been instrumental in creating that have no counterpart in American law are that judges cannot be removed by the legislature, but only by other judges; that any citizen can ask a court to block illegal action by a government official, even if the citizen is not personally affected by it (or lacks "standing" to sue, in the American sense); that any government action that is "unreasonable" is illegal ("put simply, the executive must act reasonably, for an unreasonable act is an unlawful act"); that a court can forbid the government to appoint an official who had committed a crime (even though he had been pardoned) or is otherwise ethically challenged, and can order the dismissal of a cabinet minister because he faces criminal proceedings; that in the name of "human dignity" a court can compel the government to alleviate homelessness and poverty; and that a court can countermand military orders, decide "whether to prevent the release of a terrorist within the framework of a political package deal," and direct the government to move the security wall that keeps suicide bombers from entering Israel from the West Bank.

The often-heard mantra – sung *ad nauseam* by elitists – that they stand for modernity and democracy is not shared by modern democracies. Here is what Posner has to say about it:

> But what we learn from Barak's book is that some foreign legal systems, even the legal system of a democratic nation that is a close ally of the United States, are so alien to our own system that their decisions ought to be given no weight by our courts. American judges distinguish between how they might vote on a statute if they were legislators and whether the statute is unconstitutional; they might think it a bad statute yet uphold its constitutionality. But in a Barak-dominated court, it would be very difficult to tell whether a judgment of unconstitutionality was anything more than the judges' opinion that it was a dumb statute, something they would not have voted for if they were legislators. And such an opinion would have no significance at all for the question of constitutionality.

One need not ponder why Posner has a low opinion of *The Judge in a Democracy*. In his view: "The book is, in fact, rather unsophisticated, as if written for a nonprofessional audience."

Let us note, in passing, that the reason for the "world record for judicial hubris" is that America is guided by the Biblical principles set up by the Founding Fathers, whereas the Israeli elite is made up exclusively of Cansino-Assens' German doctors.

* * *

Those who speak of democracy and snide at the Hebrew Scripture will do well to read I Samuel 8:7. The people no longer wanted to have Prophet Samuel as their leader and demanded that he step down and appoint an earthly king. Samuel thought that the people were dissatisfied with his leadership and prayed to God for guidance. "And the Lord said unto Samuel: Hearken unto the voice of the people in all that they say unto thee; for they have not rejected thee, but they have rejected Me, that I should not be king over them." A genuine democracy allows a leader to instruct the subalterns to abide by the will of the people and help them in finding a different leader than himself, even as the King of Kings instructed Prophet Samuel.

There is another reason why those who use the bench to thwart the will of the elected officers of the people may be inclined to snide at the Tora. According to *Psalm* 94, 'law' is not what lordly judges pontificate from the bench (v. 4). Judges are appointed, not anointed, to the bench. Those who use their judicial power to invest bias with legitimacy have transformed the court of justice into "a chair of violence." Addressing God, the psalmist asks: "Shall the seat of violence have fellowship with Thee, which crafts inequity by the means of law?" (v. 20)[57]

Bearing these points in mind, we may ask, respectfully: Are the Supreme Court's rejection of the Law *and* interference in the affairs of the elected government motivated by a genuine concern for democracy, human rights, etc., or are they a mere rhetorical tool, designed, as so elegantly put by Justice Cohn, "to turn everything upside down?" And now a *substantive* question: With a judiciary that does not regard the Law – contracted in a solemn covenant at Sinai by the entire nation in the Presence of God – as the Constitution of Israel, and given that the Law *is* the only documentary evidence of Israel's title to the Promised Land, is it surprising that Israel has yet to find proper consideration among the family of nations? Put differently: Would you respect a people ready to put aside a covenant that was corroborated by the tears and blood of 3,000 years of history, on behalf of a legal system that endows the judiciary with "the power to make males, females and females, males"?

57. For a full analysis of this psalm, see *Horizontal Society*, vol. 1, p. 187.

# Related Articles

# Contents

# Alphabetic Memory[1]

## *Mentalities* 19, 2005

While there is no consensus as to when alphabetic writing first appeared in ancient Greece, one thing is for sure: Greek poets, as well as the Muses inspiring them, were analphabetic. 'Memory' was the exclusive patrimony of the poet, not because he 'remembered,' but because the Muse that inspired him to sing his song helped him, again and again, to recall it. When Homer asked the Muses to help him "remember things past" (see *Iliad* II, ll. 484-492, 760-762; XI, ll. 218-220; XVI, ll. 112-113), he was not referring to historic times but to the songs he sung. Since there was no written text, to recall his songs the poet needed the assistance of the Muses.[2] Analphabetic language only apprehends the auditory contour of words, as if they were phonetic slabs. Nuance and multiple understandings are not tolerated. The poet's speech functions exactly like a slogan or

1. This is part of a book-in-progress.
2. See Marcel Detienne, *The Masters of Truth in Archaic Greece* (New York: Zone Books, 1996), pp. 39–52. At this early period 'memory' pertained to the realm of the sacred and was related to religion and rites; see ibid. pp. 44–50. It was only when Simonides (ca. 556–468 B.C.E.) developed a technique for remembering, that memory became independent from religion. For some background, see ibid. pp. 107–134, and José Faur, *Golden Doves with Silver Dots: Semiotics and Textuality in Rabbinic Tradition* (Bloomington, IN: Indiana University Press, 1986) pp. 32–33.

graffiti: once recognized it will elicit the same response from all.[3] A determining factor in analphabetic speech is the range of emotions that the speaker can elicit: fear, pity, anger, etc. These emotions do not belong to language proper, but to the irrational aspect of speech: rhythm, voice, imagery, etc. As with sorcery and the occult, skilled orators can suspend the rational and *charm* the audience. Hence the close, intimate relation between rhetoric and magic, leadership and charisma, politics and the divine, truth and the supernatural: belief is a consequence of *seduction.*[4]

Analphabetic consciousness unfolds in the realm of myth and magic. "Nothing is dearer to poets," noted Vico, "than singing the marvels wrought by sorceresses by means of incantations."[5] At this level of mental development, the word *is* the thing it signifies. The poet's speech creates; 'poets,' tells us Vico, is Greek for 'creators.'[6] To the analphabetic mind, poetic language "is the essence of language where language is, where man is bespoken, in the antique, strong sense of the word."[7] The metaphysical aspect of language constitutes the basis of myth and the mythmaking consciousness. This is how Cassirer described the mental process underlying mythmaking:

---

3. See *Golden Doves*, pp. 1–3.
4. Jacqueline de Romilly, *Magic and Rhetoric in Ancient Greece* (Cambridge, Mass.: Harvard University Press, 1975). See ed. Ignacio Gómez de Lino, *Mundo, Magia, Memoria* (N.p.: Taurus, 1981). There is a fine, highly incisive essay by Jorge Luis Borges, on the novel and magic, "El arte narrativo y la magia," in his collection, *Discusión* (Buenos Aires: Emecé, 1964), pp. 81–91. On the 'charismatic leader,' see the seminal article by George Devereux, "Charismatic Leadership and Crisis," *Psychoanalysis and the Social Sciences*, 4 (1955), pp. 145–157. This is why, popular opinion notwithstanding, Judaism does not recognize the legitimacy of such leadership. Cf. n. 214.
5. *The New Science*, #383, p. 120.
6. *New Science* #376, p. 117. Cf. Martin Heidegger, "... Poetically Man Dwells ..." in *Poetry, Language, Thought* (New York: Harper & Row, 1975), p. 214.
7. George Steiner, *Martin Heidegger* (New York: Viking Press, 1978) p. 146. Steiner himself, however, was not aware that Heidegger's 'poetry' is aggressively anti-writing.

> The notion that name and essence bear a necessary and internal relation to each other, that the name does not merely denote but actually *is* the essence of its object, that the potency of the real thing is contained in the name – that is one of the fundamental assumptions of mythmaking consciousness itself. Philosophical and scientific *mythology,* too, seemed to accept this assumption.[8]

Poets have been described as "interpreters of the gods."[9] Upon some thought, they are more than 'interpreters': they actually *create* the gods. After examining a problematic term *(kraíno)* in the "Homeric Hymn to Hermes," Émile Benveniste concluded:

> The god is singing of the origin of things and by his songs the gods 'are brought into existence'. A bold metaphor, but one which is consistent with the role of a poet who is himself a god. A poet causes to exist; things come to birth in his song.[10]

In fact, the poet creates something more durable and transcendent and potent than the greatest of all gods, without which no god could come to be: the analphabetic crowd. Beguiled by the 'spell' the contour of words – absolute, dense, and iridescent – the crowd will adore any god whom the poet sings.

To the analphabetic mind, writing/reading is a passive instrument to record/retrieve speech. Since writing cannot possibly evoke the charm and imagery of the speaker, reading is a pale and unreal shadow of the original. Staging and theatrics, so essential to poetic discourse, are designed to halt rationality and make the 'impossible' possible. To retrieve the past the poet must 'enthrall' the public and evoke a series of dramatic images designed to thwart critical analysis. Common man

---

8. Ernst Cassirer, *Language and Myth* (New York: Dover Publications, n.d.), p. 3; cf. ibid. pp. 51–57.
9. See *New Science,* #381, p. 120.
10. *Indo-European Language and Society,* p. 331.

may not remember. The public can access the past only through the office of the poet. The 'past' that the poet retrieves precludes intelligent consideration and interpretation. He, however, can only dictate the past. The public, as with a Passion play, can relive the poet's past and repossess it again and again, but can never access it or confront it. To be 'enthralled' by analphabetic discourse the public must be kept sequestered in the world of myth. This is why the ruling authorities ought to prevent the masses from accessing alphabetic discourse – at all costs and by all means.

There are political consequences to analphabetic discourse. Given that convincing is attained by manipulating the dramatic features of speech, political decisions could only be reached after long, intense debate. By excluding the dramatic aspects of speech, writing dissipates the voice of the people. Consequently, pagan political tradition associates writing with tyranny.[11] The same is the case with political representation. Like writing, it cannot possibly convey the full voice of the people in all its dramatic features. To help carry on a proper political discourse, the ideal society must provide all its citizens with unrestricted leisure to assemble, debate, and direct their civic affairs.[12] A vital requisite for achieving this ideal is slave labor. "There are some unfortunate situations," kindly explained Rousseau, "when one cannot preserve one's freedom except at the expense of others, and when the citizen can only be perfectly free if the slave is completely enslaved."[13] This ideology underlies the dichotomy *civita dei/regnum*, of Augustine; superman/masses, as proposed by Nietzsche in his groundbreaking, *Genealogy of Morals*; and countless variations of superior/inferior, present in all systems bent on effacing the horizontal society.[14]

---

11. See Deborah Steiner, The *Tyrant's Writ: Myths and Images of Writing in Ancient Greece* (Princeton, NJ: Princeton University Press, 1994), chapter 4.
12. See *The Tyrant's Writ*, chapter 5.
13. *Social Contract*, 3.15; cited in *The Tyrant's Writ*, p. 247.
14. See Richard Wolin, *The Seduction of Unreason: The Intellectual Romance with Fascism from Nietsche to Postmodernism* (Princeton, N J: Princeton University

The Hebrew alphabet excludes vowels (vocalization renders the scroll of the Tora 'ritually void'). Reading involves choice and semantic analysis. The text of Scripture is structured into semantic units known as *pesuqim* (verses/sentences; sing. *pasuq*). Unlike analphabetic terms which are immediately 'recognized' by all, the semantic value of Scripture is *deduced* on the basis of cogent linguistic data in the *pasuq*, i.e., it requires linguistic analysis and *interpretation*. Given the plurality of meanings and multiple understandings inherent in semantic analysis, consensus is a function of *persuasion*. Marginal factors, such as emotion, theatrics, and anything that could cloud rational analysis, are formally excluded from alphabetic discourse. This is true, even when coming from God Almighty. For that reason, the pact at Sinai was not ratified in the Presence of God, but on the following morning when God was conspicuously absent, and no phenomena, natural or divine, could affect the will of the people.

The linguistic apparatus of Israel is a highly alphabetized system.[15] Words are processed and broken down into their ultimate component, consonant-letters, while vowels are to be supplied mentally by the reader. In this fashion, grammatical classification, differentiation, nuance, and a whole range of linguistic analyses are possible, thus elevating the semantic sense of the *pasuq* to an order exceeding and excelling the sum total of each term in isolation.[16] At the Theophany at Sinai, the people simultaneously read/heard God's words. Commenting on the verse, "And all the people saw the voices" (Ex 20:15), R. 'Aqiba explained: "They saw, and they heard what they saw. They saw the word of fire coming out from the mouth of the Almighty being

Press, 2004).

15. An index of the alphabetization of the Jewish mind is the *Masora* tradition appended to the Hebrew Scripture – unique in textual history – where even minute orthographic irregularities, odd letters, as well as unusual morphological, phonological, vowels and accents, are accounted and catalogued. For an excellent overview of this highly complex subject, see A. Dothan, "Massorah," *EJ* vol. cols. 1402–1482.

16. See *Golden Doves*, pp. 1–2.

inscribed on the tablets."[17] Later rabbinic tradition explained this to mean that the people actually *read* the voices as they were enunciating the Ten Commandments.[18] Semantic reading warrants continuous interpretation on the basis of cognitive data. For that reason, the 'meaning' of a *pasuq* cannot be retrieved by active rehearsal and mere repetition, as with the epic recollections of poets, but by extending its semantic context and information units to the ideas, cultural conceptions, and challenges of the day.[19] The purpose of reading is not to retrieve the past but to structure the present. To make sense, interpretation must stimulate rationality and point to hitherto unnoticed nuances in the *pasuq*. Therefore, far from restricting the individual, the Scripture bestows *eloquence*. Commenting on the verse "The Tree of Life is medicine to the tongue" (Prov. 15:4), the rabbis taught:

> *Tree of Life* stands for '*Tora*' as is written: "She (the *Tora*) is (the) Tree of Life for those who uphold her" (Prov. 4:18). The tongue of the *Tora* sets free the language (of men). Let it be known that in the future God will grow fine trees from the Garden of Eden, and all those who are mute will chew of them. Immediately they would excel in the words of the *Tora*, as is written: "[And on the banks of the river (passing through the Garden of Eden) will grow], from either side [every edible tree, its leaves will not wither, and its fruit will never end]" (Ezra 47:12). *From either side* refers to the *Tora*. As it says [concerning the tablets containing the Ten Commandments] "from either side" [they were written] (Ex. 32:15).[20]

17. *Mekhilta de-R. Yishma'el, Yitro*, IX, p. 235.
18. See "Maimonides' Starting Precept," n. 11.
19. Cf. Berakhot 63b; *Pesiqta de-Rab Kahana* XII, 5, vol. 1, pp. 206–207.
20. My translation comes from the text cited by R. Moses Almosnino, in his *Tefilla le-Moshe* (Israel: Hamakhon le-Ḥeqer Yahdut Saloniki, 5748/1988), p. 147; which is substantially different than the versions in *Debarim Rabba* (Vilna) I, 1, vol. 2, p. 193; and *Debarim Rabba* (Lieberman) I, 7, p. 5.

Through active *interpretation* even the "lowliest" individual speaks with and through the voice of God. This is a fundamental doctrine. The rabbis taught:

> ...If one has heard a word (*dabbar*) from the mouth of the lowliest Israelite, he must regard it as if he had actually heard it from a great sage... he should not regard it only as if he had actually heard from a single sage, but as if he had actually heard from all the sages... and not only as if he had actually heard it from all the sages, but as if he had actually heard it from the *Sanhedrin* [Supreme Court]... and not only as if he had actually heard it from the *Sanhedrin,* but as if he had actually heard it from Moses the Shepherd... and not only as if he had heard it from Moses the Shepherd, but as if he had actually heard it from the mouth of God, blessed be He![21]

Given that the Hebrew alphabet excludes vowels, the whole gamut of theatrics intrinsic to speechmaking is fundamentally and irrevocably excluded from semantic reading.[22] It also excludes monolingualism. We had the opportunity to examine this cultural phenomenon among the Greeks. It was shared by other people, such as the Arabs, and more recently the Germans. 'Monolingualism' is the notion stipulating that there is one superior language alone which could express the truth, the whole truth, and nothing but the truth. It is central to the language of the analphabetic crowd, 'enthralled' by the 'charm' of the myth-making poet. At that state of consciousness the 'truth' is 'obvious' and will tolerate no analysis – as with a slogan and graffiti.[23] Among the most successful monolinguistic movements are those of the Greeks, Arabs, and Germans. Significantly, they each had a long

21. *Sifre* #41, p. 86; see *Golden Doves,* p. 56.
22. This may be the reason why the rabbis opposed "singing" verses of Song of Songs, or reciting a verse (from) the *Tora* in a drinking bout. See Sanhedrin 101a.
23. See *Golden Doves,* pp. 2–3.

analphabetic literature before the introduction of alphabetic writing. It is not merely haphazard that they, too, share the ideal of imperial domination, political totalitarianism, and coercive ideologies. In such civilizations, 'alphabetization' is marginal to their national ethos: cultivated intelligence and scientific thought vanish, as per magic, before the poet's song. Once possessed by the 'poetic truth,' the analphabetic crowd will march on the beat of the poet's drum, silently, obediently.

Paul Tillich (1886–1965), one of the great theologians of our times, distinguished between 'transitory groups,' bound together either by common interest or family ties, and 'a community of faith.' The former will disappear as soon as the conditions giving rise to their existence vanish. By contrast, 'a community of faith' will continue on the strength of its own faith, regardless of circumstances.

> In a community of faith these conditions are not decisive; the only condition of its continuation is the vitality of its faith. That which is based on an ultimate concern is not exposed to destruction by preliminary concerns and the lack of their fulfillment. The most astonishing proof of this assertion is the history of the Jews. They are, in the history of mankind, the ultimate and unconditional character of faith.[24]

The same distinction applies to the world of the spirit. Analphabetic crowds are 'transitory.' Although bound by common symbols, rituals, and spiritual values, since the crowd is precluded from examining them alphabetically, it will fall back into barbarism as soon as the call of the wild is heard. Witness the wholesale conversion to Islam by the Christian intelligentsia in the Ancient Near East, in the Mediterranean Basin, and in North Africa.[25] Witness the effervescence of values, morality, and ideals, characterizing European history from the High Middle Ages to the present. The return to barbarism, warned Tillich,

24. Paul Tillich, *Dynamics of Faith* (New York: Harper & Row, 1958), p. 119.
25. See Patricia Crone and Michael Cook, *Hagarism* (Cambridge: Cambridge University Press, 1977), chapter 9.

"can happen in any moment even in the highest culture."[26] The reason for this is that whatever the character of one's faith may be, unless it be processed and grasped alphabetically, it would not stand up to the call of barbarism.

Finally, underneath the call to barbarism lurks a pathological obsession with death that threatens the continuity of human life. At the end of his panegyric on Wisdom, King Solomon called attention to this overwhelming principle. "He who shall find me, [wisdom], shall find life, and will extort good-will from the Lord. And he who blunders against me, had wronged his soul. All those who hate me [wisdom] do love death" (Prov. 8:35–36). The following story illustrates King Solomon's point. It took place at the University of Salamanca, Spain, in 1936. A prominent fascist general, who had been crippled during the Spanish Civil war, had as a favorite motto: *Viva la muerte!* ("Long live death!"). As he began to deliver a speech, one of his followers shouted the motto in token of support. After the general concluded, the illustrious Miguel de Unamuno (1864–1936), Rector of the University replied.

> ... Unfortunately there are too many [war] cripples in Spain just now. And soon there will be even more of them if God does not come to our aid... A [war] cripple who lacks the spiritual greatness of a Cervantes [who had lost his arm in battle] is wont to seek ominous relief in causing mutilation around him.

As if to prove King Solomon's principle, the general retorted: "*Abajo la inteligencia!* ("Down with intelligence!"). To which Unamuno responded:

> This is the temple of the intellect.... It is you who profane its sacred precincts. You will win, because you have more than

---

26. Paul Tillich, "The Decline and the Validity of the Idea of Progress," in ed. Jerald C. Brauer, *The Future of Religions* (New York: Harper 84 Row, 1966), p. 69.

> enough brute force. But you will not convince. For to convince you need to persuade. And in order to persuade you will need what you lack: Reason and Right in the struggle. I consider it futile to exhort you to think of Spain.[27]

The shield against the call to barbarism is alphabetic discourse. The vitality of the Jewish faith noted by Tillich, rests on this simple fact: the alphabetic mind is immune to analphabetic discourse. This is why Jews withstood the barrage of analphabetic propaganda, coming from all quarters, since late antiquity to modern times. By contrast, the first step in the process of Jewish assimilation is erasure of the alphabetic mind. Soon after being 'emancipated' from alphabetic discourse, national memory will begin to falter. Caught up in a perpetual state of metamorphoses and paranoid fantasies brought about by sudden, psychological eruptions, the analphabetic Jew will begin to hear the call of the wild or poet – as you prefer. In next to no time, he will find antisemitic propaganda 'medicine to his bones and soothing balm to his spirit' – the only way to end the flooding of those ineffable memories that keep on cropping on his moods. Rapidly thereafter he will relish in anti-Jewish bashing with extra zest and passion; not to appear discombobulated and incapable of nuance, as the rest of the analphabetic crowd. As recognized by Unamuno, it is futile to exhort someone marching to the beat of *Viva la Muerte!* and *Abajo la inteligencia!* to think. He is immune to reason and all that jazz.

27. The citations proceed from Eric Fromm, *The Anatomy of Human Destructiveness* (New York: Holt, Rinehart, and Winston: 1973), pp. 331–332.

# Modern Sephardic Thought: Religious Humanism and Zionism*

*The Sephardi and Oriental Jewish Heritage*, 1982

## I. The Two Dimensions of Judaism

For the Sepharadim, Judaism is two-dimensional. One dimension is theological, grounded on the idea of the *Berit*, 'covenant', with God established with the People of Israel at the foot of Mt. Sinai; the other is political. The people of Israel are governed by their own laws and

* For the sources and references of this paper, see my "Early Zionist Ideals Among Sepharadim in the 19th Century," *Judaism*, XXV (1976), pp. 54–64; "Sepharadim in the 19th Century: New Dimensions and Old Values," *Proceedings of the American Academy*, XLIV (1977), pp. 29–52; "Vico, Religious Humanism, and the Sephardic Tradition," *Judaism*, XXVII (1978), pp. 63–71; *Rabbi Yisrael Moshe Ḥazzan: The Man and His Works* (Haifa: Academic Publishers, 1978), English introduction, pp. 3–16.

institutions. The laws are the source of government and political autonomy, not their effect.

When the biblical prophets charged the King and the Priest in the name of the *Tora,* they were, in fact, postulating the principle that the laws governing Israel *lie* beyond political authority and ecclesiastical bureaucracy. The survival of Israel is a direct result of this belief. As the people of Israel were losing all forms of earthly power, they became more and more aware that their constitutive values were not predicated upon political institutions and territorial integrity.

Heroic thinking – dominating political theory from early Antiquity until Modern times – conceives civil and natural right as an extension of might. Thus, the vanquished were regarded as godless, without civil and natural liberty. Since absolute sovereignty is the sole ground of law and justice, the conquered lost, along with their territory, the right to civil and criminal administration of justice.

Jewish survival as a vanquished people is a direct challenge to heroic political thinking. Accordingly, *galut,* 'exile', is a political concept. In its barest form, it means that the Jewish nation was not dissolved after the territorial loss of the land of Israel. It is worth noting that the Sepharadim viewed themselves as members of the Jewish nation rather than of the Jewish religion: the political dimension of Judaism is essential to the Sephardic mind. There are two implications to this idea. First, the governments serving as the hosts of the Jewish people are not the supreme legal and political authority of the Jews. The rules and legislations governing the Jewish people are not the fiat of the authority of that country over them, but of negotiations and accords arrived at by two equally autonomous parties: the Jews in exile and the host government. Secondly, as an extension, the messianic ideal expressed the hope that the Jewish nation would eventually regain full sovereignty and be established in the Promised Land.

From the above, it is clear why, traditionally, the Sepharadim viewed themselves as a nation, rather than as a mere religious group. The major objective of the rabbinic and lay leadership was to preserve the *autonomy* of the Jewish people. This autonomy expressed the theological-political dimensions of Judaism. Theologically, the ultimate source of values and criteria stem from a tradition whose roots lie at the foot of Mt. Sinai. Politically, it was the ability of the Jewish communities to administer their own internal affairs according to their own juridical institutions that gave credence to the claim of being, in fact, a nation in exile.

## II. The Enlightenment: A Challenge to Jewish Political and Ideological Autonomy

The most serious challenge to Jewish political and theological autonomy came in modern times as a result of the Enlightenment. Essentially, the Enlightenment taught that there are absolute canons of truth, valid at all times and in all places, according to which all cultures and societies are to be measured. From this perspective, all religions, and Judaism in particular, are worthless relics of a primitive past. In Voltaire's words, Jews are a "horde," "a savage and barbaric horde," a "vagabond horde of Arabs," "an Arabian horde." As for their writings, "the Jews were nothing but plagiarists." "The Jews ... treat their history and ancient fables as their peddlers treat their clothes. They turn them and sell them for new as dearly as possible." The high regard· for the Jews among the nations "is a strange example of human stupidity." Voltaire's views about the writings of the ancients in general, and the Jews in particular, may be summarized as follows:

> All these documents are curious, but they are documents of the human imagination alone, from which one cannot learn a single truth, scientific or historical. There isn't a small book of science today that isn't more useful than all the books of antiquity.

Accordingly, participation in the Enlightenment implied an abandonment of the very foundations of the Jewish faith.

At the political level, 'emancipation' meant the abdication of the

Jewish national autonomy, and the termination of the 'Jewish nation'. The question regarding the Jewish nation came to the fore when the issue of Jewish citizenship was debated in Europe. Napoleon, like all properly informed Christians, regarded the Jews as a separate nation. This point is specifically significant for an adequate understanding of the issues underlying Jewish emancipation. Christians who were in favor of granting citizenship to the Jews demanded, as a condition *sine qua non*, the abolition of the Jewish nation. Otherwise, to grant French citizenship to a Jew would be as ridiculous as granting French citizenship to an Englishman or a Dane. Likewise, those who opposed giving citizenship to the Jews argued that, since the Jews had their own autonomous nation, they were not part of the French nation.

One of the principal effects of granting citizenship to the Jews by Napoleon was the dissolution of the Jewish nation. The Jewish Sanhedrin, convoked in Paris, May 30, 1806, testified obliquely to this effect:

> At the present time, when the Jews no longer form a separate people, but enjoy the advantage of being incorporated with the Great Nation [i.e. French Empire] (which privilege they consider as a kind of political redemption) …

The sixth question put before the Sanhedrin. "Do Jews born in France and treated by the laws as French citizens, consider France as their country? Are they bound to defend it? Are they bound to obey the laws and to conform to the dispositions of the civil code?" directly concerns the issue of the Jewish nation. F.D. Kirwan, the translator of the Sanhedrin's transactions, clearly perceived the ultimate consequences of the Sanhedrin's response:

> The answer to the sixth question, by which the French Jews acknowledge France as their country, without any restrictions whatever, is still a more heinous dereliction of the tenets of Mosaic law; for they give up by it the hope of the expected Messiah, and the everlasting possession of the promised land

of Canaan which they deem a part of the sacred Covenant between God and his chosen people.

Sepharadim responded to both of these challenges.

## III. Religious Humanism and Secular Rationalism

The central figure among the Sephardic Rabbis in the 19th century, and one of the most gifted members in its long chain of intellectual tradition, was Rabbi Yisrael Moshe Ḥazzan. He was born in Izmir, Turkey, in the year 1807, and was highly respected by his contemporaries, who recognized him as the leading figure in the fields of Rabbinic Scholarship, Jewish jurisprudence, Philosophy, and Theology. He died in Beirut, Lebanon, in 1863.

Rabbi Ḥazzan advocated religious humanism as a viable alternative to the negative effects of rational secularism. He also pointed out the dangers that the ideology of the Enlightenment posed to the European establishment in general and to the Jews in particular. His views were widely known in Sephardic circles: from Morocco, Portugal, and Holland in the West, to Syria, the Holy Land, and Egypt in the East.

Before we attempt an explicit characterization of the impact of religious humanism on Sephardic life and thought, we shall touch upon the main objections made by Rabbi Ḥazzan and other Sephardic Rabbis against Jewish involvement in the ideology of the Enlightenment.

Sephardic opposition to the ideology of the Enlightenment did not reflect either opposition to participation in the non-Jewish culture, or opposition to secular education. The foremost Rabbinic authorities, such as Rabbis Yishma'el Ha-Kohen (1723–1811), Ḥayyim (1788–1869) and Abraham (1809–1899) Palaggi, Yisrael Moshe and Eliahu (1845- 1908) Ḥazzan, Yiṣḥaq ben Walid (1777–1870), Raḥamim Yosef Franco (1835–1901) and Yosef Ervaṣ (1847–1925), etc., all permitted secular subjects to be included in the curricula of the Jewish schools.

There were Rabbis, like Ḥazzan and Yehuda Bibas (1780–1852), who insisted that the Jew ought to acquire a wide humanistic education that would prepare him to face the complexities of modern society. In the view of Rabbi Bibas, proper education in the "seven wisdoms" takes precedence in modern times over the study of *Tora*:

> The seven wisdoms, or sciences, such as music, astronomy, etc., are meant. When a man is well, if he takes medicine it will do him harm; but if he will be ill, then he must put away bread and take the medicine. Now, the law is bread; but the Jews are sick, they are ignorant and degraded. You must therefore lay aside the study of the law and take the medicine, which is the seven wisdoms or sciences spoken of here.

The objections raised by Sephardic Rabbis concerned *the effects* that this brand of culture was having on *the Jewish Society*. In particular, they questioned the wisdom of the Jewish educator who used the classroom as a means of exposing tender children to the propaganda of the most attractive aspects of this new ideology.

Criticism is essential to the conceptual frame of the Enlightenment. Within this context, criticism is no longer a means to discover the truth, but, rather, an end in itself. This peculiar form of criticism is essentially negative. It finds expression in the pessimistic view of human history and of traditional institutions held by the Enlightenment. Rabbi Ḥazzan perceived the essentially negative characteristics of the Enlightenment. He stated this point in clear terms:

> The righteous know that in this low generation, reason and religion are handled indiscriminately: as an axe with which to destroy. Whatever does not pass through the [test] fire of modern civilization (which is continually inventing new decrees), they will destroy in fire.

In the eyes of the Sephardic Rabbis, the main problem of the enlightened Jew was his profound ignorance of the culture with which he became involved. His knowledge of the Enlightenment was at best ornamental and specious. Basically, he confused superficial knowledge of French with the actual understanding of French culture and civilization. Rabbi Abraham Ḥamwi of Aleppo, who flourished in the second half of the 19th century, upon visiting Europe stated:

> My heart aches because of what is happening today, in this generation. Many among the masses, those who pretend to philosophize, that have learned some French – I wish they would have learned French adequately! Upon leaving school, they already begin to speak arrogantly, mocking and making fun of our sacred sages of blessed memory....

According to Rabbi Ḥazzan, there was a basic intellectual lethargy that found expression in the naive belief that one could be converted into a modern man by reading some articles in Diderot's *Encyclopaedia*. In his book *She'erit Ha-Naḥala*, there is a dialogue between two Sephardic Rabbis from Jerusalem and a rich Sephardic merchant from Leghorn. One of the rabbis says to the merchant:

> You, too, have fallen in the trap that has seduced some Europeans of our time. This is the great desire to know every subject and topic on one foot! In the past, as now, and in this very night, we are truly sorrowed by this deplorable trend that has taken roots in this region: that by reading some volumes of the Encyclopaedia, all become scientists, etc., etc. It is truly impossible that on one foot every one could become a rabbinical philosopher and philologist. For this they require a very lengthy time!

A superficial knowledge of the newly adopted civilization resulted in ideological aggressiveness bordering on blind fanaticism. Paraphrasing Hosea 4:12, Rabbi Ḥazzan described the superstitious attitude with which the newly enlightened Jew approached modern culture.

"To the stock of Voltaire and Mirabeau he asks counsel, and the staff of Diderot declareth unto him." This becomes especially significant when one realizes that – as was brilliantly stated by Peter Gay – the main objective of the Enlightenment was "to assimilate the two pasts they had inherited, Christian and pagan, to pit them against one another and thus to secure their independence."

Obviously, whatever problems the Jew was facing at that time, they had little to do with the problems that the Enlightenment was trying to solve. Rabbi Ḥazzan pointed out this aspect of Jewish involvement in the Enlightenment. In his opinion, the secular ideals and anti-religious values proposed as solutions to the problems affecting the Jew were not grounded in a genuine understanding of the specific situation of the Jew in modern times. Rather, these solutions were "the effect of trying to imitate the ideals of Voltaire and Mirabeau."

It was the view of Rabbi Ḥazzan that European Jewry had come to a stage of total disintegration as a result of its inability to cope with Western culture, especially with the Enlightenment. He attributed this failure to what he described as "the European plague, which is the illness of 'either extreme.'" By this he meant the attitudes of either total surrender to the dictates of the Enlightenment, or total rejection of all aspects of both Jewish and Western culture. Thus, the Sephardic dissatisfaction with both the religious and the secular products of these attitudes. According to Rabbi Ḥazzan, this extremism was an extension of a superficial knowledge of either one of the two systems. Specifically, this superficiality gave rise to a chain of four attitudes intimately related to each other: (a) *Religious fanaticism*, leading eventually to (b) *hypocrisy*. These two attitudes discouraged the best elements of the Jewish population from any serious participation in the religious life and traditional institutions of Judaism. Thus (c) *religious indifference* among the Jewish elite. And finally, the atmosphere of aggressive ideology characteristic of extremism, as well as the weakening of Jewish values and institutions, gave rise to (d) *schism and internal enmity*.

About the year 1850, as a result of the foregoing analysis, Rabbi

Ḥazzan gave a gloomy picture of the future spiritual and physical well-being of European Jewry:

> Behold, there it lies before us, this great corruption that [prevails] among us [Jews] in this region of Europe. Something that we have not [dared to] imagine, or think in our hearts. It was about a hundred years since [the seeds] of corruption were sown in these countries. By our generation, [they] had grown like grass, they had taken roots, and they had covered the earth: They covered the Mountains of Ashkenaz and their shadow and many branches reached Italy. Woe unto us that this has taken place in our times! Who could extend a cure to us, since Satan is dancing among us, establishing in our Nation sects, numerous parties, and different altars... This corrupt trend, to introduce novelties, and divide the hearts, will be the cause to chase away from our Holy Tradition many of our beloved children: It would be the cause that never again will the name of Israel be mentioned there. God save us!

## IV. Vico and Sephardic Humanism

Today, Vico is recognized as a leading figure in the development of Modern Western thought. The concepts of man, culture, and history serving as the foundations of a modern humanities, are a direct outgrowth of his vision. The point to be remembered, however, is that until relatively recent times he was almost unkown. It is a credit to the insight of a small group of Sephardic rabbis, led by Rabbi Ḥazzan and Eliahu Benamozegh (1822–1900), to have discovered the deep significance of Vico's contributions. To the Jew, in particular, Vico offered a genuine alternative to vindicate his own specific spirituality and subjectivity without having to surrender to rational secularism on the one hand, or to remain confined in an intellectual ghetto, on the other hand.

We shall examine some of the most significant aspects of Vico's vision.

Voltaire conceives man as an intrinsic part of nature. Therefore, man is to be understood, exclusively, in the light of nature. There are canons, eternal and immutable, operative in all spheres of human activities, which are recognizable by human reason and valid in all times and societies. Vico conceives of man in historical terms, not in terms of nature. He rejects the notion of eternal and immutable truths, of absolute canons of thought and feeling. According to him, the canons operating in the realm of history are relative and dynamic, with a constant changing in the patterns and categories of human thought and feeling. Even the most fundamental concepts of the human mind, such as the concepts of freedom and justice, are subject to constant change. It is well to emphasize that this change is not a progress from the imperfect to the perfect, since this notion entails an absolute criterion of value. As mentioned, Vico understands man in terms of history. But history, for him, is not merely a compilation of data. For Vico, history means to grasp the specific sets of values and conventions of a group or society at a definite time, to know their categories of feeling and thoughts, what questions they asked, what they demanded of themselves, and what they expected from others. He conceives Poetry, Myth, and Religion as stages in the historical development of man. Accordingly, what for Voltaire may have been forms of unreason and human decadence, are for Vico monuments of the human past, encounters with the sublime, expressions of fear, love, hope, and doubt.

The multiformity and relativity of human values that Vico projected reduced the whole criticism of the Enlightenment against religion and Judaism to a petulant expression of naïveté. On the positive side, it helped make understandable the historical process underlying the classical Jewish texts. Rather than conceive the Jewish past as uniform and static, or to dismiss it as a mass of obscurist hocus-pocus, it provided the intellectual tools to come to grips with the historical development of Judaism as reflected in the classical texts. Rabbi

Benamozegh, in his Commentary to the Pentateuch, *Em La-Miqra* (5 volumes, Leghorn, 1862–1863), made ample use of Vico's *New Science.*

Benamozegh wrote:

> The great investigator, Vico, thanks to his vast knowledge of ancient Latin, was able to discover, through analysis of words and names, and their constitutive (elements) and origin, important concepts that were never explicitly stated in the history and antiquities of the Romans. He formulated the principle that in every language, the beliefs and early history are stored. Therefore, I thought to pursue the same method and to see whether I (too) could discover (the) fundamental aspects of our holy language. The Lord was with me and I made significant discoveries, part of which is presented in this work.

Elsewhere, he wrote:

> In my opinion, the proper method to be applied when examining the Holy Scriptures in their relation to the tradition of our Sages, is to investigate the roots of the language, and see whether it is possible to discover the connection of the verse with the law, exegesis, or event. We have learned from Vico, the great Italian sage, that the ancient languages hide ... in their idioms and expressions ... customs, beliefs, and deeds that were once known among the peoples who used them and later were totally forgotten. I too, since some time ago, have tried to follow these methods, and the Lord helped me in these pursuits.

Rabbis Ḥazzan and Benamozegh explored the juridical interpretation of a verse in light of the conventions and modes of thinking prevalent at the time. However, thanks to his superb mastery of the entire Rabbinic literature, Rabbi Ḥazzan was able to further develop this method. In this connection, it is important to note the view of Vico that in Latin "almost the whole corpus of its words had sylvan or rustic origins." Rabbi Ḥazzan accepted this principle and applied it to the biblical lexicon. Taking cognizance of the further semantic developments affecting the Hebrew language, he then attempted to show the relationship between the philological meaning of a term and the meaning that it has acquired through juridical exegesis. The complexity of the subjects prevents us from illustrating this method of analysis. It may be more appropriate, perhaps, to review the impressions on this matter that were given by one of the most distinguished Jewish scholars of the last century. When the book *Naḥala le-Yisrael* by Rabbi Ḥazzan, dealing with the laws of inheritance, reached R.S.J. Rapoport (1790–1867), he made the following comments:

> Without indulging in any form of flattery, I must say that never yet has a work of this quality come to me. He shows marvels because of his correct method of interpreting (the texts) and the way in which they were formulated, not only in the vast field of Talmudics, but also in the field of the exegesis of the verses connected with the subject of inheritance. This was done with the most pure and subtle intellect. They [i.e. the verses he explained] will suffice to show to every reader, even if he were to be a gentile scholar, what the correct and appropriate law is, without needing to have recourse to the Authority of Tradition. However, he also was able to raise it [Jewish Tradition] as if it were a flag for us, the House of Jacob, on the basis of an extraordinary erudition, deep understanding and the propositions of theories that are [logically] correct and quite plausible. This he was able to accomplish on the basis of the Talmud and all the commentaries that came after it, whether in the Codes of Law or the books of *Responsa*... He thoroughly exhausted the subject without leaving any doubts at all on the matter. I am shocked and dismayed that until now the good name of this great man, outstanding among ten thousand, was not heard throughout the globe!

The long tradition of Religious Humanism continued to develop among Sephardic Rabbis independently of Vico. This will help us to understand why Sephardic thinkers were ready to perceive the significance of Vico's vision, to accept his methodology, and to apply it to their literature and specific historical process.

## V. Sepharadim and Western Society

The image of Western Civilization projected by Voltaire was radically different from the image projected by Vico, and resulted in different attitudes among Jews regarding the unity of Western man and his culture. According to Voltaire, the great civilizations of the West were elitist civilizations imposed by enlightened oligarchies on the masses. The Jew, depending on his commitment to Judaism, developed either a subservient attitude, hoping to do one day for his backward brethren what his enlightened masters had done for him, or else developed a resentful attitude towards a civilization threatening to deprive him of his most sacred values and institutions.

It is not unreasonable to suggest that the negative attitude toward Western culture that developed in some Jewish circles may have been the result of having known Western civilization exclusively through the image of rational secularism.

The Sephardic Rabbi and layman were acquainted with the materialist trends current in the Western world. However, they never believed that these trends spoke for the whole of Western culture, or that they reflected its highest ideals. Specifically, they cautioned against those who maintained that a sound relationship between the Jew and non-Jew could be best established on the grounds of rational secularism and materialism. Knowledge of Western civilization through the image of Religious Humanism helped the Sephardi develop a more relaxed attitude towards the Western world. The Sephardi was aware that there were fundamental values and institutions common to the Jew and the Christian. However, at the same time, he recognized that there were also fundamental values and institutions separating the Jew from the Christian. Joseph Salvador (1796–1873), with Montesquieu, very adequately described this relationship as two branches stemming from the same trunk. Likewise, Rabbi Ḥazzan, referring to the relations of Jews and Christians wrote: "We Jews and Christians are two branches growing from the same trunk." The meaning is clear: we have common roots, but we have grown in different directions. It is the special duty of the Jew to contribute to the preservation and growth of the humanistic values of the society in which he lives. It was the belief of Rabbis like Ḥazzan and Bibas that only in societies whose basic institutions are grounded on religious humanism can a Jew have a modicum of spiritual and material safety.

Viewed from this perspective, the heritage of the Jew is best preserved not through spiritual and cultural isolation but by nourishing the roots from which both the Jewish and gentile civilizations grew. Rabbi Yehuda Bibas, who was rightly described as "a genuine Pharisee of the old school, rigidly observing the Jewish law," expressed the attitude of the Sephardic Rabbinate in unmistakable terms. Referring to a conversation that he had with Rabbi Bibas, Bonar reported:

> He [R. Bibas] denied that God ever meant the Jews to be a people separate from other nations, asserting that He intended them to enlighten all the earth, a duty which they must still perform whenever it shall be in their power. If they had means, like the English, they ought to send out missionaries.

Accordingly, preservation of the Jewish faith and tradition cannot imply disrespect or lack of love to the gentiles; quite the contrary. This point was eloquently expressed by Rabbi Bibas when he declared "that he loved Christians exceedingly, and that no Christian loved the Jews more than he did the Christians."

These ideas were not only operative in the intellectual realm as manifestations of social pleasantries. Rather, they found expression in the attitudes and behavior of the Jew. Eventually, they were formulated as law by the most prominent Sephardic jurists of the time.

When Rabbi Ḥazzan came to Rome in the year 1847, he discovered that certain practices connected with the synagogue services and Jewish rituals gave rise to mockery on the part of some elements of the non-Jewish population. Local Jews interpreted this mockery as an expression of disrespect toward Judaism. Rabbi Ḥazzan adjudicated on this matter. His analysis of the subject, and the conclusion at which he arrived, illustrate what we usually refer to as the humanistic approach to Jewish law among Sephardic jurists. After analyzing the content of the mockery, Rabbi Ḥazzan showed that it did not reflect any disrespect toward Judaism. Rather, it was connected with the fact that the behavior displayed by the Jews on these occasions offended the aesthetic standards of the society in which they lived. Moreover, he went on to demonstrate that the behavior in question was not prescribed by Jewish law, and in many instances was explicitly forbidden by the Rabbis. Furthermore, on the basis of an exhaustive analysis of the problem, Rabbi Ḥazzan demonstrated that according to the Jewish law, one is to take cognizance of the standards of the society in which he lives. Accordingly, he issued a series of *Responsa* prohibiting the continuation of these practices.

The following example will show the position of Sephardic jurists on the relation of Jewish Law to the aesthetic standards of the non-Jewish society. The problem of music in the synagogue gave rise to a heated controversy in the Ashkenazic communities, resulting in schism and ill feeling. We shall analyze how this problem was resolved by Sephardic jurists.

There are several legal aspects to this problem. On the problem of whether the organ may be played in the synagogue, or must be forbidden since it is traditionally associated with the liturgy of the Church, Rabbi Shem Ṭob Samun, who flourished in Leghorn, and Ya'aqob Recanatte (1759–1824) from Verona, adjudicated that it is permissible. This decision was approved, reluctantly, by Rabbi Ḥayyim 'Ayyash, the grandson of the illustrious Rabbi Yehuda

'Ayyash (died 1760) and son of the *Rishon Le-Ṣion* (Chief Rabbi of Israel). Rabbi Rephael Aharon ben Shim'on (1848–1929) analyzed the question of whether gentile instrumentalists could be engaged before the Sabbath to play on the Sabbath. His decision was that if the music is connected with religious celebration it is permitted on the basis of the principle that one may instruct a gentile to perform a work which is only forbidden by the Rabbis, if this is somehow connected with a religious act (*Shebut de-Shebut le-Shem Miṣva Muttar*). He based his view on a meticulous analysis of all the legal material on the subject. Furthermore, he pointed out the widespread custom among Sepharadim of engaging gentile musicians to play for them on the Sabbath. Rabbi Moshe Pardo (died 1888), grandson of the illustrious Rabbis David Pardo (1719–1792) and Ḥayyim David Azulai (1724–1806), referred to the practice of Sepharadim of engaging gentile musicians to play in the synagogue on Holy Days at the time that the scroll of the *Tora* is returned to the ark. Rabbi Yosef Nessim Burla (1829–1903), a member of the High Rabbinic Court in Jerusalem, adjudicated on whether gentile singers can participate in the synagogue choir. After a careful analysis of the subject, he concluded that the only grounds for proscribing gentile participation in the synagogue choir is on the technicality that one may not teach *Tora* to a· gentile. The most significant aspect of this problem was adjudicated by Rabbi Ḥazzan. He took up the question as to whether it is permitted to use church music at the synagogue services. He concluded that it is permitted, since Jewish law does not object to the aesthetics of the gentile society, even when, in a different context, these activities are used in religious services. This decision was approved by the Chief Rabbi of Tiberias, Rabbi Ḥayyim Shemuel Cohen Convorte (died 1873).

There is a major point, touching on the relationship between participation in the humanistic and aesthetic values of the gentile society and Jewish autonomy, that needs to be examined in order to thoroughly understand the position of Sephardic Rabbis on this issue. Participation in the humanistic values and aesthetic activities of the society were encouraged as long as they did not conflict with the values and institutions upon which Jewish autonomy rests. However, when conflict arises, the preservation of Jewish autonomy takes precedence. We will explore this principle within the context of Jewish law. A question was submitted to Rabbi Ḥazzan as to whether it is permitted to shave on the days between the first and last days of Passover and the Feast of the Tabernacle (*Ḥol Ha-Mo'ed*), since to remain unshaven for over a week, as Jewish law demands, comes in conflict with the standards of modern society. The Rabbi submitting the question believed that it was permitted to shave, and supported his view from the decision of Rabbi Ḥazzan to allow church music in the synagogue. The answer of Rabbi Ḥazzan deserves special attention, and it clearly defines the position of the Sephardic jurists on this matter. There are two points to be considered. The first point is that the prohibition against shaving on those days was promulgated by the highest judicial authority of the Jews, and was upheld by Talmudic and post-Talmudic tradition. On the other hand, there is no Rabbinic promulgation prohibiting gentiles' music in synagogue services. The only basis for such a prohibition was a responsum of a 17th-century rabbi, Joel Sirkes, whom Rabbi Ḥazzan characterizes as "one who finds great pleasure in creating new prohibitions and limitations on the Jewish people." After a careful analysis of Rabbi Sirkes' *responsum*, he shows that his decision was not warranted by talmudic sources. Thus, there are no grounds to issue a prohibition against church music. Moreover, on the basis of Rabbinic literature, he showed that it should be encouraged to express Jewish devotion according to the aesthetic standards of the society in which they live. The second point addresses itself obliquely to the question of Jewish autonomy: "If the values and aesthetic standards of the non-Jewish society" says Rabbi Ḥazzan, "come into conflict with our Sacred *Tora*, or with the tradition of our Sages of revered memory, we will not surrender even the point of the letter *yod*."

We may summarize the foregoing as follows:

(a) Sephardic Rabbis found in Vico a viable alternative to the specific problems that the Enlightenment presented to the Jew.
(b) Vico's vision was particularly attractive to the Sephardic Rabbi since his own intellectual tradition closely identified with Religious Humanism.
(c) Some of the methods developed by Vico were applied in the interpretation of classical Jewish texts.
(d) Religious Humanism affords a deeper understanding of Judaism and Christianity. It also allows a greater participation in the basic intellectual and cultural issues of the time without demanding that the participants surrender their spiritual autonomy and individuality. Moreover, it provides the spiritual grounds on which multiform and multidimensional values may be operative in a pluralistic society.

## VI. The Modern Idea of a Jewish Nation: A Sephardic Response

Zionist ideals among Sepharadim in the 19th century may best be understood in the light of the new cultural and political trends affecting Europe at that time. There was a profound awareness that the Jewish nation in *galut* would eventually surrender its autonomy and disintegrate under the pressures of rational secularism and political emancipation. It was the view of Rabbis such as Yehuda Bibas, Yehuda Alcalai (1798–1879), Natan 'Amram (1805–1870), Baruch Miṭrani (1847–1919), and others, that the only effective way to preserve Jewish autonomy in modern times was to establish a Jewish national home in the Holy Land.

We shall first investigate the efforts made by Sepharadim at that time to revive Hebrew as the national language of the Jewish people.

The Sepharadim were the first to realize the political role that the Hebrew language could play in promoting Jewish nationalistic feelings and political unity among Jews. In one of her essays, published in 1842, seventeen years before the birth of Eliezer Ben-Yehuda, Grace Aguilar (1816–1847) presented this point quite forcibly. She argued that "the preservation of our Law in its original purity" was a supreme duty in ancient times; "how much more requisite must it be now," in modern times. Hebrew was "the silver link that would give unity to the Jewish nation scattered throughout the earth." To this effect, it was imperative that Hebrew be taught to every Jewish man and woman. Commenting on the parental duty to educate the child, Miss Aguilar remarked:

> Ere we proceed to the remainder of this verse, may we be permitted to hint on the importance of making the Hebrew language familar to every Hebrew child?

Against those who argued that Hebrew is a dead language, she replied:

> It cannot be considered a dead language; for the nation to which it originally belonged continues to exist, and will exist forever.

In particular, she pointed out the national significance of Hebrew as a means of promoting political unity among the Jews:

> It is not indeed spoken as it would have been, had we remained in our own land; yet it might still continue the link uniting the sons of Israel wherever they may be. The sojourners in England, France, Austria, Spain, might be enabled to converse or to commune with each other in their own native tongue, though of the language of their respective homes each might be ignorant.

Grace Aguilar realized that, in order to accomplish this goal, it was necessary to bring about a change in the current method of instruction: rather than learn the language through the Hebrew classics, one should learn the Hebrew classics through the language. Hebrew ought to be spoken before it is read. The method used in Jewish schools, to confront the child who has just learned the Hebrew alphabet with the liturgy, was as ridiculous as if "as soon as a child had acquired his letters in French or Italian, the Henriade or Dante should be placed before him, and he should be desired to learn passages by rote with merely the assistance of a subjoined translation."

Her views on the effective revision of the pedagogical system in Hebrew school are specific:

> Never may we hope for the perfect attainment of this ancient and glorious language till the present system has given place to one more calculated to engage a child's fancy; till the prayer book is not the first which we place in an infant's hands; till other than words so sacred as prayer are the first we teach our children to repeat. Our aim indeed should be to enable them to address their Creator in the language of their ancestors to read His word pure and unaltered, even as it came from Heaven; but by placing it too early before them, we frustrate our own desires.

Grace Aguilar perceived the religious and political roles that only the Hebrew language could adequately perform. The sacred task of the Jewish educator was

> that every child of Israel, male or female, should perfectly understand the language of our ancestors, that in which the awful yet invisible Voice delivered His dictates to Moses, that we may indeed feel Hebrew is bound to Hebrew by a link neither oceans nor water nor spreading wastes of land can sever! … The sacred language is the silver link which, uniting them to each other, separates them from other nations, and makes them feel that they are indeed the witnesses of the Lord. And while they read in rejoicing faith the Book of Life in the language in which it was given, or in humble adoration

> prostrate themselves before God's throne, must not a glowing of the whole soul attend the addressing of the Eternal, in the same language in which His awful voice addressed His favored servants?

A few years earlier, in 1837, her friend, Abigail Abarbanel Lindo (1803–1843) had already published a Hebrew-English, English-Hebrew Lexicon, with the "object to assist those who wish to study the sacred language."

In 1845, Rabbi Yisrael Moshe Ḥazzan made an appeal for the revival of the Hebrew language. Like Grace Aguilar, he, too, emphasized the nationalistic role of Hebrew in promoting political unity among Jews. Moreover, he pointed to the Christian interest in classical languages as an example which the assimilationist Jew in particular should try to emulate by studying the language of his own classical literature. It is of great significance to note that Rabbi Ḥazzan indicated that, since the Reform movement cited among one of its objectives the promotion of greater unity among the Jewish people, they could accomplish this objective by establishing schools to teach Hebrew.

> Do you not yourself desire union and friendship among Israel? Above all, let me remind you that it is incumbent upon every Israelite, male and female, to have his children instructed in the language of your nation, viz., the sacred tongue...What nation is there on earth who have themselves neglected their language as, alas! we have neglected ours? If you were to open schools for instruction in the Hebrew and Chaldee languages, which are both indispensable to Judaism, how strongly would you cement the union and enhance the felicity of faith and peace. Do not our Christian brethren (to their credit, be it mentioned), after a thorough knowledge of their native tongue, still pursue the study of the Latin and Greek languages, because of the technical and philosophical terms met with in their literature? Much more so we, whose faith and literature

> is closely interwoven with those two languages; why should we not rather cultivate those precious plants in preference to vain toys of the imagination, which bear no fruit of joy but deep rooted discord and implacable hatred.

In a similar fashion, Rabbi Alcalai, in 1852, published a pamphlet urging the adoption of the Hebrew language as a means of fostering national unity among Jews. The need for the revival of Hebrew as the spoken language of the Jews was felt even by the semi-educated Sephardi. The following report, by Andrew Bonar, a missionary from the Church of Scotland, in 1839, illustrates our point:

> He said that… they needed to be taught their own language, for none could speak Hebrew, and few understand it. If a school were instituted, he believed it would be well attended.

It is important to note, in this connection, the upsurge of Hebrew grammars, such as *Darkhei No'am,* written in Judeo-Spanish by Rabbi Alcalai, and printed in Belgrade, 1839, and *Leḥem Ha-Bikkurim,* by Rabbi Shaul Ha-Kohen (1772–1848) of Tunis. In the introduction to this last book, published in Leghorn in 1870, one of the reasons given for the work is that among the nations there is great interest in the proper studies of their respective languages. How much more so should this be with the Jewish people, whose very existence depends on their sacred literature. Moreover, Jews go through great efforts in order to instruct their children in foreign languages, when they are neglecting the study of Hebrew.

Another Hebrew grammar, this one in Judeo-Spanish, was put out by Rabbi Menaḥem Farḥi, with the complaint

> that other spoken languages are further progressing, but our language is continuously losing ground. Therefore, I was determined to try to present before the students some of the principles of our holy language in a special book. In this way,

> perhaps, some men of wisdom of our times, those who have the power to establish something that, if well organized, will be able to benefit the youth of our people.

Among the Jewish educators who centered their curricula around the study of Hebrew, special mention should be made of R. Barukh Miṭani, whose efforts at the elementary school level, as well as the works that he composed for this purpose, make him a unique pioneer in this field of Jewish pedagogy.

Intimately connected with the efforts for the revival of Hebrew was the establishment of Hebrew magazines, such as *Daber Maslzarim* and *Karmi* (bilingual: Hebrew and Judeo-Spanish).

Rabbi Yehuda Bibas was the first Jew in modern times to give full expression to the Zionist ideal and to show the significance of the return to the land of Israel. His Zionist ideals were grounded on his interpretation of the duty of *teshuba,* repentance, whose literal meaning is 'return'. *Teshuba* is operative at two levels. At the individual level, it is spiritual, and means the recognition and abandonment of sin, followed by a 'return' to the ways of the Lord. However, Judaism also recognizes *teshuba* as a collective duty. At this level, it must be – by sheer definition – political.

The beginning of political *teshuba* is the 'return' of the Jewish people in a physical and concrete sense to the Promised Land. This ideal is intimately related to the national conception of Judaism current in the Sephardic tradition, and the political dimension of *galut*: the spiritual redemption of Israel by God is predicated upon the political repentance of the Jewish people.

Since repentance, as a collective duty, is essentially political, it depends on military means for its implementation. Rabbi Bibas saw in the Greek insurrection against the Turks (1821) a paradigm of how the Jews should take possession of their ancestral home. According to him, humanistic education would prepare the Jew to build a home in the Promised Land; in particular, he urged the Jew to be trained in military science. In his view, it was the special role of the Messiah to conduct the war of conquest of the Holy Land. Referring to Rabbi Bibas, Bonar makes the following comment:

> The young men [of Corfu] spoke with great admiration of him [R. Bibas] and of his sentiments, and especially of this one, that the Jews must be instructed in science and in arms, that they may wrest the land of Palestine from the Turks under the leadership of the Messiah, as the Greeks wrested their country.

Secular Zionism developed among Sepharadim as early as 1839. In a conversation which took place on September 10, 1839, Bonar reports:

> In conversation with the son [of Samuel Hillel, a Jewish banker of Corfu,] we soon discovered that he was one of the Jews who care little about Palestine [in the traditional religious sense] and do not expect a Messiah, believing that education and civilization alone can exalt the Jews; to which he added – "a knowledge of arms, that they may defend their land when they get possession of it."

In this connection, it is pertinent to mention the activities of Joseph Marcou Baruch, who was born in Istanbul in 1872 and died in Florence in 1899. He was an idealist who devoted all of his life and energies to promote Jewish nationalistic feelings among his people. Like Rabbi Bibas, he believed that the Jews should make military preparations for the conquest of the Holy Land from the Turks. Because of these views, he was considered by many to be an "extremist," and was even branded an "anarchist." This judgement may reflect the position formulated by Moses Mendelssohn that the Jew may not bear arms to take possession of the Promised Land. This notion was never accepted by Sephardic Rabbis. To this issue, Rabbi Moshe Ya'acob Toledano (1880–1960) addressed himself in a responsum in which, without mentioning anybody by name, he dismissed the notion promoted by many rabbis that it is forbidden to the Jewish people to bear arms. Specifically, he demonstrated that it is the sacred duty of the Jewish people to take possession of the Promised Land, if necessary by the force of arms.

Rabbi Bibas, like all Sephardic religious and lay leaders, strongly supported Jewish settlement in the Holy Land, but he objected to the parasitic tendencies of the recipients of public charity there. In his opinion, it was incumbent upon the Jews living in Palestine to work and be self-supporting:

> He [Rabbi Bibas] thought that the collections for the Holy Land ought to be given up, and that the Jews there ought to be obliged to work even were it by the bayonet.

Rabbi Alcalai was deeply affected by the personality and Zionist ideology of Rabbi Bibas, and devoted his entire life toward the development and implementation of his ideals. A detailed analysis of the numerous activities of Rabbi Alcalai and his Zionist ideology transcends the scope of this paper, but, for our purpose, it would be sufficient to point out some of his most significant projects. He believed in levying a tithe upon the Jewish people and, among the different projects to be financed by these funds, the following deserve special attention: the establishment of an organization to promote international recognition of the Jewish right to the Holy Land, a Jewish Parliament, a Jewish army, schools to teach Hebrew, Jewish settlements in the Holy Land, agricultural centers, etc.

Rabbi Bibas questioned the wisdom of purchasing land in Israel without first securing political autonomy. To this effect, he attempted to dissuade Sir Moses Montefiore on the grounds that:

> Sir Moses Montefiore's plan of purchasing land for them [the Jews] in Palestine he [Rabbi Bibas] considered useless, as long as there is no security for property there. The people must first be educated and taught the sciences.

Nevertheless, there was strong support among the Sepharadim for the establishment of a plan to purchase land in Palestine. In 1844, three years before Rabbi Alcalai made a similar proposal, Rabbi Ḥazzan had tried to persuade the Jews in Europe to purchase property in the Holy Land from the Arabs. In 1858, twenty-six years before Schapira and thirty-nine years before the First Zionist Congress, Rabbi Ḥazzan pleaded with European Jewry to establish "a *Keren Kayyemet* for the purpose of purchasing property in the Holy Land." In the following year, he published a letter in the Hebrew journal, *Hamaggid* (III, no. 13), urging the Jewish people "to establish a *Keren Kayyemet* in order to buy the property that the Arabs held in the Holy Land."

A philological note will help us put the significance of this point in the proper perspective. Currently, the term *keren kayyemet* is used in the sense of a trust whose yield is to be used exclusively for a sacred purpose. However, originally, it referred to the spiritual reward of the miṣvot in the world-to-come. In Sephardic literature the phrase is very commonly used in the former sense, while in Ashkenazic literature, *keren kayyemet* never appears in the sense of a trust of money. As a matter of fact, the term *keren kayyemet* in its current, popular sense could have developed only in a Sephardic community, since it is a translation of the technical Arabic term, *waqf*.

These Sephardic ideals of national Zionism were deeply rooted among the lay leaders and the masses. Distinguished men of the stature of Sir Moses Montefiore (1784–1874) used their financial and diplomatic resources to help their co-religionists establish a home in the Promised Land. At the same time, members of some of the most prominent Sephardic families, such as Yahuda, Manni, Agha Baba, Naḥum, Picciotto, and others responded to the call of Zionism and emigrated to Palestine. Up to the 19th century, the majority of the Jews living in the Holy Land were Sepharadim, though Ashkenazic Jewry also responded to the call of Zionism. The major waves of emigration from Eastern Europe are usually designated as the First Aliyah (1882–1903) and the Second Aliyah (1904–1918). However, many of those emigrating at that time were Sepharadim, though there are no precise figures of the number of immigrants coming in these waves. Interestingly, in the census taken in Israel in November 1948, there were 3,192 survivors from the first wave of immigration, of whom about 50% were Sepharadim. Specifically: 1,172 came from Asia, 201 from Africa, and 141 from Greece and Yugoslavia. There were 9,136 survivors of the second wave, of whom 3,600 were Sepharadim: 2,985 from Asia, 440 from Africa, and 175 from Greece and Yugoslavia. These numbers are particularly significant in view of the fact that by the end of the 19th century the Sepharadim were only 8% of the entire Jewish population.

The ideal of national autonomy as a distinct political entity, rather than a mere ethnical group, was preserved only by Jews in Arab lands. They alone perceived that the demand for 'citizenship' and 'freedom', in the sense of equal access to all the political and economic opportunities of the host country, meant the termination of the Jewish Nation in exile.

This point had escaped the attention of Jewish Scholars, who are quick to describe the position of the Jew in Arab lands as that of "a second-rate citizen," without taking into consideration the fact that in these countries the Jew never wanted to forfeit his own national autonomy. Jews in Arab lands, like other Sepharadim in Western Europe prior to the French Revolution, were not "second-rate citizens," but members of the Jewish Nation. It ought to be remembered that demand for citizenship from the host government meant the recognition of that government as the supreme legal and political authority of the Jews, and the abolition of the Jewish Nation. The modern Jew who is a citizen of the U.S.A. or U.S.S.R. enjoys the political freedom of other citizens, but he does not enjoy Jewish autonomy as did the Jewish communities in Arab lands who had their own Courts of Justice, were judged by their own laws, paid taxes as an independent corporation, and maintained their own penal and educational systems. From the point of view of national autonomy, emancipation is a betrayal of the highest interests and ideals of the Jewish Nation. Unless one maintains, as the Jews in Arab lands did, that we are an autonomous Nation, it makes no juridical sense to claim a national right to the Holy Land.

As a matter of fact, the most emphatic recognition of Jewish National Autonomy was the *formal* expulsion of the Jews from Arab lands. This expulsion, and the readiness of the Jews in these lands to abandon their wealth and homes at a moment's notice, are the clearest evidence that the Jewish Nation in Exile was a legally recognized political entity. This recognition is the primary basis for a national claim to the Holy Land: Without a Jewish Nation in Exile there could not have been a Jewish Nation in Israel.

# Early Zionist Ideals Among Sepharadim in the Nineteenth Century

*Judaism* 25, 1976

## I. Political Emancipation and the Integrity of the Jewish Nation

*Galut,* in Sephardic thought, is primarily a political concept. In its barest form it means the Jewish nation was not dissolved with the territorial loss of the land of Israel. This claim rests on the idea that Jewish national autonomy is not predicated upon the control of a particular geographical area. Rather, it is an extension of the internal legal, social, and cultural institutions governing the Jewish People.[1] It is pertinent to add, at this juncture, that the Sepharadim view themselves as members of the Jewish nation, rather than of the Jewish

1. As Vico has shown, [*The New Science of Giambattista Vico,* (Ithaca, New York: Cornell University Press, 1968), *ff.* 676, p. 255], in the heroic age the "vanquished were regarded as godless men, so that along with civil liberty they lost natural liberty as well." Essentially, this political idea dominated the world up to relatively recent times, where the *right of the sword,* the *merum imperium* or absolute

religion: the political dimension of Judaism is essential to the Sephardic mind. There are several implications to this idea: two deserve special attention. First, the governments serving as the hosts of the Jewish nation are not the supreme legal and political authority of the Jews. The rules and legislations governing the Jewish People in the host country are not the fiat of the authority of that country over the Jews, but of negotiations and accord arrived at by two equally autonomous parties: the Jewish nation in Exile, and the host government.[2] Second, as an extension of the foregoing, the messianic ideal expressed the hope that the Jewish nation would eventually establish itself in the Promised Land.

From this perspective, it is evident that the demand for citizenship from the host government meant the recognition of that government as the supreme legal and political authority of the Jews, and, thereby, the abdication of Jewish political autonomy.

The question regarding the Jewish nation came to the fore when the issue of Jewish citizenship was debated in Europe. Napoleon, like all properly informed Christians, regarded the Jews as a separate

---

sovereignty, underlay the right for civil and criminal administration of justice. Thus, the concept of *galut* is a direct challenge to the very foundations of heroic political thinking.

2. The specifics of the idea of a Jewish nation ought to be properly examined in the light of the enormous data that is available on the subject. It bears directly on many significant aspects of Sephardic history. For instance, when the small group of Jews seeking permission to settle in New Amsterdam presented a petition in January 1655, it was in the name of "the Jewish nation" [see Irving J. Sloan, "Selected Documents," *The Jews in America. 1621–1970* (New York: Ocean Publications, 1971), p. 51]. Throughout this document, they never referred to themselves as members of the Jewish religion, or as individual Jews, but as the " Jewish nation," with political connotations. (See also, Ibid., p. 53. Cf. below, note 4.) This point is of particular significance in understanding the attitudes of the official governments towards the Jews, since, strictly speaking, the problem of the Jewish nation bordered on the political, rather than on the narrow issue of religious freedom. A government may have been willing to grant religious freedom to its subjects, but still could refuse to recognize the political autonomy of a particular group living within its borders.

nation.[3] This point is especially significant for an adequate understanding of the issues underlying Jewish emancipation. Christians who were in favor of granting citizenship to the Jews demanded, as a condition *sine qua non,* the abolition of the Jewish nation. Otherwise, to grant French citizenship to the Jew would be as ridiculous as granting French citizenship to an Englishman or to a Dane. Likewise, those who opposed giving citizenship to the Jews argued that, since the Jews had their own autonomous nation, they were not part of the French nation.[4]

One of the principal effects of granting citizenship to the Jews by Napoleon was the dissolution of the Jewish nation. The Jewish Sanhedrin, convoked in Paris, May 30, 1806, testified obliquely to this effective:

> At the present time, when the Jews no longer form a separate people, but enjoy the advantage of being incorporated with the Great Nation [i.e. French Empire] (which privilege they consider as a kind of political redemption) ....[5]

The sixth question put before the Sanhedrin, *"Do Jews born in France and treated by the laws as French citizens, consider France as their country? Are they bound to defend it? Are they bound to obey the laws and to conform to the dispositions of the civil code?"*[6] was directly concerned

---

3. See Robert Anchel, *Napoléon et les Juifs,* (Paris: Les Presses Universitaires de France, 1928), p. 42, note 2; cf. ibid. pp. 63–69. On the attitude of Napoleon toward the Jews, see ibid., pp. 62–74 and below, note 7.
4. For a glimpse on this subject, see Zoza Swajkowski, "Jewish Autonomy Debated and Attacked during the French Revolution," *Historia Judaica,* 20 (1958), pp. 31–46. It should be noted, *en passant,* that the situation of the Jews, as a *separate national entity,* was fundamentally different from that of the Protestants. The Protestants were only a separate *religious* group, without any claims to national autonomy. This point has not been properly appreciated. Cf. ibid., pp. 37–38.
5. F.D. Kirwan, Esq., trans. And Diogene Tama, ed., *Transactions of the Parisian Sanhedrin* (London: Charles Taylor, 1807), p. 180.
6. Ibid., p. 181.

with the issue of the Jewish nation. F.D. Kirwan, the translator of the Sanhedrin's transactions, clearly perceived the ultimate consequences of the Sanhedrin's response:

> The answer to the sixth question, by which the French Jews acknowledge France as their country, without any restrictions whatever, is still a more heinous dereliction of the tenets of Mosaic law; for they give up by it the hope of the expected Messiah, and the everlasting possession of the promised land of Canaan which they deem a part of the sacred Covenant between God and his chosen people.[7]

---

7. Ibid. p. xv. Kirwan accused the participants of the Parisian Sanhedrin of flouting Jewish law in order to conform with the wishes of the government. His views on this matter are extremely interesting. In his preface, xiii-xv, he writes:

> But while we pay a just tribute to their talents [the members of the Parisian Sanhedrin], we must deplore the way in which they have been shamefully abused in many instances, few of them, indeed, have raised their voices against the tyrannical Regulations which have been imposed upon them; some of their answers, it is true, are highly satisfactory, and among them, those concerning usury; but, in many other cases, they have manifested a culpable readiness to accede to or even to anticipate whatever might suit the views of their government, without much regard to the precepts of their law. But for the strong opposition of the Rabbis, the assembly would, as far as its authority could have gone, sanctioned the marriages of Jews with Christians, nay, in the tumultuous debate which took place on the occasion, a member broadly declared that marriage had nothing of a divine institution, and that the first precept was increase and multiply. Nor is this the only instance in which we remark, with sorrow, that the contagious infidelity of France had crept in among the Israelites. In the festival of the 15th of August, the cyphers of *Napoleon* and of *Josephine* were profanely blended with the unutterable name of Jehovah, and the Imperial Eagle was placed over the Sacred Ark. This, we understand, has given much offence, and with very just reason, we think, to the most respectable men of that community in these kingdoms.

Elsewhere, Kirwan suggests (pp. viii-ix) that Napoleon may have entertained "the idea of re-establishing them in Palestine, and that this forms a part of his plan respecting Egypt, which he is well known never to have abandoned." The lay and religious authorities that were set up by the French government were intended to remove the Jews further from the mass of the people, and, as to the Rabbinic authorities, he makes the following remark, (p. xi):

Zionist ideals among Sepharadim in the 19th century may best be understood in the light of the new cultural and political trends affecting Europe at that time. There was a profound awareness that the Jewish nation in *galut* would eventually surrender its autonomy and disintegrate under the pressures of rational secularism and political emancipation. It was the view of Rabbis such as Yehuda Bibas (1780–1852), Yehuda Alcalai (1798–1879), Natan Amram (1805–1870), Barukh Miṭrani (1847–1919), and others, that the only effective way to preserve Jewish autonomy in modern times was by establishing a Jewish national home in the Holy Land.

We shall proceed to investigate first the efforts made by Sepharadim at that time for the revival of Hebrew as the national language of the Jewish people.

## II. The Revival of the Hebrew Language: Nationalistic and Political Considerations

The Sepharadim were the first to realize the political role that the Hebrew language could play in promoting Jewish nationalistic feelings and political unity among Jews.

In one of her essays, published in 1842, seventeen years before the birth of Eliezer Ben-Yehuda, Grace Aguilar (1816–1847) presented this point quite forcibly. She argued that "the preservation of our Law in its original purity" was a supreme duty in ancient times; "How much more requisite must it be now," in modern times. Hebrew was "the silver link" that would give unity to the Jewish nation scattered throughout the earth. To this effect, it was imperative that Hebrew be taught to every Jewish man and woman. Commenting on the parental duty to educate the child, Miss Aguilar remarked:

---

"These Regulations have another remarkable feature, common to all the recent politico-religious conceptions of the French government. The Rabbis" are by them set as spies over the Jews, like the ministers of the Roman Catholic religion over the rest of the Frenchmen.

> Here we proceed to the remainder of this verse, may we be permitted to hint on the importance of making the Hebrew language familiar to every Hebrew child?[8]

Against those who argued that Hebrew is a dead language, she replied:

> It cannot be considered a dead language; for the nation to which it originally belonged continues to exist, and will exist for ever.[9]

In particular, she pointed out the national significance of Hebrew as a means of promoting political unity among the Jews:

> It is not indeed spoken as it would have been, had we remained in our own land; yet it might still continue the link uniting the sons of Israel wherever they may be. The sojourners in England, France, Austria, Spain, might be enabled to converse or to commune with each other in their own native tongue, though of the language of their respective homes each might be ignorant.[10]

Miss Aguilar realized that in order to accomplish this goal, it was necessary to bring about a change in the current method of instruction: rather than learn the language through the Hebrew classics, one should learn the Hebrew classic through the language. Hebrew ought to be spoken before it is read. The method used in Jewish schools, to confront the child who has just learned the Hebrew alphabet with the liturgy, was as ridiculous as if "as soon as a child had acquired his

8. Grace Aguilar, *The Spirit* of *Judaism,* [3rd ed.] (Philadelphia: 5624), p. 139. All subsequent quotations and paginations are from this edition. Regarding resistance among Ashkenazic Jewry for studying or praying in Hebrew, see introduction to David Mark, *Shire Tefilla* (Rodelheim: 1815).
9. Ibid.
10. Ibid.

letters in French or Italian, the Henriade or Dante should be placed before him, and he should be desired to learn passages by rote with merely the assistance of a subjoined translation."[11]

Her views on the effective revision of the pedagogical system in the Hebrew school are specific:

> Never may we hope for the perfect attainment of this ancient and glorious language, till the present system has given place to one more calculated to engage a child's fancy; till the prayer book is not the first which we place in an infant's hands; till other than words so sacred as prayer are the first we teach our children to repeat. Our aim indeed should be to enable them to address their Creator in the language of their ancestors, to read His word pure and unaltered, even as it came from Heaven; but by placing it too early before them, we frustrate our own desires.[12]

Miss Aguilar perceived the *religious* and *political* roles that only the Hebrew language could adequately perform. The sacred task of the Jewish educator was

> that every child of Israel, male or female, should perfectly understand the language of our ancestors, that in which the awful yet invisible Voice delivered His dictates to Moses, that we may indeed feel Hebrew is bound to Hebrew by a link neither oceans nor water nor spreading wastes of land can sever! ... The sacred language is the silver link which, uniting them to each other, separates them from other nations, and makes them feel that they are indeed the witnesses of the Lord. And while they read in rejoicing faith the Book of Life in the language in which it was given, or in humble adoration

11. Ibid., p. 140.
12. Ibid.

> prostrate themselves before God's throne, must not a glowing of the whole soul attend the addressing of the Eternal, in the same language in which His awful voice addressed His favored servants?[13]

A few years earlier, in 1837, her friend, Abigail Abarbanel Lindo (1803–1848), had already published a Hebrew-English, English-Hebrew Lexicon, with the "object to assist those who wish to study the sacred language."[14]

In 1845, Rabbi Yisrael Moshe Ḥazzan (1807–1863) made an appeal for the revival of the Hebrew language. Like Miss Aguilar, he, too, emphasized the nationalistic role of Hebrew in promoting political unity among Jews. Moreover, he pointed to the Christian interest in classical languages as an example which the assimilationist Jew in particular should try to emulate by studying the languages of his own classical literature. It is of great significance to note that Rabbi Ḥazzan indicated that, since the Reform movement cited among one of its objectives the promotion of greater unity among the Jewish people, they could accomplish this objective by establishing schools to teach Hebrew.

> Do you not yourself desire union and friendship among Israel? Above all, let me remind you that it is incumbent upon every Israelite, male and female, to have his children instructed in the language of your nation, viz., the sacred tongue...
>
> What nation is there on earth who have themselves neglected their language as, alas, we have neglected ours? If you were to open schools for instruction in the Hebrew and Chaldee languages, which are both indispensable to Judaism, how strongly would you cement the union and enhance the felicity of faith and peace. Do not our Christian brethren, (to

13. Ibid., p. 143.
14. Abigail Abarbanel Lindo, *Hebrew and English, and English and Hebrew Dictionary, with Roots and Abbreviations,* (London: Samuel Meldola, 1846 [5606]) p. iv.

> their credit, be it mentioned,) after a thorough knowledge of their native tongue, still eagerly pursue the study of the Latin and Greek languages, because of the technical and philosophical terms met with in their literature? Much more so we, whose faith and literature is closely interwoven with those two languages; why should we not rather cultivate those precious plants in preference to vain toys of the imagination, which bear no fruit of joy but deep rooted discord and implacable hatred.[15]

In a similar fashion, Rabbi Alcalai, in 1852, published a pamphlet urging the adoption of the Hebrew language as a means of fostering national unity among Jews.[16] The need for the revival of Hebrew as the spoken language of the Jews was felt even by the semi-educated Sephardi. The following report, by Andrew Bonar, a missionary from the Church of Scotland, in 1839, illustrates our point:

> He said that…They needed to be taught their own language, for none could speak Hebrew, and few understand it. If a school were instituted, he believed it would be well attended.[17]

It is important to note, in this connection, the upsurge of Hebrew grammars, such as *Darkhei No'am,* written in Judeo-Spanish by Rabbi Alcalai, and printed in Belgrade in 1839, and *L.eḥem Ha-Bikkurim,* by Rabbi Shaul Ha-Kohen (1772–1818) of Tunis. In the introduction to this last book, published in Leghorn in 1870, one of the reasons given for the work is that, among the nations, there is great interest in the proper studies of their respective languages. How much more so should this be with the Jewish people, whose very existence depends

15. *Words of Peace and Truth* (London: Samuel Meldola, 5605–1845), pp. 13–14. This book is bi-lingual.
16. *Me'oded 'Anavim* (Leipzig: 5612–1852). See *Kitbei Ha-Rab Yehuda Alcalai,* ed. Y. Raphael, (Jerusalem; Mossad Harav Kook, 1970), vol. 2, p. 40.
17. Andrew Bonar and Robert Murray M'Cheyene, *Narrative of a Mission of Inquiry to the Jews,* 3rd edition (Philadelphia: Presbyterian Board of Publication), p. 380.

on their sacred literature. Moreover, Jews go through great efforts in order to instruct their children in foreign languages, when they are neglecting the study of Hebrew.

Another Hebrew grammar, this one in Judeo-Spanish, was put out by Rabbi Menaḥem Farḥi, with the complaint

> that other spoken languages are further progressing, but our language is continuously losing ground. Therefore, I was determined to try to present before the students some of the principles of our holy language in a special book. In this way, perhaps, some men of wisdom of our times, those who have the power to establish something that is well organized, will be able to benefit the youth of our people.[18]

Among the Jewish educators who centered their curricula around the study of Hebrew, special mention should be made of R. Barukh Miṭrani, whose efforts at the elementary school level, as well as the works that he composed for this purpose, make him a unique pioneer in this field of Jewish pedagogy.

Intimately connected with the efforts for the revival of Hebrew was the establishment of Hebrew magazines, such as *Dobeb Mesharim* and *Karmi* (bilingual: Hebrew and Judeo-Spanish).

## III. Political Repentance: The Return to Zion

Rabbi Yehuda Bibas was the first Jew in modern times to give full expression to the Zionist ideal and to show the significance of the return to the land of Israel. His Zionist ideals were grounded on his interpretation of the duty of *teshuba*, repentance, whose literal meaning is "return." *Teshuba* is operative at two levels. At the individual level, it is spiritual, and means the recognition and abandonment of

18. Rab Pe'alim (Constantinople: 1880 [5640]).

sin, followed by a "return" to the ways of the Lord. However, Judaism also recognizes *teshuba* as a collective duty. At this level, it must be – by sheer definition – political.

The beginning of political *teshuba* is the "return" of the Jewish people in a physical and concrete sense to the Promised Land. This ideal is intimately related to the national conception of Judaism current in the Sephardic tradition, and the political dimension of *galut*: the spiritual redemption of Israel by God is predicated upon the political repentance of the Jewish people.[19]

Since repentance, as a collective duty, is essentially political, it depends on military means for its implementation. Rabbi Bibas saw in the Greek insurrection against the Turks (1821) a paradigm of how the Jews should take possession of their ancestral home. Therefore, he considered it of primary importance that "the people must first be educated and taught the sciences."[20] The Jew ought to acquire a wide humanistic education that would prepare him to face the complexities of modern society. In his view, proper education in the "seven wisdoms" in our times takes precedence over the study of Tora:

> The seven wisdoms or sciences, such as music, astronomy, etc., are meant. When a man is well, if he takes medicine it will do him harm; but if he will be ill, then he must put away bread and take the medicine. Now, the law is bread; but the Jews are sick, they are ignorant and degraded. You must therefore lay aside the study of the law and take the medicine, which is the seven wisdoms or sciences spoken of here.[21]

According to Rabbi Bibas, humanistic education would prepare the Jew to build a home in the Promised Land; in particular, he urged

19. Our presentation of Rabbi Bibas's ideology is based on quotations made by his most ardent follower, Rabbi Y. Alcali. See *Kitbei ha-Rab Yehuda Alcalai,* vol. 1, pp. 20–99, 237, 238, 241, 276.
20. Bonar and M'Cheyene, p. 380.
21. Ibid.

the Jew to be trained in military science. In his view, it was the special role of the Messiah to conduct the war of conquest of the Holy Land. In referring to Rabbi Bibas, Bonar makes the following comment:

> The young men [of Corfu] spoke with great admiration of him [R. Biba] and of his sentiments, and especially of this one, that the Jews must be instructed in science and in arms, that they may wrest the land of Palestine from the Turks under the leadership of the Messiah, as the Greeks wrested their country.[22]

Secular Zionism developed among Sepharadim as early as 1839. In a conversation which took place on September 10, 1839, Bonar reports:

> In conversation with the son [of Samuel Hillel, a Jewish banker of Corfu] we soon discovered that he was one of the Jews who care little about Palestine [in the traditional religious sense] and do not expect a Messiah, believing that education and civilization alone can exalt the Jews; to which he added – "a knowledge of arms, that they may defend their land when they get possession of it."[23]

In this connection, it is pertinent to mention the activities of Joseph Marcou Baruch, who was born in Istanbul in 1872 and died in Florence in 1899. He was an idealist who devoted all of his life and energies to promote Jewish nationalistic feelings among his people. Like Rabbi Bibas, he believed that the Jews should make military preparations for the conquest of the Holy Land from the Turks. Because of these views, he was considered by many to be an "extremist," and was even branded an "anarchist".[24] This judgment may reflect the position

22. Ibid.
23. Ibid., p. 392.
24. There is no systematic study of all the data, sources, and material related to the work, ideology, and publications of Baruch, though there is a romanticized account of his life: Jacob Weinschel, *Yosef Marcou Baruch*, (Tel-Aviv: 1949).

formulated by Moses Mendelssohn that the Jew may not bear arms to take possession of the Promised Land.[25] This notion was never accepted by Sephardic Rabbis. To this issue, Rabbi Moshe Ya'acob Toledano (1880–1960) addressed himself in a *responsum*,[26] in which, without mentioning anybody by name, he dismissed the notion promoted by many rabbis that it is forbidden to the Jewish people to bear arms. Specifically, he demonstrated that it is the sacred duty of the Jewish people to take possession of the Promised Land, if necessary by the force of arms.

---

Invaluable information on Baruch may be found in *Yehude HaMizraḥi Be Ereṣ Yisrael*, vol 2, pp. 172–176. Mrs. Vicki Tamir, who has completed a volume of the History of the Jews in Bulgaria up to our days, sent me the following information on the impact of Baruch on Bulgarian Jewry:

In April, 1895, Yosef Marco Baruch arrived in Sofia and, in the face of enormous obstacles, erected in his path by the "notables" [the rich Jews of Bulgaria holding the reins of community life at that time], succeeded in creating peripatetic Zionist nuclei called Carmel I, Carmel II, Carmel III, etc., and in raising the necessary funds for the publication of a Zionist periodical, Carmel.

Eventually... Baruch left Bulgaria, but not without imprinting his example of revolutionary fervor in the hearts of the people.... Those who responded to Baruch's appeal for self-help, for denunciation of the antisemitic wave in Bulgaria and the inequities in Czarist Russia, for active struggle against the Sultan of Turkey dominating the Holy Land, and for an expanded Jewish national consciousness, came from all walks of life. One of them described Baruch as he appeared at their first meeting to address them in French: "Pallid, emaciated, sloppily dressed, his shoes torn, his scalp clean-shaven... But when he stood up and spoke, we no longer saw his pitiful exterior. We just devoured every word be uttered...

For the publication of Carmel, Yosef Marco Baruch sought the support of the father of Bulgarian letters, Ivan Vazov, to whom he subsequently dedicated a French language poem ("Merci, merci, noble poète!"–he exclaims), as well as that of Aleko Konstantinov, Bulgaria's foremost satirist, and even that of Prince Ferdinand, who sent him a donation of 100 leva.

25. It was a natural extension of the concept of Judaism as a religion without any political dimension. This point was crucial in order to gain political emancipation, and it was adequately understood by Christians who supported Jewish Emancipation. See Comte de Mirabeau, *Sur Moses Mendelssohn, Sur La Reforme Politique des Juifs*, (London: 1787), p. 115.
26. *Ha-Yam Ha-Gadol*, (Cairo: 5691–1931), pp. 180–186.

Rabbi Bibas, like all Sephardic religious and lay leaders, strongly supported Jewish settlement in the Holy Land, but he objected to the parasitic tendencies of the recipients of public charity there. In his opinion, it was incumbent upon the Jewish leadership to encourage the Jews living in Palestine to work and be self-supporting:

> He [Rabbi Bibas] thought that the collections for the Holy Land ought to be given up, and that the Jews there ought to be obliged to work even were it by the bayonet.[27]

Rabbi Alcalai was deeply affected by the personality and Zionist ideology of Rabbi Bibas, and devoted his entire life towards the development and implementation of his ideals. A detailed analysis of the numerous activities of Rabbi Alcalai and his Zionist ideology transcends the scope of this paper, but, for our purpose, it would be sufficient to point out some of his most significant projects. He believed in levying a tithe upon the Jewish people and, among the different projects to be financed by these funds, the following deserve special attention: the establishment of an organization to promote international recognition of the Jewish right to the Holy Land, a Jewish Parliament, a Jewish army, schools to teach the Hebrew language, Jewish settlements in the Holy Land, agricultural centers, etc.[28]

Rabbi Bibas questioned the wisdom of purchasing land in Israel without first securing political autonomy. To this effect, he attempted to dissuade Sir Moses Montefiore on the grounds that:

> Sir Moses Montefiore's plan of purchasing land for them [the Jews] in Palestine he [Rabbi Bibas] considered useless, as long

27. Bonar and M'Cheyene, p. 395.
28. For a brief summary of the main points of his ideology and career see *Encyclopaedia of Religious Zionism* [Heb.] (Jerusalem: Rav Kook Institute: 1958), vol. 1, columns 134–140.

> as there is no security for property there. The people must first be educated and taught the sciences.[29]

Nevertheless, there was a strong support among the Sepharadim for the establishment of a plan to purchase land in Palestine. In 1844, three years before Rabbi Alcalai made a similar proposal, Rabbi Ḥazzan had tried to persuade the Jews in Europe to purchase property in the Holy Land from the Arabs.[30] In 1858, twenty-six years before Schapira and thirty-nine years before the First Zionist Congress, Rabbi Ḥazzan pleaded with European Jewry to establish "a *Keren Kayyemet* for the purpose of purchasing property in the Holy Land." In the following year he published a letter in the Hebrew journal, *Hamaggid* (III, no. 13), urging the Jewish people "to establish a *Keren Kayyemet* in order to buy away the property that the Arabs held in the Holy Land."

A philological note will help us put the significance of this point in the proper perspective. Currently, the term *keren kayyemet* is used in the sense of a trust whose yield is to be used exclusively for a sacred purpose. However, originally, it referred to the spiritual reward of the *miṣvot* in the world-to-come. In Sephardic literature, the phrase is very commonly used in the former sense, while in Ashkenazic literature, *Keren Kayyemet* never appears in the sense of a trust of money.[31] As a matter of fact, the term *Keren Kayyemet* in its current popular sense could have developed only in a Sephardic community, since it is a translation of the technical Arabic term, *waqf*.

These Sephardic ideals of national Zionism were deeply rooted among the lay leaders and the masses. Distinguished men of the

---

29. Bonar and M'Cheyene, p. 395.
30. See the article of Rabbi Ḥazzan in the *Hamaggid*, III (No. 13).
31. In Rabbinic Hebrew, *keren* refers also to "a sum of money, a capital." In this sense it is used by Ashkenazic Rabbis. Occasionally, one finds the expression *"ha-keren yihye kayyam"*; i.e., "it should remain intact." The expression *keren kayyemet* is used by Ashkenazic Rabbis only in the sense that it appears in Rabbinic literature. Cf. R. Raphael Joseph Ḥazzan, *Ma'arkhe Leb*, vol. 2, p. 245d, *"she-yihye ha-keren kayyam veha-perot li-ṣdaqa."*

statute of Sir Moses Montefiore (1784–1885), Count. Abraham de Camondo (1785–1873) and Shemaya Angel (1810–1874), to mention just a few, used their financial and diplomatic resources to help their co-religionists establish a home in the Promised Land. At the same time, members of some of the most prominent Sephardic families, such as Yahuda, Manni, Agha Baba, Naḥum, Picciotto and others, responded to the call of Zionism and emigrated to Palestine. Up to the 19th century, the majority of the Jews living in the Holy Land were Sepharadim,[32] though Ashkenazic Jewry also responded to the call of Zionism. The major waves of emigration from Eastern Europe are usually designated as the First Aliyah (1882–1903) and the Second Aliyah (1904–1918). However, many of those emigrating at that time were Sepharadim, though there are no precise figures of the numbers of immigrants coming in these waves. Interestingly, in the census taken in Israel in November 1948, there were 3,192 survivors from the first wave of immigration, of whom about 50% were Sepharadim. Specifically: 1172 came from Asia, 201 from Africa, and 141 from Greece and Yugoslavia. There were 9,136 survivors of the second wave, of whom 3600 were Sepharadim: 2985 from Asia, 440 from Africa, and 175 from Greece and Yugoslavia.[33] These numbers are particularly significant in view of the fact that by the end of the 19th century the Sepharadim were only 8% of the entire Jewish population.

Finally, a note that may help us come to a better understanding of the Sephardi in relation to his host country, to the Jewish nation, and to the Holy Land.[34] No matter how well the Sephardi integrated in the host country, he felt himself, somehow, in *galut*. He yearned

32. In the census taken in 1839, only 26.2% of the Jewish population was Ashkenazic (*Encyclopeadia Judaica*, vol. 9, col. 497). It is important to note that the numbers of Jews in Palestine in the following 75 years are based on *estimates* and need to be carefully examined in the light of all of the available data.
33. M. Sicron and B. Gil. *Statistical Abstract of Israel* (Jerusalem), 1957, p. 20.
34. In my view, Elias Canetti, *Crowds and Power* (Penguin Books), pp. 208–209, when referring to the "ultimate nature of the bond they feel when they say 'I am a Jew,'" gave full expression to the feeling of "the Hebrew nation" and *galut* that is so much a part of the Sephardic mind.

for the time when he could be fully part of the Jewish nation, and live in the Holy Land. Grace Aguilar was a Jewess who enjoyed the privileges of Victorian society, and, yet, she was a stranger, an exile longing for her home. She lamented that Jerusalem was in Moslem hands, and she prayed for the day when the Lord would redeem the remnants of Judah. Here are a few lines from her poem, *"A Vision of Jerusalem,"* that she composed upon visiting a Christian shrine:

> I stood ALONE 'mid thronging crowds who fill'd that stranger shrine,
> For there were none who kept the faith I hold so dearly mine:
> An exile felt I, in that house, from Israel's native sod,
> An exile yearning for my home – yet loved still by my God.
> No exile from His love! No, no; though captive I may be,
> And I must weep whene'er I think, my fatherland, on thee!
> Jerusalem! My beautiful! My own! I feel thee still,
> Though for our sins thy sainted sod the Moslem strangers fill....
> Alas, my country! Thou must yet deserted rest and lone,
> Thy glory, loveliness, and life, a Father's gifts, are flown!
> Oh that my prayers could raise thee radiant from the sod,
> And turn from Judah's exiled sons their God's avenging rod![35]

35. *The Spirit of Judaism*, p. 221.

# תחיית הלשון העברית אצל היהודים הספרדים במאה הי"ט

(כ"ד בכסלו, תשל"ו)

היהודים הספרדים היו, לדעתי, הראשונים לציין את החשיבות הלאומית של הלשון העברית. הם השכילו להעיר את לב הקהל היהודי על התפקיד המיוחד של הלשון כגורם מדיני שיאחד את כל תפוצות ישראל.

בשנת 1842, שבע עשרה שנה לפני לידת אליעזר בן־יהודה, העירה גרייס אגילר (1,817–1,848) על החובה המוטלת על הדור הצעיר להחיות את לשוננו הלאומית. היא באה בטענה כי: אם "שמירת תורתנו בטהרתה [הלשונית] המקורית הייתה חובה עלינו" בתקופה העתיקה, "לא כל שכן" בתקופה החדשה.[1] שפתנו הלא היא "חבל כסף" שיביא את בני ישראל הנפוצים בארבע רוחות העולם לכלל אחדות. היהודים "מאנגליה, צרפת,

1. Grace Aguilar, *The Spirit of Judaism*, [4rd Edition], (Philadelphia: 1,865), p. 144

# The Revival of the Hebrew Language Among the Sephardic Jews in the 19th Century

*Judaism* 25, 1976

(24 Kislev 5736, November 28, 1975)

The Sephardic Jews were, in my opinion, the first to note the national importance of the Hebrew language. They astutely brought to the attention of the Jewish community the special role of the Hebrew language as a political instrument that could promote unity among the entire Jewish Diaspora.

In 1842, seventeen years before the birth of Eliezer Ben-Yehuda, Grace Aguilar (1816–1847) commented on the younger generation's duty to revive our national language. She argued that, if "the preservation of our Law in its original [linguistic] purity" was a supreme duty in ancient times, "how much more requisite must it be now," in modern times.[1] Our language is none other than "the silver link" that would give unity to the Jewish nation scattered throughout the four corners of the earth. The Jews "in England, France, Austria, Spain,

1. Grace Aguilar, *The Spirit of Judaism*, [3rd Edition], (Philadelphia: 1864), p. 143.

אוסטריה וספרד יוכלו לדבר ביניהם בשפתם הלאומית."[2] נגד אלה שטענו כי העברית "שפה מתה" היא, השיבה גברת אגילר כי דבר זה לא ייתכן: "הלא האומה שאליה לשון זו משתייכת קיימת ותתקיים לעד."[3] היא הבחינה כי תחיית הלשון לא תיתכן בלי שינוי יסודי בתוכנית ובסדר הלימודים בבתי הספר. במקום ללמוד את השפה מתוך הספרות המסורתית יש ללמוד את הספרות מתוך השפה: ידיעת השפה קודמת לידיעת הספרות. הנוהג לגשת לסידור התפילה ברגע שהילד מסיים את לימוד האלף־בית מגוחך, כאילו "היינו מבקשים ללמד את דאנטה לילד שסיים זה עתה את האלף־בית הלאטיני."[4] מגמת החינוך היא "שכל ילד מישראל, בין זכר ובין נקבה, ידע את לשון אבותינו על בוריה."[5]

בשנת 1,838 שנים אחדות לפני שגברת אגילר כתבה את הדברים האלה, פירסמה אחת מידידותיה, אביגיל אברבנאל לינדו (1,804–1,844), לקסיקון עברי־אנגלי־עברי עם סדרה של משפטים עברית־אנגלית,[6] "כדי לעזור לאלה שרוצים לדעת את שפתנו הקדושה."[7]

בשנת 1,846 פנה הרב ישראל משה חזן (1,808–1,864) בקריאה לתחיית הלשון. כגברת אגילר, הדגיש הרב חזן את התפקיד הלאומי והמדיני של הלשון. ראוי לציין כי הוא פנה בקריאה זו לאנשי הריפורמה. בין הטענות השונות שהם השמיעו להצדיק את הצורך לתנועה חדשה זו,

2. שם, עמ' 140
3. שם.
4. שם, עמ' 141
5. שם, עמ' 144
6. Abigail Abarbanel Lindo, *A Hebrew and English, and English and Hebrew Vocabulary; also Hebrew and English Dialogues,* (London: 1,838).
7. Abigail Abarbanel Lindo, *A Hebrew and English, and English and Hebrew Dictionary, with Roots and Abbreviations,* (London: Samuel Meldola, 1,847), p. iv.

might be enabled to converse or to commune with each other in their own native tongue."[2] Against those who claimed that Hebrew was "a dead language," Ms. Aguilar replied that this is not possible: "For the nation to which [the Hebrew language] belonged continues to exist, and will exist for ever."[3] She recognized that reviving the Hebrew language would not be possible without a fundamental change in the schools' curriculum and educational programs. Rather than learn the language through the classical literature, one should learn the classics through the language: knowing the language precedes knowing the literature. The practice of having a child start with the *siddur* as soon as he finishes learning the Hebrew alphabet is absurd, as if "as soon as a child had acquired his letters in Italian, Dante should be placed before him."[4] The educational objective is "that every child of Israel, male or female, should perfectly understand the language of our ancestors."[5]

In 1837, just a few years before Ms. Aguilar wrote these words, one of her friends, Abigail Abarbanel Lindo (1803–1843), published a Hebrew-English-Hebrew lexicon, together with a series of Hebrew-English sentences,[6] "to assist those who wish to study the sacred language."[7]

In 1845, R. Yisrael Moshe Ḥazzan (1807–1863) made an appeal for the revival of the Hebrew language. Like Miss Aguilar, R. Ḥazzan emphasized the nationalistic and political role of the Hebrew language. It is worth noting that in this appeal he was addressing the leaders of the Reform Movement. Among the various claims they had voiced to justify the need for this new movement was that it would promote

---

2. Ibid., p. 139.
3. Ibid.
4. Ibid., p. 140.
5. Ibid., p. 143.
6. Abigail Abarbanel Lindo, *Hebrew and English, and English and Hebrew Vocabulary; also Hebrew and English Dialogues,* (London: 1837).
7. Abigail Abarbanel Lindo, *Hebrew and English, and English and Hebrew Dictionary, with Roots and Abbreviations,* (London: Samuel Meldola, 1846), p. iv.

היא הטענה כי תנועתם תביא לאחדות בין הגורמים השונים בישראל, כגון הספרדים והאשכנזים. הרב חזן השיב כי אחדות עם ישראל לא תבוא על־ידי ויתורים בדת וכיו"ב, אלא על־ידי פיתוח היסוד הלאומי שחסר לנו - השפה העברית. "נודע שהאחווה המדינית תלויה בעיקר בג' דברי': א) אכילה ושתיה, ב) חיתון זה עם זה, ג) אשר ישמעו איש שפת רעהו."[8] הפירוד בישראל נובע מהעדר שפה משותפת: "והרי שתים הראשונו' הנה באו. והג' צרת הלשון מרקדת בינינו שהן בעון בלע ה' פלג לשונינו. ומי בכל עמי הארצות אשר איבדו לשונם כמונו בעוונות."[9] יש צורך להקים בתי ספר בהם יגדלו ילדי ישראל על ברכי הלשון העברית. מכאן הבקשה המיוחדת לאנשי הריפורמה: אם רצונם לתרום לעם ישראל תרומה שתביא לאהבה ואחדות, עליהם להקים בתי ספר לעברית,

"ותהיו זוכים ומזכים. הלא אם אתם מבקשים אהבה ואחדות בין האומה הישראלית יותר ויותר היה לכם לתקן שכל ישראל אנשים ונשים יגדלו בניהם בבקיאות לשון עמם הוא לשון הקודש."[10]

הרב חזן רמז כי על המתבוללים היוצאים בעקבות העמים ורואים בדרכי האומות אור לנתיבתם, חובה מיוחדת לייסד "בתי לימוד לה"ק ולשון כלדי."[11]

"והרי הנוצרים אחרי שבקיאים בלשונם עכ"ז משתדלים להתלמד לשון יוני ולשון לאטין על כנהו... מפני איזה מילות מחכמת

8. הרב ישראל משה חזן, דברי שלום ואמת, (לונדון: 1,846), עמ' 14–15
9. שם, עמ' 15
10. שם, עמ' 14
11. שם, עמ' 15

unity among the various factions in Israel, such as the Sepharadim and the Ashkenazim. R. Ḥazzan replied that unity in the nation of Israel could not be achieved through concessions in religion and the like, but through the development of the national foundation that we lack – the Hebrew language. "It is known that social fraternity depends mainly on three things: a) eating and drinking, b) marrying one another, and c) interpersonal communication."[8] Division within Israel stems from the lack of a common language: "The first two have already been achieved. But the third, the agony of the language, still plagues us; for indeed, as a result of our sins, God has ravaged us, fragmenting our language. Who among all other nations of the world has lost their language as we have ours, as a result of our sins?"[9] It is necessary to establish schools in which the children of Israel will be reared in the Hebrew language. Hence his special request to the leaders of the Reform Movement: If their desire is to promote love and unity among the people of Israel, they must establish schools for teaching Hebrew,

> and ultimately, you will have benefited both yourselves and others. For if what you seek is love and unity amongst the Jewish Nation, then it is all the more fitting that you see to it that all of Israel, men and women, raise their children with proficiency in their national tongue, namely, the holy language.[10]

Rabbi Ḥazzan hinted that the assimilationist Jews, who follow the nations of the world and see in those nations' ways a light for their own path, have a special duty to establish "educational institutions for the holy language and Aramaic."[11]

> Christians, after mastering their native languages, nonetheless eagerly pursue the proper study of Greek and Latin … merely

8. R. Yisrael Moshe Ḥazzan, *Words of Peace and Truth,* (London: 1845), pp. 13–14.
9. Ibid., p. 14.
10. Ibid., p. 13.
11. Ibid., p. 14.

הפילוסופיא הבאות בתוך לשונם. וע"ז טורחים ללמוד כל הלשון על משפטו. והאמת אתם, כ"ש אנחנו שעיקר אמונתנו וחכמתנו תלויות בב' לשונות הללו."[12]

בשנת 1,853 פירסם הרב יהודה אלקלעי (1,790-1,880) בלייפציג קונטרס "מעודד ענווים," כדי לעורר את ישראל "להקים דגל לשוננו הק' ולהעמידה על תילה ולהרגילה בפי הילדים."[13]

"אנחנו מפוזרים בקצווי ארץ ונעשה אומתנו לשבעים אומות ולשוננו לשבעים לשונות... ולכן מוכרחים אנחנו לעשות לשון אחת מדוברת בארצנו הק'.... לשון הקודש תהיה לה דין קדימה... לקבץ פזורנו שנבין לדבר איש אל רעהו."[14]

ראוי לציין כי גם האיש הספרדי שלא זכה לחינוך יהודי גבוה חש בצורך תחיית הלשון. כהן-דת נוצרי שביקר את קורפו בשנת 1,840 מסר את השיחה דלהלן:

> "הוא אמר כי... הם צריכים ללמוד את שפתם, כי אף אחד מהם לא יכול לדבר עברית, ומעטים הם המבינים אותה. אם ייסדו בית ספר, הוא האמין כי רבים ינהרו אליו."[15]

---

12. שם.
13. מעודד ענווים, (לייפציג: תרי"ב). ראה כתבי הרב יהודה אלקלעי, (ירושלים: מוסד הרב קוק, תשל"ה), כרך ב', עמ' 611
14. שם.
15. Cheyne, *Narrative of a Mission of* Andrew Bonar and Robert Murray M *Inquiry to the Jews,* [4rd Edition], (Philadelphia: Presbyterian Board of Publication, 1,846), p. 381

> to understand certain technical words from those languages that were used by the philosophers. And even still, they take pains to thoroughly learn the language in its entirety. And they are absolutely right! All the more so should it be for us, for whom the crux of our belief and wisdom depends on these two languages.[12]

In 1852, R. Yehuda Alkalai (1789–1879) published a pamphlet in Leipzig, "*Me'oded 'Anavim,*" to urge Israel to "raise the banner of our holy language, restoring it to its rightful place and accustoming our children to speaking it."[13]

> We are scattered to the ends of the earth, such that our nation has become seventy nations and our language seventy languages… and it is therefore incumbent upon us to establish one spoken language in our holy land…. The holy language ought to have a preferential status… in ingathering our dispersed brethren, that we may know to speak with one another.[14]

It is worth noting that even the semi-educated Sepharadi felt the need for the revival of the Hebrew language. A Christian missionary who visited Corfu in 1839 recounted the following conversation:

> [The Jew] said that… they needed to be taught their own language, for none could speak Hebrew, and few understand it. If a school were instituted, he believed it would be well attended.[15]

---

12. Ibid.
13. *Me'oded 'Anavim* (Leipzig: 1852). See *Kitbe ha-Rab Yehuda Alkalai* (Heb.), (Jerusalem: Mossad HaRav Kook, 5735 [1975]), vol. 2, p. 610.
14. Ibid.
15. Andrew Bonar and Robert Murray M'Cheyne, *Narrative of a Mission of Inquiry to the Jews,* [3rd Edition], (Philadelphia: Presbyterian Board of Publication, 1845), p. 380.

באותה תקופה יצאו לאור כמה ספרי דקדוק, כגון: "דרכי נועם" (בילוגראדו: 1,840) בספרדית להרב יהודה אלקלעי, ו"לחם הביכורים" (ליוורנו: 1,871), שנתחבר על ידי הרב שאול הכהן (1,773-1,849) מתוניס, אחד מספרי הדקדוק המשובחים שנתחברו בתקופה החדשה. בין הסיבות השונות שהשמיעו המוציאים לאור לצורך ספר דקדוק כזה, הם משמיעים - בסגנון הנמלץ הנהוג אצל הספרדים - כי, "כל האדם ללשונותם בארשו'תם[16] בגוייהם" שומרים הם את לשונם ואת חוקי הדקדוק שלה, "... עאכ"ו עם בני ישראל" שעצם קיומם מושתת על לשונם וספרותם.[17] וכן מתלוננים הם על ה"למדנים, שבלשון עילגים ידברו, כצפצוף העופות, מבלי שום שכל והבין במקר'א, בין פועל לשם ובין עתיד לעבר ובין זכר לנקבה וכיוצא, וחצי העם מדבר אשדודית אר'ש ערב'ה."[18] זאת ועוד, ההורים "מפזרים ממון ללימוד בנים ובנות לשונות העמים" ומזניחים את לשונם: "ע"ז תאבל ארץ מאין מנחם, שאין רודפים להכיר לשונם האמיתי, שמבלעדיו לא ירים איש את ידו אפילו בחכמי האומות, ולא יקרא חכם בשלמות."[19]

דברים דומים השמיע הרב מנחם פרחי שחי באותה תקופה. בהקדמה לספר דקדוק עברי בלשון ספרדית, "רב פעלים," הוא כתב כי:

16. בסגנון הנמלץ הנהוג אצל היהודים הספרדים, הגרש שעל האות שלפני סוף המילה הריהו סימן כי המילה אינה אלא מליצה הדומה בצלילה לביטוי מקראי. למשל, "ללשונותם בארשו'תם,' הריהו ביטוי על פי בראשית י:כ, מובנו כאן "ניב' (= ארש); וכן "והבין במקר'א' להלן, הוא על פי נחמיה ח:ח, מובנו כאן "כשהוא קורא [בספר] או מדבר עם אחר.' וכן "אר'ש ערב'ה,' הוא על פי ירמיה ב:ו, מובנו כאן "לשון (= ארש) הערבית' שהיא "ערבה' (= מתוקה) עליהם.

17. הרב שאול הכהן, לחם הביכורים, (ליוורנו: 1,871) עמ' 2 ב'הקדמת הרבנים המו־פלאים... בעיר תונס.'

18. שם, עמ' 4 ב'הקדמת נכד הרב המחבר זצ"ל.'

19. שם. עמ' 5 באותה הקדמה.

During that period, several grammar books were published, such as *Darkhe No'am* (Belgrade: 1839), written in Judeo-Spanish by R. Yehuda Alkalai, and *Leḥem Ha-Bikkurim* (Livorno: 1870), composed by R. Shaul Ha-Kohen (1772–1848) of Tunis. The latter work is amongst the finest grammar books compiled in modern times. Its publishers offered several reasons for the necessity of such a grammar book. They proclaimed – in the lyrical style customary among Sepharadim – that, "All men, with their various dialects (*li-lshonotam be-arsho"tam be-goyehem*),"[16] preserve their own language and its grammatical rules. "... How much more so should this be true of the nation of Israel," whose very existence is based on its language and literature.[17] Likewise, they complain about "scholars, who speak in broken Hebrew, twittering like birds, not knowing how to properly recite or speak (*som sekhel we-habin ba-miqr"a*), or to distinguish a verb from a noun, the future from the past tense, male from female conjugation, and the like, half speaking the Arabic language (*ere"sh 'areb"a*)."[18] Moreover, parents "squander money to educate their children in foreign languages," while neglecting their own language: "Over this does the land mourn, without consolation; for no one pursues knowledge of their true language – without which no man could raise his voice, even among non-Jewish sages, nor be considered a true *ḥakham*."[19]

Similar ideas were expressed by R. Menaḥem Farḥi, who lived

---

16. In the lyrical style customary among Sephardic Jews, the apostrophe over the letter preceding the end of the word signals that the word is a lyrical expression that sounds similar to some biblical phrase. For example, *li-lshonotam be-arsho"tam* is an expression based on Genesis 10:20, and its meaning here is "dialect" (=*eresh*). Similarly, *habin ba-miqr"a* later on is based on Nehemiah 8:8, but here means "when he is reciting [a book] or conversing with someone else." So too, *ere"sh 'areb"a* is based on Jeremiah 2:6, and refers here to "the Arabic language" (=*eresh*) which is "sweet" (*'areba*) to them.
17. R. Shaul Ha-Kohen, *Leḥem Ha-Bikkurim*, (Livorno: 1870), p. 1 of "The Preface by the Great Rabbis... of the City of Tunis."
18. Ibid., p. 3 of "The Preface by the Rabbinic Author's Grandson."
19. Ibid., p. 4 of the same preface.

״שאר שפות המדוברות הולכות קדימה, ושפתנו אתנו אזלא ומדל-דלא... לזאת אמרתי אני אל לבי, הבה אנסה נא גם אנכי לסדר לפני התלמידים מחוקי משפט-השפה הקדושה בספר מיוחד, אולי יתעוררו בזה אחרים מחכמי זמננו אשר כח בהם להוציא דבר מתוקן להועיל לנערי בני עמנו.״[20]

בקשר לתחיית הלשון, יש להזכיר את הפעילות של המחנכים הספרדים להכניס את השפה העברית לתוכנית הלימודים. הרב ברוך בן יצחק מטראני (בני״ם; 1,848–1,920),[21] מגדולי הרבנים בדור שעבר, אשר הקים ב-1,866 בעיר אדרינופולי בית ספר ״מקוה ישראל,״ שם לו למטרה לעורר

״לעמי בכלל ולאחי הספרדים בתורכיה בפרט, לאמר להם: רב לכם עמי להניח באשפת החרפה וזלות השפלות את כל דברי לאומיותנו, עם, ארץ, דת, שפה, וספרות ישראל ובעליהם. עת להתעורר ולהתעודד, להרים קרן לאומנו בכל אלה, לא ע״י דברים בלבד כי אם באמצעות פעולות נכבדות ומיושבות בדרך שלום עם כחותנו מבפנים ואחינו בני האדם מבחוץ.״[22]

תוכנית הלימודים התרכזה בשמירת לשון הקודש בטהרתה. כחלק מתוכנית הלימודים, רוב פרקי התנ״ך שנלמדו בבית הספר הוצגו במחזות על ידי

20. הרב מנחם פרחי, רב פעלים, (קושטא: 1,881) עמ׳ 9

21. ראה עליו, משה דוד גאון, יהודי המזרח בארץ-ישראל, כרך ב׳, (ירושלים: תרצ״ח), עמ׳ 405–418

22. שם, עמ׳ 408

during that same period. In the introduction to his book of Hebrew grammar in Judeo-Spanish, *Rab Pe'alim,* he wrote:

> The other spoken languages are further progressing, whereas our own language is continuously losing ground... Therefore, I was determined to try to present before the students some of the principles of our holy language in a special book. In this way, perhaps some men of wisdom of our times, those who have the power to establish something that is well organized, will be able to benefit the youth of our people.[20]

With regard to the revival of the Hebrew language, mention should be made of the attempts of the Sephardic educators to introduce the Hebrew language into their curricula. R. Barukh b. Yiṣḥaq Miṭrani (*BaNI"M*; 1847–1919),[21] one of the greatest rabbis of the previous generation, who established the "Miqve Yisrael" school in 1865 in the city of Adrianople, set for himself the goal of inspiring

> my people in general and my Sephardic brethren in Turkey in particular, saying to them: That's enough, my people, of laying to disgrace and contempt all our national matters – people, land, Law, language, and Jewish literature and its authors. The time has come to wake up and be encouraged, to raise our nation's crown in all these things, not only in words, but in action, but through serious and deliberate actions that are peaceful both amongst ourselves from within, and with our fellow human beings from without.[22]

His curriculum centered around preserving the holy language in its pure form. As part of the curriculum, most of the biblical episodes

---

20. R. Menaḥem Farḥi, *Rab Pe'alim,* (Constantinople: 1880), p. 8.
21. For more on R. Barukh b. Yiṣḥaq Miṭrani, see Moshe David Gaon, *Yehude ha-Mizraḥ be-Ereṣ Yisrael,* vol. 2, (Jerusalem: 5695 [1935]), pp. 404–417.
22. Ibid., p. 407.

תלמידי הכיתה. ההצגות נערכו באולם הקריאה והמחזות מהמקרא עובדו על ידו. הוא גם חיבר ספרים יסודיים בחינוך, שמטרתם להפיץ ידיעת לשוננו בין התלמידים. (רובם עדיין בכתב יד.) יצאו לאור: חנוכי בני״ם, (וינה: 1,878); אמן פדגוג, (וינה: 1,872); פרחי מדע, תרגומים שונים ממיטב הספרות העולמית, (וינה: 1,874); ודון יוסף ובתו, (וינה: 1,879). כמעט עד שנותיו האחרונות הקדיש הרב ברוך מטראני את כל כוחותיו לחנך את בני ישראל ולנטוע בלבם אהבת התורה, הלשון והלאום.

מחנך מעולה, שגם הוא פעל גדולות למען החייאת השפה העברית בבית הספר היהודי, היה הרב בן ציון טראגאן (1,871–1,929). הוא ניהל את עבודתו החינוכית בבית הספר היהודי באלכסנדריה. כמה מחיבוריו הוקדשו למקצוע החינוך העברי. ביניהם יש לציין ״שפת ציון,״ בשני חלקים, (נא אמון: 1,918) שזכה לכמה מהדורות.

באותה תקופה נוסדו כמה כתבי עת בעברית, כגון ״כרמי,״ ״כרם,״ ״דובב משרים,״ ועוד.

לבסוף יש להעיר, כי הרבנים הספרדים לא ראו בעין יפה את התוכן ואת הצורה של תחיית השפה והספרות העברית החדשה אצל משכילי אירופה. מחיצה של מושגים שונים, באשר לטיב תחיית השפה והספרות, הפרידה בין מחנה הספרדים והאשכנזים. כתוצאה מזה, בחרו הרבנים הספרדים להסתייג מפעולה. הרב אליהו בכור חזן (1,846–1,909), מגדולי הרבנים בדור ההוא, היה אחד המנהיגים המעולים בקרב הרבנים ואנשי התרבות בקהילות הספרדיות. הוא פעל גדולות כדי לקרב את מחנה הספרדים והאשכנזים זה לזה. דעתו באשר לטיב הספרות והלשון העברית החדשה, מסכמת את

studied in school were re-enacted in student plays. The plays were performed in the reading room and the scenes from the Bible were adapted by R. Miṭrani himself. He also authored elementary books in education, the goal of which was to propagate knowledge of our language among the students. (Most of these books are still in manuscript form.) Published works include: *Ḥinnukhe BaNI"M* (Vienna: 1877); *Amon Pedagog*, (Vienna: 1871); *Pirḥe Madda'*, various translations of the best of world literature, (Vienna: 1873); and *Don Yosef wu-Bitto*, (Vienna: 1878). Until his final years, R. Barukh Miṭrani devoted all his energy to educating the children of Israel and implanting in their hearts love for the Tora, the Hebrew language, and the Jewish nation.

Another excellent educator, who also worked hard to revive the Hebrew language in Jewish schools, was R. Ben-Zion Ṭaragan (1870–1928). He conducted his pedagogical work at the Jewish school in Alexandria. Several of his works were dedicated to the subject of Hebrew education. Among them, it is worth noting *Sefat Zion*, in two volumes, (Alexandria, Egypt: 1917), which was reprinted in multiple editions.

During that period, several Hebrew magazines were established, such as *Karmi, Kerem, Dobeb Mesharim*, among others.

Finally, it should be noted that the Sephardic rabbis did not approve of the content and form used by the European Jewish-Enlightenment thinkers in their revival of the Hebrew language and in their new Hebrew literature. The Sephardic and Ashkenazic camps were conceptually divided regarding the character of the language's revival and of its literature. As a result, the Sephardic rabbis chose to avoid participating. R. Eliyahu Bekhor Ḥazzan (1845–1908), one of the greatest rabbis of his generation and one of the Sephardic communities' greatest rabbinic leaders and cultural figures, worked hard to bring the Sephardic and Ashkenazic camps closer together. His opinion on the character of the modern Hebrew language and of its literature sums up the outlook

השקפותיהם של הרבנים ואנשי התרבות שבאותה התקופה. בספרו "זכרון ירושלים," גילה את לבו על נושא זה:[23]

"היום הזה רבו דוברי צחות בעמינו ובערי אלהינו, אך לא כל איש־שפתים יצדק. על רבים מהם קרא בגרון בן חלקיהו: 'לשוא עשו, עט שקר סופרים!'"

הרב חזן הבחין בלשונם הספרותית חוסר שורשים, כאילו שפתם ריקה היא מכל תוכן של ממש.

"יעשו שקר בנפשם להשמיע משל ומליצה, על דברים שלא יהגו בלבבם."

בעיניו, הסופרים האלה מנותקים מן העם היהודי, ושואבים את רעיונותיהם מספרי מליצות שכבר נס לחם זה דורות רבים.

"הם יושבים ספונים בביתם, ושולחנם המלא ספרי חידות מני קדם והחר'ז והמסגר"[24] לפניהם לפח, ישימו קטורה באפם, אבק נחירים [= סיגריה] ומעלה עשן בפיהם, ויעל עשנם כעשן הכבשן לעור עיני פקחים!"

הם לא ידעו לדבר בשפת העם, וחסר להם ידע בהבנת עומק הלשון, בהגיון המיוחד שלה ובניבים ובמושגים הספרותיים שבכתבי עם ישראל.

"הם לא ניסו הצג כף ידיהם על הגליון לדבר כלשון עמם. הדר שפתנו העמוקה לא חזו עיניהם, ההגיון ביפעת קדשו לא ידעו ולא יבינו, דרך החרוזית החסידה לא ידעו."

---

23. הרב אליהו בכור חזן, זכרון ירושלים, (ליוורנו: תרל'ד), עמ' 39–40

24. על פי מלכים ב כד:טז; כלומר ספרי חרוזים.

of the rabbis and cultural figures of that period. In his book *Zikhron Yerushalayim,* he revealed his thoughts on this matter:[23]

> There is nowadays a proliferation of eloquent speakers among our nation in God's cities. But not all articulate people speak truth. [Jeremiah] b. Ḥilqiyya cried out against many of them (cf. Jeremiah 8:8): "Their work is futile, the penmanship of dishonest scribes!"

R. Ḥazzan recognized a lack of traditional roots in their literary language, as if their speech was empty of any substantial content.

> They lie to themselves in producing parables and lyric, regarding things about which they have no clue.

In his view, these writers are disconnected from the Jewish people, drawing their ideas from outdated books of lyric.

> They sit tucked away in the comfort of their homes, their tables full of ancient books of riddles and rhymes (*ha-ḥere"z weha-masger*),[24] ensnaring them, incense permeating their nostrils and cigarette-smoke their mouths, as the smoke they produce rises like that of a furnace, blinding the clear-sighted!

They do not know to speak with the mannerisms of their own nation, as they lack understanding of the language's depth, of its unique resonance, and of the idioms and literary concepts found in the writings of the people of Israel.

> When putting their pen to paper, they are not accustomed to speaking as their nation does. Their eyes have never seen the beauty of our profound language, its resonance in all its

23. R. Eliyahu Bekhor Ḥazzan, *Zikhron Yerushalayim,* (Livorno: 1874), pp. 38–39.
24. A reference to II Kings 24:16, here meaning books of rhyme.

ומכאן חוסר ההתאמה בין מה שהם כותבים לבין מה שהם רוצים להגיד.

"נעו מעגלותיהם מרעיוניהם" - בלשונו של הרב, ואע"פ כן -"ובקהל סופרים ירבו דברים, ועל רום תפארת השפה ירבו מליצה, ידברו ולבם בל עמם!"

הרב רואה שהשכלתם של הסופרים האלה לקויה היא בעיקרה, ובכל זאת הם שמים עצמם לשופטי הספרות של עם ישראל.

"בארח דעת והכשר חכמה לא אחזה רגלם, שביבי קדשה לא בערו בכליותיהם, ועל חן תפארתה ירימו ראש ויתנבאו ולא יספו, יביעו ידברו, ומליציהם יענו! לא יבושו כי ידברו בגאוה ובוז, כי ידם תעוז להם, וכי לשונם עט סופר מהיר. גם ירהיבו עז בלבבם, לדבר גבוהה גבוהה על כל מליצה רמה ונשגבה!"

מעתה, להתמרמרותו על מצב הלשון והספרות בימיו:

"הה! לבי למליצי הזמן יזעק, ידכה ישוח. על השפה הרוממה ורחבה מני ים תאבל נפשי: המו מעי, חם לבי בקרבי ואש עצורה בעצמותי. איפה באו צעירים וחיללוה פרצו בה פרצות וישימו אותה למדרס רגל,

> sacred splendor they never knew or understood, nor are they familiar with the elegant style of rhyme.

Hence the discrepancy between what they write and what they would like to say.

> Their actions veer off from their inner thoughts [in R. Ḥazzan's language. Yet even so] They speak verbosely in the presence of sages. Regarding the glorious stature of the language, they lyricize excessively; they speak, but they do not mean what they say!

R. Ḥazzan recognizes that the education of these writers is fundamentally flawed, yet nevertheless they appoint themselves as the judges of the literature of the people of Israel.

> Never have they walked in the path of knowledge, the cultivating of wisdom; [the language]'s flames of sanctity never burned within them. By virtue of its charmful glory, they lift their heads up high with arrogance. They ramble to no end, chatter without pause, proclaiming their lyricisms! They unashamedly claim with hubris and contempt that their strength is self-made, their language that of an expert scribe's pen. They even have the audacity to utter speech more high falutin than any lyric, however lofty or sublime!

And now, for his resentment over the state of the Hebrew language and literature in his day:

> Alas! My heart cries out for the lyric of yore, crushed and bowed in sorrow. My soul mourns for the lofty language more expansive than the sea: my innards yearn, my heart grows hot within me, a fire rages in my bones. Who are these youth who have come and desecrated the language, who have made

> ובמושב זקנים יתהללו, כי ידם רב להם וימינם תעשה חיל. הוי נבו־
> נים נגד פניהם! מי יתן החרש תחרישון, ותהי לכם לתהלה ולכבוד."

חבל שחוזי תחיית הלשון משני המחנות לא זכו אז להביא לאיחוד גמור
את כל עם ישראל על־ידי חזיונם הנשגב אשר חזו.

> Their actions veer off from their inner thoughts [in R. Ḥazzan's language. Yet even so] They speak verbosely in the presence of sages. Regarding the glorious stature of the language, they criticize excessively; they speak, but they do not mean what they say!

R. Ḥazzan recognizes that the education of these writers is fundamentally flawed, yet nevertheless they appoint themselves as the judges of the literature of the people of Israel:

> Never have they walked in the path of knowledge, the cultivation of wisdom; [the language's] flames of sanctity never burned within them. By virtue of its charmful glory, they lift their heads up high with arrogance. They ramble to no end, chatter without pause, proclaiming their lewdness! They unashamedly claim with hubris and contempt that their strength is self-made, their language that of an expert scribe's [illegible] pen. They even have the audacity to utter speech [illegible] however lofty or sublime!

And now, for his resentment over the state of the Hebrew language and literature in his day:

> Alas! My heart cries out for the lyric of yore, crushed and bowed in sorrow. My soul mourns for the lofty language more expansive than the sea; my innards yearn, my heart glows hot within me, a fire rages in my bones. Who are these youth who have come and desecrated the language, who have made

> breaches in it and left it to be trodden upon? They even boast in the assemblies of elders of their great accomplishments and of their self-made success. Woe to the wise men sitting before them! If only the deaf would stay silent; that, for you, would be dignified and honorable.

It is a pity that the visionaries of the Hebrew language's revival, from both camps, did not succeed back then, through their grand vision, in bringing about the complete unification of the entire nation of Israel.

# Columbus: Mystic, Zionist

*Judaism* 25, 1976

## I.

Columbus (died in Valladolid on May 20, 1506) is a man shrouded in mystery. On the one hand, he is the most important individual in modern history: single handedly he changed the face of the globe. On the other hand, little is known about his background and early life. There is a twofold reason for this mystery. First, Columbus and his contemporaries deliberately clouded highly significant biographical data. Second, modern historians went out of their way to exclude key phrases used by Columbus and his contemporaries and glossed over documentary evidence concerning crucial aspects of his biography and beliefs. What is commonly taught about him is neither consistent with, nor stands up to, critical investigation. The data offered by historians does not jive with the information given by Columbus about himself, or with what his contemparies in Spain said. To avoid asking plain questions about the history and life of the great Discoverer, specialists perform all types of mental acrobatics. Both the cryptic character of Columbus' life and modern scholarship coincide in their efforts to becloud his biography; the motivation springs from a single source: prejudice. An investigation of the documentary evidence, particularly what Columbus wrote, shows that the great Discoverer came from a Jewish background. Américo Castro had shown that at the time of Columbus and throughout much of Spanish history, to acknowledge the Jewish background of anyone credited with a major contribution was anathema. Steeped in deep prejudice, Spanish historians – past and present – piously conceal the Jewish background of some of the most important minds to have graced the Iberian Peninsula.[1] For this type of historian, to acknowledge the Jewish ancestry of someone who made a monumental contribution to the development of Spain would be tantamount to a national disgrace. It took the efforts of Américo Castro and his students in America, of Marcel Bataillon and his school in France, and of a few intrepid souls in Spain, to show the enormous contributions made by people with Jewish ancestry in the religious, cultural, and scientific life of Spain.[2]

We will now proceed to probe into Columbus's biography. First, although he may have been born in Genoa, Italy, his background was *not* Italian.[3] Specifically, he did not know Italian as a first language. His numerous notes and marginal comments are either in Spanish or Latin. His entire correspondence, including what he wrote to his brother Bartolomé, who was from Genoa, and to Nicolo Oderigo, the Genoveese Ambassador to Castille, was in Spanish, not Italian. Furthermore, the grammatical and spelling errors made by Columbus in Latin are those of someone who speaks and thinks in Spanish, not of someone speaking Italian as a first language.[4] Concerning this fundamental issue, Cecil Roth remarked:

---

1. See my "Don Quixote: Talmudist and Mucho Más," *RRJ* 4 (2001), 139–157.
2. See my *In the Shadow of History: Jews and Conversos at the Dawn of Modernity* (Albany: SUNY, 1986).
3. Although this statement may appear self-contradictory to people living in a modern society, up until recent times it was not uncommon for the descent of foreigners in general, and people with a Jewish background in particular, to be regarded as aliens and be culturally and linguistically disconnected from their country of birth.
4. See Salvador de Madariaga, *Christopher Columbus* (New York: Macmillan

> Moreover, though a mass of documents written by him have survived, there is not the slightest evidence that he wrote Italian. The one document that may be brought up as evidence against this is in fact a comic concoction of Italian, Castilian and Portuguese, in which Italian words are not even in the majority. Even when he communicated with the Bank of St. George in Genoa, he used Spanish. What was more, he spoke and wrote Spanish before he came to Spain, for marginal notes from his hand, clearly dated 1481, are in that language.[5]

While in Italy, the name of the great Discoverer was "Colombo," a common appellation in Jewish onomastic. In Judeo-Spanish, *Colombo* translates as 'pigeon,' the Hebrew *yona*.[6] Indeed, the last Chief Rabbi of Leghorn before World War II was R. Samuel Colombo (1868–1923).

A final note concerning Columbus's linguistic background. He and his brother were accused of writing in "unknown characters."[7] Probably, this script was used to protect sensitive material in case it fell into enemies' hands. The script could not be the common Hebrew alphabet, as this would have been immediately recognized. Most probably, it was written in the cursive Hebrew script, known in Judeo-Spanish as *media letra* (Hebrew: *ḥaṣi qolmos*), a kind of short-hand script used by Sepharadim to write Hebrew, Arabic and Judeo-Spanish.

Summing up our discussion so far: An investigation of Columbus's linguistic background clearly shows that his first language was Spanish, and that he did not know Italian sufficiently well to maintain a correspondence in that language. This situation strongly suggests that his family was one of many Jewish families that escaped Spain after the massacres taking place during the last hundred years before the Expulsion in 1492, settling in Italy. Originally, the family name

Company, 1940), pp. 50–51.

5. Cecil Roth, *Personalities and Events in Jewish History* (Philadelphia: Jewish Publication Society, 1953), p. 197.
6. See ibid., pp. 203–05.
7. See *Christopher Columbus*, p. 349.

may have been "Colón" or "Colóm,"[8] a name that he used upon his return to Spain.

## II.

It is a remarkable fact that *all* of Columbus's supporters in the Spanish Court and close associates had Jewish background.[9] Special mention should be made of Fray Diego de Deza, the future bishop of Jaen and Palencia, Archbishop of Seville and Inquisitor General of Castile and Aragon. He was one of the main forces making sure that the Queen would grant Columbus's requests.[10] An important friend and strong supporter was the *converso* Andres Cabrera. His wife, Beatriz, was one of the closest and most intimate friends of the Queen. In a famous *copla* of the time, he was referred to as the "son of Pedro Lopez de Madrid, in Cuenca, Rabbi David."[11] Another highly influential friend was the *converso* Juan Cabrero, Chamberlain and confidant of King Ferdinand.[12]

The two high officers supporting Columbus in the Court, were Jewish. Gabriel Sánchez was the General Treasurer, and Luis de Santangel was the equivalent of the Minister of Finance. Before his conversion, Santangel's name was Azaria.[13] In the house of his first cousin, also named Luis de Santangel, was planned the assassination of Arubes, the first Inquisitor General of Spain.[14] Our Santangel and his family were always suspected of being secretly Jewish. On May

8. Concerning the possible Catalan origin of the Spanish name 'Colón' see R. Carrera Valls, *Los Catalanes Juan Caboty Cristobal Colom* (Barcelona: Impresa Altes, 1931).
9. See ibid., p. 154; and Cecil Roth, *The Jewish Contribution to Civilization* (London: The East and West Library, 1956), pp. 63–65.
10. See *Christopher Columbus*, pp. 49, 155.
11. Ibid., p. 163.
12. Ibid.
13. See ibid. pp. 60, 61.
14. See ibid.

30, 1497, in reward for his services to the Crown, the king granted Santangel and his children Fernando, Gerónimo, Alfonso, and Luisa, an official decree protecting them from any charges of heresy or apostasy. A special admonition was issued to the Inquisition of Valencia not to molest Santangel or any of his descent.[15] Finally, there were two prominent Jews in the Court, Abraham Senior and R. Isaac Abarbanel, who used their influence to champion Columbus's cause in the Court.[16] Diego de Deza introduced him to the most distinguished scientific mind of the time, the famous Jewish astronomer R. Abraham Zacuto.[17] R. Abraham Zacuto threw his scientific reputation behind the great Discoverer and fully supported his enterprise.

The standard version, depicting Columbus as an Italian newcomer, struggling alone in the Spanish Court, is impossible. No one could have assembled a powerful circle of friends like that mentioned above in three years. Like much that was circulated about Columbus, the story that the Queen had pawned her jewels is false. Neither the Queen nor the King had the funds for such an enterprise.[18] It was Santangel who advanced 1,140,000 *maravedis* to carry on Columbus's plan. Modern Spanish historians, eager to discredit anyone with Jewish ancestry, fabricated the story that he received 17,000 *maravedis* in interest for this loan. The allegation was proven false.[19 20 21] Remarkably, Columbus first announced the discovery of the New World to Luis de Santangel, *not* to the Spanish monarchs!20

After examining some of this data, a prominent Spanish historian concluded:

15. Ibid., pp. 124–25.
16. Ibid., p. 52.
17. See *The Jewish Contribution to Civilization*, p. 63.
18. See *Christopher Columbus*, p. 74.
19. Ibid., pp. 74–9.
20. Ibid., p. 100.
21. Ibid., pp. 162–62.

> [I]t is impossible to say that Colón was unknown and that he lacked friends at the Court. Later events are to show so imposing an array of powerful officials and members of the royal household on his side that it is difficult to see how Colón could be utterly devoid of some kind of a link with most of them just three years early. These friendships could not all have sprung up by a miracle at the last moment.21

In conclusion: Columbus had strong contacts with, and counted the support of *conversos* and Jews. Many of Columbus's crew were Jewish. To mention just a few: the interpreter Luis de Torres; Alonso de la Calle, who died on the island of Spañola in 1503; Rodrigo Sánchez de Segovia, a relative of Gabriel Sánchez; and the ship physician Maestre Bernal.

## III.

Columbus trusted Jewish scientific knowledge. Before Columbus nobody tried transoceanic travel, simply because sailors had no means by which to fix their position. Zacuto's *Almanach Perpetuum* made possible to determine the exact position from any place, at any time of the year; thus opening the possibility of sea exploration. Columbus used Zacuto's *Almanach Perpetuum* for his transoceanic navigation.[22] In one of his entries, Columbus acknowledged his indebtedness to this *Almanach*. Thanks to it he was able to predict an eclipse of the moon on February 29, 1504 and save his life and that of the crew.[23] An important instrument used by Columbus was the quadrant, invented by the famous R. Levi ben Gershom (1288–1334). The instrument,

---

22. For a glimpse on Zacuto's contribution to maritime navigation, see *The Jewish Contribution to Civilization*, pp. 65-67.
23. See *Cristobal Colón: Textos y documentos*, ed. Consuelo Varela (Madrid: Alianza Universidad, 1982), p. 262.

named "Jacob's Staff," served to determine the exact latitude and local hour from any place in the world, including the sea.[24]

Columbus was one of the greatest seamen of all time. A pivotal point of his enterprise was the theory that there were indeed new lands to discover. What was the basis for this theory? Columbus did not premise his theory on standard scientific observations, but, rather, on Isaiah's "the new earth" (66:22). In a letter addressed to the Spanish monarchs in 1501, he stated:

> I already told you that for the execution of the enterprise of the Indies I did not take advantage of reason, mathematics, or world maps; plainly, it was a fulfillment of what Isaiah [66:22] had said.[25]

A crucial element for the feasibility of his project was his thesis concerning the duration of the journey. Rejecting the authority of Marinus, Ptolemy and Toscanelly, the most prestigious scientists of the time, Columbus maintained, on the basis of *Esdras* 4:6, that the distance between Spain and the New World was only 2550 miles, not 8159.[26] To ascertain his absolute conviction on the validity of this information, this master seaman took provisions for only 2550 miles.[27]

Columbus was a superb seaman. For reasons unknown to us, he chartered what in fact was the best possible route. He chose the 28th parallel, faithfully and obstinately. He first sailed north east until he reached the Azores, and then at the Canary Islands he headed westward, thus discovering the two ocean routes. A modern investigator refers to this discovery as a "miracle."[28] Another monumental

24. See *The Jewish Contribution to Civilization*, pp. 56–58.
25. *Cristobal Colón*, p. 255.
26. See *Cristobal Colón*, pp. 219–20, 222; *Christopher Columbus*, pp. 100–01; and Carlos Esteban Deive, *Heterodoxia e Inquisicion en Santo Domingo* (Santo Domingo: Coleccion Ensayo, 1983), p. 19.
27. See *Christopher Columbus*, p. 327.
28. See *Christopher Columbus.*

discovery was made by Columbus on September 13. Somehow, he realized that the needle of the compass was pointing to the north west, rather than north, thus discovering the magnetic variations of the earth.[29] Obviously, Columbus was privy to a maritime tradition unknown to the West. It is reasonable to assume that he obtained this information from the Jews of Majorca. These Jews, heirs to a long scientific tradition in the fields of astronomy and mathematics, were superb cartographers and navigators. They enjoyed the highest scientific reputation, and were directly involved in the production of maps and the chartering of new routes, resulting in some of the most spectacular discoveries of the time.[30]

In conclusion, Columbus seemed to have had special regard for Jewish tradition. The conception, planning, and execution of this project were expressions of his steadfast belief in the preeminence of Jewish knowledge and Jewish scientific thought.

## IV.

We will now proceed to examine some of the behavior and ideas of the great Discoverer. Columbus was due to embark on August 2, which in that year happened to be *Tish'a be-Ab* – a day of Jewish National mourning, lamenting the Destruction of the Temple in Jersalem. Quite understandably from the Jewish point of view, but for reasons unexplained by historians, Columbus refused to leave on that day. He left the following day, Friday August 3, exactly, half an hour *before sunset*, the Jewish Sabbath. [31] As mentioned before, on the basis of *Esdras,* Columbus believed the journey to be of 2550 miles. According to this calculations he supposed he would reach land on October 12, the day which in fact he discovered the New World. It has been noted that on that year, October 12 was the day of *Hosha'na*

29. Ibid., p. 202.
30. See *The Jewish Contribution to Civilization,* pp. 59–61.
31. See *Personalities and Events in Jewish History,* p. 200.

*Rabba* – a holiday which in Jewish tradition symbolizes the apocalyptic redemption of Israel.[32]

The motivation for Columbus's discovery of the New World reveals his most intimate feelings. At the very outset we should point out that he had a contract signed by the Spanish monarchs, whereby ten percent of all his discoveries would belong to him. Manifesting deeply ingrained antisemitic feelings, Spanish historians, modern and old, accuse Columbus of greed and desire for power. Madariaga insists that these are "typically Jewish,"[33] traits peculiar to the "Jewish race"[34] appetite for gold.[35] And yet, Columbus was quite unambiguous about his reason for wanting to undertake such an enterprise and exact this payment from the Spanish monarchs. In what appears to be the first call for modern Zionism, Columbus stipulated that with the proceedings of his discoveries, he would raise a cavalry of 10,000 horsemen, and an infantry of 100,000 soldiers with the purpose of liberating Jerusalem.[36] In an unguarded moment, he wrote in his diary on Wednesday, 26 December 1492, that he hoped that the gold mine and species that he had found would help him persuade the Spanish monarchs "that within three years they would carry on and be ready to go and conquer *la Casa Sancta*."[37] The expression *Casa Sancta* (Holy House) is not Spanish. It is, however, the exact translation of the Hebrew *Bet ha-Miqdash*, designating the Temple

32. See M. Kayserling, *Christopher Columbus* (New York: Longmans, Green and Co.: 1894).
33. *Christopher Columbus*, p. 114.
34. Ibid., p. 151.
35. Ibid., pp. 90, 91, 106, 299, 301. As noted by Alexander Lee, *The Ugly Renaissance* (New York: Anchor Books, 2015), p. 298: "The very closeness of the two faiths [Christianity and Judaism] emphasized that [for Christians] the Jews would for ever be 'the other.'"
36. Quoted in Martin Fernandez de Navarrete, *Coleccion de los Viajes y Descubrimientos que hicieron por mar los espanoles*, vol. 2 (Madrid: Imprenta Real, 1825), p. 282.
37. *Cristobal Colón*, p. 101.

in Jerusalem.[38] The same hope was expressed in the famous document known as *Mayorazgo,* written by Columbus in 1498, where he stipulated that his heir should use his wealth "for the conquest of Jerusalem."[39] Columbus believed that he had been "elected" by God to undertake this mission. In a note that he wrote in 1503, during his fourth journey, he described a dream where a voice tells him:

> Since you were born, He always had a very important mission for you. When He saw you at an age that satisfied Him, wonderfully He made your name known throughout the world. The Indies, that as the richest part of the world, He gave to you as your own... and you were obeyed in many lands and you obtained honor and fame from the Christians. Did he do more for your people of Israel *(al tu pueblo de Israel)?*[40]

Columbus's position on this matter cost him dearly. The monarchs and powerful members of the Church and the Old Christian establishment were determined to dislodge the Admiral from the newly discovered territories, and have his wealth confiscated. His enemies accused him of being Jewish and demanded his dismissal.[41] With this purpose in mind, the monarchs sent Francisco de Bobadilla to "supervise" Columbus. Accompanying Bobadilla were a group of Franciscan Friars and well established Old Christians. A call was made to "Indians and *Christians*" [italics added] to rally against the Admiral. A priest in Bobadilla's entourage addressed a letter to Cardinal Cisneros in Spain, urging him to help in their fight against Columbus. Using the well known code-term "Pharao" to signal Jews, he argued that since

---

38. On the messianic ideology of Columbus, see Juan Gil, "Colón y la Casa Santa," *Historiografia y Bibliografia americanistas,* 21 (1977), pp. 125–135; A. Milhou, "Notes sur le messianism de Cristophe Colomb," *Cahiers du C. R. I. A. R.* no. 1 (Paris, 1981), pp. 121–201.
39. *Cristobal Colón,* p. 199.
40. *Cristobal Colón,* p. 199.
41. See *Heterodoxia e Inquisition en Santo Domingo,* p. 40.

the Cardinal had been instrumental in "freeing this land [i. e., Spain] from the sway of King Pharao," he should also "see that neither he [Columbus] nor any of his *nation* [italics added] ever come to these islands."[42] The term "nation" was a common appelative for Jews and "*conversos*"[43] Thus, Columbus returned home in irons.

The removal of Columbus from a position of power signaled a shift in policy towards native Americans, which culminated in the greatest genocide in recorded history.[44] Spaniards regarded native Americans as sub-human. Reflecting the Jewish position on this matter,[45] Columbus regarded the inhabitants of the New World as fullfledged humans, in no way inferior, either religiously or culturally, to Europeans. As long as he was in power, he opposed abusing the natives or taking advantage of them. Reflecting what may be properly described as the Jewish posture towards the "other," Columbus realized the moral and generous character of these people, as well as the love that they exhibited in their behavior with him and his crew. In a letter written on February 15, 1493, to Luis de Santangel, he described the high ethical standards of the natives. Once they overcame their natural shyness and fear, they were extremely amicable and generous:

> It is true, however, that once they loose that fear, they are so much free of deceit and are so generous with what they have, that it is hard to believe it unless one had seeing it. Whatever thing they may posses, if one would ask it from them, they would never say no, on the contrary they would offer it to the person, and show so much love that they would give the hearts,

---

42. See *Christopher Columbus*, pp. 355–57; *Heterodoxia e Inquisition en Santo Domingo*, pp. 40–1.
43. See *In the Shadow of History*, p. 241 note 13.
44. See my *Golden Doves with Silver Dots: Semiotics and Textuality in Rabbinic Tradition* (Atlanta, Georgia: Scholars Press, 1986), p. 44.
45. See *In the Shadow of History*, p. 7.

> whether it is something of value or of little worth, then if you would give them any thing in any manner for it they are happy.[46]

Consequently, Columbus felt that it was necessary to protect them from the abuse of Spaniards. Therefore, "I prohibited that they should be given such worthless things" in exchange for objects of value.[47]

At the same time, Columbus was convinced that if properly treated, the native Americans would become good Christians as they tilt towards the love and service of the Highness and all the Castilian nation [Latin version: *all the nations of Spain*], and they try to give that which they have in abundance and that we need.[48]

Unlike other Spaniards, Columbus did not regard native Americans to be idolatrous or religiously inferior, "They do not know any sect or idolatry, except that all believe that the power and good are in heaven."[49] He totally rejected the notion shared by his countrymen that the goodness of the natives reflected turpitude and cultural inferiority. The only difference between these people and the Spaniards, he proposed, was in their ships and they way they dress:

> And this is not because they are ignorants, but they are of very subtle genious, and men who had traveled through all those seas, and they give a good account of everything, except that they never saw people dressed or such ships.[50]

Upon the removal of Columbus from power, Spain initiated a racist policy unprecedented in recorded history. People "polluted" (*impuros*) with even partial non-Christian blood, be it Jewish or Moor, were forbidden to come to the New World. A policy of genocide – the largest both in terms of absolute and relative numbers – towards

46. *Cristobal Colón*, p. 142.
47. Ibid.
48. Ibid.
49. Ibid.
50. Ibid.

the natives was carried out with unprecedented sadism.[51] In a short time, the local native population was depleted, and there was need to export slave work from Africa. To preserve Christian "purity," the Inquisition was established throughout the Americas, thus legitimizing the persecution of people on the basis of race.

The policies of racism, persecution, violence, plain despotism and authoritarianism, lingering till the present throughout much of Latin America, is the most important legacy first initiated by Columbus's enemies.

51. See ibid., 4–5.

# From Our President

The World Institute for Sephardic Studies, a relatively young organization, was founded in 1970 and has acted ever since to meet, in three areas, the basic cultural and intellectual problems facing Sephardic communities in this country and in Israel. The WISS works to create effective organization among the various Sephardic groups, and to promote both intellectual and spiritual leadership for Sepharadim and a young Sephardic lay leadership.

Prior to the founding of WISS, there was no central Sephardic organization, no group that recognized all Sephardic problems of all the Sephardic segments, and all Sephardic opinions. We Sepharadim had neither a platform that spoke on our behalf nor a forum where all of us could meet and discuss our common concerns. One of the main objectives of the WISS has been to establish contact with all Sepharadim. We must recognize that Sepharadim were never monolithic, but were always a pluralistic community living in a pluralistic society. Therefore, in order to effect a genuine harmony and unity among us, we must include all opinions, ideologies and concerns current among us. What we strive to attain is unity of purpose, not uniformity of thought. Our spirit is one of cooperation. We must work together and help each other. We believe that it is high time for Sepharsdim in this country to reach out and try to know each other. We must speak to each other, try to convince each other and let ourselves be convinced by others. The is no valid reason for us, as Sepharadim, to be insulated from one another.

We have worked very hard in the past three years to establish an organization that would focus on and meet these needs. This year, finally, we were able to open our own office. It is not yet adequately equipped, but it is our own space. We have managed to collect and catalogue a mailing list of 18,000 names. We have received hundreds of requests for assistance. Some we were able to answer directly, some we referred to other Jewish agencies, and some we could not answer at all. But that is only the beginning. We hope that in the future we will be able to make WISS a strong, central organization which can effectively help others.

Aside from a strong, central organization, Sepharadim today are in great need of intellectual and spiritual leaders, scholars who recognize the enormous wealth and variety of the Sephardic tradition, not as outsiders but as people who have grown up in and were spiritually formed by it. They must believe in it and feel the need to transmit it to others, not as a profession but as an act of love. These scholars must grasp the complexity of our present situation – the values, the concerns, the problems affecting our youth. They must be fluent in the values of the past and the values of the present and they must know how to translate our glorious past into a vigorous present and a promising future.

Fortunately, we have been able to find such leaders. But they are too few. The need of the Sephardic community for an effective spiritual and intellectual leadership makes it an imperative for us to take the necessary measures that will ensure this quality of leadership in the near future. We examined the problem and there seemed to us to be two ways to meet this need: indirectly, by helping organizations; or directly, by helping individuals. There is no doubt that we should try to help all responsible organizations. But at the same time, it is important to realize that the problems of the Sepharadim are so complex and of such a specific nature that none of the established Jewish organizations could, by itself, adequately handle all the complexities of the Sephardic problems. Therefore, the WISS has instituted funds for scholarships. These scholarships are designed to help young men and women who are thirsty to drink of our Sephardic past and are deeply committed to Jewish life and values, and we are confident that they will grow to be a source of guidance and wisdom for all Jews.

This year we have been able to give fourteen scholarships to students who will receive a doctorate or higher degree within three years. Some will be finishing sooner. This means that in three years we will have produced fourteen top Sephardic leaders.

There is little doubt that when these Sephardic students develop intellectually, they will also improve their social and economic standings. And as their own positions improve, those of their families are certain to improve as well. No longer will they and their families be condemned to the ranks of the underprivileged. This point is of vital importance to us. We are gravely concerned with the plight of the Sepharadim in Israel.

The third problem facing Sephardic communities all over the world to which the WISS addresses itself is the lack of young Sephardic leadership. It is true that we count – and God bless them all – with important lay leaders of the Sephardic communities in this country, and have with us today perhaps their finest representative, Mr. Louis Rousso. We are very privileged. It is important to observe, however, that the Sephardic leader of today seldom has at his disposal the human resources that he needs in order to work effectively. When a moment of crisis comes, the Sephardic leader finds himself alone; very few are willing to work with him, to go down to the nitty-gritty and do the necessary work. We think that it is necessary to develop the kind of youth that will be aware of the problems facing the Sephardi communities and their leaders, youth who are committed to Sephardic life and its survival. It is essential for the well-being of our society to develop a youth that respects the leadership of its elders and is willing to work hand-in-hand with them. In order to attain this goal we have established the Young Sephardic Leadership. This movement consists of young men and women who, we hope, will be the lay leaders of tomorrow. These young men and women spend many hours of each day working for Sepharadim. As genuine Sepharadim, they respect their elders and want to work and cooperate with them. We began last year with forty such young men and women. Today we have over five hundred young members in the New York Metropolitan area. These young Sephardic men and women will eventually be the lay leaders of their respective communities. In order to produce an effective lay leadership of the future, we believe that these youngsters should be groomed in leadership and responsibility. The current practice among the Sephardic communities of not approaching men for positions of leadership until they reach their mature years is inappropriate. How can we expect that one who has had no opportunity to actively participate in the life of the community will suddenly be able to lead that community in his mature years? If we wish to have lay leaders of high quality in the future, we must prepare the ground for them today. The Young Sephardic Leadership movement of the WISS aims at this.

I would like to take this opportunity to tell you that our Young Sephardic Leadership is ready to help and assist all Sephardic communities. We believe that if we join the wisdom and expertise of our elder statesmen with the energy and vitality of the young, much can be accomplished for the benefit of all.

Let me summarize our work at the WISS: organization, scholarship and young lay leadership.

About our organization: We have been partially successful; thanks to Mr. David Barocas, we have an office. However, it is still understaffed and not properly equipped. There is much need for improvement. I hope that our office will develop in the near future with the kind of personnel and machinery needed by a genuinely effective organization.

In the area of scholarship: We have made contact with most of the Sephardic scholars the world over. In many instances, these were superficial contacts and need to be further developed. We hope to concentrate on this area and are confident that our efforts will yield positive results. We also granted fourteen scholarships in a program that is of the greatest importance and should be expanded. This year, we have already received over a hundred applications. I hope and I pray that we will be able to help most of these applicants. The more we can give now, the better and brighter our future will be.

And finally, our Young Sephardic Leadership: Our youth is terribly important. Most of our activities today are in Manhattan. However, some communities have already approached us and asked us to carry this type of activity to their communities. We will try to do it and expect to expand as much as we can.

Ours is a work of love. Our aim is to be used by the Sepharadim, rather than use the Sepharadim. I am confident that our next report will be – with the help of the Almighty – one of further progress and development. As I look at you now, Sepharadim of all different geographical backgrounds, together under one roof to discuss our future, I cannot help but feel that a very bright tomorrow is at hand for all of us.

*JOSÉ FAUR speech delivered at the annual meeting of the Board of Governors*

New York City
May 23, 1973

# The Sephardic and Oriental Communities in Israel: From Moderation to Religious Zealotry

*The Jerusalem Post*,
Friday, April 22, 1988

Traditionally, the Sephardic and Oriental communities in Israel were known for their tolerance and moderate views on both political and religious matters. Unlike Eastern European Jews, who were generally divided into two opposing camps, the "secular" and the "religious," Sepharadim never permitted this type of internal division. People on both sides of the fence were conciliatory in their views and tolerant with the dissenting party.

Religious leaders had a healthy respect for the secular establishment. They did not oppose secular education, military service or national institutions. More importantly, they did not regard modernity or material progress as a threat to Judaism and Jewish life. Most Sephardi rabbis of the last generation allowed secular education in their communities. They also respected the new sociological changes.

In an outstanding responsum, Rabbi Ben-Zion 'Uzziel, the first

Sephardic Chief Rabbi of the State of Israel, permitted women to vote and hold public office. Service in the armed forces and the defence of the state were regarded as religious duties of the highest order. There were good, well-balanced relations with the secular and less religious elements.

The secular leadership reciprocated. Unlike his Ashkenazi counterpart, the secular Sephardi never felt alienated from religion. It is a well-known fact that up to 1961, and even later, in Jerusalem and other cities, secular Sepharadim would attend Sabbath services in the morning before going to watch the football game in the afternoon.

Extremism on either side was unheard of. Indeed, many Ashkenazim admired the Sepharadim for their religious and political tolerance, and taunted their own communities for not following the Sephardi example.

This scenario has changed radically. In the last few years, Sephardi communities in Israel and the Diaspora have been swept by an unprecedented religious fervour, and are becoming more and more intolerant and extremist.

The large Sephardic *yeshivot,* such as Porat Yosef, Qol Ya'aqob and Ḥazon 'Obadia, are now controlled by ultra-Orthodox extremists. Students coming out of these institutions are more interested in changing the religious and political structure of the community than in teaching.

Since many Sephardic synagogues depend on these and similar institutions for religious guidance, the average Sephardi, particularly in Israel, is becoming deeply involved in religious extremism. Let me illustrate with an event that borders on the comic, but nonetheless reflects the new ideology.

Last summer, staying in Jerusalem, I regularly attended a Sephardi synagogue. One afternoon, a group among the congregation was agitated because the young man invited to conduct the services wore only a *kippa* in the street and not a regular hat. One of them with total disregard for the rabbi of the synagogue, got up and delivered a homily. His point was that Aaron, the high priest of Israel, had (I am quoting) a *migba'at gedola,* a large hat, and therefore it is improper for anyone to serve as a *ḥazzan* unless he, too, wears a large hat! Another charged that the man in question also had a TV set in his house. An eye witness told me that a few weeks ago, a group of students from Ḥazon 'Obadia, interrupted the Sabbath services of the same synagogue, shouting *apiqoros* (heretic) and other insults at the religious leaders.

Such scenes would have been impossible half a decade ago.

Harassed by religious terrorists and ultra-fanatics, moderate Sephardi religious leaders are intimidated and fearful of reprisals. Those who dare to speak up are branded as heretics and subjected to slander and character assassination.

What is happening? A historical perspective would be helpful in understanding the situation.

From the dawn of Zionism, the Sephardi communities failed to set up a modern organization that would enable them to participate effectively within the Jewish world, and promote their own specific interests and values. The reasons for this failure were varied. They ranged from the political and economic, that came with the collapse of the Ottoman Empire, to the cultural and educational. The overriding reason, however, was that Sephardi organizations were invariably established by lay leaders along purely secular lines. The result was dismal, especially in Israel.

All the different "Oriental" parties established along ethnic and political ideologies collapsed. The Sepharadim in Israel, as well as throughout the Diaspora, refused to identify with them, and continued to support the well-established political organizations.

This situation is presently undergoing radical change in Israel, for the first time in history, Sephardi leaders are now establishing and directing political parties along religious lines. The spiritual impetus for this movement comes from Rabbi Ovadia Yosef, the former *Rishon le-Ṣion.* He is the present spiritual leader of Shas, the ultra-Orthodox party that successfully challenged Agudat Yisrael at the last elections, receiving 70,000 votes, and is now the organ for the ultra-Orthodox

Sepharadim. (Another Sephardi religious party, Tami, competes against the NRP, representing a more liberal view.)

There are three specific factors contributing to the success of the ultra-Orthodox movement.

First, it was established by religious leaders. Accordingly, they were able to use the Sephardi *Yeshiva,* supported by all the communities throughout the Diaspora, and its fund-raising apparatus, as the basis for their political activities and organization. Since, in many instances, the fundraising campaign is conducted by the rabbi, under the auspices of the synagogue (e.g., the Sephardi synagogue in Deal, NJ), the average Sephardi Jew in the U.S. is persuaded that he is contributing to some religious institution rather than to a political party. And indeed, for income-tax purposes, they are listing it as a religious contribution. At the same time, the religious leaders are able to reach the Sepharadim who traditionally voted for the NRP and Agudat Yisrael.

Secondly, in order to tap Sephardi religiosity, as well as the frustration with the religious parties of the establishment, these leaders attacked the NRP and Agudat Yisrael for their lack of genuine religiosity. This attack was launched from the perspective of the extreme right.

Thirdly, as a consequence, the Sepharadim soon found themselves aligned with the *Ḥaredi* movement, under the control of Menachem Shach, opposing the State of Israel, Zionism, and anything to do with the secular and modern world. Inspired by this ideology, the new Sephardi found himself on the side of extremism, and against both the religious and the political establishment.

Psychologically, this position was particularly attractive to the Israeli Sephardi, as it provided him with an avenue for venting his long frustration with both the religious and the secular establishment.

In an article in *Les Temps Sepharades* last December, Prof. Moshe Bar Ascher of the Hebrew University pointed out how these Sepharadim model their religious institutions and outlooks according to ultra-Orthodox ideology: "In fact they have adopted all the concepts, particularly those of Hungarian Jews." Thus, they refuse to serve in the IDF, to celebrate Independence Day and other national holidays, and have become highly intolerant of Jews of other persuasions.

This new situation has brought about a radical change in the role of the Sephardi rabbi. The strength (as well as the weakness) of the traditional rabbi was the fact that he consistently refused to get involved in any form of politics. With the death of one of the last Talmudic luminaries of the Sephardi world, the revered Rabbi Ezra Attie, head of Yeshivat Porat Yosef, an intellectual vacuum was left at the highest institution of learning. The opportunity was seized to implement a radical change. Teachers as well as students saw their role more as political activists than as pedagogues and spiritual leaders.

In a relatively short time, many of the Sephardi *yeshivot,* led by Porat Yosef, Qol Ya'aqob and Ḥazon 'Obadia, became the mouthpieces for the new political ideology: the Sephardi institutions of higher learning became more involved in politics than education. Rabbis were evaluated in terms of political power and ideology rather than Tora-learning and personal piety. The title *Gedole Yisrael,* "the Great of Israel," never before used in Sephardi tradition, was awarded, exclusively, to the members of the political hierarchy, regardless of knowledge and personal standards: a "great" rabbi came to mean one who carries political clout. Rabbinic questions, and matters pertaining to the very essence of the Tora were treated and resolved on the basis of political expediency.

One of the consequences of this metamorphosis is the elimination of the traditional Sephardi rabbi – the *ḥakham,* or enlightened sage who embodied Tora and wisdom.

There is no doubt that some good has resulted from all this. Professor Bar Ascher pointed out how this new movement has slowed down secularization among the Sepharadim in Israel. It has also contributed to the *baale teshuva* movement, attracting many Sepharadim who had assimilated into Western culture and now seek to rediscover their Jewish roots.

On the other side of the coin, Bar Ascher noted that the Sephardi leadership "has adopted the colours and ideology of ultra-Orthodox

Ashkenazim." Many would find offensive the language and tone used in their attack against the State of Israel. In addition to their anti-Israeli and anti-Zionist diatribes, we must consider what Bar Ascher describes as their conduct "in daily life, *vis-à-vis* the non-religious, whom they treat without love or tolerance. Of particular concern is their bitter opposition to all types of general education. Again quoting the professor:

"After some time, the ḥaredim believe that all the children and young people must attend the yeshiva, without becoming involved in the [type of] learning that could produce the [future] physicians, engineers, etc... since all men, according to them, must become the prophets of God."

Professor Bar Ascher proposes that "the intellectuals must open a debate" with the ultra-Orthodox Sepharadim. But is this possible? At present, it seems highly unlikely.

Paradoxically, their very approach to Judaism and Jewish learning, so alien to the Sephardi and rabbinic tradition, makes all communication with them impossible. Instead of methodically teaching students the traditional Jewish texts, these leaders indoctrinate them with the belief that they possess the spirit of God, and have exclusive access to the truth. Indeed, by ingraining this belief in their students and followers, they have cut them off from their own tradition, from the rest of Israel, and from the study of the Tora. One cannot cite to these graduates the teachings of our rabbis, the accumulated traditions of the great sages of Israel, or the authoritative codes of Jewish law. Any idea contradicting their views – even when proceeding from the greatest sages of Israel – is automatically branded as heresy.

Last month I visited Buenos Aires. There I had the opportunity to come in contact with many of the common people, the grass-roots of the new Sephardi leaders. Upon learning of my presence, many of them came to me as a rabbi and asked me for a blessing.

When I was a young boy growing up in that same city, we would approach the rabbis and ask them to explain difficult passages of the Tora and Talmud. It seems to me that until these leaders instruct their followers to seek knowledge of the Tora and Jewish life rather than to go hunting for blessings, no meaningful dialogue can take place.

It is ironic that by subordinating the Tora to political expediency, these leaders have, in fact, betrayed the very essence of the Tora that they profess to represent.

# U.S. Policy in the Mideast: Machiavelli or Rudolph Valentino?

*The Jewish Press*, "Sephardic News," Friday, March 15, 1991

There are two possible settings that could explain current U.S. policy in the Middle East. A Machiavellian scenario would suggest that Secretary of State Baker, wanting to insure U.S. interest in the Gulf, both militarily and economically, made sure that "moderate" Iraq would get as much credit from the USA as needed to build his war machine.

With this purpose in mind, he got his friend, Senator Bob Dole, to sit with Saddam in Mosul in August 1989 to attest to his "rehabilitation." Saddam passed the test with flying colors. Senator Dole fought tooth and nail for the Iraqi dictator, dismissing the opposition as tools of Israeli and Zionist propaganda. Thus, Saddam was able to get over $4 billion dollars in credit from America.

Meanwhile the State Department turned the other cheek, while the Bank of Atlanta, in conjunction with Italy's Banco dil Lavoro – a bank with close ties to the Vatican – laundered the money we gave Saddam for "agricultural products," to pay for his military hardware.

To make sure that Saddam would not be hindered in his ambition, Baker gave the important job of Ambassador to Iraq to April Glaspie, a person with very limited qualifications, but well known for her support for any and all pan-Arabic causes. The net result is a new role for our army – U.S. military presence in the region is a foregone conclusion – and an economic boom for American companies, in the rebuilding of Kuwait. This may have been what Baker had in mind when, in an unguarded moment, he was quoted as saying that the reason for American intervention in the Gulf was "jobs!"

Although logical and self-consistent, the above scenario is too cerebral for State Department personnel. I always felt that if there is one individual responsible for our problems in the Middle East, it is Rudolph Valentino, the "king of the silent screen."

Let me explain. As a Sephardic Jew whose family was doing business with the Arabs for centuries, I was always dismayed at the romanticized notion of Arab culture and psychology promoted by our State Department. Anybody who had any personal dealings with Arabs can tell you that there is nothing romantic or noble about their life-style or value-system. Those who point to the relative good situation of Jews in Arab lands as a proof of religious tolerance, etc., forget that until the end of World War I, the political bosses of the region were the Turks and not the Arabs! Whatever good relations prevailed between Jew and Arab were the effect of the superb skills of the Jewish leadership, not of Arab "moderation."

The notion of "moderate" Arabs is an oxymoron fabricated by the Near East section of the State Department. Until yesterday, the Iraqis and the Jordanians, not to mention the P.L.O., were "moderate." Syria, who to the best available data was directly responsible for blowing up Pan Am flight 103, is today a "moderate" Arab ally. What the Iraqis did to the Kuwaitis is the minimum that any other Arab would do to any other Arab in similar circumstances. In fact, there are no differences in the patterns of thought and feelings amongst Iraqis, Kuwaitis, and Saudis. Lebanon's internecine battles represent the natural state of Arab society when not ruled by brutal dictatorship.

The only source for our State Department's views is found in the silent screen. In "The Sheik," Rudolph Valentino portrays the hero as hopelessly romantic, stately, unselfish, bountiful, loyal, and responsible. Hollywood, and the media, promoted this image in countless ways. It is this image, rather than real facts and accuracy, which govern the thinking of our policy makers. Poor Valentino! He never dreamed that "The Sheik" he portrayed would have such a deep and lasting influence in U.S. policy in the Middle East.

# The Mother of all Thanks, Anti-Jewish Invectives

## *The Jewish Press*, "Sephardic News," Friday, March 29, 1991

Arabs always complain that they are misunderstood, that somehow they are measured by canons slanted against them. Left-wing intellectuals, pan-Arabists, and the media agree. We all heard the condescending lecturing by prominent officials from the State Department with dazed expressions, high-style and a lot of hot air, explaining why we should withhold moral judgments about the Arabs. Although we were taught to believe that the rules of morality are universal, Arab supporters insist that this cannot apply when assessing the behavior of this people.

In fact, if there is one moral villain – it's Israel. Whatever may be regarded as "wrong" with the Arabs, is Israel's fault. Deep down, we are reassured by these pundits that the Arabs are jolly good fellows; if we could only eliminate Israel….

One such pundit was CBS newsman Bob Simon. From the biased way he reported the news, bending backwards to simultaneously fault Israel and sanitize the Arabs, I always suspected he was a Jew. You need a special type of uprootedness to mushroom into a Mike Wallace, an Anthony Lewis, or a Rita Hauser.

On Sunday, March 3rd, Bob Simon gave an account on the CBS

program "60 Minutes" of the harrowing experience that he and the other three members of his TV crew endured during 40 days of captivity in Iraq. They were blindfolded, held in solitary confinement, starved, and tortured. The worst moment was when an Iraqi captain grabbed Bob Simon by the face and spat at him, shouting "*Yahudi*" (Jew). I believe that this version was sanitized for public consumption.

Knowing well the Arabs, I am certain that the captain not only grabbed his face but he also made sure that Bob Simon's mouth was wide open as he spat into it. Now, don't rush to judge the captain by Western standards! Try to understand him according to his canons of propriety. So far, the media has managed to sanitize everything these misunderstood victims do – from the wanton murdering and maiming of children to the blowing up of airplanes and kidnapping. Therefore, why is it so difficult to understand that within "the mother of all cultures and civilizations," they make you swallow their sputum as they call you *Yahudi*, which is the proper manner to express to a Jew the gratitude for 25 years of slanted reporting in favor of Arab causes – Palestinian in particular.

The surreal vision of "Arab nobility" peddled by the enemies of Israel may seem exciting to those Jews who feel that the best way to prove themselves is by vilifying their own. When they are faced with the crude reality, we Jews cannot help but feel sorry for them.

At the same time, to those enamored by Arab wisdom, let us remind them of the proverb popular among Jews from Syria, *'In bizaq al-wuaḥad la-foq, 'ala wajho; la-taḥt, 'ala daqno* – (If one spits upwards, it will fall on his face; downward, it will fall on his beard). In other words, there was so much spitting towards everything Israel does, that it is not surprising that some of it backtracked!

# For The Sake of Expediency

## *The Jewish Press*, "Sephardic News," Friday, April 12, 1991

David Nassy (1747–1806), a Sephardic physician from Suriname, came to the USA in 1792, where he resided until 1795. He was the first Jew to become a naturalized U.S. citizen. In 1793, for his successful treatment of yellow fever, he became the first Jew to be elected a member of the American Philosophical Society. After returning to Suriname, he made some very interesting observations about the USA. In a book, *Lettre politico-theologico-morale sur Les Juifs* (Paramaribo, ca. 1798), he noted that the success of America was not the result of a particular political system, i.e. democracy. He pointed to democratic nations ridden by corruption and injustice, whereas some enlightened monarchies had achieved high social and political standards. In his view, what makes America unique are the people, not the political system. It is the morality of the people, the fact that Americans would not tolerate double standards, corruption at high levels, or the manipulation of values for the sake of expediency.

Without the moral fiber of her citizens, the USA would have been just another country laden with unfulfilled promises: it is the people who make the political system work, rather than the other way around.

**We are in danger of losing our moral standards.**

For the sake of expediency, the Near East section of the State Department counseled against allowing Israel, the only democratic state in the region, from participating in the liberation of Kuwait. Few believe that either Kuwait or Saudi Arabia would have preferred to remain under the grip of Saddam Hussein, than Jewish participation in the region. And if their Jewish hatred is so great, would such a people merit the spilling of a single drop of American blood?

For the sake of expediency our soldiers, Jews and non-Jews, but especially Jews, had to forfeit one of their most basic rights – the freedom to worship. Reminiscent of the Inquisition period, Jewish soldiers in the Gulf had to hide their religious symbols. The shofar could not be blown on Rosh Hashana, lest our Arab allies be offended. I wonder what decision our Supreme Court would have rendered if someone would have refused to serve under such conditions, on the grounds that it violated his or her constitutional rights. There is something ominous and foreboding when policy makers are ready to forgo the right of their citizens so as not to "offend" an "ally?"

For the sake of expediency, pressure was put on Israel to forfeit the most basic human right: the right of self-defense. Rhetoric aside, our policy makers made it crystal clear that they would not give Israel the code by which to identify her planes, therefore running the risk of being shot down by the U.S. Air Force, or what would have been infinitely more catastrophic, to shoot down one of our planes. The idea that Jews, individually or collectively, ought not to defend themselves but trust their safety to the kindness of strangers, sends chilling reverberations from a not too distant past

For the sake of expediency, the same policy makers advised our president to shake the bloodiest hand in the Middle East – that of president Hafez al-Assad from Syria.

For the sake of expediency the same elements in the State Department altered history in order to protect one of their own, April Glaspie, the former Ambassador to Baghdad. The new official line is that somehow our Ambassador had warned Saddam not to invade Kuwait, where in fact Assistant Secretary John Kelly had confirmed the accuracy of the Iraqi transcript. "The now official line," wrote William Satire of the New York Times (March 25, 1991), "is a transparent lie." And, for the sake of expediency, what have we and our Arab allies done to the Kurds? We have reneged on our implicit promises and allowed the destruction of thousands of souls.

# Loving Enemies and Stabbing Innocents

## *The Jewish Press*, "Sephardic News," Friday, April 26, 1991

Jews are often taunted for not loving the enemy. Nietzsche strongly objected to those passages in the Hebrew Scriptures, particularly the Psalms, where victims raise their voices in anger, pledging never to forget or forgive. Why could Jews not be 'evangelic' and let bygones be bygones? The Rabbis, who were superb psychologists, explained, "Whoever is compassionate with the cruel, would end up being cruel with the compassionate… Whoever becomes compassionate with cruel people, would end up falling down under them" (I used the version in Midrash Shemuel, Cracow 5653, p. 100, n. 8). The message is clear – those who love the enemy and are forgiving of the heartless and vicious, will eventually adopt their psychological traits and methods. Anna Freud, in *The Ego and the Mechanism of Defense* (New York: International Universities Press, 1946), called attention to the fact that victims often surrender part of their personality, adopting that of their foe.

In a forthcoming book, *In the Shadow of History: Jews and Conversos at the Dawn of Modernity* (New York: SUNY, 1992), I argue that in Judaism, "hating" the enemy acted as a defense mechanism, sparing the people from absorbing the values and personalities of the persecutors. By "forgiving the enemy," Christianity ended up absorbing the worst psychological traits and methods of the Roman Empire. Soon, Christianity perceived itself as the Roman Church. The "triumph" of Christianity meant that it now could switch roles, and persecute others as ruthlessly as the Romans once persecuted them.

Arabs hated and will always hate the United States, as well as all political systems standing for democracy and freedom. The Arabists in the State Department know this well. Nasser of Egypt, Syria, Iraq, Yemen, et al, were staunch supporters of the USSR. It was not merely a matter of interest but also of ideology: all of them are bitter enemies of democracy and freedom and favor despotism and authoritarianism. Arab "friendship" with the USA is a direct result of the collapse of the communist system. Following the logic of "love thine enemy," our boys at the State Department rushed to embrace the Arab nations.

We are beginning to pay the price. We are witnessing the worst moral debacle in our history. The reason why we are reneging on our promise and letting two million Kurds be decimated and dislocated by Saddam is not what you hear in the media. The official pretext that we won't intervene in the "internal affair" of a sovereign country, offends our intelligence. Our government never felt coy about intervening in Grenada and Panama. Worse, to protect Palestinian terrorists and political agitators, we persistently and consistently intervene in the internal affairs of Israel. The reason why our government is not helping the Kurds is quite simple. All of our new friends, Syria, Kuwait, Saudi Arabia, and Egypt, are as ruthless and oppressive with their own minorities as Iraq. There is no difference between the treatment of Kurds by Iraq, and of the Shiites and other minorities by the Kuwaitis, Saudis, Syrians, etc. American intervention on behalf of the Kurds would mean recognizing the rights of oppressed minorities, and the beginning of the end of the only type of government our new "allies" believed in: enslavement and despotism. Thus, the USA caved in to the demands of our "allies" and reneged on our promise. The morality of our "Desert Storm" campaign is gone with the wind. To help

760,000 Kuwaitis, we are sacrificing close to 2,000,000 innocent souls! Does it make any sense to you? "Go, tell it to the Kurds!"

A final point. The claim of respecting the "internal" affairs of countries committing atrocities against their citizens is particularly painful to us Jews, during this time as we are remembering the *Shoah*. Since our President has publicly and repeatedly compared Saddam to Hitler, his policy of non-intervention is a reaffirmation of the policy of "enlightened" Western nations refusing to halt Hitler's massacre of the Jews, on the grounds that this would constitute interfering in the "internal affairs" of another nation.

By loving our enemies we ended up stabbing many innocent people in the back. I don't mean the Israelis and other foreigners, but as Americans, from the founding fathers to every Joe and Jane, who believe in the tenets of morality and fair play upon which this great nation of ours stands.

# Facing The Enemy: Eyeball to Eyeball

## *The Jewish Press,* "Sephardic News," Friday, May 24, 1991

Rabbi Jacob Israel Algazi (1680–1756) of Izmir, Turkey, was recognized as the highest authority in all branches of Jewish studies; Talmud, jurisprudence, and mysticism. Because of his mastery of the esoteric aspects of the Tora, he was appointed head of Bet-El in Jerusalem, the most prestigious Academy of Mysticism in the Sephardic world. He was also the head of Neve Shalom, the finest Rabbinic Academy of the time. From that school graduated many outstanding Talmudists. Prominent among them were his son, Rabbi Yom Ṭob Algazi (1727–1802), and one of the greatest luminaries of all time, R. H. Y. D. Azulay (1724–1806). Finally, he was the *Rishon le-Ṣion,* Chief Rabbi of the Holy Land, representing the highest legal authority among the Sepharadim.

Rabbi Algazi was a superb expounder of the Scriptures. In one of his lectures he noted that Isaiah's verse, "Every instrument to be designed against you will not be effective, and every tongue that will stand up against you in judgment, you will convict" (Isa. 54:17) is not symmetric. In the first part, the instruments of war designed to destroy the Jewish people will fail, without the participation of the people. The second part is a commandment urging the active participation of the people. The term *tarshi'i* ("you shall convict") is an imperative to expose the *rish'ut* ("evilness") of our enemies for all to see.

We have been lax in this duty.

For the first time in our long history, we enjoy the freedom to answer our detractors. America is a free and pluralistic democracy. Within the American system it is not only a privilege, but our civic duty to expose our enemies for what they really are. It is high time for us, American Jews, to assume this responsibility, and face those directing the psychological onslaught against Israel. If there is one thing that the American public does not tolerate it is a warped sense of morality. Within this context, several issues come to mind.

Case in point. Consider the hero's welcome accorded to General Norman Schwarzkopf. It was well deserved. I, for one, greatly admire his conduct and demeanor – like a true champ – and applaud his brilliance and courage. Now compare the treatment of this hero with the vituperation with which Ariel Sharon was received in this country after his no less brilliant campaign in Lebanon. The official excuse for abusing the Jewish hero was his "indirect responsibility" for the massacre of 500 Palestinians in Sabra and Shatila, while the Israelis were in Lebanon. What about holding General Schwarzkopf and other leaders responsible for the death, starvation, and dislocation of thousands upon thousands of innocent victims taking place under our nose in Iraq?

Another case – can you think of a better example of hypocrisy and double standards than reporter Sabra Chartrand's (New York Times, April 25, 1991) indignation at the Israeli Army's intention to demolish the house of a Palestinian who tried to kill a soldier? The running argument was that since that Palestinian had died, the punishment was doubly outrageous. Reporter Leslie H. Gelb (New York Times, April 3, 1991) observed, "The State Department practically achieves rhetorical orgasms of condemnation every time Israel deports Palestinian terrorists. It rarely condemns the killing of Kurds and Shiites." He went on telling a story about a Kurd who said to a

Palestinian, "I envy you. When you die, at least the Arabs, the United States and the United Nations complain." The truth is more painful. For the State Department, Palestinians too, are worthless. They only count when they are killed by Israelis in self-defense. An important question that we must put forward to the American public – are our enemies moved by humanitarian concern for the Palestinian, or by malice towards Israel?

Yet another, case in point: The State Department prevented an American citizen from suing the Saudis for having tortured him. Mr. Scott J. Nelson was arrested and tortured by Saudi officials because he reported a safety hazard at one of their hospitals, thus embarrassing his Saudi superiors. A three-judge Federal appeal panel ruled that Mr. Nelson was entitled to sue the Saudi government for compensation. Other American workers have similar claims. Mr. Nelson was prevented by U.S. and Saudi officials from starting his claim in court. Reporter Neil A. Lewis (New York Times, April 23, 1991) quotes Senator Arlen Specter, saying that "it was 'appalling' that the Bush Administration would seek to prevent a United States citizen from being able to bring a claim that he was tortured." One need not be pro-Israel to see that there is something heinous when government officials side with a country torturing their own fellow citizens.

In our days, we have witnessed countless times the fulfillment of the first part of Isaiah's verse. It is high time to begin thinking about our duty to fulfill the second part of the verse.

# The President's Proposal: For or Against Israel?

## *The Jewish Press*, "Sephardic News," October 18, 1991

In his commentary to the Mishna (Abot 1:6), Maimonides (1135–1204) observed that just as we are counseled to give the benefit of the doubt to an individual known for his righteousness, in the case of an individual whose "malicious acts became public (Arabic: *wa-shuhrat*), and thereupon we see him doing something which, according to all external evidence (Arabic: *dalailatha Kulha),* indicates that it is good, we must be guarded from him and not believe [it] to be good, as long as there is a possibility that [it was done] for evil."

Maimonides supported his view with the verse, "Even when sweetening his voice don't trust him, because [he still bears] seven abominations in his heart" (Proverbs 26:25). Maimonides' view bears directly on how we are to construe President Bush's recent proposal to rescind the infamous act equating Zionism with racism. Was it designed to help Israel, or is it a ploy to further assail Jewish interests?

I am inclined to the latter, for the following reasons: First, it is a falsehood that the annexation of Jerusalem or that the settlements in the West Bank are "illegal." Whether something is "illegal" does not depend on the *fiat* of the State Department. International regulations "emanate from nations' own free will, as expressed in conventions, or by generally accepted usages" – not by what the officers of one nation declare.

Granted, a government could maintain that in its view something is contrary to international law, but that will not render it illegal. Only the World Court has compulsory jurisdiction, but only with signatory nations. In 1976, when Nicaragua went to the World Court against the USA, a signatory nation, the USA claimed first, that it had the right to interpret what is and what is not under the jurisdiction of the World Court, and second, that even if granting that said dispute fell under the jurisdiction of the Court, it still had the right to withdraw.

Second, the UN was deliberately vague, declaring that Israel will have to return "territories" – not all territories – for peace. Obviously, the precise perimeters of the term "territories" will have to be the subject of political negotiations. Since the USA has no claims on those territories, what are the grounds, either legal or moral, by which it assumes the right to impose its interpretation of the term "territories" on Israel? There is an element of cynicism in our government's claim that it does not recognize the right of conquest, when the very existence of these United States is based upon an act of conquest. Significantly, whereas in the case of the West Bank, Gaza, and East Jerusalem such conquest was in response to an act of war against the State of Israel, the USA's war against the Indian nations was purely for the sake of conquest.

Third, only a duly constituted nation could have a claim to a territory. The "Palestinians," however, never constituted a "nation." As a matter of fact, the USA has never recognized the Palestinians as a "nation," nor has it accorded to the Palestinian organizations the status of a "nation in exile." If so, how could our President claim that the Jewish settlements in the territories are illegal, because they "belong" to a "nation" which, according to the USA, does not exist? The last country to have held legal title to the land of Israel was Turkey, who lost it during World War I. England, however, never took title of the land of Israel, and occupied it as a colonial power – a status no longer recognized by international law. Therefore, whatever territory

Israel took possession of, it did so using a Hebrew legal term – *min ha-hefqer,* "from ownerless" lands.

For those who find it difficult to digest this kind of "ethical behavior," and wish to follow Maimonides' view, may I suggest two alternative interpretations to his recent proposal. It could have been designed to counter charges that the administration bears ill feelings towards Israel. In this case, eventually the President would "find" himself restrained by our "Arab allies" from pursuing this matter "at this moment." There is another, more ominous possibility. Until now, the President hasn't demanded that the UN take an "active" role in the "peace negotiations." The objective for rescinding the resolution would be the "rehabilitation" of the UN – not Israel! Is there any doubt that our President will then break his promise to Israel one more time, and demand that, in light of "the new situation," the UN should take an active role in the negotiations?

# *Sheloshim*: Rabbi Hillel Lieberman *z"l*

## *The National Jewish Post and Opinion*, October 18, 2000

I knew him as a child (he was a student at Flatbush Yeshiva, as were my children). I maintained close relations with his father, Rabbi Zvulun Lieberman, a family friend, and someone I respect both as a rabbi – one of the architects of Modem Orthodoxy – and as a man of great vision and integrity.

Rabbi Zvulun Lieberman arrived at Ben Gurion Airport Tuesday afternoon, Oct. 12. My wife, Esther, and I were among a small group waiting at the airport. He had been ill and had undergone a series of operations. I was worried for him and wondered how anyone, particularly at his age, could bear the loss of a son in such tragic circumstances. After a long wait, Rabbi Lieberman emerged. I hadn't seen him for six years. He looked older, but somehow (incredibly) taller, more erect. He was leaner, walking slowly but firmly. I noticed a cane. He was not leaning on it, but held it as if it were the staff of a patriarch. Later, I realized that I was witnessing a transformation: my good friend Rabbi Lieberman was in the process of becoming a saintly patriarch.

We embraced and exchanged some words erupting from a shared feeling of pain, pride, and longing. Jews will immediately know what I am talking about.

The next morning, Esther and I traveled aboard an armored bus from Bnei Brak to Elon More, where the funeral took place. On the bus people were very polite (my experience is probably idiosyncratic, but I find that generally *dati* and *masorati* people in Israel are friendly and easy going, both in the streets and on the highways). There was a level of intimacy, a self-conscious energy linking the passengers, as if we were all the protagonists of a full-blown novel.

The landscape was biblical. The sky above bore a different tone of blue. Not like that of Haifa, or even Jerusalem. It was more like the blue of Montana or Wyoming, pale and bright and soft and clean. The same sky you'd smell as a child, the first time that your parents took you to spend a day in the country.

When we arrived at Elon More, the funeral procession was on its way, carrying Hillel to the synagogue. After a short while the funeral eulogies began. The first speaker was Rabbi Lieberman. There was no anger in his speech. The voice was low. The tone intimate, as if he were sharing with you an inward looking, inconceivable moment.

In quiet, emotional wisdom, he proceeded to describe Hillel's love for Ereṣ Israel. How, from his early childhood, he knew that his destiny lay in the land of Abraham, Isaac, and Jacob. How, immediately after graduation, he had embarked on a solitary voyage to Israel in search of a dream. How he had found and married the ideal wife, the children they bore and raised together, and the bliss that they experienced learning and teaching in the area where Jacob raised Joseph. In an attempt to fathom the source of the overwhelming feeling moving Hillel from his early childhood, Rabbi Lieberman pointed to his son's illustrious ancestry of saints and sages. Perhaps? Or was there something else, more vivid and distinctive, beyond the common and the ordinary?

Yes! It was the hand of the Almighty, before Whom, he, Rabbi Zvulun Lieberman, bowed his head, accepting His decree, fully and wholeheartedly. The last speaker was Rabbi Mordechai Eliahu. In classical rabbinic fashion he began by expounding passages bearing on the concepts of isolation and exile befalling the Jewish people, on the heinous crime perpetrated on Hillel and on the rest of Israel, on the lingering nostalgia....

Suddenly, like the patriarch Joseph whom Hillel venerated so much, Rabbi Eliahu could no longer contain his tears. (Those who know Rabbi Eliahu would concur that underneath the razor-sharp mind of this distinguished halakhist kindles a soul, pure and unspoiled.) Sobbing like a child, he proceeded to delineate the incongruous events, the betrayed dreams and spiritual dislocations landscaping Israel. He finished with a cry of hope for national regeneration and salvation. It was an electrifying moment. As we left the synagogue I embraced Rabbi Lieberman for the last time. He offered *me* words of comfort and consolation. It was precisely at that moment when I realized that my good friend, old Rabbi Zvulun, had catapulted to a higher dimension – a dimension reserved for the special pious and righteous of Israel – lying somewhere between angelic beings and us mortals.

After the funeral, a long line of buses was ready to take the public to the burial grounds in Yitzhar. On the way there was a mob stoning the buses. Quickly, the stoning turned to shooting, in which three Jewish youths were injured. Wisely, our driver moved quickly away. We buried Hillel amidst the sound of shooting below and the hovering of helicopters above. The last oration was pronounced, and then one of Hillel's sons, who seemed barely ten, closed the funeral with the recitation of the *Qaddish*.

As we were leaving the site, I saw someone from ABC News interviewing the mother, Rabbanit Brakha Lieberman. She spoke calmly, with fluency and poise, with objectivity and compassion, offering a gritty and realistic account of Hillel's ideology, of the meaning of the land of Israel for us the people of Israel, and how we have always shared, and will continue to share, our bounty with *all* Jews and Muslims alike. We prayed *Minḥa* and then took our bus back home.

As we were approaching the end of the journey, I realized that we had all been privileged to share in an event invested with a timeless quality. It was something placid and fulfilling, a stream of consciousness, a step above the ordinary staircase of emotion.

Something … I know exactly what it what was. In the land of Israel, not too from where our Patriarch Joseph dwelled, Hillel lived a full and happy life. He had fulfilled his dream and enjoyed every moment of it. Before taking leave of planet Earth to meet Patriarch Joseph, he used his heavenly connections to make sure that every participant would savor an instant of his fulfilled dream, so that we could carry it with us, like a small gem, for the rest of our lives. This was Hillel's way of expressing his thanks, and of telling us: "I lived a happy life. Now you go ahead and fulfill your dream in the land of Israel!"

*The fonts used in this book are from the Arno family*

*The Library of the Jewish People*